THE OXFORD HANDBO

ANALYTICAL
SOCIOLOGY

THE OXFORD HANDBOOK OF

ANALYTICAL SOCIOLOGY

Edited by

PETER HEDSTRÖM

and

PETER BEARMAN

OXFORD

UNIVERSITY PRESS

OXFORD

UNIVERSITY PRESS

Great Clarendon Street, Oxford ox2 6dp

Oxford University Press is a department of the University of Oxford.
It furthers the University's objective of excellence in research, scholarship,
and education by publishing worldwide in

Oxford New York

Auckland Cape Town Dar es Salaam Hong Kong Karachi
Kuala Lumpur Madrid Melbourne Mexico City Nairobi
New Delhi Shanghai Taipei Toronto

With offices in

Argentina Austria Brazil Chile Czech Republic France Greece
Guatemala Hungary Italy Japan Poland Portugal Singapore
South Korea Switzerland Thailand Turkey Ukraine Vietnam

Oxford is a registered trade mark of Oxford University Press
in the UK and in certain other countries

Published in the United States
by Oxford University Press Inc., New York

British Library Cataloguing in Publication Data

Data available

Library of Congress Cataloging in Publication Data

The Oxford handbook of analytical sociology/edited by
Peter Hedström and Peter Bearman.
p. cm.
Includes bibliographical references.
ISBN 978–0–19–921536–2
1. Sociology. 2. Sociology–Philosophy.
I. Hedström, Peter. II. Bearman, Peter.
HM585.0984 2009
301–dc22   2009013905

Typeset by SPI Publisher Services, Pondicherry, India
Printed in Great Britain
by
MPG Books Group, Bodmin and King's Lynn

ISBN 978–0–19–921536–2 (hbk.)
ISBN 978–0–19–958745–2 (pbk.)

1 3 5 7 9 10 8 6 4 2

ACKNOWLEDGMENTS

This book would not have come into existence without the generous support of several individuals and institutions. We wish to thank Fletcher Haulley at Columbia for his managerial and editorial work and for his careful attention to detail. We also want to thank the Yale School of Management for organizing one of the workshops at which drafts of the chapters were presented, the participants at these workshops for their valuable comments, and the Rockefeller Foundation's Bellagio Center for providing peace and tranquility at a critical juncture. Finally we want to thank our home institutions—the Institute for Social and Economic Research and Policy at Columbia and Nuffield College at Oxford—for partial funding, and Dominic Byatt at Oxford University Press for the detailed feedback we have received from him throughout the project.

CONTENTS

PART I FOUNDATIONS

PART II SOCIAL COGS AND WHEELS

PART III SOCIAL DYNAMICS

LIST OF FIGURES

....

LIST OF TABLES

About the Contributors

Yvonne Åberg is a Research Fellow at Nuffield College, University of Oxford, and Assistant Professor of Sociology at the Swedish Institute for Social Research, Stockholm University. She received her Ph.D. in sociology from Stockholm University. Her research focuses on large-scale population based social networks, especially family networks and complex overlapping networks, models of social interactions, and family demography.

Delia Baldassarri is Assistant Professor of Sociology at Princeton University. She holds Ph.D.s in sociology from Columbia University and the University of Trento. Her work in the areas of social networks, collective behavior, political inequality, and economic development aims at capturing the attitudinal and structural bases of social integration and conflict. She is the author of a book on cognitive heuristics and political decision-making (*The Simple Art of Voting*), and has written articles on interpersonal influence, public opinion and political polarization, formal models of collective action, civil-society and inter-organizational networks.

Karen Barkey is Professor of Sociology at Columbia University. She received her Ph.D. in sociology from the University of Chicago. She studies state centralization/decentralization, state control, and social movements against states in the context of empires. Her research focuses primarily on the Ottoman Empire and recently on comparisons between Ottoman, Habsburg, and Roman empires. Her latest book is *Empire of Difference: The Ottomans in Comparative Perspective* (Cambridge: Cambridge University Press, 2008).

Peter Bearman is Director of the Lazarsfeld Center for the Social Sciences, the Cole Professor of Social Science, Codirector of the Health and Society Scholars Program, and an Associate Member of Nuffield College, University of Oxford. He holds a Ph.D. in sociology from Harvard University. A recipient of the NIH Director's Pioneer Award in 2007, Bearman is currently investigating the social and environmental determinants of the autism epidemic. Current projects also include an ethnographic study of the funeral industry and, with support from the American Legacy Foundation, an investigation of the social and economic consequences of tobacco-control policy.

Michael Biggs is Lecturer in Sociology at the University of Oxford. He studied at Victoria University of Wellington and Harvard University. His research has focused on social movements and political protest, addressing two theoretical puzzles. One is the volatility of collective protest: why a mass movement can emerge suddenly, appear powerful, and yet collapse quickly. The second puzzle is the use of self-inflicted suffering for political ends, as with hunger strikes and, most dramatically, with protest by self-immolation.

Iris Bohnet is Professor of Public Policy at the Harvard Kennedy School, Director of the Women and Public Policy Program, Associate Director of the Harvard Laboratory for Decision Science and a vice chair of the Program on Negotiation at Harvard. She holds a Ph.D. in economics from the University of Zürich. A behavioral economist, combining insights from economics and psychology, her research focuses on decision-making, and on improving decision-making in organizations and society. In particular, she analyzes the causes and consequences of trust and employs experiments to study the role of gender and culture in decision-making and negotiation.

Richard Breen is Professor of Sociology at Yale University. He received his Ph.D. in social anthropology from the University of Cambridge. He has previously held faculty positions at Nuffield College, University of Oxford, the European University Institute, and the Queen's University, Belfast. He has also held research positions at the Economic and Social Research Institute, and was Director of the Centre for Social Research at the Queen's University, Belfast. His research interests are social stratification and inequality, and the application of formal models in the social sciences.

Elizabeth Bruch is Assistant Professor of Sociology and Complex Systems at the University of Michigan, and a faculty member at the Population Studies Center. She earned her Ph.D. at the University of California, Los Angeles. Her research spans a broad array of population phenomena in which the actions of individuals and other units (such as families, couples, or neighborhoods) are dynamically interdependent. Her current work examines the conditions under which income inequality and economic factors associated with neighborhood choice can exacerbate or attenuate race segregation.

Hannah Brückner is Professor of Sociology at Yale University. She received her Ph.D. from the University of North Carolina, Chapel Hill. She works on a wide range of topics related to the life course, inequality, health, gender, and sexuality. Current research projects focus on adolescent romantic relationships, and timing and sequencing of family formation and career development. She has a long-standing interest in quantitative methodology and the integration of biological and sociological explanations of social structure and human behavior.

Ivan Chase is Professor of Sociology at the State University of New York, Stony Brook. He received his Ph.D. in sociology from Harvard University. He is interested in social organization: what forces produce it, how it comes to have its characteristic forms, and what kinds of theories are best suited to understanding it. In pursuing these problems, he works primarily with social structures that can be studied under controlled conditions in the laboratory. These social structures include networks of relationships in face-to-face groups using dominance hierarchies in fish, the distribution of material resources using resource distribution through 'vacancy chain' processes, in humans and hermit crabs, and cooperation and the coordination of effort using 'foraging decisions' in ants.

Karen S. Cook is the Ray Lyman Wilbur Professor of Sociology and Director of the Institute for Research in the Social Sciences at Stanford University, where she also received her Ph.D. in sociology. Her current research focuses on issues of trust in social relations and networks. She is also working on projects related to social justice, power-dependence relations, and social-exchange theory, in addition to collaborative research on physician–patient trust. She is the co-author of *Cooperation without Trust?* (New York: Russell Sage, 2005).

Peter Dodds is Assistant Professor of Mathematics and Statistics at the University of Vermont, and a visiting faculty Fellow at the Vermont Advanced Computing Center. He received his Ph.D. in mathematics from the Massachusetts Institute of Technology. He is working on problems in geomorphology, biology, ecology, and sociology, with a general interest in complex systems and networks.

Jon Elster is the Robert K. Merton Professor of Social Sciences at Columbia University and a professor at the Collège de France. He received his Ph.D. from the University of Paris. Before taking his current position at Columbia University, he taught in Paris, Oslo, and Chicago. His research interests include the theory of rational choice, the theory of distributive justice, and the history of social thought (Marx and Tocqueville). He is currently working on a comparative study of constitution-making processes from the Federal Convention to the present, besides being engaged in a project on the microfoundations of civil war.

Scott Feld is Professor of Sociology at Purdue University. He received his Ph.D. in sociology from the John Hopkins University and has held faculty positions at SUNY, Stony Brook, and Louisiana State University. His ongoing research interests focus on social networks, and processes of individual and collective decision-making. Currently he is studying innovations in marriage and divorce laws.

Andreas Flache is Professor of Sociology at the University of Groningen and member of the Interuniversity Center for Social Science Theory and Methodology (ICS). He received his Ph.D. in social and behavioral sciences from the University of Groningen. His general research interest concerns cooperation, social integration, and solidarity and how they are related to the structure and emergence of social networks.

Christine Fountain is Assistant Professor of Sociology at the University of South Carolina and a visiting associate research scholar at the Institute for Social and Economic Research and Policy at Columbia University. She received her Ph.D. in sociology from the University of Washington. Her work concerns the relationships between institutions and the interactions of people within those institutions. Specifically, she studies the interplay between labor markets, network structures, careers, and hiring processes.

Jeremy Freese is Professor of Sociology at Northwestern University. He previously taught at the University of Wisconsin-Madison and was a Robert Wood Johnson Scholar in Health Policy Research at Harvard University. He attained his Ph.D. in sociology from Indiana University. Freese is interested in drawing connections across biological, psychological, and social causes of divergence in individuals' lives, especially as these intersect with technological and other kinds of social change. Additionally, he has worked on social-science methods, including co-authoring a book on the analyses of categorical data.

Diego Gambetta is an Official Fellow of Nuffield College and Professor of Sociology at the University of Oxford. He previously was a Research Fellow at King's College, Cambridge, and then reader in sociology at the University of Oxford, and Fellow of All Souls College. His main interests are signaling theory; trust and mimicry; organized crime and violent extremists. He recently published (with Heather Hamill) *Streetwise: How Taxi Drivers Establish Their Customers' Trustworthiness* (New York: Russell Sage, 2005). His new book, *Codes of the Underworld. How Criminals Communicate*, will be published by Princeton University Press in the summer of 2009.

Alexandra Gerbasi is an Assistant Professor at California State University at Northridge. She received her Ph.D. in sociology at Stanford University. Her research interests include the development of trust and cooperation in exchange networks, the sources and effects of transitions in types of exchange, and the role of social-psychological incentives in social exchange.

Daniel G. Goldstein is Assistant Professor of Marketing at London Business School. He received his Ph.D. from the University of Chicago and previously he has been at Columbia, Harvard, and Stanford universities and at the Max Planck Institute in Berlin. His expertise is in psychology and decision-making, with an emphasis on business and policy. He is on the executive board of the Society for Judgment and Decision Making and is the editor of *Decision Science News*.

Bernard Grofman is Jack W. Peltason Endowed Chair and Professor of Political Science, Adjunct Professor of Economics, and Director of the Center for the Study of Democracy at the University of California, Irvine. He holds a Ph.D. in political science from the University of Chicago. His past research has dealt with mathematical models of group decision making, legislative representation, electoral rules, and redistricting. Currently he is working on comparative politics and political economy, with an emphasis on viewing the USA in a comparative perspective.

Peter Hedström is Professor of Sociology and an Official Fellow of Nuffield College, University of Oxford. He holds a Ph.D. in sociology from Harvard University, and previously held faculty positions at the University of Chicago, Stockholm University, and Singapore Management University. He recently published *Dissecting the Social: On the Principles of Analytical Sociology* (Cambridge: Cambridge University Press, 2005), and he has a special interest in analytical sociology and the analysis of complex social networks.

Stathis Kalyvas is the Arnold Wolfers Professor of Political Science at Yale, where he directs the program on 'Order, Conflict, and Violence.' He earned his Ph.D. in political science at the University of Chicago. He is the author of *The Rise of Christian Democracy in Europe* (New York: Cornell University Press, 1996) and, more recently *The Logic of Violence in Civil War* (Cambridge: Cambridge University Press, 2006). He is currently researching the micro-dynamics of civil war, with a focus on warfare, recruitment, and violence, using disaggregated data from Colombia and Vietnam, among others.

W. Brent Lindquist is Deputy Provost and Professor of Applied Mathematics and Statistics at the State University of New York, Stony Brook. He received his Ph.D. in theoretical physics from Cornell University. His research career has included quantum electrodynamics, Riemann problems in conservation laws, and numerical computation of flow in porous media. His current research concentrates on various aspects of data mining—largely in application to three-dimensional digitized images.

Freda Lynn is Assistant Professor of Sociology at the University of Iowa and received her Ph.D. in sociology from Harvard University. Her research interests include status processes, social inequality, and social networks. She is currently studying how quality uncertainty affects citation accumulation in scientific disciplines.

Michael Macy is Goldwin-Smith Professor of Sociology at Cornell University and received his Ph.D. in sociology from Harvard University. Macy pioneered the use of agent-based models in sociology to explore the effects of heterogeneity, bounded rationality, and network structure on the dynamics and stability of social systems. He is currently principal investigator for an NSF-supported team of social, information, and computer scientists who are building tools that will make the Internet archive accessible for research on social and information networks.

Robert Mare is Distinguished Professor of Sociology and Statistics at the University of California, Los Angeles and an Associate Member of Nuffield College, University of Oxford. He received his Ph.D. in sociology from the University of Michigan. His research interests focus on dynamic analysis of residential mobility and residential segregation; educational assortative mating and marriage markets; and the joint analysis of social mobility, fertility, marriage, and other demographic processes.

James Moody is Associate Professor of Sociology at Duke University, where he recently moved after teaching for seven years at Ohio State University. He attained his Ph.D. in sociology at the University of North Carolina, Chapel Hill. An expert in network analysis, he has written extensively about the implications of social network structure for health and social organization. With Peter Bearman and Katherine Stovel, Moody co-authored 'Chains of Affection: The Structure of Adolescent Romantic and Sexual Networks,' which received the Gould Prize for the best paper published in the *American Journal of Sociology* in 2004.

Trond Petersen holds a joint appointment in the Department of Sociology at the University of California, Berkeley, and the Organizational Behavior and Industrial Relations Group at the Walter A. Haas School of Business at Berkeley. He is an adjunct Professor at the Norwegian University of Science and Technology in Trondheim and an adjunct researcher at the University of Oslo. Prior to Berkeley, he taught at Harvard University. He earned his Ph.D. in sociology from the University of Wisconsin, Madison. He is interested in organizations, social stratification, inequality, economic sociology, comparative studies, and quantitative methods.

Joel Podolny is Vice President and Dean of Apple University at Apple, Inc. Prior to his current position, he was Dean of the Yale School of Management. He has also served as a professor at the Harvard Business School, Harvard Faculty of Arts and Sciences, and the Stanford Graduate School of Business. His best-known research brings the sociological conception of status to the study of market competition. In addition to his work on status, he has conducted research on the role of social networks in mobility and information transfer within organizations. His current research explores how leaders infuse meanings into their organizations.

Meredith Rolfe is a Senior Research Fellow at the Centre for Corporate Reputation, Saïd Business School, University of Oxford and a Research Fellow at Nuffield College, University of Oxford. Her recently completed book, *Voting Together*, uses conditional decision models to challenge the conventional explanation of why college-educated citizens are more likely to vote. Her current research uses the conditional choice approach to better understand why women support social welfare more than men, why ethnic minorities earn less than ethnic majorities, and why corporations rise and fall in public esteem. She holds a Ph.D. in political science from the University of Chicago.

Jens Rydgren is Associate Professor of Sociology at Stockholm University and is associated with the Linnaeus Center for Integration Studies. He received his Ph.D.

in sociology at Stockholm University and is currently doing research on radical right-wing parties in Western Europe, as well as on xenophobic attitudes among West European voters.

Matthew J. Salganik is Assistant Professor of Sociology at Princeton University. He received his Ph.D. in sociology from Columbia University. His research interests include sampling methods for hidden populations such as drug injectors and sex workers, social networks, fads, and web-based social science.

Katherine Stovel is Associate Professor of Sociology at the University of Washington and received her Ph.D. in sociology from the University of North Carolina, Chapel Hill. While her research spans a number of substantive areas, including economic sociology, adolescent health, and quantitative methods, her work is motivated by a general concern with how basic principles of social interaction are expressed in specific historical or cultural contexts, and why these expressions may result in new institutional arrangements or new identities for individuals.

Lars Udehn is Professor of Sociology at Stockholm University. He received his Ph.D. in sociology from Uppsala University. His interests include the history of ideas and sociological theory, and he recently published *Methodological Individualism: Background, History and Meaning* (London: Routledge, 2001).

Diane Vaughan is Professor of Sociology and International and Public Affairs at Columbia University. She holds a Ph.D. in sociology from Ohio State University. Her specializations include the sociology of organizations, culture, science and technology, ethnography, and analogical theorizing. Much of her work has examined 'the dark side of organizations': mistake, misconduct, and disaster. The orientation of her research is to situate individual action and meaning-making within its social context, including the organization itself and its institutional environment. She is currently working on *Dead Reckoning: Air Traffic Control in the Early 21st Century* and *Theorizing: Analogy, Cases, and Comparative Social Organization.*

Duncan J. Watts is a principal research scientist at Yahoo! Research, where he directs the Human Social Dynamics group. He is also an adjunct Senior Research Fellow at the Institute for Social and Economic Research and Policy at Columbia University, an external faculty member of the Santa Fe Institute, and an associate member of Nuffield College, University of Oxford. His research interests include the structure and evolution of social networks, the origins and dynamics of social influence, and the nature of distributed 'social' search. He is the author of *Six Degrees: The Science of a Connected Age* (New York: W.W. Norton, 2003) and *Small Worlds: The Dynamics of Networks between Order and Randomness* (Princeton, N.J.: Princeton University Press, 1999). He holds a B.Sc. in physics from the University of South Wales and a Ph.D. in theoretical and applied mechanics from Cornell University.

Christopher Winship is the Diker-Tishman Professor of Sociology at Harvard University, where he also received his Ph.D. Research interests include the Ten Point Coalition, a group of black ministers who are working with the Boston police to reduce youth violence; statistical models for causal analysis; the effects of education on mental ability; causes of the racial difference in performance in elite colleges and universities; changes in the racial differential in imprisonment rates over the past sixty years. With Steve Morgan he recently published *Counterfactuals and Causal Inference: Methods and Principles for Social Research* (Cambridge: Cambridge University Press, 2007).

PART I

FOUNDATIONS

CHAPTER 1

....

WHAT IS ANALYTICAL SOCIOLOGY ALL ABOUT? AN INTRODUCTORY ESSAY*

....

PETER HEDSTRÖM
PETER BEARMAN

INTRODUCTION

....

ANALYTICAL sociology is concerned first and foremost with explaining important social facts such as network structures, patterns of residential segregation, typical beliefs, cultural tastes, common ways of acting, and so forth. It explains such facts not merely by relating them to other social facts—an exercise that does not provide an explanation—but by detailing in clear and precise ways the mechanisms through

* We wish to thank Lars Udehn and Petri Ylikoski for their valuable comments.

which the social facts under consideration are brought about. In short, analytical sociology is a strategy for understanding the social world.

Understanding the social world is also the project of sociology in general, but the strategies used in the mainstream of the discipline differ in important respects from the analytical strategy. This book brings together some of the most prominent analytical sociologists in Europe and the United States in an effort to clarify the distinctive features of the approach and to further its development. The overarching purpose of the book is to move sociology in a more analytical direction.

In this introductory chapter we focus on some of the fundamentals of the analytical approach. Two interrelated aspects are of particular importance: the explanatory principles guiding the approach and the type of explanatory factors being evoked. Analytical sociology explains by detailing mechanisms through which social facts are brought about, and these mechanisms invariably refer to individuals' actions and the relations that link actors to one another.[1]

The chapter is organized as follows. We start by briefly describing what is to be meant by a 'mechanism' and a 'mechanism-based explanation.' These questions have more to do with philosophy of science than with sociology proper, but they have important implications for sociology. Once the explanatory principles are applied to the social world, we arrive at a position which may be referred to as 'structural individualism.' Structural individualism is a methodological doctrine according to which social facts should be explained as the intended or unintended outcomes of individuals' actions. Structural individualism differs from traditional methodological individualism in attributing substantial explanatory importance to the social structures in which individuals are embedded (see Udehn 2001: 318–19). In this chapter we explicate the details of this doctrine and we present various examples based on our own research and that of others to make the abstract principles more concrete. We conclude the chapter with a brief overview of the book.

1.1 MECHANISM EXPLANATIONS

Detailing in clear and precise ways the mechanisms through which social facts are brought about is one of the pillars of the analytical approach. During the last decade there has been a growing interest in mechanisms and mechanism-based explanations, not only in the social sciences but also in philosophy of science, particularly philosophy of biology.[2]

In philosophy, the traditional view used to be that an explanation of a phenomenon consists in showing that it is expected given a general and applicable causal law (e.g. Hempel 1965). This by now rather outdated view never played any serious role in sociology, however. Sociological explanation is all about mechanisms and statistical associations and has been so for decades.[3]

Although many sociologists use the word 'mechanism,' they often use it in an offhand casual sense without any commitment to the type of mechanism-based explanatory strategy focused upon here. The core idea behind the mechanism approach has been expressed as follows by Elster (1989: 3–4): 'To explain an event is to give an account of why it happened. Usually . . . this takes the form of citing an earlier event as the cause of the event we want to explain. . . . [But] to cite the cause is not enough: the causal mechanism must also be provided, or at least suggested.'

As observed by Mahoney (2001), there is no consensus on what is to be meant by a 'mechanism.' In fact, there appears to be almost an overabundance of definitions, and Table 1.1 describes some of the most frequently cited definitions.

These definitions differ a great deal from one another, but underlying them all is an emphasis on making intelligible the regularities being observed by specifying in detail how they were brought about. Bechtel and Richardson have expressed this core idea as follows:

> By calling the explanations mechanistic, we are highlighting the fact that they treat the systems as producing a certain behavior in a manner analogous to that of machines . . . A machine is a composite of interrelated parts . . . that are combined in such a way that each contributes to producing a behavior of the system. A mechanistic explanation identifies these parts and their organization, showing how the behavior of the machine is a consequence of the parts and their organization.   (1993: 17)

Although one should not take the machine metaphor as such particularly seriously, the idea that mechanism explanations identify component parts that jointly produce the collective outcome to be explained is at the very heart of the approach.

The currently most satisfactory discussion of the mechanism concept is found in Machamer, Darden, and Craver (2000). Following their lead, mechanisms can be said to consist of entities (with their properties) and the activities that these entities engage in, either by themselves or in concert with other entities. These activities bring about change, and the type of change brought about depends upon the properties and activities of the entities and the relations between them. A mechanism, thus defined, refers to a constellation of entities and activities that are organized such that they regularly bring about a particular type of outcome, and we explain an observed outcome by referring to the mechanism by which such outcomes are regularly brought about.

This implies that explanations should refer to the types of entities and activities through which the outcome to be explained is believed to have been brought about. As will be discussed in detail below, if we believe that actors, their properties, actions, and relations to one another are what explain social change, we should

Table 1.1 Alternative mechanism definitions

Author	Definition	Reference
Bunge	A mechanism is a process in a concrete system which is capable of bringing about or preventing some change in the system.	Bunge (1997)
Machamer, Darden, and Craver	Mechanisms are entities and activities organized such that they are productive of regular changes from start to finish.	Machamer, Darden, and Craver (2000)
Elster (I)	A mechanism explains by opening up the black box and showing the cogs and wheels of the internal machinery. A mechanism provides a continuous and contiguous chain of causal or intentional links between the explanans and the explanandum.	Elster (1989)
Elster (II)	Mechanisms are frequently occurring and easily recognizable causal patterns that are triggered under generally unknown conditions.	Elster (1999)
Hedström and Swedberg	A social mechanism is a precise, abstract, and action-based explanation which shows how the occurrence of a triggering event regularly generates the type of outcome to be explained.	Hedström and Swedberg (1998)
Stinchcombe	A mechanism is a piece of scientific reasoning which gives knowledge about a component of another, ordinarily higher-level, theory.	Stinchcombe (1991)

formulate our explanations in such terms and not in terms of various social abstractions and their relationships to one another.

This view of appropriate explanations as generative models differs in important respects from the explanatory principles used in mainstream sociology, where the emphasis rather is on statistical associations (see also Epstein 2006). As is evidenced throughout this volume, the mechanism-based approach is not in opposition to traditional experimental and nonexperimental approaches. Such methods are essential for adjudicating between rival mechanisms and for distinguishing the relevant activities and relations of a mechanism from the irrelevant ones. The difference instead centers on whether one should rest with establishing statistical associations or whether one should follow the analytical strategy and aim for models which show how a proposed mechanism generates the outcome to be explained.

The analytical agenda also embraces the idea of sociological theory as a toolbox of semigeneral mechanisms. As Hedström and Udehn discuss in their chapter, analytical sociology is firmly anchored in the Mertonian tradition. At the core of this tradition is a strong emphasis on the importance of semigeneral middle-range theories, and an equally strong skepticism towards the idea of general sociological theory.

Although there exist some celebrated examples of semigeneral mechanisms, much work remains to be done. The basic idea of theories as semigeneral mechanisms is fairly clear, however, and is related to Kitcher's idea (1981) of 'argument patterns' (but not to his idea of what an explanation entails; see also Machamer, Darden, and Craver 2000). Hedström (2005) uses the notion of an abstract mechanism scheme to highlight the defining features of various types of mechanisms. The following scheme is at the heart of Merton's theory of a self-fulfilling prophecy, for example:

$$B_i \rightarrow A_i \rightarrow B_j \rightarrow A_j \rightarrow B_k \rightarrow A_k \rightarrow \ldots \qquad (1)$$

A represents a specific action, B a belief, and the subscripts identify different actors. That is to say, in (1) the beliefs of actor i are such that they make i perform a certain action; i's action influences the beliefs of actor j in such a way that j also decides to act; and j's action in turn influences the beliefs of k, and so on.

This mechanism scheme has limited scope in that it only is relevant for explaining certain types of phenomena, but it is general in the sense that it makes no reference to time, place, identity of actors, content of beliefs, or type of actions. The abstract symbols should be thought of as placeholders for different concrete phenomena (different kinds of actions, different kinds of beliefs, different individuals, etc.) and what identifies it as a particular type of mechanism is the specific *pattern* linking the types of entities to one another. Merton (1968: 475–90) showed how the same self-fulfilling pattern could be used for partially explaining phenomena as different from one another as runs on banks and racial prejudices. (See Biggs's chapter in this volume for additional examples.)

To bring home the notion of a mechanism schema, let's use one additional example—that of a selection mechanism. Selection mechanisms have been suggested to be central for explaining a range of different phenomena such as the ecology of organizational populations (Hannan and Freeman 1989) and the evolution of individual behavior (Skryms 1996), to mention just two sociology-related examples. There are numerous subtle distinctions involved, but for our purpose it is sufficient to present the selection mechanism in its most basic form. As such it is a type of mechanism which links the property of an entity to its reproductive success in a specific environment.[4] The core scheme for the selection mechanism may be summarized as follows:[5]

1. A set of entities, e_1 to e_N, vary with respect to a property, p_i.
2. In a certain environment the benefit, b_i, bestowed on entity i is a function of its property p_i.
3. The value of b_i influences the relative frequency of entities with different properties at subsequent time periods. (Properties that perform better in the environment will become more frequent.)[6]

This mechanism can explain how and why the relative frequency of entities with different properties changes over time. As in the previous example, the abstract symbols should be thought of as placeholders for more concrete phenomena (such as individuals, organizations, organizational strategies, etc.). Because of the wide scope of the selection mechanism, it constitutes an important part of the sociological toolbox.

1.2 STRUCTURAL INDIVIDUALISM

The basic explanatory principle behind the mechanism approach thus is that proper explanations identify the entities, activities, and relations that jointly produce the collective outcome to be explained. When we apply this idea to the explanation of social facts it implies a form of structural individualism. As we define the term, structural individualism is a methodological doctrine according to which all social facts, their structure and change, are in principle explicable in terms of individuals, their properties, actions, and relations to one another. It differs from traditional notions of methodological individualism (e.g. Elster 1982) by emphasizing the explanatory importance of relations and relational structures.

We want to emphasize that structural individualism is a *methodological* position which has nothing to do with political individualism or any other form of normative position outside the scientific domain. It simply is a view of what acceptable explanations in the social sciences are all about, and it has been embraced by scholars as different as Merton, Coleman, and the analytical Marxists of the 1980s.[7]

Although structural individualism emphasizes the importance of action-based explanations, it is essential to note that it does not imply a commitment to any specific type of motive or intentional state that is assumed to explain why individuals act as they do. Thus, it does not imply a commitment to any form of rational-choice theory and in its barest form it may not make any reference to mental or intentional states whatsoever (see the chapter by Rolfe). Structural individualists share two important concerns, however, and these are the Weberian concern with action oriented towards others and the mechanism-based concern with causal depth.

1.3 ACHIEVING CAUSAL DEPTH

By causal depth we mean the explicit identification of the microfoundations, or the social cogs and wheels, through which the social facts to be explained are brought about. The central cogs and wheels of social life are actions and relations. Actions are important because all the things that interest us as sociologists are the intended or unintended outcomes of individuals' actions. Individuals' actions typically are oriented towards others, and therefore relations to others are central when it comes to explaining why individuals do what they do. In addition, as demonstrated most clearly in the literature on diffusion processes (e.g. Strang and Soule 1998), social relations are central for explaining why, acting as they do, individuals bring about the social outcomes they do. That relations are important for explaining outcomes does not mean that they are independent of individuals and their actions, however. As emphasized above, in principle all relational structures are explainable as intended or unintended outcomes of individuals' action.

Consider, for example, the case of vacancy chains as analyzed by White (1970). A retirement, motivated perhaps by a desire for a more leisurely life, creates an opportunity for others, i.e. a vacancy waiting to be filled by a new occupant. The vacancy generated by the retirement is filled by another individual whose reason for taking the job, perhaps, is to attain more status, or a higher salary, or just a change in venue, but this creates another vacancy in this person's old job, and in this way vacancy chains create social interdependencies which are important for explaining mobility. Individuals' desires—for retirement, for promotion, for status, or for a change in venue—motivate the system. Without such orientations, people may not move. But the essential cogs and wheels are not solely found in the intentions of actors. Causal depth is achieved by recognizing that action takes place in social structures that in this case channel mobility opportunities and thereby explain why we observe what we observe.

1.4 THE MICRO–MACRO LINK

Some sociologists and many traditional economists would find it attractive if all explanations were 'rock-bottom explanations' (Watkins 1957) that start from an idealized state of nature in which no social relations are assumed to exist or to matter. Such thought-experiments can be challenging and entertaining and they can be of use in normatively oriented theory, but we do not see them as serious contenders for explanations of what is observed here and now. Of course, many essential components of sociological explanations—such as norms, and networks—often are the results of long and intricate social processes. If we aim for rock-bottom explanations, such components must either be ignored, which to us seems unacceptable, or they must be endogenized, which, given the current state of social theory, is in many

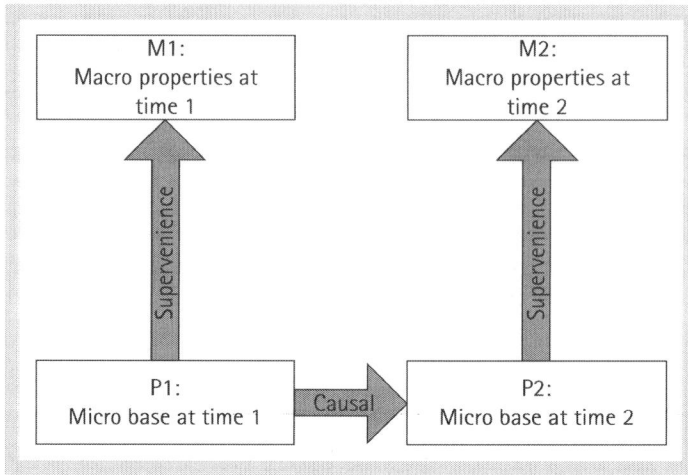

Fig. 1.1 Micro–macro relations as supervenience relations

cases impossible. For this reason, the realism and the precision of the proposed explanation will be greatly improved if we take certain macro-level properties such as relational structures as given and incorporate them into the explanation.

Making sense of the relationship between micro and macro thus emerges as a central concern of analytical sociology, and this raises the question of what we mean by a macro property. As we define the term, macro properties are properties of a collectivity or a set of micro-level entities that are not definable for a single micro-level entity. Important examples of such macro-level properties include typical actions, beliefs, desires, etc. among members of the collectivity as well as distributions and aggregate patterns characterizing the collectivity such as inequality, spatial segregation, and networks.

Our view of the relation between micro and macro is similar to what in philosophical analyses of the mind–body problem sometimes is referred to as 'supervenience' (e.g. Kim 2005), and is depicted in Figure 1.1.

Using the language of supervenience, a macro property, **M**, supervenes on a set of micro-level properties, **P**, if identity in **P** necessarily implies identity in **M**. If the macro property is supervenient upon the micro it means that, if two collectivities or societies are identical to one another in terms of their micro-level properties, then their macro-level properties also will be identical. It also implies that two collectivities that differ in their macro-level properties will necessarily differ in their micro-level properties as well. But it does *not* imply that two collectivities with an identical macro-level property will necessarily have identical micro-level properties, because identical macro-level properties can be brought about in different ways.

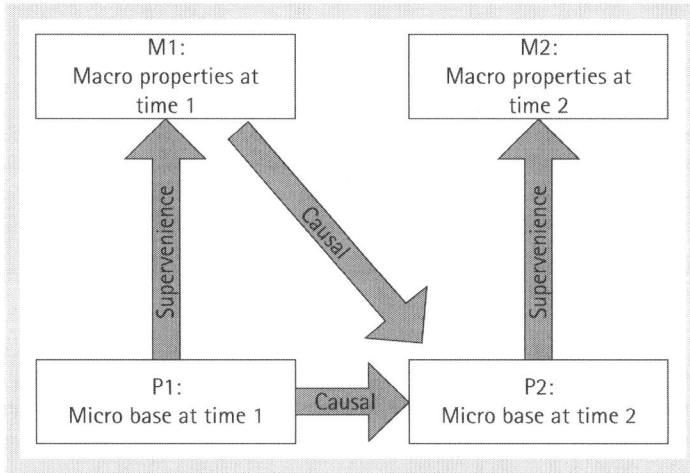

Fig. 1.2 Macro dynamics from a supervenience perspective

Although macro is dependent upon micro, micro-to-macro or P-to-M relations should not be viewed as causal relations. Macro properties are always instantiated at the same time as the micro properties upon which they supervene, and a group or a society has the macro properties it has in virtue of the properties and relations of its micro-level entities. The micro-to-macro relationship is a parts-to-a-whole relationship rather than cause-to-an-effect relationship. For example, if a set of dyadic relations exists between the members of a group, these dyadic relations do not cause the network structure linking the individuals to one another; they constitute it. Similarly, the properties of the individuals residing in different spatial locations do not cause the extent of residential segregation; they constitute it.

Yet another important implication of the supervenience perspective is that if a macro or micro property at an earlier time period, **P1** or **M1**, causally influences a macro-level property in the present, **M2**, it must do so by influencing its supervenience base, **P2** (see Fig. 1.2). Sociological examples of causal relations of the **M1**-to-**P2** kind include processes that operate 'behind the back' of individuals, such as various socialization processes, but macro-level properties also can have causal efficacy by being components which individuals consciously take into account when deciding what to do. One such example is when an individual's decision of whether or not to join a social movement is influenced by the number of other individuals who already have joined the movement (see e.g. Hedström 1994). Other examples of such decisions discussed elsewhere in this volume are those of whether to kill someone, whether to vote, whether to move to a new neighborhood, whether to buy the latest best-seller, and whether to express an opinion about wine quality.[8]

Although systematic regularities can be observed at the M level, such associations typically say little about why we observe what we observe. From this perspective such associations are surface phenomena arising from and requiring explanations in terms of deeper underlying processes. The important point is that at each instance of time, macro, M, is supervenient on micro, P, and in order to explain changes in M we must explain changes in this micro base. Until very recently we did not have the analytical tools needed for analyzing the dynamics of complex systems that large groups of interacting individuals represent. Powerful computers and simulation software have changed the picture—so much so that it is possible to have some confidence that agent-based computer simulations will transform important parts of sociological theory because they allow for rigorous theoretical analyses of large and complex social systems. (See the chapter by Macy and Flache for an overview.)

Although the social dynamics observed at the M level typically are extremely complex and hard to understand, the basic cogs and wheels of these social processes may be possible to describe with rather simple models. Thomas Schelling's segregation model (1978) is a particularly nice illustration of this. In the Schelling model we have two kinds of individuals, who we may refer to as Whites and Grays, and who are distributed on a lattice. Each individual decides where to live on the lattice, but the decision is influenced by the past decisions of others. Some constraints are present—most importantly, individuals only can move to vacant positions, and they prefer to live near at least some of their own kind. If the Whites and the Grays are randomly distributed throughout the social space represented by the lattice many of them will be dissatisfied, since they will have too few neighbors of their own kind (see Panel A of Fig. 1.3). This will prompt them to move to new locations, but on entry into the new locations they may tip the balance of the local population there, making others leave. If a few Grays move into an area, the local Whites might leave, and when they arrive at their new areas they might prompt Grays to leave, and so on.

Schelling demonstrated that even if individuals have strong preferences for mixed neighborhoods, segregation often arises as an unintended consequence. For example, if the Whites and the Grays want at least 26 percent of their own kind in their neighborhood in order to stay, they typically bring about a collective outcome where the average neighborhood consists of more than 70 percent of the same kind. (See Panel B in Fig. 1.3 for a typical example.)[9]

Schelling also showed that small and seemingly trivial differences at the micro level can make huge differences at the macro level. If the individuals inhabiting the lattice had wanted at least 25 instead of 26 percent of their own kind in their neighborhoods, we would observe a macro structure like the one in Panel C—a considerably less segregated pattern than the one in Panel B.

If we were presented with these macro-level patterns only, it is very likely that we would draw the conclusion that because the society pictured in Panel B is more

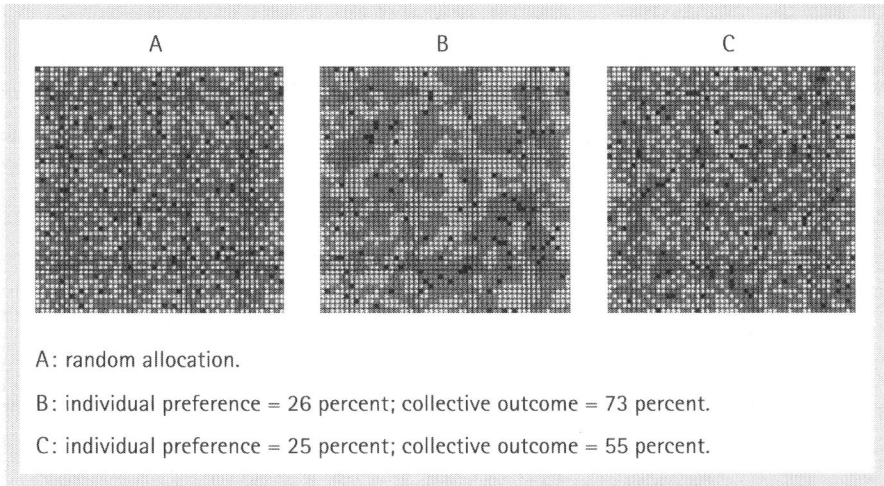

A: random allocation.

B: individual preference = 26 percent; collective outcome = 73 percent.

C: individual preference = 25 percent; collective outcome = 55 percent.

Fig. 1.3 Individual preferences and neighborhood segregation

highly segregated, those who generated this pattern must have been much more prejudiced than those who generated the pattern observed in Panel C, although the differences between the individuals in the two societies are in fact negligible and without social significance in and of themselves.

This is a very important result that extends far beyond this stylized example. It has been produced many times in many different contexts; for example, in Granovetter's work (1978) on collective action. The point is not that things tip, however interesting that may be. The point is that macro-level outcomes and relationships tell us very little about why we observe the macro-level outcomes and relationships we observe. Trying to make causal inferences on the basis of macro-level data is highly error prone.

Another important point also should be noted. If we view these simulations in the light of Figure 1.2 we can see that the complex and unexpected results do not have anything to do with the complexity of the micro-to-macro link or with any mysterious form of 'emergence'; at each instant of time the link from micro to macro simply is a supervenience relation. The complexity exclusively is due to the complex dynamics of the micro base.

An important methodological point follows from this: In order to understand collective dynamics we must study the collectivity as a whole, but we must not study it *as* a collective entity. Only by taking into account the individual entities, and most critically the relations between them and their activities, can we understand the macro structure we observe. Predicting and explaining macro-level dynamics is one of the most central goals of analytical sociology and the main focus of several chapters in this volume.

1.4.1 More complex and empirically calibrated models

When discussing macro-to-micro or M1-to-P2 relations we made a distinction between two types of relations. Macro properties can influence what individuals do either through processes that operate behind their backs or by being social facts which they consciously take into account when deciding what to do. Schelling's model is of the latter kind. Individuals observe the composition of their local environments and this is one of the key components influencing their actions. Preferences and neighborhood compositions form an interactive process that induces segregation, even if the actors are not overtly segregationist. As an example of the other kind of process, here we consider a study of the sexual and romantic networks of adolescents undertaken by Bearman, Moody, and Stovel (2006). In this case, individuals' actions are systematically influenced by norms whose existence the individuals themselves would not be able to articulate. The example also illustrates how one can go about testing alternative mechanisms by examining their degree of 'generative sufficiency' (Epstein 2006); that is, by investigating the extent to which the micro-level mechanisms can generate the type of social fact which is to be explained.

The context is a single high school of roughly a thousand students in the Midwestern United States. The macrostructure to be explained is the surprising discovery that the sexual and romantic network structure of students in the school resembles a spanning tree. Figure 1.4 reports the observed structure of relationships over eighteen months.

The observed structure is a network of relationships, some sexual, most affective, and many involving the exchange of fluid, an important factor for understanding disease diffusion. The focus is on the giant component linking 286 of the 500 or so students active in the network, and the question is simple: What is the micro-level explanans that accounts for the puzzling macro-level explanandum?

One possibility is that the spanning tree arises from a purely random process. This is not the case, however. If the degree distribution is fixed to the observed distribution, the resulting graphs bear no relationship to the structure being observed. In fact, they look significantly different. Whatever is going on in the dating world is not the outcome of a purely random process.

Another possibility is that the observed network reflects structured preferences. Students selecting partners may do so for lots of reasons. One student prefers girls who are preferred by others, another likes boys with spiky hair, a third has an aversion to acne, a fourth only selects partners with a higher (or lower) grade-point average, and so on. Despite these idiosyncrasies, there may be some characteristics of a pair that suggest increased likelihood of matching. (For matching processes in more detail see the chapter by Stovel and Fountain in this volume.) And in fact there are. It turns out that boys prefer (or have access to) girls who are younger than them and girls prefer (or have access to) boys who are older than they are. In

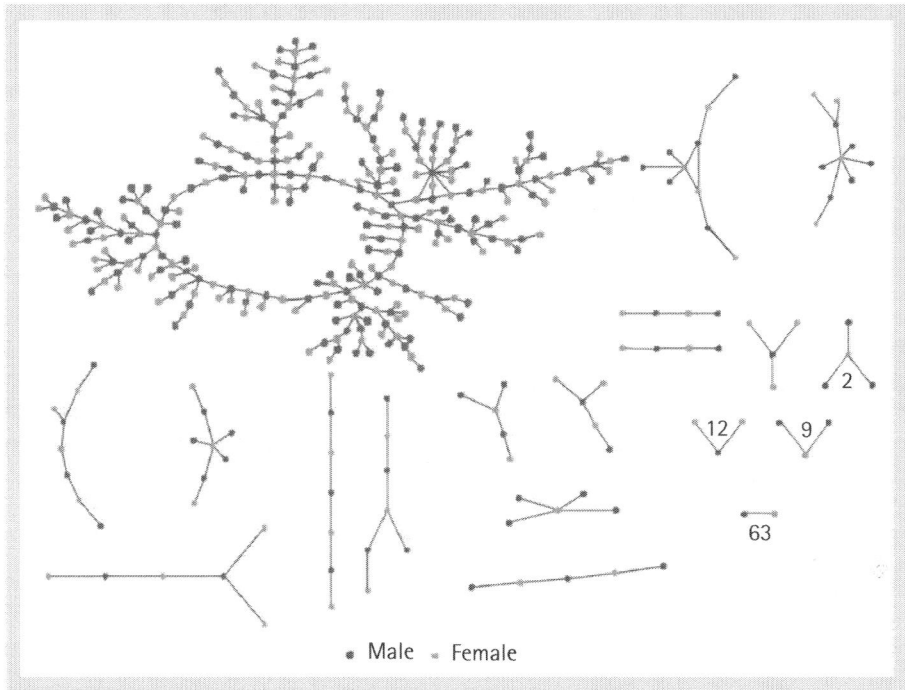

Fig. 1.4 The structure of a sexual network in an American high school

addition, nonsmokers have a strong aversion to smokers. The joint effect of these structured preferences on the macrostructure can be simulated. Fixing the degree distribution to the observed distribution, and modeling the probability of partner selection based on the observed preferences yields a network structure of course, but not one resembling the spanning tree being observed.

The characteristic features of the spanning-tree structure are the absence of a network core and that cycles are rare. (For more detail on networks and dynamic network models in general see the chapter by Moody in this volume.) A core would arise in a heterosexual network of the kind considered here if the partnerships that were formed generated cycles. The shortest possible cycle in a heterosexual network of this kind has a length of four. A cycle of length four would mean, from a boy's point of view, that he formed a partnership with his prior girlfriend's current boyfriend's prior girlfriend. If there were to be a norm prohibiting such relationships, the resulting structure would approximate a spanning tree.[10]

If one were to ask high-school students if there was such a norm, it is unlikely that the answer would be confirmatory. But the logic of the high-school context in which status loss would be associated with such relationships (not to mention the so-called yuck factor that arises from too much closeness) implies an avoidance of four-cycle relationship partners. This hypothesis is directly testable. Fixing the degree distribution as before and modeling the formation of the network under the restriction that cycles of length four should be avoided generates macrostructures that almost exactly correspond to the observed spanning-tree structure.

It seems therefore that a simple and plausible explanation at the micro level is the likely explanation for the observed structure at the macro level. The students imagine that they are freely choosing their partners on the basis of their preferences and beliefs. This is partially true, but they are just not 'free' to choose everyone because they are constrained by past actions of others and by their desire not to lose status in the eyes of their peers, and these constraints explain the spanning-tree structure of the network.

The explanatory strategy can be described as follows (see also Epstein 2006):

1. We start with a clearly delineated social fact that is to be explained.
2. We formulate different hypotheses about relevant micro-level mechanisms.
3. We translate the theoretical hypotheses into computational models.
4. We simulate the models to derive the type of social facts that each micro-level mechanism brings about.
5. We compare the social facts generated by each model with the actually observed outcomes.

In the case of the adolescent sexual network this method produced rather clear-cut results. Of the various mechanisms, only one was able to generate the social fact to be explained. Obviously this is not always the case, but the generative methodology is generally applicable and it is a crucial part of the analytical toolbox.

1.5 A Brief Overview of the Book

In the limited space that follows we briefly provide a road map to the volume and the chapters in it. The volume is organized into four parts. The second chapter in this first part continues the introductory focus of the first chapter by locating analytic sociology in the Mertonian tradition of middle-range theory, a theory tradition in which the focus is on partial explanation of phenomena observed in different social domains through identification of core causal mechanisms. The subsequent eight chapters in 'Part II: Social Cogs and Wheels' focus on the role of action and interaction in explaining diverse social processes. In 'Part III: Social Dynamics,' fifteen chapters explore the macroscopic dynamics brought on by the activation of the cog-and-wheel mechanisms. In Part IV we ask authors from other areas of social science to consider how analytic sociology relates to their programs. Consequently, we have chapters that identify the foundations for the development of game theory and new developments in experimental economics, analytic ethnography, survey research, and comparative history.

The terrain covered in this volume is vast. Below, and very briefly, we provide a rough guide to each chapter. There are many different ways the reader can move across the terrain of analytic sociology. Thus, while we believe all of the chapters should be read, the order in which one reads them is flexible. The descriptions below are designed to provide the reader with enough information to design their own path through the volume.

1.5.1 Social cogs and wheels

In the first chapter in Part II, *Emotions*, Jon Elster argues that while emotions governing action are often thought to be inaccessible to analytic social-science inquiry, this need not be the case. Even if emotions, which are occurrent events (e.g. a fit of rage), trigger actions and reactions discontinuous with prior action streams, emotions do not make the rational-actor model fail. Elster argues that emotions can determine belief, and urgency-based emotions (where urgency is the preference for earlier action over later action, as distinct from impatience, which is the preference for earlier rather than later rewards) can determine outcomes. In this regard, emotions are not inconsistent with a rational-actor model, though they may and often do induce temporary preference shifts, especially for interaction-based emotions— which are likely to yield stronger reactions than comparison-based emotions.

Jens Rydgren considers *beliefs* in the second chapter. For Rydgren, beliefs are defined as 'proposition(s) about the world in which a person is at least minimally confident.' Here Rydgren considers in depth the multiple mechanisms by which beliefs are formed—briefly, from observation, influence/socialization, induction, deduction from other beliefs, adaptation to desire (wishful thinking), and dissonance-reduction mechanisms—and identifies both the conditions under which each obtains and the characteristic processes (and problems) associated with each. For example, conformity processes occur more frequently in repeated-interaction groups and generate snowball effects on others; dissonance reduction occurs only when beliefs are part of the same belief system; and so on. While beliefs are slippery and difficult to nail down, Rydgren shows that they need to be considered in any explanation of action.

In the third chapter Jeremy Freese considers *preferences*. He shows that preferences can lead to actions that appear not to reflect the original preferences, that preferences about preferences can and often do stand at odds with abstract preferences, and that the fact of preference change means that our accounts of action need to acknowledge how actors manipulate their own (or others) preferences in subtle, not easily enumerated, and complex ways. The fluidity and manipulability of preferences carries significant implications for explanations of action, challenging rational-actor models and forcing deeper consideration of the dynamics of preference formation and expression.

In the fourth chapter Trond Petersen considers *opportunities*, and shows how opportunities, defined as the set of choices available to actors once social context is taken into account, confront actors. In considering the relationship between opportunity and inequality (broadly construed), Petersen considers how actors can both expand the opportunities that confront them and restrict the opportunities that confront others. Central to our understanding of opportunity dynamics are the ways in which opportunities shape preferences, which in turn shape the pursuit of outcomes through interaction.

Next, Dan Goldstein considers the role of *heuristics* in driving social action and argues that the focus on heuristics, which involves our rethinking 'the mind' as an effort-minimizing machine, will yield stronger explanatory theories than models of action that presume that actors weigh and assess alternative strategies for achieving outcomes. The discussion focuses on the simple heuristics that people use in their everyday lives. Goldstein shows how their different heuristics lead to different modes of inference, and why some heuristics fare better in some contexts than others. Key factors that determine whether a heuristic will be successful, from cue validity to network structure, are discussed, as are the conditions that give rise to actors' switching heuristics.

The first five chapters of this second part can be seen to focus most attention on explanations of action that are ego-centered, broadly conceived. Ego-centered explanations of actions typically refer to reasons, heuristics, emotions, or other mental states that explain why individuals do what they do in a given social situation. This is in contrast to alter-centered explanations, that primarily focus on causes that center on the actions of others. The next three chapters consider such alter-focused explanations. Of course, as all eight chapters reveal, ego- and alter-centered explanations are not mutually exclusive, and explanation is often best achieved by considering both frameworks simultaneously.

Diego Gambetta discusses *signaling* theory in Chapter 8. First, Gambetta cautions against promiscuous use of the idea of signaling, often introduced to account for actions not directly beneficial to actors—and thus deployed to explain too much. Showing that careful design of empirical studies that allows for the incorporation of signal cost and benefit is possible, Gambetta reveals how signaling theory provides a robust analytic framework for accounting for behaviors otherwise seen as irrational, from spending habits to the actions of cab drivers, prisoners, and others in complex and uncertain social contexts.

Jon Elster considers *norms* and their relationship to action in the next chapter, where he distinguishes between social and moral norms and other quasi-moral and legal norms. He defines social norms as non-outcome-oriented injunctions to act or to abstain from acting, sustained by the sanctions that others apply to norm violators. Elster suggests that avoidance of shame plays an important role in this context.

In the final chapter of this first part of the book, on *trust*, Cook and Gerbasi focus on the role trust plays as a determinant of cooperative behavior, and the conditions under which trust is a key element in our understanding of action. Cook and Gerbasi note that, like signaling, trust as a foundation for action has been 'oversold,' and that trust is just one mechanism of many for motivating cooperation—and hence inducing social order. Here they discuss how trust intercalates in formal control mechanisms, and whether trust substitutes, undermines, or supports such mechanisms. Of deep interest are the macro-level consequences of trust, especially the oft-noted decrease in trust (of persons and institutions).

1.5.2 Dynamic processes

In Part III, fifteen chapters consider dynamic processes that generate characteristic features of social structure, all of which build from elements of the basic cogs and wheels identified in Part II. Each chapter covers a vast terrain, from segregation to status, from matching to diffusion, and while each one serves to introduce readers to core issues in these subdisciplines, the central focus is on demonstration of an analytical approach to making sense of dynamics. In the first chapter Macy and Flache provide an introduction to *agent-based modeling in the social sciences*. The central intuition is that social order is built up from the unscripted actions of individual agents who constitute the social system and act in relation to others, and their actions. Macy and Flache show how an agent-based computational approach (ABC) can reveal how 'if everyone is flying by the seat of their pants, social order is possible.'

Bruch and Mare investigate *segregation dynamics*, with a special focus on the relationship between identity-based individual choices and the constraints on those choices due to others' identity-based choices. They describe various mechanisms likely to be at work and derive how they are likely to influence the extent of segregation.

Biggs focuses his lens on *self-fulfilling processes*; that is, processes in which actors, 'mistakenly think that their belief follows reality when in fact their belief creates it' (p. 299). As an unintended consequence actors thereby make an initially false belief come true.

Salganik and Watts, building on experimental studies of *social influence*, in turn explain why some cultural goods (novels, songs, movies, and so on) turn out to be successful, whereas others with equivalent attributes fail to sell, why successes are often wildly successful, and those responsible for producing such blockbusters (such as this book) have absolutely no ability to predict whether or not they will be successful.

Åberg also focuses on social influence, but her approach is nonexperimental and she is concerned with the *contagiousness of divorce*. She shows how divorces among co-workers influence individuals' divorce risks, and she reveals important gender differences in social influence.

Using an agent-based simulation approach, Stovel and Fountain focus on *matching* processes, specifically two-sided matching contexts such as marriage and job markets. Both are central for understanding macro-level social inequality and segregation outcomes in which variation in preferences and information affects the timing of matches, the sequencing of matches, and ultimately social-structural outcomes (for example extreme segregation) in the context of different network structures through which information about jobs, partners, etc. diffuses.

In the next chapter, on *collective action*, Baldassarri shifts away from traditional foci and, in an attempt to develop new links between the empirical research on movements and the analytical literature on collective action, attends to the role of social interactions and interpersonal-influence dynamics (especially dynamics relevant for polarization) in shaping collective identities and interests—that is, the core of the problem of collective action.

Conditional-choice dynamics are explored in the next chapter, by Rolfe, where the focus is on identifying model frameworks for the analysis of threshold processes in which initial states and conditional-decision rules generate observed outcomes. Attention is devoted to the ways in which outcomes are shaped by differing interaction behaviors, the location of key actors, and network size (among other factors).

In almost every chapter networks and diffusion have been central concerns; Moody attacks both *network dynamics* and diffusion directly. He examines models for how networks evolve and discusses why network-evolution dynamics matter for diffusion. The central focus concerns how the timing of relations shapes diffusion across networks by introducing switches in pathways across which goods of various sorts—ideas, diseases, beliefs, and so on—can flow.

Threshold models of social influence are taken up directly in the next chapter, where Watts and Dodds explore the consequences of simple heuristics in the context of social influence on collective decision-making processes and demonstrate how the structure of influence networks shapes the roles of individual actors (prominent or not) in the generation of collective behavior, including wild cascades of influence.

Time is the focus of the next chapter, where Winship explores *scheduling* dynamics. Noting that scheduling conflicts arise from the simple fact that if one thing is scheduled at a specific time (and place) another cannot be, Winship explores why such scheduling conflicts exist and why they are often enormously difficult to resolve. He then turns to the macro-level social outcomes arising from such conflicts, focusing attention on hierarchy, segregation, and boundary-maintenance dynamics.

In a similar manner, Feld and Grofman focus on *homophily*, but instead of simply arguing that homophily is a fixed preference (persons prefer to flock with similar persons), they show that characteristic features of social structure—the fact of multiple foci of activity—induce network autocorrelation more than expected, while at the same time providing a balance against dynamics inducing pure segregation.

Status and *dominance hierarchies* are the focus of the next two chapters. Podolny and Lynn highlight status dynamics grounded in tangible constraints and opportunities available to actors (in contrast to conceptualizations of status as a property of individuals). Similarly, Chase and Lundquist propose an array of new models (from observation of dynamics amongst animals) for understanding the generation of dominance hierarchies that explicitly reject the idea that positions achieved in hierarchies arise from, or can be linked to, characteristics of individuals.

The final chapter of this section considers *conflict* and action. Here Kalyvas focuses on the causes and consequences of interpersonal and group conflict, with special attention to the microfoundations of conflict and peace; specifically, the role of individual preferences and actions in producing conflict and the role of conflict in shaping preferences, identity, and actions.

1.5.3 Perspectives from other fields and approaches

As noted earlier, it is our hope that the analytical-sociology framework will emerge as the central template for a renewed sociology for the twenty-first century. That at present most analytical sociologists arise from the social-network and/or mathematical- and computational-modeling traditions, while not accidental, does not mean that future work will be tied as tightly to these methods. The next five chapters, written by leading experts in their fields (none of whom would necessarily identify themselves as an analytical sociologist) consider how surveys, ethnography, historical sociology, game theory, and experimental economics currently are, or could be, organized to relate to the research program described in the other chapters that comprise this volume. At the same time, each author also considers how an analytical approach could drive, and fits well with, the leading edges of their research traditions. In many respects, these five chapters collectively point to the future of analytical sociology and begin to answer the most critical question: Where do we go from here?

The first two chapters consider theoretical approaches more often thought to be akin to the analytical-sociological viewpoint, game theory and experimental economics. Breen's discussion of *game theory* shows how it can be simultaneously deployed as a tool for framing questions and for formal analytical investigation of the relationship between micro-level decisions and macro-level outcomes, and suggests that evolutionary game theory may provide an especially fecund tool for sociologists. Bohnet considers *experiments* in the lab and field that provide a framework for the study of how norms operating at the micro level can be causally linked to macro level outcomes.

The final three chapters focus in turn on surveys, ethnography, and historical sociology. Hannah Brückner first considers *surveys*, as a research-design strategy extremely well suited to allow researchers to reveal complex mechanisms at play in social life. Here Brückner shows, for example, how surveys can be used to determine motivations of actors, even motivations not seen by the respondents themselves. Likewise, Vaughan suggests that developments in *analytical ethnography* fit nicely with the goals of analytical sociology, as both focus on mechanism-based explanations of observed outcomes, thus bridging the micro and macro levels of analysis. In a similar vein, Barkey carefully investigates the use of different methods employed in *historical sociology* through which historical macro social outcomes are analyzed—comparative, institutional, relational, and cultural—and considers the enduring tension revealed by the meso-level structures that often shape outcomes. In all three chapters, new analyses and new strategies are proposed as exemplary models for historical, ethnographic, and survey-based analytical sociology.

Notes

1. The focus on actors and actions suggests to some that analytical sociology is a variant of rational-choice theory. This is not the case, however. Although some analytical sociologists are rational-choice theorists, most are not.

2. As an example of this see the special issue of *Studies in History and Philosophy of Science Part C: Studies in History and Philosophy of Biological and Biomedical Sciences*, 36 (2) (June 2005).

3. Examining all articles published in the two leading sociology journals, *American Journal of Sociology*, for the years 1895–2001, and *American Sociological Review*, for the years 1936–2004, one finds only 40 articles which refer to 'scientific law(s),' 'social law(s),' 'covering law(s),' and the like in their titles or abstracts, and only 8 of these were published after 1950.

4. A property here is broadly defined to also include relevant relational properties of the entities.

5. This characterization builds in part on Sober (1984) and Darden and Cain (1989).

6. As far as the third item is concerned it often is essential to further distinguish between learning-by-doing processes and evolutionary processes where the number of 'offspring' depends upon the properties of their b-values.

7. See the chapter by Hedström and Udehn for a discussion of Merton's form of structural individualism, Coleman (1986) for a programmatic statement of his form of structural individualism, and Roemer (1986) for examples of analytical Marxism.

8. In the philosophical literature on the mind–body problem, mental states correspond to our macro states (**M**) and the neural or physical level corresponds to our micro level (**P**). In that literature, mental causal claims and claims that attribute causal efficacy to neural or physical processes are often seen as being in competition with each other, with the former being undercut by the latter. (Kim 2005 defends such a position.) The heart of their argument is that **M**'s causal powers cannot be anything beyond the causal powers of its supervenience base, **P**, and hence **M** is superfluous from a causal standpoint once **P** has been taken into account. Since we have no expertise in neuroscience we do not wish to comment on that literature, but we want to note that such arguments carry no force in the social sciences. In the social world we observe causal relations of the **P1**-to-**P2** kind as well as causal relations of the **M1**-to-**P2** kind, and although there may be practical difficulties involved in empirically distinguishing

between the two (see Manski 2000), both types of causation are likely to be operative in most social processes.

9. The simulations are done using the NetLogo software (see Wilensky 1997). These particular simulations are based on a 52*52 grid (torus), with 1,250 Whites and 1,250 Grays, and with a neighborhood defined as the eight squares surrounding each actor. Vacant positions are colored black.

10. Prohibitions and prescriptions governing partner choice are not unusual of course. In classificatory kinship systems in which we observe generalized exchange, marriages are prescribed with one's mother's mother's brother's daughter's daughter (or MMBDD). Under such a kinship system, for example, different clans would exchange women in a perfect cycle, preventing tendencies towards splitting and opposition within the group (see Bearman 1997).

REFERENCES

BEARMAN, P. S. (1997), 'Generalized Exchange', *American Journal of Sociology*, 102 (5): 1383–415.

—— MOODY, J., and STOVEL, K. (2004), 'Chains of Affection: The Structure of Adolescent Romantic and Sexual Networks', *American Journal of Sociology*, 110: 44–91.

BECHTEL, W., and RICHARDSON, R. C. (1993), *Discovering Complexity: Decomposition and Localization as Strategies in Scientific Research* (Princeton, N.J.: Princeton University Press).

BUNGE, M. A. (1997), 'Mechanism and Explanation', *Philosophy of the Social Sciences*, 27: 410–65.

COLEMAN, J. S. (1986), 'Social Theory, Social Research, and a Theory of Action', *American Journal of Sociology*, 91: 1309–35.

DARDEN, L., and CAIN, J. A. (1989), 'Selection Type Theories', *Philosophy of Science*, 56: 106–29.

ELSTER, J. (1982), 'Marxism, Functionalism and Game Theory: The Case for Methodological Individualism', *Theory and Society*, 11: 453–82.

—— (1989), *Nuts and Bolts for the Social Sciences* (Cambridge: Cambridge University Press).

—— (1999), *Alchemies of the Mind: Rationality and the Emotions* (Cambridge: Cambridge University Press).

EPSTEIN, J. M. (2006), *Generative Social Science: Studies in Agent-Based Computational Modeling* (Princeton, N.J.: Princeton University Press).

GRANOVETTER, M. S. (1978), 'Threshold Models of Collective Behavior', *American Journal of Sociology*, 83: 1420–43.

HANNAN, M. T., and FREEMAN, J. (1989), *Organizational Ecology* (Cambridge, Mass.: Harvard University Press).

HEDSTRÖM, P. (1994), 'Contagious Collectivities: On the Spatial Diffusion of Swedish Trade Unions, 1890–1940', *American Journal of Sociology*, 99: 1157–79.

—— (2005), *Dissecting the Social: On the Principles of Analytical Sociology* (Cambridge: Cambridge University Press).

—— and Swedberg, R. (1998), 'Social Mechanisms: An Introductory Essay', in P. Hedström and R. Swedberg (eds.), *Social Mechanisms: An Analytical Approach to Social Theory* (Cambridge: Cambridge University Press), 1–31.

HEMPEL, C. G. (1965), *Aspects of Scientific Explanation* (New York: Free Press).

KIM, J. (2005), *Physicalism, or Something Near Enough* (Princeton, N.J.: Princeton University Press).

KITCHER, P. (1981), 'Explanatory Unification', *Philosophy of Science*, 48: 507–31.

MACHAMER, P., DARDEN, L., and CRAVER, C. F. (2000), 'Thinking About Mechanisms', *Philosophy of Science*, 67: 1–25.

MAHONEY, J. (2001), 'Beyond Correlational Analysis: Recent Innovations in Theory and Method', *Sociological Forum*, 16: 575–93.

MANSKI, C. F. (2000), 'Economic Analysis of Social Interactions', *Journal of Economic Perspectives*, 14: 115–36.

MERTON, R. K. (1968), *Social Theory and Social Structure* (New York: Free Press).

ROEMER, J. E. (1986) (ed.), *Analytical Marxism: Studies in Marxism and Social Theory* (Cambridge: Cambridge University Press).

SCHELLING, T. C. (1978), *Micromotives and Macrobehavior* (New York: Norton).

SKRYMS, B. (1996), *Evolution of the Social Contract* (Cambridge: Cambridge University Press).

SOBER, E. (1984), *The Nature of Selection* (Cambridge, Mass.: MIT Press).

STINCHCOMBE, A. L. (1991), 'The Conditions of Fruitfulness of Theorizing About Mechanisms in Social Science', *Philosophy of the Social Sciences*, 21: 367–88.

STRANG, D., and SOULE, S. A. (1998), 'Diffusion in Organizations and Social Movements: From Hybrid Corn to Poison Pills', *Annual Review of Sociology*, 24: 265–90.

UDEHN, L. (2001), *Methodological Individualism: Background, History and Meaning* (London: Routledge).

WATKINS, J. W. N. (1957), 'Historical Explanation in the Social Sciences', *British Journal for the Philosophy of Science*, 8: 104–17.

WHITE, H. C. (1970), *Chains of Opportunity: System Models of Mobility in Organizations* (Cambridge, Mass.: Harvard University Press).

WILENSKY, U. (1997), *NetLogo Segregation Model* (Evanston, Ill.: Center for Connected Learning and Computer-based Modeling, Northwestern University).

CHAPTER 2

....

ANALYTICAL SOCIOLOGY AND THEORIES OF THE MIDDLE RANGE*

....

PETER HEDSTRÖM

LARS UDEHN

INTRODUCTION

....

THE theories found in this book are contemporary incarnations of Robert
K. Merton's notion of middle-range theory (1968*b*: ch. 2). In this chapter we discuss
the defining characteristics of such theories and we use some of Merton's own
theories to exemplify what this type of theory is all about. The chapter is written in
a Mertonian spirit. It is not a contribution to the history of ideas but a contribution
to the systematics of sociological theory (Merton 1968*b*: ch. 1). We engage with Merton, because many of his ideas and insights are of lasting importance to analytical
sociology and because we want to give credit to those upon whose shoulders we
stand.

* We wish to thank Delia Baldassarri, Charles Crothers, Uskali Mäki, Richard Swedberg, Petri
Ylikoski, Hans Zetteberg, and Harriet Zuckerman for their useful comments and information.

Merton was one of the giants of twentieth-century sociology. He wrote with considerable depth and knowledge on a wide range of topics, including bureaucracy, deviance, mass communications, professions, social stratification, and, most extensively, on the sociology of science. He was exceptionally erudite and attached much importance to the consolidation and codification of existing sociological theories (Merton 1948: 166; 1957b: 10–16; 1968b: 69–72), but he also had a theoretical agenda of his own and this agenda has much in common with that of contemporary analytical sociology (cf. Geels 2007: 634).[1]

At the most basic level, Merton and contemporary analytical sociologists agree on the importance of clearly distinguishing sociological theory from the history of ideas:

> Schools of medicine do not confuse the history of medicine with current theory, nor do departments of biology identify the history of biology with the viable theory now employed in guiding and interpreting research. Once said, this seems so obvious as to be embarrassing. Yet the extraordinary fact is that in sociology, this distinction between the history of theory and current viable theory has not caught hold.
>
> (Merton 1948: 165)[2]

Analytical sociologists also share Merton's vision of middle-range theory as the type of theory which sociology should aim for, his emphasis on the importance of tightly linking micro and macro levels to one another, and his belief in the important role of endogenous social dynamics.

The analytical side of Merton is rarely seen in standard textbook accounts of his scholarship, however. There we instead find Merton the functionalist or Merton the structural functionalist, and almost always in the company of Parsons (see Parsons 1975: 67; Sztompka 1986: 126–43). Although the image of Merton as a functionalist is widespread, he was never a full-fledged functionalist, and he was critical of earlier versions of functionalism, Parsons's included (Crothers 1987: 70–8).[3] The view of Merton as a structuralist (e.g. Stinchcombe 1975; Sztompka 1986: 143–50) is more in line with his actual contributions to sociological theory, but, as will be discussed in more detail below, Merton's form of structuralism is similar to what we today would refer to as 'structural individualism' (Udehn 2001: 318–19), a doctrine which also is at the heart of analytical sociology (see Hedström 2005: 5).

The chapter is organized as follows. We start by explaining what Merton had in mind with his notion of middle-range theory and we seek to clarify certain aspects of such theories that were not made entirely clear in Merton's own writings. Thereafter we turn to the importance of linking micro and macro levels to one another. We discuss some of Merton's work on the macro-to-micro link and the importance he attached to unanticipated outcomes of individual action. Thereafter we discuss his theories of self-fulfilling prophecies and Matthew effects, which illustrate the importance of time and dynamic endogenous processes. These theories are important in their own right, but they also are important as ideal examples of what analytical sociological theory is all about; that is, clear and precise theories which detail the process through which individuals in interaction with one another bring about the social facts to be explained. We conclude by briefly discussing different kinds of middle-range theories and we emphasize the importance of developing theories with sufficient causal depth.

2.1 MIDDLE-RANGE THEORY

The idea of middle-range theory generally is seen as one of Merton's most important contributions to sociology (see Clark 1990: 17). We agree, but note that it is not one of his most precisely articulated ideas (see Boudon 1991: 519–20). Merton used the notion of middle-range theory mainly in a negative way, to distance himself from grand theory, on the one hand, and raw empiricism on the other (see Geels 2007: 629), but the explicit definitions he provided were rather vague.[4]

Merton introduced the idea of middle-range theory in a critical comment on a paper by Parsons. In this comment he objected to Parsons's belief in the possibility of creating a sociological *theory*, in the singular, and the corollary belief that it would be possible to develop a theory that would be general enough to treat *all phenomena* of interest to sociology. 'Sociology will advance in the degree that the major concern is with developing theories adequate to limited ranges of phenomena and it will be hampered if attention is centered on theory in the large' (Merton 1948: 165–6).

The specific term 'theories of the middle range' was introduced in the first edition of *Social Theory and Social Structure* (1949: 5), but Merton's most extensive discussion is found in the third edition, from 1968. That is also where his most precise characterization of theories of the middle range is found. They are

> theories that lie between the minor but necessary working hypotheses that evolve in abundance during day-to-day research and the all-inclusive systematic efforts to develop a unified theory that will explain all the observed uniformities of social behavior, social organization and social change.   (Merton 1968b: 39)

Merton did not discuss in detail the distinction between everyday working hypotheses and middle-range theory. He simply stated that theories of the middle-range 'transcend sheer description or empirical generalization' (1968b: 68) and that 'theory is more than a mere empirical generalization—an isolated proposition summarizing observed uniformities of relationships between two or more variables. A theory comprises a set of assumptions from which empirical generalizations have themselves been derived' (1968b: 41).

Merton was more careful in characterizing the other end of the spectrum, the all-inclusive theories. He referred to them as 'total systems of sociological theory' (1968*b*: 45 ff.) and as 'master conceptual schemes' (1948: 166; 1968: 51), and he described them as 'grand' (1968*b*: 48), 'architectonic' (1948: 166; 1968*b*: 51) and 'general' (1957*a*: 108; 1963: xxx; 1968*b*: 39). The core characteristic of such theories is that they seek to encompass 'the full scope of sociological knowledge' (1968*b*: 66) and, as such, are able to explain all social phenomena (Merton 1968*b*: 39). The main examples of all-encompassing theories that Merton discussed were Parsons's theory of the social system and Marx's historical materialism (1968*b*: 68).[5]

Implicit in the notion of a 'middle-range theory' is the idea that one can order theories along a dimension called 'range' or 'scope' (see e.g. Merton 1957*a*: 108–9). The general and all-inclusive theories represent one endpoint of this dimension. Merton's notion of a general and all-encompassing theory is somewhat ambiguous, however, and in order to make the notion of explanatory middle-range theory more precise, some basic distinctions need to be introduced.

Any explanation can be said to consist of two types of components: (1) an *explanandum* or that which is to be explained, and (2) an *explanans* or that which is to explain the explanandum. When discussing different types of explanans, Mäki (1992) introduced the notion of *isolation*.[6] Isolation is a certain kind of abstraction, which consists in focusing attention on certain explanatory factors at the expense of others. For example, if the set of possible explanatory factors consists of {a,b,c,d} and we focus exclusively on {a,b} we have performed an isolation. Using Mäki's terminology, the included set {a,b} is referred to as the *isolated field* and the excluded set {c,d} as the *excluded field*. One important dimension distinguishing different types of theories from one another is the size of the isolated field in relation to the excluded field. Some theories focus attention on a narrow set of explanatory factors while others seek a more comprehensive account.

A similar set-based distinction can be made with reference to the explanandum. Some theories explain highly specific and particularistic phenomena while others explain a wide range of phenomena (or types of phenomena). The variation along this dimension is not a matter of isolation in Mäki's sense of the term, but concerns how *general* the theory is. The larger the set of phenomena or types of phenomena a theory explains, the more general it is. If theory A explains the set {p,q,r,s} and theory B explains the set {r,s}, theory A is more general than theory B. It follows from this that theories can be compared, with respect to generality, only if the phenomena they explain are of the same type and related as set and subset. A theory of groups is more general than a theory of small groups, or of reference groups. Generality stands in an inverse relation to specificity. Unless the phenomena explained by a theory are exactly alike, the more general a theory is the less specific it has to be because one cannot be as specific about large sets of phenomena as about small sets, or about particulars.

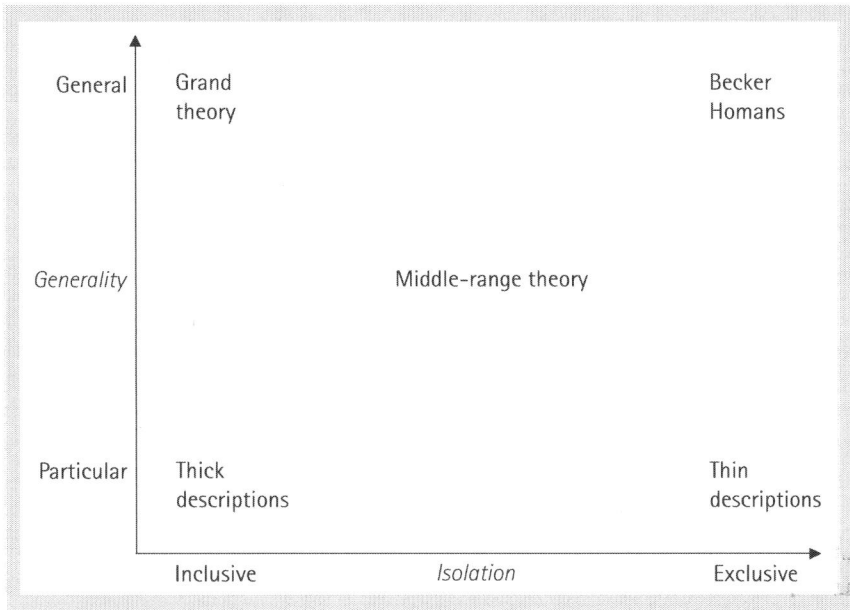

Fig. 2.1 Generality, isolation, and the defining characteristics of middle-range theories

In order to bring to the fore the defining characteristics of middle-range theory, it is necessary to take both of these dimensions into account (see Fig. 2.1). The horizontal dimension in the figure refers to the explanans and the degree of isolation, while the vertical dimension refers to the explanandum and the generality of the theory. The two dimensions are orthogonal to one another in the sense that at each level of generality theories can differ from one another in terms of their degree of isolation.

At the top of the figure we find the most general type of theories, which explain or claim to explain[7] all or virtually all phenomena of interest to sociology. Grand theory as traditionally understood and as exemplified by Parsons (1951) and more contemporary versions such as Luhmann (1995) differ from theories such as Gary Becker's rational-choice approach (1976) and George Homans's behaviorist approach (1974), not in terms of how general they are but in terms of their extent of isolation. While the explanans of the theories in the upper left-hand corner are all-inclusive and refer to society as a whole, the type of theories represented by Homans and Becker are based on an extremely small set of explanatory factors. As Becker (1976: 5) famously expressed it: 'The combined assumptions of maximizing behavior, market equilibrium, and stable preferences, used relentlessly and unflinchingly, form the heart of the economic approach.' And in Homans's case: 'the principles of behavioral psychology are the general propositions we use, whether implicitly or explicitly, in explaining all social phenomena' ([1969] 1987: 204).

At the bottom of the figure one might have expected to find historical accounts seeking to explain unique phenomenon or events, but Merton (like us) was concerned with sociology, and in sociology the opposites of general theories are 'empirical generalizations' and 'sheer descriptions.' Borrowing the terminology of Clifford Geertz (1973: ch. 1), we refer to the lower-left-hand region as 'thick descriptions' and the lower right-hand region as 'thin descriptions.' In order to clarify the distinction between these two types of descriptions, we can use the example of a run on a bank. During any specific run on a bank, many particular and unique events take place. One possibility would be to describe in detail the set of events that led to the downfall of this particular bank. This would be an example of a 'thin' descriptive account. By gradually including more information on the social, cultural, and economic environments in which the bank was embedded, 'thicker' descriptive accounts would be arrived at which may increase our understanding of why events unfolded as they did in this particular case.[8] Mainstream quantitative research as exemplified by a standard-regression model provides a description of how some behavior or other trait as measured by the dependent variable of the regression equation is related to a set of independent variables representing other traits characterizing a specific population at a specific point in time. It is located at the particularistic end of the generality dimension and its position along the horizontal dimension depends on the number and types of covariates included in the model.

The type of theories that Merton had in mind with his notion of middle-range theory is located in between the extremes represented by the four corners of this figure.[9] As far as the vertical, explanandum-related dimension is concerned, it was not detailed descriptions of particular events, processes, or patterns of association that Merton had in mind but theories 'sufficiently abstract to deal with differing spheres of social behavior and social structure, so that they transcend sheer description and empirical generalization' (Merton 1968b: 68).

He also emphasized that it would be unwise and unproductive to aim for the most general kind of theory: 'Some sociologists still write as though they expect, here and now, formulation of *the* general sociological theory... This I take to be a premature and apocalyptic belief. We are not ready. Not enough preparatory work has been done' (Merton 1968b: 45). 'Note how few, how scattered, and how unimpressive are the specific sociological hypotheses which are *derived* from a master conceptual scheme... We have many concepts but fewer confirmed theories; many points of view, but few theorems; many "approaches" but few arrivals' (Merton 1968b: 51–2).[10]

As far as the horizontal, explanans-related dimension is concerned, Merton did not have in mind theories that seek to take into account all explanatory factors that possibly could have contributed to the outcome to be explained. Although he did not use the vocabulary of isolated and excluded fields, he implicitly advocated the use of the method of isolation and argued that useful theories should focus on certain elements believed to be important and intentionally ignore others. The type of explanations thereby arrived at provide partial explanations of 'delimited aspects of social phenomena' (1968*b*: 39–40; see also Merton 1957*a*: 110; 1963: xxxiv). As will be discussed in more detail below, his theories of self-fulfilling prophecies and Matthew effects are ideal examples of this theoretical strategy. They isolate a few explanatory factors which explain important but delimited aspects of the outcomes to be explained. They do not bore the reader by trying to retell the causal story in minute detail; instead they seek to highlight the heart of the story.

Although Merton was an advocate of simple and abstract theory, he meant that the method of isolation should be used with caution and moderation, and he did not think highly of fundamentalist theories like those of Becker and Homans: 'My prime theoretical aversion is to any extreme sociological, economic, or psychological reductionism that claims to account uniquely and exhaustively for patterns of social behavior and social structure' (Merton 1994: 10).

What Merton had in mind with his notion of middle-range theory thus were theories occupying the middle regions of the two-dimensional space depicted in Figure 2.1.[11] That is to say, a clear, precise, and simple type of theory which can be used for partially explaining a range of different phenomena, but which makes no pretense of being able to explain all social phenomena, and which is not founded upon any form of extreme reductionism in terms of its explanans. It is a vision of sociological theory as a toolbox of semigeneral theories each of which is adequate for explaining a limited range or type of phenomena. In this sense his vision has more in common with the type of theories found in the life sciences than those found in the physical sciences. Contemporary biologists, for example, do not seek to develop general law-like theory but aim at identifying middle-range theory in Merton's sense of the term. As Francis Crick, who shared the Nobel Prize in 1962 for his discovery of the molecular structure of DNA, expressed it: 'What is found in biology is *mechanisms*, mechanisms built with chemical components and that are often modified by other, later, mechanisms added to the earlier ones' (1989: 138).

We have focused, so far, on the meaning of 'middle-range', but avoided the meaning of 'theory.' Merton's understanding of this term was in line with the orthodoxy of the times (see e.g. Merton 1945: 469–72; 1968*b*: 150–3). A theory, according to this orthodox view, is an axiomatic, or hypothetico-deductive, system of laws of differing generality, as suggested by analytical philosophers, such as Popper, Hempel, and Nagel, and as introduced in sociology by Zetterberg ([1954] 1965) and Homans (1967).

The paucity of universal laws in the social sciences has created widespread doubts about the fertility of this approach to theory and explanation (Giddens 1984: xviii–xx; Elster 1999: 1–2; Hedström 2005: 15 ff.). Although Merton never explicitly discussed what we today would refer to as mechanism-based explanations, from his concrete scientific work one gets the sense that he viewed sociological theories as accounts of mechanisms rather than as general axiomatic systems.[12]

In the concluding section of this chapter we will briefly discuss different types of middle-range theories. There is considerable variation between different middle-range theories in terms of their causal depth. Some are mere black-box accounts based on associations between variables or events, while others explicate in detail the social cogs and wheels through which the type of social phenomena to be explained typically are brought about. As the various chapters of this volume testify to, it is this latter type of middle-range theory that contemporary analytical sociology is all about.

2.2 MICRO–MACRO RELATIONS

It has been argued by a number of commentators, such as Stinchcombe (1975), Sztompka (1986: chs. 5–8; 1990), Crothers 1987 (1987: ch. 5), and Blau (1990: 144 ff.), that Merton, for all his skepticism towards grand theoretical systems, had a general, or systematic, theory of society himself. These reconstructions of Merton's work differ in numerous respects from one another, but they all agree that the links between macro and micro were central to Merton: 'sociology must deal successively with micro- and macro-level phenomena' and develop 'concepts, methods, and data for linking micro- and macro-analysis' (Merton 1975: 34). We agree that it is possible to detect a general theoretical framework of this kind in Merton's work, but it is not a 'theory' in his own (or our) sense of the term; it is a 'general orientation' and, as such, 'a preliminary to theory rather than theory itself' (Merton 1963: xxiv).

Merton's general orientation to sociology has much in common with James Coleman's well-known approach (1986, 1990: 6 ff.), which insists that all theories about macrophenomena must have firm microfoundations in the form of a theory of purposive action (see Fig. 2.2). It is a form of structural individualism, which differs from traditional methodological individualism in emphasizing the explanatory importance of social structures (see Udehn 2001). In the case of Merton, we have social structures constraining individuals' action and cultural environments shaping their desires and beliefs (arrow 2), and we have individuals choosing their preferred courses of action among the feasible alternatives (arrow 3), and various intended and unintended outcomes of these actions (arrow 4).

From an individual's action, the lower right-hand corner of Figure 2.2, one can move in two directions. One can move backwards to the individual's orientation to action and its social causes, or one can move forwards and examine the intended

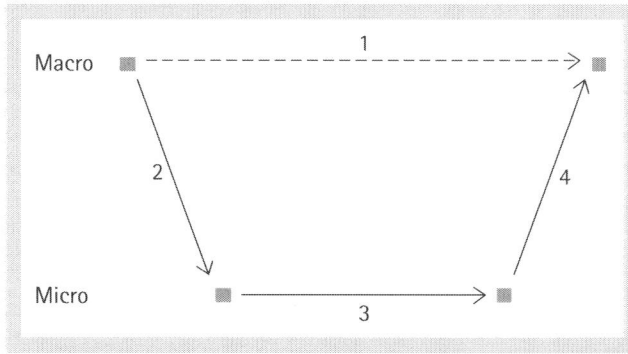

Fig. 2.2 Coleman's micro–macro scheme

and unintended consequences of the action. Existing reconstructions of Merton's general orientation have mainly looked backwards and emphasized the structural aspects of his work. This is but one side of Merton, however, the other side being his concern with the micro-to-macro link and the often unintended consequences of individual action (see Merton 1936).

2.2.1 Macro-to-micro linkages

Merton's idea of *opportunity structure* is central to his analysis of the macro-to-micro link. His first use of this idea can be found in his 1938 article on 'Social Structure and Anomie,' but it was not fully developed until the 1950s (Merton 1995: 24 ff.).[13] Merton uses the concept of 'opportunity' in the common sense of individuals' access to the means for reaching their goals. The related concept of 'opportunity structure' is introduced to focus attention on the sociologically important fact that there are differences in opportunities between social strata (see Merton 1957b: 170–6, 192–4). It is defined as '*differential access to opportunities among those variously located in the social structure*' (Merton 1995: 6).

'Opportunity' is a central concept, not only in Merton's work, but even more so in analytical sociology, where individuals are seen as making choices within constraints and according to their desires, beliefs, and opportunities.[14] Elster (1979: 113) has suggested a model in which action can be seen as the end result of two filtering processes (see Fig. 2.3). The first filter is the structural constraints, which delimit the number of 'abstractly' possible actions to the set of feasible actions. If the set of feasible actions contains only one single action, we have a case of strong situational determinism, also called a 'single-exit' situation (Latsis 1972: 207 ff.). In this limiting case, theoretical orientations as diverse as rational choice and structuralism coincide with one another (Elster 1979: 113–15; Satz and Ferejohn 1994: 77 ff.). If the opportunity set contains more than one alternative, the individual has a choice to

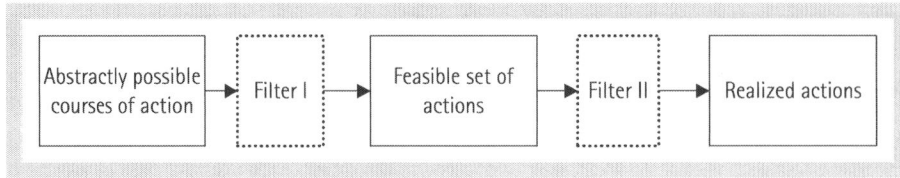

Fig. 2.3 Jon Elster's two–filter model

make, and then the second filter comes into operation. This second filter consists of mechanisms which single out which member of the feasible set of actions is to be realized.[15]

Merton did not believe that strong situational determinism is the normal case. The actions of individuals are usually constrained, but not determined, by the structures in which they are embedded. Individuals, therefore, make choices, and, as emphasized by Stinchcombe, 'the core process that Merton conceives as central to social structure is *the choice between socially structured alternatives*' (1975: 12).

Merton's theory of social structure and anomie is an example of a situational mechanism linking macro to micro (see Merton 1938; 1949: ch. 4; 1957*b*: chs. 4 and 5; 1995). It is an attempt to explain behavior that deviates from dominant social norms and values. It starts at the macro level with identifying social and cultural properties that may lead to high levels of deviance, especially for groups in the lower strata of society. Merton does not stay at the macro level, however; nor does he treat social structure as only constraining. Within the constraints there are opportunities, and this implies that individuals make choices (Merton 1995: 17), and the preferences, or desires, of individuals are shaped, in part at least, by the prevailing cultural norms of society.

Merton's theory of anomie is one part of his more general theory of reference groups. According to conventional sociological wisdom, the source of our desires, beliefs, identities, self-images, satisfaction levels, etc. is in other people. We are influenced by other people and we tend to compare our own situation with that of others. The point of departure in Merton's writings on reference groups is the idea of relative deprivation as used by Samuel Stouffer et al. in *The American Soldier* (1949; see Merton 1957*b*: 225). *The American Soldier* is most famous for having shown that soldiers with low opportunities for promotion had a more favorable opinion towards these opportunities than soldiers with high promotion opportunities (Stouffer et al. 1949: i. 250 ff.; Merton 1957*b*: 236). Belonging to a group with a high promotion rate creates excessive hopes and increases the risk that they might be dashed. This shows how a macro property, the promotion rate, influences micro-level properties such as individual sentiments and actions, and thereby it represents a macro-to-micro link.

2.2.2 Micro-to-macro linkages

As mentioned above, the micro-to-macro link refers to the link between individual actions and the collective outcomes that these actions bring about. Merton's first treatment of this theme is found in his essay 'The Unanticipated Consequences of Purposive Social Action' (1936). This essay contains numerous ideas that are central for understanding the micro-to-macro link, and it is a nice example of Merton the analytical sociologist. In this essay he dissects an important process and identifies various conditions under which unanticipated consequences are likely to be important (see Fig. 2.4).

Merton starts by making a distinction between unintentional 'behavior' and purposeful 'action' (1936: 895). An example used by Gilbert Ryle (1968: 1) can be used to pinpoint the difference between these two categories: If a person's eyelids contract because of an involuntary twitch, it is an example of unintentional behavior, but if the same individual intentionally contracts her eyelids to signal something to another person, it is an example of an action. From the bodily movement as such it would not be possible to know whether it was a twitch or a wink; the distinction hinges on whether it was intentionally brought about or not.

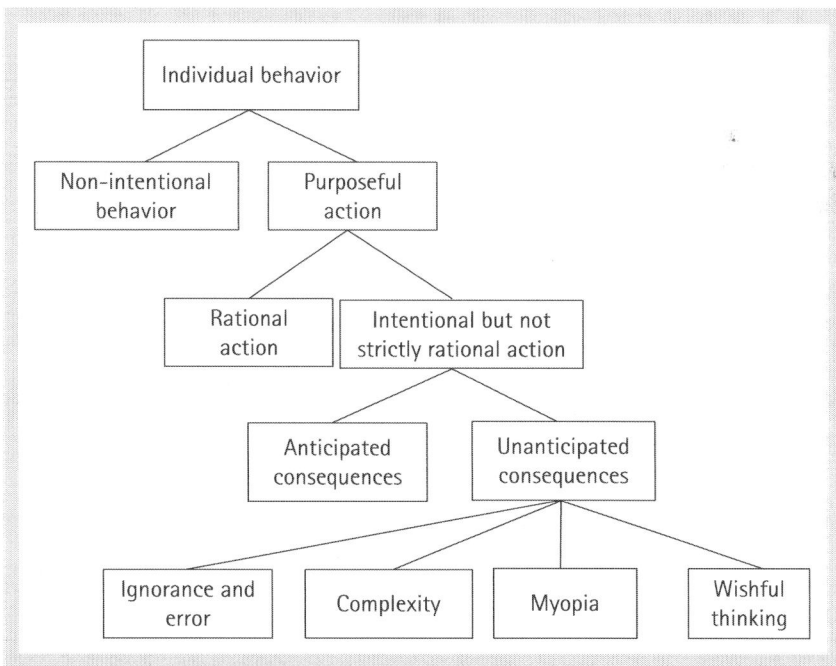

Fig. 2.4 Analytical distinctions introduced in Merton's analysis of the unanticipated consequences of social action

Merton fully appreciated the importance of clearly distinguishing between rational action and purposeful or intentional action: 'it must not be inferred that purposive action implies "rationality" of human action (that persons always use the objectively most adequate means for the attainment of their end)' (1936: 896). 'It is as much a fallacious assumption to hold that interested action in fact necessarily entails a rational calculation of the elements of the situation as to deny rationality any and all influence over such conduct' (1936: 902).

The next distinction introduced by Merton is the core distinction between anticipated and unanticipated consequences. Since an analyst cannot know for sure the purpose that motivates the action of another individual, this makes it difficult for the analyst to distinguish between anticipated and unanticipated consequences. Merton did not think that these difficulties were insurmountable, however:

> Ultimately, the final test is this: does the juxtaposition of the overt action, our general knowledge of the actor(s) and the specific situation and the inferred or avowed purpose 'make sense,' is there between these, as Weber puts it, a 'verständliche Sinnzusammenhang'? If the analyst self-consciously subjects these elements to such probing, there is substantial probability that his conclusion in respect to purpose is not too far afield in the majority of instances.   (1936: 897)

Although this form of plausibility test is crucial, we are not sure that Merton the mature scholar would have considered introspection to be 'the final test.'

The last and final set of distinctions concerns the causes or reasons for an action not resulting in the consequences which motivated it, and Merton distinguished between four different sources: (1) ignorance and error, (2) complexity, (3) myopia, and (4) wishful thinking. In the first category he included sheer ignorance on the part of the acting individual as well as true stochasticity. In the second category he included environmental elements which make the assessment of likely consequences complex and time-consuming, and he partly anticipated Simon's later work on 'satisficing' (Simon 1982): 'it is manifestly uneconomic behavior to concern ourselves with attempts to obtain knowledge for predicting the outcomes of action to such an extent that we have practically no time or energy for other pursuits' (Merton 1936: 900). The fact that decision-making is costly in terms of time and energy means that individuals often act on the basis of imperfect information and as a result their actions often bring about unexpected results.

Similarly, his discussion of myopia and wishful thinking anticipated some of Elster's later work (e.g. Elster 1979, 1983). Wishful thinking (or wish-fulfillment, as Merton called it) leads 'to a distortion of the objective situation and of the probable future courses of events; such action predicated upon "imaginary" conditions must inevitably evoke unexpected consequences' (1936: 901). And myopia, or the 'imperious immediacy of interest,' generates unanticipated consequences because an individual then is excessively concerned 'with the foreseen immediate consequences' to the neglect of 'further or other consequences of the same act' (1936: 901).[16]

Merton thus identified a range of factors which act as wedges between individual intentions and actual outcomes. The existence of such wedges did not make him abandon the type of explanatory framework described in Figure 2.2, however, because only by grounding the macro in the purposeful actions of individuals is it possible to understand why we observe the macro-level outcomes we observe.

2.3 SOCIAL DYNAMICS

So far we have mainly focused on static relations between different kinds of properties and events. Social processes unfold over time, however, and, particularly when individuals' actions in part depend upon what others do, small and seemingly unimportant differences can influence the course of development in unexpected ways. In such situations it is essential to have a theory which allows for an explicit analysis of the likely dynamics.

In some of his best and most influential work, such as his theories of self-fulfilling prophecies and Matthew effects, Merton analyzed social dynamics using the type of approach depicted in Figure 2.2, i.e. by successively linking macro and micro levels to one another. He not only identified the static cogs and wheels of the causal machinery, he also examined the dynamics that the causal machinery was likely to give rise to. In addition to being important theories in their own right, these theories, like the theories of Schelling (1978), are ideal-typical icons of what analytical sociological theory is all about.

The basic idea at the heart of Merton's theory of the self-fulfilling prophecy (1949: ch. 7) is what he referred to as the Thomas Theorem: 'If men define situations as real, they are real in their consequences' (1938: 331–2; 1968: 475; see Thomas and Thomas 1928: 572). Self-fulfilling prophecies can arise in situations characterized by a great deal of uncertainty, and, as Michael Biggs shows in his chapter in this volume, self-fulfilling prophecies are relevant for explaining a range of different types of phenomena. The common denominator in all of these cases is that individuals 'mistakenly think that their belief follows reality when in fact their belief creates it' (p. 299 below). Merton focused on the process through which an initially false belief evokes behavior that eventually makes the false belief come true. The example he used was a run on a bank. Once a rumor of insolvency gets started, some depositors are likely to withdraw their savings, acting on the principle that it is better to be safe than sorry. Their withdrawals strengthen others' beliefs that the bank is in financial difficulties, partly because the withdrawals may actually hurt the financial standing of the bank, but more importantly because the act of withdrawal in itself signals to others that something might be wrong with the bank. This produces even more withdrawals, which further strengthens the belief, and so on. By this mechanism, even an initially sound bank may go bankrupt if enough depositors withdraw their money in the (initially) false belief that the bank is insolvent.

The theory of the Matthew effect derives its name from the 'Gospel According to St Matthew':

> For unto every one that hath shall be given, and he shall have abundance: but from him that hath not shall be taken away even that which he hath.[17]

It has much in common with the theory of the self-fulfilling prophecy and it refers to a cumulative advantage process, which makes the rich richer and the poor poorer.

The Matthew effect mostly has been used for explaining reward and prestige distributions in science (see Merton 1968a; 1988), and, as detailed by Zuckerman (1998: 146),

> the Matthew Effect amplifies processes of accumulation of advantage and disadvantage. It heightens the extent of inequality in scientists' standing and the influence of their work. In the case of accumulative advantage and disadvantage, inequalities derive, at least in part, from actual differences in the extent of contribution, differences which make the reward system appear to be effective and just. In the special case of the Matthew Effect, however, such differences derive mainly from judgments scientists make which are shaped by prior experience and features of the stratification and communication systems of science, both being unrelated to reliable information about the extent and quality of contributions of the various scientists involved in these conjoint events.

The mechanism is of considerable generality, however, and has been used in a range of other domains as well. DiPrete and Eirich (2006) provide a detailed overview of its actual and potential use for explaining various stratification outcomes. Cumulative-advantage processes are important in this domain because they can lead to heightened inequalities. Ideas about Matthew effects and self-fulfilling prophecies also are at the heart of Roger Gould's theory of status hierarchies (2002). According to Gould, the hierarchical differentiation observed in most groups can be partially explained by the social nature of status: we accord a certain level of status or respect to another person *because* of the status or respect accorded to this person by others. Our status-conferring gestures are cues to others who seek guidance for their own judgments, and 'the uncertainty and subjectivity inherent in quality judgments gives rise to a self-reinforcing process in which collective adherence to socially provided assessments reproduces and thereby validates those very assessments' (Gould 2002: 1148).[18]

As an unintended by-product, the self-reinforcing nature of Matthew-like processes brings about highly skewed distribution of outcomes unless they are opposed by other countervailing processes. Merton (1988) and Zuckerman (1998)

Self-fulfilling prophecy

$$B_A \longrightarrow A_A \longrightarrow B_E \longrightarrow A_E$$

Matthew effect

$$B_A \longrightarrow A_A \longrightarrow O_E \longrightarrow A_E$$

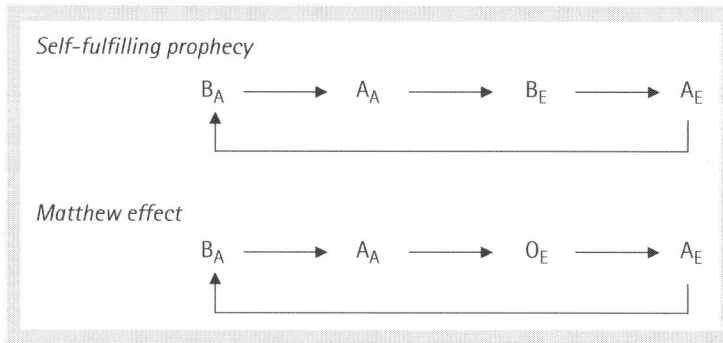

Fig. 2.5 The logic of self–fulfilling prophecies and Matthew effects. The subscripts identify the individuals in question, Ego and Alter(s), and B, A, O represents the beliefs, actions, and opportunities of the relevant individuals

discuss various concrete countervailing processes observed in the world of science, while Gould (2002) suggests a general reciprocity-based mechanism which is likely to dampen the distributional impact of the Matthew effect:

> Someone who pays less attention to you than you pay to her implicitly asserts that she is superior to you in status. If you do not respond by withdrawing your attention, you have implicitly agreed. . . . There is thus a tension between the self-reproducing character of status attributions and people's desire to have their attributions recipro-cated: the more faithfully you follow the existing status ranking in distributing your attributions, the greater the likelihood that your expressions of esteem for high-status alters will be asymmetric.   (Gould 2002: 1151)

The theory of the self-fulfilling prophecy and the theory of the Matthew effect thus have several core characteristics in common: (1) they refer to dynamic processes that (2) are operative in environments characterized by a great deal of uncertainty; (3) the collective outcomes are unintended by the individuals who bring them about; (4) the processes are driven by social interactions between individuals; and (5) the processes are endogenous and self-reinforcing. In their pure forms, they differ from one another in one important respect, however; one is belief-centered while the other is opportunity-centered (see Fig. 2.5).

The self-fulfilling prophecy has the following general argument pattern: The beliefs of one or several alters are such that they decide to perform a certain action; their actions influence ego's belief about the value of performing the act in such a way that ego also decides to act; and ego's action in turn strengthens the beliefs of others in the value of performing the act. This type of self-reinforcing and belief-centered cycle then is repeated as described above in the case of the run on a bank.

The Matthew effect is built upon a slightly different argument pattern: ego performs an action in a manner that exceeds what normally is expected; this influences others' beliefs and actions in such a way that ego's opportunities for excellent performance are further enhanced. In the context of reward distributions in science, Merton (1988: 616) expressed the core idea behind this self-reinforcing and opportunity-centered cycle as follows:

> When the scientific role performance of individuals measures up to or conspicuously exceeds the standards of a particular institution or discipline—whether this be a matter of ability or chance—there begins a process of cumulative advantage in which those individuals tend to acquire successively enlarged opportunities for advancing their work (and the rewards that go with it) even further.

These theories are icons of analytical sociology because they are clear, simple, and action-based theories which dynamically integrate micro- and macro-level phenomena and are sufficiently general to be applicable in a range of different domains. Although they are general, it is important to note that they are designed to explain delimited aspects of the social.

Concluding Remarks

Middle-range theories are 'middle' both in terms of the range of phenomena that they are intended to explain and in terms of the set of factors included in their explanans. A middle-range theory is a theory capable of partially explaining phenomena observed in different social domains, and it is a simple type of theory in the sense of being a theory which seeks to tell the heart of a causal story rather than the full story. Middle-range theories make no pretense of being able to explain all phenomena of sociological interest, and they are not founded upon any extreme form of reductionism in terms of their explanans.

As hinted at above, there is considerable heterogeneity among theories that are middle-range according to these defining characteristics, and sociologists of very different persuasions have appropriated the term for their own particular uses. In concluding this chapter, we briefly bring to the fore what from an explanatory point of view appears to be the most important characteristic distinguishing one type of middle-range theory from another.

Middle-range theories, like all explanatory theories, can be said to consist of two types of components: an explanandum and an explanans. To explain something is to provide information that justifies the claim that the explanans explains the explanandum, and middle-range theories differ from one another in the kind of information they consider sufficient for justifying such claims. In the sociological and philosophical literature one can identify information on four different kinds of relationships that have been used to justify such claims:[19]

1. causal laws;
2. statistical associations;
3. counterfactual dependencies; and
4. causal mechanisms.

The first and strongest requirement is that the relationship between the explanans and the explanandum must be an instance of a general causal law. Although this idea is most closely associated with writings of Hempel (1965), the same basic idea was formulated in the following way by John Stuart Mill: 'An individual fact is said to be explained, by pointing to its cause, that is, by stating the law or laws of causation, of which its production is an instance' (1874: 332). It is far from clear what should be meant by a 'causal law.' The traditional philosophical view is 'that laws have many or all of the following features: they are universally quantified conditional statements, describing exceptionless regularities that contain no reference to particular individuals, times, or places, contain only "purely qualitative" predicates, are confirmable by their instances, and support counterfactuals' (Woodward 2003: 167). These kinds of laws clearly are not found in the social sciences and probably not anywhere outside of basic physics, and therefore they are irrelevant from the perspective of the social sciences.

Since strict causal laws do not exist in the social sciences, many have settled for a weaker version of the same idea, that of a statistical association between the explanans and the explanandum. As Paul Lazarsfeld once expressed this idea: 'If we have a relationship between x and y; and if for any antecedent test factor the partial relationships between x and y do not disappear, then the original relationship should be called a causal one' (1955: 124–5). That is to say, if the statistical association between x (the explanans) and y (the explanandum) persists even after controlling for possible confounders, this is said to justify the claim that x explains y. The strengths and weaknesses of this approach have been discussed in detail elsewhere (see Hedström and Swedberg 1998; Hedström 2005), and we will not repeat that here. In brief, however, partial correlations and other forms of statistical associations are rarely as unequivocal and easily interpretable in causal terms as this view would seem to suggest. As Stinchcombe (1968: 13) once expressed it: 'A student who has difficulty thinking of at least three sensible explanations for any correlation that he is really interested in should probably choose another profession.' Hence, statistical associations in and of themselves rarely are sufficient to warrant explanatory claims. They must be backed by more fine-grained evidence.

The core idea behind the third alternative is that information on invariant counterfactual dependencies between the explanans and the explanandum is what warrants such claims. In James Woodward's terms, 'the explanation must enable us to see what sort of difference it would have made for the explanandum if the factors cited in the explanans had been different in various possible ways' (2003: 11). This is an improvement over the second alternative in that it properly handles cases such as the 'flagpole example' often referred to in the philosophical literature. That is, if a flagpole casts a shadow, we can explain the length of the shadow by appealing to facts such as the height of the flagpole, but from the perspective of the statistical-association alternative there is nothing that prevents us from also explaining the height of the flagpole with reference to the length of its shadow, although we all agree that that would be unintuitive. The counterfactual approach avoids this problem because an ideal intervention which changes the length of the shadow will have no effect on the length of the flagpole, while a change in the length of the flagpole will change the length of the shadow.

The fourth alternative, causal mechanisms, should not necessarily be seen as an alternative to the counterfactual approach, but rather as adding further requirements. As emphasized by Woodward (2002) and Morgan and Winship (2007) there is nothing in the counterfactual approach as such which guarantees sufficient causal depth, because perceptions of sufficient depth are discipline-specific while the counterfactual approach is not.[20] To make this point more concrete, we can return to Figure 2.2. There is nothing in the counterfactual approach which suggests that an explanation in terms of the macro-micro-macro path is preferable to the macro-to-macro path (arrow 1). As long as an intervention which changes a macro property (the explanans) invariably leads to a change in another macro property (the explanandum), a strict counterfactualist would be satisfied, although a relationship at that level is a black box which offers no information on why the properties are related to one another. In this respect the causal-mechanisms alternative differs from the counterfactual alternative in that it insists that the link between the explanans and the explanandum should be expressed in terms of the entities and activities through which the relationship is believed to have been brought about, i.e. in this case in terms of individuals and their actions. As Elster (1989: 3–4) expressed it: 'To explain an event is to give an account of why it happened. Usually...this takes the form of citing an earlier event as the cause of the event we want to explain.... [But] to cite the cause is not enough: the causal mechanism must also be provided, or at least suggested.' In order for a claim to be explanatory it is not enough to show *that* macro-level properties are systematically related to one another, it also is necessary to show *why* this is so and this we do by showing *how* the explanans is likely to have brought about the explanandum.[21]

As most clearly expressed in his theories of self-fulfilling prophecies and Matthew effects, Merton's notion of middle-range theory is built on the fourth type of link between explanans and explanandum. It represents the same vision of sociological theory as that of analytical sociology. That is to say, that there is no general sociological theory in the singular but that sociological theory consists of a toolbox of mechanism-based theories each of which is capable of partially explaining a range of phenomena observed in different social settings.

NOTES

1. Merton participated in the 1996 conference on social mechanisms which resulted in Hedström and Swedberg (1998), which in certain respects is as an early predecessor to the current volume. During this conference Merton made it clear that he viewed analytically oriented and mechanism-based theorizing as indisputably Mertonian in its spirit. As Harriet Zuckerman, who also attended the conference, recently expressed it in an email to one of us: 'It was clear to me how much in tune Bob was with the explicit effort to identify classes of mechanisms that would account for various kinds of consequences.' Similarly, in a letter to Richard Swedberg in which he discussed Coleman's work Merton drew attention to the centrality of mechanism-based theorizing in his own 'Columbia-style' sociology: 'Jim's recurrent emphasis on the importance of *specifying social mechanisms* may be another expression of "Columbia-style sociology".'

2. That this continues to be an embarrassing fact of the discipline is illustrated in a statement of Craig Calhoun, the former editor of *Sociological Theory*, where he notes that the submissions he received to the journal all too often were 'summaries of what dead people said (with no indication of why living ones should care or how the revered ancestor's work would advance contemporary analytic projects)' and 'criticisms of what other people have said that dead people said (with no more indication of why we should care than that those criticized are famous)' (1996: 1).

3. Besides his functional interpretation of the Democratic political machine (Merton 1949: 70–81) there is little in the form of full-fledged functional analysis to be found in his work.

4. This fuzziness undoubtedly has contributed to its popularity, since it made it possible for sociologists of various persuasions to appropriate the term for their own particular purposes, often in a noncommittal way (see Pawson 2000: 283).

5. Other examples mentioned were the philosophical systems of German idealism (1968*b*: 45), the early sociology of Comte and Spencer (Merton 1948: 165; 1968*b*: 46), and the grandiose theories of historical development proposed by Sorokin and Toynbee (Merton 1957*a*: 107).

6. Isolation is the method advocated by Max Weber in the construction of ideal types (see Weber [1904] 1949: 42 ff., 90 ff.).

7. As noted by Merton, what often is presented as grand theories are not, strictly speaking, theories at all, but conceptual schemes, or general orientations (Merton 1948: 166; 1968*b*: 52). At best such 'theories' can identify some factors that are important to consider, but typically they are too vague and too far removed from reality to be of even such limited use (Merton 1957*a*: 109–10; 1968*b*: 39).

8. We are of course aware that thick description, in the sense of Geertz, involves a great deal of generalization.

9. Middle-range theories are not, as some social scientists seem to believe (see e.g. Hunter 1989: 216; Billing and Alvesson 1993: 31), located at some meso level in between the macro and micro levels.

10. This does not mean that Merton was insensitive to the value of generalization. On the contrary, he advocated the consolidation of middle-range theories into more general theories (1948: 166; 1957*b*: 10–16; 1968*b*: 69–72), and he saw the development of one

unified theory, capable of explaining all social phenomena, as an attractive but distant goal (1968*b*: 45).

11. We are of course aware that the location of Merton's wide-ranging theoretical work varied along the two dimensions of Figure 2.1, and that his theories of self-fulfilling prophecies and Matthew effects probably are somewhat further towards the north-east corner of this conceptual space than was the bulk of his theoretical work.

12. Merton's most extended treatment of mechanisms is found in his discussion of role sets, where 'social mechanisms' are defined as 'processes having designated effects for designated parts of the social structure' (Merton 1957*b*: 111–12). According to Merton, a middle-range theory of role sets is concerned 'with the analytical problem of identifying the social mechanisms which produce a greater degree of order or less conflict than would obtain if these mechanisms were not called into play' (1968*a*: 45). This mechanism-based view of theory is strikingly similar to that of contemporary analytical sociologists.

13. The term 'opportunity structure' first appeared in print in the second edition of *Social Theory and Social Structure* (1957*b*: 176).

14. Opportunities are but the other side of constraints. As Peter Blau has observed, constraints and opportunities are correlative concepts: 'restricted opportunities become constraints; fewer constraints enlarge opportunities' (1990: 145).

15. Two interesting twists of this model, elaborated in great detail by Elster, are that individuals may constrain themselves (Elster 1979: 2000) and that they may adapt their preferences to their opportunities (Elster 1983).

16. See Chabris, Laibson, and Schuldt (2008) for a review of recent work on myopia and other forms of time-discounting.

17. Quoted from Merton (1968*a*: 58).

18. See the chapter by Chase and Lindquist in this volume for a brief discussion of Gould's theory. The Matthew effect also is at the core of Podolny's analysis of status processes in markets. See Podolny (2005) and Podolny's and Lynn's chapter in this volume for more details.

19. Traditionally many philosophers also have insisted that explanations must take the form of sound deductive arguments. We believe that all sound explanations can be expressed in the form of deductive argument, but, as argued by Woodward and others, 'when explanations are deductive, we should see their deductive structure as having explanatory import only to the extent that it traces or represents an independently existing causal order or set of dependency relations' (Woodward 2003: 361).

20. The discipline-specific nature of what is considered to be sufficient causal depth can be seen in that what we as sociologists may take for basic explanans—such as actions and the intentions that motivate them—is seen as major explanandum by other disciplines such as psychology and cognitive science.

21. What is required for these deeper explanations may not be different in kind from the sort of information on which the counterfactual approach focuses. When adjudicating between rival mechanisms (Morgan and Winship 2007) and when distinguishing between relevant and irrelevant entities and activities of a mechanism (Craver 2006), the counterfactual approach seems useful. For an alternative take on this see Bogen (2004, 2005). See also the chapter by Macy and Flache in this volume for a discussion of tools useful for establishing that a proposed mechanism can generate the outcome to be explained.

REFERENCES

BECKER, G. S. (1976), *The Economic Approach to Human Behavior* (Chicago, Ill.: University of Chicago Press).

BILLING, Y. D., and ALVESSON, M. (1993), *Gender, Managers, and Organizations* (Berlin: de Gruyter).

BLAU, P. (1990), 'Structural Constraints and Opportunities: Merton's Contribution to General Theory', in J. Clark, C. Modgil, and S. Modgil (eds.), *Robert K. Merton: Consensus and Controversy* (London: Falmer), 141–55.

BOGEN, J. (2004), 'Analysing Causality: The Opposite of Counterfactual is Factual', *International Studies in the Philosophy of Science*, 18: 3–26.

—— (2005), 'Regularities and Causality, Generalizations and Causal Explanations', *Studies in History and Philosophy of Biological and Biomedical Sciences*, 36: 397–420.

BOUDON, R. (1991), 'What Middle-Range Theories Are', *Contemporary Sociology*, 20: 519–22.

CALHOUN, C. J. (1996), 'What Passes for Theory in Sociology?', *Sociological Theory*, 14: 1–2.

CHABRIS, C. F., LAIBSON, D. I., and SCHULDT, J. P. (2008), 'Intertemporal Choice', in S. N. Durlauf and L. E. Blume (eds.), *The New Palgrave Dictionary of Economics Online* (Palgrave Macmillan), at <http://www.dictionaryofeconomics.com>, accessed 2008.

CLARK, J. (1990), 'Robert Merton as a Sociologist', in J. Clark, C. Modgil, and S. Modgil (eds.), *Robert K. Merton: Consensus and Controversy* (London: Falmer) 13–23.

COLEMAN, J. S. (1986), 'Social Theory, Social Research, and a Theory of Action', *American Journal of Sociology*, 91: 1309–35.

—— (1990), *Foundations of Social Theory* (Cambridge, Mass.: Harvard University Press).

CRAVER, C. F. (2006), 'When Mechanist Models Explain', *Synthese*, 153: 355–76.

CRICK, F. (1989). *What Mad Pursuit: A Personal View of Scientific Discovery* (London: Penguin).

CROTHERS, C. (1987), *Robert K. Merton* (London: Tavistock).

DIPRETE, T. A., and EIRICH, G. M. (2006), 'Cumulative Advantage as a Mechanism for Inequality: A Review of Theoretical and Empirical Developments', *Annual Review of Sociology*, 32: 271–97.

ELSTER, J. (1979), *Ulysses and the Sirens: Studies in Rationality and Irrationality* (Cambridge: Cambridge University Press).

—— (1983), *Sour Grapes: Studies in the Subversion of Rationality* (Cambridge: Cambridge University Press).

—— (1989), *Nuts and Bolts for the Social Sciences* (Cambridge: Cambridge University Press).

—— (1999), *Alchemies of the Mind: Rationality and the Emotions* (Cambridge: Cambridge University Press).

—— (2000), *Ulysses Unbound* (Cambridge: Cambridge University Press).

GEELS, F. W. (2007), 'Feelings of Discontent and the Promise of Middle Range Theory for STS', *Science, Technology and Human Values*, 32: 627–51.

GEERTZ, C. (1973), *The Interpretation of Cultures* (New York: Basic).

GIDDENS, A. (1984), *The Constitution of Society* (Cambridge: Polity).

GOULD, R. V. (2002), 'The Origins of Status Hierarchies: A Formal Theory and Empirical Test', *American Journal of Sociology*, 107: 1143–78.

HEDSTRÖM, P. (2005), *Dissecting the Social: On the Principles of Analytical Sociology* (Cambridge: Cambridge University Press).

HEDSTRÖM, P., and SWEDBERG, R. (1998) (eds.), *Social Mechanisms: An Analytical Approach to Social Theory* (Cambridge: Cambridge University Press).

HEMPEL, C. G. (1965), *Aspects of Scientific Explanation* (New York: Free Press).

HOMANS, G. C. (1961), *Social Behavior* (London: Routledge & Kegan Paul).

—— (1967), *The Nature of Social Science* (New York: Harcourt, Brace & World).

—— [1969] (1987), *Certainties and Doubts: Collected Papers, 1962–1985* (New Brunswick, N.J.: Transaction).

—— (1974), *Social Behavior: Its Elementary Forms* (New York: Harcourt, Brace & World).

HUNTER, D. (1989), 'Organizing and Managing Health Care: A Challenge for Medical Sociology', in S. Cunningham-Burley and N. P. McKegagney (eds.), *Readings in Medical Sociology* (London: Tavistock/Routledge), 213–36.

LATSIS, S. J. (1972), 'Situational Determinism in Economics', *British Journal for the Philosophy of Science*, 23: 207–45.

LAZARSFELD, P. (1955), 'Interpretation of Statistical Relations as a Research Operation', in P. Lazarsfeld and M. Rosenberg (eds.), *The Language of Social Research* (New York: Free Press), 115–25.

LUHMANN, N. (1995), *Social Systems* (Stanford, Calif.: Stanford University Press).

MÄKI, U. (1992), 'On the Method of Isolation in Economics', *Poznan Studies in the Philosophy of the Sciences and the Humanities*, 26: 319–54.

MERTON, R. K. (1936), 'The Unanticipated Consequences of Purposive Social Action', *American Sociological Review*, 1: 894–904.

—— (1938), 'Social Structure and Anomie', *American Sociological Review*, 3: 672–82.

—— (1945), 'Sociological Theory', *American Journal of Sociology*, 50: 462–73.

—— (1948), 'Discussion', *American Sociological Review*, 13: 164–8.

—— (1949), *Social Theory and Social Structure* (Glencoe, Ill.: Free Press).

—— (1957a), 'The Role-Set: A Problem in Sociological Theory', *British Journal of Sociology*, 8: 106–20.

—— (1957b), *Social Theory and Social Structure*, rev. and enlarged edn. (Glencoe, Ill.: Free Press).

—— (1963), introd. to A. Barton (ed.), *Social Organization Under Stress: A Sociological Review of Disaster Studies* (Washington, D.C.: National Academy of Sciences/National Research Council).

—— (1968a), 'The Matthew Effect in Science: The Reward and Communication Systems of Science Are Considered', *Science*, 159: 56–63.

—— (1968b), *Social Theory and Social Structure*, enlarged edn. (New York: Free Press).

—— (1975), 'Structural Analysis in Sociology', in P. M. Blau (ed.), *Approaches to the Study of Social Structure* (New York: Free Press), 21–52.

—— (1988), 'The Matthew Effect in Science: Cumulative Advantage and the Symbolism of Intellectual Property', *ISIS*, 79: 606–23.

—— (1994), 'A Life of Learning' (Charles Homer Haskins Lecture for 1994), American Council of Learned Societies, occasional paper no. 25, pp. 2–10.

—— (1995), 'Opportunity: The Emergence, Diffusion, and Differentiation of a Sociological Concept, 1930s–1950s', in W. S. Laufer (ed.), *The Legacy of Anomie Theory* (New Brunswick, N.J.: Transaction), 3–78.

MILL, J. S. (1874), *A System of Logic, Ratiocinative and Inductive, Being a Connected View of the Principles of Evidence and the Methods of Scientific Investigation* (New York: Harper).

MORGAN, S. L., and WINSHIP, C. (2007), *Counterfactuals and Causal Inference: Methods and Principles for Social Research* (Cambridge: Cambridge University Press).

PARSONS, T. (1951), *The Social System* (London: Routledge & Kegan Paul).

—— (1975), 'The Present Status of Structural-functional Theory in Sociology', in L. A. Coser (ed.), *The Idea of Social Structure: Papers in Honor of Robert K. Merton* (New York: Harcourt Brace Jovanovich), 67–83.

PAWSON, R. (2000), 'Middle-Range Realism', *Archives Européennes de sociologie*, 41: 283–325.

PODOLNY, J. M. (2005), *Status Signals: A Sociological Study of Market Competition* (Princeton, N.J.: Princeton University Press).

RYLE, G. (1968), 'The Thinking of Thoughts: What is "Le Penseur" Doing?' University of Saskatchewan lecture no. 18, repr. in Ryle, *Collected Papers* (London: Hutchinson, 1971).

SATZ, D., and FEREJOHN, J. (1994), 'Rational Choice and Social Theory', *Journal of Philosophy*, 91: 71–87.

SCHELLING, T. C. (1978), *Micromotives and Macrobehavior* (New York: Norton).

SIMON, H. A. (1982), *Models of Bounded Rationality*, 2 vols. (Cambridge, Mass.: MIT Press).

STINCHCOMBE, A. L. (1968), *Constructing Social Theories* (New York: Harcourt, Brace & World).

—— (1975), 'Merton's Theory of Social Structure', in L. A. Coser (ed.), *The Idea of Social Structure: Papers in Honor of Robert K. Merton* (New York: Harcourt Brace Jovanovich), 11–53.

STOUFFER, S. A., et al. (1949), *The American Soldier* (Princeton, N.J.: Princeton University Press).

SZTOMPKA, P. (1986), *Robert K. Merton: An Intellectual Profile* (Basingstoke: Macmillan).

—— (1990), 'R. K. Merton's Theoretical System: An Overview', in J. Clark, C. Modgil, and S. Modgil (eds.), *Robert K. Merton: Consensus and Controversy* (London: Farmer), 53–64.

THOMAS, W. I., and THOMAS, D. S. (1928), *The Child in America: Behavior Problems and Programs* (New York: Knopf).

UDEHN, L. (2001), *Methodological Individualism: Background, History and Meaning* (London: Routledge).

WEBER, M. [1904] (1949), *The Methodology of the Social Sciences* (New York: Free Press).

WOODWARD, J. (2002), 'What is a Mechanism? A Counterfactual Account', *Philosophy of Science*, 69: 366–77.

—— (2003), *Making Things Happen: A Theory of Causal Explanation* (Oxford: Oxford University Press).

ZETTERBERG, H. [1954] (1965), *On Theory and Verification in Sociology* (Totowa, N.J.: Bedminster).

ZUCKERMAN, H. (1998), 'Accumulation of Advantage and Disadvantage: The Theory and Its Intellectual Bibliography', in C. Mongardini and S. Tabboni (eds.), *Robert K. Merton and Contemporary Sociology* (New Brunswick, N.J.: Transaction), 139–62.

PART II

SOCIAL COGS
AND WHEELS

CHAPTER 3

....

EMOTIONS

....

JON ELSTER

INTRODUCTION

....

THE term 'emotion' harbors various complexities.

First, it may refer to an occurrent event (a fit of rage) or to a standing disposition (irascibility or irritability). The disposition may be strong and yet rarely be triggered, if others learn about it and take care not to provoke it or if the agent is aware of it and avoids situations in which it might be triggered. Both occurrent emotions and emotional dispositions may, therefore, enter into the explanation of behavior. In this chapter the focus will mainly be on occurrent emotional events.

Second, one may be 'in the grip' of an emotion, in the sense of displaying the characteristic behavioral and physiological patterns of the emotion, and yet be unaware of it. If the culture lacks the concept of depression, a man whose woman-friend has just left him may state, non-self-deceptively, that he is 'tired' (Levy 1973). An emotion such as anger or love may 'sneak up' on the agent without her being aware of it, until it suddenly bursts into consciousness. In such cases, we may talk of 'proto-emotions.' Although they do affect behavior, proto-emotions usually have less of a causal impact than the full-blown emotions that are conceptualized by society and acknowledged by the individual. The fact that animals can only have proto-emotions sets limits to the relevance of animal psychology for the study of human emotions. It is possible, for instance, that the apparent absence of the sunk-cost fallacy in animals other than humans (Arkes and Ayton 1999) is due to the fact that they are not subject to pride and *amour-propre*.

Third, the term 'emotion' should not be identified with the older term 'passion' or with the more recent term 'visceral factor' (Loewenstein 1996). Passions include most emotions, but hardly sadness, boredom (if that counts as an emotion), and other low-intensity states. At the same time the passions include strong nonemotional disturbances, such as madness, intoxication, or addictive cravings. The ancients even thought of inspiration as a passion, because of its involuntary and unbidden character (Dodds 1951). Visceral factors form an even broader class, including pain, intense thirst or hunger, and an overwhelming desire to sleep or to urinate. Some of the claims made about emotions in this chapter are also valid for these broader classes, whereas others are not.

Fourth, emotion theorists disagree on what emotions are and on what emotions there are. I shall not try to survey the controversy or offer my own solution. Rather, I want to point to what may be an emerging consensus: the *emotions do not form a natural kind*. Two emotions, such as anger and love, may be related as bats and birds or as sharks and whales rather than as bats and whales (both mammals). Although most of the states that we preanalytically classify as emotions tend to have a number of features in common, none of these is invariably present. For any alleged basic feature, such as sudden onset or rapid decay (Ekman 1992*a*), one can provide counterexamples. The implication is that the appeal to emotions in explaining behavior is likely to take the form of mechanisms rather than laws (Elster 1999*a*: ch. 1).

Finally, emotion theorists also disagree on what emotions are *for*. With regard to the handful of emotions that are uncontroversially observed in all societies, it is tempting to assume that their universal character points to an evolutionary function. It is, however, a temptation to be resisted. Although it is valid to assume that a universally observed feature of human beings has an evolutionary explanation, the latter could well take the form of showing that the feature is a by-product of adaptation (pleiotropy) rather than adaptive in and of itself. It seems clear that fear is adaptive, but less obvious that envy or regret is. Many of the proposed evolutionary accounts are little more than just-so stories. An example is the idea that post-partum depression should be understood as a female bargaining tool in the battle of the sexes (Hagen 2003).

3.1 RATIONAL CHOICE AND EMOTIONAL CHOICE

To understand the role of emotions in the explanation of behavior, it will be convenient to begin with a brief statement of the rational-choice theory of action.

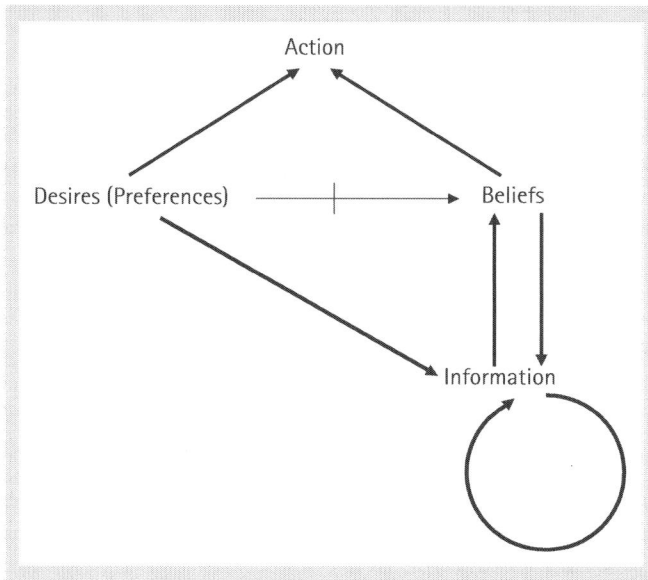

Fig. 3.1 The standard model of rational choice

Emotions and rationality are not necessarily opposed to each other. A person may act rationally on desires that are shaped by emotion. Acting on beliefs that are shaped by emotion will, however, typically be irrational. Although it is sometimes stated that emotions can enhance the rationality of beliefs, no plausible mechanism has been proposed.

What I take to be the standard model of rational choice is defined in terms of the relation among four elements: action, beliefs, desires (or preferences), and information (Fig. 3.1).

The arrows in the diagram have a double interpretation: they stand for relations of causality as well as of optimality. The desires and the beliefs of a rational agent cause him or her to choose the course of behavior that they rationalize. In this Humean approach, no arrows lead to the desires: they are the unmoved movers of behavior. This is not to say, of course, that desires are uncaused, only that they are not the result of any optimizing operation.

The rational agent optimizes in three separate dimensions. He chooses the action that best realizes his desires, given his beliefs about what his options are and about the consequences of choosing them. These beliefs are themselves inferred from the available evidence by the procedures that are most likely, in the long run and on average, to yield true beliefs. The blocked arrow reflects the fact that desires are not allowed to have any direct impact on beliefs, as they have in wishful thinking or in counterwishful thinking (see Sect. 3.5). Finally, prior to belief formation the agent gathers more evidence in an amount that is optimal in light of the agent's desires and the expected costs and benefits of gathering more information. The loop reflects the fact that the expected benefits may be modified by what is found in the search itself. We may note for future reference that the costs of information-gathering are of two kinds: direct costs (e.g. buying a catalogue) and opportunity costs (e.g. the risk of being bitten by a snake while trying to decide whether it is a snake or a stick).

In the rational-choice model of action the role of beliefs is limited to that of informing the agent about how best to realize his or her desires. The emotion-based model relies on the fact that beliefs can also generate emotions that have consequences for behavior. With qualifications to be set out below, the general mechanism is:

$$\text{cognition} \longrightarrow \text{emotion} \longrightarrow \text{action tendency}$$

Among the couple of dozen emotions that can be robustly identified, each has a specific set of cognitive antecedents that tend to trigger it. Examples (spelled out more fully in Elster 1999*a*) are shown in Table 3.1.

An important distinction is between the emotions that are triggered by beliefs about *actions* (anger, Cartesian indignation, guilt, gratitude) and those that are triggered by beliefs about *character* (hatred, contempt, shame). Another important distinction is between *interaction-based* emotions (e.g. anger) and *comparison-based* emotions (e.g. envy).

The third-party emotion that I refer to as 'Cartesian indignation' was first identified by Descartes (1985: art. 195), with the important proviso that if B *loves* C the indignation is transformed into anger (ibid. art. 201). Descartes was also the first to identify (in a letter to Princess Elisabeth of Bohemia from January 1646) what we

Table 3.1 Cognitions and emotions

Belief	Emotion
A imposed an unjust harm on B	B feels anger towards A
A imposed an unjust harm on C in the presence of B	B feels 'Cartesian indignation' towards A
A is evil	B feels hatred towards A
A is weak or inferior	B feels contempt towards A
B feels contempt towards A	A feels shame
A has behaved unjustly or immorally	A feels guilt
A has something that B lacks and desires	B feels envy
A is faced with impending danger	A feels fear
?	B loves A
A suffers unmerited distress	B feels pity towards A
A has helped B	B feels gratitude towards A

might call 'third-party gratitude'; that is, B's positive feeling towards A caused by A's helpful behavior towards C.

As noted in Table 3.1, the cognitive antecedents of love are unclear. According to Stendhal (1980: 279), B's belief that A may (but also may not) love B is a necessary condition for B's loving A. It is clearly not a sufficient condition. In some cases, at least, B's love is triggered by B's *perception* of A as beautiful or gracious rather than by B's beliefs about A. Although B may come to believe that A has all sorts of wonderful qualities, the belief tends to be an effect of the emotion rather than its cause (ibid. 287). Sexual desire, if that counts as an emotion, often requires no cognitive triggers.

It is in fact an important truth about emotions that they can be triggered by perceptions with no propositional content. In a standard example, the mere sight of a snake-like shape on the path may cause fear through a pathway that goes directly from the sensory apparatus to the amygdala, without passing through the cortex (LeDoux 1996). From the point of view of the social sciences, however, the more important effect of perception occurs when it is added to cognition rather than substituting for it. Abstract knowledge gains in vividness and motivating power when it is accompanied by visual cues. Some ex-smokers who are afraid of relapsing keep color photographs of smokers' lungs on the walls of their apartment. The sight of a beggar in the street may trigger more generosity than the knowledge of starving children in Africa. Propaganda often relies more on images than on words. Petersen (2005) illustrates this effect with a picture showing a graphic image of a happy and grinning Serb cutting the throat of a young Albanian boy. The caption urges the reader not to let Serbs return to Kosovo. The poster provided no new information, since everyone knew that the Serbs committed atrocities; it only made the information more vivid and present. As will be shown below, memory of past injustice has more power to trigger current emotion if the harm has left visible traces in the present.

There may be some indeterminacy in the triggering and the targeting of emotions. In one case, A intentionally causes B to kill C. Will the relatives or neighbors of C feel anger towards A or towards B? Assume that A is a resistance movement in a German-occupied country, B is the occupational force and C is the as-yet uncommitted population. If the Italian resistance movement kills a German officer and the Germans respond by killing a hundred civilians chosen at random, the anger of the population may be directed towards the resistance and not, as the resistance leaders may have hoped, towards the Germans (Cappelletto 2003). In another case, A offers a privilege to B but not to C. Will C feel anger towards A or envy towards B? Assume that A is the French king before 1789, B the French nobility, and C the French bourgeoisie. Tocqueville argued that the bourgeoisie predominantly felt envy towards the nobility. (See Elster 1999: 192–9 for references and discussion.) In both cases the emotion experienced by C and/or its target are subject to indeterminacy, which may of course be lifted if the relevant features of the situation are identified.

Figure 3.2 offers a way of thinking about 'emotional choice.' Here the thick arrows represent only causal effects of the emotions, without implying optimality.

The feedback relation between emotion and belief is clear from the diagram. In some cases the effect of emotion is to strengthen the belief that triggered it, which in turn strengthens the emotion itself. Consider the proverb 'Fear increases the danger'; that is, the perceived danger. Ekman (1992b) refers to this mechanism as an emotional 'wildfire.' A historical example is the Great Fear that developed independently in seven different parts of France in the spring and early summer of 1789, a process in which the people *scared itself*, 'se faisait peur à lui-même' (Lefebvre 1988: 56). From an evolutionary point of view, such behaviors are puzzling: Why would the tendency to exaggerate the danger enhance the fitness of the organism? Or to take another example, why would natural selection favor the tendency to perceive nonexistent virtues in the object of one's affection, thereby causing the affection to gain strength? As these remarks suggest, it may be wiser to stick to the search for proximate causes and to remain agnostic about ultimate ones.

References to fear can be ambiguous (Gordon 1987: 77). Sometimes they refer to *prudential fear*, as when I stay at home because I fear it's going to rain. In this case my decision to stay home is explained by the simple belief–desire model in Figure 3.1. Americans who fear an attack by terrorists may take appropriate (rational) precautions. After the first anthrax cases in 2001, for instance, it may have been quite rational to take precautions when opening letters of unknown origin. In other cases talk about fear clearly refers to *visceral fear*, in which fear as an emotion is involved in one of the ways shown in Figure 3.2. The idea of hope is also open to these two interpretations.

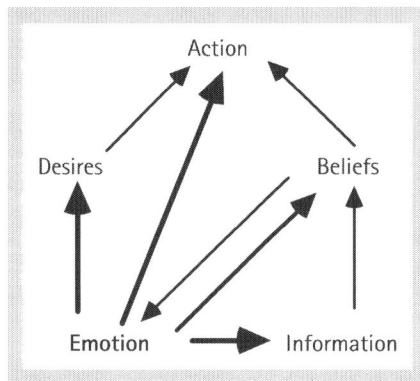

Fig. 3.2 **A model of emotional choice**

Fleeing danger out of visceral fear can be irrational, if it causes us to go from the frying pan into the fire. A plausible example is provided by the estimated 350 excess deaths caused after 9/11 by Americans using their car instead of flying to wherever they were going (Gigerenzer 2004). By contrast, it appears that no excess deaths were caused by people switching from train to car after the attacks in Madrid on 11 March 2004. One reason may be that the Spanish were habituated to terror by decades of ETA actions, and had come to adopt an attitude of prudential rather than visceral fear (López-Rousseau 2005). This is perhaps also how one may understand those who refer to *familiarity* as a factor reducing the perceived seriousness of risk (Slovic 2000: 141; Sunstein 2005: 43). Regular exposure to a danger transforms the visceral fear that occurred on the first occasion into prudential fear.

In the following sections I will spell out the nature of the causal relations identified by the bold arrows in Figure 3.2. In doing so, I will disaggregate 'desires' into 'substantive preferences' and 'formal preferences.' The former are everyday objects such as a preference for apples over oranges or for ten dollars over five dollars. The latter include risk aversion, impatience (i.e. time-discounting), and urgency. The last idea will be unfamiliar, and is in fact the only original notion presented in the chapter. In brief anticipation, urgency is the preference for earlier action over later action, to be distinguished from a preference for earlier reward over later reward (impatience). As will be seen, there is a close relation between urgency and the investment in information.

3.2 A Direct Impact of Emotion on Action?

There is a venerable tradition in philosophy for arguing that passion can cause agents to behave contrary to what, *at the time of action*, they believe would be the best thing to do, all things considered (e.g. Davidson [1969] 1980). 'I do not do the good I want, but the evil I do not want is what I do' (St Paul); 'I see the better, and approve it, but follow the worse' (Medea). Although I do not want to deny the possibility of weakness of will in this synchronic sense, the idea has serious conceptual and empirical problems (Elster 1999*b*).

It seems hard, in the first place, to envisage this combination of extreme passion and extreme lucidity, such as that found in Racine's Phèdre (Bénichou 1948: 230). It is often more plausible to assume that the emotion which induces the desire to do wrong also clouds or biases cognition, to obscure the wrongness of the action or to make it appear good. This is, for instance, the pattern of Racine's Hermione (ibid.).

Moreover, how could one distinguish empirically between this synchronic case and one in which a preference reversal occurred prior to the action, perhaps only a few milliseconds before? Finally, what is the causal mechanism by virtue of which the emotion bypasses the considered judgment of the agent? References to a 'partition of the mind' (Davidson 1982) are, so far, little more than hand-waving.

Many alleged instances of synchronic weakness of will may instead be due to a temporary *preference reversal* (Elster 2006, 2007). The mechanisms capable of generating such reversals include hyperbolic time-discounting, cue dependence, and, as we shall see in the next section, emotion.

3.3 THE IMPACT OF EMOTION ON SUBSTANTIVE PREFERENCES

Each action has associated with it a specific action tendency, which may also be seen as a temporary preference. Here I use the word 'preference' in a somewhat large or loose sense. Strictly speaking, an agent can be said to have a preference for A over B only if both options are mentally present for him or her and the agent, weighing them against each other, arrives at a preference for one of them. Consider, however, the following case. An agent knows that he is going to find himself in a dangerous situation and prefers, ahead of time, to stand fast in the face of the danger. This might, for instance, be an impending battle. Under enemy fire, however, he panics and flees. In this case, there may be no explicit comparisons of options, only an urge to run away that is so strong that everything else is blotted out. I shall nevertheless describe the action as resulting from a preference for fleeing over fighting, reversing the earlier preference for fighting over fleeing. In actual cases it will always be hard to tell whether the alternative of fighting makes a fleeting appearance on the mental screen.

Table 3.2 illustrates some of the action tendencies associated with emotions. We see that the relation is one–many rather than one–one. Fear, for instance, may cause either fight or flight. If a guilty person is unable to 'redress the moral balance of the universe' by undoing the harm he has caused, he may try to achieve the same result by imposing a comparable harm on himself.

Action tendencies may differ in strength. Historical examples suggest (Elster 2004: ch. 8) and experiments confirm (Fehr and Fischbacher 2004) that the two-party emotion of anger induces a greater willingness to impose harm on the offender than does the three-party emotion of Cartesian indignation.

In these cases willingness to impose harm may be measured either by the severity of the punishment one is willing to impose (keeping the cost of punishing constant)

Table 3.2 Emotions and action tendencies

Emotion	Action Tendency
Anger/Cartesian indignation	Cause the object of the emotion to suffer
Hatred	Cause the object of hatred to cease to exist
Contempt	Ostracize; avoid
Shame	'Sink through the floor'; run away; commit suicide
Guilt	Confess; make repairs; hurt oneself
Envy	Destroy the envied object or its possessor
Fear	Flee; fight
Love	Approach and touch the other; help the other; please the other
Pity	Console or alleviate the distress of the other
Gratitude	Help the other

or by the cost one is willing to assume (keeping the severity constant). Often the cost of punishment and the severity go together. The cost to society of keeping someone in prison for ten years is presumably twice the cost of keeping the person in prison for five years. The use of the death penalty, which is typically less costly than life imprisonment, provides an exception.

If we compare anger and indignation with contempt, a further difference appears. An agent A may be more willing to suffer a loss by ostracizing B than to suffer a same-sized loss by punishing B. The reason is that the loss to the ostracizer takes the form of utility forgone, caused by the renunciation of mutually profitable transactions, whereas the loss to the punisher takes the form of a direct reduction of utility due to the fact that punishment is costly or risky. As we know from prospect theory (Kahneman and Tversky 1979), people usually evaluate direct costs as about twice as important as opportunity costs. Hence, people should be more willing to ostracize than to punish, given the same objective loss in both cases.

By the same token ostracism should be less painful to the ostracized. That statement, however, misses an important aspect of ostracism. The reason it is painful to be excluded from interacting with others is not or not only the loss of objective opportunities for improving one's well-being. The pain is also caused by the knowledge that others think so badly about the agent that they are willing to give up *their* opportunities for improvement rather than have dealings with him or her. Schematically, for B it might be worse if A chooses (3, 5) over (6, 6) than if A chooses (4, 4) over (6, 6), where the first number in each pair stands for the material welfare of A and the second for that of B.

Interaction-based emotions tend to trigger stronger reactions than comparison-based emotions. In ultimatum-game experiments (see Fig. 3.3), for instance, subjects seem less willing to punish on the basis of envy than on the basis of anger. In this game, one subject (the proposer) offers a division of ten dollars between himself and another subject (the responder). The latter can either accept it or reject it; in

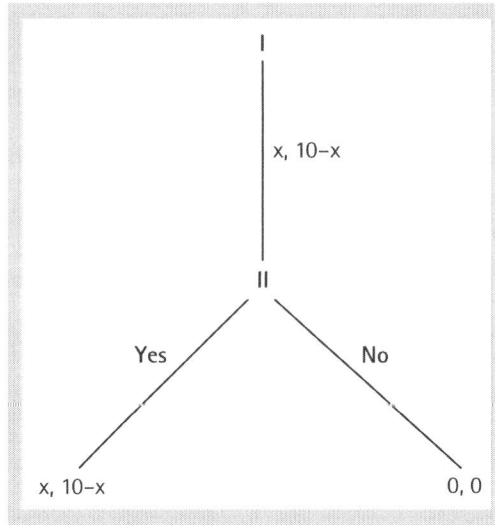

Fig. 3.3 The ultimatum game

the latter case neither gets anything. A stylized finding is that proposers typically offer around (6, 4) and that responders reject offers that would give them 2 or less (see Camerer 2003 for details and references). To explain these findings, we might assume that responders will be motivated by *envy* to reject low offers, and that self-interested proposers, anticipating this effect, will make offers that are just generous enough to be accepted. If this explanation were correct, we would expect that the frequency of rejection of (8, 2) would be the same when the proposer is free to propose any allocation and when he is constrained—and known to be constrained—to choose between (8, 2) and (2, 8). In experiments, the rejection rate is lower in the latter case. This result suggests that responder behavior is more strongly determined by the interaction-based emotion of anger than by the comparison-based emotion of envy.

These emotion-based action tendencies are often characterized in terms of three properties: quick decay, a cold-to-hot empathy gap, and a hot-to-cold empathy gap. For the first I refer again to Ekman (1992*a*); for the last two one may consult Loewenstein (1996, 2005). I shall briefly describe these claims and then point to some exceptions.

The quick decay of emotion is what enables us, in many cases, to refer to the emotion-induced preference reversal as a *temporary* one. In some cases the emotion disappears together with its cause. When you flee from a danger, the fear abates because you have removed yourself from the threat. In other cases the emotion simply loses momentum even though the cause is still present. Nothing seems to be known concerning the rate of decay of emotion, or of the various emotions. As

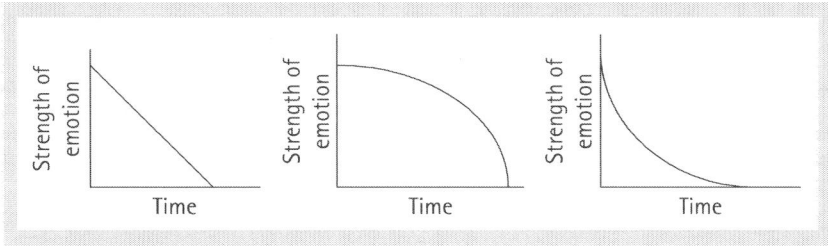

Fig. 3.4 Patterns of decay of emotion

observed by Roger Petersen (personal communication) any of the above patterns might occur (see Fig. 3.4).

Some examples follow. The short half-life of anger underlies the advice of counting to ten. (Whether an angry person could remember that advice is another matter.) The typical duration of romantic love, or *amour-passion*, is from eighteen months to three years (Tennov 1979.) Grief for a dead spouse usually abates after a year or two. After September 11 2001 the number of young American men who expressed an interest in serving in the army increased markedly, but there was no increase in actual enlistment (*USA Today*, 25 Sept. 2001). In countries that had been occupied by Germany during World War II the collaborators that were tried shortly after liberation were sentenced more severely, for the same crimes, than those who were tried one or two years later. It seems very likely that the spontaneous abatement of emotion was a major cause of this trend (Elster 2004: ch. 8).

If emotion induces immediate action, it may sometimes be reversed later when the emotion abates. Some of the severe sentences for collaborators who had been tried early were commuted in the light of the more lenient practice that developed later. Among the 200,000 men who deserted the Union army during the American Civil War, presumably out of fear, 10 percent returned voluntarily (Costa and Kahn 2007). In some cases, however, action taken on the basis of emotion-induced temporary preferences is irreversible. Some collaborators who received the death penalty were executed before the tide turned. When young men and women enlist in a guerilla movement in a moment of enthusiasm and later want to leave it, they may find that this option is closed to them (a lobster-trap situation).

While these and other examples show that emotion-induced preference reversals can be relatively short-lived, there are counterexamples. Unrequited love and unsatisfied desire for revenge may endure for decades (Elster 1999a: 305). Hatred and envy seem more impervious than anger to spontaneous decay. The emotion may also stay alive for a very long time if the abstract knowledge of injustice done to oneself or to one's ancestors is reinforced by constant visual reminders. Although we might think that killings would leave stronger memories than confiscation of property, the opposite can be the case. Referring to the twentieth-century descendants of those who had their property confiscated in the French Revolution, one historian writes that 'Generations forget more quickly spilled blood than stolen goods. By their continued presence under the eyes of those who had been despoiled of them, the fortunes arising out of the national estates maintain an eternal resentment in the souls' (Gabory 1989: 1063).

A cold-to-hot empathy gap arises when an agent, in a nonemotional state, is incapable of anticipating the impact of an emotion he might experience on some future occasion. A hot-to-cold empathy gap arises when the agent, in an emotional state, is incapable of anticipating that it may not last forever. Both effects may be illustrated by the example of the six Frenchmen who killed themselves in June 1997 after they had been exposed as consumers of pedophiliac materials. Had they been able to anticipate the devastating impact of shame, they might have abstained from becoming consumers in the first place. Had they been able to anticipate that their shame (and the contempt of others) would decay with time, they might not have killed themselves.

In some cases people have been able to anticipate the decay of their emotions and to act on the basis of that anticipation. During the Second World War the desire to contribute to the American war effort was strong only immediately after hearing radio appeals for funds. A study of contributors revealed that some listeners telephoned at once because they wished to commit themselves to a bond before their generosity waned (Cowen 1991: 363, citing Merton 1946: 68–9). A similar case arose in the Belgian war trials after World War II. On the basis of the experience from World War I it was believed that after a while the popular willingness to impose severe sentences on the collaborators would give place to indifference. Hence some Belgians wanted the trials to proceed as quickly as possible, before anger was replaced by a more dispassionate attitude (Huyse and Dhondt 1993: 115). In these cases, the anticipation of decay produced the same effect as urgency: a desire for immediate action. In other cases it may counteract urgency. In Holland after 1945 some jurists argued that the death penalty was to be avoided because 'in collaboration cases the court, and the public, tended to become less severe as the memories of the occupation faded' (Mason 1952: 64).

3.4 THE IMPACT OF EMOTION ON FORMAL PREFERENCES

Among formal preferences I include risk aversion, impatience, and urgency. Whereas the first two have been widely discussed, the third is relatively marginal in the literature. Yet I believe it is of comparable importance in its impact on behavior.

In many psychological studies of emotions *valence* (position on the pleasure–pain dimension) is used as the independent variable. In this paradigm it has been found that positive emotions tend to make people more risk-averse (Isen and Geva 1987), whereas negative emotions cause them to be more risk-seeking (Leith and Baumeister 1996). At the same time, positive and negative emotions generate, respectively, optimistic and pessimistic cognitive biases (Isen and Patrick 1983). Hence, when subjects are not explicitly told the odds of winning and losing, but have to assess them from the evidence available to them, cognitive bias and risk attitudes work in opposite directions. Thus, happy people assess the odds as more favorable, but for given odds are less willing to risk their money. The net effect is in general indeterminate.

Compared to the fine-grained classifications of emotions based on cognitive antecedents or action tendencies, valence is a coarse-grained category. In studies that use cognitive antecedents as the independent variable, the impact of emotion on risk attitudes appears in a different light. Lerner and Keltner (2001) found that whereas fearful people expressed pessimistic risk estimates and risk-averse choices, angry people expressed optimistic risk estimates and risk-seeking choices. In this case, emotion-induced risk attitudes and emotion-induced cognitive bias work in the same direction.

I define *impatience* as a preference for early reward over later reward, i.e. some degree of time-discounting. I define *urgency*, another effect of emotion, as a preference for early action over later action. The distinction is illustrated in Table 3.3.

In each case the agent can take one and only one of two actions, A or B. In case 1 these options are available at the same time, in cases 2 and 3 at successive times. In case 2 the rewards (whose magnitude is indicated by the numbers) occur at the same later time, in cases 1 and 3 at successive later times. Suppose that in an unemotional state the agent chooses B in all cases, but that in an emotional state he chooses A. In case 1 the choice of A is due to emotionally induced impatience.

Table 3.3 Urgency and impatience

t1	t2	t3	t4
	Case 1: impatience		
A	3		
B		5	
	Case 2: urgency		
A		3	
B	4		
	Case 3: impatience and/or urgency		
A		3	
B			6

In case 2 it is due to emotionally induced urgency. In case 3 it could be due to either or to the interaction of the two. In practice, the tendency for early action to be correlated with early reward makes it hard to isolate the two effects. One can, however, imagine experiments that would allow one to do so. It might be more difficult, however, to isolate the urgency effect from the anticipation of the decay of emotion.

In impatience, there is a two-way trade-off between the size of the reward and the time of delivery of the reward. In urgency, there is a three-way trade-off: the urge to act immediately may be neutralized if the size of the reward from acting later is sufficiently large or if that reward is delivered sufficiently early.

There is scattered evidence (e.g. Tice, Braslasvky, and Baumeister 2001) and some speculation about how occurrent emotions may cause increased rate of time-discounting. There is also evidence (Ostaczewski 1996) that emotional *dis-positions* such as introvert/extrovert may be correlated with differential rates of time-discounting. The change in the formal preferences of the agent may, in turn, induce a reversal of substantive preferences, causing the agent to prefer front-loaded options, in which the benefits are delivered first and the costs come later, over options that have the opposite pattern.

The case of urgency is more complicated. The first to have clearly stated the idea may have been Seneca: 'Reason grants a hearing to both sides, then *seeks to postpone action*, even its own, in order that it may gain time to sift out the truth; but anger is precipitate' (*On Anger*, 1.17). Seneca praises the Roman general Fabius, called the Cunctator (hesitator) for his delaying tactics, asking:

> How else did Fabius restore the broken forces of the state but by knowing how to loiter, to put off, and to wait—things of which angry men know nothing? The state, which was standing then in the utmost extremity, had surely perished if Fabius had ventured to do all that anger prompted. But he took into consideration the well-being of the state, and, estimating its strength, of which now nothing could be lost without the loss of all, he buried all thought of resentment and revenge and was concerned only with expediency and the fitting opportunity; he conquered anger before he conquered Hannibal.   (*On Anger*, 1.11)

Although the emotion-induced tendency to prefer immediate action to delayed action has not been much discussed or recognized by psychologists, I shall offer some observations to suggest that it is actually quite important.

In many cases, the preference for early action may also be thought of as an *inability to tolerate inaction*. It is hard to do nothing when we are under the sway of emotions. In a book on 'how doctors think,' Bernard Groopman discusses 'commission bias' in the following terms:

> This is the tendency toward action rather than inaction. Such an error is more likely to happen with a doctor who is overconfident, whose ego is inflated, but it can also occur *when a physician is desperate and gives in to the urge to 'do something'*. The error,

not infrequently, is sparked by pressure from a patient, and it takes considerable effort for a doctor to resist. 'Don't just do something, stand there', Dr Linda Lewis, one of my mentors once said when I was unsure of a diagnosis.

(Groopman 2007: 169; emphasis added)

Economists talk about an 'action bias' (Patt and Zeckhauser 2000), as illustrated for instance by goalkeepers facing a penalty kick in soccer (Bar-Eli et al. 2007). The goalies almost always throw themselves to the left or to the right before the ball is kicked, even though the optimal strategy is (apparently) to stand still in the middle of the goal. The explanation offered for this fact is that in some circumstances people would rather be blamed for a mistake caused by an action than for a mistake caused by inaction. An alternative account, which is the one I am suggesting here, would focus on how 'the goalie's anxiety at the penalty kick' induces an urge to act rather than to wait.

The behavior of terrorists and suicide attackers may be illuminated by the notion of urgency. Crenshaw (1972: 392) suggests that in the Algerian war of independence terrorism 'relieve[d] the tension caused by inaction.' Yet if terrorist attacks result from an urge to act immediately, they risk being inefficient. Before they kill themselves suicide attackers are presumably in a state of high emotional tension. According to one kamikaze pilot, the stress of waiting was 'unbearable' (Hill 2005: 28) To counteract the urge to take immediate and premature action, 'The first rule of the Kamikaze was that they should not be too hasty to die. If they could not select an adequate target, they should return to try again later' (ibid. 23). Suicide attackers in the Middle East are also screened carefully for emotional instability that might interfere with their effectiveness (Ricolfi 2005: 107). In Afghanistan, organizers sometimes prefer the technique of remote detonation, which 'reduces mistakes caused by attacker stress, such as premature detonation' (UNAMA 2007: 50).

Let me cite a few more examples of urgency at work. As suggested by the proverb 'Marry in haste, repent at leisure,' the emotion of love can induce a desire for immediate action. The perception of the dangers of haste and of the short half-life of emotions may explain why in many countries one has to give notice of an intended marriage. More generally, many 'delay legislations' may be seen in this perspective, whether they involve handgun sales, abortion, divorce, or voluntary sterilization (Elster 2007: 116–25). The simple switch from bottles to blister packs has contributed to the reduction of the number of suicides and of severe liver damage from paracetamol poisoning (Turvill et al. 2000). Although strong, the urge to kill oneself is so short-lived that by the time one has managed to open all the bubbles it may have subsided. Reducing the maximum number of tablets that can be available in individual preparations has also reduced the likelihood of severe poisonings (Gunnell et al. 1997). By the time one has done the round of pharmacies to buy enough bottles, the urge may have subsided.

Or consider the tendency of guilt to induce an overwhelming urge to confess even when, as in an extramarital affair, confession may hurt the spouse and simply putting an end to the affair would be more appropriate. The agent may tell himself that he acts morally, whereas in reality he is merely ridding himself of a tension. The emotion of guilt seems to have a *momentum* that causes the agent to take immediate action. This fact seems to be well known to interrogators of suspected criminals:

> Interview rooms should be of plain color, should have smooth walls, and should not contain ornaments, pictures, or other objects that would in any way distract the attention of the person being interviewed. Even small, loose objects, such as paper clips or pencils, should be out of the suspect's reach so that he cannot pick up and fumble with anything during the course of the interview. Tension-relieving activities of this sort can detract from the effectiveness of an interrogation, especially during the critical phase *when a guilty person may be trying desperately to suppress an urge to confess*. If pictures or ornaments are used at all, they should be only on the wall behind the suspect. If there is a window in the room, it, too, should be to the rear.
>
> (Inbau et al. 2005: 29; emphasis added)

The desire to punish a defeated enemy can be so strong that normal time-consuming procedures of due process are neglected. In a dissenting Supreme Court opinion on the trial of General Yamashita, Frank Murphy wrote that 'in all this needless and unseemly haste there was no serious attempt to charge or prove that he committed a recognized violation of the laws of war' (*Yamashita v. Styer* [1946] 327 US 1). The crucial fact is that the haste was *needless*: I return to this point. Transitional justice exhibits many other examples of 'wild justice' that were not justified by any imminent danger (Elster 2004: ch. 8). James Fitzjames Stephen refers critically to commissions of martial law that 'authorize not merely the suppression of revolts by military force, which is undoubtedly legal, but the subsequent punishment of offenders by illegal tribunals, which is ... forbidden by the Petition of Rights' (1883: i. 210).

Urgency can be highly adaptive. In threatening situations, immediate reaction is often crucial. The opportunity costs of urgency are often far less than the opportunity costs of waiting. In many of the cases I have cited, however, waiting is costless. After the enemy has been defeated, haste in condemning and executing him is indeed 'needless.' In typical cases, delaying a proposal of marriage or postponing a confession of adultery cannot harm and might help. Whatever the causes of maladaptive urgency, it seems clear that it exists and matters. The reasons it has been ignored are probably that the effects of urgency are easily confused with those of impatience and that urgency is easily assumed to be adaptive in all cases simply because it is adaptive in some cases.

A contentious but important example is provided by the reactions of the western governments after the attacks on September 11 2001. The unprecedented haste in which the antiterrorist laws were adopted (Haubrich 2003) suggests that emotion may have been at work. It is not clear which emotion dominated: anger or fear. Nor is it clear whose emotions were in play: those of the executive and legislative leadership or those of the population at large. Bracketing these issues, and assuming that the urgency of the measures that were taken had some emotional source, were they adaptive or maladaptive? I shall return to that question in the next section.

3.5 THE IMPACT OF EMOTION ON BELIEF FORMATION AND INFORMATION-GATHERING

As suggested by Figure 3.2, emotions can affect beliefs in two ways: directly, and indirectly via the gathering of information. The result is, respectively, biased beliefs and low-quality beliefs. I shall consider them in turn.

A French proverb states: 'We believe easily what we fear and what we hope.' The second part of the statement refers to the well-known phenomenon of emotion-induced wishful thinking. In a state of *amour-passion* a person will find all sorts of wonderful qualities in the object of the emotion. As Stendhal says, 'From the moment he falls in love even the wisest man no longer sees anything *as it really is*. . . . He no longer admits an element of chance in things and loses his sense of the probable; judging by its effect on his happiness, whatever he imagines becomes reality' (1980: ch. 12) As a different kind of example, one may cite the numerous rumors among Napoleon's followers about his impending return after his two defeats in 1814 and 1815 (Ploux 2003).

This familiar effect is entirely unsurprising. The phenomenon of emotion-induced 'counterwishful thinking' is more puzzling. Why should we believe that a danger is greater than it actually is? Why, for instance, would a husband believe that his wife is unfaithful to him, when both the evidence and his desires point in the opposite direction? What's in it for the organism? The outcome is dissonance production, not reduction. This 'Othello effect,' as we might call it, does not seem to have attracted the attention of psychologists, although a few philosophers (e.g. Mele 1999) have offered some (to my mind unconvincing) speculations. Yet the phenomenon is undeniable, as shown by many cases of panicky rumor formation. After the insurrection of the workers in Paris in June 1848, for instance, two men who were observed on the side of a country road became first 10, then 300 and 600 in the telling and retelling, until finally one could hear that three thousand 'levelers' (*partageux*) were looting, burning, and massacring. Thirty thousand soldiers were sent out to counter the threat. An investigation revealed that one of the two was insane and that the other was his father who was in charge of him (Ploux 2003).

I now turn to the impact of emotion on belief that is mediated by information-gathering. The crucial mechanism is that of urgency. The preference for early action over delayed action may prevent the agent from gathering the amount of information that would have been optimal from a rational point of view. In itself, this mechanism does not induce biased beliefs, only low-quality beliefs. It may, however, *prevent de-biasing* of beliefs. Often bias and urgency coexist. In love, we observe both the bias described by Stendhal and the urgency described by the proverb about marrying in haste. If it had not been for the urgency, the agent might have gathered more information about the other person that would have made it harder to sustain the rose-tinted perceptions. The same interaction between bias and urgency can occur in fear and anger. After September 11 2001 emotion may both have induced an exaggerated perception of the danger and prevented the gathering of information that would have produced a more accurate perception.

Typically, urgency generates low-quality beliefs by causing the agent to ignore long-term consequences of present choice, because *the calculation of long-term and indirect effects is itself a time-consuming process*. One reason why legislatures scrutinize bills for a long time—sometimes several years—before enacting them into law is the desire to identify possible indirect or 'perverse' effects. If they focus on the immediate—and more quickly identifiable—short-term effects only, they run the risk of making serious mistakes. After September 11 2001 western governments may have done exactly this. It has now become a commonplace to observe that the violation of human rights symbolized by Guantanamo Bay and Abu Ghraib led to more terrorists being recruited than were deterred or apprehended. As Minister of the Interior, Nicholas Sarkozy opposed the French law banning the veil in schools on these grounds. In an interview with *Le Nouvel Observateur* on 19 October 2003 he stated his 'fear that a law adopted in such a hurried way (*dans l'urgence*) would be viewed by the Muslim community as a punishment or a humiliation. This would only produce the opposite of the desired effect, and might risk triggering confrontation or radicalization. . . . Let us not open up a new war of religion.'

Impatience reinforces the tendency to underinvest in information about long-term consequences. Since an impatient agent cares little about the future, he has little incentive to find out what it is going to be like. Because of the emotion-induced urgency, he invests little in information-gathering of *any* kind. As shown in Figure 3.5, both urgency and impatience tend to cause 'short-termism.'

As noted earlier, urgency can be adaptive. The cost of ignoring long-term consequences may be less than the cost of delaying action. In nonemotional states, loss aversion induces a tendency to *disregard* opportunity costs and to pay more attention to out-of-pocket expenses. Faced with a possible risk, an agent might be dissuaded from taking extensive precautions because of their direct cost, while not giving enough weight to the fact that inaction might also be costly. The urgency of

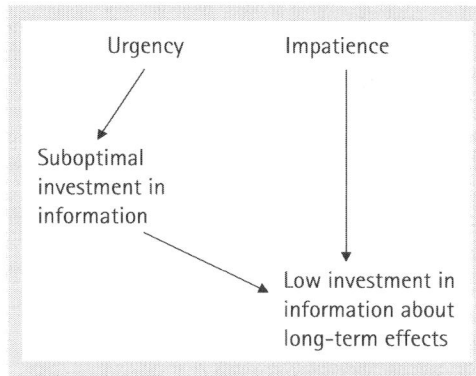

Fig. 3.5 Causes of 'short–termism'

emotion may sometimes provide a useful corrective to this irrational tendency. Yet, as also noted, urgency is often maladaptive. Panic reactions or instant retaliation ('shoot first, ask later') may be less adaptive in complex modern societies than they were at the stage when evolution fixed them in our genes.

REFERENCES

ARKES, H., and AYTON, P. (1999), 'The Sunk Cost and Concorde Effects: Are Humans Less Rational than Lower Animals?', *Psychological Bulletin*, 125: 591–600.

BAR-ELI, M., et al. (2007), 'Action Bias among Elite Goalkeepers: The Case of Penalty Kicks', *Journal of Economic Psychology*, 28: 606–21.

BÉNICHOU, P. (1948), *Morales du grand siècle* (Paris: Gallimard).

CAMERER, C. (2003), *Behavioral Game Theory* (New York: Russell Sage).

CAPPELLETTO, F. (2003), 'Public Memories and Personal Stories: Recalling the Nazi-fascist Massacres', paper presented at the workshop on 'Memory of War', Department of Political Science, MIT, January 2003.

COSTA, D., and KAHN, M. (2007), 'Deserters, Social Norms, and Migration', *Journal of Law and Economics*, 50: 323–53.

COWEN, T. (1991), 'Self-constraint Versus Self-liberation', *Ethics*, 101: 360–73.

CRENSHAW, M. (1972), 'The Concept of Revolutionary Terrorism', *Journal of Conflict Resolution*, 16: 383–96.

DAVIDSON, D. (1969), 'How is Weakness of the Will Possible', in Davidson, *Essays on Actions and Events* (Oxford: Oxford University Press).

—— (1982), 'Paradoxes of Irrationality', in R. Wollheim and J. Hopkins (eds.), *Philosophical Essays on Freud* (Cambridge: Cambridge University Press), 289–305.

DESCARTES, R. (1985), 'Passions of the Soul', in *The Philosophical Writings of Descartes*, i, trans. John Cottingham, Robert Stoothoff, and Dugald Murdoch (Cambridge: Cambridge University Press).

DODDS, E. R. (1951), *The Greeks and the Irrational* (Berkeley/Los Angeles, Calif.: University of California Press).

EKMAN, P. (1992*a*), *Telling Lies* (New York: Norton).

—— (1992*b*), 'An Argument for Basic Emotions', *Cognition and Emotion*, 6: 169–200.

ELSTER, J. (1999*a*), *Alchemies of the Mind* (Cambridge: Cambridge University Press).

—— (1999*b*), 'Davidson on Weakness of Will and Self-deception', in L. Hahn (ed.), *The Philosophy of Donald Davidson* (Chicago, Ill.: Open Court), 425–42.

—— (2004), *Closing the Books* (Cambridge: Cambridge University Press).

—— (2006), 'Weakness of Will and Preference Reversal', in J. Elster et al. (eds.), *Understanding Choice, Explaining Behavior: Essays in Honour of Ole-Jørgen Skog* (Oslo: Oslo Academic Press).

—— (2007), *Agir contre soi* (Paris: Jacob).

FEHR, E., and FISCHBACHER, U. (2004), 'Third-party Punishment and Social Norms', *Evolution and Human Behavior*, 25: 63–87.

GABORY, A. (1989), *Les Guerres de Vendée* (Paris: Laffont).

GIGERENZER, G. (2004), 'Dread Risk, September 11, and Fatal Traffic Accidents', *Psychological Science*, 15: 286–7.

GORDON, R. M. (1987), *The Structure of Emotions* (Cambridge: Cambridge University Press).

GROOPMAN, B. (2007), *How Doctors Think* (Boston, Mass.: Houghton Mifflin).

GUNNELL, D., et al. (1997), 'Use of Paracetamol for Suicide and Non-fatal Poisoning in the UK and France: Are Restrictions on Availability Justified?', *Journal of Epidemiology and Community Health*, 51: 175–9.

HAGEN, E. H. (2003), 'The Bargaining Model of Depression', in P. Hammerstein (ed.), *Genetic and Cultural Evolution of Cooperation* (Cambridge, Mass.: MIT Press).

HAUBRICH, D. (2003), 'September 11, Anti-terror Laws and Civil Liberties: Britain, France and Germany Compared', *Government and Opposition*, 38: 3–28.

HILL, P. (2005), 'Kamikaze 1943–1945', in D. Gambetta (ed.), *Making Sense of Suicide Missions* (Oxford: Oxford University Press).

HUYSE, L., and DHONDT, S. (1993), *La répression des collaborations, 1942–1952: Un passé toujours présent* (Bruxelles: CRISP).

INBAU, F., et al. (2005), *Criminal Interrogation and Confessions* (Sudbury, Mass.: Jones and Bartlett).

ISEN, A., and PATRICK, R. (1983), 'The Effects of Positive Feeling on Risk-taking', *Organizational Behavior and Human Performance*, 31: 194–202.

—— and GEVA, N. (1987), 'The Influence of Positive Affect on Acceptable Level of Risk and Thoughts About Losing', *Organizational Behavior and Human Decision Processes*, 39: 145–54.

KAHNEMAN, D., and TVERSKY, A. (1979), 'Prospect Theory', *Econometrica*, 47: 263–92.

LeDOUX, J. (1996), *The Emotional Brain* (New York: Simon & Schuster).

LEFEBVRE, G. (1988), *La grande peur de 1789* (Paris: Colin).

LEITH, K., and BAUMEISTER, R. (1996), 'Why do Bad Moods Increase Self-defeating Behavior? Emotion, Risk-taking, and Self-regulation', *Journal of Personality and Social Psychology*, 71: 1250–67.

LERNER, J. S., and KELTNER, D. (2001), 'Fear, Anger, and Risk', *Journal of Personality and Social Psychology*, 81: 146–59.

LEVY, R. (1973), *The Tahitians* (Chicago, Ill.: University of Chicago Press).

LOEWENSTEIN, G. (1996), 'Out of Control: Visceral Influences on Behavior', *Organizational Behavior and Human Decision Processes*, 65: 272–92.

—— (2005), 'Hot–cold Empathy Gaps and Medical Decision-making', *Health Psychology*, 24: S49–S56.

LÓPEZ-ROUSSEAU, A. (2005), 'Avoiding the Death Risk of Avoiding a Dread Risk: The Aftermath of March 11 in Spain', *Psychological Science*, 16: 426–8.

MASON, H. L. (1952), *The Purge of Dutch Quislings* (The Hague: Nijhoff).

MELE, A. (1999), 'Twisted Self-deception', *Philosophical Psychology*, 12: 117–37.

MERTON, R. K. (1946), *Mass Persuasion* (Westport, Conn.: Greenwood).

OSTACZEWSKI, P. (1996), 'The Relation between Temperament and the Rate of Temporal Discounting', *European Journal of Personality*, 10: 161–72.

PATT, A., and ZECKHAUSER, R. (2000), 'Action Bias and Environmental Decisions', *Journal of Risk and Uncertainty*, 21: 45–72.

PETERSEN, R. (2005), 'The Strategic Use of Emotion in Conflict: Emotion and Interest in the Reconstruction of Multiethnic States', unpublished MS, Dept. of Political Science, MIT.

PLOUX, F. (2003), *De bouche à oreille: Naissance et propagation des rumeurs dans la France du XIXe siècle* (Paris: Aubier).

RICOLFI, L. (2005), 'Palestinians, 1981–2003', in D. Gambetta (ed.), *Making Sense of Suicide Missions* (Oxford: Oxford University Press).

SLOVIC, P. (2000), *The Perception of Risk* (Sterling, Va.: Earthscan).

STENDHAL (1980), *De l'amour*, ed. V. Del Litto (Paris: Gallimard).

STEPHEN, J. F. (1883), *A History of English Criminal Law* (London: Macmillan).

SUNSTEIN, C. (2005), *Laws of Fear* (Cambridge: Cambridge University Press).

TENNOV, D. (1979), *Love and Limerence* (New York: Stein & Day).

TICE, D., BRASLASVKY, E., and BAUMEISTER, R. (2001), 'Emotional Distress Regulation Takes Precedence over Impulse Control', *Journal of Personality and Social Psychology*, 80: 53–67.

TURVILL, J., BURROUGHS, A., and MOORE, K. (2000), 'Change in Occurrence of Paracetamol Overdose in UK after Introduction of Blister Packs', *The Lancet*, 355: 2048–9.

UNAMA (United Nations Assistance Mission to Afganistan) (2007), 'Suicide Attacks in Afganistan', at <http://www.unama-afg.org/docs/_UN-Docs/UNAMA%20-%20SUICIDE%20ATTACKS%20STUDY%20-%20SEPT%209th%202007.pdf>, accessed 2008.

CHAPTER 4

···

BELIEFS*

···

JENS RYDGREN

INTRODUCTION

···

SOCIETY consists of people doing things, and in order to understand how social reality works we have to explain social action. This is true not only for understanding micro-sociological issues, but also complex macro-sociological phenomena such as capitalism and globalization, which ultimately consist of people doing things in certain ways. Action, as it is understood in this chapter, is what people do *intentionally*, in contrast to behavior, which is what they do *unintentionally* (see Hedström 2005: 38). In order to explain action, which by definition is to provide an intentional explanation, we need to specify the future state the action was intended to bring about (Elster 1983a). In order to do this we have to take people's desires and beliefs into account.

Of particular interest for the explanation of action are beliefs about the causal relationship between goals and the means of reaching these goals (cf. Elster 1983a). If an actor desires *y*, we may assume that s/he will act in a way that s/he believes will lead to *y*, for instance by doing *x*, in particular if *x* is seen as satisfyingly effective in reaching *y* compared to other action alternatives s/he can think of, and in particular if the actor believes that *x* is not interfering with fundamental values shared within his or her social surround. Hence, we may assume that—given their desires and beliefs—people act intentionally and with reason, if by reason we mean the 'human

* I would like to thank Pär Bendz, Peter Hedström, Stefan Svallfors, Ryszard Szulkin, Christopher Winship, and participants at the Nuffield Analytical Sociology Workshop (15–16 June 2007) for valuable comments on earlier drafts of this chapter.

process of seeking, processing, and drawing inferences' (Lupia et al. 2000: 1–2; cf. Hedström 2005: 61).[1]

However, as Elster emphasized (1983a: 70), since people's 'beliefs and desires are themselves in need of explanation . . . intentional explanation is far from a rock-bottom analysis.' With this in mind, the aim of this chapter is to contribute to a better understanding of belief formation.

If beliefs—which can be defined as propositions about the world in which a person is at least minimally confident (see Kruglanski 1989; Hedström 2005: 39)[2]—could always be inferred from people's situations in a perfect way, that is if beliefs were always congruent with reality, belief-formation processes would be transparent and of little interest to explanatory sociology. On the other hand, if beliefs were always incorrect and flawed in a uniquely idiosyncratic way, beliefs would be of little interest to analytical sociology because what needs to be explained is not the concrete actions of single individuals but rather the typical actions of typical individuals or why certain groups or categories of people act in certain ways. As will be demonstrated below, beliefs are sometimes biased and flawed, but these biases are not always random and unpredictable. This fact points to the need to identify patterns in belief-formation processes and, by doing this, to stake out a middle ground between the universalistic ambitions of much rational-choice theory, which may be analytically useful but sometimes too unrealistic to be sociologically meaningful, and subjectivist approaches, which are of scant analytical value. Because of the patterned character of belief biases, it is also unlikely that deviations from well-founded beliefs (derived from a strong assumption about rationality and perfect knowledge) are like random terms that cancel in the aggregate, as has often been proposed from Stinchcombe (1968) and onwards.

Consequently, this chapter will focus on common, relatively universal mechanisms of belief formation. We may analytically distinguish between six principal, albeit slightly overlapping, ways in which beliefs are formed: (1) by observation; (2) by relying on information received from others (including school teachers and the mass media, etc.), and here we also include socialization; (3) by inferences that go beyond direct observation, in using inductive strategies; (4) by deduction from other beliefs; (5) by adapting beliefs to fit desires (e.g. wishful thinking); and (6) by dissonance-reducing mechanisms, such as when beliefs are modified or rationalized to bring them into line with one's action or other beliefs (see Fishbein and Ajzen 1975; Holland et al. 1986: 22; Elster 1979, 1983b; Bar-Tal 1990; Festinger 1957). Often, however, beliefs are formed by combinations of these mechanisms. In the following sections I will further discuss most of these different types of belief formation.

Much of the following discussion will be set in a socio-cognitive framework. This framework is based on the assumption that individuals are motivated by an 'effort after meaning' (Bartlett 1995: 44); they are 'meaning-seeking' beings in the sense that they strive to obtain cognitive closure. Not being able to understand what is happening in one's surround—or what is likely to happen in the near future—results in negative emotions such as stress and frustration, something that most people try to avoid. As a consequence of this inherent effort after meaning, people inevitably, and usually unconsciously, form beliefs in order to obtain cognitive closure.

It should moreover be emphasized that individuals are socially situated, and that the conceptual schemes, knowledge, and information that shape people's views of the world are socially mediated. Only by specifying the situations in which people are embedded may we fully assess the reasons for their beliefs and understand group-specific uniformities in belief formation.

In addition, it should be noted that although beliefs are a fundamental component of intentional explanations of action, beliefs are themselves usually the result of unintentional—and often even unconscious—processes (see Hedström 2005: 43). Within the socio-cognitive framework in which this chapter is largely set, it is assumed that people are not only meaning seekers but also 'cognitive misers'; that is, motivated by a drive to save time and cognitive energy. This often leads them to use cognitive strategies that are vital for belief formation—and to rely on ready-made beliefs—without much reflection. In fact, people often do not become conscious of the beliefs they hold until they come to perceive doubt about their correctness and/or desirability. From a person's own perspective, all beliefs can be placed on a continuum ranging from absolute certainty to profound doubt (cf. Boudon 1989: 104), and the more certain people are about a belief's correctness the less likely they are to change the belief, or to even reflect on that belief and on possible alternative beliefs. Hence, doubt is one of the principal driving forces of belief change (cf. Peirce 1957a); unless doubt is triggered, few people will change beliefs. This chapter, therefore, will try to answer the question why people sometimes tend not to doubt dubious or false beliefs.

The remainder of this chapter will be structured in the following way. In Section 4.1 I will discuss the role of categorization in belief formation, something that is important for understanding how beliefs are formed both by observations and as a result of inferences. In the following two sections I will discuss two other fundamental mechanisms of belief formation by inferences: inductive reasoning and analogism. In Section 4.4 I will discuss the conditions under which people's beliefs are particularly likely to be influenced by others, and Section 4.5 will discuss the mechanism of dissonance reduction.

4.1 THE ROLE OF CATEGORIZATION IN BELIEF FORMATION

As noted above, observations are one of the ways in which beliefs are formed. Observations are also an important reason for group-specific uniformities in belief formation. People who share observations—who have similar experiences—are more likely to share beliefs (see Rydgren 2009). However, it is important to emphasize that observations are often the result of a complex process, not merely mimetic transcripts of reality. Within the socio-cognitive framework of this chapter, it is assumed that there are no 'pure' observations; in order to make sense of the 'blooming, buzzing confusion' of raw experience (James 1890) people have to use the universal mechanism of categorization. Hence, the basic assumption is that reality is usually too complex to be perceived and apprehended without the help of categories. Categorization is a linguistic tool—we categorize by labeling—and we are largely unconscious of using categorization schemes that are not of our own choosing, but are by-products of joining, or being born into, a particular language or linguistic culture or subculture. This implies that our perceptions of the world are to some extent dependent on a priori knowledge structures, and that perceptions are always to some extent simplifications of a more complex reality. In a given situation, for example, few of us see two hundred individual flying objects; we just see birds—or maybe starlings, sparrows, and crows, if we are moderately interested in birds. Granted, there are different levels of categorization, where some are very broad and crude and some allow for subtle distinctions, but, because of our limited cognitive capacity, none of us uses fine-grained categorization levels for all domains and in all situations, although we may assume that there is considerable individual variation (see Brown 1958; Holland et al. 1986: 184; McGarty 1999).

However, it is not always evident how complex reality should be categorized. Sometimes a given object can be fitted into different categories. In the duck-rabbit figure, to take a well-known example, some people immediately see a duck where other people immediately see a rabbit. It usually takes more effort, though, to see it as a duck *and* a rabbit (see Jastrow 1900; cf. Wittgenstein 1997). Being cognitive misers, people often fail to perceive the complexity of particular observations, and risk ending up with a one-sided understanding around which beliefs are formed. It also means that two people witnessing the same thing may form very different beliefs around their observations. For reasons discussed below, this is in particular likely for observations of social reality. Let us assume a situation where, in the South Bronx, two young African American men rob an old lady. Whether this event is categorized as a 'race problem,' a 'youth problem,' an 'urban problem,' a 'problem of masculinity,' or a 'class problem'—that is, a problem of socioeconomic marginality—is likely to play a large role in how beliefs are formed around the (direct or mediated) observation of this event. In each of these categorizations some particular features of the situation are highlighted, whereas others are de-emphasized. Which categories people choose is partly determined by the context and partly by the disposition of the categorizer. In the former case, some categorizations may be more salient and/or legitimate than others because they are more widely shared by significant others and/or promoted by 'epistemic authorities' (the concept is from Kruglanski 1989 and will be defined below) who 'frame' the event in certain ways (cf. Chong and Druckman 2007). Framing effects are likely to result from situations of ambiguous categorization; that is, beliefs are strongly influenced by the way the problem is presented by others.[3] In the latter case, the beliefs held a priori by the observer are likely to play a large role, as does 'priming.' If an event 'has occurred very recently which is evocative of a particular categorization then it is likely that subsequent events or situations will also be interpreted in terms of that same category system' (Brown 1995: 66–7; cf. McGarty 1999: ch. 4). Hence, once a particular category has been mobilized in meeting an object, event, situation, or person, further perception and understanding of the object will partly be dictated by the characteristics of the category (Kahneman and Tversky 1982).

As implied in the discussion above, categorization is not only fundamental for observations, but is also a basic mechanism for inferences. By categorizing object a (of which we know relatively little) as an instance of category A (of which we know relatively much) we very often generalize from the wider class to the instance. Hence, if objects belonging to category A usually share characteristics p, q, and r, we tend to infer that object a also has characteristics p, q, and r. As will be further discussed below, this kind of thinking constitutes the basis for induction and analogisms. Moreover, as argued by Holland et al. (1986: 89), generalizations from categorizations constitute an important type of *abduction*; that is, the tendency when encountering problematic reality to formulate an explanatory hypothesis that explains the problem inductively or deductively (see Peirce 1957b).[4]

How sound the inferences generated by inferential categorization are depends on how accurate our knowledge is of category A, the certitude with which object a is categorized as an instance of category A, how specific and fine-grained category A is, and, relatedly, how heterogeneous it is—that is, if objects belonging to category A share many or only a few characteristics. At best, this way of making inferences through categorization is a parsimonious cognitive mechanism for predicting, relatively accurately, unknown characteristics of specific objects (or persons, events, situations, etc.). At worst, however, it restrains people from using more sophisticated tools to make inferences, and makes them prone to stereotypical beliefs. There are good reasons to assume that this risk is particularly pronounced with regard to inferences involving social categorizations. In the physical world, according to Nisbett and Ross (1980: 38–9), it is an approximate truth to say that 'if you've seen one oak tree, you've seen them all.' Here we only need a limited number of properties to define objects as belonging to one category rather than another, and once we have correctly placed an object in the category of oak trees, we can with extremely high probability predict that 'the tree will provide shade and acorns, [and] that it's wood will be hard and burn slowly' (ibid.). In the social world, however, this is rarely the case. Here the observed properties of an object are less diagnostic and not so sharply delineated. As noted above, there are usually many possible categories into which the object may be placed, and once the categorization has taken place, further predictions of properties of the categorized object are likely to fail. Hence, in the social world, categorizations should be no more than 'tentative guides for perception and behavior. When they are relied on heavily, there are bound to be inferential errors and misguided actions' (Nisbett and Ross 1980: 8–9; cf. McGarty 1999).

4.2 THE ROLE OF INDUCTIVE REASONING IN BELIEF FORMATION

When making inferences that go beyond direct observation, people often rely on various inductive strategies. While induction is problematic from a philosophical point of view, human thinking could not do without it (see Boudon 1994: 64). In everyday thinking, inductive strategies very often lead to reasonably satisfying results (seen from a person's own perspective). However, as will be discussed below, sometimes these strategies go awry and lead to incorrect inferences. Yet when people use such well-tried strategies they tend to rely on the results without much reflection, something that may help explain why people sometimes fail to doubt dubious or even false beliefs.

First, even for logically valid reasoning such as *modus ponens* and *modus tollens* the validity of the inferences depends on how well the process of categorization works. And, as discussed above, categorization may sometimes be problematic, in particular concerning objects in the social world. One important problem, identified by Holland et al. (1986: 231), is the tendency to take for granted that 'a property observed in an object is a constant, stable one.' When making inferences about swans being white or not, for instance, it is usually expected that 'a particular swan, once observed to be white, will continue to be white.' However, in particular for social entities and phenomena, such as persons or behavior, it is far from generally the case that properties stay constant—something that may lead to erroneous inferences. Second, people sometimes employ logically invalid inductive strategies. Such strategies often help them make inferences that are 'good enough,' or at least better than what would have otherwise been arrived at. However, because they are similar in form to logically valid inductive strategies, people tend to be overconfident about beliefs that result from such inferences. Arguably, the two most common, and important, forms of such logically invalid inductive strategies are the 'affirmation-of-the-consequent induction'; that is,

1. If p, then always q
2. q
_____
3. Therefore, p

and the 'denying-the-antecedent induction,' that is

1. If p, then always q
2. *Not-p*

---

3. Therefore, *not-q* (Holland et al. 1986: 267).

Whether such logically invalid inductive modes of reasoning turn out to useful or not largely depends on the conditional probability of p|q. Everything else being equal, a high probability of p|q will lead to less erroneous inferences than will be the case with a low probability of p|q. Since the probability of p|q is much higher in Example A than in Example B (below), the conclusion drawn from the line of reasoning in Example A seems more plausible than the inference drawn in Example B:

A:

1. If it is cold (p), people wear a lot of clothes (q).
2. People wear a lot of clothes (q).

---

3. Therefore, it is cold (p).

B:

1. Pneumonia (p) causes fever (q).
2. I have a fever (q).

---

3. Therefore, I have pneumonia (p). (See Rydgren 2004.)

Although we cannot be sure that our inferences lead to correct beliefs in the first example (people could, for instance, wear a lot of clothes because it is fashionable), it is a useful guiding principle to look out of the window to see what people are wearing in order to determine whether it is cold out or not. (If fashion dictated a lot of clothes, people would probably have noted it earlier.) Stated differently: based on earlier experiences most people 'know' that the conditional probability of p|q is high. The second example, however, is considerably less certain as a guiding principle because my fever could have been caused by a multitude of other ills. However, since most people have had the opportunity to experience that this is the case, they 'know' that the conditional probability of p|q is low. This is probably why few people draw the conclusion drawn in Example B.

In Examples A and B it is relatively easy to assess the probability of p|q because they involve events and properties that are repetitive. People have a good chance to assess probability over time, and to modify initial misconceptions. As Ayer (1963: 202) has argued, 'in order to estimate the probability that a particular individual possesses a given property, we are to choose as our class of reference, among those to which the individuals belongs, the narrowest class in which the property occurs with an extrapolable frequency.' However, as discussed above, categories and classes of references—in particular in the social world—are often arbitrary and not so sharply delineated. A given object (or person, event, situation, etc.) can often be placed in a range of different categories, and there are occasionally several 'narrowest reference categories' to choose between. As a result, in many cases people do not know whether the conditional probability of p|q is high or low, in particular in cases where we cannot easily choose between different, equally narrow reference classes, or when the event in question is unique. In such cases people may come to rely on flawed estimations of the conditional probability of p|q, which leads to erroneous inferences and makes them ascribe too much certainty to beliefs that result from such thought processes. Under certain circumstances people may even come to believe inferences similar to the one in Example B (above).

This may be exemplified by the many daycare sex-abuse scandals in the USA in the 1980s and early 1990s (Oberschall 2000). These all began when parents of one or two children suspected that a daycare provider had 'touched' their child; gradually, this developed into accusations of 'dozens of adults victimizing many children in hundreds of acts of oral and anal sex, ritual torture of animals and babies...and killing unspecified babies with knives and guns' (Oberschall 2000: 297–8). There were no eyewitnesses to the abuse, and in addition no physical evidence from medical examinations. Still, not only the parents, but members of the juries, too, believed that the abuse had really taken place. One important reason for this, I would argue, was the lack of prior experience and relevant information, which made it difficult to estimate the conditional probability of p|q. The only 'authorized' information came from the therapists and child-protection workers who were in charge of the interrogation of the children, and who therefore greatly influenced the belief-formation process. The therapists and the child-protection workers presented 'a huge list of "symptoms"' indicating abuse. Everything 'from bed wetting and nightmares to fears and aggressive play, excessive interest in sex, being uncooperative and uncommunicative, spending too much time on the toilet' were all viewed as signs of sexual abuse (Oberschall 2000: 303). To put this into the logical form presented above:

1. If children have been sexually abused (p), they wet their beds (q) *or* have nightmares (r) *or* play aggressively (s), etc.
2. Since my child wets his/her bed (q) *or* has nightmares (r) *or* plays aggressively (s),

---

3. s/he has been sexually abused (p).

Since all these symptoms can be caused by a multitude of other things, the fact that the inference drawn from this line of reasoning became significant in the determination of guilt is unacceptable from a logical perspective. Yet this is what happened.

However, in order to fully understand this case we have to take into account the dilemma of choosing between possible Type 1 errors (that is, to believe something is incorrect while it is actually correct) and Type 2 errors (that is, to believe something is correct while it is actually incorrect) (see Rydgren 2004). This dilemma was succinctly formulated by Pascal (1995: 121–5) in his famous passage on 'the wager.' In deciding whether or not to believe in the existence of God, it is according to Pascal a better bet to choose to believe than to disbelieve. If your belief in God's existence turns out to be incorrect, you lose nothing at all, whereas you gain eternal bliss if it turns out to be correct; and if your disbelief in God's existence turns out to be correct you gain nothing at all, whereas you lose everything, by being subjected to eternal damnation, if you erroneously believe that God does not exist. In decision-theoretical terms, therefore, to believe in God is superdominant over disbelieving. This argument has rightly been criticized on many grounds (see Hájek 2004 for a review), but it formulates an important mechanism for how everyday thinking in situations of uncertainty often works (cf. Mackie's discussion (1996) on the 'belief trap,' which is essentially the same mechanism). In the example above, which admittedly is trickier than Pascal's wager since it lacks an evident superdominant strategy, the risk of committing a Type 1 error (that is, disbelieving in sexual assaults that actually took place, which might lead to more abuses in the future) might for the people involved—in particular for the parents—have consequences that override the risk of committing a Type 2 error (that is, incorrectly believing that sexual assaults had been committed, and risking condemning an innocent person). Granted, beliefs are only occasionally formed consciously as implied by these examples; most of the time we do not decide to believe what we believe. However, this mechanism may also work unconsciously, sometimes together with the drive to make one's beliefs fit with one's desires, such as in wishful thinking.

4.3 ANALOGISM

Another common and, in fact, indispensable way of making inferences that goes beyond direct observations is to rely on analogical reasoning. Like the 'affirmation-of-the-consequent induction' and the 'denying-the-antecedent induction,' as discussed above, analogism is invalid from a logical point of view. Yet it is potentially very useful and it often helps people reach better conclusions—around which beliefs are formed—than would otherwise have been arrived at (see Holyoak and Thagard 1999: 7).

We have an analogism when we draw the conclusion from

1. the fact that object A has properties p and q
2. and the observation that object B has the property p

---

3. that object B also has property q.

Hence, analogism is fundamentally an inference based on categorizations and it may be a relatively parsimonious way for people in ambiguous situations to make sense of what is going on and what to expect in the near future. Analogism may thus be an important mechanism in belief formation. In order to be effective, analogies must follow two criteria. They must concern *significant* and *pertinent* properties that are common to the objects (or persons, situations, events, etc.), and they must not ignore significant or pertinent dissimilarities between the objects (see e.g. Pratkanis and Aronson 2002: 90). The problem, of course, is that it is sometimes difficult to determine which properties are pertinent—in particular with regard to categories in the social world.

Analogism is particularly useful for employing 'knowledge' about the past to understand the present or predict the future (see Rydgren 2007). Such 'knowledge' may consist of beliefs based on one's own earlier observations, or on beliefs received from others. Nevertheless, in situations of uncertainty it is often tempting to rely on 'the lessons of the past' (see Boudon 1989: 105). This is true both of mundane, commonplace decisions and decisions of vital importance. If one does not know much about wine, for instance, and is going to have some friends over for dinner, it is likely that one will follow the line of reasoning that

1. since the bottle I bought last time (A) was a Bordeaux (p) and tasted good (q),
2. there are good reasons to believe that, among all the possible alternatives in the store, bottle B which also is a Bordeaux (p),

---

3. will taste good as well (q).

Although this analogism is error prone, the likelihood of making sound predictions will probably be higher than would have been the case without any guiding principle. In this case categorization (i.e. that A and B in fact share p) does not cause much of a problem, and it is relatively easy, through practical experience or theoretical learning, to identify additional pertinent properties of wine that will increase the chances of making sound predictions by enabling us to use a narrower reference category (see Rydgren 2004). However, as discussed above, categorization may sometimes cause greater problems, and it is not always obvious which properties are pertinent or not. In such cases, the likelihood of making sound predictions when using the analogism is much lower, and there is often little consensus over which of several possible 'lessons of the past' one should rely on.

After the Iraqi occupation of Kuwait in 1990, for instance, both leading advocates for and against sending American troops to the Gulf based their understanding of the situation—and their predictions about the future—on analogisms. However, whereas those who advocated sending troops relied on the World War II analogism, comparing Saddam Hussein to Hitler and warning of a politics of appeasement (i.e. 'if Chamberlain and others had taken a tough stance against German aggression earlier, the war would not have needed to become as widespread and protracted'), those who were against sending troops to the Gulf relied on the Vietnam War analogy (Schuman and Reiger 1992). As shown by Khong (1992), analogisms of this kind are often used when making decisions of vital importance, even in war situations, although it is not at all evident that they involve all (or even most) pertinent aspects—and pertinent aspects only.

In addition to the problem of categorization, there are a variety of fallacies associated with analogism, of which two will be discussed here (see Rydgren 2007 for further discussion and additional biases). First, there is the problem of overreliance. Because analogisms are often applied to nonrepetitive events, which makes it difficult for people to falsify them within the realms of everyday epistemology, people often rely on analogisms more uncritically than they should. Similarly, although analogical inferences are at best probabilistic, people often make the erroneous inference 'from the fact that A and B are similar in some respect to the false conclusion that they are the same in all respects' (Fischer 1970: 247).

Second, there is the problem of selection bias. For the first step of the analogism—that is, past events with which to compare the present—people tend to select events that are easily available to memory (cf. Khong 1992: 35). In other words, people tend to rely on the *availability heuristic* (Tversky and Kahneman 1982). The availability heuristic is often useful, because people tend to remember significant events better than insignificant ones. However, there are several factors affecting availability that may lead to bias. One important example is the risk of an 'egocentric bias'; that is, the tendency to be insensitive to one's limited knowledge of the world that lies outside one's experiences. Because of their location in the social structure and their lifestyles and personal preferences, people encounter specific but limited slices of the social world—something which 'may funnel unrepresentative evidence or information to them in a thousand different domains' (Nisbett and Ross 1980: 262–3). Another important bias is that vivid information tends to be better remembered and is more accessible than pallid information. Information that is likely to attract and hold our attention because it is emotionally interesting, concrete, and imagery-provoking, and/or proximate in a sensory, temporal, or spatial way may be deemed vivid (Nisbett and Ross 1980: 44–5). This implies that common routine events—which although dull are often highly representative—are forgotten, whereas spectacular, unique, and unexpected events—which are often highly unrepresentative—are easily accessible to memory. A particular type of pallid information that people tend to overlook is null information, about potential events that did not occur. This not only leads to availability-heuristic biases; more generally it also leads to flawed inferences about causation. To assess the probability that A causes B we should not only take positive cases into account (i.e. those instances in which A is followed by B) but also negative cases (i.e. those instances in which A is not followed by B). Numerous experiments have shown that people often fail to do this in their everyday thinking. (See Boudon 1994: 68–9 for a discussion of this literature.)

4.4 THE ROLE OF SOCIAL INFLUENCE ON BELIEF FORMATION

As implied above, people often get their beliefs from others. From early childhood on, others try to impose their beliefs on us. This is as true of parents, friends, and teachers as it is of state institutions or the media, to mention just a few examples.[5] Hence, as Peirce (1957a: 16) emphasized, to the extent that people are not hermits they will necessarily influence each other's beliefs. Belief formation through social influence takes place more or less constantly, and is usually unconscious from an actor's perspective. Yet I will argue that two situations in particular are likely to make people receptive to social influence: (1) so-called black-box situations, that is situations of uncertainty (Boudon 1989) when people face new situations that their standard cognitive strategies fail to handle; and (2) when a person's beliefs deviate from those held by most others in his or her social surround.

Let us start with the former. Because of our limited cognitive resources as well as time limitations none of us has deep knowledge of all domains. We may know a lot about French literature or car motors, for instance, but little or nothing about quantum physics or international law. If that is the case, the latter two areas are black boxes for us. As has been argued by Boudon (1989: 84), it is often a reasonable strategy—and sometimes even rational—for people in such situations to avoid examining what is inside these black boxes, 'but rather to rely on authoritative arguments and judgements.' Most of the time, we may assume, people's navigation through black-box situations is not haphazard. Whom one relies on in a black-box situation largely depends on whom one trusts and whom one views as authoritative—and people tend to view certain actors and sources as more authoritative than others. For instance, people tend to be more confident in information coming from *epistemic authorities* (Kruglanski 1989), and more likely to adopt beliefs espoused by such actors, whose authority often derives from their social role, often associated with a position of power. Elite actors such as political, intellectual, and religious leaders are typical examples of epistemic authorities (see

Bar-Tal 1990: 71), as are experts more generally. Moreover, people are more likely to view somebody belonging to the same social group or social category as themselves as an epistemic authority (Raviv et al. 1993: 132).

However, people not only rely on epistemic authorities in black-box situations, but also on each other, particularly in situations in which no expert or other epistemic authority is readily available. There are numerous examples of this in mundane everyday action, as when one glances at other diners for information about which fork to use for the first course, or when the choice of restaurant is based on the number of other people already eating there (Granovetter 1978; Hedström 1998). Similarly, invoking the same mechanism of *social proof*, studies of consumption behavior have often observed that people are more likely to buy a product if they believe it is popular. As Neill (2005: 192) noted, this is why McDonald's 'advertises "billions and billions" of hamburgers sold.' In all these cases people base their beliefs on the assumption that what most others do is likely to be correct and that these people have good reasons for acting as they do. However, one risk associated with the strategy of imitation is that everyone may imitate the others, and that everyone may think that they alone are uncertain and confused or feel doubt. Sometimes, however, as in Merton's discussion (1968) of the self-fulfilling prophesy, an initially false belief may become true as enough people act upon it. A rumor about a bank's insolvency is likely to activate the Type 1/Type 2 dilemma (as discussed above), and many people will find it a better strategy to believe in the rumor and possibly be wrong than to incorrectly disbelieve it (because there are greater personal costs associated with the latter alternative). As a result, people will start to withdraw their savings from the bank, which will on the one hand reduce the bank's solvency and on the other hand be likely to influence other people to withdraw their money—and so on, until the bank actually goes bankrupt. We may assume that the likelihood of such an outcome will increase if the initial rumor originates from an epistemic authority, or if a trusted high-status person acts on the rumor.

However, sometimes—as in Hans Christian Andersen's story, 'The Emperor's New Clothes' (2001)—people in black-box situations may even come to follow a majority that actually does not exist; they may all come to believe that everyone else has understood something important of which they themselves are ignorant, and refrain from questioning the consensus out of fear of ridicule or ostracism. I will come back to this phenomenon—which is known as *pluralistic ignorance* (Allport 1924)—below.

Hence, it is not only in black-box situations that people are particularly receptive to social influence, but also in situations in which they discover that the beliefs they hold deviate from those of most others in their social surround. In fact, as implied above, we may assume that beliefs are particularly likely to be influenced by the social surround in situations in which these two conditions combine. As noted by Festinger (1950, 1954), in situations of subjective uncertainty in which people lack objective reference points for their beliefs, they tend to compare their beliefs to those of significant others.[6] The more their beliefs harmonize with those of significant others, the more valid the beliefs are judged to be. When people discover that their beliefs harmonize with those held by most others in the group, they tend to become confident in their rightness and seldom change their opinion. Situations in which people's beliefs harmonize poorly with those held by significant others, on the other hand, tend to exacerbate the feeling of subjective uncertainty. To remedy this situation, people may change the group they belong to, and thus their significant others (which, however, often is difficult to do), or either try to change the beliefs held by the others in the group, or change their own beliefs to better reflect those of the group, which is often far easier.

However, the pressure to increase consistency between oneself and others is likely to vary between different structural situations. In particular, it is important to take 'loci of activity' into account (Feld 1981; Feld and Grofman 2009). Such loci (e.g. workplaces or neighborhoods) are important, as they bring people together in repeated interaction and thus organize people's social relations. We may assume that people will feel less pressure to increase consistency between oneself and others when interacting with people with whom they share only one or two loci, as compared to people with whom they share many loci. In the first case, more inconsistencies may be allowed for.

Nevertheless, this kind of conformity process was demonstrated by Asch (1956) in a series of highly influential experiments. Individuals were asked to match the length of a line with other lines of different length. All but one of the individuals in the group was instructed to make a match that was obviously wrong. When the last uninformed individual in each group was asked to make a match, one third of them yielded to the obviously erroneous judgment of the majority. Among the conforming subjects, a majority said they conformed because they lacked confidence in their own judgment and concluded that they must have been mistaken and the majority correct. The second most common reason was to persist in the belief that the majority was wrong, but to suppress this knowledge because of an unwillingness to deviate from the group. Asch showed that a majority of three persons was sufficient to have this effect. However, it is of crucial importance that the majority be unanimous, otherwise conformity decreases dramatically: conformity decreased from about a third to only five percent when a single individual deviated from the group by giving the correct answer (Allen 1975; cf. Bond 2005).

As shown by Asch's experiments, it is important to distinguish between belief conformity, on the one hand, and conformity in action, on the other. In order to escape negative sanctions, or to be rewarded economically or socially, people may change their action in order to conform to the group (see e.g. Deutsch and Gerard 1955), without giving up deviant beliefs held privately. Festinger (1953) emphasized this distinction by distinguishing between *internalization*—that is, both belief conformity and conformity in action—and *compliance*—that is, conformity in action but not in beliefs (see also Brown 2006). According to Festinger, compliance is more likely if a person is restricted from leaving a group or society and when there is a threat of social, economic, or physical punishment for noncompliance. The likelihood for internalization, on the other hand, increases if the person is attracted to the group and wishes to remain a member.

It is important to emphasize that people who suppress their true beliefs in order to conform to the majority view, or what they perceive to be the majority view (something that Kuran 1995 has called *preference falsification*) are likely to have an influence on other people's beliefs in the manner discussed above. This fact is of great importance for understanding diffusion processes. One poignant example is how conflicts escalate. As demonstrated by Kuran (1998), the pressure on people to conform to the 'in-group' increases in polarized situations in which the cost of remaining a deviant or even a passive bystander increases—because of both the risk of being branded a traitor by the in-group and the risk of being left unprotected from assaults from the 'out-group.' As a result, moderates may suppress their true beliefs, which gives radical or fanatical elements disproportionate influence. At the same time, because of the people who comply, others may get the impression that the majority is bigger than it actually is, which will increase the likelihood that they will comply as well—or that they will actually change beliefs. And so on.

Above I briefly introduced this kind of phenomenon as *pluralistic ignorance*. In situations of pluralistic ignorance people comply with the majority action while suppressing their true beliefs; at the same time, however, they believe that other people's actions reflect *their* true beliefs. There are numerous examples of pluralistic ignorance in all spheres of social life. As argued by Miller and McFarland (1991: 305), for instance, racial segregation in the USA may have persisted 'long after the majority opposed it because those who held anti-segregationist positions mistakenly believed they were in the minority' (see O'Gorman 1975 for a well-known study showing this). Even today, as shown by Shelton and Richeson (2005), racial segregation is partly upheld by pluralistic ignorance. Even though 'members of different racial groups would like to have more contact with members of other groups, they are often inhibited from doing so because they think out-group members do not want to have contact with them.' Pluralistic ignorance may also explain why totalitarian regimes may stay in power despite weak popular support and without having to use much direct violence. In states such as the Soviet Union, where there was little open communication among citizens (i.e. where public meetings were forbidden and where people feared informers), people 'lacked reliable information on how many of the fellow citizens favored radical political change—to say nothing of knowing others' readiness to react' (Kuran 1995: 125; see also Coser 1990). Because few people wanted to act against the regime if not enough other people were prepared to do the same, this impeded collective action (see Granovetter 1978).

As implied by the last example, the principal way out of pluralistic ignorance is communication. However—and this lies at the heart of the problem of pluralistic ignorance—people commonly refrain from communicating their true beliefs to others whom they do not fully trust, out of fear of negative sanctions. Hence, only under certain circumstances is communication likely to lead to 'common beliefs' (Bar-Tal 1990) or 'common knowledge' (Chwe 1999, 2001)—that is, to a situation in which people believe that their beliefs are shared by others with a high degree of certitude, and also believe that other people 'know' that they believe that is the case. Communication is more likely to lead to common beliefs among people in close contact with one another, and especially among cliques of people constituting so-called interlocked triads (that is, situations in which A knows B and C, and B and C also know one another). Strong ties are thus more likely to foster common beliefs than are weak ties; however, the problem is that such beliefs are likely to spread much more slowly through strong ties than through weak ones since weak ties are more likely to bridge different clusters (Chwe 1999; cf. Granovetter 1973). Common beliefs among a mass of people are more likely to emerge through various mass events, such as demonstrations or mass-media reports, that are shared by many people simultaneously. To understand the fall of Communism in the Soviet Union and the Eastern Bloc, one should not underestimate the fact that demonstrations organized by 'true believers,' in Leipzig for instance, were not violently repressed, something that attracted more people to subsequent demonstrations, which in turn created common beliefs about the fact that a considerable number of people were prepared to act against the regime (cf. Kuran 1995; Beissinger 2002).

4.5 DISSONANCE AND CONSISTENCY-SEEKING

As discussed above, people sometimes experience dissonance when they compare their beliefs with those held by significant others. However, even comparison with one's own other beliefs or with the ways in which one acts may create dissonance (Festinger 1957). The assumption of this theory is that humans are *consistency seekers*; dissonance is assumed to lead to negative emotions from which people are relieved once they have restored consistency between action and beliefs and/or between different beliefs by unconsciously changing one or more of their beliefs (Festinger 1957; Harmon-Jones and Mills 1999).

We find this mechanism in many classic explanations. For instance, the gist of Hannah Arendt's argument (1958) about how racism emerged as an ideology was that it was a way of reducing the dissonance between merciless exploitation due to imperialist expansion and the belief in humanity as the measure of everything. By dehumanizing the exploited group, imperialist expansion came to be seen as relatively natural and unproblematic. More generally, we often see this mechanism at work in processes of 'blaming the victim.' When treating another person badly, we commonly seek a way of justifying the action such as by adopting the belief that the person in question 'is stupid or careless or evil . . . and therefore deserved our maltreatment' (Pratkanis and Aronson 2002: 229; see Davis and Jones 1960 for a sociopsychological experiment showing this process).

However, the obvious objection to the theory of cognitive dissonance is that 'people do in fact tolerate a fair amount of inconsistency' (Fiske and Taylor 1991: 11). It is not uncommon for people to hold contradictory beliefs, apparently without experiencing any serious dissonance. And people sometimes do blame themselves after mistreating another person. As a result, we should be cautious not to exaggerate the motivational force provided by the search for consistency. This is not to say that consistency-seeking and dissonance reduction is not an important mechanism in many situations, only that it is far from universal and that we must understand why some inconsistencies rather than others activate the mechanism of dissonance reduction (cf. Kuran 1995: 183). In order to approach this important question, I would argue that we need to distinguish between beliefs according to their *centrality* and *tightness*.

Beliefs are often interconnected in various belief systems in which different beliefs imply each other (see e.g. Borhek and Curtis 1983). Such belief systems may concern politics or religion, for instance, and for some people politics and religion are different belief systems (that is, one's religious beliefs do not imply one's political beliefs) and for some people politics and religion are the same belief system. Beliefs that are subjectively deemed to belong to different belief systems and therefore do not imply one another possess no or only low tightness, whereas beliefs deemed to belong to the same belief system possess higher tightness (Martin 2002). As emphasized by Martin (ibid. 872), epistemic authorities play an important role in creating such belief tightness in authorizing certain webs of implications between beliefs and precluding others. I would argue that the mechanism of dissonance reduction needs belief tightness to be activated. We may assume that people without much reflection tolerate inconsistency between beliefs belonging to different belief systems, whereas cognitive dissonance is considerably more likely to result from inconsistency between beliefs belonging to the same belief system.

Moreover, beliefs are of different degrees of centrality within belief systems (Rokeach 1973). While a change in central beliefs has implications for many other beliefs, a change in more peripheral beliefs does not seriously affect other beliefs (Bar-Tal 1990: 16). With Rokeach (1973), we may assume that the more central a belief is, that is the more connected it is with other beliefs, the more resistant it is likely to be to change. This implies two important things. First, when dissonance occurs as a result of inconsistency between a central belief and one or more peripheral beliefs, people are more likely to change the latter than the former in order to reduce the dissonance. Second, people may leave central beliefs unchanged even if they cause inconsistencies and dissonance, because to change them would cause greater emotional distress than that caused by the dissonance. Moreover, similar to the logic of Kuhn's argument about paradigm shifts (1962), we may assume that people do not change beliefs, and in particular not central beliefs, unless there are available alternative beliefs that are perceived to be better.

CONCLUSION

The focus of this chapter has been on common, relatively universal mechanisms of belief formation, and it should be clear from the discussion above that beliefs cannot be inferred from strong assumptions about rationality—that is, that actors have perfect knowledge about the world and about optimal courses of action in given situations. Beliefs are not transparent, but should be taken seriously in the explanation of action. People tend to rely on beliefs that work, beliefs that are subjectively deemed to be good enough (see Simon 1979), even if these beliefs are biased and flawed. Priming, framing effects, and processes of social influence affect people's beliefs, and these need to be considered when assessing the beliefs groups of people hold in specific situations. This fact also points to the need to be cautious with making assumptions about Bayesian updating processes (see e.g. Breen 1999) unless empirical evidence justifying the assumption can be presented. In some situations it may be a realistic assumption; in many others it is not.

NOTES

1. So the line of argument taken in this chapter is that people act the way they do *because* of their beliefs (and desires); however, an alternative line of argument—proposed by Pareto (1935)—is that people act the way they do because of sentiments and self-interests, and that beliefs are mere rationalizations—that is, explanations constructed a posteriori in order to make their behavior seem reasonable (see also Fonesca 1991: 198; cf. Margolis 1987: 22). Although I agree with Pareto that action is not always—or even mostly—preceded by conscious calculations of possible action alternatives, it is difficult for me to conceive of action that does not involve a priori beliefs.

2. It is useful to distinguish between *descriptive beliefs* or *factual beliefs*, which imply truth or falsity, and *evaluative beliefs*, which have to do with believing something is good or bad (see e.g. Bar-Tal 1990). Both descriptive beliefs and evaluative beliefs can be about objects as well as relations between objects.

3. In such a way, for instance, about 20 percent of Americans believed that too little was spent on welfare, whereas 65 percent believed too few public resources were spent on 'assistance to the poor' (Chong and Druckman 2007: 104).

4. For instance, when pondering on the reason why my boss all of a sudden seems irritable towards me, I hypothesize that he is overworked—because that would explain his change in behavior.

5. One should not underestimate the role of the mass media—and in particular television—in this context. Writing in the early 1990s, Iyengar (1991: 1) observed that television 'takes up more of the typical American waking hours than interpersonal interaction.'

6. As argued by Goethals et al. (1991: 153), such social comparisons are often forced: whether we want it or not, most of us compare with other people 'who are salient or available, or with whom we interact.'

References

ALLEN, V. L. (1975), 'Social Support for Nonconformity', in L. Berkowitz (ed.), *Experimental Social Psychology Advances* (New York: Academic).

ALLPORT, F. H. (1924), *Social Psychology* (New York: Houghton Mifflin).

ANDERSEN, H. C. (2001), *Fairy Tales from Andersen* (Oxford: Oxford University Press).

ARENDT, H. (1958), *The Origin of Totalitarianism* (New York: Harcourt Brace).

ASCH, S. E. (1956), 'Studies of Independence and Conformity: A Minority of One Against a Unanimous Majority', *Psychological Monographs*, 70.

AYER, A. J. (1963), 'Two Notes on Probability', in Ayer (ed.), *The Concept of a Person and Other Essays* (London: Macmillan).

BAR-TAL, D. (1990), *Group Beliefs: A Conception for Analyzing Group Structure, Processes, and Behavior* (New York: Springer).

BARTLETT, F. C. (1995), *Remembering: A Study in Experimental Social Psychology* (Cambridge: Cambridge University Press).

BEISSINGER, M. R. (2002), *Nationalist Mobilization and the Collapse of the Soviet State* (Cambridge: Cambridge University Press).

BOND, R. (2005), 'Group Size and Conformity', *Group Processes and Intergroup Relations*, 8 (4): 331–54.

BORHEK, J. T., and CURTIS, R. F. (1983), *A Sociology of Belief* (Malabar, Fla.: Krieger).

Boudon, R. (1989), *The Analysis of Ideology* (Oxford: Polity).

——(1994), *The Art of Self-Persuasion: The Social Explanation of False Beliefs* (Oxford: Polity).

BREEN, R. (1999), 'Beliefs, Rational Choice and Bayesian Learning', *Rationality and Society*, 11 (4): 463–79.

BROWN, R. (1958), 'How Should a Thing Be Called?', *Psychological Review*, 65: 14–21.

——(1995), *Prejudice: Its Social Psychology* (Oxford: Blackwell).

——(2006), *Group Processes: Dynamics Within and Between Groups* (Oxford: Blackwell).

CHONG, D., and DRUCKMAN, J. N. (2007), 'Framing Theory', *Annual Review of Political Science*, 10: 103–26.

CHWE, M. S. (1999), 'Structure and Strategy in Collective Action', *American Journal of Sociology*, 105: 128–56.

—— (2001), *Rational Ritual: Culture, Coordination, and Common Knowledge* (Princeton, N.J.: Princeton University Press).

COSER, L. A. (1990), 'The Intellectuals in Soviet Reform: On "Pluralistic Ignorance" and Mass Communications', *Dissent*, 37: 181–3.

DAVIES, K., and JONES, E. E. (1960), 'Changes in Interpersonal Perception as a Means of Reducing Dissonance', *Journal of Abnormal and Social Psychology*, 61: 402–10.

DEUTSCH, M., and GERARD, H. B. (1955), 'A Study of Normative and Informational Social Influence upon Individual Judgement', *Journal of Abnormal and Social Psychology*, 51: 629–36.

ELSTER, J. (1979), *Ulysses and the Sirens: Studies in Rationality and Irrationality* (Cambridge: Cambridge University Press).

—— (1983a), *Explaining Technical Change: A Case Study in the Philosophy of Science* (Cambridge: Cambridge University Press).

—— (1983b), *Sour Grapes: Studies in the Subversion of Rationality* (Cambridge: Cambridge University Press).

FELD, S. (1981), 'The Focused Organization of Social Ties', *American Journal of Sociology*, 86 (5): 1015–35.

—— and GROFMAN, B. (2009), 'Homophily and the Focused Organization of Ties', in P. Hedström and P. Bearman (eds.), *The Oxford Handbook of Analytical Sociology* (Oxford: Oxford University Press), 521–43.

FESTINGER, L. (1950), 'Informal Social Communication', *Psychological Review*, 57: 271–82.

—— (1953), 'An Analysis of Compliant Behaviour', in M. Sherif and M. O. Wilson (eds.), *Group Relations at the Crossroads* (New York: Harper).

—— (1954), 'A Theory of Social Comparison Processes', *Human Relations*, 7: 117–40.

—— (1957), *A Theory of Cognitive Dissonance* (Stanford, Calif.: Stanford University Press).

FISCHER, D. H. (1970), *Historians' Fallacies: Toward a Logic of Historical Thought* (New York: HarperPerennial).

FISHBEIN, M., and AJZEN, I. (1975), *Belief, Attitude, Intention and Behavior* (Reading, Mass.: Addison-Wesley).

FISKE, S. T., and TAYLOR, S. E. (1991), *Social Cognition* (New York: McGraw-Hill).

FONESCA, E. G. (1991), *Beliefs in Action: Economic Philosophy and Social Change* (Cambridge: Cambridge University Press).

GOETHALS, G. R., MESSICK, D. W., and ALLISON, S. T. (1991), 'The Uniqueness Bias: Studies of Constructive Social Comparison', in J. Suls and T. A. Wills (eds.), *Social Comparison: Contemporary Theory and Research* (Hillsdale, N.J.: Erlbaum).

GRANOVETTER, M. S. (1973), 'The Strength of Weak Ties', *American Journal of Sociology*, 78 (6): 1360–80.

—— (1978), 'Threshold Models of Collective Behavior', *American Journal of Sociology*, 83: 1420–43.

HÁJEK, A. (2004), 'Pascal's wager', in *Stanford Encyclopedia of Philosophy*, at <http://plato.stanford.edu/entries/pascal-wager/>, accessed 2008.

HARMON-JONES, E., and MILLS, J. (1999) (eds.), *Cognitive Dissonance: Progress on a Pivotal Theory in Social Psychology* (Washington, D.C.: American Psychological Association).

HEDSTRÖM, P. (1998), 'Rational Imitation', in P. Hedström and R. Swedberg (eds.), *Social Mechanisms: An Analytical Approach to Social Theory* (Cambridge: Cambridge University Press).

HEDSTRÖM, P. (2005), *Dissecting the Social: On the Principles of Analytical Sociology* (Cambridge: Cambridge University Press).

HOLLAND, J. H., et al. (1986), *Induction: Processes of Inference, Learning, and Discovery* (Cambridge, Mass.: MIT Press).

HOLYOAK, K. J., and THAGARD, P. (1999), *Mental Leaps: Analogy in Creative Thought* (Cambridge, Mass.: MIT Press).

IYENGAR, S. (1991), *Is Anyone Responsible? How Television Frames Political Issues* (Chicago, Ill.: University of Chicago Press).

JAMES, W. (1890), *The Principles of Psychology* (New York: Holt, Rinehart & Winston).

JASTROW, J. (1900), *Fact and Fable in Psychology* (Boston, Mass.: Houghton Mifflin).

KAHNEMAN, D., and TVERSKY, A. (1982), 'Subjective Probability: A Judgment of Representativeness', in D. Kahneman, P. Slovic, and A. Tversky (eds.), *Judgment under Uncertainty: Heuristics and Biases* (Cambridge: Cambridge University Press).

KHONG, Y. F. (1992), *Analogies at War: Korea, Munich, Dien Bien Phu, and the Vietnam Decisions of 1965* (Princeton, N.J.: Princeton University Press).

KRUGLANSKI, A. W. (1989), *Lay Epistemics and Human Knowledge: Cognitive and Motivational Bases* (New York: Plenum).

KUHN, T. S. (1962), *The Structure of Scientific Revolutions* (Chicago, Ill.: University of Chicago Press).

KURAN, T. (1995), *Private Truths, Public Lies: The Social Consequences of Preference Falsification* (Cambridge, Mass.: Harvard University Press).

—— (1998), 'Ethnic Dissimilation and its International Diffusion', in D. A. Lake and D. Rothchild (eds.), *The International Spread of Ethnic Conflict* (Princeton, N.J.: Princeton University Press).

LUPIA, A., McCUBBINS, M. D., and POPKIN, S. L. (2000), 'Beyond Rationality: Reason and the Study of Politics', in Lupia, McCubbins, and Popkin (eds.), *Elements of Reason: Cognition, Choice, and the Bounds of Rationality* (Cambridge: Cambridge University Press).

McGARTY, C. (1999), *Categorization in Social Psychology* (London: Sage).

MACKIE, G. (1996), 'Ending Footbinding and Infibulation: A Convention Account', *American Sociological Review*, 61 (6): 999–1017.

MARGOLIS, H. (1987), *Patterns, Thinking, and Cognition* (Chicago, Ill.: University of Chicago Press).

MARTIN, J. L. (2002), 'Power, Authority, and the Constraint of Belief Systems', *American Journal of Sociology*, 107 (4): 861–904.

MERTON, R. K. (1968), *Social Theory and Social Structure* (New York: Free Press).

MILLER, D., and McFARLAND, C. (1991), 'When Social Comparison Goes Awry: The Case of Pluralistic Ignorance', in J. Suls and T. A. Wills (eds.), *Social Comparison: Contemporary Theory and Research* (Hillsdale, N.J.: Erlbaum).

NEILL, D. B. (2005), 'Cascade Effects in Heterogeneous Populations', *Rationality and Society*, 17 (2): 191–241.

NISBETT, R., and ROSS, L. (1980), *Human Inference: Strategies and Shortcomings of Social Judgment* (Englewood Cliffs, N.J.: Prentice-Hall).

OBERSCHALL, A. (2000), 'Why False Beliefs Prevail: The Little Rascals Child Sex Abuse Prosecutions', in J. Baechler and F. Chazel (eds.), *L'Acteur et ses raisons: mélanges en l'honneur de Raymond Boudon* (Paris: Presses Universitaires de France).

O'GORMAN, H. J. (1975), 'Pluralistic Ignorance and White Estimates of White Support for Racial Segregation', *Public Opinion Quarterly*, 39: 313–30.

PARETO, V. (1935), *The Mind and Society, iii. Theory of Derivation* (New York: Harcourt, Brace).

PASCAL, B. (1995), *Pensées* (London: Penguin).

PEIRCE, C. S. (1957a), 'The Fixation of Belief', in Pierce, *Essays in the Philosophy of Science* (New York: Bobbs-Merrill).

—— (1957b), 'The Logic of Abduction', in Pierce, *Essays in the Philosophy of Science* (New York: Bobbs-Merrill).

PRATKANIS, A., and ARONSON, E. (2002), *Age of Propaganda: The Everyday Use and Abuse of Persuasion* (New York: Owl).

RAVIV, A., BAR-TAL, D., and ALBIN, R. (1993), 'Measuring Epistemic Authority: Studies of Politicians and Professors', *European Journal of Personality*, 7: 119–38.

ROKEACH, M. (1973), *The Nature of Human Values* (New York: Free Press).

RYDGREN, J. (2004), 'The Logic of Xenophobia', *Rationality and Society*, 16 (2): 123–48.

—— (2007), 'The Power of the Past: A Contribution to a Cognitive Sociology of Ethnic Conflict', *Sociological Theory*, 25 (3): 225–44.

—— (2009), 'Shared Beliefs About the Past: A Cognitive Sociology of Intersubjective Memory', in P. Hedström and B. Wittrock (eds.), *The Frontiers of Sociology* (Amsterdam: Brill).

SCHUMAN, H., and RIEGER, C. (1992), 'Historical Analogies, Generational Effects, and Attitudes toward War', *American Sociological Review*, 57 (3): 315–26.

SHELTON, J. N., and RICHESON, J. A. (2005), 'Intergroup Contact and Pluralistic Ignorance', *Journal of Personality and Social Psychology*, 88 (1): 91–107.

SIMON, H. A. (1979), *Models of Thought* (New Haven, Conn.: Yale University Press).

STINCHCOMBE, A. L. (1968), *Constructing Social Theories* (New York: Harcourt, Brace & World).

TVERSKY, A., and KAHNEMAN, D. (1982), 'Judgment Under Uncertainty: Heuristics and Biases', in D. Kahneman, P. Slovic, and A. Tversky, *Judgment Under Uncertainty: Heuristics and Biases* (Cambridge: Cambridge University Press).

WITTGENSTEIN, L. (1997), *Philosophical Investigations* (Cambridge, Mass.: Blackwell).

CHAPTER 5

....

PREFERENCES

....

JEREMY FREESE

INTRODUCTION

....

ANALYTIC social science endeavors to explicate iterative connections between the
properties of a social system and the action of individuals. In a celebrated example
from Schelling (1978), patterns of racial segregation are connected to an individual's
either staying where they live or moving (see also Bruch and Mare, this volume).
Such projects require a logic of how actors respond to circumstances. In Schelling's
model, actors moved if the proportion of neighbors 'unlike' themselves exceeded
a threshold. This can be expressed as a simple rule ('If more than two-thirds of
neighbors are unlike oneself, move; otherwise, stay'), and analytic work might
simply model actor behavior as following rules. Yet our appreciation of the exercise
as telling us something instructive about human affairs is greatly enhanced if the
behaviors implied by the rules can be interpreted in a way that makes sense to
us as human action (Hedström 2005). Schelling's model becomes intelligible as
a model of meaningful, understandable action when we suppose that individuals
are *deciding* whether to stay or move, and these decisions are influenced by their
wanting at least a specified proportion of neighbors to be like themselves.

Understanding behavior as *intentional* pervades everyday life. We experience
ourselves as wanting things and acting on those wants. We apprehend others as
having wants of their own, sometimes overlapping with ours and sometimes not,
and our beliefs about what others want influence our interactions with them. Our
sense of people as pursuing purposes feels 'natural' and works reasonably well in
everyday life, and social scientists do not leave this sense behind when we come

to the office. Social science does not use intentional interpretation just in giving meaning to agents in simulations like Schelling's, but also in explaining and predicting action. For example, toward explaining the observed network of romantic relationships in a high school, Bearman, Moody, and Stovel (2004) invoke a model in which adolescents want partners with characteristics like themselves and want to avoid negative implications that might follow from dating an ex-partner's current partner's ex-partner.

As commonplace as it is to talk about wants, reflection quickly indicates that their incorporation into social-scientific explanation is not straightforward. The wants of others are not directly observable; instead we often seem to infer them from the very phenomena (their behavior) that we are otherwise trying to explain. Moreover, we know that we often feel uncertain or ambivalent about what we want, that we can feel we want something but not act like it, and that we are not always honest to others about what we believe we want. How, then, should social scientists think about the place of wants in explaining action? How do wants fit into efforts to explain large-scale social phenomena partly by reference to the actions of individuals?

Social scientists use a constellation of terms to characterize wants and closely related counterparts, including desires, tastes, preferences, goals, values, aspirations, purposes, objectives, appetites, needs, motives, ends, drives, attractions, orientations, and wishes. Of these, analytic social science has made the most use of 'preferences,' and so 'preferences' serves as the focal term for this essay. The preference for 'preference' stems partly from 'preference' implying alternatives. We desire things in their own right, but we prefer things to other things. We can desire both X and Y and still prefer X to Y. We also can desire neither X nor Y and still prefer X to Y. Preferences thus become an especially sensible term of art if one regards the world as full of trade-offs and regards actors as wanting many things (and a pony, too!) but only being able to obtain some of them.

The concept of preferences can be tightened with assumptions to yield rational-actor models in which actions are posited to be optimal. Rational-actor models dominate economic thinking, but they have been used less in sociology. 'Preference' here is not meant to presume invocation of rational-actor theory. Instead the relationship between 'preference' generally and its specific usage in rational-choice theories will be recurrently considered in what follows. More broadly, beyond its appropriateness to comparison of undesired alternatives, I do not make any working distinction in this essay between 'preferring' X to Y and 'desiring more' or 'wanting more.' Certainly, 'desire' is often used to convey more the experience of wanting, and 'values' are regularly intended to orient attention to basic moral wants, but these distinctions are not my focus here.

This essay considers four basic issues regarding 'preferences' as an explanatory concept in analytical sociology. First, I take up how the ontology of preference should be understood; that is, the question of what preferences are. I argue against both the ideas that preferences are 'mental events' and that they are 'behavioral tendencies.' Second, given that real-world alternatives may be characterized by numerous different attributes, I consider how to approach the question of which attributes may be most salient to understanding action. Third, I discuss applying 'preferences' to organizations, and, while I contend there is no principled reason why preferences are more naturally a property of persons than of organizations, I maintain that the orientation of sociology to the preferences of each is rightly different. Finally, I discuss preference change over time, with especial focus on the preferences of actors being a target of purposive action by others and by actors themselves.

5.1 WHAT ARE PREFERENCES?

For purposes here, *explaining* action is understood as constructing narratives that make the occurrence of action *y*—when and how and by whom it occurs—intelligible to an audience by reference to causes. *Causes* of *y* are events and states of the world for which, if different at the pertinent point in time, we assert that (the probability distribution for) *y* would be different.[1] *Immediate causes* of *y* are causes whose place in the explanation is narratively contiguous to *y*. Immediate causes are of course themselves caused, and causes of causes are caused, and so on. Explaining particular actions is thereby an indefinite project, in which the narrative network may extend *backward* in time, *inward* to the psychology/physiology/neurology of actors, and *outward* to the social and physical environments in which actions are determined (Freese 2008). Explanations are never 'full' or 'complete' in any essential sense but rather at best adequate to the practical purpose of providing understanding for some audience.

From this perspective, preferences may be understood in the first instance as being among the prototypic immediate causes of actions understood as intentional. Say someone offered vanilla or chocolate ice cream chooses vanilla. 'Why?' 'She prefers vanilla.' This is not an empty statement given possible alternatives: 'She actually prefers chocolate, but that chocolate scoop is already half melted.' As explanations go, the statement suffices in the same sense in which Boudon (1998) says that rational action is its own explanation. Given this preference and a set of background conditions, the action *follows*, and so the explanation provides a causal narrative that is logically continuous in the sense that there is no narrative gap intervening between explanans and explanandum. Offering 'She prefers vanilla' as sufficient suggests 'Under the circumstances, had she preferred chocolate, she would have chosen chocolate.' The psychology of the actor is asserted to be decisive, and 'preference' is the way in which the decisive difference is characterized. While sufficient in this sense, the explanation might be regarded as (obviously) practically deficient, in that we may feel inadequately informed without knowing more about why the person prefers vanilla to chocolate or why the person came to be offered chocolate and vanilla instead of some different set of flavors or no choice at all.

What does it mean to say someone prefers vanilla to chocolate? Clearly, preferences are deployed in explanations as attributes of actors, as something actors *have*. One possibility is that preferences may be identified with some physically real characteristic of brains. Maybe to say someone prefers vanilla to chocolate is to say that a prototypic vanilla scoop stimulates a stronger dopamine-reward response in the brain (or whatever) than a prototypic chocolate scoop. While one hope of 'neuroeconomics' is to lend insights into the internal processes involved in choice comparisons (Camerer, Loewenstein, and Prelec 2005), a large amount of philosophical and cognitive-science argument provides abundant reason to doubt that preferences (or desires abstractly) can be reduced to any kind of physical definition (see Dennett 1987; Ross 2005). I will not rehearse the arguments here, but simply consider that it is unlikely that all people who prefer chocolate to vanilla could be said to do so for the same reason, or that all manner of preferences (amongst foods, jobs, leisure activities, romantic partners) could be reduced to the same internal differentiating process. Indeed, preferring vanilla to chocolate does not even imply that a person experiences vanilla as better-tasting, as one might think chocolate tastes better yet prefer vanilla for other reasons (e.g. a belief that vanilla is healthier, an aversion to brown foods).

A different possibility is that preferences are characterizations of a behavioral pattern or tendency, so that 'I prefer vanilla' is just another way of saying 'I tend to choose vanilla.' In addition to possibly conflating attributes of actors with those of situations, identifying preferences as behavioral patterns undermines their status as causes and thus their relevance to explanation. Saying 'I tend to choose vanilla' articulates a pertinent statistical regularity, but a statistical regularity in itself is not a cause (though it possibly reflects a common underlying cause that produces the regularity). Revealed-preference theory in rational-actor theory takes actions as manifestations of a transitive ordering of preferences over all outcomes (Samuelson 1947). In some interpretations (e.g. Gintis 2007) this implies preferences are part of a redescription of action and so no more explanatory than 'I chose vanilla because I chose vanilla.' Clearly, either revealed-preference theory or that interpretation of it must be rejected if preferences are to remain part of one's explanatory vocabulary. Nonetheless, reference to recurrent choice and behavioral patterns seems *close* to what preferences might be, especially since considering past actions would seem to provide the plainest grounds on which preferences may be inferred.

The solution might seem to regard preference as a disposition to choose one alternative over another, but this raises the question of just what we mean by 'disposition.' Clearer would be to consider preference as making reference to the alternative that would be selected in *a counterfactual situation of abstract, hypothetical choice.* To say an actor prefers vanilla to chocolate is to say that either the actor will choose vanilla over chocolate or there will be some reason(s)—drawing upon other preferences, beliefs, or circumstances—the actor does not. A statement of an abstract preference of X over Y bears affinities to an idea of a 'default setting' in computer science or an 'unmarked form' in linguistics. Preferences thereby specify a default expectation about choice that may be part of a sufficient immediate explanation when it is consistent with observed choice and prompt further explanatory elaboration when it is not.

In this view, preferences are not to be reduced to any specific property inside an actor's head. The preferences of individuals may appear to be 'mental states,' but they are not mental states in the sense that we would imagine neuroscience or any other enterprise to eventually be able to describe specific circumstances of the brain in a way that maps unproblematically onto what social science means when it says an individual prefers X to Y. Instead preferences are *holistic simplifications* of the internal workings of actors that are used when making sense of behavior as intentional. Put another way, when we interpret action as intentional, we take the actor to be a system, and preferences are attributed as a property of the operations of that system treated as a whole (Dennett 1987). Philosophers often refer to preferences as part of our 'folk psychology,' but better for understanding their explanatory role in social science is to understand them as *black-boxing psychology*, as simplifying the messy and mysterious internal workings of actors. Preferences accomplish this simplification by representing inner complexity in the most immediately action-implicative terms, by distilling complexity through the bottleneck provided by hypothetical decision. Whatever goes on in the brains of actors, the question of whether they prefer chocolate or vanilla comes down to the resulting implication for our expectation about a hypothetical choice. (Although outside the purview of this chapter, one can take a similar stance regarding beliefs, considering them as propositions about what hypothetical choices imply for what an intentional actor apparently regards as true. Rydgren, this volume, though, adopts a more introspective and cognitivist perspective on belief that fully decouples it from choice and action.)

Preferences and beliefs thereby serve as a model to whatever complicated machinery produces the action of the systems to which they are applied. Even so, if the model is to work in any kind of consistent way, attributes of preferences characterize real, internal operations of the actor, even though only at the emergent level of choices. To be sure, understanding exactly what is going on internally to yield a particular preference takes us to a more explicitly cognitive or neurological vocabulary and may be wildly different for different actors. But if we reduce preference only to its usefulness for predictive claims, we lose it as a matter of causal claim and thereby as a term for explanation. Preferences can be used in explanation so long as we recognize that we are understanding ourselves as using a simplification that characterizes holistically a more complicated (and multiply realizable) underlying reality. When we say a preference caused an action, we are asserting that if the internal operations were such that an alternative characterization of the preference would instead apply, then the action would be different.

'Preferences,' along with beliefs and the rest of the intentional idiom, stands as both partition and interface between analytic social science and psychology. Preferences are useful for efficient, parsimonious characterization of the behavior of what Coleman (1990) calls 'natural persons.' Schelling's model implies psychological processes that yield a preference to have at least some neighbors like oneself, but we do not have to know what these processes are to render the action in his model intelligible. Psychologists, meanwhile, may take a preference as a starting point, and want to pursue why the system works as it does. That research is unlikely to find holistic concepts like 'preference' to be enduringly useful, except as an object of explanation. As analytic social science develops, points at which inadequate models yield empirical anomalies and failure may prompt efforts toward models of the actor that are less parsimonious and readily intelligible, but more internally realistic and behaviorally accurate. Appeals to more elaborate models of cognition in agent-based modeling, for example, may manifest just such a push for elaboration (Macy and Flache, this volume), as may all the efforts of the 'heuristics and biases' work across cognitive psychology and behavioral economics (Kahneman and Tversky 2000; Camerer and Loewenstein 2004). Emphatically: intentional explanations are not cognitive explanations—and preference is not a cognitive concept—because, like rational-choice explanations more generally, intentional explanations simplify precisely what the cognitive idiom complicates. Even so, and even as cognitive psychology and neuropsychology continue to make 'folk psychology' obsolete for their own purposes, we should not be surprised if the simple power of the concept of preferences sustains its vitality in analytic social science.

At the same time, analytical sociology may benefit from keeping the pragmatic justification for preferences in view for at least three reasons. First, we should not be surprised that interrogation can reveal all kinds of murkiness about exactly where preferences end and beliefs, capacities, emotions, etc. start, and we should not expect this murkiness to be subject to any tidy scientific resolution. Second, conceptualizing preferences as choice in a hypothetical 'default' situation is a transparent fiction, and thereby highlights that real situations of choice are never abstract and never semantically empty. 'Eliciting' preferences is not a matter of psychological excavation but of practical and social construction (Lichtenstein and Slovic 2006). Consequently, the idea of what to take as an individual's preference for any normative or scientific purpose rests on a defense of the procedure used that is not to be adjudicated by reference to 'real' preference but to other criteria. Third, we should not be especially troubled by failings of individuals to exhibit the coherence and consistency that application of the language of preferences would imply. The language of intentionality is the characterization of a system as a *unified subject*; whether natural persons act like unified subjects is fundamentally an empirical and contingent question. In other words, we should recognize that even as 'preference' undergirds a powerful, ubiquitous idiom for understanding action, it is ultimately a logical concept loosely coupled to the actual acting organism, and so 'preference' should be used when useful and unsentimentally discarded when some alternative idiom serves better instead. Likewise, in considering the rational (or reasonable) action theories versus more elaborate alternatives, we should keep in view that this is more a practical choice in terms of usefulness and parsimony for specific projects than any debate about what actor psychology is 'really' like.

5.2 PREFERENCE AND PERSONALITY

In analytic social science, preferences are often assumed to be the same across persons. In Schelling's model, for instance, all actors were presumed to have the same preferences, and all variation in individual behavior in the model followed from variation in actors' immediate situations (the proportion of 'like' neighbors). Especially when trying to explain variation in real behavior, however, social science regularly confronts actors behaving differently in *similar* situations. Variation in preferences serves as one candidate explanation.

Explaining choices with defensibly attributed preferences implies connecting the present choice to past choices or other evidence by virtue of abstract commonalities. One does not choose between an abstract apple and an abstract orange, but rather between *this* apple and *this* orange at *this* time under *these* conditions. Alternatives in real choices index abstract attributes that actors are asserted to have preferences regarding. When a student chooses to accept a scholarship at Northwestern instead of Yale, the explanation 'I prefer Northwestern' suffices in one logical sense but is also obviously wanting for elaboration of *what it is* about Northwestern and Yale that caused the actor to choose one over the other.[2] Here a useful distinction perhaps might be drawn between 'preferences' and 'tastes,' with the latter being a more elemental subspecies of the former. That is, we might consider 'taste' to index the attributes of alternatives leading one to be preferred to another, and 'preference' to index the alternatives themselves (see Elster, this volume, on 'substantive' versus 'formal' preferences).

For decisions like what college to attend or where to live, alternatives obviously have many different attributes, and rarely is one alternative best in every respect. We thus need some way of talking about how tastes over different attributes of alternatives can explain the choice itself. In early utilitarianism concrete preferences were posited as deriving from an ultimate preference to maximize happiness, and so preferences for concrete things in the world could be interpreted via the expected consequences of their combination of attributes for happiness. Rational-actor models have since come to discard the psychologism of 'happiness' for the pure abstraction of 'utility,' which is nothing but what is maximized by a weighting of the preferences revealed by behavior (Friedman 1953; Schoemaker 1982). The 'utility function' is the function by which are weighted the different abstract 'commodities' or 'goods' that are manifested in different concrete alternatives. Following earlier arguments, the idea of an actual mathematical function precisely characterizing a long series of real-world individual behaviors quickly becomes quixotic, but, even then, utility functions provide a useful fiction for conceptualizing choices as the result of trade-offs among abstract attributes. Even when sociologists eschew the formality of rational-actor theories by proposing that actions are 'reasonable' instead of 'rational,' a relaxed counterpart to the notion of a weighted function seems to be how they imagine different aspects of alternatives influencing ultimate choice (Boudon 1989; Hedström 2005).[3]

Exactly what are the abstract commodities indexed by a utility function is left vague. Even if we could articulate some specifiable commodity like 'happiness' that served as the pertinent attribute of the utility function, it would remain to be explained what it is about choosing Northwestern over Yale that yields the difference in expected 'happiness.' In explaining an action by reference to a preference as indicated by past choices, the explanation may be more satisfying the more extensive the past choices it invokes. Granted, some specific choices may be hard to understand beyond quite concrete tastes (as in a taste for vanilla), but others may manifest a more abstract pattern quite readily (as when a person makes a series of specific job decisions that manifest a taste for autonomy). If we want to make sense of heterogeneity in larger individual patterns of action, we might thus look for abstract tastes that are pertinent to choices across many situations.

Broadly relevant and abstract tastes that vary across persons may capture a large part of what we understand as *personality*.[4] Sociology's own literature on 'social structure and personality' (House 1977) has shown only intermittent interest in the consequences of personality and has held a limited, unusual view of what personality is. Indeed, many sociologists persist in understanding their discipline as fundamentally about decrying constructs like personality as overrated for explaining action, and, accordingly, consequences of personality differences per se have been mostly left to psychologists. Yet perhaps personality psychology can provide analytical sociology with insight in *parameterizing the actor*; that is, perhaps it will help articulate what differences in abstract preferences may be especially useful in developing models for explaining behavioral differences.

Personality psychology has long sought a concise characterization of the dimensions of individual variation that have been salient and pervasive enough to become part of everyday language. Presently, the most highly regarded outcome of this effort is the five-factor model of personality (FFM) (John and Srivastava 1999; McCrae and Costa 2003). The FFM is not intended to 'reduce' personality to five numbers, but it does propose that other personality constructs are associated with at least one of these five and that the FFM provides a useful simplification of the independent dimensions of individual variation. The dimensions of the FFM, sometimes called the Big Five, are extraversion, openness to experience, emotional stability (also called neuroticism), agreeableness, and conscientiousness.

Each dimension has facets. Inspecting a widely used FFM inventory (the NEO PI-R) indicates that many facets resonate with abstract tastes suggested by sociological work on social order or status attainment (Hitlin and Piliavin 2004). Examples are facets that at least roughly index the value one attaches to the well-being of others, fulfilling commitments, obedience to traditional authorities, immediate gratification, social relations, achievement, dominance in a situation, and being honest.

While many studies exist on the relationship between personality dimensions and individual outcomes of broader social-science interest (see McCrae and Costa 2003: 216–33; Roberts et al. 2003: 580 for reviews and references), far less work has sought to integrate personality into the effort to understand connections between local interactions and larger social-level phenomena that characterizes the aspiration of analytic social science. Granted, in exercises focused on particular decisions—especially if they only are intended as illustrative, using simulacra of actors—considering preferences only in more superficial, specific terms may be more useful anyway. The abstract tastes indexed by personality traits may be most valuable when trying to understand patterns of substantively diverse choices or outcomes that are thought to be the result of a diversity of choices over the life course. The measurement of such tastes may be most useful in data-collection efforts that are intended to serve many purposes and so may place a premium on extensively validated measures with possibly broad application.

At the same time, abstract tastes are only useful insofar as they actually cleave decision-making at its joints. Rational-choice models of decision-making commonly invoke the concepts of *risk preference* and *time preference*. Although risk preference is often misunderstood by sociologists (see Freese and Montgomery 2007), the concept refers to the relative valuation of a gamble with an expected value of x dollars versus a certain payoff of y dollars. An actor who requires $x > y$ to choose the gamble is *risk-averse*, one who will take the gamble when $x < y$ is *risk-loving*, and one who is indifferent between the gamble and uncertain payoff when $x = y$ is *risk-neutral*. Risk preference can be posited as important to all kinds of different decisions, but some evidence suggests that individuals do not exhibit especially strong stability of risk preference across different domains (Berg, Dickhaut, and McCabe 2005; Freese and Montgomery 2007). Time preference refers to rate at which future rewards are discounted, as in the magnitude of the difference between x and y for which a respondent would be indifferent between receiving y dollars now and receiving x dollars in a year.[5] As with risk preferences, evidence seems to indicate that time preferences differ for different domains (Frederick, Loewenstein, and O'Donoghue 2002). Consequently, it remains unclear how useful it will prove to attempt to characterize individuals as having a general risk or time preference, even though the constructs hypothetically are applicable to a wide range of human decisions.

The relative neglect of the consequences of personality differences by sociologists may contribute to a broader underappreciation of how these consequences are determined by larger social processes. For example, analytic models demonstrate that the expected consequences of altruistic preferences vary depending on the number of fellow altruists among one's interactants. Tendencies toward impulsive or sensation-seeking behavior may have more negative outcomes for adolescents from disadvantaged backgrounds (Shanahan et al. 2008). Policies emphasizing lightly regulated individual choice may yield greater returns to conscientiousness, and periods of rapid technological advance may especially advantage those with high openness to experience (Freese and Rivas 2006). Additionally, although ample evidence exists for assortative mating and homophily of other familial and social ties by personality traits, little explicit consideration has been given to how this network clustering may amplify or dampen the effects of individual differences. (A tendency for the gregarious to associate with one another, for instance, might imply a much greater effect of gregariousness on number of *second*-degree ties than if people formed such ties randomly, which might amplify whatever positive effects such ties provide.) Studies of the import of individual differences warrant complementary consideration of what conditions make differences more or less important, and this kind of inquiry demands a more sustained sociological imagination than studies by psychologists provide. In sum, analytical sociology's interest in modeling actor variation may find conceptualizing this variation as following from variation in preferences obviously appealing; reflective consideration of the root tastes involved may make possible theoretical and empirical connection to well-studied concepts in personality psychology; and analytical sociology should consider as part of its project understanding how social dynamics can make preference variation more or less consequential for ultimate outcomes.

5.3 WHO HAS PREFERENCES?

In everyday life we use intentionalist language promiscuously. We say 'Sally wants to go to Europe' and also that 'Walmart wants to expand into Europe.' The commonsense understanding is that we are using the language of intentionality literally when talking about 'natural persons' and figuratively when talking about 'collective subjects.' An upshot of Section 5.1, however, is that it may be more apt to consider that preferences are always being used figuratively, at least if by 'literally' we mean to be referring to identifiable internal states of actors. Consequently, that preferences only really apply to individuals because preferences are properties of 'a' brain cannot be defended. If preferences are characterizations of intentional systems, then the appropriateness of saying that a system is acting intentionally would seem to rest less on intuitions about the system's ontology and more on how well the application fits the system's behavior (Tollefson 2002; King, Felin, and Whetten 2007).

In some cases attributions to collective subjects, like 'Asian American adolescents value achievement and connectedness more than do Caucasian Americans' (Hitlin and Piliavin 2004: 369), are based just on a simple aggregation of individual behavior; there is no pretense of a system whose action is being explained. Why this tendency among individual persons exists can be taken as a matter of sociological explanation, perhaps drawing on some specific experience, identity, or goal held in common. Other collective subjects, however, are understood as exhibiting coordination among constituent individuals. The activities of workers on an assembly line can be made collectively intelligible as 'building a car.' Coleman (1990) uses 'corporate actors' to refer to constructed relations of multiple natural persons that may be otherwise characterized as 'actors,' and the prototype for such actors might be the corporation, at least as classically envisaged as a kind of intelligent, purposive social machinery.

Talking about organizations as acting according to preferences is a way of making sense of organizational behavior while black-boxing the internal dynamics that result in their behavior as intentional systems. In many cases that black-boxing may be undesirable to social science, as understanding the internal process that leads to an organization doing one thing rather than another may be precisely the object of a sociological inquiry. Nonetheless, in principle, interpreting an organization's activities as those of a unified subject is sustainable so long as those activities collectively support the attribution of either stable or intelligibly changing beliefs and preferences. Indeed, by this standard, organizations may exhibit action more coherent and consistent with attributed preferences than do natural actors. Applications of rational-choice theories, notably, often characterize actions of firms and political parties much more effectively than those of natural persons for several reasons (Satz and Ferejohn 1994; Clark 1997). First, organizations are typically brought into being for accomplishing a specific purpose, like enriching their principals, which then might serve as dominating the preferences of the actor. Second, organizations may exist in environments that strongly discipline actions that stray from purposes necessary for continued existence of the organization (e.g. earning a profit). By contrast, natural people can tolerate a very broad range of nonruinous preferences in typical environments. Third, while we may have the experience of there being some place in our brains where 'everything comes together' for deliberative decision-making, strong indications from cognitive science are that decision-making is much more decentralized (Dennett 1991). Organizations, on the other hand, commonly have a centralized decision-making unit that can explicitly direct action, monitor the effectiveness of different coordinated parts in implementing actions, and amend its structure to better realize actions. Fourth, in making decisions and coordinating actions, organizations may develop more externalized, coherent, and binding statements of identity that become a guide for subsequent action (King, Felin, and Whetten 2007). Finally, in bringing together multiple decision makers and specialists, organizations may be less prone to simple 'performance errors' in trying to figure out the best course of action.

Nonetheless, organizations often fail to exhibit the stability of purpose that fits the characterization of them as a unified subject. From the outside such failures may look like instability of purpose over time, a lack of coordination among parts, ineffective pursuit of purposes, failure to engage in seemingly obvious opportunities, or incoherence of various parts of the organization. Explaining the failure of an organization to act like a unified subject will often then proceed by opening up the organization and looking at the actions of its agents from the standpoint of considering those members as intentional systems acting in structural relationships with one another. Of course, when organizations *do* act like unified subjects, exactly how this is accomplished *also is a matter for inquiry.*

When talking about the preferences of natural persons, we considered how intentionality provided a partition and interface between the labors of analytic social scientists and psychologists. With respect to the preferences of organizations, sociologists are often interested precisely in understanding why the organization acts as it does. More quickly than with natural persons, social scientists perceive intentionalist language as applied to organizations as inadequate and look for explanatory tools that talk about how structure and process within the organization produce behaviors only intermittently characterized as those of a unified subject. However, such a tendency need not reflect any actual fact of nature, but instead just the questions that the social scientist is asking and the availability of information on internal processes. The membership of an organization, the structure of their relations, and the content of their interactions are components of organizational functioning that do not take place in the heads of individual members, and these provide core materials for social scientists interested in the internal dynamics of organizational behavior.

At the same time, our promiscuity in using intentionalist language does not only extend to units of analysis larger than ourselves. We sometimes say things like 'part of me wants to quit my job.' People regularly characterize their own deliberation as manifesting various kinds of internal tension, inner dialogue, and 'of-two-mindedness.' The notion of people possessing multiple intentionalities has been the anchor of one prominent line of sociological social psychology (Mead 1934), and discussions of 'the unconscious' by both psychological and sociological theories has often proceeded as though it were a separate intentional system inside us. When talking about conflict within organizations, we can readily understand outcomes as the product of a negotiation between two or more opposing subjects in conflict, and our sense of the reality of such conflict is enhanced by the sides being manifested in real persons with 'real' intentions. When talking about inner conflict, it seems unclear what comprise these sparring ghosts in the machine.[6] Perhaps this is all just misleading introspection, or we may actually be able to look at moment-to-moment behaviors in our lives and find it hard to reckon that we have acted with an overarching unity of purpose, as opposed to appearing to dither over vacillating dominant ideas of what we want.

Some theorists have suggested that we might usefully think about natural persons as a squabbling 'parliament' of interests, which can be thought of as a narrow set of preferences (Ainslie 2001; see also essays in Elster 1985).[7] Dynamics among these interests may then provide a better characterization of behavior than any alternative wed to our being a truly unified subject, as opposed to just sometimes looking like one. Useful here also may be that culture provides schema for the intentionality implied by different identities, and one can have preferences about manifesting these identities quite apart from the preferences that comprise them ('I don't enjoy peer-reviewing papers, but it's part of being an active member of the research community'). Identity theories often conceive of the self as an internalized hierarchy of self-categorizations (Stryker 1980; Stets and Burke 2000) that bears no small affinity to a preference ordering, and each of these categorizations carries socially acquired understandings of the kind of behavior an intentional system appropriate to that categorization would manifest (as in understanding how the *performance* of an ideal member of this identity would be carried out, à la Goffman 1959). In this respect, instability as a unified subject would follow from the uncertain resolution of conflicts, not just about what we want but about what kind of person we want to be. Indeed, Winship (2006) offers the metaphor of puzzle-solving to describe the actual muddling work of policy design—an effort to engineer solutions that satisfy competing preferences as well as possible—and perhaps the same kind of puzzle-solving is characteristic of the individual engineering of a busy life. In sum, sociologists should find no discomfort in using preferences to refer to collective subjects, and sociologists interested in the complexity of selves may profit from trying to consider more systematically how individuals may manifest multiple intentionalities.

5.4 PREFERENCE FORMATION AND CHANGE

In analytic social science, preferences are commonly posited not just to be the same across persons but also unchanging over time. The immutability of preferences has received especially vigorous defense in economics, as the ability of models to generate unique, precise predictions is much complicated by preferences being endogenous to unfolding events. Stigler and Becker (1977: 76) provide an especially rousing description of the working premise that 'tastes neither change capriciously nor differ importantly between people. On this interpretation one does not argue over tastes for the same reason that one does not argue over the Rocky Mountains—both are there, will be there next year, too, and are the same to all men.' This statement might seem remarkable for how it is flatly contradicted by even casual observation—the very notions of personality and socialization, for instance, depend on preferences differing nontrivially across people and over time. For that matter, discussions of emotion and action often afford interpretation as transient changes in preferences, as in the idea of rage involving an alteration in the preference for immediate versus delayed outcomes and in preferences regarding the well-being of others (Elster, this volume).

Stigler and Becker's ultimate position is far less radical than the above-quoted pronouncement. As discussed earlier, the tangible objects of choice are taken only to be *indirect* means of obtaining the commodities that are the *real* objects of preference in an analysis. Stigler and Becker discuss several ways that experiences might affect various stocks of psychological 'capital,' which in turn modify the extent to which tangible choices provide the commodities sought. So specific music preferences change but the abstract preference for activities yielding 'appreciation' remains the same; the specific preference for, for example, 'Blue Danube' over 'Well-Tempered Clavier' changes over time because experience allows the actor to appreciate 'Well-Tempered Clavier' more than before.[8] These abstract preferences are what I have been here calling 'tastes.' By emphasizing abstract tastes for commodities, the model allows analysis to proceed with the assumption these tastes are unchanged, but at the same time offering what can be interpreted as a simple model of learning or socialization. Indeed, the model is ultimately quite consonant with the familiar sociological emphasis on past experience as explaining psychological variation across persons. Far more incompatible with the approach is behavioral genetics, with its body of evidence that close to half of intrapersonal variation in personality traits may be accountable by genetic variation between persons (Loehlin 1992). Ironically, then, even as many sociologists express antipathy toward both neoclassical economics and behavioral genetics, the greater the relevance of genetics for understanding behavioral variation, the greater the challenge to orthodox economic assumptions about preferences.

Sociology is distinct from both behavioral genetics and economics in the extent to which the malleability of preferences over the life course has played a central role in theorizing. For instance, crucial to arguments about the importance of norms is not just that norms influence behavior by affecting incentives (i.e. via the threat of sanctions), but that they are *internalized*, experienced by the person as reflecting right and wrong, good and bad. *Association* models provide the dominant means of conceptualizing how preferences change by social scientists. In the prototypic example, actors are (repeatedly) exposed to some X and also to some Y for which they have a strong preference or otherwise positive affective reaction. As a result, they come to have a preference for X even in the absence of Y. This Y is sometimes thought of as some kind of more fundamental preference ('need' or 'drive'). As described by Coleman (1990: 516):

> [T]he course of events and action creates over time a whole superstructure of interests [i.e. preferences] that were originally pursued as paths toward the satisfaction of more central needs. These come to be autonomous interests insofar as they satisfy, over some period of time, the more central needs.

Structural functionalism's faith in the great power of relatively simple conditioning led to Wrong's complaint (1961) of an 'oversocialized' conceptualization of actors and Garfinkel's complaint (1967) of actors being taken for 'cultural dopes.'

While structural functionalism has fallen somewhere beyond mere disrepute, sociologists still grant 'socialization agents' considerable capacity to purposively influence the preferences of young actors (Hitlin and Piliavin 2004). Parents have preferences regarding the preferences their children develop, and variation across parents may dampen intergenerational mobility. Kohn (1969) presents evidence that upper-class parents emphasize teaching their children self-direction while lower-class parents emphasize obedience; these preferences are speculated to be useful for subsequent status attainment and thereby set the stage for reproduction of the same divergence of socialization practices and attainment in the next generation. Status-attainment theory posits that parental encouragement influences aspirations, which in turn influences choices about investing in schooling (Sewell and Hauser 1975). Bourdieu's theory of investments by parents in the cultural capital of children highlights the possible contribution of aesthetic preferences to subsequent status attainment (Bourdieu and Passeron 1990).

Bourdieusian theory also reflects a longtime recognition by sociologists that preferences are used by others to make broader inferences about an actor. As Bourdieu (1984: 6) famously put it, 'Taste . . . classifies the classifier.' Individuals make favorable attributions toward others perceived as having either preferences associated with high status or preferences like their own. Indeed, a standard protocol for in-group-bias experiments in social psychology involves asking respondents to express a preference between paintings by Kandinsky and Klee, and subjects exhibit favoritism toward others that they are led to believe expressed the same preference (Tajfel et al. 1971).[9] The social significance of preferences provides incentives for actors to lie about their preferences, or to selectively and conspicuously advertise those preferences that are associated with esteem or similarity to others.[10] Actors also have an incentive to invest in purposive cultivation of preferences consonant with a preferred identity or set of social affiliations.[11] In other words, purposive manipulation of preferences is not just for socialization agents, but can also be self-directed, as in someone who takes a course about wines out of a desire to appear more sophisticated or to be able to banter knowledgeably with vino-erudite consociates. That said, it is unclear how much of the influence of identity on preference development can be characterized as something like 'investment' in 'appreciation,' as opposed to a person's having aesthetic preferences being more fundamentally tied to the idea of those perceived as like or unlike them. The distaste that contemporary educated adults have toward names for newborns like 'Crystal' and 'Jimmie,' for instance, seems to derive *fundamentally* from the déclassé connotations these names have acquired (Lieberson 2000).

Preferences may provide the most convincing signals for identity precisely when they are, in a sense, 'unnatural.' Preferences that require motivation or work to cultivate, and perhaps even are hard to cultivate at all without an extensive background base of knowledge and experience, can service cultural boundaries well (i.e. preferences provide a kind of signal; see Podolny and Lynn, this volume).[12] This observation can be juxtaposed with the point that something like a default 'human nature' is implicit in many considerations of preference change.[13] Roughly, this natural state is something more selfish, hedonic, and immediate-reward-oriented than that of the mature actor whose preferences have been shaped by various socialization and other civilizing processes of contemporary society. 'Incomplete' socialization was at one time prominent in sociological explanations of deviant behavior (e.g. Dubin 1959), and self-control-based theories posit that preferences for delayed reward are something that institutions cultivate in actors. Bowles and Gintis's account (1976, 2000) of the educational system may be thought of as attempted preference modification away from a state of nature and toward preferences more suitable for a capitalist economy. In short, 'unnatural' preferences may be rewarded in social systems—perhaps partly because they are unnatural—and these rewards may prompt investment in their cultivation, making preferences endogenous to the demands of society. Sociobiologically minded scholars have frequently contended that 'human nature' serves to keep societal variation 'on a leash' (Lumsden and Wilson 1981: 13; Udry 2000). An important counterpoint is that social competition may create incentives for cultivating and otherwise engineering the self toward extremes.

As suggested earlier, identities may prompt individuals to engage in actions indicative of a preference for a different set of preferences than what their behaviors to that point imply. If we use *goals* in a fairly restrictive sense to refer to non-immediate, articulable attainments that actors can express (possibly sporadic and floundering) commitment to pursue, then the same can be said of goals as well. An actor having preferences about preferences is a tricky notion—after all, if we really wanted not to want something, haven't we already succeeded?—but goals and identities carry implications for preferences and can be objects of preference in their own right.[14] As such, these implications can stand in conflict with one another and with tastes for abstract commodities like 'hedonic pleasure.' Internal processes by which these conflicts are handled may lead to introspective experiences and behaviors that undermine easy characterization as a unified subject in folk-psychological terms. Such internal processes also have external counterparts in efforts of others to commit actors to different goals or identities and to shape belief about what different goals and identities oblige. Sociology's openness to preference change allows for a much more nuanced consideration of *manipulation* of actors—whether by others or by actors themselves—than what orthodox rational-actor models allow.

Notes

1. Hedström (2005: 39) defines desires as mental *events*, perhaps because he wants to consider desires as causes and recognizes that many philosophers quarrel with causes that are not events (p. 14). Yet social-science invocations of 'desire' and 'preference' in explanations—including the examples in Hedström's book—refer overwhelmingly to continuing conditions or states of actors. Either some term other than 'cause' needs to be available for discussing the counterfactual implications of different states, or social science needs to resist the idea that only events are causes.
2. 'Cause' here is used loosely. The statement does sustain a counterfactual, in that we are asserting that if specified attributes of Northwestern were different, the actor would perhaps prefer Yale instead. Yet, unlike usual understandings of 'cause,' attributes do not temporally precede what they are attributes of.
3. The chief difference between 'rational' versus 'reasonable' action appears to be the uniqueness with which preferences can be said to determine actions.
4. This implies that the basic problems of considering preferences as causes also apply to personality traits as causes.
5. That discount rates are typically nonlinear can be quickly intuited from considering that the difference required for an actor to be indifferent between y dollars now versus x dollars in a year is perhaps much larger than between receiving y dollars in 1 year and x dollars in 2 years.
6. Speaking of ghosts in the machine, Coleman (1990: 526) speculates about modeling the lack of unity of purpose in natural persons as multiple intentionalities based on internalized models of primary-socialization agents, akin to having the wishes of your mother and first-grade teacher fighting inside your head.
7. While perhaps more evocative of simply scattered rather than multiple but discrete intentionalities, Gould (2003) offers some especially intriguing speculations about using network ideas to talk about the coherence of temporally successive actions.
8. The example is from Bourdieu (1984).
9. Valuing the well-being of another person more after forming social ties with them is a species of preference change.
10. Elster's writings on rationality proceed by copious, conspicuous reference to high-culture sources for examples about human life (e.g. Elster 2000, 2007); an interesting

thought-experiment is to imagine how the same logical arguments would read differently if examples from television or other popular-culture sources were used instead.

11. Entrepreneurs have strong incentives to devise and engineer associations among individuals between proprietary goods and preferred identities and affiliations. How goods come to have the implications for identity and affiliation that they do is itself an important topic for the sociology of consumption.

12. If a preference that distinguishes a group also confers status within it, this might promote runaway processes that culminate in claims of finding beauty in stimuli so extreme that an outside observer might wonder whether everyone who professes to the preference is just pretending. In this respect, aesthetic preferences within subcultures may manifest phenomena similar to sectarian splits and zealotry in religious belief.

13. 'Human nature' is most commonly invoked for explaining preferences held in common among persons, such as the desire for status or social affiliations (Turner 1987). Evolutionary historical explanations are commonly provided for why we have such preferences, although the fundamentally speculative character of many such accounts is well known.

14. Indeed, *setting a goal* implies a desire to produce actions that one would not otherwise produce, and then consistency with goals becomes another attribute to influence choices.

References

AINSLIE, G. (2001), *Breakdown of Will* (Cambridge: Cambridge University Press).

BEARMAN, P. S., MOODY, J., and STOVEL, K. (2004), 'Chains of Affection: The Structure of Adolescent Romantic and Sexual Networks', *American Journal of Sociology*, 110: 44–91.

BERG, J., DICKHAUT, J., and McCABE, K. (2005), 'Risk Preference Instability Across Institutions: A Dilemma', *Proceedings of the National Academy of Sciences*, 102: 4209–14.

BOUDON, R. (1989), 'Subjective Rationality and the Explanation of Social Behavior', *Rationality and Society*, 1: 173–96.

—— (1998), 'Social Mechanisms without Black Boxes', in Peter Hedström and Richard Swedberg (eds.), *Social Mechanisms* (Cambridge: Cambridge University Press), 172–203.

BOURDIEU, P. (1984), *Distinction: A Social Critique of the Judgement of Taste* (Cambridge, Mass.: Harvard University Press).

—— and PASSERON, J.-C. (1990), *Reproduction in Education, Society and Culture* (Newbury Park: Sage).

BOWLES, S., and GINTIS, H. (1976), *Schooling in Capitalist America* (New York: Basic).

—— (2000), 'Does Schooling Raise Earnings by Making People Smarter?', in K. Arrow, S. Bowles, and S. Durlauf (eds.), *Meritocracy and Economic Inequality* (Princeton, N.J.: Princeton University Press).

CAMERER, C. F., and LOEWENSTEIN, G. (2004), 'Behavioral Economics: Past, Present, and Future', in C. F. Camerer, G. Loewenstein, and M. Rabin (eds.), *Advances in Behavioral Economics* (Princeton, N.J.: Princeton University Press).

—— —— and PRELEC, D. (2005), 'Neuroeconomics: How Neuroscience Can Inform Economics', *Journal of Economic Literature*, 43: 9–64.

CLARK, A. (1997), *Being There: Putting Mind, Body, and World Together Again* (Cambridge, Mass.: MIT Press).

COLEMAN, J. S. (1990), *Foundations of Social Theory* (Cambridge, Mass.: Harvard University Press).

COSTA, P. T., and MCCRAE, R. R. (1992), *NEO PI-R Professional Manual* (Lutz, Fla.: Psychological Assessment Resources).

DENNETT, D. C. (1987), *The Intentional Stance* (Cambridge, Mass.: MIT Press).

—— (1991), *Consciousness Explained* (New York: Little, Brown).

DUBIN, R. (1959), 'Deviant Behavior and Social Structure: Continuities in Social Theory', *American Sociological Review*, 24: 147–64.

ELSTER, J. (1985) (ed.), *The Multiple Self* (Cambridge: Cambridge University Press).

—— (2000), *Ulysses Unbound: Studies in Rationality, Precommittment, and Constraints* (Cambridge: Cambridge University Press).

—— (2007), *Explaining Social Behavior: More Nuts and Bolts for the Social Sciences* (Cambridge: Cambridge University Press).

FREDERICK, S., LOEWENSTEIN, G., and O'DONOGHUE, T. (2002), 'Time Discounting and Time Preference: A Critical Review', *Journal of Economic Literature*, 40: 351–401.

FREESE, J. (2008), 'Genetics and the Social Science Explanation of Individual Outcomes', *American Journal of Sociology*, 114: S1–S35.

—— and MONTGOMERY, J. D. (2007), 'The Devil Made Her Do It?: Evaluating Risk Preference as an Explanation of Sex Differences in Religiousness', in Shelley J. Correll (ed.), *Advances in Group Processes: The Social Psychology of Gender* (Oxford: Elsevier), 187–230.

—— and RIVAS, S. (2006), 'Cognition, Personality, and the Sociology of Response to Social Change: The Case of Internet Adoption', CDE working paper (Culture, Development, Enviroment, at Sussex) no. 2006-07.

FRIEDMAN, M. (1953), 'The Methodology of Positive Economics', in his *Essays in Positive Economics* (Chicago, Ill.: University of Chicago Press), 3–43.

GARFINKEL, H. (1967), *Studies in Ethnomethodology* (Englewood Cliffs, N.J.: Prentice Hall).

GIERYN, T. F. (1999), *Cultural Boundaries of Science: Credibility on the Line* (Chicago, Ill.: University of Chicago Press).

GINTIS, H. (2007), 'A Framework for the Unification of the Behavioral Sciences', *Behavioral and Brain Sciences*, 30: 1–61.

GOFFMAN, E. (1959), *The Presentation of Self in Everyday Life* (Garden City, N.Y.: Doubleday).

GOULD, R. V. (2003), *Collison of Wills: How Ambiguity About Social Rank Breeds Conflict* (Chicago, Ill.: University of Chicago Press).

HEDSTRÖM, P. (2005), *Dissecting the Social: On the Principles of Analytical Sociology* (Cambridge: Cambridge University Press).

HITLIN, S., and PILIAVIN, J. A., 'Values: Reviving a Dormant Concept', *Annual Review of Sociology*, 30: 359–93.

HOUSE, J. S. (1977), 'The Three Faces of Social Psychology', *Sociometry*, 40: 161–77.

JENSEN, M. C., and MECKLING, W. H. (1976), 'Theory of the Firm: Managerial Behavior, Agency Costs, and Ownership Structure', *Journal of Financial Economics*, 3: 305–60.

JOHN, O. P., and SRIVASTAVA, S. (1999), 'The Big Five Trait Taxonomy: History, Measurement, and Theoretical Perspectives', in L. A. Pervin (ed.), *Handbook of Personality Theory and Research* (New York: Guilford), 102–38.

KAHNEMAN, D., and TVERSKY, A. (2000), *Choices, Values, and Frames* (Cambridge: Cambridge University Press).

KING, B., FELIN, T., and WHETTEN, D. A. (2007), 'What Does It Mean to Act?: The Theoretical Foundations of the Organization as a Rational Actor', working paper, Brigham Young University.

KOHN, M. L. (1969), *Class and Conformity: A Study in Values* (Homewood, Ill.: Dorsey).

LICHTENSTEIN, S., and SLOVIC, P. (2006), 'The Construction of Preference: An Overview', in Lichtenstein and Slovic (eds.), *The Construction of Preference* (Cambridge: Cambridge University Press), 1–40.

LIEBERSON, S. (2000), *A Matter of Taste* (New Haven, Conn.: Yale University Press).

LOEHLIN, J. C. (1992), *Genes and Environment in Personality Development* (Newbury Park, Calif.: Sage).

LUMSDEN, C. J., and WILSON, E. O. (1981), *Genes, Mind, and Culture: The Coevolutionary Process* (Cambridge, Mass.: Harvard University Press).

MCCRAE, R. R., and COSTA, P. T. (2003), *Personality in Adulthood: A Five-Factor Perspective*, 2nd edn. (New York: Guilford).

MARWELL, G., and OLIVER, P. E. (1993), *The Critical Mass in Collective Action: A Micro-social Theory* (Cambridge: Cambridge University Press).

MEAD, G. H. (1934), *Mind, Self, and Society from the Standpoint of a Social Behaviorist* (Chicago, Ill: University of Chicago Press).

ROBERTS, B. W., et al. (2003), 'Personality Trait Development in Adulthood', in J. T. Mortimer and M. J. Shanahan (eds.), *Handbook of the Life Course* (New York: Kluwer), 579–95.

ROSS, D. (2005), *Economic Theory and Cognitive Science: Microexplanation* (Cambridge, Mass.: MIT Press).

SAMUELSON, P. A. (1947), *Foundations of Economic Analysis* (Cambridge, Mass.: Harvard University Press).

SATZ, D., and FEREJOHN, J. (1994), 'Rational Choice and Social Theory', *Journal of Philosophy*, 91: 71–87.

SCHELLING, T. C. (1978), *Micromotives and Macrobehavior* (New York: Norton).

SCHOEMAKER, P. J. H. (1982), 'The Expected Utility Model: Its Variants, Purposes, Evidence and Limitations', *Journal of Economic Literature*, 20: 529–63.

SEWELL, W. H., and HAUSER, R. M. (1975), *Education, Occupation, and Earnings: Achievement in the Early Career* (New York: Academic).

SHANAHAN, M. J., et al. (2008), 'Environmental Contingencies and Genetic Propensities: Social Capital, Educational Continuation, and a Dopamine Receptor Polymorphism', *American Journal of Sociology*, 110: S260–86.

STETS, J. E., and BURKE, P. J. (2000), 'Identity Theory and Social Identity Theory', *Social Psychology Quarterly*, 63: 224–37.

STIGLER, G. J., and BECKER, G. S. (1977), 'De Gustibus Non Est Disputandum', *American Economic Review*, 67: 76–90.

STRYKER, S. (1980), *Symbolic Interactionism: A Social Structural Version* (Menlo Park, Calif.: Cummings).

TAJFEL, H., et al. (1971), 'Social Categorization and Intergroup Behavior', *European Journal of Social Psychology*, 56: 364–73.

TOLLEFSON, D. (2002), 'Organizations as True Believers', *Journal of Social Philosophy*, 33: 395–410.

TURNER, J. H. (1987), 'Toward a Sociological Theory of Motivation', *American Sociological Review*, 52: 15–27.

UDRY, J. R. (2000), 'Biological Limits of Gender Construction', *American Sociological Review*, 65: 443–57.

WINSHIP, C. (2006), 'Policy Analysis as Puzzle Solving', in M. Moran, M. Rein, and R. E. Goodin (eds.), *The Oxford Handbook of Public Policy* (Oxford: Oxford University Press), 109–23.

WRONG, D. H. (1961), 'The Oversocialized Conception of Man in Modern Sociology', *American Sociological Review*, 26: 183–93.

CHAPTER 6

OPPORTUNITIES*

TROND PETERSEN

INTRODUCTION

THE concept of opportunity arises in a variety of ways in social sciences analysis, but two are especially important. First, the concept arises in analyses of the choices people make. Opportunities consist of the possible choices available once political, social, economic, and technical constraints have been taken into account. For example, a young person's opportunity for attending medical school depends on the number of students to be admitted, the number of other students applying for admittance, her qualifications relative to others, and sometimes her financial situation. While the opportunities available usually are seen as fixed and outside an agent's control, there are important situations where agents restrict their opportunities and situations where they actively seek to modify and expand the opportunities they face.

Second, the concept of opportunity arises in analyses of social inequality and civil rights. Extensive debates address whether one should strive for equality of opportunities, resources, outcomes, or welfare. A key concern has been equality of opportunity by sex and race in access to education, employment, health, and more. Legislation in many countries over the last fifty years has focused on such equality, as have social-sciences analyses. But, as has become increasingly clear, equality of opportunity does not guarantee equality of outcomes or of welfare, simply because

* I draw on materials previously published in Petersen (1994, 2004a, 2004b) and Petersen and Saporta (2004).

people differ in their talents, preferences, and the constraints they face, and these considerations enter into analysis of inequality as well.

In this chapter I will outline both uses of the concept of opportunity. I proceed by discussing its role in analyzing choices. I first distinguish between choices made without attention to what other agents do versus choices made strategically taking into account the possible actions of others, and then turn to a discussion of how agents may act to shape the constraints and opportunities they face, and finally how available opportunities may shape preferences.

These abstract ideas are then applied to the substantive field of inequality, first in the context of civil-rights legislation and debates in theories of justice, and next in an analysis of differential labor market outcomes. For the latter I address career opportunity and opportunity hoarding in the professions. I end with a discussion of opportunities for employers to discriminate on the basis of race and sex in the current legal environment, showing how explicit attention to choice opportunity may inform one on specific inequality outcomes.

The concept of opportunity thus provides multiple services, from the broad to the narrow, and does so covering many substantive domains. In all the analysis of inequality below, the role of choice is central, and, as such, the concept of opportunity as used in analysis of choice enters there too.

The key insights are that opportunities often depend on the actions of others, that they sometimes shape preferences, that some agents may be able to expand the opportunities they face and conversely restrict the opportunities others face, and that legal interventions may do the same.

6.1 OPPORTUNITY IN CHOICES

The concept of opportunity arises integrally in analyzing the choices agents make. Sometimes choices are made in isolation, other times they are made while considering what other agents will do. The first situation is referred to as classical decision-making, the second as interdependent decision-making.

For the role of opportunities in choice, it is useful first to cite Elster's analysis of rational choice (1979: 86) as the outcome of a two-step process:

> To explain why a person in a given situation behaves in one way rather than in another, we can see his action as the result of two successive filtering processes. The first has the effect of limiting the set of abstractly possible actions to the feasible set, i.e. the set of actions that satisfy simultaneously a number of physical, technical, economic and politico-legal constraints. The second has the effect of singling out one member of the feasible set as the action which is to be carried out.

(See also Hedström and Udehn 2009.)

6.1.1 Classical decision-making

In many settings choices are made in isolation, without taking into account what other agents might do or not do. This is the typical situation in consumers' markets, such as buying groceries, gasoline, and more. One needs to know the agents' preferences, the constraints they face, and the opportunities open to them, and an analysis of their choices can be made. It is the context of choice addressed in classical decision-making analysis.

The core idea is that given the agent's preferences and available opportunities she will choose the opportunity that best satisfies her preferences. Consider for example a farmer who needs to choose when to harvest her crop. In a region with stable weather, with no uncertainty whether the sun will shine or not next week, she will harvest once the crop is optimally ripe. This would be classical decision-making under certainty. But in most regions the weather is variable, and the best time for harvesting will depend on uncertain future weather conditions. Her course of action will then be guided by guesses of future conditions. The agent can no longer choose the best opportunity, because the agent does not know what it will be. But she may choose the opportunity that maximizes her expected outcome, given her guesses of future conditions. This would be classical decision-making under uncertainty. She chooses against an unknown future environment, but not against the unknown choices made by other agents.

6.1.2 Interdependent decision-making

In a self-subsistence agrarian economy opportunities would depend on one's plot of land, and then on weather conditions, one's health, and more, but not integrally on the choices and actions of other farmers. This is very different in modern large-scale societies. Opportunities available to an agent often depend not only on endowments and conditions of nature, but also on what everyone else does, through interactions and interdependencies. In assessing one's opportunities one thus needs to assess what others are likely to do, thereby engaging in strategic reasoning and interaction. And even in agrarian societies each farmer may on occasion be affected by the actions of people far away, as in the case of pests, where fungus originating on one continent spreads to other continents over a period of one to two years through exports of seeds and travel. A prominent example is the Irish potato famine of 1845–6, where events in the USA led to famine in Ireland. These were however events that no farmer could have reacted to strategically.

For analyzing opportunities and choice in strategic settings, game theory provides the appropriate framework. Students of game theory investigate strategic interaction among two or more actors, individual, corporate, or of other kinds.[1] In Elster's words (e.g. 1985: 10), game theory is a theory for studying interdependent decisions where two or more actors act intentionally. There are four types of interdependencies. First, the reward of each depends on the choices of all, through general social causality. Second, the reward of each depends on the rewards of all, through envy, altruism, and solidarity. Third, the choice (i.e. action) of each depends on the choices of all, through strategic reasoning. Fourth, the desires of each depend on the actions of all, through the fact that individual preferences and plans are social in their origins. Game theory cannot deal with the social origins of preferences, but it deals well with the three other kinds of interdependencies. And even when it comes to the social origins of preferences, game theory can at least give some insight into what kinds of social situations are likely to lead the actors to change their preferences, as when sympathy for one's coactors arises in repeated interactions (e.g. Elster 1985: 362).

Since the action of each then depends on what he or she expects everyone else to do, the opportunities of each also depend on what everyone else does. For example, when college students migrate from one field of study to another, in the short run this opens up more opportunities for study in the fields being vacated and restricts opportunities in the fields being populated.

It is obvious that strategic interaction is important and occurs in many parts of social life. And even when the goal is to reach consensus and common understanding, which Habermas terms 'communicative interaction,' (1981), strategic elements may enter. So game theory seems to offer a particularly apt framework for analyzing social situations, and to understand how opportunities evolve in an interdependent world. Weber ([1922–3] 1978: 4) states that sociology is the interpretive understanding of social action and that 'Action is "social" insofar as its subjective meaning takes account of the behavior of others and is thereby oriented in its course.' Game theory analyzes action where the behavior of others is taken into account.

In strategic settings the opportunities faced by the individual agent are thus not fixed, but evolve as the results of the actions taken by all the involved agents. Perceptive agents choose actions while trying to anticipate how others will act, as well as trying to influence how others will act.

6.1.3 Changing the opportunities: restriction and expansion

In most analyses the opportunities an agent faces are taken as being beyond the agent's control and influence, seen as provided to the agent through physical, technical, economic, social, and political constraints. In some settings agents may however act to modify the opportunities available (see Winship 2009). Similarly, legal interventions often result in opportunity restriction or expansion and sometimes both. They may restrict opportunities for some groups, open up opportunities for other groups, and generally rule on what can and cannot legally be done.

The most thoroughly discussed case of opportunity restriction is where individuals and institutions deliberately act to remove opportunities—that is, to restrict the choice set. The behavior is referred to as self-binding or precommitment (Elster 1979, 2007). The principal rationale for such behavior is that 'less may be more.' A person craving chocolate but prone to weight gain may avoid the candy section in the grocery store and keep no supply at home. There are a variety of motives and attendant techniques for self-binding. Motives include desire to tame passions, to prevent weakness of will, and to guard against misjudgment. Techniques include avoiding settings that trigger passions or weakness of will and which thus may induce one to choose the opportunity one would like to avoid. Oftentimes institutions impose restrictions by removing opportunities through legislation. For example, married couples seeking divorce are legally required to enter into a separation period, the idea being that they for a period need to be protected against rash actions from possibly passing troubles before divorce can be granted.

The opposite of self-binding is to expand one's opportunities. In some settings agents can act upon and modify the constraints they face, and thereby open up novel opportunities. Also a common phenomenon, though not yet analyzed in the same detail, and certainly not as psychologically intriguing, it characterizes behavior by creative agents and in periods of change. Entrepreneurs, artists, and inventors often achieve their successes by changing the opportunity set most others would view as given. On a large scale, science and technology expand our opportunities, as they have in information technology during the last thirty years, and as is likely to occur on an even larger scale in biology, neuroscience, and energy during the next half century. On a smaller scale, Claudio Monteverdi created the opera, Joseph Haydn the string quartet, and so on. Geck (2006: 136) describes how Johann Sebastian Bach acted to change his constraints, and characterizes his outlook as follows:

> A pragmatist in the post of St Thomas cantor would reason as follows: I have the school's pupils, the council musicians, and a few students at my disposal; I will adapt my music to those resources. Bach's reasoning goes this way: I have the school's pupils, the council musicians, and a few students at my disposal, and the St Matthew Passion in my head; therefore I need better conditions.

6.1.4 Interactions of opportunities and preferences

A common phenomenon is that agents may adapt their preferences to the opportunities they face. If a particular option in the choice set gets removed, an agent may adapt her preferences so that the option no longer is seen as valuable. This phenomenon has been analyzed by Elster (1984) in the appropriately titled book *Sour Grapes*. Alternatively there may be counteradaptive preferences. An option that gets removed may become more highly valued. Or an available option may become defined as 'forbidden fruit' and then removed from the actual set of perceived opportunities. Preferences can thus adapt to opportunities in many ways: 'People can align their preferences with what they do not have, with what they cannot have, and with what they are forbidden to have' (Elster 1999: 22).

6.1.5 Opportunity and choice: a summary

The concept of opportunity as used in analyzing choice behavior traverses many issues: the role of other agents in shaping one's opportunities, the rigidity of opportunities, how opportunities may influence preferences, how agents may act to change the opportunities they face, and legal restrictions and expansions of opportunities, such as when civil-rights legislation has opened up new opportunities for women and minorities and restricted the opportunities for employers to engage in discrimination. I shall now apply some of these ideas to the area of social inequality.

6.2 OPPORTUNITY AND INEQUALITY: PREFERENCES AND TALENTS

The concept of opportunity is central in studies of inequality and in equality legislation throughout the entire western world during the last fifty years, legislation that led to the most far-reaching social changes in this part of the world since World War II.

The core concern in policies for equality is to achieve equality of opportunities for various groups, such as in employment through access to jobs, wages, and promotions. Equality of opportunity is then usually understood as equal treatment: equally qualified persons should have equal chances of access to education, of being hired or promoted, and so on, and there should be no differential treatment by sex, race, or other irrelevant characteristics. Equality of opportunity in this sense—unquestionably the first and most basic notion of equality—is often associated with a libertarian position, where equality of basic rights is sought (Sen 1992: ch. 1), and the position has been enshrined in equality legislation in most modern nations.

Equality of opportunity in the sense of equal treatment is however sometimes seen as too narrow a goal in modern societies. In many contexts, and by many political thinkers, achieving equality of opportunity is not sufficient for reaching social goals of value. One simple reason is, as Goldthorpe (1980: 30) once pointed out, that unequal outcomes could 'be regarded as a situation of inequality' or 'as one in which equal opportunities were unequally taken.' Preferences and constraints faced may prevent agents from fully realizing the opportunities they are offered. For example, even with no differential treatment of men and women by employers, women may be constrained by their family situation from reaping the full benefits of equal opportunity in the workplace, or they may have preferences that differ from men with respect to work hours, choice of occupation, and educational tracks to pursue. These may lead to inequality of outcomes even in presence of equality of opportunity in terms of equal treatment to reach outcomes.

For such reasons, researchers sometimes argue that the goal of equality of opportunity should be supplemented with three other notions of equality. A second notion of equality holds that agents should be given equal resources for achieving outcomes (Dworkin 1981*a*, 1981*b*). Resources are inputs that agents use to achieve material, psychological, and other outcomes. In a narrow version one focuses on equality of material resources. Differences by for example birth need then be compensated; children from less-well-off families receive compensation to aid them compete on an equal footing with children from better-off families, such as receiving educational scholarships tied to family income or wealth. What is sought equalized is material resources for achieving outcomes, not necessarily equal treatment for reaching outcomes. Equalizing material resources, coupled with equal treatment, is then tantamount to a broader definition of equality of opportunity. This is referred to as a resource-egalitarian position (Sen 1992: ch. 1), but a narrow version in that it focuses only on material resources.

As a practical matter it can be difficult to equalize material resources, in which case equal treatment usually will lead to worse outcomes and hence arguably lower opportunities for those with fewer resources. For example, families with higher incomes can send their children to better schools, hire tutors, enroll them in extra courses, and thus give them advantages in the educational and employment domains that children from less-well-off families do not enjoy. In such situations, institutions sometimes engage in unequal treatment, thereby creating inequality of opportunity in the equal-treatment sense of the concept in order to compensate for inequality of resources. This occurs in college and university admissions when students from poorer families are given extra points in admissions. Such practices are known as affirmative action in the USA. By engaging in unequal treatment, and hence deviating from the basic notion of equality of opportunity, the institutions compensate for unequal resources and thus achieve more equality of outcomes.

But even where equality of material resources is an achievable goal, it does not necessarily lead to equality of outcomes, an observation that gives rise to a third notion of equality. The central point is that some agents may be better able to utilize a given material-resource bundle due to superior talents or physical strength or better networks to other central agents. A person's resource bundle for functioning in society consists not only of alienable material resources but also of the inalienable resources talent, health, dispositions, and more (Dworkin 1981*a*, 1981*b*). Hayek (1960: 76–7) writes: 'It is just not true that humans are born equal...if we treat them equally, the result must be inequality in their actual position ... [thus] the only way to place them in an equal position would be to treat them differently. Equality before the law and material equality are, therefore, not only different but in conflict with each other.' If the goal is equality of material outcomes, or at least equality of opportunity to reach equal material outcomes, then equality of material resources will be insufficient, and those less favorably positioned to utilize a given material-resource bundle due to lack of talents or handicaps may have to be allocated more material resources to achieve same outcomes. This is a broader version of resource egalitarianism in that it encompasses alienable as well as inalienable resources, and aims at equalizing the total-resource bundle by also compensating for deficits in inalienable resources, and is the version argued by Dworkin (1981*b*).

Others again raise the criticism that equality of outcomes, especially in material terms, is the incorrect metric, and that what ought to be equalized is welfare or the subjective experience of life, yielding yet a fourth notion of equality. To achieve equality of welfare, there must be inequality of resources and material outcomes not only to compensate those less fortunate in material, physical, and mental endowments, but also to compensate the agents with less fortunate or optimistic outlooks on life and preferences. Two equally endowed agents in terms of health and talents and with equal material resources may experience very different levels of welfare. One agent may be occupationally more ambitious than the other, but not occupationally more successful, and since the distance between ambition and achievement will be wider for the more ambitious person, she may subjectively experience lower welfare. Dworkin (1981*a*: 188–9) articulated the position as follows:

> For the concept of welfare was invented or at least adopted by economists precisely to describe what is fundamental in life rather than what is merely instrumental. It was adopted, in fact, to provide a metric of assigning a proper value to the resources: resources are valuable so far as they produce welfare. If we decide on equality, but then define equality in terms of resources unconnected with the welfare they bring, then we seem to be mistaking means for ends and indulging in a fetishistic fascination for what we ought to treat only as instrumental.

In aiming for equality of welfare one thus focuses on the subjective aspects of life, how it is experienced by the agents, and seeks to equalize these. The position is referred to as welfare egalitarianism.

Each of these four conceptions of equality—of opportunity, resources, outcomes, and welfare—argues for equality in one dimension, they just differ in the dimension chosen (Sen 1992: ch. 1). But equality in one dimension cannot be attained without simultaneously inducing inequality in other dimensions. There is broad agreement in modern liberal societies on the principle of equality of opportunity in the equal-treatment sense. But it accepts inequality of resources by birth, and leads to inequality of outcomes due to different material resources and capabilities for utilizing equal opportunities, and to inequality of welfare due to differences in needs and preferences.

Central to these discussions is the role of responsibility and of motivation (Dworkin 1981*a*, 1981*b*). It makes sense to compensate agents for handicaps, poor health, and other conditions from birth or outside their control. But it appears undesirable to compensate agents for having expensive preferences, for having ambitions that cannot reasonably be satisfied and which hence may lead to dissatisfaction, or for having failed to develop their talents in attainable ways, or other aspects of their acquired dispositions. A miser needs fewer resources to achieve same welfare as the spendthrift, but there is no argument or public policy that resources should be transferred from misers to spendthrifts in order to equalize their welfares. Nor is there a policy to transfer resources from the optimist Panglossian to the pessimist misanthrope to equalize welfares. One compensates for unfortunate conditions outside the agent's control, but not for unusual preferences or actions that did not lead to the desired outcomes. Dworkin (1981*b*) thus argues for resource egalitarianism, encompassing alienable (material) resources as well as inalienable ones (e.g. talents), and against welfare egalitarianism, since the latter seeks to compensate agents for situations for which they should be held responsible. Closely related to responsibility is motivation. One needs systems of opportunity that encourage and motivate responsible behavior. The need arises because production and distribution often are hard to separate, in that agents may not have the incentives to produce if they at the same time are not assured compensation when the product gets distributed.

Many of these distinctions were touched upon by Karl Marx in the *Critique of the Gotha Program* ([1875] 1972: 16–17). In the early part of socialism there would be equality of material resources, since ownership of the means of production and of land would be socialized. But since people have different talents, the results would still be inequality of outcomes. As Marx put it, the early part of socialism would recognize unequal ownership of individual talents but not inequality of physical holdings such as factories and land, corresponding to what today is called resource egalitarianism, in its narrow version. According to Marx, recognizing differences in outcomes due to differences in talents is necessary because of motivational problems during this period; that is, such inequality encourages responsible behavior, as echoed by Davis and Moore (1945) seventy years later from an entirely different political viewpoint. Under communism, in contrast, motivational problems are absent, since human mentalities have changed, and inequality of outcomes due to inequality of talent would no longer be needed, and resources should be allocated according to needs, corresponding to a state of welfare egalitarianism.

6.3 CAREER OPPORTUNITIES FOR EMPLOYEES: RIGID OPPORTUNITY STRUCTURE

While the broad literatures discussed above play a clear role in sociological analyses, for understanding the role of opportunity in creating inequality, research in sociology with its empirical orientation typically has a more limited focus, leaving the more abstract discussions to political theorists and philosophers. The core focuses of interest are instead on the mechanisms and causes of inequality in occupational position, wages, promotions, educational outcomes, and less on welfare outcomes or resource bundles. Underlying much sociological research is a concern with equality of opportunity, in the sense of equal treatment, but also a concern with compensation for disadvantaged position due to social background and birth, leading to a preoccupation with compensatory mechanisms such as affirmative action.

One important strand of sociological research with a focus on opportunity addresses occupational career opportunity in modern organizations. Sørensen (1977, 1979) pulled together and expanded on many of the central contributions (e.g. White 1970) and set the agenda for research. His goal was to analyze differences in career outcomes and how these arise due to differences in opportunities, now to be summarized.[2]

6.3.1 The vacancy competition model

Sørensen (1977) proceeded from five central building blocks describing both social structure and individual resources:

(1) There is a fixed occupational structure, characterized by a distribution of jobs.
(2) Opportunities to get ahead will be determined by the rate at which vacancies in the occupational structure open up, through turnover, job creation, and more.
(3) People differ in the job-relevant resources they possess (e.g. human capital, experience), which help them compete for positions in the occupational structure.
(4) People want to get ahead in the structure (the action part).
(5) The rate at which opportunities to get ahead in the occupational structure open up varies systematically between demographic groups.

From these five features characterizing a stratification system, his analysis focuses on the immediate implication that individual success depends not only on (3) individual resources, but also on the (1) distribution of positions, (2) the rate at which positions open up, and (5) which group one is in and when one entered the labor market. The last point highlights that variations in opportunities to get ahead depend on differences between demographic groups in abilities to utilize the opportunities, due to inequality in resources or unequal treatment and especially when a group first entered the labor market.

Sørensen referred to this particular conceptualization of inequality as the *vacancy-competition model*. Several features are noteworthy, but two call for further comments. First, wages and rewards in a job are not determined by the incumbent's individual resources and productivities. They are determined by the job, being attached to titles or positions. Individuals get access to jobs by competing for these, and then their amount of individual resources is relevant. To understand inequality, and to assess whether it can be justified or not, one needs to focus not only on inequality of resources and of opportunity, but also on the more rigid aspects of the occupational system. This is a common conception in the stratification literature. Second, and also important, with respect to analyzing the role of personal resources, one must account for interdependencies between agents. Since positions, with their associated rewards, in many settings are occupied by agents for long periods of time, without being open to competition from other and possibly more qualified agents, for explaining inequality it might be as illuminating to focus on who got access to opportunities when as on the distribution of personal qualifications. A highly qualified agent may end up being poorly rewarded simply because the advantageous positions are occupied by other agents.

In the human-capital model of inequality (e.g. Becker 1964), which was a target of critique for Sørensen, the rewards that agents receive are 'deserved' in the sense that no one receives any unearned advantages. In Sørensen's vacancy chain model, in contrast, as people progress through the occupational structure they may be held up because there are no opportunities for them to advance. They may possess the skills needed for advancement to higher positions, but when these are already occupied they cannot progress, and hence suffer a structural disadvantage. Their disadvantage is offset exactly by the structural advantage held by the sometimes less accomplished agent currently occupying the position.

6.3.2 Rigidity of the opportunity structure

In the conceptualization discussed above, the structure of opportunity is rigid. There is a fixed set of positions to which people are allocated and with each position there is a fixed reward (see e.g. White 1970).

How well does this conceptualization capture reality? In a stable economy, with little growth and innovation, this may be the correct conceptualization. The same holds for many stable organizations. As Sørensen writes: 'the vacancy competition model might offer a more plausible theory of the earnings attainment process in the large sectors of the economy where earnings are attributes of jobs and not of persons' (1979: 383, see also p. 365). But for a more dynamic economy this is only a partial characterization. It can take account of the fact that some positions disappear and others are created, so that the number and mix of jobs in an economy change. But it does not reflect how individuals sometimes create their own jobs, either through self-employment or through initiatives vis-à-vis their employers, as in many professional jobs. An important characteristic of contemporary labor markets is that many people don't sit around and wait for opportunities to arrive. Instead they modify the constraints faced and create and expand their opportunities, as in the quote on Johann Sebastian Bach above.

The imagery of individuals competing for open vacancies needs thus to be supplemented with one where individuals create positions, and where, in the end, part of the occupational distribution reflects the distribution of initiatives of individuals. Using Sørensen's terminology (1983a), there has been a shift from so-called closed to more open positions. The occupational structure has probably become less rigid, and the relative role of individual qualifications may have become more important for success and the role of vacancies less so.

6.4 OPPORTUNITY HOARDING: EXPANSION AND RESTRICTION OF OPPORTUNITY

Another important way in which the concept of opportunity is used in inequality research is for analyzing opportunity hoarding and rents, where agents position themselves in order to reap economic and positional advantages that could not be had under conditions of free exchange. Many authors have contributed to this line of research (e.g. Tilly 1998), but here I take up again a particular line advanced by Sørensen.

From Weber ([1922–3] 1978: 43–6, 341–3), Sørensen (1983b) made the observation that some positions in society are open to competition, whereas other positions are less so. In the part of the labor market with so-called open positions, the opportunities for upward movement in the occupational structure should also be more favorable. These themes were developed in Sørensen's work on structural inequality, rents, and class (1996, 2000). In an economy with open positions, the distribution of inequality will closely mirror the distribution of individual resources. But with many closed positions the fit is less tight, and individuals and groups earn rents, unrelated to their resources and merits, as a function of structural advantages gained at fortuitous earlier points in historical time. Agents are thus able to hoard opportunities due to advantages gained at prior points in time and to the advantages accruing from positions closed to competition from more qualified agents.

It is in the study of professions that the concept of opportunity hoarding arises most forcefully. This research addresses how professional associations introduce licensing requirements and restrict the unlicensed from practicing the profession, thereby creating positions closed to competition from other agents. Such strategies are justified by the need to protect the public from charlatans and unqualified practitioners, for example in the medical profession. At the same time these practices give rise to monopoly earnings for the professionals (e.g. Weeden 2002). Opportunity hoarding in the professions has many times emerged from complex and decade-long interactions involving professionals, their organizations, educational institutions, and the state and the judicial system (Abbott 1988). Professional groups often struggle over who should retain jurisdiction over a given professional domain. For example, in many countries lawyers and accountants fought over who should be certified for delivering business-accounting services. The state clearly has an interest in the quality of business accounting, in that accounting practices must match the tax code, and the efficiency of this match is important for tax collection. In many countries therefore the courts and legislative apparatus have intervened in and settled interprofessional disputes, as they did in the case of business accounting in France, England, Norway, the USA, and other countries during the twentieth century. Similar disputes may be found between medical doctors, psychologists, and psychiatrists with respect to who may give psychological advice and administer and prescribe psychopharmacological drugs. For the professions involved, the disputes are often about opportunity hoarding, though rarely articulated as such, and the same may hold for the educational institutions certifying the professionals. For the state and legislative apparatuses the conflicts are principally about the need to regulate certain activities and protect the broader public.

The professions thus raise intriguing analytic questions. One need understand not only the self-interest of professionals and their organizations, but also how professions often have norms and codes of conduct to restrict self-interest and hence to protect the public interest, and may be explicit about these norms through their professional associations, and sometimes create incentives for proper professional conduct. The public good then gets guarded both by the professional association and the state. Professions may thus engage in both opportunity hoarding through restricting the opportunities of competing professional groups and exclusion of unlicensed practitioners, and at the same time restricting own choices and opportunities, in the sense of self-binding through professional codes. It may be that the very practice of restricting the choice and opportunities of others also compels the professions to put restrictions on own choices and opportunities. This is an arena where opportunities are not taken as given by any party, but are actively sought modified by the competing professions, the state, and sometimes clients, as has increasingly become the case in health care over the last two decades.

6.5 LEGAL RESTRICTIONS: OPPORTUNITY STRUCTURE FOR DISCRIMINATION FOR EMPLOYERS

Having addressed the supply side of the labor market—how employees face variations in opportunities—it is instructive to turn to the demand side: how employers face variations in opportunities for treating men and women differentially, to engage in discrimination by sex and race.

The focus below on the opportunities for discrimination mirrors the focus in civil-rights legislation in most OECD countries. That focus is precisely on restricting the opportunities available for employers to discriminate between employees on the basis of race and sex and other characteristics seen as illegitimate in employment, thereby restricting the choice set of employers, making certain previously available choice options illegal.[3] And once in place, the hard constraints induced by legislation and the practice of law may induce new soft constraints through social norms that further restrict what employers view as legitimate behavior. As in the case of the professions and opportunity hoarding, this is another instance of self-binding, in part through legislation where some opportunities are removed from the legal choice set, in part through self-restriction where some opportunities no longer are seen as socially legitimate to pursue. And while the goal of the legislation was to expand opportunities for women and minorities, the instrument for accomplishing the goal was to restrict the opportunities of employers to treat groups differentially. Legislation simultaneously resulted in opportunity expansion and restriction.

The starting point for understanding the role of legislation for restricting employer behavior is the three distinct arenas for discrimination in employment (Petersen 2004b). Wage and career differences between men and women caused by discrimination from employers can come about by several mechanisms. In the first, women are differentially allocated to occupations and establishments that differ in the wages they pay. This involves discrimination in the matching process at the point of hire, in subsequent promotions, and through differential dismissal. I call these processes 'allocative discrimination.' In the second, women receive lower wages than men within a given occupation within a given establishment. I call this process 'within-job wage discrimination.' In the third, female-dominated occupations are paid lower wages than male-dominated ones, although skill requirements and other wage relevant factors are the same. This is the issue addressed by comparable-worth initiatives. I call this process 'valuative discrimination.'

Analytic frameworks for these processes mostly focus on the motivations for employers to discriminate, such as prejudice, stereotypes, and statistical discrimination (e.g. England 1992: ch. 2; Petersen 2004b). While these are important and relevant, my goals are different. As a device for theorizing, I take as a central premise that employers discriminate and that discrimination, consciously or non-consciously, in fact is widespread.[4] I then proceed from a massive fact, much discussed but not from the current vantage point, that such actions take place in an extensive legal environment making them illegal. This creates considerable variations across contexts in opportunities to discriminate. So rather than analyzing the motivations for discriminatory behaviors, it becomes relevant and even critical to ask: If employers discriminate, for whatever reasons, where would they most likely succeed in this? I thus elucidate where in the employment relationship discriminatory behaviors most likely would occur, addressing so to speak the 'opportunity structure' for discrimination in the current legal environment.

My conceptual errand is thus to provide a framework identifying the structural conditions under which discrimination is feasible, where employers thus have opportunities to discriminate, leading to a comparative analysis of the relative importance of the three forms of discrimination in contemporary organizations.

6.5.1 Three central dimensions

In order to understand the relative prevalence and importance of the three forms of discrimination, the central step is to identify the conditions required for discriminatory practices to be feasible and successful. One then needs to theorize not primarily the behaviors of employers but the ability of employees, firm-internal adjudication organs, and the judicial system to fight and withstand instances of employer discrimination. To this end I distinguish three dimensions that may inhibit or facilitate unjustified differential treatment of men and women.

The *first* dimension that may mitigate against discriminatory behaviors is the ease with which information about such practices can be assembled and documented. When information is hard to collect and document, discriminatory practices are also more likely to succeed. The importance of information—its availability, amount, and type—has been extensively researched in the social-psychological literature on stereotypes (e.g. Heilman 1995). It addresses how employers may be more likely to stereotype employees when acting on limited information. I approach this somewhat differently. I focus on how the ease of assembling documentation may facilitate whether employers can succeed in discriminating and whether employees and legal or quasi-legal bodies can successfully counter attempts at discrimination.

The *second* dimension concerns the ambiguity of assembled documentation. Unless a piece of information can be interpreted in a relatively unambiguous manner across potential evaluators with different orientations and values, it need not be helpful in establishing the existence of discrimination. This will hold for firm-internal adjudication procedures, through affirmative action boards, which, when the evidence is ambiguous, may not follow up complaints from employees. But it will hold even more for external agencies, such as the legal system, who may be asked to pass judgment on the basis of ambiguous information.[5] Again, there is an extensive social-psychological literature addressing how ambiguity of information may lead to the use of stereotypes and hence discrimination, with a focus on motives rather than opportunities for discrimination (Heilman 1995: 11–12; see also Reskin 1998: 29–31).

The *third* dimension concerns the availability of a plaintiff or complainant who may press charges regarding discrimination. If such individuals or groups of individuals are not forthcoming, discriminatory practices are more likely, as one might expect to be the case in employment relationships involving illegal immigrants. The number of instances of discrimination likely is far greater than those that are brought to the attention of the courts or other parties. At issue here is the proposition that discrimination will be more prevalent when the party discriminated against is less likely to complain. So it may even obtain that the fewer cases of a given type that are brought to the courts the more prevalent this form of discrimination may be.

The first two dimensions pertain to aspects of the information needed—ease of documentation and ambiguity of information—the third to the availability of a complainant. Each of these is a prerequisite for a complaint to be made and is thus fundamental. But clearly other factors are important as well, such as costs of complaining, be they monetary, psychological, or social, the expected payoffs to complaining, what the available redress procedures are, firm-internal organs versus the judicial system, and more.

Even so, by focusing on essentials only, I can from the three dimensions provide a forceful conceptual analysis of what to expect in terms of the relative importance of the three forms of discrimination. The central step is to identify the opportunity structure for discrimination in an environment where discrimination is illegal.

I use the conventional definition of discrimination. Differential-treatment discrimination occurs when applicants and employees with equal qualifications and productivities are differentially treated because of their sex (Reskin 1998: 23). Disparate-impact or structural discrimination occurs when men and women are treated equally within the given set of rules and procedures but where the latter are constructed so that they favor one sex over the other (ibid. 32). My principal concern is with differential treatment, though I also address disparate-impact discrimination, such as in recruitment procedures and in valuative discrimination.

6.5.2 Within-job wage discrimination

As regards within-job wage discrimination: where a man and a woman, equally qualified and productive, doing the same work for the same employer are paid unequally, the situation is straightforward. Such cases are in principle easy to document, the evidence is mostly unambiguous, and there is a clear potential complainant, the woman discriminated against. This form of discrimination is illegal since 1963 in the USA, and is likely to be infrequent, simply because it is a particularly transparent form of differential treatment most easily pursued in the legal system and elsewhere. For example, such disparate treatment may be pursued through firm-internal grievance procedures, which is much less costly than litigation. As Freed and Polsby (1984: 1080) write: 'Such cases certainly must arise, but as a practical matter they are undoubtedly settled before litigation.'

The main difficulty arises when pay depends not only on the job occupied but also on the qualifications, merit, or productivity of the incumbent. These can justify wage differences even within jobs. But they can be hard to assess. Sometimes it may also be difficult to identify whether two jobs are substantially equal or not, and hence whether the Equal Pay Act applies, in which case it may be easier for the employer to pay unequal wages (Freed and Polsby 1984).

6.5.3 Allocative discrimination

As regards allocative discrimination, the situation is more complex. It gives rise to sex segregation in jobs and firms (see Bielby and Baron 1986; Petersen and Morgan 1995; Reskin 1998) and involves three types: in hiring, in promotion, and in dismissal or firing.

The *first* type of allocative discrimination, at the point of hire, entails the most intricate set of issues, with three processes to be analyzed. The first concerns the recruitment process itself—for example, whether it occurs through newspaper ads, employment agencies, or social networks (e.g. Granovetter [1974] 1995; Bloch 1994). The second concerns who gets offers or gets hired and who does not when a job is being filled (Bloch 1994). The third concerns the conditions under which those hired get hired or the quality of the offers given (e.g. pay, level, and tasks).

In terms of the recruitment process, discrimination is hard to document. For example, if recruitment to a large extent takes place through information networks, these may operate in a manner discriminatory against women, such as by operating through male job and referral networks. These processes are difficult to document, and there is the complex issue of whether one can show discriminatory intent, not only disparate impact (England 1992: ch. 5). With limited documentation, its level of clarity versus ambiguity is irrelevant and incentives to complain are weak.

In terms of who gets offers or is hired, discrimination is also difficult to document. Information on the applicant pool is rarely available and all that may be accessible to outsiders is information on those hired. Even in large firms, information on the hiring process tends to be incomplete. And even when the relevant information is available, it likely is ambiguous, open to many interpretations.

As for the availability of a complainant, this is most problematic. Those not hired and possibly discriminated against will rarely know what occurred, and even when they do, it may be impossible to gather the relevant evidence. And those turned down often have applied for other jobs and may have gotten those, in which case the incentives for complaining or filing suits are small, in particular when this kind of discrimination typically requires litigation. Jencks (1992: 53) writes: 'laws and regulations that bar discrimination in hiring are harder to enforce than those that bar discrimination against workers who are already on a firm's payroll.'

When it comes to quality of offers made and to placement at hire, it is easy to document the identities of the parties hired and often also the conditions under which they were hired but less so the conditions offered to those who declined the offers. But the subjective element in deciding which conditions to offer is usually high, simply because less is known at the point of hire than at later promotion. As Gerhart (1990: 419) writes, 'differential treatment in salary setting is more likely for new hires than for longer-tenure employees, for whom observation of actual performance is possible.' So unless an employer determines the conditions offered at initial hire exclusively on the basis of formal qualifications such as degree, grades, and experience, this is a stage where differential treatment of men and women can easily occur in that it will be relatively easy to justify. And even when conditions are determined primarily on the basis of formal qualifications, there is still the difficulty of lack of comparability, such as comparing grades and degrees from different schools. The subjective element is thus likely to be pronounced. But one should expect less disparate treatment here than in who gets offers and who does not. This is so because conditions at initial employment among those hired often become known among colleagues and may hence form the basis for comparison processes and feelings of injustice as well as complaints, which management likely wants to avoid.

The *second* type of allocative discrimination, in promotion, is easier to analyze. Although deciding which employee is more qualified for promotion usually involves some degree of subjective judgment, on which there may be disagreements among various assessors, one is typically still in a position where one can document in a comparatively unambiguous manner the relative qualifications of those promoted and those passed over, given the promotion rules of the organization (e.g. Spilerman 1986). As long as the relative qualifications can be compared and verified vis-à-vis a third party, claims about the occurrence of discrimination can in principle be settled. Potential complainants are readily available, those passed over for promotion. And, again, many firms have internal due-process and grievance procedures that can deal with such cases, rather than through costly litigation.

Once employees are in the 'system' there are strong incentives for firms to treat them equally. Promotion discrimination is no doubt more difficult to deal with than within-job wage discrimination, but is not fraught with major complications.

The *third* type of allocative discrimination, in dismissal, is more straightforward to analyze. Here the information is usually easy to assemble, is less ambiguous, and there is a clear complainant, the person fired. It can be dealt with either through firm-internal grievance procedures or through litigation, and the incentives to pursue wrongful dismissal are usually high. By 1985 most lawsuits in the civil-rights area were filed by fired employees, followed by current employees (about 10 percent of cases), while fewest cases were filed by those not hired (see Donohue and Spiegelman 1991: 1016, 1031). This may well reflect the greater difficulty of pursuing discrimination in hiring, not differences in the prevalence of the types of discrimination.

6.5.4 Valuative discrimination

Turning to the third form, valuative discrimination, the situation is the most complex (e.g. Nelson and Bridges 1999: ch. 2). Here the discrimination is not against any specific individual but against classes of jobs held primarily by women. Documentation of such cases is difficult, the evidence is highly ambiguous, and the availability of a complainant can but need not be lacking, depending on whether a group of employees or a party acting on their behalf will press for re-evaluation of wages. The employer and sometimes the courts are asked to assess the relative worth of various jobs, a task that is difficult and on which there typically will be disagreements. Its legal status is unclear and it is by many not considered discrimination at all, arising rather from market processes that in principle should be fair (see e.g. Rhoads 1993). Precisely for these reasons one should expect valuative discrimination to be quite prevalent. This is where employers are most likely to succeed in differential treatment of men and women in that their actions consist of treating classes of jobs in a differential manner, but classes on which the sexes are unequally distributed.

6.5.5 Implications

I now summarize, in the text and in Table 6.1, the ranking of the three forms of discrimination in terms of prevalence and importance for explaining the gender wage and attainment gap in employment. This gives the relevant predictions and hypotheses for what to expect to find in empirical investigations (col. 4).

Within-job wage discrimination should be the least prevalent and least important. It is easy to document, the evidence is relatively unambiguous, and plaintiffs

Table 6.1 Dimensions facilitating discrimination, result thereof, and research evidence, by type of discrimination

Type of discrimination	Dimensions of discrimination			Result	Research evidence	
	Ease of documentation	Clarity of evidence	Availability of plaintiff	Ease of discrimination	Amount of evidence	What it shows
	1	2	3	4	5	6
Within-job wage	High	High	High	Low	Some	Little
Allocative:						
Recruitment	Low	Medium	Low	High	None	Unknown
Who gets hired	Low	Medium	Low	High	Some	Little
Conditions at hire	Medium	Medium	Low	High	Some	Some
Promotion	High	Medium	High	Medium	Some	Little
Dismissal	High	High	High	Low	None	Unknown
Valuative	Low	Low	Medium	High	Much	Much

Note: See Section 6.5 for discussion. The far-left column lists the three types of discrimination, and within the second type—allocative discrimination—the various forms thereof. The heading 'Dimensions of discrimination' provides in columns 1–3 the three dimensions that facilitate or hinder discriminatory practices, where each dimension is ranked high, medium, or low with respect to how easy it is to document, the clarity of documentation, and the availability of a plaintiff. Column 4 gives the net result from the three dimensions with respect to how easy it is to discriminate on the basis of gender. Columns 5 and 6 summarize the research evidence. Column 5 indicates the amount of evidence available, from none, through some, to much. Column 6 reports what the research shows with respect to the amount of discrimination of a given type, ranked from little, through some, to much, as well as unknown in the cases where there is no research.

are available. Allocative discrimination in promotion as well as dismissal should be more significant, but still not the most prevalent, for the same reasons. The main difference from within-job wage discrimination is that the evidence often is more ambiguous. Allocative discrimination at the point of hire, in contrast, should be considerably more widespread. This holds for recruitment procedures, for who gets offers and who does not, and for quality of offers made. Finally, valuative discrimination should be the most widespread. Here the documentation is most difficult to assemble, most ambiguous, and the availability of a plaintiff can be troublesome.

All of this leads to the conclusion that with respect to discrimination against identifiable individuals as opposed to classes of jobs, the point of hire is where differential treatment should be most widespread.[6] This view is also found among legal practitioners. Wymer and Sudbury (1992: 624) comment that 'employers have been forced to become more systematic and careful when making their promotion, demotion, salary, and discharge decisions. In most cases, employers have developed and implemented fairly reliable procedures to reduce—if not eliminate—the extent to which non-job-related biases and prejudices enter into these decisions.' They continue: 'Simply because discharged employees are far more likely to sue than rejected job applicants, employers historically have not been quite so careful in the *hiring* process. Although the possibility of a failure-to-hire lawsuit is not new, it has not been the type of claim with which employers are confronted frequently in the employment discrimination arena.'

Concerning resultant inequality, whatever discrimination takes place at initial hiring and assignment may have effects for subsequent career developments. Blau and Ferber (1987: 51) write: 'Once men and women are channeled into different types of entry jobs, the normal everyday operation of the firm will virtually ensure sex differences in productivity, promotion opportunities, and pay.' Observed differences in wages may thus largely be a result of differential hiring and initial placement. An overall gender wage gap will remain even with fair promotion and wage-setting policies within firms as long as there is differential treatment in the hiring process (see also Stinchcombe 1990: 259).

One controversial prediction emerging from this framework is that women do not necessarily face more severe career disadvantages as they progress within an organization, precisely because it becomes more difficult to discriminate as more information becomes available. The opportunities for discrimination thus decline. This contrasts to much current thinking, where female career blockages are thought to increase with seniority, the classic glass-ceiling hypothesis, as well as the recent social-psychological theorizing stressing that 'a succession of small events, such as not getting a good assignment, result in large discrepancies in advancement and achievement' (Valian 1998: 18). The two views lead to opposite orderings of the interaction between gender and seniority, one hypothesizing a declining gender effect with seniority, the other an increasing effect.

CONCLUSIONS

Opportunity is a central concept in analyzing choices. I distinguished between choices made without attention to what other agents do and choices that take into account the possible actions of others, and then turned to a discussion of how agents may attempt to shape the constraints and opportunities they face, and finally how available opportunities may shape preferences. These are central concerns in much of economics, philosophy, and the parts of psychology addressing choice behavior, but less central in sociological analyses.

Opportunity is also a central concept in analyses of social inequality. I first addressed its use in theories of justice and civil-rights legislation, and next in analyses of differential labor-market outcomes in the contexts of careers and professions. I ended with a discussion of opportunities for employers to discriminate on the basis of race and sex in the current legal environment, showing how explicit attention to choice opportunity may inform one on specific inequality outcomes. Attention to variation in and creation of opportunities is the cornerstone in analyses of social inequality, and is important for understanding the operation of both sides of the market, first for employees seeking the best available opportunities and second for employers figuring out which constraints they face and where there are opportunities for treating employees differentially, when an employer is so inclined.

In understanding inequality, sociologists have paid careful attention to the opportunities available, through analysis of discrimination, affirmative action, and more. Less attention has been given to the role of choice and strategic behavior, the concerns in the literatures using the concept of opportunity in understanding choices. As I hope the present chapter has illustrated, in analysis of inequality there is much to be gained by incorporating the role of choice: how interdependencies are important, the role of strategic reasoning, how agents try to modify the constraints they face, and not least legal interventions, which simultaneously can expand and restrict opportunities.

NOTES

1. In the rest of this subsection I draw extensively on Petersen (1994).
2. In this subsection I draw extensively on Petersen (2004a).
3. I draw here extensively on Petersen and Saporta (2004). To make the text here consistent with the text in earlier sections I write in the first person, even though I draw extensively on joint work with Saporta.
4. Many researchers will also attest to the empirical correctness of this assertion (e.g. Reskin 1998: 88; Rhode 1997: ch. 7). Others will strenuously deny it (e.g. Epstein 1992: ch. 18).

5. Cases reaching the legal system will rarely be factually simple, but will rather contain elements of ambiguity and will call for interpretation. Otherwise, they should in principle be possible to settle through firm-internal grievance procedures. At stake conceptually and empirically is thus the level not the presence of ambiguity. Sometimes there may be more ambiguity than the courts are willing to accept, as when they were asked to pass judgments on the correct rate of pay for male- and female-dominated work in early comparable-worth litigation (see e.g. Nelson and Bridges 1999: 12–13).

6. Lazear (1991: 13–14) offers the same sentiment: 'My view is that hiring is most important; promotion is second; and wages are third.' (He gives no sustained argument why this likely is the case.) Or, as Epstein (1992: 58) writes, 'most firms prefer the risk of litigation with initial hires, instead of with promotion and dismissal.' Olson (1997: 61) states: 'one should expect bigotry to manifest itself more in refusals to hire people than in the self-defeating practice of hiring them only to turn around and fire them.'

REFERENCES

ABBOTT, A. D. (1988), *The System of Profession* (Chicago, Ill.: University of Chicago Press).

BECKER, G. S. (1964), *Human Capital: A Theoretical and Empirical Analysis, with Special Reference to Education* (Chicago, Ill.: University of Chicago Press).

BIELBY, W. T., and BARON, J. N. (1986), 'Men and Women at Work: Sex Segregation and Statistical Discrimination', *American Journal of Sociology*, 91 (4): 759–99.

BLAU, F., and FERBER, M. (1987), 'Occupations and Earnings of Women Workers', in K. S. Koziara, M. H. Moskow, and L. D. Tanner (eds.), *Working Women: Past, Present, Future* (Washington, D.C.: Bureau of National Affairs), 37–68.

BLOCH, F. (1994), *Antidiscrimination Law and Minority Employment* (Chicago, Ill.: University of Chicago Press).

DAVIS, K., and MOORE, W. E. (1945), 'Some Principles of Stratification', *American Sociological Review*, 10 (2): 242–9.

DONOHUE III, J. J., and SPIEGELMAN, P. (1991), 'The Changing Nature of Employment Discrimination Litigation', *Stanford Law Review*, 43 (5): 983–1033.

DWORKIN, R. (1981a), 'What Is Equality? Part 1: Equality of Welfare', *Philosophy & Public Affairs*, 10: 185–246.

—— (1981b), 'What is Equality? Part 2: Equality of Resources', *Philosophy & Public Affairs*, 10: 283–345.

ELSTER, J. (1979), *Ulysses and the Sirens* (New York: Cambridge University Press).

—— (1984), *Sour Grapes* (New York: Cambridge University Press).

—— (1985), *Making Sense of Marx* (New York: Cambridge University Press).

—— (1999), *Alchemies of the Mind: Rationality and the Emotions* (New York: Cambridge University Press).

—— (2007), *Ulysses Unbound* (New York: Cambridge University Press).

ENGLAND, P. (1992), *Comparable Worth: Theories and Evidence* (Hawthorne, N.Y.: de Gruyter).

EPSTEIN, R. A. (1992), *Forbidden Grounds: The Case Against Employment Discrimination Laws* (Cambridge, Mass.: Harvard University Press).

FREED, M. G., and POLSBY, D. D. (1984), 'Comparable Worth in the Equal Pay Act', *University of Chicago Law Review*, 51 (4): 1078–111.

GECK, M. (2006), *Johann Sebastian Bach: Life and Work* (New York: Harcourt).

GERHART, B. (1990), 'Gender Differences in Current and Starting Salaries: The Role of Performance, College Major, and Job Title', *Industrial and Labor Relations Review*, 43 (4): 418–33.

GOLDTHORPE, J. (1980), *Social Mobility and Class Structure in Modern Britain* (Oxford: Clarendon).

GRANOVETTER, M. [1974] (1995), *Getting a Job: Study of Contacts and Careers*, 2nd edn. (Chicago, Ill.: University of Chicago Press).

HABERMAS, J. (1981), *Theorie des kommunikativen Handelns* (Frankfurt am Main: Suhrkamp).

HAYEK, F. (1960), *The Constitution of Liberty* (Chicago, Ill.: University of Chicago Press).

HEDSTRÖM, P., and UDEHN, L. (2009), 'Analytical Sociology and Theories of the Middle Range', in Peter Hedström and Peter Bearman (eds.), *The Oxford Handbook of Analytical Sociology* (Oxford University Press), 25–47.

HEILMAN, M. E. (1995), 'Sex Stereotypes and Their Effects in the Workplace: What We Know and What We Don't Know', *Journal of Social Behavior and Personality*, 10 (6): 3–26.

JENCKS, C. (1992), *Rethinking Social Policy* (Cambridge, Mass.: Harvard University Press).

LAZEAR, E. P. (1991), 'Discrimination in Labor Markets', in E. Hoffman (ed.), *Essays on the Economics of Discrimination* (Kalamazoo, Mich.: Upjohn Institute), 9–24.

MARX, K. [1875] (1972), *Critique of the Gotha Program* (Peking: Foreign Languages Press).

NELSON, R. L., and BRIDGES, W. P. (1999), *Legalizing Gender Inequality: Courts, Markets, and Unequal Pay for Women in America* (New York: Cambridge University Press).

OLSON, W. K. (1997), *The Excuse Factory: How Employment Law Is Paralyzing the American Workplace* (New York: Free Press).

PETERSEN, T. (1994), 'On the Promise of Game Theory in Sociology', *Contemporary Sociology*, 23 (3): 498–502.

—— (2004a), 'Aage B. Sørensen's Contribution to Modeling Social Inequality: From Studying Structure to Studying Process', *Research in Social Stratification and Mobility*, 21: 27–44. (Special issue, ed. Arne L. Kalleberg et al. entitled *Inequality: Structures, Dynamics and Mechanisms: Essays in Honour of Aage B. Sørensen*.)

—— (2004b), 'Discrimination, Social Measurements in', in K. Kempf-Leonard (ed.), *Encyclopedia of Social Measurement* (New York: Academic).

—— and MORGAN, L. A. (1995), 'Separate and Unequal: Occupation–Establishment Segregation and the Gender Wage Gap', *American Journal of Sociology*, 101 (2): 329–65.

—— and SAPORTA, I. (2004), 'The Opportunity Structure for Discrimination', *American Journal of Sociology*, 109 (4): 852–901.

RESKIN, B. F. (1998), *The Realities of Affirmative Action in Employment* (Washington, DC: American Sociological Association).

RHOADS, S. E. (1993), *Incomparable Worth: Pay Equity Meets the Market* (Cambridge/New York: Cambridge University Press).

RHODE, D. L. (1997), *Speaking of Sex: The Denial of Gender Inequality* (Cambridge, Mass.: Harvard University Press).

SEN, A. (1992), *Inequality Reexamined* (Cambridge, Mass.: Harvard University Press).

SØRENSEN, A. B. (1977), 'The Structure of Inequality and the Process of Attainment', *American Sociological Review*, 42 (6): 965–78.

—— (1979), 'A Model and a Metric for the Process of Status Attainment', *American Journal of Sociology*, 85 (2): 361–84.

—— (1983a), 'Processes of Allocation to Open and Closed Positions in Social Structure', *Zeitschrift für Soziologie*, 12: 203–24.

—— (1983b), 'Conceptual and Methodological Issues in Sociological Research on the Labor Market', *Work and Occupations*, 10: 261–87.

—— (1996), 'The Structural Basis of Social Inequality', *American Journal of Sociology*, 101 (5): 1333–65.

—— (2000), 'Toward a Sounder Basis for Class Analysis', *American Journal of Sociology*, 105 (6): 1523–58.

SPILERMAN, S. (1986), 'Organizational Rules and the Features of Work Careers', *Research in Social Stratification and Mobility*, 5: 41–102.

STINCHCOMBE, A. L. (1990), *Information and Organizations*, (Berkeley, Calif.: University of California Press).

TILLY, C. (1998), *Durable Inequality* (Berkeley/Los Angeles, Calif.: University of California Press).

VALIAN, V. (1998), *Why So Slow? The Advancement of Women* (Cambridge, Mass.: MIT Press).

WEBER, M. [1922–3] (1978), *Economy and Society* (Berkeley/Los Angeles, Calif.: University of California Press).

WEEDEN, K. A. (2002), 'Why Do Some Occupations Pay More Than Others?', *American Journal of Sociology*, 108 (1): 55–101.

WINSHIP, C. (2009), 'Time and Scheduling', in Peter Hedström and Peter Bearman (eds.), *The Oxford Handbook of Analytical Sociology* (Oxford: Oxford University Press), 498–520.

WHITE, H. C. (1970), *Chains of Opportunity* (Cambridge, Mass.: Harvard University Press).

WYMER III, J. F., and SUDBURY, D. A. (1992), 'Employment Discrimination "Tester"—Will Your Hiring Practices "Pass"', *Employee Relations Law Journal*, 17 (4): 623–33.

CHAPTER 7

HEURISTICS

DANIEL G. GOLDSTEIN

I see your face in every flower,
Your eyes in stars above.
It's just the thought of you,
The very thought of you, my love.

('The Very Thought of You')[1]

INTRODUCTION

LOVERS, it has been remarked, see the faces of those they love in the natural world. Scientists, it has been remarked, fall in love with tools, and see them in the phenomena they investigate (Gigerenzer 1991). For example, one of the most popular statistical tools in the experimental social sciences is analysis of variance, or ANOVA. In the 1970s, a full 70 percent of articles in experimental-psychology journals used this one technique (Edington 1974). In a psychological theory of how the mind attributes a cause to an effect, Kelly (1967) suggested that minds perform causal attribution the same way social scientists do; that is, by means of analysis of variance. The ANOVA theory seems to have resounded well with the scientific audience, racking up more than 900 references in a decade (Kelly and Michaela 1980). Still, today, causal attribution is a leading question in social psychology. Scientific tools transformed into theories again in the years following the introduction of the computer to university departments. In the *cognitive revolution* of the 1970s and 1980s the new field of cognitive science was born based on the idea that the mind is analogous to a computer (Gigerenzer and Goldstein 1996). In the words of a founder of this movement, Herbert Simon (1979: 363), 'The fundamental reactions of the mental chemistry employ elementary information processes that operate upon symbols and symbol structures: copying symbols, storing symbols, retrieving symbols, inputting and outputting symbols, and comparing symbols.' These continue to serve as the basic verbs of cognitive psychology today.

In the field that is the topic of this volume James Coleman proposed the following explanation of why, in the second half of the twentieth century, sociology became decidedly less social:

> One may ask just why there came to be such a radical shift toward a focus on individual behavior in a discipline whose subject matter, after all, is the social system. Part of the answer lies in the invention of techniques. The statistical tools of survey design and analysis began in the 1940s to make possible quantitatively precise statements about samples of independent individuals and the populations (again of independent individuals) they represent, as well as analysis of factors affecting individual behavior. There was no comparable development of tools for analysis of the behavior of interacting systems of individuals or for capturing the interdependencies of individual actions as they combine to produce a system-level outcome. The far greater complexity required of tools for these purposes constituted a serious impediment to their development and continues to do so (though some methods such as those generally labelled 'network analysis' move in that direction).   (1986: 1316)

Coleman suggests that tools for analyzing social systems failed to develop because of their complexity. However, some complex tools, such as computers, have both developed at a rapid rate and influenced scientific models. We might take Coleman to mean that it was the complexity of *applying* system-analysis tools that kept them from influencing his field, perhaps due to the reluctance of scientists to adopt them. It has been observed (Gigerenzer 1991; Gigerenzer and Goldstein 1996) that tools are transformed into successful theories only after the tools have achieved widespread adoption. If there ever was a simple, widespread tool in the social sciences, it is the one that we focus on in this chapter: the linear model.

Linear models are everywhere in social science, where they serve as near-universal tools for estimation, modeling, designing experiments, and testing hypotheses. One would be pressed to find a social scientist who has not used ANOVA, multiple regression, the general linear model, or the generalized linear model for statistical analysis. The most frequently used linear models make use of optimization techniques, arriving at coefficients in a way that minimizes error.

Given the prevalence of linear models and the tendency of scientists to turn tools into theories, are we, as social scientists, at risk of seeing the world through the lens of a linear model? I would argue that in my area of specialization, the psychology of decision-making, this is the case. In particular, I think that scholars of decision-making gravitate towards models that *weigh and combine* all available evidence, and towards models that *optimize* based on the information given, much like multiple-regression models.

As a prescriptive norm, there are old and abundant examples of weighing and combining evidence being equated with good reason. Consider the image of blind justice holding a scale, or Darwin's deliberations about whether to marry (Darwin [1887] 1969: 232–3), psychological theories based in making trade-offs (e.g. Fishbein and Ajzen 1975), or the moral algebra Benjamin Franklin ([1772] 1987) offered as decision-making advice to a friend:

> [M]y Way is, to divide half a Sheet of Paper by a Line into two Columns, writing over the one Pro, and over the other Con. Then during three or four Days Consideration I put down under the different Heads short Hints of the different Motives that at different Times occur to me for or against the Measure. When I have thus got them all together in one View, I endeavor to estimate their respective Weights; and where I find two, one on each side, that seem equal, I strike them both out: If I find a Reason pro equal to some two Reasons con, I strike out the three. If I judge some two Reasons con equal to some three Reasons pro, I strike out the five; and thus proceeding I find at length where the Ballance lies; and if after a Day or two of farther Consideration nothing new that is of Importance occurs on either side, I come to a Determination accordingly. And tho' the Weight or Reasons cannot be taken with the Precision of Algebraic Quantities, yet when each is thus considered separately and comparatively, and the whole lies before me, I think I can judge better, and am less likely to make a rash Step; and in fact I have found great Advantage from this kind of Equation, in what may be called Moral or Prudential Algebra.

Moving from the prescriptive towards the descriptive, psychologists in recent theories of decision-making have commonly assumed that the mind works like a linear model, summing and weighing the evidence at hand. These range from multiple-regression-inspired 'lens model' applications (Hammond, Hursch, and Todd 1964) to the popular neural-network models of the 1980s and 1990s (Rumelhart, McClelland, and the PDP Research Group 1986), which weighed and combined evidence, and minimized error, much like multiple regression. In fact, simple neural networks are functionally equivalent to multiple regression. Under the view that minds make elaborate trade-offs, the modeling of decision behavior can be achieved in a straightforward way by simply fitting linear models to choice or ratings data. For example, one can present people with descriptions of apartments (rent, distance from city center, square footage, etc.) and ask them to rate the attractiveness of each apartment on a 100-point scale. Based on the ratings, one can simply run a multiple regression and interpret the resulting beta weights as the psychological 'decision weights' that the mind assigns to rent, square footage, and so on. This type of modeling is appealing because it is straightforward, and provides useful models that predict what kinds of apartments a person will prefer.

In sociology, certain rational-choice models embody the same spirit. For instance, an individual making a choice in accordance with subjective expected utility seeks all available options, considers the aspects (or possible outcomes) of each alternative, and assigns a weight to each. Stopping rules for gathering information, when present, can be optimization problems in their own right (e.g. 'stop at the point at which the cost of seeking out another alternative outweighs the benefits of having one'), and thus not address how a limited mind might make such a calculation. (For a discussion of the merits and limitation of rational-choice theory in sociology see Hechter and Kanazawa 1997 and Green and Shapiro 1994.)

Limitations of the rational, linear model view of cognition emerge in practice. In laboratory experiments people are usually given all the information they are supposed to consider in a decision, but outside the lab gathering information is expensive and getting all relevant information is impossible. Search costs often need to be paid with time or money. When a doctor needs to diagnose a patient who is on the verge of dying from an unknown cause, there are fifty tests she could run, but running all of them would bankrupt the patient, and could take more time than the patient has to live. A diagnosis based on limited information must be made. Similarly, search in memory takes time and people cut costs there as well— we don't pause in the grocery store, recalling our life experiences with each of the available brands of butter. In addition to information and memory-search costs, making trade-offs and optimal decisions invokes cognitive costs. In a split second, a computer can run a regression and return a set of weights that not only allow for predictions of the outcome variable, but that take into account how each predictor variable might correlate with all the others. People, however, have tremendous difficulty keeping track of intercorrelations between cues (Armelius and Armelius 1974). Roger Shepard (1967) looked into the question of whether people integrate information like linear models do. While he noted that the perceptual system (i.e. the visual or auditory system) seems to carry out impressive feats of information integration, when it comes to higher-level cognition (i.e. reasoning about propositions) he found that people had trouble considering or combining even a few pieces of information. It has been noted that several schools of psychology have embraced the surprising thesis that higher-level cognition might work by simpler laws than lower-level cognition. Perhaps the eye and ear can weigh and integrate information better than the logical mind can (Todd and Gigerenzer 2000). The view of the mind as an optimal linear model is a view that ignores search costs and cognitive effort. It can at best be an 'as if' model.

Starting in the 1950s, this classical view of the mind was challenged by Herbert Simon, who proposed looking for models of 'bounded rationality' instead of classical rationality. Simon (1956) postulated that the time, information, and cognitive constraints of organisms necessitate that they 'satisfice' rather than optimize. Satisfice, a Scottish word blending 'satisfy' and 'suffice' means to settle for good-enough solutions, rather than for optimal ones. In the last 35 years the rational, optimizing view of the mind also came under attack by proponents of the successful heuristics-and-biases program (Kahneman, Slovic, and Tversky 1982), who argued that much thinking is achieved through mental shortcuts or heuristics, which by their very nature do not gather and combine all available information. The heuristics-and-biases program has retained the normative kernel of the classical view, for instance that weighing and combining all available information is what one *ought* to do, but rejects the idea that people can stand up to these ideals. Explanations in this research program have invoked rather high-level accounts for how people make judgments. A few of the program's constructs, such as *availability* and *representativeness*, and *anchoring and adjustment*, have been used as explanations in thousands of articles in psychology. In the early 1990s two new research programs introduced more precise, testable models of decision-making heuristics. Payne, Bettman, and Johnson's *adaptive decision maker* program (1993) forwarded the view that decision makers draw from a toolbox of heuristic strategies, and introduced process-tracing techniques to identify which individuals were using which strategy when. Following their lead, Gerd Gigerenzer, myself, and present and past colleagues from the Adaptive Behavior and Cognition research group at the Max Planck Institute for Human Development in Berlin have forwarded a view, based on what I have termed 'fast and frugal' models of cognition. Where the *heuristics and biases* program was more focused on departures from rational norms, the *fast and frugal* program rejected these norms as normative, and asked instead how well simple heuristics will fare when making inferences in real-world environments. While the adaptive-decision-maker program concentrated on identifying strategy use, the fast and frugal program concentrated more on the accuracy/effort consequences of the strategy selected. Finally, while both the adaptive-decision-maker and the *rational choice* paradigm of sociology concentrate on individuals making choices to satisfy their preferences, the fast-and-frugal program has chiefly looked at inferences; that is, minds making guesses about the world (and other minds).[2]

The goal of the fast-and-frugal program is to design and test computational models of heuristics that are (a) ecologically rational (i.e. they exploit structures of information in the environment), (b) founded in evolved psychological capacities such as memory and the perceptual system, (c) fast, frugal, and simple enough to operate effectively when time, knowledge, and computational might are limited, (d) precise enough to be modeled computationally, and (e) powerful enough to model both good and poor reasoning (Goldstein and Gigerenzer 2002). As with Simon's notion of satisficing, these models have *stopping rules* to limit search for information. As opposed to classical models, they do not weigh and combine information. While sacrificing the generality and intuitive appeal of linear models, fast-and-frugal models aim to offer robustness, transparency, and psychological plausibility.

In this chapter I describe the two heuristics that started the fast-and-frugal research program—the Recognition Heuristic and the Take-the-best

Heuristic—and then move on to describe how fast-and-frugal heuristics are being employed as models not just of individual decision-making, but of group decision-making as well. The problems that have been analyzed with the simple heuristics have been varied, including models that predict homelessness, high-school dropout rates, parental investment, obesity, attractiveness, mortality, house prices, rent, professor's salaries, fuel consumption, car accidents, pollution levels, mate search, stock-market returns, nonverbal social interactions, and beyond (Gigerenzer, Todd, and the ABC Research Group 1999). One chapter is not enough space to cover all aspects of judgment and decision-making, so the focus will be on the topic of inference.

7.1 RECOGNITION-BASED INFERENCE

Imagine that you have made it to the final round of 'Who Wants to Be a Millionaire.' You will either leave the show with nothing or with a million dollars, based on your answer to the following question: 'Which city has a larger population: Milwaukee or Detroit?'

As it turns out, we put this very question to two groups (though not for a million dollars). One was from the University of Chicago and the other from Munich, Germany. Which group was more accurate?

Naturally, more Americans than Germans should know that Detroit is the much larger city. Not only are University of Chicago students some of the best and brightest, but Chicago is rather close to both Milwaukee and Detroit, so first-hand experience and memory should prove useful. The Germans, on the other hand, knew little about American cities—in fact one-third of them had never even heard of Milwaukee before. Who did better? A pitiful 40 percent of the Americans (slightly worse than chance) answered correctly. However, the vast majority of the Germans (about 90 percent) got it right.

In a variation on this experiment we quizzed American students on the twenty-two largest cities in both the USA and Germany (Goldstein and Gigerenzer 2002). We were surprised again: Americans did slightly better with foreign cities (73 percent correct) than with domestic ones (71 percent correct). We refer to these situations, in which lesser states of knowledge can outperform greater states, as *less-is-more effects*.

How can people who clearly know less about a given domain nonetheless do better than those who know more? Consider the following thought-experiment. Three American siblings sit down to take a test on the hundred largest cities in Germany. The test consists of pairs of cities, and in each pair the larger city must be identified. Assume the youngest sibling has never even heard of Germany before, and recognizes none of the cities on the quiz. The eldest sibling recognizes them all. The middle sibling recognizes half of the hundred cities from what she has overheard. The cities she recognizes are larger than those she doesn't recognize in 80 percent of paired comparisons (a realistic assumption, as it turns out). Now assume (i) that the children know nothing about the cities beyond recognizing their names, and (ii) that they attack the test using a strategy called the *recognition heuristic*:

> Recognition heuristic: If one of two objects is recognized and the other is not, then infer that the recognized object has the higher value with respect to the criterion.

How will the three children perform at the task? Since the recognition heuristic is only applicable when exactly one object is recognized, the youngest and eldest child will not be able to use it. These children will have to guess on every question and thus score 50 percent correct. (Why will the eldest child have to guess? Recall, the children know nothing about the cities beyond recognizing their names.)

For the middle child, who recognizes half of the objects, the questions will fall into three categories. In one quarter of the questions she will recognize neither city and have to guess. In another quarter of the questions she will recognize both cities and also have to guess. However, in the remaining half of the cities she will recognize one city but not the other. For these items she will pick the city she recognizes and score 80 percent correct. Achieving 80 percent correct on half the items and 50 percent correct (by guessing) on the other half, this child will attain 65 percent correct overall, counterintuitively outperforming even her elder sibling. The bottommost curve in Figure 7.1 shows how the three siblings, and all intermediate knowledge states, would perform on the quiz.

The recognition heuristic lends itself to mathematical modeling. If an individual uses the rule, the proportion correct on a paired comparison task is

$$2 \left(\frac{n}{N} \right) \left(\frac{N-n}{N-1} \right) \alpha + \left(\frac{N-n}{N} \right) \left(\frac{N-n-1}{N-1} \right) \frac{1}{2} + \left(\frac{n}{N} \right) \left(\frac{n-1}{N-1} \right) \beta$$

where N is the number of objects in a reference class (for example 100 cities), n is the number of recognized objects (for example 50 cities), α is the probability of getting a correct answer when only one object is recognized, β is the probability of getting a correct answer when both objects are recognized, and 0.5 is the probability of getting a correct answer when guessing. If α and β remain constant as n varies, and $\alpha > \beta$, this function takes on an inverted-U shape, predicting that intermediate states of recognition knowledge can outperform more complete states. Figure 7.1 plots this function for 3 levels of β (0.5, 0.6, 0.7). Since these levels of β are less than α (which is 0.8 in the figure), the resulting curves achieve maximum accuracy when fewer than all the objects are recognized.

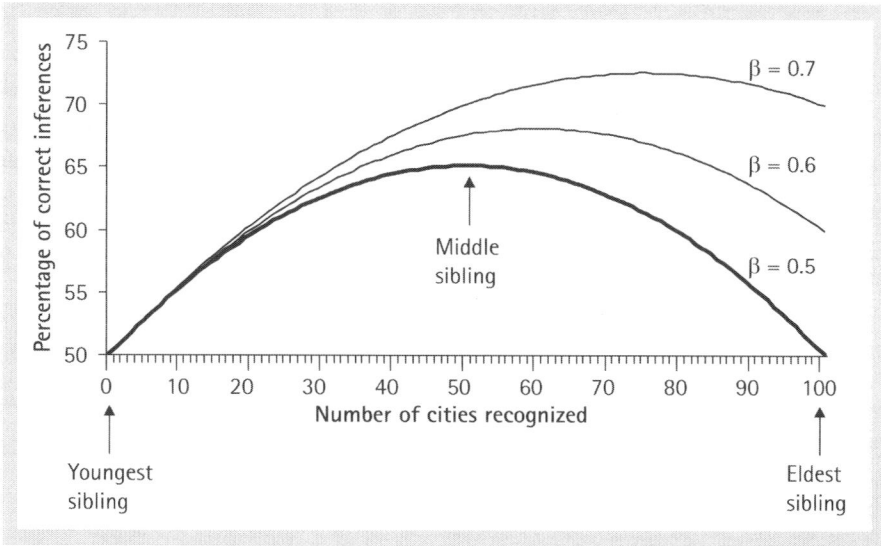

Fig. 7.1 Three siblings' responses to a test on the hundred largest cities in Germany. The accuracy of the three siblings from the thought-experiment, and of all intermediate knowledge states, is plotted on the bottom curve. To see what happens when we relax the assumption that the siblings know nothing about the cities beyond their names, we plot two lines depicting the case in which they have a 60 percent or 70 percent ($\beta = 0.6$ or 0.7) chance of making a correct inference when both objects are recognized. All three curves show how a less-complete state of recognition knowledge can, under the stated assumptions, lead to more correct inferences than a greater state of knowledge

The recognition heuristic is a simple model of two-alternative choice. It does not weigh or combine information. It limits search through a simple stopping rule ('Stop searching for cues if only one object is recognized') and it limits cognitive costs by having a simple choice rule ('Choose the alternative favored by recognition'). Despite its simplicity, in the interaction with natural environments it can make accurate inferences, predict choice behavior, and explain counterintuitive phenomena like the less-is-more effect.

Precisely defined heuristics can easily be coded into computer simulations to test hypotheses. We have used simulations to check whether the less-is-more effect derived above would arise when α and β are not fixed, but are allowed to vary in a real-world environment. The simulation learned to recognize German cities in the order of how well known they are. In addition to just learning to recognize cities, we ran conditions in which 0, 1, 2, or 9 pieces of information were learned in addition to city names. An example of a cue was the *soccer-team cue*: the simulation learned whether each city has a soccer team in the major league (an excellent predictor of population). After learning about each city, the simulated participant was quizzed on all pairs of cities, guessing when neither city was recognized and applying the recognition heuristic when exactly one city was recognized. When both cities were recognized, further cue knowledge, if any was available, was used to make an inference by means of another heuristic (named take-the-best, which we will look at later). Unlike the eldest sibling, who had to guess when both objects were recognized, our simulation could make a more informed inference in these cases. Would this cause the less-is-more effect to disappear? When the simulation had no knowledge beyond recognition, the less-is-more effect persisted. However, unlike the smooth curve in Figure 7.1, here we saw a jagged curve, but with the same inverted-U shape, reflecting the variation in α one might find when learning about cities in the real world. With one piece of information learned in addition to recognition, the simulation scored about 62 percent correct when all cities were recognized. However, when only three-quarters of the cities were recognized, the score was about 70 percent correct: a less-is-more effect. A similar pattern held when two or more pieces of information were available. Finally, with nine cues, the less-is-more effect flattened out.

As opposed to an all-purpose tool like a linear model, the recognition heuristic, or any simple heuristic, is domain specific. Instead of being unboundedly rational, it is *ecologically rational*, with respect to some environments but not others. There are domains in which the recognition heuristic will not work; for instance, to infer a US city's distance from Chicago. And there are domains in which people will not apply it. For instance, Oppenheimer (2003) presented people with pairs consisting of fictional cities with foreign-sounding names (e.g. 'Heingjing') compared to nearby small towns and found that participants chose the fictional, unrecognized cities 50 to 80 percent of the time. People may suspend use of the recognition heuristic when they believe test items constitute a biased sample or are drawn from an unknown reference class (e.g. the conjunction of neighboring towns and foreign cities) for which the validity of recognition is unknown. People might also not use the recognition heuristic when they have knowledge of the target variable (population), such as when they know that the town has less than 10,000 people. They might suspend use of the heuristic when they know that they recognize something from an artificial or uninformative context, such as from a lab experiment. The recognition heuristic is a model that lowers information-search costs, accordingly people might not use it when making inferences from information given to them on paper. In addition, the recognition heuristic is certainly not something that all people use in all situations. In every experimental test there are some participants whose decisions are best fit by recognition even in the face of conflicting cue information, and those who switch strategies in such cases. The *adaptive toolbox* view of cognition is one in which people learn, select, and switch between simple strategies, as opposed to update parameters in general-purpose models.

We have seen how simple heuristics can enable the specification of precise models and testing via analysis and computer simulation. To test models of behavior, experimental data can be compared to the heuristics' predictions. For example, to see how well the recognition heuristic predicts inferences, one can ask people which objects they recognize, give them paired-comparison questions, and then compute how often they choose recognized over unrecognized objects. Our studies on foreign cities found that despite having no free parameters, the recognition heuristic predicted choice in 90 to 100 percent of applicable cases. Other investigations have looked at the validity and adherence rates of the recognition heuristic for domains including predicting which athlete or team will win a competition, which party will win an election, which musician will sell more records, which stock will show higher growth, and beyond (Snook and Cullen 2006; Pachur and Biele 2007; Scheibehenne and Bröder 2007; Serwe and Frings 2006).

Herbert Simon made the following observation of an ant walking on the beach:

> Viewed as a geometric figure, the ant's path is irregular, complex, hard to describe. But its complexity is really a complexity in the surface of the beach, not a complexity in the ant...The ant, viewed as a behaving system, is quite simple. The apparent complexity of its behavior over time is largely a reflection of the complexity of the environment in which it finds itself.   ([1969] 1996: 51–2)

Simple heuristics are able to make complex predictions by exploiting complexity that is inherent in the environment, such as the correlations between recognition and objects in the environment, and how these change between people, between domains, or over time. We turn now to show how a similar approach can be taken to a somewhat more difficult problem: making inferences with knowledge beyond recognition.

7.2 KNOWLEDGE-BASED INFERENCE

What is the simplest way to make smart choices between recognized alternatives? Sticking with our example domain, assume someone's knowledge about four German cities can be represented as in Table 7.1.

The table represents subjective knowledge. A plus in the top row means that the person recognizes that city, while a minus means they do not. We use the term 'cue' to mean a piece of information, and the cues in this table take on three values: plus, minus, or question mark. For the recognized cities, a plus means that the person believes the city has a feature; for instance, this person believes that city A was once an exposition site and believes that city B has a major-league soccer team. A minus represents the belief that a feature is lacking, so this person believes that city A is not

Table 7.1 A subjective knowledge matrix

	City			
	A	B	C	D
Recognition	+	+	+	−
Cue 1: Exposition site	+	−	?	?
Cue 2: Soccer team	?	+	?	?
Cue 3: Intercity train	−	+	+	?
Cue 4: State capital	?	−	−	?
Cue 5: University	?	?	−	?

on the intercity train line, city B is not a State capital, and city C lacks a university. If a person does not know whether a city has a particular feature, it is represented by a question mark. Note that the unrecognized city has question marks for all features, which is an assumption we made in our simulations, though one could think of situations in which a person could infer or deduce the cue values of an unrecognized object.

How might a mind or machine make an inference from basic knowledge such as this? A model could embrace the Enlightenment notion of classical rationality, and assume that when making a decision all information will be searched for, weighed, and combined optimally. On the other hand, a modeler could ask what the simplest possible mechanism might look like. We took the latter approach in designing what we have called the minimalist heuristic and the take-the-best heuristic.

7.2.1 Minimalist heuristic

The minimalist heuristic proceeds as follows:

Step 0. If applicable, use the recognition heuristic; that is, if only one object is recognized, predict that it has the higher value on the criterion. If neither is recognized, then guess. If both are recognized, go on to Step 1.

Step 1. Random search: Draw a cue randomly (without replacement) and look up the cue values of the two objects.

Step 2. Stopping rule: If one object has a positive cue value (+) and the other does not (i.e. either − or ?) then stop search. Otherwise go back to Step 1 and search for another cue. If no further cue is found, then guess.

Step 3. Decision rule: Predict that the object with the positive cue value has the higher value on the criterion.

For instance, when deciding whether City B or City C is larger, the minimalist heuristic might first try cue 4 at random. Since it doesn't discriminate between the two cities (neither is a state capital), another cue is drawn, say cue 3. This cue also doesn't discriminate, and so now cue 2 might be drawn. Since City B has a professional soccer team and City C may or may not, the stopping rule is satisfied, and City B is chosen.

7.2.2 Take-the-best heuristic

The minimalist heuristic certainly is simple. However, it is safe to assume that organisms know that not all cues are created equally. Even pigeons can learn the relationship between a cue and a criterion, so a model that tries cues in a particular order may be warranted. But which order? The take-the-best heuristic orders cues by *subjective cue validity*, which is a subjective estimate of *objective cue validity*. Objective cue validity is a feature of the environment. It is the relative frequency with which a cue correctly predicts the criterion defined with respect to the reference class. For instance, in the set of German cities we studied (Gigerenzer and Goldstein 1996), when inspecting all pairs of cities in which one has a soccer team and the other does not, the cities with teams have a larger population 87 percent of the time. Thus, the objective validity of the soccer team cue is 0.87. Take-the-best only differs from minimalist in one way. Instead of step 1 being random search, in take-the-best we have:

Step 1. Ordered search: Choose the cue with the highest subjective validity that has not been tried before. Look up the cue values of the two objects.

Heuristics are composed of building blocks. By changing one step, a very different model can emerge. Minds, we hypothesize, can alter the building blocks of cognitive strategies to match new task environments. These are the building blocks of the take-the-best heuristic:

- Search rule: Look up cues in order of validity
- Stopping rule: Stop search after the first cue discriminates between alternatives
- Decision rule: Choose the alternative that this cue favors

There are many contexts in which a mind might need rules for searching, stopping the search, and for choosing. While these categories of rules are rather general, the specific instantiation of the rules (e.g. random versus ordered search) may vary from situation to situation. In some domains, where abundant reasons are needed to justify a decision, instead of using take-the-best, a decision maker might search for cues until two are found that point to the same alternative. This modifies the stopping and decision rules, but still provides a precise, plausible model.

Why are minimalist and take-the-best fast and frugal? Search costs are reduced by only looking for as much information as is needed to discriminate between the alternatives. Cognitive costs are reduced because neither model deals with the correlations between the cues, neither tries to weigh and combine predictors. Both have a very simple choice rule: choose the object to which the first discriminating cue points.

Gerd Gigerenzer and I compared the performance of take-the-best and minimalist to that of strategies that use more information, carrying out a 'horse-race' simulation in which strategies competed (Gigerenzer and Goldstein 1996). The contestants included:

1. The minimalist heuristic;
2. The take-the-best heuristic;
3. Dawes's rule: Give each object a score, which is the number of positive cues minus the number of negative cues. Choose the object with the higher score;
4. Franklin's rule: Give each object a score, which is the sum of the cue validities of the positive cues minus the sum of the cue validities of the negative cues. Choose the object with the higher score;
5. Multiple regression: Fit a multiple-regression model to the matrix of cues and criterion values, and use the resulting linear model to arrive at a score for each object based on its cue values. Choose the object with the higher score.

The environment used was a set of German cities with more than 100,000 inhabitants (83 cities at the time). Exhaustive pairs of objects were drawn from this reference class and each competing strategy attempted to infer the larger object in each pair, based on the cue values. Missing knowledge was simulated in two ways. First, there were states of limited recognition knowledge in which 0 to 83 cities were recognized. As in the above thought-experiment, and consistent with our empirical estimates, the recognized cities were larger than the unrecognized cities in 80 percent of all possible pairs. The second dimension of missing knowledge was missing knowledge about cue values. From the complete matrix, we randomly replaced cue values with missing values, such that 0, 10, 20, 50, 75, or 100 percent of the original cue values remained. At each state of limited recognition knowledge and limited cue knowledge the results of many trials were averaged so that the subsets of recognized cities and missing cues would be different from trial to trial.

How well did the strategies perform? Before looking at their accuracy, let us consider the disadvantage the two fast-and-frugal heuristics faced. Unlike the linear models (contestants 3–5), the heuristics used limited information to make inferences. The linear models looked up all 10 cues per object, while take-the-best looked up only 3 on average, and minimalist only 2.8. How well can a heuristic do if it uses less than one-third of the available information? Table 7.2 shows the accuracy of all the competitors, averaged across all states of missing knowledge. Despite having access to all the cues, Dawes's rule and Franklin's rule were actually outperformed by the fast-and-frugal heuristics. Multiple regression, which has the benefit of all the information in addition to optimized weights, did as well as take-the-best.

Table 7.2 Two fast-and-frugal heuristics versus three linear models

Strategy	Frugality (Number of cues looked up)	Knowledge about cues	Accuracy (% correct)
Take-the-best heuristic	3	Rank order	65.8
Multiple regression	10	Beta weights	65.7
Franklin's rule	10	Cue validities	62.3
Dawes's rule	10	Direction	62.1
Minimalist heuristic	2.8	Direction	64.7

Note: The number of cue values looked up is calculated per object in the comparison. The 'direction' of a cue is its sign: positive or negative.

The above contest looked at only one environment, and was a fitting, rather than a prediction, task. That is, the models got to train themselves on the same data on which they were later tested. If scientific models are to help us predict the future and generalize to new situations, they should be judged on their ability to predict new data, not merely on how well they fit available data. Jean Czerlinski, Gerd Gigerenzer, and I increased the number of environments from 1 to 20, so that, instead of looking only at German cities, we drew upon statistical databases and made inferences about a diverse set of topics, ranging from sociology to psychology to biology (Gigerenzer, Todd, and the ABC Research Group 1999). Environments varied in size from 11 objects to 395 objects and from 3 cues to 18 cues. The predictive quality of the strategies was tested using cross-validation: each environment was split in half randomly, and models were trained on one half, and tested the other. (A thousand random splits were carried out for each environment.) 'Training' has different meanings for different models, as some estimate more parameters than others. Training for multiple regression means determining a set of weights. For take-the-best it means determining a cue order. For Dawes's rule and minimalist, training only involves figuring out the direction of the cues (for example, figuring out whether having a soccer team correlates with being a large or small city). In contrast to the previous simulations, all objects were recognized. If the good performance of the heuristics in the previous simulation was overly due to the recognition heuristic, in these twenty environments there would be no such advantage.

How did the various strategies perform across more data sets and cross-validation? Looking at frugality, the heuristics maintained their advantage. Multiple regression and Dawes's rule each looked up 7.7 cue values on average while minimalist and take-the-best looked up 2.2 and 2.4 respectively. Figure 7.2 shows accuracy in both fitting and prediction. In fitting, multiple regression comes in first at 77 percent correct. Take-the-best again beat Dawes's rule. When moving from fitting to prediction all strategies suffered, but regression's accuracy decreased the

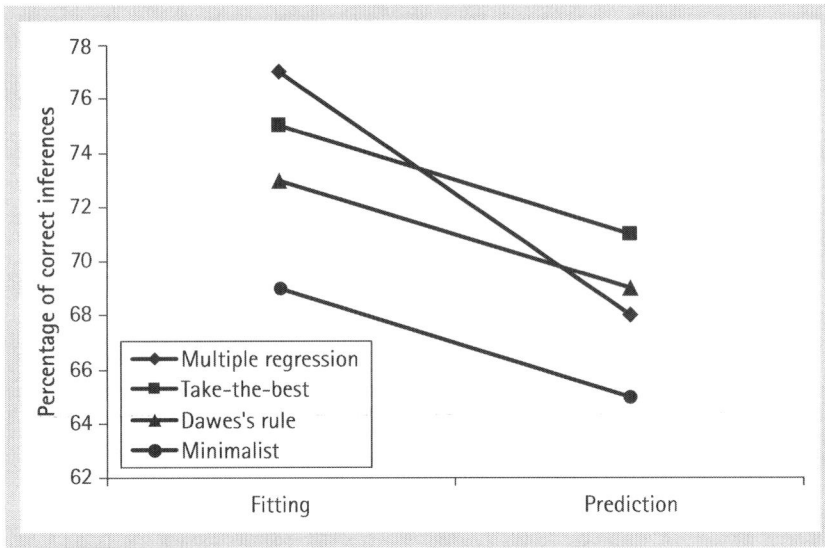

Fig. 7.2 Accuracy of the decision rules tested by Czerlinski, Goldstein, and Gigerenzer (1999) in fitting (training and testing on the same data) versus prediction (training on half the data and testing on the other half). Because of the tendency of models with more free parameters to overfit the training data, multiple regression loses the most accuracy when moving from fitting to prediction

most. As a result, take-the-best won the predictive competition, Dawes's rule came in second, and multiple regression dropped to third.

How can a strategy that uses partial information (like take-the-best), and a strategy that gives equal weight to all cues (like Dawes's rule), outpredict multiple regression, which determines its weights in an error-minimizing way? One reason is that more complex models, especially models with many free parameters, run the risk of overfitting training data. The training set can be thought of as having both structure and noise. A good model treats the structure as structure and regards the noise as noise, but an overparameterized model will treat the noise as part of the structure. When facing a prediction task, in which the structure will be the same but the random noise will be different, this overparameterized model can make worse predictions than a simpler variant. When a model performs well in generalizing from test sets to training sets, it is called robust. Robyn Dawes, for whom Dawes's rule is named, published an excellent paper in 1979 entitled 'The Robust Beauty of Improper Linear Models in Decision Making.' The simple 'unit' weights (+1 and −1) in Dawes's model allow for robust predictions because noise in the training data usually does not affect the weight. The worst that could happen is that the weight would change sign (i.e. go from + to − or vice versa) if the training data were very different than the test data. Take-the-best uses a cue ordering instead of unit weights or beta weights, and we have seen that it often relies on only a few cues. These results suggest that the cues which are highly valid in the training set tend also to be highly valid in the test set.

Much of the research in the field of judgment and decision making has historically involved decision-making at the individual level. In the interests of this volume, I'll turn now to recent research in which simple heuristics are being used to model social behavior.

7.3 Social Heuristics

Research on social heuristics tests the assumption that models of group decision-making can be created with the same building blocks (stopping rules, choice rules, etc.) that individual heuristics employ. Since the building blocks were designed to be as simple as possible, this approach to modeling may allow us to discover the minimal level of complexity needed to model complicated social behaviors.

7.3.1 The recognition heuristic in groups

Many important decisions, for instance who gets the Nobel Prize, are made by groups. It has been observed that people seem to win prizes for winning prizes, that is the rich get richer, which has been called 'Matthew effect' in science (Merton 1968; see also the chapters by Podolny and Lynn, and Hedström and Udehn in this volume). How might this arise? Consider that many prize committees are interdisciplinary, and since the members come from different fields, they may not be familiar with the same candidates. In fact, they may not even recognize the names of many potential candidates. If the group is guided by an invisible heuristic that says 'only give the prize to a candidate whose name is recognized by all the committee members,' it may lead to awarding the prize to an already famous person, since any promising candidate who is unanimously recognized by an interdisciplinary group has a good chance of already being famous.

Could a group's inferences be guided by a simple recognition-based heuristic? Torsten Reimer and Konstantinos Katsikopoulos (2004) looked at what inferences groups make when some of the members only recognize some of the alternatives. In the first part of their experiment, German students were given a recognition test on American cities, and asked which city is larger in all pairs of recognized cities. In the second session participants were placed into groups of three and given pairs of cities, now with the opportunity to discuss before arriving at a group decision of which is larger. Since the experimenters knew precisely which cities each member

Table 7.3 Three individuals' responses to two cities in a group decision-making task

Member	Recognize Milwaukee	Recognize Detroit	Belief
1	Yes	Yes	Milwaukee is larger
2	Yes	Yes	Milwaukee is larger
3	No	Yes	–

recognized, and what each member believed about the relative populations of the recognized cities, hypotheses concerning group recognition could be tested.

Consider the case in Table 7.3. The question is to infer whether Milwaukee or Detroit has a larger population. Members 1 and 2 recognize both cities, and believe that Milwaukee is larger. Member 3, however, only recognizes Detroit. What will the group decide? The opinions of numbers 1 and 2 ought to carry considerable weight, as recognizing both cities implies impressive knowledge of US geography. If the group were to vote based on their previously expressed beliefs, the majority of members would vote for Milwaukee. However, in these situations, the experimental groups *rejected* the majority belief about 60 percent of the time. Partial ignorance (incomplete recognition) by one group member spoke louder than majority recognition.

If we change Table 7.3 such that member 2 recognizes neither city, a similar situation occurs. This is a case in which one person, who knows more about the objects, has expressed a belief which goes against the prediction of a recognition-based heuristic. Much like in the previous example, when these cases were analyzed the group chose the object recognized by the less-knowledgeable member about 60 percent of the time. When two group members had incomplete recognition, and the third believed that the city not recognized by the other two is larger, the group chose the object recognized by those with partial recognition about 75 percent of the time. A lack of knowledge can speak louder than expressed beliefs in certain instances of group decision-making.

7.4 Knowledge Aggregation in Groups

Anyone who has served on committees can attest that groups do not always make the best decisions. One example problem, which has captured the attention of social psychologists for years, is the *hidden profile* task. Suppose a group of four members must choose which of two job candidates to hire: Candidate A or Candidate B. There are facts (henceforth *cues*) that speak in favor of each candidate, numbered 1 to 12, and shown above the line in Figure 7.3. Examples of cues might be proficient typing ability, the ability to speak French, a university degree, and so on. Cues 1 through 4 are common knowledge; that is, all four group members know these facts. In addition, Cues 1 through 4 support candidate A. The remaining cues 5–12 are not shared (i.e. each is known only by one person), and support Candidate B.

Numerous experiments have been conducted in which groups of participants are assembled, given shared and unshared cues by the experimenter, and asked to choose a candidate. What might the groups decide? If the group were to pool all available information about candidates A and B, the collective knowledge of the group would be as represented below the line in Figure 7.3. Candidate A would have four supporting reasons, while Candidate B would have eight, suggesting, *ceteris paribus*, that B should be chosen. Because the candidates can only be seen

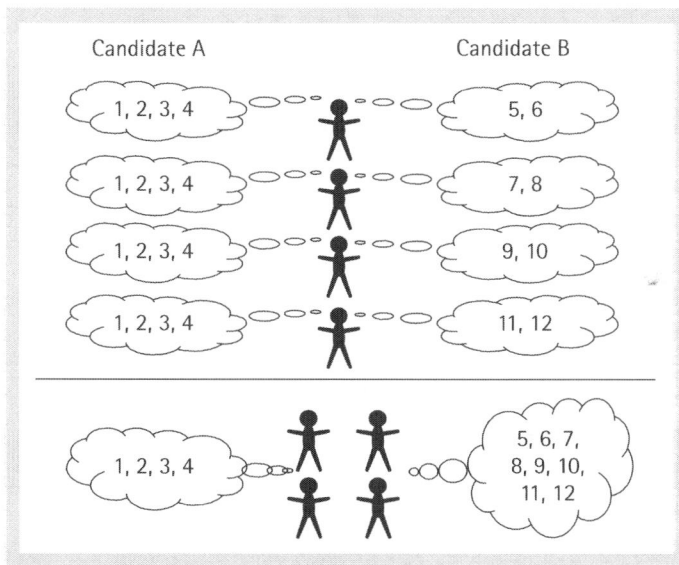

Fig. 7.3 Distribution of knowledge in a 'hidden profile' scenario. Cues (numbers 1 through 12) concerning two job candidates (A and B) are distributed among four group members who must decide to hire one candidate. Each individual has knowledge that suggests Candidate A is better than Candidate B, but if they were to pool their knowledge as a group—the situation depicted below the line at bottom—they would see there are more cues supporting Candidate B

in this light after pooling information, the full representation is called a 'hidden profile.'

What if the group members do not pool their information? From the point of view of each committee member, Candidate A has four pros while Candidate B only has two, so each individual might arrive at the opinion that A is better. Were the group to vote, one can see how Candidate A could be chosen over Candidate B. When such problems are given to groups of people in experiments, the typical result is that Candidate A is chosen. One characteristic finding is that groups tend to talk more about candidate A than B; that is, they focus more on shared than unshared information (Stasser and Titus 1987; Wittenbaum and Stasser 1996; Gigone and Hastie 1997).

One explanation of groups' failure to detect hidden profiles is that they do not invest sufficient time and effort gathering and processing information. Is it true that extensive information-processing is needed to solve this problem? Are there simple strategies groups might employ to make fast, frugal, and accurate decisions? Torsten Reimer, Ulrich Hoffrage, and colleagues have extended the family of simple heuristics to address this task and found that a modified version of the take-the-best heuristic could effectively detect hidden profiles in computer simulation, suggesting that extensive information-processing is not necessary to solve the hidden-profile task. This result also poses new research questions. Why, if simple strategies exist, do real groups fail? How common are hidden profiles, anyway? When there is a hidden profile, how often is it the best choice? Reimer and Hoffrage (2005) found, when randomly generating scenarios (that is, creating simulated individuals who possess varying amounts of knowledge about the candidates) that only 456 in 300,000 environments contained a hidden profile—not very often, considering the amount of attention they have received in the literature. Detection failures could be significant if the hidden alternative (which groups typically do not choose) is almost always the best one. By running their simulations using a criterion of quality, Reimer and Hoffrage found that out of three alternatives, the hidden profile was the highest-valued one from 41 to 71 percent of the time, meaning that in a number of cases it could be wise *not* to choose it. In addition, they found that hidden profiles were most likely to arise when cues were low in validity or steeply decreasing in validities, and they found that hidden profiles were much more likely to be the best alternatives when cues were compensatory and high in validity. All these results are useful to predict when hidden profiles can be a cause for concern in applied settings.

Another example of heuristic methods for group problem-solving comes from research by Mason, Jones, and Goldstone (2005). Using sophisticated software, laboratory participants sitting at computers were connected to one another through lattice, 'small world,' full, and random network structures. Individuals were given a difficult problem of trying to find the maximum value of an unknown function by trial and error. They could submit guesses (numbers in the range of 1 to 100) to the computer and receive as feedback the value of the function for that guess, but with random noise added to make matters difficult. In addition, they could see the guesses and feedback of their immediate neighbors in the network. In an initial test the function to be maximized was unimodal, and perhaps not surprisingly people in fully connected networks got close to the maximum fastest. Since every player could see every other player's guesses, people likely imitated best guesses, leading all players to do their prospecting in an ultimately favorable region of the search space. However, a different picture emerged in a second condition in which the unknown function was not unimodal, but had a global maximum and two broad local maxima that could trap guessers. One might expect that, again, the greater amount of information available in the fully connected network would help its members. Surprisingly, in the trimodal problem the small-world network was the quickest to approach the global maximum. Individuals in the fully connected network were less exploratory and a strategy of imitation often led them into suboptimal local solutions. People in the small-world network were motivated to explore their local parts of the problem space, but since they were connected by 'shortcuts' to other locally working groups, they could be made aware of better solutions. Here we can see how the success of a simple heuristic like imitation depends not just on the structure of the information environment (unimodal versus multimodal), but on the social networks that exist between decision makers. We also observe an instance in which less information leads to better decisions through its effect on local exploratory behavior.

7.5 LEARNING CUE ORDERS SOCIALLY

Heuristics like take-the-best search for cues in a particular order. In earlier work (Gigerenzer and Goldstein 1996) we did not put forward theories of how cue orders were learned. Our hunch at the time was that it happened through cultural transmission. Todd and Dieckmann (2005) have modeled the cue-order learning process, and run simulations in which decision makers try to learn on their own. They found that when decision makers learned in isolation, they arrived at good cue orders slowly. Even after feedback on a hundred paired comparisons, accuracy rose only modestly above that obtained with a random cue ordering. A similar result was found in the lab as well: Todd and Dieckmann (in press) gave people feedback on a hundred items and noted they exhibited slow progress in learning cue orderings.

How might many minds work together to speed up individual learning? Garcia-Retamero, Takezawa, and Gigerenzer (2006) created a 'social learning' simulation that consisted of two alternating phases. In one phase individuals attempted to learn on their own, getting feedback from the environment. After a certain number of trials, individuals would come together in the other phase to share what they had learned. After this, they would go back to making inferences on their own with an (ideally) improved cue ordering and repeat the cycle. Figure 7.4 shows the situation in the Todd and Dieckmann simulation at the top, in which people learn as individuals and do not communicate, and that of the Garcia-Retamero, Takezawa, and Gigerenzer simulation, in which people alternate between individual and social learning phases, at the bottom.

In the social-learning simulation, individuals start out on their own (lower-left section of Fig. 7.4) making inferences with a random cue ordering. Supposing there are five cues called A, B, C, D, and E, this initial ordering might be D, C, A, E, B. After learning individually, each person might reorder the cues according to a specific criterion; for instance, the success rate of each cue when it was used. When coming together (lower-right section of Fig. 7.4), the members must decide on an ordering collectively. The individuals will each take this ordering back into the world (back to the lower-left of Fig. 7.4), modify it, and repeat.

As a group, there are many knowledge-aggregation rules that might be used to arrive at a new cue ordering for all to adopt. Several combination rules were tested in simulation, including majority voting, Condorcet voting, as well as averaging the cue-validity estimates of all members. These all involved combining information from all the members into the final decision. A very simple rule, which ignores the input of all but one member, is having everyone simply imitate the cue ordering of the individual that was most successful on his or her own. Though this rule was simplest and most frugal, it had the surprising result of exhibiting the fast learning rate and greatest accuracy, as Figure 7.5 shows. This social learning can be very rapid. One simulation found that if a group of 10 individuals meets just once (after each getting feedback on 50 paired comparisons), the accuracy is as high as that obtained when ordering cues according to their true ecological validities. Mechanisms like these help us see how potentially difficult aspects of applying individual heuristics (such as arriving at a cue ordering on one's own) can be plausibly modeled through simple social interaction. The success of imitation strategies, however, depends on the rational abilities of each agent to faithfully record, and the honesty of each agent to faithfully report, its individual success, as well as the ability of agents to adjust for the possibly biased or dishonest information coming from others. (For further discussion of the consequences of biased agents for simulations see the chapter by Macy and Flache, and for more on the issue of whom to trust see the chapters by Bohnet and by Cook and Gerbasi, all in this volume.)

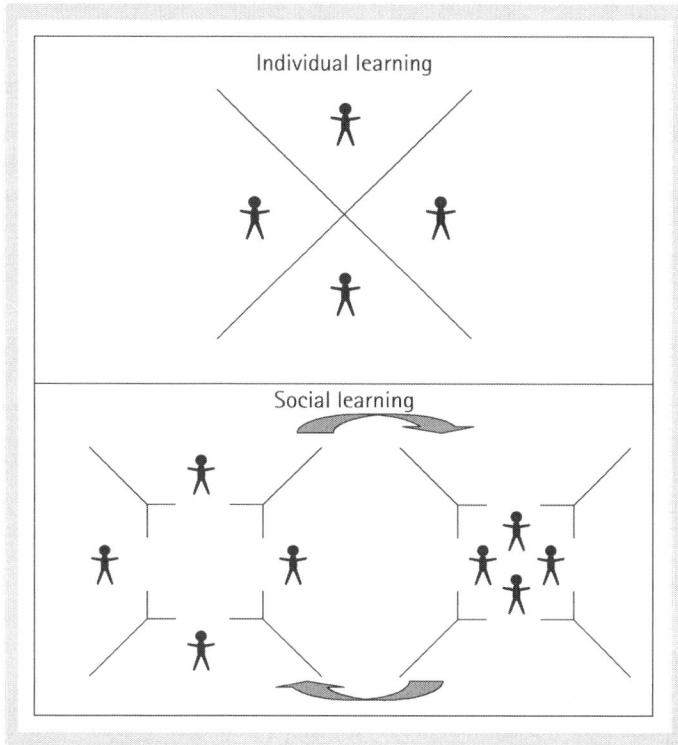

Fig. 7.4 Individual and social learning as modeled by Todd and Dieckmann (2005) and Garcia-Retamero, Takezawa, and Gigerenzer (2006). The objective is to learn a cue ordering for take-the-best. At top, in individual learning, decision makers get feedback from the environment only, but not from each other. In social learning, at bottom, the simulation alternates between an individual learning phase at left, and a social exchange phase at right. In social exchange, group members communicate the experiences they had during individual learning, in order to collectively arrive at new cue ordering as a group. Once a new ordering is found, all individuals test it out alone and the cycle repeats

CONSIDERATIONS

The fast-and-frugal approach has some limitations. In order to keep the definitions of heuristics precise, they may need to deal with operational definitions that can gloss over subtleties of psychological experience. The recognition heuristic, for

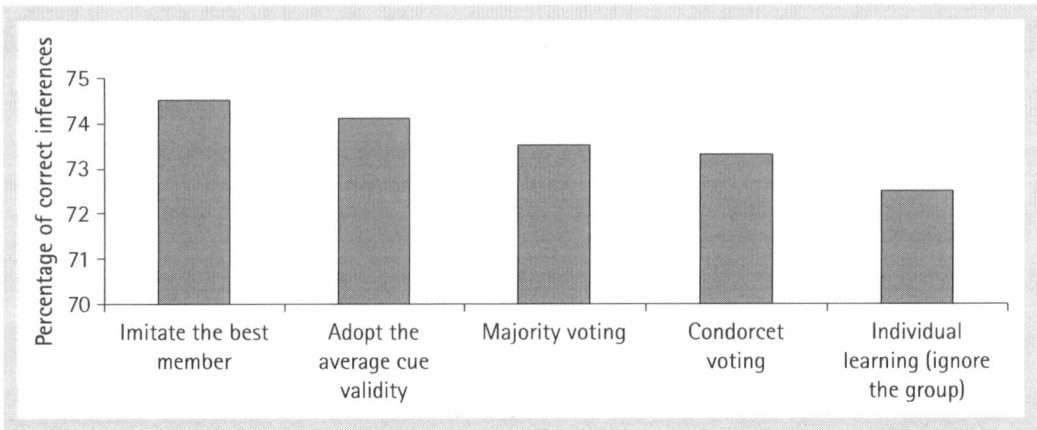

Fig. 7.5 Correct inferences under various social learning rules after a hundred paired comparisons (adapted from Garcia-Retamero, Takezawa, and Gigerenzer 2006). A frugal strategy of ignoring all the input except that of the most successful member fared best. As benchmarks, the minimalist heuristic achieved 70% correct, and take-the-best (using the true ecological validities) scored 74.1% correct

instance, uses as an input a yes/no judgment concerning whether an object is recognized. This judgment, however, can be influenced by numerous moderating factors (Dougherty, Franco-Watkins, and Thomas 2008; Gigerenzer, Hoffrage, and Goldstein 2008). For instance, a slightly familiar name may be rated as recognized in the context of unfamiliar names, but unrecognized in the context of very famous names. These shifts in recognition judgments can lead to changes in inference. One needs to look beyond the simple recognition heuristic to model how recognition judgments change according to context. Similarly, contextual cues may cause a person to switch from using one heuristic to using another. A person might use the recognition heuristic for items that are naturally sampled from the environment, but suspend its use on perceived trick questions. Reinforcement learning can cause people to switch between heuristic strategies as well, and Rieskamp and Otto (2006) have recently put forward a promising theory of how people learn to do so.

It is tempting to criticize simple and noncompensatory heuristics because one can easily identify 'corner' cases in which they should make incorrect predictions. Take-the-best or the recognition heuristic may arrive at the wrong answer when the first cue points towards one alternative and all the other cues point to the other. Furthermore, in such cases simple heuristics may mispredict behavior as well. However, models should be evaluated not on the capacity to mispredict in theory, but on the number and consequence of mispredictions in realistic tests. Linear models mispredict, too; it is just harder for humans to notice a priori when and where they will break down. It is also difficult at first glance to appreciate that simpler models can be more robust—the results of Figure 7.2 come as a surprise to many.

For every heuristic there are kind and unkind environments. A heuristic that works well in the natural world, for instance, may fail in social situations in which players are trying to mislead each other. Perhaps more than general-purpose models, the accuracy and efficiency of heuristics are tightly linked to properties such as cue validities, the cost of information, cue intercorrelations, rates of change, likelihood of false information, local maxima, network structure, and more. Through computer simulation, mathematical analysis, and laboratory experimentation, the science of heuristics is getting a clearer picture of how the success of strategies depends on the structure of the environment (Katsikopoulos and Martignon 2006; Hogarth and Karelaia 2007; Todd, Gigerenzer, and the ABC Research Group, in preparation).

This chapter provides examples of how simple heuristics might account for complex behavior, how they can serve as robust models, and how they can make counterintuitive predictions. Perhaps the greatest benefit of this heuristic-based approach is its precision. Hedström and Swedberg (1998) have decried vagueness in social theory, noting a tendency 'to label, relabel, and describe rather than to explain,' and similar critiques have been aimed at explanation by redescription in psychology (Gigerenzer 1996). When developing the models in the book *Simple Heuristics That Make Us Smart* (Gigerenzer, Todd, and the ABC Research Group 1999), our research group was guided by the maxim 'if you can't write it as a simple computer program, it's not a simple heuristic.' While coding something is not a high hurdle (anything can be written as a program with enough assumptions), and while not all computer programs clarify matters (e.g. complex neural networks which remain opaque even to their creators), the rule turned out to be valuable in practice. Not only did it lead to models that were more precise, but the maxim led to accidental discovery as well. For instance, while coding a variant of take-the-best called take-the-last (which tries cues in order which cue last discriminated), we were surprised when this simple mechanism won the competition by a full 10 percentage points (Gigerenzer and Goldstein 1996: 661). We had absentmindedly presented the questions in a systematic (as opposed to random) order that only this heuristic, and none of the more complex models like multiple regression, could exploit. Simon famously noted that rationality is bounded by a scissors whose two blades are 'the structure of task environments and the computational capacities of the actor' (1990: 7). Modeling simple heuristics and information environments in code leads one to notice the interaction of both blades.

There is a long tradition of viewing the mind as a generalized maker of trade-offs, a prudent judge that weighs and combines all available information through mysterious optimizing processes. However, there is promise in coming at the problem from the opposite direction. By combining the simple building blocks of search rules, stopping rules, and choice rules, one can account for the complexities of behavior with models that are transparent, robust, and psychologically plausible.

NOTES

1. The song is by Ray Noble (1934) and has been covered by Bing Crosby, Doris Day, Nat King Cole, Billie Holiday, and others.
2. All these approaches have, as one might imagine, addressed the questions that the others have posed. I arrive at these high-level characterizations by considering the kinds of data that each program has chosen to collect. For instance, heuristics-and-biases research often computes the proportion of people deviating from a normative answer, the adaptive-decision-maker program has collected ample process and preference data, and the fast-and-frugal approach has focused on algorithmic speed and accuracy.

REFERENCES

ARMELIUS, B., and ARMELIUS, K. (1974), 'The Use of Redundancy in Multiple-cue Judgments: Data from a Suppressor-variable Task', *American Journal of Psychology*, 87: 385–92.

COLEMAN, J. S. (1986), 'Social Theory, Social Research, and a Theory of Action', *American Journal of Sociology*, 91 (6): 1309–35.

CZERLINSKI, J., GOLDSTEIN, D. G., and GIGERENZER, G. (1999), 'How Good Are Simple Heuristics?', in G. Gigerenzer, P. M. Todd, and the ABC Research Group (eds.), *Simple Heuristics that Make Us Smart* (New York: Oxford University Press).

DARWIN, C. [1887] (1969), *The Autobiography of Charles Darwin, 1809–1882* (New York: Norton).

DAWES, R. M. (1979), 'The Robust Beauty of Improper Linear Models in Decision Making', *American Psychologist*, 34: 571–82.

DOUGHERTY, M. R., FRANCO-WATKINS, A. M., and THOMAS, R. (2008), 'The Psychological Plausibility of the Theory of Probabilistic Mental Models and Fast and Frugal Heuristics', *Psychological Review*, 115: 199–211.

EDINGTON, E. S. (1974), 'A New Tabulation of Statistical Procedures Used in APA Journals', *American Psychologist*, 29: 25–6.

FISHBEIN, M., and AJZEN, I. (1975), *Belief, Attitude, Intention, and Behavior: An Introduction to Theory and Research* (Reading, Mass.: Addison-Wesley).

FRANKLIN, BENJAMIN [1772] (1987), *Writings* (New York: Library of America).

GARCIA-RETAMERO, R., TAKEZAWA, M., and GIGERENZER, G. (2006), 'How to Learn Good Cue Orders: When Social Learning Benefits Simple Heuristics', in R. Sun and N. Miyake (eds.), *Proceedings of the Twenty-eighth Annual Conference of the Cognitive Science Society* (Mahwah, N.J.: Erlbaum), 1352–8.

GIGERENZER, G. (1991), 'From Tools to Theories: A Heuristic of Discovery in Cognitive Psychology', *Psychological Review*, 98: 254–67.

—— (1996), 'On Narrow Norms and Vague Heuristics: A Rebuttal to Kahneman and Tversky', *Psychological Review*, 103: 592–6.

—— and GOLDSTEIN, D. G. (1996), 'Mind As Computer: The Birth of a Metaphor', *Creativity Research Journal*, 9: 131–44.

—— HOFFRAGE, U., and GOLDSTEIN, D. G. (2008), 'Fast and Frugal Heuristics are Plausible Models of Cognition: Reply to Dougherty, Franco-Watkins, and Thomas (2008)', *Psychological Review*, 115 (1): 230–7.

—— TODD, P. M., and the ABC Research Group (1999), *Simple Heuristics That Make Us Smart* (New York: Oxford University Press).

GIGONE, D., and HASTIE, R. (1997), 'The Impact of Information on Small Group Choice', *Journal of Personality and Social Psychology*, 72: 132–40.

GOLDSTEIN, D. G., and GIGERENZER, G. (2002), 'Models of Ecological Rationality: The Recognition Heuristic', *Psychological Review*, 109: 75–90.

GREEN, D. P., and SHAPIRO, I. (1994), *Pathologies of Rational Choice Theory: A Critique of Applications in Political Science* (New Haven, Conn.: Yale University Press).

HAMMOND, K. R., HURSCH, C. J., and TODD, F. J. (1964), 'Analyzing the Components of Clinical Inference', *Psychological Review*, 71: 438–56.

HECHTER, M., and KANAZAWA, S. (1997), 'Sociological Rational Choice Theory', *Annual Review of Sociology*, 23: 191–214.

HEDSTRÖM, P., and SWEDBERG, R. (1998), 'Social Mechanisms: An Introductory Essay', in Hedström and Swedberg (eds.), *Social Mechanisms: An Analytical Approach to Social Theory* (Cambridge: Cambridge University Press), 1–31.

—— and UDEHN, L. (2009), 'Analytical Sociology and Theories of the Middle Range', in P. Hedström and P. Bearman (eds.), *The Oxford Handbook of Analytical Sociology* (Oxford: Oxford University Press), 25–47.

HOGARTH, R. M., and KARELAIA, N. (2007), 'Heuristic and Linear Models of Judgment: Matching Rules and Environments', *Psychological Review*, 114 (3): 733–58.

KAHNEMAN, D., SLOVIC, P., and TVERSKY, A. (1982) (eds.), *Judgment Under Uncertainty: Heuristics and Biases* (Cambridge: Cambridge University Press).

KATSIKOPOULOS, K. V., and MARTIGNON, L. (2006), 'Naïve Heuristics for Paired Comparisons: Some Results on their Relative Accuracy', *Journal of Mathematical Psychology*, 50: 488–94.

KELLY, H. H. (1967), 'Attribution Theory in Social Psychology', in D. Levine (ed.), *Nebraska Symposium on Motivation* (Lincoln, Nebr.: University of Nebraska Press), 192–238.

—— and MICHAELA, I. L. (1980), 'Attribution Theory and Research', *Annual Review of Psychology*, 31: 457–501.

MACY M., and FLACHE, A. (2009), 'Social Dynamics from the Bottom Up: Agent-based Models of Social Interaction', in P. Hedström and P. Bearman (eds.), *The Oxford Handbook of Analytical Sociology* (Oxford: Oxford University Press), 245–68.

MASON, W., JONES, A. and GOLDSTONE, R. L. (2005), 'Propagation of Innovations in Networked Groups', in M. Bucciarelli, B. G. Bara, and L. Barsalou (eds.), *Proceedings of the*

Twenty-Seventh Annual Conference of the Cognitive Science Society, 2005 (Mahwah, N.J.: Erlbaum).

MERTON, R. K. (1968), 'The Matthew Effect in Science', *Science*, 159 (3810): 56–63.

OPPENHEIMER, D. M. (2003), 'Not So Fast! (And Not So Frugal!): Rethinking the Recognition Heuristic', *Cognition*, 90: B1–B9.

PACHUR, T., and BIELE, G. (2007), 'Forecasting From Ignorance: The Use and Usefulness of Recognition in Lay Predictions of Sports Events', *Acta Psychologica*, 125: 99–116.

PAYNE, J. W., BETTMAN, J. R., and JOHNSON, E. J. (1993), *The Adaptive Decision Maker* (Cambridge: Cambridge University Press).

PODOLNY, J., and LYNN, F. (2009), 'Status', in P. Hedström and P. Bearman (eds.), *The Oxford Handbook of Analytical Sociology* (Oxford: Oxford University Press), 544–65.

REIMER, T., and HOFFRAGE, U. (2005), 'Can Simple Group Heuristics Detect Hidden Profiles in Randomly Generated Environments?', *Swiss Journal of Psychology*, 64: 21–37.

—— and KATSIKOPOULOS, K. (2004), 'The Use of Recognition in Group Decision-making', *Cognitive Science*, 28 (6): 1009–29.

RIESKAMP, J., and OTTO, P. E. (2006), 'SSL: A Theory of How People Learn to Select Strategies', *Journal of Experimental Psychology: General*, 135: 207–36.

RUMELHART, D., McCLELLAND, J., and the PDP Research Group (1986), *Parallel Distributed Processing: Explorations in the Microstructure of Cognition, i. Foundations* (Cambridge, Mass.: MIT Press).

SCHEIBEHENNE, B., and BRÖDER, A. (2007), 'Predicting Wimbledon 2005 Tennis Results by Mere Player Name Recognition', *International Journal of Forecasting*, 23 (3): 415–26.

SCHOOLER, L. J., and HERTWIG, R. (2005), 'How Forgetting Aids Heuristic Inference', *Psychological Review*, 112: 610–28.

SERWE, S., and FRINGS, C. (2006), 'Who Will Win Wimbledon 2003? The Recognition Heuristic in Predicting Sports Events', *Journal of Behavioral Decision Making*, 19 (4): 321–32.

SHEPARD, R. N. (1967), 'On Subjectively Optimum Selections among Multi-attribute Alternatives', in W. Edwards and A. Tversky (eds.), *Decision Making* (Baltimore, Md.: Penguin), 257–83.

SIMON, H. A. (1956), 'Rational Choice and the Structure of the Environment', *Psychological Review*, 63: 129–38.

—— [1969] (1996), 'The Sciences of the Artificial', Karl Taylor Compton Lectures, MIT, 1968, 3rd edn. (Cambridge, Mass.: MIT Press).

—— (1979), 'Information-processing Models of Cognition', *Annual Review of Psychology*, 30: 363–96.

—— (1990), 'Invariants of Human Behavior', *Annual Review of Psychology*, 41: 1–19.

SNOOK, B., and CULLEN, R. M. (2006), 'Recognizing National Hockey League Greatness with an Ignorance-based Heuristic', *Canadian Journal of Experimental Psychology*, 60: 33–43.

STASSER, G., and TITUS, W. (1987), 'Effects of Information Load and Percentage of Common Information on the Dissemination of Unique Information during Group Discussion', *Journal of Personality and Social Psychology*, 53: 81–93.

TODD, P. M., and DIECKMANN, A. (2005), 'Heuristics for Ordering Cue Search in Decision-making', in L. K. Saul, Y. Weiss, and L. Bottou (eds.), *Advances in Neural Information Processing Systems*, xvii (Cambridge, Mass.: MIT Press), 1393–400.

—————— (in press). 'Simple Rules for Ordering Cues in One-reason Decision Making', in P. M. Todd, G. Gigerenzer, and the ABC Research Group (eds.), *Ecological Rationality: Intelligence in the World* (New York: Oxford University Press).

—— and GIGERENZER, G. (2000). 'Précis of Simple Heuristics that Make Us Smart', *Behavioral and Brain Sciences*, 23: 727–41.

—————— and the ABC Research Group (in preparation), *Ecological Rationality: Intelligence in the World* (New York: Oxford University Press).

WITTENBAUM, G. M., and STASSER, G. (1996), 'Management of Information in Small Groups', in J. L. Nye and A. B. Bower (eds.), *What's Social About Social Cognition?* (London: Sage), 3–28.

CHAPTER 8

SIGNALING*

DIEGO GAMBETTA

INTRODUCTION

SIGNALING theory (ST) tackles a fundamental problem of communication: How can an agent, the receiver, establish whether another agent, the signaler, is telling or otherwise conveying the truth about a state of affairs or event which the signaler might have an interest to misrepresent? And, conversely, how can the signaler persuade the receiver that he is telling the truth, whether he is telling it or not? This two-pronged question potentially arises every time the interests between signalers and receivers diverge or collide *and* there is asymmetric information; namely, the signaler is in a better position to know the truth than the receiver is.

The state of affairs or event about which communication can occur could be anything. As it happens, in the literature it often has to do with the signaler's unobservable qualities, or, as it is sometimes said, her 'type'; for example, in a famous early study by Michael Spence (1974) the quality refers to a worker's productivity, which can be either of two types, high and low, and which the employer cannot directly observe. An 'honest' signaler would like to persuade the receiver that he is the good type, but the problem is that a 'dishonest' signaler too would like to do the same. How can the receiver decide and what should the signaler do?

Signaling theory, which is only a little more than thirty years old, has now become a branch of game theory. In economics it was introduced by Michael Spence in

* I am grateful to Macartan Humphreys, Ekaterina Korobtseva and Margaret Meyer for their specialized advice and to Michael Biggs, Valeria Pizzini-Gambetta, and the editors for their comments on an earlier version of this chapter.

1973. In biology it took off not so much when Amotz Zahavi first introduced the idea in 1975, but only since 1990, when Alan Grafen proved formally through game theory that 'honest' signals can be an evolutionarily stable strategy (ESS).[1] In both biology and microeconomics it has had considerable success and is now found in textbooks (e.g. Kreps 1990: ch. 17; Krebs and Davies 1998: ch. 14). Since its inception it has attracted a robust following in political science and more recently also among anthropologists, especially those with an interest in evolution. It is hard to think of any other theory that in recent times has been developing so fast across *all* behavioral sciences. Unfortunately, despite some lonely practitioners, sociologists are still largely oblivious to its existence. However, the theory's potential to make sense of many human interactions commonly investigated by sociologists is arguably large and the theory should become an important element in the toolbox of analytical sociology.

In the rest of the Introduction I will describe some key concepts. In Section 8.1 I will introduce the basic principles in nonformal terms. In Section 8.2 I will illustrate different ways in which the cost of the signal and the quality being signaled are related, and mention some of the theory's limitations. In Section 8.3 I will then briefly introduce some of its applications and lastly in Section 8.4 provide some information on its origins. This chapter is a mere introduction to a complex topic, and makes no claim to be exhaustive of all that scholars should know before using it properly.

Unobservable properties and signs

Much of what is important to know about others is not easily knowable. People have properties that affect how we decide to interact with them: loyalty, fidelity, trustworthiness, innocence, generosity, resilience, fighting ability, fertility, tolerance, determination, competence, intelligence—to name some examples. People also have intentions towards us that we would like to know before deciding how to interact with them.

The problem however is that these properties are not observable. We cannot directly see or otherwise perceive people's honesty or resilience. We cannot read their intentions as if they were written in an open book. They know and we do not. Sometimes we do not even know if they are who they say they are. Identity too can be an unobservable property. The problem extends to the goods that people trade and whose quality can be established only through experience. But how can we decide prior to experience whether to buy them or how can we persuade others that our goods are of good quality?

We can however perceive (and display) other things. We can see if people are handsome, if they smell nice, and if their voice sounds relaxed. We can observe how they move or dress, whether they have tattoos, and with whom they go out, how much money they spend and on what items, whether their hands are smooth or callous, and whether they blush easily or look us in the eye. We can see what they do or gather evidence on what they have done in our absence. We can memorize their individual traits, such as face or email address, and we reidentify them on seeing those traits again. We can of course hear what they say and the accent with which they say it.

Sometimes what we perceive conveys no information on properties that interests us; sometimes we mistake an innocent gesture for a sign or a signal of some property. Still, our best chance to find out something about people's unobservable properties is by establishing a connection between their perceivable features and their unobservable properties. Whenever interests are potentially at odds, this connection is the object of signaling theory.

Signs and signals

People's perceivable features come in two forms: signs and signals. The difference and links between the two are complex, but in the limited space I have I will only mention the main distinctions, drawing on Bacharach and Gambetta (2001).

Signals are the stuff of *purposive* communication. Signals are any observable features of an agent which are intentionally displayed for the purpose of raising the probability the receiver assigns to a certain state of affairs. 'Features' of an agent that make up a signal could be anything: they include parts or aspects of his body, pieces of behavior by him, and his appurtenances.

Signs are a different concept from signals. Signs can be just anything in the environment that is perceptible and by being perceived happens to modify our beliefs about something or someone. But signs are dormant potential signals. They are the raw material of signals. The basic form of the sign–signal transformation is that a signaler takes steps to display the sign. We cannot take for granted that signs are noticed. A duelling scar may be not on the face but the thigh or chest. The crowded tables of a restaurant may be invisible from the street unless we devise some system for outsiders to see them. One way of signaling is to take steps to make apparent a sign that would not otherwise be observed: to bare the chest to display a tattoo, to glaze the restaurant façade to reveal the crowds inside. One trigger of this transformation is the bearer's realization of the meaning of certain actions in the eyes of an observer. I may be unaware that my accent is informing others of some quality of mine, until some observer acts in a way that makes me aware and at which point I may choose to display it intentionally. We often produce the raw material of signals innocently by going about our lives, without planning for them to become signals. Most of our actions and observable traits will never become signals, but some will. Even checking one's email on one's home computer at a certain time can later become a verifiable alibi we can display, should we be accused of having perpetrated a crime somewhere else at that time.

The transformation goes also in the opposite direction and yesterday's signal can become today's sign. Consider a tattoo on my wrist, which induces beliefs in others that I am a sailor. Once I have had it done, in each subsequent encounter with someone it is a fait accompli and so a sign. I am not thinking about its effects every time someone sees it. But the day I chose to have it done, the action I took was a signal. Moreover, from the perspective of that day, on which I foresaw and intended an endless string of tattoo-induced beliefs in my nautical quality, it was a signal on all these future occasions too. So whether a tattoo is a signal or a sign on a particular occasion depends on the temporal perspective from which the agent regards that occasion.

> If the same signalling situation arises day after day, what is at first a conscious intention tends to become habitual and internalised. But it remains an intention for all that, on this simple test: were one to be made aware of the issue—for example, by losing a suitcase containing all one's clothes—one would choose to re-outfit oneself with similar items—for example, with new clothes in the same style—with the explicit intention of signalling one's qualities. In short, the intention does not have to be 'occurrent', but only 'triggerable'. So conforming to the dress codes and outward practices of one's group can be explained as a broadly intentional act, with the purpose of signalling membership of that group. (Bacharach and Gambetta 2001: 174)

Finally, it is important to notice that the understanding of signals in biological models does not require intentionality, but rests on natural selection and can be applied to all organisms (Searcy and Nowicki 2005: 3–5). While arguably many signals among humans are intentionally emitted and responded to, humans too like any other animals develop, display, and respond to behaviors and morphological features which have communicative value unthinkingly. Thus, for instance, it seems that human males prefer females with a higher waist–hip ratio (see e.g. Singh and Young 2001).[2] This is a 'preference' they manifest in very different human groups without knowing its source; namely, that it would be a signal of fertility with which the ratio would be positively correlated. Those with that preference would be rewarded by more offspring, which via genetic transmission are more likely to carry that preference, which will then spread in the population. In the biological sense, the ratio and the response are considered a 'signaling system.' Unlike other animals, though, humans can learn, and unconscious signals can potentially shift to a greater or lesser extent under the domain of culture and intentionality. Women, for instance, can learn that the waist–hip ratio makes them more attractive without knowing why and can take steps both to display it 'honestly' and more effectively by wearing figure-hugging dresses and to enhance it by squeezing their waist in a corset or bustle, in which case they would silence the biological signaling system as the waist–hip ratio would no longer be a reliable signal.

8.1 THE THEORY'S BASIC PRINCIPLES

When we believe that our interests and those of others are identical, establishing a connection between signals and states of affairs can be relatively easy. In many of our exchanges we simply believe what others want us to believe by what they do or say. This is the case when we deal with an individual with whom we have reasons to believe that we share our interests either generally or in a given situation.

A child who is told by his father to jump from a wall—'Jump, I'll catch you'—has no reason to disbelieve his father. The father's words mean what he says; they describe his true intentions because of who he is. The underlying problem here is one of coordination: both need to understand given utterances or gestures in the same way. They need to know the conventions, whether linguistic or related to other gestures. The main threat to communication here is *misunderstanding*.

Yet, as a Sicilian anecdote indicates, even in this case one cannot be entirely sure. A Mafioso once said to his son 'Jump, I'll catch you!' and when the son did he let him fall to the ground. 'Now,' he said, 'you'll learn that you cannot trust anyone.' This grim lesson reminds us of the threat of misrepresentation, by which others wilfully lead us to make the wrong connection: they emit false signals. The son understood the meaning of the message correctly and acted accordingly, but the message was false. Whether people truly share their interests with us is also not directly observable, itself a property that may be misrepresented.

When our interests are not necessarily identical, as in courtship or in business, or worse they openly clash, as in conflicts, the risk of strategic misrepresentation is potentially rife. Can we believe the pitiful story of a beggar asking us for money in the street, a suitor promising marriage, or that Iraq has weapons of mass destruction? From the minor daily encounters to the grand interactions between nations, the question of what to believe is ubiquitous. We cannot trust what people say or do to persuade us that they are trustworthy by default; or when they try to persuade us that it is not to our advantage to fight them because they are stronger than us. And yet not all signalers are lying. The honest among them—by 'honest' here I simply mean that they mean what they say or signal to us—are eager for us to know that they are honest. Is there a way in which truth can be transmitted even when interests are not aligned and knowledge is asymmetrical?

Typical situations that signaling theory covers have two key features:

  (i) There is some action the receiver can do which benefits a signaler, whether or not he has the quality k, for instance marry him, but
  (ii) this action benefits the receiver if and only if the signaler truly has k, and otherwise hurts her—for instance, marry an unfaithful man.

This applies to conflict situations too: if we know that our opponent is going to win a fight, we may choose to yield without fighting at a lesser cost for both. Thus k signalers and receivers share an interest in the truth, but the interests of non-k signalers and receivers are opposed: non-k signalers would like to deceive receivers into thinking they have k, in order to receive the benefit, while receivers have an interest in not being deceived. (The interests of ks and non-ks are also usually opposed because the activity of the latter damages the credibility of the signals of the former.)

The main result in signaling theory is that *there is a solution in which at least some truth is transmitted, provided that among the possible signals is one, s, which is cheap enough to emit, relative to the benefit, for signalers who have k, but costly enough to emit, relative to the benefit, for those who do not. If s is too costly to fake for all or most non-k signalers then observing s is good evidence that the signaler has k.*

If the cost relationship is such that all and only k signalers can afford to emit s, the solution in which they do so, often referred to in the literature as 'equilibrium,' is called 'separating' or 'sorting.' In this equilibrium signals are unambiguous, and the receiver is perfectly informed. All those with k will be perfectly separated from those without k by being able to emit s. No poisoner (normally) seeks to demonstrate his honesty by drinking from the poisoned chalice. Drinking is a signal that one is not a poisoner. At the opposite extreme both k and non-k signalers can afford to emit s relative to their respective benefits. In this case s is uninformative and the equilibrium is said to be 'pooling'; that is, once s is emitted the receiver knows nothing more about who has and who has not k than she did before, and should disregard s. (In Monty Python's *Life of Brian* there is a humorous rendition of a pooling signal. The Romans accept the mob request to free Brian, who is being crucified with a dozen others, and ask 'Who's Brian?' Brian answers 'I am Brian,' but so do all the others. The Romans are none the wiser and Brian is crucified.)

The cost condition may also give rise to intermediate equilibria, so-called semi-sorting ones. In a semisorting equilibrium there is a signal s which is emitted by all k signalers, but not only them; a certain proportion of non-k signalers emit it too. Here although observing s is evidence for the receiver in favor of k, it is not conclusive evidence; it makes it more likely that the signaler has k, but does not imply that he does. The higher the proportion of non-k signalers who use this signal the less conclusive is the evidence.

Signals that approach near perfection exist but are rare. Architects set up offices in the early skyscrapers to show that they trusted them not to collapse. Boatbuilders sailed on the first voyages to show they trusted their boats not to sink. Tim Spicer, a mercenary chief, said he always fought alongside his men to show his trust in their quality.[3] However, most signals in real life are only semisorting: they inform, but not perfectly. We rarely encounter a fully mimic-proof signal. Most of the time someone looking like a Hasidic Jew will be a Hasidic Jew. But occasionally he is a Palestinian suicide bomber disguised as one. Virtually everybody who boards a plane gives a signal, mostly unthinkingly, that he is not intent on causing it to crash. But, as we know only too well, suicide terrorists may be prepared to do just that and can afford to mimic a normal passenger simply by boarding. Some can drink from a poisoned chalice.

When the contamination of the signal is partial it remains credible enough for the majority of honest signalers to keep using it and for a minority of mimics to gain from using it too. In it, at least some truth can be transmitted. In many instances weak signals induce receivers to probe and seek more credible signals, or k signalers to spend resources protecting their signals from the threat posed by dishonest non-k signalers. When the contamination is complete the signal stops being informative, and rational receivers should ignore it.

8.1.1 A classic example

To understand how signaling theory works I will now discuss a classic case of a perfectly discriminating signal reported by Livy, the Roman historian. The Etruscans were besieging Rome, and a brave man known as Caius Mucius infiltrated the enemy's camp aiming to kill Porsena, the King of the Etruscans.

> Afraid to ask which of the two was the king, lest his ignorance should betray him, Mucius struck as fortune directed the blow and killed the secretary instead of the king. . . . He was seized and dragged back by the king's bodyguard to the royal tribunal. Here, alone and helpless, and in the utmost peril, he was still able to inspire more fear than he felt.

Rather than being cowed, Mucius threatens Porsena, hinting at the fact that many more like him are queueng up to try and kill him.

> The king, furious with anger, and at the same time terrified at the unknown danger, threatened that if [Mucius] did not promptly explain the nature of the plot which he was darkly hinting at he should be roasted alive. 'Look,' Mucius cried, 'and learn how lightly regard their bodies those who have some great glory in view.' Then he plunged his right hand into a fire burning on the altar. Whilst he kept it roasting there as if he were devoid of all sensation, the king, astounded at his preternatural conduct, sprang from his seat and ordered the youth to be removed from the altar. 'Go,' he said, 'you have been a worse enemy to yourself than to me . . . I send you away exempt from all rights of war, unhurt, and safe.'   (Livy 1912: 2. 12)[4]

The case of Mucius, who later gained the nickname Scaevola (left hand), shows us the basic principle at work, and makes very clear all the fundamental elements that need to be identified to describe a genuine signaling episode.

> *The main characters*: Mucius is the signaler and Porsena the receiver.
> *The property*: Porsena cannot observe Mucius' resistance to pain for the sake of loyalty to his Romans compatriots.

The signaler's gain if truth is transmitted: Mucius' interest is to avoid being tortured or killed.

The receiver's gain if truth is transmitted: Porsena's interest is to know Mucius' quality to avoid torturing him in vain.

The information asymmetry: Mucius knows whether he has the property, but Porsena does not.

The weak signal: Mucius could just say that he will not give in to torture. But words are cheap in this case, they do not meet the cost condition. Porsena knows that anyone could say that, and would in the circumstance. The question for Mucius is: Is there a signal that I can afford which is less costly than being tortured to death, but which is such as to leave Porsena in no doubt? Is there a signal that someone who merely pretends to have the resilience that I have could not afford?

The persuading signal: Incinerating his hand is just that signal. Mucius loses his right hand but keeps his life and honour, while Porsena, who is neither vengeful nor a sadist, avoids a pointless act. Mucius pays a high cost, in terms of pain and of inflicting a permanent handicap on himself, but still better than open-ended torture that could result in death. Both gain given the situation.

The cost condition: The high cost endured by Mucius is what persuades Porsena. 'If Mucius can do that to himself then there is little more that I can do to him,' he infers. 'He would die rather than betray his countrymen.' Cost is the crucial variable. Or, more accurately, it is the difference between that cost and the cost that a hypothetical mimic could afford to pay. When such a difference cannot be bridged, the signal is perfectly discriminating. No feeble man pretending to be tough could have endured Mucius' feat.

Any analysis that fails to identify *all* the above elements—and in the several sloppy applications that exist this is often the case—cannot with any certainty claim to be truly describing a signaling episode.

8.1.2 Differential costs

When considered carefully a signaling episode has at least two notional signalers rather than one. Even if the receiver faces just one person, he is uncertain whether that person is the one that has k or is the mimic, the bad or low-quality type who claims he has k but does not. The problem for the receiver is to distinguish between them, and for the honest signaler the problem is to make sure that he is not confused with the mimic.

Suppose there are two notional signalers, the Mucius type and a weaker type, let's call him Lucius. Porsena does not know whether the man in front of him is the Mucius or Lucius type. If he is the Lucius type then it pays Porsena to torture

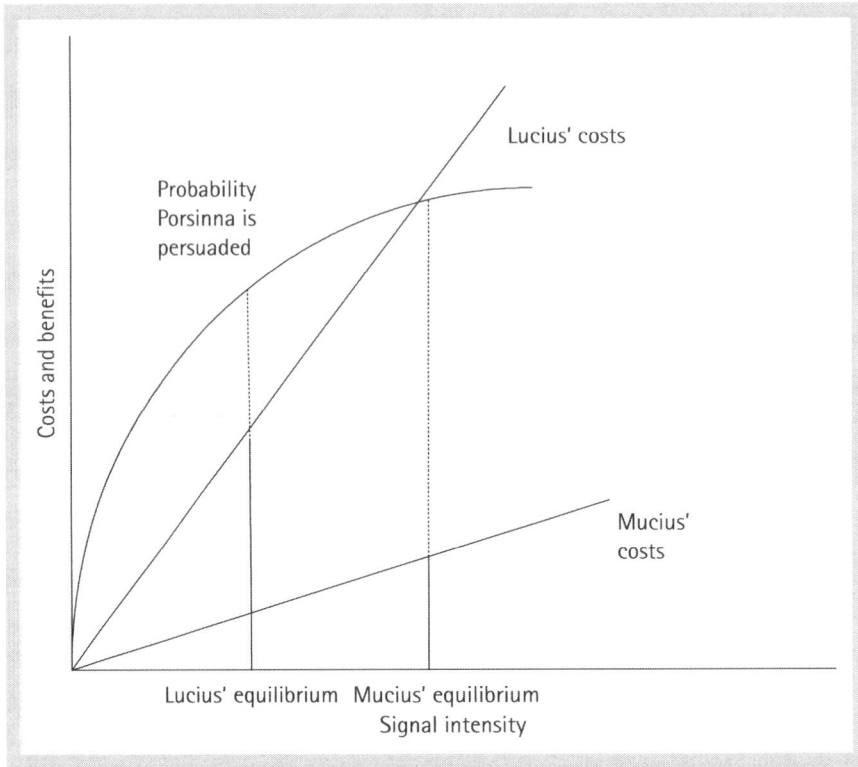

Fig. 8.1 A signaling model in which two signalers face different costs to emit the same signal intensity (after Johnstone 1997)

him, for he may obtain information on the Romans' plans, while it does not pay to torture Mucius. Both types would like Porsena to believe that they are resilient to torture.

Suppose there is a continuous signal whose cost for the signaler is positively correlated with the property the signaler wants to signal: the longer you can keep your hand in a burning fire the higher the cost and the more intense the signal becomes. The Mucius type is more resilient, and this implies that for him the same length of time with his hand in the fire is less costly than it is for the weaker type. Lucius can burn the tip of his fingers, Mucius a whole hand. Lucius and Mucius are on two different cost lines, as represented in Figure 8.1. For the same intensity they have different costs, Mucius can thus emit a more intense signal, a signal that Lucius cannot afford.

In Figure 8.1 I represent the signaler's benefits as a continuous variable for ease of exposition and generality. One can think of it as the probability that Porsena assigns to facing a type who is resilient to torture rather than someone who just pretends to be, a probability that grows as the signal intensity grows. The higher that probability is, the higher are also the probability that Porsena will choose not to torture and the related expected benefit for the signalers. If both signalers are maximizers, they will stop at their equilibrium point, where the distance between their respective cost line and the benefit line peaks (the dotted lines in Fig. 8.1). In the situation depicted in the graph, even if Lucius pushed it to the limit, to the right of his equilibrium line, he would not be able to reach Mucius' signaling intensity at equilibrium, as it would be unbearable for him. On witnessing the highest level of signal intensity Porsena can rest assured that he is facing the Mucius type.

8.1.3 Differential benefits

Let us consider now the case in which the relationship between signal cost and signal intensity is the same for both types of signalers, whereas the benefit of signaling rises more rapidly for the signaler who has a higher need and receives more satisfaction from the receiver's response. Does it mean that the cost condition does not obtain and thus informative signaling cannot occur?

Suppose we have a loving creature, Don Ottavio, and a philanderer, Don Giovanni. Don Ottavio is more desirous of Donna Anna and in greater need than Don Giovanni to quell his loving thirst. Donna Anna is wondering who truly depends on her love most, and knows that both of them want to persuade her that they are the one. Following the conventions of their time, they manifest their desire by serenading Donna Anna. Both are equally skilled at serenades, so the cost is the same for them. However, Don Ottavio has an advantage for, given the higher benefits he expects, he can afford an extra cost and serenade her more and more frequently. We can think of the benefits in terms of the warmth of Donna Anna's response to her suitors which goes from ignoring to flirting and lastly to having sex.

In Figure 8.2 Don Giovanni could afford to do just as much, but if he is a maximizer, as we expect a Don Giovanni to be, he will serenade her only up to his equilibrium point in which the distance between the cost and the benefits for him is at its maximum. By contrast, Don Ottavio can serenade her more not because it is easier for him but because he gains more from her positive responses. The differential cost condition, the key to the reliability of the signal, is still achieved. So if Donna Anna wanted to yield more to the suitor who most depended on her love and from whom she can thus expect more loyalty, on observing the differential frequency of serenading she should decide that Don Ottavio is her man.

This is an illustrative example and it does not quite reflect how the story goes in Mozart's opera! It also does not take into account that persistence may sort the opposite effect and be taken as a sign of desperation. Yet there is some evidence that women looking for a long-term mate are responsive to 'serenading' persistence—in

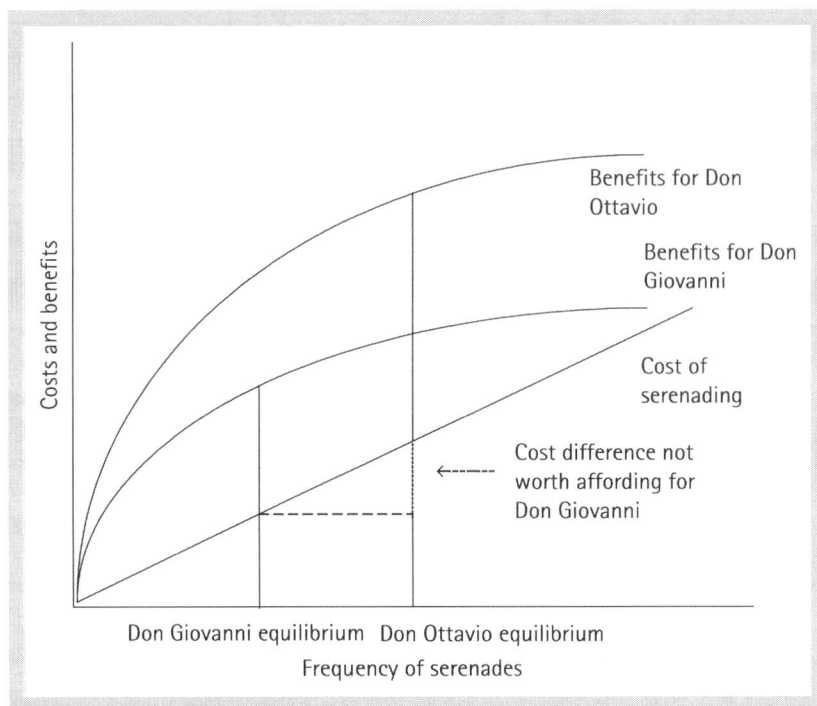

Fig. 8.2 A signaling model in which two signalers obtain different bene-fits from the same receiver's response (after Johnstone 1997)

the form of 'spending a lot of time with the woman, seeing her more often than other women, dating her for an extended period of time, calling her frequently on the phone, and writing her numerous letters' (Buss 2003: 102).[5]

8.2 SOURCES OF SIGNAL COST

In order to identify a signaling episode it is essential to know the link between the property being signaled and the cost of the signal. There are several types of links, the main ones of which I will now describe.

8.2.1 Receiver's independent cost: 'wasting' key resources

In animal behavior 'the concept of signal costs requires that signaller fitness go down as the signalling goes up' (Searcy and Nowicki 2005: 14); in other words, the signaling animal has to sacrifice or, as it is sometimes said, 'waste' resources, and the resources sacrificed have to be correlated with the information which is to be conveyed. A classic example is that of the stotting gazelle when detecting a lion on the hunt. Gazelles that stot, that is jump up and down, show to the lion that they have lots of physical energy, so much of it in fact that they can 'waste' it in display. The gazelle is signaling that it can outrun the lion should it choose to give chase (Zahavi and Zahavi 1997: 6–7). The lion, if persuaded, will be less likely to chase an energetic gazelle, for stotting is correlated with running potential. (The 'honesty' of the signal is maintained provided that lions occasionally put it to the test.)

A classic human example of a signal with this source of cost can be found in Ovid's *Fasti*, in which the poet describes how the Romans came to worship Jupiter Pistor or Jupiter the Baker. When the Gauls were besieging Rome in 387 BC Jupiter instructed the Romans 'to throw down among the enemy the last thing you'd wish to yield!' The Romans

> shook off sleep, and troubled by the strange command, asked themselves what they must yield, unwillingly. It seemed it must be bread: they threw down the gifts of Ceres [loaves of bread], clattering on the enemy helms and shields. The expectation that they could be starved out vanished. The foe was repulsed, and a bright altar raised to Jove the Baker.   (bk. 6: June 9: The Vestalia)[6]

Here the cost of the signal to the signaler comes from the fact that he 'wastes' in display the precise resource he would need most were the receiver to attack, 'the last thing you'd wish to yield'—energy for the lion-stalked gazelle, bread for the Gaul-besieged Romans. (The difference is that the Romans took a desperate risk and bluffed!) These examples are about conflict, but wasting the resource the property of which one wants to signal applies more broadly. The classic Veblen's case, which I will mention below, comes under this heading: a rich man who wants to show that he is rich can choose conspicuous ways to 'waste' his money, for instance.

8.2.2 Receiver-dependent cost: exposure to risk

Another category of signal cost is, by contrast, *dependent* on the receiver's response. Here the signal does not require an expenditure of resources. Consider the alarm calls that many animals, birds, and marmots for instance, emit on spotting a predator. The traditional interpretation of this behavior is altruism: the animal alerts its companions of the impending danger. However, Amotz Zahavi (1997: ch. 12), one of the theory's founders, suggested a different interpretation of the call compatible with self-interest: the warning effect would be a by-product while the primary motive would be to inform the predator that one has seen it and that one is not scared. By increasing the risk of predator detection and attack, the caller would signal that it has confidence in its ability to escape or fight back, thereby reducing the risk of an attack.

To understand the difference between receiver-dependent and receiver-independent costs, consider two types of signals aimed at dissuading opponents from fighting. One consists in threatening the opponent by moving very close to him or in showing one's back to him, either way signaling that one is not afraid of the opponent's attack, so much so that one makes it easier for the opponent to strike. Here there is no loss of resources, the cost is merely potential and due to the increased risk the individual incurs of suffering should the receiver attack. In the other case one can try to dissuade the opponent by tying one's hand behind one's back and thus depriving oneself of a resource which would be essential for one to fight. In both cases one shows confidence in one's ability to overcome the opponent, in the former by facilitating the opponent's attack, in the latter by handicapping oneself.[7] (The name used in zoology to refer to signaling theory, *the handicap principle*, is derived from this type of case and thus to receiver-independent costs.)

8.2.3 Third party-dependent cost

I do not know if it occurs among other animals, but among humans we also have signals the cost of which is dependent on a third party's response, which the communicating agents can exploit. Divine Brown, a Los Angeles prostitute who achieved her fifteen minutes of fame for administering oral sex to British actor Hugh Grant in 1995, revealed her particular kind of test to make sure that the prospective customer was not an undercover policeman. Before agreeing to trade, she asked Grant to expose himself in the street. The reason, she said, is that an undercover policeman would not do that. Divine believed that exposing oneself is an action with information value because only a real customer can afford to do it while an undercover policeman would not break the law for he would risk losing his job. In this case the signal cost for the 'dishonest' signaler is imposed by a third party, the law and the police authorities.

The same reasoning inspires a tougher test applied by drug dealers in New York. Since the mid-nineties

> as police have intensified their assault, the dealers have also adopted more perilous tactics. Five or six times each month, undercover investigators are now forced to use cocaine or heroin at gunpoint, to prove to dealers that they can be trusted. At least twice a month, an officer [who refuses] is shot or otherwise wounded during a staged purchase, say police commanders, who spoke on condition of anonymity.
>
> (*New York Times*, 21 January 1998; Gambetta 2009: ch. 1)

8.2.4 Multiple sources of cost

We often find signals that have more than one source of costs. These are harder to handle, for they can signal more than one property to more than one type of receiver. In animals the classic example of multiple costs is the peacock's tail: costly to grow in terms of developmental resources and nutrients, costly to fan and display, costly to maintain free of parasites, costly to carry, as it both makes the animal more noticeable to predators and hampers its ability to run away. It could serve to attract mates as well as to discourage predators. For humans, consider the tattoo as an example of multiple costs: when extensive and done according to traditional needle techniques, tattoos are produced at the cost of some considerable pain, a cost independent of receivers, which testifies to a certain endurance of the individual, à la Mucius. However, a tattoo can also generate cost from the receiver's response. If it cannot be washed out or veiled and if it is conventionally associated with belonging to a gang, the display of the tattoo can increase the likelihood of attacks by rival gangs, thus testifying to the signaler's loyalty to the gang and disregard for danger. (Here we can appreciate how even a name or a logo, once permanently etched on someone's body, can in certain conditions be costly to display. Not all words or symbols are necessarily cheap.)

8.2.5 Signals costless to honest signalers

A frequent mistake is to think that only signals that are costly for the honest signaler are informative. We often read sentences such as 'Signaling theory argues that expense of the signal ensures the honesty of that which is being signaled,' and the literature refers to 'costly' signals as being persuasive. In many cases, however, persuasive signals have little or no cost for the genuine possessors. We need to bear in mind that it is not the absolute cost per se that informs, but the cost differential between what the k signaler can afford relative to what the non-k signaler can afford (and both costs relative to the respective benefits obtained from the receiver's response if the receiver is persuaded). Only if this difference is large enough to discriminate between the two does the signal inform well. In many cases we obtain that difference perfectly well with costless signals, which work because it is the dishonest signaler who cannot afford them. Social life is interwoven with cheap yet reliable signals, so reliable in fact we do not even notice. If the property to be signaled is your identity, the cost of showing that it is you, if it is you, can be negligible. If I say on a low-quality interphone 'Hi, it's Diego' this is costless for me, but is also uninformative, for others could say that too. But if the sound transmission is good, then my statement will come with my voice and accent clearly attached, and this again is still costless for me but more informative, for it would be more costly for someone else to imitate my voice and accent accurately. And if the medium of communication allows it I can just do what no one else can: show my face, which will be still costless for me and impossible to do for mimics. If being a woman works as a signal of nonaggression, for example, then the cost of being one and displaying it are high only for men who would like to mimic 'woman-ness,' while costless for genuine women. Drinking from a nonpoisoned chalice has no cost for the nonpoisoner. In short, not all honest signals imply a cost for the honest signaler.

8.2.6 Knowing costs, benefits, and incidence of deception

Signaling theory is a powerful tool that can deliver specific answers to the questions when and how much false signaling will occur. However, crucial for the existence of the solutions which it offers are strong assumptions about the players' background knowledge: they must know the sizes of the benefits and of the cost of emitting s, for both k signaler and non-k signalers; and a receiver must also know the base-rate probabilities that a signaler is k and non-k.

> When she peers through the Judas hole and sees a stranger in a UPS uniform, as she wonders whether to confer the benefit of opening the door she needs to have in mind the ease or difficulty of acquiring a UPS disguise, and the value to a criminal of what he would get from securing entry, and have some idea of the general incidence of criminality.   (Bacharach and Gambetta 2001: 161)

These measures are of course not necessarily easy to obtain, and imperfect knowledge often explains the occurrence of successful deception.

What thus counts as a signal as well as what makes it more or less costly for different types of signalers is particular to the context in which it is used, and this is one of the reasons why the theory, while powerful in abstract terms, is often hard to apply without a fine-grained appreciation of the domain in which signals are emitted and received. To identify German spies British interrogators asked the results of famous cricket matches, the knowledge of which was costless to acquire for a genuine British man by simply living in the country, but hard to know and costly to memorize for even a well-trained German spy.

8.2.7 When signaling fails

Even without deception and even if the right cost conditions are present, there are still ways in which signaling can fail. In general, this is because signaling and asking for certain signals may reveal more than we would wish and thus prove confusing or backfire. I shall mention only two members of a larger family. To reflect on them is important, for it reveals some of the theory's limitations.

8.2.8 Social norms and conventions

Suppose you want to signal that you have a lot of energy. Does running around in circles persuade people that you do? It might, but it also persuades them that you are a very odd person. Or suppose that you want to persuade people that you have lots of financial resources: would, literally, burning a stack of banknotes persuade them? Once again it might, but it would also persuade them that you may also be mad. Or suppose further that you want to persuade a potential partner that you love them. Would giving them the equivalent in cash of the cost of an engagement ring serve the purpose? Which signals really work is not uniquely determined by the cost conditions posited by the theory. Signals that succeed need to be emitted within the constraints of what is acceptable, traditional, and considered normal. Nouveaux riches, for instance, by displaying their wealth prove they have it, but by doing so crassly they also display their uncouthness.

8.2.9 Receiver's demands

In the standard model the signaler chooses to send a signal somehow knowing the receiver has an interest in the information it conveys. But in a richer model the receiver herself when in doubt initiates the communicative exchange by probing and asking for further signals. But asking is not necessarily a neutral move. Consider the folk story of the woman who asks her fiancé to prove his love for her by bringing her his mother's heart. If he does, he signals that he is indeed prepared to do anything for her, but at the same time he gives a sign that he is a cruel man who stops at nothing to get what he wants. At the same time, by asking for such a love test she too gives a sign that she is a monster. Asking for a signal may lead us to say something about ourselves in the process which turns the signaler away. The signal can only work as intended if neither cares about the other's cruelty. To avoid side effects some shared understanding of what is permissible or acceptable to ask in the circumstance must exist. Often, when fishing for signals one pretends not to be, precisely to avoid offending the other.

8.3 APPLICATIONS

Without aiming to be exhaustive, I will now briefly describe the various fields of applications in descending order of the theories' popularity.

The longest strides, bridging theory and empirical research with equal vigor, have been made in studies of animal behavior and morphology, concerning mating, feeding, cooperation, and intra- and interspecific conflict. Here I have no space to dwell on this, while encouraging the reader to look up the excellent overview by Searcy and Nowicki (2005).

Signaling theory is now a fundamental part of microeconomics[8] and game theory. Various theoretical refinements have been published over the last twenty years (e.g. Cho and Kreps 1987; Kreps and Sobel 1994). Although to a lesser extent than in animal studies, several empirical tests have also been carried out: on Spence's early model of education as a signal of productivity (see Logren, Persson, and Weibull 2002 for a review and Kübler, Müller, and Normann 2005 for an experimental test), and on a variety of practices, such as product guarantees, financial markets, advertising,[9] charity donations (Glazer and Konrad 1996), and scientific publications funded by private firms (Belenzon and Patacconi 2008).

Recent theoretical developments in economics include[10] a model by Feltovich, Harbaugh, and To (2002), backed by some experimental evidence, which tries to explain a puzzle that is at once of interest to sociologists and may seem a challenge to signaling theory, so-called 'countersignaling':

> Why do the nouveaux riches flaunt their wealth, while the old rich scorn such gauche displays? Why do mediocre students often outperform talented students? Why are moderate quality goods advertised heavily, while high-quality goods rely on their reputation? Why do minor officials prove their status through petty displays of authority, while the truly powerful prove their strength by avoiding such displays?[11]

With respect to the standard model, two realistic modifications are introduced: first, in addition to low- and high-quality signalers there are medium-quality ones; next, receivers have additional incomplete information about the signaler's quality that is independent of the signal. For instance, the signaler's wealth is

> inferred not just from conspicuous consumption, but also from information about occupation and family background. This extra information is likely to be only partially informative, meaning that types of medium quality may still feel compelled to signal so as to separate themselves from low types. But even noisy information will often be sufficient to adequately separate high types from low types, leaving high types more concerned with separating themselves from medium types. Since medium types are signaling to differentiate themselves from low types, high types may choose to not signal, or countersignal, to differentiate themselves from medium types. While it might seem that the sender is just saving signaling costs by not signaling, we show that countersignaling can be interpreted as a signal of confidence that the extra information about the sender is favorable.[12]

In political science, apart from Jervis's early study (1970) written before signaling theory was first formalized, there have been both theoretical developments (e.g. Austen Smith and Banks 1998) and many applications.[13] The topics tackled using the theory range widely, and cannot possibly all be mentioned here. They include ways of credibly signaling foreign-policy interests (Fearon 1997); trying to explain why sometimes mass political action affects politicians' choices (Lohmann 1993); how different political arrangements can favor more discriminating signals of high-quality politicians (e.g. Besley 2005; Humphreys and Weinstein 2008); under what conditions bargaining mediators are credible (Kydd 2003); whether the size of terrorist attacks can be a signal of terrorist organizations' resources (Overgaard 1994); and whether the theory can shed light on ethnic mimicry (Habyarimana et al. 2007).

Anthropologists too have started to use signaling theory, especially to make sense of seemingly 'wasteful' or 'inefficient' practices in premodern cultures, such as redistributive feasts, big-yam displays, and hunting difficult prey. Closer to the interests of sociologists, they have also used the theory to investigate the cooperative effects of differentially costly rituals and requirements in religious groups (see e.g. Sosis and Bressler 2003). Making sense of established human practices, an understandable ambition, is arduous, for they are often sustained by a whole gamut of other mechanisms. Still, in this literature there is now much attention paid to measuring the payoffs of both signalers and receivers, and attempts at testing the theory against other hypotheses. A good overview of studies in anthropology is in Bliege Bird and Smith (2005).

Finally, in sociology, as I said, the use of signaling theory has been scant and not of uniformly high quality. On the theory front, Breen and Cooke (2005; cf. Breen's chapter in this volume), in an article on the marriage market, develop a model of simultaneous signaling by three types of men and three types of women, before women decide whether to marry. Raub (2004) has a model of 'hostage posting' as a signal of commitment aimed at inducing trust. The late Michael Bacharach (who was an economist) and I developed the analytical links between trust decisions and signaling theory, and extended the signaling model to cover identity signaling (Bacharach and Gambetta 2001) and identity mimicry (Gambetta 2005).

On the empirical front, Hamill (2001) tried to explain, in terms of status signaling within their group, the peculiar attraction that a group of deviant youth in West Belfast displayed for the punishment beatings they received from the IRA. Kaminski (2004), in an ethnographic study of Polish prisons, employs signaling theory to make sense of prisoners' self-harm and initiation rituals. Podolny (2005) makes some use of signaling theory, with reference to status interpreted as a signal of a firm's quality (see also the chapter by Podolny and Lynn in this volume). Hamill and I (2005) try to test some signaling-theory predictions on the signals taxi drivers rely on when deciding whether to pick up hailers or callers in Belfast and New York, which are both dangerous cities for drivers in which paramilitary and ordinary criminals pose as bona fide passengers. On trust and signaling there is also a recent experimental paper by Diekmann and Przepiorka (2007). Finally, I use the theory to explain criminals' strategies to identify bona fide criminals; the patterns of prison fights; and the use of self-harm among criminals (Gambetta 2009: ch. 5).

8.4 ORIGINS

Although as a formally defined and well-developed tool signaling theory is relatively young, in a loose sense the core idea has ancestors, the most notable of which is Thorstein Veblen's *The Theory of the Leisure Class* (see Fig. 8.3), published in 1899.[14] The idea came as a solution to a grand empirical puzzle: How can we explain the widespread occurrence of wasteful activities, self-harming practices, gifts, and nonanonymous altruism? How can we make sense of practices that do not produce material goods for the direct enhancement of well-being, but seem to waste useful goods, or waste the time that could be helpfully spent in productive activities? Why, was Veblen's question, should our fundamental instinct for workmanship, frugality, efficiency, and the pursuit of self-interest be violated on such a large scale by seemingly irrational and costly practices? (The question of waste is also at the centre of the theory in biology: 'The Handicap Principle is a very simple idea: waste can make sense, because by wasting one proves conclusively that one has enough assets to waste and more. The investment—the waste itself—is just what makes the advertisement reliable,' Zahavi and Zahavi 1998: 229.)

The analytical reach of the modern version of the theory has become broader, in that it includes, as we have seen, costs that are not produced only by wasteful use of resources, and its foundations have become deeper and more precise, capable of producing testable propositions. However, it is worth giving a brief account of the ancestors, not only because it is interesting as intellectual history, but because it reveals some of the pitfalls of using the theory which even some contemporaries still incur.

8.4.1 Veblen and his progeny

Veblen was at pains to make clear that he was using the term 'waste' as a 'technical term,' and 'for want of a better term': 'It is here called "waste" because this expenditure does not serve human life or human well-being on the whole, not because it is waste or misdirection of effort or expenditure as viewed from the standpoint of the individual consumer who chooses it' ([1899] 1994: 60).

His answer to the question of what waste is for relies on three assumptions: (i) we want more prestige rather than less; (ii) other people want to know how much of it we deserve; and (iii) prestige is, in contemporary societies, also a function of how much wealth we have. But since wealth is not an easily observable property of individuals and families, people display their real wealth by wasting time, goods, and money in a visible way, conspicuously that is:

> The growth of conspicuous leisure and consumption, it appears that the utility of both alike for the purposes of reputability lies in the element of waste that is common to

Thorstein Veblen 1899
Conspicuous consumption as
status signal

Marcel Mauss
1924
Gift giving

Thomas Schelling
1960
Threats and committments

Robert Jervis
1970
Signals in international
relations

Pierre Bourdieu
1972
Symbolic capital

Amotz Zahavi
1975
Various animal
behaviors

Michael Spence
1974
Market signaling

Alan Grafen
1990
Formalizes signals
as ESS

Economics

Biology

Other social
sciences

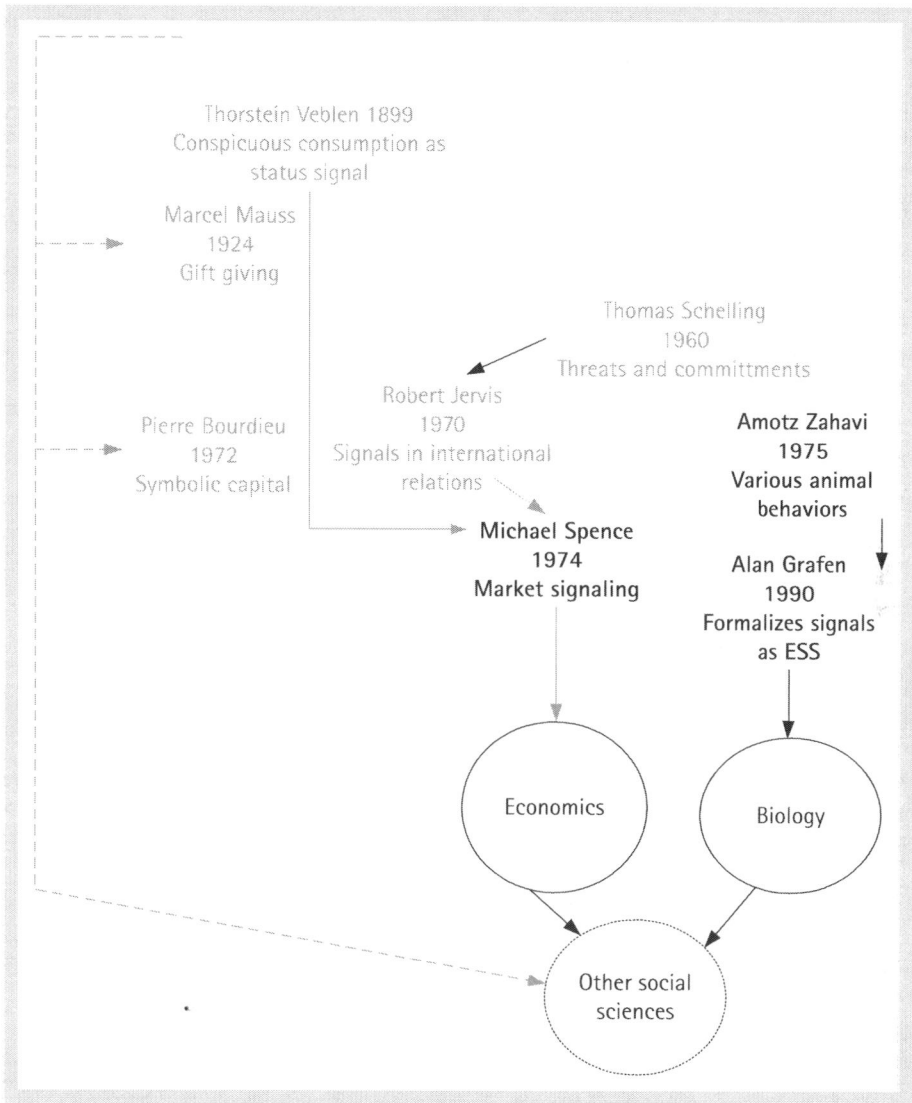

Fig. 8.3 Genealogy of signaling theory (ancestors in gray)

both. In the one case it is a waste of time and effort, in the other it is a waste of goods. Both are *methods of demonstrating the possession of wealth.*

([1899] 1994: 53, emphasis added)

Veblen tried to fit into his model a monumental array of human practices, from dress to artistic efforts, from religious objects to leisurely pursuits, from rituals to hedonistic activities. Nearly anything that does not serve basic economic purposes becomes a conspicuous way of informing others of one's wealth. While his book is still a brilliant read and an inspiration for new work (e.g. Bagwell and Bernheim 1996; Becker, Murphy, and Glaeser 2000), he has little to say on what his model cannot explain.[15]

Whether by influence or coincidence, Veblen's idea has progeny, which include Marcel Mauss and Pierre Bourdieu, and whose latest descendant is Eric Posner. In the *Essais sur le don* Marcel Mauss never cites Veblen, but his core observations bear a striking similarity to Veblen's theory:

> In some potlatch systems [in northwest America] one must spend everything one possesses and keep nothing. The highest prestige will be gained by the richest man who is also capable of squandering his wealth recklessly... Everything is conceived as if it was a 'war of wealth'... Sometimes it is not a question of giving and of receiving in return, but of destroying in order not even to appear desirous of receiving something back. Whole cases of candlefish or whale oil, houses, and blankets by the thousands are burnt; the most valuable coppers are broken and thrown into the sea in order to crush, 'flatten' a rival. In this way, not only does one improve one's position on the social ladder, but also that of one's family.   (Mauss [1924] 1954: 35)[16]

Bourdieu never mentions Veblen or Mauss, but in *Esquisse d'une theorie de la practique* ([1972] 1977), as well as later in *La Distinction*, he moves onto the same turf. Just like Veblen, and declaring himself to be reacting to reductive 'economism,' he wants to 'extend economic calculation to *all* the goods, material and symbolic, without distinction' (p. 178). 'Symbolic capital, in the form of the prestige and renown attached to a family and a name is readily convertible back into economic capital' (p. 179). The acquisition of prestige, he writes in reference to his fieldwork in Algeria, implies

> substantial material and symbolic investments, in the form of political aid against attack, theft, offence, and insult, or economic aid, which can be very costly, especially in times of scarcity. As well as material wealth, *time* must be invested... *giving or squandering time* being one of the most precious of gifts... [S]ymbolic capital can only be accumulated at the expense of the accumulation of economic capital.

> (Bourdieu [1972] 1977: 180)

Grand theory relying on the core idea has reemerged recently with Eric Posner's *Law and Social Norms* (2000). Posner attempts something very ambitious; namely, to explain social norms as signaling equilibria. He believes that the key property humans want to signal is their ability to postpone gratification. In the language of economics, this is referred to as the 'discount rate'; that is, how much a good is valuable tomorrow relative to its value today. Those who signal a low discount rate are perceived as better partners in repeated cooperative endeavours, for they feel relatively less tempted to cheat. Posner interprets an extravaganza of practices as signals of a low discount rate: manners, fashion, gift-giving, conspicuous consumption, marriage and family, obedience to law, shaming of criminals, deferred sex, unprotected sex, voting, patriotic displays, self-censorship, race discrimination, nationalism. He never cites Bourdieu, and mentions Mauss only once, in passing (p. 50), and Veblen in a footnote. However, as McAdams points out in an extensive critical essay, just like Veblen, 'at no point does [Posner] identify a particular norm or a type of norm behavior that his theories cannot explain' (2001: 654).

The manner in which the core idea of signaling is used by these authors shares a problem: they interpret anything that looks like waste of resources, anything that seems to contradict standard economic efficiency and has costs for the self-interested agent, as being motivated by the intent to signal either wealth or low discount rates. This tendency to explain too much before careful testing—aptly captured by the phrase 'when you have a hammer everything starts looking like a nail'—has a paradoxical consequence: it makes economic theory always true. This criticism does not apply to Veblen only but, as McAdams points out, to Posner too: 'If people refrain from costly behavior X, we say that they are maximising their utility by avoiding costs. But if people routinely engage in costly behavior X, we can now say that they are signaling their low discount rate and producing a net gain' (2001: 641). An analogous criticism has been voiced of Zahavi's rendition of the theory in biology: if a trait works cheaply and equally in everyone we can call it a standard Darwinian adaptation that maximizes fitness; if it is expensive and highlights individual differences we can call it a Zahavian adaptation that maximizes fitness via signaling. Together they 'explain everything and thus nothing' (Miller 1998: 345).

In theory there is nothing intrinsically wrong in the idea that waste can be a signal of wealth. Michael Spence deals with this in a chapter of his book: 'The status signalling model works, that is to say, signalling takes place, because the real opportunity costs of signalling via conspicuous consumption are negatively correlated with income, which is what consumption is supposed to signal' (1974: 68).

Generally, it is potentially fruitful to entertain the notion of symbolic capital as Bourdieu does; but one cannot proceed by fiat, for one needs criteria to separate what is investment in symbolic capital from costly human activities that have a different origin (cf. Cronk 2005: 609). We need criteria by which to establish how a practice can escape from this trap whereby everything that is real is, in one way or another, rational. What one can extend is not a conclusion, but a method that analyzes human action including waste with a presumption of rationality.

The solution to what Geoffrey Miller called 'the Panglossian temptation' is careful empirical design, which derives from the theory testable predictions liable to be disproved without assuming that all costly activities are *ipso facto* signals. We must obtain measures of the key variables—in particular the costs of the signal, and the benefits that accrue to both the signalers from the signal and the receivers in responding to a given signal. We could thus rule out, as McAdams writes, 'signalling claims when the measured returns were less than the measured costs' (2001: 641).

To test empirically whether people really spend their money on lavish objects to signal their wealth, whether they succeed and how, and who their audience really is and what it gains from responding in one way or another to the signal, for a start we could search for variations in Veblen's assumptions. For instance, we could test whether for domains in which wealth is not valued very much, and in which other properties confer prestige, as for example among academics or priests, we observe lower proportions of conspicuous expenditure. We could further measure whether domains in which wealth is more or less easily observable yield corresponding differences in conspicuous consumption. For instance, in Norway people can now see each other's income-tax returns online, while, say, in Southern Italy many are too engaged in the black economy (or, worse, in the 'black and blue' economy) for anyone to be able to easily know their real wealth, and people should thus spend proportionally a lot more than in Norway displaying it. Research along these lines is only just beginning (e.g. Kerwin, Hurst, and Roussanov 2007), and the extensive range of options that comes to mind with regard to wealth displays epitomizes the potential that this genuinely cross-disciplinary theory has in many other domains of human behavior.

Notes

1. An ESS is a strategy which, if adopted by a population of players, cannot be invaded by any alternative strategy. It is a Nash equilibrium which is 'evolutionarily' stable, meaning that once it is fixed in a population, natural selection alone is sufficient to prevent alternative (mutant) strategies from successfully invading.
2. This hypothesis is controversial; see, for instance, Buller (2005), who challenges the evidence for the cross-cultural applicability of the waist–hip-ratio preference.
3. Interview with Lt. Col. Tim Spicer, *Cambridge Review of International Affairs*, 13 (1) (1999), 165–71.
4. I am not the first to use this as an example of an extreme signal: see Austen Smith and Banks (2000).
5. 'One strong signal of commitment is a man's persistence in courtship. It can take the form of spending a lot of time with the woman [etc.] . . . These tactics are extremely effective in courting women as permanent mates, with average effectiveness ratings of 5.48 on a 7-point scale, but only a moderately effective 4.54 at courting casual sex partners. Furthermore, persistence in courtship proves to be more effective for a man than for a woman because it signals that he is interested in more than casual sex' (Buss 2003: 102).
6. The translated text of *Fasti* can be found online at A. S. Kline's free archive of poetry website, at <http://www.tonykline.co.uk/PITBR/Latin/OvidFastiBkSix. htm#BkVIJune9>, accessed 2008.
7. A related category of signals draws its cost from defying not the risk of the receiver's attack, but the risk posed by impersonal forces. Some games of daring come into

this category: teenagers in England for instance have been known to put their heads on the railway tracks and compete on who moves away last as the train approaches. Here they are all signalers and receivers of each other's actions. Modern technology allows youth to play this game of daring solo and film themselves, so as to build a lasting record-signal that they can display to a wider audience rather than only to witnesses. One such case ended up, briefly, on YouTube and was reported in the British press in January 2008; <http//:www.dailymail.co.uk/pages/live/articles/news.html?in_article_id=507592&in_page_id=1770>, accessed 2008.

8. An entertaining illustration from an economist's point of view can be found in Frank (1988: chs. 5–6).

9. See Bolton and Dewatripont (2005: 125–7) for an overview of these applications.

10. For another development concerning a phenomenon of interest to sociologists see Austen Smith and Fryer (2005) in which 'The key idea is that individuals face a two audience signaling quandary: behaviors that promote labor market success are behaviors that induce peer rejection.'

11. This quotation and the following one are taken from the authors' extended abstract available at <http://www.zhongwen.com/cs/index.html>, accessed 2008.

12. See also Daley and Green (2007), who generalize a signaling model in which the receiver is also partially informed of the qualities of the signaler by means other than the latter's costly signal, and has some idea of the signaler's 'grades'; that is, any imperfect public message about the signaler's type.

13. A sign of the theory's success is that a useful early book on asymmetric information models in political science by Banks (1991) is, at the time of writing this chapter, cited by nearly a hundred articles, according to Google Scholar.

14. Two ancestors of signaling theory are Thomas Schelling's *The Strategy of Conflict* (1960), in particular in his discussion of threats and credible commitments, and Robert Jervis's *The Logic of Images in International Relations* (1970). By contrast, Ervin Goffman—of whom most sociologists knee-jerkily think whenever the topic of signaling comes up—while of course dealing with communication, often brilliantly so, does not refer to the signaling principle, although he comes close. He circles around the problem of what he calls 'credibility' of statements (1969: 103 ff.), but does not offer the signaling principle as a solution. Following Schelling, he refers to 'commitment' (pp. 112–13), which is a different solution to the problem of credibility: rather than signaling that he has the property to do X, in commitment an agent finds a way to *bind himself* to do X at a later time. The closest Goffman got to signaling theory was to say the following (also quoted by Jervis):

> knowing that the individual is likely to present himself in a light that is favourable to him, the others may divide what they witness into two parts; a part that is relatively easy for the individual to manipulate at will, being chiefly his verbal assertions, and a part in regard to which he seems to have little concern or control, being chiefly derived from the expressions he gives off. The others may then use what are considered to be the ungovernable aspects of his expressive behaviour as a check upon the validity of what is conveyed by the governable aspects. ([1959] 1990: 18)

Goffman picks up one strand of ST by pointing out that people will not attend to easy-to-fake signals, such as words, but then points to their attempts to catch whether the others are truthful by observing giveaways, which would include emotional expressions (1969: 127).

15. For some penetrating criticisms of Veblen's theory see Veyne (1976: 94 ff.) and Elster (1983: 66 ff.).

16. Although I use the translation in the 1954 English edition as a basis, I have modified this quotation to make it more faithful to the original and correct some misinterpretations. For a modern study of gifts as economic signals see Camerer (1988).

REFERENCES

AUSTEN SMITH, D., and BANKS, J. F. (2000), 'Cheap Talk and Burnt Money', *Journal of Economic Theory*, 91: 1–16.

——and FRYER, R. (2005), 'An Economic Analysis of "Acting White" ', *Quarterly Journal of Economics*, 120 (2) 551–83.

BACHARACH, M. O. L., and GAMBETTA, D. (2001), 'Trust in Signs', in Karen Cook (ed.), *Trust in Society* (New York: Russell Sage).

BAGWELL, L. S., and BERNHEIM, B. D. (1996), 'Veblen Effects in a Theory of Conspicuous Consumption', *American Economic Review*, 86 (3): 349–73.

BANKS, J. S. (1991), *Signaling Games in Political Science* (New York: Harwood).

BECKER, G. S., MURPHY, K. M., and GLAESER, E. (2000), 'Social Markets and the Escalation of Quality: The World of Veblen Revisited', in G. S. Becker and K. M. Murphy (eds.), *Social Economics: Market Behavior in a Social Environment* (Cambridge, Mass.: Harvard University Press), 84–104.

BELENZON, S., and PATACCONI, A. (2008), 'Open Science as a Signaling Device: Evidence from Firm Publications', unpublished paper, March.

BESLEY, T. (2005), 'Political Selection', *Journal of Economic Perspectives*, 19: 3–60.

BLIEGE BIRD, R., and SMITH, E. A. (2005), 'Signaling Theory, Strategic Interaction, and Symbolic Capital', *Current Anthropology*, 46 (2): 221–48.

BOLTON, P., and DEWATRIPONT, M. (2005), *Contract Theory* (Cambridge, Mass.: MIT Press).

BOURDIEU P. [1972] (1977), *Outline of a Theory of Practice* (Cambridge: Cambridge University Press).

BREEN, R., and COOKE, L. P. (2005), 'The Persistence of the Gendered Division of Domestic Labour', *European Sociological Review*, 21 (1): 43–57.

BULLER, D. (2005), *Adapting Minds: Evolutionary Psychology and the Persistent Quest for Human Nature* (Cambridge, Mass.: MIT Press).

BUSS, D. M. (2003), *The Evolution of Desire: Strategies of Human Mating* (New York: Basic).

CAMERER, C. (1988), 'Gifts as Economic Signals and Social Symbols', *American Journal of Sociology Organizations and Institutions: Sociological and Economic Approaches to the Analysis of Social Structure*, 94 (supplement): S180–S214.

CHO, I. K., and KREPS, D. (1987), 'Signaling Games and Stable Equilibria', *Quarterly Journal of Economics*, 102: 179–221.

CRONK, L. (2005), 'The Application of Signalling Theory to Human Phenomena: Some Thoughts and Clarifications', *Social Science Information*, 44: 603–20.

DALEY, B., and GREEN, B. (2007), 'Market Signaling with Grades', unpublished paper, Graduate School of Business, Stanford University, December.

DIEKMANN, A., and PRZEPIORKA, W. (2007), 'Signaling Trustworthiness: Evidence from Lab Experiments', unpublished sociology paper, ETH Zurich, November.

ELSTER, J. (1983), *Sour Grapes* (Cambridge: Cambridge University Press).

FEARON, J. D. (1997), 'Signaling Foreign Policy Interests', *Journal of Conflict Resolution*, 41 (1): 68–90.

FELTOVICH, N., HARBAUGH, R., and To, T. (2002), 'Too Cool for School? Signalling and Countersignalling', *RAND Journal of Economics*, 33: 630–49.

FRANK, R. H. (1988), *Passions Within Reason* (New York: Norton).

GAMBETTA, D. (2005), 'Deceptive Mimicry in Humans', in S. Hurley and N. Chater (eds.), *Perspectives on Imitation: From Neuroscience to Social Science* (Cambridge, Mass.: MIT Press), ii. 221–41.

——(2009), *Codes of the Underworld: How Criminals Communicate* (Princeton, N.J.: Princeton University Press).

—— and HAMILL, H. (2005), *Streetwise: How Taxi Drivers Establish Customers' Trustworthiness* (New York: Russell Sage).

GLAZER, A., and KONRAD, K. (1996), 'A Signaling Explanation for Private Charity', *American Economic Review*, 86 (4): 1019–28.

GOFFMAN, E. [1959] (1990), *The Presentation of Self in Everyday Life* (London: Penguin).

——(1969), *Strategic Interaction* (Philadelphia, Pa.: University of Pennsylvania Press).

GRAFEN, A. (1990), 'Biological Signals as Handicaps', *Journal of Theoretical Biology*, 144: 517–46.

HABYARIMANA, J., et al. (2007), 'Placing and Passing: Evidence from Uganda on Ethnic Identification and Ethnic Deception', paper presented at the annual meeting of the American Political Science Association, Chicago, August.

HAMILL, H. (2001), 'Hoods and Provos: Crime and Punishment in West Belfast', D.Phil. thesis (Oxford University).

HUMPHREYS, M., and WEINSTEIN, J. (2008), 'Policing Politicians: Citizen Empowerment and Political Accountability in Uganda', unpublished manuscript, February.

JERVIS, R. (1970), *The Logic of Images in International Relations* (New York: Columbia University Press).

JOHNSTONE, R. A. (1997), 'The Evolution of Animal Signals', in J. R. Krebs and N. B. Davies (eds.), *Behavioural Ecology* (Oxford: Blackwell), 155–78.

KAMINSKI, M. (2004), *Games Prisoners Play* (Princeton, N.J.: Princeton University Press).

KERWIN, K. C., HURST, E., and ROUSSANOV, N. (2007), 'Conspicuous Consumption and Race', NBER working paper no. 13392, September.

KREBS, J. R., and DAVIES, N. B. (1998), *An Introduction to Behavioural Ecology* (Oxford: Blackwell).

KREPS, D. M. (1990), *A Course in Microeconomic Theory* (New York: Harvester Wheatsheaf).

—— and SOBEL, J. (1994), 'Signalling', in R. J. Aumann and S. Hart (eds.), *Handbook of Game Theory with Economic Applications* (Amsterdam: North-Holland), ii. 849–67.

KÜBLER, D., MÜLLER, W., and NORMANN, H. T. (2005), 'Job Market Signaling and Screening in Laboratory Experiments', *Games and Economic Behavior*, 64 (2008), 219–36.

KYDD, A. (2003), 'Which Side Are You On? Bias, Credibility and Mediation', *American Journal of Political Science*, 47 (4): 597–611.

LIVY (1912), *History of Rome*, trans. W. L. Roberts (New York: Dutton); at <http://www.perseus.tufts.edu/cgi-bin/ptext?lookup=Liv.++2.+12>, accessed 2008.

LOGREN, K. G., PERSSON, T., and WEIBULL, J. W. (2002), 'Markets with Asymmetric Information: The Contributions of George Akerlof, Michael Spence and Joseph Stiglitz', *Scandinavian Journal of Economics*, 104 (2): 195–211.

LOHMANN, S. (1993), 'A Signaling Model of Informative and Manipulative Political Action', *American Political Science Review*, 87 (2): 319–33.

McADAMS, R. H. (2001), 'Signaling Discount Rates: Law, Norms, and Economic Methodology', *Yale Law Journal*, 110: 625–89.

MAUSS, M. [1924] (1954), *The Gift: Forms and Functions of Exchange in Archaic Societies* (London: Cohen and West).

MILLER, G. F. (1998), 'Review of "The Handicap Principle" by Amotz and Avishag Zahavi', *Evolution and Human Behavior*, 19 (5): 343–47.

OVERGAARD, P. B. (1994), 'The Scale of Terrorist Attacks as a Signal of Resources', *Journal of Conflict Resolution*, 38 (3): 452–78.

PODOLNY, J. M. (2005), *Status Signals* (Princeton, N.J.: Princeton University Press).

POSNER, E. (2000), *Law and Social Norms* (Cambridge, Mass.: Harvard University Press).

RAUB, W. (2004), 'Hostage Posting as a Mechanism of Trust: Binding, Compensation, and Signaling', *Rationality and Society*, 16 (3): 319–65.

SCHELLING, T. (1960), *The Strategy of Conflict* (Cambridge, Mass.: Harvard University Press).

SEARCY A. W., and NOWICKI, S. (2005), *The Evolution of Animal Communication. Reliability and Deception in Signalling Systems* (Princeton, N.J.: Princeton University Press).

SINGH, D., and YOUNG, R. K. (2001), 'Body Weight, Waist-to-Hip Ratio, Breasts, and Hips: Role in Judgments of Female Attractiveness and Desirability for Relationships', *Ethology and Sociobiology*, 16: 483–507.

SOSIS, R., and BRESSLER, E. R. (2003), 'Cooperation and Commune Longevity: A Test of the Costly Signaling Theory of Religion', *Cross-cultural Research*, 37 (2): 211–39.

SPENCE, M. (1973), 'Job Market Signaling', *Quarterly Journal of Economics*, 87: 355–74.

—— (1974), *Market Signaling* (Cambridge, Mass.: Harvard University Press).

VEBLEN, T. [1899] (1994), *The Theory of the Leisure Class* (New York: Dover).

VEYNE, P. (1976), *Le pain et le cirque* (Paris: Seuil).

ZAHAVI, A. (1975), 'Mate Selection: A Selection for a Handicap', *Journal of Theoretical Biology*, 53: 205–14.

—— and ZAHAVI, A. (1998), *The Handicap Principle* (Oxford: Oxford University Press).

CHAPTER 9

NORMS

JON ELSTER

INTRODUCTION

THERE is no general agreement among scholars about how to define social norms. I shall stipulate a definition, which will be justified, I hope, by its rough correspondence with ordinary as well as scholarly usage and by its usefulness in generating questions and suggesting answers.

Consider two statements:

(1) Always wear black clothes in strong sunshine.
(2) Always wear black clothes at a funeral.

The first injunction is a matter of instrumental rationality, since the air between the body and the clothes circulates more rapidly when the garments are black. The second expresses a social norm, which has no obvious instrumental significance. The existence and importance of social norms cannot be doubted. The proximate causes involved in their operation, which will be the focus of this chapter, are reasonably well understood. Yet their ultimate origin and function (if any) remain controversial.

There is a pervasive tendency in much of the literature to view social norms as socially useful. Norms are supposed to be society's way of coping with market failures (Arrow 1971), a mechanism for internalizing externalities (Coleman 1990), or a welfare-maximizing device (Ellickson 1991). There are no doubt cases in which norms have these effects, and probably some cases in which they owe their existence to these effects. Yet against this Panglossian view I believe that many norms are sources of pointless suffering. When a small girl comes home crying because her friends ridicule her purchase of the wrong sort of pram for her doll, no useful function is served. Codes of honor and norms of revenge may cause more murders than they prevent. Anti-achievement norms (see below) are obviously not socially desirable. Moreover, many social norms that would be socially useful are in fact not observed, examples being the absence in overpopulated societies of a social norm to have few children or, in developed societies, the absence of a norm against driving an SUV. The fact that social norms seem to exist everywhere suggests that an evolutionary explanation might be forthcoming, but so far none has been proposed that goes beyond the just-so-story level.

Social norms are *social* both because they are maintained by the sanctions that others impose on norm violators and because they are shared—and known to be shared—with others. Their social character does not, however, violate methodological individualism. A social norm is simply a shared expectation that others will react to a given behavior in a way that is painful for oneself.

I distinguish social norms from *moral norms* in terms of the emotions sustaining them and the causal structures that link emotions to norm violations. I represent this distinction in Figure 9.1, which also includes the action tendencies of the emotions generated by norm violations.

As shown in Figure 9.1, the operation of social norms depends crucially on the agent *being observed by others*. The anticipation of being observed may cause her to abstain from the norm-violating behavior or to hide it carefully. Actually being observed may trigger one of the action tendencies of shame: hide, run away, or kill oneself (see my chapter on emotions, this volume). Thus, in 1997 six people killed themselves in France after being exposed as consumers of pedophiliac material: presumably the shame was too much to bear. Prior to the exposure, however, these people may have led more or less normal lives. The same comment applies to the American admiral who killed himself in 1996 when he was exposed as not entitled to the combat decorations he was wearing (Boyer 1996). In experiments, the mere display of two stylized eye-like shapes on the desktop background induces significantly more generous offers in a dictator game (Haley and Fessler 2005).

I also distinguish social norms from what I call the *quasi-moral norms* that are triggered by the agent *observing the behavior of others*. To see how these differ from social and moral norms, take the case of littering in the park. An agent following a moral norm will abstain from littering even when alone in the park. If she follows a quasi-moral norm and observes that others are carefully putting their ice-cream wrappers in their pockets or in a wastebasket, she will do so too even if she could drop it on the ground unnoticed. An agent who is subject only to a social norm will litter unless observed by others. The important research project of Ernst Fehr and his collaborators largely centers on the role of quasi-moral norms in generating cooperation, either by the mechanism of conditional cooperation or by that of punishment of noncooperators (see Elster 2005 for a survey).

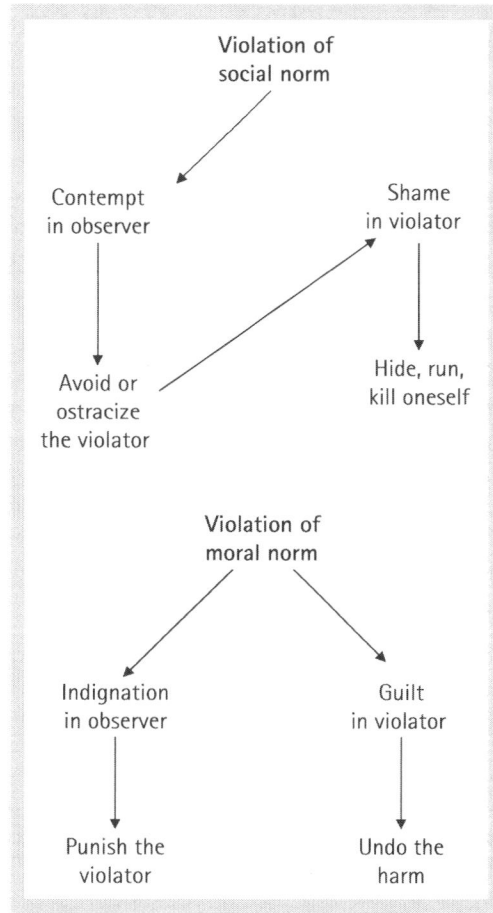

Fig. 9.1 Social and moral norms

I further distinguish social norms from *legal norms* by the fact that the latter depend on the existence of specialized enforcers rather than on the more diffuse sanctions that sustain social norms. To see how legal norms differ from social, quasi-moral, and moral norms, consider reactions to water scarcity in a community. As a legal measure, the municipal council may enact an ordinance forbidding watering lawns or filling up swimming pools, and send out inspectors to verify compliance. When there is a water shortage in California, social norms operate to make people limit their consumption. Indoor consumption, in particular, is monitored by visitors, who may and do express their disapproval if the toilet bowl is clean. In Bogotá, under the imaginative mayorship of Antanas Mockus, people followed a quasi-moral norm when reducing their consumption of water. Although individual monitoring was not feasible, the aggregate water consumption in the city was shown on TV. People complied when they observed that others were for the most part complying. A (weak) moral norm is presumed to operate when toilets have two push buttons dispensing different amounts of water for different uses.

I also distinguish social norms from *conventions*, in the sense explored by Schelling (1960) and Lewis (1969). An example is the convention regulating inter-rupted phone calls, according to which it is the person who made the call in the first place who is to call up again. Unlike legal and social norms, conventions do not, for their efficacy, require any kind of sanctioning of violators. Given the convention, it is in the self-interest of each agent to follow it.

Finally, I distinguish norms from *equilibria* in repeated games. Hume (1978: 520–1) spells out the following dilemma.

> Your corn is ripe to-day; mine will be so tomorrow. It is profitable for us both, that I should labour with you to-day, and that you should aid me to-morrow. I have no kindness for you, and know you have as little for me. I will not, therefore, take any pains upon your account; and should I labour with you upon my own account, in expectation of a return, I know I should be disappointed, and that I should in vain depend upon your gratitude. Here then I leave you to labour alone: You treat me in the same manner. The seasons change; and both of us lose our harvests for want of mutual confidence and security.

This dilemma can be resolved if the farmers know they will need each other's help over the indefinite future. Suppose farmer A's corn will be ripe in September and farmer B's in August. Then farmer A will help farmer B in August 2008 without being afraid that B will not help him in September 2008, since A knows that if B does not help him in September 2008 A will not help B in August 2009, and so on. This equilibrium is similar to a social norm in that it is sustained by sanctions. The conditionality of the equilibrium behavior—help your neighbor with his harvest if and only if he helped you with yours—is also found in some social norms, such as 'Send a Christmas card to your friend if and only if he sent one to you last Christmas.' The difference between an equilibrium strategy in repeated interactions and a social norm is that the former is outcome-oriented, while the latter is not. In an experimental study, Falk, Fehr, and Fischbacker (2005) found that nonstrategic sanctioning is more important than the strategic variety. Also, of course, many social norms are unconditional.

Analytically, these six categories are clearly distinguishable. In practice, they may converge on the same behavior. The rule of driving at (say) the right side of the road could, in theory, subsist as a mere convention. It is of course also a legal norm, a social norm (violators may be harassed by other drivers), a moral norm (a truck driver may be concerned about the welfare of those he might injure if he moved into the opposite lane to overtake another vehicle), and, possibly, a quasi-moral norm. An equilibrium may be enforced by social norms, as when a farmer who does not reciprocate with help in harvest time is ostracized by the local community.

Also, in some cases it may be impossible to tell whether a given norm is a social or a moral norm. If addressed to oneself, the question 'What if everybody did that?' expresses the moral norm of 'everyday Kantianism.' If addressed to others, it conveys a social norm. The line between indignation and contempt may, in a given case, be hard to draw. In principle, the first emotion targets an *action* and the second the *character* of the agent, but in the observer's mind the two may well go together. I shall mostly stay away from these complications, by focusing on relatively clear-cut cases of social norms, but they cannot be eluded altogether.

A final conceptual issue concerns the relation between social norms and *identity*. In my opinion, the explanatory value of the idea of identity remains to be established. Bracketing this question, and assuming that identity is somehow related to an agent's idea about what she ought to be and ought to do, it should be sharply distinguished from her idea about what others ought to do. Akerlof (2007: 8) and Akerlof and Kranton (2005: 12) systematically conflate these ideas.

9.1 THE OPERATION OF SOCIAL NORMS

On my account of social norms, they are maintained by the interaction of contempt in the observer of a norm violation and shame in the norm violator. It remains to spell out how this idea is related to that of sanctions. There are two main possibilities: either the expression of contempt *constitutes* a (nonmaterial) sanction, or the contempt *causes* the observer to impose material sanctions on the violator. Although I mainly subscribe to the first idea, I begin with the second and more commonly held one.

The action tendency of contempt is *avoidance* (see my chapter on emotions, this volume). Anticipated contempt generates what one might call *avoidance avoidance*; that is, abstaining from behavior that might trigger avoidance in the observer. Actual contempt, as explained above, generates shame and its associated action tendencies. One may also use the sharper term *ostracism*, which, however, is perhaps too close to *punishment* to capture the core reaction to violations of a social norm.

Avoidance behavior has the important potential for causing losses for both parties, if the observer refrains from undertaking mutually profitable interactions with the violator. In a traditional society, a father might let his daughter remain unmarried rather than consent to her marrying a man who has violated an important social norm. In a modern society, an employer might refrain from hiring a member of a minority group, not because he is racist but because he fears that other businessmen might think him a 'Jew-lover' or 'nigger-lover' and, as a consequence, refuse to deal with him.

Avoidance may go unnoticed by the norm violator, in which case it would not be capable of producing shame or of shaping behavior. This statement needs to be qualified, however, since it seems likely that some reactions to norm violations shape behavior by psychological reinforcement rather than by conscious perception. I have in mind, for instance, the culture-specific norms that define the appropriate 'interpersonal distance' in social interactions. If I come closer than (say) 50 cm to a person at a cocktail party, he or she may view my behavior as inappropriately aggressive or amorous and, as a consequence, take a step back. Although my conscious mind may fail to register the cause–effect relationship, repeated experience may induce a tacit knowledge of the norm.

Often, however, the victim of avoidance cannot fail to register the fact that others are avoiding him. 'Why didn't he accept my invitation or at least tell me he couldn't make it?' 'Why does nobody join me for lunch in the office cafeteria?' Moreover, very frequently the avoidance is accompanied by some verbal or nonverbal action signifying contempt. When the observer's contempt is observable, the target knows that he may incur material losses, as a result of being denied interaction opportunities. The anticipation of this eventuality may then deter him from violating the norm. When indignation and contempt blend or fuse together, the observer may impose a direct punishment on the violator (see my chapter on emotions, this volume). Anticipation of this possibility may also act as a deterrent.

The motivation behind this view of social norms is usually to turn norm-governed behavior into a species of rational behavior (see e.g. Coleman 1990: ch. 11). Norms, it is argued, shape behavior if and only if the material costs incurred by a norm violation exceed the material gains. Employers will hire members of minority groups if and only if their greater productivity or lower salaries more than offset the loss of contracts with firms that refuse to deal with such employers. In that case, however, we are immediately led to ask why these other firms would behave in this way. The first answer that comes to mind is that they punish because if they didn't they would be punished in turn. Among schoolchildren, a child might be more willing to interact with a 'nerd' when not observed by her classmates. In a society with strong norms of revenge one might expect that a person who fails to shun someone who fails to take revenge would himself be shunned.

In his discussion of the tyranny of the majority, Tocqueville (2004: 294) offered an eloquent analysis of such second-order avoidance behavior:

> The master no longer says: You will think as I do or die. He says: You are free not to think as I do. You may keep your life, your property, and everything else. But from this day forth you shall be a stranger among us. You will retain your civic privileges, but

they will be of no use to you. For if you seek the votes of your fellow citizens, they will withhold them, and if you seek only their esteem, they will feign to refuse even that. You will remain among men, but you will forfeit your rights to humanity. When you approach your fellow creatures, they will shun you as one who is impure. And even those who believe in your innocence will abandon you, lest they, too, be shunned in turn.

Yet if we go on to ask whether the nonshunners of the nonshunners would themselves be shunned, it is evident that the argument soon runs out of steam. Social life simply does not have this relentless transitivity. A child who abstains from joining the mob in harassing a child who is friendly towards the nerd is unlikely to be harassed. Experimentally, the question might be examined by seeing whether third parties would punish responders who, by accepting very low offers in an ultimatum game, fail to punish ungenerous proposers. I would be surprised if they did, and even more surprised if fourth-party observers punished nonpunishing third parties.

The signaling theory of social norms offers an alternative account of why people are willing to incur the costs of ostracizing others. To signal that they belong to a 'good' type, people have to engage in costly behavior, including not only costly gift-giving, but also 'the costly action of shunning people who act in an unusual way' (Posner 2000: 25–6). This argument seems inconsistent, however. The theory assumes that people who behave in unusual ways, by violating social norms, signal that they belong to a bad type. Since dealing with bad types is likely to be costly (they cheat, break promises, sell products of substandard quality, etc.), shunning them is likely to be *beneficial* rather than costly. That fact does indeed provide a reason for shunning them, but not the reason the theory claims to identify.

I believe that these instrumental considerations are misguided. When people shun first-order violators, most of the time they act emotionally and spontaneously, not to avoid punishment or to signal their type. Moreover, it is precisely by virtue of its spontaneity that such avoidance or punishment behavior is capable of inducing the strong feeling of shame in its targets. If the latter knew that their punishers were motivated merely by instrumental concerns, they might feel anger but surely not shame. Among writers not blinded by rational-choice theory there is a strong consensus that being the object of contempt causes an almost intolerable feeling of shame. Thus, Lovejoy (1961: 181, 191, 199) quotes Voltaire as saying that 'To be an object of contempt to those with whom one lives is a thing that none has ever been, or ever will be, able to endure. It is perhaps the greatest check which nature has placed upon men's injustice,' Adam Smith that 'Compared with the contempt of mankind, all other evils are easily supported,' and John Adams that 'The desire of esteem is as real a want of nature as hunger; and the neglect and contempt of the world as severe a pain as gout and stone.'

The emotional meaning of sanctions was recognized by Aristotle, who wrote that 'Shame is the imagination of disgrace, in which we shrink from the disgrace itself and *not from its consequences*' (*Rhetoric* 1384^a; emphasis added). In the seventeenth century, the English naturalist John Ray expressed the same ideas as follows:

> I cannot but admire the Wisdom and Goodness of God, in implanting such a Passion in the Nature of Man, as Shame, to no other Use or Purpose, that I can imagine, than to restrain him from vicious and shameful actions. . . . Now Dishonour is nothing else but men's ill opinion of me, or Dislike and condemnation of my Actions, in some way declared and manifested to me; which, why I should have such an Abhorrence of, and why it should be so grievous and tormenting to me, there seems to be not a sufficient Ground and Foundation in the Nature of Things, supposing such as have this Opinion have neither Power nor Will to hurt my body.
>
> (cited after Lovejoy 1961: 165)

In his discussion of this issue Nico Frijda (1986: 274) initially hesitates when he writes that 'Being rejected from the group and other forms of social isolation are potent sources of distress; they may lead to suicide or voodoo death. . . . However, they are perhaps to be understood as exemplars of loss of satisfying, or merely of familiar, conditions.' But the last suggestion can't be right: the emotional reactions of outcasts and of emigrants are not the same. The latter are affected only by their state of isolation from others, the former also and mainly by the way it is brought about. Later, Frijda (1986: 351) recognizes as much, when he writes that in western cultures 'social rejection constitutes severe punishment, and most likely not merely because of its more remote adverse consequences.'

Situations triggering social norms can involve three distinct costs: the material cost incurred by the ostracizer, the material cost incurred by the person who is ostracized, and the emotional suffering of the latter. Almost by definition, the intensity of the suffering caused by shame increases with the intensity of contempt. Plausibly, the best measure of the intensity of contempt is how much the ostracizer is willing to give up of material benefits. It follows that *the ostracized is worse off emotionally the more the ostracizer makes himself worse off materially*. If we accept the views of the authorities cited by Lovejoy, it also follows that from the point of view of the ostracized, the material loss he might suffer from the avoidance behavior matters less than the loss incurred by the ostracizer. What can be more humiliating than seeing that another person is willing to incur considerable expenses in order not to have to deal with me? All these effects are of course intensified if one is the target of *many* acts of ostracism, because then it is impossible to persuade oneself that the ostracizer simply acted out of irrational dislike.

To pursue the last observation, let me distinguish between high-stake dyadic interactions and low-stake triadic interactions, using the vendetta as an example. If B does something that can be interpreted as an insult to A or to A's family, the code of honor requires A to take revenge, often at considerable risk to himself. If A violates this norm, an observer C may react by avoiding or ostracizing A. Although C's reaction to A's perceived cowardice may not in itself amount to much, either in emotional or in material terms, the presence of other third parties D, E, F...that have the same reaction creates a multiplier effect. The sum total of many small 'acts of snubbing' may be devastating (Coleman 1990: 284). The person who fails to carry out a mandated revenge may suffer 'a thousand small insults' that amount to a kind of civic death (Busquet 1920: 357–8).

Obviously the physical presence of D, E, F, etc. on the scene is not necessary; what matters is that they somehow gain knowledge about A's failure to abide by the norm. Often, such knowledge is spread by *gossip*. In much of the literature on norms there is a tendency to explain the phenomenon of gossip by the benefits it brings to the collectivity, on the assumption that gossip is costly for the gossiper (Coleman 1990: 285; Ellickson 1991: 173; Fehr and Fischbacher 2002: 18). This appears to be a needless piece of functionalist reasoning. Casual observation suggests that people gossip because of the direct benefits it provides—it's *fun*. Or, as the French moralists would have it, gossip is due to the malignity and weakness·of human nature. According to La Rochefoucauld, 'If we had no faults we should not find so much enjoyment in seeing faults in others' (1665: maxim 31).

9.2 SOME IMPORTANT SOCIAL NORMS

Some of the statements and analyses proposed so far may seem excessively stark. While space does not allow for a full-scale treatment (for a wider range of examples see Elster 1989*a*; 1989*b*; 2007: ch. 22), a selective survey of some important or representative social norms will permit more nuanced views. These are

- Work norms
- Tipping norms
- Queueing norms
- Fairness norms
- Political norms

Work norms. I shall consider two well-studied instances of norms related to work: involuntary unemployment and rate-busting. Concerning the first, I shall discuss two separate arguments. In one, Clark (2003) tries—paradoxically but plausibly—to explain the persistence of unemployment by the 'norm of employment.' Although Clark does not define the term, it is clear from the context that he has in mind the stigma associated with unemployment. The more strongly felt the stigma, the more eager the individual will be to seek employment. In addition—and this is the central piece of causal machinery in the argument—the higher the rate of unemployment in the individual's reference group, the lower the stigma. (An experimental confirmation of this tendency is found in Gächter and Fehr 1999.)

Thus, if an external shock throws a large number of individuals out of work, the very fact that there are so many of them might reduce their incentive to get back to work, so that unemployment might persist even when economic conditions improve (hysteresis).

Another argument addresses the question of why the unemployed do not seek employment by underbidding the employed workers. In a complex model, Akerlof (1980) argued that behavior is guided by three forces: ordinary economic utility, 'custom' (social norms), and a concern for reputation that may be damaged by disobeying the custom. One such custom may be a norm prohibiting employers from hiring workers at lower wages because each of his current workers would refuse to train them, as 'by doing so he would suffer a loss of reputation according to the norms of his society.' The model also incorporates changes in the custom over time as a result of the interaction between those who believe in the norm and those who obey it without believing in it.

Subsequently, Lindbeck and Snower (1988) argued that involuntary unemployment can occur by virtue of 'insiders' issuing rational threats to harass 'outsiders' hired at lower wages. In response, several authors (Elster 1989b; Fehr 1990; Naylor 1994) claimed that since harassment is costly and thus generates a free-rider problem, this threat would not be credible unless sustained by a social norm. In response, Lindbeck and Snower (2001: 179) claim that 'These assertions do not hold water when insiders also threaten to harass colleagues who cooperate with, or do not harass underbidding outsiders,' thus neglecting the issue whether *that* threat would be any more credible.

Although Akerlof (2003: 28) asserts that he accepts the insider–outsider theory, his acceptance is contradicted by his assimilation of harassing underpaid outsiders to harassing overperforming rate busters. Summarizing a classic study by Roy (1952) of an Illinois machine shop where 'insiders established group norms concerning effort and colluded to prevent the hiring of rate-busting outside workers,' Akerlof claims that 'workers who produced more than the level of output considered "fair" were ostracized by others.' Although Akerlof's rendering of Roy's study is inaccurate in several respects, the norm against rate-busting is indeed a central idea in the original work. The argument the workers in Roy's shop used to justify the norm was that rate-busting would induce management to lower piece-rates, so that everybody would have to run faster and faster to stay in the same place. Management, it seems, has no credible way of precommitting itself to maintaining piece-rates if workers put in a greater effort.

This example may provide a case of an externality-induced norm. Each worker who exceeds the standard increases by some small amount the probability that management will reduce piece-rates, to the detriment of everybody. Although her effort may be individually rational, it is collectively undesirable. In any given case, however, one would have to consider whether the ostracism might not be due to *envy* felt towards hard-working workers. The *anti-achievement norm,* 'Don't stick your neck out,' known from small towns everywhere (Sandemose 1936; Thomas 1973: 43) might also operate in the workplace, and the alleged ratchet effect (Carmichael and MacLeod 2000) might be no more than a rationalization of this response.

Tipping norms. Tipping for service is not a negligible phenomenon (Azar 2007). Estimates of tips in US restaurants range from 5 billion to 27 billion dollars a year; adding tips to taxi drivers, hairdressers, and the other thirty or so professions in which tipping occurs would yield a larger figure. Estimates of the fraction of income that waiters derive from tips range from 8 percent (the IRS assumption) to 58 percent for waiters serving full-course meals. In some contexts tipping may seem puzzling, in others less so. If you go to the same hairdresser each time you need a haircut, you tip to ensure good service; the same applies for meals in your favorite restaurant. These behaviors are plausibly seen as equilibria in iterated interactions. Tipping in one-shot encounters, such as a taxi ride or a meal in a restaurant you do not expect to visit again, is more paradoxical. These behaviors are in fact doubly puzzling: they cannot be sustained by two-party interaction over time, nor by third-party sanctions at the time of the encounter. If you are the only passenger in the taxi, other people are rarely in a position to know whether you tip the taxi driver adequately, nor are other customers in the restaurant likely to notice how much you tip your waiter. In the following I limit myself to such cases.

As in other cases (harassing rate busters or outsiders, voting in national elections), rational choice and social norms have been offered as alternative explanations of tipping. Tipping, it has been argued, is an efficient way of remunerating waiters (Jacob and Page 1980). It is obviously easier for the client to monitor the quality of service than it is for the restaurant owner. Hence, decentralizing the monitoring function and linking reward to observed performance is a way of overcoming the 'principal–agent problem' (how to prevent workers from shirking) that besets many contractual relationships. Tipping, therefore, might be part of an 'implicit contract' for the purpose of enhancing efficiency. This explanation of management behavior leaves customer behavior unexplained, however. Given that customers tip as a function of the quality of service, delegating the monitoring of the service to the customer makes sense, but why would customers tip at all? Moreover, the argument fails to explain the common norm in many restaurants that waiters should pool their tips. Finally, it cannot explain why we tip an independent taxi driver who has no boss to report to.

A social-norm explanation obviously cannot rely on avoidance and ostracism in these one-shot interactions. Instead, it can cite the fact that people simply do not like the idea that others, for example a disappointed taxi driver, might disapprove of them, even if they do not expect to meet them again. Being the object of the contemptuous stare of the other is not necessary. It may be enough simply to know or have reason to believe that the other feels contempt. In the words of Conlin, Lynn, and O'Donoghue (2003: 311), perhaps a tipping restaurant customer simply 'dislikes having someone disapprove of her, even someone with whom she will never interact again.'

Queueing norms. Like the workplace, the queue is a norm-ridden social system. At the same time, the queue is a transient phenomenon, unlike the workplace, which, as an ongoing entity, would seem to have much greater potential for sanctioning. Before I proceed to discuss queueing norms, let me pursue this contrast for a moment.

It is probably a common intuition that norms have less impact on behavior in communities with high turnover.

> Men who live in democracies are too mobile to allow some group of them to establish and enforce a code of etiquette. Each individual therefore behaves more or less as he pleases, and manners are always to some extent incoherent because they are shaped by each individual's feelings and ideas rather than conforming to an ideal model held up in advance for everyone to imitate.   (Tocqueville 2004: 711–12; see also p. 736)

Earlier, I referred to the small-town norm of 'Don't stick your neck out,' with the implication that in more anonymous interactions deviant behavior would be less severely sanctioned. In light of this intuition, it is interesting that as communities grow larger and more mobile, we observe the emergence of *norms regulating the behavior among strangers*. This remark strengthens the interpretation of norms in terms of emotion rather than material sanctions. Under most circumstances, it is difficult to impose material sanctions on a person who violates a queue norm. People can give full rein, however, to expressions of contempt or indignation.

There is a norm, I believe, against walking up to the person at the head of a bus queue and offering him or her money in exchange for the place (for evidence, see Shiller, Boycko and Korobov 1991: 393). This norm is obviously inefficient: if the person who is asked accepts to move to the back of the line in exchange for the money, both agents benefit and nobody is hurt. According to Tocqueville (2004: 204), such norms against open display of wealth in public are specific to democratic societies: 'Do you see this opulent citizen? ... His dress is simple, his demeanor modest. Within the four walls of his home, luxury is adored.' There may also be an underlying idea that the use of queueing is a valuable counterweight to the pervasive use of money in allocating scarce goods. To prevent the rich from getting everything, ordinary citizens might prefer to have some goods be allocated by a mechanism that puts the rich at a disadvantage, because of their greater opportunity costs of queueing (Calabresi and Bobbit 1978: 93).

In communist Poland, where queueing was endemic, there was no norm against purchasing a place in a queue (Hrada 1985), probably because this practice was seen as one of many necessary forms of jockeying for position. Other forms included hiring people to stand in line for oneself or moving back and forth between several queues while asking people in each of them to 'hold the place.' (We may note in passing the Pareto inefficiency of the latter practice.) There were norms regulating these activities, and deviations were sanctioned. A surprising norm was the rule against reading while queuing. '[W]omen do not want to be told, even by implication, that they are actually wasting time in queues. If one reads or works in the queue, this implicitly reminds others that they are wasting time. The response is to scold the deviant, putting the reminder out of sight and mind' (Hrada 1985: 396). In addition, people reading or working would shirk their duty of monitoring violations of queue norms.

A different kind of violation occurs when someone intrudes in a queue, whether at the head of the line or somewhere in the middle. In this case, negative reactions of other people in the queue (behind the intruder) might be due to considerations of cost, be it in the form of time costs or (if they are queueing for a scarce good) material costs. Alternatively, they might be due to outrage or indignation. Milgram et al. (1986) and Schmitt, Dubé, and Leclerc, (1992) find that although both factors may be at work, subjects usually have a stronger reaction to illegitimate intrusions than to legitimate ones that impose equal costs. (A telling fact in both these studies is that the confederates of the experimenter who were asked to intrude in the queue felt the task to be highly aversive.) There is often a norm to the effect that responsibility for rejecting intruders lies with the person immediately behind him or her (Mann 1969: 348; Milgram et al. 1986: 688). In Australian football queues, more people jump the queue during the hours of darkness, because 'the knowledge that one cannot be seen easily undermines social pressure and shaming as a technique' (Mann 1969: 347).

There are also norms regulating place-holding in queues. In my supermarket, the norm seems to be that it is acceptable to leave the shopping cart in the line to go to pick up one item from the shelves, but not several. In Australian football queues 'the norm in leaving position markers is that one must not be absent for periods longer than two to three hours' (Mann 1969: 346).

As a transition to the next set of norms, let me note the trade-off between efficiency and perceived justice in queues. Although it would often be more efficient if most people placed a marker in the queue and then went home for a while, this practice would violate equality since the people who remained in the queue to maintain it would be disfavored (Mann 1969: 345). The basic principle of fairness in queueing, 'First in, first out,' can be violated when there are multiple and independent queues. Thus, reported customer satisfaction is higher in the single-queue Wendy's restaurants than in the multi-queue Burger King and McDonald's restaurants, although the latter average half the waiting time of Wendy's (Larson 1987: 896). At Houston airport, customers with checked luggage complained about the baggage delay (a 1-minute walk to the carousel and a 7-minute wait at the carousel), compared to passengers with hand luggage who could proceed directly to the taxi stand. When the airport authorities changed the disembarking location so that all customers had to walk six minutes, complaints dropped to nearly zero (ibid. 897).

Fairness norms. Many fairness norms are quasi-moral rather than social norms. The person who watches TV in Bogotá and tells herself that 'since most people are consuming less water, it is only fair that I should do so too' is abiding by a quasi-moral norm. Other forms of such conditional compliance include voting in national elections and reporting one's income correctly to the tax authorities. In the following I shall be concerned with some of the social norms of fairness observed in the labor market.

Kahneman, Knetsch, and Thaler (1986) recorded perceived fairness by asking subjects over the telephone to assess the fairness of various economic transactions. One pair of vignettes was the following:

> **Question 2A**: A small photocopying shop has one employee who has worked in the shop for six months and earns $9 per hour. Business continues to be satisfactory, but a factory in the area has closed and unemployment has increased. Other small shops have now hired reliable workers at $7 an hour to perform jobs similar to those done by the photocopy shop employee. The owner of the photocopying shop reduces the employee's wage to $7.
>
> (N = 98)   Acceptable 17%   Unfair 83%
>
> **Question 2B**. A small photocopying shop has one employee ... [as in Question 2A] ... The current employee leaves, and the owner decides to pay a replacement $7 an hour.
>
> (N = 125)   Acceptable 73%   Unfair 27%

The responses demonstrate the importance of *entitlements* in perceptions of justice. What exists easily acquires a normative force merely by existing. At the first day of a conference each participant may find his or her seat more or less randomly. On the second day a convention has been created: people converge to their chosen seats because this is the obvious (focal-point) allocative mechanism. On the third day the convention has hardened into an entitlement norm: I get angry if another participant has taken 'my' seat.

Similar norms exist in employment relations, as shown by the responses to these vignettes:

> **Question 9A**. A small company employs several workers and has been paying them average wages. There is severe unemployment in the area and the company could easily replace its current employees with good workers at a lower wage. The company has been making money. The owners reduce the current workers' wages by 5 percent.
>
> (N = 195)   Acceptable 23%   Unfair 77%
>
> **Question 9B**. ... [as in Question 9A] The company has been losing money. The owners reduce the current workers' wages by 5 percent.
>
> (N = 195)   Acceptable 68%   Unfair 32%

These and other findings show that there is a reference norm of wages, a reference norm of profits, but that in the case of conflicts the latter takes precedence over the former. The last intuition is probably shaped by the (apparent) fact that if the firm is not allowed to lower wages in bad economic times it may go bankrupt and thus not be able to pay any wages at all. Yet the norm creates a problem of moral hazard, if management knows that in the case of a bad result they can always make the workers pay for the losses. This fact may explain why Sweden adopted the Rehn-Meidner system of 'equal pay for equal work' across firms in an industry, combined with generous retraining programs for workers if their firm goes bankrupt.

At the same time, the reference norm for wages has been put in question. In classical capitalism, firms did not suffer from paying wages above the going rate, as long as they posted satisfactory—albeit not maximal—profits. In the era of hostile takeovers, however, firms that do not maximize are at risk. There is nevertheless a widely shared social norm that profitable firms should not dismiss workers or reduce their wages. In France, the announcement by Michelin in 1999 that the firm was laying off 451 workers in one factory while making record profits created a huge outcry. In 2005 France adopted 'satisficing' legislation that prevents firms from laying off workers unless it is necessary to 'safeguard' profits (Cahuc and Carcillo 2007).

In a field study of wage negotiations between school boards and teachers' unions in Pennsylvania, Babcock, Wand, and Loewenstein (1996) demonstrated that real-life negotiators make a *strategic use* of the norm of fairness. They asked negotiators on both sides in 500 school districts to name districts comparable to their own for the purpose of determining a fair wage. In their analysis of the 75 districts in which they obtained a response from each side they found that school boards tended to choose districts with lower wages for teachers than the wages in districts chosen by the unions. They found a similar self-serving bias in the responses to a question whether the teachers in neighboring districts or nonteachers in the same district were the most relevant group. Moreover, the greater the discrepancy between the choices of the school board and those of the unions, the greater the likelihood of a strike in that district, confirming the experimental results of Babcock, Wand, and Loewenstein (1995).

Political norms. Usually the study of social norms does not include political behavior. I shall look at a subset of political norms, (unwritten) constitutional *conventions* (Avril 1997; Jaconelli 1999, 2005) to argue that some of them fall under the heading of social norms as defined here. At the same time, I argue that other constitutional conventions are more plausibly seen as conventions in the Schelling-Lewis sense or as equilibria in repeated games. (In the following I use 'convention' to refer to constitutional conventions and 'Schelling-Lewis convention' to refer to that particular idea.) Although the space allocated to this topic may seem surprising, I believe it is warranted precisely by the fact that it is almost completely ignored in the literature on norms.

Almost all contemporary countries have a written constitution. Great Britain is the main exception. In that country, conventions form the tacit yet robust framework of political life (Turpin 2002). The following conventions are representative. The monarch cannot refuse to sign a bill that has been passed by both Houses of Parliament. Assent has not been withheld since 1708. Parliament should meet at least once a year. The House of Lords does not originate any money bills. When the House of Lords acts as an appellate court, only Law Lords take part. Conversely, Law Lords stay away from politically contentious matters. The House of Lords does not vote against the principle of a bill that has been announced in the manifesto of the governing party. The Prime Minister must be a member of the House of Commons. The Cabinet cannot instruct the Attorney General. The rules of parliamentary procedure require some degree of fair play between the majority and the minority, for example in the assignment of committee seats and of speaking time.

Conventions can stand in one of three relations to the written document: canceling it, violating it, or supplementing it. If the constitution says that an organ is allowed (but not required) to take certain actions, a convention may forbid it from doing so. In Canada and Australia, the Governor-General cannot exercise his legal power to dismiss the Prime Minister and to veto legislation. In neither country is the Senate allowed to use its constitutional right to veto money bills. In the French Third Republic, a convention was established almost from the beginning that the President could not exercise his constitutional right to dissolve Parliament. In the USA, there seems to be a convention that Congress cannot use its constitutional right to limit the jurisdiction of the Supreme Court.

If the constitution requires that a certain action only be done in a certain way, a convention may violate the constitution by allowing it to be done otherwise. I only know of two clear-cut cases, both from France. After de Gaulle, contrary to the constitutional clauses regulating amendment, submitted an amendment to the constitution to popular referendum in 1962, there is now (probably) a convention allowing this to happen. In France, it has also become accepted that there may be proxy voting by members of the *Assemblée Nationale*, notwithstanding that Article 27 of the 1958 Constitution provides that the right to vote is personal.

If the constitution has a gap, it may be filled by a convention. In Norway (until recently) and in the Netherlands, the basic principle of parliamentarianism—that the government must step down if it receives a vote of no confidence—has been a matter of convention only. The right of the US Supreme Court to review the constitutionality of federal laws and of the Norwegian Supreme Court to review laws passed by Parliament exists only by convention. The Canadian principle that a member of the opposition chairs the parliamentary committee that oversees public accounts (Heard 1991: 79) and the Australian principle that an incoming government does not open the archives of its predecessor (Cooray 1979: 71) obtain by convention. Until 1940 there was a convention in the USA that no one could be president for a third successive term. In that country there is a convention that all members of a state delegation to the electoral college vote for the candidate who received most votes in their state.

Before I proceed to an analysis of the mechanisms sustaining these norms, let me briefly mention the unwritten 'fundamental laws of France' (Mousnier 1996: i. 503–5) that were in effect until 1789. The most important was perhaps the Salic law: upon the death of the monarch the crown passes to the closest legitimate male relative in the male line. Arguably, this law operated as a Schelling-Lewis convention to prevent civil war, just as the convention of driving on the right side of the road serves to prevent accidents:

> The most unreasonable things in the world become the most reasonable because men are so unbalanced. What could be less reasonable than to choose as ruler of a state the oldest son of a queen? We do not choose as captain of a ship the most highly born of those aboard. Such a law would be ridiculous and unjust, but because men are, and always will be, as they are, it becomes reasonable and just, for who else could be chosen? The most virtuous and able man? That sets us straight away at daggers drawn, with everyone claiming to be most virtuous and able. Let us then attach this qualification to something incontrovertible. He is the king's eldest son: that is quite clear, there is no argument about it. Reason cannot do any better, because civil war is the greatest of evils.   (Pascal 1991: *Pensée* no. 786)

Few constitutional conventions, however, are conventions in the Schelling-Lewis sense. The classical view was that constitutional conventions are upheld by the 'blame or unpopularity' (Dicey 1915: cxlii) that will attach to anyone who violates them. More specifically, the 'remedy for alleged convention-breaking is generally recognized to be, in the main, political. Either the government can be shamed by publicity and political debate into conceding error or changing its course of action, or its misdeeds can be made the subject of argument at the next General Election' (Marshall 1986: 27). Although many conventions are, as we shall see, enforced in this way, there is also an important set of conventions that are related to the fundamental fact of modern democracies that political parties *alternate in power*. They are upheld by long-term self-interest rather than by fear of blaming and shaming.

These conventions have the structure (more or less) of a repeated prisoner's dilemma. Each political party would, when in power, prefer to use its power to the hilt, were it not for the fact that its successor could then be expected do the same. I have already cited two modern conventions to this effect: the practice of not opening the archives of the previous government and the fair allocation of committee seats and speaking time in parliament. The reason why Congress abstains from using its power to limit the jurisdiction of the Supreme Court may be that 'once one political faction uses certain means that threaten judicial independence, other factions will be more willing to use those devices in the future' (Wilson 1992: 693). Similar conventions in Canada and Norway ensure that a member of the opposition chairs the parliamentary committee overseeing the government. In France, there may now be an emerging convention that a member of the opposition chairs the finance committee.

Other constitutional conventions conform more closely to the views I cited from Dicey and Marshall. They are, I believe, nothing but social norms applied to political behavior. For an example, consider the following description of what might happen to someone who violated the convention regulating members of the electoral college:

> There has been no instance within living memory of any failure to obey the party's behest, but everyone is agreed that, if such a thing happened, the culprit, however technically innocent of any violation of the law, would suffer severe penalties. According to Professor J. A. Woodburn, any Presidential Elector who voted independently for a candidate of his own choice 'would probably not find it comfortable to return home.' He 'would be ostracized and despised and would be visited with the social condemnation and contempt due to one who had been guilty of an infamous betrayal of public trust; and a Presidential candidate elected by such betrayal would probably not accept the office.' Benjamin Harrison, indeed, goes so far as to predict that 'an Elector who failed to vote for the nominee of his party would be the object of execration, and in times of very high excitement might be the subject of a lynching.'   (Horwill 1925: 37–8)

The crucial question (see below) is whether such a person would be ostracized even by those who shared his preference for the candidate in question.

For another example, consider what would happen to someone who violated the convention against a third-term presidency. This rule was mainly enforced by the nominating bodies, on the assumption that a candidate who violated it was unlikely to be elected. Yet direct action was also possible. When Theodore Roosevelt stood for a third term after a split in the Republican Party, which had failed to nominate him, feelings ran high. On one of his speech-making tours, Mr Roosevelt was shot at by a man of unbalanced mind, who said: 'I shot Theodore Roosevelt because he was a menace to the country. He should not have a third term. I shot him as a warning that men must not try to have more than two terms as President' (Horwill 1925: 95). Once again, this motivation is consistent with the belief that Roosevelt would have been the best person for the position.

Voting can provide a very effective sanctioning mechanism for the violation of political norms. Moreover, under conditions of the secret ballot voters cannot have an instrumental motive (the fear of being sanctioned for not sanctioning). Before the introduction of the secret ballot, that motive may sometimes have operated. General Grant declined to run for President for a third term, fearing that the voters would punish him for violating the two-term convention by turning against him. It is at least conceivable (although in my view improbable) that the voters would have voted against him because they would have been afraid of being observed (and sanctioned for) voting for him.

By the time Theodore Roosevelt stood for a third term, and was defeated, the secret ballot had been introduced for presidential elections. The reason for his defeat may have been the violation of the two-term convention. The example is not unambiguous, however, since it was doubly unclear whether he *was* violating the convention: he had only been *elected* once before (his first term began when he was Vice-President and the President died) and he was not standing for a third term *in a row*. I do not know of any clear-cut cases.

Yet even if there were clear-cut cases in which a candidate who violated a convention was defeated, it does not follow that he was defeated *for* violating the convention. This raises an issue mentioned earlier, whether even those who shared his substantive preferences would ostracize a defector from the electoral college. When voters confront a candidate or a policy proposal that violates a convention, they have to weigh the procedural importance they attach to the convention against their substantive preferences. A negative vote might be due mainly to the latter, in which case the norm against violating the convention would do no causal work. Some might claim that except in extreme cases substantive preferences will always trump procedural preferences. Yet this idea is hard to square with the fact that in 1896 the two-term convention was sufficient for the Democrats to deny the nomination to their best candidate. They clearly thought, and we'd be hard put to say that they were wrong, that voters would be very attentive to a violation of the convention.

Politicians routinely claim that electoral victory in procedurally contested cases vindicates their behavior. In 1975, the Labor government in Australia had a majority in the Lower House, while the Liberals and their allies from the Country Party had a majority in the Senate (Cooray 1979). The Senate had delayed voting the budget, which by convention it is required to accept without amendments. The Governor-General then called new elections, which by convention he is not allowed to do. The elections resulted in a Liberal landslide. The Liberal/Country Party throughout the election campaign asked the people to focus on economic issues and not the constitutional ones, but after the election claimed that the people had spoken and justified the actions of the Senate and the Governor-General. In 1962, de Gaulle read the outcome of the referendum as (i) the adoption of the direct election of the President, (ii) an approval of constitutional amendment by referendum, and (iii) a vote of confidence in himself.

9.3 SOCIAL NORMS VERSUS OTHER MOTIVATIONS TO ACT

The set of human motivations is a pie that can be sliced in many ways. In other writings (Elster 1999, 2007) I have used the trichotomy interest/reason/passion to contrast the motivational bases of different behaviors. For the present purposes

I shall contrast social norms with presocial ('raw') emotions and with consequentialist motivations.

I have argued that social norms are ultimately sustained by the emotions of contempt (or indignation) and shame. Yet the influence of emotion on behavior is much larger than the impact mediated by social norms. Emotion-induced vengeance, for instance, is not limited to revenge induced by social norms. If I stumble over a stone and hurt my foot, I may kick it in return, thus compounding the pain. Social norms may amplify the spontaneous desire for revenge, as they do in societies guided by codes of honor, or dampen it, as in societies that profess the norm of turning the other cheek.

Each society, in fact, has a normative hierarchy of motivations that include some emotional states. In classical Athens, for instance, it seems that motivations to act were ranked in roughly the following order. First came patriotism in defense of the city; then came the desire for glory in competitive activities, from athletics to playwriting; next came vengeance; then self-interest; and at the bottom we find envy and hubris (the desire to humiliate others). Such metamotivations can induce a strong pressure to hide one's emotion from others or even from oneself (Elster 1999: ch. 5). Thus, envy is often transmuted into the more acceptable feeling of righteous indignation, or self-interest misrepresented as a desire for revenge. According to Tocqueville (2004: 611), the Americans he met were 'pleased to explain nearly all their actions in terms of self-interest properly understood. They will obligingly demonstrate how enlightened love of themselves regularly leads them to help one another out and makes them ready and willing to sacrifice a portion of their time and wealth for the good of the state.' This 'norm of self-interest' (Miller 1999) may still be at work in American society.

In many cases, social norms and consequentialist motives pull in opposite directions. Although acting rationally for the sake of one's material self-interest is one consequentialist motive, it is far from the only one. Even when acting in a consequentialist mode, people may be prone to 'cold' cognitive mistakes (Gilovich, Griffin, and Kahneman 2002). Also, consequentialist reasoning may be perfectly other-regarding, as when I ask myself which charitable institution will best ensure that my donations go to the needy rather than to bureaucrats or dictators. Finally, self-interest may be associated with immaterial goods such as posthumous fame or salvation. For simplicity, however, I shall limit myself to the issue of 'social norms versus the rational pursuit of material self-interest' or, for short, 'norms versus interest.'

I have argued against the idea that norms can be *reduced* to interest, in the sense that norm followers are 'nothing but' rational sanction avoiders. This is not to deny that people often take steps to avoid sanctions, by refraining from a forbidden act, by hiding it, or by performing a mandatory one. What I resolutely deny is the idea that the sanctioners have a consistently consequentialist motivation. The infinite regress involved in individuals sanctioning each other for not sanctioning for not sanctioning for not sanctioning . . . norm violators is absurd on theoretical as well as on empirical grounds, Akerlof (1976) and Abreu (1988) notwithstanding. Moreover, once an observed norm violation has taken place, the reaction of the violator is often disproportionate, due to the 'hot–cold empathy gap' (see my chapter on emotions, this volume). Also, even the rational anticipation of sanctions can be very difficult. In arenas as different from one another as norms of etiquette and norms of vengeance, the agent may be unable to tell whether she is doing too much or too little, or even whether there is a standard that defines what is too much and too little. Due to the 'cold–hot empathy gap,' the agent may also be unable to anticipate how horribly bad it will feel when he is caught cheating on an exam or on his spouse.

In many cases the agent will trade obedience to norms and material rewards off against one another. A person who really needs to catch the first train may be willing to suffer the contemptuous glares and remarks that others will direct to him if he intrudes in the queue. If he could persuade them that his need is truly acute, they might accept the intrusion, but such pleas are easily dismissed as 'cheap talk.' (A visibly pregnant woman, by contrast, can credibly claim to have a greater need.) Up to a certain point, a customer might refuse to deal with a store that once took advantage of a snowstorm to raise the price of snow shovels (Kahneman, Knetsch, and Thaler 1986), but an urgent need for a thermometer to measure the temperature of a sick child might override her reluctance. As these two examples illustrate, the trade-off operates in norm violators as well in observers of norm violations.

References

ABREU, D. (1988), 'On the Theory of Infinitely Repeated Games with Discounting,' *Econometrica*, 56: 383–96.

AKERLOF, G. (1976), 'The Economics of Caste and of the Rat Race and other Woeful Tales', *Quarterly Journal of Economics*, 90: 599–617.

——— (1980), 'A Theory of Social Custom, of which Unemployment may be One Consequence', *Quarterly Journal of Economics*, 94: 749–75.

——— (2003), 'Behavioral Macroeconomics and Macroeconomic Behavior', *American Economist*, 47: 25–47.

——— (2007), 'The Missing Motivation in Macroeconomics', *American Economic Review*, 97: 5–36.

——— and KRANTON, R. (2005), 'Identity and the Economics of Organization', *Journal of Economic Perspectives*, 19: 9–32.

ARROW, K. (1971), 'Political and Economic Evaluation of Social Effects and Externalities', in M. Intriligator (ed.), *Frontiers of Quantitative Economics* (Amsterdam: North-Holland), 3–25.

AVRIL, P. (1997), *Les conventions de la constitution* (Paris: Presses Universitaires de France).

AZAR, O. (2007), 'The Social Norm of Tipping: A Review', *Journal of Applied Social Psychology*, 37: 380–402.

BABCOCK, L., WANG, X., and LOEWESTEIN, G. (1996), 'Choosing the Wrong Pond: Social Comparisons in Negotiations that Reflect a Self-serving Bias', *Quarterly Journal of Economics*, 111: 1–19.

BOYER, P. (1996), 'Admiral Boorda's War', *New Yorker*, 16 September.

BUSQUET, J. (1920), *Le droit de la vendetta et les paci corses* (Paris: Pedone).

CAHUC, P., and CARCILLO, S. (2007), 'Que peut-on attendre de l'interdiction de licencier pour améliorer la compétitivité des enterprises?', *Revue Economique*, 58: 221–46.

CALABRESI, G., and BOBBIT, P. (1978), *Tragic Choices* (New York: Norton).

CARMICHAEL, H., and MACLEOD, W. (2000), 'Worker Cooperation and the Ratchet Effect', *Journal of Labor Economics*, 18: 1–19.

CLARK, A. (2003), 'Unemployment as a Social Norm', *Journal of Labor Economics*, 21: 323–51.

COLEMAN, J. (1990), *Foundations of Social Theory* (Cambridge Mass.: Harvard University Press).

CONLIN, M., LYNN, M., and O'DONOGHUE, T. (2003), 'The Norm of Restaurant Tipping', *Journal of Economic Behavior & Organization*, 5: 297–321.

COORAY, L. (1979), *Conventions: The Australian Constitution and the Future* (Sydney: Legal).

DICEY, A. V. (1915), *The Law of the Constitution*, 8th edn. (Indianapolis, Ind.: Liberty).

ELLICKSON, R. (1991), *Order Without Law* (Cambridge Mass.: Harvard University Press).

ELSTER, J. (1989a), *The Cement of Society* (Cambridge: Cambridge University Press).

—— (1989b), 'Social Norms and Economic Theory', *Journal of Economic Perspectives*, 3: 99–117.

—— (1999), *Alchemies of the Mind* (Cambridge: Cambridge University Press).

—— (2005), 'Fehr on Altruism, Emotion, and Norms', *Analyse und Kritik*, 27: 197–210.

—— (2007), *Explaining Social Behavior* (Cambridge: Cambridge University Press).

FALK, A., FEHR, E., and FISCHBACHER, U. (2005), 'Driving Forces Behind Informal Sanctions', *Econometrica*, 73: 2017–30.

FEHR, E. (1990), 'Cooperation, Harassment, and Involuntary Unemployment: Comment', *American Economic Review*, 80: 624–30.

—— and FISCHBACHER, U. (2002), 'Why Social Preferences Matter—the Impact of Nonselfish Motives on Competition, Cooperation and Incentives', *Economic Journal*, 112: C1–C33.

FRIJDA, N. (1986), *The Emotions* (Cambridge: Cambridge University Press).

GÄCHTER, S., and FEHR, E. (1999), 'Collective Action as a Social Exchange', *Journal of Economic Behavior and Organization*, 39: 341–69.

GILOVICH, T., GRIFFIN, D., and KAHNEMAN, D. (2002) (eds.), *Heuristics and Biases* (Cambridge: Cambridge University Press).

HALEY, K., and FESSLER, D. (2005), 'Nobody's Watching? Subtle Cues Affect Generosity in an Anonymous Economic Game', *Evolution and Human Behavior*, 26: 245–56.

HEARD, A. (1991), *Canadian Constitutional Conventions* (Oxford: Oxford University Press).

HORWILL, H. (1925), *The Usages of the American Constitution* (Oxford: Oxford University Press).

HRADA, J. (1985), 'Consumer Shortages in Poland', *Sociological Quarterly*, 26: 387–404.

HUME, D. (1978), *A Treatise on Human Nature* (Oxford: Oxford University Press).

JACOB, N., and PAGE, A. (1980), 'Production, Information Costs and Economic Organization: The Buyer Monitoring Case', *American Economic Review*, 70: 476–8.

JACONELLI, J. (1999), 'The Nature of Constitutional Convention', *Legal Studies*, 24: 24–46.

—— (2005), 'Do Constitutional Conventions Bind', *Cambridge Law Journal*, 64: 149–76.

KAHNEMAN, D., KNETSCH, J., and THALER, R. (1986) 'Fairness as a Constraint on Profit-Seeking', *American Economic Review*, 76: 728–41.

LA ROCHEFOUCAULD, F., DUC DE (1665), *Réflexions ou sentences et maximes morales*.

LARSON, R. (1987), 'Perspectives on Queues: Social Justice and the Psychology of Queuing', *Operations Research*, 35: 895–905.

LEWIS, D. (1969), *Convention* (Cambridge, Mass.: Harvard University Press).

LINDBECK, A., and SNOWER, D. J. (1988), 'Cooperation, Harassment and Involuntary Unemployment', *American Economic Review*, 78: 167–88.

—— —— (2001), 'Insiders Versus Outsiders', *Journal of Economic Perspectives*, 15: 165–88.

LOVEJOY, A. O. (1961), *Reflections on Human Nature* (Baltimore, Md.: Johns Hopkins University Press).

MANN, L. (1969), 'Queue Culture: The Waiting Line as a Social System', *American Journal of Sociology*, 75: 340–54.

MARSHALL, G. (1986), *Constitutional Conventions* (Oxford: Oxford University Press).

MILGRAM, S., et al. (1986), 'Response to Intrusion into Waiting Lines', *Journal of Personality and Social Psychology*, 51: 683–9.

MILLER, D. (1999), 'The Norm of Self-interest', *American Psychologist*, 54: 1053–60.

MOUSNIER, R. (1996), *Les institutions de la France sous la monarchie absolue* (Paris: Presses Universitaires de France).

NAYLOR, R. (1994), 'On the Credibility of Harassment in the Insider–Outsider Model', *European Journal of Political Economy*, 11: 725–32.

PASCAL, B. (1991), *Pensées*, ed. Sallier (Paris: Garnier).

POSNER, E. (2000), *Law and Social Norms* (Cambridge, Mass.: Harvard University Press).

ROY, D. (1952), 'Quota Restriction and Goldbricking in a Machine Shop', *American Journal of Sociology*, 57: 427–42.

SANDEMOSE, A. (1936), *A Fugitive Crosses his Track* (New York: Knopf).

SCHELLING, T. S. (1960), *The Strategy of Conflict* (Cambridge Mass.: Harvard University Press).

SCHMITT, B., DUBÉ, L., and LECLERC, F. (1992), 'Intrusions into Waiting Lines: Does the Queue Constitute a Social System', *Journal of Personality and Social Psychology*, 63: 806–15.

SHILLER, R., BOYCKO, M., and KOROBOV, V. (1991), 'Popular Attitudes towards Free Markets', *American Economic Review*, 81: 385–400.

THOMAS, K. (1973), *Religion and the Decline of Magic* (Harmondsworth: Penguin).

TOCQUEVILLE, A., COMTE DE (2004), *Democracy in America* (New York: Library of America).

TURPIN, C. (2002), *British Government and the Constitution*, 5th edn. (Colchester: Butterworths).

WILSON, J. G. (1992), 'American Constitutional Conventions', *Buffalo Law Review*, 40: 645–738.

CHAPTER 10

....

TRUST

....

KAREN S. COOK

ALEXANDRA GERBASI

INTRODUCTION

....

DURING the past two decades trust has become a major object of study in the
social sciences. Several writers have proposed various reasons for this focus of study.
Sztompka (2006: 905–6) has recently identified two: (1) a shift in the social sciences
from a major focus on the macro-societal level to closer analysis of the 'microfoundations of social life,' and (2) 'the changing quality of social structures and
social processes in . . . later modernity.' Among the changes he lists as most relevant
are: the shift to democracy in many sectors of the world and the concomitant
increased role of human agency, globalization and the attendant uncertainty inherent in the 'unfamiliar, non-transparent and distant' linkages it entails, as well as
increasingly rapid social change. Under such uncertainty, he argues, trust becomes
problematic in ways unprecedented in human history, increasingly important in
people's everyday lives and thus to sociologists as a 'hot' topic of study.

Others have echoed similar themes in their discussions of the rise of interest in
the role of trust in society and in social life (e.g. Luhman 1979, 1988; Fukuyama
1995; Uslaner 1998, 2002; Putnam 2000; Warren 2006). Some of the macro-social
factors that create conditions of uncertainty and an expansion of the types of
risk individuals face include migration to urban centers, immigration, rapid social
change, increasing inequality, political and economic transitions, violence, civil war,
terrorist activity, and other forms of political unrest.

In this chapter we address the question: What role does trust play as a determinant of cooperative behavior in social relations and social organizations, under what conditions? We argue that: (1) trust is only one mechanism by which we motivate cooperation and manage social order (there are significant alternatives, often more important than trust—especially under increased uncertainty and risk), and (2) the role of trust in society has been radically oversold as a necessary and wholly positive force. Like social capital, it can lead to negative consequences that have been overlooked in current research. In fact, there are many situations in which distrust (not trust) is merited—thus it can't be simply 'good' to trust or even generally good for a society to be more trusting despite macro-level claims by some authors to this effect (e.g. Fukuyama 1995).

Building on recent work on trust as a relational phenomenon (as reflected in the 'encapsulated interest' conceptualization of trust developed by Hardin 2002, 2006 and his collaborators, Cook, Hardin, and Levi 2005), we analyze the role of trust in various contexts. In the process we review and comment on some of the current empirical research concerning the significance of trust in social relations and social organizations and we conclude with a brief statement about the role of trust at the macro-social level.

10.1 Some Issues of Definition, Scope, and Measurement

Let us begin with a brief definitional exercise. Trust is clearly linked to risk and uncertainty (or to vulnerability, as Heimer 2001 notes). I am less likely to trust someone when uncertainty is high, especially when I am vulnerable because I am at risk of exploitation (as in the case in which someone might possess knowledge that would be damaging to me if, for example, it were shared with my employer). The kind of 'thick' trust that Luhman wrote about, which arises in social relations that are close and familiar such as familial or kinship ties and long-term friendships, represents an important category of social relations in which trust is relevant, but we are less concerned with analysis of these relationships than in the study of what is often referred to as 'thin' trust, more common in organizational and institutional settings. One reason for this focus is that the larger claims about the role of trust in most societies focus on thin trust, not relations of thick trust. Second, in relations characterized by 'thick' trust there is often little uncertainty or risk involved. Familiarity and strong connections create an environment in which there is heavy normatively based social control. What Cook and Hardin (2001) have called 'communal norms' produce social control. In fact, it is the existence of strong norms about trust in close personal relationships that makes violations of trust so noteworthy. Examples include well-known and frequent violations of trust between partners (especially long-term partnerships like those of married or cohabiting couples) or the less common violations of trust between parents and their children either in the form of elder abuse or child abuse. In these cases the problem is the *violation of trust* (or the failure of parties to be trustworthy) and less so the actual role of trust in facilitating social cooperation—especially since strong norms exist in these relationships concerning the extent to which one party must take the other's welfare into account. In reality there are very few people that we trust in this general way—with respect to many or all aspects of our relationship. Thus, while a very important category of trust relations, we set them aside in this chapter for the purpose of dealing with the more general claims about the role of trust in society that have little to do with familial, and very close personal, relations such as these.

We treat trust as an aspect of a relationship between two or more actors and thus refer to it as *relational trust. Trust exists when one party to the relation believes the other party has incentive to act in his or her interest or to take his or her interests to heart.* This view of trust has been called the 'encapsulated interest' conception of trust relations (see Hardin 2002; Cook Hardin, R., and Levi, M 2005). It emphasizes the importance of an interest in maintaining the relationship into the future, or an interest in maintaining one's reputation for trustworthiness in a network of relations, as the primary foundation of the trustworthiness of each party in the relationship. This view of trust differs from a more psychological orientation that treats trust as purely cognitive, not relational.

A trust relation emerges out of mutual interdependence (as is typical of cooperation and exchange relations) and the knowledge developed over time of reciprocal trustworthiness. Because this conceptual framework allows for variation in trusting relationships over time and across persons and situations it can be used in explanations of social phenomena. In this framework trust is not a simple disposition or psychological trait; it is a characteristic of a social relation. Various factors determine the extent to which I will trust you, including my knowledge of your trustworthiness in specific situations with respect to particular domains of action (e.g. I might trust you with my dog, but not my wallet), as well as situational factors (such as level of uncertainty and risk).

In this model, trust is a three-part relation. *A trusts B with respect to a particular issue (or domain of activity) or set of issues x, y . . .* A is very unlikely to trust B with respect to all issues of importance to him or her. (Such relations, as we claim above, are very rare.) Note that in this model what matters most is the nature of the relationship between the actors; thus, characteristics of the relationship affect levels of trust between the actors (e.g. relation duration, status inconsistencies, power asymmetries, network embeddedness, etc.). Individual attributes of each actor may matter (e.g. gender, education level, or occupation) and trust may vary over these dimensions, but usually these factors are relevant primarily as determinants of trustworthiness. That is, our beliefs about actors' levels of trustworthiness may relate to cognitions about the relevant characteristics of actors in specific settings. And such judgments concern not only the competence or reliability of the actor, but also their motivation to 'do no harm' (or take one's interests to heart). Pressures toward homophily in social relations also imply that individual attributes affect who we are likely to enter relationships with in most settings (see e.g. Blau 1964).

Trust relations are not only dyadic, as this conception implies, but they can be embedded in a broader network of relations (e.g. with actors C, D, E . . . N) that have implications for levels of trust and trustworthiness between the actors engaged in exchange or cooperation. Thus, there may also be positional determinants of trust relations. Here what matters is the location of the relationship in a network of social relations between individuals or organizational units. In addition, factors such as density of the network and the strength of ties in the network may have implications for the emergence of trust and for the diffusion of trustworthiness within the network. They can also affect the speed at which distrust spreads throughout a network.

In the simplest three-party network, for example, Burt and Knez (1995) have explored the effects of the 'third-party observers' on relational trust. They begin with the premise that third parties often observe interactions between individuals in the focal relationship. The nature of the relationships between the individuals involved and these third parties can have substantial effects on trust.

Burt and Knez (1995) examined third-party effects on trust relations using network data on manager success. Trust was measured in terms of confidences shared among the trusted parties and distrust was measured in terms of disrupting behavior or unhelpful work-related behavior. They found effects for both the strength of an individual's relationship with the person to be trusted, and for whether the focal relationship was observed by a third party. A strong focal relationship (exhibiting long tenure, frequent contact, and strong emotions) has a positive effect on trust: the stronger one's relationship the more likely one is to trust the other party. One is also less likely to distrust that person when there is a strong positive relationship. But the presence of third parties modifies these results. When the focal relationship is deeply embedded, that is the actors in the network have a high degree of indirect contact (i.e. their contacts know each other), trust is significantly more likely than when the actors in the network have little indirect contact with each other (i.e. the degree their friends know each other is low). The presence of third parties increases the likelihood of distrust in the focal relationship when there is little direct contact in the network, but does not appear to have an effect in relationships with a high level of direct contact.

Burt and Knez also found that the type of third party has an effect on trust. Mutual third parties, those individuals well-known to both ego and alter, have a positive effect on trust. On the other hand, exclusive third parties, those well-known either by ego or alter, but not both, increase the likelihood of distrust. The distinction between strong and weak relationships in this study may actually be close to the distinction between 'thick' and 'thin' trust in the trust literature.

Often we take specific behaviors as our *indicators of trustworthiness* (or as measures of trust). As Molm (2006) notes in her review of Cook et al. (2005), assessments of a party's trustworthiness are reflected in behaviors that indicate that a party does take what is in my best interest into account, such as the physician who is always available, competent, reliable, and who demonstrates that she/he 'cares' about my well-being through significant behaviors that directly benefit me. There can be many different types of evidence of trustworthiness that allow us to build trust relations with those we come to know (see Cook, Hardin, and Levi 2005: ch. 2).

In fact, these *behavioral* indicators are likely to be the most important category of measures of trustworthiness (and thus our propensity to trust). The more common measures, based on attitudinal surveys, are less likely to be good indicators of trustworthiness (given the lack of strong correlations between attitudes and behavior in many settings and the vagueness of the actual questions posed in surveys of trust—e.g. 'Do you think most people can be trusted?' See Rotter 1967, 1971, 1980; Kosugi and Yamagishi 1998). And, my knowledge that you are more trusting of strangers than I am does not really provide me with evidence of your trustworthiness with respect to me in a particular domain of activity. These attitudinal measures may reveal the extent to which I am likely to trust 'most people,' but they do not do a good job of revealing who most people are or in allowing us to predict the extent to which someone would actually trust another specific person in a particular situation.

10.2 DIMENSIONS OF TRUST AND TRUSTWORTHINESS

Trust is typically granted to those we find trustworthy; thus, assessments of trustworthiness are central determinants of our objects of trust. The literature is divided on the extent to which there are distinct dimensions that compose our judgments of trustworthiness. There is some empirical evidence that there are at least two relevant dimensions that are sometimes distinguishable in empirical settings. These two key dimensions are (1) competence or reliability (Can you be trusted to complete the task or action at hand in an appropriate manner?), and

(2) integrity, honesty, and the commitment to 'do no harm' at least with respect to me in a specific situation (Jeffries and Reed 2000; Cook Hardin, R., and Levi, M 2005; Cook et al. 2009).

There is a fairly large literature relating competence to trust (Giffin 1967; Kee and Knox 1970; Rosen and Jerdee 1977; Gabarro 1978; Cook and Wall 1980; Lieberman 1981; Good 1988; Butler 1991; Sitkin and Roth 1993; Mishra 1996). In addition to competence, the actor must also be highly likely to complete the assigned task to be perceived as trustworthy or reliable (Ouchi 1981; Gabarro 1978; Kirkpatrick and Locke 1991). This dimension is often referred to in the literature as cognitive-based trust (Rempel, Holmes, and Zanna 1985; Jeffries and Reed 2000). These concepts reference the ability of the trustees to fulfill their obligations (Jeffries and Reed 2000). When decision-making entails a high level of uncertainty, such as when buying expensive goods (Cook et al., forthcoming), selecting a physician (Cook Hardin, R., and Levi, M 2005), or hiring a lawyer, perceived competence of the trustee is often the main factor in the decision.

The other identifiable component of trust is motivation. Besides ability or expertise, Peters, Covello, and McCallum (1997), in their study of trust and communication, find that two of the three main components predicting trust are (1) perceptions of openness and honesty, and (2) perceptions of concern and care. Integrity and honesty are key to building trust in the world of business as well: 'Nothing is noticed more quickly and considered more significant than a discrepancy between what executives preach and what they expect their associates to practice' (Nanus 1989: 102). Such discrepancies are viewed as indicators of lack of integrity.

Issues of integrity, honesty, and the commitment to 'do no harm' become increasingly important when there is a power difference between individuals. In Kramer's study of faculty members and graduate students (1996) he finds that students attend to detail and recall negative behaviors and actions more than do their advisors, which is typical of those with less power in a relationship. The findings from Kramer (1996) and Nanus (1989) are common in the relationship literature (see also Cook Hardin, R., and Levi, M 2005), and they highlight the difficulty of developing trust in power-asymmetric relationships, in which the higher-power actors' behaviors can substantially diminish trust, unless they reflect honesty and integrity. The multidimensional nature of trustworthiness thus has some empirical support in the existing literature, but debate persists over the extent to which trust is unidimensional (with psychologists often treating it as unidimensional—Uslaner 1998; Tazelaar, Van Lange, and Ouwerkerk 2004; Mulder et al. 2006). When not treated as unidimensional, trust is often categorized as either cognitive or affective. We discuss this particular distinction before reviewing some of the empirical work on the role of trust in social organizations and social relations.

Cognitive trust is based on past experience that allows an individual to predict the likelihood of a partner following through on an agreement or living up to her obligations (Rempel et al. 1985; McAllister 1995). It is sometimes referred to as predictability or the capacity to be reliable. This knowledge is often based on reputation or it is derived directly from observations of prior interactions. On the other hand, *affective* trust is the confidence an individual places in a partner on the basis of feelings generated by the interaction (Johnson-George and Swap 1982 and Rempel, Holmes, and Zanna 1985). Affective trust is the strength of an individual's reliance on a partner based primarily on emotions. Reputation can also influence affective trust, but it is primarily based on personal experiences with the focal partner.

As might be expected, cognitive and affective trust are interrelated. McAllister (1995) argues that some level of cognitive trust is necessary for affective trust to develop. An individual must find that the other lives up to her expectations concerning reliability and dependability before she invests further in the relationship. He also mentions an important caveat: 'as affective trust matures the potential for decoupling and reverse causation increases' (1995: 30). That is, affective trust influences cognitive trust. This implies, for example, that once a high level of affective trust develops, the individual may discount information that should decrease cognitive trust. The specific empirical relationship between cognitive and affective trust under different circumstances needs further investigation.

Recent work by Molm and her colleagues (Molm, Collett, and Schaefer 2007) also suggests that different types of interaction should lead to the development of different levels of cognitive and affective trust. Based on a hypothesized continuum of expressive value displayed in different types of exchange (e.g. negotiated versus reciprocal exchange), the level of affective trust displayed should also vary. In binding negotiated exchange, where there is little expressive value of the interaction, cognitive trust may develop, but affective trust should be low, they argue. On the other hand, in reciprocal exchange the expressive value of the interaction is higher; thus, the level of affective trust should be much higher in reciprocal exchange than in negotiated exchange. These hypothesized relationships between types of exchange and types of trust (cognitive versus affective) have not yet been investigated empirically, but they are implied by the existing research on trust relations in various types of exchange.

It should be noted that the encapsulated-interest account of relational trust is primarily a cognitive conception of trust, though once trust develops it may have implications for level of affect in the relationship. And affective ties may influence the nature of the assessments of encapsulated interest that enter into cognitive judgments concerning whom to trust. There is much more work to be done to spell out these relationships between cognitive and affective factors in trust relations. We move from this general definitional exercise to a discussion of the actual role of trust in society and some of the unresolved debates.

10.3 SOME EVIDENCE ON THE ROLE OF TRUST IN SOCIAL RELATIONS AND SOCIAL ORGANIZATIONS

In support of the encapsulated-interest account of trust, experimental evidence indicates that trust emerges in ongoing relationships when both parties have an incentive to fulfill the trust (e.g. Molm, Takahashi, and Peterson 2000; Malhotra and Murnighan 2002). One major source of this incentive is the implicit commitment to the relationship itself, based in part on a concern with maintaining future interaction opportunities. In a dyadic relation both parties must have a desire to continue the relationship for it to remain viable. Over time mutual dependence on the relationship may develop and secure some degree of commitment to the relationship.

In a relationship in which there is a power difference between the actors, however, the degree of commitment to the relationship may be asymmetric, as in the faculty–student example above. The less powerful actor in such a relationship may offer greater commitment as a way of 'balancing' the power differential (Leik and Leik 1977). This is only one way in which power differences between actors affect commitment and the possibility for a trust relationship. As Cook and Emerson (1978), Lawler and Yoon (1993, 1996), Kollock (1994), and Yamagishi, Cook, and Watabe (1998) have demonstrated, commitment is more likely to occur between power equals, as a result of frequent, positive exchange, and in response to uncertainty (either in terms of resource or service quality, access to exchange opportunities, or the potential for exploitation). Power inequalities thus may inhibit trust.

As an example, in physician–patient relationships mutual dependence can emerge between the parties to the exchange even though there is an inherent power inequality in the relationship, which derives in part from the differential competencies of the parties involved with respect to medical issues (the domain of relevance in this potential trust relation). Patients generally receive better care in the context of an ongoing dyadic relationship in which the physician gets to know their health history and general life circumstances (McWilliam, Brown, and Stewart 2000; Leisen and Hyman 2001). And many physicians prefer to treat patients they trust, since they are typically more compliant with medical regimens and less likely to resort to litigation. Hence, maintaining the relationship over time is an important factor in both the emergence of trust and the quality of care. Organizational-level factors, however, have reduced the longevity of physician–patient relations, so that many interactions with physicians are not repeated. One of the negative consequences of managed care, for example, is that frequent renegotiation of employer–insurance-provider contracts results in high turnover. This reality increases the extent to which physician–patient encounters are 'one-shot' interactions, blocking even the possibility of repeat interactions in which mutual trust can develop.

As Cook Hardin, R., and Levi, M (2005: 47) argue, under uncertainty, reliance on interpersonal mechanisms for maintaining trust often gives way to the imposition of organizational mechanisms that are believed to ensure trustworthiness more effectively through increased monitoring and sanctioning, ironically reducing the possibility for ongoing trust relations. A number of studies indicate clearly that various forms of formal control reduce the effectiveness of informal mechanisms of cooperation. For example, in the literature on relational contracting there is evidence that pressure to formalize contracts and make them as complete as possible serves to signal lack of trust and thus undermines the possibility of developing a trusting relationship that fosters greater flexibility and adaptability under environmental uncertainty (see Macaulay 1963).

Similarly, both experimental and organizational field studies indicate that monitoring and sanctioning (especially the imposition of sanctioning systems) as external mechanisms of social control reduce (or 'crowd out') internal motivations to engage in cooperative behaviors (as a result of the development of a trust relationship). Bohnet and Baytelman (2007: 99) have recently reported experimental results that support the conclusion that 'all settings that offer tighter institutional constraints compared to anonymous one-shot [trust] games decrease intrinsically motivated trust.' Mulder et al. (2006), in their work on 'the paradox of sanctioning systems,' demonstrate that subjects exposed to no sanctioning at all trust others more than do those first exposed to a sanctioning system, which is subsequently removed. And Molm, Takahashi, and Peterson (2000) and Malhotra and Murnighan (2002) demonstrate that trust relations are more likely to emerge when the situation allows for actions that clearly reveal or at least 'signal' the trustworthiness of each party to the exchange.

In several laboratory studies Maholtra and Murnighan (2002), for example, demonstrate that 'the use of binding contracts to promote or mandate cooperation' leads 'interacting partners to attribute others' cooperation to the constraints imposed by the contract rather than to the individuals themselves thus reducing the likelihood of trust developing.' Molm's work also reflects this critique of contracts and binding negotiations. By comparing negotiated (highly contractual and relatively certain) exchange with reciprocal exchange (with no contracts and greater uncertainty) she demonstrates that trust is higher among the parties to reciprocal exchange (assuming they develop a relationship over time) than among the parties engaged in a series of negotiated exchanges that are binding. Her findings are consistent with those of Malhotra and Murnighan. Contractual exchange leaves little room for relatively unambiguous demonstrations of personal trustworthiness. Molm also focuses on another important feature of the comparison between negotiated and reciprocal exchange, and that is the salience of conflicting interests over cooperative interests or the explicit distributive aspects of the bargaining situation versus the implicit negotiation that occurs in reciprocal exchange.

One key issue that is not well addressed in this particular literature is the extent to which trusting behavior begets trustworthiness. That is, does the simple act of trusting another induce trustworthy behavior on the part of that actor? The answer to this question has important implications for organizational design (and for decisions about monitoring and sanctioning—processes that are costly for organizations to implement). Cook Hardin, R., and Levi, M (2005) addressed this question in one set of experiments using the PD/D paradigm,[1] in which actors can clearly signal their trustworthiness by investing incrementally over time in the relationship and thus signaling their willingness to trust that a partner will reply with a trusting response (i.e. will honor the trust placed in them). By allowing participants to choose their level of risk (i.e. the amount they entrust to their partner), they can signal their level of trust in their partner. When interacting with the same partner over time, increasing the level of risk they were willing to take was clearly associated with perceptions of stronger trust for both partners. The amount of risk taken and the resulting higher levels of perceived trust also induced more cooperation between the partners. The results indicate that the capacity to signal one's trust of another person does increase the extent to which they behave in a trustworthy manner by honoring the trust placed in them. (In the experimental setting this entails returning a portion of the funding that was entrusted to them on each action opportunity and thus initiating or sustaining a trust relationship.)

10.4 TRUST: MAIN AND MODERATING EFFECTS IN THE CONTEXT OF ORGANIZATIONS

In the literature on organizations there is some evidence that interpersonal or relational trust among employees and between employees and their supervisors (or employers) increases discretionary actions that benefit the organization. These actions are often referred to as organizational citizenship behaviors (OCBs). In this sense trust does facilitate a type of prosocial behavior, but typically only under a particular set of conditions (Whitener et al. 1998; Leana and Van Buren 1999; Dirks and Ferrin 2001). While trust has a main effect on OCBs, it serves more commonly as a *moderator* of other factors (intensifying the effect, for example, of certain types of incentives; see Dirks and Ferrin 2001). There are few other clear examples of the direct effect of trust on behavior in organizations (e.g. on factors such as individual or group performance, etc.). The one exception is attitudinal effects. Trust does seem to have a positive effect (or negative in the case of its absence) on workplace satisfaction.

Trust serves to moderate (and typically enhance or mitigate) the effects of other factors in organizations such as information-sharing, risk-taking, and working toward group or collective goals versus individual goals. Dirks and Ferrin (2001) more generally argue that trust affects how one assesses the future behavior of an individual with whom one is interdependent. Trust affects how one interprets the actions of the other party as well as the motives behind their behavior. They argue that trust serves to reduce the uncertainty involved in relationships. When looking at the effect of incentive systems on cooperation, they argue that incentives are not enough to produce cooperation within the group. The individuals with low levels of trust in the group are more likely to pursue individual goals than group goals, while those with high levels of trust are more likely to cooperate with the group.

Kimmel et al. (1980) find that trust moderates the effect of aspiration levels on negotiation outcomes. Under high trust, high aspiration levels lead to high levels of information-sharing and cooperative negotiation behavior. Under low trust, high aspiration levels lead to low levels of information-sharing and less cooperative negotiation behavior. Read (1962) finds that trust also mediates the relationship between motivation to be promoted and the likelihood of sharing information with one's boss. Among individuals with a strong desire to be promoted the likelihood of sharing information decreases greatly when the individual does not trust her boss. The role of trust as a mediating factor in Dirks and Ferrin's model (2001) is closely associated with risk. Those who are motivated to attain some goal, and who trust their group, boss, or organization, are more likely to engage in risky behaviors (i.e. those that may affect their individual goals) than are those with low levels of trust, who are more likely to attempt to minimize risk.

In the arena of interorganizational relations (not intra-organizational phenomena), strategic alliances between organizations are often facilitated directly by trust relations between individuals in the organizations involved. Such alliances based on trust allow the organizations flexibility and the capacity to adapt to rapid change and environmental turbulence. Strategic alliances (see Young-Ybarra and Wiersema 1999), a special category of interorganizational relations, are nimble and relatively short-lived relations between organizations that meet mutual needs but do not lead to the negative consequences of 'lock-in' or more formal structures that are harder to exit when the situation requires it.

Trust relations sometimes facilitate other types of transactions between organizations. Brian Uzzi (1997) identifies two types of relationships common among firms in the manufacturing business: (1) close relations and (2) arms-length relations. Individuals connected by 'close' relationships were more likely to be trusting and cooperative, even though the same individuals could be self-interested and businesslike in their arms-length relations. In the close relationships the individuals would more often engage in joint problem-solving, transfer finer-grained information to one another, and generally be more trusting. In contrast, the arms-length relationships were more typically economic relations characterized by lack of reciprocity, less continuity, and a focus on narrowly economic matters. Trust developed in relations between manufacturers when extra effort was initially offered voluntarily and then reciprocated, in much the same way that Blau (1964) suggests that trust emerges in social-exchange relations. Uzzi notes that this extra effort might involve giving an exchange partner preferred treatment, offering overtime, or placing an order before it was needed to help a partner during a slow time. Trust relations involved less monitoring and thus reduced organizational costs.

Powell (1996) identifies a number of types of business networks in which trust plays a role in the organization of economic activity. For example, in research and development networks such as those in Silicon Valley, trust is formed and maintained through professional memberships in relevant associations, a high degree of information flow across the network, and by frequent shifting of employees across organizational boundaries. In another example Powell explores the role of trust in business groups such as the Japanese *keiretsu* and the Korean *chaebol*. In these business groups trust emerges out of a mixture of common membership in the group, perceived obligation, and vigilance. Long-term repeat interactions are key to establishment of trust relations in this context as well as in most circumstances in which trust relations emerge. Repeat interactions provide the opportunity for learning, monitoring, dyadic sanctioning, and increasing mutual dependence which reinforces the basis for trust.

The use of personal ties as the basis for business relations, however, does not always have positive consequences. In a study of commercial bankers and their corporate customers, Mizruchi and Stearns argue that uncertainty creates 'conditions that trigger a desire for the familiar, and bankers respond to this by turning to those with whom they are close' (2001: 667). They hypothesize that uncertainty leads bankers to rely on colleagues with whom they have strong ties for advice and for support of their deals. Their findings reveal that the tendency of bankers to rely on their approval networks and on those they trust leads them to be less successful in closing deals. In this case reliance on trust relations leads to lower organizational efficiency.

There are other examples of interorganizational phenomena that seem to be facilitated by trust relations, though the extent to which trust is essential is not clear, since in most cases some form of contract (informal or formal) and often monitoring at some level are also entailed in these interactions or the transactions are embedded in a larger network of multidimensional ties between the actors (either as principals or as agents for organizations) that reduce risk. While the general finding is that trust between organizations reduces the need for formal agreements between parties, reduces transaction costs, and increases efficiency, there are contradictory results, and we do not have evidence that trust alone provides backing for these relations. Instead we mainly have anecdotes and some field studies that highlight the significance of trust relations between the principals or their agents. What we do not have is evidence that trust *substitutes* for more formal agreements or even informal modes of contracting (or of completing the relevant transactions). In addition, there is some evidence that too much reliance on trust relations (or trust networks) has negative consequences.

In settings in which there are weak institutional safeguards and higher levels of risk and uncertainty, however, contracts are relatively meaningless and the actors must rely on trust networks or close personal relations in which reciprocity is likely. This is the case in many transitional economies. An example is the use of personal relations, some involving trust, as the basis for commerce between individuals and organizations in Russia because corruption is commonplace (Lonkilia 1997). Since formal channels were not only overly bureaucratic, rigid, and inefficient but also highly ineffective, many individuals under Communist regimes accomplished various tasks and engaged in barter and exchange outside normal routines through networks of relations built up of trusted associates (e.g. Marin 2002). Civil society had declined under Communist rule (Neace 1999).

The rise of a barter economy (exchange often based on interpersonal trust relations) is one mechanism for dealing with the risk and uncertainty entailed when there is low liquidity in the market and an absence of institutional-level trust (Marin 2002: 73). Noncash transactions increase when there is less confidence in the institutions that facilitate cash transactions in the economy. Russia's transition from central planning to a decentralized market economy, according to Rock and Solodkov (2001), has been so chaotic and fraught with corruption that confidence in all financial institutions, especially banks, was extremely low. Although based to some extent on existing social structures (e.g. trust networks), the barter economy of exchange persists in response to this banking failure in the countries in the former Soviet Union and contributes to what is called the 'banking-development trap.' In the presence of stronger banking and credit institutions the noncash sector of the economy should have declined steadily. While it has declined somewhat in the twenty-first century in Russia, for example, it is still estimated to compose around 50 percent of the transactions. Barter allows for 'softer' pricing and thus for coverage of what are called credit-enforcement costs (i.e. the costs of opportunism) in such risky environments. The trust networks that exist clearly facilitate barter, though they may not facilitate further economic development, since they serve as an alternative to the establishment of more formal credit systems that might foster an increase in cash transactions. (This general trend toward barter is referred to as the 'demonetization' of the economy.)

The significance of trust networks derives from the long-term climate of distrust that existed in these countries and that set the terms of the relations between individuals and state enterprises. Individuals created trust relations as a means of coping with a pervasive generalized environment of distrust. In China the weak effect of law is argued by Luo (2007) to be one of the reasons for the strong effect of personal relationships in business transactions and interorganizational alliances. Often in such settings when there has been a weak tradition of the rule of law and strong centralized power structures personal networks and informal trust relations provide the 'security' that is missing from the institutional framework.

10.5 TRUST AND SOCIETY: MACRO-LEVEL EFFECTS

In the larger society the role of *trust* is complex. Several macro-level theorists claim that trust is 'required,' not in the sense that it fills the gaps in existing macro-level social-control mechanisms (that is, in the gray areas which are not covered by law, institutional regulation, or norms), but in the stronger sense that it actually facilitates market transactions, organizational efficiency, and thus economic productivity and growth (cf. Arrow 1974; Fukuyama 1995; and Zak and Knack 2001).

Moving beyond the relational level, 'social trust' (i.e. the kind of generalized trust that has been written about most at the macro level and that is reflected in typical survey items) has been the focus of much research, but little that clarifies the mechanisms by which such generalized trust works to create the conditions conducive to a more prosperous economy (with the possible exception of Zak and Knack 2001) or other general outcomes at the societal level. Trust may facilitate market processes and cooperation between organizations, but precisely how this works is not spelled out; nor is the extent to which trust is necessary for market functioning and interorganizational commerce known. At the level of market processes it may simply be that general trust allows extension of the forms of interaction that support markets—buyers and sellers connect more easily because they are less concerned about possible exploitation. But in those settings in which trust matters most (under high uncertainty and clear risks) individuals are least likely to rely on trust and most likely to require that more formal mechanisms of cooperation and control be in place.

When these more formal mechanisms come into existence to manage uncertainty and risk, they are subsequently likely to 'crowd out' trust (and other internalized forms of cooperative motivation) as we have suggested. Thus, it can be imagined that over time societies become less dependent on trust relations and informal mechanisms of social control (e.g. communal norms of cooperation that foster collective goal-orientation) and more reliant on formal institutional guarantees and safeguards. This argument fits with recent empirical work by Paxton (1999), for example on social capital, in which she finds that (among other things) trust in *institutions* as a general indicator of 'legitimacy' has not declined (once scandals in specific institutional settings for particular years are included as controls), but that trust in *individuals* has declined in the USA. Paxton reports a strong and consistent decline in trust in individuals from 1975 to 1994 (a drop of about 0.5 percent per year).[2]

Some of the standard survey measures of general trust would then be picking up confidence in these more formal and institutional safeguards and, thus, ironically, serving as indicators of less 'need' for relational trust (or trust in individuals you know). You can 'trust' or, more precisely, take a risk on a stranger in such environments precisely because there is strong rule of law and institutions that function well to manage exploitation and insure against failures of trust. Generalized trust (in strangers) on this notion would therefore be relatively high in the USA, Western Europe, and some East Asian countries (as the data suggest) and low where there is weak rule of law and corrupt institutions as reflected in low trust scores in Eastern European countries and parts of South America and south-east Asia, for example.

A reduction in this type of general trust over time would reflect a weakening of the institutions of social control or of the rule of law and would be cause for alarm, not because social capital (in the most general sense) is declining (if general trust is taken as one indicator of social capital), but because such a decrease might induce increased reliance on contracts and other forms of assurance (e.g. hostage posting or other credible commitment strategies) which in turn could further diminish reliance on trust relations in those sectors in which they were still viable as the primary basis for interpersonal transactions. It is this 'Catch-22' that is problematic for modern society, rather than the hypothesized reduction in social capital per se (i.e. less time for collective activities, fewer association memberships, smaller social networks, etc.). Additional empirical research is needed to investigate the conditions under which this proposition (regarding the negative correlation between formal and informal modes of social control and mechanisms for facilitating cooperation) holds, with what specific interpersonal, organizational, and societal-level consequences. In addition, we do not yet have good evidence on the extent to which reliance on relational trust is an effective form of social control and cooperation in contrast to alternative mechanisms for assuring cooperation, compliance, and the control of corruption or other types of malfeasance.

10.6 TRUST NETWORKS: NEGATIVE CONSEQUENCES

While trust networks can emerge to facilitate social and economic exchange under uncertainty (DiMaggio and Louch 1998; Guseva and Rona-Tas 2001), such networks can also emerge to support corruption and other forms of illegal activity. Like social capital, trust networks can be put to bad uses as well as good. In addition, since they tend to closure (Coleman 1998) they may limit opportunity. Corrupt networks are embedded in social structures just as other markets are (Cartier-Bresson 1997). In a discussion of corruption networks and illegal social exchange, Cartier-Bresson argues that in purely economic exchanges corruption arises in the limited dealing of impersonal agents who do not know each other. In such cases exploitation can occur, and there is uncertainty about the resulting prices and the outcome of the exchange. In social exchanges corruption can be organized and regular because the parties are likely to have repeat dealings through social networks. It is this organization of corruption by social networks that, Cartier-Bresson argues, enables 'a real institutionalization of procedures' and the persistence of this type of 'embedded' corruption (p. 466). In his view the regularization of corruption through networks can lead to its normalization. Illicit activities become commonplace and thus are often left unchallenged.

Illegal forms of behavior also result in risk and uncertainty and can lead to the formation of similar trust networks. This is the type of trust built up in closed associations such as the Mafia (Gambetta 1993), which are highly exclusionary networks. In the Mafia the network includes only those who are members of the association, and strong norms exist that determine the nature of acceptable behavior as well as the rules of trade. Only insiders can participate; outsiders are excluded from the perquisites of 'membership.' Where governments have failed or where general institutions are corrupt, alternative organizations like the Mafia may take over the economic arena and subsequently make it difficult to establish general market mechanisms. In such a situation, risk and uncertainty for those outside the organization may remain high because it is in the interest of the Mafia to mediate economic transactions through its 'trust networks.' Creating mechanisms to break down the control of the Mafia may be very problematic.

Nee and Sanders (2001) provide some additional insight into the downside of the use of trust networks. In this case the networks are formed through immigration flows as immigrants move across borders into 'safe havens' most often in urban settings. These relatively closed trust networks (often formed by 'strong ties' to relatives or friends in the receiving community), which draw immigrants into an ethnic enclave for access to jobs and other resources, may actually lock these employees into low-wage jobs with little spare time to develop the human capital that would be needed to move up and out of the protective environment of their enclave. In such settings relying on trust relations in the short run may result in longer-term negative outcomes for the individuals involved (Cook 2005).

10.7 ALTERNATIVES TO TRUST

Cook Hardin, R., and Levi, M (2005) treat trust as only one possible source of cooperative, prosocial behavior, and not the most common source of such behavior. In fact, they argue that reliance on alternatives to trust is more common in society.

These alternatives to the production of cooperation (and other forms of prosocial behavior) include organizational and institutional mechanisms for creating incentives for cooperative behavior and coordination of activity, as well as safeguards against the failure of cooperation and forms of exploitation or corruption.

In related work, Bradach and Eccles (1989), for example, view trust as only one type of control system, to be distinguished from price and authority, building on Arrow's treatment (1974) of governance mechanisms. Reliability and flexibility are important aspects of business relations, and Bradach and Eccles (1989) associate these characteristics with trust relations. Especially under uncertainty, trust becomes an important determinant of transactions as exchange partners seek out those who are trustworthy and likely to be reliable in continued exchange. In the experimental literature, noted above, Kollock (1994) and Yamagishi, Cook, and Watabe (1998),[3] among others, demonstrate that uncertainty leads to commitment among exchange partners as they attempt to avoid opportunism and potential exploitation or defaults.[4] The tendency to form committed relations and to 'lock-in' has some associated opportunity costs, since committed exchange partners may not explore new relations that might yield better terms. It is this 'stickiness' to certain partnerships often created by trust and commitment that may have significant negative effects on economic outcomes, especially if there are fundamental changes in the economy such as may be created by new technologies and new or rapidly expanding markets for trade and production.

The commitment between exchange partners that emerges, especially under conditions of risk and uncertainty, can be the basis for trust between those involved in the ongoing relationship as the parties develop more accurate assessments of each party's trustworthiness. While Cook (2005) argues that these trust networks may yield 'lock-in' over time and failure to explore alternatives, Yamagishi and Yamagishi (1994) argue that ongoing relations lead to commitment, similarly creating 'lock-in' and the avoidance of alternatives. For Yamagishi this is called an 'assurance' structure, since trustworthiness is assured not by 'trust relations' but by the capacity to monitor and sanction one another in close personal networks. In such structures actors do not need to invest in the 'ability to detect' cheaters. Trust of strangers in Yamagishi's treatment of trust is the result of a kind of social intelligence that gives some individuals greater capacity to take a risk on a stranger and be right. Those with low social intelligence avoid such risks due to low trust and thus lose out on opportunities for profitable exchange. For Yamagishi and Yamagishi (1994) trusting is a characteristic of an individual and not a social relationship, which makes it distinct from the encapsulated-interest view of trust which is distinctly relational. The two views are not incompatible, since those involved in trust relations may indeed vary in their levels of social intelligence, which may affect their initial willingness to enter a trust relation with another party, absent good information about their trustworthiness (either through prior experience or reputation).

In an interesting historical study of the US economy between 1840 and 1920 Lynne Zucker (1986) identified three basic modes of trust production in society. First, there is process-based trust that is tied to a history of past or expected exchange (e.g. gift exchange). Reputations work to support trust-based exchange because past exchange behavior provides accurate information that can easily be disseminated in a network of communal relations (Cook and Hardin 2001). Process-based trust has high information requirements and works best in small societies or organizations. The second type of trust she identifies is characteristic-based trust, in which trust is tied to a particular person depending on characteristics such as family background or ethnicity. The third type of trust is institution-based trust, which ties trustworthiness to formal societal structures that function to support cooperation. Such structures include third-party intermediaries and professional associations or other forms of certification that remove risk. Government regulation and legislation also provide the institutional background for cooperation, lowering the risk of default or opportunism. High rates of immigration, internal migration, and the instability of business enterprises from the mid-1800s to the early 1900s, Zucker argues, disrupted process-based trust relations. Cook Hardin, R., and Levi, M (2005) similarly treat these institutional mechanisms as alternatives to reliance on trust relations.

Thus, in Zucker's view the move to institutional bases for securing trustworthiness was historically inevitable. Interestingly, this thesis represents a direct link to studies by Greif et al. (1995) and other economic historians of the emergence of various institutional devices for securing cooperation in long-distance trade in much earlier periods. Similarly, anthropologists have studied the production of trust in primarily economic relations. An example is Ensminger's study (2001) of the emergence of fictive kin relations among the Orma in Kenya as a device for securing trustworthiness and economic reliability in nomadic cattle-herding, where monitoring is difficult if not impossible. Zucker's discussion supports the general argument that institutional alternatives to relational trust are more commonly used to motivate social cooperation under increased uncertainty and the risk of opportunism.

10.8 CONCLUSION AND A RESEARCH AGENDA

In our view trust is rarely 'necessary' in the strictest sense of this term for the production of social order but it can facilitate cooperation (under various circumstances) and it can extend the reach of alternative mechanisms of social control and often reduce transaction costs. However, like social capital, it may have negative consequences. Examples include trust networks that undermine formal authority or institutional regulations, or trust networks that tend to closure and cut off links to new opportunities or that operate in an exclusionary fashion. Rather than summarize findings, we will simply point to some of the unresolved research questions that we define as part of the open agenda for trust research.

Some of the open research questions include: (1) When does trust actually substitute for more formal mechanisms of social control and when is it required to facilitate cooperation? More importantly: (2) Is there a negative correlation between formal and informal mechanisms of control and does reliance on formal mechanisms of control or of producing cooperation 'crowd out' trust and internally motivated cooperation or social restraint? Specifically, does monitoring and sanctioning reduce intrinsic motivation to cooperate in much the same way that extrinsic rewards have been shown to reduce intrinsic motivation to perform? (3) What are the organizational-design implications of the answers to these research questions? (4) What are the consequences of too much reliance on trust relations and trust networks for social structure and society at large, and for the individuals involved in such networks of trust? (5) What are the macro-level effects of a decrease of 'trust in individuals' or of 'trust in institutions'? Do the survey items we rely on actually provide valid evidence that trust in individuals has declined or simply that fear (and risk) has increased? An indicator that the latter is partially true in the USA and in some other countries is the gated-community phenomenon that Paxton (1999) highlights in her research. And, what are the implications of this decline for economic activity, democratic politics, and collective well-being (or the collective commitment to the provision of collective goods)? Do trust networks limit the boundaries of such activity? These research questions remain at the heart of the research agenda for those interested broadly in understanding the role of trust in society.

NOTES

1. This game is a modification of the prisoner's dilemma (PD) in which the players can choose the amount to entrust to their partner, and is thus similar to the investment game used in experiments on trust.
2. Paxton (1999) cites as indicators of this trend the increased investment in security devices and the increase in 'gated' communities in many locales in the USA.
3. For Yamagishi and Yamagishi (1994) commitment leads to a kind of 'assurance' that obviates the need for trust (see subsequent discussion).
4. This same phenomenon is called 'relational contracting' in an older literature (see Macaulay 1963).

References

Arrow, K. J. (1974), *The Limits of Organization* (New York: Norton).

Blau, P. M. (1964), *Exchange and Power in Social Life* (New York: Wiley).

Blendon, R. J., and Benson, J. M. (2001), 'Americans' Views on Health Policy: A Fifty-year Historical Perspective', *Health Affairs*, 20: 33–46.

Bohnet, I., and Baytelman, Y. (2007), 'Institutions and Trust: Implications for Preferences, Beliefs and Behavior', *Rationality and Society*, 19: 99–135.

Bradach, J. L., and Eccles, R. G. (1989), 'Price, Authority, and Trust: From Ideal Types to Plural Forms', *Annual Review of Sociology*, 15: 97–118.

Burt, R., and Knez, M. (1995), 'Kinds of Third-party Effects on Trust', *Rationality and Society*, 7 (3): 255–92.

Butler, J. K. (1991), 'Toward Understanding and Measuring Conditions of Trust: Evolution of a Trust Inventory', *Journal of Management*, 17: 643–63.

Cartier-Bresson, J. (1997), 'Corruption Networks, Transaction Security and Illegal Social Exchange', *Political Studies*, 45 (3): 463–76.

Coleman, J. (1998), 'Social Capital in the Creation of Human Capital', *American Journal of Sociology*, 94: 95–120.

Cook, J., and Wall, T. (1980), 'New Work Attitude Measures of Trust, and Personal Need Nonfulfillment', *Journal of Occupational Psychology*, 53: 39–52.

Cook, K. S. (2005), 'Networks, Norms and Trust: The Social Psychology of Social Capital', *Social Psychology Quarterly*, 68: 4–14.

——— and Emerson, R. M. (1978), 'Power, Equity and Commitment in Exchange Networks', *American Sociological Review*, 43: 721–39.

——— and Hardin, R. (2001), 'Norms of Cooperativeness and Networks of Trust', in M. Hechter and K.-D. Opp (eds.), *Social Norms* (New York: Russell Sage), 327–47.

——— Hardin, R., and Levi, M. (2005), *Cooperation Without Trust* (New York: Russell Sage).

——— et al. (2005), 'Trust Building Via Risk Taking: A Cross-Societal Experiment', *Social Psychology Quarterly*, 68 (2): 121–42.

——— et al. (2009), 'Assessing Trustworthiness in Online Goods and Services', in K. S. Cook et al. (eds.), *Trust and Reputation* (New York: Russell Sage).

DiMaggio, P., and Louch, H. (1998), 'Socially Embedded Consumer Transactions: For What Kinds of Purchases Do People Most Often Use Networks?', *American Sociological Review*, 63: 619–37.

Dirks, K. T., and Ferrin, D. L. (2001), 'The Role of Trust in Organizational Settings', *Organization Science*, 12: 450–67.

Ensminger, J. (2001), 'Reputations, Trust, and the Principal Agent Problem', in K. S. Cook (ed.), *Trust in Society* (New York: Russell Sage), 185–201.

Fukuyama, F. (1995), *Trust: The Social Virtues and the Creation of Prosperity* (New York: Simon & Schuster).

Gabarro, J. (1978), 'The Development of Trust, Influence and Expectations', in A. G. Athos and J. Gabarro (eds.), *Interpersonal Behavior: Communication and Understanding in Relationships* (Englewood Cliffs, N.J.: Prentice Hall), 290–303.

Gambetta, D. (1993), *The Sicilian Mafia* (Cambridge, Mass.: Harvard University Press).

GIFFIN, K. (1967), 'The Contribution of Studies of Source Credibility to a Theory of Inter-personal Trust in the Communication Department', *Psychological Bulletin*, 68: 104–20.

GOOD, D. (1988), 'Individuals, Interpersonal Relations and Trust', in D. Gambetta (ed.), *Trust: Making and Breaking Cooperative Relations* (New York: Blackwell), 31–48.

GREIF, A., MILGROM, P., and WEINGAST, B. R. (1995), 'Coordination, Commitment and Enforcement: The Case of the Merchant Guild', in J. Knight and H. Sened (eds.), *Explaining Social Institutions* (Ann Arbor, Mich.: University of Michigan Press), 27–56.

GUSEVA, A., and RONA-TAS, A. (2001), 'Uncertainty, Risk, and Trust: Russian and American Credit Card Markets Compared', *American Sociological Review*, 66: 623–46.

HANLON, G. (1998), 'Professionalism as Enterprise: Service Class Politics and the Redefini-tion of Professionalism', *Sociology*, 32: 43–63.

HARDIN, R. (2002), *Trust and Trustworthiness* (New York: Russell Sage).

—— (2006), *Trust* (Cambridge: Polity).

HEIMER, C. (2001), 'Solving the Problem of Trust', in K. Cook (ed.), *Trust in Society* (New York: Russell Sage), 40–88.

JEFFRIES, F. L., and REED, R. (2000), 'Trust and Adaptation in Relational Contracting', *Academy of Management Review*, 25: 873–82.

JOHNSON-GEORGE, C., and SWAP, W. C. (1982), 'Measurement of Specific Interpersonal Trust: Construction and Validation of a Scale to Assess Trust in a Specific Other', *Journal of Personality and Social Psychology*, 43 (6): 1306–17.

KEE, H. W., and KNOX, R. E. (1970), 'Conceptual and Methodological Considerations in the Study of Trust', *Journal of Conflict Resolution*, 14: 357–66.

KIRKPATRICK, S. A., and LOCKE, E. A. (1991), 'Leadership: Do Traits Matter?', *Academy of Management Executive*, 5: 48–60.

KOLLOCK, P. (1994), 'The Emergence of Exchange Structures: An Experimental Study of Uncertainty, Commitment, and Trust', *American Journal of Sociology*, 100: 313–45.

KOSUGI, M., and YAMAGISHI, T. (1998), 'General Trust and Judgments of Trustworthiness', *Japanese Journal of Psychology*, 69: 349–57.

KIMMEL, M., et al. (1980), 'Effects of Trust, Aspiration, and Gender on Negotiation Tactics', *Journal of Personality and Social Psychology*, 38: 9–22.

KRAMER, R. M. (1996), 'Divergent Realities and Convergent Disappointments in the Hier-archic Relation: Trust and the Intuitive Auditor at Work', in R. M. Kramer and T. R. Tyler (eds.), *Trust in Organizations: Frontiers of Theory and Research* (Thousand Oaks, Calif.: Sage), 216–45.

LAWLER, E. J., and YOON, J. (1993), 'Power and the Emergence of Commitment Behavior in Negotiated Exchange', *American Sociological Review*, 58: 465–81.

—— (1996), 'Commitment in Exchange Relations: Test of a Theory of Relational Cohesion', *American Sociological Review*, 61: 89–108.

LEANA, C. R., and VAN BUREN III, H. J. (1999), 'Organizational Social Capital and Employ-ment Practices', *Academy of Management Review*, 24: 538–55.

LEIK, R. K., and LEIK, S. K. (1977), 'Transition to Interpersonal Commitment', in Robert L. Hamblin and John H. Kunkel (eds.), *Behavioral Theory in Sociology* (New Brunswick, N.J.: Transaction), 299–322.

LEISEN, B., and HYMAN, M. R. (2001), 'An Improved Scale for Assessing Patients' Trust in their Physician', *Health Marketing Quarterly*, 19: 23–42.

LIEBERMAN, J. K. (1981), *The Litigious Society* (New York: Basic).

LONKILIA, M. (1997), 'Informal Exchange Relations in Post Soviet Russia: A Comparative Perspective', *Sociological Research Online*, 2, at <http://www.socresonline.org.uk/2/2/9.html>, accessed Feb. 2009.

LUHMANN, N. (1979), *Trust and Power* (New York: Wiley).

—— (1988), 'Familiarity, Confidence, Trust: Problems and Alternatives', in D. Gambetta (ed.), *Trust* (Oxford/New York: Blackwell).

LUO, Y. (2007), *Guanxi and Business* (Singapore: World Scientific).

MCALLISTER, D. J. (1995), 'Affect- and Cognition-based Trust as Foundations for Interpersonal Cooperation in Organizations', *Academy of Management Journal*, 38 (1): 24–59.

MCWILLIAM, C. L., BROWN, J. B., and STEWART, M. (2000), 'Breast Cancer Patients' Experiences of Patient–Doctor Communication: A Working Relationship', *Patient Education and Counseling*, 39: 191–204.

MACAULAY, S. (1963), 'Non-contractual Relations in Business: A Preliminary Study', *American Sociological Review*, 28: 55–67.

MALHOTRA, D. and MURNIGHAN, J. K. (2002), 'The Effects of Contracts on Interpersonal Trust', *Administrative Science Quarterly*, 47: 534–59.

MARIN, D. (2002), 'Trust Versus Illusion: What is Driving Demonetization in the Former Soviet Union?', *Economics of Transition*, 10 (1): 173–200.

MISHRA, A. K. (1996), 'Organizational Responses to Crisis: The Centrality of Trust', in R. Kramer and T. Tyler (eds.), *Trust in Organizations* (Newbury Park, Calif.: Sage), 261–87.

MIZRUCHI, M. S., and STEARNS, L. B. (2001), 'Getting Deals Done: The Use of Social Networks in Bank Decision Making', *American Sociological Review*, 66: 647–71.

MOLM, L. D. (2006), Review of K. S. Cork, R. Hardin, and M. Levi, *Cooperation Without Trust*, *Administrative Science Quarterly*, 51: 305–7.

—— COLLETT, J., and SCHAEFER, D. (2007), 'Building Solidarity through Generalized Exchange: A Theory of Reciprocity', *American Journal of Sociology*, 113: 205–42.

—— TAKAHASHI, N., and PETERSON, G. (2000), 'Risk and Trust in Social Exchange: An Experimental Test of a Classical Proposition', *American Journal of Sociology*, 105: 1396–427.

MULDER, LAETITIA, B., et al. (2006), 'Undermining Trust and Cooperation: The Paradox of Sanctioning Systems in Social Dilemmas', *Journal of Experimental Social Psychology*, 42: 147–62.

NANUS, B. (1989), *The Leader's Edge: The Seven Keys to Leadership in a Turbulent World* (Chicago, Ill.: Contemporary).

NEACE, M. B. (1999), 'Entrepreneurs in Emerging Economies: Creating Trust, Social Capital, and Civil Society', *Annals of the American Academy of Political and Social Science*, 565: 148–61.

NEE, V., and SANDERS, J. (2001), 'Trust in Ethnic Ties: Social Capital and Immigrants', in K. S. Cook (ed.), *Trust in Society* (New York: Russell Sage).

OUCHI, W. (1981), *Theory Z: How American Business Can Meet the Japanese Challenge* (Reading, Mass.: Addison-Wesley).

PAXTON, P. (1999), 'Is Social Capital Declining in the United States? A Multiple Indicator Assessment', *American Journal of Sociology*, 105: 88–127.

PETERS, R. G., COVELLO, V. T., and McCALLUM, D. B. (1997), 'The Determinants of Trust and Credibility in Environmental Risk Communication: An Empirical Study', *Risk Analysis*, 17: 43–54.

POWELL, W. W. (1996), 'Trust-based Forms of Governance', in Roderick Kramer and Tom R. Tyler (eds.), *Trust in Organizations: Frontiers of Theory and Research* (Thousand Oaks, Calif.: Sage), 51–67.

PUTNAM, R. (2000), *Bowling Alone: The Collapse and Revival of American Community* (New York: Simon & Schuster).

READ, W. H. (1962), 'Upward Communication in Industrial Hierarchies', *Human Relations*, 15: 3–15.

REMPEL, J. K., HOLMES, J. G., and ZANNA, M. P. (1985), 'Trust in Close Relationships', *Journal of Personality and Social Psychologist*, 49: 95–112.

ROCK, C., and SOLODKOV, V. (2001), 'Monetary Policies, Banking and Trust in Changing Institutions: Russia's Transitions in the 1990s', *Journal of Economic Issues*, 25: 451–8.

ROSEN, B., and JERDEE, T. H. (1977), 'Influence of Subordinate Characteristics on Trust and Use of Participative Decision Strategies in a Management Simulation', *Journal of Applied Psychology*, 62: 628–31.

ROTTER, J. B. (1967), 'A New Scale for the Measurement of Interpersonal Trust', *Journal of Personality*, 35: 1–7.

—— (1971), 'Generalized Expectancies for Interpersonal Trust', *American Psychologist*, 26: 443–50.

—— (1980), 'Interpersonal Trust, Trustworthiness and Gullibility', *American Psychologist*, 35: 1–7.

SITKIN, S. B., and ROTH, N. L. (1993), 'Explaining the Limited Effectiveness of Legalistic "Remedies" for Trust/Distrust', *Organization Science*, 4: 367–92.

SZTOMPKA, P. (2006), 'New Perspectives on Trust', *American Journal of Sociology*, 112: 905–19.

TAZELAAR, M. J. A., VAN LANGE, P. A. M., and OUWERKERK, J. W. (2004), 'How to Cope with "Noise" in Social Dilemmas: The Benefits of Communication', *Journal of Personality and Social Psychology*, 87: 845–59.

USLANER, E. M. (1998), 'Social Capital, Television, and the "Mean World": Trust, Optimism and Civic Participation', *Political Psychology*, 19: 441–67.

—— (2002), *The Moral Foundations of Trust* (Cambridge: Cambridge University Press).

UZZI, B. (1997), 'Social Structure and Competition in Interfirm Networks: The Paradox of Embeddedness', *Administrative Science Quarterly*, 42: 35–67.

WARREN, M. E. (2006), 'Democracy and Deceit: Regulating Appearances of Corruption', *American Journal of Political Science*, 50: 160–74.

WHITENER, E. M., et al. (1998), 'Managers as Initiators of Trust: An Exchange Relationship Framework for Understanding Managerial Trustworthy Behavior', *Academy of Management Review*, 23: 513–30.

YAMAGISHI, T., COOK, K. S., and WATABE, M. (1998), 'Uncertainty, Trust and Commitment Formation in the United States and Japan', *American Journal of Sociology*, 104: 165–94.

—— and YAMAGISHI, M. (1994), 'Trust and Commitment in the United States and Japan', *Motivation and Emotion*, 18: 129–65.

YOUNG-YBARRA, C., and WIERSEMA, M. (1999), 'Strategic Flexibility in Information Technology Alliances: The Influence of Transaction Cost Economics and Social Exchange Theory', *Organization Science*, 10: 439–59.

ZAK, P. J., and KNACK, S. (2001), 'Trust and Growth', *Economic Journal*, 111: 295–321.

ZUCKER, L. G. (1986), 'Production of Trust: Institutional Sources of Economic Structure, 1840–1920', in B. M. Staw and L. L. Cummings (eds.), *Research in Organizational Behavior* (Greenwich, Conn.: JAI), 53–112.

PART III

SOCIAL DYNAMICS

···

CHAPTER 11

SOCIAL DYNAMICS FROM THE BOTTOM UP

AGENT-BASED MODELS OF SOCIAL INTERACTION*

···

MICHAEL MACY

ANDREAS FLACHE

INTRODUCTION

···

THE 'Hobbesian problem of order' is a fundamental question across the social sciences. The problem arises because individuals are interdependent yet also autonomous. If there were a 'group mind,' 'collective conscience,' 'managerial elite,' or 'bureaucratic hierarchy' that directed individual behavior like cogs in

* This chapter builds on and extends Macy and Willer (2002), Centola and Macy (2005), Flache and Macy (2006), and Macy and van de Rijt (2006). We wish to acknowledge their many contributions to the ongoing research program on which this chapter is based. We thank the National Science Foundation (SBR-0241657 and SES-0432917, and SES-0433086) and Netherlands Organization for Scientific Research (NWO-VIDI-452-04-351) for support during the time that this research was conducted.

a vast machine, then the explanation of order might appear less problematic. Nevertheless, a growing number of social scientists recognize that social life is a complex system—more like an improvisational jazz ensemble than a symphony orchestra. People are not simply incumbents of social roles; we each chart our own course on the fly. How then is social order possible? The problem is compounded by scale. In a small jazz ensemble, each musician is aware of everyone else and knows that everyone else is aware of her. But imagine an improvisational group with thousands of members, each of whom is only aware of her immediate neighbors. If every player is an interdependent yet autonomous decision maker, why do we not end up with a nasty and brutish cacophony, a noisy war of all against all?

This chapter will describe a new approach to formal theory that can help find the answer: agent-based computational (ABC) modeling. We begin, in Section 11.1, by introducing ABC modeling as a computational implementation of 'methodological individualism,' the search for the microfoundations of social life in the actions of intentional agents. Section 11.2 then shows how the method differs from an earlier generation of modeling approaches. On the one side, ABC modeling differs from game theory in relaxing the behavioral and structural assumptions required for mathematical tractability. On the other, it differs from equation-based methods of computer simulation (such as system dynamics) in modeling population behavior not as resulting from a unified system but as an emergent property of local interaction among adaptive agents. In Section 11.3 we offer an overview and conclusion that addresses potential weaknesses of ABC modeling and proposes research strategies to cope with them.

11.1 THE MICROFOUNDATIONS OF SOCIAL LIFE

ABC modeling originated in computer science and artificial intelligence to study complex adaptive systems composed of large numbers of autonomous but interdependent units. Agent models of self-organized behavior have been applied with impressive success in disciplines ranging from biology to physics to understand how spontaneous coordination can arise in domains as diverse as computer networks, bird flocks, and chemical oscillators. Increasingly, social scientists are using this same methodology to better understand the self-organization of social life as well.

These models are *agent-based* because they take these individual units as the theoretical starting point. Each agent can perform its own computations and have its own local knowledge, but they exchange information with and react to input from other agents. The method is *computational* because the individual agents and their behavioral rules are formally represented and encoded in a computer program, such that the dynamics of the model can be generated through step-by-step iteration from given starting conditions.

Despite their technical origin, agents are inherently social. Agents have both a cognitive and a social architecture (Wooldridge and Jennings 1995; Gilbert and Troitzsch 1999). Cognitively, agents are heuristic and adaptive. Socially, agents are autonomous, interdependent, heterogeneous, and embedded. *Heuristic* means that agents follow simple behavioral rules, not unlike those that guide much of human behavior, such as habits, rituals, routines, norms, and the like (Simon 1982). *Adaptive* means that actions have consequences that alter the probability that the action will recur, as agents respond to feedback from their environment through learning and evolution. *Autonomous* agents have control over their own goals, behaviors, and internal states and take initiative to change aspects of their environment in order to attain those goals. Autonomy is constrained by behavioral and strategic *interdependence*. Behavioral interdependence means agents influence their neighbors in response to the local influence that they receive. More precisely, each agent's actions depend on a configuration of inputs that correspond to what the agent perceives in its local environment, and these actions in turn have consequences, or outputs, that alter the agent's environment. Strategic interdependence means that the payoffs of a player's strategy depend in part on the strategies of other players. *Heterogeneity* relaxes the assumption common to most game-theoretic and system-dynamics models that populations are composed of representative agents.

Finally, and perhaps most importantly, agents are *embedded* in networks, such that population dynamics are an emergent property of local interaction. This does not preclude the possibility that each agent has every other agent as a neighbor, but this is a special case. Agent models also allow for the possibility that agents change structural locations or break off relations with some neighbors and seek out others.

ABC models have been applied to the emergence and dynamics of social segregation (Fossett and Warren 2005), cultural differentiation (Axelrod 1997; Mark 2003), political polarization (Baldassarri and Bearman 2007), network structures (Stokman and Zeggelink 1996; Eguíluz et al. 2005), collective action (Heckathorn 1990; Macy 1990), informal social control (Centola, Willer, and Macy 2005), and the emergence of cooperation through evolution (Axelrod 1984) and learning (Macy and Flache 2002). Some recent overviews and assessments of this work are Macy and Willer (2002), Moretti (2002), and Sawyer (2003). Growing interest among sociologists is reflected in a recent special issue of the *American Journal of Sociology* devoted to 'Social Science Computation' (Gilbert and Abbott 2005).

Although ABC models can also be used to generate predictions that can be empirically tested, it is the application to theoretical modeling that is most relevant for a handbook on analytical sociology. Agent models use a dynamic or processual understanding of causation based on the analytical requirement that causes and effects must be linked by mechanisms, not just correlations. This link is primarily located in the actions of agents and their consequences. Thus, the agent-based approach replaces a single integrated model of the population with a population of models, each corresponding to an autonomous decision maker. This reflects the core methodological-individualist interest in the emergence of population dynamics out of local interaction. Although methodological individualism is older by many decades, ABC modeling can be characterized as its fullest formal representation. Yet ABC modeling has also fundamentally altered the explanatory strategy in methodological individualism, as we elaborate below.

11.1.1 Methodological individualism and ABC modeling

Methodological individualism is most closely identified with Schumpeter and Hayek, but can be traced back to classical social thinkers like Hume and Smith, and later to Max Weber's interpretative method. Weber summarized the core idea, that 'in sociological work...collectivities must be treated as solely the resultants and modes of organization of the particular acts of individual persons, since these alone can be treated as agents in a course of subjectively understandable action' (1968: 13). There are two key ideas here: (1) the *bottom-up idea* that macrosocial patterns must be understood as the outcome of processes at the microsocial level, and (2) the *action principle* that what aggregate up from micro to macro are not attributes of individuals but consequential decisions.

These two principles of methodological individualism are illustrated by a wide range of paradoxical phenomena where individual intentions produce unexpected aggregate results:

- 'Rational herding,' in which everyone crowds into an inferior restaurant because each assumes that the food must be superior if so many people want in
- The 'free rider problem,' in which collective action fails because everyone assumes that it will succeed without them
- The 'bystander problem,' in which everyone observing cries for help assumes that someone else will respond, despite the trivial cost of helping and the dire consequences when no one does
- Residential segregation that emerges in a population that prefers diversity
- An arms race among countries who each prefer to spend on health and education but respond with fear to the escalating armament of their neighbors
- A spiral of retaliatory sectarian, ethnic, or clan violence between groups who once intermarried and lived and worked together peacefully
- Self-destructive adolescent behaviors, such as substance abuse, in response to peer pressures that increase with the rate of compliance

Models based on methodological individualism fall into two broad classes, depending on how they specify the mechanisms by which local interactions generate population dynamics. Expected-utility theory posits a forward-looking deductive mechanism, while evolution and learning provide a backward-looking experiential link (Heath 1976). That is the Janus face of methodological individualism. In much of economics and game theory Janus is facing forward—actions are consciously directed toward their future consequences, based on the ability to predict outcomes through the exercise of rationality. It is this expectation that explains the action, not the actual consequences, which need not even occur (Heath 1976: 3; Scott 2000).

11.1.2 Backward-looking rationality

In ABC models, in contrast, Janus sometimes faces backward, for example in models based on evolution (Axelrod 1984) or learning (Macy and Flache 2002). Backward-looking models replace choices with rules, and intention with repetition. 'Choice' refers to an instrumental, case-specific comparison of alternative courses of action. In contrast, 'rules' are behavioral routines that 'provide standard solutions to recurrent choice problems' (Vanberg 1994: 19). These rules are structured as input–output functions, where the input is a set of conditions of varying complexity and the output is an action. 'The primary mental activity involved in this process,' according to Prelec (1991), 'is the exploration of analogies and distinctions between the current situation and other canonical choice situations in which a single rule or principle unambiguously applies.' This cognitive process contrasts with the forward-looking evaluation of the utility that may be derived from alternative choices.

Backward-looking problem solvers may act as if with deliberate and purposeful intention, but they look forward by rehearsing the lessons of the past. In backward-looking models *repetition*, not prediction, brings the future to bear on the present, by recycling the lessons of the past. Through repeated exposure to a recurrent problem, the consequences of alternative courses of action can be iteratively explored, by the individual actor (learning) or by a population (evolution), in which positive outcomes increase the probability that the associated rule will be followed, while negative outcomes reduce it.

Evolution alters the frequency distribution of rules carried by individuals competing for survival and reproduction. Biological evolution involves genetically hard-wired rules that spread via replication, based on how well the carrier is adapted to survive and reproduce. Social and cultural rules are usually not encoded genetically but are instead 'softwired,' in the form of norms, customs, conventions, rituals, protocols, and routines that propagate via role-modeling, formal training, social influence, imitation, and persuasion.

A classic example of an agent-based evolutionary model is Axelrod's *Evolution of Cooperation* (1984). Axelrod explored whether cooperation based on reciprocity can flourish in a repeated prisoner's dilemma game played in the 'shadow of the future.' In his computational tournament, the winner was a simple strategy of conditional cooperation named 'tit for tat.' Axelrod's work was highly influential far beyond the game-theory community (Etzioni 2001) and has triggered a number of follow-up studies that have supported and extended his findings (e.g. Gotts, Polhill, and Law 2003).

Nevertheless, critics such as Binmore (1998) have pointed out that the performance of any strategy in Axelrod's artificial evolutionary competition might have been very different had the strategy faced another set of contestants or another initial distribution. Recognizing this limitation, Axelrod ran a follow-up tournament using a genetic algorithm (1997: 14–29). The genetic algorithm opens up the set of strategies that are allowed to compete by allowing 'nature' to generate entirely new strategies, including some that might never have occurred to any game theorist. Genetic algorithms are strings of computer code that can mate with other strings to produce entirely new and potentially superior programs by building on partial solutions. Each strategy in a population consists of a string of symbols that code behavioral instructions, analogous to a chromosome containing multiple genes. A set of one or more bits that contains a specific instruction is analogous to a single gene. The values of the bits and bit combinations are analogous to the alleles of the gene. A gene's instructions, when followed, produce an outcome (or payoff) that affects the agent's reproductive fitness relative to other players in the computational ecology. Relative fitness determines the probability that each strategy will propagate. Propagation occurs when two mated strategies recombine. If two different rules are both effective, but in different ways, recombination allows them to create an entirely new strategy that may integrate the best abilities of each 'parent,' making the new strategy superior to either contributor. If so, then the new rule may go on to eventually displace both parent rules in the population of strategies. In addition, the new strings may contain random copying errors. These mutations restore the heterogeneity of the population, counteracting selection pressures that tend to reduce it.

Critics of genetic algorithms have raised probing questions about modeling cultural evolution as a genetic analog (Chattoe 1998). What is the mechanism that eliminates poor performers from the population and allows others to propagate? 'Imitation of the fittest' may be more applicable than starvation and reproduction but, unlike survival of the fittest, mimetic selection replicates only observed behavior and does not copy the underlying (unobservable) rules. Biological analogs paper over the importance of this distinction.

Concerns about the looseness of the evolutionary metaphor have prompted growing interest in relocating the evolutionary selection mechanism from the population level to the cognitive level. Reinforcement learning assumes that actors tend to repeat successful actions and avoid those that were not. Hence, the more successful the strategy, the more likely it will be used in the future. This closely parallels the logic of evolutionary-selection at the population level, in which successful strategies are more likely to be replicated (via higher chances to survive and reproduce or by greater social influence as a role model). However, this similarity need not imply that adaptive actors will learn the strategies favored by evolutionary-selection pressures (Fudenberg and Levine 1998; Schlag and Pollock 1999). The selection mechanisms are not the same. Learning operates through processes like stochastic reinforcement, Bayesian updating, best reply with finite memory, or the back-propagation of error in artificial neural networks. Like a genetic algorithm, an artificial neural network is a self-programmable device, but instead of using recombinant reproduction, it strengthens and weakens network pathways to discover through reinforcement learning the optimal response to a given configuration of inputs. In contrast to evolutionary models, the selection process operates *within* the individuals that carry them, not *between* them. Learning models operate on the local probability distribution of strategies within the repertoire of each individual member, while evolutionary models explore changes in the global frequency distribution of strategies across a population.

Whether selection operates at the individual or population level, the units of adaptation need not be limited to human actors but may include larger entities such as firms or organizations that adapt their behavior in response to environmental feedback. For example, a firm's problem-solving strategies improve over time through exposure to recurrent choices, under the relentless selection pressure of market competition, as inferior routines are removed from the population by bankruptcy and takeover. The outcomes may not be optimal, but we are often left with well-crafted routines that make their bearers look much more calculating than they really are (or need to be), like a veteran outfielder who catches a fly ball as if she had computed its trajectory.

11.2 ABC MODELING, GAME THEORY, AND SYSTEM DYNAMICS

ABC modeling can be located relative to an earlier generation of approaches to formal social theory. It differs on the one side from forward-looking game-theoretic models, although both are methodologically individualist. On the other side, it also differs from macrosocial system-dynamics modeling, although both are computational.

11.2.1 Game theory

Like ABC modeling, game theory is a formal method that deduces in a systematic and rigorous way macrosocial implications from assumptions about microsocial behavior. Based on these assumptions, game theory has identified conditions in which social order can emerge out of individually rational actions. These include the opportunity for ongoing interaction and the opportunity to learn about the reputation of a stranger (Binmore 2007).

The game paradigm obtains its theoretical leverage by modeling the social fabric as a matrix of interconnected autonomous agents guided by outcomes of their interaction with others, where the actions of each depend on, as well as shape, the behavior of those with whom they are linked. Viewed with that lens, game theory appears to be especially relevant to sociology, the social science that has been most reluctant to embrace it. This reluctance reflects in part a set of behavioral and structural assumptions that sociologists find empirically implausible. ABC models allow these assumptions to be greatly relaxed, while preserving the formalism and logical precision of game theory.

Behavioral assumptions

Orthodox game theory typically relies on two controversial behavioral assumptions—unlimited calculating ability and unlimited access to information. These assumptions were imposed not because they are empirically plausible but as simplifications that can aid in identifying equilibrium outcomes. Nevertheless, game theory confronts a growing number of laboratory experiments that reveal systematic violations of those behavioral assumptions (Camerer 2003). These studies suggest that decision-making may be best described by a set of behavioral heuristics that may change across decision contexts (Vanberg 2002; Todd and Gigerenzer 2003) and frames (Tversky and Kahneman 1981) and do not necessarily maximize individual decision outcomes (Fehr and Gächter 2000).

These empirical discrepancies have been excused on the grounds that backward-looking adaptive mechanisms like learning and evolution can be expected to constrain actors to behave 'as if' they were fully rational decision makers with unlimited calculating power and perfect information. In short, we do not need to worry about the plausibility of the behavioral assumptions so long as the population *predictions* are accurate. Unfortunately, the 'as if' principle has not held up well. Laboratory studies of human decision-making have revealed widespread deviations not only from the behavioral postulates but also from the predictions, suggesting the very real possibility that the errors do not necessarily cancel out in the aggregate.

Moreover, even when the predictions are identical across models with different behavioral assumptions, we cannot be sure that the causal mechanisms are the same. For example, both forward-looking and backward-looking models predict higher levels of cooperation when the prisoner's dilemma game is played repeatedly in small densely clustered neighborhoods rather than large random networks where two strangers might never meet again. However, the mechanisms are very different, depending on the behavioral assumptions. In a prisoner's dilemma played by forward-looking game theorists, the mechanism is the concern for reputation and the prospect of cumulative payoffs in future interaction with neighbors. Thus, cooperation becomes more likely as the expectation of future encounters increases. However, in agent-based learning models the mechanism is the coordination complexity for random walk from a self-limiting noncooperative equilibrium into a self-reinforcing cooperative equilibrium (Macy and Flache 2002). And in agent-based evolutionary games the mechanism is the probability that a strategy of conditional cooperation will encounter like-minded others (Cohen, Riolo, and Axelrod 2001). In short, generalizing results obtained under different simplifying assumptions can be highly misleading, even when the predictions are robust as the behavioral assumptions are relaxed.

Concerns about robustness of equilibrium solutions to variation in behavioral assumptions have motivated efforts to develop more cognitively realistic models of the actors (Boudon 1996; Lindenberg 2001). Recent advances in evolutionary game theory (e.g. Bendor and Swistak 2001), formal theories of learning in strategic interaction (e.g. Fudenberg and Levine 1998), stochastic evolutionary models (Young 1998) and sociophysics (e.g. Helbing and Huberman 1998) have successfully incorporated backward-looking decision heuristics into game-theoretic equilibrium analysis. Despite the advances, these approaches retain the requirement of mathematical tractability, imposing restrictive assumptions in both the model of behavior and the model of social structure that they employ.

ABC models extend the effort to relax restrictive behavioral assumptions. With computational solutions it is possible to use backward-looking models of boundedly rational adaptive actors, based on learning and evolution. Rationality can be bounded in two ways: incomplete information, and limited cognitive ability to process the information. Adaptive agents typically have some capacity for gradient search, through processes like reinforcement learning or evolutionary selection, but without the assumption that they will always arrive at the global maximum. Agents can also be entirely nonpurposive, based on expressive or normative rules that are responses to environmental conditions, including behaviors of others. Information can be limited by memory, perceptual constraints, and deception. Agents can also be limited to local information by the structure of social and physical networks, the problem to which we now turn.

Structural assumptions

Closed-form mathematical solutions also require simplifying assumptions about the structure of networks in which games are played. Game theorists generally assume interaction occurs within randomly or completely connected networks. These structures are much more amenable to mathematical solutions than the complex networks observed in most empirical studies. More complex structures, including 'small world' (Watts 1999) and 'scale free' (Barabasi 2002) networks, pose formidable challenges to equilibrium analysis that have discouraged efforts to relax the structural assumptions in most game-theoretic models.

The problem is compounded by the need to assume that networks are static. Fixed networks are a reasonable assumption for communication, transportation, and power grids, but in most social networks the nodes can decide with whom to interact or whether to move to a new location and change all their neighbors in a single stroke. There has been recent progress in modeling dynamic networks as equilibrium strategies among actors seeking to maximize utility by making and breaking ties (Jackson 2004). However, in relaxing the assumptions of fixed networks, these studies bring back in the behavioral assumptions of orthodox game theory.

Moreover, in theorizing network structure as a Nash (1950) equilibrium, the network remains static. Nash equilibrium is the fundamental solution concept in game theory and refers to a configuration of strategies such that no player has an incentive to deviate unilaterally. Once the equilibrium obtains, the population remains there forever. This applies not just to equilibrium models of network structure but to the strategy profile for any game. Nash equilibrium tells us which strategic configurations are stable, but, as Aumann argues (1987; see also Epstein 2006: ch. 3), this does not tell us whether the equilibrium will ever be reached, or with what probability. And when there are multiple equilibria, we do not know the probability distribution over possible states or the transition probabilities should the system be perturbed. Further still, there are almost no games with a unique equilibrium, and in games involving ongoing interactions the number may be infinite, which means game theory can tell us little more than that almost any outcome might persist, should it ever obtain.[1]

As a consequence of these behavioral and structural limitations, the need for a more powerful modeling tool was growing at the same time that advances in computational technology were making one widely available. ABC modeling offers the possibility to relax the restrictive behavioral assumptions of classical game theory, provides a dynamic alternative to static Nash-equilibrium analysis, and extends network analysis to heterogeneous populations embedded in complex and dynamic networks. This allows agent models to extend the reach of game theory while retaining the power to model social order as it emerges out of local interactions—but carried out by agents following nonlinear behavioral heuristics, who are embedded in complex network structures. ABC models make it possible to relax not only the forward-looking behavioral assumptions but also the macrosocial assumptions of random mixing, fixed network structures, and static equilibrium. Agents can decide heuristically not only how to act but also with whom they want to do it, within the constraints of a complex and dynamic network structure. These decisions can then aggregate to create a wide range of population-level regularities, including Nash equilibrium, punctuated equilibrium, saddle points, homeostasis, as well as complex landscapes with attractor basins of varying depth and location.

11.2.2 Equation-based models

ABC also differs from an earlier generation of equation-based models. These models begin with a set of assumptions about the functional relationships among variables characterizing population-level distributions, based on parameters that are estimated from empirical observations or posited from theoretical assumptions. From this set of equations we can then derive predictions, such as the equilibrium of the population dynamics or the expected change in the distribution of some attribute, given changes in the distributions of others.

In the 1960s the first wave of innovation used computers to simulate control and feedback processes in organizations, industries, cities, and even global populations. With roots in structural functionalism, 'system dynamics' models typically consisted of sets of differential equations that predicted a population distribution of interest as a function of other system-level processes. Applications included the flow of raw materials in a factory, inventory control in a warehouse, state legitimacy and imperialist policy, urban traffic, migration, disease transmission, demographic changes in a world system, and ecological limits to growth (Meadows et al. 1974; Forrester 1988; Hanneman, Collins, and Mordt 1995).

Equation-based models often assume individuals are representative agents who interact with everyone else with equal probability. For example, in the original Kermack and McKendrick (1927) SIR model, an epidemic is modeled as a system of three coupled nonlinear ordinary differential equations, by assigning representative actors to classes of 'susceptibles,' 'infectives,' and 'removed' who randomly mix and move from one class to another based on probabilities of transmission, death, and recovery. Moreover, the models assume that awareness of a deadly epidemic does not change population behavior, such as fleeing to uninfected areas or moving the family to the basement. Instead, people continue to go about their normal behavior, randomly mixing with everyone else.

Agent-based modeling replaces a single unified model of the population with a population of models, each of which is a separately functioning autonomous entity. These entities can be embedded in any network structure, and the structure itself can change, through processes like homophily, structural balance, or third-party information about the trustworthiness of a partner. Interactions among these agents then generate the system dynamics from the bottom up, shifting the focus to the relationships among *actors* instead of the relationships among *factors*, like education and social liberalism, the problem to which we now turn.

11.2.3 Multivariate linear models

Equation-based approaches are also used for statistical modeling, in which population parameters are estimated from the distribution of empirically measured individual attributes. For example, a multivariate regression model of social liberalism might include survey responses to a battery of items measuring attitudes like ethnic tolerance, abortion rights, and gay marriage, along with measures of demographic attributes like age, education, and income. The model can then be used to estimate the extent to which college graduates are more socially liberal, and, if so, whether this difference is a direct effect of exposure to liberal ideas in the classroom, an indirect effect via greater access to a 'self-directed occupation' (Kohn 1969), or a spurious effect of differences in social background (e.g. growing up in a liberal household with parents who are college grads).

A key difference between this approach and an ABC model is that the regression model assumes that observations are independent. The problem is that 'politically correct' opinions are likely to be influenced by the attitudes and beliefs of peers, violating the independence assumption.

A simple ABC model illustrates the problem. Consider a population of N agents, half of whom are college graduates. Each agent has opinions on a variety of social issues ranging continuously from -1 (indicating strong conservative views) to $+1$ (indicating strong liberal views). Using this model, we can manipulate social influence to find out what happens when the independence assumption is unwarranted. In the 'baseline' condition all opinions are randomly distributed at the outset and never change. Hence, there is no peer influence and no ideological difference between grads and non-grads. In the 'independent observations' condition (as assumed in regression and structural-equations models) there is also no peer influence. Instead we assume college grads are more liberal on social issues, implemented as a parameter p which is the proportion of grads whose opinions on all issues are always liberal, no matter what views are held by others. In the 'social influence' condition, college grads do not have a liberal bias ($p = 0$). Instead agents adjust their opinions to be similar to the opinions of those whom they admire or whose approval they desire, and they distance themselves from those regarded as politically incorrect. A fourth condition is a hybrid: it is identical to the influence condition, but in addition there is also a small ideological effect of attending college ($p > 0$).

As assumed in most influence models with continuous opinions (e.g. French 1956; Abelson 1964), we assume agents shift their opinion on each issue in the direction of a weighted average of the opinions of others on that issue. Technically,[2]

$$o_{ik,t+1} = o_{ik,t} + \frac{1}{2(N-1)} \sum_{i \neq j} w_{ij}(o_{jk,t} - o_{ik,t}) \tag{1}$$

where k refers to the kth issue (e.g. abortion rights) and $o_{ik,t}$ is agent i's opinion on k at time t, $-1 \leq o_{ik,t} \leq 1$. The weight w_{ij} corresponds to the social distance between i and j, where distance is measured in the D-dimensional state space consisting of demographic attributes (like education, age, ethnicity, etc.) and opinion attributes. The distance between two agents i and j is zero if they are identical on all D dimensions, and the distance is 2 if they differ on all dimensions. The weight w_{ij} is then simply 1 minus the distance; hence $-1 \leq w_{ij} \leq 1$. A positive weight means i is attracted to j and thus seeks to reduce the distance from j in the opinion space. A negative weight means i seeks to increase the distance by differentiating from j. Equation 2 formalizes the weight for the case where education ($e = \pm 1$) is the sole demographic attribute and there are K opinions (hence $D = K + 1$):

$$w_{ij,t+1} = 1 - \frac{\left|e_j - e_i\right| + \sum_{k=1}^{K} \left|o_{jk,t} - o_{ik,t}\right|}{K + 1} \tag{2}$$

For purposes of illustration, we chose one of the simplest versions of this model, with only a single demographic attribute (college education) and only $K = 2$ opinions. (With more demographic or opinion dimensions to the state space the qualitative results we report for the simpler version can still be obtained for a large range of initial distributions of opinions and demographic attributes.) We imposed no exogenous restrictions on who may influence whom—the network structure is entirely determined by the interaction preferences of the agents. We initialized the model by randomly distributing opinions and college degrees, and then set initial weights according to equation 2. Opinions and weights were updated in discrete time steps. In every time step an agent i was randomly selected to update either i's opinions or weights. Updating continued until the population reached equilibrium. We then measured 'social liberalism' by averaging the measures on each of the two opinions to get a composite score.

The simplified model with social influence and $p = 0$ allows analytical identification of the possible equilibrium states. The simplest equilibrium is agreement by all agents on all issues, at which point there is zero pressure on anyone to change. At this equilibrium, linear regression will show zero correlation between education and social liberalism, since there is no variance in either attribute. With $p = 0$, zero correlation is the correct result. So far so good. There is also an equilibrium with some large number of profiles. To simplify the exposition, let us assume that everyone ends up with strong views to the left or right (close to ± 1). Using GLL to refer to a consistently liberal college grad and NCC to refer to a consistently conservative non-grad, there could be an equilibrium in which the population self-organizes into eight profiles: GLL, GLC, GCL, GCC, NLL, NLC, NCL, and NCC. If each profile has sufficient membership, the positive ties within each profile will outweigh any imbalance in the relative influence from incumbents of other profiles.

At this equilibrium, education will still be uncorrelated with social liberalism when $p = 0$, hence peer influence will not create a spurious association.

So far, we have considered an equilibrium with only one group, and equilibria with a large number of groups. There is also an equilibrium in which the population polarizes into two opposing camps, one liberal on both social issues and one conservative, and each camp has the same number of college grads. The fact that a liberal and a conservative have the same education (hence they are identical on one dimension out of three) is not sufficient to overcome their ideological hostility (maximal disagreement on the other two dimensions). And the fact that two agents with identical opinions differ in education (hence they are similar on two dimensions out of three) is not sufficient to drive them apart ideologically. Thus, the population stabilizes, again with a zero correlation between education and social liberalism—as it should be. With all these possible equilibria considered so far, there is still no problem with the assumption that the observations are independent, even though the assumption is wrong.

The problem arises if the population splits into two opposing camps with different numbers of college grads in each camp. For example, suppose everyone in one camp is a grad and there are no grads in the other. At this equilibrium there is a perfect correlation between education and social liberalism, even though education has no effect on opinion. However, this is an extreme case. From a random start, if the population ends up with everyone in agreement, or ends up with a large number of camps of about equal size, or ends up in two camps with about the same number of grads in each camp, there will be no problem. A regression model that assumes independent observations will give the correct result—zero correlation between education and liberalism—even though the independence assumption is violated. The regression result will be incorrect only if there are two camps and the two camps differ sharply in the number of grads. Given our assumption that education has no effect on liberalism, how likely is it that such a difference might obtain at equilibrium?

To find out, we ran fifty realizations from a random start, in which opinions were subject to peer influence but education had no effect on opinion ($p = 0$). Each realization proceeded until equilibrium obtained. We then measured the magnitude of the correlation between education and social liberalism (regardless of sign) at each equilibrium and averaged these results over all fifty realizations. The undirected-magnitude measure tests whether education appears to cause changes in social liberalism in any direction (left or right). We also measured the direction of the correlation, to see if education appears to increase social liberalism. The directed measure can be zero even if education is highly correlated with opinion, so long as the correlation is as likely to be strongly positive as strongly negative.

Note that our purpose here is not to explain how people become socially liberal, and our results do not do that. On the contrary, we could relabel the 'social liberalism' opinions to refer instead to musical preferences or table manners or any arbitrary attribute that can be influenced by others. And we could relabel

Table 11.1 How peer influence affects the association between education and social liberalism

Peer influence	Proportion of grads with liberal bias	Directed correlation	Undirected correlation
No	0	0.002	0.08
No	0.1	0.052	0.088
No	0.2	0.108	0.122
Yes	0	−0.031	0.709
Yes	0.1	0.292	0.860
Yes	0.2	0.696	0.915

'education' to be gender or eye color or any attribute that cannot be influenced by others. The effect of education on social liberalism is simply an illustration of the possible danger of linear statistical models that assume independence of the observations.

The results reported in Table 11.1 reveal this danger very dramatically.[3] When $p = 0$, college grads are not assigned a liberal bias. Thus, the observed correlation between education and liberalism should be zero, and indeed it is very close to that ($r = 0.08$) when the statistical assumption of independent observations is realized in the model by precluding peer influence. However, when we allowed peer influence, in violation of the independence assumption, the magnitude of the correlation soars, to $r = 0.709$. This very strong correlation is entirely an artifact of the self-organization of the population into liberal and conservative camps with unequal numbers of college grads. Although there are many other possible equilibria in which the correlation would remain close to zero, the population dynamics strongly favor the polarized outcome with unequal numbers of college grads in each camp—even though the model assumes that education has no effect on beliefs. The 0.709 correlation is thus entirely spurious.

The imbalance is highly stable—once a population tips in one direction, it never tips back—but when $p = 0$ tipping is equally likely in either direction. The population dynamics of peer influence then make college graduates highly liberal or highly conservative (the undirected correlation is $r = 0.709$), but with equal probability (the directed correlation is $r = -0.031$). In some populations grads will be much more liberal, and in others much more conservative, but it will be hard to find a population in which grads and non-grads have similar opinions.

When $p > 0$ the population will tend to tip toward social liberalism among college grads. For example, $p = 0.2$ biases college grads such that the correlation between education and opinion is $r = 0.108$ in the absence of social influence, and the effect is almost always in the same direction (hence the directed and undirected measures are nearly identical). At this level of liberal bias, education explains only 1 percent of the variance in opinion. Yet even this relatively weak nonspurious effect is sufficient to tip the population into what appears (incorrectly) to be a powerful effect of education, with $r = 0.696$. The population will now consistently tip toward social liberalism among college grads, and the correlation is so strong that this one binary variable alone can explain half the variance in social liberalism. That is because peer influences have greatly exaggerated what is in fact a very weak liberal bias among grads. By assuming independence of observations, a regression model attributes all this effect of peer influence to differences in education.

Of course, a multiple-regression model could show that these educational differences were spurious, due to the prior effects of social background (e.g. grads' children may be more likely to attend college and already liberal before they enter). Ironically, this result—showing that the ideological effects of education were spurious—would itself be spurious! Peer influences can greatly exaggerate the effects of all demographic (fixed) attributes, whether these are causally prior to educational attainment (e.g. parents' education) or causally subsequent (e.g. occupational self-direction). One can only wonder how many published regression results are largely an artifact of social-influence processes that were assumed away by the statistical requirement for independence of the observations.

ABC modeling makes it possible to see how peer influences can interact with the effects of individual experience in shaping behavior. To assess from empirical data how much variation in behavior can be accounted for by influences from peers and how much can be attributed to individuals' sociodemographic characteristics, a modeling tool is needed that can handle the mutual interdependency of behaviors of multiple socially interconnected actors. Moreover, the model needs to take into account that actors may make or break social relationships, depending on their own and others' behavior. For example, an observed association between opinion similarity and the presence of friendship relations in an empirical network can be attributed to contagion (friends influence each other) or selection (similar people become friends) or both. Stochastic actor-oriented models proposed by Snijders (2001) and implemented in the SIENA[4] toolkit are a class of ABC models that allow investigators to disentangle statistically these simultaneous mechanisms, using longitudinal data about the change of network relations and of actors' behaviors or attributes. For example, in the problem just considered, if we entered panel data on individual opinions, educational attainment, and network structure, SIENA could tell us whether college grads were more socially liberal, and, if so, the extent to which this difference was due to peer influence, network structure, or a liberal bias among college graduates.

Stochastic actor-oriented models combine ABC modeling with statistical estimation and testing of the mechanisms assumed by the modeler. The general model assumes that agents choose their social ties and their behavior by myopically optimizing a random utility function. The modeler specifies which 'effects' are assumed to drive the decision-making of agents. In our example we assumed that agents are influenced by friends, and that they tend to establish positive social ties to those who agree with them. To test this in an actor-oriented stochastic model we would include in the submodel of the opinion dynamics the effect of the number of friends one agrees with after having changed an opinion on the likelihood that the corresponding opinion change can be observed. Correspondingly, we would include in the submodel of the network dynamics the same effect on the likelihood that an agent establishes or breaks a particular network tie. The statistical estimation and test of the corresponding parameters is based on computer simulation of the specified agent-based model. Broadly, SIENA finds the parameters for the effects specified by the modeler by simulating the distribution of the networks and actor attributes for a range of selected parameter values. The program then selects the set of parameters for which the simulation yields the best match with the observed dynamics of network and behavior.

11.3 METHODOLOGICAL PRINCIPLES

'If you didn't grow it, you didn't explain it.' Joshua Epstein calls this 'the bumper sticker reduction of the agent-based computational model.' Epstein is one of the founders of ABC modeling, and his 'bumper sticker' challenges social scientists to raise the bar for what constitutes an explanation of social change. Structural equations and system-dynamics models, even with longitudinal data, are not sufficient, because they tell us only about the interactions among the attributes of the actors but not the actors themselves, who are typically assumed to be fully independent. Nor are game-theoretic models sufficient, because the Nash equilibrium only explains why a population pattern persists, and not how it obtains or changes.

Nor, even, are ABC models sufficient for an explanation, according to Epstein, for three related reasons. First, there may be alternative specifications that can generate the same observed population dynamics. This limitation closely parallels the multiple-equilibrium problem in game theory. 'Growing' the pattern shows that an explanation is possible but does not tell us how much confidence to place in it or how many other explanations may also be possible. Second, even when there is only one way that can be found to generate the population pattern, the necessary behavioral assumptions may be highly implausible. Third, even if there is only one model that can generate an empirical pattern, and the model is sensible, if it is overly complicated we may be unable to uncover the underlying causal process. This is an important disadvantage of computational modeling compared with game theory. A deductive proof of equilibrium requires knowledge of the causal process, which is not required to generate a pattern computationally. Unlike game-theoretic models, in which the causal mechanisms are necessarily explicit, computational models generate input–output patterns in which the causal linkages cannot be derived from inspection of the source code but must instead be unraveled through close observation of events as they unfold. It is not enough to show which parameter values are responsible for the outcome, we need to know the sequence of *actions* that are responsible. Without this, we cannot rule out the possibility that the results are nothing more than artifacts of particular modeling technologies or even bugs in the source code.

In sum, the ability to generate a population pattern from the bottom up is a necessary step, but it is not sufficient. The most we can say is that ABC models can take us well beyond what we can know using discursive models based on theoretical intuition or statistical models of interactions among variables or mathematical models of interactions in a static equilibrium.

How far ABC models can take us depends decisively on two things: the macro-social complexity and the microsocial simplicity. Generally speaking, highly complex and nonlinear population patterns can be very difficult to generate from the bottom up, which makes any model that succeeds worthy of attention. The more complex the target pattern—such as a population dynamic characterized by phase transitions, nonmonotonicity, or punctuated equilbrium—the harder it becomes to find a relatively simple model that can generate the pattern, and thus the more compelling it becomes when we succeed.

At the micro level it is the other way around. The simpler the set of assumptions about agent behavior, the less likely that the results depend on theoretically arbitrary parameters whose effects are poorly understood, and the more likely we can identify the underlying causal mechanism. Suppose we can generate a complex population pattern with a relatively simple agent model. We have now identified a set of conditions that are sufficient to produce the pattern, and we can test which conditions are necessary by systematically exploring the parameter space, but we do not know *why* these conditions are necessary or sufficient. What is the mechanism that explains how the conclusions follow from the assumptions and why the conclusions follow from some sets of assumptions but not from others?

Schelling's (1978) classic ABC model of residential segregation illustrates the importance of keeping things as simple as possible. The model generates an equilibrium that can also be generated by models with 'top-down' assumptions about mortgage bank redlining and institutional racism. Nevertheless, because the model is highly transparent, it provides insight into a tipping process that was not previously apparent to researchers. The model is therefore useful, despite the inability to rule out alternative explanations, because it reveals a heretofore hidden mechanism that may account for the persistence of segregation forty years after passage of the Fair Housing Act and despite pronounced increases in ethnic tolerance. In short, the goal is to generate a complex population pattern, using a simple and transparent model with a small number of assumptions about local interaction.

This goal poses a dilemma. Like statistical modelers trying to boost the explained variance by throwing in more variables, computational modelers may be tempted to improve the empirical fit by adding new assumptions, leading to models that are too complex to be understood independently from their particular implementation. While game-theoretic models may sometimes be too simple to explain the dynamics of a complex system, ABC models can easily become too complex to explain the dynamics of a simple system. Little is gained by reliance on multivariate regression to see which of the model's many parameter combinations have the most effect on population behavior. The primary benefit of ABC modeling is that it allows us to identify the causal processes that underlie observed correlations. That benefit is lost when it becomes as difficult to explain the patterns generated by the model as it is to explain the corresponding patterns observed in nature. Simply put, Epstein's bumper sticker is fine for the front of the car, but we need a different one for the back: 'If you don't know *how* you grew it, you didn't explain it.'

The 'kitchen sink' temptation in ABC modeling not only obscures causal mechanisms but also limits the ability to test the numerical robustness. Unlike the deductive conclusions in closed-form mathematical models, the results of ABC models depend on numerical values. The number of numerical combinations explodes as the number of parameters increases, making a full exploration of the parameter space impractical. To make matters worse, when the model is stochastic, it is also necessary to test robustness over many realizations, no two of which may be identical, and for which none may resemble the mean of the distribution. Unlike experimental manipulations, where results are expected to change with the parameters, a sensitivity analysis is used to demonstrate the stability of the results and to rule out the possibility that the results of the experimental manipulations are nothing more than an artifact of arbitrary parameter combinations or an idiosyncratic random seed (see Saam 1999; Chattoe, Saam, and Möhring 2000). Models that are designed to make accurate predictions are likely to have so many parameters that rigorous sensitivity-testing is simply not possible, even with very fast computers.

We recognize that models can also be too simple. For example, critics might regard our reinforcement learning model as overly simplistic in its behavioral assumptions, preferring instead more elaborate models of human cognitive processes (Conte et al. 2001) with situation-specific modes of cognition, such as repetition, imitation, deliberation, and social comparison (Jager et al. 2000). Here again the enormous speed and power of modern computers reinforces the temptation to make models that are cognitively and/or behaviorally realistic. For example, Younger (2004) models hunter-gatherer societies that include such intricacies as when the agents fall asleep and what it takes to get them to wake up. When models become so complicated that researchers can only report input–output covariance with a long list of parameters, the value of experimental methods is largely undermined.

In contrast, analysis of very simple and abstract models can reveal new theoretical insights that have broad applicability, beyond the stylized models that produced them. While important discoveries can be made by open-ended exploration of theoretical possibilities, researchers need to resist the temptation to become freewheeling adventurers in artificial worlds. Careful, systematic mapping of a parameter space may be less engaging, but it makes for better science. This requires theoretically motivated manipulation of parameters, based on careful review of current theoretical and empirical knowledge, and a clear statement of the hypotheses that guided the experimental design. Models should start out simple, and complications should be added one at a time, making sure that the dynamics are fully understood before proceeding. Coleman (1990) advises modelers to begin with observable relationships between well-specified macrosocial phenomena, such as the relationship between network clustering and the rate at which an innovation diffuses. Computational experiments can then be used to test hypotheses about the microsocial causal mechanism that underlies the macrosocial relationship.

In conclusion, agent-based computational modeling combines the rigor of formal model-building with behavioral and structural complexity that would not be mathematically tractable with orthodox game theory. ABC models provide an ideal test bed for deriving testable implications for macrosocial dynamics of behavioral principles such as social rationality (Lindenberg 2001) and 'fast and frugal' decision heuristics (Todd and Gigerenzer 2003). Agent-based models can also be used to perform computational experiments that test the effects of structural conditions such as network topology, including networks that evolve as actors seek more attractive neighbors. With the adoption of a standard methodology, we believe that agent-based computational modeling will lead to significant advances in the bottom-up approach to the study of social order and change.

NOTES

1. Game theorists have responded to the problem by proposing procedures that can winnow the set of possible equilibria. For example, the solution set can be narrowed by identifying equilibria that are risk-dominant (which eliminates any equilibrium that does not pay at least the maximin), Pareto-dominant (which eliminates any equilibrium that is less preferred by at least one player), trembling-hand-perfect (strategies must remain in equilibrium even if one player should accidentally deviate from equilibrium behavior), and subgame-perfect (the strategy profile constitutes a Nash equilibrium in every subgame). However, these equilibrium selection methods are theoretically arbitrary (e.g. there is no a priori basis for risk-dominant behavior) and they often disagree about which equilibrium should be selected (e.g. in assurance, Pareto dominance

and subgame perfection identify mutual cooperation while risk dominance points to mutual defection).

2. We limit opinions to the unit interval in absolute value ($-1 \leq o_{ik} \leq 1$) by truncating at ± 1. Assuming a smoother approach to the interval limits would not result in qualitatively different model behavior.

3. For simplicity, we illustrate the effects of the independence assumption using zero-order product-moment correlation instead of multiple regression. Both methods assume independence and both give misleading results for these data when the assumption is violated.

4. SIENA (for 'simulation investigation for empirical-network analysis') is a computer program for statistical estimation of models of the evolution of social networks, based on Snijders' stochastic actor-oriented model (2001).

References

ABELSON, R. (1964), 'Mathematical Models of the Distribution of Attitudes Under Controversy', in N. Frederiksen and H. Gulliken (eds.), *Contributions to Mathematical Psychology* (New York: Holt, Rinehart, & Winston), 142–60.

AUMANN, R. (1987), 'Correlated Equilibrium as an Expression of Bayesian Rationality', *Econometrics*, 55: 1–18.

AXELROD, R. (1984), *The Evolution of Cooperation* (New York: Basic).

—— (1997), *The Complexity of Cooperation* (Princeton, N.J.: Princeton University Press).

BALDASSARRI, D., and BEARMAN, P. (2007), 'The Dynamics of Polarization', *American Sociological Review*, 72: 784–811.

BARABASI, A. (2002), *Linked: The New Science of Networks* (Cambridge, Mass.: Perseus).

BENDOR, J., and SWISTAK, P. (2001), 'The Evolution of Norms', *American Journal of Sociology*, 106: 1493–545.

BINMORE, K. (1998), Review of R. Axelrod, *The Complexity of Cooperation: Agent-based Models of Competition and Collaboration*, *Journal of Artificial Societies and Social Simulation*; <http://www.soc.surrey.ac.uk/JASSS/1/1/review1.html>, accessed Feb. 2009.

—— (2007), *Game Theory: A Very Short Introduction* (Oxford: Oxford University Press).

BOUDON, R. (1996), 'The "Cognitivist Model": A Generalized Rational-Choice Model', *Rationality and Society*, 8: 123–50.

CAMERER, C. (2003), 'Behavioral Game Theory', *Experiments in Strategic Interaction* (New York: Russel Sage).

CENTOLA, D., and MACY, M. (2005), 'Social Life in Silico: The Science of Artificial Societies', in S. Wheelan (ed.), *Handbook of Group Research and Practice* (Thousand Oaks, Calif.: Sage).

—— WILLER, R., and MACY, M. (2005), 'The Emperor's Dilemma: A Computational Model of Self-Enforcing Norms', *American Journal of Sociology*, 110: 1009–40.

CHATTOE, E. (1998), 'Just How (Un)realistic are Evolutionary Algorithms as Representations of Social Processes?', *Journal of Artificial Societies and Social Simulation*, 1, <http://www.soc.surrey.ac.uk/jasss/1/3/2.html>, accessed Feb. 2009.

CHATTOE, E., SAAM, N., and MÖHRING, M. (2000), 'Sensitivity Analysis in the Social Sciences: Problems and Prospects', in R. Suleiman, K. G. Troitzsch, and N. Gilbert (eds.), *Tools and Techniques for Social Science Simulation* (Heidelberg: Physica).

COHEN, M., RIOLO, R., and AXELROD, R. (2001), 'The Role of Social Structure in the Maintenance of Cooperative Regimes', *Rationality and Society*, 13: 5–32.

COLEMAN, J. (1990), *Foundations of Social Theory* (Cambridge, Mass.: Harvard University Press).

CONTE, R., et al. (2001), 'Sociology and Social Theory in Agent-based Simulation: A Symposium', *Computational and Mathematical Organization Theory*, 7: 183–205.

EGUÍLUZ, V., et al. (2005), 'Cooperation and Emergence of Role Differentiation in the Dynamics of Social Networks', *American Journal of Sociology*, 110: 977–1008.

EPSTEIN, J. (2006), *Generative Social Science: Studies in Agent-based Computational Modeling* (Princeton, N.J.: Princeton University Press).

ETZIONI, A. (2001), 'On Social and Moral Revival', *Journal of Political Philosophy*, 9: 356–71.

FEHR, E., and GÄCHTER, S. (2000), 'Cooperation and Punishment in Public Goods Experiments', *American Economic Review*, 90: 980–94.

FLACHE, A., and MACY, M. (2006), 'Bottom-up Modelle Sozialer Dynamiken: Agentenbasierte Computermodellierung und Methodologischer Individualismus. Kölner Zeitschrift für Soziologie und Sozialpsychologie', in A. Diekmann (ed.), *Methoden der Sozialforschung: Sonderheft 44/2004 der Kölner Zeitschrift für Soziologie und Sozialpsychologie* (Wiesbaden: Verlag für Sozialwissenschaften), 536–60.

FORRESTER, J. (1988), *Principles of Systems* (Taylor & Francis).

FOSSETT, M., and WARREN, W. (2005), 'Overlooked Implications of Ethnic Preferences for Residential Segregation in Agent-based Models', in D. Sallach (ed.), *Social Dynamics: Interaction, Reflexivity and Emergence* (Argonne, Ill.: Argonne National Laboratory).

FRENCH, J. (1956), 'The Formal Theory of Social Power', *Psychological Review*, 63: 181–94.

FUDENBERG, D., and LEVINE, D. (1998), *The Theory of Learning in Games* (Boston, Mass.: MIT Press).

GILBERT, N., and ABBOTT, A. (2005), 'Introduction', *American Journal of Sociology*, 110: 859–63 (special issue on 'social-science computation').

—— and TROITZSCH, K. (1999), *Simulation for the Social Scientist* (Milton Keynes: Open University Press).

GOTTS, N. M., POLHILL, J., and LAW, A. (2003), 'Agent-based Simulation in the Study of Social Dilemmas', *Artificial Intelligence Review*, 19: 3–92.

HANNEMAN, R., COLLINS, R., and MORDT, G. (1995), 'Discovering Theory Dynamics by Computer Simulation: Experiments on State Legitimacy and Imperialist Capitalism', *Sociological Methodology*, 25: 1–46.

HEATH, A. (1976), *Rational Choice and Social Exchange: A Critique of Exchange Theory* (Cambridge: Cambridge University Press).

HECKATHORN, D. (1990), 'Collective Sanctions and Compliance Norms: A Formal Theory of Group Mediated Social Control', *American Sociological Review*, 55: 366–84.

HELBING. D., and HUBERMAN, B. (1998), 'Coherent Moving States In Highway Traffic', *Nature*, 396: 738–40.

JACKSON, M. (2004), 'A Survey of Models of Network Formation: Stability and Efficiency', in G. Demange and M. Wooders (eds.), *Group Formation in Economics: Networks, Clubs and Coalitions* (Cambridge: Cambridge University Press).

JAGER, W., et al. (2000), 'Behavior in Commons Dilemmas: Homo economicus and Homo psychologicus in an Ecological–Economic Model', *Ecological Economics*, 35: 357–79.

KERMACK, W., and MCKENDRICK, A. (1927), 'A Contribution to the Mathematical Theory of Epidemics', *Proceedings of the Royal Society of London*, series A, 115: 700–21.

KOHN, M. (1969), *Class and Conformity: A Study in Values* (Homewood, Ill.: Dorsey).

LINDENBERG, S. (2001), 'Social Rationality versus Rational Egoism', in Jonathan Turner (ed.), *Handbook of Sociological Theory* (New York: Kluwer), 635–68.

MACY, M. (1990), 'Learning Theory and the Logic of Critical Mass', *American Sociological Review*, 55: 809–26.

—— and FLACHE, A. (2002), 'Learning Dynamics in Social Dilemmas', *Proceedings of the National Academy of Sciences of the USA*, 99: 7229–36.

—— and WILLER, R. (2002), 'From Factors to Actors: Computational Sociology and Agent-based Modelling', *Annual Review of Sociology*, 28: 143–66.

—— and RIJT, A. VAN DE (2006), 'Game Theory', in B. Turner (ed.), *The Cambridge Dictionary of Sociology* (Cambridge: Cambridge University Press).

MARK, N. (2003), 'Culture and Competition: Homophily and Distancing Explanations for Cultural Niches', *American Sociological Review*, 68: 319–45.

MEADOWS, D. L., et al. (1974), *The Dynamics of Growth in a Finite World* (Cambridge, Mass.: MIT Press).

MORETTI, S. (2002), 'Computer Simulation in Sociology: What Contribution?', *Social Science Computer Review*, 20: 43–57.

NASH, J. (1950), 'Equilibrium Points in N-Person Games', *Proceedings of the National Academy of Sciences of the USA*, 36; 48–9.

PRELEC, D. (1991), 'Values and Principles: Some Limitations on Traditional Economic Analysis', in A. Etzioni and P. Lawrence (eds.), *Perspectives on Socioeconomics* (London: Sharpe).

SAAM, N. (1999), 'Simulating the Micro–Macro Link: New Approaches to an Old Problem and an Application to Military Coups', *Sociological Methodology*, 29: 43–79.

SAWYER, R. (2003), 'Artificial Societies: Multiagent Systems and the Micro–Macro Link in Sociological Theory', *Sociological Methods and Research*, 31: 325–63.

SCHELLING, T. (1978), *Micromotives and Macrobehavior* (New York: Norton).

SCHLAG, K., and POLLOCK, G. (1999), 'Social Roles as an Effective Learning Mechanism', *Rationality and Society*, 11: 371–97.

SCOTT, J. (2000), 'Rational Choice Theory', in G. Browning, A. Halcli, and F. Webster (eds.), *Understanding Contemporary Society: Theories of the Present* (London: Sage), 126–38.

SIMON, H. (1982), *Models of Bounded Rationality* (Cambridge, Mass.: MIT Press).

SNIJDERS, T. (2001), 'The Statistical Evaluation of Social Network Dynamics', in M. E. Sobel and M. P. Becker (eds.), *Sociological Methodology* (Boston/London: Blackwell), 361–95.

STOKMAN, F., and ZEGGELINK, E. (1996), 'Self-organizing Friendship Networks', in B. G. Liebrand and D. M. Messick (eds.), *Frontiers in Social Dilemmas Research* (Berlin: Springer), 385–418.

TODD, P., and GIGERENZER, G. (2003), 'Bounding Rationality to the World', *Journal of Economic Psychology*, 24: 143–65.

TVERSKY, A., and KAHNEMAN, D. (1981), 'The Framing of Decisions and Psychology of Choice', *Science*, 211: 453–8.

VANBERG, V. (1994), *Rules and Choice in Economics* (London: Routledge).

VANBERG, V. (2002), 'Rational Choice vs. Program-based Behavior: Alternative Theoretical Approaches and their Relevance for the Study of Institutions', *Rationality and Society*, 14: 7–54.

WATTS, D. (1999), 'Networks, Dynamics, and the Small-world Phenomenon', *American Journal of Sociology*, 105: 493–527.

WEBER, MAX (1968), *Economy and Society*, trans. and ed. G. Roth and C. Wittich (Berkeley, Calif.: University of California Press).

WILLER, R., KUWABARA, K., and MACY, M. (2005), 'The Emperor's Dilemma II: False Enforcement of Unpopular Norms', *American Journal of Sociology*, 110 (4): 1009–40.

WOOLDRIDGE, M., and JENNINGS, N. (1995), 'Intelligent Agents: Theory and Practice', *Knowledge Engineering Review*, 10: 115–52.

YOUNG, P. (1998), *Individual Strategy and Social Structure: An Evolutionary Theory of Institutions* (Princeton, N.J.: Princeton University Press).

YOUNGER, S. (2004), 'Reciprocity, Normative Reputation, and the Development of Mutual Obligation in Gift-giving Societies', *Journal of Artificial Societies and Social Simulation*, 7, at <http://www.soc.surrey.ac.uk/jasss/7/1/5.html>, accessed Feb. 2009.

···

SEGREGATION DYNAMICS

···

E L I Z A B E T H B R U C H

R O B E R T M A R E

INTRODUCTION

···

A pervasive property of social organization is that persons with similar social characteristics tend to cluster in close physical and social proximity. Racial and ethnic groups in the USA tend to reside in separate communities (Massey and Denton 1993). Throughout the world, men and women are segregated into distinct jobs and occupations (Charles and Grusky 2004). And small-scale social units such as marriages and families tend, by processes of assortative mating, to bring together individuals with similar religion, education, age, social-class background, and other traits (Kalmijn 1998). A central goal of sociological inquiry is to understand the segregation of people in physical and social space and the processes through which these patterns arise and persist. Segregation may occur through benign processes, such as the concentration of married people in small towns or babies in parks on sunny afternoons. But it may also reflect the workings of social hierarchies. For instance, disadvantaged ethnic minorities often live closest to areas of environmental pollution; neighborhoods reflect hierarchies of income and wealth; and the scarcity of women in executive positions results from the different behaviors of men and women and the different ways that men and women are treated. A common feature of segregation processes is that they are self-reinforcing. That is, the characteristics of settings across which groups are segregated are interdependent with the actions of individuals within the groups. If low rents draw poor people to less desirable neighborhoods, government may more easily dispose of waste in these already disadvantaged areas. This deters in-migration by more affluent individuals and reinforces neighborhood economic segregation. Segregation also tends to limit the choices available to individuals. For example, a white family that prefers to live in an integrated community may be limited to either virtually all-white or all-black neighborhoods. Given a limited set of choices, they opt to remain with their own group, further sustaining segregation.

This chapter is concerned with models of segregation processes and the methods and data for studying these processes empirically. We describe segregation in general terms and discuss the key parts of segregation processes: the actors, dimensions of clustering, and universe in which clustering occurs; focus on residential segregation and review measures, data, and models for investigating the dynamic interdependence of individual action and neighborhood characteristics; and briefly consider how multiple segregating processes may amplify or attenuate one another.

12.1 ANALYSIS OF SEGREGATION

Segregation is the nonrandom allocation of people who belong to different groups into social positions and the associated social and physical distances between groups. Segregation *per se* is a static property of a population, whereas segregation *processes* are the actions that create and sustain segregation.

12.1.1 Single and multiple sets of actors and dimensions of segregation

In principle, segregation may result from individuals' behaviors at a single level of social organization. For example, individuals may choose dwellings in a simple real-estate market where the only other actors are buyers, sellers, and their neighbors. More realistically, however, individual actions are coordinated in a more complex way. Buyers, sellers, renters, landlords, agents, lenders, and politicians all affect real-estate transactions. In the interests of presenting the current state of the art, we focus here mainly on segregating processes that are produced primarily through the behavior of individuals at one level of social organization (e.g. individuals who decide where to move), but we recognize the importance of other actors as well.

Social research typically examines segregation processes in only one social dimension or social context, but in fact people are segregated in multiple dimensions and contexts. For example, the same socioeconomic criteria by which children are distributed across neighborhoods may also funnel them into schools, peer groups, and eventual occupational trajectories. These contexts may overlap and amplify the inequality-producing effects of segregation in other environments. For example, residential segregation, political boundaries, and the structure of school taxation may affect human-capital formation and lifelong inequalities (Benabou 1996; Durlauf 1996). In addition, a change in segregation along one dimension (e.g. poverty status) may exacerbate or mitigate segregation on another dimension (e.g. race) (Wilson 1987). Further, segregation occurs in contexts other than residential neighborhoods, including differential sorting in marriages, occupations, peer groups, lunchrooms, dormitories, prisons, church congregations, and even chat rooms in cyberspace. Winship (this volume) proposes that time as well as physical or social space is yet another dimension along which segregation may occur. Variations in the models and methods discussed here for residential segregation are potentially useful in these other contexts as well.

The analysis of segregation consists of summarizing how a population that is differentiated into groups (e.g. economic strata, race, language, or gender groups) is distributed across social locations (e.g. neighborhoods, congregations, marriages, college dormitories, or jobs) and of discovering the processes that establish and maintain that distribution. The social groupings of interest usually reflect normative concerns with barriers between socioeconomic, ethnic, cultural, gender, and other groups. The social locations of interest also reflect normative concerns with segregation in work, residence, leisure, worship, and other contexts.

12.1.2 Segregation of groups across social locations

We can classify the locations across which groups are segregated along two dimensions. First, segregation may be across groups of fixed or variable size. Examples of locations of relatively fixed size include marriages, jobs in a workplace, housing units in neighborhoods, and dinner seating at a wedding reception (assuming a fixed number of chairs per table). Locations of variable size include cliques in high school, church congregations, or picnickers on a beach. Second, segregation may involve the formation and dissolution of new locations, or entries and exits from enduring groups. New locations are formed when people marry, picnic on the beach, or form a friendship group. Often these locations are temporary and exits result in their dissolution. On the other hand, some locations endure beyond the lives of their incumbents. Enduring groups include work organizations, church congregations, or residential neighborhoods. Together these dimensions combine into four ideal types: (1) fixed transitory, (2) fixed permanent, (3) variable transitory, and (4) variable permanent. These types of locations vary in the segregation and segregation processes that they create. Segregation across transitory locations comprises not only the uneven distribution across these locations, but also differential participation. For example, the homogamy of marriages is affected not only by who marries whom given marriage, but also by who marries and which marriages persist (Schwartz and Mare 2003). In contrast, segregation across permanent locations usually comprises only the uneven distribution across locations. For example, residential neighborhoods are relatively permanent arrangements and all individuals live in some kind of neighborhood. The dynamics of segregation across fixed-size locations are, by definition, mediated by vacancies. One person cannot enter a neighborhood unless another person leaves. The pattern of segregation can only change by individuals' coordinated entries and exits from the neighborhood. In variable-sized locations, in contrast, segregation may evolve through growth and decline as well as exchanges of dwellings between new and departing residents. Residential neighborhoods and job locations within firms have elements of all four locations, although in the short to medium term they are fixed permanent locations.

12.2 THE PROBLEM OF SCALE

Segregation is created and maintained through the interdependent actions of individuals. The mechanisms that link individual action and aggregate segregation may work on multiple scales (Levin 1992). For example, although segregation may occur across rectangular neighborhoods of 20 blocks, individuals may be aware of 1 or 2 block areas, or their overall metropolitan environments, or social networks that are only loosely tied to geography. In addition, behavioral regularities may vary across geographical scales, and thus micro-level processes may not aggregate in a simple way. For example, the factors governing individual residential preferences may vary across different levels of geography and individual actions may affect segregation at these geographic levels in different ways. A challenge to segregation research is to identify and account for these variations.

12.2.1 Social interactions and segregating processes

Segregation processes result from interdependence between the actions of individuals and the characteristics of groups. Segregation may arise from a process in which individuals have preferences about a population statistic (for example, the proportion of white households in a neighborhood), and their own characteristics or actions also contribute to that statistic (Schelling 1971, 1978). (For discussion of the explanatory status of preferences see Freese, this volume.) When a person leaves a neighborhood because she cannot tolerate its ethnic composition, she marginally changes the ethnic makeup of both the neighborhood that she vacates and also the neighborhood into which she moves. This may induce other individuals to move because the relative attractiveness of neighborhoods has changed. The makeup of neighborhoods results from the individuals' past cumulative and interdependent choices. In the short run, individuals respond to their environments; in the longer run, individuals' responses change the environment for everyone. There may be no straightforward way to infer patterns of neighborhood segregation from the tolerance, intentions, or behaviors of individuals. Micro-level preferences and actions may generate a range of possible neighborhoods. Even a relatively tolerant population, for example, may collectively create highly segregated neighborhoods (Schelling 1971). Models that seek to explain such aggregate outcomes of interdependent behavior must represent feedback between individuals' actions and neighborhood characteristics.

Models for feedback effects can also describe segregation in other contexts. Occupations may 'tip' from predominantly male to predominantly female (and vice versa). Although exogenous forces such as a shortage of men during times of war may effect massive shifts in the sex composition of jobs, changes in the sex composition of jobs may also be governed by endogenous processes (Reskin and Roos 1990). An initial change toward feminization of an occupation may make it less attractive to men, which further lowers the number of men who work in that occupation, creating a cascade of female entrances and male exits from the position. Male-to-female turnover may be associated with a decline in the job's skill, status, and wages, which further affects the job's relative appeal (e.g. Kalleberg, Wallace, and Althauser 1981).

The creation of marriages also entails interdependent behavior. Hernes (1972) examines the transition of individuals in a birth cohort from being single to married, and shows how the aggregate transformation of marital statuses results if the pressure to marry is proportional to the fraction already married in the same cohort and the rate of marriage is proportional to this pressure. An extension of this model can incorporate the effects of not only the fraction of a cohort that is already married, but also the homogamy of existing marriages (on, for example, race). The marriage behavior of the cohort depends on both the race-specific proportions of persons who are already married, and also the normative climate for inter- and intraracial marriage established by those already married.

Interdependent actions also determine the specific marriages that occur through 'two-sided matching' (Roth and Sotomayor 1990). The preferences of one sex define the marriage opportunities of the other. A match only occurs if no man that the eligible woman prefers to her potential husband-to-be also prefers her to his current match. Changing even one person's preferences may affect the whole system of stable matches. Taken together, the diffusion of marital statuses through cohorts of men and women; the norms about whether, when, and whom to marry established by those who are already married; and the coordinated actions of the two-sided marriage markets determine the numbers and types of marriages. Patterns of homogamy on such social characteristics as race, educational attainment, social-class background, and religion are a key form of segregation.

12.2.2 Units of analysis in segregation research

When analyzing segregation and other dynamic processes, one must determine the scale at which to model the process, and face the related problem of determining the level of aggregation of the relevant components in time, space, or organization (Pascual 2001). In empirical work these choices are often guided by practical considerations. Administrative boundaries, for example, may define neighborhoods for the researcher, but may not correspond to people's notions of neighborhoods or local communities (e.g. Grannis 1998). Similarly, analyses of marriage patterns may define a marriage 'market' as a census labor-market area. One's inferences about segregation and segregation processes may depend on these assumptions.

Individuals may act alone or in concert. Marriages are (typically) two-person events, firms go through hiring cycles, and entire families change their residences. A related consideration is the units of time in which behavior occurs. Smaller units of time reveal finer-grained transitions. A company may hire 10 employees in a month, but at most only 1 person per day. A neighborhood may lose 50 households per year, but only 1 or 2 households move in a week. The units of time in which we observe decisions may conceal important segregation processes. For example, if individual interactions are a key component of neighborhood change, gross annual population flows between neighborhoods may conceal important behavior. Similarly, if people choose homes first on the basis of housing-unit attributes and secondly on the basis of the neighborhood, correlations between population flows and the aggregate properties of housing stocks may conceal key behavioral mechanisms.

Segregation may result from overlapping and interrelated processes on multiple dimensions. Although residential patterns are governed by race, income, age, the presence of children, home-ownership status, and other dimensions, different dimensions of segregation may be more salient at different scales. Race and income may segregate individuals across neighborhoods, whereas religious affiliation, age, birthplace, and political beliefs may segregate individuals across larger regions. Neighborhoods may be relatively homogeneous in race but relatively heterogeneous in income, and cities may be relatively homogeneous in political affiliation but heterogeneous in race.

Different segregation processes may play out on different scales. For example, the degree of job segregation by sex may differ substantially at the firm, occupation, or industry levels (Bielby and Baron 1984). Similarly, explanations of segregation across neighborhoods may depend on individuals' ethnic tolerance and preferences for local amenities, whereas racial differentiation across cities may be caused by labor-market processes, population composition, and political behavior. In addition, large and small populations or groups of locations may follow different dynamics. If human behavior is governed by random as well as systematic influences, lower levels of aggregation tend to exhibit more randomness than higher levels (e.g. small towns versus large cities). For a fixed neighborhood size, changing the size of the population may affect segregation (Bruch and Mare 2006, 2009). The size of groups relative to population size may also affect the process. For example, the same level of ethnic tolerance or discriminatory behavior may produce low levels of segregation when we define neighborhoods as census tracts, but higher levels of segregation when we define neighborhoods as contiguous housing units.

Finally, it is necessary to specify the universe where segregating processes occur. This includes the physical or spatial units along which we measure segregation (e.g. neighborhoods, married pairs, or occupations), the population at risk of segregation (e.g. all women between the ages of 25 and 49), and the spatial universe (e.g. Los Angeles County).

12.2.3 Markets and other institutions

For analytical simplicity, researchers often assume that individual actions, unconstrained by market imperfections, affect segregation. In fact, people are constrained by space, social organization, and time (e.g. social networks, career trajectories, or speed-dating rules). In the housing market, for example, an individual's chances of hearing about a vacant housing unit may depend on its distance from her current residence or on whether it is located where the neighbors are members of the individual's ethnic group or social class (e.g. Krysan 2006). Similarly, in a labor market a member of an ethnic minority may be relatively more likely to hear about job openings at firms or in occupations where minorities are well represented (Montgomery 1991). More generally, organizational structures, such as internal labor markets, may channel access to mobility opportunities (e.g. Doeringer and Piore 1971). Barriers to communication or mobility among firms and the seniority rules that govern job trajectories may affect job and occupational segregation. Social organization and communication patterns may arise exogenously or may themselves be a function of segregation patterns and processes (Moody, this volume).

12.2.4 Models of segregation processes

We next consider some models for how people are allocated to positions through coordinated action. These models vary in their assumptions about the structure of positions and the key actors in the allocation process.

Queueing

In a simple queueing model, a heterogeneous population is available for entry into a set of social locations, such as desirable jobs or occupations. Actors who control those locations, such as employers, rank potential employees by their task-related qualifications, such as education or prior experience, and their ascriptive traits, such as race or sex (e.g. Huffman and Cohen 2004). Employers hire top-ranked individuals in sufficient numbers to fill available positions, forcing lower-ranked individuals to take less desirable positions. Employers also rank their current employees and, during economic downturns, lay off workers who are at the bottom of that queue. This model can account for variations in group differences in unemployment and for the occupational segregation of groups defined by traits that affect rank in the queue. In this model employers are the only actors, and their actions are limited to following a queueing rule.

Vacancy chains

In vacancy models open positions, such as job or housing vacancies, 'move' within a hierarchical system (White 1970; Marullo 1985; Abbott 1990). Mobility occurs when a position opens and the next individual 'in line' for this position moves to fill it. Vacancy chains occur when the initial opening sets off a series of individual moves, possibly governed by a queueing mechanism, each filling the vacancy left by the previous occupant. The chain stops when the last position is either filled by a new entrant into the system or eliminated. Thus, opportunities for mobility depend on the availability of empty positions, and the mobility of any one person affects the opportunities available to others. In these models the dynamics are governed by a fixed set of rules and positions. Although the mobility opportunities of individuals are interdependent, the model does not allow for coordinated individual choices.

Matching

Matching models assume that people are allocated to positions via markets, in which actors on both sides (e.g. buyers and sellers, men and women, etc.) compete for the most desirable match. The preferences and characteristics of actors on each side of the market simultaneously establish the opportunities of the other side. Gale and Shapley (1962) derived a matching equilibrium under the assumption that both sides of the market have full information about and ranked preferences for items available on the other side of the market. In this equilibrium, no actor on one side of the market can break his match and find a preferred partner who also prefers him to whomever she is already with. The likelihood that any man ends up with his preferred mate depends on not only his preferences and the preferences of his potential partner, but also on the preferences of all other actors in the market. Extensions of this model allow for incomplete information and sequential rather than simultaneous search processes (e.g. Mortensen 1988). Matching models represent market mechanisms that govern the allocation of people into jobs, houses, or interpersonal relationships, and thus hold potential for understanding segregation processes. Use of these models in empirical work has been hampered by lack of suitable data in individuals' preferences and search behaviors. Logan et al. (2008) propose statistical models of two-sided choice that enable one to estimate the underlying behavioral model using data only on existing matches (rather than complete data on individual preferences and search).

Location choice

Models of location choice represent the effects of individuals' preferences and choices on the distribution of individuals across social locations. In these models individuals face a range of possible location choices (e.g. vacant dwellings, peer groups, job openings) in groups that have fixed characteristics in the short run. Their choices are governed by available vacancies and the costs and benefits of entering a location. In the longer run, the choices of individuals affect the opportunity structures of other individuals, not only by altering the vacancy distribution, but also by changing the characteristics of the locations they leave and enter. The result is a dynamic relationship between individual choices and the distribution of a population across locations. These models share with vacancy-chain models the interdependence of mobility opportunities among individuals, but differ in allowing for change in the characteristics of these opportunities via shifting population composition. They share with matching models the coordinated choices of individuals, but differ in allowing for multisided rather than two-sided matching.

12.3 RESIDENTIAL SEGREGATION

Three key processes generate ethnic segregation: individuals' preferences for their own ethnic group (or avoidance of other groups) (see e.g. Clark 1986); economic inequalities among ethnic groups combined with price differences in housing; and discrimination in such forms as redlining and racial steering by real-estate agents (see e.g. Yinger 1995). Absent theoretical understanding of how neighborhoods change, it is difficult to identify the relative effects of these several mechanisms. Much research on segregation trends is based on census-based cross-sectional studies of cities (see e.g. Massey and Denton 1993). Other studies, based on survey attitude data, investigate the willingness of individuals to live in neighborhoods of varying race/ethnic composition (see e.g. Farley et al. 1994). Still others audit the responses of real-estate agents to potential home 'buyers' with varying social characteristics who are in fact accomplices of the researcher (see e.g. Turner et al. 2002). Although these data are informative, they do not directly show the dynamics of neighborhoods. Censuses do not show the intercensal behavior that governs trends in segregation. Individuals' stated preferences about neighborhoods do not alone explain residential patterns, because they do not show their link to mobility behavior and aggregate segregation. Audit studies can demonstrate discrimination, but do not reveal how much segregation would occur in the absence of discrimination. Thus, models are needed to bridge the inference gap between processes at the individual, neighborhood, and city-wide levels of observation and analysis.

12.3.1 Measuring residential segregation

Summary measures of segregation establish the criteria for judging how well models of segregation processes explain aggregate residential patterns. Segregation is multidimensional in both concept and measurement. Massey and Denton (1988) identify five dimensions: *evenness*, the over-/underrepresentation of groups in different parts of a city; *exposure*, contact between groups; *concentration*, confinement of one group in a small area; *centralization*, confinement of a group in the inner city; and *clustering*, residence in one contiguous space. Traditional segregation measures capture one or more of these dimensions. Measures of evenness include the index of dissimilarity, the Gini coefficient, and the entropy index (see e.g. James and Taeuber 1985). Exposure is captured by isolation indices (ibid.), whereas clustering is measured by White's spatial-proximity index (1983). Reardon and Firebaugh (2002) extend the two-group segregation measures to multigroup comparisons. For segregation of quantitative traits such as household income, researchers often rely on measures that are based on the relative sizes of between- and within-neighborhood variability (Jargowsky 1996).

Most commonly used segregation measures are *aspatial* in that they summarize the population composition of areas but do not take account of the spatial relationships among these areas. This may create a 'checkerboard problem,' in which a measure yields the same value where a racial minority is segregated into a single spatially contiguous region and where minority neighborhoods are interspersed with white areas (White 1983). Reardon and colleagues (e.g. Reardon and O'Sullivan 2004; Reardon et al. 2006) develop spatial measures of segregation and show that once distance between areas is taken into account, the five dimensions of segregation reduce to two: spatial exposure and spatial evenness. Their spatial-segregation scores give more weight to the population of nearby locations than more remote locations. They also consider the role of scale in understanding segregation processes. Segregation may look different when examining lower or higher levels of aggregation (e.g. neighborhoods defined as the area surrounding a household with a radius of 500 versus 400 meters), and information about the degree to which segregation changes with scale may shed light on the underlying processes governing segregation. *Segregation profiles* show the level of segregation by scale in a given area, and the degree to which segregation changes with scale (e.g. blocks versus census tracts).

12.3.2 Models of residential choice

We can formalize our discussion of the key elements in segregation processes, including the residential-opportunity structures of individuals or families, their tastes and preferences, the effects of their evolving knowledge and sentiments, and the links between the actions of individuals and the composition and segregation of neighborhoods (McFadden 1978). Although we refer to the choices of 'individuals,' the decision makers may be other units such as families or agents acting on behalf of organizations such as firms or schools. We refer to 'neighborhoods,' but the model is potentially applicable to choices among specific dwelling units as well as larger community areas; and, with modification, to other types of social locations (jobs, church congregations, marriage partners, etc.) where segregation occurs.

Denote by U_{ijt} the (latent) utility or attractiveness that the ith individual attaches to the jth neighborhood at time t. Let p_{ijt} denote the probability that the ith individual moves to the jth neighborhood at time t. The utility of a neighborhood for an individual depends on characteristics of the neighborhood and on the individual's own characteristics. To the analyst, these characteristics may be observed or unobserved, but these characteristics are known to the actors to whom they apply. Denote by Z_{jt} the observed characteristics of the jth neighborhood at time t (for example, the race/ethnic makeup of the neighborhood, the prices and rents of vacant houses, and the location of the neighborhood within a city, including distance from other neighborhoods with varying amenities and demographic characteristics). Let X_{it} denote observed characteristics of the ith individual at time t. These personal characteristics include fixed demographic characteristics such as race and sex and variable characteristics such as income as well as personal employment, family, and residential histories. Personal characteristics, including tastes and preferences, may result from past residential experiences. Let η_{jt} and ε_{it} be unobserved characteristics of neighborhoods and individuals respectively. Then the attractiveness of neighborhoods is

$$U_{ijt} = F(Z_{jt}, X_{it}, \eta_{jt}, \varepsilon_{it}). \tag{1}$$

If F is a linear random utility model, then, for example, for a single observed neighborhood and personal characteristic (Z and X respectively), a model is

$$U_{ijt} = \beta Z_{jt} + \gamma X_{it} + \delta Z_{jt} X_{it} + \eta_{jt} + \varepsilon_{it} + a Z_{jt} \varepsilon_{it} \tag{2}$$

where β, γ, δ, and a are parameters. This model incorporates a rich set of effects of observed and latent characteristics of persons and neighborhoods. When individuals choose where to live they implicitly compare neighborhoods in their choice set; that is, neighborhoods that they know about and where they may move with a nonzero probability. The comparison between the jth and the j'th neighborhood is

$$U_{ijt} - U_{ij't} = \beta_i^*(Z_{jt} - Z_{j't}) + \delta(Z_{jt} - Z_{j't})X_{it} + \varphi_{jj't} \tag{3}$$

where $\beta_{it}^* = \beta + a\varepsilon_{it}$ and $\varphi_{jj't} = \eta_{jt} - \eta_{jt}$. Utility differences between neighborhoods are a function of differences in their observed and unobserved characteristics (Z and η respectively). The characteristics of individuals do not affect the utility comparison additively because the comparison is within individuals, but they may interact with neighborhood characteristics. For example, the effect of differences in the proportion of persons in a neighborhood in a given ethnic group on the relative attractiveness of the neighborhood is likely to differ between individuals who are members of that ethnic group and those who are not. Unmeasured characteristics of individuals may also modify the effects of neighborhood characteristics. These unmeasured characteristics (ε_{it}) induce random variation in the β_i^* around the effects of measured neighborhood characteristics β. For example, the effect of the proportion of persons in the neighborhood who are ethnic minorities may depend on an individual's level of tolerance, which is unobserved to the analyst.

Given data on the characteristics of individuals and neighborhoods and the behaviors or stated preferences of individuals for neighborhoods, and an assumed probability distribution of the unobserved characteristics of individuals and neighborhoods, it is possible to estimate the parameters of the discrete choice model. If the $\varphi_{jj't}$ follow an extreme value distribution, we obtain a *discrete choice* conditional logit model:

$$p_{ijt}(Z_{jt}, X_{it}, C_{(i)}) = \frac{\exp(\beta_i^* Z_{jt} + \delta Z_{jt} X_{it})}{\displaystyle\sum_{k \in C_{(i)}} \exp(\beta_i^* Z_{kt} + \delta Z_{kt} X_{it})} \tag{4}$$

where $C_{(i)}$ denotes the set of neighborhoods available ('choice set') for the ith individual which may be restricted to incorporate discrimination, prices, or information constraints. For example, the choice set may be restricted to units within a given radius of a person's current home, to units in neighborhoods that are at least 10 percent own-race, or to units where monthly rent or mortgage payments would be less than some fraction of an individual's income. Although this model is a variant of standard choice models for consumer demand, it is possible to extend it so as to take account of special features of residential choice and mobility. Some of these extensions are as follows:

Price effects

Prices reflect aggregate housing demand and may be a positive function of the expected number of people who seek to move into each neighborhood. Lower prices offset the unattractive traits of some neighborhoods and thus attract residents. Housing markets 'clear' when prices adjust such that for any unit of time the expected number of households moving into any dwelling unit is 1 (if the number of dwellings is less than or equal to the number of households) or the ratio of households to housing units (if dwellings exceed households).

The choice not to move

Individuals may evaluate their current location differently from other possible destinations. For example, whites may tolerate a higher level of racial integration in their current neighborhood, because neighbors are already known. Alternatively, people may assess neighborhood characteristics in their current location in the same way that they respond to possible destination areas, but moving costs deter mobility and make the current residence more attractive, *ceteris paribus*.

The effects of neighborhood change and individual experience

Individuals may respond not only to the current characteristics of neighborhoods, but also to how those characteristics have changed in the recent past. People may use past information about neighborhood change to forecast future neighborhood change, a phenomenon reflected in popular parlance that 'the neighborhood is changing.' Additionally, individuals' own residential histories may change their preferences. People who have lived in integrated neighborhoods, for example, may be more or less tolerant of diversity.

Supply of housing

Whether an individual can move into a housing unit or geographic area depends on the supply of vacant housing. If the discrete choice model applies to specific dwellings, then the choice set consists of available (vacant or soon to be vacant) units and mirrors the supply of housing. However, if the choice model applies to aggregations of dwelling units such as neighborhoods, then it is necessary to take an indirect approach to housing supply by including the log of the number of vacancies or the number of dwelling units as a regressor in equation (4) (McFadden 1978).

12.3.3   Some specific behavioral models

Using the general model of location choice we can examine specific behavioral rules. A variant of Schelling's notion that people are willing to live in neighborhoods as long as they are the local majority yields the model:

$$p_{ijt}(Z_{jt}) = \frac{\exp(1^*\{Z_{jt} \geq 0.5\})}{\sum\limits_{k \in C_{(i)}} \exp(1^*\{Z_{jt} \geq 0.5\})} \tag{5}$$

where Z_{jt} is the own-race proportion in neighborhood j, and $1^*\{\}$ is an indicator function that equals 1 if the expression in brackets is true, and 0 otherwise. This threshold function assumes that people only differentiate between neighborhoods above and below 50 percent own-group and are indifferent to compositional differences among neighborhoods that do not cross the threshold. Alternatively, individuals may prefer to be the local majority, but respond to small changes in neighborhood composition, yielding a continuous function in the proportion within an ethnic group:

$$p_{ijt}(Z_{jt}) = \frac{\exp(Z_{jt})}{\sum\limits_{k \in C_{(i)}} \exp(Z_{kt})}. \tag{6}$$

Equations (5) and (6) are illustrated in Figure 12.1. These two functions have the same average level of tolerance, but make different assumptions about how people evaluate neighborhoods. These and other specifications can be tested for their adequacy in fitting individual data on residential choice and investigated for the type of aggregate segregation patterns that they imply.

12.3.4   Strategies for linking residential mobility and neighborhood change

Three related strategies for linking data at the individual and neighborhood level to test hypotheses about the causes of segregation are Markov models, general-equilibrium models with prices, and agent-based models. Each of these models blends individuals' neighborhood choices with aggregate neighborhood change. Given individual preferences and initial neighborhood conditions, these approaches treat both the demographic composition of neighborhoods and mobility behavior as endogenous. Whereas Markov models are a form of

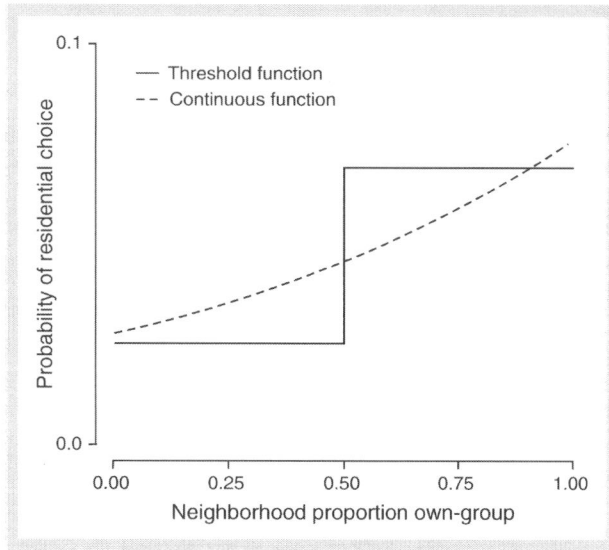

0.1 —

Probability of residential choice

— Threshold function
-- Continuous function

0.0 —

0.00   0.25   0.50   0.75   1.00
Neighborhood proportion own-group

Fig. 12.1 Two hypothetical decision rules

macrosimulation (mobility occurs through expected rates of transition), agent-based modeling is a form of microsimulation (individuals move according to stochastic realizations of probabilistic choice) (Macy and Flache, this volume). The general-equilibrium approach relies on expected rates of mobility, but is computed from individual-level cross-section data.

These strategies combine data at the individual and aggregate levels, including estimated variants of the discrete choice models from survey data, observations of neighborhood conditions from census or other administrative data, and estimated probabilities of mobility between neighborhoods. Administrative data define the initial population distribution, as well as fixed attributes of neighborhoods. The models generate subsequent and equilibrium neighborhood distributions implied by a set of individual choice probabilities. The model equilibrium is a distribution of individuals across neighborhoods such that no person can expect to improve his situation, given the decisions of all other individuals. For a wide range of residential-choice functions there are one or more population-level equilibria (e.g. Brock and Durlauf 2001). Equilibria may be static (the expected distribution of people across neighborhoods is unchanging) or dynamic (the distribution of people across neighborhoods cycles through a finite set of states). They may be unique (only one distribution of individuals across neighborhoods is an equilibrium) or nonunique (individual behavior implies multiple possible stable distributions). They may be robust to small random perturbations or, alternatively, small departures from equilibrium may cumulate, ultimately moving the system into a new equilibrium.

Markov models

Markov models link a set of individual- or group-specific residential-mobility probabilities to expected patterns of neighborhood turnover. A Markov model has a finite set of K states, $S = \{s_1, s_2, \ldots, s_k\}$. The states can be specific neighborhoods (for example, census tracts in a city) or neighborhood types (for example, poor versus nonpoor neighborhoods). The expected distribution of the population across the K states at time t, is

$$m[t] = [m_1^1(t), \ldots, m_K^1(t), m_1^2(t), \ldots, m_K^2(t), \ldots, m_1^G(t), \ldots, m_K^G(t)], \qquad (7)$$

where superscript $g = 1, 2, \ldots, G$ indexes group membership (e.g. ethnic groups). We also specify a GK by GK matrix $\mathbf{P}$ of conditional probabilities that a member of group g moves to state j at time $t + 1$ conditional on being in state i at time t. Markov models assume that the distribution of the population at time $t + 1$ depends only on characteristics and locations of the population at time t (and no prior time periods). The population distribution at time $t + 1$ is therefore

$$m[t + 1] = \mathbf{P}m[t]. \qquad (8)$$

Markov models usually assume time-invariant constant probabilities (P) of moving between states (e.g. Quillian 1999). However, if individuals react to and transform their neighborhoods through their mobility behavior, then their behavior follows an *interactive* Markov model (Conlisk 1976) where the elements of $\mathbf{P}$ depend on the population distribution at time t:

$$m[t + 1] = \mathbf{P}(m[t])m[t]. \qquad (9)$$

If, for example, $m[t]$ represents the distribution of blacks and whites across neighborhoods, then the probability of moving into a given neighborhood is a function of its race composition. In this model, preferences for neighborhood characteristics are fixed, but the attractiveness of specific neighborhoods changes as a result of their changing characteristics. (In principle, the same model may be represented as a fixed-rate Markov model of mobility between neighborhood *types*, but an interactive Markov model of mobility between specific neighborhoods.) Mare and Bruch (2003) investigate residential segregation using an interactive Markov model. The transition matrix $\mathbf{P}$ is based on rates of residential mobility estimated from longitudinal survey data. Each iteration of the model represents a unit of time, and with sufficient iterations the neighborhoods reach an equilibrium distribution. The equilibrium, however, results from the simplified conditions represented in the model. Actual cities seldom reach an equilibrium distribution because they are subject to external shocks (for example, new housing construction or immigration).

A Markov model predicts the implications of a given profile of behavior for a specified state space. The state space is typically neighborhoods or neighborhood types, and the population moving between states is typically described by a limited number of discrete characteristics (for example, black/white and poor/nonpoor). Although the state space may, in principle, include an arbitrary number of dimensions of individual and neighborhood characteristics, multidimensional models are unwieldy because the state space increases dramatically with each added dimension (Van Imhoff and Post 1998). Microsimulation approaches such as agent-based modeling may be a more useful method in these cases.

General-equilibrium models with price effects

A second approach to linking individual behavior with population dynamics is through general-equilibrium models with prices. This approach allows the entire population to adjust to the new environment, thereby changing the makeup of neighborhoods. Bayer and colleagues (e.g. Bayer, McMillan, and Rueben 2004) apply this framework to examine the degree to which ethnic preferences affect patterns of ethnic segregation. Their approach consists of a model of residential choice at the individual level and a simulation of the implications of that model for patterns of neighborhood change. It includes a discrete choice model for the probability of choosing a housing unit, conditional on its price and other attributes (e.g. owned versus rented, number of rooms, elevation) and neighborhood characteristics (e.g. air quality, ethnic composition, average household income). Some housing unit and neighborhood attributes, such as size and air quality, are fixed, whereas others, such as neighborhood ethnic composition, are endogenous to the sorting process. Each household optimizes its location given the set of alternatives and the decisions of other households. (Thus, the parameters are estimated assuming the distribution of households is in equilibrium.)

The estimated behavioral model is a tool for examining how neighborhoods achieve different equilibria depending on variation in preferences or population composition. A change in preferences or household characteristics (e.g. an elimination of race preferences) yields a new equilibrium distribution of households across neighborhoods via the mechanisms of price-regulated changes in supply and demand for housing. The model adjusts housing prices so that markets clear; that is, the expected number of households moving into each housing unit is 1. The model (1) generates neighborhood housing prices that clear the market; (2) given new prices, predicts the probability that each household chooses each housing unit; (3) aggregates housing-choice probabilities at the neighborhood level to estimate the revised socioeconomic composition of each neighborhood; (4) estimates the new socioeconomic composition of each neighborhood; and (5) repeats steps 1–4 until convergence. Unlike Markov models, which show how neighborhoods change en route to equilibrium, the general-equilibrium approach compares old and new equilibria following a change in model inputs. The latter approach assumes equilibrium at the beginning of the simulation, whereas Markov models do not make this assumption.

Agent-based models

These represent neighborhood change as the result of the interdependent decisions of individuals ('agents') who follow specified rules of behavior. For example, agents obtain information about neighborhoods and decide whether to move to a new housing unit or stay in their current housing unit. Each agent's decision changes the social landscape for other agents, thus affecting their subsequent behavior. Agents' decisions about where to move are individual-level stochastic realizations of transition probabilities governed by a discrete choice model (5). Given the characteristics of the agent and the housing vacancies to which it is exposed, the agent's decision is determined by a random draw from the probability distribution generated by the discrete choice model (Bruch and Mare 2006, 2009). Because agent models represent all information at the individual level, including an individual's complete residential history, they allow for a more flexible specification of the state space and more complex interactions between an agent and its environment than Markov models (Van Imhoff and Post 1998).

Schelling (1971, 1978) used a simple agent-based model for residential segregation in which two groups ('blacks' and 'whites') are distributed across a grid in accordance with their preferences about neighborhood racial makeup. Each agent wishes to live where at least 50 percent of its neighbors are members of its own group. Irrespective of how agents are initially distributed, they try to move whenever they are surrounded by a majority of their own color. This model predicts a resulting pattern of segregation more severe than any individual alone would prefer. Zhang (2004) and Pancs and Vriend (2007) show that ethnic segregation occurs even when agents prefer to live in an integrated neighborhood. Bruch and Mare (2006, 2009) simulate the segregation dynamics when individuals have the same average tolerance as Schelling's threshold, but differ in how they respond to small changes in neighborhood composition (see Fig. 12.1 above). Whether preferences follow a continuous or threshold function affects segregation outcomes. When the decision-making process has some degree of randomness, threshold functions lead to higher levels of segregation. When agents make finger-grained distinctions among neighborhoods that vary in racial composition, preferences alone may not lead to segregation because the segregating effects of changes in the size of the population at risk of entering a neighborhood are offset by a corresponding change in that neighborhood's desirability. Other studies link Schelling's behavioral model to empirical studies of racial tolerance and residential choice (Bruch and Mare 2006, 2009; Fossett 2006) or more realistic geography and population composition (Benenson 2004; Bruch 2006, 2009).

Agent-based models are also valuable for exploring the sensitivity of conclusions about segregation to alternative assumptions about individual behavior, neighborhood size, and population size. Holding the size of agents' neighborhoods fixed, the same preference function can produce a low level of segregation in a large population, but a high level of segregation in a small population. In a small population, when agents evaluate neighborhoods according to a continuous function, changes in the size of the population at risk of entering a neighborhood may be too large to offset the change in that neighborhood's desirability (Bruch and Mare 2006, 2009).

12.4 MULTIPLE SEGREGATION PROCESSES

Notwithstanding the focus of this chapter on racial residential segregation, people sort on many factors, including age, income, and lifestyle, and may be segregated across multiple sets of locations, including schools, workplaces, families, and others. Insofar as characteristics of individuals or households are correlated, processes that increase segregation in one grouping may reinforce or attenuate segregation across other groupings. Similarly, residential segregation may reinforce or attenuate segregation across other sets of social locations.

12.4.1 Residential segregation by race and income

We illustrate the process of segregation on two dimensions, race and income. Figure 12.2 illustrates a possible relationship between housing costs and the probability of choosing a dwelling. Suppose that the probability of moving into a given housing unit increases with the unit price up to a threshold c^*. People want to live in the best housing they can afford, but by definition cannot live at all in unaffordable housing. Thus, they distinguish among affordable but not unaffordable dwellings. Given a level of racial tolerance and income inequality among races, sorting by income may exacerbate or attenuate ethnic segregation. The distributions of race and income together can produce more *or* less segregation than race alone (depending on the ethnic group). For example, in Los Angeles, whites are less tolerant toward blacks than other ethnic groups, but Hispanics have on average substantially lower incomes than either blacks or whites. As a result, whites live closer to blacks than their ethnic preferences alone would imply (Bruch 2006, 2009). Similarly, a reduction in income disparities between blacks and whites may *increase* race segregation because an enlarged black middle-class may sustain segregated black middle-class neighborhoods that would not otherwise be possible (Sethi and Somonathan 2004; Bayer, Fang, and McMillan 2006).

12.4.2 Overlapping social locations

Segregation also occurs across overlapping sets of social locations. Residential segregation may, for example, be interdependent with marriage markets and patterns

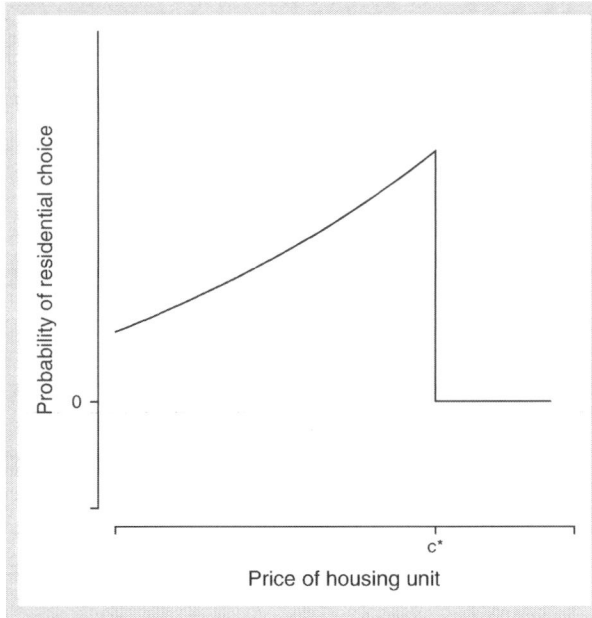

Fig. 12.2 Hypothetical relationship between housing costs and household resources

of assortative mating, friendship networks in high schools, job-referral networks, and occupational segregation. These connections arise because of the social ties created by both opportunities for contact provided by physical propinquity and the creation of normative expectations.

Residential segregation and marriage

Although people may meet their future partners in a variety of locations (Kalmijn and Flap 2001), the neighborhood is a key context in which they form romantic ties. Proximity to potential partners with similar social characteristics contributes to marital homogamy on those characteristics. Norms about intergroup contact may depend on opportunities for contact among different groups and patterns of assortative mating—for example, if people living in educationally integrated neighborhoods may be less likely to form relationships and, if they do marry, are more likely to marry heterogamously. Conversely, educationally homogeneous neighborhoods tend to narrow the range of potential partners that an individual meets. Single persons in homogeneous neighborhoods may be more likely to marry and, when they marry, to marry homogamously. (Married couples in homogeneous neighborhoods, however, may also be more likely to separate, given high rates of contacts with other desirable mates.) Single persons may move to neighborhoods where there are people who are demographically similar to themselves, thereby reinforcing residential segregation along demographic lines. Once married, a homogamous couple may also be more likely to reside in a neighborhood that is demographically homogeneous and similar to the couple themselves—more so than if the couple is heterogamous and is forced to choose a heterogeneous neighborhood or one that resembles one spouse more than the other. In short, the combined marriage choices and residential decisions of single and married persons may mutually reinforce marital homogamy and residential homogeneity. Of course, some people do marry heterogamously and live in neighborhoods with persons demographically different from themselves. When this behavior occurs often enough, it may offset the mutually reinforcing segregative effects of marriage and residential patterns. Heterogeneous neighborhoods provide, through both propinquity and norm formation, a catalyst for heterogamous marriages, and heterogamous couples may contribute to desegregation. Which of these competing effects dominate the marriage and housing markets depends on the strength of marital and residential preferences. Their dynamics is a fertile ground for segregation research.

Residential segregation, school segregation, and friendships

Because children are assigned to school districts based on where they live and parents choose neighborhoods in part on the basis of the quality of available schools, residential and school segregation are closely linked. Because schools foster friendships, neighborhood segregation may affect the segregation of children into ethnically or economically homogeneous peer groups. Thus, residential segregation may affect children's friendships and peer groups both directly because of geographic propinquity and indirectly through school segregation and its effects on children's environments (e.g. Mouw and Entwisle 2006). However, whereas attending a racially diverse school may increase opportunities for contact, it may also increase ethnic tension and therefore decrease the likelihood of forming a bond conditional on contact. Thus, residential integration can reduce peer segregation by increasing opportunities for interracial contact, but increase peer segregation by decreasing the likelihood of friendship conditional on contact.

Residential and workplace segregation

Residential segregation may affect workplace segregation and unemployment in two ways. First, neighborhood segregation places disadvantaged populations further from job opportunities, thus increasing job search costs and commuting times (Holtzer 1991). Physical distance between work and home may affect employment outcomes. Second, residential segregation may isolate disadvantaged populations from social networks that lead to job referrals, regardless of the physical location of the job (e.g. Mouw 2002). Both mechanisms mutually reinforce residential and occupational segregation. If individuals cannot obtain well paying jobs, they are less likely to be able to afford to move into neighborhoods more proximate to better employment opportunities, further reinforcing both physical separation along socioeconomic lines and differential access to information about jobs.

Conclusion

The models and methods required for advancing knowledge about segregation processes are well within the sights of researchers working in the field, and much can be learned by carrying out empirical work using the analytic strategies discussed here. Yet our knowledge of segregation processes remains in its infancy. We can identify many of the behaviors and environments that may influence levels and trends in segregation in a variety of empirical contexts. But much more research is needed to show which factors matter most in various empirical applications or to judge the sizes of their effects. This research requires painstaking and creative attention to model refinement at both micro and macro levels along with rigorous empirical validation every step of the way.

References

ABBOTT, A. (1990), 'Vacancy Models for Historical Data', in R. Breiger (ed.), *Social Mobility and Social Structure* (New York: Cambridge University Press), 80–102.

BAYER, P., MCMILLAN, R., and RUEBEN, K. (2004), 'Residential Segregation in General Equilibrium', NBER working paper no. 11095.

——— FANG, H., and MCMILLAN, R. (2006), 'Separate When Equal? Racial Inequality and Residential Segregation', NBER working paper no. 11507.

BENABOU, R. (1996), 'Heterogeneity, Stratification, and Growth: Macroeconomic Implications of Community Structure and Educational Finance', *American Economic Review*, 86: 584–609.

BENENSON, I. (2004), 'Agent-based Modeling: From Individual Residential Choice to Urban Residential Dynamics', in M. Goodchild and D. Janelle (eds.), *Spatially Integrated Social Science* (New York: Oxford University Press), 67–95.

BIELBY, W., and BARON, J. (1984), 'A Woman's Place is with Other Women: Sex Segregation within Organizations', in B. Reskin (ed.), *Sex Segregation in the Work Place* (Washington, D.C.: National Academy Press), 27–55.

BROCK, W., and DURLAUF, S. (2001), 'Discrete Choice with Social Interactions', *Review of Economic Studies*, 68: 235–60.

BRUCH, E. E. (2006), *Dynamic Models of Ethnic and Economic Segregation*, Ph.D. thesis (UCLA).

——— and MARE, R. D. (2006), 'Neighborhood Choice and Neighborhood Change', *American Journal of Sociology*, 112: 667 709.

———— (2009), 'Preferences and Pathways to Segregation: Reply to Van de Rijt, Siegel, and Macy', *American Journal of Sociology*, 114: 1181–98.

CHARLES, M., and GRUSKY, D. B. (2004), *Occupational Ghettos* (Stanford, Calif.: Stanford University Press).

CLARK, W. (1986), 'Residential Segregation in American Cities: A Review and Reinterpretation', *Population Research and Policy Review*, 5: 95–127.

CONLISK, J. (1976), 'Interactive Markov Chains', *Journal of Mathematical Sociology*, 4: 157–85.

DOERINGER, P., and PIORE, M. (1971), *Internal Labor Markets and Manpower Analysis* (Lexington, Mass.: Heath).

DURLAUF, S. (1996), 'A Theory of Persistent Income Inequality', *Journal of Economic Growth*, 1: 75–93.

FARLEY, R., et al. (1994), 'Segregation and Stereotypes: Housing in the Detroit Metropolitan Area', *American Journal of Sociology*, 100: 750–80.

FOSSETT, M. (2006), 'Ethnic Preferences, Social Distance Dynamics, and Residential Segregation: Theoretical Explorations Using Simulation Analysis', *Journal of Mathematical Sociology*, 30: 185–273.

GALE, D., and SHAPLEY, L. S. (1962), 'College Admissions and the Stability of Marriage', *American Mathematical Monthly*, 69: 9–14.

GRANNIS, R. (1998), 'The Importance of Trivial Streets: Residential Streets and Residential Segregation', *American Journal of Sociology*, 103: 1530–64.

HERNES, G. (1972), 'The Process of Entry into First Marriage', *American Sociological Review*, 37: 173–82.

HOLZER, H. (1991), 'The Spatial Mismatch Hypothesis: What Has the Evidence Shown', *Urban Studies*, 28: 105–22.

HUFFMAN, M., and COHEN, P. (2004), 'Racial Wage Inequality: Job Segregation and Devaluation across US Labor Markets', *American Journal of Sociology*, 109: 902–1036.

JAMES, D., and TAUEBER, K. (1985), 'Measures of Segregation', *Sociological Methodology*, 15: 1–32.

JARGOWSKY, P. (1996), 'Take the Money and Run: Economic Segregation in US Metropolitan Areas', *American Sociological Review*, 61: 984–98.

KALLEBERG, A., WALLACE, M., and ALTHAUSER, R. (1981), 'Economic Segmentation, Worker Power, and Income Inequality', *American Journal of Sociology*, 87: 651–83.

KALMIJN, M. (1998), 'Intermarriage and Homogamy: Causes, Patterns, Trends', *Annual Review of Sociology*, 24: 395–421.

—— and FLAP, H. (2001), 'Assortative Meeting and Mating: Unintended Consequences of Organized Settings for Partner Choices', *Social Forces*, 79: 1289–312.

KRYSAN, M. (2006), *Does Race Matter in the Search for Housing? Search Strategies, Locations, and Experiences*, paper presented at the annual meeting of the Population Association of America, Los Angeles, Calif.

LEVIN, S. (1992), 'The Problems of Pattern and Scale in Ecology: The Robert H. MacArthus Award Lecture', *Ecology*, 6: 1943–67.

LOGAN, J., HOFF, P., and NEWTON, M. (2008), 'Two-sided Estimation of Mate Preferences for Similarities in Age, Education, and Religion', *Journal of the American Statistical Association*, 103 (482): 559–69.

MCFADDEN, D. (1978), 'Modelling the Choice of Residential Location', in A. Karlqvist et al. (eds.), *Spatial Interaction Theory and Planning Models* (Amsterdam: North-Holland).

MARE, R. D., and BRUCH, E. E. (2003), 'Spatial Inequality, Neighborhood Mobility, and Residential Segregation', California Center for Population Research working paper no. 003-03, University of California, Los Angeles.

MARULLO, S. (1985), 'Housing Opportunities and Vacancy Chains', *Urban Affairs Quarterly*, 20: 364–88.

MASSEY, D., and DENTON, N. (1988), 'The Dimensions of Residential Segregation', *Social Forces*, 67: 281–315.

——(1993), *American Apartheid: Segregation and the Making of the Underclass* (Cambridge, Mass.: Harvard University Press).

MONTGOMERY, J. (1991), 'Social Networks and Labor Market Outcomes: Toward an Economic Analysis', *American Economic Review*, 81: 1408–18.

MORTENSEN, D. (1988), 'Matching: Finding a Partner for Life or Otherwise', *American Journal of Sociology*, 94: S215–S240.

MOUW, T. (2002), 'Are Black Works Missing the Connection? The Effect of Spatial Distance and Employee Referrals on Interfirm Racial Segregation', *Demography*, 39: 507–28.

——and ENTWISLE, B. (2006), 'Residential Segregation and Interracial Friendship in Schools', *American Journal of Sociology*, 112: 394–441.

PANCS, R., and VRIEND, N. (2007), 'Schelling's Spatial Proximity Model of Segregation Revisited', *Journal of Public Economics*, 1: 1–24.

PASCUAL, M. (2001), 'Scales that Matter: Untangling Complexity in Ecological Systems', in S. Fitzpatrick and J. Bruer (eds.), *Carving our Destiny: Scientific Research Faces a New Millennium* (Washington, D.C.: National Academy of Science/Joseph Henry).

QUILLIAN, L. (1999), 'Migration Patterns and the Growth of High-poverty Neighborhoods, 1970–1990', *American Journal of Sociology*, 105: 1–37.

REARDON, S., and FIREBAUGH, G. (2002), 'Measures of Multigroup Segregation', *Sociological Methodology*, 32: 33–67.

——and O'SULLIVAN, D. (2004), 'Measures of Spatial Segregation', *Sociological Methodology*, 34: 121–62.

——et al. (2006), 'Segregation and Scale: The Use and Interpretation of Spatial Segregation Profiles for Investigating the Causes, Patterns and Consequences of Residential Segregation', paper presented at the 2006 meeting of the Population Association of America, New York.

RESKIN, B., and ROOS, P. (1990), *Job Queues, Gender Queues: Explaining Women's Inroads into Male Occupations* (Philadelphia, Pa.: Temple University Press).

ROTH, A. E., and SOTOMAYOR, M. (1990), *Two-sided Matching: A Study in Game-theoretic Modeling and Analysis* (Cambridge: Cambridge University Press).

SCHELLING, T. C. (1971), 'Dynamic Models of Segregation', *Journal of Mathematical Sociology*, 1: 143–86.

——(1978), *Micromotives and Macrobehavior* (New York: Norton).

SCHWARTZ, C. R., and MARE, R. D. (2003), 'The Effects of Marriage, Marital Dissolution, and Educational Upgrading on Educational Assortative Mating', CCPR working paper no. 026-03.

SETHI, R., and SOMANATHAN, R. (2004), 'Inequality and Segregation', *Journal of Political Economy*, 112: 1296–321.

TURNER, M., et al. (2002), *Discrimination in Metropolitan Housing Markets: Phase I— National Results from Phase I of the HDS 2000* (Washington, D.C.: US Department of Housing and Urban Development).

VAN IMHOFF, E., and POST, W. (1998), 'Microsimulation Methods for Population Projection', *Population: An English Selection*, 10: 97–138.

WHITE, H. (1970), *Chains of Opportunity* (Cambridge, Mass.: Harvard University Press).

WHITE, M. (1983), 'The Measurement of Spatial Segregation', *American Journal of Sociology*, 88: 1008–18.

WILSON, W. J. (1987), *The Truly Disadvantaged* (Chicago, Ill.: University of Chicago Press).

YINGER, J. (1995), *Closed Doors, Opportunities Lost: The Continuous Costs of Housing Discrimination* (New York: Russell Sage).

ZHANG, J. (2004), 'A Dynamic Model of Residential Segregation', *Journal of Mathematical Sociology*, 28: 147–70.

CHAPTER 13

....

SELF-FULFILLING PROPHECIES*

....

MICHAEL BIGGS

INTRODUCTION

....

THE term 'self-fulfilling prophecy' (SFP) was coined in 1948 by Robert Merton to describe 'a *false* definition of the situation evoking a new behavior which makes the originally false conception come *true*' (Merton [1948] 1968: 477). He illustrated the concept with a run on a bank (a fictitious 'parable'); his main application was to racial discrimination. The term has since entered social science and even everyday English, a rare feat for a sociological neologism. The concept has been subsequently rediscovered or renamed as the 'Oedipus effect' (Popper 1957), 'boot-strapped induction' (Barnes 1983), or 'Barnesian performativity' (MacKenzie 2006). SFP has been discerned in a congeries of processes (see e.g. Henshel 1978): within an individual, as with placebo response; in relations between individuals, such as teacher and student; in relations between collective actors, like states; underlying institutions, such as banks and financial markets; and, most provocatively, between social theory and social reality.

SFP is a particular type of dynamic process. It is not the truism that people's perceptions depend on their prior beliefs (Rydgren, this volume). Nor is it the truism that beliefs, even false ones, have real consequences. To count as SFP, a belief

* The editors, Diego Gambetta, John Goldthorpe, Rob Mare, Federico Varese, and Duncan Watts all helped to sharpen the argument.

must have consequences of a peculiar kind: consequences that make reality conform to the initial belief. Moreover, I argue that there is an additional defining criterion. The actors within the process—or at least some of them—fail to understand how their own belief has helped to construct that reality; because their belief is eventually validated, they assume that it was true at the outset. This misapprehension is implicit in Merton's account. His examples are social pathologies, but not merely in the sense that they are socially undesirable. They are 'pathological' for being predicated on misunderstanding. Depositors fail to realize that their own panicked withdrawals cause the bank to collapse; whites fail to realize that their own racial discrimination makes African Americans seem intellectually inferior.

The mirror image of SFP is the 'suicidal prophecy' (Merton 1936), in which the initial belief leads to behavior that makes the belief untrue. This kind of dynamic process has attracted little attention, although it may have considerable importance, as for example in the pursuit of positional goods. It is excluded due to limitations of space.

The chapter opens by proposing an explicit definition of SFP. I argue that the concept is best used to demarcate a narrow range of social processes rather than to encompass all of social life (Barnes 1983). Conceptualization underlines just how difficult it is to empirically demonstrate the existence and significance of SFP. The next two sections reflect my conviction that analytical sociology must be empirical as well as theoretical: a summary of methods for investigating SFP is followed by a review of systematic evidence for selected phenomena. The final two sections offer explanations for why self-fulfilling prophecies occur: why false or arbitrary beliefs are formed and why they are subsequently fulfilled. My aim is to demonstrate commonalities among substantively diverse phenomena, and to identify the conditions which are most likely to give rise to SFP.

13.1 CONCEPT

Conceptualizing SFP will clarify its essential elements and differentiate it from other kinds of dynamic processes. There are two criteria. The first is a causal sequence like the following:

(1) X believes that 'Y is p.'
(2) X therefore does b.
(3) Because of (2), Y becomes p.

To illustrate, X is a teacher, Y is a student, and p stands for someone with great academic ability; b is the behavior—perhaps providing better teaching or expressing greater emotional warmth—that actually causes Y to fulfill the expectations of high achievement. The third step requires it to be true that Y becomes p rather than X incorrectly perceiving that 'Y becomes p.' SFP is not merely confirmation bias.

The second criterion is a misapprehension of this causal sequence. X and Y (or at least one of them) wrongly assume that the causal order is as follows:

(0) Y is p.
(1) Because of (0), X believes that 'Y is p.'
(2) X therefore does b.
(3) Because of (0), Y manifests p.

To continue the illustration, teacher and student assume that the teacher's expectations simply reflect the fact that the student has great ability. They assume that this ability—and not the teacher's behavior—causes the subsequent high achievement. This assumed causal sequence will be called the 'inductively derived prophecy' (IDP). This term is inelegant but will prove useful shorthand.

So SFP comprises a causal sequence whereby an actor's belief motivates behavior that turns it into reality, while at the same time the actor(s) misapprehend the causal sequence as one whereby belief simply reflects reality. This misapprehension is not unreasonable; after all, IDP is common.

The distinction between the two causal sequences can be sharpened by specifying a counterfactual. SFP requires that alteration of X's belief would alter the outcome:

(1) X believes that 'Y is q.'
(2) X therefore does c.
(3) Because of (2), Y becomes q.

If the teacher were to believe that the student is mediocre, then the teacher would behave very differently, and this would cause the student to perform poorly. By contrast, the counterfactual in IDP requires that a different belief held by X has no effect on Y:

(0) Y is p.
(1) Despite (0), X believes that 'Y is q.'
(2) X therefore does c.
(3) Because of (0), Y manifests p.

In this case the teacher's belief would have no effect on the student's performance.

I have defined the causal sequence of SFP without specifying Y's 'real' state at the outset (corresponding to step 0 of IDP). Merton's stipulation that X's belief be false raises epistemological difficulties in cases where it is hard to conceive of Y's state prior to interaction with X (Miller 1961; Krishna 1971). Consider police indiscriminately attacking an unruly crowd, who then react by fighting back (Stott and Reicher 1998). Does it make sense to conceive the crowd as inherently peaceable? This difficulty is circumvented by resort to the counterfactual: If the police had instead shown restraint, then the crowd would have dispersed without violence.

Therefore I will refer to X's beliefs as false or *arbitrary*: arbitrary because a different belief would create a different reality.

Thus far I have considered SFP involving two individual or collective actors (X and Y). This is readily generalized to a causal sequence involving multiple individuals (X_i) and an abstract social institution (Y):

(1.1) X_1 believes that 'Y is p.'
(2.1) X_1 therefore does b.
    (1.2) Because of (2.1), X2 believes that 'Y is p.'
    (2.2) X_2 therefore does b.
        (1.3) Because of (2.1) and (2.2), X_3 believes that 'Y is p.'
        (2.3) X_3 therefore does b.
        . . .
  (3) Because of (2.1), (2.2), (2.3) . . . , Y becomes p.

In Merton's parable of a bank run, X_i are the depositors, Y is the bank, and p stands for insolvency; b is the behavior—withdrawing money—that actually causes the bank to fail. The iteration of the first two steps in the sequence is a process of positive feedback: as more depositors withdraw their money from the bank, the remaining depositors will be more likely to believe that the bank is insolvent.

Having offered a precise definition, I will now put it to use. First, let me show how this definition helps to distinguish SFP from superficially similar dynamic processes. Take the first criterion, causal sequence. According to Merton, whites deprived African Americans of education because they believed them to be intellectually inferior; given such inadequate education, blacks became academically inferior. Is the belief (step 1) sufficient to explain the behavior (step 2)? One suspects that this belief was more of a rationalization for hatred and fear of blacks. The question may be sharpened by considering the counterfactual: Is altering those beliefs in intellectual inferiority, leaving everything else unchanged, conceivable? If whites came to believe that blacks were equally intelligent, would they have devoted resources to providing equal educational facilities? Only if the answer is affirmative would this fall under my definition of SFP.

Equally important is the second criterion, misapprehension. This distinguishes SFP from self-enforcing conventions and similar phenomena. Take the example of driving on the left in Great Britain. Each driver believes that others will drive on the left and therefore drives on that side of the road. Leaving aside the difficulty of envisaging a plausible counterfactual (How many drivers would have to simultaneously switch their beliefs to reverse the convention?), there is no misapprehension of causation. Drivers are quite aware that they drive on the left only because everyone else in Britain does. After all, they have no difficulty comprehending that the convention reverses as soon as they arrive in France.

My definition thus serves to demarcate a particular type of dynamic process. It nevertheless encompasses a diverse range of phenomena. This chapter selects a

Table 13.1 Examples of SFP

Placebo response
(1) Y believes: 'I have received a treatment that relieves pain.'
(2) Because of (1), Y experiences pain relief.

Interpersonal expectancy
(1) X believes that 'Y has great ability.'
(2) X therefore gives Y challenging material and communicates high expectations.
(3) Because of (2), Y performs well on tests.

Reactive conflict
(1) X believes that 'Y is aggressive.'
(2) X therefore attacks Y.
(3) Because of (2), Y attacks X.

Bank run
(1.1) X_1 believes that 'Y is insolvent.'
(2.1) X_1 therefore withdraws deposits.
      (1.2) Because of (2.1), X_2 believes that 'Y is insolvent.'
      (2.2) X_2 therefore withdraws deposits.
            (1.3) Because of (2.1) and (2.2), X_3 believes that 'Y is insolvent.'
            (2.3) X_3 therefore withdraws deposits.
        ...
(3) Because of (2.1), (2.2), (2.3) ..., Y fails.

Investment bubble
(1.1) X_1 believes that 'Y generates high returns.'
(2.1) X_1 therefore invests in Y.
      (1.2) Because of (2.1), X_2 believes that 'Y generates high returns.'
      (2.2) X_2 therefore invests in Y.
(3.1) Because of (2.2), Y pays high returns to X_1.
            (1.3) Because of (2.1), (2.2), and especially (3.1), X_3 believes that 'Y generates
                high returns.'
            (2.3) X_3 therefore invests in Y.
            (3.2) Because of (2.3), Y pays high returns to X_2.
        ...

Social theory
(1) $X_1 ... X_n$ believe that 'Y is a true model of society.'
(2) $X_1 ... X_n$ therefore act accordingly.
(3) Because of (2), society conforms to Y.

few of these for consideration, summarized in Table 13.1. Interpersonal expectancy and reactive conflict are straightforward.[1] Placebo response is rather different. It is SFP when caused by response expectancy—'anticipations of one's own automatic responses to various stimuli' (Kirsch 2005: 794)—rather than by unconscious conditioning (Stewart-Williams and Podd 2004). While placebo response occurs 'within' the individual undergoing treatment, it is important to note that the individual's belief derives from situational encounters with someone assumed to possess expertise.[2] Placebo response deserves attention because it has been investigated so extensively and rigorously. The bank run exemplifies SFP with positive feedback. Positive feedback also occurs in the investment bubble, though the causal sequence is more elaborate. As more people invest in the scheme, their investment increases the scheme's credibility. Moreover, subsequent investment enables the scheme to provide initial investors with the promised returns; these returns further enhance the credibility of the scheme. All this leads to further investment. The process can last for some time, but it eventually proves unsustainable. The ultimate outcome is the same as in the bank run: financial failure. The crucial difference is that in the investment bubble this outcome refutes rather than fulfills the prophecy. What is self-fulfilling—albeit temporarily—is the belief that the investment yields high returns.

The final example to be considered is self-fulfilling theory. What distinguishes social science from natural science is the potential for reality to be altered by theory. A theory of society could, in principle, prove self-fulfilling. Marxism predicts that capitalism is fated to end in revolution; if many people believe in the theory, then they could foment revolution. For self-fulfilling theory, misapprehension is more ambiguous than for other phenomena, for individuals may be partly cognizant of their own role in making reality conform to theory. Nevertheless, the ability of theory to motivate action surely requires a conviction that the theory expresses some underlying truth about society, however imperfectly instantiated in actually existing social arrangements.

These varied phenomena are alike in that SFP is very hard to distinguish from IDP. Indeed, social life provides plenty of genuine examples of the latter: patients experience pain relief because they have been given morphine; students perform well because they have genuine talent; enemies attack because they are aggressive; banks fail because they are insolvent; investments yield high returns because the asset is productive; theories are confirmed because they are true. In all these cases, beliefs follow reality. And because such cases exist, actors are naturally prone to misapprehend the causal sequence of SFP: they mistakenly think that their belief follows reality, when in fact their belief creates it.

13.2 METHOD

Identifying SFP in reality poses an immense challenge. If the actors involved cannot discriminate between IDP and SFP, how can a sociologist know any better? One method is to manipulate actors' beliefs in order to see whether those beliefs have causal effect. The experimental method (see Bohnet, this volume) is worth discussing for its probative value, and also because it reveals how beliefs are not easily manipulated—a point of some sociological interest.

Placebo research exemplifies the experimental method. Randomly assign patients to two groups. Convince the first that they are getting a painkiller such as morphine, while injecting an inert substance. Leave the second group untreated altogether; this control group is necessary to exclude spontaneous remission and regression to the mean. The difference in pain experienced by the two groups (placebo minus control) is placebo response. There is also an alternative experimental design. Administer the painkiller to the first group, as with any treatment. Covertly administer the painkiller to the second group without them realizing what has happened; in practice, this can be done when patients are constantly hooked to an intravenous drip (Levine et al. 1981). The difference in pain experienced by the two groups (treatment minus covert) is placebo response.[3] Each design allows the effects of subjective belief to be disentangled from the inherent physical powers of the treatment. Similar manipulation is used to study interpersonal expectancy. The most informative experiments are those conducted outside the psychology laboratory, in natural social situations. Randomly select a small proportion of students in a class. Convince the teacher that these students have especially high potential. At the end of the school year, compare this select group with the control group. The difference in performance measures the effect of the teacher's positive expectations (Rosenthal and Jacobson 1968).

The logic of experimental design is straightforward; putting it into practice is surprisingly difficult. The norm of informed consent constrains manipulation in medical research. In the double-blind clinical trial, patients in the so-called placebo group are *not* deceived into thinking that they are getting the treatment; they know that placebo and treatment are equally likely. In fact, blinding is rarely if ever achieved; well over half the patients correctly guess whether they are getting placebo or treatment (Shapiro and Shapiro 1997). Informed consent must attenuate placebo response.

Even without this normative constraint, manipulation is difficult to accomplish. Experimental subjects expect to be duped. In a typical experiment looking at the effects of caffeine, one third of the subjects in the control group—given placebo and told exactly that—believed incorrectly that they had received caffeine (Kirsch and Rosadino 1993). Similar problems may attend experiments in natural settings. The initial findings on teachers' expectations were widely reported in the press. In subsequent replications, teachers may well have become suspicious when educational psychologists arrived with a list of students deemed to be exceptionally talented.

The difficulties of manipulating belief do not vitiate experimental findings, of course. Rather, we should consider these findings as establishing a *lower bound* on the causal effect of belief. The point is illustrated by a novel surgical technique for angina pectoris, which initially demonstrated impressive success in reducing pain (Beecher 1961; Benson and McCallie 1979). Subsequent placebo surgery demonstrated that the operation was physically ineffective; it also induced a less potent placebo response. In other words, being treated 'for real' by an enthusiastic surgeon amplified placebo response. Consider another example, an experiment showing that listeners are more likely to download a song from a website if they believe it is popular with other users (Salganik and Watts 2007). We may infer that the effect of popularity would be far greater if someone believed that the song was the number-one hit in the country.

The experimental method provides the strongest proof that false or arbitrary beliefs can become self-fulfilling. In most processes of concern to sociologists, however, experiment is not possible; even where it is feasible in some fashion, there may be doubts about its ecological validity. An alternative is to find a 'natural experiment,' where real life has provided a situation where we know—in retrospect—that beliefs were false, analogous to the surgery for angina pectoris. Ponzi schemes offer a neat natural experiment for investment bubbles, inasmuch as the investment is inherently incapable of generating value. The name comes from a scheme created by Charles Ponzi in Boston after the First World War (Zuckoff 2005). He initially promised a 40 percent return after 90 days; the rate of return was soon raised to 50 percent in 45 days. This spectacular profit supposedly came from arbitraging the value of international reply coupons in different countries. He would buy coupons in Italy, where postal costs were low, then ship the coupons to the USA and exchange them (somehow) for dollars. This premise was so absurd that Ponzi made no attempt to implement it.

An alternative method is statistical analysis of longitudinal data. For interpersonal expectancy, use teachers' expectations of ability at time t_1 to explain performance at t_2, controlling for performance at t_0. This has been done with data from schools in Michigan, which include many potentially confounding variables; the statistical identification of the causal effect of teachers' beliefs is therefore convincing (Jussim, Eccles, and Madon 1996; Madon, Jussim, and Eccles 1997). Statistical analysis is possible even if the data do not include measures of beliefs. Economic historians use data on banks to test whether failure can be predicted from the institution's previous financial characteristics (e.g. the extent to which liquidity is maintained by borrowing) and from exogenous economic shocks. SFP is thus treated as a residual—plausible if failure cannot be predicted by these economic variables (e.g. Calomiris and Mason 1997, 2003).

13.3 EVIDENCE

Empirical investigation must answer two questions. The first is whether SFP can occur. An affirmative answer requires evidence that a false or arbitrary belief can have a causal impact on behavior, so as to make that behavior conform to the belief. It is one thing to discern a causal effect in the requisite direction, another thing to demonstrate that the effect's magnitude is substantial. If SFP can occur, there follows a less obvious but equally important question: whether it occurs often enough—outside the context of experimental manipulation—to be socially significant. An affirmative answer requires evidence that false or arbitrary beliefs are prevalent. Such an answer cannot be provided by experiments, and so in this respect statistical evidence is more valuable. I will review three bodies of systematic research—on placebo response, interpersonal expectancy in education, and bank runs—and then note evidence on Ponzi schemes and music popularity.

There is a huge body of research on placebos. Evidence is compelling for pain, depression, and anxiety. The outcome is subjective experience as reported by the patient (e.g. pain on a scale from 1 to 10); there are sometimes associated physical measurements, as with facial inflammation after dental surgery (Hashish et al. 1988). For pain, a meta-analysis of conventional clinical trials, comparing the placebo group with the control group, finds a standardized mean difference of 0.27 (Hróbjartsson and Götzsche 2001). Thus, placebo reduced pain by about a quarter of a standard deviation, which is modest. But these trials undermine placebo response by informed consent, as mentioned above. A meta-analysis of experimental studies, where subjects in the placebo group had been told that they were getting an effective analgesic, finds a standardized mean difference of 0.85 (Vase, Riley, and Price 2002). This is substantively large. For depression, a meta-analysis of clinical trials of anti-depressants finds that the placebo group experienced about 80 percent of the benefits of the treatment group (Kirsch et al. 2002).[4]

Placebo response is ubiquitous in medical treatment. What is interesting for the sociologist is that 'treatments' *without* inherent physical powers can survive thanks to placebo response, along with spontaneous remission and other factors that cannot be discerned without experimental control. Until the nineteenth century at the earliest, the vast majority of medical treatments had no inherent physical powers—or at least none that were beneficial (Shapiro and Shapiro 1997). Treatments that flourished were surely those that induced a powerful placebo response; for instance, cures composed of rare or repugnant ingredients, like viper's flesh. Today, the massive market for 'alternative' therapies can be attributed in many cases to placebo response. Less obviously, perhaps, technologically advanced equipment may also induce a powerful placebo response (Kaptchuk et al. 2000). Ultrasound apparatus, for example, relieves muscular pain equally well when it is turned off (Hashish et al. 1988).

There is an extensive literature on interpersonal expectancy in education (Jussim and Harber 2005). The outcome is typically the result of a standardized written test. It is sometimes an IQ test, but this need not imply that expectations alter 'intelligence'; test-taking performance is sufficiently important, given its impact on students' life chances. A meta-analysis of experiments using an IQ test finds that under the most favorable conditions (when expectations are manipulated at the beginning of the school year) the standardized mean difference between the 'high expectations' group and the control group is 0.32 (Raudenbush 1984). In other words, 63 percent of the former group performed above the latter group's median. Similarly modest effects were found in statistical analysis of students learning mathematics in Michigan. These data also show, however, a much greater effect of expectations on lower-class and especially African American students (Jussim, Eccles, and Madon 1996). For the latter, the standardized mean difference was 1.35. To put this more concretely, moving from the lowest to the highest expectation is predicted to raise the student's grade from C to B+. For trainees in the Israeli army, a meta-analysis of several experiments finds a standardized mean difference of 0.86 (Eden 1990; Kierein and Gold 2000). All these figures are averages across all levels of ability. The less able are more sensitive to teachers' expectations than the more able (Kierein and Gold 2000; Madon, Jussim, and Eccles 1997). In addition, expectations that are overestimated appear more powerful than expectations that are underestimated. Happily, then, SFP is most likely to *raise* the performance of those who are *below* average.

The prevalence of inaccurate expectations is another matter. Systematic evidence suggests that teachers' expectations are usually accurate, in the sense that they conform to objective indicators of prior performance such as test scores (Jussim and Harber 2005). One might be tempted to argue that prior performance is simply the result of prior expectations, and so ultimately students' trajectories depend on the expectations of their initial teacher. To the contrary, the effects of expectations seem to diminish rather than accumulate over subsequent years (Smith, Jussim, and Eccles 1999). What is most important is whether inaccurate expectations are correlated with social categories such as race or class, which would vindicate Merton's original application of SFP. The Michigan data show that teachers were biased neither against African Americans nor lower-class students: differences in expectations for these groups matched differences in prior performance (Jussim, Eccles, and Madon 1996).[5] We cannot, of course, conclude that biased expectations have never existed. Systematic studies on teachers have been conducted in America in recent decades, in a time when racism was becoming unacceptable in the teaching profession. One might doubt whether the same results would have been obtained in Michigan classrooms in the 1950s, for example.

There are a number of statistical studies of bank runs in the USA before the adoption of federal deposit insurance. Bank failure was far more common than in other countries, due to the prohibition of large-scale banks. A crucial distinction is between suspension and failure: some banks that suspended withdrawals eventually reopened, while others failed. There is clear evidence that a run could lead to suspension. Event-history analysis of banks during the panic of 1893 cannot distinguish between those that were suspended but reopened and those that remained unscathed (Carlson 2005). This suggests that runs beset banks that were fundamentally sound. An indirect approach is to examine the effect of state deposit insurance (introduced by some states and not others), which should reduce or eliminate runs. In the 1920s, it is estimated that insurance halved the number of suspensions due to runs, as diagnosed by regulators at the time (Chung and Richardson 2006). These suspensions, however, represented only a small proportion of all suspensions. When it comes to failure, moreover, there is scant evidence that runs often caused solvent banks to fail. Event-history analysis of banks in the 1930s—including the Chicago panic of 1932, the setting for Merton's parable—reveals fundamental preexisting differences between those that survived and those that failed (Calomiris and Mason 1997, 2003). Solvent banks could survive (even after suspension) because they maintained the confidence of large depositors, who had better information about their financial position.

The literature on financial bubbles is huge and contentious. It is not a simple matter to establish that an investment boom is really a bubble. To take a salutary example, 'tulipmania' has passed into social-scientific folklore as the exemplary bubble, and yet the original evidence can be interpreted as showing rational investment in an intrinsically valuable commodity (Garber 1989). Therefore I will focus on the original Ponzi scheme as a natural experiment proving the possibility of a pure bubble, inflated by SFP. As mentioned above, the underlying investment scheme—arbitrage on postal vouchers—was not feasible, let alone productive. Yet the scheme succeeded in attracting a huge volume of investment. Ponzi appointed an Italian grocer as agent (on 10 percent commission). By January 1920 the agent had persuaded seventeen individuals, his customers and friends, to invest an average of a hundred dollars each. Crucially, the trickle of investors continued over the following month, so that Ponzi could pay the returns owed to the original investors. Once investors gained such extraordinary high yields, they told their friends and family; they also often reinvested what they had gained. Figure 13.1 traces the total

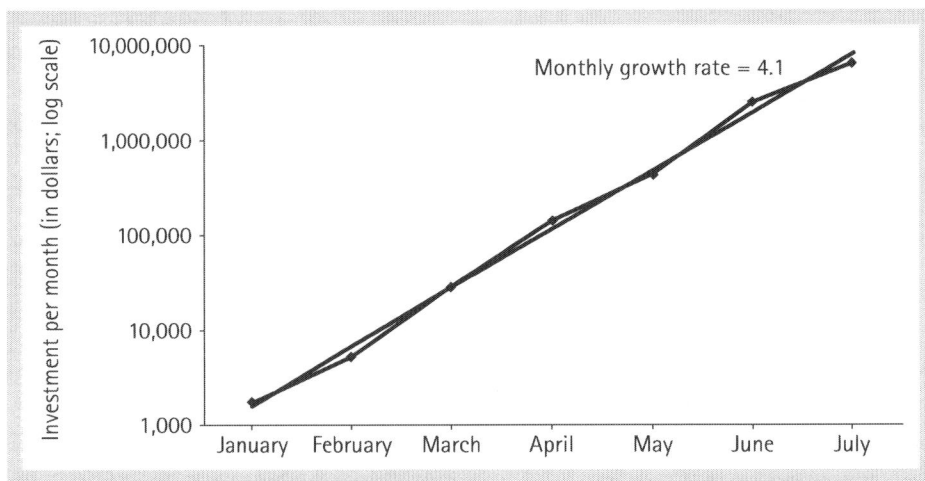

Fig. 13.1 Sums invested in Ponzi's scheme, 1920

Source: Zuckoff (2005).

invested each month. (Unfortunately reinvestment is not distinguished.) Investment grew exponentially, represented by a straight line on the graph's logarithmic scale; it quadrupled every month. In July, about twenty thousand people invested in the scheme. By the end of that month, people waited in line for hours outside Ponzi's office, eager for their chance to get rich quick. Under investigation by the financial authorities, he voluntarily halted deposits. Even then, however, there was no panic; most investors did not withdraw their money. The scheme collapsed some weeks later when a newspaper discovered his earlier arrest for fraud. Without these two interventions, it seems that the scheme would have continued for longer.

Ponzi schemes should be most viable where people have little or no experience in investment, like the shopkeepers and workers in 1920. Therefore these schemes flourished in Russia and Eastern Europe in the 1990s, during the transition to a market economy; Albanian investors lost the equivalent of half the country's annual GDP (Bezemer 2001). More surprising is the recent discovery that thousands of experienced investors in the United States and Western Europe had been similarly fooled. As this chapter went to press, Bernard Madoff admitted running a Ponzi scheme from the early 1990s to 2008, which consumed many billions of dollars (statement to U.S. District Court in New York, 12 March 2009). His fraud departed from the classic Ponzi model, however, in that the returns were not extraordinarily high and there was no wholesale recruitment of investors. Aside from pure Ponzi schemes, conventional investment booms—like Internet stocks in the 1990s or house prices in the 2000s—owe something to self-fulfilling expectations (Shiller 2000).

Finally, a recent study is noteworthy for exploiting the Internet to conduct an experiment in a natural setting (Salganik and Watts 2007). Songs from real music groups were made available for listening and downloading. The popularity of each song, indicated by the number of previous downloads, was visible to users. In one condition, popularity was inverted part way through the experiment: users were deceived into thinking that the most popular song was the least popular, and so forth. This dramatically affected subsequent usage, making the 'worst' (indicated by previous downloads) songs more popular and the 'best' songs less popular. Over time, however, the very best songs gradually rose in rank, showing that appreciation depends on intrinsic qualities as well as perceived popularity.

13.4 EXPLANATIONS: BELIEF

I now turn to the overarching theoretical problem, explaining *why* SFP occurs. The problem can be broken down into two questions. First, why does X form false or arbitrary beliefs (step 1 of the causal sequence) and behave accordingly? Second, why does X's behavior subsequently fulfill those beliefs (step 3)? Answering these questions involves, at the same time, describing the conditions in which SFP is likely to arise. There is no single answer to each question, of course, because SFP encompasses such diverse processes. However, we can identify explanations of sufficient generality to apply to more than one substantive phenomenon.

The first question—how to explain false or arbitrary beliefs—is thrown into relief by contrasting SFP with IDP. In IDP, X's belief about Y is derived from evidence about Y. In SFP, by contrast, X formulates a false or arbitrary belief without waiting for evidence. The former scenario may seem naive (Rydgren, this volume), but it is what the actor imagines is happening. The teacher, for example, considers her belief about the student's ability to be based on observation. I will identify three explanations for behavior based on false or arbitrary beliefs.

One explanation is that X has power over Y or that Y accepts X's expertise. X then has considerable latitude in forming beliefs about Y, whether or not they are justified by evidence. Y cannot challenge false or arbitrary beliefs due to this power imbalance, or—more insidiously—Y accepts those beliefs as true. At one extreme, consider the example of a prisoner who is tortured as long as he refuses to admit being a terrorist; at the other extreme, consider a student who accepts the teacher's judgment that he is poor at mathematics. In both cases X's belief may be completely false and yet will remain uncontested; X has therefore no reason to revise or even question it. The belief can survive long enough to become self-fulfilling.

A second explanation is that the cost of making a mistake is asymmetric and the cost of waiting is high. This situation is exemplified by the bank run. If a depositor is uncertain whether to believe a rumor that the bank is about to collapse, there is a vast difference in the cost of making a mistake. On the one hand, withdrawing savings is a relatively low-cost action, even if the bank turns out to be sound. On the other, inaction will mean losing everything if the rumor is true. Waiting for more evidence of the bank's financial condition simply increases the likelihood, if it really is unsound, of losing everything. Therefore the rational action is to withdraw savings immediately.[6] The same logic applies to reactive conflict, insofar as the cost of mistaken aggression is outweighed by the cost of mistaken passivity. When police are deciding whether to attack an unruly crowd, the cost (to them) of attacking people who would have dispersed peacefully may be far lower than the cost of allowing a violent mob to get out of control.

A third explanation is that someone stands to gain by inculcating false or arbitrary beliefs. Purveyors of medical remedies or Ponzi schemes are obvious examples. Politicians too may gain from provoking international conflict. Where the instigator intentionally decides to mislead others, this still counts as SFP insofar as it requires others to misapprehend the causal sequence. The politician may cynically provoke another state, but gains only if the populace believe that their country is the victim of unprovoked aggression. While this explanation depends on intentional deception, it is also possible to suggest a more elaborate version where 'deception' is unintended. After all, the most convincing advocates are those who genuinely believe. It is crucial, however, for such an explanation to specify how rewards shape action in the absence of intentionality; in short, to avoid the problem of functionalism. A selectionist explanation may be plausible. Consider several homeopaths dispensing (ineffective) remedies to patients. Those who are most enthusiastic about the potency of a remedy will—by inculcating a false belief in the patient and hence inducing placebo response—enjoy the best results. Over time, those homeopaths will thrive while their more cautious colleagues fail. In this scenario, the fact that homeopaths are rewarded for inculcating false beliefs helps to explain why this particular SFP occurs, but there is no conscious deception by practitioners.

These three explanations are sufficiently general to cover a range of SFPs. They do not, however, exhaust the possible explanations for false or arbitrary beliefs. Two processes—investment bubbles and self-fulfilling theories—demand other explanations. While the logic of asymmetric costs helps to explain a bank run, it makes an investment bubble more puzzling. If the investment turns out to be bogus, then the investor will lose everything. How then could such an investment be explained? It is possible to conceive of an inordinately sophisticated investor who knows that the investment is a bubble and who is able to calculate when it will burst; such an investor can exit with a handsome profit. A bubble created by such sophisticates alone would not, of course, fall within my definition of SFP. There is ample evidence that bubbles attract naive investors in considerable numbers. This can be demonstrated for Ponzi's scheme, because after Ponzi closed it to new depositors he continued to redeem existing certificates. Anyone knowing that it was a bubble would have immediately withdrawn their money. Because the vast majority of investors did not, they must have believed that the scheme was intrinsically capable of generating extraordinary returns. To explain this belief, it is necessary to refer to learning. They had seen other investors receiving—in cash—the promised rate of return; some had experienced this for themselves on previous iterations. 'Each satisfied customer became a self-appointed salesman,' recalled Ponzi (Zuckoff 2005: 116). 'I admit that I started a small snowball downhill. But it developed into an avalanche by itself.'

Self-fulfilling theory demands a particular explanation. It is easy to see why social scientists adhere to theories that are false or arbitrary: the interlocking system of propositions is almost impervious to countervailing evidence, and scientists are far more committed to their theory than are (say) depositors to their belief about the bank. What is harder to discern is why some theories motivate their adherents to act in the world outside academia.[7] Powerful motivation is created by the conflation of descriptive and normative claims. Neoclassical economics and Marxism share this character. On one hand, they are ostensibly hard-headed scientific theories of reality, possessing unique rigor. On the other hand, they specify—and also justify— a normative ideal, immanent in capitalism or imminent in history. The combination seems logically contradictory, but it is nonetheless highly productive. Markets are natural, and so we should create them! The revolution is inevitable, and so we should foment it! Motivation can also spring from a more venal source. Neoclassical economics promises tangible gain to those who deploy it in the real world. Anyone who believes its predictions about prices should use those predictions in their own market trading.

13.5 EXPLANATIONS: FULFILLMENT

After explaining why X behaves on the basis of false or arbitrary beliefs, there follows a second question: Why does that behavior cause Y to fulfill those beliefs? After all, action on the basis of incorrect beliefs is widespread—but it is rare for the consequences of action to bring reality into alignment with the initial beliefs, as with SFP. The explanation may be straightforward where Y is an institution. A bank by definition does not have sufficient liquidity to repay all its depositors simultaneously; a Ponzi scheme can obviously thrive if the volume of new investment is sufficient to repay earlier investors. Explanation poses a much greater challenge where Y is an actor. Potential explanations can be classified according to the degree to which Y accepts X's belief about Y. I will focus on three types of explanation.

One type of explanation depends on Y believing in the validity of X's expectations. In some circumstances, this invidious belief could simply have its effect by means of altering Y's perceived payoffs. A student accepting the teacher's low opinion of his ability would rationally choose to reduce the time spent on study or practice. A more intriguing explanation is 'response expectancy,' originally proposed to explain placebo response. Here Y's belief has its effect beneath the actor's consciousness. Believing that you have been given morphine leads to pain relief, but you are not aware of the causal connection. Researchers on pain have actually discovered a chemical substance that enhances placebo response, by interacting with the brain's endogenous opioid system (Colloca and Benedetti 2005). This substance has no inherent physical powers to relieve pain—demonstrated by the fact it has no effect when administered covertly. It simply amplifies the effect of belief. While the precise mechanisms can be left to biologists, response expectancy may have unappreciated significance for sociology. Anxiety and depression are subject to placebo response, and these have socially important effects. A student who accepts the teacher's low expectations may suffer from anxiety when taking a test, and anxiety will necessarily degrade performance.[8]

At the opposite extreme is a type of explanation that does not require Y to accept (or even know about) X's belief. Rather, X's behavior alters the payoff structure for Y. Torture will almost inevitably elicit a confession even when the victim knows that he is innocent. Reactive conflict has the same logic: once the police attack the crowd, they will fight back even though they do not accept the police's characterization of them as a violent mob. In some circumstances Y's behavior need not involve a decision. A student who does not accept the teacher's low opinion is nonetheless hindered by being assigned less challenging material. For a less hypothetical example, consider the observation that a gang member's status predicted his bowling performance when the gang bowled together, even though some of the low-ranking individuals showed considerable skill when bowling alone (Whyte [1943] 1993). If someone with low rank began performing well, other gang members (especially those at the bottom of the hierarchy) would deliberately throw him off his game. It is no wonder, then, that the gang's beliefs proved self-fulfilling. Response expectancy may also have contributed, if the individual himself expected poor performance and this interfered with his concentration.

A third type of explanation falls in between the other two. There is a gap between Y's self-image and (Y's perception of) X's belief about Y; this gap leads Y to behave in ways that conform to X's belief. In short, Y intentionally lives up—or down—to X's expectations. When X has higher expectations, it is easy to envisage how Y would be motivated not to disappoint X. Experiments in the Israeli army show that when the instructor (falsely) believed that trainees were promising, he behaved in ways that made the trainees feel that they were being treated better than they deserved; this motivated them to increase their own effort in return, which in part explains their superior performance (Eden 1990). When X has lower expectations, however, it is not altogether clear (at least to me) why Y would fulfill those expectations rather than striving to reverse them. There is experimental evidence, however, that trust lives down as well as up to expectations; those who believe that they are mistrusted are less likely to behave in a trustworthy manner (Bacharach, Guerra, and Zizzo 2007).

Self-fulfilling theory again demands separate consideration. Theory can be made real by shaping institutions (outside academia) which in turn direct the action of numerous individuals. As an example, neoclassical economics postulates that firms maximize profits, or equivalently shareholder value (Blinder 2000). Half a century ago this proposition was contradicted by empirical evidence. Some economists modified the theory to make it more realistic (e.g. maximizing revenue or satisficing), but strict neoclassical economists argued that it was reality that needed revising: managers should be given appropriate incentives to maximize profits, namely stock options. Thanks in part to their argument, companies now adopt this form of compensation. Moreover, it is now taken for granted that the sacred duty of managers is to maximize shareholder value. As a result, short-term profit maximization—as neoclassical theory predicts—is surely more often true now than it was half a century ago. Even when it is not true, the fact that managers invariably claim to be maximizing shareholder value gives the theory superficial plausibility.

Theory can also be made real when its predictions are used to guide self-interested action. Neoclassical economists insist that prices in capital markets incorporate all relevant information; this is the 'efficient-market hypothesis.' Yet initial econometric testing revealed significant anomalies, like the finding that small firms provided higher returns than large firms. Anyone who believed this finding could make excess profits by investing in smaller firms, and that is exactly what some market participants—including the author of the hypothesis—did. As a result, the anomaly disappeared in subsequent empirical investigation (Schwert 2003; MacKenzie 2006). This example is structurally similar to the bank run: the belief provides incentives for action that makes it become true. It is less demanding than the bank run, however, because the effect can be produced by a tiny minority of market participants. Another example is analogous to the investment bubble, in that it enjoyed only temporary success. Economists formulated a model of stock-option prices before a formal market was institutionalized, and indeed the model helped to legitimize the creation of such a market. Traders in this new market then used the model to calculate expected returns, assisted by datasheets sold by one of the model's authors. Option prices, when investigated econometrically, were eventually found to closely match the model's predictions. All this changed with the 1987 crash, when traders discovered to their cost that the model underestimated the volatility of stock prices (MacKenzie 2006). On this account, the model was self-fulfilling for a time, in part because it enjoyed such widespread use as a predictive tool.

Conclusion

This chapter has proposed a conceptualization that explicates the essential characteristics of SFP; it has reviewed systematic empirical evidence on the possibility and prevalence of SFP; and it has sketched a variety of explanations for SFP, which at the same time suggest conditions under which this process is likely to occur. All this could be condensed into a checklist for analyzing a dynamic process as SFP. First, establish the causal sequence. This can be checked by considering the counterfactual: Is it plausible that a change in the initial belief would alter the outcome? Second, establish misapprehension by at least some of the participants. Sketch their assumed IDP. Enlightenment can be employed as a diagnostic: Is it plausible that making participants understand the actual causal sequence would alter the outcome? Third, gather evidence on the magnitude and prevalence of SFP. Even if systematic evidence is not available, it is certainly helpful to broaden the focus to include IDP as well as SFP in this particular context. To clarify this with an example, consider not only the bank run causing a solvent institution to fail, but also the bank run that responds to the institution's real insolvency. Fourth, explain why the false or arbitrary belief was formed. Why did the individual(s) act on the basis of this belief rather than waiting for evidence (as with IDP)? Fifth, explain why this belief became self-fulfilling. Remember that most incorrect beliefs do not have such an effect.

I have argued for a restricted definition of SFP, which makes misapprehension of the causal process an essential criterion. Clearly this definition excludes many dynamic processes in which false beliefs have important consequences. However, it is more useful to restrict SFP to denote a very particular type of process than to extend it to wide swathes of social life. Indeed, it is arguable that SFPs can exist because they are unusual, being 'parasitic' on the frequency of IDP. These two processes would stand in the same relation as forged to authentic banknotes; the former are more likely to go undetected when rare. I have also argued for the importance of empirical research. Psychologists and economists (and medical researchers) have done much more than sociologists to systematically demonstrate the occurrence of SFP. To be sure, empirical investigation poses a huge challenge. The most compelling evidence pertains to processes (like placebo response) that are of less interest to sociologists, whereas the grandest claims for SFP (like self-fulfilling theory) are extremely difficult to investigate. This challenge will test the ingenuity of analytical sociologists.

One final lesson can be drawn from SFP. My emphasis on misapprehension underlines the importance of 'folk sociology,' how social actors themselves under-stand the causal processes which lead to their action and which flow from it. This understanding is usually tacit and often confused, but no less significant for all that. The abiding fascination of SFP is the notion that social actors are caught in a web of their own making; they reify social reality, failing to realize that they are responsible for creating it. Analytical sociologists typically wield Occam's razor to whittle the individual actor down to the simplest decision function. Sometimes explanation requires a more complex—and admittedly less analytically tractable—notion of the individual actor, as someone whose own (mis)understanding of social process has to be taken into account.

NOTES

1. Worth noting is a variant of reactive conflict where X's behavior creates or at least expands Y as a collective entity. Naming an enemy such as 'the Mafia' or 'al-Qaeda' and attributing to it extraordinary powers is liable to encourage many other groups to jump on the 'brandwagon' and identify themselves accordingly (Gambetta 2004).

2. It is telling that ultrasound equipment produces a placebo response only when it is applied by someone else; self-massage with the same apparatus has no effect (Hashish et al. 1988).

3. This assumes that the treatment's inherent powers and the placebo response have an additive effect in the treatment group.

4. This fraction includes spontaneous remission and regression to the mean as well as placebo response; on the other hand, placebo response is attenuated by informed consent.

5. How can that be reconciled with the finding that teachers' expectations had a greater effect on students from these groups? When a teacher underestimated the ability of an African American student, that had a significantly detrimental effect on the student's performance (and a more detrimental effect than on a white student); yet teachers on average were no more likely to underestimate the ability of African Americans than that of white students.

6. This situation (as in clinical trials with informed consent) requires a more elaborate specification of belief. Rather than X believing in a simple proposition, X has a probabilistic belief: 'There is probability π that the bank is unsound' and hence 'There is probability $1 - \pi$ that the bank is sound.' The decision to withdraw deposits may be rational even if the probability π is small.

7. Anyone who adheres to a theory is motivated to seek supporting evidence, of course, but mere confirmation bias is not SFP. To count as such, the theory must alter the social reality that it describes.

8. This is not trivial: merely labeling a test an 'intelligence test' significantly degrades the performance of African American students relative to white students (Steele and Aronson 1995).

References

BACHARACH, M., GUERRA, G., and ZIZZO, D. J. (2007), 'The Self-fulfilling Property of Trust: An Experimental Study', *Theory and Decision*, 63: 349–88.

BARNES, B. (1983), 'Social Life as Bootstrapped Induction', *Sociology*, 17: 524–45.

BEECHER, H. K. (1961), 'Surgery as Placebo: A Quantitative Study of Bias', *Journal of the American Medical Association*, 176: 1102–7.

BENSON, H., and McCALLIE, D. P., JUN. (1979), 'Angina Pectoris and the Placebo Effect', *New England Journal of Medicine*, 300: 1424–9.

BEZEMER, D. J. (2001), 'Post-socialist Financial Fragility: The Case of Albania', *Cambridge Journal of Economics*, 25: 1–23.

BLINDER, A. S. (2000), How the Economy Came to Resemble the Model', *Business Economics*, 1: 16–25.

CALOMIRIS, C. W., and MASON, J. R. (1997), 'Contagion and Bank Failures During the Great Depression: The June 1932 Chicago Banking Panic', *American Economic Review*, 87: 863–83.

—— (2003), 'Fundamentals, Panics, and Bank Distress During the Depression', *American Economic Review*, 93: 1615–47.

CARLSON, M. (2005), 'Causes of Bank Suspensions in the Panic of 1893', *Explorations in Economic History*, 42: 56–80.

CHUNG, C.-Y., and RICHARDSON, G. (2006), 'Deposit Insurance and the Composition of Bank Suspensions in Developing Economies: Lessons from the State Deposit Insurance Experiments of the 1920s', NBER working paper no. 12594.

COLLOCA, L., and BENEDETTI, F. (2005), 'Placebos and Painkillers: Is Mind as Real as Matter?', *Nature Reviews: Neuroscience*, 6: 545–52.

EDEN, D. (1990), *Pygmalion in Management: Productivity as a Self-fulfilling Prophecy* (Lexington, Mass.: Lexington).

GAMBETTA, D. (2004), 'Reason and Terror: Has 9/11 Made it Hard to Think Straight?', *Boston Review*, 29 (2): 32–6.

GARBER, P. M. (1989), 'Tulipmania', *Journal of Political Economy*, 97: 535–60.

GRACELY, R. H., et al. (1985), 'Clinicians' Expectations Influence Placebo Analgesia', *Lancet*, 325: 43.

HASHISH, I., et al. (1988), 'Reduction of Postoperative Pain and Swelling by Ultrasound Treatment: A Placebo Effect', *Pain*, 33: 303–11.

HENSHEL, R. L. (1978), 'Self-altering Predictions', in J. Fowles (ed.), *Handbook of Futures Research* (Westport, Conn./London: Greenwood), 99–123.

HRÓBJARTSSON, A., and GØTZSCHE, P. C. (2001), 'Is the Placebo Powerless? An Analysis of Clinical Trials Comparing Placebo with No Treatment', *New England Journal of Medicine*, 344: 1594–602.

JUSSIM, L., ECCLES, J., and MADON, S. (1996), 'Social Perception, Social Stereotypes, and Teacher Expectations: Accuracy and the Quest for the Powerful Self-fulfilling Prophecy', *Advances in Experimental Social Psychology*, 28: 281–388.

——and HARBER, K. D. (2005), 'Teacher Expectations and Self-fulfilling Prophecies: Knowns and Unknowns, Resolved and Unresolved Controversies', *Personality and Social Psychology Review*, 9: 131–55.

KAPTCHUK, T. J., et al. (2000), 'Do Medical Devices Have Enhanced Placebo Effects?', *Journal of Clinical Epidemiology*, 53: 786–92.

KIEREIN, N. M., and GOLD, M. A. (2000), 'Pygmalion in Work Organizations: A Meta-analysis', *Journal of Organizational Behavior*, 21: 913–28.

KIRSCH, I. (2005), 'Placebo Psychotherapy: Synonym or Oxymoron', *Journal of Clinical Psychology*, 61: 791–803.

——et al. (2002), 'The Emperor's New Drugs: An Analysis of Antidepressant Medication Data Submitted to the US Food and Drug Administration', *Prevention and Treatment*, 5: art. 23.

——and ROSADINO, M. J. (1993), 'Do Double-blind Studies with Informed Consent Yield Externally Valid Results? An Empirical Test', *Psychopharmacology*, 110: 437–42.

KRISHNA, D. (1971), ' "The Self-fulfilling Prophecy" and the Nature of Society', *American Sociological Review*, 36: 1104–7.

LEVINE, J. D., et al. (1981), 'Analgesic Responses to Morphine and Placebo in Individuals with Postoperative Pain', *Pain*, 10: 379–89.

MACKENZIE, D. A. (2006), *An Engine, Not a Camera: How Financial Models Shape Markets* (Cambridge, Mass./London: MIT Press).

MADON, S., JUSSIM, L., and ECCLES, J. (1997), 'In Search of the Powerful Self-fulfilling Prophecy', *Journal of Personality and Social Psychology*, 72: 791–809.

MERTON, R. K. (1936), 'The Unanticipated Consequences of Purposive Social Action', *American Sociological Review*, 1: 894–904.

—— [1948] 1968, 'The Self-fulfilling Prophecy', in Merton, *Social Theory and Social Structure*, 2nd edn. (New York: Free Press), 475–90.

MILLER, C. (1961), 'The Self-fulfilling Prophecy: A Reappraisal', *Ethics*, 72: 46–51.

POPPER, K. (1957), *The Poverty of Historicism* (London/New York: Routledge).

RAUDENBUSH, S. W. (1984), 'Magnitude of Teacher Expectancy Effects on Pupil IQ as a Function of the Credibility of Expectancy Induction: A Synthesis of Findings From 18 Experiments', *Journal of Educational Psychology*, 76: 85–97.

ROSENTHAL, R., and JACOBSON, L. (1968), *Pygmalion in the Classroom: Teacher Expectation and Pupils' Intellectual Development* (New York: Holt, Rinehart & Winston).

SALGANIK, M. J., and WATTS, D. J. (2007), 'An Experimental Approach to Self-fulfilling Prophecies in Cultural Markets', Paper presented to the 2006 ASA.

SCHWERT, G. W. (2003), 'Anomalies and Market Efficiency', in G. M. Constantinides, M. Harris, and R. Stulz (eds.), *Handbook of the Economics of Finance*, vol. 1A (Amsterdam/London: Elsevier/North-Holland), 937–72.

SHAPIRO, A. K., and SHAPIRO, E. (1997), *The Powerful Placebo: From Ancient Priest to Modern Physician* (Baltimore, Md.: Johns Hopkins University Press).

SHILLER, R. J. (2000), *Irrational Exuberance* (Princeton, N.J.: Princeton University Press).

SMITH, A. E., JUSSIM, L., and ECCLES, J. (1999), 'Do Self-fulfilling Prophecies Accumulate, Dissipate, or Remain Stable Over Time?', *Journal of Personality and Social Psychology*, 77: 548–65.

SPITZ, H. H. (1999), 'Beleaguered *Pygmalion*: A History of the Controversy Over Claims that Teacher Expectancy Raises Intelligence', *Intelligence*, 27: 199–234.

STEELE, C. M., and ARONSON, J. (1995), 'Stereotype Threat and the Intellectual Test Performance of African Americans', *Journal of Personality and Social Psychology*, 69: 797–811.

STEWARD-WILLIAMS, S., and PODD, J. (2004), 'The Placebo Effect: Dissolving the Expectancy Versus Conditioning Debate', *Psychological Bulletin*, 130: 324–40.

STOTT, C., and REICHER, S. (1998), 'How Conflict Escalates: The Inter-group Dynamics of Collective Football "violence" ', *Sociology*, 32: 353–77.

VASE, L., RILEY III, J. L. and PRICE, D. D. (2002), 'A Comparison of Placebo Effects in Clinical Analgesic Trials Versus Studies of Placebo Analgesia', *Pain*, 99: 443–52.

WHYTE, W. F. [1943] (1993), *Street Corner Society: The Social Structure of an Italian Slum*, 4th edn. (Chicago, Ill.: University of Chicago Press).

ZUCKOFF, M. (2005), *Ponzi's Scheme: The True Story of a Financial Legend* (New York: Random House).

CHAPTER 14

SOCIAL INFLUENCE

THE PUZZLING NATURE OF SUCCESS IN CULTURAL MARKETS*

MATTHEW J. SALGANIK

DUNCAN J. WATTS

THIS chapter is motivated by a puzzling aspect of contemporary cultural markets: successful cultural products, such as hit songs, best-selling books, and blockbuster movies, are orders of magnitude more successful than average; yet which particular songs, books, and movies will become the next 'big thing' appears impossible to predict. Here we propose that both of these features, which appear to be contradictory at the collective level, can arise from the process of social influence at the individual level. To explore this possibility empirically we constructed a website where participants could listen to, rate, and download new music, and more importantly, where we could control the information that these participants

* The authors are grateful to Peter Hausel for developing the MusicLab website; to Jason Booher-Jennings for graphical-design assistance; to Bolt Media for assistance recruiting participants; and to Delia Baldassarri, Peter Bearman, Peter Dodds, Andrew Gelman, and the members of the Collective Dynamics Group for helpful conversations. This research was supported in part by the National Science Foundation (SES-0339023, SES-0092162 and a graduate research fellowship) and the James S. McDonnell Foundation.

had about the behavior of others. Using a novel experimental design we found support for our ideas in a series of four experiments involving a total of 27,267 participants.

INTRODUCTION

One of the striking features of contemporary cultural markets is that 'successes,' such as hit songs, best-selling books, and blockbuster movies, are orders of magnitude more successful than average. Examples of extreme inequality abound. Michael Jackson's 'Thriller' has sold more than 41 million copies, while thousands of bands struggle to even release an album (Vogel 2004); the seven books in the Harry Potter series have collectively sold more than 300 million copies at a time when most authors only achieve sales in the thousands; and the 1997 blockbuster movie *Titanic* grossed 600 million dollars at the US box office alone, nearly fifty times the average US box-office take for movies produced in that year. Although each case is unique, they are all part of a generic pattern in cultural markets: most entrants do poorly while a few successes stand out. This pattern—which occurs for pop music (Chung and Cox 1994; Krueger 2005), trade publishing (Hirsch 1972; Sorensen 2007), television (Bielby and Bielby 1994), and movies (Faulkner and Anderson 1987; De Vany and Walls 1999; Vogel 2004)—leads cultural markets to be called 'superstar' (Rosen 1981) or 'winner-take-all' (Frank and Cook 1995) markets.

Such large differences in success seem to suggest that these 'superstar' objects are somehow intrinsically different from their peers. Yet, if that is so, why is it that even experts are routinely unable to predict which of the many entrants will become the superstars? As with inequality of success, examples of unpredictability abound. The first book in the Harry Potter series, which went on to sell tens of millions of copies, was rejected by eight publishers before finally being accepted for publication (Lawless 2005).[1] The megahit television show 'American Idol,' which is currently in its sixth season and regularly attracts millions of viewers, was initially rejected by three major television networks (Carter 2006).[2] *Star Wars*—now regarded as the very archetype of the blockbuster movie—was widely viewed by Fox insiders as an all-but-certain flop, right up until the day of its release (Seabrook 2000). And in music, Bob Dylan's 'Like A Rolling Stone,' which was recently named the greatest rock and roll song of all time by two major pop-music magazines, was almost never released because executives thought it was too long (Considine 2004).

Incorrect predictions, moreover, are not limited to misjudging future superstars; sometimes products that are predicted to become superstars fail. For example, Carley Hennessy was a young Irish pop singer whose demo recording greatly impressed the president of MCA Records. Expecting her to become a superstar, MCA invested more than two million dollars in the production and marketing of her first album, *Ultimate High*. Despite this support, in its first three months the album sold just 378 copies (Ordonez 2002). Stories of such flops are often unknown to those outside of cultural industries, and this sampling bias seriously distorts outsiders' intuition about cultural markets. For example, those outside of cultural industries are often surprised to learn that failures greatly outnumber successes; it is estimated that about 80 percent of movies and that 90 percent of musicians lose money for their parent companies (Ordonez 2002; Vogel 2004).

Perhaps not surprisingly, industry executives routinely talk about the unpredictability of success (Peterson and Berger 1971; Hirsch 1972; Denisoff 1975; Gitlin 1983), and even prominent ones refer to their work as 'a crap game' (Denisoff 1975). In the film business one successful producer described the work as 'rather like being a wildcat oil driller. You hit a lot of dry wells hoping for a gusher' (Faulkner and Anderson 1987), and the well-respected screenwriter William Goldman wrote that 'the single most important fact, perhaps, of the entire movie industry is that "nobody knows anything" ' (1983). Similar sentiments are heard from both television and publishing executives. For example, Leslie Moonves, Chairman of CBS, said, 'You never really do know what will work or not work. Most of your big hits come out of nowhere' (Hirschberg 2005), and, according to Judith Regan, President of ReganBooks, the same rule applies to publishing: 'You know, nobody knows' (Williams 2005). These impressions of industry executives about unpredictability are also supported by outside research. A study of over two thousand movies found that the budget of a movie, the name recognition of its stars, its genre, and most other obvious characteristics explained relatively little of the variation in success, leading the authors to conclude that in film 'revenue forecasts have zero precision' (De Vany and Walls 1999). Bielby and Bielby (1994) found similar results in a study of the success of television shows.

It is this paradox of cultural markets—that success is at once unequal and unpredictable—that we investigate here. We propose a conceptual model that shows that social influence, a process well studied at the individual level, leads to unanticipated consequences at the collective level, including inequality and unpredictability of success. Then we review results from a series of four experiments—details of which have been published elsewhere (Salganik, Dodds, and Watts 2006; Salganik and Watts 2008, 2009)—that were designed to explore various aspects of the conceptual model. These experiments, summarized in Table 14.1, involved more than 27,000 participants and provide strong support for the proposed model.

Table 14.1 Description of four experiments

	Participants	
	www.bolt.com	Electronic small–world experiment
Weaker influence	Experiment 1 (n = 7,149)	
Stronger influence	Experiment 2 (n = 7,192)	Experiment 3 (n = 2,930)
Manipulation		Experiment 4 (n = 9,996)

Note: The experiments are nested, in the sense that each experiment changes one thing from the experiment that precedes it.

14.1 SOCIAL INFLUENCE

The existence of social influence on individual decisions has been well established by sociologists and experimental social psychologists since the 1930s (Sherif 1937; Asch 1952; Katz and Lazarsfeld 1955) and there has been a substantial body of research attempting to understand the origins of social influence (Cialdini and Goldstein 2004). Based on this research there are a number of reasons to believe that social influence operates on individuals' choices in cultural markets. First, in all these markets individuals are faced with an overwhelming number of options; for example, a typical 'big-box' bookstore currently stocks between 40,000 and 100,000 books, and those shopping on the Internet see their choices increased by a factor of 10 (Brynjolfsson, Hu, and Smith 2003). Out of a huge mass of objects, and with no information about most of them, an individual must pick one to consider. In making this decision, individuals are probably more likely to consider objects that are already successful (Adler 1985; Hedström 1998; Goldstein and Gigerenzer 2002). This mimicry could derive from individuals using the behavior of others as a signal of the quality of the objects— a phenomenon known as 'social' or 'observational' learning (Banerjee 1992; Bikhchandani, Hirschleifer, and Welch 1992; Hedström 1998)—or occur because in the quest for discussion partners individuals benefit from compatibility with the choices of others (Adler 1985). Also, the opinions of others could affect the individual's evaluation of the object—for example, individuals laugh longer and more often at jokes when others are laughing, even when the laughter is canned (Fuller and Sheehy-Skeffington 1974).

These individual tendencies to mimic the behavior of others are often reinforced by structural features of many cultural markets. For example, booksellers order more copies of best-selling books, give them more prominent in-store placement, and sell them at lower prices. Similar patterns appear in music markets when radio stations preferentially play whatever songs are 'hot,' thereby increasing the amount that people like these songs through a process that psychologists call the 'mere-exposure effect' (Cutting 2003). Without even knowing the popularity of the objects, in other words, individuals can be influenced by the opinion of others via these indirect processes.

14.2 CUMULATIVE ADVANTAGE

As the above discussion suggests, the social-influence process can depend on a combination of individual and structural factors. In order to understand the collective dynamics of cultural markets, however, we must switch our attention from the *origins* of social influence at the individual level to the *consequences* of social influence at the collective level. Because many of the influence processes presented so far have the effect of making successful objects more successful, cultural markets can be understood with the help of a large body of research on what have come to be called 'cumulative advantage' models (DiPrete and Eirich 2006).[3] These models have been studied in a variety of fields and under a variety of names—rich-get-richer, success-breeds-success, preferential attachment, Gibrat's principle, constant or increasing returns to scale, and 'the Matthew effect'—and this body of literature can be roughly divided into two distinct classes.

One part of the literature, mostly produced by statisticians and physicists, is concerned with inequality in the distribution of *outcomes for a set of objects*. Work in this stream of literature, beginning with Yule (1925), and later Simon (1955), Price (1976), and more recently Barabási and Albert (1999) and many others, suggests that cumulative advantage processes generate inequality in outcomes for objects that are otherwise indistinguishable. These dynamic models, while differing in their specifics, share the feature that objects that have become successful tend to become more successful still; thus, initially small differences—possibly the result of random fluctuations—grow into large differences over time. Taken together, this body of work suggests that the observed inequality in cultural markets is consistent with a cumulative-advantage process.

The second part of the cumulative-advantage literature, mostly produced by economists, focuses, instead, on the *outcomes for specific objects*. The prototypical example of this work is that on competing technology standards—for example the QWERTY versus Dvorak keyboards (David 1985). Research in this literature, for example Arthur (1989), emphasizes that in situations where cumulative advantage operates it is not possible to predict ahead of time which technology standard will become dominant. Because of 'path dependence' and 'lock-in,' one realization of the process will produce one winner, but the next realization, performed under

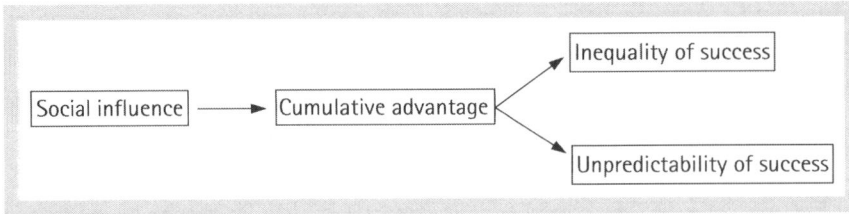

Fig. 14.1 Schematic of proposed cumulative–advantage model

identical conditions, will produce a different winner. Models of this kind, therefore, suggest that if social influence leads to cumulative advantage, then the outcomes in cultural markets will never be precisely predictable because these outcomes vary from realization to realization (Watts 2002, 2003). Thus, the inability of industry executives to predict successful objects may not stem from a lack of competence, but rather from the inherent impossibility of the task.

14.3 TESTING THE MODEL: AN EXPERIMENTAL APPROACH

The conceptual model presented above, and shown in Figure 14.1, is grounded in existing literature and suggests a solution to the paradoxical nature of success in cultural markets: the inequality and unpredictability in cultural markets, which superficially seem to be at odds with one another, could both stem from social influence at the level of the individual. Unfortunately, for several reasons, this model is difficult to test, even though there are excellent data on the sales of books, music, and movies. First, all observed outcomes in cultural markets are generated in the presence of an unknown amount of social influence; thus, it is difficult to convincingly estimate what would have happened in the absence of social influence. Further, with observational data it is hard to argue that outcomes are truly unpredictable. For example, the fact that eight publishers rejected the first Harry Potter book seems to suggest that outcomes are unpredictable, but one could also argue that the book's success followed directly from its 'quality' and that the eight publishers who rejected the book were simply too stupid to realize that they were reading a future best-seller. To convincingly show that outcomes are truly unpredictable one would need to observe multiple 'histories' or 'realizations' of the same process. If Harry Potter became popular in all of these histories then we could conclude that there is something special about the book, but if Harry Potter became popular in one of these histories, but not the others, then we could conclude that there was some inherent unpredictability in the outcome. Without observing these counterfactual outcomes, any tests of cumulative-advantage models with observational data will be open to multiple, conflicting interpretations.

In order to resolve these methodological issues, we have adopted an experimental approach. Specifically, we examined the effect of social influence on the success of cultural objects by creating an artificial cultural market in the form of a website where participants could listen to, rate, and download songs by unknown bands, but also where we could control the information that participants had about the behavior of others. Naturally, our website lacked many of the features of real cultural markets, but our purpose was not to reproduce a real cultural market, rather it was to observe the effects of social influence under controlled conditions (Zelditch 1969).[4] Our artificial market, therefore, allowed us to clearly and directly test our prediction that social influence could lead to both inequality and unpredictability of success.

Upon arriving at our website participants were presented with a welcome screen informing them that they were about to participate in a study of musical tastes and that in exchange for participating they would be given a chance to download some free songs by up-and-coming artists. Next, participants provided informed consent,[5] filled out a brief survey, and were shown a page of instructions. Finally, participants were presented with a menu of 48 songs by unknown artists.[6] Having chosen to listen to a song, they were asked to rate it on a scale of 1 star ('I hate it') to 5 stars ('I love it'), after which they were offered the opportunity to download the song. Because of the design of our site, participants could only download a song after listening to and rating it. However, they could listen to, rate, and download as many or as few songs as they wished in a single session.

Also upon arrival, participants were randomly assigned (without being informed of the assignment) to one of two experimental conditions—independent and social-influence—that differed only by the availability of information on the past behavior of others. Participants in the social-influence condition were also further assigned at random to one of a number of independently evolving groups that we will call 'worlds' to emphasize that they represent parallel histories. Participants in the independent condition chose which songs to listen to based solely on the names of the bands and their songs, while participants in the social-influence condition could also see how many times each song was downloaded by previous participants in their world. Thus, although the presence or absence of download counts was not emphasized, the choices of participants in the social-influence worlds could clearly be influenced by the choices of previous participants, whereas no such influence was possible in the independent condition. By comparing outcomes across these conditions, therefore, we can directly isolate the effect of social influence on collective outcomes. This 'macrosociological' research design, presented in Figure 14.2, differs from those common in economics and psychology because rather than focusing on the origins of social influence at the individual level, it focuses on how the

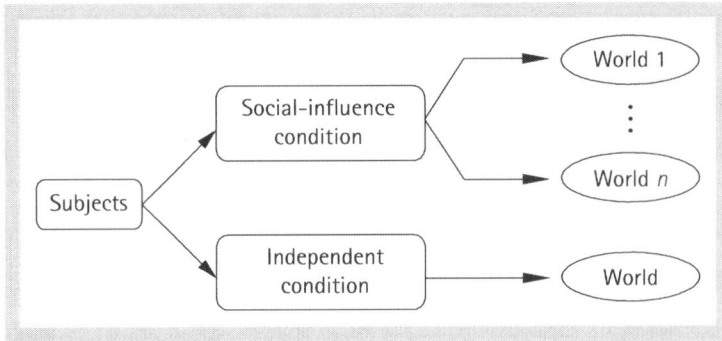

Fig. 14.2 Schematic of the experimental design for experiments 1–3

social-influence process aggregates to produce collective outcomes (Schelling 1978; Coleman 1990; Hedström 2005, 2006).

14.4 EXPERIMENTS 1 AND 2: VARYING THE STRENGTH OF THE SOCIAL SIGNAL

To explore the effects of social influence on the inequality and unpredictability of success we conducted two experiments that were similar except for the strength of social influence to which participants were exposed. In experiment 1, participants (n = 7,149) were presented the songs in a three-column menu (Fig. 14.3) in a random order that was fixed for each participant (i.e. the songs were not sorted by popularity). In experiment 2, however, participants (n = 7,192) were presented the songs in a single column sorted by popularity (Fig. 14.3). This change in layout was intended to increase the salience of the information regarding the behavior of other participants and thus increase the strength of social influence.

In both experiments participants were assigned either to one of eight social-influence worlds or to the independent condition. Further, in both experiments the same 48 songs were used, and, as much as possible, we recruited our subjects from the same source: the website www.bolt.com, a web community for teens and young adults. As a result of our recruiting strategy, participants were predominately teenagers living in the USA; a more complete demographic description of the participants in both experiments is presented in Salganik, Dodds, and Watts (2006). All songs started with zero downloads and the counts were updated in real time as the experiment progressed.

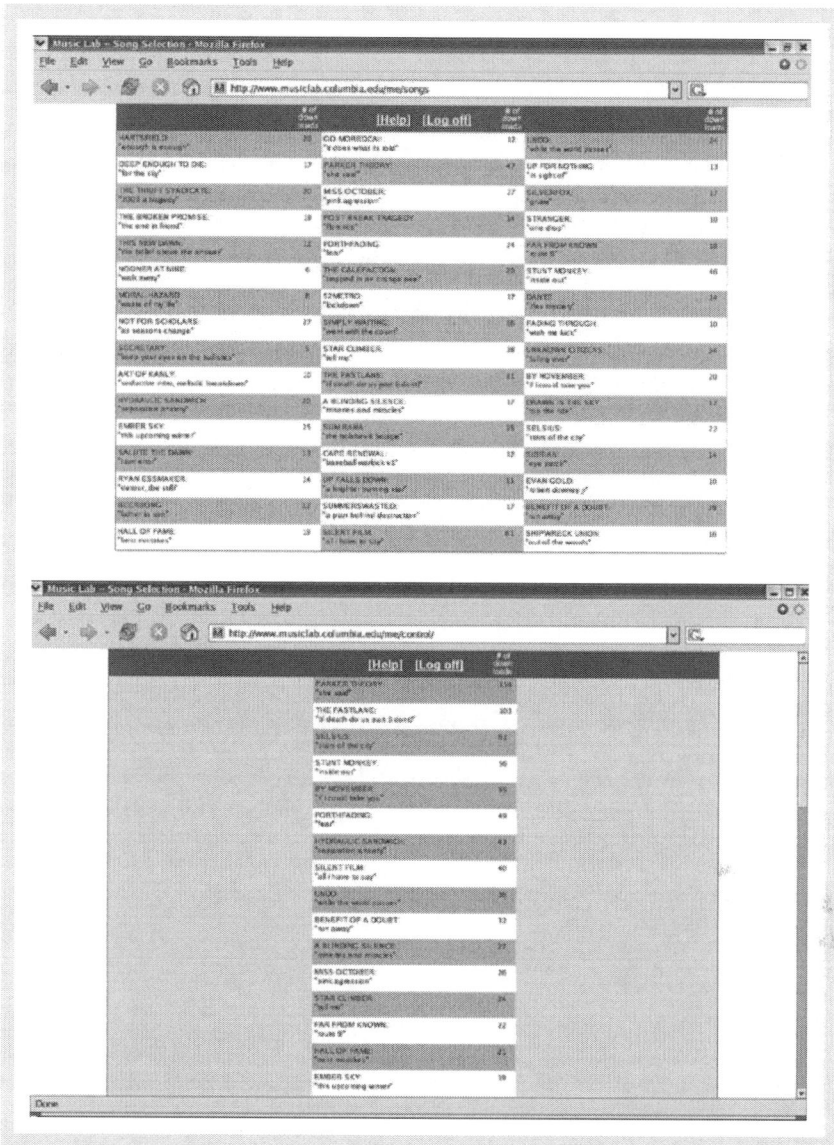

Fig. 14.3 Screenshots of song menu from experiments 1 (top) and 2–4 (bottom)

Based on the conceptual model discussed previously, we proposed two related hypotheses: first, we expected that in both of the experiments the success of the songs in the social-influence condition would be more unequal and more unpredictable than the success of songs in the independent condition; and second, because participants in experiment 2 were exposed to a stronger form of social influence, we expected that success in the social-influence condition in experiment 2 would be more unequal and more unpredictable than success in the social-influence condition in experiment 1.

14.4.1 Individual behavior

Within our experimental framework there are three main ways that participants' behavior can be affected by the behavior of others: first, the participant must decide which of the 48 available songs to listen to; then, while listening to a song, the participant must decide which rating to assign the song; finally, the participant must decide whether or not to download it. Information about the popularity of the songs could affect all of these decisions, but here we will focus our attention on the effect of popularity on participants' listening decisions.[7]

At the time each subject participated, every song in his or her world had a specific download count and market rank. (For example, the song with the most downloads had a market rank of 1.) It is therefore straightforward to calculate the probability that a participant chose to listen to the song of a given market rank (independent of which song occupied that rank at the time). Figure 14.4a shows that in the social-influence condition in experiment 1 participants were more likely to listen to more popular songs. For example, a participant had a 20 percent chance of listening to whatever was the most popular song but only a 7 percent chance of listening to a song of middle market rank. This behavior can be contrasted with the behavior in the independent condition where, as expected given our design, listening decisions were unrelated to popularity.

Recall that because of the design of the song menu we expected more social influence in experiment 2, and this pattern was indeed observed (Fig. 14.4b). For example, in experiment 1, participants were about 3 times more likely to listen to the most popular song than a mid-level song; in experiment 2, participants were about 8 times more likely.[8] We don't know exactly why participants were more likely to listen to popular songs, but our concern here is not to understand and differentiate the specific mechanisms that lead to social influence at the individual level. Rather, we want to explore the effects of social influence at the aggregate level. It is sufficient for our purposes, therefore, to simply show that participants' choices were affected by the choices of other participants. Now we will turn our attention to the aggregate outcomes.

14.4.2 Inequality

The first aggregate level feature of success that we were interested in exploring was inequality of success. Here we measure the success of a song in terms of its market share of downloads (i.e. the fraction of all downloads in a world that belong to a

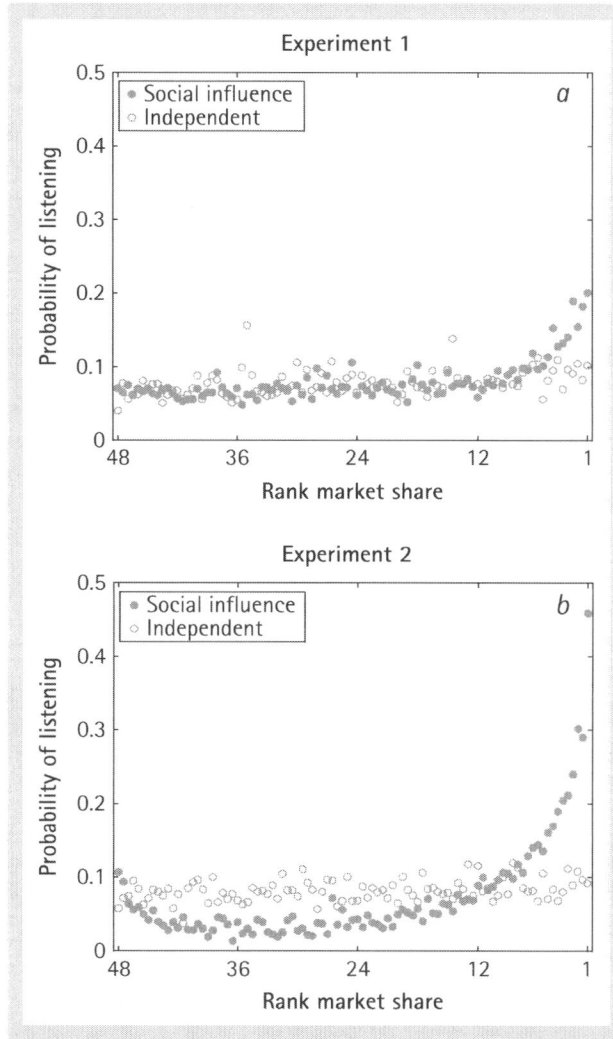

Fig. 14.4 **Listening–choice plots for experiments 1 and 2**

specific song) and we measure the inequality of success using the Gini coefficient, one of the most common measures of inequality; other measures of inequality yield qualitatively similar results (Salganik 2007).

In Figure 14.5 we plot the Gini coefficients from experiment 1 and experiment 2. In experiment 1, the Gini coefficients for the eight social influence worlds ranged from 0.28 to 0.42, with mean 0.34, while the independent world had a Gini coefficient of 0.26. The probability of observing a difference this large between the two conditions due only to chance was small ($p < 0.01$), so the results are statistically significant.[9] We see a similar pattern in experiment 2, where the Gini coefficients in

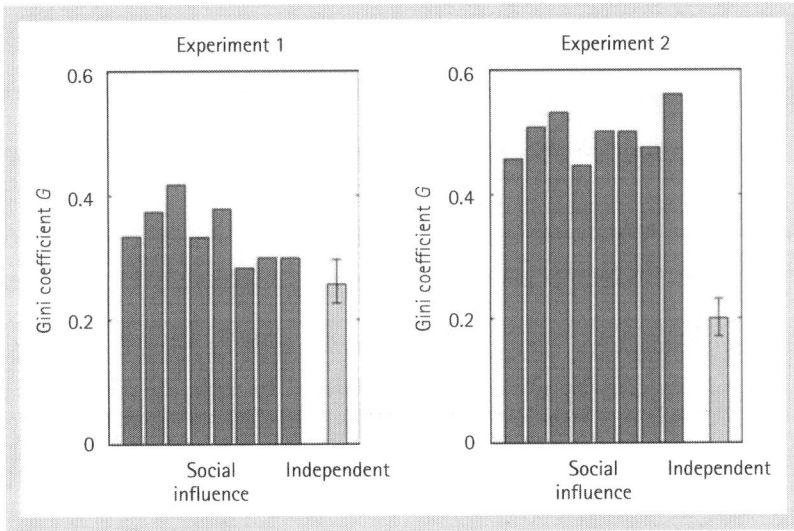

Fig. 14.5 Inequality in success, as measured by the Gini coefficient, in experiments 1 and 2

the social-influence world range from 0.45 to 0.56, with mean 0.50. These are much larger than the Gini coefficient in the independent world of 0.20. Again, differences this large are not likely due to chance (p < 0.01).

Finally, turning our attention to the comparison across experiments, we see that all the social-influence worlds in experiment 2 are more unequal than the most unequal social-influence world in experiment 1. The difference across experiments is both statistically significant (p < 0.001) and substantively significant. To understand the size of this difference we can make a comparison to current levels of income inequality. The difference in inequality between the social-influence worlds in experiment 1 and experiment 2 is of similar magnitude to the difference in income inequality in Western European nations (G ~ 0.34), and income inequality in developing nations like Nigeria, Peru, and Venezuela (G ~ 0.50) (UNDP 2004).

14.4.3 Unpredictability

Now we turn to the question of unpredictability of success. Here we conceptualize unpredictability as the variation in success across different realizations of the same process. If success is the same in all realizations, then the outcome is, at least in theory, predictable, and its unpredictability is defined to be 0. If outcomes differ across realizations, however, precise predictions about market share become increasingly difficult. Therefore, we define the unpredictability of specific song u_i

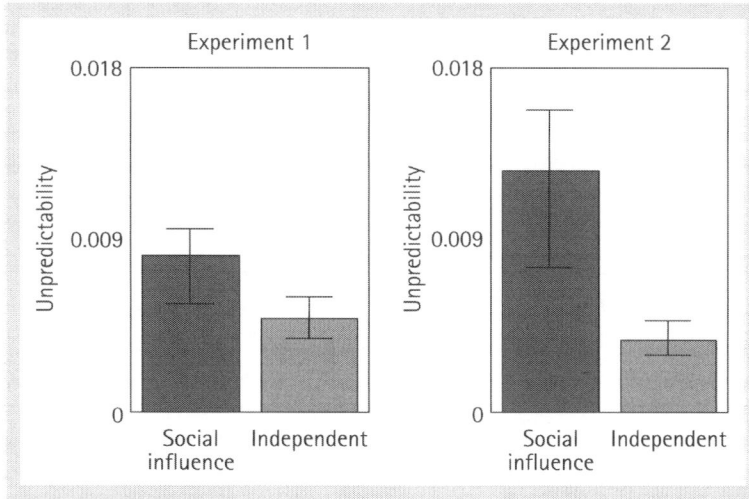

Fig. 14.6 Unpredictability of success in experiments 1 and 2

to be the average difference in market share between two randomly chosen success outcomes. That is,

$$u_i = \frac{\sum_{i=1}^{R} \sum_{j=i+1}^{R} \left| m_{ij} - m_{ik} \right|}{R\left(R-1\right)/2}$$

where m_{ij} is the market share of song i in world j and R is the number of realizations. A larger value of u_i implies more difference between two randomly chosen realizations, and thus greater unpredictability. Once we have measured the unpredictability of a song, we calculate the unpredictability of an entire experimental condition, U, by averaging the unpredictability of all songs in that condition.

Recall that the conceptual model suggests that increased social influence at the individual level should lead to greater unpredictability at the aggregate level. In Figure 14.6, we plot the unpredictability measure U in experiment 1 and experiment 2. We observe that, as expected, in both experiments the unpredictability is greater in the social-influence condition than in the independent condition (both p < 0.01).[10] Further, increasing the amount of social influence at the individual level increased the unpredictability by about 50 percent—a difference that is unlikely to have resulted from chance, although it falls just short of standard levels of statistical significance (p = 0.06). Social influence, therefore, generates unpredictability that is inherent to the aggregation process itself in the sense that it cannot be reduced simply by knowing more about either the songs or the preferences of individuals.

Overall, the results from experiments 1 and 2 strongly suggest that social influence at the micro level leads to inequality and unpredictability of success at the macro level. Together they show a 'dose–response' relationship, whereby we are able to manipulate an individual-level process and yield predictable results at the aggregate level. A comparison of experiments 1 and 2 also highlights a surprising effect of social influence. On the one hand, increasing the social influence, by changing the song menu from an unordered grid to a ranked list, increased the inequality of outcomes; thus, 'the winners' in any particular realization seemed more distinguishable from 'the rest.' On the other hand, however, this same change also increased differences between the realizations. Increasing social influence, in other words, increased the appearance of predictability while simultaneously decreasing the actual (i.e. *ex ante*) predictability. Critically, because individual participants only ever experience one outcome, the increase in unpredictability is largely invisible to them.

14.4.4 The role of appeal

Our experimental design permits us to measure inequality and unpredictability as a function of social influence without requiring any measure of the 'quality' of the songs. This feature is advantageous because the 'quality' of cultural products is very hard to measure, since it is largely, if not completely, a social construction (Gans 1974; Becker 1982; Bourdieu 1984; DiMaggio 1987; Cutting 2003). Nevertheless, given the central role that 'quality' is frequently assigned in explaining success (Rosen 1981), the relationship between the two deserves some further consideration.

While we cannot measure quality for the reasons described above, our experimental design permits us to measure something related that we call 'appeal.' Because the behavior of the participants in the independent condition reflects only their individual preferences (i.e. they were not subject to social influence), the appeal a_i of each song i can be defined as the market share of downloads that song earned in the independent condition, $a_i = d_i / \sum d$, where d_i is the number of downloads for song i in the independent condition.

We now return to a slightly modified version of our original question and ask about the role of appeal in the success of cultural objects. Earlier in the chapter we found that success in the social-influence worlds was unpredictable, *but this does not mean that the success of the songs was purely random*; instead success was positively related to appeal. Figure 14.7 plots the relationship between the appeal of the songs, as measured in the independent condition, and the success of the songs in the eight influence worlds. A clear pattern emerges that, on average, songs of higher appeal were more successful; however, this average trend was quite noisy. Further, while appeal was positively associated with success in both experiments,

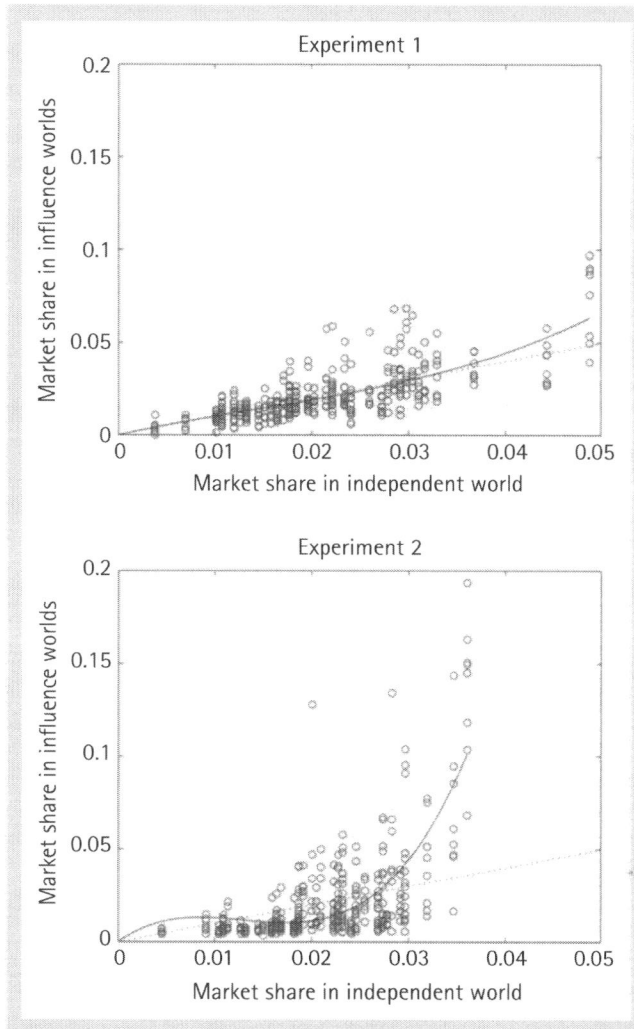

Fig. 14.7 Relationship between appeal and success (The dotted line indicates the appeal–equals–success line and the solid line is a third–degree polynomial fit to the data)

this relationship was highly nonlinear in experiment 2, as seen in the solid line in the figures that represents the best-fit third-degree polynomial to the data. This nonlinearity means that for the highest appeal songs a small increase in appeal was associated with a large increase in success. Another pattern in Figure 14.7 is that the range of observed market shares increased as the appeal increased. In other words, the highest-appeal songs were most unpredictable.

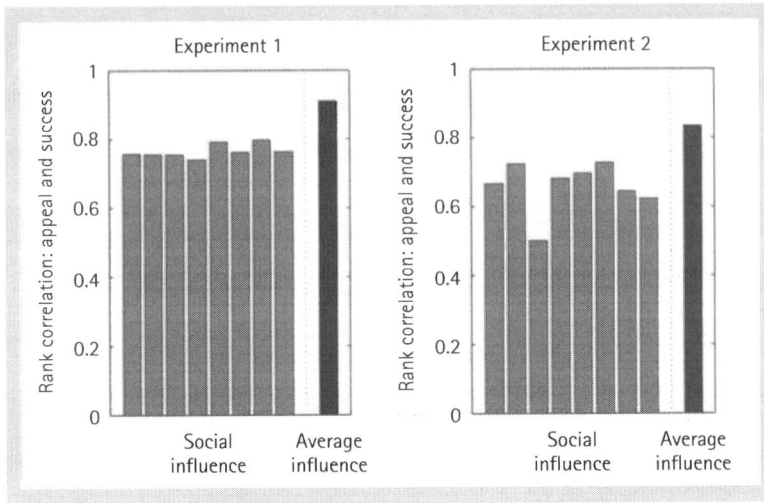

Fig. 14.8 Spearman's rank correlation between appeal and success

Further, the relationship between appeal and success can be quantified using Spearman's rank correlation.[12] As seen in Figure 14.8, the relationship between appeal and success was stronger in each of the eight influence worlds in experiment 1 than in the eight influence worlds in experiment 2, suggesting that social influence weakened the relationship between appeal and success. In addition, we constructed a measure of average success for each song by averaging its market share across the eight influence worlds. In both experiments the relationship between appeal and this average success measure was stronger than the relationship between appeal and success in any specific realization (Fig. 14.8)—a result that suggests that each outcome is a combination of *signal* (based on the appeal of the songs) and *noise* (based on the effects of social influence). By averaging over many realizations, the noise tends to cancel, revealing a signal that is related to appeal. We suspect, therefore, that if we had had 800 social-influence worlds instead of 8, the rank correlation between appeal and average success would be very close to 1. Thus, in our experiments, the intuition that the 'best' songs become the most successful is valid, but only on average; in any particular realization the 'best' songs were not necessarily the most successful.

The ratio of signal to noise in outcomes in actual cultural markets is an interesting open question. It may be hard to establish empirically, however, not only because the real world rarely presents multiple realizations of the same process, but also because our measure of appeal is based on the behavior of the people in the independent condition, and therefore is unaffected by success in the influence worlds. In real cultural markets, however, appeal is likely to be *endogenous*. For example, Cutting (2003) has shown that because of what psychologists call the mere-exposure effect, the more exposure people have to a specific painting, the more they like it. Therefore, as an object becomes more successful and people are increasingly exposed to it, the appeal of that object increases. This endogenous nature of appeal may have the effect of increasing the observed correlation between appeal and success in real cultural markets, thereby complicating attempts to separate them. Rather than appeal leading to success, however, we would conjecture that it is often also the case that success leads to appeal.

14.5 EXPERIMENT 3: THE SETUP AND REPLICATION

Experiments 1 and 2 provide strong support for the argument that social influence at the individual level leads to inequality and unpredictability of success at the collective level. There are risks, however, in drawing sweeping conclusions based solely on studies of American teenagers, a population that may be particularly susceptible to peer influence or unusual in other ways. Therefore, we attempted to replicate the results with a different pool of participants by sending an email to 13,546 participants from the electronic small-world experiment (Dodds, Muhamad, and Watt 2003), a previous, unrelated research project. These emails, along with the web postings that they generated, yielded 2,930 participants for experiment 3—participants that were older, more often male, and more international than the participants in the first two experiments (Salganik and Watts 2009). These participants were assigned into two social-influence worlds and one independent world, yielding worlds of similar size to experiments 1 and 2.[13] As with experiments 1 and 2, all download counts started at zero and were incremented in real time.

In experiment 3, as in the first two experiments, participants' listening decisions in the social-influence condition were affected by information about the popularity of the songs (Fig. 14.9). Turning to the collective level, Figure 14.10 shows that the inequality and unpredictability of success were larger in the social-influence condition than the independent condition (Fig. 14.10). Thus, both of our main hypotheses held in this different study population, suggesting that the effects of social influence that were observed in experiments 1 and 2 cannot be attributed to some special characteristics of the teenagers from www.bolt.com.[14] Additonal comparisons between experiment 2 and 3 are available elsewhere (Salganik and Watts 2009).

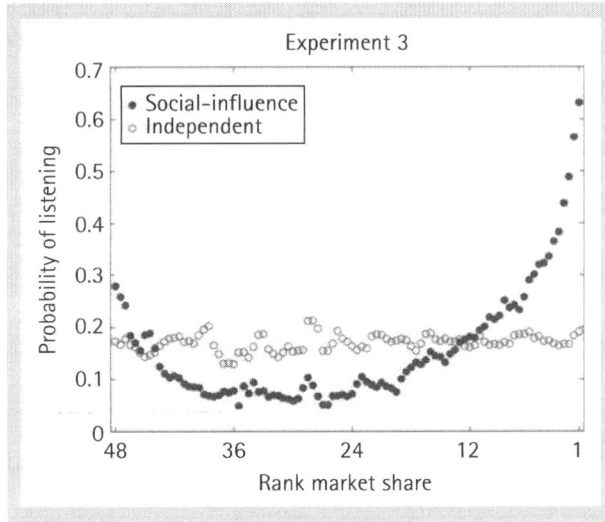

Fig. 14.9 Listening–choice plots for experiment 3

14.6 EXPERIMENT 4: SELF-FULFILLING PROPHECIES

In the first three experiments we allowed the popularity of the songs to emerge naturally, without any intervention. In real cultural markets, however, firms and artists actively intervene in this process by marketing and promoting their products, often attempting to distort the perceived popularity of objects. For example, the authors Michael Treacy and Fred Wiersma surreptitiously purchased thousands of copies of their book *The Discipline of Market Leaders* in an attempt to artificially boost it on the *New York Times* best-seller list (Stern 1995). A natural way to think about the effects of these attempts to change the perceived popularity of objects is in the context of the work on self-fulfilling prophecies developed by Robert K. Merton. As defined by Merton (1948), '[a] self-fulfilling prophecy is, in the beginning, a *false* definition of the situation evoking a new behavior which makes the originally *false* conception come *true*.' Thus, given the frequent attempts at manipulation, and the relevant theoretical framework, a natural area of investigation is the effect of false perceptions of the popularity of the cultural objects on their subsequent popularity.

Despite some recent studies (Hanson and Putler 1996; Sorensen 2007), we know very little about the possibilities of self-fulfilling prophecies in cultural markets, in part because of the limitations of observational data (Biggs 2009). For example, Treacy and Wiersma's book ultimately made the best-seller list and remained

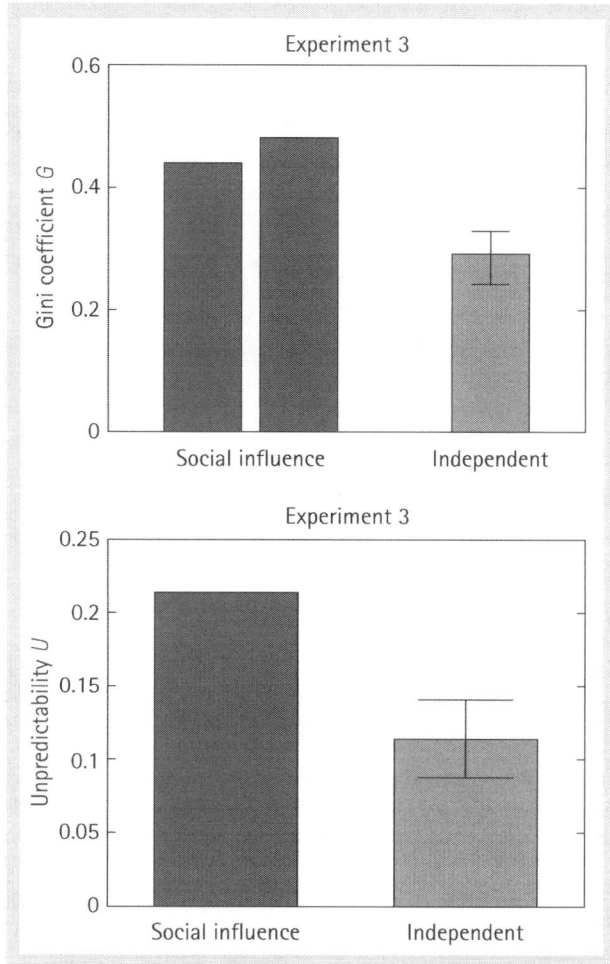

Fig. 14.10 Inequality and unpredictability of success in experiment 3

there for fifteen weeks. But how much of its success could be attributed to the manipulation and how much could be attributed—as the authors themselves insisted—to the 'quality' of the book itself? Answering this question requires comparing actual sales to the sales that would have occurred in the absence of manipulation, an outcome that we cannot observe. As this discussion illustrates, the problem of self-fulfilling prophecies in cultural markets is difficult with observational data, but naturally suited to a 'multiple-worlds' experiment.

To recruit participants for experiment 4 we sent emails to the remaining 50,800 participants from the electronic small-world experiment. These emails, in addition to the web postings they generated, yielded 9,996 new participants who were randomly assigned into either a social-influence or an independent condition. In

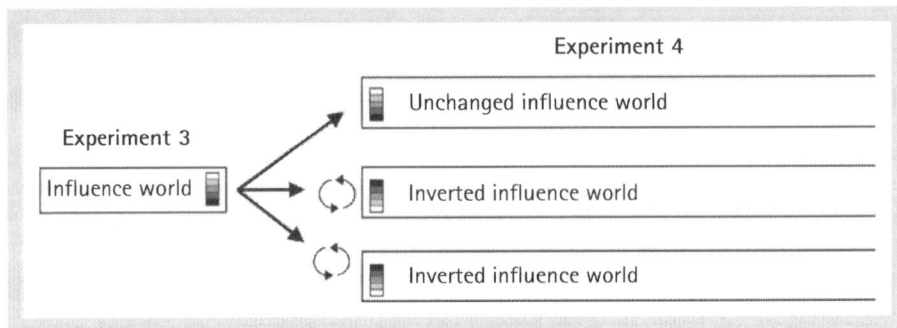

Fig. 14.11 **Schematic of social–influence worlds in experiment 4**

the previous experiments the number of downloads for the songs always started at 0. In experiment 4, however, we had three social-influence worlds, some of which had different initial conditions in order to give some participants a *false* sense of the popularities of the songs. In one of the social-influence worlds—the unchanged social-influence world—the initial download counts were set to be the final downloads counts from one of the social-influence worlds in experiment 3. This unchanged world, therefore, can be thought of as a control condition that allowed us to observe success in the absence of manipulation. In the other two social-influence worlds we set the initial download counts by *inverting* the success from the unchanged world. For example, at the beginning of experiment 4 in the unchanged social-influence world 'She Said' by Parker Theory had the most downloads, 128, while 'Florence' by Post Break Tragedy had the fewest, 9.[15] In the inverted worlds these download counts were swapped so that participants had the *false* impression that 'She Said' had 9 downloads and 'Florence' had 128. In this manner we also swapped the download counts for the 47th and 2nd songs, the 46th and 3rd songs, and so on. After this one-time intervention all download counts were updated accurately as the 9,996 participants listened to and downloaded songs in the four worlds—one unchanged social-influence world, two inverted social-influence worlds, and one independent world (Figure 14.11).

In Figure 14.12*a* we can follow the number of downloads over time for the initially most popular song in the unchanged world, 'She Said' by Parker Theory (song 1), and the initially least popular, 'Florence' by Post Break Tragedy (song 48). As expected, in the unchanged world, where the popularity of the songs was not manipulated, the download trajectories during experiment 4 continue the linear-growth pattern of experiment 3. In the two inverted worlds, however, we observe different dynamics. First, 'Florence' was downloaded about seven times more often in the inverted worlds (where it was ranked first) than the unchanged world (where it occupied a much lower rank). Clearly, the perception of success led to future success for 'Florence.' Similarly, the perception of less success led to decreased success for 'She Said'; in the inverted worlds (where it was not ranked first) it

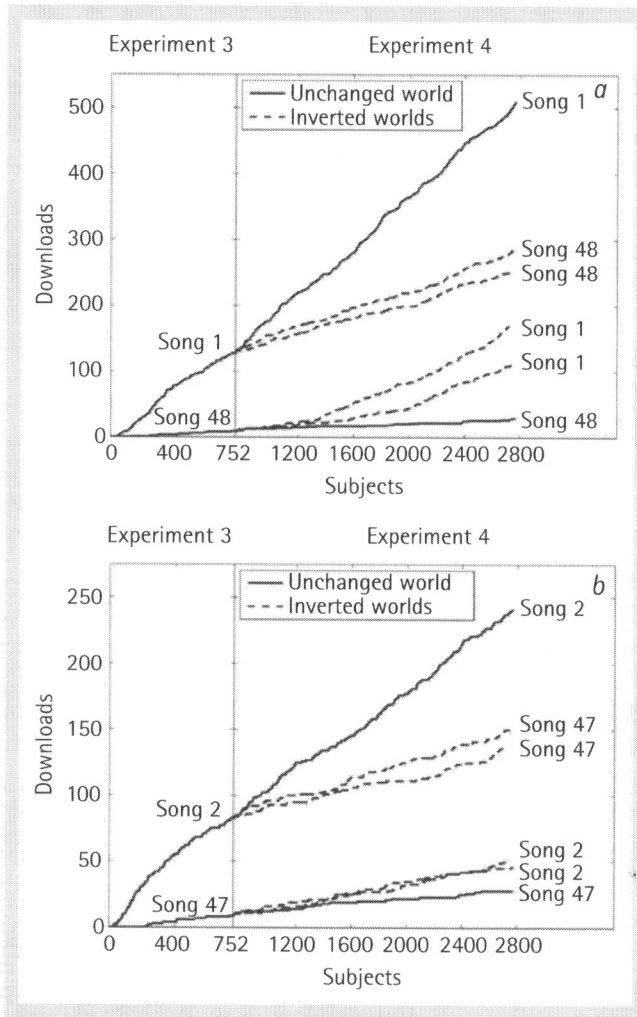

Fig. 14.12 Success dynamics for song 1 and song 48 (top) and for song 2 and song 47 (bottom)

was downloaded a third as often as the unchanged world (where it was ranked first). Although the misperception of success was *transiently* self-fulfilling for these songs, it was not *stably* self-fulfilling. Growth projections—described more fully in Salganik and Watts (2008)—suggest that if the experiment had continued for thousands more participants 'She Said' would have eventually overtaken 'Florence' and returned to its original spot as the most popular song. For some pairs of songs, however, the inversion appeared to be *stably* self-sustaining, as seen in Figure 14.12*b*, which plots the success dynamics of 'Went with the Count' by Simply Waiting (the original 2nd song) and 'For the Sky' by Deep Enough to Die (the original 47th song). In this case, growth projections suggest that in both inverted worlds 'For the Sky' will always stay more popular than 'Went with the Count.' That is, in this case, once participants believed that 'For the Sky' was more popular their behavior reinforced this pattern. These results suggest that one-time interventions in cultural markets, either random or intentional, can harden to create a new social reality. Additional results about subsequent system dynamics are presented in Salganik and Watts (2008).

14.7 THE *MONA LISA*

In experiment 4 we found that, at least in our artificial cultural market, one-time exogenous shocks in the popularity of the songs could lead to self-fulfilling prophecies: once participants believed that 'For the Sky' was more popular than 'Went with the Count' their behavior reinforced that pattern. But could this self-reinforcing dynamic happen in real cultural markets? In fact, we think it already has, and it has happened for one of the most famous paintings in the world: the *Mona Lisa*.

By many measures the *Mona Lisa* is the most famous work of art in the world; but why? Reading the opinion of an art critic like Kenneth Clark, the answer would appear to be simple: because the *Mona Lisa* is 'the supreme example of perfection' (Clark 1973). According to the historian Donald Sassoon (2001), however, the *Mona Lisa*'s rise to iconic status is far less straightforward than a simple 'it is the most famous because it is the best' explanation would suggest. Sassoon notes, for example, that until about 1900 the *Mona Lisa* was 'just' a well-respected painting by a famous old master (Leonardo da Vinci) hanging in one of the greatest museums in the world (the Louvre). That is, the painting had achieved a status that few paintings ever reach, but the painting was not yet a global icon; in fact, it wasn't even the most valued painting in the Louvre. In 1849 the painting was valued at 90,000 francs, a large amount at the time, but easily dwarfed by the values placed on other paintings in the museum, including Titian's *Les Pèlerins d'Emmaüs* (150,000 francs), Raphael's *La Vierge, l'Enfant Jesus, et Saint Jean* (400,000 francs), and Raphael's *Sainte Famille* (600,000 francs) (Sassoon 2001).

Then, on 11 August 1911, something happened that set into motion a series of events that were crucial in the painting's ascent to the status of global icon: the *Mona Lisa* was stolen. On that Monday, the day that the museum was closed, Vincenzo Peruggia, an unemployed Italian painter, took the painting out of its frame and walked out of the museum. The theft created a huge burst of publicity for the painting, as its image, as well as descriptions of its importance, were printed on the front pages of newspapers all over France. After the theft, the painting remained missing for two years until it was recovered when Peruggia tried to sell the painting to an antique dealer in Florence. The recovery of the painting, just like the theft, generated another burst of newspaper coverage, this time in both France and Italy.

The publicity brought on by the theft and recovery of the painting meant that in 1919 when Marcel Duchamp was looking for something famous to parody, the *Mona Lisa* was a natural choice. *L.H.O.O.Q.*, his mustached parody of the *Mona Lisa*, did not hurt the painting, but rather served to reinforce its fame, making it even more likely to be parodied in the future (Biel 2005; Sassoon 2006). In fact, since Duchamp, the *Mona Lisa* has been parodied by hundreds of artists, including such luminaries as Jasper Johns, Robert Rauschenberg, René Magritte, Salvador Dali, and Andy Warhol. The *Mona Lisa* has also crossed over to mainstream culture: it has appeared in numerous advertisements for firms ranging from Chanel to Air India; it has graced the cover of magazines from the *New Yorker* (twice) to *Le Figaro*; and it was featured prominently on the cover of Dan Brown's mega-best-selling novel, the *Da Vinci Code* (Sassoon 2006). In each case, the image was chosen because it was already well known, and in each case the use of the image served to reinforce its fame.

This brief sketch raises a number of questions: What if Peruggia had stolen *Sainte Famille* instead of *Mona Lisa*; or what if Duchamp had decided to parody a different woman with an enigmatic expression painted by a different old master (e.g. Vermeer's *Girl with a Pearl Earring*)? Unfortunately, we cannot answer these questions with certainty. A careful reading of the history, however, suggests that the next time you are in the Louvre and you see a crowd swarming around one specific painting, you might want to consider that had history turned out slightly differently that mob could very easily be standing somewhere else.

NOTES

1. Interestingly, Nigel Newton, the chief executive of Bloomsbury and the man who purchased the rights to the first Harry Potter book, attributes the discovery of Harry Potter not to any forethought on his part, but to his daughter who read the manuscript and liked it; she was able to convince him to pay a mere 2,500 pounds for the rights to publish the book. On the phenomenal success of the book and its sequels, the publisher said, 'We hit it lucky' (Lawless 2005).

2. The story of how 'American Idol' eventually made it onto the air bears some surprising parallels to the story of Harry Potter's publication. The key person in getting 'American Idol' on the air was not the show's agent, producer, or star, but rather Liz Murdoch, daughter of Rupert Murdoch, the owner of Fox Networks. After she told her father that she liked the British version of the show, 'Pop Idol,' Mr Murdoch ordered his executives to sign and air the show despite their hesitations (Carter 2006).

3. Although the details of the influence process may matter for collective outcomes in some cases (Dodds and Watts 2004, 2005), we argue that for the issues of interest here—inequality and unpredictability—only the most general features of social influence are relevant.

4. Additional discussion of differences between our website and real cultural markets, and how these differences might have affected our results, is presented in Salganik, Dodds, and Watts (2006).

5. The research protocols used were approved by the Columbia University Institutional Review Board (protocol numbers IRB-AAA5286 and IRB-AAAB1483).

6. The music was sampled from the website www.purevolume.com. Additional details about the sampling and screening procedures are available in Salganik, Dodds, and Watts (2006) and Salganik (2007).

7. For a discussion about measuring social influence on participants' other decisions see Salganik (2007).

8. Another interesting pattern in the listening probabilities in experiment 2, and not present in experiment 1, was the slight increase in the propensity for participants to listen to the least popular songs, those ranked 45th to 48th. This pattern could be an artifact of the list format used in experiment 2, or instead could reflect a real tendency for anticonformist behavior (Simmel 1957). Further experiments would be required to adjudicate between these possibilities.

9. A more detailed description of the procedure to assess statistical significance is described in Salganik, Dodds, and Watts (2006).

10. A more detailed description of the procedure to assess statistical significance is described in Salganik, Dodds, and Watts (2006).

11. For more on the limitations of our measure of appeal see Salganik and Watts (2008).

12. We use Spearman's rank correlation instead of the more familiar Pearson correlation because of the nonlinear relationship between appeal and success in experiment 2. Spearman's rank correlation is not affected by this nonlinearity because it is a measure of monotonic association not linear association.

13. We chose to have only three worlds so that we could save as many email addresses as possible for the recruitment of participants for experiment 4.

14. It was also the case that the level of inequality and unpredictability in experiment 3 was less than that in experiment 2. We suspect that these differences are because in experiment 3 participants listened to more songs on average than in experiment 2: 7.7 versus 3.6 out of 48 possible songs. This issue is discussed further in Salganik (2007).

15. 'Florence' by Post Break Tragedy was tied with 10 other songs that also had 9 downloads. This tie, and all other ties during the inversion, was broken randomly.

References

ADLER, M. (1985), 'Stardom and Talent', *American Economic Review*, 75 (1): 208–12.

ARTHUR, W. B. (1989), 'Competing Technologies, Increasing Returns, and Lock-in by Historical Events', *Economic Journal*, 99 (394): 116–31.

ASCH, S. E. (1952), *Social Psychology* (Englewood Cliffs, N.J.: Prentice Hall).

BANERJEE, A. V. (1992), 'A Simple Model of Herd Behavior', *Quarterly Journal of Economics*, 107 (3): 797–817.

BARABÁSI, A., and ALBERT, R. (1999), 'Emergence of Scaling in Random Networks', *Science*, 286 (5439): 509–12.

BECKER, H. S. (1982), *Art Worlds* (Berkeley, Calif.: University of California Press).

BIEL, S. (2005), *American Gothic* (New York: Norton).

BIELBY, W. T., and BIELBY, D. D. (1994), ' "All Hits are Flukes": Institutionalized Decision-making and the Rhetoric of Network Prime-time Program Development', *American Journal of Sociology*, 99 (5): 1287–313.

BIGGS, M. (2009), 'Self-fulfilling Prophecies', in P. Hedström and P. Bearman (eds.), *The Oxford Handbook of Analytical Sociology* (Oxford: Oxford University Press), 294–314.

BIKHCHANDANI, S., HIRSHLEIFER, D., and WELCH, I. (1992), 'A Theory of Fads, Fashions, Customs, and Cultural Change as Information Cascades', *Journal of Political Economy*, 100 (5): 992–1026.

BOURDIEU, P. (1984), *Distinction*, trans. R. Nice (Cambridge, Mass.: Harvard University Press).

BRYNJOLFSSON, E., HU, Y., and SMITH, M. D. (2003), 'Consumer Surplus in the Digital Economy: Estimating the Value of Increased Product Variety at Online Booksellers', *Management Science*, 49 (11): 1580–96.

CARTER, B. (2006), *Desperate Networks* (New York: Doubleday).

CHUNG, K. H., and COX, R. A. K. (1994), 'A Stochastic Model of Superstardom: An Application of the Yule Distribution', *Review of Economics and Statistics*, 76 (4): 771–5.

CIALDINI, R. B., and GOLDSTEIN, N. J. (2004), 'Social Influence: Compliance and Conformity', *Annual Review of Psychology*, 55: 591–621.

CLARK, K. (1973), 'Mona Lisa', *Burlington Magazine*, 115 (840): 144–51.

COLEMAN, J. S. (1990), *Foundations of Social Theory* (Cambridge, Mass.: Harvard University Press).

CONSIDINE, S. (2004), 'The Hit We Almost Missed', *New York Times*, 3 December.

CUTTING, J. E. (2003), 'Gustave Caillebotte, French Impressionism, and Mere Exposure', *Psychonomic Bulletin & Review*, 10 (2): 319–43.

DAVID, P. (1985), 'Clio and the Economics of QWERTY', *American Economic Review*, 75 (2): 332–7.

DE VANY, A., and WALLS, W. D. (1999), 'Uncertainty in the Movie Industry: Does Star Power Reduce the Terror of the Box Office', *Journal of Cultural Economics*, 23: 285–318.

DENISOFF, R. S. (1975), *Solid Gold* (New Brunswick, N.J.: Transaction).

DIMAGGIO, P. (1987), 'Classification in Art', *American Sociological Review*, 52 (4): 440–55.

DIPRETE, T. A., and EIRICH, G. (2006), 'Cumulative Advantage as a Mechanism for Inequality: A Review of Theoretical and Empirical Developments', *Annual Review of Sociology*, 32: 271–97.

DODDS, P. S., and WATTS, D. J. (2004), 'Universal Behavior in a Generalized Model of Contagion', *Physical Review Letters*, 92 (21): 218701.

—— (2005), 'A Generalized Model of Social and Behavioral Contagion', *Journal of Theoretical Biology*, 232: 587–604.

—— MUHAMAD, R., and WATTS, D. J. (2003), 'An Experimental Study of Search in Global Social Networks', *Science*, 301: 827–9.

FAULKNER, R. R., and ANDERSON, A. B. (1987), 'Short-term Projects and Emergent Careers: Evidence from Hollywood', *American Journal of Sociology*, 92 (4): 879–909.

FRANK, R. H., and COOK, P. J. (1995), *The Winner-take-all Society* (New York: Free Press).

FULLER, R. G. V., and SHEEHY-SKEFFINGTON, A. (1974), 'Effect of Group Laughter on Responses to Humorous Materials: A Replication and Extension', *Psychological Reports*, 35: 531–4.

GANS, H. (1974), *Popular Culture and High Culture* (New York: Basic).

GITLIN, T. (1983), *Inside Prime Time* (New York: Pantheon).

GOLDMAN, W. (1983), *Adventures in the Screen Trade* (New York: Warner).

GOLDSTEIN, D. G., and GIGERENZER, G. (2002), 'Models of Ecological Rationality: The Recognition Heuristic', *Psychological Review*, 109 (1): 75–90.

HANSON, W. A., and PUTLER, D. S. (1996), 'Hits and Misses: Herd Behavior and Online Product Popularity', *Marketing Letters*, 7 (4): 297–305.

HEDSTRÖM, P. (1998), 'Rational Imitation', in P. Hedström and R. Swedberg (eds.), *Social Mechanisms: Analytical Approach to Social Theory* (Cambridge: Cambridge University Press).

—— (2005), *Dissecting the Social* (Cambridge: Cambridge University Press).

—— (2006), 'Experimental Macro Sociology: Predicting the Next Best Seller', *Science*, 311: 786–7.

HIRSCH, P. M. (1972), 'Processing Fads and Fashions: An Organization-set Analysis of Cultural Industry Systems', *American Journal of Sociology*, 77 (4): 639–59.

HIRSCHBERG, L. (2005), 'Giving Them What They Want', *New York Times Magazine*, 4 September.

KATZ, E., and LAZARSFELD, P. F. (1955), *Personal Influence* (Glencoe, Ill.: Free Press).

KRUEGER, A. B. (2005), 'The Economics of Real Superstars: The Market for Rock Concerts in the Material World', *Journal of Labor Economics*, 23 (1): 1–30.

LAWLESS, J. (2005), 'Nigel Newton: Is there Life After Harry? You Can Bet Your Hogwarts There Is', *Independent*, 3 July.

MERTON, R. K. (1948), 'The Self-fulfilling Prophecy', *Antioch Review*, 8: 193–210.

ORDONEZ, J. (2002), 'Behind the Music: MCA Spent Millions on Carly Hennessy—Haven't Heard of Her?', *Wall Street Journal*, 26 February.

PETERSON, R. A., and BERGER, D. G. (1971), 'Entrepreneurship in Organizations: Evidence from the Popular Music Industry', *Administrative Science Quarterly*, 16 (1): 97–106.

PRICE, D. (1976), 'A General Theory of Bibliometric and Other Cumulative Advantage Processes', *Journal of the American Society for Information Science*, 27 (5): 292–306.

ROSEN, S. (1981), 'The Economics of Superstars', *American Economic Review*, 71 (5): 845–58.

SALGANIK, M. J. (2007), 'Success and Failure in Cultural Markets', Ph.D. thesis (Columbia University).

—— and WATTS, D. J. (2008), 'Leading the Herd Astray: An Experimental Study of Self-fulfilling Prophecies in an Artificial Cultural Market', *Social Psychology Quarterly*, 71 (4): 338–55.

—— (2009), 'Web-based Experiments for the Study of Collective Social Dynamics in Cultural Markets', *Topics in Cognitive Science*.

—— DODDS, P. S., and WATTS, D. J. (2006), 'Experimental Study of Inequality and Unpredictability in an Artificial Cultural Market', *Science*, 311: 854–6.

SASSOON, D. (2001), *Becoming Mona Lisa* (New York: Harcourt).

—— (2006), *Leonardo and the Mona Lisa Story* (New York: Overlook).

SCHELLING, T. C. (1978), *Micromotives and Macrobehavior* (New York: Norton).

SEABROOK, J. (2000), *Nobrow* (New York: Vintage).

SHERIF, M. (1937), 'An Experimental Approach to the Study of Attitudes', *Sociometry*, 1 (1): 90–8.

SIMMEL, G. (1957), 'Fashion', *American Journal of Sociology*, 62 (6): 541–8.

SIMON, H. A. (1955), 'On a Class of Skew Distribution Functions', *Biometrika*, 42 (3/4): 425–40.

SORENSEN, A. T. (2007), 'Bestseller Lists and Product Variety', *Journal of Industrial Economics*, 55 (4): 715–38.

STERN, W. (1995), 'Did Dirty Tricks Create a Best-seller?', *Business Week*, 7 August.

UNDP (2004), *Human Development Report* (New York: United Nations Development Programme).

VOGEL, H. L. (2004), *Entertainment Industry Economics* (Cambridge: Cambridge University Press).

WATTS, D. J. (2002), 'A Simple Model of Global Cascades in Random Networks', *Proceedings of the National Academy of Sciences of the USA*, 99 (9): 5766–71.

—— (2003), *Six Degrees* (New York: Norton).

WILLIAMS, A. (2005), 'Feeding the Hunger for the Next Diet Book', *New York Times*, 17 April.

YULE, G. U. (1925), 'A Mathematical Theory of Evolution based on the Conclusions of Dr J. C. Willis, FRS', *Philosophical Transactions of the Royal Society of London, Series B*, 213: 21–87.

ZELDITCH, M. (1969), 'Can You Really Study an Army in the Laboratory?', in A. Etzioni and E. W. Lehman (eds.), *A Sociological Reader on Complex Organization* (New York: Holt, Rinehart, & Winston).

CHAPTER 15

THE CONTAGIOUSNESS OF DIVORCE*

YVONNE ÅBERG

INTRODUCTION

RESEARCH on the risk of divorce has attracted a great deal of interest over the past several decades, mostly due to a very rapid increase in divorce rates in most western societies. In the USA, for example, although there are considerable variations in divorce rates by race, education, and age at marriage, on average about half of all marriages end in divorce (see Raley and Bumpass 2003). We have a fairly detailed picture of the many characteristics of individuals and couples that influence the risk of divorce, such as number of children, education, income, age at marriage, and ethnicity (see White 1990). We know much less about how the characteristics of those with whom the individuals interact influence the stability of their marriages.

A large body of sociological and social-psychological research shows that individuals' actions are often influenced by the people with whom they interact (see e.g.

* I am particularly grateful to Peter Hedström for his many helpful comments. In addition I wish to thank Peter Bearman, Eva Bernhardt, Magnus Bygren, Andrew Cherlin, Carrie Conaway, Andreas Diekmann, Ann-Zofie Duvander, Michael Gähler, Carl le Grand, Jan Hoem, the late Mia Hultin, Jan Jonsson, Peter Marsden, Gigi Santow, Annemette Sørensen, Richard Swedberg, Ryszard Szulkin, Elizabeth Thomson, and Lisa Wallander for valuable comments.

Cialdini and Trost 1998), and this is also a recurrent theme throughout this book. The actions of significant others have been shown to be important for explaining a vast array of phenomena, including involvement in social movements (see e.g. McAdam and Paulsen 1993), virginity pledges (see e.g. Bearman and Bruckner 2001), lynching (see e.g. Tolnay, Deane, and Beck 1996), sexual behavior (see e.g. Billy, Brewster, and Grady 1994), contraceptive use (see e.g. Brewster 1994; Rosero-Bixby and Casterline 1994), and suicide (see e.g. Phillips 1974; Bearman and Moody 2004; Hedström, Liu, and Nordvik 2008).

Demographers have also paid some attention to social interactions and the contagious processes they may give rise to. An early study focusing on social-interaction effects on divorce was that of Dean and Bresnahan (1969). They mapped the spatial patterning of divorce in a mid-sized city in the state of Ohio, and found that it resembled a 'measles pattern'; that is, that divorce was spatially clustered. The pattern they found was suggestive and indicated that divorce may be contagious, but they did not have access to the type of data needed to test whether this was indeed the case. A more recent study, partially in the same tradition, is that of South and Lloyd (1995). They found that the risk of divorce for young people was substantially influenced by contextual factors. Most importantly, they found the sex ratio among singles residing in the same geographic area as the respondent to be important. This finding suggests that the supply of spousal alternatives in the local marriage market significantly influences the risk of marital dissolution.

Social interactions have also been the focus of some of the research on the 'inheritance' of divorce. As McLanahan and Bumpass (1988), Wolfinger (1999), and others have shown, children of divorce are more likely to divorce than comparable others. As noted by Diekmann and Engelhardt (1999), this is a potentially important factor contributing to the upward trend in marriage dissolution rates during the post-World War II period. Other recent examples include Kohler's analysis of fertility (2001) and Nazio and Blossfeld's analysis of cohabitation (2003). On the whole, these are noteworthy and interesting exceptions, however. Most demographic researchers pay little or no attention to the role of social interactions and the endogenous processes they can give rise to.

The analyses presented in this chapter suggest that interactions with others are crucial when it comes to explaining divorce; the marital status of those with whom individuals interact at work strongly influences their divorce risks. These results are based on data from a unique Swedish longitudinal database including all employees at approximately 1,500 randomly selected workplaces. The database allows for detailed analyses of how the sex, age, and marital status of a person's coworkers influence his or her risk of divorce, when one controls for other known risk factors. The core finding is that divorce is contagious, but that the patterns of influence differ significantly between men and women.

This chapter is organized as follows. I start with a discussion of various mechanisms that suggest that the marital status of significant others influences an individual's decision to divorce. Then I present the data and the results from the empirical analysis, and I conclude by discussing some implications of these findings for future research.

15.1 THE MARITAL STATUS OF OTHERS AND THE DECISION TO DIVORCE

The demographic composition of an individual's social context may influence the risk of marital disruption in a variety of ways. To better understand how this influence may operate, it is essential to try to specify various mechanisms likely to generate a relationship between the marital status of others and an individual's decision to divorce. As suggested by Wright (1971), Elster (1989), Hedström (2005), and others, the cause of an action like this may be seen as the constellation of opportunities, desires, and beliefs in the light of which the action appears reasonable. Given this conceptual framework, the mechanisms of relevance may be grouped under the following four headings:

1. opportunity-based mechanisms;
2. desire-based mechanisms;
3. belief-based mechanisms;
4. trigger mechanisms.

The fourth type of mechanism, trigger mechanisms, refers to events that make divorce a consciously reflected upon alternative and thereby, indirectly, make the other mechanisms causally efficacious. In the following pages I will briefly discuss specific examples of these types of mechanisms which make an individual's decision to divorce contingent upon the individual's local demographic context.[1]

15.1.1 Opportunity-based mechanisms

For an action to take place, the individual must have an opportunity to perform the act; that is, the conditions must be such that the action is part of the individual's opportunity set. Strictly speaking, all married persons in most western countries have the opportunity to divorce, although there may be legally imposed delays. In this section I will therefore not focus on the opportunities to divorce as such, but on how variations in other aspects of an individual's opportunity structure may influence how desirable a divorce is likely to appear. One such opportunity is the opportunity to meet a new partner.

The probability of becoming involved with a new partner before a divorce and the prospect of finding a new partner in the future are probably greater the larger the proportion of persons in the individual's local context who are of the opposite sex and of relevant age. (For bisexual and homosexual persons the spousal alternatives may obviously be of the same sex.) Some previous research indeed strongly suggests that the availability of spousal alternatives increases the risk of marital disruption. Udry (1981), for example, found that wives' perceptions of how easily their husbands could be replaced with a man of comparable quality increased the risk of divorce independently of marital happiness. As mentioned above, South and Lloyd (1995) showed that the risk of divorce for young people is higher when there is an unbalanced sex ratio among singles residing in their residential area. In addition they found that many divorced persons had been romantically involved with someone other than their spouse just before the marriage ended. Similarly, McKinnish (2004) found that the risk of marital disruption varies with the proportion of persons of the opposite sex in the same industry and occupation.

All else being equal, we should for reasons such as these expect individuals to be more likely to initiate a divorce if they are embedded in contexts with a relative abundance of potential spousal alternatives. It is also likely that the marital status of these persons matters, because single persons are probably perceived to be more available as spousal alternatives than are married persons. This opportunity-based mechanism implies that the risk of marital disruption should be higher if the local demographic context consists to a large extent of individuals of the opposite sex; particularly if these are single or divorced.

In addition to variations in the opportunities to find a new partner, opportunities to find and/or maintain friends after a divorce are likely to be important. Because of social homophily, married couples often socialize with other married couples, whereas single persons often socialize with other single persons (Verbrugge 1977).[2] Therefore, divorced persons often lose contact with some of their married mutual friends as a consequence of their new single status. In addition, the size of a divorcee's friendship network often decreases after a divorce, because friends choose to be loyal to and maintain contact with only one of the former spouses (Gerstel 1988). The risk of losing friends is a social cost that may prevent an individual from deciding to initiate a divorce. Single friends, primarily of the same sex, can often compensate for the loss of married friends after a divorce (Milardo 1987). For this reason, the opportunity to socialize with single friends is likely to increase the risk of marital disruption by reducing the likely social costs of the divorce. All else being equal, this mechanism suggests that the more that a person's friends and acquaintances are single, the greater the person's risk of divorce—especially if those friends are of the same sex.

15.1.2 Desire-based mechanisms

In addition to these opportunity-based mechanisms, the strength of marriage norms is likely to influence the desirability of divorce by influencing the focal person's attitudes toward divorce.[3] As the majority of adults are married, being married constitutes the norm, especially for middle-aged and older persons, and this norm is likely to be stronger among married persons than among divorcees. Normative pressure against divorce is thus likely to weaken the more people get divorced, and a person considering a divorce is therefore likely to experience fewer moral or normative qualms if there are many divorcees among his/her significant others. An unhappily married person who refrains from divorce on normative or moral grounds may be influenced by the frequency of divorcees among friends and acquaintances. Booth, Edwards, and Johnson (1991) found that the risk of marital disruption is increased by having a divorced friend or sibling. They interpreted this as an effect of weakened marriage norms. This suggests that divorce is likely to be a more desirable option the more divorced individuals there are among the person's significant others, especially if they are of the same sex as the focal individual.

15.1.3 Belief-based mechanisms

An individual's beliefs about the opportunities and the desirability of different action alternatives may be crucial in their own right for explaining why individuals do what they do.[4] In such situations it is essential to consider how the individual came to hold these beliefs.

The decision to divorce is a decision taken under conditions of imperfect information. As much experimental social-psychological research has shown, it is in uncertain decision situations that a decision maker's beliefs are likely to be particularly influenced by other people (e.g. Cialdini and Trost 1998). A married person cannot know exactly what his or her life will be like after a marital disruption. One way to reduce this uncertainty is to gather information from divorced friends and acquaintances. If they seem to manage well after their divorces, they are likely to influence the individual's beliefs in such a way that the likelihood that the individual will initiate a divorce will increase. On the other hand, if they seem to be unhappy in their new status, they are likely to influence the individual's beliefs in the opposite direction and thereby serve as deterrents. Much research has found that the majority of divorcees view their divorces favorably, especially a few years after the divorce (Pettit and Bloom 1984; Wadsby and Svedin 1992). It is therefore likely that divorcees more often serve as positive reinforcers than as negative deterrents. A married person with many divorced friends is therefore likely to be more optimistic about life as a divorcee than is a person with few divorced friends, even if the actual quality of life after divorce will be the same. Thus, all else being equal, the more divorcees a person encounters, the more likely it is that he or she will divorce.

In addition, as Raley and Bumpass (2003) argue with reference to Becker's theory of the family (1981), there may be a positive-feedback effect from the aggregate divorce rate at one point in time and individuals' divorce risks at later points in time. Observing the dissolution of other individuals' marriages is likely to increase individuals' awareness of the fact that marriages are seldom for a lifetime, and this may decrease the investments they are willing to make in the relationship. The lower level of investment may in turn lower their threshold for leaving the relationship.

15.1.4 Trigger mechanisms

Each day of our lives we are faced with an almost infinite number of possible action alternatives; however, we consciously reflect upon only a small subset of all these alternatives. What I refer to as trigger mechanisms are events that change the cognitive status of an action alternative from being a mere theoretical possibility to a consciously reflected upon alternative.

At any particular point in time divorce is a theoretical possibility for most married individuals, but far less often is it a consciously reflected upon alternative. The decline in the quality of a marriage can often be a slow and gradual process (Vaughan 1986). In deteriorating marriages an event that deviates from normal routine may act as a trigger that causes a shift in perspectives and turns divorce into a more salient decision alternative (Willén 2001). The triggering event may, for example, be an unusually strong marital conflict, but it may also be the divorce of a friend or acquaintance. News of someone else's divorce can therefore be a trigger that initiates a process of marriage evaluation that may in the end result in another marital disruption. Thus, all else being the same, divorces among friends and acquaintances may turn divorce into a consciously reflected upon alternative, and thereby increase the risk of a divorce.

15.1.5 Endogenous processes

The aforementioned mechanisms imply that individuals' choices to remain married or not depend in part on whether those with whom they interact are divorced, single, or married. The mechanisms discussed above are interesting and important in their own right because they allow us to better understand individuals' decisions to divorce. In addition, they are important because they play a rather special role in the process that causes changes in divorce rates. To the extent that mechanisms like these are operative, the causal process is likely to be partly endogenous. That is to say, divorces may lead to more divorces through an endogenous contagion or diffusion process.

Contagion, as here defined, exists when the probability of divorce is causally influenced by divorces of other individuals. The term *contagion* does not refer to one specific causal mechanism. Divorce may be contagious because of opportunity-based mechanisms, belief-based mechanisms, desire-based mechanisms, trigger mechanisms, or, more likely, because of a combination of different types of mechanisms. For example, A and B are unhappily married. A gets an attractive job offer and starts a full-time job with better pay than her previous part-time job. The job offer is an exogenous event that enables her to support herself and to divorce B. Her friend C is unhappily married to D, but has refrained from divorce for fear of becoming socially isolated. The divorce of A is part of the endogenous process that causes the divorce of C, and C may in a similar way influence yet others. The main implication of this is that social interactions can set in motion chain reactions that greatly magnify the effects of an initial exogenous event.

15.2 COWORKERS AS A LOCAL DEMOGRAPHIC CONTEXT

The mechanisms and hypotheses discussed above refer to how the marital status of those with whom individuals interact is likely to influence their own risk of divorce. In order to test these various hypotheses I will focus on one particular type of context: the workplace.

For a range of different reasons a focus on the workplace seems appropriate. First of all, many studies show that people interact with their coworkers many hours per week both inside and outside the workplace. According to a Swedish study, 50 percent of all employed persons socialize with their colleagues during off-hours (Statistics Sweden 1992). Furthermore, when a person seeks to build a new friendship network, after a divorce for example, single coworkers are often readily available. Despite existing gender segregation, workplaces are also important marriage 'markets' (Laumann et al. 1994). Similarly, in a 1992 Finnish survey, 49 percent of men and 40 percent of women had at least once fallen in love with a colleague or other person they met at work, despite their being married (Kontula and Haavio-Mannila 1995). The workplace is therefore a potentially important contributor to strains in many marriages.

In addition to this direct influence of coworkers, workplaces are likely to shape individuals' beliefs about the world at large. Research by Tversky and Kahneman (1973) and others has shown that individuals often draw biased conclusions about larger social contexts based on information from their immediate social environ-ments. To the extent that this 'availability heuristic' is operative, individuals in workplaces with many divorcees are likely to overestimate the number of divorcees in society at large.[5] This may in turn influence the individuals' decisions whether or not to remain married via the mechanisms discussed above.

15.3 DATA AND METHOD

Most network-oriented research on the family uses surveys with information on rather small ego-centered networks of friends (Lee 1979; Milardo 1988). A disad-vantage of this approach is the possibility of selection bias. Because of this, I use coworkers rather than friends as the reference group. The risk that persons will select themselves into different workplaces on the basis of their divorce propensities is likely to be much smaller than the risk of their selecting friends on the same basis.

In this chapter a unique Swedish database is used (see Vilhelmsson 2003 for a description). The database consists of a random sample of workplaces and it contains information on all the individuals who worked at any of these workplaces. It includes detailed demographic and socioeconomic information obtained from various governmental registers for the years 1987 to 1995, such as employment registers, tax registers, and registers of completed education. In addition, it contains the exact date of marriages, divorces, deaths, and deaths of spouses if such events occurred during the years 1987–1995. There is also information on the date of the last change in marital status that occurred prior to 1988, which means that the exact duration of all marriages can be calculated. As these records are col-lected from official registers instead of from the individuals themselves, they are of much higher quality than data based on surveys typically are, and there are no missing data.

Previous research by South and Lloyd (1995) on how the availability of spousal alternatives influenced the risk of divorce used data on so-called labor-market areas to measure the relevant demographic contexts. Since the average population in these areas is greater than 500,000, they include many individuals who the focal individual will never have seen nor heard about. Since the primary interest here is to analyze whether individuals are influenced by other individuals whom they know and with whom they interact rather frequently, workplaces with more than 75 employees have been excluded. The size of the average workplace is therefore about 27 persons. Although only about one-third of the working-age population work in workplaces with less than 75 employees, the process being analyzed here is not likely to differ much between workplaces of different sizes. Table 15.4, in the Appendix to this chapter, provides some descriptive statistics on the sample being analyzed.

So-called piecewise exponential-hazard-rate models with time-varying covariates, shared frailty at the workplace level, and fixed effects at the level of industrial sector are used to analyze how the hazard of divorce is influenced by various workplace and individual-level characteristics.[6] Although it seems unlikely that individuals select themselves into different workplaces on the basis of how divorce-prone they are, we cannot ignore this possibility. To reduce the risk of finding spurious effects of coworker variables because of workplace-specific unobserved heterogeneity, models with shared frailty at the workplace level are used.[7] The type of model being estimated looks like this:

$$h_{ijt} = w_j \exp(a + \beta C_{ijt-1} + \gamma X_{ijt-1} + \tau T_{it})$$

where h_{ijt} is the hazard of individual i in workplace j divorcing at time t, w_j is the shared-frailty parameter of workplace j, C_{ijt-1} is a vector of variables describing the demographic composition of individual i's coworkers at workplace j at time $t-1$, X_{ijt-1} is a vector of control variables measured at time $t-1$, and T_{it} is a vector of dummy variables measuring time since the onset of marriage for individual i. a is the intercept, and β, γ, and τ are parameters to be estimated. As the influence of the local demographic context as well as individual characteristics may differ between men and women, separate models are estimated for men and women.

To avoid problems of causal order, all relevant covariates are lagged by one calendar year. The variables describing the local demographic contexts refer to the situation at the end of the previous year. The risk group consists of married individuals. I have excluded employees with only a marginal attachment to the workplace. Persons with an income of less than 44,000 kronor per year—approximately 6,400 US dollars in 2008—are excluded from the analyses. Persons are also censored when they reach sixty-five, which is the general retirement age in Sweden. Furthermore, individuals are censored when they die, become widowed, or leave one workplace in the sample without resuming work at another one. Divorced and widowed individuals reenter the risk set the exact date when they remarry. Censored individuals also reenter the risk set when they fulfill the aforementioned criteria.

The period being analyzed runs from 1 January 1988 to 31 December 1995. Duration dependence, that is the length of marriage, is controlled for by including a set of dummy variables measuring the time that has elapsed since the year of entry into marriage. For marriages that started later than 1 January 1988 the individuals enter the risk set at the date of marriage. Persons who were still married at the end of 1995 are considered right-censored.

15.3.1 Coworker variables

Individuals of all marital statuses who fulfill the criteria discussed above regarding workplace affiliation are included when constructing variables that measure the demographic composition of the workplace. The following procedure is used: First, the number of individuals of each combination of sex, age, and marital status are counted for each workplace and year; for example, the number of 37-year-old single men, in 1992, in workplace *j*. Then these variables are adjusted so that the focal person is not included when counting his or her coworkers. Finally, these counts are used to construct variables describing the proportion of coworkers belonging to different demographic categories, as described below. I use proportion instead of number of coworkers because the larger the workplace, the lower the probability that two coworkers will interact and influence each other's behavior.

As the data used in these analyses are collected from governmental records, there is no information on cohabitation for childless persons, and it is therefore impossible to distinguish cohabiting childless persons from single childless persons. In the dichotomous categorization of single versus nonsingle coworkers, cohabiting coworkers without children are therefore by necessity classified as singles, while cohabiting coworkers in intact families with children are classified as nonsingles. In Sweden, in virtually all respects, legal as well as social, cohabiting persons with children are seen and treated the same way as are married people. However, the risk of divorce is not estimated for nonmarried cohabitants, only for formally married persons.[8]

Seven coworker variables are used in the analyses:

The variable *Proportion opposite sex and relevant age among all coworkers* describes the proportion of coworkers who are of the opposite sex and of relevant age as far as spousal alternatives are concerned. A female coworker of relevant age is considered to be between 15 years younger and 5 years older than the focal man, and a male coworker of relevant age is considered to be between 5 years younger and 15 years older than the focal woman.

The variables *Proportion singles among coworkers of the opposite sex and relevant age* and *Proportion singles among coworkers of the same sex* describe the marital status of the coworkers. A coworker is considered to be single if he or she is unmarried, widowed, or divorced, but not if he or she is cohabiting in an intact family with children.

The contagion of divorce is examined with the variables *Proportion divorced among coworkers of the opposite sex and relevant age* and *Proportion divorced among coworkers of the same sex*. Coworkers who have divorced but are no longer single are not included in this category. The variables *Proportion recently divorced among coworkers of the opposite sex and relevant age* and *Proportion recently divorced among coworkers of the same sex* are included to test whether the contagion effects are

Table 15.1 Combination of coworker variables and causal mechanisms, and their hypothesized effects on the risk of divorce

Variables	Mechanisms				
	Opportunity-based		Desire-based	Belief-based	Trigger
	find new partner	find single friends			
Proportion of the opposite sex and relevant age among all coworkers	+				
Proportion singles among coworkers of the opposite sex and relevant age	+				
Proportion singles among coworkers of the same sex		+			
Proportion divorced among coworkers of the opposite sex and relevant age	+				
Proportion divorced among coworkers of the same sex		+	+	+	
Proportion recently divorced among coworkers of the opposite sex of relevant age	+				+
Proportion recently divorced among coworkers of the same sex		+	+	+	+

time-dependent. A coworker who divorced during the previous calendar year is considered to be recently divorced.

Table 15.1 relates each of these variables to the most relevant mechanisms discussed above. A plus sign in a cell indicates that the variable is expected to have a positive effect on the risk of divorce.

Controls for factors that are known to affect the risk of divorce are included as covariates in the models.[9] This reduces the risk of finding spurious effects of the coworker variables caused by a selection of persons into different workplaces based on their individual characteristics. The control variables are described in the Appendix to this chapter.

15.4 RESULTS

I have estimated four different models for each gender, with different sets of coworker variables. The models for men, 1m, 2m, 3m, and 4m, are shown in Table 15.2*a*, and the models for women, 1 w, 2 w, 3 w, and 4 w, are shown in Table 15.2*b*. The control variables are the same for men and for women.

As expected, models 1 m and 1 w suggest that the proportion of coworkers who are of the opposite sex and of relevant age increases the risk of marital disruption. A man is about 83 percent more likely to divorce if all of his coworkers are female and of relevant age, and a woman is more than twice as likely to divorce if all of her coworkers are male and of relevant age, compared to when all coworkers are either of the same sex as the focal person, or outside the relevant age-span. This result strongly suggests that the opportunity to find spousal alternatives increases the risk of divorce.

Somewhat surprisingly, models 2 m and 2 w suggest that the proportion of singles among coworkers of the opposite sex and of relevant age does not have any significant effect on the risk of marital disruption once I have controlled for the other variables in the model. Thus, on the face of it, there is no support for the hypothesis that single coworkers are perceived as being more available as spousal alternatives than married coworkers, and thereby have a greater impact on divorce risks. Since the effect of the sex-composition variable remains just as strong after controlling for the proportion of singles, these results seem to imply that married persons influence coworkers of the opposite sex just as effectively as do single persons.[10]

The proportion of singles among coworkers of the same sex, on the other hand, increases the risk of divorce, at least for men. The risk of marital disruption is about 51 percent higher for men (see model 2 m) and about 46 percent higher for women (see model 2 w) if all coworkers of the same sex are single as opposed to married.[11] These results imply that the marital status of the same sex is more important than the marital status of the opposite sex, and they offer support for the hypothesis that the potential availability of single friends increases the risk of divorce, particularly for men.

Models 3 and 4 (m and w) include variables measuring the proportion of divorcees among coworkers of the same and of the opposite sex. Model 4 (m and w) includes variables measuring both the proportion of divorced coworkers as well as the proportion of *recently* divorced coworkers. When both types of variables are included in the same model the variable measuring the proportion of divorced coworkers captures the effect of the proportion of coworkers who have been divorced for more than one year.

As can be seen in model 3 m, the proportion of divorcees among female coworkers of relevant age significantly increases the risk of divorce for men. However, when including a variable measuring the proportion of *recently* divorced women of relevant age in model 4 m, an important time dimension of the contagion process is made visible. The proportion of *recently* divorced women has a significant effect, but the variable measuring the overall proportion of divorced women loses its significance. Thus, it is only recent divorces among female coworkers that seem to influence men's divorce risks. The pattern is similar for women. When including

Table 15.2a Piecewise exponential–hazard–rate models of the risk of divorce among men, with shared frailty at the workplace level. Hazard ratios with Z-statistics in parentheses

Variable	Model			
	1 m	2 m	3 m	4 m
Proportion of the opposite sex and relevant age among all coworkers	1.835 (2.28)**	1.883 (2.35)**	1.768 (2.14)**	1.795 (2.21)**
Proportion singles among coworkers of the opposite sex and relevant age		0.987 (−0.11)		
Proportion singles among coworkers of the same sex		1.506 (2.05)**		
Proportion divorced among coworkers of the opposite sex and relevant age			1.535 (2.27)**	1.277 (1.15)
Proportion recently divorced among coworkers of the opposite sex and relevant age				2.535 (2.26)**
Proportion divorced among coworkers of the same sex			3.189 (3.14)***	2.279 (2.01)**
Proportion recently divorced among coworkers of the same sex				4.853 (2.08)**
High-school education	1.054 (0.42)	1.058 (0.45)	1.051 (0.40)	1.052 (0.41)
College education	0.820 (−1.29)	0.839 (−1.14)	0.828 (−1.24)	0.829 (−1.22)
Pedagogic education	0.983 (−0.08)	0.980 (−0.09)	0.996 (−0.02)	0.998 (−0.01)
Administrative education	0.893 (−0.79)	0.896 (−0.78)	0.896 (−0.77)	0.896 (−0.78)
Technical education	0.878 (−1.10)	0.885 (−1.04)	0.878 (−1.11)	0.883 (−1.06)
Health education	0.729 (−1.06)	0.738 (−1.02)	0.727 (−1.08)	0.711 (−1.16)
Log income	1.146 (1.19)	1.154 (1.25)	1.149 (1.21)	1.151 (1.23)
Partly unemployed	1.427 (2.02)**	1.424 (2.01)**	1.438 (2.07)**	1.434 (2.06)**
Nordic immigrant	1.343 (1.54)	1.328 (1.48)	1.353 (1.58)	1.349 (1.57)
Other immigrant	0.970 (−0.18)	0.954 (−0.27)	0.961 (−0.23)	0.965 (−0.21)
Number of children	0.381 (−19.80)***	0.382 (−19.74)***	0.384 (−19.70)***	0.384 (−19.81)***
Age at marriage	0.883 (−3.45)***	0.884 (−3.42)***	0.885 (−3.40)***	0.886 (−3.39)***
Square of age at marriage	1.001 (1.95)	1.001 (1.94)	1.001 (1.83)	1.001 (1.85)
Duration dependence, 16 dummies	Yes***	Yes***	Yes***	Yes***
New at the workplace	1.061 (0.62)	1.059 (0.59)	1.059 (0.59)	1.056 (0.57)
Spouse is coworker	0.492 (−3.37)***	0.487 (−3.41)***	0.503 (−3.27)***	0.504 (−3.26)***
Industrial sector 20 dummies	Yes	Yes	Yes	Yes
Dispersion, θ	0.051	0.044	0.008	0.000
Probability $\theta = 0$	0.160	0.194	0.439	1.000
Log likelihood	−2072	−2070	−2065	−2061

* significant at 10%; ** significant at 5%; *** significant at 1%; two-tailed tests.

Table 15.2b Piecewise exponential–hazard–rate models of the risk of divorce among women, with shared frailty at the workplace level. Hazard ratios with Z–statistics in parentheses

Variable	Model			
	1 w	2 w	3 w	4 w
Proportion of the opposite sex and relevant age among all coworkers	2.328 (2.95)***	2.346 (2.96)***	2.247 (2.82)***	2.261 (2.83)***
Proportion singles among coworkers of the opposite sex and relevant age		0.998 (−0.02)		0.988 (−0.05)
Proportion singles among coworkers of the same sex		1.462 (1.85)*		
Proportion divorced among coworkers of the opposite sex and relevant age			1.198 (0.85)	3.183 (2.36)**
Proportion recently divorced among coworkers of the opposite sex and relevant age				1.945 (2.03)**
Proportion divorced among coworkers of the same sex			1.632 (1.52)	
Proportion recently divorced among coworkers of the same sex				0.055 (−2.02)**
High-school education	1.097 (0.86)	1.096 (0.85)	1.097 (0.86)	1.100 (0.88)
College education	1.075 (0.52)	1.076 (0.53)	1.074 (0.51)	1.074 (0.51)
Pedagogic education	0.667 (−2.59)***	0.673 (−2.54)**	0.671 (−2.56)**	0.672 (−2.55)**
Administrative education	0.737 (−2.95)***	0.738 (−2.93)***	0.735 (−2.97)***	0.735 (−2.97)***
Technical education	0.888 (−0.60)	0.882 (−0.64)	0.887 (−0.61)	0.885 (−0.62)
Health education	0.724 (−2.59)***	0.727 (−2.56)**	0.723 (−2.60)***	0.722 (−2.61)***
Log income	1.954 (6.20)***	1.928 (6.07)***	1.931 (6.09)***	1.938 (6.11)***
Partly unemployed	1.590 (3.99)***	1.596 (4.02)***	1.592 (4.00)***	1.592 (3.99)***
Nordic immigrant	1.410 (2.45)**	1.403 (2.41)**	1.411 (2.45)**	1.415 (2.47)**
Other immigrant	0.919 (−0.49)	0.916 (−0.51)	0.916 (−0.51)	0.916 (−0.51)
Number of children	0.666 (−9.22)***	0.668 (−9.16)***	0.666 (−9.21)***	0.665 (−9.23)***
Age at marriage	0.891 (−3.36)***	0.891 (−3.39)***	0.889 (−3.43)***	0.890 (−3.40)***
Square of age at marriage	1.001 (2.10)**	1.001 (2.14)**	1.001 (2.15)**	1.001 (2.13)**
Duration dependence, 16 dummies	Yes***	Yes***	Yes***	Yes***
New at the workplace	1.292 (3.23)***	1.287 (3.18)***	1.288 (3.19)***	1.291 (3.22)***
Spouse is coworker	0.469 (−3.56)***	0.476 (−3.49)***	0.476 (−3.49)***	0.475 (−3.50)***
Industrial sector 20 dummies	Yes***	Yes***	Yes***	Yes***
Dispersion, θ	0.026	0.013	0.010	0.028
Probability θ = 0	0.273	0.385	0.413	0.268
Log likelihood	−2513	−2511	−2511	−2506

* significant at 10%; ** significant at 5%; *** significant at 1%; two-tailed tests.

both types of variables in the model, women's divorce risks increase with the proportion of recently divorced male coworkers, but are not affected by the proportion of male coworkers who have been divorced for more than one year (see model 4 w). The short duration of the effect suggests that it is the act of divorce rather than the divorced state per se that influences divorce decisions of coworkers of the opposite sex.

These models also include the corresponding types of variables for coworkers of the same sex. Model 3 m suggests that the proportion of divorcees among male coworkers has a strong and highly significant effect on other men's divorce risks. Thus, there is a contagion effect of divorce among men. If all male coworkers of a married man were divorced, these results suggest that his divorce risk would be more than three times higher than if none of his male coworkers were divorced. This contagion effect seems to be especially strong when the divorced male coworkers are recently divorced (see model 4 m).

Among women the pattern of contagiousness differs radically from that among men. As model 4 w shows, the proportion of female coworkers who have been divorced for more than one year increases the risk of marital disruption among other women, while the proportion of female coworkers who are recently divorced *reduces* the divorce risk. These patterns of same-sex divorce contagion are summarized in Table 15.3.

In sum, these results imply that divorced men encourage other men to divorce. This effect is long-lasting, but strongest shortly after the marital disruption. Recently divorced women, on the other hand, seem to *deter* other women from divorcing. Over time, this effect seems to be transformed, however. The presence of female coworkers who have been divorced for more than one year seems to encourage other women to seek divorce.

As emphasized by Manski (2000), selection effects can easily be mistaken for contagious or contextual effects. However, log-likelihood tests show that the shared frailty-dispersion parameter, θ, is not significantly different from zero in any of the models. This means that there are no signs of a latent workplace-level effect once I have controlled for the other covariates included in the models.[12]

Table 15.3 Gender differences in the patterns of same-sex divorce contagion

| | Contagion | |
	Short-term	Long-term
Men	++	+
Women	−	+

15.4.1 Effects of control variables

On the whole, the effects of the control variables are as expected or some-what weaker than one would expect given previous research (see Tables 15.2a–b). However, a few of them may be worth a comment. The type of education affects the risk of marital disruption for women but not for men. The results suggest that women who aim for traditional female types of occupations have a lower risk of divorce than women who aim for traditionally male occupations.

The results also suggest that the risk of divorce is dramatically reduced if the spouse works in the same workplace. Married couples who work at the same workplace run only about half the risk of a marital breakup as compared to other couples. This effect may be because divorce is more difficult to cope with or to initiate when both partners work at the same workplace (see Ackerman 1963; Booth, Edwards, and Johnson 1991). For example, opportunities to find new partners and new single friends among the coworkers are probably lower if the spouse is present at the workplace. The effect could also be due to different types of selection effects.

There is no significant effect of industrial sector on men's risk of divorce, while including the twenty industrial-sector dummy variables significantly improves the fit of the model for women. The two industrial sectors with the highest divorce risks are 'hotels and restaurants,' and 'manufacture of textiles and textile products.' The two industrial sectors with the lowest risks are 'retail trade' and 'banking.'

CONCLUDING REMARKS

In this chapter I have analyzed how the local demographic context, in the form of coworkers' sex, age, and marital status, influences the risk of divorce for men and women. The initial theoretical discussion suggested that the risk of marital disruption is likely to be high if the context is such that it offers ample opportunities for married persons to find spousal alternatives, and/or single friends. The local demographic context is also likely to influence the risk of divorce by making divorce appear as a more desirable alternative than it otherwise would, and divorces of others can act as a trigger that makes divorce into a more salient alternative and thereby increases the risk of divorce.

Using statistical models which take into account time-varying factors at the individual as well as the contextual level, the empirical results strongly suggest that the local demographic contexts in which individuals are embedded are of considerable importance for divorce decisions. By and large, the empirical results support the hypotheses developed above concerning systematic relationship between the local demographic context of an individual and his/her risk of divorce. In addition, they add a more nuanced picture of the patterns of influence.

The empirical analyses suggest that divorces are contagious in the sense that the probability of divorce is influenced by divorces of other people, but they reveal that the contagion processes operate differently for men and women. If married men interact with divorced men, their divorce risks seem to increase, and this influence is strongest if the divorced men are recently divorced. If married women interact with divorced women, their divorce risks also seem to increase, but only in the long run. Recently divorced women seem to deter other women from divorcing.

The differing results for men and women may be due to gender differences in social, psychological, and economic adjustments to marital disruption. It is well known that women fare economically worse than men after a marital disruption (Weitzman 1985; Peterson 1996; Gähler 1998). Research on gender differences in the social and psychological consequences of divorce is more ambiguous (Gerstel, Riessman, and Rosenfield 1985; Kitson and Morgan 1990; Wadsby and Svedin 1992). However, some studies have found gender differences in the temporal aspects of the adjustment to divorce. Bloom and Caldwell (1981) showed that women reported more severe psychological symptoms than did men shortly before separation, while men reported more severe symptoms shortly after separation. Gähler (1998) found that for women, mental well-being was lowest shortly before and after the divorce, while for men mental well-being was lowest several years after the divorce. As women more often than men take the main responsibility for the children, the lower well-being of women at the time of divorce may also reflect problems for the children in adapting to their new family circumstances.

The gender differences in divorce contagion may also be explained by differences in how men and women portray their divorces to others. As women often self-disclose more than men (Cozby 1973; Hill and Stull 1981), they may confide more in their female coworkers and reveal more about the distress caused by their marital disruption than do men. If that is the case, friends of divorcing women would be led to believe that divorce is a more distressing event than friends of divorcing men, even if the divorcing men and women had equally distressing experiences.

Yet another possible interpretation is that these results may be caused by a gender-based selection effect. Women who are dissatisfied with being divorced might remarry sooner than women who are more content with their divorced state. The subgroup of recently divorced women would then consist of relatively more women who are dissatisfied than the entire group of divorced women. There may be a selection in the opposite direction among men, as suggested by Niemelä, Myyrä, and Lento (1985). They found that women who have remarried have lower self-esteem than women who live alone after divorce, while among men the pattern is the opposite: those who have remarried have the highest self-esteem. See also Hemström (1996), who reports similar results for changes in mortality ratios.

All in all, the differing results for men and women suggest that there is an important gender dimension that influences mechanisms and divorce contagion that deserves to be explored in much more detail than has been possible here.

One plausible interpretation and implication of these results is that there is an important endogenous component in the causal process explaining divorces; that is, that divorces lead to more divorces through an endogenous feedback process. The strong increase in divorce rates in most western countries during the postwar period is probably partly caused by exogenous factors, such as changing labor markets for women and changing legislation, but it is probably also partly caused by an endogenous contagion process that multiplied the effects of the external causes.

Another implication of the results is that they suggest a potentially important link between the sex segregation of workplaces and divorce risks. As the sex segregation in the workforce declined, especially during the 1970s and 1980s (Reskin 1993), encounters between men and women at work increased, and this may have contributed to the rise in divorce rates observed during this period (Cherlin 1992).

The data being used in this study has many unique features, but it has some shortcomings nonetheless. The most important shortcoming is that there is no data on the subjective beliefs and desires of these individuals. Therefore one cannot always know which micro-level mechanisms have been at work. The analyses suggest that the opportunities to find new friends and partners are important. However, it is less obvious how to interpret the finding that individuals are influenced by divorces among those of the same sex. Is it for desire- or belief-related reasons? Given the fact that divorce is common in Sweden, the desire-based mechanisms are not likely to be as important as the belief-based ones. In countries where divorce is less common, and where there are strong normative sanctions against divorce, desire-based mechanisms of this kind are likely to be more important.

To summarize, these results on the contagiousness of divorce underscore the importance of an analytical-sociology approach to demography, which pays close attention to patterns of social interaction. Much of sociological and social-psychological research suggests that to understand individual actions it is essential to relate them to the actions of others with whom they interact. Divorces appear to be no exception to this rule.

NOTES

1. For a more detailed discussion of 'conditional choice' see Rolfe's chapter in this volume.
2. See McPherson, Smith-Lovin, and Cook (2001) for a detailed review of the role of homophily in the formation of ties. See also the chapter by Feld and Grofman in this volume.

3. See Freese's chapter on preferences and Elster's chapter on norms in this volume for a more detailed discussion about the role of desires and norms in explaining actions.

4. For a more detailed discussion about the role of beliefs in explaining actions see Rydgren's chapter in this volume.

5. For a more detailed discussion about the role of the availability heuristic in explaining actions see Goldstein's chapter in this volume.

6. Stata 10 was used to estimate the models.

7. Shared-frailty models are the equivalent of random-effect models in ordinary regression analyses. A 'shared frailty' is a latent multiplicative effect on the hazard function which is identical for all individuals in the same workplace. The frailty is assumed to be gamma-distributed with a mean equal to 1 and a variance equal to θ, and it is estimated along with the other parameters of the model (see Gutierrez 2002).

8. One reason for this decision is that there is no information on the duration of cohabitation before 1988. Since it is likely that cohabitants are more influenced by their coworkers than are married persons, the strategy adopted here can be considered cautious. Focusing on the risk of divorce for married persons only is likely to reduce the likelihood of finding significant effects of coworkers.

9. See e.g. Morgan and Rindfuss (1985), White (1990), Waite and Lillard (1991), Lillard and Waite (1993), Forthofer (1996), Andersson (1997), Hoem (1997), and Rogers (1999) for analyses suggesting the importance of the variables included here.

10. As mentioned above, however, it is not possible to distinguish between true singles and cohabiters without children, which, at least partially, may explain this result.

11. If cohabiting coworkers without children had not been defined as singles, the effect would probably have been even higher. The result for women is on the borderline of being significant, however, with a p-value of 0.065. It is difficult to decide which is the most appropriate model to estimate, and this decision influences the significance of this variable. In a model without the 20 dummy variables for industrial sector, for example, the effect estimate is considerably stronger (64%), and the p-value is 0.012.

12. Also, in models without any coworker variables (not shown) the dispersion parameter is not significantly different from zero.

APPENDIX

Table 15.4 below shows some descriptive statistics of the data.

Control variables

The control variable 'high-school education' identifies individuals with high-school education or vocational training at the secondary-educational level, and 'college education' is a dummy variable that identifies persons who have completed a college education. (The reference category is education at a lower level than high school.) In addition to controlling for the level of education, the models also control for the type of education by including dummy variables for the four most common types of education or training; 'pedagogic education,' which prepares for jobs such as teaching and child care; 'administrative education,' which

Table 15.4 Descriptive statistics

	Men	Women
Number of individuals	16,854	20,278
Number of divorces	789	928
Number of workplaces (1,516 in total)	1,365	1,390
Mean number of employees per workplace	26.5	26.5
Mean number of persons at risk per workplace and gender and year	7.8	8.9

prepares for jobs in wholesale and retail sales, secretarial and office work, administration, business, law, social and behavioral sciences, etc.; 'technical education,' which prepares for jobs in manufacturing, construction, science, engineering, computing, etc.; and 'health education,' which prepares for jobs in medicine, nursing, dentistry, pharmaceuticals, social work, etc. (The reference category is all other types of education or training, which include compulsory education.)

I use the variable 'log income' to estimate the effect of income on the risk of marital disruption. It measures the logarithm of annual taxable income, standardized for inflation, and is centered around the mean of the logarithm. The variable 'partly unemployed' indicates whether the person received any unemployment benefits during the previous calendar year. 'Nordic immigrant' identifies persons who were born in Denmark, Finland, Iceland, or Norway. Persons born outside the Nordic countries are identified with the variable 'other immigrant,' and the reference category is persons born in Sweden.

The 'number of children' is known to be an important factor that enhances marital stability, and is therefore controlled for here. (The database only includes information about the number of children for the years 1987, 1991, and 1995. The values for the intervening years are estimated by linear interpolation.) 'Age at marriage' and the 'square of age at marriage' control for possible curvilinear effects of how old the person was at the start of the marriage. The length of time under which the individual has been at risk of experiencing a divorce—that is, the 'duration of marriage'—is controlled for by including a set of 16 dummy variables.

The variable 'new at the workplace' identifies persons who started to work at their current workplace the previous year. The variable 'spouse is coworker' indicates whether or not the spouse works at the same workplace as the focal person. The selection of individuals into different 'industrial sectors' is controlled for by including dummy variables identifying the 20 largest industrial sectors for men in the models for men, and the 20 largest industrial sectors for women in the models for women. 86 percent of the men and 94 percent of the women worked in one of these sectors.

REFERENCES

ACKERMAN, C. (1963), 'Affiliations: Structural Determinants of Differentials Divorce Rates', *American Journal of Sociology*, 69 (1): 13–20.

ANDERSSON, G. (1997), 'The Impact of Children on Divorce Risks of Swedish Women', *European Journal of Population*, 13: 109–45.

BEARMAN, P. S., and BRUCKNER, H. (2001), 'Promising the Future: Virginity Pledges and First Intercourse', *American Journal of Sociology*, 106 (4): 859–113.

——and MOODY, J. (2004), 'Suicide and Friendships among American Adolescents', *American Journal of Public Health*, 94: 89–95.

BECKER, G. S. (1981), *A Treatise on the Family* (Cambridge, Mass.: Harvard University Press).

BILLY, J. O. G., BREWSTER, K. L., and GRADY, W. R. (1994), 'Contextual Effects on the Sexual Behavior of Adolescent Women', *Journal of Marriage and the Family*, 56 (2): 387–404.

BLOOM, B. L., and CALDWELL, R. A. (1981), 'Sex Differences in Adjustment During the Process of Marital Separation', *Journal of Marriage and the Family*, 43 (3): 693–701.

BOOTH, A., EDWARDS, J. N., and JOHNSON, D. R. (1991), 'Social Integration and Divorce', *Social Forces*, 70 (1): 207–24.

BREWSTER, K. L. (1994), 'Neighborhood Context and the Transition to Sexual Activity among Young Black Women', *Demography*, 4: 603–8.

CHERLIN, A. J. (1992), *Marriage, Divorce, Remarriage* (Cambridge, Mass.: Harvard University Press).

CIALDINI, R. B., and TROST, M. R. (1998), 'Social Influence: Social Norms, Conformity, and Compliance', in D. T. Gilbert, S. T. Fiske, and G. Lindzey (eds.), *The Handbook of Social Psychology*, ii (New York: McGraw-Hill), 151–93.

COZBY, P. C. (1973), 'Self-disclosure: A Literature Review', *Psychological Bulletin*, 79: 73–91.

DEAN, D. G., and BRESNAHAN, B. S. (1969), 'Ecology, Friendship Patterns, and Divorce: A Research Note', *Journal of Marriage and the Family*, 31 (3): 462–3.

DIEKMANN A., and ENGELHARDT, H. (1999), 'The Social Inheritance of Divorce: Effects of Parent's Family Type in Postwar Germany', *American Sociological Review*, 64: 783–93.

ELSTER, J. (1989), *Nuts and Bolts for the Social Sciences* (Cambridge: Cambridge University Press).

FORTHOFER, M. S. (1996), 'Associations Between Marital Distress and Work Loss in a National Sample', *Journal of Marriage and the Family*, 58: 597–605.

GÄHLER, M. (1998), *Life After Divorce: Economic, Social and Psychological Well-being among Swedish Adults and Children Following Family Dissolution* (Stockholm: Swedish Institute for Social Research).

GERSTEL, N. (1988), 'Divorce, Gender, and Social Integration', *Gender and Society*, 2 (3): 343–67.

——RIESSMAN, C. K., and ROSENFIELD, S. (1985), 'Explaining the Symptomatology of Separated and Divorced Women and Men: The Role of Material Conditions and Social Networks', *Social Forces*, 64 (1): 84–101.

GUTIERREZ, R. G. (2002), 'Parametric Frailty and Shared Frailty Survival Models', *Stata Journal*, 2: 22–44.

HEDSTRÖM, P. (2005), *Dissecting the Social: On the Principles of Analytical Sociology* (Cambridge: Cambridge University Press).

——LIU, K. Y., and NORDVIK, M. K. (2008), 'Interaction Domains and Suicides: A Population-based Panel Study of Suicides in Stockholm, 1991–1999', *Social Forces*, 87 (2): 713–40.

HEMSTRÖM, Ö. (1996), 'Is Marriage Dissolution Linked to Differences in Mortality Risks for Men and Women?', *Journal of Marriage and the Family*, 58: 366–78.

HILL, C. T., and STULL, D. E. (1981), 'Sex Differences in Effects of Social and Value Similarity in Same-sex Friendships', *Journal of Personality and Social Psychology*, 41 (3): 488–502.

HOEM, J. M. (1997), 'Educational Gradients in Divorce Risks in Sweden in Recent Decades', *Population Studies*, 51: 19–27.

KITSON, G. C., and MORGAN, L. A. (1990), 'The Multiple Consequences of Divorce: A Decade Review', *Journal of Marriage and the Family*, 52 (4): 913–24.

KOHLER, H. P. (2001), *Fertility and Social Interactions: An Economic Perspective* (Oxford: Oxford University Press).

KONTULA, O., and HAAVIO-MANNILA, E. (1995), *Sexual Pleasures: Enhancement of Sex Life in Finland 1971–1992* (Aldershot: Dartmouth).

LAUMANN, E., et al. (1994), *The Social Organization of Sexuality: Sexual Practices in the United States* (Chicago, Ill.: University of Chicago Press).

LEE, G. R. (1979), 'Effects of Social Networks on the Family', in W. R. Burr, et al. (eds.), *Contemporary Theories about the Family* (New York/London: Free Press), 27–56.

LILLARD, L. A., and WAITE, L. J. (1993), 'A Joint Model of Marital Childbearing and Marital Disruption', *Demography*, 4: 653–81.

McADAM, D., and PAULSEN, R. (1993), 'Specifying the Relationship between Social Ties and Activism', *American Journal of Sociology*, 99: 640–67.

McKINNISH, T. G. (2004), 'Occupation, Sex-integration, and Divorce', *American Economic Review*, 94 (2): 322–5.

McLANAHAN, S., and BUMPASS, L. (1988), 'Intergenerational Consequences of Family Disruption', *American Journal of Sociology*, 94: 130–52.

McPHERSON, M., SMITH-LOVIN, L., and COOK, J. M. (2001), 'Birds of a Feather: Homophily in Social Networks', *Annual Review of Sociology*, 27: 415–44.

MANSKI, C. F. (2000), 'Economic Analysis of Social Interactions', *Journal of Economic Perspectives*, 14 (3): 115–36.

MILARDO, R. M. (1987), 'Changes in Social Networks of Women and Men Following Divorce: A Review', *Journal of Family Issues*, 8 (1): 78–96.

—— (1988), 'Families and Social Networks: An Overview of Theory and Methodology', in R. M. Milardo (ed.), *Families and Social Networks* (Newbury Park, Calif.: Sage), 13–47.

MORGAN, S. P., and RINDFUSS, R. R. (1985), 'Marital Disruption: Structural and Temporal Dimensions', *American Journal of Sociology*, 90 (5): 1055–77.

NAZIO, T., and BLOSSFELD, H. P. (2003), 'The Diffusion of Cohabitation Among Young Women in West Germany, East Germany and Italy', *European Journal of Population*, 19: 47–82.

NIEMELÄ, P., MYYRÄ, J., and LENTO, R. (1985), 'A New Approach to Marriage: Coping Strategies After Divorce', in L. Cseh-Szombathy, et al. (eds.), *The Aftermath of Divorce: Coping with Family Change: An Investigation in Eight Countries* (Budapest: Ákadémia).

PETERSON, R. R. (1996), 'A Re-evaluation of the Economic Consequences of Divorce', *American Sociological Review*, 61 (3): 528–36.

PETTIT, E. J., and BLOOM, B. L. (1984), 'Whose Decision Was It? The Effects of Intiator Status on Adjustment to Marital Disruption', *Journal of Marriage and the Family*, 46 (3): 587–95.

PHILLIPS, D. P. (1974), 'The Influence of Suggestion on Suicide: Substantive and Theoretical Implications of the Werther Effect', *American Sociological Review*, 3: 340–54.

RALEY, R. K., and BUMPASS, L. (2003), 'The Topography of the Divorce Plateau: Levels and Trends in Union Stability in the United States After 1980', *Demographic Research*, 8: 245–60.

RESKIN, B. (1993), 'Sex Segregation in the Workplace', *Annual Review of Sociology*, 19: 241–70.

ROGERS, S. J. (1999), 'Wives' income and Marital Quality: Are There Reciprocal Effects?', *Journal of Marriage and the Family*, 61: 123–32.

ROSERO-BIXBY, L., and CASTERLINE, J. B. (1994), 'Interaction Diffusion and Fertility Transition in Costa Rica', *Social Forces*, 73 (2): 435–62.

SOUTH, J. S., and LLOYD, K. M. (1995), 'Spousal Alternatives and Marital Dissolution', *American Sociological Review*, 60: 21–35.

Statistics Sweden (1992), *Social Relations 1988–89: Living Conditions Report No. 72*, at <http://www.scb.se>, accessed 2008.

TOLNAY, S. T., DEANE, G., and BECK, E. M. (1996), 'Vicarious Violence: Spatial Effects on Southern Lynchings, 1890–1919', *American Journal of Sociology*, 3: 788–815.

TVERSKY, A., and KAHNEMAN, D. (1973), 'Availability: A Heuristic for Judging Frequency and Probability', *Cognitive Psychology*, 5: 207–32.

UDRY, J. R. (1981), 'Marital Alternatives and Marital Disruption', *Journal of Marriage and the Family*, 43 (4): 889–97.

VAUGHAN, D. (1986), *Uncoupling* (New York: Vintage).

VERBRUGGE, L. M. (1977), 'The Structure of Adult Friendship Choices', *Social Forces*, 56 (2): 576–97.

VILHELMSSON, R. (2003), 'Super APU—A Swedish Matched Employer–Employee Data Set', working paper, Swedish Institute for Social Research, Stockholm University.

WADSBY, M., and SVEDIN, C. G. (1992), 'Divorce: Different Experiences of Men and Women', *Family Practice*, 9: 451–60.

WAITE, L. J., and LILLARD, L. A. (1991), 'Children and Marital Disruption', *American Journal of Sociology*, 4: 930–53.

WEITZMAN, L. J. (1985), *The Divorce Revolution: The Unexpected Social and Economic Consequences for Women and Children in America* (New York: Free Press).

WHITE, L. K. (1990), 'Determinants of Divorce: A Review of Research in the Eighties', *Journal of Marriage and the Family*, 52: 904–12.

WILLÉN, H. (2001), 'The Creation of a Realizable Option in the Face of Marital Distress: Application of a Perspective Model for Decision-making on Divorce', in C. M. Allwood and M. Selart (eds.), *Decision-making: Social and Creative Dimensions* (Dordrecht: Kluwer).

WOLFINGER, N. H. (1999), 'Trends in the Intergenerational Transmission of Divorce', *Demography*, 36: 415–20.

WRIGHT, G. H. VON (1971), *Explanation and Understanding* (Ithaca, N.Y.: Cornell University Press).

CHAPTER 16

···

MATCHING*

···

KATHERINE STOVEL
CHRISTINE FOUNTAIN

What I have been describing is the problem of moving from a model of individual behavior to a theory of the behavior of a system composed of these individuals, taking social organization explicitly into account in making this transition, rather than assuming it away. This, I believe, is the central intellectual problem in the social sciences.

(James Coleman 1984: 86)

INTRODUCTION

···

MATCHING is a crucial yet often invisible process through which social structure is translated into the experiences of individuals and social organizations (Coleman 1991). By matching, we refer to the process by which social actors form mutually exclusive pairs from a pool of potential partners, or, as Mortensen describes it, 'voluntary pairing under competitive conditions' (1988: S216). Matching may be accomplished via a centralized decision maker, in which case the rules that govern allocation can be understood as an articulation of collective values, or through two-sided matching processes in which actors sort and sift through alternatives while seeking a mutually agreeable match. Some variant of matching is evident in a wide range of substantive domains, including the assignment of employees to

* Research for this chapter was supported by the National Science Foundation (SES-0351834).

postings within a firm, the college-application process, organ transplants, residential choice, and in modern monogamous marriage and job markets. Because matching processes frequently link individuals with social positions or opportunities, the institutions that rely on matching play a central role in stratification and intergroup relations (Gangl 2004). Understanding how actual individuals are matched in these arenas (rather than simply knowing the structure of association between traits) is therefore fundamental for sociological analysis of social organization (Solga and Konietzka 1999). Beyond this substantive import, models of matching offer an exemplary analytic example of how social organization is shaped by, and shapes, individual experience.

This chapter is organized as follows: we begin with a conceptual discussion of matching processes, introducing key features of matching problems and the range of empirical institutions that resolve them. We then turn to formal models designed to describe matching processes. Developed primarily in economics, matching models are equilibrium models that describe stable systems. Here we note that while economists have recognized the implications of information limits on matching solutions, to date the literature has not integrated insights from the field of social-network analysis into approaches to this problem. In the final section we describe an agent-based simulation model that remedies this problem. Our model, designed to shed light on labor-market segregation, incorporates social-network structure into an individual-level matching model.

16.1 A Conceptual Introduction to Matching Processes

In many social circumstances actors seek to form voluntary, mutually exclusive relationships with one another. Examples include marriage, of course, but also employment (Coleman 1991; Witte and Kalleberg 1995; Werum 2002), school placement (Elster 1993; Chen and Sonmez 2006), and, in some respects, housing decisions. The nature of these relations, in terms of their durability and the obligations and expectations associated with them, may vary by time and place, but in all matching problems actors seek pairings from a pool of alternatives, constrained by the fact that each must find a partner who is also willing to accept them. For instance, fifty years ago there were millions of men who would have been thrilled to marry Marilyn Monroe, but only a lucky few were able to pull off this feat, and even they had to wait their respective turns. Thus, while individual desires are a necessary condition for making a match, the fact that a match must be acceptable to both parties means an individual's ability to meet her desires is ultimately limited by the structure of others' desires, and the distribution of others in the population. Furthermore, before any match can be made, actors must have some means of learning about their potential partners, for one cannot marry someone that one is not aware of (even in arranged marriage systems there is an information path linking potential brides to potential grooms). Thus, matching processes are also highly dependent on the structure of information flow within a population.

Matching problems share some features with economic exchange in markets, most notably the idea of two actors among many agreeing to engage in a transaction. And certainly many matching problems have been analyzed in terms of economic exchange, largely by introducing the fiction of a price mechanism into the process (see e.g. Becker 1981). The idea here is that bundles of traits can be evaluated and valued, much as the quality of a good can be valued, and that exchanges occur when 'buyers' find 'sellers' who are willing to exchange equivalent values. However, as Coleman points out, matching problems are 'very different from a neoclassical perfect market ... [since] the role of "price" as an allocation mechanism is greatly altered; and the entities exchanged are not fungible—there is not a market in trading of wives' (1984: 86). Another crucial distinction between matching processes and many economic exchanges is the stickiness of the pairing: quite often, there are significant costs or risks associated with changing partners, and these costs shape the temporal dynamics of matching.

At the macro level, the outcome of a constrained and competitive process of matchmaking is known as assortative mating, an aggregate phenomenon in which particular traits are more (or less) likely to pair with one another. Studies of assortative mating in marriage markets in the USA reveal a general tendency toward positive assortative mating with respect to race, and negative assortative mating with respect to age (Hayes and Jones 1991; Mare 1991; Kalmjin 1994; Blackwell and Lichter 2004). While many interpret such findings as revelatory of individual preferences, these findings are also consistent with clustered opportunity structures. In the end, all that analyses designed to assess the strength of assortative mating in US marriage markets show us is that whites are more likely to marry other whites.[1] Without a model that takes into account individual behavior, such analyses, which fail to bridge the gap between individuals and social structure, are analytically inadequate.

Thus, following in the tradition of matching models, we treat matching as a process that must begin at the individual level, and build from there. From this perspective it is possible to identify four key analytic features that define a matching process: the preferences actors have over characteristics (of alters or of pairings), the distribution of (relevant) characteristics in the population, the information structure that allows actors to know about potential matches and alternatives, and the operative rules or norms about matching. Variation in these features—especially in preferences and information—affect the role sequencing and timing play in which matches are made.

16.1.1 Preferences over characteristics

Lay explanations for outcomes often begin with individual preferences: Why did I marry this person? I fell in love with him. Why do I live in this neighborhood? I want my children to go to good schools. In everyday life, actors often express preferences over sets of alternatives, and though they may exaggerate preferences' role in accounting for outcomes, this does not mean that preferences are purely fictive. Frequently, preferences are expressed in terms of characteristics of the possible outcomes: an employer may prefer to hire a college graduate, a landlord may prefer tenants with good credit records, parents may prefer brides with a large dowry, and a worker might prefer to work part-time. Within a given matching arena, particular characteristics may organize the preferences of most participants; for those looking for housing, relevant features might include location, age, quality, or size of dwelling, racial profile of neighborhood, rating of nearby schools, price, etc., as well as, typically, some idiosyncratic preferences (e.g. a preference for yellow houses). Individual buyers will have different preferences across these basic features, which enables them to evaluate houses.

Beyond the features of potential matches, however, actors may have preferences for characteristics of the search process (they prefer it to be short, or exhaustive), or the match itself (in courtship, some may simply prefer the one who adores them). It goes without saying that in two-sided matching arenas, agents on each side may have preferences over characteristics of agents on the other side.

One specific type of preference plays a key role in understanding matching processes: the reservation point. Borrowed from labor economics, a reservation point is defined as the boundary below which a potential match is deemed so unattractive that the actor would prefer to remain unmatched than accept a match with this feature. For instance, a worker laid off from a job paying twenty dollars an hour might prefer to stay out of the labor market rather than take a job paying ten dollars. The existence of reservation points contributes to the idea that matchings are voluntary rather than coerced. Even economists recognize that an individual's reservation points may change: when young, a woman might be picky when choosing dates, though as she ages she might be willing to take a chance with a less desirable partner. Reservation points are important for individuals because they provide a mechanism for quickly screening alternatives; in the aggregate, they define classes of unacceptable matches.

Debates about the origins and durability of preferences divide disciplines; for theoretical and practical reasons, economists assume fixed preferences (at least in the short run), while many sociologists recognize (1) that preferences themselves may be formed through interaction, and (2) that persons may develop preferences to align with their opportunities. These sociological insights are nicely revealed in the social dynamics of matching, for one commonly observed outcome of the matching process is a shift in preferences (e.g. Solga and Diewald 2001). For our purposes, because preferences can be articulated at the individual level—even if they are socially produced—they ground our discussion of matching processes with a plausible microfoundation.

The concept of preferences advances our understanding of matching processes for several reasons. Preferences can be conceptualized as weights on possibly observed characteristics, and thus can be combined to produce an evaluation (and ranking) of the overall desirability of particular potential matches. In simple commodity-allocation problems, the preferences of actors, combined with constraints on availability of goods, is sufficient to describe allocation. Matching is more complex, however, because *both sides* have preferences and the matching process is contingent upon both sides accepting a pairing. Yet because the structure of observed matches is rarely consistent with a unique preference structure (and, in any case, preferences are notoriously difficult to discern empirically), variation in the structure of preferences is insufficient to describe variation in matching outcomes across contexts.

16.1.2 Distribution of characteristics in the population

Matching is pairing under competitive conditions, which focuses our analytic gaze on the pools from which matches are made. The empirical pool of potential partners constrains the ability of actors to realize their preferences. In most research, pools are described in terms of the distribution of key features that organize actors' preferences. In some matching arenas—such as romance, or housing—a number of characteristics are invoked as relevant while in others only a few features structure the matching process. To follow the example of housing markets, the stock of housing in a specific metropolitan area could be described in terms of its age, its size, the quality/condition of dwellings, etc., and the relationship between this empirical distribution and buyers' desires allows us to predict price and duration on the market.

Actual matches are in part determined by the composition of the pool. Agents with preferences for characteristics that are very rare will face stiff competition—in the sense that the other sides' preferences for their characteristics will come to dominate the matching process. A young school child might enjoy the company of a child from a different ethnic background, but if she attends an all-white school, her friends will be white (or she will be isolated). This example rests on simple availability: actors are unable to realize their preferences if they prefer things that do not exist in their choice set. But in matching models the duality of choice introduces a second level of complexity: if all whites prefer cross-race friends, but there are only a few blacks in the population, only those whites who are desirable to these particular blacks will be able to realize their preference for cross-race friendships. This symmetry constraint, which is at the heart of Rytina and Morgan's simple yet elegant work on the mathematics of social relations (1982), implies a strong matching process. The consequence of matching in this example is a network of friendships in which most whites have largely white peer groups, while blacks have more integrated networks. This same insight serves as the basis of the paradox recognized by Raymond Boudon (1973) in his analysis of the value of a college degree: as more and more people with college degrees enter the labor market, this credential is no longer sufficient to differentiate a candidate and make her a top choice for many jobs.

16.1.3 Information

To find a spouse or to get a job—or to conclude any other kind of match—one must have information about potential spouses or jobs, and be able to evaluate this information. Potential spouses and jobs that are not known about might as well not exist, while sometimes it is difficult to assess, a priori, the merits of a potential match. As some wise parents of children choosing among highly selective colleges recognize, perhaps the biggest consequence of choosing one school over another is that college defines the pool from which lifelong friends and romantic partners are most often drawn. Information is equally important in other matching arenas, and demand for scarce and high-quality information frequently drives the market for matchmakers and other brokers. Information matters for matching processes for two reasons: some high-quality matches may not be made, simply because the potential partners are unaware of each other, while other matches turn out differently than expected because signals are noisy and hard to read.

This latter insight is developed most fully in Stiglitz's and Spence's work on screening and signaling (Stiglitz 1975; Spence 1973, 1974). Screening is particularly important when the matching arena is flooded with too much information (as in a very large number of applicants for a single low-skill position), or because it is difficult to predict the future from the past (such as with promising Ph.D.s who flame out at prestigious universities). Under these conditions, actors may weigh information from known sources more heavily than information from unknown sources. As we show below, the consequences of such responses to information overload have implications at the macro level: if actors rely on networks for reliable information, and these networks are biased with respect to some attribute, the resulting matching can reproduce clustering across domains and maintain segregation.

Signaling models incorporate the insight that actors are rarely able to pick and choose from a set of offers without first making their quality and availability known to potential partners. So somehow participants in matching arenas need to simultaneously gather information about alternatives and convey information about their own value as matches (Spence 1973, 1974). Severe information asymmetries concerning the reliability of these signals may create a classic 'lemon' market (Akerlof 1970); avoiding this trap involves investing extensively in screening, hiring, training, and evaluating prospects (Spence 1973, 1974).

In matching arenas, the consequences of information overload, costs of screening signals, or simple constraints on the information available about alternatives can limit individuals' opportunities. These constraints effectively shrink the pool of competitors—and may shift its composition as well—and therefore will benefit the remaining individuals, at the expense of those unknown. When matches are sticky, the consequences of information asymmetries are particularly significant: those who are able to match early may face systematically better (or worse) opportunities later—because of additional experience they gain, or because they are trapped. Thus, it is in matching arenas when decoupling is difficult (marriages, some jobs) that economists most often lament the prevalence of 'mismatch.'

The basic neoclassical model of exchange recognizes the importance of information: full and perfect information is typically considered a condition for the proper functioning of markets. Deviations from perfect information may result in suboptimal sorting of sellers and buyers (for an empirical example, see Fountain 2005). Yet while many economic models presume perfect information, in most real settings information is noisy and flows through a variety of socially structured channels, including educational institutions, organizations and secondary associations, newspapers, websites, headhunters, and word-of-mouth. Each of these channels constrains access to information—in terms of both the number of persons who might hear about available options, and which particular persons hear about them. One additional channel through which a great deal of information flows is personal contacts, or social networks.

If networks were socially equivalent to other information sources, they would not merit further discussion here. And yet there is ample evidence to suggest that networks are, in some fundamental ways, distinct from more generalized information channels. Consider job searching: If an individual's personal-contact network is disproportionately composed of others who share a particular trait, then this individual may disproportionately hear about jobs held by (or known about by) other workers with the same trait (Fernandez and Fernandez-Mateo 2006). From the employer's perspective, this creates a pool of potential employees that mirrors the contact network of current employees; selection from this pool will amplify the level of segregation in employment. Further, using networks to find and evaluate possible matches creates 'bilateral asymmetries' in information (Granovetter 2005) which can amplify the fragility of the matching process. Thus, in and of itself, a constraint on the flow of information—combined with a segregated network structure—could produce and maintain segregation within jobs or neighborhoods, without any discriminatory action on the part of individual employers (ibid.). Similar effects can occur in housing and marriage markets when information about neighborhoods or potential spouses diffuses through religiously or ethnically structured networks. Surprisingly, very little research has explicitly connected the structure of communication networks with formal matching processes, though Granovetter and others have argued for the theoretical import of this connection.

16.1.4 Rules or norms about matching

The final analytic feature of matching is the set of rules or norms governing the process. These rules or norms can be understood as encoded values: they reflect and produce priorities about fairness and control. In empirical contexts, the informal rules governing matching processes describe how interaction between actors is coordinated; different kinds of rules place different pressure on preferences and information structures. There are two major families of matching regimes: centralized and decentralized systems. Centralized regimes are typically introduced either to maintain authority of a decision maker (patronage systems) or to improve efficiency (e.g. assignment of organs to donors; Healy 2006). We consider them briefly, and then turn to decentralized matching.

In centralized matching systems some central agent assigns partnerships. The classic example here is a matchmaker in a marriage market, whose role is to arrange partnerships between people or families (Dissanayake 1982; Ahuvia and Adelman 1992; Bloch and Ryder 2000). The main analytic feature of centralized matching systems is that after entering the arena one or both sides gives up the right to refuse a match. Centralized matching is most commonly found either when information constraints are particularly acute (e.g. quality is particularly difficult to discern) or when power is highly centralized (as in traditional Indian marriage markets, or Soviet labor markets).

An interesting empirical case of centralized matching rules is the matching of organs to donors, which is a formalized brokerage situation in the sense that there is an intermediary who resolves information asymmetries and coordinates transfer. Although families of donors might have preferences about who their loved ones' organs go to, this possibility is eliminated in centralized organ-donation systems. (Once the decision to donate is made, the family has no say in who receives it.) Rather, characteristics of recipients are identified (e.g. general health, age, stage of disease, geographic location), and when organs become available they are assigned to patients based on an established protocol (Elster 1993; Healy 2006). In this case, patients in need of an organ have a relatively low reservation point: by joining a waiting list they are agreeing to accept an offered organ—though the agency that administers the list implicitly promises to certify the quality of the offered organs. The actual rules of allocation are often a stratified first-come, first-served model (or a lottery), within equivalency classes. Centralized allocation regimes emerge in contexts like organ donation in part because of signaling problems (it is very difficult for patients to discern the quality of the organs in a timely fashion), and distributional asymmetries (demand for organs is massive relative to supply). Finally, in many western countries there are ethical concerns about using a price-based bargaining process to allocate organs because it creates incentives for the poor to sell their body parts.

Decentralized matching dominates empirical matching arenas. Here actors navigate the terrain of possible alternatives more or less on their own, guided by their preferences, what they know about what is available, and their understanding of the rules of the game. Matching rules are institutionalized to the extent that actors reproduce them through their own action. Within informal (decentralized) matching systems, key features of the rules involve (1) whether one side dominates the choice process; (2) whether it is possible to simultaneously hold multiple offers; and (3) the expected durability of matches once made (their 'stickiness').[2]

In some matching arenas it is conventional for one side to initiate the matching process. The classic example here is monogamous courtship and marriage: in most western societies, men (or their agents) take the lead on making a proposal to a particular woman. While women can signal interest, they have traditionally been forced to wait for a man to ask for their hand. This asymmetry reflects an underlying power difference; though women can refuse a particular proposal, under these norms they cannot express their own preferences or use the matching arena to learn their value. The consequence of this rule is particularly detrimental to women (at least with respect to their ability to realize preferences for particular types of partners) because they cannot collect and hold multiple offers simultaneously. Two sides of the same coin, the norm for male-led courtship often coincides with weak female economic power, which means that women may have a low reservation point for husbands (e.g. they prefer marriage to an undesirable spouse over remaining single), thus if they wish to find a mate, they must choose quickly from a restricted set of possible offers. Empirically, a macro-level consequence of the male-dominated matching norm is substantial asymmetry in status within marriages—and a larger pool of unmatched higher-status women (Rose 2005).

Contrast this market for wives with a typical job or residential-housing market. As in the marriage market, one side monopolizes the offer stage (employers or buyers) but there is no normative prohibition against recipients simultaneously holding multiple offers. Instead, desirable candidates (or sellers) may collect and compare offers, gaining valuable information about characteristics of potential matches and about their own bargaining position. Employers or sellers may try to regain the upper hand by imposing a time limit on the offer (analogous to an engagement period), but high-demand candidates are frequently able to string employers along while they evaluate their alternatives (or wait for even better offers). Note that, as in many matching arenas, the relative power of each side in the match is in part a function of demand and supply; if many workers are chasing few jobs, employers can put candidates on short leashes. One important consequence of such tight markets is a shift in the reservation point, a change that can have long-term consequences when matches are sticky.

The final important feature of matching rules is the extent to which matches are durable. Here we observe great variation across empirical contexts: some matches are expected to be short (rental housing) while others have longer-term implications (some jobs, marriage). In general, the longer matches are expected to last, the more individuals are willing to invest in search (in order to avoid a bad, lasting match). One way to accomplish this is to be choosy—i.e. to have a high initial reservation point. And yet because these durable partnerships are often the means by which collateral social resources or position are allocated (status, wages), remaining unmatched may ultimately drive down an individual's private reservation point. Thus, individuals' preferences are likely to be more sensitive to waiting time when matches are sticky, with reservation points coming in to play much more frequently. Sticky matches also shape the population distribution, since early matches take desirable players out of the matching arena. Thus, new entrants may perceive that 'all the good ones are already gone,' and, in a sense, they may be right.

16.2 FORMAL MATCHING MODELS

Formal models of matching processes come mainly from economics, where equilibrium solutions dominate. While some (e.g. Becker) study matching with market models, a better economic model of matching processes is a queueing model, proposed by Thurow (1975) in the context of labor markets. The idea here is that rather than workers and employers negotiating over price, workers compete for jobs with fixed characteristics. Workers queue up for jobs in order of desirability (in the eyes of employers), and are selected based on their position in the queue. Once selected, workers receive the rewards associated with the position. Because employers in large organizations can rarely evaluate workers effectively, Thurow argues that position in the queue is based on employers' assessment of the 'typical' productivity of workers of a particular type. The result, according to Thurow, is 'statistical discrimination' against certain types of workers, particularly low-skilled blacks. The basic queueing model was used to explain labor market experiences of women by Reskin and Roos (1990) and has more recently been applied to local labor markets (e.g. Bluestone and Stevenson 1999).

Extending from a basic queueing model, Sørensen (1977) and Sørensen and Kalleberg (1981) develop a model that focuses on the implications of queues combined with contracts between employers and workers. As in the basic queueing model, wages are a function of holding a particular job (rather than marginally related to productivity), and workers compete for access to vacancies in the labor market (see also Baron 1984). Here the 'stickiness' of the match distinguishes such a vacancy-competition model from a spot market for labor. In this respect, the analytic features of Sørensen's queueing and contract model more closely mirror empirical features of many matching arenas, including marriage and housing, than do traditional market models.

By far the most well-known and commonly used formal model of two-sided matching was introduced by Gale and Shapley (1962). It shares many analytic features with queueing and contract models, including a fixed set of positions with defined rewards (i.e. it is not a bargaining model). The basic logic of Gale–Shapley is a deferred-acceptance model, with one side proposing and the other accepting. Given a rank ordering of all actors in the system for actors of the other type, one proposer is randomly selected to propose a match to her most preferred match. This recipient provisionally accepts the match, as long as it is in his ranked set (e.g. is above his reservation point). Then another proposer is randomly selected to make an offer to her most preferred match. Again, the offer is provisionally accepted, contingent on the proposer being in the recipient's ranked set. However, if the recipient has already provisionally accepted a match, but the new offer comes from a preferred partner, the new offer is provisionally accepted and the first proposer returns to the pool of unmatched proposers. The matching proceeds in this fashion until all proposers have made offers to all the potential partners they prefer over remaining unmatched. Some recipients may receive no offers, and some proposers may remain unmatched.

It has been shown that given a fixed set of preferences, the conventional Gale–Shapley matching algorithm produces a stable, optimal (but not necessarily unique) match (see Roth and Vande Vate 1990). The Gale–Shapley procedure has been frequently used in two-sided matching models—including to match medical students to residencies (Roth 1990)—and its properties are fairly well understood. Extensions of this and other matching models (Becker 1973; Jovanovic 1979) have been developed in economics that allow for time and search costs (see e.g. Shimer and Smith 2000; Rogerson, Shimer, and Wright 2005; Atakan 2006; Hoppe, Moldovanu, and Sela, 2006; Smith 2006) and uncertainty in quality (Mortensen and Pissarides 1994; Mortensen 1998; Moscarini 2005).

Our review shows that many features of the matching process are well described in the analytic and empirical literature. The largest gap, however, concerns one of the more sociological aspects of matching, the structures over which information flows. Given the significance of information for altering the outcomes of matching processes, it is somewhat surprising that the vast literature on social networks and information diffusion (e.g. Granovetter 1995; Watts 1999) has not been explicitly integrated into social-scientific matching models (see Calvo-Armengol and Zenou 2005). Studies of networks reveal a great deal of local homogeneity in networks (McPherson, Smith-Lovin, and Cook 2001), which could result in highly clustered opportunities for matching (Granovetter 2005). In the remainder of this chapter we describe an agent-based matching model that demonstrates the utility of combining models of network structure with matching models.

16.3 AN ILLUSTRATION: SOCIAL NETWORKS AND LABOR-MARKET SEGREGATION

While those who study matching processes have become increasingly interested in modeling the consequences of limited information, very little research integrates a sophisticated sense of social networks into matching models. This is unfortunate, since, like matching models, the study of social networks is explicitly oriented toward building models of social structure from actual social behavior—in this case, networks of relations. We address this lacuna with a model that focuses explicitly on the link between social networks and the dynamics of matching; this exercise reveals that fundamentally different macro-level conditions are produced by varying preferences or information structure. The model we describe here is motivated by questions about the persistence of segregation in the labor market, but the basic finding extends to other two-sided matching arenas with fixed positions. Simulated results based on this model reveal how network homophily can result in acute segregation, even when employers do not have discriminatory preferences and workers are equally qualified. The key insight is that information flows are frequently socially structured (in some cases as the result of previous matching), and that the nature of these information flows can profoundly affect the macro-level patterns generated by the matching process.

16.3.1 Model overview

Our basic strategy is to build a very simple artificial world populated by workers who want to find jobs and managers who want to staff jobs. Empirical evidence reveals that labor markets are often highly segregated with respect to the ascribed attributes of workers. Many occupations are sex-typed, while in heterogeneous societies certain fields are often dominated by specific ethnic groups. Various explanations have been proposed to account for segregation in labor markets. On balance, most of these explanations can be classified as essentially *supply-side* arguments, emphasizing differences in human-capital distributions between groups, or *demand-side* accounts, based on employer preferences. Yet labor-market stratification is actually produced via a matching process where outcomes are a function of preferences, distributions, rules, and information structure.

While real labor markets are multidimensional and complex, our goal in designing the artificial world is to capture (and vary) core features of theoretical interest. Thus, our workers are heterogeneous with respect to only two characteristics: a binary attribute (e.g sex or race) and a quantitative measure that captures variation in qualification (e.g education or skill). Managers' preferences about potential workers are reflected in utility equations that operationalize various employer-based decision rules. The primary source of information about job vacancies is a social network that links workers and managers. Within each iteration of the model, workers become aware of a set of job openings, and managers select among their pool of available candidates. Workers are assigned to a job or are left unmatched via the basic Gale–Shapley matching algorithm, labor-market features are adjusted in response to the new conditions, and the process begins again. We use this basic simulation framework to conduct experiments contrasting different labor-market conditions. We vary three families of parameters: employer preferences; characteristics of populations; and the information regime.

Employer preferences

Employer preferences for—or against—certain classes of workers are often identified as an important source of labor-market segregation. We compare employers who are indifferent to workers' characteristics to two distinct types of employer preferences: a preference for more skilled workers, and a discriminatory preference. These preferences are controlled in a utility calculation: in the most general form, an employer i's utility for a worker j is a linear function of characteristics of the worker, the employer, and the current labor market conditions.[3]

$$U_{ij} = \alpha X_{ij} + \beta LM_t + \varepsilon_j \qquad (1)$$

In this conceptualization, X_{ij} includes a variety of worker and job characteristics, LM_t contains current labor-market conditions, and ε_j is a small employer-specific noise term. The sets of parameters α and β can be thought of as preferences for characteristics: a higher relative value of a parameter means a stronger employer preference for this characteristic.

In the first preference condition, all workers are fully equivalent in the eyes of employers and selection among candidates is essentially random.[4] In practice, this means that the αs associated with workers' skill and attributes are set to zero.

The second condition is designed to capture employers' preferences for more skilled workers. Here we set the α associated with workers' skill to a value > 0, while keeping the α associated with workers' attributes equal to zero. This means that *ceteris paribus*, workers who present with higher skills will be preferred over workers who present with lower skills.

The third condition introduces a discriminatory preference. The general thinking here is that employers may prefer to hire workers who are like them in salient ways: women managers prefer women employees, Irish foremen prefer Irish workers, and black business owners prefer black employees. We call this an *in-group bias*, and operationalize it by introducing a binary X_{ij} term that indicates whether the worker and manager are in the same attribute category. When this preference is operative, the α assigned to this indicator variable is set to > 0, so that managers will select same-group candidates over candidates who do not share the attribute.

Population structure

While employer preferences may be an important source of labor-market segregation, there is reason to believe that their significance is contingent on the structure and characteristics of the supply of labor that employers confront. At the most basic level, a highly skewed population distribution could make it very difficult for some employers to exercise a discriminatory preference, simply because workers matching their desired profile are scarce. Drawing from the logic of economists' arguments concerning human capital, we compare scenarios where workers' skills and attributes are correlated to scenarios where these two characteristics are independent of one another.

Information regimes

While employer preferences and the association between skill and attribute dominate discussions of labor-market segregation, the key contribution of this model is its focus on how access to information about vacancies and candidates affects labor-market processes. We have two aims here: first we model the effects of randomly restricting the amount of information available to all actors in the labor market. Second, and more importantly, we examine the relationship between the structure of networks through which information flows and labor-market outcomes.

As a baseline comparison, we evaluate the model under a condition of full information. Full information is an important assumption of neoclassical micro-economic models of markets, and, while it is empirically unrealistic, it offers a theoretical benchmark against which we can compare outcomes derived from models capturing key features of social processes that influence labor markets.

Once we move away from a full information regime, agents in the model have access to jobs primarily via a social network linking workers and managers.[5] A substantial body of research shows that informal social networks are an important vector for the diffusion of information about jobs; here we concentrate directly on whether network homophily translates into labor-market segregation. By homophily we refer to the tendency of like to choose like as a relationship partner (McPherson, Smith-Lovin, and Cook 2001). The primary question we ask

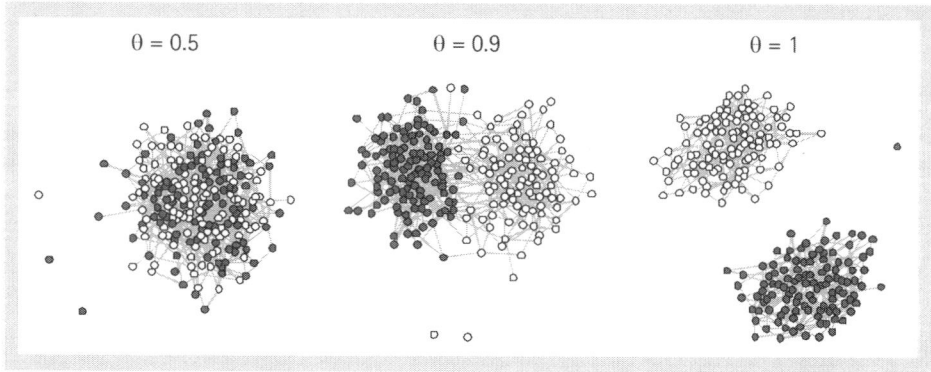

Fig. 16.1 Representative simulated networks at varying levels of homophily

is: Are there levels of network homophily that can generate substantial segregation in employment, even absent explicitly discriminatory preferences on the part of employers?

We fix the network at the outset, and vary the level of homophily across trials. We control the level of homophily in the network with a simple function that governs the probability P_{ij} of a tie between two actors i and j.

$$P_{ij} = (1 - 2p)((1 - \theta)H_{ij} + \theta(1 - H_{ij})) + p \qquad (2)$$

The key parameter here is θ, which controls the strength and direction of the network bias. H_{ij} is a binary measure that indicates if i and j share an attribute, and p is a very small underlying probability of a tie. When $\theta = 0.5$, the probabilities of in- and out-group ties are equal, and the graph approximates a Bernoulli random graph. As θ approaches zero, most ties will cross group boundaries, while as θ approaches 1, in-group ties will dominate. Figure 16.1 depicts networks generated with θ values of 0.5, 0.9, and 1.0. One nice feature of this expression is that in the case of equally sized groups θ can be interpreted as the proportion of all ties that are within the group.

In our network-restricted information scenarios, workers have access to information about any jobs controlled by managers they are tied to directly, as well as about those jobs controlled by managers connected to their network partners.

16.3.2 Outcomes

Our outcome is the level of segregation in the simulated labor market. Because we have implemented a simple two-group model, we use the familiar index of dissimilarity to measure segregation (Reardon and Firebaugh 2002), with the cluster of jobs controlled by a single manager as our unit of aggregation. Substantively, the index of dissimilarity measures the proportion of workers who would have to shift from one manager to another in order make the distribution across managers proportional to the distribution in the population. A value of zero means that workers are distributed in proportion to their representation in the population; higher values mean greater segregation.

16.3.3 Results

The experimental design varies three families of parameters: preferences, population, and information.[6] To establish the baseline, we consider how employer-preference regimes interact with different population structures under conditions of full information. We then restrict information via social networks, and examine what happens when networks are more or less structured by our attribute variable. The results show that several combinations of parameters generate substantial levels of segregation in the artificial labor market, including scenarios in which employers are indifferent to workers' characteristics.

16.3.4 Full-information regime

The first scenarios we examine give all actors full information about each other, but employer-preference regimes vary. This verifies the model, and reveals some preliminary comparisons about the mechanisms of interest.

Figure 16.2 plots results of 50 trials for each of 5 distinct employment-preference/population-structure scenarios. Each unique constellation of parameter values is arrayed along the x-axis, while the level of labor-market segregation from the resulting trials (measured with the dissimilarity index) is plotted on the y-axis. Variability within each scenario comes from the stochastic aspects of the model.

In the first employer-preference regime, managers are completely indifferent to all types of worker heterogeneity (skill and attribute). Further, they are aware of all workers. We consider this scenario a baseline; it produces a dissimilarity index centered about 25 percent, with very little variability. This is the minimum level of segregation possible in our model; what segregation remains is driven largely by small numbers and technical features of the model.

The second scenario adds in a taste for discrimination. In the absence of any other structure in the model, when managers prefer workers who share their attribute over workers who don't, segregation becomes extremely high. In trials run under this scenario, close to 100 percent of workers are employed in fully segregated firms. Again variability is relatively low.

The third scenario is a variation on discrimination. In this case, rather than preferring to hire workers that are similar to themselves, all managers prefer to hire

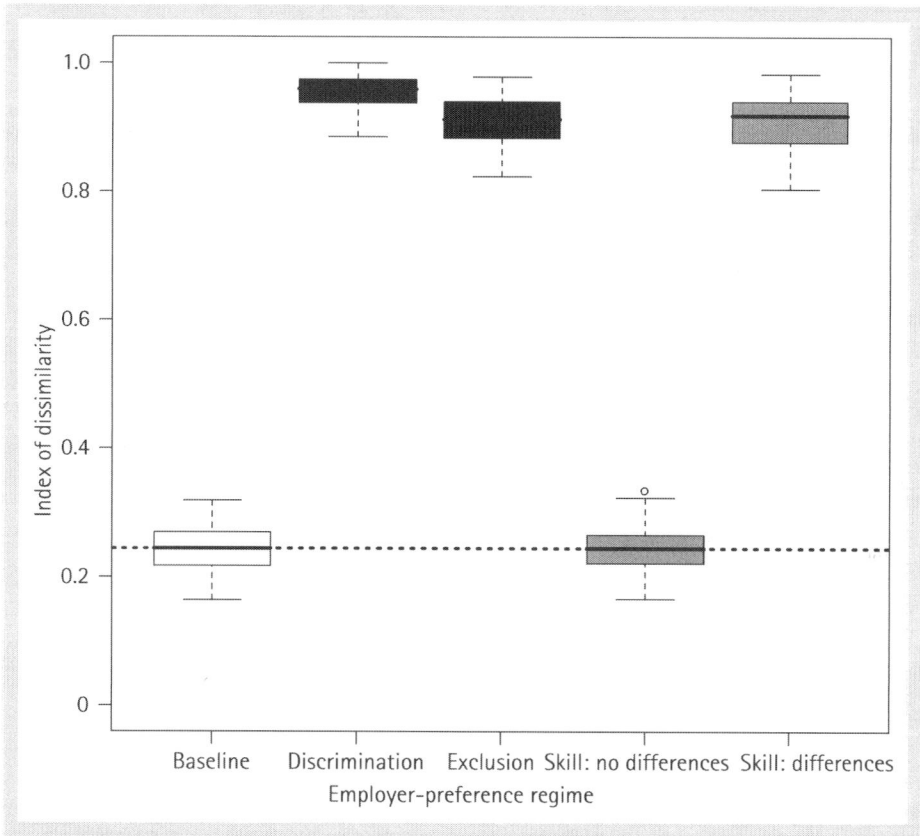

Fig. 16.2 Employer–preference regimes and labor–market segregation under full information

one group over the other, regardless of their own attribute. In this case, the level of segregation is similar to that of the other type of discrimination.

In the fourth scenario, employers prefer higher-skilled workers and are indifferent to attribute. However, worker skill and attribute are independent of one another. This scenario represents what some would consider a labor market *ideal*, in the sense that employers are seeking the most competitive workers, but whatever process produces skill in the population is not associated with ascribed attribute. In our model, this scenario produces levels of segregation that are statistically indistinguishable from the baseline model.

The final scenario combines an employer preference for higher-skilled workers with an association between skill and attribute. This regime generates substantially higher levels of segregation than the baseline model, though there is a bit more variability than in the discriminatory regime. In this scenario, human capital is rewarded, but since it is unevenly distributed between the two groups, one group enjoys better labor-market outcomes.

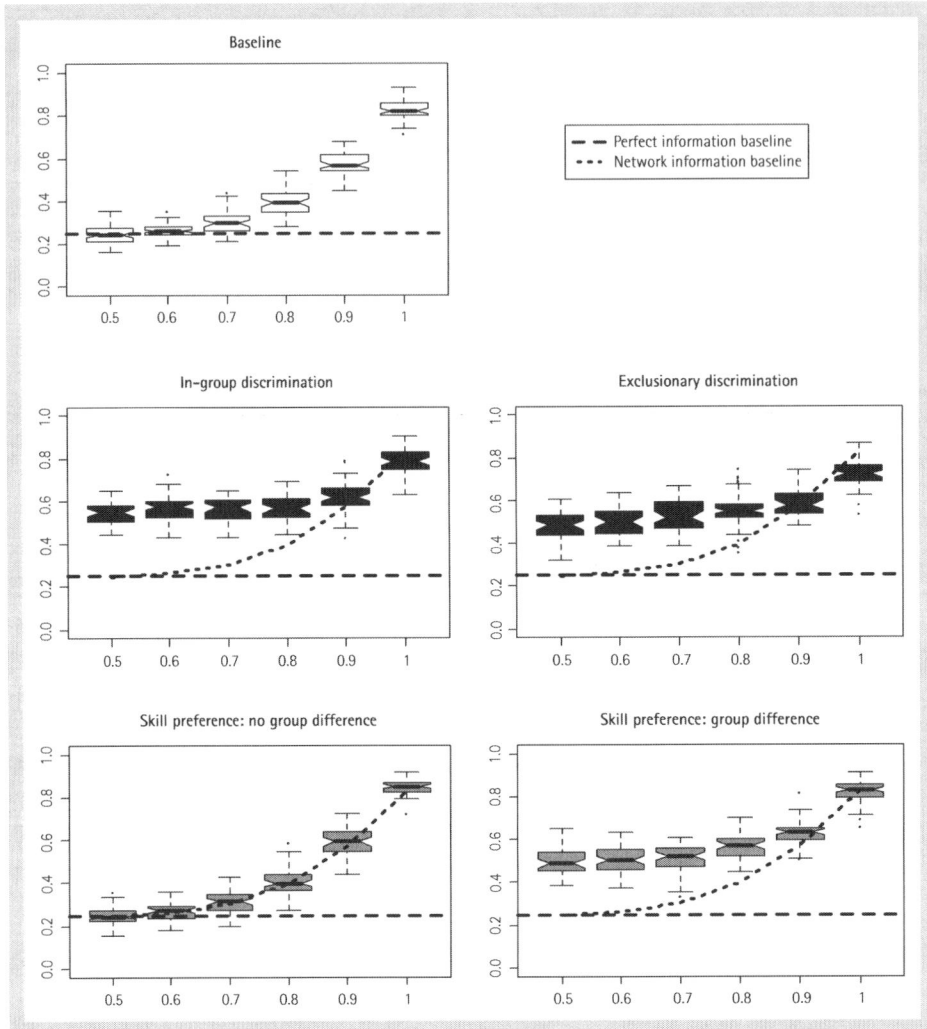

Fig. 16.3 Levels of firm segregation across five experimental regimes

16.3.5 Network-information regimes

We now turn to scenarios in which information flows primarily through a social network that links workers and managers. Figure 16.3 displays the level of segregation resulting from the same experimental regimes shown in the previous figure, however here we connect workers and managers through social networks characterized by varying levels of homophily with respect to the binary attribute.

The baseline scenario, found in the top panel, contains boxplots for sets of 50 trials (at each parameter combination) when employers are indifferent to worker characteristics. While the index of dissimilarity is still plotted along the y-axis, the x-axis now arrays trials characterized by various levels of network homophily. On the far left the graphs are random with respect to attribute ($\theta = 0.5$); as we move toward the right, networks' in-group biases become more pronounced. This figure reflects the baseline association between network homophily and labor-market segregation in our network-restricted models. It is evident that when networks are integrated, the level of segregation is comparable to our full-information baseline. However, as networks become more homophilous ($\theta \geq 0.7$), the level of labor-market segregation begins to rise quite dramatically. When networks are largely segregated into two distinct clusters, the average level of segregation in the simulated data is almost four times greater than in the baseline model. The implication of this result is that high levels of segregation are possible even when employers are indifferent to any worker characteristics. The mechanism generating segregation when networks have a strong in-group bias is a selective pool: if job-relevant information flows through networks, and networks are disproportionately composed of those in the same attribute category, workers will predominantly hear about jobs controlled by in-group managers, and managers will be forced to choose from a pool that disproportionately reflects their own attribute identity.

The second row of Figure 16.3 shows analogous plots for trials when employers exhibit an active preference for workers who share their own attribute (left) or belong to a single sought-after category (right). For reference, we indicate the level of segregation for the full-information baseline as well as the segregation trajectory for the baseline model under varying network conditions. Results here are substantially different from the baseline: When networks are random, discriminatory preferences increase labor-market segregation substantially over baseline levels (D—the index of dissimilarity—is roughly three times higher than the baseline). However, the index of dissimilarity for these trials is not as high as in the full-information discrimination regime, because the restriction on information means that some employers are 'forced' to choose workers they don't prefer, simply because there are no others in their randomly generated pool. As the network bias gets stronger, the level of labor-market segregation rises. However, even at the highest levels of in-group bias, segregation does not rise above the network-restricted baseline levels. This suggests that when networks are highly segregated ($\theta \geq 0.9$), the network itself is the cause of extremely high levels of labor-market segregation, rather than any existing employers' discriminatory preferences. Interestingly, in the exclusionary regime employers are unable to segregate the firms to quite the same high level as in the in-group-discrimination regime.

The last row reports results of trials where employers prefer higher-skill workers, but skill and attribute are independent (left), as well as where there are skill differences between groups (right). When skill and attribute are independent, the pattern in the level of segregation is identical to our network-baseline model. While segregation does rise, it is purely as a result of changes in the level of in-group bias in the underlying network through which job-related information flows. In contrast, when groups differ in their average skill, the pattern is closer to that generated by the discriminatory-preference regime—though the level of segregation observed for low levels of θ is somewhat lower. As in the discriminatory case, when networks have a strong in-group bias, the level of labor-market segregation is substantially higher, though again the values do not rise above those generated in the baseline model.

When comparing the impact of employer preferences and population characteristics on segregation, the results from the network-restricted-information trials mimic the crude pattern observed in the full-information trials. Specifically, discriminatory preferences are extremely effective at generating segregated labor markets, while the combination of skill preferences and group differences in skill levels is almost as effective. However, the network-restricted scenarios reveal that these well-known mechanisms for creating segregation are not necessary conditions: When networks reveal strong in-group biases, these biased networks themselves are sufficient to segregate the artificial labor market. In fact, adding either of the segregating mechanisms to a homophilous network does not result in an increase in labor-market segregation above the level observed with the homophilous network alone.

Concluding Comments

The study of social life requires understanding how individuals form relations with one another, and how these relations structure access to positions and other resources. Neither individual preferences nor the structure of opportunities alone is sufficient to explain this complex process. Treating the link between person and position as a matching process, however, enables scholars to explicitly model the interplay between individuals and social positions and provides an analytic foundation for understanding the reproduction of institutionalized patterns of interaction. Substantively, this orientation sheds light on one of the major sources of segregation, since empirically both norms and information constraints effectively restrict individual choice in the matching processes. The result is local clustering, and the development of subsequent preferences and capacities that may reinforce this pattern.

In this chapter we have reviewed some of the core features of matching processes, discussed formal models describing matching regimes, and presented results from a simulation that brings a network model into the matching literature. We now offer some additional comments on various endogenous aspects of matching processes.

At some fundamental level matching is governed by preferences, and to the extent that we are willing to treat individual preferences as fixed and exogenous, matching may be relatively straightforward. However, sociologists recognize that this conceit is little more than an analytic convenience: it flies in the face of empirical investigations of behavior. Though this direction has not been well developed, there is ample reason to believe that studies of matching may contribute to our understanding of how some preferences are structured and constrained by local opportunities. The idea here rests on three important facets of matching processes: that matches are constrained by others' preferences, the strength of local rules about the importance of being matched, and the costs of decoupling. Each of these factors may cause actors to *come to prefer* that which is available to them (Baron 1984; Solga and Konietzka 1999). Thus, matching arenas may best be understood as settings in which actors' preferences are, at least in some respects, endogenously produced.

Matching processes may also play a role in structuring the production of actors with particular characteristics. Key here are the complex temporal dynamics that operate in matching arenas. Particular matches occur at a given moment in time, but the operative rules frequently have a longer life span. For any actors watching the process, 'made matches' (and failed matches) offer the best guide of what to expect. These later actors read the outcomes of those ahead of them and attempt to position themselves accordingly. Consider a labor market that rewards (or ignores) educational credentials. If this reward structure is stable over the medium term, actors who anticipate entering this labor market may invest in (or avoid) acquiring credentials in order to be more competitive in the matching arena. This proactive investment will alter then the subsequent distribution of potential employees over which employers choose, and may ultimately change the rewards to the credential—often to the detriment of those who thought they were acting in their own best interest (Boudon 1973; Stovel, Savage, and Bearman 1996). The general point here is that because matching systems have a large number of 'moving parts,' there are numerous possibilities for feedback loops. Frequently these are self-reinforcing, though they may also result in significant disruptions.

Our investigations into the interactions between network structures and matching processes point to another form of reinforcement that may occur as actors are matched to position. We have shown that homogeneous networks are sufficient to generate segregated workplaces. But what if segregated workplaces themselves increase the level of homophily of networks? This would clearly have implications for subsequent job-finding (Stovel and Fountain 2006), but it could also have implications for how persons navigate other matches as well. Consider the substantive domains in which matching plays a prominent role: marriage, school assignment, housing markets, finding a job. These are exactly the places where people's networks are formed. Because networks can play such an important role in structuring the type and amount of information that individuals have access to, networks stitch these matching domains together, and changes in one domain may have significant implications for adjacent domains.

Obviously the feedback inherent in matching processes has implications for the individuals: as actors observe matching, they may prospectively adjust their behavior or attitudes, thus shaping their own prospects. Yet this feedback can also have consequences at the macro level, where these cumulative effects will often appear as more than a simple aggregation of individual changes. Rather, if actors fail to appreciate the two-sided nature of most matching processes, the combination of interdependence and uncertainty can trigger a cascade that profoundly alters the structural landscape. Consider a common finding in evolutionary game theory: When actors are randomly paired, exploitative strategies easily dominate, but if actors are paired via competitive matching, something interesting occurs. Initially, exploiters dominate, but over time they are surpassed by more cooperative players (Yamagishi, Hayashi, and Jin 1994; Skyrms and Pemantle 2000; Hauk and Nagel 2001; Chiang 2008). This result is a direct consequence of the two-sided nature of the matching process: exploiters benefit from playing with altruists, but altruists prefer other altruists over exploiters. Because matches must be *mutually* acceptable, the exploiters are unable to find altruists willing to play with them, and vanish as a consequence.

Pairings such as those described throughout this chapter are a basic building block of social structure, so understanding the matching processes that link us to one another as well as to opportunities and positions should be of central importance to sociologists. The primary social institutions in which we participate, including families, schools, the labor market, the economy, religious organizations, neighborhoods, and other social groupings, are all built in part from these processes. The advantage of the matching model is that it neglects neither choice nor constraint, while directing analytical focus on the interdependence of actors on the preferences, attributes, information, and actions of others in the matching arena. Matching models can provide a useful tool with which to describe and build theory about the complex, interdependent processes through which individuals' choices create—and are constrained by—social structures.

Notes

1. John Logan's two-sided matching model (Logan 1996; Logan, Hoff, and Newton 2008) is an attempt to incorporate the population marginals into the choice structure of individuals, and therefore is an improvement over existing log-linear models of net association. However, these models also confound individual preferences and the local choice set that individuals confront.

2. A fourth element of the rules of matching concerns whether actors regularly hire agents to represent them. Agents or brokers are most common when information asymmetries are acute and matches are relatively sticky; that is, when the costs of mismatch are high. When actors choose agents to represent them, matching can proceed as in other contexts though search times may decline (see Levitt 2005). Matching arenas in which brokers gain complete control may be indistinguishable from centralized matching.

3. We also calculate an analogous set of utilities from the workers' perspectives. This allows us to use the two-sided matching algorithm.

4. In all trials reported here the model does include a slight preference for previous employees; this 'stickiness' is included to reduce the overall amount of turnover in the labor market and serves to crystallize observed patterns more quickly (Fountain and Stovel 2005).

5. We also distribute a small amount of random information, to simulate non-network recruitment strategies.

6. All trials are based on labor markets with 200 workers and jobs, and 20 managers, k = 5, 100 iterations per trial with 50 representatives in each θ by regime configuration. There is 0.005 random information (except with the perfect-information regime) and two equally sized worker categories with mean skill 70 and 30 (s.d. = 5) when relevant.

References

Ahuvia, A. C., and Adelman, M. B. (1992), 'Formal Intermediaries in the Marriage Market: A Typology and Review', *Journal of Marriage and the Family*, 54: 452–63.

Akerlof G. (1970), 'The Market for "Lemons": Quality Uncertainty and the Market Mechanism', *Quarterly Journal of Economics*, 84 (3): 488–500.

Atakan, A. E. (2006), 'Assortative Matching with Explicit Search Costs', *Econometrica*, 74: 667–80.

Baron, J. N. (1984), 'Organizational Perspectives on Stratification', *Annual Review of Sociology*, 10: 37–69.

Becker, G. S. (1973), 'A Theory of Marriage: Part I', *Journal of Political Economy*, 81: 813–46.

—— (1981), *A Treatise on the Family* (Cambridge, Mass.: Harvard University Press).

Blackwell, D. L., and Lichter, D. T. (2004), 'Homogamy among Dating, Cohabiting, and Married Couples', *Sociological Quarterly*, 45: 719–37.

Bloch, F., and Ryder, H. (2000), 'Two-sided Search, Marriages, and Matchmakers', *International Economic Review*, 41: 93–115.

Bluestone, B., and Stevenson, M. (1999), 'Racial and Ethnic Gaps in Male Earnings in a Booming Urban Economy', *Eastern Economics Journal*, 25: 209–38.

Boudon, R. (1973), *Mathematical Structures of Social Mobility* (San Francisco, Calif.: Jossey-Bass).

Calvo-Armengol, A., and Zenou, Y. (2005), 'Job Matching, Social Network and Word-of-mouth Communication', *Journal of Urban Economics*, 57: 500–22.

Chen, Y., and Sonmez, T. (2006), 'School Choice: An Experimental Study', *Journal of Economic Theory*, 127: 202–31.

CHIANG, Y. (2008), 'A Path Towards Fairness: Preferential Association and the Evolution of Strategies in the Ultimatum Game', *Rationality and Society*, 20 (2): 173–201.

COLEMAN, J. S. (1984), 'Introducing Social Structure into Economic Analysis', *American Economic Review*, 74: 84–8.

—— (1991), 'Matching Processes in the Labor Market', *Acta Sociologica*, 34: 3–12.

DISSANAYAKE, W. (1982), 'Newspapers as Matchmakers—A Sri Lankan Illustration', *Journal of Comparative Family Studies*, 13: 97–108.

ELSTER, J. (1993), *Local Justice: How Institutions Allocate Scarce Goods and Necessary Burdens* (New York: Russell Sage).

FERNANDEZ, R. M., and FERNANDEZ-MATEO, I. (2006), 'Networks, Race, and Hiring', *American Sociological Review*, 71 (1): 42–71.

FOUNTAIN, C. (2005), 'Finding a Job in the Internet Age', *Social Forces*, 83: 1235–62.

—— (2006), 'Labor Market Structure, Networks Dynamics, and Economic Change', Ph.D. thesis (University of Washington).

—— and STOVEL, K. (2005), 'Turbulent Networks', unpublished manuscript, Department of Sociology, University of Washington.

GALE, D., and SHAPLEY, L. S. (1962), 'College Admissions and the Stability of Marriage', *American Mathematical Quarterly*, 69: 9–15.

GANGL, M. (2004), 'Institutions and the Structure of Labour Market Matching in the United States and West Germany', *European Sociological Review*, 20: 171–87.

GRANOVETTER, M. (1995), *Getting a Job: A Study of Contacts and Careers*, 2nd edn. (Chicago, Ill.: University of Chicago Press).

—— (2005), 'The Impact of Social Structure on Economic Outcomes', *Journal of Economic Perspectives*, 19: 33–50.

HAUK, E., and NAGEL, R. (2001), 'Choice of Partners in Multiple Two-person Prisoner's Dilemma Games', *Journal of Conflict Resolution*, 45 (6): 770–93.

HAYES, B. C., and JONES, F. L. (1991), 'Education and Marriage Patterns in Australia', *International Journal of Sociology and Social Policy*, 11: 1–16.

HEALY, K. (2006), *Last Best Gifts: Altruism and the Market for Human Blood and Organs* (Chicago, Ill.: University of Chicago Press).

HOPPE, H. C., MOLDOVANU, B., and SELA, A. (2006), *The Theory of Assortative Matching Based on Costly Signals*, CEPR discussion paper no. 5543, available at SSRN website <http://www.ssrn.com/abstract=909614>, accessed 2008.

JOVANOVIC, B. (1979), 'Job Matching and the Theory of Turnover', *Journal of Political Economy*, 87: 972–90.

KALMIJN, M. (1994), 'Assortative Mating by Cultural and Economic Occupational Status', *American Journal of Sociology*, 100: 422–52.

LEVITT, S. (2005), *Freakonomics* (New York: HarperCollins).

LOGAN, J. A. (1996), 'Rational Choice and the TSL Model of Occupational Opportunity', *Rationality and Society*, 8: 207–30.

—— HOFF, P., and NEWTON, M. (2008), 'Two-sided Estimation of Mate Preferences for Similarities in Age, Education, and Religion', *Journal of the American Statistical Association*, 103 (482): 559–69.

MCPHERSON M., SMITH-LOVIN, L., and COOK, J. M. (2001), 'Birds of a Feather: Homophily in Social Networks', *Annual Review of Sociology*, 27: 415–44.

MARE, R. (1991), 'Five Decades of Educational Assortative Mating', *American Sociological Review*, 56: 15–32.

MORTENSEN, D. (1988), 'Matching: Finding a Partner for Life or Otherwise', *American Journal of Sociology*, 94: S215–S240.

—— and PISSARIDES, C. A. (1994), 'Job Creation and Job Destruction in the Theory of Unemployment', *Review of Economic Studies*, 61: 397–415.

MOSCARINI, G. (2005), 'Job Matching and the Wage Distribution', *Econometrica*, 73 (2): 481–516.

REARDON, S. F., and FIREBAUGH, G. (2002), 'Measures of Multigroup Segregation', *Sociological Methodology*, 32: 33–67.

RESKIN, B., and ROOS, P. (1990), *Job Queues, Gender Queues: Explaining Women's Inroads into Male Occupations* (Philadelphia, Pa.: Temple University Press).

ROGERSON, R., SHIMER, R., and WRIGHT, R. (2005), 'Search-theoretic Models of the Labor Market: A Survey', *Journal of Economic Literature*, 43 (4): 959–88.

ROSE, E. (2005), *Education, Hypergamy, and the Success Gap*, Center for Statistics and the Social Sciences working paper no. 53, University of Washington.

ROTH, A. E. (1990), 'New Physicians: A Natural Experiment in Market Organization', *Science*, 250: 1524–8.

—— and VANDE VATE, J. H. (1990), 'Random Paths to Stability in Two-sided Matching', *Econometrica*, 58: 1475–80.

RYTINA, S., and MORGAN, D. L. (1982), 'The Arithmetic of Social Relations: The Interplay of Category and Network', *American Journal of Sociology*, 88: 88–113.

SHIMER, R., and SMITH, L. (2000), 'Assortative Matching and Search', *Econometrica*, 68 (2): 343–69.

SKYRMS, B., and PEMANTLE, R. (2000), 'A Dynamic Model of Social Network Formation', *Proceedings of the National Academy of Sciences of the USA*, 97 (16): 9340–6.

SMITH, L. (2006), 'The Marriage Market with Search Frictions', *Journal of Political Economy*, 114: 1124–44.

SOLGA, H., and DIEWALD, M. (2001), 'The East German Labour Market after German Unification: A Study of Structural Change and Occupational Matching', *Work, Employment and Society*, 15: 95–126.

—— and KONIETZKA, D. (1999), 'Occupational Matching and Social Stratification: Theoretical Insights and Empirical Observations Taken from a German–German Comparison', *European Sociological Review*, 15: 25–47.

SØRENSEN A. B. (1977), 'The Structure of Inequality and the Process of Attainment', *American Sociological Review*, 42 (6): 965–78.

—— and KALLEBERG, A. L. (1981), 'An Outline of a Theory of the Matching of Persons to Jobs', in I. Berg (ed.), *Sociological Perspectives on Labor Markets* (New York: Academic).

SPENCE, A. M. (1973), 'Job Market Signaling', *Quarterly Journal of Economics*, 87 (3): 355–74.

—— (1974), *Market Signaling: Informational Transfer in Hiring and Related Screening Processes* (Cambridge, Mass.: Harvard University Press).

STIGLITZ, J. E. (1975), 'The Theory of "Screening", Education, and the Distribution of Income', *American Economic Review*, 65 (3): 283–300.

STOVEL, K., and FOUNTAIN, C. (2006), *Hearing About a Job: Employer Preferences, Networks and Labor Market Segregation*, unpublished manuscript, Department of Sociology, University of Washington.

—— SAVAGE, M., and BEARMAN, P. (1996), 'Ascription into Achievement: Models of Career Systems at Lloyds Bank, 1890–1970', *American Journal of Sociology*, 102: 358–99.

THUROW, L. (1975), *Generating Inequality: Mechanisms of Distribution in the US Economy* (New York: Basic).

TOMIYAMA, Y. (1992), 'Social Matching Theory and College Admission Institutions', *Riron to Hoho/Sociological Theory and Methods*, 7: 61–83.

WATTS, D. (1999), 'Networks, Dynamics and the Small World Phenomenon', *American Journal of Sociology*, 105 (2): 493–527.

WERUM, R. (2002), 'Matching Youth and Jobs? Gender Dynamics in New Deal Job Training Programs', *Social Forces*, 81: 473–503.

WITTE, J. C., and KALLEBERG, A. L. (1995), 'Matching Training and Jobs: The Fit between Vocational Education and Employment in the German Labour Market', *European Sociological Review*, 11: 293–317.

YAMAGISHI, T., HAYASHI, N., and JIN, N. (1994), 'Prisoner's Dilemma Networks: Selection Strategy Versus Action Strategy', in U. Schulz, W. Albers, and U. Mueller (eds.), *Social Dilemmas and Cooperation* (Berlin: Springer-Verlag), 233–50.

CHAPTER 17

···

COLLECTIVE ACTION*

···

DELIA BALDASSARRI

Let us weigh the gain and the loss in wagering that God is. Let us estimate these two chances. If you gain, you gain all; if you lose, you lose
nothing.... But there is an eternity of life and happiness. And this being
so, if there were an infinity of chances, of which one only would be for
you, you would still be right in wagering one to win two, and you would
act stupidly, being obliged to play, by refusing to stake one life against
three at a game in which out of an infinity of chances there is one for you,
if there were an infinity of an infinitely happy life to gain.

(Pascal, *Pensées*)

INTRODUCTION

···

THE notion of collective action comprises the broad range of social phenomena
in which social actors engage in common activities for demanding and/or providing collective goods. Some social phenomena—e.g. grass-root activism, social
movements, or revolutions—strongly denote this concept, others belong to a more
extensive understanding of what collective action is about—e.g. orchestra concerts,

* I thank Mario Diani, Charles Tilly, Michael Macy, Matthew Salganik, and the editors for helpful
comments.

soccer games, open-source software. Some forms of collective action are rare, others very common; some arise in the context of social conflicts, others simply require cooperation. A collective good is something that, by definition, a single individual cannot produce relying exclusively on his own means. Its achievement is instead possible through the independent, interdependent, or coordinated contribution of many people.

Analytical models

In the analytical-sociology tradition, the problem of collective action lies in 'the disparity between individual optimization and collective optimality' (Coleman 1989: 5), of which the free-rider problem (Olson 1965) and the tragedy of the commons (Hardin 1968; Ostrom 1990) are two popular incarnations. Accordingly, over the last fifty years most analytical research has focused on the cognitive, dispositional, and structural conditions under which cooperation becomes the preferred strategy for rational, self-interested individuals whose 'primitive' strategy would instead be free-riding. Like the many philosophers who devoted their intellect to the demonstration of the existence of God in a world where religion could not be stronger, analytical-sociology scholars have provided various insightful explanations of how cooperation can arise from self-interested actors in a world where cooperation appears to be common in several domains of human life.

Behavioral experiments

Although scholars recognized long ago that cooperation occurs more often than a rational-choice approach would suggest, observational evidence was not considered sufficient to assess between egoistic and altruistic models of human behavior, because in real life (seemingly) altruistic/nonselfish behavior can always be explained as covertly oriented to increase one's reputation or psychological well-being or as being enforced by internalized social norms and fear of social sanctions. In contrast, in more recent years experimental evidence has put in jeopardy the micro foundation of the rational-choice approach by documenting people's predisposition to reciprocity, cooperation, and punishment of defectors, as well as recognizing the distinctive role of communication, face-to-face interaction, and personal(ized) relationships in fostering and maintaining cooperation (Ostrom 1998, 2000; Fehr and Gintis 2007). Consequently, the contextual and institutional dynamics that favor reciprocity, reputation, and trust have gained more prominence, shifting the explanatory focus from the psychological dispositions of the actors to the relational dynamics and institutional settings that affect human behavior.

Empirical research

While the analytical tradition has pursued the study of collective action by modeling actors' interdependent behavior in abstract, highly simplified scenarios, other scholars have dedicated themselves to the empirical study of collective action, social movements, and contentious politics, casting a new light on the role of the masses in social change (Tilly 1978; McAdam [1982] 1999; della Porta and Diani 2006). Their work was crucial in many ways. First, they contributed to finally overthrowing the old belief that crowds and gatherings are nothing more than irrational (or hysterical) expressions of collective behavior (LeBon [1895] 1896; Park 1930; Blumer 1951). Second, they also moved away from explanations according to which social movements erupt as a response to disruptive psychological states (e.g. deprivation, frustration, alienation, or normative ambiguity) induced by the structural strains of contemporary societies (Kornhauser 1959; Smelser 1962; McAdam [1982] 1999; McPhail 1991).

Instead of digging into psychological states, social-movements scholars shifted the explanation of collective action to the political level, analyzing the political process and political-opportunities structure (Tilly 1978; McAdam [1982] 1999; Tarrow 1994). Rather than being viewed as an irrational or emotional outbreak, collective action was understood, especially by proponents of the resource-mobilization theory (McCarthy and Zald 1973, 1977), as a goal-seeking activity strategically deployed by social actors—individuals or groups. The collection of events catalogues and the classification of different mobilization repertoires were used to understand the alternative deployment of diverse political strategies (Tilly 1978, 2007). Research extended to the study of mobilizing structures, formal and informal organizations, networks, forms of recruitment, and interorganizational coordination (McAdam 1988; Obershall 1993; Diani 1995, 2003). Finally, framing analysis and the cultural approach were used to capture the cognitive and affective aspects fundamental to the construction of shared meanings and collective identities (Snow et al. 1986; Melucci 1989).

It is from this copious, if not always coherent, research that the empirical field of collective action and social movements took form. Over the years it has hosted structural, rational, and cultural approaches as well as some attempts to overcome or integrate such diverse standpoints (Lofland 1996; McAdam, McCarthy, and Zald 1996), the most recent of which, contentious politics, calls for mechanisms-based explanations (McAdam, Tarrow, and Tilly 2001). Although not exactly of the kind advocated by the current generation of analytical sociologists (Hedström and Swedberg 1998; Hedström 2005), the social-mechanisms program that scholars of contentious politics have embraced is similarly critical of 'correlational analysis' and variable-based explanations, and interested in causal explanations and in the link between different levels of analysis.

Nonetheless, the analytical-sociology (AS) and contentious-politics (CP) perspectives diverge broadly. Methodologically, while AS refuses the search for general laws but maintains its faith in statistical inference, CP opts instead for few-cases comparisons. Substantively, while CP concentrates mainly on historical dynamics, macro phenomena, and processes of identity formation and transformation that take place *during* the unfolding of collective action episodes, the AS micro-founded approach has a good grasp on individual attitudes and purposes, but hardly accounts for institutional changes and structural dynamics, because macro-level states are generally considered exogenous to the model (Baldassarri 2006).

Not surprisingly, the analytical and empirical research traditions have grown apart, estranged from each other. As a by-product, formal models of collective action have focused on a narrow range of problems concerning the cognitive and structural conditions that enable self-interested actors to overcome the free-rider problem, while collective-action and social-movements scholars have pursued the broader task of providing comprehensive accounts of actual collective-action phenomena, taking little advantage of the methodological insights and analytical tools provided by formal theory.

In sum, while most of the research on formal models has revolved around the disparity between individual interest and collective optimality, both experimental and empirical research have consistently shown that such incongruence is not the rule. Moreover, actors' levels of cooperation are contingent on relational dynamics and contextual factors that favor the emergence of social norms and sanctioning systems. Therefore, to capture the distinctive nature of collective action, we need to start from a model of human action that goes beyond the give-and-take of individual and collective interest and captures the interplay between these two dimensions. Class *in se* becomes class *per se* when individual interest and group consciousness combine (Marx [1852] 1963): any consistent course of (collective) action ultimately depends on the availability of a shared representation of what constitutes the collective good (Pizzorno 1983).

Accordingly, the basic understanding that inspires this chapter is that collective action is made possible by the co-occurrence of individuals' interest and group identity, by, first, producing a shared representation of the collective good, and, second, inducing a consistent course of action. While scholars have mostly focused on the latter aspect, debating the consequentiality (or lack thereof) between common interest and collective action, this chapter shifts the focus to the first aspect, questioning what is usually taken for granted, namely the definition of the collective good, and discusses the role of social interactions, interpersonal influence, and conflict in shaping the formation and transformation of collective identities and interests. This shift will contribute to reducing the gap between analytical and empirical research.

In the next section I argue in favor of a synergy between formal models and empirical knowledge, with a specific focus on rare and conflictual forms of collective action (Sect. 17.1). I then summarize the scholarship on formal models of collective action and its main achievements in addressing the problem of cooperation among self-interested actors (Sect. 17.2). In the light of the most recent experimental findings and the legacy of empirical research, I sketch the lines of an understanding of collective-action phenomena that goes beyond the classical free-rider problem (Sect. 17.3) to account for the emergence of shared interests and collective identities (Sect. 17.4), by focusing on the role of conflict, social networks, and interpersonal influence, (Sects. 17.5 and 17.6), and of multiple levels of decision-making and actors' consciousness (Sect. 17.7).

17.1 ANALYTICAL MODELS FOR THE STUDY OF EXTRAORDINARY FORMS OF COLLECTIVE ACTION

Collective action is a quite heterogeneous concept, which entails a wide range of social phenomena. If asked to name cases of collective action, people usually refer to such rare cases as riots, revolutions, or coups d'état, while more frequent events, like blood donations or petitions, or examples from their everyday life, such as participation in voluntary associations, are less likely to come to mind.

This holds also for social scientists. Empirical research on collective action is disproportionately concerned with extraordinary events, usually involving a large and diverse pool of political actors, contentious issues, and some threat to the extant sociopolitical order.[1] There are good reasons to concentrate on singular, exceptional events that make the newspapers, among which is the fact that they have the potential to induce drastic rather than incremental changes, and have larger consequences on social and political assets.

Nonetheless, we should be aware of the difficulties entailed in the study of exceptional social phenomena. In fact, the regularity and predictability of events have an important role in guiding people's behavior as well as social research. Our capacity of inferring regularities from empirical data varies according to the frequency and predictability of the phenomena under investigation. There are two main reasons for this. The first is 'statistical': If the probability of observing a given event is low, it is extremely difficult to investigate the explicative factors that make such a phenomenon more or less likely to happen (Lieberson 1997). In other words, one needs a certain number of cases in order to disentangle regularity from contingency.

While this aspect concerns frequency, a second argument refers to the predictability of individuals' behavior. If actors have already engaged in a certain form of collective action, their behavior will be more predictable than the behavior of others acting under conditions they have never experienced before. Actors in ordinary cases of collective action can better select their means, and anticipate others' reactions and the consequences of their own action. In contrast, actors involved in nonordinary cases, such as revolutions, are less likely to know the outcome of their action, as very few of them have taken part in a revolution before (Kiser and Welser 2005). Actually, they do not even know that they are part of a revolutionary movement, or a revolt, or just a riot. It follows that in nonordinary cases contingency is higher than in ordinary cases, and therefore it is harder to discern robust mechanisms from case-specific factors.

In sum, it appears that those singular cases that are of greater interest to scholars are also more difficult to study empirically. Formal modeling, when informed by theoretical speculation and empirical evidence, can help. In general, the use of formal modeling is commendable in many fields of sociology (White 1963; Coleman 1973; Gilbert 1999; Edling 2002; Macy and Willer 2002; Baldassarri 2005; Hedström 2005; and in this book Breen; Macy and Flache), but there are additional, specific reasons for which it is crucial in advancing our understanding of collective-action phenomena. Among them is the fact that while empirical reality is, by definition, the single realization of a set of possible outcomes, formal modeling—especially when pursued through computer simulations—allows the exploration of the entire range of alternative outcomes. Traditionally this is achieved through 'computational experiments' in which researchers manipulate initial parameters and speculate about the necessary conditions that bring about a certain outcome. Alternatively, one can keep the initial set of parameters fixed and rely on stochastic processes to produce a multiplicity of outcomes and then study the source of such variability.[2] In both cases the advantage of an analytic approach is that social dynamics that are rarely observed in reality can be reproduced as many times as scholars want.

Granted that a formal model is useful as long as the assumptions on which it is based are simplifications but not complete distortions of reality,[3] collective-action research can greatly profit from the level of generalization that formal models require. By abstracting the behavior of individuals from their specific ideologies and other contextual factors, the analytical approach forces scholars to step away from case-specific and *ad hoc* explanations, test the robustness of their explanatory schemes, and define the scope conditions of their deployment. At the same time, formal models are informative to the extent that they capture the key features of those rare but denotative cases. There is little value in coming up with a highly formalized explanation of why people dress up for carnivals and parades, sing in choruses, or join the Elks (it will always remain a mystery anyway), while it is worth investigating through analytical tools those aspects of collective action—e.g. interpersonal influence and large-scale cascades of activism, conflict escalation and structural polarization, ideological commitment and shifting alliances—that are difficult to map empirically.

17.2 FORMAL MODELS OF COLLECTIVE ACTION AND THE PROBLEM OF COORDINATION

Analytical sociologists have mainly thought of collective action as a problem of coordination between self-interested actors (Elster 1989). In this framework, collective action has the characteristics of a social dilemma—which is 'a situation in which actions that are individually rational can lead to outcomes that are collectively irrational' (Heckathorn 1996: 250)[4]—and researchers' goal is to reveal the conditions under which rational, self-interested actors can overcome this dilemma.

The study of collective action was originally framed in these terms by Olson in *The Logic of Collective Action* (1965). Breaking with the previous research tradition based on the assumption that the presence of a common interest would (unproblematically) lead actors to mobilize, Olson argued that

> unless the number of individuals is quite small, or unless there is coercion or some other special device to make individuals act in their common interest, *rational, self-interested individuals will not act to achieve their common or group interests.*
>
> (1965: 2)

This is for the reason that, in a context in which public goods are nonexcludable, rational, self-interested actors would rather free-ride on others' contribution (Olson 1965; see also Hardin 1982; Oliver 1993). For years to follow, the main puzzle for collective-action scholars—and not only rational-choice ones[5]—became to explain under which conditions cooperation can emerge among self-interested actors. Olson himself offered a first solution to the problem, suggesting that rational actors are induced to contribute to the provision of public goods by the presence of 'selective incentives'—exclusive, private incentives that either reward participants or punish noncooperators. This solution, however, was shown to be tautological: since someone has to pay for selective incentives, their provision is a collective good itself, and thus subject to the free-rider problem.[6]

Indeed, very few aspects of Olson's seminal work were exempt from criticism. (For a summary see Oliver 1993; Ostrom 2003; Baldassarri 2005.) Nonetheless, virtually all subsequent formal models of collective action took on the free-rider problem while introducing important modifications to Olson's basic assumptions. First of all, scholars included *interdependence* between actors. To this goal, game theory provided a parsimonious framework for investigating the strategic choices of interdependent agents (Hardin 1982; Axelrod 1984, 1997; Coleman 1990; Ostrom 1990; Lomborg 1996). While an exhaustive account of this research can be found elsewhere (see Breen's chapter in this volume), here it is worth mentioning the influential contribution of Axelrod's *The Evolution of Cooperation* (1984), in which he showed how in a two-person *iterated* prisoner's dilemma cooperation among self-interested actors can eventually emerge.[7] Subsequently, Heckathorn extended the application of game theory to other social dilemmas[8] and studied the dynamics of these games in a two-dimensional game space, thus providing a comprehensive and elegant way to frame collective-action problems in game-theoretical terms (1996, 1998). Finally, Macy proposed a stochastic learning model of iterated prisoner's dilemma in which players adopt adaptive, backward-looking—instead of purposive, forward-looking—strategies, thus relaxing some of the strong rationality assumptions of previous models (Macy 1991a).

Analytically speaking, these are remarkable achievements. Nonetheless, one might ask to what extent our understanding of collective-action phenomena has been improved by referring to a 'situation between two individuals, . . . in which two people hurt each other more than they help themselves in making self-serving choices and could both be better off if obliged to choose the opposite' (Schelling 1978: 110). In other words, beside its elegance and power in framing the problem of cooperation in a two-actors system, one has to recognize the limitations of this analysis of strategic interaction when applied to events that unfold over time and involve large heterogeneous groups (Abbott 2001; Oliver and Myers 2002). According to Abbott,

> [g]ame theory won't get us far, because it is ignorant, except in the most general terms, of a serious concern with structure and with complex temporal effects. But simulation may help us understand the limits and possibilities of certain kinds of interactional fields, and that would be profoundly sociological knowledge.   (2001: 124)

Indeed, game theory is not the only formal approach to the study of collective action. Several scholars have used decision equations to further investigate individual dispositions and structural features that induce social actors to contribute to the provision of public goods.[9] Scholars working in this vein have strongly relaxed Olson's rational-choice assumptions and, generally, moved away from conceiving collective action as the mere by-product of the pursuit of private interest. Research has developed in many different directions (see Oliver 1993 for a summary). Extant formal models of collective action consider a range of foci including: the effect of compliance norms, group sanctions, and mutual influence (Obershall 1973; Heckathorn 1990, 1993; Gould 1993); population heterogeneity in resources, interest, and power and the shape of the production function (Marwell and Oliver 1993); processes of stochastic, adaptive-learning decision-making (Macy 1990, 1991b); threshold models and cascades (Granovetter 1978; Schelling 1978; Chwe 1999; Watts and Dodds 2007); network structure and actor's position (Macy 1990; Gould 1993; Marwell and Oliver 1993; Kim and Bearman 1997).

It is now common understanding among scholars that there is no 'single and simple' solution to the problem of collective action, and that substantial theoretical advances are more likely to occur when scholars break it down into more specific research issues. In general, distinct features of the collective-action phenomena give rise to different problems and related solutions. For instance, while free-riding is arguably the central problem in the provision of public goods—goods that are characterized by nonexcludability and jointness in consumption—we should also consider problems of over appropriation and over crowding if considering the provision of common-pool resources—situations in which one person's use reduces the amount of good available to others (Ostrom 1990, 2002). Another example in which the nature of the good affects the solution of the collective-action problem is Marwell and Oliver's finding (1993) that the role of early contributors depends on the shape of the production function:[10] a critical mass of original contributors is likely to trigger the participation of other people in a context in which the production function is accelerating, while when the production function is decelerating, early contributors are likely to provide enough good to induce everyone else to free-ride.

In all these studies collective action has been treated primarily as a problem of coordination. Despite the variety of arguments provided, the common explanatory strategy is to show how it is that individuals whose nonstrategic rationality suggests inaction are induced to adopt some sort of strategic view in which individual and collective interest come to coincide. Cooperation from self-interested actors is therefore induced through a modification of their cost/benefit calculus. In other words, the 'trick' is to show that the course of action induced by individuals' private interest is an action that leads toward the achievement of the collective good.

Durkheimians and functionalists, as well as lay observers, might be willing to question the fact that private and public interests can be told apart in the first place and label the conceptual distinction between individual interest and public good as purely fictional. But even scholars, like us, willing to ground our explanation in individuals' beliefs, actions, and interactions, might have something to gain from a proper understanding of the relation between individual and collective interests.

17.3 BEYOND THE FREE RIDER

While, on the one hand, the mere presence of shared interest is not sufficient condition for collective action (Marx [1852] 1963; Olson 1965), we do see collective action more often than suggested by the Olsonian model of self-interested actor. In recent years experimental research has accumulated consistent evidence of the fact that free-riding is not the default option for a large part of the population, even in the absence of selective incentives, normative pressure, or relational history.

For instance, let's consider the main findings of a classical public-goods game, where players are free to decide what part (if any) of their given endowment to contribute to the public good in a context in which when someone makes a contribution each player receives a proportion (i.e. 50 percent) of such a contribution. While the optimal group outcome would be for everyone to give their entire endowment, the optimal strategy for rational egoists is to contribute nothing. Ostrom, reviewing numerous experimental replications of this game, listed seven general findings:

(1) Subjects contribute between 40 and 60 percent of their endowments to the public good in a one-shot game as well as in the first round of finitely repeated games.
(2) After the first round, contribution levels tend to decay downward, but remain well above zero. . . .
(3) Those who believe others will cooperate in social dilemmas are more likely to cooperate themselves. . . .
(4) In general, learning the game better tends to lead to more cooperation, not less. . . .
(5) Face-to-face communication in a public good game—as well as in other types of social dilemmas—produces substantial increases in cooperation that are sustained across all periods including the last period. . . .
(6) When the structure of the game allows it, subjects will expend personal resources to punish those who make below-average contributions to a collective benefit, including the last period of a finitely repeated game. . . .
(7) The rate of contribution to a public good is affected by various contextual factors including the framing of the situation and the rules used for assigning participants, increasing competition among them, allowing communication, authorizing sanctioning mechanisms, or allocating benefits.   (2000: 140–1)

These findings require a theory of micro behavior based on something different from the fictional antagonism between actors' selfishness and group interest. In fact, a consistent proportion of individuals act in favor of the collective interest, sacrificing their own in order to contribute to the common good and/or punish defectors, even in contexts lacking selective incentives of any sort. In other words, the collective interest is shown to be an inherent—perhaps ancestral—part of individuals' choice. At present, most scholars have opted for assuming the existence of different types of individuals: according to Ostrom, in addition to *rational egoists*, there are *conditional cooperators* and *willing punishers*. Similarly, Fehr and Gintis (2007) came to the conclusion that

> self-regarding and norm-regarding actors coexist and that the available action opportunities determine which of these actors types dominate the aggregate level of social cooperation.   (p. 43)

Strong reciprocity, which is the predisposition to cooperate conditionally on others' cooperation and to punish defectors (Fehr and Gintis 2007), has become the alternative to selfishness as a basic building block of human behavior.[11]

Nonetheless, the fact that rational-choice theory is in troubled waters does not mean that an alternative is already available. In search of a new theoretical framework, some scholars have turned to evolutionary theories. Ironically, in the Darwinian tradition based on the idea of individual selection, altruism was viewed as an aberrant behavior. In contrast, more recent developments in evolutionary biology based on kin or group selection argue that the presence of some altruists might favor the survival of genes or group (Hamilton 1963; Price 1970; Trivers 1971; Dawkins 1976). Similarly, evolutionary psychologists suggest that different personality traits have developed over time and such phenotypic variation produces selective advantages at the group level (Sober and Wilson 1998). Finally, empirical evidence has been provided in favor of the 'social-brain hypothesis,' according to which primates' brains evolved to handle the complexity of their social system (Dumbar 1998) and to perform social functions like tactical deception (Whiten and Byrne 1988) and coalition formation (Harcourt 1989), rather than, as generally believed, to process ecological information.

Ostrom adopts an 'indirect evolutionary approach' to explain how norm-regarding actors have emerged and survived in a world of rational egoists, and assumes that (a) 'modern humans have inherited a propensity to learn social norms' (p. 143) and (b) actors evolve and adapt their preferences to material rewards.[12] The key idea here is that 'social norms may lead individuals to behave differently in the same objective situation depending on how strongly they value conformance with a norm' (Ostrom 2000: 144). While self-interested actors respond exclusively to objective payoff structures and are indifferent to the context, conditional cooperators value norms of reciprocity and change their intrinsic preferences according to their experiences. In this perspective, the study of the contextual and institutional aspects that favor the emergence and maintenance of social norms becomes central to the collective-action research agenda (Ostrom 1990, 1998, 2000).

While evolutionary theory can provide a systemic account for the existence of a basic tendency toward altruistic behavior, it is ill suited to capture the fine-grained contextual differences that determine the occurrence of collective action in certain settings rather than others, or to enlighten the specific mechanisms through which social norms are created, diffused, and internalized. In more general terms, evolutionary theory does not provide an alternative micro foundation for collective-action phenomena; it simply provides a framework that allows scholar to bypass the free-rider problem, without having to find a real alternative to the assumption of self-regarding actors.[13]

In contrast, a promising alternative comes from the empirical research that does not take individual interest and social norms as given, but rather investigates the process of their emergence and transformation. In a nutshell, according to this perspective, the distinctive feature of collective-action phenomena lies in the co-occurrence of identity and interest (Gamson 1990; Bearman 1993; Gould 1995). Without rejecting the idea that actors mobilize to pursue their interest, scholars working in this vein assume that 'most individuals act routinely to safeguard and sustain the central sources of meaning and identities in their lives' (McAdam [1982] 1999: xiii). Instrumental behavior occurs within the boundaries of what is admitted and considered possible in the social contexts to which individuals belong. Instead of assuming social norms or pre-existing identities as given, interstitial entities useful to explain deviations from selfish behavior, this approach regards dynamics of identity construction and group identification as part of the process that leads to the definition of both the individual and group interest.

The overlap between individual and collective interest that makes collective action possible is therefore the by-product of the emergence of collective identities from patterns of social interaction. Any consistent course of (collective) action ultimately depends on the availability of a shared representation of the collective good, and only the presence of a collective identity can generate a confidence in the individual that s/he will be capable of fulfilling her/his own interest in the long as well as in the short run (Pizzorno 1983).

A collective identity is a function of both the patterns of social relations experienced by the actors and its salience in the current political circumstances. Individuals lie at the intersection of multiple, even alternative, social spheres that contribute to shape their interests and define what is politically salient to them. Here is where we need an approach capable of accounting not only for people's willingness to cooperate, but also for dynamics of interest formation. What becomes politically salient to individuals emerges from the interplay of their own preferences and the patterns of relations in which they are embedded. At the macro level, 'participation identities,' which are identities capable of mobilizing collective action,

> are those that optimize on the trade-off between comprehensiveness (offering the advantage of a broad-band constituency) and social integration (ensuring sufficient levels of internal social linkage to make mobilization possible).   (Gould 1995: 202–3)

Formal organizations boost the scale of collective action by linking local collectivities and organizing multiple grievances into coherent narratives.

In this perspective, there is no need to assume norms or ideology (or some other metaphysical entity) as the driving force of people's commitment; the specific interest that becomes relevant to the individual and shared among group members is elicited through interaction and the experience of group affiliation. The local context—the proximate others—functions to activate certain interests and reduce the significance of others.

So far, formal models of collective action have assumed the public good, the common goal for which people mobilize, as an aspect exogenous to the model, something given, and nonproblematic. While for ordinary forms of collective action this is a plausible assumption, in the case of extraordinary forms the definition of what becomes *the* public good is likely to be the *endogenous* product of the collective action itself (Calhoun 1991; Loveman 1998).[14] This, as we will see, has consequences not only for the definition of the collective interest but also for shaping the structural and ideational preconditions that lead to collective action.

17.4 THE ORIGIN OF SHARED INTERESTS AND COLLECTIVE IDENTITIES

When they first started in October 1989, street demonstrations in Berlin were dominated by the hope of political reforms. East Germans wanted the reestablishment of the original socialist values. One of the most popular slogans was 'Wir sind das Volk' (We are the people). A Few weeks later the slogan changed into 'Wir sind ein Volk' (We are one citizenry/country) and the call for the reunification of East and West Germany overcame all the other demands (Corni 1995: 437–8). What happened in those few weeks? How is it possible that from a call for social reforms the movement shifted toward the request for reunification?

Quite often, during the earlier stages of collective action the definition of what is the common good—what it is that people are mobilizing for—is far from clear. From rebellious movements to the rise of new parties, the formation and transformation of public opinion, the political arena, and institutional settings are due to complex dynamics (e.g. group solidarity and political alignment, conflict escalation, cascades of activism) that simultaneously alter both the micro conditions and the macro contexts in which social actors operate. Individuals' hold composite and often alternative sets of preferences about social assets, and their primary interest and allegiance is shaped during the unfolding of the collective enterprise: actors' desires and preferences are modified, new issues substitute for old ones, and different sets of people enter the public arena eventually changing overall patterns of alliances (Tilly 1978; Kuran 1989; Lindemberg 1989). This makes collective action different from market situations. In pure economic transactions individuals' interest can be taken as given. In contrast, in phenomena of collective action what constitutes interest, the goal for which people mobilize, is a by-product of the mobilization itself (Calhoun 1991).

Questions like 'How does a collective good become collective?' 'How does a social identity emerge as a distinctive trait of a group of individuals?' can be addressed, allowing changes in the macrostructural configuration of people's preferences, and modeling local patterns of interaction as generative processes that affect and modify both micro behaviors and the emergent macrostructure. In doing so, formal modelers will be able to treat as endogenous aspects that are usually assumed as exogenous, such as the selection of the public good, the overall distribution of actors' interest and preferences, and the structural properties of the relational network in which people are embedded.

Scholars who have posed collective interest and identity as something that has to be explained have quite often stressed the importance of tangible relations—the network of multiple ties in which individuals are embedded—in determining collective identities and actors' sense of commitment (McAdam 1988; Calhoun 1991; Bearman 1993; Gould 1995). For instance, in his study of Parisians' protests Gould describes the interplay between actors' interaction and the construction of a collective identity in this way:

> the collective identity of workers as workers only emerges if the social networks in which they are embedded are patterned in such a way that the people in them can plausibly be partitioned into 'workers' and 'non workers'; but once this is possible, social conflict between collective actors who are defined in terms of this partition will heighten the salience and plausibility of the partition itself. The intensification of the boundary's cognitive significance for individuals will, in other words, align social relations so that becomes even more real.   (1995: 15)

Shared interest and collective identity arise from the interplay of patterns of micro relations and the alignments they generate at the macro level. Consequently, neither individual dispositions nor structural features can be assumed as stable properties, because their changes are constitutive aspects of collective-action phenomena. The next section speculates on some specific aspects of potential interest for modeling the emergence of collective interest and group identity. The goal here is not to come up with a generic 'wish list' of realistic elements that would be realistically impossible to translate into formal language or, even if that were technically possible, would end up changing the nature of the problem itself. Instead the intention is to elicit ideas for extending existing models, as well as inspiring new ones. Their formalization is only one step away.

17.5 CONFLICT, INTERPERSONAL INFLUENCE, AND NETWORK STRUCTURE

Models of collective action usually assume a pool of actors who will gain from the production of a certain good. Nonetheless, in a nontrivial part of collective-action phenomena there are also actors who could lose from its production, gain more from the pursuit of alternative goods, or who are initially truly indifferent to its provision. In studying such contentious cases we should start by assuming a set of potentially attainable goods (e.g. a park, free Internet access, and a new electoral law) and actors who hold different preferences on each of them. That is, actors can be for or against a certain good, or they can prefer an alternative good, like a parking area instead of a park. Indeed, many have argued that the essence of politics lies in the bipolar and inherently conflictual nature of the issues at stake (Schmitt [1927] 1996; Downs 1957; Hinich and Munger 1994), and more often than not collective decisions are dictated by the trade-off between alternative social choices. This is even more true for contentious episodes such as rebellions, popular uprisings, or revolutions, where mobilization presents itself as an alternative to the status quo.

Assuming actors that hold multiple and alternative views seems therefore a commendable strategy, as well as modeling social interactions and dynamics of interpersonal influence that affect and simultaneously are affected by such a multi-faceted set of interests. Olson aside, virtually all formal models of collective action have assumed some form of interdependence among actors and some have already explicitly included social networks and influence dynamics (Gould 1993; Kim and Bearman 1997). In addition, several scholars have investigated the dynamics of interpersonal influence to model group consensus and social cohesion (French 1956; Harary 1959; Abelson 1964; Friedkin and Johnsen 1990; Friedkin 1999), dynamics of ideological polarization (Abelson 1979; Nowak, Szamrej, and Latané 1990; Hegsel-mann and Krause 2002; Macy et al. 2003), collective decision-making (Marsden 1981), diffusion of fads (Watts and Dodds 2007), and the persistence of cultural differences (Axelrod 1997) and political disagreement (Huckfeld, Johnson, and Sprague 2004).

In modeling interpersonal relations and influence dynamics, two factors deserve close consideration: the selection of interaction partners which determines the structure of the actors' social network, and the process of interpersonal influence which determines the directionality of opinion change. Let us consider the first aspect. Structural differences (differences in the distribution of social relations) can induce populations with similar interest distributions at the individual level but very different collective behaviors because

> actors subject to cross-pressures of one kind or another are less likely to participate in collective decisions than people who receive consistent signals from their social environments. (Marsden 1981: 1216)

For instance, if actors' likelihood to join a movement is a function of the number of activists they personally know, then the distribution of movement activists across the population is extremely important. In general, while empirical research seems to suggest that dense social networks (Obershall 1973; Tilly 1978; McAdam 1988; Gould 1995; Diani 1995) and closely interconnected niches of activists (Pfaff

1996; Osa 2001) facilitate collective action, the results from formal models lead to discordant conclusions with respect to the impact of different network structures and the structural position of core activists on collective-action outcomes. Marwell and Oliver (1993) have found that network density and, under certain conditions, centrality favor collective action; Gould (1993) has suggested instead a complex relation between network centrality and mobilization that depends on the structural position of early initiators. According to Macy (1991a), collective action has more chance in sparse networks, because random defection is less likely to spread through the population. For Kim and Bearman, instead, social-network density always facilitates collective action; nonetheless, fundamental to mobilization 'is the organization of motivated actors into a densely linked activist core that is insulated from counter-pressures encouraging defection' (1997: 90). While most of the discordance derives from substantial differences in their core assumptions, all these models share the limit of relying on a *static* relational structure.

A promising alternative is to model *dynamic* networks as they emerge from the unfolding of social interactions (see Moody's chapter in this volume). In real life, people have some freedom in choosing their interaction partners, and even greater liberty in deciding what they want to talk about; in sum, actors adapt their behavior to the characteristics of their interactants. This 'ability to tell people apart' (Macy 1991a: 833) can be modeled by giving people the option of 'exit' or remaining 'loyal' to an interaction partner (or probabilistically, becoming more or less likely to interact with a certain actor) depending on the outcome of previous interactions (Macy 1991a), and on their similarities (Macy et al. 2003; Baldassarri and Bearman 2007). This has the double effect of introducing an element of historicity and human agency into the model.

A similar sensitivity to the relational dimension of social phenomena should be introduced when modeling processes of interpersonal influence. Social influence is not an accidental phenomenon, like a sneeze, or an unintentional one, like a yawn. While the diffusion of a disease occurs through physical contact, the modification or reinforcement of someone's interest or identity implies sustained forms of interaction. Many models of diffusion are mechanic (either deterministic or probabilistic) consequences of actors' contact: encounters induce changes in status. Such models are of limited use for collective-action dynamics. Most empirical studies of group dynamics and persuasive communication suggest that while interaction with similar (or liked) others reduces distance, interaction with dissimilar others may increase distance leading to group polarization (Kitts 2006). The direction of opinion changes should be modeled as contingent on interactants' relative position. Mechanisms of dissonance reduction (Festinger 1957) might in fact both work in favor of *compromise* and feed *conflict*, depending on whether individuals will be more balanced by reducing or exacerbating the differences between them.

17.6 FROM CONFLICT, COOPERATION

To give a suggestion of how these ideas can be implemented, I adapt to our discussion of the origin of collective goods results from a model of interpersonal influence over political attitudes that Peter Bearman and I have developed to study the simultaneous evolution of interest and social relations in a context in which people hold preferences on multiple issues.[15] Let us assume a context in which people have preferences on four different public goods, such as use of public spaces, provision of public services, security, and so on. For each good, actors' preferences range from a strong interest in one outcome to a strong interest in the alternative outcome (e.g. use a public space to build a park versus a parking area). Preferences are originally normally distributed, which means that at the outset the majority of people have only very mild preferences for the one or the other outcome.

In general, actor a's likelihood of getting into a discussion with actor b depends both on his personal level of interest in public goods and on the affinity of interests between them. Specifically, the mechanisms that govern interaction are:

- for each actor, the frequency of interaction is proportional to the overall level of interest in public goods
- actors tend to interact with others that have preferences similar to their own
- actors can change interlocutors from time to time
- actors retain information about others' preferences and adjust their future behavior accordingly
- actors are likely to discuss the public good that is most salient to them

These interactions provide the foundation for personal influence, which might operate to bring people closer together or induce greater distance. That is, when interlocutors share the same view, interaction leads to a *reinforcement* of their belief. Where discussants differ, either *compromise* or *conflict* can result. If they have contrasting views on the focal good, but share similar opinions on the remaining goods, they compromise by reducing their interest on the focal good. In contrast, if disagreement is across the board, their interest on the focal issue is reinforced and their respective positions diverge further.

Influence is bidirectional, opinion change is incremental, and its magnitude is inversely related to actor's interest. In sum, we model opinion change as an interpersonal process, where the intensity and direction of the change depends on the relative position of discussion partners. Intensity is a function of the difference in the level of interest of the two interlocutors. Direction is determined by the signs of their preferences.

We studied the model through computer simulations. Due to stochastic processes, the model generates qualitatively different outcomes. In a large majority of cases goods are discussed at comparable rates and interactions give rise to a cohesive discussion network. In contrast, in some rare cases we observe a very different dynamic. Discussions disproportionally focus on a single public good (e.g. use of a public space), people's interest in that good grows, the interest distribution becomes bipolar (i.e. people are either strongly for the park or strongly for the parking area), and their patterns of relation crystallize into a polarized network. When a single good dominates public discourse, actors segregate themselves into homogeneous niches of dense interaction, reinforcing each other's commitment and reducing the chances to get in touch with actors that have an alternative view on the focal good.

As interest grows, of course, actors' likelihood of mobilizing will rise as well. According to this model, the attitudinal and social polarization associated with the takeoff of a single good is a precondition to collective action. That is, the emergence of a collective interest—an interest that dominates the public discussion—and the formation of social identities, in the form of sustained niches of social interaction,[16] occur together. These two dimensions are interdependent. Meaningful social partitions are less likely to arise in the absence of polarizing goods. At the same time, interest polarization on a specific good is of little consequence if it is not encoded into crystallized relational patterns. In sum, the model shows that collective action is made possible by the simultaneity of collective identity and interest.

At the micro level, the model reveals an interesting irony. The emergent relational network tends to minimize individual exposure to disagreement, independent of its overall macrostructural features. This induces a selective perception of the external reality—individuals are disproportionately exposed to people who share their attitudes—that can transform, in the context of the action over the long run, otherwise negligible changes into tangible achievements. In other words, actors interacting on the basis of their individual interest in public goods are capable of self-segregating into homogeneous 'ideological enclaves' where collective action is nurtured. This is, of course, exactly why shared interests and identities play such a strong role in fostering actors' commitment to their political beliefs and consequent action.

Finally, this model provides a basic intuition of the role played by contentious dynamics in shaping collective interest. Collective-action scholars, 'chasing' cooperation, never thought of finding its roots in social conflict. But by allowing actors to have multiple and alternative preferences it is possible to show how a distinct collective interest can coalesce from dynamics of social interaction and interpersonal influence in which people learn to 'tell each other apart' and split into opposite camps, thus producing the motivational and structural preconditions for local cooperation. In the next section I speculate on the dynamics through which these niches of local cooperation can cumulate in large-scale-collective-action phenomena.

17.7 GROUPS, MULTIPLE LEVELS OF DECISION-MAKING, AND ACTORS' CONSCIOUSNESS

By definition, collective action is characterized by noncentralized decision-making: while a strong leader or institution can be very effective in forcing individuals to contribute to the provision of public goods, phenomena characterized by such binding decisions do not belong to the collective-action domain. Nonetheless, noncentralized decision-making processes do not necessarily imply 'disorganized' choices, although this seems to be standard for formal modelers.

This is in sharp contrast with empirical reality. Granted that macro outcomes emerge from the composition of individuals' behavior, such composition does not necessarily occur as the 'algebraic' sum of individuals' decisions. Common strategies, selection of means, timing, division of labor, leadership, are all aspects of collective action that imply organization and harmonization of multiple actors. Organizations, associations, and groups, regardless of their grade of institutionalization and bureaucratization, are the critical movers between single actors and their common goal. On the one hand, they satisfy members and shape their attitudes, on the other, they introduce discontinuity between micro and macro dimensions—they solve problems of coordination. In sum, organizations mediate, translate, and synchronize individuals' efforts.

Formal models of collective action seldom consider the role of groups and other agencies of intermediation. This is a limitation, especially in modeling high-risk, large-scale phenomena for which it is necessary to take into account the scale and temporal discontinuities induced by multiple layers of decision-making. While collective action problems of the kind: 'the residents of Maple Street generally agree that they would like it to be cleaner than the city keeps it' (Gould 1993: 183) can be properly modeled by questioning the behavior of other neighbors if Betty volunteers an hour picking up refuse, this simple focus on the action and reaction of individual actors is not sufficient when referring to nonordinary forms of collective action.

Organized groups might have a nonlinear impact on the aggregation of individual participants, thus leading to qualitatively different collective-action outcomes. Social-movement organizations not only provide people with a reason to believe that their small contribution would not be wasted, but also create the preconditions for the incremental cumulation of mobilizing efforts—if nobody has written a petition, it is not possible to sign one (Gould 1993). Moreover, in many contexts the group's rationality is higher than the individuals' and therefore decision-making processes at the organizational level can be modeled in purely instrumental terms (McAdam [1982] 1999). Finally, if we adopt Coleman's dynamic view of 'long-term social change' as a process 'in which social organization comes to be the creation of human intelligence' (Coleman 1989: 9), civil-society and social-movement groups should be regarded as corporate actors that have an autonomous impact on social outcomes, by mediating between individuals' desires and common interest.

Of course, when introducing new features into a model, it is not sufficient to evaluate their realism, one should ask to what extent they might lead to new results. The explicit consideration of multiple levels of decision-making can help reformulate the debate on the effectiveness of small and large groups (Oliver 1980; Ostrom 2003) by showing how intermediate actors are able to bring together the narrow interest of small, relatively homogeneous groups and generate significantly larger and more heterogeneous mobilizing collectives (cf. Hedström, Sandell, and Stern's concept (2000) of meso-level networks). Along this line, coalition theories, cooperative games, and public-choice models can be used to model dynamics of group formation, intergroup alliances, and interest realignment (Neumann and Morgenstern 1944; Gamson 1961; Riker 1962; Axelrod 1970; Laver and Schofield 1998; Bandyopadhyay and Chatterjee 2006).

A second reason why collective action cannot be reduced to the aggregation of individual choices concerns the consciousness collective actors have of the necessity to be 'many.' Too often, explanatory models of cooperative behavior

> assume that the process leading to collective action occurs behind actors' backs, i.e., that actors' understanding of how collective action works is less accurate than the modelers' understanding.   (Gould 1993: 194)

Instead of purposive actors (Weber 1922; Coleman 1990), formal models are often populated by interest-driven automata with limited or no agency. In contrast, empirical research and experimental evidence have suggested that persuading other actors and sanctioning defectors are constituent parts of individuals' behavior that should be modeled in their individual-interest function. This has consequences not only for actors' mobilization but also for the definition of the collective good itself. Consider a trivial example: three friends want to spend the entire week-end sailing, but at least six people are needed in order to handle the boat. Our three friends invite other acquaintances to join them. While the organizers are strongly interested and motivated, the pool of other potential participants is less enthusiastic and their participation is contingent on the weather, alternative schedules, etc. Likely, to recruit others, the three organizers will limit their sail to Sunday afternoon.

Quite often, the number of earliest actors available for mobilization does not reach the number needed to produce the collective good. To facilitate the participation of others, earliest actors are likely to change their immediate goals. But the pool of new joiners might differ from the original set of activists with respect to their attitudes and desires, and this change in the composition of the overall-attributes distribution might have consequences on the group strategy and eventually modify the ultimate goal of the collective enterprise.

In problems of aggregation, changes in the size and composition of the pool of potential joiners are often unimportant. A market transaction is a market transaction and it does not matter to the buyer and seller whether thousands of others are exchanging goods or not.[17] The exchanges made by other people need simply to be 'parameterized' in the individual-decision function. In contrast, when actions are not only interdependent—in the sense that they have consequences on other actors' utility functions—but the goal of a specific action is collective, the pool characteristics—the characteristics and desires of potential activists—become relevant in defining the action itself. It follows that at the aggregate level we do not observe the simple composition of individual actions, or of interdependent actions. At the aggregate level we observe an outcome that is somehow consciously drifted by a—more or less explicit—bargaining process. While people buying and selling, or neighbors moving in and out (Schelling 1971) do not feel responsible for the construction of markets or the process of shaping the class or ethnic characteristics of a neighborhood, people involved in collective action do act consciously toward a goal that is reached together or not reached at all. This makes the macro outcome less likely to be a by-product of individual choices than a deliberate decision that is based on actors' rational understanding of the situation.

Conclusion

The formal approach to collective action sketched in these pages builds on a theory of action according to which instrumental action occurs within the boundaries of what is defined as meaningful and worth pursuing by the situation and social context in which actors are embedded. Such an approach is simultaneously less and more rational than the one currently in use among analytical sociologists. It is less rational—better, differently rational—in the sense that individual interest cannot be disentangled from group interest and is partly defined by group expectations. In this perspective, the collective good is neither a social construction, in the sense that it is based on real, material interests, nor the mere consequence of objective conditions. What comes to be perceived as a collective good is the by-product of individual preferences and patterns of social relations.

At the same time, this approach implies higher rationality in the sense that individuals are assumed capable of foreseeing the benefit of collective action and consciously acting to achieve it. Collective action among purposive actors who hold multiple and often alternative sets of preferences involves dynamics of persuasion, alignment, and coalition-building. To fully capture these aspects of human agency, we needed a model in which individuals' attitudes, social structure, and the collective interest itself are not fixed, predefined aspects exogenous to the model; rather, they are shaped in interaction sequences.

Overall, this framing shifts the analytical focus from coordination problems to key features of collective-action phenomena that have been, so far, largely neglected; namely, the origin of collective goods, the role of conflict, the interplay between individual attitudes and social networks, multiple levels of decision-making, actors' consciousness, and the incorporation of collective interest into the definition of individual interest. This shift has the potential to enrich analytical sociology's repertoire of explanatory mechanisms.

NOTES

1. Empirical research is also subject to a second bias, concerning the specific content of collective-action phenomena. In the last few decades scholars have devoted dispro-portionate attention to mobilization on progressive issues; e.g. civil-rights, minority, antiglobalization, and peace movements, compared to the rare scholarship on army recruitment, pro-war movements, and traditional religious groups. Similarly, scholars have privileged topics concerning different aspects of globalization, shifting their research attention away from the myriads of ordinary activities that (still) take place at the local level and are local in scope.

2. See e.g. Medina (2005) for an innovative use of evolutionary game theory to generate probabilistic predictions, such as 'the *relative likelihoods* of cooperation and defection' (p. 425).

3. In this regard, the 'as if' condition, according to which a model is useful as long as it produces accurate predictions, without necessarily being based on 'realistic' assumptions (Friedman 1953), is not an acceptable standard. Since we are in the business of revealing the social mechanisms that underlie certain social phenomena, we need to make sure that not only the results but also the building blocks of our models are reasonable.

4. For a more rigorous (and restrictive) definition of the concept of social dilemma see Van de Rijt and Macy, working paper.

5. As Oliver observes (1993), the influence of Olson's argument was not limited to rational-choice scholars. Even resource-mobilization and political-opportunity theo-ries (McCarthy and Zald 1973; McAdam [1982] 1999) did not assume collective action as a natural consequence of collective interest, but rather as something that is hard to achieve.

6. This is commonly known as the second-order free-rider problem (Frohlich and Oppenheimer 1970; Oliver 1980; Heckathorn 1989).

7. 'What the Prisoner's Dilemma captures so well is the tension between the advantages of selfishness in the short run versus the need to elicit cooperation from the other player to be successful in the longer run' (Axelrod 1997: 6).

8. Specifically, he linked the problem of trust to the prisoner's dilemma, coordination to the assurance game, bargaining to the chicken game, and overcooperation to the altruist's dilemma.

9. It is worth noticing that the two analytical strategies have often been combined.

10. The production function is a function that relates individual contributions to group outcomes. A linear function implies that each individual contribution translates into a constant unit of public good (and therefore that the effect of an individual contribution does not depend on the level of public good that has already been provided). Instead we would use an accelerative production function if initial contributions are assumed to provide disproportionately more collective benefit than later contributions, while if the reverse is true, a decelerative production function is appropriate.

11. Similar conclusions have been reached with respect to the study of empathy (Davis, Luce, and Kraus 1994; Sautter, Littvay, and Bearnes 2007) and altruism (Andreoni, Harbaugh, and Vesterlund 2007) in prisoner's-dilemma games.

12. Under these assumptions, if actors were to have complete information about the other players, conditional cooperators would get the higher payoff, while with no information only rational egoists would survive. In the (real) world of incomplete information, cooperative types will survive in substantial numbers.

13. Similarly, looking at the empirical and historical research on collective action, structuralists and culturalists have moved numerous critiques to the rational-choice approach, but they have not yet elaborated real alternatives (McAdam [1982] 1999).

14. Indeed, to explain social revolutions, even rational-choice theorists had to recognize the socially constructed nature of individuals' preferences; that is, the fact that actors' perception of their own influence on the production of a collective good is larger than the actual influence (Klandermans 1984; Muller and Opp 1986; Lindenberg 1989).

15. The model and its results are extensively described elsewhere (Baldassarri and Bearman 2007).

16. Such niches are the necessary context in which collective sanctions and compliance norms, norms of fairness, or selective incentives can effectively operate.

17. Although the size of the market has to be large enough to guarantee exchangeability of actors.

REFERENCES

ABELSON, R. P. (1964), 'Mathematical Models of the Distribution of Attitudes under Controversy', in N. Frederiksen and H. Gulliksen (eds.) *Contributions to Mathematical Psychology* (New York: Holt, Rinehart, & Winston), 142–60.

—— (1979), 'Social Clusters and Opinion Clusters', in P. W. Holland and S. Leinhardt (eds.), *Perspectives on Social Network Research* (New York: Academic), 239–56.

ABBOTT, A. (2001), *Time Matters: On Theory and Method* (Chicago, Ill.: University of Chicago Press).

ANDREONI, J., HARBAUGH, W. T., and VESTERLUND, L. (2008), 'Altruism in Experiments', in S. Durlauf and L. Blume (eds.), *The New Palgrave Dictionary of Economics*, 2nd edn. (Basingstoke/New York: Palgrave Macmillan) and at <http://www.dictionaryofeconomics.com/dictionary>, accessed 2008.

AXELROD, R. (1970), *Conflict of Interest* (Chicago, Ill.: Markham).

—— (1984), *The Evolution of Cooperation* (New York: Basic).

AXELROD, R. (1997), 'The Dissemination of Culture: A Model with Local Convergence and Global Polarization', *Journal of Conflict Resolution*, 41: 203–26.

BALDASSARRI, D. (2005), 'Oltre il free rider: l'utilizzo di modelli formali nello studio dell'azione collettiva', *Rassegna Italiana di Sociologia*, 40 (1): 125–56.

—— (2006), 'A Relational Approach to Collective Action: Analytical and Empirical Investigations', Ph.D. thesis (University of Trento).

—— and BEARMAN, P. (2007), 'Dynamics of Political Polarization', *American Sociological Review*, 72: 784–811.

BANDYOPADHYAY, S., and CHATTERJEE, K. (2006), 'Coalition Theory and Its Applications: A Survey', *Economic Journal*, 116 (509): F136–55.

BEARMAN, P. (1993), *Relations into Rhetorics: Local Elite Social Structure in Norfolk, England: 1540–1640* (New Brunswick, N.J.: Rutgers University Press).

BLUMER, H. (1951), 'Collective Behavior', in A. M. Lee (ed.), *New Outline of the Principles of Sociology* (New York: Barnes & Noble), 167–222.

CALHOUN, C. (1991), 'The Problem of Identity in Collective Action', in Joan Huber (ed.), *Macro–Micro Linkages in Sociology* (Newbury Park, Calif.: Sage), 51–75.

CHWE, M. S. (1999), 'Structure and Strategy in Collective Action', *American Journal of Sociology*, 105: 128–56.

COLEMAN J. J. (1973), *The Mathematics of Collective Action* (London: Heinemann).

—— (1989), 'Rationality and Society', *Rationality and Society*, 1: 5–9.

—— (1990), *Foundations of Social Theory*, (Cambridge, Mass.: Harvard University Press).

CORNI, G. (1995), *Storia della Germania* (Milano: Il Saggiatore).

DAVIS, M., LUCE, C., and KRAUS, S. J. (1994), 'The Heritability of Characteristics Associated with Dispositional Empathy', *Journal of Personality*, 62: 371–91.

DAWKINS, R. (1976), *The Selfish Gene* (Oxford: Oxford University Press).

DELLA PORTA, D., and DIANI, M. (2006), *Social Movements: An Introduction* (Malden: Blackwell).

DIANI, M. (1995), *Green Networks: A Structural Analysis of the Italian Environmental Movement* (Edinburgh: Edinburgh University Press).

—— (2003), 'Network and Social Movements: A Research Program', in M. Diani and D. McAdam (eds.), *Social Movements and Networks: Relational Approaches to Collective Action* (Oxford/New York: Oxford University Press), 299–319.

DOWNS, A. (1957), *An Economic Theory of Democracy* (New York: Harper & Row).

DUMBAR, R. I. M. (1998), 'The Social Brain Hypothesis', *Evolutionary Anthropology*, 6 (5): 178–90.

EDLING, C. R. (2002), 'Mathematics in Sociology', *Annual Review of Sociology*, 28: 197–220.

ELSTER, J. (1989), *The Cement of Society: A Study of Social Order* (Cambridge: Cambridge University Press).

FEHR, E., and GINTIS, H. (2007), 'Human Motivation and Social Cooperation: Experimental and Analytical Foundations', *Annual Review of Sociology*, 33: 43–64.

FESTINGER, L. (1957), *A Theory of Cognitive Dissonance* (Evanston: Row, Peterson).

French, J. R. (1956), 'A Formal Theory of Social Power', *Psychological Review*, 63: 181–94.

FRIEDKIN, N. E. (1999), 'Choice Shift and Group Polarization', *American Sociological Review*, 64: 856–75.

—— and JOHNSEN, E. C. (1990), 'Social Influence and Opinions', *Journal of Mathematical Sociology*, 15: 193–206.

FRIEDMAN, M. (1953), 'The Methodology of Positive Economics', in Friedman, *Essays in Positive Economics* (Chicago, Ill.: University of Chicago Press), 3–43.

Frolich, N., and OPPENHEIMER, J. A. (1970), 'I Get By With a Little Help From My Friends', *World Politics*, 23: 104–20.

GAMSON, W. A. (1990), *The Strategy of Social Protest*, 2nd edn. (Homewood, Ill.: Dorsey).

GILBERT N. (1999), 'Simulation: A New Way of Doing Social Science', *American Behavioral Scientist*, 42: 1485–8.

GINTINS, H., et al. (2003), 'Explaining Altruistic Behavior in Humans', *Evolution and Human Behavior*, 24: 153–72.

GOULD, R. V. (1993), 'Collective Action and Network Structure', *American Sociological Review*, 58: 182–96.

—— (1995), *Insurgent Identities: Class, Community, and Protest in Paris from 1948 to the Commune* (Chicago, Ill.: University of Chicago Press).

GRANOVETTER, M. (1978), 'Threshold Models of Collective Behavior', *American Journal of Sociology*, 6: 1420–43.

HAMILTON, W. D. (1963), 'The Evolution of Altruistic Behaviour', *American Naturalist*, 97: 354–6.

HARARY, F. (1959), 'A Criterion for Unanimity in French's Theory of Social Power', in D. Cartwright (ed.), *Studies in Social Power* (Ann Arbor, Mich.: Institute for Social Research).

HARCOURT, A. H. (1989), 'Sociality and Competition in Primates and Non-primates', in V. Standen and R. Foley (eds.), *Comparative Socioecology* (Oxford: Blackwell), 142–52.

HARDIN, G. (1968), 'The Tragedy of the Commons', *Science*, 162: 1243–8.

HARDIN, R. (1982), *Collective Action* (Baltimore, Md.: Johns Hopkins University Press).

HECKATHORN, D. (1989), 'Collective Action and the Second-order Free-rider Problem', *Rationality and Society*, 1: 78–100.

—— (1990), 'Collective Sanctions and Compliance Norms: A Formal Theory of Group Mediated Social Control', *American Sociological Review*, 55: 366–84.

—— (1993), 'Collective Action and Group Heterogeneity: Voluntary Provision Versus Selective Incentives', *American Sociological Review*, 58: 329–50.

—— (1996), 'The Dynamics and Dilemmas of Collective Action', *American Sociological Review*, 61 (2): 250–77.

—— (1998), 'Collective Action, Social Dilemmas and Ideology', *Rationality and Society*, 10 (4): 451–79.

HEDSTRÖM, P. (1996), 'Rational Imitation', in P. Hedström and R. Swedberg (eds.), *Social Mechanisms* (Cambridge: Cambridge University Press), 306–27.

—— (2005), *Dissecting the Social: On the Principles of Analytical Sociology* (Cambridge: Cambridge University Press).

—— and SWEDBERG, R. (1998), *Social Mechanisms* (Cambridge: Cambridge University Press).

—— SANDELL, R., and STERN, C. (2000), 'Mesolevel Networks and the Diffusion of Social Movements: The Case of the Swedish Social Democratic Party', *American Journal of Sociology*, 106 (1): 145–72.

HEGSELMANN, R., and KRAUSE, U. (2002), 'Opinion Dynamics and Bounded Confidence: Models, Analysis, and Simulation', *Journal of Artificial Sciences and Social Simulation*, 5 (3), at <http://www.jasss.soc.survey.ac.uk/index_by_issue.html>, accessed 2008.

HINICH, M., and MUNGER, M. (1994), *Ideology and the Theory of Political Choice* (Ann Arbor, Mich.: University of Michigan Press).

HUCKFELD, R., JOHNSON, P. E. and SPRAGUE, J. (2004), *Political Disagreement: The Survival of Diverse Opinions within Communication Networks* (Cambridge: Cambridge University Press).

KIM, H., and BEARMAN, P. S. (1997), 'The Structure and Dynamics of Movement Participation', *American Sociological Review*, 62: 70–93.

KISER, E., and WELSER, H. T. (2007), 'The Microfoundations of Analytic Narratives', *Sociologica*, 3.

KITTS, J. A. (2006), 'Social Influence and the Emergence of Norms Amid Ties of Amity and Enmity', *Simulation Modeling Practice and Theory*, 14: 407–22.

KLANDERMANS, B. (1984), 'Mobilization and Participation: Social Psychological Expansions of Resource Mobilization Theory', *American Sociological Review*, 49: 583–600.

KORNHAUSER, W. (1959), *The Politics of Mass Society* (Glencoe, Ill.: Free Press).

KURAN, T. (1989), 'Sparks and Prairie Fires: A Theory of Unanticipated Political Revolution', *Public Choice*, 61: 41–74.

LAVER, M., and SCHOFIELD, N. (1998), *Multiparty Government—The Politics of Coalition in Europe* (Ann Arbor, Mich.: Ann Arbor).

LEBON, G. [1895] (1896), *The Crowd: A Study of the Popular Mind* (New York: Macmillan).

LIEBERSON, S. (1997), 'Modeling Social Processes: Some Lessons from Sports', *Sociological Forum*, 12: 11–35.

LINDENBERG, S. (1989), 'Social Production Functions, Deficits, and Social Revoutions', *Rationality and Society*, 1 (1): 51–77.

LOFLAND, J. (1996), *Social Movement Organizations: Guide to Research on Insurgent Realities* (New York: de Gruyter).

LOMBORG, B. (1996), 'Nucleus and Shield: The Evolution of Social Structure in the Iterated Prisoner's Dilemma', *American Sociological Review*, 61: 278–307.

LOVEMAN, M. (1998), 'High-risk Collective Action: Defending Human Rights in Chile, Uruguay, and Argentina', *American Journal of Sociology*, 104 (2): 477–525.

MCADAM, D. [1982] (1999), *Political Process and the Development of Black Insurgency: 1930–1970* (Chicago, Ill.: University of Chicago Press).

—— (1988), *Freedom Summer* (New York: Oxford University Press).

—— MCCARTHY, J., and ZALD, M. N. (1996), *Comparative Perspectives on Social Movements: Political Opportunities, Mobilizing Structures and Cultural Framing* (Cambridge: Cambridge University Press).

—— TARROW, S., and TILLY, C. (2001), *Dynamics of Contention* (Cambridge: Cambridge University Press).

MCCARTHY, J. D., and ZALD, M. (1973), *The Trend of Social Movements in America: Professionalization and Resource Mobilization* (Morristown, N.J.: General Learning).

—— (1977), 'Resource Mobilization and Social Movements: A Partial Theory', *American Journal of Sociology*, 82: 1212–41.

MCPHAIL, C. (1991), *The Myth of the Madding Crowd* (New York: de Gruyter).

MACY, M. W. (1990), 'Learning Theory and the Logic of Critical Mass', *American Sociological Review*, 55: 809–26.

—— (1991a), 'Learning to Cooperate: Stochastic and Tacit Collusion in Social Exchange', *American Journal of Sociology*, 97: 808–43.

—— (1991*b*), 'Chains of Cooperation: Threshold Effects in Collective Action', *American Sociological Review*, 56: 730–47.

—— and WILLER, R. (2002), 'From Factors to Actors: Computational Sociology and Agent-based Modeling', *Annual Review of Sociology*, 28: 143–66.

—— et al. (2003), 'Polarization in Dynamic Networks: A Hopfield Model of Emergent Structure', in R. Breiger, K. Carley, and P. Pattison (eds.), *Dynamic Social Network Modeling and Analysis* (Washington, D.C.: National Academy Press).

MARSDEN, P. V. (1981), 'Introducing Influence Processes into a System of Collective Decision', *American Journal of Sociology*, 86: 1203–35.

MARWELL, G., and OLIVER, P. E. (1993), *The Critical Mass in Collective Action: A Microsocial Theory* (New York: Cambridge University Press).

MARX, K. [1852] (1963), *The Eighteenth Brumaire of Louis Bonaparte* (New York: International).

MEDINA, L. F. (2005), 'The Comparative Statics of Collective Action: A Pragmatic Approach to Games with Multiple Equilibria', *Rationality and Society*, 17 (4): 423–52.

MELUCCI, A. (1989), *Nomads of the Present* (Philadelphia, Pa.: Temple University Press).

MULLER, E. N., and OPP, K.-D. (1986), 'Rational Choice and Rebellious Collective Action', *American Political Science Review*, 80: 471–89.

NEUMANN, J. VON, and MORGENSTERN, O. (1944), *Theory of Games and Economic Behavior* (Princeton, N.J.: Princeton University Press).

NOWAK, A., SZAMREJ, J., and LATANÉ, B. (1990), 'From Private Attitude to Public Opinion: A Dynamic Theory of Social Impact', *Psychological Review*, 97 (3): 362–76.

OBERSHALL A. (1973), *Social Conflict and Social Movements* (Englewood Cliffs, N.J.: Prentice Hall).

—— (1993), *Social Movements: Ideologies, Interests and Identities* (New Brunswick, N.J.: Transaction).

OLIVER, P. E. (1980), 'Rewards and Punishments as Selective Incentives for Collective Action: Theoretical Investigations', *Americal Journal of Sociology*, 85: 1356–75.

—— (1993), 'Formal Models of Collective Action', *Annual Review of Sociology*, 19: 271–300.

—— and MYERS, D. J. (2002), 'Formal Models in Studying Collective Action and Social Movements', in B. Klandermans and S. Staggenborg (eds.), *Methods of Research in Social Movements* (Minneapolis, Minn.: University of Minnesota Press).

OLSON, M. (1965), *The Logic of Collective Action* (Cambridge, Mass.: Harvard University Press).

OSA, M. (2001), 'Networks in Opposition: Linking Organizations Through Activists in the Polish People's Republic', in M. Diani and D. McAdam (eds.), *Social Movements and Networks: Relational Approaches to Collective Action* (Oxford/New York: Oxford University Press), 77–104.

OSTROM, E. (1990), *Governing the Commons: The Evolution of Institutions for Collective Action* (New York: Cambridge University Press).

—— (1998), 'A Behavioral Approach to the Rational Choice Theory of Collective Action', *American Political Science Review*, 92 (1): 1–22.

—— (2000), 'Collective Action and the Evolution of Social Norms', *Journal of Economic Perspectives*, 14 (3): 137–58.

—— (2003), 'How Types of Goods and Property Rights Jointly Affect Collective Action', *Journal of Theoretical Politics*, 15 (3): 239–70.

PARK, R. E. (1930), 'Collective Behavior', in Edwin R. Seligman (ed.), *Encyclopedia of the Social Sciences* (New York: McMillan), iii: 631–3.

PFAFF, S. (1996), 'Collective Identities and Informal Groups in Revolutionary Mobilization: East Germany in 1989', *Social Forces*, 75 (1): 91–118.

PIZZORNO, A. (1983), 'Sulla razionalità della scelta democratica', *Stato e Mercato*, 7: 3–46.

PRICE, G. R. (1970), 'Selection and Covariance', *Nature*, 227: 520–1.

RIKER, W. H. (1962), *The Theory of Political Coalitions* (New Haven, Conn.: Yale University Press).

SAUTTER, J. A., LITTVAY, L. and BEARNES, B. (2007), 'A Dual-edged Sword: Empathy and Collective Action in the Prisoner's Dilemma', *ANNALS of the American Academy of Political and Social Science*, 614 (1): 154–71.

SCHELLING, T. (1978), *Micromotives and Macrobehavior* (New York: Norton).

SCHMITT, C. [1927] (1996), *The Concept of the Political*, trans. George D. Schwab (Chicago, Ill.: University of Chicago Press).

SMELSER, N. J. (1962), *Theory of Collective Behavior* (New York: Free Press).

SNOW D. A., et al. (1986), 'Frame Alignment Processes, Micromobilization, and Movement Participation', *American Sociological Review*, 51: 464–81.

SOBER, E., and WILSON, D. S. (1998), *Unto Others: The Evolution and Psychology of Unselfish Behavior* (Cambridge, Mass.: Harvard University Press).

TARROW, S. (1994), *Power in Movement: Social Movements, Collective Action, and Politics* (Cambridge: Cambridge University Press).

TILLY, C. (1978), *From Mobilization to Revolution* (Reading: Addison/Wesley).

—— (2008), 'Describing, Measuring, and Explaining Struggle', *Qualitative Sociology*, 31 (1): 1–13.

TRIVERS, R. L. (1971), 'The Evolution of Reciprocal Altruism', *Quarterly Review of Biology*, 46: 35–57.

VAN DE RIJIT, A., and MACY, M. 'Social Dilemmas: Neither More nor Less', working paper.

WATTS, D., and DODDS, P. (2007), 'Influentials, Networks and Public Opinion Formation', *Journal of Consumer Research*, 34 (4): 441–58.

WEBER, M. [1922] (1968), *Economy and Society*, trans. and ed. G. Roth and C. Wittich (New York: Bedminster).

WHITE, H. (1963), 'Uses of Mathematics in Sociology', in J. C. Charlesworth (ed.), *Mathematics and the Social Sciences: The Utility and Inutility of Mathematics in the Study of Economics, Political Science, Sociology* (Lancaster: American Academy of Political and Social Sciences), 77–94.

WHITEN, A., and BYRNE, R. (1988), 'Tactical Deception in Primates', *Behavioral Brain Science*, 12: 233–73.

....

CHAPTER 18

CONDITIONAL CHOICE*

....

MEREDITH ROLFE

INTRODUCTION

....

WHAT do buying a pair of jeans (Bearden and Rose 1990), expressing political attitudes or choosing a political candidate (Berelson, Lazarsfeld, and McPhee 1954; Niemi 1974; Zuckerman 2005), prescribing tetracycline (Coleman, Katz, and Menzel 1966), implementing a policy reform (Mintrom 1997; Simmons and Elkins 2006), clapping in a standing ovation (Miller and Page 2004), eating bagels or other foods (Latané 1996), wearing belts (Axelrod 1997), choosing a restaurant (Granovetter and Soong 1988), and liking the latest hit on the radio (Salgarik, Dodds, and Watts 2006) all have in common? The people involved—consumers, voters, doctors, policy makers, or radio listeners—are influenced by the people around them. Their actions, in other words, are conditionally dependent: what one person does depends in part on what others are doing.

Conditional decision-making research spans many disciplines and analytical approaches, yielding a rich but unruly proliferation of specialized literatures that have defied orderly synthesis. Previous reviews are limited to a particular decision model (e.g. diffusion) and are often organized around empirical variables used

* Special thanks for comments or special assistance go to Scott Blinder, Peter Bearman, Adrienne LeBas, Michael Dawson, Tom Snijders, Anne Shiu, and Nick Collier. Portions of this chapter are based upon work supported by the National Science Foundation under Grant No. 0453076.

in research (Valente 1995; Strang and Soule 1998; Rogers 2003; Greenhalgh et al. 2005). This chapter takes a different approach, identifying theoretical explanations of variation in the trajectory and outcome of conditional decision-making processes from a review of the various formal literatures, both mathematical and simulation-based.

When individuals make conditional decisions, only a limited number of formal mechanisms can explain variation in the resulting social activity. Obvious explanations stem from variation in individual decision-making: what individuals do before observing others (initial activity); how individuals respond to the observed actions of those around them (conditional decision rules); and how resistance to influence is introduced into the process. Less intuitive explanations, meanwhile, invoke social networks: the size of a group; the structure of the relevant networks of influence; social cleavages; and the location of particularly influential individuals within a social network.

This chapter introduces and details each of these formal mechanisms. Section 18.1 provides a brief introduction to conditional decision-making, defining key words and concepts used throughout the chapter. Section 18.2 introduces conditional decision rules and initial states of activity, describing how together they shape the basic trajectory and outcome of a conditional decision-making process. Section 18.3 reviews possible sources of resistance to influence, describing how unconditional actors pull all other group members towards their position, and how individual variation in resistance to influence can stop a process from reaching complete conformity. Section 18.4 addresses patterns of social interaction, which work in combination with resistance to influence to explain variation in activity among individuals or groups.

18.1 WHAT IS CONDITIONAL DECISION-MAKING?

Conditional decision-making refers to both the set of models that assume conditional decisions, and the process generated by that assumption. Just as game theory is not limited to prisoners' dilemmas or coordination games, conditional decision-making is not limited to diffusion or threshold models. Numerous specific models described in the literature (see Table 18.1 at the end of this chapter for examples) meet the sole requirement for classification as a conditional decision model: actors make decisions using rules that are conditional on the actions of others.[1]

Conditional decision-making also refers to a dynamic decision-making process or sequence of states of activity. When individuals base their actions or opinions on what other people do or say, any small change (initial activity) sets off a chain reaction of conditional decision-making. If ten people decide to buy a new iPod, some of their friends will buy one as well, and then the friends' friends will join in, and so on. This dynamic trajectory of changes in activity will eventually settle down to a stable outcome state. Stable states may be characterized by convergence to complete or partial conformity, where everyone does the same thing or holds the same opinion, or multipeaked outcomes, in which there is a greater diversity of social action.

Empirical research generally seeks to explain variation in outcomes or trajectories of change in activity. Explaining outcomes might involve understanding why some innovations that inspire initial activity spread successfully (e.g. iPods), while others fizzle out (e.g. Beta VCRs). We wonder why in some situations all actors eventually adopt the same approach (e.g. use of the Australian ballot in American elections (Walker 1969)) but in others they do not (e.g. not everyone wears the same brand of jeans, or votes for the same political candidates). Alternatively, why is the same outcome reached in processes that follow very different trajectories? For example, the tipping point leading to widespread adoption may come only after a long and steady buildup of activity (e.g. public support for recycling), or it may occur virtually overnight (e.g. cultural fads).

To identify possible explanations, I develop a systematic framework to organize and synthesize results from a range of conditional decision models. Game theory again provides a helpful parallel, isolating four key aspects of a strategic situation: players, strategies, payoffs or utility functions, and information. Similar key components fully describe a conditional decision situation: actions, decision rules, information, and networks. Brief descriptions of the key components and related parameters of conditional decision models appear in the Glossary, while Table 18.1 characterizes well-known models using the same framework.

GLOSSARY

(a) Important terms

Basic dynamic The likely trajectory and outcome of a conditional decision-making process, ignoring the impact of model factors related to resistance to influence and social networks. Depends on three factors: type of action, conditional decision rules, and initial activity (Sect. 18.2).

Conditional decision model factors or parameters Formal elements of a conditional decision-making model that can take on different values. These parameters are classified as aspects of: (1) action, (2) decision rules, (3) information about others, and (4) networks of social interaction (see App. (b)).

Critical point or mass Proportion of the population that must adopt an action before a particular conditional decision-making process tips from one likely outcome to another.

Initial activity Actual state of activity prior to observation of the choices of other people. May be described as initial-opinion distribution, or situation where only initial actors are active. Examples of initial actors: first movers, unconditional actors, innovators, index case.

Outcome Stable state of activity, in which no one changes what they are doing; equilibrium.

Complete Conformity An outcome state in which all actors do the same thing.

Partial Conformity An outcome state in which most actors do the same thing (binary action) or the distribution of attitudes is unimodal (continuous action).

Multipeaked An outcome state in which the distribution of attitudes is multimodal (continuous action) or a substantial portion of actors are engaged on both sides of a binary action or in more than one categorical action.

Resistance to influence Umbrella term for model factors which decrease conditional responsiveness. Includes unconditional actors, partial resistance, fixed decisions, deterministic threshold rules, and memory (Sect. 18.3).

State of activity Complete description of what all actors are doing at a particular moment in time.

Trajectory Dynamic set of all states of activity between initial state and outcome state.

(b) Conditional decision model parameters

Action The decision, behavior, or attitude statement to be modeled or explained. A better term to use is practice (Strang and Soule 1998; Wedeen 2002), but the term 'action' will be used in keeping with the rest of the volume. Examples: joining in a riot, adopting a new technology, contributing money to a campaign, expressing support for health-care spending.

Type of action The metric in which the action is expressed. Includes binary, continuous, ordinal-categorical, nominal-categorical (Sect. 18.2.1).

Fixed action An actor might have repeated opportunities to change her mind. If so, the length of time after which an action can be changed or revised is specified. If there is no chance to change her mind, the action is fixed. Fixed actions are found in threshold, diffusion, and herding models (Sect. 18.3.4).

Decision rules Decision rules tell the actor to engage in an action with some probability.

Initial activity rules Rules which assign actors to their initial state of activity. Rules may assign activity randomly, or according to some characteristic of the actor (e.g. conditional or unconditional decision rules, attributes, social location) (Sect. 18.2.3).

Conditional decision rule A rule that assigns a probability of action as a function of what other people are doing. Includes threshold or stochastic focal point rules, linear mean matching rules, and less frequently uses rules incorporating unimodal or decreasing functions (Sect. 18.2.2).

Unconditional decision rule A rule that assigns a constant probability of engaging in an activity. Actors rely either partially or completely on unconditional rules (Sects. 18.3.1 and 18.3.2).

Heterogeneous distribution Specifies which decision rules are used and by what proportion of the population, when all actors do not use the same rule (Sect. 18.2.2).

Stochastic rule A decision rule that allows for random fluctuation or errors, as opposed to deterministic rules as often found in threshold models (Sect. 18.3.3).

Information Parameters specifying what an actor can observe about other people.

Actor attributes Actors may have particular attributes, which might or might not be observable by other actors (Sect. 18.4.3).

What is observed What information about an individual is available to other actors. Includes attributes, actions, decision rules (Sect. 18.3.4).

Updating sequence In parallel or synchronous updating, actors revise their decisions simultaneously. In asynchronous updating, one or several actors at a time make a decision at each time point (and others can observe these changes immediately).

Memory Do actors respond only to behavior observed during the present time step? If decision rules are conditional on observed behavior extending back over several time steps, a memory rule is required for updating across multiple observations (Sect. 18.3.4).

Networks Umbrella term for factors which change the patterns of social interaction among actors.

Interaction space The topology of potential interactions (e.g. all-see-all, grid/torus, specific-network-structure). Actors who choose interaction partners are limited by this space (Sect. 18.4.2).

Active choice of interactions Do actors choose their friends? If yes, specify rules for selection (Sect. 18.4.3).

Actor movement Can actors move in space? If yes, specify rules for movement (Sect. 18.4.3).

Social location Particular actors (e.g. early movers, strong leaders) may be placed into particular social locations (e.g. near other early movers, on the end of a full or partial cleavage, in well-connected-network positions) (Sect. 18.4.4).

18.2 THE BASIC DYNAMIC

When conditional decision-making characterizes an action or opinion expression, everyone in the group will (theoretically) end up agreeing on an opinion or doing the same thing. Of course, political opinions, consumer choices, and other social practices are often characterized by the coexistence of social influence with lasting variation in opinion or behavior. Resistance to influence and breaks in network connectivity can keep a system of conditional decision-makers from reaching complete agreement (Abelson 1964). While these obstacles to agreement are considered later in the chapter, this section looks at the basic dynamic of conditional decision models absent these complications. Three factors shape the basic trajectory and likely outcome states produced by a conditional decision-making process: the type of action, the distribution of decision rules, and the initial state of activity.

18.2.1 Action types: binary, categorical, and continuous

As with any empirical variable, actions may be classified as binary, categorical, or continuous; examples of each appear in Table 18.1. Given the inherently binary nature of action (you either do something or you don't), many social situations can be represented as offering a binary choice (or string of such choices) of whether or not to engage in some activity—such as protesting in the street, putting a campaign sign in the front yard, or voting in an election. A continuous action goes beyond a simple yes-or-no decision; examples include donations of money or time to volunteer organizations.

Categorical choice sets, either ordinal or nominal, are less common, but do have clear empirical analogues. Examples of ordinal actions include a voter choosing between multiple political parties aligned in a left–right issue space (Downs 1957) or a consumer choosing between products assessed along multiple dimensions (Bettman, Luce, and Payne 1998). Nominal categories are also intuitively appealing as a representation of cultural practices or social identities (Axelrod 1997; Lustick, Miodownik, and Eidelson 2004).

The key mathematical distinction between action types is between actions that produce linear or nonlinear dynamics.[2] A system with nonlinear elements such as discrete actions (binary, nominal, or categorical) or nonlinear decision rules (fixed or stochastic focal point) does not change outcome states gradually, but may suddenly shift from one likely outcome to another (or one stable state to another) at a particular critical point, also known as the tipping point or critical mass.[3] The sudden shifts, or phase transitions, are difficult to predict in real-life examples of nonlinear decision-making, but they are mathematically well understood (i.e. we know when they will occur in mathematical models and what sorts of changes in model parameters produce them). In any specific nonlinear decision model, the expected impact of changes in resistance to influence and social networks depends in part on the location of critical points.

Despite this significant difference between standard continuous-opinion models and other forms of conditional decision-making, the formal mechanisms driving these processes are similar. Both types of decision processes converge to a single point in the absence of resistance to influence or network cleavages; initial activity and the distribution of decision rules determine the likely trajectory and outcome; and only assumptions that introduce resistance to influence or changes in social interaction alter this basic dynamic. Differences are noted throughout the chapter: the initial trajectory of binary actions is more complex, a single unconditional actor has less influence over the outcome of binary models, and different assumptions produce partial and/or multipeaked convergence.

18.2.2 Distribution of conditional decision rules

Conditional decision rules are both the defining element of conditional choice models and the key factor affecting the likely outcome and trajectory of the decision-making process. This section introduces the three most common functional forms used to represent conditional decision rules and discusses empirical and motivational justifications for each. Next, I consider how decision-rule distributions affect the likely trajectory and outcomes of conditional action, and discuss how decision rules are used in empirical research.

A conditional decision rule expresses an actor's decision as a function of what others around her are doing (e.g. definitely vote for Labour if the majority of her friends are voting Labour). Most research incorporates conditional decision-making using one of three rules: (1) fixed or threshold focal point matching, (2) stochastic focal point matching (often median matching), or (3) linear matching (often mean matching).[4] Figure 18.1 provides an example of each of these rules, where the graphically represented rule gives the continuous opinion point or probability that a focal actor will engage in some action (y-axis) as a function of the average decision of her friends (x-axis).

Both fixed threshold (Fig. 18.1(a)) and stochastic (Fig. 18.1(b)) focal point matching rules are often described as a preference for conformity, but actors using focal point rules might be engaged in rational imitation (Hedström 1998) or contributing to a public good with an accelerating production function (Oliver 1993), rather than bandwagoning or bowing to social pressure. Members of a crowd who will only join in a riot once others have started rioting, people who change their minds if three of their neighbors agree, and decision makers who try to imitate the majority can be modeled using threshold focal point rules (see Table 18.1). Similar in spirit to threshold rules, stochastic or continuous focal point matching rules assume that even actors with a focal point of participation in mind (say 20 percent of their friends, or half of the crowd) may not change actions at that exact focal point every time. Subjects in public-goods experiments use focal point matching rules when making decisions about continuous actions, such as deciding how much money to contribute (Fischbacher, Gächter, and Fehr 2001).

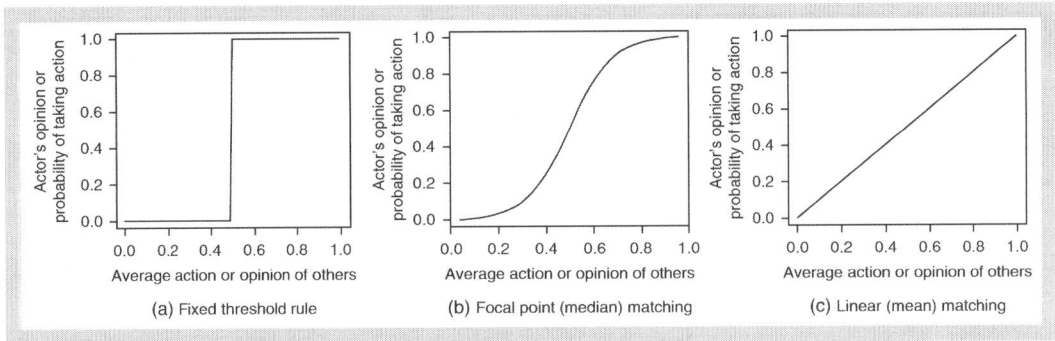

Fig. 18.1 Three common conditional decision rules

The linear mean matching rule (see Fig. 18.1(c)) maps an individual's decision to the average of her friends' opinions, and is often used to describe changes in continuous opinions (see Table 18.1). Gould (1993) proposed that neighbors facing a social dilemma might respond fairly to the contributions of others using egocentric linear matching rule (with slope less than 1). Group members facing public goods with decelerating production functions, and who nonetheless wish to claim full credit for doing their fair share, may also rely on linear rules. Evidence confirms that up to half of all subjects rely on the 'fair share' mean matching rule in public-goods experiments (Ledyard 1995). Linear matching may also describe actors in a status competition who desire to 'keep up with the Joneses'.[5]

Many of the models featured in Table 18.1 include homogeneous actors using the same decision rule; however, empirical evidence favors heterogeneous rule distributions. Individuals facing the same decision situations use different conditional rules (Ledyard 1995; Offerman, Sonnemans, and Schram 1996): some people might be wholly or largely immune to influence, while others quickly adopt new habits from friends. Different situations might also yield different rule distributions even among similar populations (Fehr and Gächter 2000; Casari and Plott 2003). A distribution of rules allows for multiple types of decision makers (e.g. innovators, crowd followers, elite adopters), and numerous potential motives (e.g. guilt, fairness, conformity) in the same situation. Cutting-edge formal work addresses how heterogeneity of conditional responses affects the likely trajectory and outcome of conditional decision processes (Delre, Jager, and Janssen 2007; Young 2007).

While all conditional decision-making processes follow a basic trajectory toward conformity, the shape of this trajectory depends on the conditional rules in use. In models of continuous opinions the decision rule determines whether a group is more likely to move towards an average or more extreme point on the continuum. Individuals responding linearly to the average opinion of those around them converge to the mean of the initial distribution of opinions (Abelson 1964; Hegselmann and Krause 2002), while focal point rules move opinion towards the extremes. Situationally specific use of linear versus nonlinear decision rules by actors expressing (continuous) opinions may be a potent explanation of varying outcomes of group decision-making processes. Juries and other deliberative groups often polarize when participants hold similar positions on one side of an issue, but moderate when initial opinions are evenly distributed (Isenberg 1986; Sunstein 2002). This pattern might reflect differential usage of decision rules in the two situations: nonlinear rules within a group with a shared identity, and linear rules when groups cross identity boundaries. The use of nonlinear rules may capture the effects of competition for status or power within a social group.

Meanwhile, binary choices produce one of three possible types of trajectories (Dodds and Watts 2004). In 'critical mass' models—where only a few people are spurred into action by the initial adopters of a new idea—the adoption curve is initially flat, and the behavior will fizzle out unless there is a sufficient critical mass of early adopters. In 'vanishing critical mass' models where people respond quickly to the actions of others, the curve shoots up faster, as a smaller critical mass is required for widespread diffusion. 'Epidemic' models are particularly responsive in the early stages (e.g. some or all people respond exponentially to exposure), thus resulting in an assured epidemic within the population even with low levels of initial activity. In general, widespread diffusion is more likely when people facing binary decisions rely on unconditional adoption, linear matching (at the mean or above) or low focal point rules. A larger proportion of high focal point or self-regarding linear rules make diffusion less likely, as these rules reduce early responsiveness.

Conditional rules are therefore a vital element of any explanation involving conditional decision-making. Research may start with an empirical assessment of decision rules in a particular situation. These assessments are used in conjunction with either simulations of conditional decision-making in the particular situation or the rules of thumb outlined in the preceding paragraphs to gain substantial insight into the dynamics of influence in that situation. Section 18.4 contains several examples of theory-testing using dynamics predicted from observed conditional responsiveness.

When conditional responses cannot be directly observed, creative approaches can incorporate the impact of decision rules on the likely trajectory and outcome of conditional decision processes. For example, Young (2007) compares the curve produced by two different individual-level models of conditional decision-making (social learning and simple imitation) to data on when farmers adopt a new hybrid corn. He finds that farmers are directly influenced by the decisions of other farmers, regardless of the payoffs of those decisions. Similarly, Axtell and Epstein (1999) compare real data on the age of retirement for people affected by a change in retirement law to the predicted retirement decisions made on the basis of rational choice and conditional decision-making. These data support the claim that most of the gradual shift to earlier retirement age was produced by social imitation, not rationality. In both cases the authors generate precise estimates of the decision-making dynamic and compare these estimates to observed behavior to assess theories of individual decision-making.

18.2.3 Initial state of activity affects the basic outcome

While the distribution of decision rules sets the basic trajectory of opinion change in a given situation, the initial state of activity determines the likely outcome of the conditional decision-making process. In a simple binary choice or diffusion model, initial activity that meets or exceeds the critical-mass level (as dictated by the degree of conditional responsiveness of decision-making) will ensure widespread diffusion, while lower levels of initial activity will eventually fizzle out. Initial activity can also be used to predict the outcome of continuous-opinion processes. For example, as noted above, when jury members update their opinions by averaging across the opinions of other jurors, all juror opinions will converge to the average of the group's initial statements about the appropriate size of the award.

In applied research, the initial state of activity can either be estimated on the basis of observed data or assumed for the purposes of theory-testing. In some cases initial activity is observed, for example the first American state or states adopting a new policy, or the first farmers adopting hybrid corn. In other cases researchers might model variation in initial activity to explore whether it can explain variation in the trajectory or outcome of a given conditional decision process. For example, Rolfe (2005a) examines whether variation in voter turnout in different populations might stem from different levels of initial, unconditional activity.

What empirical factors influence the level of initial activity? Initial activity may vary with properties of the action itself; some products or ideas may simply be more appealing than others. Buying an iPod is fun; volunteering to clean up litter is not. Thus, we expect more initial or early adopters for the iPod. It is tempting to extend this analogy and assume that popular products are always intrinsically better than their competitors, and thus initially chosen by more people. While this may well be true for the iPod, the popularity of an activity is not a simple function of its intrinsic qualities.

Initial adoption rates may also stem from characteristics of the people making choices, rather than the choice itself. As a possible example, in the USA those under the age of forty have led the way in pursuing ethical consumer goods and a 'green lifestyle,' while baby boomers have lagged behind. The younger population may contain more people willing to adopt new consumption patterns and lifestyles than the older demographic group with well-established habits and less time or motivation to seek out new consumption options. Thus, the same action might have a higher baseline probability of initial adoption in one population than another, generating greater diffusion in the younger population, even if members of both groups respond to initial activity at similar rates. Finally, if the initial activity level in a group is assumed to be random, some groups will randomly end up with more initial activity than others. Thus, different outcomes across different groups may be due to chance. The luck of the draw in initial states is linked to explanations based on group-size effects, as discussed below.

18.3 RESISTANCE TO INFLUENCE

In this section I review several ways of incorporating resistance to influence into mathematical models of conditional decision-making, highlighting situations in which these approaches are (or are not) empirically plausible. First, unconditional actors resist influence entirely, and can alter the likely outcome of a conditional decision-making process. Second, individuals who refuse to completely abandon their own initial opinion may slow down or completely halt the process of convergence, although partial resistance to influence is not a complete explanation of polarized opinions. Third, fixed decision rules produce multipeaked outcomes that are not robust to small changes in the model. Fourth, fixed actions capture resistance to influence of a different form, and thus threshold models are a reasonable approximation of decision-making in some situations.

18.3.1 Unconditional actors affect the direction of convergence

Even in conditional decision-making processes some people may make decisions independently of others' actions. Unconditional action is characteristic of innovators of a new idea or product (Rogers 2003), first movers in collective action (Elster 1989), altruistic cooperators in social dilemmas (Ledyard 1995), and committed ideologues in political debates. Unconditional action may be motivated by personal preferences, but these preferences need not be innovative or prosocial; strategic actors following an equilibrium strategy may also be unconditional actors. As detailed below, individual differences in learning or information-processing might also produce differences in unconditional action. For example, unconditional actors might be slow to update opinions, or struggle to interpret social signals, or have strong prior reasons for believing they are correct, either habitually or in a particular situation.

Unconditional actors can alter the expected outcome of a conditional decision-making process in several ways. In conditional decision-making processes involving binary actions, unconditional actors may provide the critical mass required to ensure diffusion and thereby determine the outcome of the process. Unconditional opposition to a new idea or behavior, however, will increase the size of the necessary critical mass and thus reduce the likelihood of widespread adoption. In continuous-opinion dynamics, one person who refuses to change her mind drags everyone else in the population towards her position, as long as those other people are even partially open to influence (Friedkin and Johnsen 1997). Multiple unconditional actors produce multipeaked outcome states (Boccara 2000; Flache and Torenvlied 2001). Psychological studies of influence are consistent with this result. Both consistent minorities (Bond and Smith 1996) and self-confident individuals (Zarnoth and Sniezek 1997) can influence the positions of other subjects, even when the influentials hold an incorrect view.

18.3.2 Partial resistance to influence

In many cases individual resistance to influence is distributed in smaller doses throughout the population instead of being concentrated in a few unconditional actors. Partial resistance may be captured by an unconditional element in the decision rule, or by a gradual increase in weight put on one's own former opinion. Partial resistance to influence produces partial convergence to the expected outcome in continuous choice models, but usually only slows down convergence in binary choice models. Individual differences in experiences and beliefs (Friedkin 1999; Hegselmann and Krause 2002) or preferences and payoffs (Bikhchandani, Hirshleifer, and Welch 1992) may result in independent, individual predispositions to particular attitudes or choices. In such cases conditional decision-making rules incorporate a weighted, unconditional element (see Table 18.1). This modeling approach can help recover the hidden dynamics of conditional decision-making that lie beneath stable patterns of observed opinions (Friedkin 1999, 2001). It is less satisfying as an explanation of cultural emergence, as it assumes the pre-existence of the diverse opinions it purports to explain.

Individuals may vary in the strength with which they hold onto their prior opinions. Some models allow opinions to 'harden', as actors who are initially open to influence place progressively larger weights on their own current opinion (Chatterjee and Seneta 1977).[6] Latané and Nowak (1997) use a related technique to capture variation in personal conviction in a binary choice model, allowing actors to put a substantial weight on their own prior (but not necessarily initial) opinion. Either modeling approach could be justified on the basis of Bayesian learning, the tendency of opinions to become more fixed with age (Visser and Krosnick 1998), or differences in lay theories of personality (Dweck and Leggett 1988).[7]

Crucially, if a substantial portion of the population facing a continuous choice is even partially resistant to influence, the group will never converge completely (Friedkin 1999; Hegselmann and Krause 2002). Incomplete convergence in combination with linear decision rules produces opinions centered on a single opinion or action, but with some distribution around the mean opinion (partial convergence). In contrast, partial resistance to influence does not prevent nearly complete convergence to uniform positions in a binary choice model (Lewenstein, Nowak, and Latané 1992; Dodds and Watts 2004), although it slows down the process substantially and may produce a series of semi-stable steps along the way. Just as a single unconditional actor could change the direction of convergence in a continuous (but not binary) opinion model, partial resistance to influence changes the final outcome of continuous (but not binary) choice processes.

18.3.3 Fixed decision rules

Some simulated conditional decision models produce diverse outcome states (e.g. Latané and Nowak 1997; Huckfeldt, Johnson, and Sprague 2004; Lustick, Miodownik, and Eidelson 2004), although analytical results from the same models predict complete conformity (Lewenstein, Nowak, and Latané 1992; Klemm et al. 2003; Dodds and Watts 2004). Why do the simulation results differ from analytical expectations? It is tempting to attribute the difference to the impact of local community, but this is not the complete answer (Lewenstein, Nowak, and Latané 1992). Simulated binary (and probably categorical) choice models that combine threshold or fixed focal point rules and local network structure produce multipeaked outcomes, but such outcomes are generally not robust.[8]

When minority clusters result from a combination of fixed thresholds and local interactions, they will disappear if actors make stochastic decisions or interact in irregular formations or with randomly selected long-distance neighbors (San Miguel et al. 2005). Latanés social impact theory (see Table 18.1), however, allows for both of these possibilities and continues to produce minority clusters. In this case the social impact theory is the exception that points us to the more important principal driving the maintenance of local minority clusters: boundary protection. Local clusters are sustained by individuals who are strongly resistant to influence, and thus form a stable boundary between majority and minority groups (Latané 1996), often surrounded by other strong-minded or easily influenced actors who reinforce their commitment. These individuals effectively cut off communication between the majority and minority groups in the network, and function as a break in network connectivity (see Sect. 18.4).

Although boundary protection is unlikely to work in such a literal fashion, other forms of boundary policing do protect the distinctive character of social groups. Punishment of norm violation is typically seen as prosocial or altruistic (Boyd et al. 2003), but both political leaders and ordinary citizens punish group members who take moderate political positions.[9] Parties use partisan whips to control legislators while in session, and may even use deliberate violence to bloody the hands of moderate party leaders (LeBas 2006). African American students actively resist and even censure black conservatives (Harris-Lacewell 2004), and partisan citizens censure candidates who move to the middle on core party issues (Morton, Postmes, and Jetten 2007). Pressure to adhere to the norms of a particular social identity can undermine the moderating influence of generalized social interaction. As mentioned earlier, people may even use different decision rules when responding to others with a shared social identity.

While it is easy to account for the difference between simulations and formal analysis of binary choice models, a considerable disjunction remains between the actions of real people facing binary decisions and those of simulated actors following conditional decision rules. If people make conditional decisions but remain partially resistant to influence, we would expect continuous opinions to partially converge to a single point while binary opinions largely converge to a uniform position. While it is true that responses to continuous measures such as political ideology appear partially convergent, vote choice and responses to binary questions that probe party identification are multipeaked and not uniform. Future research should distinguish conditional decision-making in controlled responses to questions about personal attitudes from conditional decision-making in the affective, implicit responses that govern binary evaluations and actions.

18.3.4 Thresholds: fixed actions and memory

The previous section showed that fixed threshold rules introduce a nonrobust form of resistance to influence, and may produce misleading results when used in simulations. Nonetheless, stochastic conditional decision-making produces threshold dynamics when: (1) actions are fixed for the course of the decision-making process, or (2) memory of past observations shapes actors' choices. A multipeaked or partial-conformity outcome is likely when initial activity is at or below the critical point of the model.

Actions are clearly fixed when: a decision is difficult to revise (e.g. legislative adoption of an innovative policy reform); an individual expresses verbal or written commitment to an action (McAdam 1986; Ostrom, Walker, and Gardner 1992); or subsequent decisions are not interesting to the researcher (e.g. whether doctors stopped prescribing tetracycline). Repeated decisions may still exhibit threshold dynamics in any given 'round' of decision-making if a person is unable or unlikely to change her mind within a given period of time. Opinion statements made during the course of a single discussion might follow this type of path-dependent process (Wood 2000), as group members defend statements they made early in the discussion. Group members reflecting back on the discussion several days later, however, may undergo lasting opinion change better represented by simultaneous updating of mutable opinions.

Threshold models may also capture stochastic decision-making when people respond conditionally to expectations of others based on memories of previous interactions.[10] Most people decide whether or not to be helpful and fair multiple times a day. Should I wash the dishes or leave them for someone else; get paper for the copier or leave it for a coworker? While each decision is binary, memories of repeated decisions fall along a continuous scale. Thus, when people base conditional decisions on memories of past activity, two outcomes are likely. First, greater levels of cooperation are likely than might be expected on the basis of a single interaction (Chwe 1999). Second, behavioral diversity is more likely in groups where a large portion of the population relies on linear conditional decision rules.

Not all repeated decisions are characterized by threshold dynamics. Repeated decisions that can be revised on the basis of instant feedback may produce conformity, even when memory-based responses produce behavioral diversity. For example, subjects faced with a public-goods dilemma contribute around 50–60 percent of the maximum possible in a one-shot game or in the first round of a repeated game (Ledyard 1995). When the public-goods game is repeated several times with the same group of subjects, however, contributions partially converge towards zero. This behavior can be reproduced almost exactly by simulated actors who draw on the same distribution of conditional contribution rules used by real-life subjects (Ledyard 1995; Fischbacher, Gächter, and Fehr 2001). Threshold models produce an average contribution rate of 50–60 percent, while revisable, stochastic decision processes almost completely converge to the noncooperative equilibrium (Rolfe 2005a).

18.4 THE CONTINGENT EFFECT OF LOCAL NETWORKS

Social influence requires social interaction. Not surprisingly, then, the structure of social interaction greatly affects social dynamics. Changes in patterns of social interaction can speed up or slow down the conditional decision-making process, but rarely alter the baseline outcome unless the connectivity of a network is fundamentally altered (Abelson 1964). Below, I consider the four factors, either alone or in conjunction with resistance to influence, most likely to impact conditional decision-making processes: group size, local-network structure, social cleavages and friendship selection, and social location of influential actors.

18.4.1 Group size

In some situations individuals in groups have information about large numbers of others, such as crowds at a protest or fans at a soccer game. In these situations larger groups will conform more closely to the expected trajectory and outcome of the basic dynamic than smaller groups. For example, when the baseline dynamic of a diffusion model supports widespread adoption, larger groups will be more likely to follow this trajectory. When the baseline dynamic works against widespread diffusion, however, innovations may be sustained in smaller groups purely through good luck. Any particular group is a sample from a population distribution, and larger samples are more likely to be representative than small ones.

A brief example clarifies the logic driving the group-size effect. Granovetter's original threshold model of joining a riot (1978) assumes a uniform distribution of threshold-decision rules. The basic dynamic of this process is complete diffusion as long as there is some initial activity. Although Granovetter showed that rioting was still unlikely in most finite groups of a hundred people, larger groups are much more likely to riot given the same distribution of thresholds. For example, widespread rioting occurs in only 1 percent of simulated groups with a hundred people, while complete participation is the outcome in 10 percent of simulated groups of a thousand (Rolfe 2005b). When riot participation is averaged across all the simulated outcomes, only 12 percent of actors in groups of a hundred ultimately join in, while 34 percent of those in groups of a thousand participate. Larger crowds are thought to inspire more contagious phenomena because of psychological tendencies or emotional activation that is distinctly present in large crowds versus smaller groups or one-on-one interactions (LeBon [1895] 1995). However, in this example crowds of a hundred riot less often than crowds of a thousand not because individual behavior or psychology varies between the two groups, but simply because of the statistical properties of samples.

18.4.2 Local-network structure

The basic dynamic of conditional decision-making assumes that all decision makers are influenced by everyone else, as in 'all see all' networks (Granovetter 1978). People often respond most to the actions of those close to them, whether closeness is defined in terms of cohesiveness, physical location, similarity, or frequency of contact (Festinger, Schachter, and Back 1950; Festinger 1954; Homans 1958). A decision maker might respond to close relations because she has more information about their actions or opinion; because sanctioning and rewarding occurs more often in close relationships; or perhaps because of some other quality of face-to-face contact.[11]

The precise impact of local networks depends on both the network itself and the basic dynamic of the decision-making process. In general, local networks that are sufficiently large and that contain many random or long-distance ties (e.g. random, small-world, or large and loosely knit biased random networks) increase the likelihood that the model will conform to the basic dynamic, while small or highly structured personal networks (grids, scale-free networks, or small and dense biased random networks) work against the basic dynamic. Random networks often have little impact on expected trajectory aside from speeding up convergence to the expected outcome in some cases (San Miguel et al. 2005). Long-range ties typical of small-world networks counteract the dampening effects of dense local communities, and speed back up the convergence process (Guzmán-Vargas and Hernandez-Perez 2006). Scale-free networks, in which some actors have thousands of ties while most actors have only a handful, can slow down convergence (San Miguel et al. 2005). Networks with dense local communities, such as spatial grids or strongly biased random networks (Skvoretz 1985; Jin, Girvan, and Newman 2001), generally decrease the speed and extent of convergence. The impact of local networks may be nonlinear when initial activity is near the critical point of the model. Small personal networks slow down convergence in many circumstances (Klemm et al. 2003), but sometimes incubate nascent activity that might otherwise die out.

Local networks figure prominently in empirical explanation of variation in both the trajectory and outcome of conditional decision-making processes. In Coleman, Katz, and Menzel's classic diffusion study (1966) the authors argue that doctors adopted tetracycline as a conditional response to the decisions of those close to them in medical-advice networks. Burt (1987) challenged these findings, arguing that doctors responded conditionally to other doctors occupying structurally equivalent network positions. Hedström (1994) shows that unionization in Sweden diffused through networks of geographic proximity, and that conditional decision-making did not reflect countrywide unionization activity (all-see-all networks). Andrews and Biggs (2006) argue that geographic networks of media coverage were more essential than networks of personal communication and social interaction in bringing the novel technique of lunch-counter sit-ins to the attention of potential protestors (primarily black male college students) in the southeastern United States during the civil-rights movement. Gould (1991) and Hedström, Sandell, and Stern (2000) provide evidence that long-range ties, whether formal or informal, can reinforce the spread of political activity through and between local communities. Rolfe (2005a) argues that larger social networks, not increased propensity to vote conditionally or unconditionally, account for the higher rate of voter turnout among the college educated. Bearman, Moody, and Stovel (2004) find that negative conditional preferences in the selection of sexual partners affect sexual-network structure, and in turn impact the likelihood that sexually transmitted diseases will spread.

18.4.3 Social cleavages and friendship selection

When there is no path through personal relationships that links each individual in the network to all other members, the network is not fully connected, and conditional decision-making will produce multipeaked outcomes. Each subgroup may converge to a single point, but rarely converge to the same point (Abelson 1964; Friedkin and Johnsen 1990). However, even one tie between the two subgroups ensures a shared point of convergence. It remains an open question which networks of personal relationships exhibit the six degrees of separation thought to characterize the small world of acquaintanceship (Sola Pool and Kochen 1978), but complete social cleavages are unlikely to explain much variation in contemporary social activity.[12]

In contrast, incomplete social cleavages in combination with resistance to influence may play a major role in explaining social phenomena. Incomplete social cleavages reduce the chances of observing unimodal distributions of activity in the outcome state when actors are partially resistant to influence. Friedkin (2001) describes a small group of wire connectors who are working in the same wiring room. The workers socialize in two distinct cliques with little contact between them. Members of both groups partially converge on a shared norm of work rate within the group, but one group converges on a substantially higher rate than the other.

Conditional decision-making models often produce complete social cleavages when actors select interaction partners with similar traits or opinions. While homophily may characterize many friendships (McPherson, Smith-Lovin, and Cook 2001), self-selection of friends theoretically produces complete social cleavages. The basic dynamic is familiar from Schelling's work (1973), which shows that even weak preferences for homophily lead to completely segregated communities.[13] Friendship selection is an integral feature of many models of emergent culture (see Table 18.1), but diversity is not robust when based on a complete social cleavage (Klemm et al. 2003; Flache and Macy 2006).

Active selection of potential sources of influence may still break up the flow of information without a complete social cleavage, and thus contribute to variation in observed opinions. Baldassari and Bearman (2007) allow actors to select discussion topics as well as friends, and diversity is preserved when friends avoid contentious discussion topics. Bounded-confidence models (Hegselmann and Krause 2002) posit that actors are only influenced by people whose (continuous) opinions are not dramatically different from their own. Opinions are multipeaked when network connectivity is broken via the bounded-confidence mechanism. Either approach fits with the increase in strongly partisan opinions among those with enough political knowledge to screen incoming information that is inconsistent with their political beliefs (Zaller 1992).

18.4.4 Social location of influentials

The 'two-step flow' theory of opinion formation (Lazarsfeld, Berelson, and Gaudet 1944) popularized the concept of influentials: individuals who have a disproportionate impact on those around them. While other scholars have identified influentials by the number of people they might be able to influence (e.g. Watts and Dodds 2007) or their structural location (Burt 1999), in this section I look at people who can change the outcome of social-influence processes. Earlier we saw that influentials arise endogenously when people who resist influence (unconditional decision makers) pull everyone else towards their position.[14] Influentials may also alter the dynamic of conditional decision-making through either (1) their location relative to both other influentials and decision makers who are easily influenced (clustering), or (2) their location relative to social cleavages.

When initial activity is close to or below the critical mass needed for diffusion, clustering of influentials (unconditional actors) and early adopters (e.g. those using linear decision rules) can provide a local critical mass large enough to generate widespread diffusion (Chwe 1999; Watts and Dodds 2007). Clustering of influentials has successfully encouraged reductions in tobacco use among teens (Valente et al. 2003) and the growth of new businesses (Stoneman and Diederen 1994). In situations where initial activity falls short of the critical point, nascent innovations cannot build substantial support if the influence of first movers is diluted. Therefore, small groups, kept effectively smaller by inward-turning ties, best support new ideas or behaviors under these circumstances. Successful diffusion here requires either planning or luck in sampling, clumping together first movers or early adopters who reinforce each others' behavior. Self-sustaining clusters can be created deliberately by handpicking individuals who are already committed to an action and isolating them in small, close-knit groups—a strategy employed by armed forces and terrorist organizations.

The location of influentials relative to social cleavages can also affect the course of decision-making in a group. In a continuous-opinion model with unconditional actors, Friedkin and Johnsen (1997) show that two friends who influence one another but lie along the cleavages of two cliques will develop divergent opinions. This is precisely the pattern of political disagreement found along partial cleavages within personal networks (Huckfeldt, Johnson, and Sprague 2004). As mentioned earlier, uncompromising influentials who police group boundaries may preserve cultural diversity by insulating minority groups from outside forces.

CONCLUSION

Human decision makers are inherently social: what most people do, say, or believe depends on what those around them do, say, or believe, even when individuals do not consciously frame their choices with reference to social pressure, desire to help others, or other social motives. Given that conditional decision-making is an omnipresent fact of social life, what sorts of general mechanisms can explain variation in observable social activity? As a formal approach to decision-making, conditional choice provides a systematic framework for examining links between social action and individual behavior when individual decisions are conditional or interdependent. Whereas rational choice explanations rely on variation in costs, benefits, probabilities, and information to generate variation in predicted outcomes, the conditional choice framework points toward variation in the factors detailed above: the initial activity or distributions of decision rules that constitute the basic dynamic, resistance to influence, social network structure, and the location of key actors in those networks as means of explaining variation in outcomes and trajectories.

Thus, conditional choice as described in this chapter is neither a stand-alone theory nor a set of specific empirical mechanisms; rather, it is a framework for explanation of social action. From this formal framework researchers can develop precise more mid-range theories of particular phenomena by drawing links between the formal mechanisms identified in this chapter (initial activity, decision rules, resistance to influence, network size) and empirical variables in the real world. How might this work in practice? Strang and Soule (1998) show that new management practices often diffuse from prestigious firms to more peripheral ones. The conditional choice framework suggests several possible explanations for this phenomenon, drawing on several of the formal mechanisms it identifies. Does the pattern of diffusion occur because leaders of prestigious companies are more likely to be first movers? Or do the innovations of less-prestigious firms fail to spread, either because the status of the early adopter leads to a different distribution of decision rules or because less prestigious firms are less favorably located in the relevant network structure? By identifying the range of possible formal mechanisms at play, the conditional choice framework encourages the development and testing of mid-range theories across different substantive areas that nonetheless fit into a coherent explanatory framework, while pushing research towards a precise treatment of theoretical issues.

Notes

1. Although I borrow the terminology of dynamical systems, I describe individuals (not systems) as following rules determining change over time (as in agent-based modeling). Individual decision-making is better suited to social-science research, and

it is fairly easy to translate from one form of expression to the other (López-Pintado and Watts 2006).

2. Axelrod (1997) claims that culture (as he defines it) is more likely to emerge when actors face nominal choices along several dimensions. However, this claim is misleading, as it attributes the impact of non-robust modeling assumptions to an intrinsic property of nominal choices (Klemm et al. 2003; Flache and Macy 2006). Nominal choices modeled as linked binary actions produce complete conformity in both herding models (Banerjee 1992) and the Sznajd opinion model (Sznajd-Weron and Sznajd 2000), unless the number of nominal choices is exceedingly large in proportion to the size of the group. When actions are ordinal, the basic dynamic occupies a middle ground between continuous- and binary-choice models (Amblard and Deffuant 2004; Stauffer and Sahimi 2006).

3. Despite the empirical appeal of categorical actions, this chapter will focus on binary and continuous actions—the relevant formal mechanisms work in similar ways across the action types, and more research exists on binary and continuous actions.

4. Conditional responses may take on other functional forms, such as: exponentially increasing (Banerjee 1992; Dodds and Watts 2004), decreasing, or unimodal (hump-shaped) (Elster 1989; López-Pintado and Watts 2006).

5. Thanks to Jeff Grynaviski for this point.

6. Convergence still occurs if positions harden too slowly (Hegselmann and Krause 2002).

7. People who believe personality is fixed are less likely to update opinions on the basis of new information (Heslin, Latham, and VandeWalle 2005; Molden, Plaks, and Dweck 2006).

8. Semi-stable diverse states are produced when actors get 'stuck.' For example, take an audience member facing a standing ovation decision. He has 8 neighbors, 4 of them standing up and 4 remaining seated. This actor is stuck if using a majority threshold-decision rule, he will never sit down if he is standing, or vice versa.

9. Friedman and Podolny (1992) suggest that a less harmful form of boundary policing may be effectively implemented through the dual boundary-spanning roles of gatekeeper and representative.

10. Thanks to Michael Dawson for this point.

11. Face-to-face contact is more effective at increasing turnout than other forms of mobilization (Gerber and Green 2000; Green, Gerber, and Nickerson 2003). Face-to-face contact also changes contributions in social dilemmas, even when there is no opportunity to reward or punish group members (Ostrom, Walker, and Gardner 1992).

12. An obvious exception is complete geographic isolation, or the reproduction of variation associated with historical cleavages rooted in geographic isolation.

13. However, there is ample evidence of institutional discrimination in the USA in real estate and job markets (Massey and Denton 1993; Sidanius & Pratto 1999).

14. Even when persuasive ability is manipulated directly (Latané 1996), resistance to change determines actual influence over process outcomes (Holyst, Kacperski, and Schweitzer 2000).

Table 18.1 Conditional-decision-making models

		Model											
		Continuous opinion *DeGroot*	Continuous opinion *Abelson*	Continuous opinion *Friedkin and Johnsen*	Bounded confidence *Hegselmann and Krause*	Identity and Culture *Axelrod, Lustick*	Herding/Information cascade *Banerjee, Bikchandani et al.*	Sznajd majority *Sznajd and Sznajd*	Majority (morals) *Bainbridge*	Social impact *Latané et al.*	Political disagreement *Huckfeldt*	Threshold *Granovetter*	Contagion/Infection *Dodds and Watts*	Segregation *Schelling*
Action														
	Number of actions possible	1 continuous	1 continuous	1 continuous	1 continuous	f nominal ($k \times f$ binary)	1 nominal (linked binary)	Binary or ordinal	1 binary	1 binary	f nominal ($k \times f$ binary)	1 binary	1 binary	1 binary
	When action can be changed	Next decision	Next decision	Next decision	Next decision	Next decision	Fixed	Next decision	Next decision	Next decision	Next decision	Fixed	Varies	Next decision
Rule Distribution														
	Initial-activity rule	Random	Random	Random	Uniform random	f Random (1 of k traits on f features)	Random first mover	Random	Random (50%)	Random, varies	Random	First movers only	First movers	No
	Conditional decision rule(s)	Weighted average	Weighted average	Weighted average	Average	Imitate 1		Thresholds (2, 3, 4)	Majority +1	Weighted mean or majority +1	Majority +1	Thresholds	Thresholds	Thresholds
	Unconditional actors/rules	No	+ e	+ e	+ e or time-variant self-weight	No	+ e (private signal)	No	No	No or + e	No	First movers	No	Tags only
	Heterogeneous distributions	–	+ e	w_{ij} and + e	No	Klemm et al. (2003)	+ e	No	No	Weights	No	Uniform, normal	Young (2007)	Tags only
	Stochastic rule?	No	No	No	No	No	No or + e	No	No	No or + e	No	No	Yes	No

Information

Actor attributes	No	No	No	No	No	No	No	No	Weight	–	–	–	Binary tag
What is observed	opinion	opinion	opinion	opinion	Actions	Actions	Actions	Actions	Actions	Actions	Action only	Action	Tag
Updating sequence	Synchronous	Continuous	Synchronous	Synchronous	Asynchronous random	Asynchronous sequential	Varies	Synchronous	Synchronous		Threshold order	Synchronous	
Memory of past observations	No	No	No	No	No	Yes	No	No	No	No	–	Varies	No
Who is observed?													
Interaction space	Weights	All see all, weights	Weights	All see all	Grid	All see all	Grid	Grid/ torus (8)	Grid/torus	Grid or Multiple grids	All see all	Nearest neighbors	Grid/ torus (8) move on grid
Active choice of interactions	No	No	No	On action	On action	No	No	Yes	No	Shared actions	No	No	
Agents move in space?	–	–	–	–	No	–	No	Yes	No	No	No	No	Yes
Social location of.... (initial activity, rules, cleavages)									Holyst et al. (2001)		Chwe (1999), Watts (2002)		Yes

References

ABELSON, R. P. (1964), 'Mathematical Models of the Distribution of Attitudes under Controversy', in N. Frederiksen and H. Gulliksen (eds.), *Contributions to Mathematical Psychology* (New York: Holt, Rinehart, & Winston), 42–160.

AMBLARD, F., and DEFFUANT, G. (2004), 'The Role of Network Topology on Extremism Propagation with the Relative Agreement Opinion Dynamics', *Physica A: Statistical Mechanics and its Applications*, 343: 725–38.

ANDREWS, K. T., and BIGGS, M. (2006), 'The Dynamics of Protest Diffusion: Movement Organizations, Social Networks, and News Media in the 1960 Sit-Ins', *American Sociological Review*, 71: 752–77.

AXELROD, R. (1997), *The Complexity of Cooperation* (Princeton, N.J.: Princeton University Press).

AXTELL, R., and EPSTEIN, J. (1999), 'Coordination in Transient Social Networks: An Agent-based Computational Model of the Timing of Retirement', in H. J. Aaron (ed.), *Behavioral Dimensions of Retirement Economics* (Washington, D.C.: Brookings Institution Press).

BALDASSARI, D., and BEARMAN, P. (2007), 'Dynamics of Political Polarization', *American Sociological Review*, 72: 784–811.

BANERJEE, A. V. (1992), 'A Simple Model of Herd Behavior', *Quarterly Journal of Economics*, 107 (3): 797–817.

BEARDEN, W. O., and ROSE, R. L. (1990), 'Attention to Social Comparison Information: An Individual Difference Factor Affecting Consumer Conformity', *Journal of Consumer Research*, 16: 461–71.

BEARMAN, P. S., MOODY, J., and STOVEL, K. (2004), 'Chains of Affection: The Structure of Adolescent Romantic and Sexual Networks', *American Journal of Sociology*, 110: 44–91.

BERELSON, B., LAZARSFELD, P. F., and McPHEE, W. N. (1954), *Voting: A Study of Opinion Formation in a Presidential Campaign* (Chicago, Ill.: University of Chicago Press).

BETTMAN, J. R., LUCE, M. F., and PAYNE, J. W. (1998), 'Constructive Consumer Choice Processes', *Journal of Consumer Research*, 25: 187–217.

BIKHCHANDANI, S., HIRSHLEIFER, D., and WELCH, I. (1992), 'A Theory of Fads, Fashion, Custom, and Cultural Change as Informational Cascades', *Journal of Political Economy*, 100 (5): 992–1026.

BOCCARA, N., (2000), 'Models of Opinion Formation: Influence of Opinion Leaders', *International Journal of Modern Physics*, C 11: 1157–65.

BOND, R., and SMITH, P. B. (1996), 'Culture and Conformity: A Meta-analysis of Studies Using Asch's (1952 B, 1956) Line Judgement Task', *Psychological Bulletin*, 119: 111–37.

BOYD, R., et al. (2003), 'The Evolution of Altruistic Punishment', *Proceedings of the National Academy of Sciences*, 100: 3531–5.

BURT, R. S. (1987), 'A Note on Strangers, Friends and Happiness', *Social Networks*, 9 (4): 311–31.

—— (1999), 'The Social Capital of Opinion Leaders', *ANNALS of the American Academy of Political and Social Science*, 566: 37–54.

CASARI, M., and PLOTT, C. R. (2003), 'Decentralized Management of Common Property Resources: Experiments with a Centuries-old Institution', *Journal of Economic Behavior & Organization*, 51: 217–47.

CHATTERJEE, S., and SENETA, E. (1977), 'Towards Consensus: Some Convergence Theorems on Repeated Averaging', *Journal of Applied Probability*, 14: 89–97.

CHWE, M. SUK-YOUNG. (1999), 'Structure and Strategy in Collective Action', *American Journal of Sociology*, 105 (1): 128–56.

COLEMAN, J. S., KATZ, E., and MENZEL, H. (1966), *Medical Innovation: A Diffusion Study* (Indianapolis, Ind.: Bobbs-Merrill).

DELRE, S. A., JAGER, W., and JANSSEN, M. A. (2007), 'Diffusion Dynamics in Small-world Networks with Heterogeneous Consumers', *Computational & Mathematical Organization Theory*, 13 (2): 185–202.

DODDS, P. S., and WATTS, D. J. (2004), 'Universal Behavior in a Generalized Model of Contagion', *Physical Review Letters*, 92: 218701.

DOWNS, A. (1957), *An Economic Theory of Voting* (New York: Harper).

DWECK, C. S., and LEGGETT, E. L. (1988), 'A Social-cognitive Approach to Motivation and Personality', *Psychological Review*, 95: 256–73.

ELSTER, J. (1989), *The Cement of Society* (New York: Cambridge University Press).

FEHR, E., and GÄCHTER, S. (2000), 'Cooperation and Punishment in Public Goods Experiments', *American Economic Review*, 90 (4): 981–94.

FESTINGER, L. (1954), 'A Theory of Social Comparison Processes', *Human Relations*, 7: 17–140.

—— SCHACHTER, S., and BACK, K. (1950), *Social Pressures in Informal Groups* (Stanford, Calif.: Stanford University Press).

FISCHBACHER, U., GÄCHTER, S., and FEHR, E. (2001), 'Are People Conditionally Cooperative? Evidence from a Public Goods Experiment', *Economics Letters*, 71 (3): 397–404.

FLACHE, A., and TORENVLIED, R. (2001), 'Persistent Instability in Polarized Opinion Formation and Collective Decision-making', Paper presented at the fourth summer school on 'Polarization and Conflict', 23–7 July 2001, San Sebastian, Spain.

—— and MACY, M. W. (2006), 'What Sustains Cultural Diversity and What Undermines It? Axelrod and Beyond'; at <http://www.arxiv.org/abs/physics> accessed 2008.

FRIEDKIN, N. E. (1999), 'Choice Shift and Group Polarization', *American Sociological Review*, 64: 856–75.

—— (2001), 'Norm Formation in Social Influence Networks', *Social Networks*, 23: 167–89.

—— and JOHNSEN, E. (1990), 'Social Influence and Opinions', *Journal of Mathematical Sociology*, 15: 193–205.

—— —— (1997), 'Social Position in Influence Networks', *Social Networks* 19: 209–22.

FRIEDMAN, R. A., and PODOLNY, J. (1992), 'Differentiation of Boundary Spanning Roles: Labor Negotiations and Implications for Role Conflict', *Administrative Science Quarterly*, 37: 28–47.

GERBER, A. S., and GREEN, D. P. (2000), 'The Effects of Canvassing, Telephone Calls, and Direct Mail on Voter Turnout: A Field Experiment', *American Political Science Review*, 94 (3): 653–63.

GOULD, R. (1991), 'Multiple Networks and Mobilization in the Paris Commune, 1871', *American Sociological Review*, 56: 716–29.

—— (1993), 'Collective Action and Network Structure', *American Sociological Review*, 58 (2): 182–96.

GRANOVETTER, M. (1978), 'Threshold Models of Collective Behavior', *American Journal of Sociology*, 83 (6): 1420–43.

GRANOVETTER, M., and SOONG, R. (1988), 'Threshold Models of Diversity: Chinese Restaurants, Residential Segregation, and the Spiral of Silence', *Sociological Methodology*, 18: 69–104.

GREEN, D. P., GERBER, A. S., and NICKERSON, D. W. (2003), 'Getting Out the Youth Vote in Local Elections: Results from Six Door-to-door Canvassing Experiments', *Journal of Politics*, 65 (4): 1083–96.

GREENHALGH, T., et al. (2005), 'Storylines of Research in Diffusion of Innovation: A Meta-narrative Approach to Systematic Review', *Social Science & Medicine*, 61: 417–30.

GUZMÁN-VARGAS, L., and HERNANDEZ-PEREZ, R. (2006), 'Small-world Topology and Memory Effects on Decision Time in Opinion Dynamics', *Physica A: Statistical Mechanics and its Applications*, 372: 326–32.

HARRIS-LACEWELL, M. (2004), *Barbershops, Bibles, and BET: Everyday Talk and Black Political Thought* (Princeton, N.J.: Princeton University Press).

HEDSTRÖM, P. (1994), 'Contagious Collectivities: On the Spatial Diffusion of Swedish Trade Unions, 1890–1940', *American Journal of Sociology*, 99: 1157–79.

—— (1998), 'Rational Imitation', in P. Hedström and R. Swedberg (eds.) *Social Mechanisms: An Analytical Approach to Social Theory* (Cambridge: Cambridge University Press), 306–28.

—— SANDELL, R., and STERN, C. (2000), 'Mesolevel Networks and the Diffusion of Social Movements: The Case of the Swedish Social Democratic Party', *American Journal of Sociology*, 106: 145–72.

HEGSELMANN, R., and KRAUSE, U. (2002), 'Opinion Dynamics and Bounded Confidence: Models, Analysis and Simulation', *Journal of Artificial Societies and Social Simulation*, 5 (3); at <http://www.jasss.soc.survey.ac.uk/5/3/2.html>, accessed 2008.

HESLIN, P. A., LATHAM, G. P., and VANDEWALLE, D. (2005), 'The Effect of Implicit Person Theory on Performance Appraisals', *Journal of Applied Psychology*, 90: 842–56.

HOLYST, J. A., KACPERSKI, K., and SCHWEITZER, F. (2000), 'Phase Transitions in Social Impact Models of Opinion Formation', *Physica A: Statistical Mechanics and its Applications*, 285: 199–210.

HOMANS, G. C. (1958), 'Social Behavior as Exchange', *American Journal of Sociology*, 63: 597–606.

HUCKFELDT, R. R., JOHNSON, P. E., and SPRAGUE, J. D. (2004), *Political Disagreement: The Survival of Diverse Opinions within Communication Networks* (Cambridge/New York: Cambridge University Press).

ISENBERG, D. J. (1986), 'Group Polarization: A Critical Review and Meta-analysis', *Journal of Personality and Social Psychology Bulletin*, 50: 1141–51.

JIN, E., GIRVAN, M., and NEWMAN, M. (2001), 'The Structure of Growing Social Networks', *Physical Review*, E 64: 046132.

KLEMM, K., (2003), 'Nonequilibrium Transitions in Complex Networks: A Model of Social Interaction', *Physical Review*, E 67: 026120.

—— et al. (2005), 'Globalization, Polarization and Cultural Drift', *Journal of Economic Dynamics and Control*, 29: 321–34.

LATANÉ, B. (1996), 'Dynamic Social Impact: The Creation of Culture by Communication', *Journal of Communication*, 46: 13–25.

—— and NOWAK, A. (1997), 'Self-organizing Social Systems: Necessary and Sufficient Conditions for the Emergence of Clustering, Consolidation, and Continuing Diversity', in

G. A. Barnett and F. J. Boster (eds.), *Progress in Communication Sciences* (Greenwich, Conn.: Ablex), 43–74.

LAZARSFELD, P. F., BERELSON, B., and GAUDET, H. (1944), *The People's Choice: How the Voter Makes up his Mind in a Presidential Campaign* (New York: Columbia University Press).

LEBAS, A. (2006), 'Polarization as Craft', *Comparative Politics*, 38: 419–38.

LEBON, G. [1895] (1995), *The Crowd: A Study of the Popular Mind* (New Brunswick, N.J.: Transaction).

LEDYARD, J. (1995), 'Public Goods', in J. Kagel and A. Roth. (eds.), *Handbook of Experimental Economics* (Princeton, N.J.: Princeton University Press), 111–94.

LEWENSTEIN, M., NOWAK, A., and LATANÉ, B. (1992), 'Statistical Mechanics of Social Impact', *Physical Review*, A 45 (2): 703–16.

LÓPEZ-PINTADO, D., and WATTS, D. J. (2006), 'Social Influence, Binary Decisions and Collective Dynamics', working paper, Columbia University.

LUSTICK, I., MIODOWNIK, D., and EIDELSON, R. J. (2004), 'Secessionism in Multicultural States: Does Sharing Power Prevent or Encourage It?', *American Political Science Review*, 98 (2): 209–30.

McADAM, D. (1986), 'Recruitment to High-risk Activism: The Case of Freedom Summer', *American Journal of Sociology*, 92 (1): 64–90.

McPHERSON, M., SMITH-LOVIN, L., and COOK, J. M. (2001), 'Birds of a Feather: Homophily in Social Networks', *Annual Review of Sociology*, 27: 415–44.

MASSEY, D. S., and DENTON, N. A. (1993), *American Apartheid: Segregation and the Making of the Underclass* (Cambridge, Mass.: Harvard University Press).

MILLER, J. H., AND PAGE, S. E. (2004), 'The Standing Ovation Problem', *Complexity*, 9 (5): 8–16.

MINTROM, M. (1997), 'Policy Entrepreneurs and the Diffusion of Innovation', *American Journal of Political Science*, 41: 738–70.

MOLDEN, D. C., PLAKS, J. E., and DWECK, C. S. (2006), ' "Meaningful" Social Inferences: Effects of Implicit Theories on Inferential Processes', *Journal of Experimental Social Psychology*, 42: 738–52.

MORTON, T. A., POSTMES, T., and JETTEN, J. (2007), 'Playing the Game: When Group Success is More Important than Downgrading Deviants', *European Journal of Social Psychology*, 37: 599–616.

NIEMI, R. G. (1974), *How Family Members Perceive Each Other: Political and Social Attitudes in Two Generations* (New Haven, Conn.: Yale University Press).

OFFERMAN, T., SONNEMANS, J., and SCHRAM, A. (1996), 'Value Orientations, Expectations and Voluntary Contributions in Public Goods', *Economic Journal*, 106 (437): 817–45.

OLIVER, P. E. (1993), 'Formal Models of Collective Action', *Annual Review of Sociology*, 19: 271–300.

OSTROM, E., WALKER, J., and GARDNER, R. (1992), 'Covenants With and Without a Sword', *American Political Science Review*, 86: 404–17.

ROGERS, E. M. (2003), *Diffusion of Innovations* (London: Collier Macmillan).

ROLFE, M. (2005a), 'A Social Theory of Voter Turnout', Ph.D. Thesis (University of Chicago).

—— (2005b), 'Social Networks and Simulations', in C. M. Macal, D. Sallach, and M. J. North (eds.), *Proceedings of Agent 2004 Conference on Social Dynamics: Interaction, Reflexivity, and Emergence* (Chicago, Ill.: University of Chicago Press), 483–99.

SALGANIK, M. J., DODDS, P. S., and WATTS, D. J. (2006), 'Experimental Study of Inequality and Unpredictability in an Artificial Cultural Market', *Science*, 311: 854–6.

SAN MIGUEL, M., et al. (2005), 'Binary and Multivariate Stochastic Models of Consensus Formation', *Computing in Science & Engineering*, 7: 67–73.

SCHELLING, T. C. (1973), 'Hockey Helmets, Concealed Weapons, and Daylight Saving: A Study of Binary Choices with Externalities', *Journal of Conflict Resolution*, 17 (3): 381–428.

SIDANIUS, J., and PRATTO, F. (1999), *Social Dominance: An Intergroup Theory of Social Hierarchy and Oppression* (Cambridge: Cambridge University Press).

SIMMONS, B., and ELKINS, Z. (2006), 'The Globalization of Liberalization: Policy Diffusion in the International Political Economy', *American Political Science Review*, 98: 171–89.

SKVORETZ, J. (1985), 'Random and Biased Networks: Simulations and Approximations', *Social Networks*, 7: 225–61.

SOLA POOL, I. DE, and KOCHEN, M. (1978), 'Contacts and Influence', *Social Networks*, 1: 5–51.

STAUFFER, D., and SAHIMI, M. (2006), 'Discrete Simulation of the Dynamics of Spread of Extreme Opinions in a Society', *Physica A: Statistical Mechanics and its Applications*, 364: 537–43.

STONEMAN, P., and DIEDEREN, P. (1994), 'Technology Diffusion and Public Policy', *Economic Journal*, 104: 918–30.

STRANG, D., and SOULE, S. A. (1998), 'Diffusion in Organizations and Social Movements: From Hybrid Corn to Poison Pills', *Annual Review of Sociology*, 24: 265–90.

SUNSTEIN, C. R. (2002), 'The Law of Group Polarization', *Journal of Political Philosophy*, 10: 175–95.

SZNAJD-WERON, K., and SZNAJD, J. (2000), 'Opinion Evolution in Closed Community', *International Journal of Modern Physics*, C 11: 1157–65.

VALENTE, T. W. (1995), *Network Models of the Diffusion of Innovations* (Creskill, N.J.: Hampton).

——— et al. (2003), 'Effects of a Social-network Method for Group Assignment Strategies on Peer-led Tobacco Prevention Programs in Schools', *American Journal of Public Health*, 93: 1837–43.

VISSER, P. S., and KROSNICK, J. A. (1998), 'Development of Attitude Strength over the Life Cycle: Surge and Decline', *Journal of Personality and Social Psychology*, 75: 1389–410.

WALKER, J. L. (1969), 'The Diffusion of Innovations among the American States', *American Political Science Review*, 63: 880–99.

WATTS, D. J., and DODDS, P. S. (2007), 'Influentials, Networks, and Public Opinion Formation', *Journal of Consumer Research*, 34: 441–58.

WEDEEN, L. (2002), 'Conceptualizing Culture: Possibilities for Political Science', *American Political Science Review*, 96 (4), 713–28.

WOOD, W. (2000), 'Attitude Change: Persuasion and Social Influence', *Annual Review of Psychology*, 50: 539–70.

YOUNG, H. P. (2007), 'Innovation Diffusion in Heterogeneous Populations', economics series working paper no. 303, Department of Economics, University of Oxford.

ZALLER, J. (1992), *The Nature and Origins of Mass Opinion* (New York: Cambridge University Press).

ZARNOTH, P., and J. A. SNIEZEK (1997), 'The Social Influence of Confidence in Group Decision Making', *Journal of Experimental Social Psychology*, 33: 345–66.

ZUCKERMAN, A. S. (2005), *The Social Logic of Politics: Personal Networks as Contexts for Political Behavior* (Philadelphia, Pa.: Temple University Press).

CHAPTER 19

NETWORK DYNAMICS*

JAMES MOODY

INTRODUCTION

MUCH of social-network research treats network structure as fixed and enduring. This is clear in canonical definitions: 'Network models conceptualize structure...as lasting patterns of relations among actors' (Wasserman and Faust 1994: 4). Of course, this static conception has never been taken entirely seriously by those working on networks. We all know that relations change over time (Dunphy 1963; Hallinan and Hutchins 1980; Wellman et al. 1997; Burt 2002) and that sequence and ordering matter for myriad social outcomes (Abbott 1995, 1998). Similarly, many in the networks field have lamented the focus on structure over dynamics, and research on changes in network features has continuously bubbled to the surface (Roy 1983; Weesie and Flap 1990; Bearman and Everett 1993; Suitor, Wellman, and Morgan 1997; Leskovec, Kleinberg, and Faloutsos 2005; Powell et al. 2005). Still, the conceptual tools, data-collection instruments, and analysis methods at our disposal funnel network terms (and thus

* This work is supported by NSF: HSD 0624158 and NICHD DA012831-05. An earlier version of this chapter was presented at a number of talks and colloquia. Thanks to participants at the SCANCOR seminar, the joint Harvard/MIT networks seminar, and the Stanford sociology department. Much of this work stems from conversations and joint work with Peter Bearman, Martina Morris, Dan McFarland, and Skye Bender-deMoll. Special thanks to the Center for Advanced Studies in Behavioral Science and the National Forest Service for residency during the writing.

thinking) toward static conceptions of social structure. For example, the language of graph theory that forms the basis of most network measures describes networks as linked sets: G(V, E) of vertices (V) and edges (E). Where is time in this formalization?

In this chapter I propose to examine dynamic networks and diffusion. I want to extend our thinking about networks from static structures (G(V, E)) to the ongoing, evolving traces of enacted social relations: G(V, E, T), where T indexes start- and end-time sets on edges. Doing so will proceed in three steps. First, I will review models for the evolution of networks over time (Sect. 19.1). This section is about how and why networks change. I cannot catalogue the set, but I hope to highlight many ways that time can be incorporated into networks. Second, I will review how network timing affects the flow of things across networks (Sect. 19.2). This section asks 'when is a network'—by showing that edge timing reshapes the set of paths potentially useful for diffusion. Third, I will combine these two approaches and ask how our extant models for network change affect our understandings of diffusion and vice versa (Sect. 19.3).

I hope this survey of the intersection of time and structure will point to a new way of thinking about networks as linked temporal events. That is, there is a clear intersection of two types of 'structure' in dynamic networks: structure as contact pattern and structure as the unfolding of edges linked together in time. I think if we modify the classic tools of structural analysis we can make this dual linkage apparent in a scientifically profitable way. At the moment, however, much of this work is provisional: I'll be hinting at a fairly broad set of ideas that all point to the need for integration, rather than providing this integration directly.

19.1 MODELS FOR NETWORK CHANGE

Here I use 'model' to describe rules or tendencies that govern the formation and evolution of networks. These rules range from very specific algorithms, such as Chase's 'double attack' strategy for dominance relations (1980), to expressions of general tendencies in pair formation ('like with like' statements of homophily). For ease of exposition, I distinguish between 'node-based' and 'edge-based' models. Node-based models specify edge creation and deletion as some function of the dyad members' characteristics.[1] Edge-based models specify edge creation and deletion as a function of adjacent edges, thus creating a dependence of edges within one dyad on edges in another.

19.1.1 Node-based models

The most common node-based models are based on fixed exogenous features of nodes, such as their race, sex, or age (McPherson and Smith-Lovin 1987; Moody 2001) and encompass a long body of work on homophily (Cohen 1977; Tuma and Hallinan 1979; McPherson and Smith-Lovin 1987; Suitor and Keeton 1997). These models express the common observation that relations tend to form in a like-with-like manner. In friendship and romance, for example, we see strong age and race similarity in tie formation.[2]

Models based on static node attributes have a limited and typically indirect relation to network evolution. In a world where attributes were randomly distributed, we would expect a process of forming relations with those similar to oneself to quickly sort actors into adjacent regions of the attribute space, evolving a network toward a steady state where the probability of a tie was a direct function of attribute distance. The classic Schelling residential-segregation models (1971) follow this logic.[3] Furthermore, most empirical settings are presorted in a manner correlated with node attributes (Feld 1981), so wider patterns of social organization often reinforce (and predispose) node similarity.

The strongest dynamic effects of fixed node attributes are on the stability of relations over time. Cross-category ties are not only less frequent (Moody 2001), but typically less stable (Hallinan and Williams 1987; Burt 2002). As such, we expect them to have shorter duration, suggesting more 'churning' of cross-category than within-category relations.[4]

When node attributes are not fixed, homophily will predict relational changes consistent with emerging social differences. Since homophily models predict tie formation of like with like, and people change many relevant social states at different rates over time, there is some natural network evolution that will occur across the 'developmental' life of a population (Dunphy 1963). In school settings, for example, we would expect network ties between differentially maturing students to be less stable, with new ties forming as students become similarly mature. In general, any time-varying node attribute with intra-individual variance will create a time-shifting attribute space, and we expect ties to follow a similar shifting pattern.

In a diffusion context, however, we can also expect time-varying node attributes to evolve as a result of changes in the network, such as when friendships influence a behavior that in turn affects tie formation with others (Cohen 1977, 1983; Hallinan and Williams 1990; Bauman and Ennett 1994; Haynie 2001). While data limitations often make the independent effects hard to detect, it is analytically possible to model network formation where a 'bit' flows through the net and changes node states which in turn make partners more or less attractive (Mark 1998; Snijders 2002). As such, we would see a partially endogenous model of network change, where the change results from a negotiation of ties and attributes, with each capable of shifting (Baldassarri and Bearman 2007).

19.1.2 Edge-based models

The second major class of network-evolution models focuses on how edges emerge or dissolve as a function of surrounding edges. These are typically either *order rules* for the formation and dissolution of new ties based on past ties or *pattern rules* that make relations conditional on ties among surrounding nodes. The distinction turns on timing: order rules guide relational activity by a set of steps conditional on earlier steps. These have the form 'After doing x, next do y.' Pattern rules guide action as a function of actions among surrounding dyads in the network, and thus have the form 'If surrounding relations are of pattern x, do y.' White's vacancy-chain model for intrafirm mobility (1970) and Chase's model for the formation of dominance hierarchies (1980) are two clear examples of order rules. Chase's model also helps introduce some important pattern elements, so I focus on that here.

In studying the emergence of dominance hierarchies among hens, Chase notes that pure linear hierarchies always emerge. That is, we can always identify a top hen who dominates every other, and then one under her who dominates everyone but the top hen, and so forth down the line to a single hen dominated by all others. However, among hens, node-level attributes (weight, aggressiveness, etc.) do not correlate strongly enough with position to account for the stability of the structure. Moreover, when disrupted, the hen hierarchy will always re-emerge in a perfect linear hierarchy, but with individual chickens occupying different positions in the structure. How can we account for the macro-level stability in the face of these micro-level fluctuations? Chase shows that a simple actor-based order rule, called the 'double-attack strategy' will generate a perfectly linear hierarchy.

The double-attack strategy is stated as: Given any group of three, any time you attack one, quickly turn to attack the second. By quickly establishing dominance over two neighbors, the resulting dominance relation among *them* becomes irrelevant for the structure. It doesn't matter what they do, in either case you get a perfectly linear ordering of the triad. This rule is sketched schematically in Figure 19.1 below.

The universe of all dominance triads is the state-space for the model (all triads containing only asymmetric or null dyads, here labeled with the standard MAN labeling; Wasserman and Faust 1994). The double-attack rule constrains the transitions through this state-space. This strategy takes us from the situation of a single dominance relation (the 012 triad) to two dominance relations (the 021D triad) *in a way that must necessarily lead* to a linear hierarchy (the 030T triad). If, instead of the double-attack rule, hens followed an 'attack the bystander' rule, where once attacked they attacked whoever was left, this would be equivalent to arriving at the 021C triad. This, in turn, would leave open the potential for cyclic dominance structures (030C), which would undercut the observed linear hierarchy. Experimental evidence confirmed that hens follow a double-attack rule, giving rise to all transitive triads and thus a perfect linear hierarchy. The key point, for our

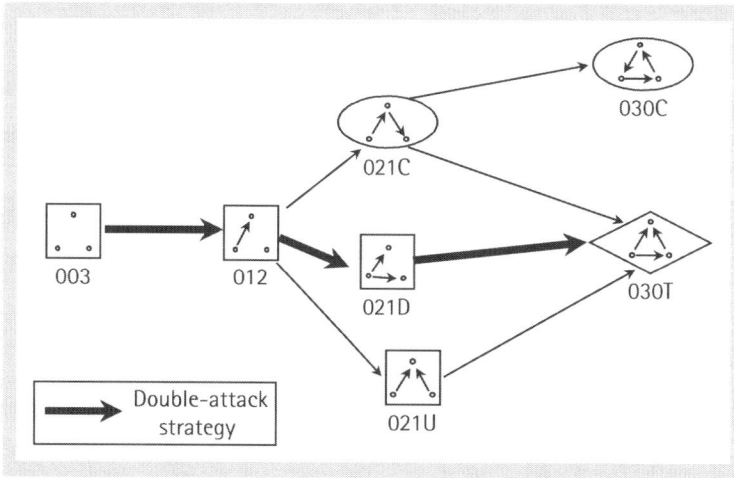

Fig. 19.1 An order–rule model for dominance hierarchy

purposes, is that a simple behavior rule based on order (attack twice) is sufficient to produce a clear macrostructure, independent of node attributes.

Other order rules for network formation relate to the timing and duration of ties. In American romantic relations, for example, monogamy is normative: one should not start a new sexual relation until the last one is finished. In practice, of course, populations vary widely on the level of monogamy practiced and many relations overlap in time (Laumann et al. 2004). So a typical pattern may be to start a new relation while still involved with a prior partner, and only drop the first relation after the second seems promising. Or, one may have a steady partner with short relations on the side. Each of these variants from pure monogamy can be expressed as a behavior rule on the temporal order of relations. As with dominance relations among chickens, the normative pressures for and against such romantic rules will produce specific global structures, which have a clear effect on features of the resulting macrostructure, such as diffusion potential (see below).

Perhaps the most studied *pattern* rule for network formation is social balance. In its original formation (Heider 1946; Cartwright and Harary 1956; Holland and Leinhardt 1977), balance models sought to explain the development of groups from an individual-level model of social dissonance. Considering triads of positive and negative relations, we say a triad is balanced whenever 'a friend of a friend is a friend' or 'an enemy of an enemy is a friend.' Violations of these patterns are hypothesized as stressful for actors, who thus have an incentive to change their relations toward a less stressful pattern. Figure 19.2 below outlines the potential resolutions of one unbalanced state to one of any three balanced states (the result depending on which relation ultimately changes).

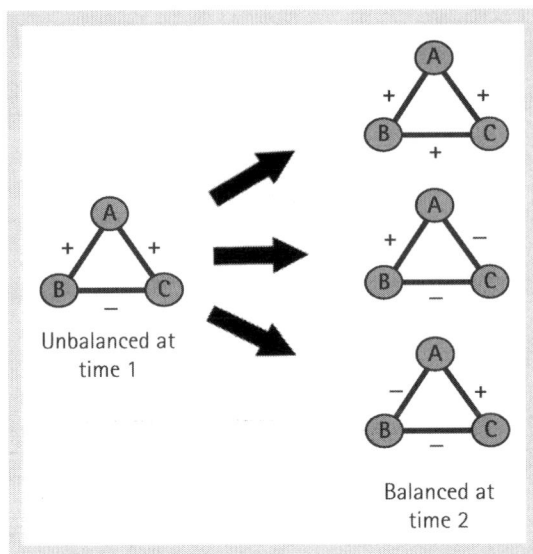

Fig. 19.2 Potential resolutions of an unbalanced triad

While explicitly dynamic, the classic social-balance theory is an equilibrium 'crystallization' model. In theory, consistent balanced action on the part of actors negotiating positive and negative ties should lead to one of two ultimate states: a single positively connected set or two competing sets. But, *once these sets have emerged*, there is no endogenous-*pattern* reason for the network to change. Chase's dominance model (1980) and Schelling's neighborhood-segregation model (1971) similarly have fixed endpoints of stability: once the rules are followed by all, there is no more change expected. In this sense, then, they are only temporarily dynamic, becoming static once the equilibrium has been met.

Balance models have been generalized to directed relations by focusing on tendencies for transitivity (if $i \rightarrow j$, and $j \rightarrow k$, then $i \rightarrow k$) or peer influence in nomination structure (if $i \rightarrow j$, and $i \rightarrow k$, then $j \rightarrow k$) (Johnsen 1986). For the most part, these models have been treated empirically as equilibrium models, by comparing an observed network against an ideal-typical network with no instances of inconsistent triads. While there is general support for these models, they almost always also contain 'excess' intransitivity: a statistical overrepresentation of states the model predicts to be rare. I suspect that at least part of the lack of fit is that the models are, in practice, not crystallizing but instead fully dynamic.

In contrast to crystallizing models, some rules for network evolution should lead to systems where actors' positions are not fixed, but instead they have new reasons to change relations as the system evolves. A simple example would be the norms guiding a cocktail-party-conversation network. In such settings it is considered rude to dominate conversation with a small number of people. You are expected to engage quickly, mingle freely, and never spend too much time in one conversation. If most actors follow this rule, the network should bubble continuously and never crystallize in a single structure (see Ingram and Morris 2007). In a perhaps more interesting substantive case, Ron Burt's model for structural holes (1992, 2005)—if taken as a guide for strategic action—would likely lead to a continuously shifting social network.[5] If at time t actor i collects a rent by bridging actors j and k, then at time t + 1 j and k have an incentive to form a direct relation. But closing this triad removes the profit motive for i, who is now less likely to maintain his relation to j or k. This span–close-span cycle is built into the competing interests of actors through relations: if rent is to be had by bridging holes, it comes at a cost to those bridged, who thus have an incentive to close the hole. But once closed, there is incentive to minimize redundancy and thus open new holes. Or, if one combines the substantive claim of Gould (2002), that people will not maintain asymmetric relations indefinitely, with the balance-model prediction that close friends agree on the status of thirds, asymmetric nominations will be coordinated, leading to hierarchy in the cross section, but one that will be unstable over time.

Finally, models that appear to have crystallizing implications may in fact be fully dynamic if either small levels of randomness are introduced or coordination difficulties in the process of implementing relational change limit global resolution in realistic time spans. That is, when viewed as a dynamic social process, the dyad-level state changes that actors seek may differ from the system-level features seen as the ultimate expression of those goals. For example, social-balance models 'forbid' certain triads, and if actors managed to completely avoid these triads the system would crystallize around a fixed macrostructure with no endogenous incentives to change. But can actors make choices that actually avoid such triads? The state-space for changes in triads in fact requires movement through forbidden triads, and thus their emergence in the system is very likely. This is because actors experience the *transition* to or from a given triad in multiple ways, and a state that is balanced from one actor's point of view may not be from another's. As such, there are many routes through the triad state-space, with different implications for each actor, which can often result in the production of triads seen as undesirable at the global-model level. In Figure 19.3 below I sketch one such system.

The crystallized version of the model suggests that, eventually, all actors will arrive at one of the fully transitive triads (diamonds) and stay there. But the edge-level *transition* from state to state makes some intransitive triads attractive for some actors (the solid paths leading to circled triads), which means that one actor's move to create a locally consonant social system creates dissonance for others, who now have to adjust their relations.[6] In realistic time spans or when combined with other social features that also introduce random changes in the network it is unlikely that an observed network will ever converge on the hypothesized crystallized structure, *even if* all actors are following balance-like rules for behavior.

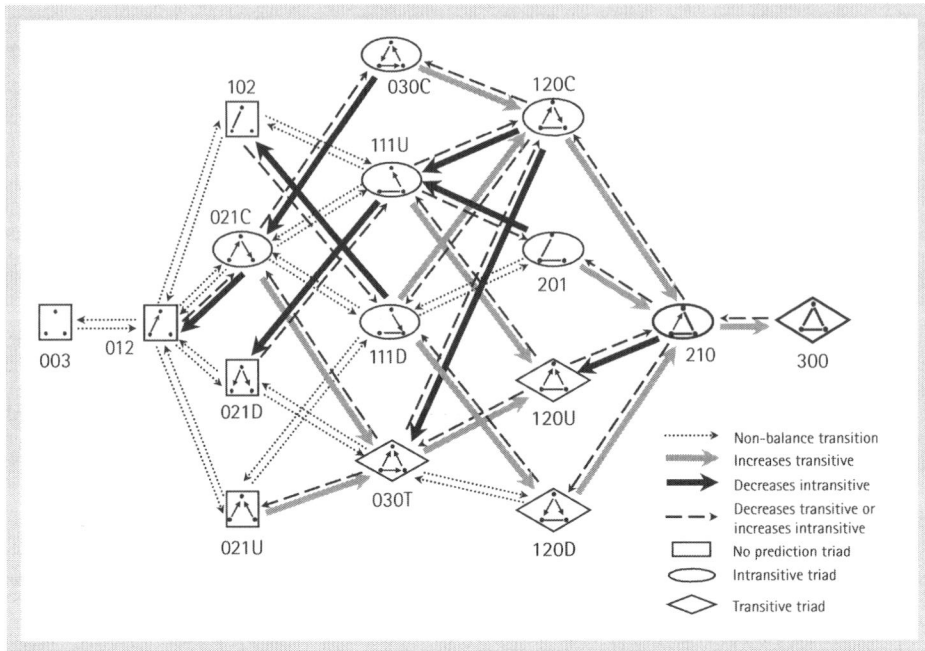

Fig. 19.3 Transition space for directed relations (Some transitions will both increase transitivity and decrease intransitivity. They are shaded here for net effect. If transitions from different actors in the triad have different effects, multiple lines are given)

I suspect that these sorts of fully dynamic models are much more common than equilibrium models tending toward crystallized states. In most complex settings there are likely multiple formation rules (transitivity, reciprocity, no returning to past breakups, etc.), changing node attributes, aging populations, and complex pattern rules with multiple consistent 'routes' through the state-space. Together these create a fluid social network that only rarely crystallizes.

19.1.3 Summary of models for network change

Models for network change can be described as either *node*- or *edge*-based. Edge-based rules can be further partitioned into *order* rules governing relational timing relative to one's own prior actions and *pattern* rules governing the dependencies of one's current relations on relations of those nearby in the network. As I highlight below with an extension of four-cycle rules for romance, these may overlap. The dynamism of node-based rules depends crucially on the dynamics of the attributes governing change. When they are stable; the network is stable. But in many substantively interesting cases ranging from politics to health behavior node attributes are an endogenous function of network ties, creating complex connections between attributes and structure. Edge-based rules are almost always minimally dynamic, providing a mechanism to move from randomness in ties to order. But many such models impose uniform-action assumptions that lead to equilibrium outcomes which are rarely realistic. I expect that future work will highlight ways in which such models maintain an orderly change, allowing both micro flexibility and macro stability. Finally, some models not assumed to be dynamic (such as motivations to seek structural holes) could easily be generalized to dynamism.

Taking a dynamic view of network structure has at least two crucial implications. First, the timescale for thinking about 'structure' becomes critical. If we care about networks for position effects (rather than flow effects), then knowing the relevant position (leader, isolate, group member, etc.) depends on the timescale over which dynamic relations are viewed. It also makes clear that a given position reflects a trajectory as much as a state. Second, in thinking about how networks act as conduits for flow, we must understand how timing constrains diffusion opportunities. This takes us directly to the subject of Section 19.2: effects of network dynamics on diffusion.

19.2 NETWORK DYNAMICS AND DIFFUSION

In this section I review the structure requirements for network diffusion and demonstrate how these requirements are affected when we assume edges come and go over time. Because things can only flow over a currently connected tie, goods held by actors can only move across current and future ties. This simple limit has dramatic implications for how tie order affects diffusion potential. After reviewing this direct effect I discuss how network structure moderates this effect.

19.2.1 Graph features controlling diffusion

Diffusion refers simply to the transmission of some 'bit' from node to node over the network. The content of the bit can range widely from ideational content (beliefs and opinions) to information, physical goods, or infectious agents. While the content is never irrelevant, we can abstract from content-specific features by identifying how network structures provide pathways for the bit to travel. Content-specific features can then be recovered by specifying the likelihood that nodes pass the bit to adjacent partners and the types of paths that are favored for transmission (see Borgatti 2005).

Conditional on the pairwise probability of transmission (P_{ij}), the key general features governing diffusion in a network are connectivity, distance, and redundancy. Connectivity is binary: a path from i to j in the network exists or not. If so, then it is *possible* for a good to travel from i to j. Given connectivity, the likelihood of transmission is governed jointly by the length of the path(s) connecting i and j and the number of paths available. The probability of transmission L steps along a single path is $P_{ij}L$, and since P_{ij} is typically much less than 1, transmission over long distances along any single path is unlikely.[7] In most networks, however, there are multiple routes between two nodes, and thus the probability increases with each additional path. This increase is roughly additive if the paths are independent, and is also a key reason that multiple connectivity increases social cohesion (Moody and White 2003).[8]

The redundancy provided by multiple paths represents a trade-off: if the probability of transmission is high, then the most efficient networks will approach spanning trees—as extra edges are connecting nodes that will get the bit anyway. If transmission is uncertain, or the system is likely to be disrupted at either the nodes or edges, then multiple connectivity provides a route around transmission breaks. Short-distance redundancy—as with direct clustering—usually slows diffusion unless P_{ij} is extremely small (which is the insight resting behind the strength of weak ties; Granovetter 1973). When P_{ij} is reasonably high, then having multiple direct contacts to the same source is purely redundant with minimal diffusion advantage.

19.2.2 Timing effects on diffusion

Time matters for network diffusion because of what it means for the dyadic transfer of a specific bit at a specific time and because of how it changes the set of paths open for diffusion of any bit. The first way that time matters is through the time-sensitive nature of the bit-diffusing and how this temporal sensitivity affects P_{ij}. Bits traveling over a network are often time-sensitive: information about a job is only useful so long as the job is unfilled, secrets are only important so long as they've been kept secret by others, hot stock tips matter only so long as the price is low. In a more concrete case, sexually transmitted infections (STI) are most contagious shortly after being transferred. This means that P_{ij} is high when one first gets the bug, but it declines steadily over time as the body's immune system combats the disease.[9] Or, shortly after one hears a new joke (or secret, or idea) it's fresh in one's mind and thus more likely to be spread, but as it comes to be replaced with new ideas it is less likely to come to the forefront. Unlike information about a job, in these instances the decay in transmission value is relative to the last transmission, and thus gets 'refreshed' at each passing.

In these cases time affects the likelihood that the good will be passed from node to node and thus structural connectivity and timing must mesh. While we have good models for an epidemic threshold in static graphs, a similarly relevant dynamic instance is less obvious. If the graph is fully connected at each instance, then connectivity is complete and timing is unproblematic. However, in many cases that we care about (such as sexual networks) this high level of immediate connectivity is unlikely, as the momentary degree distribution implies a graph well below that required for a giant component (Palmer 1985). We thus need a time-sensitive measure that captures whether new edges are being formed fast enough to consistently fall 'in front' of the infectivity window. The image here is similar to an old Road Runner cartoon, where the coyote is frantically laying track just ahead of the rapidly approaching train: for a bit that is time-sensitive relative to last transmission, the next transmission edge must be laid quickly. I am unaware of any closed-form solutions for this problem.

The second way in which timing matters is in determining transmissibility paths, since goods can only flow forward in time. This is true regardless of the dyadic probability of transfer. For example, in thinking about STD risk, we are at risk from our sexual partners' past partners, but not future partners after they leave us. This idea is captured by the notion of a *time-ordered path*. A time-ordered path consists of a standard graph path, with the added stipulation that the finish time for each additional step along the path is greater than or equal to the starting time of the previous step (Moody 2002). Once time order is considered, contact paths—the chains of edges linked by nodes we are familiar with—become illusory with respect to diffusion. Seemingly connected components when time is ignored become fractured once time is introduced. Consider as an example Figure 19.4 below, which consists of a simple circle graph of 8 nodes. In panel (a) all edges occur at the same time, and reachability (the proportion of ordered pairs that could reach each other) is complete. In the rest of the panels, edges exist at the times listed next to them (here treated as discrete intervals). Here the same set of edges result in a nearly twofold difference in diffusion potential based solely on when relations occur.

Reachability in a timed network thus ranges from complete, when all edges in a connected-contact component exist at the same time, to a graph-specific minimum achieved when edges are timed to break long paths into shorter ones. This minimum occurs when paths have an 'early–late–early' timing sequence. If every actor has only 2 direct contacts, then the minimum reachable would be 3 others, as seen in Figure 19.5 below. The closed-form solution for this minimum is known for graphs with constant degree (Moody 2002), but identifying a minimum-reachability graph for any arbitrary degree distribution requires algorithmic search.[10] This minimum is analytically useful as a baseline for disentangling the diffusion effects of relational timing from the diffusion effects of contact structure.

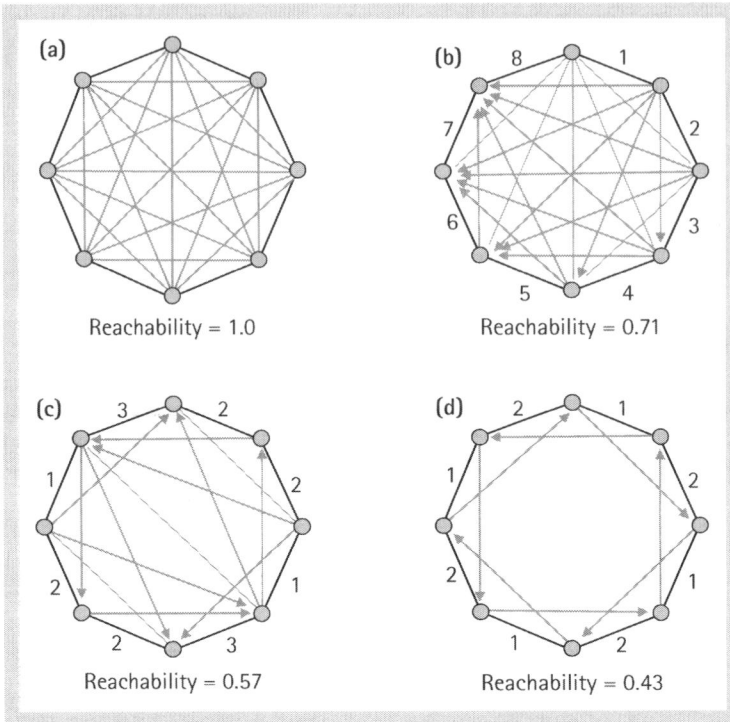

Fig. 19.4 Effect of edge timing on diffusion potential

19.2.3 The duality of concurrency and cycles

The level of concurrency and the number of cycles are two key determinants of diffusion in a dynamic network. Since both of these features are likely affected by local (node-level) rules for relational behavior, they are prime targets for linking network evolution and diffusion. Concurrency exists whenever two edges sharing a node exist at the same time. Concurrency in sexual relations occurs when one starts

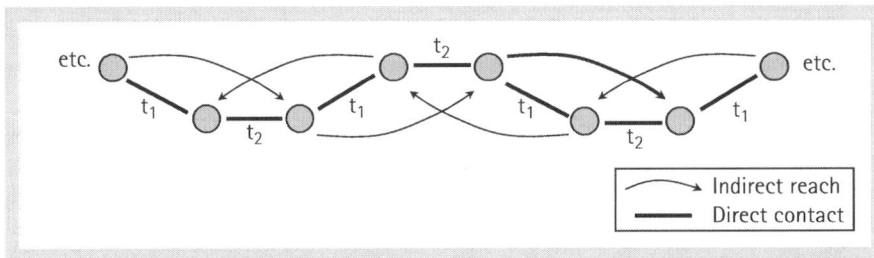

Fig. 19.5 A time ordering for a two-regular graph that minimizes reachability

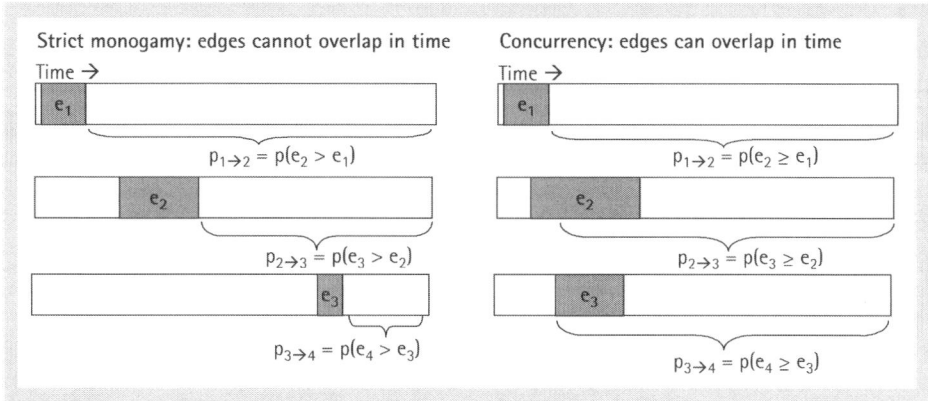

Fig. 19.6 Time–sample space for monogamy and concurrency

a second relation before ending the first. Concurrency is complete in graphs such as electricity-transmission wires, plumbing-pipe systems, or highways, where every edge is ongoing with those adjacent.

The level of concurrency increases diffusion for three reasons. First, overlapping relations minimize the amount of time a bit is trapped in a given dyad, making infectivity windows unimportant.[11] Second, for any fixed observation window, concurrency increases the probability of drawing a later edge from the set of all possible edges in the graph state-space, thus creating longer diffusion paths. Consider Figure 19.6, which portrays the emergence of edges along a four-step path over a period of time. When concurrency is not allowed, each new edge must be drawn from a pool of edges that shrinks over time, since you can only draw new edges from the future. But with concurrency, each new edge can be drawn from anywhere in the time space.[12] Since the probability of the chain· is the product of each step, the joint probability is higher in the concurrency case, and we should find more long paths when concurrency is high.

Finally, and I think most significantly, concurrent relations make asymmetric time-ordered paths symmetric, rapidly increasing the set of nodes mutually at risk to transmission. Consider Figure 19.7 below.

When relations do not overlap, a can reach c, but not vice versa. This implies that every future partner of a (and all their future partners) is safe from any infection introduced by c to b. But when the relations overlap in time, the formerly asymmetric-path becomes symmetric, and the set of all nodes following a are now at risk to a bit introduced by c (and vice versa). From a reachability standpoint, a graph with no concurrency will have almost entirely asymmetric paths; as concurrency increases the reachability matrix becomes more symmetric and correspondingly denser.

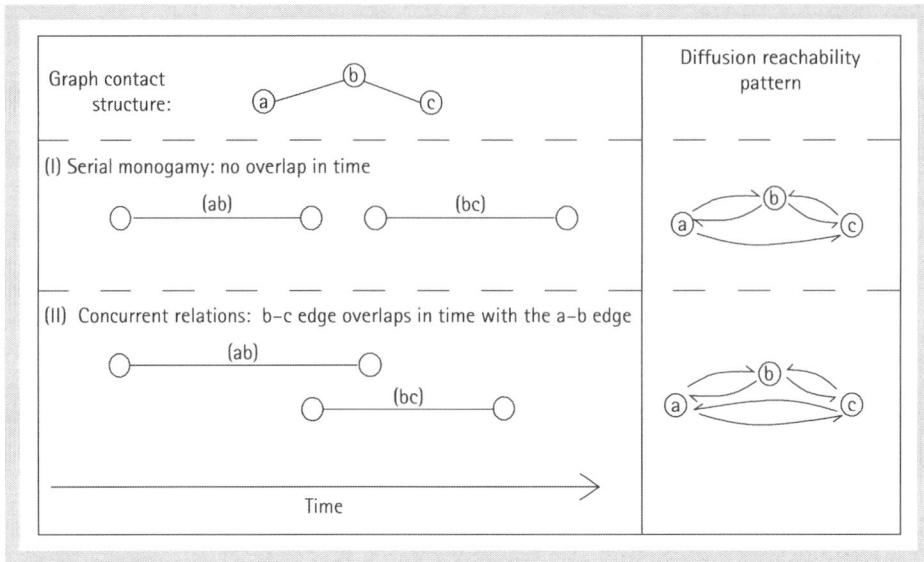

Fig. 19.7 Effect of concurrency on the symmetry of indirect relations

Cycles in graphs are paths that start and end in the same node. At the dyad level, we can also imagine repeated contact as a type of temporal cycle, in the sense that a path exists from i to j then later from j to i through repeated contact. Cycles in the contact and timing structure have much the same effect as concurrent ties, bringing a bit from 'downstream' back to an 'upstream' source. The link between concurrency and cycles is actually somewhat deeper. One can imagine slicing a network into very small time sets—moments—where it would be exceedingly rare to see two relations overlapping in time. In such a set, a relation termed 'concurrent' at one level of time aggregation (an i–j–k triple) would be seen as a sequence of dyadic cycles (i–j, j–k, j–i, . . . , etc.) at a lower level of time aggregation. Thus, concurrency at a higher level of aggregation is simply a cycle at a finer time scale.

Cycles are substantively interesting because there are likely strong content-based rules that govern the likelihood of seeing cycles of different lengths. For example, strong in-group preferences for minority populations will decrease the number of potential partners and thus, for the same average degree, increase the number of cycles.[13] Results from Bearman, Moody, and Stovel (2004) suggest that adolescents avoid short cycles in romantic ties, which through a constraint mechanism similar to the minority mixing example above must increase the number of long-distance cycles.

A final timing feature that intersects with contact structure is relational scheduling (Gibson 2005). While analytically distinct from the edge-timing features discussed thus far, in most substantive settings there are strong content features for either the bit or the node that create scheduling constraints. For example, while one can send an email to thousands of people simultaneously, one can read them only one at a time. Similarly, while commercial sex workers may have many sexual partners, there are limits to the number at any given moment. Since the most typical scheduling problems are based on sorting high volume, these factors can make star nodes bottlenecks for diffusion rather than shortcuts that route a bit instantaneously to many others.

19.2.4 Summary of dynamic effects on diffusion

Time shapes diffusion by changing the within-dyad likelihood of transmission and limiting potential diffusion paths. These simple effects have profound implications for systems features of networks, since most analysis programs designed to identify reach (and thus diffusion potential) treat all adjacencies as concurrent, greatly inflating diffusion potential (see examples below). Within-network position measures that rest on path structure, such as centrality or block position, are likely also misleading. Pure timing effects, however, can never be disentangled from the contact structure, since every structure requires some minimum connectivity. In addition, since rules for constructing and ending relations must be enacted dynamically, there is a strong substantive reason to link diffusion dynamics to network diffusion, which I address next.

19.3 LINKING NETWORK EVOLUTION
TO DIFFUSION

There is little work that explicitly links network evolution and diffusion. The linkage is implicit in models of social outcomes resulting from network change, such as work on networks and markets (Baker 1984; White 2002), opinion formation (Friedkin 1998), and iterated game theory. The clearest line of work in this vein allows both the ideation and the network to co-evolve (Mark 1998; Baldassarri and Bearman 2007). I now explore this linkage by first describing how micro-level behavior rules affect diffusion capacity, and then move to the system level to briefly explore how timing changes our view of otherwise well-known structural models. This section is largely exploratory, suggesting new ways we might think about how networks and time intersect with diffusion. It is meant to suggest future directions for a wide-open field, and makes no claim to cover the scope of all possible questions in this area.

19.3.1 Micromechanisms linking timing and structure

In most empirical settings the presence of normative rules about relation timing likely shapes relational patterns as well. For example, since concurrency in romantic ties is normatively sanctioned, actors seek to hide these relations to avoid detection, which may take them to socially distant partners, which in turn widens the risk network (Adams 2007). Or, in cases where concurrency is crucial to the relational activity, such as brokering structural holes, actors need to bridge multiple social worlds to extract information and arbitrage benefit, but likely need to minimize the visibility of the hole spanned to maintain a real profit.

Explicit timing models that would govern the formation and dissolution of ties for network relations are rare. Balance models predict which ties should be unstable, but do not specify how long they will last (but see Burt 2002). Homophily models suggest that the risk of dissolution increases as homophily decreases, but again this is not explicitly linked to tie timing. Empirically we have information on the duration of romantic (Cate, Levin, and Richmond 2000) and friendship (Suitor, Wellman, and Morgan 1997) ties across different settings, but little theory about a 'life course' for relations per se. While we typically expect sanctions for concurrent romantic relations, the interaction factors governing this norm have attracted less attention than simple demographic profiles of those most likely to have concurrent relations (Laumann et al. 2004). In general, there is much work to be done on specifying families of timing rules: ways that actors coordinate and sequence multiple relations across different types of relational domains.

The second way to approach the linkage is to incorporate time into structural models. For example, Bearman, Moody, and Stovel (2004) found that high-school romantic relations tend to avoid four-cycles. This avoidance is based on an analog to an incest taboo: the relation that would create a four-cycle becomes too relationally close. Dynamically this is an interesting type of node-attribute prohibition since the off-limit status is one that emerges over time: a node that at time 1 would have been an acceptable partner becomes unacceptable as relations unfold in time. From a diffusion standpoint, the prohibition for short cycles will (in any network of fixed density) increase the number of long cycles, which increases general-diffusion potential.

Since a potential four-cycle can only form after a three-step chain has emerged, one could build time into the model by asking if particular temporal patterns for the unfolding of three-chains are more or less visible, and thus more or less salient for the formation of future relations. Figure 19.8 presents the set of all possible timed three-chains, with numbers on edges denoting order. The top row consists of all nonconcurrent patterns, the bottom of all patterns that contain concurrency.[14]

While empirical research on these unfolding chains has yet to be done, we can build hypotheses based on the information content implied by the ordering. That is, we could imagine that actors know of their current partner's most recent other

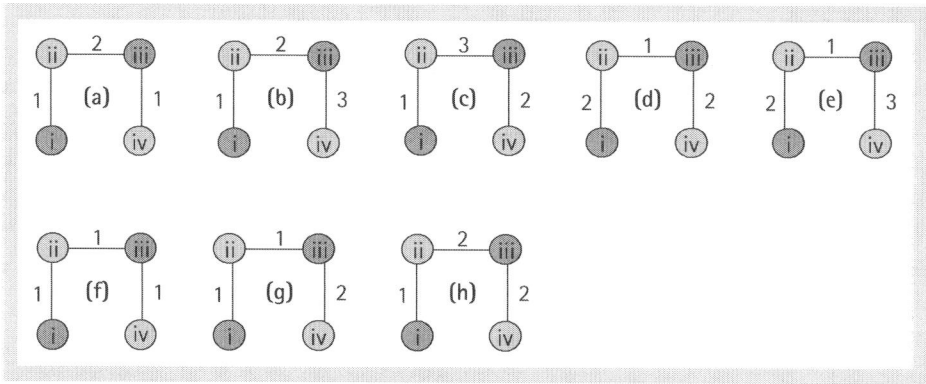

Fig. 19.8 Possible time sets for potential four-cycles

partner. This would suggest that pattern (d) would be more visible than pattern (a), since in (d) the nodes that could create a four-cycle (i and iv) would know their t2 partner's history, but in (a) they may not. Similarly, I imagine that the chains arising from concurrency are generally less visible, as actors may be either actively hiding them or drawing partners from otherwise disconnected social worlds. However, pattern (g) is likely least visible—particularly if node iii was left unaware of ii's concurrent relation with i.[15] Alternatively, an unfolding that links pattern considerations could make cycles unlikely. So, for example, if nodes search for homophily on at least one dimension, but seek a new partner after a breakup that is different than their last, then in sequences such as (d) or (e) the tail nodes may be quite distant in the attribute space and thus unlikely to form a relation based purely on homophily. In any event, careful readings of the temporal unfolding of local patterns could be built into our structure models for networks to inform diffusion.

We can build a similar process for the popular preferential-attachment models (Barrabasi and Albert 1999), by adding limits on edge duration or concurrent partners. In the standard model, as new nodes enter the population they attach to the most active nodes already there, and thus first movers should acquire more ties quickly, and cumulative degree should correlate with time in the network. If current degree is limited by either scheduling or resource issues, then as new ties are added, old ties are dropped. This simple dynamic has three immediate implications for diffusion. First, the set of people exposed through an 'attractor' node decreases with the speed of new-tie acquisition, since these become effectively short-duration edges, and thus only a narrow time-range of bits can pass through those chains onto other nodes. Second, the reachability becomes asymmetric around the attractor node, as his new contacts are at risk to bits introduced by the first set, but not vice versa. Third, since those who first attach to the attractor nodes are themselves likely to be high degree later in time, if the ties between the stars have ended, then what appear to be linked shortcuts capable of fast transmission are not connected in time, thus limiting overall diffusion. Thus, a seemingly efficient and rapid transition system may be highly constrained due to the limiting effects of immediate degree.

We could extend this general strategy—of linking a time-dependent feature of the pattern behavior to local diffusion—in multiple directions. In the markets-and-networks field, a niche-filling model should favor new ties that span long distances (see Powell et al. 2005 for the biotech case), which should link information from widely disparate areas of the network. If edges are very short-lived, however, then the information will likely not move far (see simulation results below). Or, if knowledge acquired through a contact affects your attraction to new contacts, then this could create a self-reinforcing opinion network that, if the initial contact patterns are distinct, can create bifurcations in the idea space. In general, the key to linking diffusion processes to network evolution rests on carefully thinking about how a local-level attachment rule intersects with edge timing to string together edges that form properly time-ordered diffusion paths. This is a ripe area for future research.

19.3.2 Macromodels and emergent contact dynamics

In the next two sections I want to demonstrate how simple behavior rules for networks will generate dynamic networks that ultimately constrain diffusion, even though the analogous case without timing would suggest rapid and complete diffusion potential. In the first case I seek a model that is a close dynamic analog to simple random graphs, which may thus form a baseline for future work. In the second I want to ask how replacing a static assumption for edges with a simple random-duration parameter affects fundamental conclusions of the structural model.

19.3.3 The cocktail-party problem

Barabassi (2002) opens his book on the power of networks with a fun example. Having invited over a group of acquaintances, the host lets a few close friends know that there's an unmarked bottle of fine wine behind the bar. Although he tells only a few people, a short time later he finds that the wine bottle is empty and many people he did not tell complement him on the great wine and how generous it is to bring out the good stuff. This is, obviously, a clear story about network diffusion: from a small number of 'seed' nodes, the news spread throughout the party and the wine was quickly consumed.

We might call this situation the 'cocktail-party problem': given a fully dynamic network, where nodes converse for only a short time, how likely is it that the network will become fully connected—capable of spreading information to and from all partygoers? One abstraction of the situation would be to distribute nodes

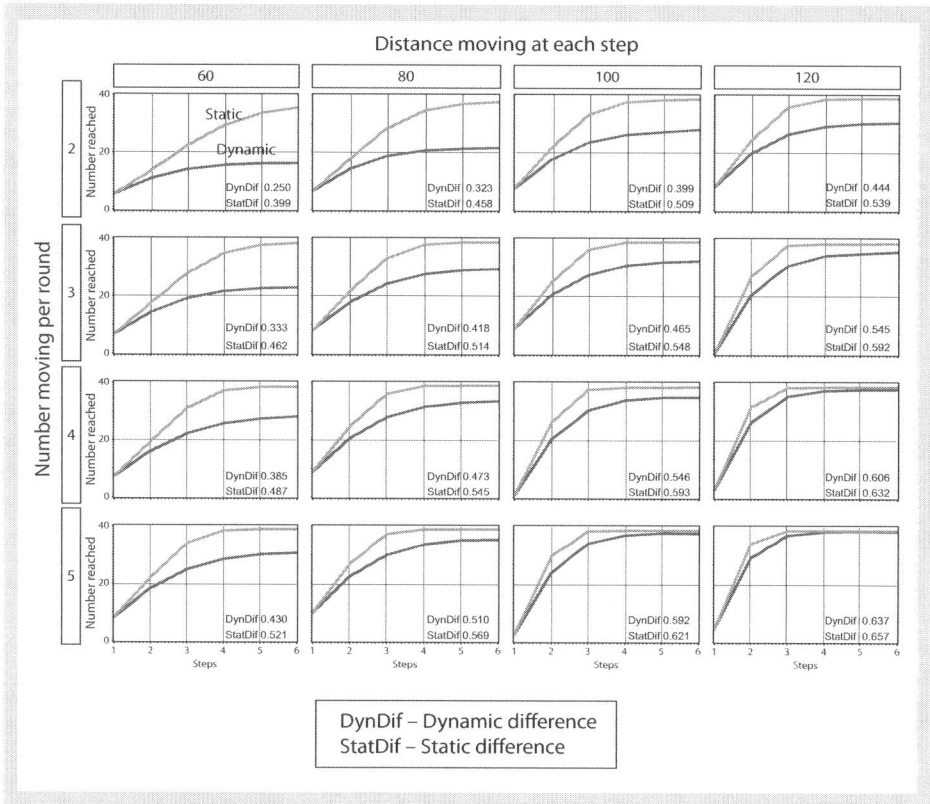

Fig. 19.9 Cocktail-party mean reachability

randomly across a space and let them move randomly, forming edges to those they are close to. Nodes wander at each iteration—they typically don't move much, but every so often they do, moving away from their current conversation partners into the orbits of others. This model thus has two dynamic parameters: the relative frequency of long-distance moves and the length of those moves. A third (static) parameter describes the 'orbit' size: how many people they can talk with at any give time.

At any moment, the graph consists of a set of disconnected conversation cliques; as people mingle they break groups and form new ones.[16] The two dynamic parameters have different effects on the construction of the network. As people take long steps more frequently, they are more likely to change relations quickly; duration thus drops but degree increases. But if the distance moved is short, they will ultimately stay in the same general region of the space for most of the time, ultimately meeting the same people. As the length of moves increases, actors come into entirely new worlds. Figure 19.9 summarizes a set of typical results for this setup.

A trace through a network plots the cumulative number of people reachable within a given number of steps (Pool and Kochen 1978). Figure 19.9 plots the mean of traces for all forty actors across the simulation space. Because potential diffusion paths are truncated when relations end, dynamic traces falls under the static (i.e. contact-ignoring-time) curve. The two dynamic parameters both contribute independently to increasing connectivity, and, even though they work through different underlying mechanisms, have a roughly parallel effect on ultimate reachability and diffusion. As people start moving further in the space (across the columns), they build long-distance bridges and thus increase connectivity. Similarly, when actors move often, they create new ties at a faster rate and similarly increase overall diffusion. Thus, as in our discussion of the general properties of dynamic diffusion, we can generate a great deal of network connectivity *either* by increasing numbers of partners *or* by building long-distance alternate routes around dynamic breaks. Of course, the effect is strongest when both features operate simultaneously (moving down the diagonal).[17]

This is a simple dynamic-network model: the rules govern random movement in a social space, and the key interaction features (duration, overlap, cycles) all emerge 'accidentally' from those parameters. This is, then, effectively the dynamic equivalent of the simplest random graph, which has formed the foundation of most statistical approaches to networks. A simple dynamic model of this sort may provide some key insights into how diffusion emerges in random graphs. Of key interest will be understanding how rates of partner change, duration, and so forth affect the sustainability of diffusion in dynamic networks.

19.3.4 Dynamic models with contact structure: rethinking the small-world effect

Some of the most influential recent work in social networks is based on Duncan Watt's 'small-world model' of social networks (1999). The heart of the model rests on a seeming paradox: while most of our contacts are directly connected to each other, we can nonetheless reach (nearly) everyone on the planet in a few relational steps. How is this possible? Watts shows clearly that in networks constructed to have very high levels of connection among friends—high local clustering—the addition of a small number of random ties will dramatically shorten the average distance between everyone in the network.

These random shortcuts lower average distance, making diffusion more likely. Importantly, the returns to new random ties are decreasing at the margins: the first few ties make a dramatic reduction in average distance, but additional ties have only a small effect. We can think of this rapid return to shortcuts as the functional signature of the small-world mechanism. This implies that it doesn't take much random activity to lower the average distance, and thus presumably increase the diffusion potential of a network. Most of the work building on the small-world

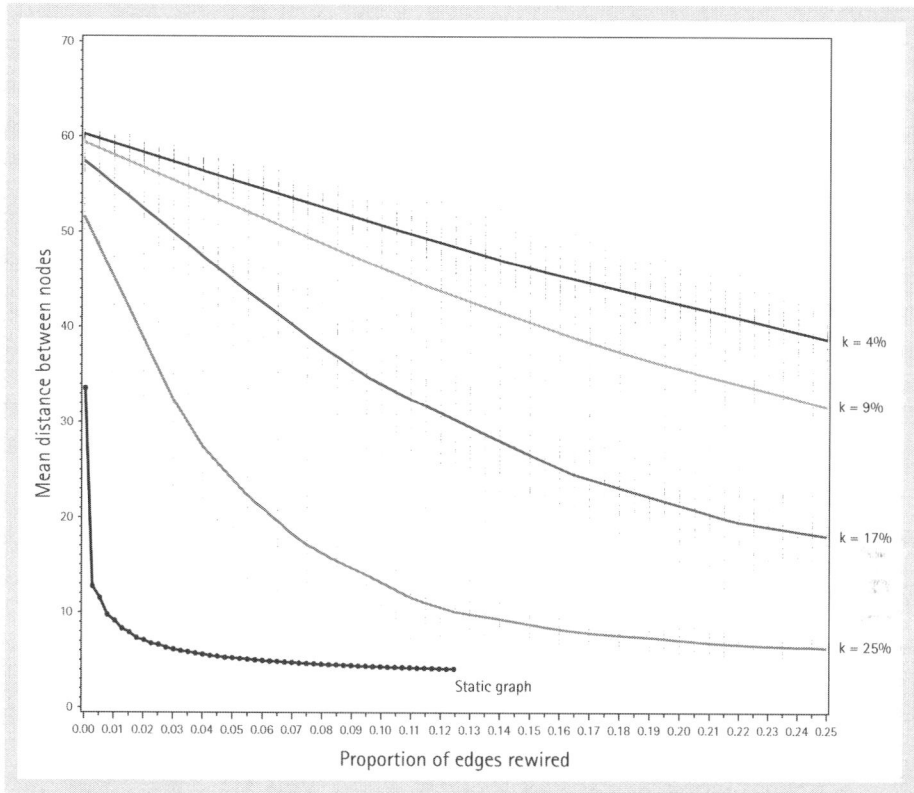

Fig. 19.10 Effect of rewiring on mean distance in a dynamic small-world model

model treats the underlying network as static. But what happens when we relax this assumption?

Figure 19.10 provides results of a simulation experiment designed to answer this question. Here I construct a degree = 6, nearest-neighbor ring lattice of 200 nodes.[18] Each edge in the graph has a start time drawn from a uniform distribution over the observation window and a randomly assigned duration drawn from a skewed distribution. The extent of concurrency in the graph is controlled by adjusting the dispersion of start times, here chosen to create four levels between 4 percent and 25 percent edge concurrency. These are substantively high levels of concurrency for many empirical settings. For this network, a 4 percent edge-concurrency rate implies that nearly 50 percent of nodes are involved in a concurrent relation. In contrast, Laumann et al. (2004) reports that around 30 percent of males and 16 percent of females in Cook County had concurrent relations with their most recent sex partner. When edge concurrency is 25 percent, every node is involved in concurrent relations.[19] The bottom line gives the effect of rewiring in a similar static graph.

Rewiring of the dynamic graph does not show the immediate returns to shortcuts characteristic of the static small-world model. Instead, rewiring lowers the average distance between nodes in a linear fashion unless concurrency is very high. However, even at the highest concurrency levels, the effect is slower than would be expected in a static graph. This suggests that the diffusion effect of small amounts of randomness will be limited in dynamic network settings and thus to effectively lower the distance in the graph we need many more random ties.

The rewiring effect fails in these dynamic networks because the shortcut ties, in addition to linking otherwise disconnected sets, must also occur at the right time in the path sequence; a shortcut that lands on a node with few future ties will have no substantive effect on the network. Thus, it takes either very high levels of concurrency (as assumed in a static graph) or many more rewirings to have an effect similar to that observed in static graphs. Note as well that this model makes no substantive distinction between the duration of local or rewired ties. We might expect, however, that rewired ties are structurally weak and thus of shorter duration. If so, their role in creating diffusion potential will be even lower.

Conclusion and Extensions: What's Next?

Dynamic networks pose challenges for all sorts of classic social-network methods, ranging from visualizing dynamic graphs (Moody, McFarland, and Bender-deMoll 2005), to measuring and modeling the underlying network. In this chapter I have attempted to identify how thinking about graphs as linked sets of nodes, edges, and times—as $G(V, E, T)$ instead of $G(V, E)$—is critical for our understanding of the development of structure and the diffusion of things through those structures. The general problems associated with dynamic graphs are larger, and will create many opportunities for new advances in our work.

For example, since diffusion depends on properly time-ordered paths, it may make sense to give more thought to how edges are linked to each other in time, rather than how nodes are linked through edges, which suggests using a dynamic version of the line graph.[20] Every edge in the contact graph is converted to a node in the line graph, and a directed edge is drawn from an earlier to a later contact edge. This time-defined version of the line graph, as a structural projection of all three elements of a dynamic graph, holds all of the information we care about for dynamic diffusion. But it is a somewhat odd projection substantively, since it removes the nodes we are used to thinking about from the picture entirely (though this does fit with some movements in current social theory; Emirbayer 1997).

The fundamental features of graphs that make them systems are paths: linked sets of edges. As such, most of our substantively important measures on networks—centrality, blocking, cohesion, and so forth—rest explicitly or implicitly on the underlying path structure. Since this set of paths is truncated in a timed graph—and done so in ways that change features such as the transitive nature of distance between nodes—most of our measures of network properties must be rethought for dynamic graphs. Some of these extensions are simple—just reworking the standard statistics with a time-based version of the path/reachability matrix. But others offer substantive challenges, such as creating trajectory-based measures or blockings of times instead of nodes to capture ritualized action in network dynamics (see McFarland 2004, 2006).

Finally, statistical models are now emerging that can handle both the evolution of the network and the influence of the network on a given node property (Snijders et al. 2005; Snijders, Steglich, and Schweinberger 2007). These statistical models use network evolution as part of the estimation routine, evolving a graph through a Markov space. In principle, these models should make it possible to carefully specify action rules for network evolution that we can then easily evaluate for diffusion potential. Substantively, I suspect that by admitting time to networks we will be forced toward more particular, substance-based network models rather than the 'one-structure-fits-all' solutions we have been used to (such as small-world models, scale-free models, or balance models). That is, while the networks field has vaunted generality for most of its history, the particulars of how goods flow, how relations form, and how these interact to form dynamic diffusion systems all suggest that substance-specific methods and models will be required.

NOTES

1. For those familiar with the exponential-random-graph framework, this term largely encompasses 'dyad independence' models.
2. Such models also include attribute-based relational restrictions, such as the propensity for cross-sex ties in romantic relations, culturally defined age difference between sex partners, or incest taboos against close-kin sexual relations.
3. Shelling's models were not based on networks, but the translation from neighbors in geography to neighbors in networks is transparent.
4. Though the literature is strangely silent about how such relations must be forming faster as well, to maintain a fairly constant cross-section distribution.
5. It should be noted that Burt does not propose his model as a strategic guide for social relations. Structural holes are valuable, in his settings, just to the extent that they bridge otherwise fixed holes.

6. The dashed transitions are those that actors should avoid due to balance theory: they decrease transitivity or increase intransitivity. These two effects are distinguishable, and it appears that avoiding intransitivity is more powerful for actors than seeking transitivity (Moody 1999), but they are collapsed in this figure in the interests of visual simplicity.

7. Per act, probability of transfer for many sexually transmitted diseases is less than 1/1000. This makes within-dyad transmission crucially dependent on the duration of the relation, as even rare transmission events are likely given enough time. However, relational duration also plays directly into the other order features outlined here, likely creating extremely interesting dependencies that I leave to future work.

8. The probability that a good passes from i to j given k independent paths connect them is equal to the sums of the probability that it passes along each path minus the probability that it passes over multiple paths. When paths are not independent, this calculation is not trivial.

9. In cases like HIV, infectivity increases again toward the end of the virus's life cycle in the host, creating a two-peak curve.

10. The minimum depends on the degree distribution because actors must be able to pass a bit to their direct contacts and they must make those contacts at some moment in time, so anything that was passed to them by their first contact must put all subsequent contacts at risk. The length of these chains is determined by how the ordering is sequenced.

11. Technically, this effect is due to the fact that concurrent relations shorten the time between acquiring a bit and passing it on to zero. One can imagine a relational system where at the moment the bit is passed from i to j, j ends the relation with i and forms a new relation with k—like an old-fashioned bucket brigade. This would create zero concurrency but also minimize the time a bit is stuck in the host. This only works, however, for degree = 2; if degree > 2 then scheduling makes it impossible to make the transmission delay zero for all partners.

12. The notion of a time-space to draw edges from is most relevant when our interest is on diffusion within a particular observation window, though it is also relevant for any real-world data-collection space, where the observed window is some time prior to the interview.

13. The maximum number of independent cycles in any component is the number of edges minus the number of nodes minus 1 (Harary 1969).

14. These are time-isomophic patterns, so they are robust to flips or rotation. So, for example, pattern (b) is equivalent to a timing such as 3–2–1. Since order is all that matters, pattern (a) would be the same if it were 2–3–2 instead of 1–2–1.

15. Of course, if the concurrency itself is the reason for the relation to end, then these patterns would be most visible.

16. For a fully dynamic visualization of the simulation see <http://www.soc.duke.edu/~jmoody77/cparty1.mov>, accessed 2008.

17. The inset statistics are a simple summary of diffusion potential in any network. For each dyad, the score is reachable × (1/distance), which is then averaged over the entire graph.

18. I have used other network structures. When degree is lower even at the highest concurrency levels rewiring has a linear, rather than decreasing-marginal-return, effect on distance. Results available on request.

19. Since temporal ordering breaks up strong components, many dyads will be unreachable and thus infinitely distant. I set the distance between unreachable pairs to the maximum distance in the static nonrewired graph. Since edge timing is randomly assigned, each trial produces somewhat varying results, and Figure 19.10 plots a LOESS regression line over the observed data points.

20. The idea of using a line graph for dynamic networks was first introduced by Morris and Kretzschmar (1995, 1997); the extension to a directed version is my building on a suggestion by Scott Feld.

References

Abbott, A. (1995), 'Sequence Analysis: New Methods for Old Ideas', *Annual Review of Sociology*, 21: 93–113.

—— (1998), 'The Causal Devolution', *Sociological Methods & Research*, 27: 148–81.

Baker, W. (1984), 'The Social Structure of a National Securities Market', *American Journal of Sociology*, 89: 775–811.

Baldassarri, D., and Bearman, P. S. (2007), 'Dynamics of Political Polarization', *American Sociological Review*, 72: 784–11.

Barabassi, A. (2002), *Linked: How Everything Is Connected to Everything Else and What It Means* (New York: Perseus).

—— and Albert, R. (1999), 'Emergence of Scaling in Random Networks', *Science*, 286: 509–12.

Bauman, K. E., and Ennett, S. T. (1994), 'Peer Influence on Adolescent Drug Use', *American Psychologist*, 49 (9): 820–2.

Bearman, P. (1997), 'Generalized Exchange', *American Journal of Sociology*, 102 (5): 1383–415.

—— and Everett, K. (1993), 'The Structure of Social Protest', *Social Networks*, 15: 171–200.

—— Moody, J., and Stovel, K. (2004), 'Chains of Affection', *American Journal of Sociology*, 110: 44–91.

Borgatti, S. P. (2005), 'Centrality and Network Flow', *Social Networks*, 27: 55–71.

Burt, R. S. (1992), *Structural Holes: The Social Structure of Competition* (Cambridge, Mass.: Harvard University Press).

—— (2002), 'Bridge Decay', *Social Networks*, 24: 333–63.

—— (2005), *Brokerage and Closure: An Introduction to Social Capital* (Oxford: Oxford University Press).

Cartwright, D., and Harary, F. (1956), 'Structural Balance: A Generalization of Heider's Theory', *Psychological Review*, 63: 277–93.

Cate, R. M., Levin, L. A., and Richmond, L. S. (2000), 'Premarital Relationship Stability: A Review of Recent Research', *Journal of Social and Personal Relationships*, 19: 261–84.

Chase, I. D. (1980), 'Social Process and Hierarchy Formation in Small Groups: A Comparative Perspective', *American Sociological Review*, 45: 905–24.

Cohen, J. M. (1977), 'Sources of Peer Group Homogeneity', *Sociology of Education*, 50: 227–41.

—— (1983), 'Peer Influence on College Aspirations', *American Sociological Review*, 48: 728–34.

Doreian, P., et al. (1996), 'A Brief History of Balance Through Time', *Journal of Mathematical Sociology*, 21 (1–2): 113–31.

DUNPHY, D. C. (1963), 'The Social Structure of Urban Adolescent Peer Groups', *Sociometry*, 26: 230–46.

EKEH, P. P. (1974), *Social Exchange Theory: The Two Traditions* (Cambridge, Mass.: Harvard University Press).

EMIRBAYER, M. (1997), 'Manifesto for Relational Sociology', *American Journal of Sociology*, 103: 281–317.

FARARO, T. J. (1981), 'Biased Networks and Social Structure Theorems', *Social Networks*, 3: 137–59.

FELD, S. L. (1981), 'The Focused Organization of Social Ties', *American Journal of Sociology*, 86: 1015–35.

FRIEDKIN, N. E. (1998), *A Structural Theory of Social Influence* (Cambridge: Cambridge University Press).

GARNETT, G. P., and JOHNSON, A. M. (1997), 'Coining a New Term in Epidemiology: Concurrency and HIV', *AIDS*, 11: 681–3.

GIBSON, D. R. (2005), 'Concurrency and Commitment: Network Scheduling and Its Consequences for Diffusion', *Journal of Mathematical Sociology*, 29: 295–323.

GOULD, R. (2002), 'The Origins of Status Hierarchies: A Formal Theory and Empirical Test', *American Journal of Sociology*, 107: 1143–78.

GRANOVETTER, M. (1973), 'The Strength of Weak Ties', *American Journal of Sociology*, 81: 1287–303.

HALLINAN, M. T., and HUTCHINS, E. E. (1980), 'Structural Effects on Dyadic Change', *Social Forces*, 59 (1): 225–45.

——and KUBITSCHEK, W. N. (1990), 'The Formation of Intransitive Friendships', *Social Forces*, 69 (2): 505–19.

——and WILLIAMS, R. A. (1987), 'The Stability of Students' Interracial Friendships', *American Sociological Review*, 52: 653–64.

——(1990), 'Students' Characteristics and the Peer-influence Process', *Sociology of Education*, 63: 122–32.

HARARY, F. (1969), *Graph Theory* (Reading, Mass.: Addison-Wesley).

HAYNIE, D. (2001), 'Delinquent Peers Revisited: Does Network Structure Matter?', *American Journal of Sociology*, 106: 1013–57.

HEIDER, F. (1946), 'Attitudes and Cognitive Organization', *Journal of Psychology*, 21: 107–12.

HOLLAND, P., and LEINHARDT, S. (1977), 'A Dynamic Model for Social Networks', *Journal of Mathematical Sociology*, 5: 5–20.

INGRAM, P., and MORRIS, M. (2007), 'Do People Mix at Mixers? Structure, Homophily, and the Pattern of Encounter at a Business Networking Party', *Administrative Science Quarterly*, 52: 558–85.

JOHNSEN, E. C. (1986), 'Structure and Process: Agreement Models for Friendship Formation', *Social Networks*, 8: 257–306.

KANDEL, D. B. (1985) 'On Processes of Peer Influences in Adolescent Drug Use', in B. Stimmel (ed.), *Alcohol and Substance Abuse in Adolescence* (New York: Haworth).

LAUMANN, E. O., et al. (2004), *The Sexual Organization of the City* (Chicago, Ill.: University of Chicago Press).

LESKOVEC, J., KLEINBERG, J., and FALOUTSOS, C. (2005), 'Graphs Over Time: Densification Laws, Shrinking Diameters and Possible Explanations', *Procedings of the 11th ACM SIGKDD International Conference on Knowledge Discovery and Data Mining*, at <http:// www.cs.cornell.edu/home/kleinber/kdd05-time.pdf>, accessed Feb. 2009.

McFARLAND, D. (2004), 'Resistance as a Social Drama—A Study of Change-oriented Encounters', *American Journal of Sociology*, 109 (6): 1249–318.

—— (2006), 'Curricular Flows: Trajectories, Turning Points, and Assignment Criteria in High School Math Careers', *Sociology of Education*, 79 (3): 177–205.

McPHERSON, J. M., and SMITH-LOVIN, L. (1987), 'Homophily in Voluntary Organizations: Status Distance and the Composition of Face-to-face Groups', *American Sociological Review*, 52: 370–9.

McPHERSON, M., and RANGER-MOORE, J. (1991), 'Evolution on a Dancing Landscape: Organizations and Networks in Dynamic Blau Space', *Social Forces*, 70: 19–42.

MARK, N. (1998), 'Birds of a Feather Sing Together', *Social Forces*, 77: 453–85.

MOODY, J. (1999), *The Structure of Adolescent Social Relations: Modeling Friendship in Dynamic Social Settings* (Chapel Hill, N.C.: University of North Carolina Press).

—— (2001), 'Race, School Integration, and Friendship Segregation in America', *American Journal of Sociology*, 107: 679–716.

—— (2002), 'The Importance of Relationship Timing for Diffusion', *Social Forces*, 81: 25–56.

—— McFARLAND, D. A., and BENDER-deMOLL, S. (2005), 'Dynamic Network Visualization', *American Journal of Sociology*, 110: 1206–41.

—— and WHITE, D. R. (2003), 'Social Cohesion and Embeddedness: A Hierarchical Conception of Social Groups', *American Sociological Review*, 68: 103–27.

MORGAN, D. L., NEAL, M. B., and CARDER, P. (1997), 'The Stability of Core and Peripheral Networks Over Time', *Social Networks*, 19 (1): 9–25.

MORRIS, M., and KRETZSCHMAR, M. (1995), 'Concurrent Partnerships and Transmission Dynamics in Networks', *Social Networks*, 17 (special issue on 'Social Networks and Infectious Disease: HIV/AIDS'): 299–318.

—— (1997), 'Concurrent Partnerships and the Spread of HIV', *AIDS*, 11: 641–8.

PALMER, E. N. (1985), *Graphical Evolution: An Introduction to the Theory of Random Graphs* (New York: Wiley).

POTTERAT, J. H., et al. (1999), 'Chlamydia Transmission: Concurrency, Reproduction Number and the Epidemic Trajectory', *American Journal of Epidemiology*, 150: 1331–9.

POWELL, W. W., et al. (2005), 'Network Dynamics and Field Evolution: The Growth of Interorganizational Collaboration in the Life Sciences', *American Journal of Sociology*, 110 (4): 1132–205.

RAPOPORT, A., and HORVATH, W. J. (1961), 'A Study of a Large Sociogram', *Behavioral Science*, 6: 279–91.

ROY, W. G. (1983), 'The Unfolding of the Interlocking Directorate Structure of the United States', *American Sociological Review*, 48: 248–57.

SCHELLING, T. (1971), 'Dynamic Models of Segregation', *Journal of Mathematical Sociology*, 1: 143–86.

SNIJDERS, T. A. B. (2002), 'A Multilevel Network Study of the Effects of Delinquent Behavior in Friendship Evolution', unpublished manuscript.

—— et al. (2005), 'New Specifications for Exponential Random Graph Models', *Sociological Methodology*, 32: 301–37.

—— STEGLICH, C. E. G., and SCHWEINBERGER, M. (2007), 'Modeling the Co-evolution of Networks and Behavior', in K. V. Montfort, H. Oud, and A. Satorra (eds.), *Longitudinal Models in the Behavioral and Related Sciences* (Mahwah, N.J.: Lawrence Erlbaum).

SOLA POOL, I. DE, and KOCHEN, M. (1978), 'Contacts and Influence', *Social Networks*, 1: 5–51.

Suitor, J. J., and Keeton, S. (1997), 'Once a Friend, Always a Friend? Effects of Homophily of Women's Support Networks Across a Decade', *Social Networks*, 19 (1): 51–62.

——Wellman, B., and Morgan, D. L. (1997), 'It's About Time: How, Why and When Networks Change', *Social Networks*, 19 (1): 1–7.

Tuma, N. B., and Hallinan, M. T. (1979), 'The Effects of Sex, Race, and Achievement on Schoolchildren's Friendships', *Social Forces*, 571 (4): 1265–85.

Wasserman, S., and Faust, K. (1994), *Social Network Analysis* (Cambridge: Cambridge University Press).

Watts, D. J. (1999), 'Networks, Dynamics, and the Small-world Phenomenon', *American Journal of Sociology*, 105: 493–527.

Weesie, J., and Flap, H. (1990), *Social Networks Through Time* (Utrecht: ISOR).

Wellman, B., et al. (1997), 'A Decade of Network Change: Turnover, Persistence and Stability in Personal Communities', *Social Networks*, 19 (1): 27–50.

White, H. C. (1970), *Chains of Opportunity* (Cambridge, Mass.: Harvard University Press).

——(2002), *Markets From Networks: Socioeconomic Models of Production* (Princeton, N.J.: Princeton University Press).

——Boorman, S. A., and Breiger, R. L. (1976), 'Social Structure From Multiple Networks, 1', *American Journal of Sociology*, 81: 730–80.

CHAPTER 20

....

THRESHOLD MODELS OF SOCIAL INFLUENCE*

....

DUNCAN J. WATTS

PETER DODDS

INTRODUCTION

....

THE study of social influence in decision-making has a long history in social science, dating back at least a century, to when economic philosophers like Rae (1905) and Veblen (1912) became concerned with what Veblen labeled 'conspicuous consumption'—a form of consumption whose primary purpose is to signal wealth to others. Although one could, in principal, signal wealth in very direct ways— say by burning piles of cash in public—Rae and Veblen noted that the wealthy typically prefer to purchase mansions and luxury items. To be acceptable, in other words, conspicuous consumption depends not only on the scarcity of the goods in question, but also on their social desirability (Robinson 1961)—an elusive and at times arbitrary-seeming quality that, like clothing fashions (Barber and Lobel 1952; Simmel 1957; Crane 1999), is driven by individual tendencies of both imitation

* The authors gratefully acknowledge the support of the National Science Foundation (SES-0094162 and SES-0339023) and the James S. McDonnell Foundation.

and also differentiation. Analogous connections between micro-level social influence and macro-level social change have been made subsequently to account for a wide range of phenomena, including scientific trends (Sperber 1990), business management (Blumer 1969), consumer and cultural fads (Johnstone and Katz 1957; Aguirre, Quarantelli, and Mendoza 1988); voting behavior (Lazarsfeld, Berelson, and Gaudet 1968), the diffusion of innovations (Katz, and Lazarsfeld 1955; Coleman, Katz, and Menzel 1957; Bass 1969; Valente 1995; Strang and Soule 1998; Young 2009) and word-of-mouth marketing (Gitlin 1978; Weimann 1994; Earls 2003).

A separate—and even earlier—root of social-influence studies appears to have been inspired by the observations of crowd behavior by early writers like Charles Mackay (1852), Gustave Le Bon (1895), and Gabriel Tarde (1903). At the risk of oversimplification, we suggest that this early work inspired at least two broad streams of productive research that have continued along different lines, and in different academic disciplines, to the present. The first such stream, carried out largely within experimental social psychology, deals with the micro-level psychological mechanisms leading to social conformity, as well as its converse, differentiation. The second stream, meanwhile, has focused on the more macroscopic question of collective action—for example, the dynamics of social movements or the provision of public goods—and has been largely the domain of sociologists, economists, and political scientists. We comment briefly on each of these fields in turn.

Since the 1930s, social psychologists (Sherif 1937; Asch 1953; Bond and Smith 1996; Cialdini and Goldstein 2004) have investigated the origins and effects of majority influence over individual members of the minority, as well as the converse problem (minority influence over the majority). The various manifestations of conformity and compliance, moreover, have been attributed to a multiplicity of psychological mechanisms (Deutsch and Gerard 1955; Cialdini and Goldstein 2004)—principally, desire for accuracy; desire to affiliate; and desire for positive self-image. In practice, it is usually unclear which of these mechanisms is responsible for observed behavior, or even if the different mechanisms are analytically distinct (Cialdini and Goldstein 2004). Nevertheless, the tendency (whether conscious or unconscious) of individuals to conform to group norms and behavior has been invoked to account for a wide range of social phenomena, including local variability in crime rates (Glaeser, Sacerdote, and Scheinkman 1996; Kahan 1997), economic conventions (Young and Burke 2001), 'bystander inactivity' (Cialdini 2001), obedience to authority (Milgram 1969), residential segregation (Schelling 1971), and herd behavior in financial markets (Shiller 2000; Welch 2000).

The related literature on collective action is concerned less with the individual-level psychology of group participation, and more with the conditions under which groups of individuals can coordinate to achieve collective goals. As a result, collective-action studies tend to be theoretical, rather than experimental, and are often framed in terms of the relative costs and benefits of coordinated action, rather than in terms of conformity per se. Nevertheless, the same psychological mechanisms of social influence, such as desire to affiliate with a cause, and inferring its likely success from the participation of others, appear to be at least in part responsible for individual decisions to join in, or abstain from, collective action. Variations on these arguments, therefore, have been invoked to account for the success or failure of social movements (Kim and Bearman 1997), political uprisings (Kuran 1991; Lohmann 1994), contributions to public goods (Oliver and Marwell 1985; Ostrom et al. 1999), and other forms of collective behavior (Granovetter 1978; Chwe 1999; Macy and Flache 2002).

Finally, while much of the social-influence literature is concerned with non-market behavior, such as social movements, conformity to reference groups, and fashion, a related body of work that has attracted the attention of economists deals with a class of technology markets that exhibit what have been called 'network externalities' (Katz and Shapiro 1985), or somewhat more generally 'network effects' (Liebowitz and Margolis 1998). Both terms are meant to imply that the utility to an individual of a particular product (e.g. a fax machine) or skill (e.g. a language) is positively related to the number of other compatible products in use; that is, the size of the relevant 'network' associated with the product or skill. Katz and Shapiro (1985) further differentiated 'direct' from 'indirect' network effects, where the former refers to physical networks, such as the telephone network, which can presumably be owned, and the latter refers to virtual or metaphorical networks, like the population of users of some particular computer-operating system for whom availability of auxiliary products like compatible software, as well as support services, may influence purchasing decisions.

Social influence is thus not a singular phenomenon, or even (yet) a well-defined family of phenomena, but rather a blanket label for a loose congregation of social, psychological, and economic mechanisms, including: identifying with, or distancing oneself from, certain social groups; avoiding sanctions; obeying authority; reducing the complexity of the decision-making process; inferring otherwise inaccessible information about the world; gaining access to a particular network; or reaping the benefits of coordinated action. Precisely what these different mechanisms have in common, and to what extent their differences, when they exist, can be overlooked for the purpose of constructing models of individual choice, ought therefore to be a matter of considerable interest to 'analytical sociology.'

20.1 Social-Influence and Threshold Models

Answering this question in general, however, is extremely difficult—the class of decisions under consideration is simply too broad to tackle all at once. In order to make some concrete progress, therefore, we restrict our analysis of social influence to the class of 'binary choices,' by which we mean choices between precisely two discrete alternatives. Although simple, binary-choice models can illuminate the dynamics of a surprising range of decisions, from the trivial (to dress in costume for the party or to dress normally; to cross the street or to wait for the walk sign) to the consequential (to join a strike or to keep working; to leave a neighborhood or to remain). Even decisions that involve choices between more than two alternatives—for example, which car to buy or which movie to see—may sometimes be represented as a sequence of binary choices (Borghesi and Bouchaud 2007)—say, to buy a car or not; to look for new or used cars; to buy through a dealer or privately; to prefer sedans to SUVs; and so on. Moreover, as Schelling (1978) argued, even quite complex decision-making processes, such as drafting a treaty on climate change, often culminate in binary choices—for example, to sign or not to sign. Binary choices have therefore received considerably more theoretical attention than other kinds of choices, and a wide range of models have been proposed by sociologists and economists; for example, diffusion models (Bass 1969); segregation models (Schelling 1971); coordination models (Schelling 1973; Morris 2000); social-learning models (Bikhchandani, Hirshleifer, and Welch 1992); threshold models (Granovetter 1978), and generalized contagion models (Dodds and Watts 2004, 2005).

Unfortunately, this proliferation of models has not yet produced an equivalently encompassing theoretical framework; thus, it is often unclear how one should relate the assumptions or findings of similar-sounding models to one another. For example, some social-influence models (e.g. Friedkin 1998) assume, in effect, that when A influences B the total quantity of opinion between A and B is conserved (in the manner of a gas diffusing between chambers); thus A's strength of opinion must diminish in order for B's to increase. Other models, meanwhile, are motivated instead by analogy with the spread of an infectious disease (e.g. Bass 1969); thus, A can 'infect' B with a new opinion, while A's strength of opinion remains undiminished. Either one of these assumptions may or may not be justified in any particular circumstance, but both models cannot be valid descriptions of the same process. Likewise, models of social learning that are typically studied in the 'information cascade' literature in economics (Bikhchandani, Hirshleifer, and Welch 1992) are formally quite different from the class of threshold models that have been studied by Granovetter (1978) and others—in a nutshell, the former assume that the particular order in which an individual observes the actions of others is important, whereas the latter assumes that it is not. Once again, in any given situation, it is either the case that the order of signals matters (in which case an information-cascade model is appropriate) or it does not (in which case an influence-response function is)—both models cannot be equally relevant to the same application. In practice, however, authors consistently invoke the same motivating examples—crowd behavior, group conformity, voting, diffusion of innovations, social movements, and herding in financial markets—regardless of what kind of model they then proceed to analyze.

Clarifying what assumptions are required in order for any given model to be a valid representation of the phenomenon in question, and how the various assumptions of different models can be related would therefore be extremely helpful steps towards a theoretically consistent and substantively interpretable theory of social-influence processes. Recently, Lopez-Pintado and Watts (2008) have proposed that a number of mechanism-specific models are equivalent in the sense that they can all be described in terms of an 'influence-response function'—a one-dimensional function that maps the number of others choosing alternative A versus B into a probability that the focal actor i will choose A. By making explicit the assumption that signal order is unimportant, this framework excludes certain existing classes of models (e.g. social-learning models), and hence presumably certain interesting phenomena (i.e. those in which signal order does matter). In restricting itself to certain phenomena and not others, however—by identifying clearly what it cannot explain—the explanatory power of the approach is arguably increased. For example, it can be shown that superficially quite different kinds of choices—inferring quality from observations of others versus deciding whether or not to contribute to a public good—can be shown to correspond to similar influence-response functions, and therefore may result in similar kinds of collective dynamics.

In other recent work Dodds and Watts (2004, 2005) have further partitioned the class of influence-response functions according to the importance of interactions between successive signals. In epidemiological models of contagion, for example— models that have been invoked by Bass (1969) and others as models of the diffusion of innovations—successive contacts between 'infected' and 'susceptible' individuals result in a new infection with constant probability; thus, infection 'events' are treated independently of one another. In threshold models, by contrast—models that are also used to model the diffusion of innovations—the probability that an additional positive signal will trigger adoption depends extremely sensitively on how many other signals have been observed: just below the threshold, a single observation can increase the adoption probability from near zero to near one, where otherwise it will have little effect. Epidemiological and threshold models of contagion are therefore quite distinct with respect to their (again, typically unstated) assumptions regarding the mechanism by which influence spreads from one person to another. What Dodds and Watts showed was that these differences can be captured in the shape of the influence-response function, and that, in fact, an entire family of contagion models can be specified in between the two cases. The shape of the influence-response function, moreover, can have important consequences for the conditions under which contagious entities, whether diseases, products, or ideas, can spread.

Whether or not a particular domain-specific example of social influence can be adequately described in terms of an influence-response function, say, and if so what the shape of the corresponding function should be, are ultimately empirical questions. Although empirical progress in this area is limited, some recent developments are promising. By reanalyzing aggregate-diffusion curves (Griliches 1957), for example, Young has demonstrated that the diffusion of hybrid corn in the USA during the 1940s is better explained by a threshold model of adoption than by a Bass-style model of diffusion (Young 2009). Leskovec, Adamic, and Huberman (2007), moreover, have attempted to reconstruct the individual-level influence-response functions themselves, using online recommendations for books and movies. In general, such experiments are extremely difficult to perform; thus, it is still the case that formal models of social influence suffer from a dearth of realistic psychological assumptions. Nevertheless, a successful experimental program must be predicated on asking the right empirical questions, and in this respect a systematic formal-modeling approach of the kind we describe here is worth pursuing, if only as a means to focus empirical attention on the assumptions and parameters of greatest importance.

Bearing in mind this last objective, the subspace of social-influence models that can be represented as influence-response-functions influence models in turn exhibits a number of dimensions that ought to be of interest to the field of analytical sociology. Early work by Schelling (1978), and later Granovetter and Soong (1983), for example, indicated that binary decisions for which the corresponding decision 'externality' is negative—that is, when others' choice of A makes one less likely to choose A—generate qualitatively different dynamics than when the influence is positive—a result that has been studied in greater detail recently (Lopez-Pintado and Watts 2008). Models of social influence, moreover, tend to assume (often implicitly) that all actors involved are of the same kind, whereas in reality individuals may be influenced by a variety of actors—for example, peers, role models, media organizations, and high-profile individuals like critics, celebrities, or increasingly 'bloggers'—each of which may exert a different kind of influence, and may in turn be influenced differently.[1] Bloggers, for example, exploit online media to share information and opinions with a potentially global audience, yet frequently engage in two-way, unfiltered conversations with readers; thus, they may be expected to exert influence that is neither like word of mouth, nor like mass media. Some recent modeling work (Lopez-Pintado and Watts 2009) has begun to consider the effects of combined media and interpersonal influence, but this aspect of social-influence modeling is as yet poorly explored.

Another important yet understudied element of social influence—and the one that we focus on here—is that of influence networks. If it matters that people pay attention to one another, in other words, then surely it might also matter who pays attention to whom. Unfortunately, in spite of recent interest in the topic (Newman, Barabási, and Watts 2006), it is still the case that little is known about the structure of large-scale social networks, let alone how influence propagates on them. Kossinets and Watts (2006), for example, have studied the evolution of a relatively large network of email exchanges among the members of a university population. But this network is, at best, a representation of who *talks* to whom—it tells us very little about who *pays attention* to whom, or with respect to what. Similar problems arise with other empirical examples of social networks, which typically utilize some proxy for social interaction, like co-membership of corporate boards (Davis 1991) or co-authorship of a scientific paper (Newman 2004), rather than the social interactions themselves. It is plausible, in other words, that two people who sit on a board together might influence one another's opinions, but it is equally plausible that they do not, or that they do so with respect to only some issues, or that they are also influenced by numerous other unrecorded social relations. In the absence of relevant empirical data, therefore, we instead posit a series of theoretical models of networks, all of which are simple and unrealistic, but some of which are more realistic than others.

In order to make progress, we further narrow our focus to a special case of influence-response functions—namely, deterministic-threshold functions, according to which individuals adopt a new 'state' (e.g. wearing seat belts or joining a political uprising) based on the perceived fraction of others who have already adopted the same state. We choose to study threshold models for the practical reason that the collective dynamics of threshold models is already well understood in certain limiting cases—in particular, the 'all-to-all approximation' (Granovetter 1978), in which all individuals are influenced equally by the states of all others. Although the main purpose of this chapter is to consider the dynamics of social influence on networks, it is nevertheless helpful to anchor our results by reviewing the main features of Granovetter's model (Sect. 20.2). In the spirit of analytical sociology, we then proceed systematically up the chain of complexity, reviewing first the dynamics of 'cascades' of influence on random networks (Watts 2002) in which each individual i is exposed only to a fixed neighborhood of k others, drawn randomly from the population. We then introduce two models of networks that advance on the random-network model by including some simple notions of group structure (Sect. 20.3), and consider how these changes affect the likelihood of cascades for different seeding strategies. Although with each step up this chain the tractability of the corresponding models decreases, we are nevertheless able to make progress by leveraging our understanding of the simpler models that we have already considered.

20.2 INFLUENCE CASCADES ON COMPLETE AND RANDOM NETWORKS

Inspired by Schelling's seminal work on neighborhood segregation and coordination games (1969, 1973), Granovetter (1978) proposed a method, novel to sociology, for analyzing the outcomes of collective action when individuals are faced with a choice to adopt some new ('active') state—a behavior, belief, or even an innovation—or else to remain in their existing ('inactive') state. Granovetter illustrated the model with the example of a hypothetical crowd poised on the brink of a riot. Because all involved are uncertain about the costs and benefits associated with rioting, each member of the crowd is influenced by his peers, such that each of them can be characterized by some threshold rule: 'I will join a riot only when sufficiently many others do; otherwise I will refrain.' Granovetter did not specify an explicit theory of human decision-making from which the threshold model could be derived, and, as we have discussed, other kinds of rules are clearly possible (Dodds and Watts 2004; Lopez-Pintado and Watts 2008). For the purpose of this analysis, however, we will accept Granovetter's informal reasoning that under some circumstances at least, a threshold rule is a plausible rule of thumb for an individual to follow, and instead focus on the consequences for collective dynamics of changing the influence network—that is, who pays attention to whom.

20.2.1 Granovetter's 'all-to-all' model

With respect to this last question, Granovetter made the simplest possible assumption—namely, that every individual in the population pays attention equally to all others—which in network terms corresponds to a 'complete' or an 'all-to-all' network. He then completed the model by allocating to each individual in the population a threshold ϕ_i^*, according to some probability distribution $f(\phi)$ (see Figs. 20.1a and 20.1b for an example), where the value of ϕ_i^* is assumed to capture all the relevant psychological attributes of individual i with respect to the particular decision at hand, and the distribution $f(\phi)$ represents both the average tendencies and also the heterogeneity present in the population. Lowering or raising the mean of $f(\phi)$, for example, would therefore correspond to raising or lowering the general susceptibility of the population, while increasing or decreasing the variance would correspond to an increase or decrease in variability in susceptibility across individuals.

Commencing in a population in which some fraction a_0 is assumed to have been activated by some exogenous process (and the remainder of the population $1 - a_0$ is therefore inactive), at each subsequent time step t, each individual i compares a_{t-1}, the active fraction of the population during time step $t-1$, with their own threshold ϕ_i^*, becoming (or remaining) active if $a_{t-1} \geq \phi_i^*$. The fraction of the population a_t that is active at any time t can then be described simply in terms of the active fraction at the previous time step, a_{t-1}, and the one-dimensional 'map' $a_t = F(a_{t-1})$, shown in Figure 20.1(c). The function F can be derived easily by observing that at any point in time t, a_t is just the fraction of the population whose thresholds fall below a_{t-1}; thus F is given by $F(a_{t-1}) = \int_{\phi=0}^{a_{t-1}} f(\phi)d\phi$, which

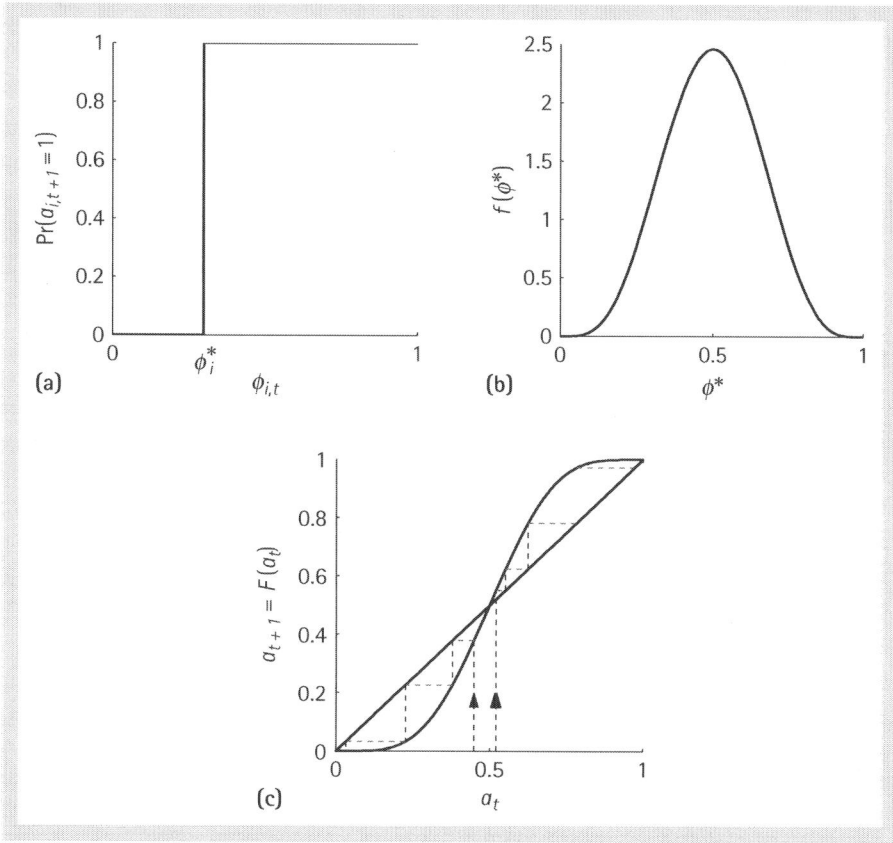

Fig. 20.1 Granovetter's threshold model of collective action

is simply the cumulative-distribution function of f (the threshold distribution) evaluated at a_{t-1}.

Once the system has been represented in this manner, its dynamics and equilibrium properties are surprisingly easy to compute using a simple graphical technique known as a 'cobweb' diagram—a common technique from the field of nonlinear dynamics (Strogatz 1994). Starting from any initial condition, a_0, the fraction of active individuals at the next time step, $t = 1$, is $a_1 = F(a_0)$ which can be found by drawing a vertical line on Figure 20.1(c) to intersect $F(\phi)$ at a_0. This fraction now becomes the input for the next 'iteration' of the map, which is achieved graphically by drawing a horizontal line from the map to the diagonal, also shown in Figure 20.1(c). The process now repeats, thus generating values for $a_2 = F(a_1)$, $a_3 = F(a_2), \ldots$, and so on until some equilibrium value a_∞ is reached, at which no further changes occur; that is, $a_\infty = F(a_\infty)$.

Equilibrium values of the map F are easy to identify graphically, as they are simply the points at which F intersects with the diagonal (i.e. where it maps onto itself). Figure 20.1(c), for example, exhibits three equilibria—one at $F(0) = 0$, one at $F(1) = 1$, and one at an intermediate value $F(a_*) = a_*$. The last of these equilibria, however, is different from the first two: as can be verified using the cobweb technique, any initial condition will eventually converge on one of the first two equilibria, but will diverge from the intermediate value no matter how close to it one starts. The two extreme equilibria are therefore *stable*, whereas the intermediate value a_* is *unstable*. The equilibrium at a_* therefore acts as a kind of switch—small changes in the initial condition near a_* can result in polar-opposite outcomes, whereas away from a_* even large changes in the initial condition will converge on the same outcome.

Although extremely simple, this model already yields an important insight: that in the presence of social influence collective outcomes are not easily intuited from the individual attributes of the population itself.[2] In his hypothetical example of a crowd poised on the brink of a riot Granovetter observed that if the distribution of thresholds is precisely uniform—that is, one person will riot spontaneously, one person will join in when he observes one other rioter, another will join when he observes two others, and so on—the entire crowd will end up in the riot. This result, however, is exceedingly fragile with respect to perturbations in the distribution of thresholds (which in turn alters the number and nature of the corresponding equilibria). If, for example, no one has a threshold of three, and instead two individuals have a threshold of four, then the cascade will terminate after only three people have joined in. The two crowds would be indistinguishable in terms of their individual attributes, but their collective behavior could not be more different: rather than witnessing an all-out riot, an observer would see just three troublemakers jostling an otherwise orderly crowd. Consequently, small changes in individual preferences may lead to large and unpredictable system-level changes (a point that has also been made by Kuran 1991).

20.2.2 Extension to random networks

Recently, Watts (2002) has adapted Granovetter's threshold model to a network framework where, in contrast to the all-to-all assumption of Granovetter's model, individuals are assumed to be influenced directly only by a small subset of immediate 'neighbors'—a more realistic assumption for large populations. As with Granovetter's model, Watts (2002) considered a population of N individuals that is initially in a state of universal inactivity, and in which each individual i is randomly assigned a threshold ϕ_i^*, drawn from the distribution $f(\phi)$. Each individual is then assigned k_i neighbors, whom it both influences and is influenced by, where k_i is drawn at random from the distribution p_k. For the purpose of tractability, Watts considered networks in which neighbors were drawn at random—an unrealistic assumption in light of what is known about real social networks, but one that provided a natural first step away from the all-to-all case. In the simplest case that Watts considered—that is, where all individuals have the same threshold—the population can therefore be characterized completely by just three parameters: N, ϕ^*, and k, where k is the mean degree (i.e. the average number of neighbors influenced directly by each individual). Even in such a simple case, however, the analysis is nontrivial and the results are counterintuitive.

At time $t = 0$ Watts assumed that the population would be 'shocked' by choosing some individual i_0 to be activated exogenously, meaning that their state is switched from inactive to active regardless of their threshold $\phi^*_{i_0}$ or their degree of influence k_{i_0}. If as a result of i_0's activation any of its neighbors' thresholds are now exceeded, those neighbors will also activate in the next time step, after which their neighbors may, in turn, activate, and so on, thus generating a 'cascade' of activations. At some time $T > 0$, where T is the duration of the cascade, some fraction of the population $S \leq 1$ will have been activated, and no more activations will be possible. (Once an individual is activated, we assume they remain so for the duration of the cascade.) Thus, the impact of every cascade can be quantified by its size S. Repeating this numerical experiment many times, it is possible to study the distribution of cascade sizes $g(S)$ for any particular population (as defined by the parameters N, ϕ^*, and k), and also to study the properties of $g(S)$ as a function of N, ϕ^*, and k.

Watts's (2002) main finding is illustrated in Figure 20.2: On random networks, 'global' cascades of influence can only take place within a certain region of the (ϕ^*, k) parameter space, called the 'cascade window,' whereas outside this region cascades are typically small.[3] The extra condition of the cascade window is a major difference between Granovetter's all-to-all approximation and the more realistic case of sparse-influence networks, as now the success of a cascade depends not only on the individual attributes of the population (as captured by Granovetter in the threshold distribution), but also on the connectivity of the influence network. Who pays attention to whom, in other words, is potentially every bit as important as how susceptible individuals are to a particular innovation or idea. The cascade window, moreover, has a particular shape, which Watts also explained in a manner that is illustrated in Figure 20.3. In brief, a cascade in its early stages can only spread via 'vulnerable' individuals who can be activated by only a single active neighbor. In order for a cascade to spread globally, therefore, the population must contain a connected network of vulnerable individuals that 'percolates,' in the sense that it 'reaches' the entire population even though it may only be a small subset of the total (Stauffer and Aharony 1992). Global cascades can therefore occur if and only if the network contains what Watts called a 'percolating vulnerable cluster' (Watts 2002), but which might also be thought of as a 'critical mass,' meaning a relatively small population that, once activated, triggers a disproportionately large change in public opinion.[4]

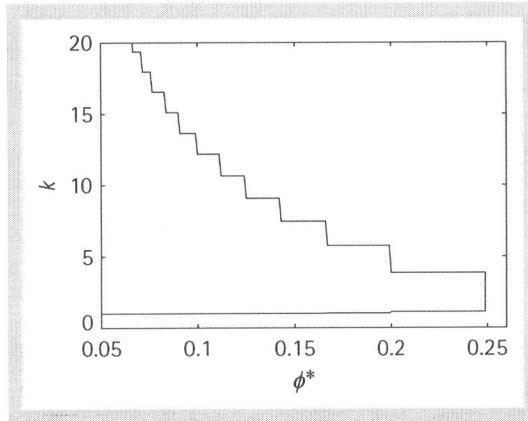

Fig. 20.2 The cascade window for random networks, where all members of the population have the same critical threshold ϕ^*, and k is the average degree of the influence network

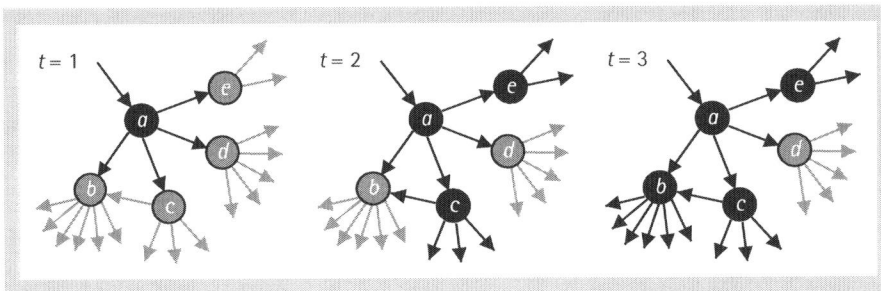

Fig. 20.3 Spread of influence throughout a network via vulnerable nodes. Black indicates a node or edge is active, and gray indicates inactive. All nodes in this example have a threshold $\phi^* = 0.18$, which means they are vulnerable if they have degree $k \leq 5$. At time $t = 1$ node a becomes active, as do its outgoing edges. At time $t = 2$ nodes e and c register that their thresholds have been exceeded and also become active. Node b, a nonvulnerable, switches on in time step $t = 3$, since now $2/8 = 25\%$ of its neighbors are active

Since an individual's threshold is exceeded only when a specified *fraction* of its network neighbors are activated, the condition to be vulnerable is $\phi_i^* < 1/k_i$, where k_i is the degree of node i. Thus, influential (i.e. high-k_i) nodes are less likely than low-k_i nodes to be vulnerable. However, in order to *propagate* influence, an individual must be capable both of being influenced (which requires at least one neighbor) and also of influencing someone other than the source of the influence (requiring at least one additional neighbor); thus, only individuals with $k_i \geq 2$ can contribute to the initial spread of influence. The upshot of these countervailing requirements is that a percolating vulnerable cluster—hence a critical mass—will only exist, and global cascades occur, when the average density k of the influence network is neither too low nor too high. For low k, although most nodes are vulnerable in the sense defined above, no large connected clusters exist, and cascades are confined to the small, isolated clusters in which they begin. On the other hand, when k is sufficiently large, the network will always exhibit a globally connected cluster (in graph-theoretic language, a giant component: Bollobas 2001), but too few of these nodes will be vulnerable. Lying in between these extremes is the cascade window, within which global cascades are possible.[5]

20.3 CASCADES IN NETWORKS WITH GROUP STRUCTURE

As interesting as they are from an analytical perspective, random networks are probably poor approximations of real social networks, for the simple reason that randomness overlooks the obvious importance of groups (Breiger 1974; Feld 1981; Blau and Schwartz 1984). People come together in well-defined, localized contexts—workplaces, schools, places of worship, clubs, and so on—that enhance the formation and maintenance of social connections. One might therefore expect not only that networks of influence relations will exhibit numerous characteristics of group structure, but also that these properties will have important consequences for the transmission of social influence across a network.[6] In this section we describe and analyze two models that emphasize, in different ways, the importance of social groups in the formation of influence networks.

20.3.1 Random-group networks

Consistent with our modeling strategy, our first class of networks with group structure constitutes only a modest departure from standard random networks (Newman, Strogatz, and Watts 2001), thus permitting us to test the effects of incorporating groups, while benefiting from our understanding of cascades on random networks. To build a random-group network we first create a standard random network with an average degree k_g (see Fig. 20.4). In two stages, we then replace each node in this network with a group of n_g nodes and then add edges between nodes: first, within each group, each pair of individuals is connected with

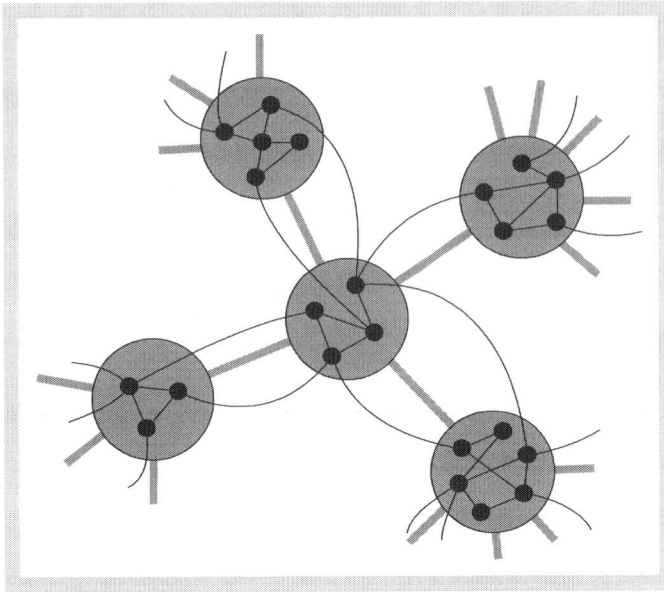

Fig. 20.4 Example of a random–group network. The gray disks and edges represent the underlying random network of groups

probability p, as per the typical construction of a standard random graph; and second, links between each pair of nodes that belong to adjacent groups on the underlying random network are created with probability q.

20.3.2 Generalized-affiliation networks

Our second class of networks with group structure is based on a model, first introduced by Watts, Dodds, and Newman (2002), that captures the effects of homophily (McPherson, Smith-Lovin, and Cook 2001) and group affiliation (Feld 1981) in determining social networks. In this model, each individual is allocated coordinates in each of H 'social dimensions' such as profession or geographic location, and 'social distance' d between two individuals is taken to be the minimum of all distances between their attributes. (For any given dimension, the distance between two attribute values is measured as the number of levels to the lowest common ancestor.) For example, in Figure 20.5 nodes i and j belong to the same group in the $h = 2$ attribute but are maximally far apart in the $h = 1$ attribute. The social distance d_{ij} is therefore 1 (we define two nodes sharing the same group to be a distance 1 apart) because i and j match in at least one attribute. Two individuals being socially 'close' is assumed to make a connection more likely; thus, for a

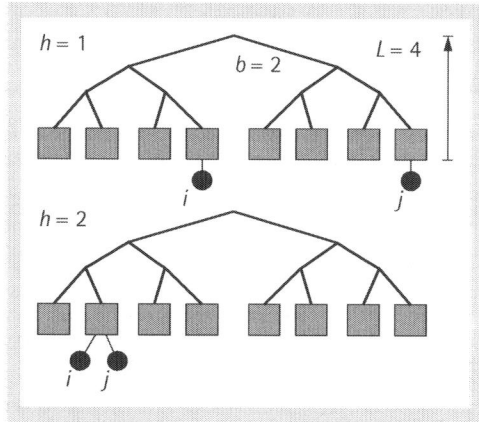

Fig. 20.5 Example of the generalized–affiliation model, where each node has attributes in two dimensions

population of individuals with identities assigned as above we realize a network by connecting each pair of individuals with probability $e^{-\alpha d}$ where d is the distance in a randomly chosen dimension, and α is defined as the 'homophily parameter'—for high α, ties are almost always made between people who strongly match on at least one attribute, and for low α, ties may be made between more distant individuals. Finally, we depart from the original Watts, Dodds, and Newman (2002) formulation by allowing individuals who share a common acquaintance to connect with each other with probabilities β_1 and β_2, depending on whether they are in the same, or different, groups respectively. The more acquaintances in common, the greater the chance of connection (Kossinets and Watts 2006); thus, we assume that any pair of unconnected individuals that are affiliated with the same group and have m mutual acquaintances within that group will have a connection probability of $1 - (1 - \beta_1)^m$.

20.3.3 Cascade-seeding strategies

In Figure 20.6 we show cascade windows for random-group networks, and generalized-affiliation-model networks, where, for purposes of comparison, we overlay the cascade windows of standard random networks (solid line) on those of the two networks with group structure. Our main interest here concerns seeding strategies that target multiple individuals simultaneously, in part because it is artificial to restrict seeding to a single individual, and in part because single-individual seeds do not exploit the presence of group structure. Nevertheless, we include the single-seed strategy in order to provide a direct comparison between networks with group structure and the random networks studied previously. Figures 20.6a and 20.6d therefore show cascade windows for random-group networks and generalized-affiliation-model networks, for cascades that are triggered by a single-seed node, where the gray scale indicates the average size of cascades generated by a single, random node activated at time $t = 0$ (i.e. darker shade corresponds to larger cascades).

We find that both classes of networks involving group structure yield cascade windows different to that for standard random networks. For both classes of networks we see that the upper boundary of the cascade window exceeds that of standard random networks; that is, group-based networks can be vulnerable to activation cascades even when their average degree is significantly higher than that of the most vulnerable node. By enabling close-knit clusters of nodes to reinforce each others' adoptions, the introduction of groups therefore serves to push the upper bound of k well beyond its previous limit, where insufficiently many vulnerable nodes existed to form a critical mass. At the lower limit of the cascade window, however, we observe that the two classes of networks with group structure begin to differ: generalized-affiliation-model networks are similar to ordinary random networks; but, for reasons that we do not yet fully understand, the lower boundary for random-group networks is raised considerably.

The clear increase in the width of the cascade window in the presence of group structure also suggests a further question: Can seeds consisting of entire (albeit still small) groups trigger global cascades even under conditions where single-node seeds would fail? Figure 20.6 therefore also shows results for two other seeding strategies: (1) a random set of n_g nodes (Figs. 20.6b and 20.6e), and (2) a cohesive group of n_g nodes (Figs. 20.6c and 20.6f). A cohesive-group seed is a natural choice of seed in the current context as it uses the structure of the underlying network in an obvious manner—a marketer, for example, might provide a close-knit group of people with some free samples, or pay a team to use or endorse a particular product. It is also natural, however, to target an equal-size set of n_g individuals but scattered randomly throughout the network. Because it is not a priori obvious which of these two strategies will perform better, we compare them directly.[7] In both cases we also include (again for comparison purposes) the outline of the cascade window for the same seeding strategy employed on ordinary random networks (i.e. those studied previously).

On ordinary random networks the addition of larger seeds—created by first selecting a random node and then adding $n_g - 1$ of its nearest neighbors to the seed—can easily be shown to increase the frequency of global cascades when the network is inside the cascade window. It is also easy to show, however, that for standard random networks all three types of seed choices—cohesive-group, random-set, or a lone individual—lead to *exactly* the same cascade windows (Figs. 20.6(a)–(f)). The reason is that a random network either does or does not

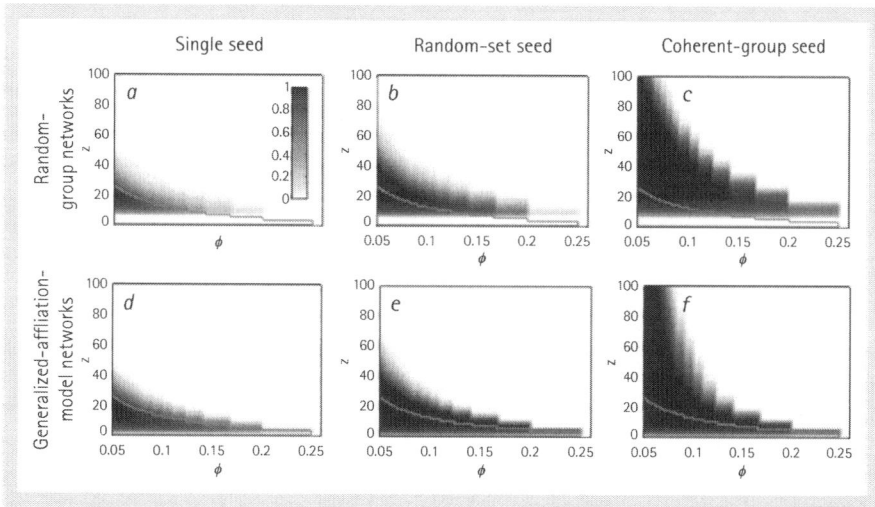

Fig. 20.6 Mean size of activation events for random–group networks and generalized–affiliation networks for three seeds: (*a*) single randomly chosen node; (*b*) a random set of $n_g = 10$ nodes; and (*c*) a cohesive group of $n_g = 10$ nodes. The solid line indicates the equivalent cascade window for standard random networks

have a vulnerable cluster, and a finite seed in a random network with no vulnerable cluster cannot generate a cascade. Within the boundaries of the cascade window, a larger seed, be it a cohesive group or a random set, has a better chance of hitting the percolating vulnerable cluster; thus, when global cascades are possible, the probability of generating a cascade is increased for larger seeds. At the same time, however, the nature of any finite seed does not alter the possibility of a cascade occurring in the first place; thus, the window remains invariant for random networks regardless of seeding strategy.

In networks with group structure the situation is different. First, we observe that for our two types of group-based networks activation cascades are generally more likely to occur over a broad range of k when the initial seed is a randomly chosen cohesive group of size n_g (Figs. 20.6*c* and 20.6*f*) as opposed to a randomly chosen set of n_g individuals (Figs. 20.6*b* and 20.6*e*). In particular, Figures 20.6*c* and 20.6*f* show that for both classes of networks, cohesive-group seeds can generate spreading when the average degree is an order of magnitude greater than that of the most connected vulnerable individual. Networks with group structure may therefore be highly vulnerable to influences initiated by cohesive groups, even when they are extremely resilient to social contagion, as we have modeled it here, when initiated by single seeds. Moreover, since we have assumed little knowledge of the networks in our simulations—only at the level of group membership—our results suggest easily implemented methods for increasing the spread of an influence in real populations. Rather than targeting individuals who are thought to be influential (Katz, and Lazarsfeld 1955; Weimann 1994), for example, a more successful strategy may be to target cohesive groups. Finally, these results also indicate that spreading is possible in group-based networks even when there are relatively few or even no vulnerable individuals (i.e. those individuals who are activated when only one neighbor is active), and certainly when there is no percolating vulnerable cluster.

Social influence in group-based networks therefore spreads in a way that is qualitatively distinct from spreading in all-to-all and random-network versions where, respectively, a nonzero vulnerable fraction and a percolating vulnerable cluster are needed for activation to spread. In the case of random networks, the largest vulnerable cluster can be interpreted as the *critical mass* of the system: when an individual in this cluster is activated, the rest of the cluster begins to follow in short order, whereupon nonvulnerables are also activated. Clearly, however, the vulnerable-cluster notion of critical mass on a network is insufficient to understand the dynamics of cascades in the presence of groups. Rather, it appears that when groups are the medium of transmission it is important to think of a critical mass in terms of the arrangement of vulnerable versus nonvulnerable *groups*, not individuals—a kind of 'renormalized' version of the previous conception. If an initial group is activated, the process within that group becomes self-reinforcing, since high levels of clustering within groups naturally maintain activation. Providing that neighboring groups have sufficient connections between them, activation will be able to spread, even when the individuals in question—when examined in isolation—would not appear vulnerable in the previous sense of being susceptible to activation by a single neighbor.

The vulnerability of group-based networks to social contagion is as yet a poorly understood phenomenon, but it clearly opens up new research questions as well as suggesting new possibilities for triggering, or preventing, cascades of social influence. As the results presented in this chapter make clear, changing the connectivity and topology of the influence network—even in possibly quite subtle ways—can have important implications both for the scale of cascades that may propagate throughout a population, and also the manner in which those cascades may be seeded. In addition to pursuing experimental studies of social influence at the level of individuals, therefore, we would argue that sociology in the analytical tradition espoused in this volume requires a more comprehensive theoretical understanding of the dynamics of social-influence networks—advanced, for example, through a systematic program of formal modeling—along with a tighter coupling between theory development and empirical testing. Aside from its interest to sociologists, moreover, a better understanding of the structure and dynamics of social-influence networks could be of value to marketers, public-health authorities, and indeed anyone concerned with affecting or understanding changes in public opinion, cultural beliefs, or social norms.

NOTES

1. A number of diffusion models (e.g. Strang and Tuma 1993; Myers 2000) incorporate spatial and temporal heterogeneity; however, here we are making the somewhat different point that the actors involved in the diffusion process can themselves be heterogeneous.

2. At the broadest level, this insight is essentially the same as that derived from Schelling's much earlier work on residential segregation and coordination games (Schelling 1969, 1978). Nevertheless, Granovetter's model was considerably more transparent than Schelling's, allowing for individual heterogeneity and easy computation of equilibria; thus, it is Granovetter's model that we generalize here.

3. Strictly speaking, a 'global' cascade is one that occupies a finite fraction of the entire population in the theoretical limit of the population size $N \to \infty$, whereas nonglobal cascades are always finite in size. In practice, however, global cascades can be detected in finite populations simply by considering only cascades that exceed a prespecified cutoff size (where the precise choice of cutoff is unimportant).

4. Our use of the term is thus broadly consistent with Rogers's (1995) definition as 'the point at which enough individuals have adopted an innovation so that the innovation's further rate of adoption becomes self-sustaining' (p. 313), but adds analytic power to the concept by specifying precise conditions under which a critical mass exists, regardless of whether any successful cascade is actually observed.

5. Recently, Whitney (2007) has shown that global cascades can also occur in a narrow region just above the upper limit of the cascade window, and that these cascades—which according to Watts's calculations should not take place—are driven by a slightly different mechanism than the one Watts proposed. Specifically, Whitney showed that cascades can occur outside of the theoretical cascade window as a consequence of triadic structures that he calls 'motifs,' which can arise in sufficiently dense random networks. The local clustering implied by motifs can cause otherwise stable nodes to be vulnerable to the combined influence of two neighbors—a situation that does not arise in less dense random networks until the entire vulnerable cluster has been activated. Because motifs appear to matter only in a narrow region outside the cascade window, Whitney's findings are largely consistent with Watts's. Nevertheless, they suggest that even small variations away from pure randomness can lead to considerable additional complexity in the dynamics of social influence—a point we also make in Section 20.3.

6. Chwe (1999) has, in fact, made precisely this point in the context of somewhat smaller simulated networks than we consider here.

7. To ensure comparisons are fair, in all simulated networks the population size is $N = 10^4$, all groups are of size $n_g = 10$, and individuals have a uniform threshold of $f_i = 0.15$ (meaning nodes of degree six or less are vulnerable). The parameters for the generalized affiliation networks shown are $H = 2$, $b = 10$, $L = 4$, $f_i = 2$, $b_1 = b_2 = 0.5$.

REFERENCES

AGUIRRE, B. E., QUARANTELLI, E. L., and MENDOZA, J. L. (1988), 'The Collective Behavior of Fads: The Characteristics, Effects, and Career of Streaking', *American Sociological Review*, 53: 569–84.

ASCH, S. E. (1953), 'Effects of Group Pressure upon the Modification and Distortion of Judgments', in D. Cartwright and A. Zander (eds.), *Group Dynamics: Research and Theory* (Evanston, Ill.: Row, Peterson), 151–62.

BARBER, B., and LOBEL, L. S. (1952), ' "Fashion" in Women's Clothes and the American Social System', *Social Forces*, 31: 124–31.

BASS, F. M. (1969), 'A New Product Growth for Model Consumer Durables', *Management Science*, 15: 215–27.

BIKHCHANDANI, S., HIRSHLEIFER, D., and WELCH, I. (1992), 'A Theory of Fads, Fashion, Custom, and Cultural Change as Informational Cascades', *Journal of Political Economy*, 100: 992–1026.

BLAU, P. M., and SCHWARTZ, J. E. (1984), *Crosscutting Social Circles* (Orlando, Fla.: Academic Press).

BLUMER, H. (1969), 'Fashion: From Class Differentiation to Collective Selection', *Sociological Quarterly*, 10: 275–91.

BOLLOBAS, B. (2001), *Random Graphs* (New York: Academic).

BOND, R., and SMITH, P. B. (1996), 'Culture and Conformity: A Meta-analysis of Studies Using Asch's (1952b, 1956) Line Judgment Task', *Psychological Bulletin*, 119: 111–37.

BORGHESI, C., and BOUCHAUD, J.-P. (2007), 'Of Songs and Men: A Model for Multiple Choice with Herding', *Quality and Quantity*, 41 (4): 557–68.

BREIGER, R. (1974), 'The Duality of Persons and Groups', *Social Forces*, 53: 181–90.

CHWE, M. SUK-YOUNG (1999), 'Structure and Strategy in Collective Action', *American Journal of Sociology*, 105: 128–56.

CIALDINI, R. B. (2001), *Influence: Science and Practice* (Needham Heights, Mass.: Allyn & Bacon).

——and GOLDSTEIN, N. J. (2004), 'Social Influence: Compliance and Conformity', *Annual Review of Psychology*, 55: 591–621.

COLEMAN, J. S., KATZ, E., and MENZEL, H. (1957), 'The Diffusion of an Innovation among Physicians', *Sociometry*, 20: 253–70.

CRANE, D. (1999), 'Diffusion Models and Fashion: A Reassessment', *Annals of the American Academy of Political and Social Science*, 566: 13–24.

DAVIS, G. F. (1991), 'Agents without Principles? The Spread of the Poison Pill through the Intercorporate Network', *Administrative Science Quarterly*, 36: 583–613.

DEUTSCH, M., and GERARD, H. B. (1955), 'A Study of Normative and Informative Social Influences upon Individual Judgment', *Journal of Abnormal Social Psychology*, 51: 629–36.

DODDS, P. S., and WATTS, D. J. (2004), 'Universal Behavior in a Generalized Model of Contagion', *Physical Review Letters*, 92: 218701.

—— (2005), 'A Generalized Model of Social and Biological Contagion', *Journal of Theoretical Biology*, 232: 587–604.

EARLS, M. (2003), 'Advertising to the Herd: How Understanding Our True Nature Challenges the Ways We Think About Advertising and Market Research', *International Journal of Market Research*, 45: 311–36.

FELD, S. L. (1981), 'The Focused Organization of Social Ties', *American Journal of Sociology*, 86: 1015–35.

FRIEDKIN, N. E. (1998), *A Structural Theory of Social Influence*, (Cambridge: Cambridge University Press).

GITLIN, T. (1978), 'Media Sociology: The Dominant Paradigm', *Theory and Society*, 6: 205–53.

GLAESER, E. L., SACERDOTE, B., and SCHEINKMAN, J. A. (1996), 'Crime and Social Interaction', *Quarterly Journal of Economics*, 111: 507–48.

GRANOVETTER, M. S. (1978), 'Threshold Models of Collective Behavior', *American Journal of Sociology*, 83: 1420–43.

—— and SOONG, R. (1983), 'Threshold Models of Diffusion and Collective Behavior', *Journal of Mathematical Sociology*, 9: 165–79.

GRILICHES, Z. (1957), 'Hybrid Corn: An Exploration of the Economics of Technological Change', *Econometrica*, 25: 501–22.

JOHNSTONE, J., and KATZ, E. (1957), 'Youth and Popular Music: A Study in the Sociology of Taste', *American Journal of Sociology*, 62: 563–8.

KAHAN, D. M. (1997), 'Social Influence, Social Meaning, and Deterrence', *Virginia Law Review*, 83: 349–95.

KATZ, E., and LAZARSFELD, P. F. (1955), *Personal Influence: The Part Played by People in the Flow of Mass Communications* (Glencoe, Ill.: Free Press).

KATZ, M. L., and SHAPIRO, C. (1985), 'Network Externalities, Competition, and Compatibility', *American Economic Review*, 75: 424–40.

KIM, H., and BEARMAN, P. S. (1997), 'The Structure and Dynamics of Movement Participation', *American Sociological Review*, 62: 70–93.

KOSSINETS, G., and WATTS, D. J. (2006), 'Empirical Analysis of an Evolving Social Network', *Science*, 311: 88–90.

KURAN, T. (1991), 'Now Out of Never: The Element of Surprise in the East European Revolution of 1989', *World Politics*, 44: 7–48.

LAZARSFELD, P. F., BERELSON, B., and GAUDET, H. (1968), *The People's Choice: How the Voter Makes Up His Mind in a Presidential Campaign* (New York: Columbia University Press).

LE BON, G. (1895), *The Crowd* (New Brunswick, N.J.: Transaction).

LESKOVEC, J., ADAMIC, L. A., and HUBERMAN, B. A. (2007), 'The Dynamics of Viral Marketing', *ACM Transactions on the Web*, 1: article 5.

LIEBOWITZ, S. J., and MARGOLIS, S. E. (1998), 'Network Effects and Externalities', in P. Newman (ed.), *The New Palgrave Dictionary of Economics and the Law* (New York: Macmillan), 671–5.

LOHMANN, S. (1994), 'The Dynamics of Informational Cascades: The Monday Demonstrations in Leipzig, East Germany, 1989–91', *World Politics*, 47: 42–101.

LOPEZ-PINTADO, D., and WATTS, D. J. (2008), 'Social Influence, Binary Decisions, and Collective Dynamics', *Rationality and Society*, 20: 399–443.

———— (2009), 'Mass Media Versus Word of Mouth', paper, Institute for Social and Economic Research and Policy, Columbia University.

MACKAY, C. (1852), *Memoirs of Extraordinary Popular Delusions and the Madness of Crowds* (London: Office of National Illustrated Library).

McPHERSON, M., SMITH-LOVIN, L., and COOK, J. M. (2001), 'Birds of a Feather: Homophily in Social Networks', *Annual Review of Sociology*, 27: 415–44.

MACY, M. W., and FLACHE, A. (2002), 'Learning Dynamics in Social Dilemmas', *Proceedings of the National Academy of Sciences of the USA*, 99: 7229–36.

MILGRAM, S. (1969), *Obedience to Authority* (New York: Harper & Row).

MORRIS, S. (2000), 'Contagion', *Review of Economic Studies*, 67: 57–78.

MYERS, D. J. (2000), 'The Diffusion of Collective Violence: Infectiousness, Susceptibility, and Mass Media Networks', *American Journal of Sociology*, 106: 173–208.

NEWMAN, M. E. J. (2004), 'Coauthorship Networks and Patterns of Scientific Collaboration', *Proceedings of the National Academy of Sciences of the USA*, 101: 5200–5.

—— BARABÁSI, A.-L., and WATTS, D. J. (2006) (eds.), *The Structure and Dynamics of Networks* (Princeton, N.J.: Princeton University Press).

—— STROGATZ, S. H., and WATTS, D. J. (2001), 'Random Graphs with Arbitrary Degree Distributions and their Applications', *Physical Review*, E 6402: 026118.

OLIVER, P. E., and MARWELL, G. (1985), 'A Theory of the Critical Mass, 1. Interdependence, Group Heterogeneity, and the Production of Collective Action', *American Journal of Sociology*, 91: 522–56.

OSTROM, E. et al. (1999), 'Revisiting the Commons: Local Lessons, Global Challenges', *Science*, 284: 278–82.

RAE, J. (1905) *The Sociological Theory of Capital* (London: Macmillan).

ROBINSON, D. E. (1961), 'The Economics of Fashion Demand', *Quarterly Journal of Economics*, 75: 376–98.

ROGERS, E. M. (1995), *Diffusion of Innovations* (New York: Free Press).

SCHELLING, T. C. (1969), *Neighborhood Tipping* (Cambridge, Mass.: Harvard University Institute of Economic Research).

—— (1971), 'Dynamic Models of Segregation', *Journal of Mathematical Sociology*, 1: 143–86.

—— (1973), 'Hockey Helmets, Concealed Weapons, and Daylight Saving: A Study of Binary Choices with Externalities', *Journal of Conflict Resolution*, 17: 381–428.

—— (1978), *Micromotives and Macrobehavior* (New York: Norton).

SHERIF, M. (1937), 'An Experimental Approach to the Study of Attitudes', *Sociometry*, 1: 90–8.

SHILLER, R. J. (2000), *Irrational Exuberance* (Princeton, N.J.: Princeton University Press).

SIMMEL, G. (1957), 'Fashion', *American Journal of Sociology*, 62: 541–58.

SPERBER, I. (1990), *Fashions in Science: Opinion Leaders and Collective Behavior in the Social Sciences* (Minneapolis, Minn.: University of Minnesota Press).

STAUFFER, D., and AHARONY, A. (1992), *Introduction to Percolation Theory* (London: Taylor & Francis).

STRANG, D., and SOULE, S. A. (1998), 'Diffusion in Organizations and Social Movements: From Hybrid Corn to Poison Pills', *Annual Review of Sociology*, 24: 265–90.

—— and TUMA, N. B. (1993), 'Spatial and Temporal Heterogeneity in Diffusion', *American Journal of Sociology*, 99: 614–39.

STROGATZ, S. H. (1994), *Nonlinear Dynamics and Chaos: With Applications in Physics, Biology, Chemistry, and Engineering* (Reading, Mass.: Addison-Wesley).

TARDE, G. (1903), *The Laws of Imitation* (New York: Holt).

VALENTE, T. W. (1995), *Network Models of the Diffusion of Innovations* (Cresskill, N.J.: Hampton).

VEBLEN, T. (1912), *The Theory of the Leisure Class: An Economic Study of Institutions* (New York: Macmillan).

WATTS, D. J., DODDS, P. S., and NEWMAN, M. E. J. (2002), 'Identity and Search in Social Networks', *Science*, 296: 1302–5.

—— (2002) 'A Simple Model of Information Cascades on Random Networks', *Proceedings of the National Academy of Sciences of the USA*, 99: 5766–71.

WEIMANN, G. (1994), *The Influentials: People Who Influence People* (Albany, N.Y.: State University of New York Press).

WELCH, I. (2000), 'Herding Among Security Analysts', *Journal of Financial Economics*, 58: 369–96.

WHITNEY, D. E. (2007), 'Exploring Watts' Cascade Boundary', working paper, Massachusetts Institute of Technology.

YOUNG, H. P. (2009), 'Innovation Diffusion in Heterogeneous Populations: Contagion, Social Influence, and Social Learning', *American Economic Review* (forthcoming).

—— and BURKE, M. A. (2001), 'Competition and Custom in Economic Contracts: A Case Study of Illinois Agriculture', *American Economic Review*, 91: 559–73.

CHAPTER 21

....

TIME AND
SCHEDULING*

....

CHRISTOPHER WINSHIP

INTRODUCTION

....

As the *New Yorker* cartoon opposite suggests, coordinating schedules can be a difficult and frustrating experience. The fact that the cartoon is among the *New Yorker*'s most famous indicates how ubiquitous such conflicts are. Perhaps more significantly, the cartoon also suggests a possible consequence of scheduling conflicts. It appears that the two individuals on the phone are likely never to get together. A relationship that once existed is about to dissolve.

As Eric Leifer (1990) has forcefully argued, social relations do not simply exist in the abstract. They must be enacted in real time and space. With respect to relations built on face-to-face interaction, there must be both specific times and places at which interaction occurs (Winship 1978). This implies that two or more people need to agree on both when and where to meet. What we see in the cartoon is a

* Special thanks to Peter Bearman for encouragement in the writing of this chapter. I also owe a singular thanks to Harrison White, who many years ago tricked me into getting started on this chapter by telling me just a month prior he wanted me to give a presentation on scheduling at a conference. Peter Hedström, Peter Bearman, Elizabeth Bruch, and Ezra Zuckerman gave helpful comments on an earlier version of the chapter. Miller McPherson was most generous in helping me understand the relationship between his work and mine. Lin Tao provided able research assistance. Lastly, Genevieve Butler, as usual, provided extraordinary assistance in helping produce the final typescript.

"No, Thursday's out. How about never—is never good for you?"

Source: Robert Mankoff, *New Yorker*, 3 May 1993

social relation whose enactment appears impossible. More generally, Leifer (1990) argues that enactment can be constrained or even infeasible. Social relations occur in a concrete physical world in which particular patterns of social relationships may or may not be possible.

In this chapter I argue that scheduling conflicts are potentially important barriers to the enactment of social relations. As such, scheduling conflicts have a number of important implications. First, conflicts affect the potential for certain types of groups to exist. A local tennis club's team involving middle-aged men whose matches take place on Saturday afternoons may or may not be viable as a result of conflicts with family commitments. A group of individuals interested in establishing a choral group may struggle with whether there is any regular time during a week when they can all meet to practice. Parents who work different shifts in order to share child-care responsibilities may find themselves more prone to divorce as a result of the minimal amount of time they can find to spend with each other.

In constraining social interactions, scheduling problems also have the potential to affect who interacts with whom. Attempts to synchronize schedules can lead to the segregation of groups of different types of individuals in time, if not in space. Individuals who work different shifts are less likely to become friends, or be able to maintain friendships. Conversely, students who eat lunch at the same time have greater opportunity to become friends, thus potentially interacting with each other at other times. Individuals who are 'morning people' are likely to find it difficult to work with 'night people' unless they live in different time zones and interact over the phone or the Internet.

At an organizational level, scheduling constraints may limit the types of larger social systems or structures that are possible. A high school may attempt to structure itself so that students are provided with a range of small-classroom experiences across a range of topics with the goal that students take classes with a mixed and diverse group of other students. It may find, however, that because of scheduling conflicts, de facto tracking occurs, with groups of students with similar abilities and interests all taking their courses together. A professional sports association may find it difficult if not impossible to schedule games so that some teams are not disadvantaged by playing a disproportionate share of their games against stronger teams.

Scheduling constraints, however, are less likely to be binding when individuals have identical or parallel time commitments; that is, where there is mechanical solidarity and congruence exists. Children in an elementary-school class may engage in a diverse set of activities, but the fact that they generally do the same activities at the same time obviates scheduling conflicts. Individuals with nine-to-five work schedules may also find it easy to schedule work meetings and family time.

While congruence may solve scheduling issues in some contexts, in others hierarchical structures may make scheduling less problematic. If there is a single top individual whose preferences take precedence, then she or he can independently figure out how much time to allocate to each activity and when to do the activity. Others will then be expected to coordinate their schedules with respect to that individual.

As the above examples show, scheduling constraints have the potential to affect social phenomena at multiple levels and in multiple ways. In this chapter I first explore why scheduling problems logically are so difficult to resolve. A subsequent goal is to then examine the potential consequences of scheduling problems on social life.

Before discussing why scheduling constraints are so problematic, I briefly discuss traditional approaches to the study of time in the social sciences (Sect. 21.1). These include an extensive literature across a number of disciplines on how societies conceptualize time; work that has examined how the organization of time has changed over history; work on the female labor force, the household division of labor, and time budgets more generally; and, finally, research by the Swedish geographer Torsten Hägerstrand and his collaborators that explicitly focuses on the temporal, as well as spatial, location of individuals.

After formally examining why scheduling conflicts are problematic (Sect. 21.2), I examine how they can affect the viability of specific relations and groups (Sect. 21.3). I then discuss how scheduling constraints both are a cause and can be a mechanism for maintaining, group boundaries and thus groups segregated from each other (Sect. 21.4). I then examine the effectiveness of different types of organizational structures for coordinating schedules (Sect. 21.5).

21.1 TIME IN THE SOCIAL SCIENCES

Over the years there have been repeated calls for the establishment of a sociology of time (e.g. Sorokin and Merton 1937; Zerubavel 1981; Hassard 1990). Such a subfield arguably now exists, though it is quite small (see Bergmann 1992 for reviews). More generally, scholars in different social-science disciplines have been concerned with time in distinctly different ways. I briefly review four schools of scholarship that are relevant to the present chapter.

Probably the largest body of research has focused on cultural differences in the conception of time. Key examples would be Malinowski's study (1927) of the Trobriand Islanders or Bourdieu's work (1963) on the Kabyle. As would be expected, much of this research is found in anthropology (see Gell 1996 for a review), though these issues have been of interest to a broad swath of scholars in the social sciences and humanities (see Bender and Wellbery 1991 for papers from authors from a diverse set of disciplines). The key idea in this literature is that time is socially constructed; as such, it may be constructed in a variety of ways. The importance of this line of research here is that this chapter turns the social-constructivist perspective on its head. Without denying the importance of how societies think about time, my purpose here is to analyze how time, because of its physical properties, constrains and affects social interaction by individuals and groups as they attempt to coordinate schedules.

There is also a vast literature on how throughout history conceptions of time, and how it is organized, have changed. The primary focus has been on the Industrial Revolution, with E. P. Thompson's book *The Making of the English Working Class* (1976) providing the classic analysis. Important work, however, has focused on earlier periods, most notably David Landes's *Revolution in Time: Clocks and the Making of the Modern World* (1983). A key theme in this literature is that as society has become more complex, and in order to allow society to be more complex, the technical means needed for people to coordinate their interactions more closely has needed to be invented. Thus, we have had the invention of calendars, clocks, shared time zones, scheduling programs, etc. (Zerubavel 1981; Hassard 1990). What this research importantly demonstrates is how critical and basic the social coordination of time is to social organization. The argument of Thompson and others is that for the Industrial Revolution to have occurred, it was essential that the way people thought about time, particularly the working classes, had to change, and that there had to be the necessary technical tools (e.g. calendars, clocks, shared time zones) to make coordination possible. One simply cannot run a large factory where the tasks of different workers are highly integrated if people are coming and going at random times. An obvious extension of this literature would consider the importance of alternative means of communication (from mail, to the phone, to email, and video-conferencing) in allowing for more complex organizational forms. I do not pursue this topic here.

Two related literatures have had a more contemporary US focus. With the rise in female labor-force participation, economists in particular have been interested in how adult females decide about how to allocate time between work and family commitments (for a review see Killingsworth and Heckman 1987). For similar reasons, a massive amount of work has been done by sociologists on how the household division of labor has and has not changed with the increased employment of women. In recent years there has been a host of new books by prominent sociologists on this topic: Arlie Hochschild's *The Second Shift* (1989); Jerry A. Jacobs and Kathleen Gerson's *The Time Divide: Work, Family, and Gender Inequality* (2004); *Fighting for Time: Shifting Boundaries of Work and Social Life*, edited by Cynthia Fuchs Epstein and Arne L. Kalleberg (2006); and *The Changing Rhythms of American Life*, by Suzanne M. Bianchi, Melissa Robinson, and John Mikic (2006).[1]

The above research on the family is complemented by a growing literature on how individuals use their time more generally. This research has primarily been empirically driven, involving the multitude of time-budget surveys that have been done in the USA and in other countries. Herz and Devens (2001) and Hammermesh and Pfann (2005*b*) provide discussions of this data and current research. Hammermesh and Pfann (2005*a*) provide a collection of recent work by economists in this area.

Common to these lines of research has been the conception of time as a fixed resource: like money, an individual only has a finite amount available for use. The classic analysis of time from this perspective is Becker (1965). Instead of having an income constraint, as is traditional in economics, an individual is faced with a time constraint and a decision about how to divide it between work and leisure. The amount one works then determines the income that is available. Totally absent from this perspective is the notion that doing things in time requires a specific time to do them in. In this sense, time is quite unlike money. Whereas in buying a good it typically does not matter to either the seller or buyer what money is used as long as it is money; in doing something in time, we need to decide exactly what time to do it. Furthermore, if a social interaction is involved, then all parties must agree on a specific time. (For further discussions of the differences between time and money see Melbin 1987 and Winship 1992.) A time-budget perspective only asks 'How much time should I spend doing something?' It does not consider the

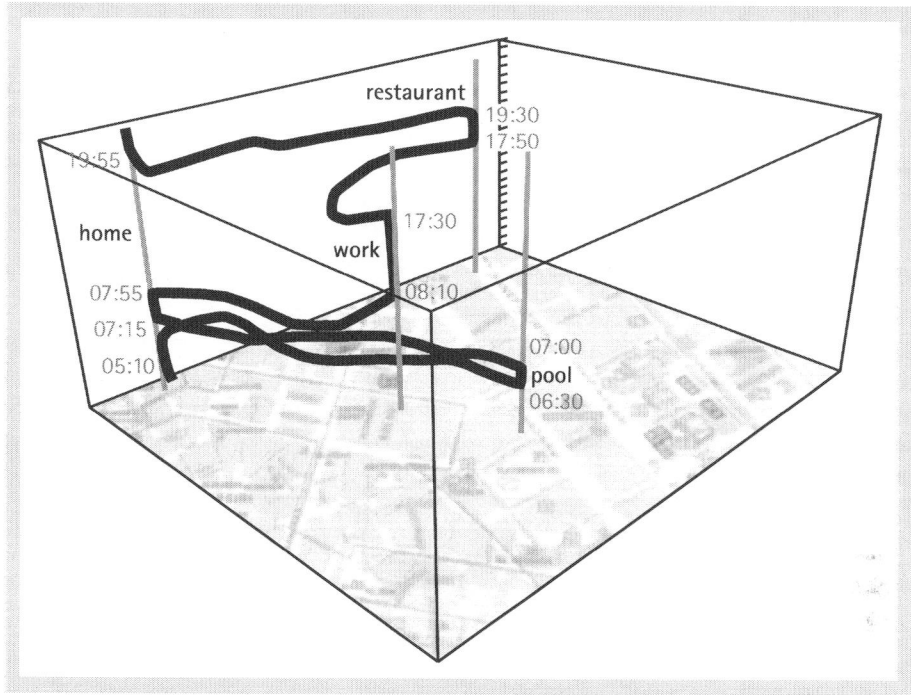

Fig. 21.1 Example of a space–time cube (from Kraak 2003: 1989)

question of 'When should I do this?' It is the later question and its implications that are the focus of this chapter.

Perhaps the research tradition that comes closest to the concerns of this chapter is that of the Swedish geographer Torsten Hägerstrand and his colleagues, with their focus on space–time geography (Hägerstrand 1970, 1973, 1975; Pred 1977; Kellerman 1989). A key assumption in their work is that individuals and individual action are not simply located in space, but also in time. The fact that individuals can only be in one location at any one time is then a critical constraint on social interaction. Most famously, Hägerstrand has represented this idea in terms of what is called a space–time cube. Figure 21.1 taken from Kraak (2003)—which provides a detailed discussion of the importance of the cube—illustrates the key idea that individuals only 'meet' when their positions within the cube intersect both in time and space.

Hägerstrand's group has used this perspective in conducting a host of applied studies investigating issues of accessibility (Miller 1991; Kwan 1998): job opportunities, the coordination of work and family responsibilities, interaction with children (Mårtensson 1979), as well as the role of space and time in creating a sense of place, region, and nation (Pred 1977, 1984; Thrift 1983). In important ways, the goal of this chapter is to bring Hägerstrand's focus on the importance of the intersection of time and space to the sociological study of relationships, groups, and organizations.

21.2 WHY IS SCHEDULE COORDINATION SUCH A PROBLEM? FORMAL INSIGHTS

We all experience scheduling conflicts in our daily lives. There may be two colloquia being held simultaneously, both of which we want to attend. More simply, we may have problems finding a time to have lunch with a friend because of each of our individual prior commitments. Often we think of this problem as one of a time-budget constraint—that there is simply not enough time to do all the things we want to do. However, the problem is also potentially one of a scheduling conflict—that other activities are scheduled at the same time. The fact that individuals face time constraints is analogous to the fact that they experience income-budget constraints in making purchase decisions. The existence of scheduling conflicts, however, indicates that individuals potentially face a coordination problem that involves other individuals. The individual in our cartoon is not frustrated because he cannot find the time to have lunch. He is frustrated because he and the person on the other end of the line cannot agree on a specific time to have lunch together.

In order to make the distinction between a time constraint and a scheduling conflict more precise, define a schedule as a two-dimensional matrix where the rows are people and the columns are times or time slots (e.g. 10–10.30 a.m.). Let activities that are done alone be indicated by a lower-case letter. Let unique joint activities be represented by capital letters. In cases where it is useful to use the same letter to represent the same type of activity, for example two colloquia, capital letters may be subscripted, e.g. C_1 versus C_2.

Consider the following example with three individuals, Tom, Dick, and Harry, and four possible activities, opera (O), symphony (S), theater (T), which are all activities each would want to do jointly, if at all; and a fourth activity, reading (r), which each would do alone, if they were to do it. Assume that there are three weekend nights for these activities: Friday, Saturday, and Sunday. Further assume that, without any coordination, each, in order of preference (e.g. Tom's first preference is opera, then theater), would like to do the activities as shown in Table 21.1.

Table 21.1 Hypothetical event schedule

	Friday	Saturday	Sunday
(1) Tom	O	T	r
(2) Dick	r	T	S
(3) Harry	S	r	O

Table 21.2 Rearranged event schedule

	Friday	Saturday	Sunday
(1) Tom	O	T	r
(2) Dick	r	T	S
(3) Harry	O	r	S

If each individual only wants to do three of the four activities as indicated in the schedule, then none of them has a time-budget-constraint problem. For example, Tom can go to the opera (O) on Friday night, theater (T) on Saturday night, and read (r) on Sunday night. We could say that the above schedule is *individually feasible*. Each individual has enough time to do all activities they would like to do. If, however, one or more of them wants to do all four activities, they are faced with a time-budget constraint. There are four activities, but there are only three time periods available. In this case the schedule would be *individually infeasible*. There simply would not be enough time slots available to do all the activities that were desired.

As I have specified in the above example, the individuals want to do all of the activities *jointly*, except reading (r). For an activity to be done jointly, it must by definition occur at the same time for all individuals involved; that is, it must be assigned to a single column within a schedule. Assume that Tom has no interest in symphony, Dick has no interest in opera, and Harry has no interest in theater. Is it possible for the three individuals in Table 21.1 to do things in pairs if they are willing to be flexible about what is done on which night? Table 21.2 shows that it is.

Tom and Harry can go to the opera on Friday night, Tom and Dick to the theater on Saturday night, and Dick and Harry to the symphony on Sunday night. As such, we can say that the above schedule is not only individually feasible, but is also *collectively feasible*. The schedule is collectively feasible in that it is possible to find a unique common time that is feasible for each individual to do each joint activity. More generally, the schedule is feasible in that it is possible to arrange the timing of events so that each unique joint event is assigned to a single column; that is, a single time slot.

Now assume that opera, symphony, and theater only occur on Friday and Saturday nights. As a result, each individual has Sunday night to read. Without loss of generality, we can simply ignore Sunday. Consider Table 21.3.

It is easy to see that at the individual level the schedule within Table 21.3 is feasible for each individual: each individual has two joint activities that they would like to pursue and two nights (Friday and Saturday) within which to do them.

A closer look at Table 21.3 reveals that there is no way to rearrange the three joint activities so that the scheduling table is collectively feasible; that is, so each joint

Table 21.3 Restricted event schedule

	Friday	Saturday
(1) Tom	O	T
(2) Dick	T	S
(3) Harry	S	O

activity is assigned to a single column.[2] If Tom and Harry go to the opera on Friday night and Tom and Dick go to the theater on Saturday night, there is no night for Dick and Harry to go to the symphony. Because interests in activities overlap, there is no way to find a unique time for each activity. If any two pairs of individuals agree to an activity, there will be no night available for the third pair to go out. There are three overlapping joint activities, but only two time slots available. Thus, although the schedule in Table 21.3 is individually feasible, there is no arrangement of activities that makes it collectively feasible. In general, although every individual may separately have enough time available for the activities that they want to carry out, it may be impossible to find a way to schedule those activities so that they can be done jointly as desired.

Because scheduling involves individuals coordinating times with each other and subsequently affects what times are available for other joint activities, schedules are a type of public good. In our example above, there are in fact only three possible schedules, assuming that individuals do not have preferences over whether an activity is done on either a Friday or Saturday night. As such, the three of them as a group need to decide which one of the three possibilities in Table 21.4 will be agreed to.

The individuals' preferences over these three schedules are shown in Table 21.5. The preferences in Table 21.5 are an example of the classic Condorcet (1785) cycle. There is no equilibrium solution here. Assume that as a group they randomly decide to choose S1. Then both Dick and Harry are better off if they defect from the agreement and choose schedule S3. Similarly, if S2 or S3 is chosen, two individuals are always better off by choosing a third alternative.

Table 21.4 Possible event schedules

	Friday	Saturday
S1	O	T
S2	T	S
S3	S	O

Table 21.5 Preferences over schedules

Tom	Dick	Harry
S1	S2	S3
S3	S1	S1
S2	S3	S2

A solution to the above problem would be to make the weekend three instead of two nights long—say, going to the opera, theater, and then the symphony. This was the original case that we considered in Table 21.1. In fact, as we know from our personal experience, when there are scheduling conflicts we often simply delay doing something to a later time. More generally, the problem of time conflicts can be resolved by having many possible time slots in which to schedule activities. Dinner and breakfast meetings can be seen as an attempt to accomplish this. In the extreme, any scheduling problem can be resolved by having as many time periods as events and assigning each event to a unique time slot. This, however, is likely to be highly inefficient for individuals. Unless an individual is interested in participating in most events, they will spend much of their time alone. As such, there will be considerable incentive for them and others to get together during times in which they plan not to attend the scheduled event.

More sophisticated and formal analyses of the time-scheduling problem have been carried out in the graph-theory literature in mathematics. The scheduling problem is equivalent to what is known as the vertex-coloring problem in graph theory.[3] The major focus here has been on determining across different situations the minimum number of time periods needed to eliminate all scheduling conflicts. As discussed in the Appendix (see n. 3), there are two key points that are of sociological interest. First, it is the local structure of specific events that is critical. If k time slots are needed to resolve a scheduling conflict then there must be at least k events that are each tied to k − 1 other events. Second, it is always possible to construct a graph with a fixed degree of sparseness, defined in a specific way, that needs an arbitrarily large number of time slots to resolve all time conflicts.

Work in operations research on combinatorial optimization has been concerned with finding actual assignments that resolve scheduling conflicts. Most of this literature has considered the problem for universities in assigning exam or class times to either eliminate or minimize the number of time conflicts (i.e. students who are scheduled to take more than one exam or class at the same time). Here the number of exams is typically in the hundreds if not thousands and the number of students is in the thousands if not tens of thousands. As a result, scheduling solutions are typically nonobvious and often the problem is to find solutions that minimize the number of conflicts as opposed to eliminating them. Numerous algorithms have been proposed for finding time schedules that eliminate or minimize the number of conflicts. Carter (1986) provides a very concise and accessible summary of past work in this area. Typically, when the number of classes and individuals is large, the computer time can be considerable, since computational time grows exponentially with the number of classes. Generally, in large problems algorithms cannot find solutions when the number of time slots available is close to the minimum number that is theoretically needed. If the number of time slots available is nearly twice this, however, at least in random graphs, most algorithms will find a solution (Grimmett and McDiarmid 1975). It seems reasonable to assume that people probably can do no better than computational algorithms and in fact are likely to do worse. Thus, in real life solving scheduling problems is likely to be exceedingly complex either for humans or for sophisticated algorithms implemented on high-speed computers.

21.3 SOCIAL IMPLICATIONS I: UNREALIZED RELATIONS AND RELATIONS ABANDONED

If two events take place at the same time, then in most cases an individual cannot do both. A student cannot take two courses that are offered at the same time. A person who works the night shift will find it difficult to be friends with someone who works during the day. Families with children in different schools may find that they are unable to travel together if the schools' vacations occur at different times. Prevention programs may find it difficult to keep individuals from dropping out because of scheduling conflicts (Fox and Gottfredson 2003).

One would expect that the problem of scheduling conflicts would be particularly troubling for voluntary groups, since presumably for many individuals work and family commitments would take top priority, leaving potentially few, if any, time slots available for groups to meet. Several papers (Warrener 1985; Tipps 2003) discuss the challenge of scheduling conflicts to the viability of singing groups. Probably no scholar has studied voluntary organizations more thoroughly than Miller McPherson (McPherson and Ranger-Moore 1991; Popielarz and McPherson 1995; McPherson and Rotolo 1996), who points to the fact that time is an important resource for voluntary groups and time constraints can limit voluntary-group involvement. McPherson and colleagues however do not explicitly consider the implications of time-scheduling problems. As discussed in Section 21.4, scheduling conflicts can lead to group segregation. In McPherson's model, voluntary groups compete with each other over individuals with similar interests and characteristics. Thus, two choral groups in a city might compete over the same individuals and their time. What McPherson doesn't consider is how scheduling constraints may actually benefit similar groups. In general it is to the advantage of groups that interest very different individuals to schedule activities at the same time, since they are unlikely to lose many interested potential members to the other group. Groups that are potentially attractive to the same individuals obviously should schedule activities at different times. As discussed in greater detail in the next section, the consequence of this is that we may find that similar individuals have similar schedules as do groups which compete for the same individuals and attempt to find nonoverlapping time periods in which to meet. As a result, individuals with similar interests and thus similar schedules may segregate into nonoverlapping clusters of groups.

The organization in which time constraints and scheduling conflicts have been most extensively studied is the family. As noted earlier, the vast majority of work in this area has focused on the constraints in the amount of time family members commit to different activities, rather than examining in detail scheduling conflicts per se. A few studies have looked explicitly at the effects of scheduling conflicts. Staines and Pleck (1983) used the 1977 US Quality of Employment survey, and found that for married couples shift work led to problems in arranging family activities. Moreover, working weekends or rotating days was associated with greater family conflict. Another study, based on a national longitudinal sample by White and Keith (1990), found 'entry into shift-work significantly increased marital disagreements and quitting shift work significantly increased marital interaction and decreased child-related problems. Looking specifically at marital breakup, the investigators found that being a shift-work couple in 1980 significantly increased the likelihood of divorce by 1983—from 7 percent to 11 percent' (Presser 2003: 82–3).

Harriet Presser, in her book *Working in a 24/7 Economy: Challenges for American Families* (2003), provides the most extensive analysis of the effects of shift work on families. Presser is interested in the effects of nonstandard work schedules on American families, both in terms of hours worked during the day, and days worked during the week. Specific to my interests, she examines consequences of non-standard work schedules along a variety of dimensions when both parents work. Presser's analysis is based on a supplement to the May 1977 Current Populations survey.

Presser first points out that nonstandard schedules are quite common. Approximately 20 percent of Americans do not have fixed daily hours and nearly 24 percent work at least in part on weekends. For dual-earner couples, about one quarter work different shifts. In approximately a third of this group, one spouse, but not both, works on weekends. Furthermore, she finds that having children further increases the chances that parents will work a nonstandard schedule.

In terms of consequences, Presser finds few statistically significant effects, though this may be due to her relatively small sample size and more importantly the detailed way in which she has parsed her data. When a husband works in the evening and wife during the day, as compared to marriages where both spouses work days, it appears to have no effect on general marital happiness, quality of time together, whether a marriage is perceived to be in trouble, or whether a marriage is perceived to have a high chance of ending in divorce. When this pattern is reversed, however, the couple with the wife working in the evening has a considerably more negative marital outcome, with some differences being statistically significant. The results are mixed when the husband or wife works nights. The marital outcomes are generally quite negative and in many cases statistically significant when either the husband or wife has rotating work hours.

Presser also used the *National Survey of Families and Households* to examine divorce rates. Here the results were also mixed. Only marriages where one spouse had fixed night-work hours or rotated hours were more likely to end in divorce.

Looking beyond marital quality, Presser finds that the more a spouse is at home when the other spouse is at work, the more likely they are to do housework. This is true for husbands as well as wives. Furthermore, she finds that parents who have nonstandard work hours are much less likely to eat dinner, but more likely to eat breakfast, with their children.

Although Presser's results are provocative, they should be interpreted with caution. Obviously individuals within couples are not assigned at random to different work schedules. As such, the associations or lack of associations she finds should not be assumed to necessarily represent causal effects. If possible, couples probably choose work schedules that are most beneficial to their marriages. If this is correct, then one might well find no or little association between couples' work schedules and the quality of their marriages when in fact there are substantial causal effects.

21.4 Social Implications II: Segregation in Time

The study of segregation in the social sciences in general and in sociology in particular has almost exclusively focused on geographical segregation, especially geographical residential segregation. As noted earlier in this chapter, the major exception to this is the work of the Swedish geographer Torsten Häagerstand and colleagues. Of course, individuals and/or groups may occupy the same space over the course of a day, but never interact because they are present in that space at different times. In Boston, a park on Washington Street in North Dorchester near one of my field sites is used by day by families with children and at night by drug dealers and prostitutes. Because these two groups are segregated in time (but not space) they seldom interact and thus there is little conflict. Similarly, in office buildings a white-collar workforce and a predominantly minority cleaning staff may work in the same space, but seldom see or interact with each other, because their work schedules have been purposely designed so that they do not overlap.

More generally, time has the potential to segregate. If science labs and athletic practice both occur on the same afternoons, there will be no athletes majoring in science, and athletics and science majors will have reduced contact. Teenagers may choose to sleep during the day and be active at night on weekends in order to avoid overly controlling parents (Melbin 1987). Within many animal species, sex segregation is maintained by males and females having alternating waking and sleeping hours. (See Ruckstuhl and Neuhaus 2005 for a discussion of the recent literature.)

In the US context, few researchers have examined the importance of segregation in time by contrasting the difference between residential and work segregation. Drake and Cayton's seminal work, *Black Metropolis* (1945), describes the far greater contact between whites and blacks at work than in their residential neighborhoods. Kornblum (1974) made the same observation for a much later period. Much more recently, the geographers Mark Ellis and Virginia Park, using the 1990 Census, have examined the difference in the patterns of residential and employment segregation in Los Angeles (2004). They find that employment is substantially less segregated than residence. This contrast is particularly sharp between whites and Mexicans. For these two groups, as well as all other pairs, they find that the difference in the degree of segregation between employment and residential segregation is far greater for men than women.

Of course, the segregation we observe in time is often not an accident. Zerubavel (1981) discusses a variety of situations in which scheduling conflicts are used instrumentally to create segregation. By segregating groups in time, group boundaries are established and maintained, with the result that in-group solidarity is enhanced. He points to the fact that Benedictine monks were required to rise early in the morning and to retire early in the evening, which minimized the opportunity for contact with the outside world. He describes how early Christian groups purposely declared Sunday as the sabbath, in order to dissociate themselves from Jews, whose sabbath is Saturday. The First Council of Nicaea, in AD 325, declared that Easter should be held on the first Sunday after the full moon so that Easter would be dissociated from the Jewish Passover holiday, despite the fact that the Last Supper was a Passover Seder.

The use of scheduling or time conflicts can be particularly effective in that introduction of one conflict that segregates two groups is likely to create others. If two groups participate in one type of activity at different times, this is likely to lead, and in some cases even force, them to participate in other types of activities at different times. Consider the children of Orthodox Jews in New York. Because of the Jewish sabbath, they cannot participate in the public-sports leagues, which typically have their games on Saturdays. In response, and because there is a significantly large

Orthodox population in New York, the Orthodox Jewish sports leagues have their games on Sundays, the Christian sabbath. Honoring the Jewish sabbath has not only resulted in separating Jews and Christians on Saturdays, but on Sundays as well. (Attendance at Orthodox day schools during the week makes the separation of the two populations nearly complete.) Similarly, it is probably no accident that elite private schools typically choose to have one two-week school vacation in March rather than a week-long break in February and another week in April as public schools do.

More generally, the establishment of separate schedules in the form of different calendars has the ability to nearly totally dissociate two groups. Zerubavel (1981: 80) discusses at length how the Dead Sea sect established a calendar distinctly different from the Jewish calendar, apparently to make it impossible for sect members to participate in Jewish life. He also discusses how both the French and Bolshevik Revolutions attempted to dissociate themselves from the Christian calendar. Specifically, after the French Revolution there was an attempt to establish a ten-day week with one fixed day of rest, the *Décadi*. The specific goal was to make it difficult if not impossible for workers to regularly honor Christian holidays, most importantly the Sunday sabbath (p. 73). Similarly, the prophet Mohammed's establishment of a lunar calendar with a 364-day year led to the dissociation of Islamic holidays from earlier Pagan ones.

The point here is that differences in schedules make it difficult for individuals or groups to interact. This is just the obverse of the point made earlier in the chapter and studied by so many scholars: that synchronization of schedules is critical for social coordination and social interaction. Thus, as many scholars have shown, as society becomes more complex, shared calendars and time-reckoning are essential to people being able to coordinate in time. However, to the degree that individuals or groups are involved in one particular activity at different times, it may be difficult, if not impossible, to engage in other activities at the same time. The commitment to use particular time slots for one activity necessarily implies that the available time slots for other activities have been reduced. The fewer the time periods available, potentially the more difficult coordination becomes.

21.5 Social Implications III: Organizational Feasibility

It has long been recognized that organizations play critical coordination functions. Perhaps the most well known and celebrated work is Oliver Williamson's book *Markets and Hierarchies: Analysis and Antitrust Implications* (1975), with its argument that organizations efficiently internalize market-transaction costs. The world of business is of course replete with scheduling problems: time to market for a product; timing of stages in construction processes; maintaining the appropriate flow of goods in time for inventory; product development; the coordination of the timing of different components so the necessary pieces are complete at specified times. The considerable literature on time and capitalism discussed very briefly above can be seen as the story of how different institutional structures and technologies involving time (calendars, time zones, clocks, etc.) developed in order to allow increasingly large organizations to coordinate their workers' schedules.

Obviously most if not all organizations have to solve time-scheduling problems. At a fundamental level, their existence depends on this. Universities need to schedule when semesters will begin and end. Furthermore they need to determine when classes will meet. To be able to offer a large number of classes but be efficient, multiple classes need to be offered at the same time. This of course then means course schedules that involve courses that meet at the same time cannot be realized. At the simplest level, organizations need to schedule meetings. For higher-level executives, this often means having an assistant whose primary task is to maintain the executive's schedule.

It is beyond the scope of this chapter to consider all the types of scheduling problems organizations face and the methods they use to resolve them. This is an enormous area of research within operations research. There is a huge literature within this field, and management systems more generally, that deals with scheduling.[4] My goal in this section is to discuss the implications of a few ideal types of organizational structures for scheduling problems. In doing so, I hope to illustrate several basic principles about what types of structures best facilitate scheduling and what types make it difficult.

Scheduling problems can be trivially solved if individuals have fully congruent schedules. The simplest example is perhaps an elementary-school class. A teacher organizes each day into a set of sequential activities and in the simplest situation all students engage in the same activity at one specific time. The only problem for the teacher is to figure out how much time to allocate to different activities and how to sequence them. She or he faces a time-budget constraint in terms of the total number of school hours in the day. However, there is no scheduling problem in terms of deciding which students will be involved in which activity when.

Perhaps the second simplest type of structure is what might be called a parallel integrated structure. In this type of structure individuals engage in the same type of activity at the same time, sometimes in the same specific activity and at other times not. The standard nine-to-five work week is the prototypical example. In the case where parents both work, they go to work at the same time, but in most cases to separate jobs and organizations. They then come home and share a common period of family time. At the societal level, activities flip between a distinct set of work groups during the day and a different set of family groups in the evening. With the exception of family businesses, sets of individuals are typically not simultaneously part of the exact same groups. For example, two people are unlikely to both work in the same place and be members of the same family. If one spouse is a homemaker, then that activity becomes the structural equivalent of work. For children, school becomes the structural equivalent of work. Small differences between a child's school and parents' work hours, however, can result in serious supervision problems and the phenomenon of latchkey kids.

Symmetrical scheduling problems, however, do not always have simple, efficient solutions, as we saw with the example of Tom, Dick, and Harry. Although each individual only needs two time periods for the activities she or he is interested in, three periods are needed in order to enact their joint activities. As discussed in the Appendix (see n. 3), situations where there are odd numbers of activities interconnected through joint membership (in graph-theoretical terms, when there are odd cycles) require more time periods to be collectively feasible than are needed to be individually feasible. Thus, in the Tom, Dick, and Harry example we have three activities, symphony, theater, opera, with each pair of activities having one individual interested in both. In this case, it takes three time periods to avoid a scheduling problem although each individual is only interested in two of the three activities.

It is perhaps not surprising that situations in which individuals are in symmetric, equal positions and/or the goal is to produce a scheduling solution with this property are difficult to achieve. In such cases there is no logical way to give any one person's scheduling goals priority. Rissman (2000) describes the attempt to create a new high school in St Paul, Minnesota with small learning environments consisting of heterogeneous mixes of students. He describes how initial efforts failed, primarily due to scheduling conflicts.

Eric Leifer (1990) has examined a related set of issues in depth. Leifer's concern is not simply to find schedules that are feasible in the collective sense defined above, but to find schedules that are fair in that they treat all individuals (units) in the same way. His analysis focuses on the problem of creating a game schedule for the National Football League. The core of the problem is that teams on average are more likely to win when they play at home than when they are away. A fair schedule is one where no team is favored by when it has home games. At minimum this means that each team should have the same numbers of home and away games. Meeting this constraint is not problematic. More demanding is that no team should be favored by having a majority of its home games early in the season. That would create the potential for a team to develop momentum. Leifer discusses cases of particularly successful teams that had most of their home games at the beginning of the season. In general the NFL has never been able to create schedules that are fully fair with respect to this criterion; that is, in any season some teams have had more home games initially than others. As Leifer reports, the same two individuals have constructed the schedule every year since 1970, typically spending eight weeks, including evenings, doing so. In his article Leifer describes his attempts to improve on their efforts by using a very sophisticated computer algorithm. Like them, he finds it impossible to create a schedule that is fair in that it provides an equal balance across teams in the sense described above of when teams play home and away games. Leifer's research reiterates the point made earlier when I discussed operation-research solutions to general scheduling problems—scheduling problems are generally extremely difficult to solve even with high-speed computers and sophisticated algorithms.

Hierarchical structures seem ideally suited to solving scheduling problems in that there is an obvious rule as to whose scheduling preferences should take priority: individuals lower-down in the organization should adjust their schedules to those above them in terms of meeting and coordinating activities. In a classic article Schwartz (1974) examines the relationship between who waits in social interactions and power. He looks at a plethora of examples from doctors to CEOs. His basic point is that power determines who waits and who doesn't. It is normative and common for the subordinate who comes to meet with his superordinate to be kept waiting. The reverse, that the subordinate should be late for a meeting, is totally unacceptable and if it happens too often may be grounds for firing. Schwartz provides a detailed analysis of why this asymmetry exists, from differences in supply and demand, who comes to whom, and the ways in which waiting itself defines who is in power.

What Schwartz does not consider is how differences in power, and thus the presence of hierarchy, act to solve schedule-coordination issues. The question of who will or should wait is also one of how scheduling conflicts between two people could be resolved. In the case where there is a clear status differential the answer is obvious. If the higher-status person is not immediately available when the lower-status person arrives, the lower-status person will have to wait; that is, the higher-status person's schedule will take precedence. If the lower-status person would like to meet with the higher-status person, the assumption is that they will adjust their schedule to accommodate to the times when the higher-status person is available.

Winship (1978) showed that where a hierarchical structure existed, not only would an equilibrium exist, but it would be Pareto-optimal. That is, there would be no other agreement about the time pairs of individuals would spend together that all individuals would either prefer or find just as acceptable.[5] Specifically, if we considered a situation in which individual B is said to be dominated by individual A, if in equilibrium B would like to spend more time with A than A is willing to spend with B and this relationship formed a hierarchy (or more precisely a partial ordering), then the equilibrium would be Pareto-optimal. That is, there would be no allocation of time between the individuals that the person at the top of the hierarchy would prefer to the equilibrium allocation.

Undeveloped in that paper is the simple insight that if there were a pre-existing hierarchy (partial ordering), and the people only need to interact with those who are above or below them, then there is a simple mechanism for solving scheduling conflicts. Specifically, the scheduling preferences of the person(s) at the top of the hierarchy should determine when the activities they need to participate in should occur. Taking those times as fixed, the scheduling preferences of the individuals below them should determine when the next set of activities should occur. And so on.

Schwartz's description (1974) of many different settings is consistent with the above allocation mechanism. This mechanism is also consistent with his general insight: that people with power, that is people higher-up in the hierarchy, are able to use their time more efficiently and fully—they will spend less time waiting. What we can see here is that a key reason for this is the way that hierarchies are likely to lead to potential scheduling conflicts being resolved.

CONCLUSION

Social relations do not simply exist as abstract entities. They need to be enacted in real time and space. In this chapter I have argued that enactment can be constrained and even be infeasible because of scheduling conflicts. Furthermore these constraints can have important implications for social relations, grading, and organizations.

After reviewing previous work on the social science of time, I provided a basic formal analysis of why scheduling conflicts exist and more importantly why they can be difficult to resolve. Because the decision to schedule an event at one time affects the time other events might be scheduled, schedules become a type of public good. As with public goods in general, it may be impossible to determine an allocation that is consistent with individual preferences (Arrow 1951).

I went on to show that scheduling constraints can have important social implications. First, they can simply prevent specific relations or groups from occurring or may cause others to dissolve. A potential choral group that cannot find a common time to practice may simply never come into existence. Two individuals may find it difficult to maintain a marriage if they can never find time to be together. Second, I show how time segregates groups and reinforces group boundaries. Parents with children and drug dealers may coexist peacefully if they use a public park at different times. Calendars may be purposefully structured so that it is difficult for individuals to engage with members of other groups: different sabbaths separate Jews and Christians; different vacation times public- and private-school students. Finally,

I discussed how organizations in order to be feasible have to be able to resolve scheduling problems. Time schedules where all individuals have the same schedule or their schedules have parallel structures are the easiest to manage. More complex forms of equality can make scheduling conflicts difficult to resolve. In contrast, hierarchies provide a simple mechanism for dealing with scheduling issues: the schedules of those higher-up in the hierarchy are given precedence over the ones of those lower-down.

The immediate impact of scheduling conflicts is easy to see: concerts not attended, lunches not had, meetings that take forever to schedule. As individuals we can readily recognize how scheduling conflicts affect our lives. Understanding how scheduling conflicts more generally affect the nature and organization of social relations can be difficult. I have suggested several important ways that they do so. It is to be hoped that other researchers will be able to identify additional ways in which time and our attempt to organize it through schedules shape social life.

Notes

1. Both of these literatures are part of an even broader literature on time use. Most important in the last several decades has been the development of time-use surveys (see Herz and Devens 2001 for a survey of recent results).
2. Note that there is no problem with there being multiple events assigned to the same column/time period. Multiple events can occur at the same time. People cannot participate in more than one event at the same time.
3. An appendix to this chapter, which is available on the author's website—<http://www.wjh.harvard.edu/soc/faculty/winship/oxford_handbook_analytical_sociology _appendix.pdf>—provides a discussion of some of the basic theorems in this literature.
4. Amazon.com listed more than 3,500 books on scheduling as of February 2008.
5. Winship's result (1978) only examined the problem of individuals allocating time among each other under the constraint that the amount of time one individual spent with another was equal. He did not consider the complicated scheduling problem that is the focus of this chapter.

References

Arrow, K. J. (1951), *Social Choice and Individual Values* (New York: Wiley).

Becker, G. S. (1965), 'A Theory of the Allocation of Time', *Economic Journal*, 75: 493–517.

Bender, J., and Wellbery, D. E. (1991) (eds.), *Chronotypes: The Construction of Time* (Stanford, Calif.: Stanford University Press).

Bergmann, W. (1992), 'The Problem of Time in Sociology: An Overview of the Literature on the State of Theory and Research on the "Sociology of Time", 1900–82', *Time and Society*, 1 (1): 81–134.

BIANCHI, S. M., ROBINSON, J. P., and MIKIE, M. A. (2006) *The Changing Rhythms of American Life* (New York: Russell Sage).

BOURDIEU, P. [1963] (1990), 'Time Perspectives of the Kabyle', in J. Hassard (ed.), *The Sociology of Time* (New York: St Martin's), 219–37.

CARTER, M. W. (1986), 'A Survey of Practical Applications of Examination Timetabling Algorithms', *Operations Research*, 34: 193–202.

CONDORCET, M. DE (1785), *Essai sur l'application de L'analyse à la probabilité des décisions rendues a la pluraliste des voix* (Paris).

DRAKE, S. C., and CAYTON, H. B. (1945), *Black Metropolis: A Study of Negro Life in a Northern City* (New York: Harcourt).

ELLIS, M., and PARKS, V. (2004), 'Work Together, Live Apart? Geographies of Racial and Ethnic Segregation at Home and at Work', *Annals of the Association of American Geographers*, 94 (3): 620–37.

EPSTEIN, C. F., and KALLEBERG, A. L. (2006) (eds.), *Fighting for Time: Shifting Boundaries of Work and Social Life* (New York: Russell Sage).

FOX, D. P., and GOTTFREDSON, D. C. (2003), 'Differentiating Completers from Non-completers of a Family-based Prevention Program', *Journal of Primary Prevention*, 24 (2): 111–24.

GELL, A. (1996), *The Anthropology of Time: Cultural Constructions of Temporal Maps and Images* (Oxford: Berg).

GRIMMETT, G. R., and McDIARMID, C. J. H. (1975), 'On Colouring Random Graphs', *Mathematical Proceedings of the Cambridge Philosophical Society*, 77: 313–24.

HÄGERSTRAND, T. (1970), 'What About People in Regional Science?', *Papers and Proceedings of the Regional Science Association*, 24: 7–21.

—— (1973), 'The Domain of Human Geography', in R. J. Chorley (ed.), *Directions in Geography* (London: Methuen).

—— (1975), 'Space, Time and Human Conditions', in A. Karlqvist and E. F. Snickars (eds.), *Allocation of Urban Space* (Farnborough: Saxton House).

HAMMERMESH, D. S., and PFANN, G. A. (2005*a*) (eds.), *The Economics of Time Use* (Amsterdam: Elsevier).

—— (2005*b*), 'Introduction: Time-use Data in Economics', in Hammermesh and Pfann (eds.), *The Economics of Time Use* (Amsterdam: Elsevier).

HASSARD, J. (1990), *The Sociology of Time* (London: Macmillan).

HERZ, D., and DEVENS, R. M. (2001), 'The American Time-use Survey', *Industrial Relations*, 40 (3): 526–9.

HOCHSCHILD, A. (1989), *The Second Shift* (New York: Avon).

JACOBS, J. A., and GERSON, K. (2004), *The Time Divide: Work, Family, and Gender Inequality* (Cambridge, Mass.: Harvard University Press).

KELLERMAN, A. (1989), *Time, Space and Society: Geographical Societal Perspectives* (Dordrecht: Kluwer).

KILLINGSWORTH, M. R., and HECKMAN, J. J. (1987), 'Female Labor Supply: A Survey', in O. Ashenfelter and R. Layard (eds.), *Handbook of Labor Economics* (North-Holland: Elsevier), 103–204.

KORNBLUM, W. (1974), *Blue Collar Community* (Chicago, Ill.: University of Chicago Press).

KRAAK, M. (2003), 'The Space–Time Cube Revisited From a Geovisualization Perspective', proceedings of the 21st International Cartographic Conference, Durban, South Africa, 16 October.

Kwan, M. P. (1998), 'Space–Time and Integral Measures of Individual Accessibility: A Comparative Analysis Using a Point-based Framework', *Geographical Analysis*, 30 (3): 191–216.

Landes, D. (1983), *Revolution in Time: Clocks and the Making of the Modern World* (Cambridge, Mass.: Harvard University Press).

Leifer, E. M. (1990), 'Enacting Networks: The Probability of Fairness', *Social Networks*, 12 (1): 1–25.

McPherson, J. M., and Ranger-Moore, J. R. (1991), 'Evolution on a Dancing Landscape: Organizations and Networks in Dynamic Bias Space', *Social Forces*, 70: 19–42.

McPherson, M., and Rotolo, T. (1996), 'Testing a Dynamic Model of Social Composition: Diversity and Change in Voluntary Groups', *American Sociological Review*, 61: 179–202.

Malinowski, B. (1927), 'Lunar and Seasonal Calendars in the Trobriands', *Journal of the Anthropological Institute of Great Britain and Ireland*, 57: 203–15.

Mårtensson, S. (1979), 'On the Formation of Biographies in Space–Time Environments', *Lund Studies in Geography*, 47: 151–62.

Melbin, M. (1987), *Night as Frontier: Colonizing the World After Dark* (New York: Free Press).

Miller, H. J. (1991), 'Modeling Accessibility Using Space–Time Prism Concepts Within Geographical Information Systems', *International Journal of Geographical Information Systems*, 5: 287–301.

Popielarz, P. A., and McPherson, J. M. (1995), 'On the Edge or In Between: Niche Position, Niche Overlap, and the Duration of Voluntary Association Memberships', *American Journal of Sociology*, 101 (3): 698–720.

Pred, A. (1977), 'The Choreography of Existence: Comments on Hagerstrand's Time-geography and its Usefulness', *Economic Geography*, 53: 207–21.

—— (1984), 'Place as a Historically Contingent Process: Structuration and the Time-geography of Becoming Place', *Annals of the Association of American Geographers*, 74 (2): 279–97.

Presser, H. B. (2003), *Working in a 24/7 Economy: Challenges for American Families* (New York: Russell Sage).

Rissman, J. (2000), 'Same As It Never Was: Realizing the Vision of Smaller Communities of Learners at Arlington High School', executive summary, Arlington High School, St Paul, Minn.

Ruckstuhl, K. E., and Neuhaus, P. (2005) (eds.), *Sexual Segregation in Vertebrates— Ecology of the Two Sexes* (Cambridge: Cambridge University Press).

Schwartz, B. (1974), 'Waiting, Exchange and Power: The Distribution of Time in Social Systems', *American Journal of Sociology*, 79: 841–70.

Sorokin, P., and Merton, R. (1937), 'Social Time: A Methodological and Functional Analysis', *American Journal of Sociology*, 42: 615–29.

Staines, G. L., and Pleck, J. H. (1983), *The Impact of Work Schedules on the Family* (Ann Arbor, Mich.: Institute for Social Research).

Thompson, E. P. (1976), *The Making of the English Working Class* (London: Gollancz).

Thrift, N. (1983), 'On the Determination of Social Action in Space and Time', *Environment and Planning D: Society and Space*, 1: 23–57.

Tipps, J. W. (2003), 'A Preliminary Study of Factors that Limited Secondary School Choral Involvement of Collegiate Choral Singers', *International Journal of Research in Choral Singing*, (1): 22–8.

WARRENER, J. J. (1985), 'Making Junior–Senior Band Succeed', *Music Educators Journal*, 72 (2): 42–4.

WHITE, L., and KEITH, B. (1990), 'The Effect of Shift Work on the Quality and Stability of Marital Relations', *Journal of Marriage and the Family*, 52: 453–62.

WILLIAMSON, O. (1975), *Markets and Hierarchies: Analysis and Antitrust Implications* (New York: Free Press).

WINSHIP, C. (1978), 'The Allocation of Time Among Individuals', *Sociological Methodology*, 9: 75–99.

—— (1992), 'Social Relations and Time', paper presented at the *Sunbelt Social Network Conference*, San Diego, Calif., 14–16 February.

ZERUBAVEL, E. (1981), *Hidden Rhythms: Schedules and Calendars in Social Life* (Chicago, Ill.: University of Chicago Press).

—— (1982), 'The Standardization of Time: A Sociohistorical Perspective', *American Journal of Sociology*, 88: 1–23.

CHAPTER 22

HOMOPHILY AND THE FOCUSED ORGANIZATION OF TIES*

SCOTT FELD

BERNARD GROFMAN

INTRODUCTION

IT is a well-known and well-documented fact of social life that people tend to inter-act with others like themselves more often than one would expect from random association among people (McPherson, Smith-Lovin, and Cook 2001). However, the finding of greater similarity than would be expected by chance may not be nearly as surprising as the finding that there is a lot *less* similarity among people who interact than one might expect to arise from the powerful social processes of social influence and selective attraction. We suggest that it is important to understand structures and processes that encourage similar people to interact and interacting

* The first author wishes to acknowledge support for the community-parenting study from a postdoctoral fellowship from NIMH to the Family Violence Research Program at the University of New Hampshire (Murray A. Straus, PI), 1987. We also want to acknowledge thoughtful comments on earlier drafts of this chapter by Peter Hedstrom, Robert Mare, and Min Yimm.

people to be similar; *and* that it is important to understand structures and processes that limit and constrain this type of consistency in social life.

'Homophily' is a term that has been often used to describe the tendencies for people with similar characteristics to interact with one another (see McPherson, Smith-Lovin, and Cook 2001). According to Kandel (1978), 'Lazarsfeld and Merton (1954) first proposed the term "homophily" to refer to the tendency for similarity on various attributes among persons who affiliate with each other (427).' However, the term 'homophily' prejudges the source of such correlations to be in the liking (phily) of similarity (homo). Preference for interacting with similar others is certainly a factor that contributes to the positive correlation between similarity and interaction, as people both choose to interact with others like themselves, and change themselves to become more similar to their interaction partners (see Kandel, 1978; McPherson, Smith-Lovin, and Cook 2001). Although some analysts may reserve the term homophily to describe either 'selective attachment' (changing interactions) or 'influence' (changing behaviors), we want to be clear that we use the term homophily as motivation for both types of individual changes.

Nevertheless, to the extent that other factors affect how people both behave and interact, one cannot necessarily infer homophily (personal *preferences* for interacting with similar others) from the empirical findings of correlations. For example, McPherson and Smith-Lovin (1987) found that the correlation could be produced by the 'restricted opportunity structure' offered by groups.

Consequently, we are careful to use the word *homophily* specifically for the personal preferences for interacting with similar others, and we use the term *network autocorrelation* to describe the correlation between similarities and interaction, irrespective of the processes that underly that correlation. *Network autocorrelation* is defined as the 'linking among similars' as a descriptive term for the tendency for similar people to be linked and linked people to be similar. Recognizing the possibility of other sources of network autocorrelation will allow us to more objectively examine various processes, including but not limited to the exercise of personal preferences, that encourage or discourage network autocorrelation in particular respects.

Before proceeding any further in our analysis of these structures and processes, it is useful to recognize (as Davis 1963 emphasized nearly fifty years ago) that strict consistency at the individual level (individuals interacting only with others like themselves) implies strict clustering at the aggregate level (completely disconnected homogeneous clusters of people). The only way that similar individuals interact and dissimilar individuals do not interact is for all of the individuals with the same characteristic to form their own cluster such that individuals interact within clusters and not across clusters. The fact that societies are not so segmented is the most obvious indication that many people must be interacting with others different from themselves.

In addition to examining network autocorrelation with respect to various individual traits/characteristics, we will also consider one specific type of behavioral network autocorrelation that has received a great deal of attention, autocorrelation with regard to interactions with other people. If individuals interact with others who have the same set of social relations to further others, then people are friends with their friends' friends. The words 'transitivity' and 'balance' have been often used to describe this type of internal consistency among sets of social relations. Researchers have repeatedly found a disproportionate amount of this particular form of consistency over a broad array of conditions. However, as with network autocorrelation more generally, complete transitivity and balance implies complete clustering. The only way for each person to be friends with all the friends' friends is for the person and those friends to be contained within a separate complete cluster.

As mentioned above, the absence of such stark separation into cliques indicates that there is far from complete transitivity and balance in society. In fact, we suggest that even though people are much more likely to be friends with their friends' friends than would be expected by chance, people are still very *unlikely* to be friends with most of their friends' friends. The great number of intransitivities indicates that whatever pressures may exist toward transitivity must be relatively weak and/or counteracted by other factors.

22.1 INDIVIDUAL ACTIONS INCREASING LOCAL CONSISTENCY AND GLOBAL SEGMENTATION

There are two distinct processes by which network autocorrelation can arise from people acting consistently with homophily, their preferences to interact with people like themselves. They can change themselves or they can change their interaction partners. Individuals can come to behave more like those with whom they interact (the effect of differential association/influence), and individuals can selectively interact with people who are already similar to themselves (selective attachment). Both of these processes lead to distinct homogeneous clusters within particular social networks and in society.

22.1.1 Changing to be similar to one's associates

We can begin by considering the effects of differential association/influence: people coming to behave like those particular others with whom they are interacting.

The overall effect of such social influence is a tendency toward homogenization of behavior, as increasing numbers of people come to behave like most people in the population. However, it is common to find that the homogenization is less than complete, as there come to be pockets of deviance from the overall norm. If people who begin with the minority behavior happen to be in contact with a majority of others with the minority behavior who are in contact with a majority of others with the minority behavior, then those minority behaviors tend to be stable. In fact, those who are surrounded by those with minority behavior may be converted in that direction. If everyone has a large number of relatively random ties, then it is unlikely that anyone would be surrounded by a majority of minority behaviors. However, many people do not have large numbers of ties, and it is likely that many people have ties to a set of alters that is very unrepresentative of the overall population, especially when that set of alters is small. Also, ties are disproportionately local, so the ties of one's alters are disproportionately likely to be redundant. If there is this type of redundancy, then if a minority-behaving person has other minority-behaving people nearby, that increases the chances of them sharing the same minority-behaving neighbors and so supporting and maintaining the minority behaviors of one another.

The 'Morals' module of Bainbridge's *Sociology Laboratory* (1986) produces a simple but powerful visual simulation that provides a clear illustration of the effects of influence through differential association. In that simulation there are 190 individuals arranged in 10 rows of 19 each. Each may be tied to any or all of 6 neighbors (2 each above and below, and 1 on each side). Beginning with a random distribution of ties among their neighbors, and with a minority of individuals randomly assigned to using drugs, individuals are assumed to change to/from drug use to be consistent with a majority of their associates. Figure 22.1 shows results of the effects of differential association that are typical of these types of effects: the drug users become highly clustered.

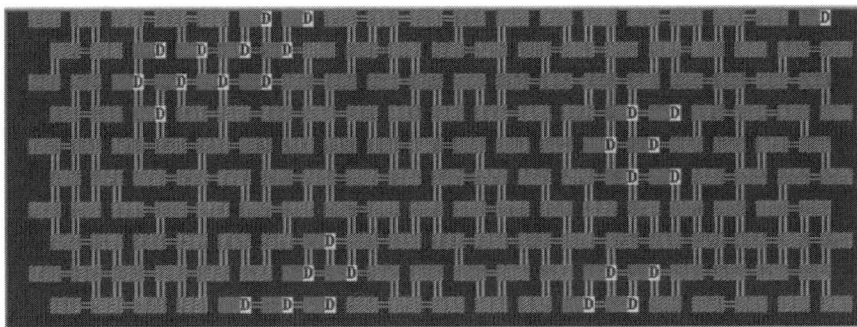

Fig. 22.1 Equilibrium resulting from differential association

Thus, the effect of these individual consistency processes is not the elimination of deviance as much as its reduction and segregation. Deviance can flourish under these conditions, but the deviants tend to have little or no contact with the conformists.

22.1.2 Choosing to associate with similar others

Individuals can increase the extent to which they interact with people behaving similarly to themselves both by (a) changing their behavior to become similar to their associates (as discussed and illustrated above), and by (b) changing their interactions by increasing their interactions with those who behave like them and decreasing their interactions with those who behave differently. This latter phenomenon is often referred to as *selective attachment*.

Bainbridge (1986) incorporated the possibility for selective attachment into his 'Morals' simulation described above. When the selective-attachment process is activated, people drop those ties to dissimilar neighbors and pick up ties to similar neighbors over time. The effect of this process can be seen in Figure 22.2, containing a random assignment of a minority of people to using drugs. The results are separate clusters of drug users and nonusers that arise entirely from selective attachment. Selective attachment alone produces no change in the drug-use behavior of any individuals, but the drug users are segregated into multiple clusters separate from the rest of the population.

One consequence of selective attachment is the protection of deviance from social pressures toward conformity that would otherwise be produced by social-influence processes. Although it is relatively easy to describe and illustrate this abstract process, as shown above, observers may overlook one or the other of these important processes in analyzing particular situations. Specifically, one of the

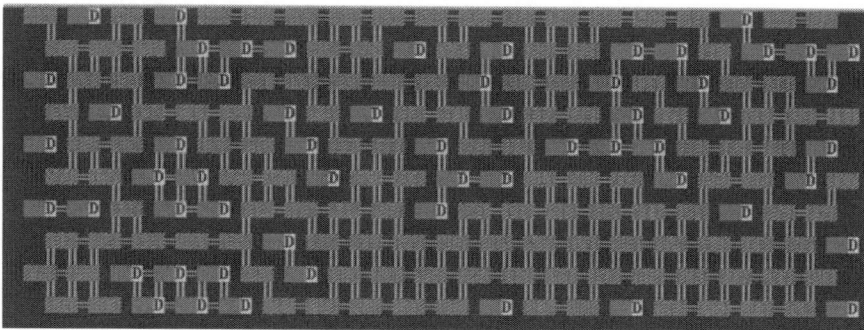

Fig. 22.2 Equilibrium resulting from selective ties

authors conducted a study several years ago for the specific purpose of demonstrating the effects of conformity processes within a community, but he had not anticipated that the powerful effects of selective attachment would subvert the homogenizing effects of social influence.

22.1.3 An empirical example: child-rearing in one small, dense student community

Based upon Festinger, Schachter, and Back's classic theory of *Social Pressures in Informal Groups* (1950), Feld (1988) hypothesized that young parents living in a spatially dense student family-housing community of other young parents would come to follow a community norm concerning parenting, and corporal punishment in particular. After interviewing about thirty mothers of young children, he realized that no such conformity process was occurring. He could find no indication of an overall norm. Rather, there were different types of people with different beliefs, and those people tended to interact with similar others who shared and reinforced their beliefs.

Specifically, there were three distinct groups of mothers. There were undergraduate-student single mothers who tended to engage in relatively low levels of child supervision consistent with their demanding lifestyles as single mothers and full-time students themselves. They were generally not punitive and especially tended not to use corporal punishment. They tended to interact largely with other single mothers and their children in the little free time they had.

In the strongest contrast, there were the conservative religious mothers married to student husbands who believed in the strictest parenting, often explicitly requiring frequent corporal punishment. They tended to belong to a particular local fundamentalist Christian church and spend time with other members of their church who had similar beliefs and practices to themselves. They had little reason to question their own beliefs and practices, and may not have even been aware that their beliefs and practices were in a relatively small minority in their community.

There was also a group of mothers married to student husbands who were not involved with that particular church. They tended to believe in a much more involved parenting style than the single mothers, with strict supervision but relatively little punishment. To the extent that they interacted with others in the community, it would mostly not be with single mothers, who were often busy students, or with the members of the fundamentalist church, who were heavily involved in that church, but more likely with others like themselves with time and interest in spending time with their children out in this neighborhood. Because they were the ones most often out and about in the community, they sometimes observed unsupervised children that seemed to them to indicate negligent parenting, but they were aware that they were not in any position to affect it.

It was clear that everyone in this community took parenting very seriously and had strong views about it, but everyone was pretty well protected from social pressures to change their own points of view. Many seemed to be relatively unaware of others' points of view and/or did not care. To the extent that some became aware of behavior that they did not approve, they were generally in no position to affect it. To the extent that some were concerned that their behaviors might be disapproved by others, they tended to avoid being observed rather than modifying their behaviors. For example, one single mother explained that she 'yelled quietly' at her daughter to avoid being monitored by some married parents in an adjacent apartment with whom she otherwise had little interaction.

So the individual beliefs and behaviors within this one small, dense community managed to avoid social pressures. The effects of social networks in this community were not to create community conformity, but rather to protect against it.

Notice that the interactions among the women in this community did seem to fall in relatively distinct clusters, but the separation did not arise either from choices to interact with others with similar parenting behaviors, or from choices to adopt parenting behaviors similar to those of interaction partners. The church group definitely had other origins, and undoubtedly had the effect of protecting its members from pressures from outsiders regarding many values and behaviors that were not necessarily popular in the larger community. The single mothers tended to have lifestyles in common (largely being students in the same programs) that made them especially likely to interact. They also experienced common circumstances as single parents and students that led them to have similar needs, values, and behaviors of various types. Given their availability to one another, they also had a tendency to rely more on one another than on others. The married mothers not involved in the fundamentalist church generally shared common circumstances of a two-parent family with the husband being a student, but they did not have any particular context (like a church or common classes) that brought them into regular contact with one another. Nevertheless, they probably ran into one another (e.g. at a local playground or market) more than they encountered the other two types of mothers, who were heavily involved elsewhere (e.g. in their classes or their church).

22.2 THE SOCIAL-STRUCTURAL INFRASTRUCTURE OF CONFORMITY—FOCI OF ACTIVITY

The community study described above illustrates how separation into homogeneous clusters can protect people against social influence. People did not either choose their associates on the basis of their parenting attitudes and behaviors, or change their behaviors to be like their associates. Rather, their friendships were based upon pre-existing foci of activity (Feld 1981). The most obvious example was the fundamentalist church. The parents in the study community that were members of that church came into repeated contact with one another in the context of church activities. They developed friendships with one another (and with other church members outside of this community) as a result of the repeated interaction. The parenting attitudes were among their shared similarities but were neither causes nor effects of the interactions among these people.

In general, foci of activity (Feld 1981) bring people together in repeated interactions that tend to create personal relationships and further interaction between the individuals involved. The effect is that there is a 'group' composed of the people who share a particular focus of activity. Selection into association with that focus of activity leads to certain types of homogeneity within the group (Feld 1982). Focused groups are important sources of network autocorrelation, because they foster interaction among a set of people who are homogeneous in particular ways. Pairs of individuals who share participation in a focus of activity will tend to both be similar in certain respects and interact with one another, even if the individuals involved do not necessarily prefer to interact with people who are similar to themselves in these respects and are not influenced by the people with whom they interact.

In fact, in the context of larger groups, the process of dyadic choice and dyadic influence may be considerably less important than the selection into the group, interaction fostered by the group, and conformity to larger-group norms. Kurt Lewin's famous statement (as paraphrased by Festinger, Schachter and Back: 1950: 6) that 'it should be easier to change a whole group at once than to change one individual and leave the rest of the group unchanged' should apply well to dyads acting and interacting within the context of a group. Action and interaction within the context of a group are guided by the nature of selection into the group, by the group activities, and by the group norms. Pairs of people within a group tend to share group behaviors with the group as a whole and therefore also with one another, and often find it more difficult to avoid interaction with others in the group than to interact with one another.

Thus, shared foci of activity are the cause of much interaction and similarity and much of the association between the two. However, foci of activity in modern society are increasingly specialized, and their impact is not in terms of linking people who are similar in all respects, but in terms of linking people who are similar in the particular respects that characterizes the particular focus. At the same time, individuals generally participate in many different foci of activity that may not overlap very much if at all in terms of membership or types of homogeneity. As Simmel (1955) argued half a century ago, the multiplicity of groups facilitates individual freedom, as the groups are homogeneous in different respects, and an individual has some freedom to choose the nature and extent of participation in the different foci of activity.

The similarity of behavior between interacting individuals that arises from an underlying focus of activity is likely to be largely confined to the context in which both the interaction and the behavior take place; and the nature of the similar behavior is likely to be that which is most relevant to that context. Tied individuals who also participate in different other contexts are likely to feel relatively few pressures to reconcile their different behaviors in those other outside contexts. Thus, people can live or work together or be in the same family and still have very different preferences for ethnic food, dance styles, or sports teams, unless the neighborhood, work, or family activities specifically come to involve shared food, dance, or sports enthusiasm.

The fact that much network autocorrelation originates within foci of activity has the implication that many of the tendencies toward consistency are conditional. For example, in terms of friends of friends, it is usually true that you are friends of your friends' friends within the same context, but not necessarily so when your friends' relations with their friends are from a different focus of activity than that underlying your friendship. For example, you probably don't even know most of your neighbors' coworkers or your cousin's fraternity brothers. There is almost no transitivity there, even though you know most of your coworkers' coworkers and your neighbors' neighbors.

Network autocorrelation is conditional with respect to other types of behavior as well. Your lawn-cutting behavior may conform to that of your neighbors but not to that of your coworkers, and your working behaviors may conform more to those of your coworkers than to those of your kin.

The importance of the focused origins of network autocorrelation is that its nature, presence, and absence is often predictable based upon understanding the focused sources. To the extent that network autocorrelation is based upon homophily, preferences for interacting with similar others, and choices of behavior or attachments based upon such preferences, one would expect a general diffuse undifferentiated tendency for people to act similarly to their interaction partners. However, to the extent that network autocorrelation is based upon the underlying structures of foci of activity, one can predict the nature of the similarities—for example, that people will have similar religious beliefs and behaviors to their families, similar work behaviors to their work associates, and similar yard maintenance to their neighbors.

At the same time, the origins of ties also have implications for encouraging interaction with others with certain differences. Specifically, heterogeneity of people associated with a focus of activity leads us to expect particular differences within those contexts; for example, the multiple generations included in families lead people to interact with family members of very different ages from themselves.

22.2.1 Some principles of focused organization of local consistency

The focused organization of social ties has the following salient characteristics:

(1) Individuals associated with the same focus of activity tend to interact with one another.

(2) People associated with a particular focus of activity tend to have certain traits, values, and behaviors associated with that focus of activity.

(3) Each individual tends to draw associates from several different foci of activity.

These characteristics of foci of activity lead to network autocorrelation of particular limited and predictable forms. Specifically, network autocorrelation means that people who are tied to one another will tend to behave similarly to one another and have ties to others in common. The focused organization as a source of network autocorrelation implies that the source of the tie between two individuals is an important determinant of and guide to which behaviors they are likely to share, and which ties to others they are likely to have in common.

(4) Two people whose relationship originated within a particular focus of activity tend to have similar traits, values, and behaviors to the extent that those traits, values, and behaviors are associated with that focus of activity.

(5) Two people whose relationship originated within a particular focus of activity tend to know, interact with, and have close relationships with several of the same others also associated with that focus of activity.

(6) Two interacting people whose relationship originated with a particular focus of activity and who are also associated with other separate foci of activity are likely to have different traits, values, and behaviors associated with those other foci and likely to have ties to others from those other foci that they do not share.

22.2.2 Visualizing the limited segmentation of focused organization

The Bainbridge simulations illustrated above show influence processes and selective attachment in the absence of foci of activity. The activating mechanism for influence with regard to any behavior is for each individual to take all alters equally into account. We suggest it is more reasonable that when people are determining behavior within a context they take account of the behaviors within that context but generally do not consider the behaviors of alters from other contexts. Thus, an individual will use fellow church members for guidance on religious practice, but not be influenced much by neighbors' religious practices.

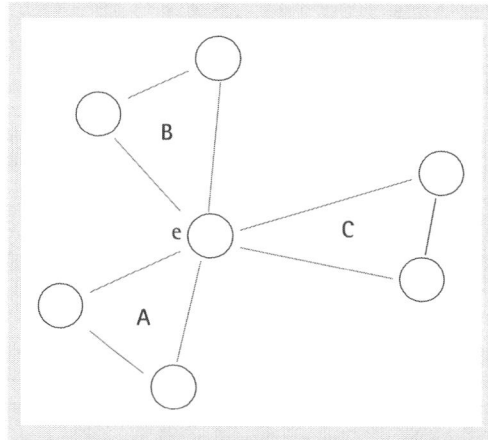

Fig. 22.3 An individual (e) participating in three foci (A, B, C) with other people

And an individual will use neighbors for guidance on landscaping, but not be influenced much by fellow church members for that purpose. Also, the person may especially use church members for guidance in choosing to interact with further church members, and neighbors for guidance in choosing to interact with further neighbors. At the individual level, this may look as shown in Figure 22.3.

Person *e* may have all the critical characteristics associated with foci A, B, and C, and *e* undoubtedly has associations with some others from A, some from B, and some form C. There is generally no compelling reason to bring individuals from these different contexts together or to try to make them 'consistent' in any way. If every one of those other individuals is also associated with multiple foci, it becomes difficult to represent these connections. However, as shown in Figure 22.4, (which illustrates the duality of people and groups—Breiger 1974; Feld 1981; McPherson 1982—that constitutes the structure of people interacting through foci of activity) the visual representation can be somewhat simplified by representing foci of activity (dark ovals) as well as individuals (small circles), and then indicating ties between individuals and foci. Individuals tied to the same focus are likely to be tied to one another and share the particular focus characteristics; for example, *g* and *c* are tied to one another and share many things associated with their common focus. However, *g* also is tied to *h* and *i* through a different focus and shares other characteristics with them; and *c* is tied to *d*, *a*, and *h* through another focus, and to *a* and *b* through still another focus. Consequently, we expect *g* and *c* to have some ties to others in common and to be similar in some regards, but we also expect that they each have many ties to others not in common, and are likely to be different from one another in many ways.

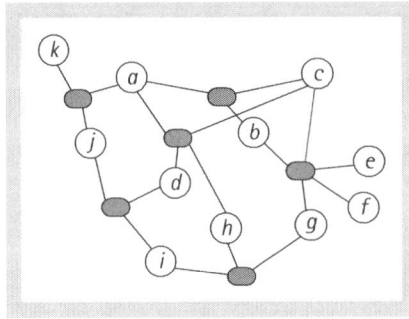

Fig. 22.4 Individuals *a* through *k* connected to one another through foci (Note that a more complete image would include many different foci for each individual, with some of those foci bridging long physical and/or social distances)

22.3 REPRESENTING THE TRIPLEXITY OF SOCIAL STRUCTURE

Milgram's often-cited conclusion in 'The Small World Problem' (1967) was that every individual is within six steps of every other individual. However, it may be more important to show that every individual is within a much shorter distance of *some* individual with most any specified trait. This could be tested by modifying Milgram's study to have targets of 'a lawyer' or 'a pot smoker' or 'a Catholic.' We should note, however, that this modified small-world technique will only be able to find the short paths for relatively visible traits, because individuals will generally need to identify the social location of people with the target traits to effectively choose paths to those targets.

Milgram's original study was about people, and their connections to one another. Feld (1981) suggested including foci of activity as intermediaries between the people, such that individuals are associated with foci of activity which are associated with other people, and consequently people are associated with other people through foci.

We can now explicitly add traits to this model to represent the triplex structure of people, foci, and traits; and then more explicitly show how this triplex structure creates a structural basis for network autocorrelation. People are associated with traits. People are associated with foci. Therefore foci are associated with traits through their people. The traits are associated with other traits because they are attached to people who are linked to people through foci.

Abstractly, the matrix of associations between people and foci can be called F, with p rows (number of people) and g columns (number of groups). The matrix of associations between people and traits can be called T, with c rows (number of characteristics) and p columns. Then, the association between traits and foci is just H (indicating the homogeneity and heterogeneity of the foci in each respect), where

$$H = T^*F.$$

The extent of network autocorrelation due to the focused organization of ties is the extent to which a particular trait is associated with itself through individuals associated with foci. The network autocorrelation matrix indicating the similarities, matrix S, is just

$$S = H^{t^*}H.$$

The main diagonal of this network-autocorrelation matrix indicates the extent to which a trait is associated with itself through individuals being associated with foci. For example, consider race. It might be represented by the three specific characteristics of white, black, other race. The main diagonal of the S matrix would show the number of whites associated with other whites, blacks associated with other blacks, and other races associated with other races, through people associated with common foci. We might also want to examine the entry s_{wb} to indicate the association of whites with blacks to contrast with the association among whites and among blacks to quantify the extent of disproportionate network autocorrelation through foci.

Note that the critical structural basis of network autocorrelation through foci is the H matrix, and one might even analyze the structural bases of network autocorrelation through foci by examining the mix of traits associated with foci of activity even without breaking it down through people. This is a mere introduction to the idea and representation of triplexity of people, groups, and traits, leaving much room for further development of both theory and application.

22.3.1 A hypothetical illustration of the triplexity of social structure

With many individuals, many foci, and many traits, the structure of interrelations can readily get complex. Nevertheless, a relatively simple example can illustrate how the specific types of homogeneity of sets associated with foci lead to particular types and amounts of network autocorrelation.

Figure 22.5 shows individuals *a* through *f* with a variety of traits represented by different colors and connected to one another through three foci (F1, F2, and F3).

Focus 1 connects three individuals, *abc*, who are all alike in their yellowness. They also share some green and some orange, but that is all. Focus 2 connects three individuals, *bcd*, who are all alike in their orangeness, and share some yellow, but

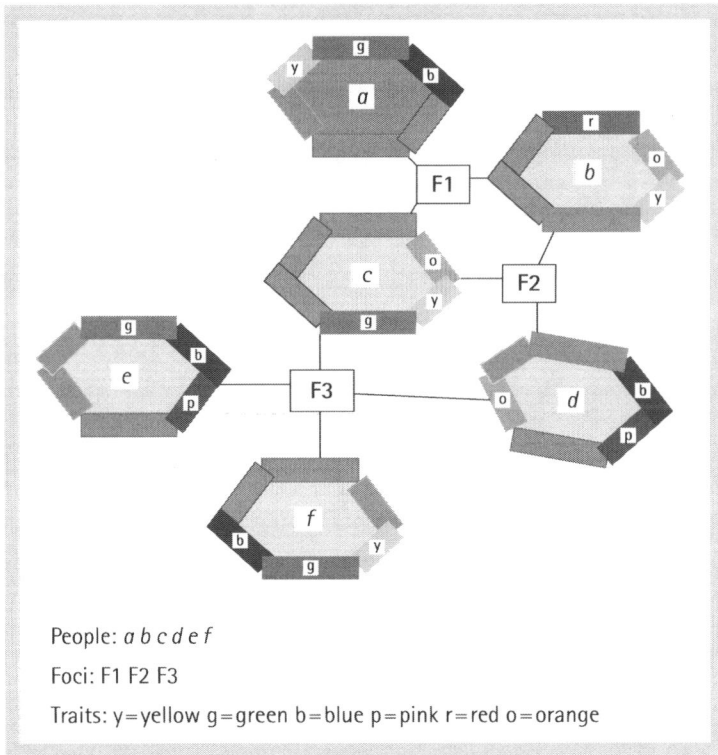

Fig. 22.5 Six individuals with combinations of six traits connected by three foci

are otherwise quite different from one another. Focus 3 connects four individuals who are mostly alike in their greenness and blueness, and have a little pinkness, orangeness, and yellowness in common.

The Appendix to this chapter presents the details of the relationships between individuals and foci (the F matrix) and traits of individuals (the T matrix), and calculates the distribution of the various traits of people associated with each of the foci (the H matrix). Then we also show how the homo-/heterogeneity of the foci determines various numbers of contacts within traits and across different combinations of traits (the S matrix). These calculations include self-contacts (i.e. contacts of people with themselves), which are not of any substantive interest and should be counted and removed as described in the Appendix. The resulting adjusted matrix (the S^a matrix) indicates the numbers of structurally-induced contacts between different people with particular traits. For example, it indicates the number of yellows with contacts with blues through foci. It also shows the number of yellows with contacts with other yellows, and all contacts between people with the same traits, which is of primary interest when examining the extent of network autocorrelation through foci.

The extent to which the structures facilitate disproportionate network autocorrelation is indicated by the extent to which there is greater structurally induced contact than would have been expected from random contact. Actual interaction may not correspond perfectly with the interaction that is anticipated from these foci. It is possible that not all individuals associated with a focus actually interact with one another, and it is possible for individuals who do not share any of these foci to nevertheless interact. Any more network autocorrelation than would have been expected by this structurally induced contact indicates some combination of effects of other unmeasured structures (e.g. homogeneous blocks within neighborhoods, or homogeneous work groups within classrooms) and personal choices based upon homophily that lead people to choose to disproportionately associate with similar others and/or to become similar to those with whom they interact.

22.4 HETEROGENEITY WITHIN AND AMONG AN INDIVIDUAL'S FOCI OF ACTIVITY

The argument above indicates how network autocorrelation depends upon the homogeneity within foci of activity. It is useful to consider how contact between people with particular different traits can also arise from the focused organization of interactions.

First, as discussed earlier, people associated with the same focus may vary widely on traits that are not core to the activities of the focus. For example, church members can have widely varying occupations, and members of professional organizations can have widely varied places of residence and ages. Traits not central to the focus will not necessarily vary widely, but there is often little that precludes such wide variation.

Second, variation in certain types of characteristics can even be inherent in particular types of foci. As previously noted, variation in gender and age are integral to families. Workplaces typically (but not always) involve varieties of complementary jobs (e.g. executives, managers, secretaries, factory workers). Voluntary organizations may seek out members with particular skills and resources (e.g. some who can provide work hours, others that can provide money, and still others that can provide particular types of expertise, products, or services). Professional organizations bring together people in different locations with potentially complementary information. Legislatures intentionally represent at least geographical diversity among the citizenry, and often intentionally represent ideological and other types of diversity. The United Nations was created to bring together representatives of all nations; the diversity is essential to its mission of facilitating coordination and reducing conflict and war among nations.

Third, the people associated with one focus of activity are pulled in various directions by the different other foci with which they are associated. This was even apparent in Festinger, Schachter, and Back's study (1950), that was intended to show the homogenizing effects of groups. Their finding that people in residences at the edges in residential groupings were more likely to be deviant from the group norm than others could well indicate that those people in those end residences were more likely to also be effective members of other outside groupings pulling them in other directions. In general, an awareness of the multiple focus sources of each individual's ties would lead us to expect that some apparent 'deviance' within a group would be a result of conformity to norms of other groups to which these individuals belong.

Fourth, the above three reasons lead us to expect that people are exposed to variation in many traits even within their focused sets. Even with some tendency *toward* homogeneity in certain central respects, there is still variation; and in less central respects people may be exposed to even more variation. In addition, since each individual is typically associated with many different foci, that individual may be exposed to different types of variation from each different focus of activity.

22.4.1 Individuals choose bundles of individuals and bundles of traits

We have been emphasizing the fact that much network autocorrelation arises from the foci of activities constraining the interactions. However, we should recognize that people do make choices to associate with particular foci of activity; and some of those choices of contexts are made specifically to facilitate interaction with certain types of people. That does not mean that they necessarily get what they want. They can generally choose from among a relatively small set of alternative foci that are available to them. They may well have to settle for more or less homogeneity on particular characteristics than they would prefer.

Ironically, there are several processes that lead to more homogeneity than many people would prefer. For example, people in a life stage often have a preference to live among people in the same life stage. People with children tend to want other children nearby, and people without children might well want not to have too many children nearby. However, as Schelling (1978) famously showed, even weak preferences for some similarity can lead to neighborhoods that are much more homogeneous than most of the people prefer. The simple process is that families with children will tend to move out of neighborhoods with few children, leaving those neighborhoods with even fewer children. People without children tend to move out of neighborhoods with too many children, leaving those neighborhoods with even more children. Thus, there tend to be two distinct types of neighborhoods, those with lots of children, and those with very few. The effect is that settings gravitate toward being more homogeneous than individuals prefer, and individuals choosing neighborhoods only have choices between extremes on these types of traits, either those homogeneously similar to them or those homogeneously different from them. Given such a stark choice, most people choose the neighborhood composed of people like themselves, even if they would prefer less homogeneity.

An individual who enters a group is confronted with the whole set of people and their whole set of social characteristics. Even as the individual maintains some freedom of choice of interaction partners and behavioral options within a group, those options are severely constrained. Thus, when people move into a neighborhood, they get all the neighbors, not just the ones they would prefer, and all the local customs. In fact, it seems that people often select into groups on the basis of only a few primary features (e.g. join a workplace primarily for the content of the job and the pay) and accept the bundle of other people and norms that are part of the package.

Thus, even as we acknowledge that individuals do make homophilous choices both in terms of choosing particular foci of activity and choosing to associate with certain individuals within those contexts, the present emphasis remains upon the structural features that affect the extent of network autocorrelation (consistency between social relations and behavior).

22.4.2 Data on individuals, foci, traits, and interpersonal relations

The most common type of social-science data includes information about traits of *individuals*. In contrast, social-network analysts generally collect data on relations between *pairs of individuals*. Despite the challenges that confront collecting both types of data, many analysts of homophily have found ways to collect and combine data on interpersonal relations and individual traits in ways that allow them to examine the nature and extent of network autocorrelation. Including information on the foci of activity that organize social interaction and underlie these network autocorrelations presents further challenges.

There are various ways to organize such data. The simplest starting point using standard software like SPSS would be to create two data files. The first file would include a record for each individual person with (1) a variable for each trait (e.g. race with its categories, political preference with its categories, etc.), and (2) an index variable (no/yes) for each potential focus of activity. These data can be used to construct the matrix relating individuals to traits, and the matrix relating each individual to foci of activity. These together are sufficient to determine the extent to which one should expect network autocorrelation with respect to each of the trait variables resulting from the pattern of shared participation in these foci of activity.

The second file would include a record for each pairwise relationship identified by ID numbers of the two participants, and a variable characterizing each aspect of the relationship between the individual and the alter (e.g. frequency of face-to-face contact, whether the person is a family member, subjective 'closeness' from the perspective of each individual). For the present purposes, this second file is to be used to determine which pairs of people have a particular type of relationship.

22.4.3 Increasing consistency over time?

Theorists focusing on personal consistency often suggest that cognitive pressures toward consistency lead all individuals to act to increase the consistency of their own relations over time (see Davis 1963; Hallinan 1974). The implication would seem to be the expectation that relations should become more consistent over time for the individuals and for society as a whole.

In fact, much of classical sociology is built upon the observation that the overall trend for modern societies is in the opposite direction, moving away from the narrow similarity-based interpersonal interaction of mechanical solidarity and toward more complementarity-based interpersonal interaction of organic solidarity (Durkheim 1933). It would seem that foci of activity are generally becoming more heterogeneous, and that individuals are increasingly involved in more different foci of activity that overlap less with one another.

There have been some times and places where nearly all foci of activity have been homogeneous in the same particular respect. For example, racial homogeneity has pervaded families, workplaces, neighborhoods, and voluntary organizations for hundreds of years in the USA in particular. Under those conditions a society becomes effectively segmented by race. However, even in that case the direction of recent change in America has certainly been away from this extreme form of local network autocorrelation and global segmentation on race. As long as there are multiple forces that bring people together in various foci of activity, there is no reason to expect any general tendency toward increasing overall network autocorrelation and segmentation over time.

So when we recognize that there is more network autocorrelation in social life than one would expect by chance, we should focus more attention on the fact that there is much less than one might expect from individual preferences for interacting with similar others. We do not observe any general tendencies toward increasing overall consistency over time that would seem to be predicted by consistency theorists (see Davis 1963; Hallinan 1974). Rather, increases and decreases in the extent of particular types of consistency reflect all of the forces that create foci of activity, determine their selection processes and relevant norms and conformity processes, and determine people's associations with them.

It may be fortunate for society that there has not been more network autocorrelation and segmentation, especially that which might foster large-scale costly social conflict between segments. Sociological theorists from Simmel (1955) through

Coser (1956), Coleman (1957), and Blau (1977) have recognized the societal benefits of crosscutting dimensions that involve major social inconsistencies. Social processes that create crosscutting ties and limit the extent of network autocorrelation may be both common and beneficial, and as worthy of our attention as processes that encourage network autocorrelation and segmentation.

Appendix: Detailed Analysis of the Triplexity of Persons, Foci, and Traits

Figure 22.5 presents one hypothetical example containing six individuals, three foci, and six personal characteristics. Here we show how we can determine the extent of structurally-induced opportunities for semilinking and for other contact between people with particular traits.

The relationships between the people and the foci can be represented by the focus matrix, F (Table 22.1).

Table 22.1 Matrix F

		People					
---	---	a	b	c	d	e	f
Foci	F1	1	1	1			
	F2		1	1	1		
	F3			1	1	1	1

The characteristics of the individuals can be represented by the trait matrix, T (Table 22.2).

Table 22.2 Matrix T

		Personal characteristics					
---	---	Yellow	Green	Blue	Pink	Red	Orange
People	a	1	1	1			
	b	1				1	1
	c	1	1				1
	d			1	1		1
	e		1	1	1		
	f	1	1	1			

The distribution of the personal characteristics within each of the foci of activity can be represented by the homo-/heterogeneity matrix, H (Table 22.3), which is determined by multiplying the F matrix by the T matrix. The H matrix is shown below.

Table 22.3 Matrix H

		Personal characteristics					
		Yellow	Green	Blue	Pink	Red	Orange
	F1	3	2	1	0	1	2
Foci	F2	2	1	1	1	1	3
	F3	2	3	3	2	0	2

This matrix indicates, among other things, that there are concentrations of yellows in F1, concentrations of oranges in F2, and especially both greens and blues in F3. The H transpose matrix, H^t (not shown), obtained by flipping this matrix over, shows how many of each color are located in each focus. Multiplying H^t by H shows the number of different ways that a person with each trait is put into contact with a person of another specific trait through all of the different foci together. For example, the 2 greens in F1 are in contact with 3 yellows in F1 giving $2 \times 3 = 6$ green-yellow contacts there, and $1 \times 2 = 2$ such contacts through F2, and $3 \times 2 = 6$ such contacts in F3, making a total of 14 such green-yellow contacts through all three foci. The S matrix shows the total intertrait contacts through all of the foci together: Matrix $S = H^{t*}H$ (Table 22.4).

Table 22.4 Matrix S

		Personal characteristics					
		Yellow	Green	Blue	Pink	Red	Orange
	Yellow	17	14	11	6	5	16
	Green	14	14	12	7	3	13
Personal	Blue	11	12	11	7	2	11
characteristics	Pink	6	7	7	5	1	7
	Red	5	3	2	1	2	5
	Orange	16	13	11	7	5	17

However, this matrix includes contacts of people with themselves within these foci, which are not the type of encounters that concern us. In a very large system these types of self-contacts would be such a small portion of the contacts that they could easily be ignored. However, in this small-play system they can severely distort the picture of contacts between different people. This problem can be addressed by simply computing the numbers of self-contacts of each type by computing the number of meaningless trait contacts between individuals and themselves. Thus, if person a is a yellow-green (among other things), then person 1 would create one yellow-green contact for every focus that contains person a. For all, the total number of meaningless self-trait contacts is: $M = T^{t*}N^*T$ where N is a vector indicating the number of foci in which each individual participates. The N vector (Table 22.5) here is just:

Table 22.5 N vector

	a	1
	b	2
People	*c*	3
	d	2
	e	1
	f	1

The number of meaningless self-trait contacts is indicated as matrix $M = T^{t*}N^{*}T$ (Table 22.6).

Table 22.6 Matrix M

		Personal characteristics					
		Yellow	Green	Blue	Pink	Red	Orange
	Yellow	7	4	2	0	2	4
	Green	4	6	3	1	0	3
Personal	Blue	2	3	5	3	0	2
characteristics	Pink	0	1	3	3	0	2
	Red	2	0	0	0	2	2
	Orange	4	2	2	2	1	7

Table 22.7 Matrix S^a

		Personal characteristics					
		Yellow	Green	Blue	Pink	Red	Orange
	Yellow	10	10	9	6	3	11
	Green	10	8	9	6	3	10
Personal	Blue	9	9	6	4	2	9
characteristics	Pink	6	6	4	2	1	5
	Red	3	3	2	1	0	3
	Orange	12	11	9	5	3	10

Consequently, the number of interpersonal contacts with the pairs of traits excluding the meaningless self-contacts is the adjusted S matrix $S^a = S - M$. (Table 22.7).

We should note that the structurally induced contact calculated here includes multiple contacts between the same people if they share more than one focus. We think that is appropriate for indicating the amount of contact that is facilitated by the structure. In this particular situation, the three orange people are each in multiple foci with one another, and the structure especially facilitates disproportionate network autocorrelation among them.

There are many ways to use this information. As a start, we suggest that one can compare the amounts of structurally induced contacts between people with particular traits with both the amounts that would be expected in the absence of the foci, and with the actual amounts of observed social interaction.

One can determine whether the foci of activity are disproportionately providing contact opportunities between people with particular traits, by comparing the amount of structurally induced contact between people with particular traits as calculated above with the amounts of contact that would be expected in a random network with this same distribution of traits among individuals but no foci structuring the interaction.

One could also determine the extent to which people are choosing interaction with disproportionately similar others among the contact opportunities available, by measuring the actual amount of interaction among individuals with particular traits, and comparing that with the amount of structurally induced contacts computed above.

This is a three-mode network, based upon persons, foci, and traits. Analysts have been increasingly developing ways to consider two-mode networks—for example, of corporations and individuals on their boards of directors. This theoretical approach provides reason to extend these developments to facilitate further consideration of three-mode networks.

REFERENCES

BAINBRIDGE, W. S. (1986), *Sociological Laboratory* (Belmont, Calif.: Wadsworth).

BLAU, P. M. (1977), *Inequality and Heterogeneity* (New York: Free Press).

BREIGER, R. L. (1974), 'Duality of Persons and Groups', *Social Forces*, 53: 181–90.

COLEMAN, J. S. (1957), *Community Conflict* (Glencoe: Free Press).

COSER, L. A. (1956), *Functions of Social Conflict* (Glencoe: Free Press).

DAVIS, J. A. (1963), 'Structural Balance, Mechanical Solidarity, and Interpersonal Relations', *American Journal of Sociology*, 68: 444–62.

DURKHEIM, E. (1933), *The Division of Labor in Society* (New York: Free Press).

FELD, S. L. (1981), 'The Focused Organization of Social Ties', *American Journal of Sociology*, 86: 1015–35.

—— (1982), 'Social Structural Determinants of Similarity Among Associates', *American Sociological Review*, 47: 797–801.

—— (1988), 'Social Pressures on Parenting in a Small Community', paper presented at the Sunbelt Social Networks Conference, San Diego.

FESTINGER, L., SCHACHTER, S., and BACK, K. (1950), *Social Pressures in Informal Groups* (Stanford, Calif.: Stanford University Press).

HALLINAN, M. (1974), *The Structure of Positive Sentiment* (New York: Elsevier).

KANDEL, D. B. (1978), 'Homophily, Selection, and Socialization in Adolescent Friendship', *American Journal of Sociology*, 84: 427–36.

LAZARSFELD, P. F., and MERTON, R. K. (1954), 'Friendship as a Social Process', in M. Berger, T. Abel, and C. H. Page (eds.), *Freedom and Control in Modern Society* (Princeton, N.J.: Van Nostrand).

MCPHERSON, J. M. (1982), 'Hypernetwork Sampling: Duality and Differentiation Among Voluntary Organizations', *Social Networks*, 3: 225–49.

—— and SMITH-LOVIN, L. (1987), 'Homophily in Voluntary Organizations: Status Distance and the Composition of Face-to-face Groups', *American Sociological Review*, 52: 370–9.

—— —— and COOK, J. M. (2001), 'Birds of a Feather: Homophily in Social Networks', *Annual Review of Sociology*, 27: 415–44.

MILGRAM, S. (1967), 'The Small World Problem', *Psychology Today*, 1: 61–7.

SCHELLING, T. C. (1978), *Micromotives and Macrobehavior* (New York: Norton).

SIMMEL, G. (1955), *Conflict and the Web of Group Affiliations*, trans. K. H. Wolff and R. Bendix (Glencoe: Free Press).

CHAPTER 23

··

STATUS

··

JOEL PODOLNY
FREDA LYNN

INTRODUCTION

THE first act of the opera *Margaret Garner* draws to a close with Edward Gaines, a Kentucky plantation owner, hosting a lavish reception to celebrate the engagement of his daughter, Caroline. Feeling forgotten after a twenty-year absence from the community, Gaines has invited the local gentry and views the celebration as an opportunity to re-establish his family and plantation in local society. Margaret Garner, the Gaines's household slave and the lone servant tending the party, offers champagne to the guests. The year is 1856; the guests accept the champagne but ignore her person entirely.

During the celebration, Gaines, Caroline, and Caroline's fiancé engage in a public exchange on the meaning of love. Unable to reach an agreement, Caroline turns to Margaret and asks for her view on the matter. Having been the recipient of Margaret's care and affection for nearly her entire life, Caroline feels that Margaret can contribute meaningfully to the conversation. The guests, however, are shocked that the daughter of their host would ask a slave to opine on the significance of love, and leave the reception immediately.

The deference that Caroline showed to the slave was a sign not only of the questionable nature of Caroline's character, but of her father's as well. Likewise, had any of the guests remained at the reception, their characters too would have been judged by the community. Gaines, no doubt, is left enraged by the party's abrupt demise. While the event did indeed provide Gaines with the opportunity to establish a position for himself in the local society, the position was much lower in status than the one he coveted.

In this chapter we will review a broad array of research on status dynamics to show that what may seem so particular (and indeed peculiar) to this scene is in fact quite general. Whether one focuses on a social gathering in the antebellum South, underwriting contests among modern investment banks, or the invisible colleges of social scientists, at least four common patterns arise. First, actors look to others' status as a signal of their underlying quality. In the above scene, all guests at the party rely on status to infer who is capable of opining on love and who is not. A plantation owner who hosts an event attended by the local social elite is assumed to have high-quality advice on the significance of love; a slave is not.

Second, an actor's status influences the rewards that she receives. In the scene above, the primary reward is the (positive) attention that an individual receives for contributions to the group. At the beginning of the reception Gaines and his future son-in-law received considerable positive attention for rather simplistic theories of the meaning of love. In contrast, no praise was given to the slave Margaret Garner for her more heartfelt expression of love's meaning nor for the service of champagne; she was instead completely ignored.

Third, an individual's status position is not fixed, but arises from the exchange relations between individuals. In the *Margaret Garner* example Caroline lowers her status when she enters into a conversation on the meaning of love with a slave, and in so doing lowers the status of those with whom she is associated (i.e. her father). The only way that the father could avoid his own status being lowered would be to disown his daughter (i.e. refuse to associate with her), and the only way that the guests could avoid their status being lowered was to leave the party. While more implicit than explicit, there is also a fourth pattern or theme manifest in the above example: actors are especially likely to rely on status queues to make inferences about quality when there is considerable uncertainty about that underlying quality. Because Gaines and his daughter are essentially new to the local community, Caroline's 'shocking' display of deference to the slave is a stronger signal of her character than had she been a long-standing member of the community.

What follows is a review of the broad array of research supporting these propositions. Much of the research that we will review has been published in the last decade. The focus on status dynamics is part of a broader trend in structural sociology, from interpreting structure as a latent constraint on action to a manifest input into actors' decisions. When the 'new structuralism' arose in the 1970s and early 1980s, sociologists focused on the significance of structure in determining the probability that an actor would come into contact with some opportunity, resource, or piece of information. Such a focus can be found in the manifestos of Mayhew (1980) and Granovetter (1985), the approach that Blau pioneered in *Inequality and Heterogeneity* (1977), the theoretical underpinnings of blockmodel analysis (White, Boorman, and Brieger 1976), as well as much of the other structural work at the time (e.g. Cook and Emerson 1978; Burt 1982; Marsden 1982). In the work of this period some actors may have been cognizant of structure and its effects on shaping interaction, but the effects of structure did not depend on the actors being cognizant of them. Structure channeled action regardless of whether actors were aware of the impact of these channels.

However, as the new structuralism evolved, those working within this tradition increasingly began to understand structure as an informational input that guided action. One of the earliest prominent examples of this new approach to structural analysis was Burt's work on diffusion (1987); he distinguished cohesion and structural equivalence as alternative mechanisms of diffusion. Whereas diffusion of a behavior via cohesion did not depend on actors being cognizant of the structure in which they were embedded, diffusion of a behavior via structural equivalence most certainly did. By 1990 Krackhardt was writing about cognitive networks and providing evidence that the accuracy of an actor's perception of structure was itself a determinant of the opportunities, resources, and information that an actor was able to obtain.

The focus on status as a signal is part of this broader underlying trend in the structural tradition. White's model of production markets (1981) conceptualized the volume/revenue combinations of producers as structural choices that signaled realizable market opportunities for participating producers. Others in the structural tradition have made a similar point even if they have not always been as explicit in invoking the concept of signal. For example, Baum and Oliver (1991, 1992) discuss how the presence or absence of a tie to a legitimate institution affects the likelihood that the organization's constituencies regard it also as legitimate. In effect, the tie to a legitimate institution is the signal. Rao, Davis, and Ward (2000) discuss how corporations will selectively affiliate with a particular exchange (e.g. NYSE or NASDAQ) because the affiliation is a signal of particular underlying qualities. Moreover, we would contend that Zuckerman's work (1999, 2000) can be interpreted in a similar light. Zuckerman argues that potential exchange partners of an actor have difficulty making sense of the identity of an actor when that actor's exchange relations or affiliations cut across common categorical distinctions. To the degree to which the potential exchange partners cannot make sense of the actor's boundary spanning across categories, they will be less likely to attend to and therefore enter into an exchange relation with that actor. In this case, boundary spanning across categories is a signal to potential exchange partners that the actor is of at least questionable quality.

In each of these works an actor's ability to demonstrate quality above some threshold is endogenous to the structural position that the actor occupies. Because potential exchange partners rely on position as a signal of quality, their willingness to direct resource flows to an actor is contingent on the position that the actor occupies. So, in the case of Baum and Oliver's work on day-care centers, a day-care center with a tie to a legitimate institution such as church or government agency is more likely to garner resources that will, in turn, allow it to deliver quality above some threshold. Or, in Zuckerman's work, if a firm diversifies in a way that its activities spread across categorical boundaries to which investors attend, the firm's cost of capital will be higher; this higher cost of capital, in turn, will mean that it is more expensive for the firm to deliver products and services at a given quality.

There is an obvious and important causality issue in the argument that quality is endogenous with respect to structure. While we assert that structural position shapes quality, it is also possible that differences in quality affect the position that actors are able to obtain. For example, maybe the reason that a given day-care center has a tie to a church or government agency is that the center is simply better than a randomly drawn counterpart without such a tie. Accordingly, any rigorous investigation of the structural determinants of actor quality must seek to disentangle the potential reciprocal impact of structure and quality upon one another.

The rest of this chapter can be divided into three parts. The first reviews the sociological conception of status as a signal. This conceptualization has its roots in the economic understanding of a signal but departs from that foundation in some important ways. After highlighting those lines of departure, we then discuss studies that demonstrate the broad applicability of the four propositions laid out above. In the last part of this chapter we explore a new line of research on status dynamics. While the lion's share of the extant research focuses on how actors rely on status to infer the quality of potential exchange partners, attention to structural cues may also affect the way in which actors experience the value of the exchange itself. For example, if an actor 'sees' a group of objects as comparable items on a status continuum rather than as unique, incommensurate entities, does this framework of comparability enhance or detract from her experience/interaction with any one of these objects? We address this question by reviewing the research on commensuration and value (Dewey 1980; Espeland and Stevens 1998; Bolla 2001), which suggests that rankings lead to a depreciation of value.

23.1 THE CONCEPT OF STATUS AS A SIGNAL

We begin by defining status in terms of accumulated acts of deference, where we view status as the 'stock' to which deference is the 'flow.' Acts of deference can differ in their level of formality, ritualism, and self-awareness. Bowing before royalty, for example, is formal, ritualistic, and implies a high degree of self-awareness; one generally does not bow without consciously thinking to do so. Consider instead what happens when an esteemed scholar arrives late to a research seminar and all the seats are taken. Typically, someone—often a graduate student—will give up his or her seat. Such behavior is sufficiently common to be considered ritualistic, and certainly deliberate enough to imply self-awareness, but the behavior is informal. There is no prescribed etiquette for how the graduate student must give up his or her seat. In contrast to these first two types of deference, other acts involve actors who are largely incognizant of their behavior. When guests in a restaurant look repeatedly at the table of a famous individual, for example, such behavior is not only informal but generally unintentional.

Aside from variation in the type of act, deference behaviors can also be characterized by the extent to which they are specific to a group, culture, or time period. Some acts of deference, like paying particularly close attention to someone when they speak, are obviously quite general and likely interpreted the same way in the majority of settings. Other acts are common in many settings but vary in the specific form. For example, while it is often customary in business settings to seat individuals around the table according to status, some countries (e.g. Japan) seat the highest-status person in the middle of the table while in others (e.g. the USA), the highest-status person is seated at the head of the table. Other acts of deference, of course, are highly idiosyncratic to a particular context and therefore require that individuals be knowledgeable about that context to appreciate the deference being conveyed. The ordering of actors' names on a movie poster or marquee, for instance, is influenced not only by the size of the roles in the movie itself, but by the relative status of the actors within the larger community of actors. An actor's (un)willingness to accept a certain billing position can thus be interpreted with regard to deference relations. The ability to appreciate the billing order, however, is clearly tied to one's knowledge of how the order is negotiated, and industry insiders are likely more attuned to the deference component than outsiders.

Finally, deference can be allocated by individual actors as well as by groups (i.e. when a group of actors bestows deference on a single actor). Similar to the different forms of deference acts at the individual level, aggregated acts of deference likewise vary in terms of formality, ritualism, and self-awareness. In the science profession, for example, the selection and awarding of the Nobel Prize would seem to represent the extreme in terms of formality, ritual, and self-awareness as a process for collectively defining who has highest status in a particular field. However, in fields that lack such prizes, status differences are more emergent, arising over time from differences in the degree to which a work is acknowledged and cited as important.

For all the types and forms of deference behavior, society generally conceives of deference as a reward for an actor's quality or her contribution(s). True deference cannot be 'seized' by an individual but rather is something awarded by others (Ridgeway 1984: 62), and theories of distributive justice and western ideals suggest that the exchange of status for quality is considered more just when the exchange is roughly proportional. In a strict sense, quality refers to any attribute, performance, or service that is highly prized within a group or community (Gould 2002: 1153; Ollivier 2004: 198), and thus the constituent elements of quality will obviously vary depending on the context.

In a task group, for example, quality is likely grounded in advice or effort that is conducive to the task that the group is trying to accomplish. In a close-knit community, quality may refer to aspects of character that help to reinforce the aspects of daily life that the community generally values. In a market, quality usually refers to the features of a product or service that—through producer advertising, consumer purchasing, the typologies of third parties like trade publications, and so on—become understood as the basis for differentiating good products and services from bad.

Researchers working in the expectation states and status characteristics tradition, however, have carefully pointed out that deference is often allocated in accordance with attributes or characteristics that are *not* necessarily relevant to any particular task or community goal. Nominal distinctions, such as gender and race, can become culturally associated with superior and inferior states of being (e.g. male versus female, white versus nonwhite) and, as such, can shape expectations of competence and subsequently the distribution of deference—even when the characteristic itself is not directly related to any context-specific task (Berger et al. 1977). Through a process of belief formation, social interaction, and diffusion, *nominal* distinctions can become consensually *valued* distinctions in the broader culture (Ridgeway 1991; Ridgeway and Balkwell 1997; Ridgeway and Erickson 2000). Once these beliefs have spread through a population and are prevalent at the cultural level, we will more likely see a correlation emerge between an actor's position vis-à-vis these nominal distinctions and the amount of deference she receives.

Regardless of the rationale used to allocate deference, the key principle is that actors who receive more deference are actors who are collectively understood as being higher status. Actors and objects in any given setting can be organized according to the amount of deference each has accumulated.[1] What this chapter is primarily concerned with is how an actor's position in a given status-ordering can, in turn, serve as a signal of quality. That is, regardless of how an actor comes to occupy a position in a given deference hierarchy, an actor's ranking can influence how her future contributions or demonstrations of quality are evaluated. In general, those who occupy a coveted status position are evaluated more positively (for a given performance of quality output) than those in inferior positions.

Research from a broad array of settings describes instances of how an individual's social-structural position within the group becomes an important consideration in others' evaluation of what the individual says or does. In *Street Corner Society* Whyte (1943) illustrates the importance of status in local gangs and the informal interactions among their members. Regardless of why or how an individual becomes a leader, once established as a leader his opinion is automatically considered more valuable and more 'right' than that of his followers. When a follower offers a suggestion or shares an opinion, the quality of his contribution is generally in doubt until approved in some way by the leader, at which point the entire collective agrees that the suggestion is worthwhile. During leadership transitions or periods of leadership instability, however, the deference hierarchy between followers and leaders is called into question by followers, and bosses become subject to the same kind of scrutiny applied normally only to followers. In short, when the security of a leader's position is in jeopardy, so too is the quality of his opinions and actions.

Blau (1955) documents a similar dynamic in his study of a government bureaucracy. Drawing a distinction between an agent's official status (i.e. his status based on job title) and unofficial status (i.e. the number of times the agent was contacted by other agents in a given period of time), Blau describes how an agent's unofficial status becomes the basis on which colleagues make inferences about the quality of that agent's advice or information. Colleagues were more likely not only to seek the advice of agents who occupied a high position in the peer-deference hierarchy, but also to follow his recommendations.

More recent, larger-scale studies of reward allocation and status positions suggest that this dynamic is not unique to small groups. While the ethnographies mentioned shed light on the social-psychological underpinnings of status signaling, larger-scale studies reveal the pervasiveness of this dynamic. In an artificial online music market with nearly 15,000 participants, Salganik, Dodds, and Watts (2006) find that subjects relied on a song's status position (i.e. its popularity among all previous buyers) to guide their buying decisions. When songs' download histories were released to subjects, there was significantly more inequality in the distribution of purchases than when ranking data were not released. Because the same songs were used in both conditions of the experiment, the findings provide clear evidence that the presence of status rankings was the key to the change in purchasing patterns.[2]

In addition, several observational and experimental studies contrasting 'blind' versus nonblind interactions provide evidence of how status cues in the form of nominal characteristics or formal titles can affect performance evaluations. When attribute information is available, it appears that actors who occupy high-deference positions receive better performance evaluations if their status is revealed than if their status remains hidden to the evaluator. Studies of the academic-review process, for example, show that articles and abstracts written by authors employed by prestigious institutions are more likely to be accepted under nonblind review than under blind review (Blank 1991; Ross et al. 2006). Similarly, using an experimental setup, Leahey (2004) shows that a given method of 'cleaning' messy qualitative data is perceived as being more/less objectionable depending on the academic rank of the individual proposing the strategy (i.e. professor versus graduate student). Her evidence suggests that subjects relied on rank to infer the quality of the product in question, where professors were essentially able to 'get away with more' than those less established. The core idea in all of these studies is that actors rely on status/positional cues (e.g. leadership position, popularity, institutional affiliation, tenure) to infer quality; actors associated with high-value positions tend to receive more favorable performance evaluations than actors of lower status, even in the absence of observable differences in performance level.

In his seminal work on economic signaling Spence (1973) wrote that in order for something observable to truly be a signal of some unobservable characteristic it must be less difficult or less costly for actors possessing the unobservable characteristic to display the signal. A warranty is a signal of a product's quality because the expense of the warranty to a manufacturer of low-quality products is higher than the expense of the warranty to a manufacturer of high-quality products. The manufacturer of low-quality products will have to make good on the warranty with greater frequency than will the manufacturer of the high-quality products. A college degree is a signal of an individual's productivity because a highly productive individual will find it less difficult to obtain the degree than a less productive individual.

If we focus on this particular feature of a signal which Spence explicated, it is fair to say that the sociological understanding of status meets the economic definition of signal. In general, it will be more difficult for lower-quality actors to attract acts of deference than it is for higher-quality actors to attract the same acts of deference. For example, the CEOs and senior executives of lower-quality firms are less likely to receive acts of deference, like media attention, than the CEOs and senior executives of higher-quality firms. So, in equilibrium, there will generally be a positive relationship between possessing the signal of status and an actor's underlying quality.

23.2 THE MATTHEW EFFECT

However, if the equilibrium relationship between status and quality is consistent with the economic conception of a signal, the sociological account of the dynamics underlying this relationship differs from the standard economic account. The standard economic account begins by positing heterogeneity in terms of an unobservable quality, and when there is meaningful variance in the performance implications of this underlying quality then the signal itself has value as basis for economic decisions. In his stylized example of education signaling, for example, Spence (1973) takes meaningful differences in productivity as given and then shows how the earning of a college degree can provide a basis for differentiating those who are more productive and those who are less productive. In effect, quality is assumed to be essentially exogenous with respect to the signal. In Spence's model, obtaining a college degree does not have an effect on one's productivity.[3]

In contrast, in the sociological account of status as a signal there is considerable interest in how small, initial differences in status—which may be due to luck or to factors uncorrelated with the potential to demonstrate quality—affect the flow of resources that give rise to significant quality differences, which in turn heighten the initial status differences. Invoking the term 'the Matthew effect' as a label for this fundamental dynamic (1968), Merton was essentially concerned with (a) how signals (in this case status or prestige) could be acquired in the absence of quality differences and (b) how status, in turn, can affect the subsequent production of quality.

Merton developed the idea of the Matthew effect from his observations of reward inequality in the sciences (1968). Specifically, he and Harriet Zuckerman observed that when two scientists offer the same scientific contribution (either through collaboration or in multiple independent discoveries), the more eminent scientist tends to receive a disproportionate amount of credit for the discovery. This observation led Merton to theorize more broadly about processes of cumulative advantage and the long-term consequences of the Matthew effect.

Suppose, for example, that two newly minted Ph.D.s of approximately the same quality working in the same research area are pursuing an academic position, and there is only one position available in that area among the more prestigious universities. The individual who does not receive that position must accept a post at a less prestigious institution. While their quality may be close enough that a 'coin toss' ultimately determines who gets the position at the prestigious university, the fact that one receives the better position will have a significant impact on their ability to demonstrate quality over time. The one employed by the prestigious university will likely have her work taken more seriously by the larger research community. She will likely have access to better doctoral students with whom to work, and her affiliation with the prestigious university will be a signal on which grant-giving institutions will rely when trying to judge the quality of work that she is capable of producing. Over time, the differences in quality between the scientists will increase in a way that reflects and thereby reinforces the status differences between the institutions.

Much of the early empirical work on the Matthew effect, not surprisingly, analyzed the career trajectories of scientists, in terms of both productivity and recognition (e.g. Cole and Cole 1973; Allison and Stuart 1974; Allison, Long, and Krauze 1982). Researchers have generally concluded that a scientist's ties to a prestigious faculty advisor and affiliations with prestigious academic departments (doctoral origin or employer) have a significant, nonspurious effect on a Ph.D.s ability to acquire scarce resources, such as tenure-track university jobs and publication opportunities (Caplow and McGee 1958; Hargens and Hagstrom 1967; Crane 1970; Long 1978; Reskin 1979). Likewise, scientists employed by more prestigious institutions are better able to attract citations, net of observable differences in training and productivity (Hargens and Hagstrom 1982; Lynn 2006).

The appeal of the Matthew-effect idea, of course, has not been confined to studies of the science profession. Researchers from numerous other domains have drawn on the idea, in some form or another, that rewards can accrue to status, independent of quality. Within organizations, for example, Kanter (1977) references the Matthew effect as an underlying determinant of intra-organizational power differences. Blau's previously mentioned study of a government bureaucracy (1955) predated Merton's article on the Matthew effect, but documented the same dynamic: the high-status agents felt more confidence from being widely respected, which allowed them to focus their concentration on accomplishing job tasks, thereby further outperforming low-status agents. Wahlberg and Tsai (1983) and Kerckhoff and Glennie (1999) apply the concept of the Matthew effect to the evolution of educational inequalities (see DiPrete and Eirich 2006 for a review), while Dannefer (1987) finds the general dynamic to be helpful in understanding the life course. The common theme across these varied applications is that higher-status actors receive more deference and resources, which ultimately translates into future quality differences that confirm—and at times, augment—initial status distinctions.

In the last decade or so some of the more quantifiable demonstrations of the Matthew effect have arisen in the context of the market. Drawing on pricing data from the investment-banking industry, Podolny (1993) argues that higher-status investment banks are able to provide underwriting services of a given quality at a lower cost. He argues that higher-status banks are more trusted by clients and industry partners, and accordingly their due-diligence costs (the time and monetary expenditures involved in examining a potential purchase to be sure that its quality is consistent with expectations) are lower. Moreover, to the degree that employees of a given quality prefer to be associated with a higher-status firm, the cost of maintaining a workforce of a given quality level is lower for high-status firms. In effect, lower-status firms will need to offer higher salaries to attract away the employees of the higher-status firms.

In a study of law firms Phillips (2001) in fact documents this relationship between firm status and labor costs. He finds that lower-status firms promote associates to partner level at a faster rate. He argues that they do so because the firm's lower status implies worse opportunities and rewards for employees of a given quality. The lower-status firm promotes earlier because the removal of uncertainty about promotion is a way of compensating for the fact that the opportunities and rewards *subsequent to promotion* will be less than those offered by a higher-status firm. Of course, in offering promotion earlier, the lower-status firm is necessarily making an earlier bet than its higher-status counterpart as to which employees are likely to be more productive, and presumably the earlier the bet, the more likely the bet is wrong. Wrong bets in turn translate into lower-quality partners.

So higher-status actors in the market find it easier or less expensive to provide services or products of a given level of quality than their lower-status counterparts, and this difference reinforces and augments any initial status differences. Of course, one might reasonably wonder whether these status effects are really just lagged quality effects. In the earlier example of the newly minted Ph.D.s we posited that they were of roughly comparable quality at the time they received their degree, and then we discussed how random assignment to institutions of different status could lead to quality differences among the scientists that are isomorphic with the status differences between institutions. However, one might reasonably wonder whether the status differences between banks or law firms are simply a function of quality differences. Podolny (1993), for example, attempts to control for quality difference in his investment-banking study by regressing price on status *and* firm size, a firm attribute that is believed to be highly correlated with a firm's quality. The control variable is imperfect but does suggest that the status effect is not entirely spurious.

Benjamin and Podolny (1999) are able to find more rigorous controls for quality differences in their study of California's wine industry. The question in this context is whether a high-status winery is able to command a higher price for a bottle of wine of a given quality. A winery's status is measured in terms of a winery's affiliation with high- and low-prestige appellations (e.g. Napa Valley, Alexander Valley), and the quality of its wine is assessed from the results of blind taste tests conducted by industry professionals. Because the evaluation of wine quality is conducted in a blind setting and the assessment procedure itself is highly standardized within the industry, this analysis comes close to isolating the impact of status on price (i.e. the impact of status net of quality) in an observational setting. As hypothesized, the authors show that higher-status wineries obtain greater returns from a given quality wine—a result that is clearly consistent with Merton's theory of scientific recognition and the distribution of resources. Just as the audience for scientific work is more willing to accept that a paper is above a given quality threshold if the scientist is high-status, so too the audience for wine is more willing to accept that the wine is above a given quality threshold if it is produced by a winery with a history of high-status affiliations.

The greater willingness of the audience to accept a claim of higher quality from a higher-status producer in turn translates into a willingness to pay more for a given-quality bottle. With greater returns from quality, higher-status wine producers can essentially outbid lower-status producers for higher-quality grapes as well as the land on which the grapes can be grown, which effectively allows higher-status wineries to 'lock in' a quality advantage over lower-status wineries. In summary, status distinctions can actually induce quality distinctions, which then can lead to the reinforcement or augmentation of initial status distinctions. Given that the significance of status seems to hold even in the presence of reasonable controls for quality differences, one would be hard-pressed to argue that these status effects are simply spurious effects of quality differences.

23.3 EXCHANGE RELATIONS AND STATUS

Of course, if status differences cannot be simply reinterpreted as quality differences, a natural question that follows is: What are the determinants of status differences? One answer is exchange relations. In Elias and Scotson's work *The Established and the Outsiders* (1965) the quality of an individual's character is inferred from that individual's position in the social structure of the larger community. In an account that bears strong similarities to the scene from *Margaret Garner* discussed earlier, Elias and Scotson capture how an individual's status within a community is affected by the status of those with whom the individual associates. They recount the tale of a newcomer's arrival at and subsequent ostracism from one of the better-off sections of town:

> Newcomers who settled in the 'good streets' of the village were always suspect unless they were obviously 'nice people'. A probationary period was needed to reassure good families that their own status would not suffer by association with a neighbor whose standards were uncertain. The ostracized 'black sheep' was in this case a woman who had recently moved into the neighbourhood and who made the following comments when she herself was asked about her relations with her neighbours: 'They're very reserved. They speak on the streets but nothing else.' She then told how she had asked the 'dustmen for a cup of tea one cold day,' soon after she arrived . . . 'They saw it. That shocked them around here.'

Status essentially 'leaks' through exchange relations. When a low-status actor enters into an exchange relation with a high-status actor, the former gains status, and the latter loses status. The pattern of exchange relations affects who receives deference and attention and who does not.

Imagine walking into a room filled with people. In the corner you see a large number of people crowded around a single individual, listening to that individual speak. It is, of course, natural to assume that the individual is high-status, because of the deference being shown to him. Now suppose that the same individual then begins a conversation with just one person in the crowd around him; this exchange would almost undoubtedly lead one to assume that particular individual is of higher status than the others. One might expect that target of the high-status individual's attention would perhaps get a following of his own now that he has been singled out for attention.

Podolny and Phillips (1996) find evidence of status transfer in an examination of how the status of investment banks changed between 1981 and 1986 in the market for high-yield debt (more colloquially known as 'junk' debt). Controlling for a bank's status in 1981 and its market performance between 1981 and 1986, they find that the status of a bank's co-management partners has an effect on the bank's status in 1986. In effect, the higher the status of a bank's exchange partners at an earlier time point, the higher the bank's subsequent status, net of performance. These results, combined with the results from Podolny's study (1993) of how status affects a bank's costs for underwriting at a given level of quality, illustrate how cumulative advantage unfolds in at least one industry. First, the status of a bank's exchange relations affects the bank's own status, which in turn affects the economic rewards to which the bank has access. The more resources acquired by the bank, the more likely it is to attract high-status exchange partners, which further solidifies its status position in the industry.

Stuart, Hoang, and Hybels (1999) provide another account of the 'leakage' of status through exchange relations, in a very different domain. Studying the flow of capital to startups in the biotechnology industry, they find that entrepreneurial startups in strategic alliances with prominent partners are able to make a public offering sooner and receive more capital upon going public, net of several controls for a firm's objective performance level (e.g. number of patent applications, progress with regard to human trials). While Stuart, Hoang, and Hybels use the term 'prominence' as opposed to 'status,' it is clear that the exchange relations with prominent others affect attention and rewards in a manner that is similar to the contexts observed by Elias and Scotson (1965) and Podolny and Phillips (1996).[4]

23.4 STATUS AND UNCERTAINTY

Finally, if status is a signal of quality, then status should be of greater value when quality is more difficult to observe. Conversely, if quality differences are relatively transparent, the potential for status cues to influence quality perceptions ought to be diminished. Reflecting on the occupational discrimination faced by black Americans in the mid-1900s, for example, Blalock (1962) theorized that discrimination against minorities by employers would be lower in work settings where it is 'easier to accurately evaluate an individual's performance level' (p. 245). The motivation for this idea came from his observations of American baseball in the 1950s and the extraordinary success of black players—once Jackie Robinson broke the initial racial barrier—relative to other occupations. Discrimination on the basis of skin color, Blalock argued, was less of a disadvantage for blacks in baseball as opposed to in traditional occupations precisely because baseball performance is easily quantified (e.g. batting average, the number of strikeouts, the number of home runs, etc.) *and* objectively evaluated:

> a salesman's performance—also easily evaluated—depends to a large extent on his ability to persuade a prospective client. If the client is prejudiced, the [black] sales-man is especially handicapped ... the [black] athlete's performance is not as directly dependent on the good-will of whites as would be the case in most managerial-type positions.   (1962: 244)

The difficulty in documenting the impact of quality uncertainty on status-signaling, however, is that it requires measurement of the extent of uncertainty. To find that status matters when quality is uncertain is not enough evidence to establish that the importance of status cues increases with quality uncertainty. Several studies, however, have made a concerted effort to document a correlation between the variability in uncertainty and variability in the importance of status. For example, in the above-mentioned study of biotechnology startups, Stuart, Hoang, and Hybels (1999) provide two measures of the uncertainty associated with a new startup's quality: the age of the startup and the amount of pre-IPO financing that the startup has received. They find that the effect of prominent affiliations is greater for those firms that are younger and that lack pre-IPO financing.

Podolny, Stuart, and Hannan (1996) also find evidence to this effect in their analysis of patent citations. Based on citation networks in the semiconductor indus-try, the authors develop a measure of the degree to which a firm finds itself in a technological niche where there is considerable uncertainty about quality. When a firm is located in a niche characterized by high uncertainty, then the patent citations from other firms—which the authors contend can be taken as a form of deference towards technological achievement—have a positive effect on a firm's sales. In contrast, when a firm is located in a low-uncertainty niche, then this measure of deference is not positively correlated with firm sales.

To summarize, we believe that there is considerable evidence from a variety of domains that actors look to status as a signal, where status can be defined in terms of accumulated acts of deference. A number of these studies, moreover, show that the signaling effects of status persist even when a control for quality is included in the analysis. Longitudinal analyses of status also support Merton's idea of the Matthew effect and cumulative advantage. Status attracts rewards and rewards attract resources; resources can then be invested in the production of quality and, in turn, augment any initial differences in status. Embedded in this process is the role of exchange relations: an actor's status is affected by the status of those with whom the actor enters into exchange relations, where ties to higher-status others tend to increase an actor's status. Finally, the signaling power of status appears to be stronger when there is considerable uncertainty about underlying quality.

23.5 STATUS AND THE DEPRECIATION
OF QUALITY

We wish to devote the rest of this chapter to discussing an underappreciated angle regarding the importance of status in social life. In the work on signaling described above, the main concern is the way in which actors rely on status to choose exchange partners and the consequences of this behavior with regard to the distribution of rewards. What has not received attention, however, is whether a reliance on status cues affects how actors experience the quality of whatever is obtained in the exchange.

The extant literature generally assumes that regardless of whether an actor picks an exchange partner by relying on status or simply by coming to the partner by chance, the experience with that partner is unaffected by how the actor arrived at the partnership. For example, we generally assume that an individual's experience working with, say, a law firm is the same whether she picked the firm by attending to status distinctions or picked the firm randomly from a phone book. We wish to challenge this assumption. Not only do actors rely on status to infer the quality of potential exchange partners, the attention to structural cues can also affect the way in which actors experience the value of the exchange itself. In particular, we believe that the attention to structural cues leads to a depreciation of quality.

To make this argument, we draw on the analytical construct of commensuration, introduced by Espeland and Stevens (1998). Commensuration is a social process by which different qualities are transformed into a common metric, such as utility, price, or rankings. Rankings of colleges, for example, organize and present otherwise unique institutions on a singular numerical scale. By definition, commensuration reduces complexity by compressing or distilling multidimensional differences into a single dimension, thereby creating explicit (vertical) relations between entities.

With regard to status rankings, the question that arises is whether the act of making a set of entities commensurable alters the potential value derived from any given entity. We believe that it does: When actors attend to structural signals in searching for exchange partners, they invoke a framework of comparability that abstracts from the qualitative distinctiveness of those potential exchange partners. That is, the recognition of status differences introduces a metric of comparability across potential alters that likely changes how an actor 'understands' his choices, which we refer to as an actor's 'value orientation.' In particular, when a framework of comparability is established, actors searching for partners become less sensitive to the value that underlying qualitative differences are capable of engendering when structural cues are present. Stated somewhat differently, to rely on status as a basis for inferring quality is a form of 'satisficing' behavior that ultimately desensitizes the searching actor to the full value that can be derived from a particular exchange relation.

In the sociological literature it is possible to draw an analytical distinction between a value orientation in which an individual embraces the unique essence of an exchange opportunity and a value orientation in which the individual downplays the defining elements of that opportunity because the individual is primarily concerned with establishing a framework of comparability across a set of necessarily dissimilar opportunities. Such a distinction in value orientations can be linked to the distinction that Marx ([1867] 1990) draws between use value and exchange value. Simmel invokes a similar distinction in *Philosophy of Money* (1978) as does Marcuse in *One-dimensional Man* (1991).

The literature on aesthetics helps illustrate the experiential differences associated with the two orientations. In his work *Art as Experience* (1980) Dewey for example draws a distinction between an aesthetic and an instrumental orientation using the example of an epicure. He writes:

> [T]he pleasures of the palate are different in quality to an epicure than in one who merely likes his food as he eats it. The difference is not of mere intensity. The epicure is conscious of much more than the taste of the food. Rather, there enter into the taste, as directly experienced, qualities that depend upon reference to its source and its manner of production in connection with the criteria of excellence.   (p. 49)

Peter de Bolla (2001) captures the aesthetic orientation similarly:

> [M]oments of aesthetic experience are qualitatively different from other kinds of experience. Such experiences do not, necessarily, come easily; they may not be available on demand. We have to work toward them, and as will become clear, work them through.   (p. 12)

Both Dewey and de Bolla place great emphasis on the fact that an aesthetic orientation obliges one to work through a detailed, nuanced understanding of the particularities of the object and the circumstances of the object's creation, whereas an instrumental orientation does not. An aesthetic orientation requires an embrace of the object's uniqueness, drawing on the individual's own knowledge of such aspects as the challenges involved in the object's creation, the intention behind the creation of the object, and the broader context of other objects that have sought to engender a similar response from the individual. In short, an aesthetic orientation is incompatible with the process of commensuration.

When commensuration occurs, the likelihood that actors can maintain an aesthetic orientation diminishes. Insofar as value arises from the active contemplation of uniqueness, we believe that the introduction of *any* common metric for valuation—for example, a rating of objects in terms of some formally defined criteria—interferes with an aesthetic orientation. Put another way, defining entities as incommensurate is a statement regarding the value of the uniqueness of those entities (Espeland and Stevens 1998: 326). The act of commensuration, however, introduces comparability and therefore explicitly denies uniqueness, and thus potentially lowers the value actors derive from engaging with ranked versus nonranked products. While empirical support for this hypothesis is currently lacking, we believe that this is a fruitful avenue for future empirical research.

CONCLUSION

We would like to conclude this chapter by summarizing its central components. In this chapter we have reviewed four dynamics that underlie the sociological conception of status and elaborated on a fifth, underappreciated assumption. We began by defining status with regard to deference relations. We posited that the building blocks of any social hierarchy are the gestures and behaviors actors use to confer deference, and that a group's status queue is based on the distribution of these gestures. A key point that we have tried to convey throughout is that status orders are not merely an epiphenomenal reflection of quality orders. While no one disputes that quality can affect an actor's ability to attract deference, we argue here that the ranking of actors into status positions, once established, becomes an independent influence on subsequent actions and outcomes.

First, we reviewed how an actor's status position can be used as a proxy for quality (dynamic 1), distinguishing between the original economic conception of a signal and the sociological interpretation. In the economic tradition, status is a signal of quality because the acquisition of status is related to underlying quality. While sociologists do not deny that quality influences an actor's chances of becoming high-status, there is a greater concern for how the connection between quality and status can be easily blurred by chance, uncertainty, and lag effects. From this perspective, status often becomes a proxy for quality simply because status cues are generally more observable than underlying quality distinctions.

We then reviewed what is perhaps the central insight from the sociological work on status, which involves the Matthew effect and the mechanisms that allow status to feed on itself (dynamic 2). Drawing from early work in the sociology of science as well as from recent advances in the sociology of organizations and markets, we described how higher-status actors are able to produce a given level of quality for a lower cost than lower-status actors. That is, an actor's position within a status order has an independent effect on the quality that an actor is able to subsequently produce. Moreover, this dynamic is likely exacerbated when quality is more difficult to observe (dynamic 4).

Another key theme reviewed is that an actor can acquire or lose status based on the status positions of those with whom they affiliate (dynamic 3). That is, regardless of how an actor comes to occupy a given status position, establishing relations with others of higher status will likely enhance her own position, while ties to lower-status others can effectively jeopardize her status. To the extent that there is some initial disjuncture between underlying quality and the status position an actor obtains, exchange relations can thus further decouple status from quality.

Finally, we highlight a fifth aspect of status dynamics that has yet to become central to the research domain. As we have reviewed in this chapter, researchers to date have been chiefly concerned with (a) why and when actors rely on status to infer quality and (b) how status affects the production of quality and formation of exchange relations. What has rarely been considered, however, is how the presence of structural cues affects the way quality is *valued*. That is, when actors search for exchange partners, does the attention to status cues affect how actors experience the exchange itself? Drawing from research on commensuration and value, we argue that the presence of structural cues likely leads to the depreciation of quality. Structural cues introduce a framework of comparability that desensitizes actors to the qualitative distinctiveness of the objects and actors in question. While there is some suggestive research pointing toward this dynamic, more is needed.

NOTES

1. This measure thus captures an actor's informal or sociometric status within a group, which is distinct from the type of official status an actor acquires as the incumbent of a formal hierarchical position. A formal status-ordering refers to an institutionally delineated set of positions (e.g. supervisor, worker, intern), where rewards are attached to the position itself and not the position's incumbent. In many situations the informal and formal dimensions of an actor's status are correlated: a worker who is highly respected by her colleagues is more likely to be considered for an official promotion; a slave receives very little deference precisely because of her formal status. The two dimensions, however, remain distinct, as there can be a mismatch between the amount of deference an actor receives and the formal position she occupies.

2. This experimental finding is entirely consistent with Becker's theory of tastes (1991, 1996), which argues that an individual's demand for a good is positively influenced by the aggregate demand for the good. For example, the extent to which a restaurant is packed with customers is used by potential customers as a signal of restaurant quality. Even though the wait for service and food would be shorter in a near-empty restaurant, Becker's model suggests that customers would still prefer the busier restaurant, presumably because the potential gain from faster service does not outweigh the potential loss from a lower-quality dining experience.

3. Among sociologists who have discussed the application of Spence's signaling model to racial inequality, some have interpreted the model as implying endogeneity. Generally,

there are two variants of the endogenous account. First, if black teenagers and their parents have fewer financial resources to afford a college education and if education has an effect on productivity, then employers will offer black employees lower wages, which will make it harder for them to send their children to college. An equilibrium arises in which black employees are seen as less productive and lack the resources to prove that they can be as productive as white employees. However, in a personal communication Spence noted that this dynamic is actually not derivable from his signaling model. In this particular account, education is not just a signal but a determinant of quality, and that is not a feature of Spence's model.

There is a second variant, that is closer to Spence's signaling model. Under this variant, quality is exogenous and uncorrelated with race, but the educational system still perpetuates racial inequality. Employers pay higher wages to those with college degrees because the pool of college-educated individuals is more productive than the pool that is not college-educated. Insofar as they lack financial resources to go to college, blacks are lumped into the noncollege-educated pool even though there are highly productive blacks in that pool. As blacks receive lower wages, they cannot send their children to college. Wage inequality persists across races despite the fact that there are no inherent productivity differences and despite the fact that race is exogenous. However, under this variant, a little experimentation on the part of employers (e.g. offering blacks higher wages than noncollege-educated whites) can over time lead to a separating equilibrium where there exist high-productivity blacks with the financial resources to signal that productivity. In effect, the signaling equilibrium is what is called 'knife-edged': slight (and reasonable) departure from the formally prescribed behavior in the model leads to the equilibrium breaking down.

4. One question that arises is the issue of asymmetry in the direction in which status leaks. In the case of the exchange between Caroline and Margaret in *Margaret Garner* there is a net loss of status: Caroline and Mr Gaines both lose status while Margaret does not win it. In the case of Baum and Oliver's study of day-care centers, however, there is a net gain of status: a day-care center with a tie to a church or government agency gains status while the agency suffers no loss of status. While no systematic theory exists to our knowledge, the direction in which status leaks appears to be tied to the uncertainty or instability of an actor's position in the status ordering. That is, the exchange partner occupying the less secure position will experience a loss or gain in status. Thus, if the relatively secure position is a low-status position (e.g. Margaret, the slave) and the insecure position is high (Caroline and Mr Gaines), we expect a net loss in status for the incumbents of the insecure position. On the other hand, if the secure entity occupies a higher position than the insecure entity (e.g. well-established government agency versus new day-care center), we expect a net gain in status for the insecure entity.

REFERENCES

ALLISON, P. D., and STEWART, J. A. (1974), 'Productivity Differences among Scientists: Evidence for Accumulative Advantage', *American Sociological Review*, 39: 596–606.

ALLISON, P. D., LONG, J. S., and KRAUSE, T. K. (1982), 'Cumulative Advantage and Inequality in Science', *American Sociological Review*, 47: 615–25.

BAUM, J. A. C., and OLIVER, C. (1991), 'Institutional Linkages and Organizational Mortality', *Administrative Science Quarterly*, 36: 187–218.

—— (1992), 'Institutional Embeddedness and the Dynamics of Organizational Populations', *American Sociological Review*, 57: 540–59.

BECKER, G. S. (1991), 'A Note on Restaurant Pricing and Other Examples of Social Influences on Price', *Journal of Political Economy*, 99: 1109–16.

—— (1996), *Accounting for Tastes* (Cambridge, Mass.: Harvard University Press).

BENJAMIN, B. A., and PODOLNY, J. M. (1999), 'Status, Quality, and Social Order in the California Wine Industry', *Administrative Science Quarterly*, 44: 563–89.

BERGER, J., et al. (1977), *Status Characteristics and Social Interaction* (New York: Elsevier).

BLALOCK, H. M. (1962), 'Occupational Discrimination—Some Theoretical Propositions', *Social Problems*, 9: 240–7.

BLANK, R. M. (1991), 'The Effects of Double-blind Versus Single-blind Reviewing: Experimental Evidence from *The American Economic Review*', *American Economic Review*, 81: 1041–67.

BLAU, P. M. (1955), *The Dynamics of Bureaucracy: A Study of Interpersonal Relations in Two Government Agencies* (Chicago, Ill.: University of Chicago Press).

—— (1977), *Inequality and Heterogeneity* (New York: Free Press).

BOLLA, P. DE (2001), *Art Matters* (Cambridge, Mass.: Harvard University Press).

BURT, R. S. (1982), *Toward a Structural Theory of Action* (New York: Academic).

—— (1987), 'Social Contagion and Innovation: Cohesion vs. Structural Equivalence', *American Journal of Sociology*, 92 (6): 1287–335.

CAPLOW, T., and McGEE, R. (1958), *The Academic Marketplace* (New York: Doubleday).

COLE, J. R., and COLE, S. (1973), *Social Stratification in Science* (Chicago, Ill.: University of Chicago Press).

COOK, K. S., and EMERSON, R. M. (1978), 'Power, Equity, and Commitment in Exchange Networks', *American Sociological Review*, 43 (5): 721–39.

CRANE, D. (1970), 'Academic Marketplace Revisited—Study of Faculty Mobility Using Cartter Ratings', *American Journal of Sociology*, 75: 953–64.

DANNEFER, D. (1987), 'Aging as Intracohort Differentiation: Accentuation, the Matthew Effect, and the Life Course', *Sociological Forum*, 2: 211–36.

DEWEY, J. (1980), *Art as Experience* (New York: Penguin).

DIPRETE, T. A., and EIRICH, G. M. (2006), 'Cumulative Advantage as a Mechanism for Inequality: A Review of Theoretical and Empirical Developments', *Annual Review of Sociology*, 32: 271–97.

ELIAS, N., and SCOTSON, J. L. (1965), *The Established and the Outsiders: A Sociological Enquiry into Community* (London: Cass).

ESPELAND, W. N., and STEVENS, M. L. (1998), 'Commensuration as a Social Process', *Annual Review of Sociology*, 24: 313–43.

GOULD, R. V. (2002), 'The Origins of Status Hierarchies: A Formal Theory and Empirical Test', *American Journal of Sociology*, 107: 1143–78.

GRANOVETTER, M. S. (1985), 'Economic Action and Social Structure: The Problem of Embeddedness', *American Journal of Sociology*, 91 (3): 481–510.

HARGENS, L. L., and HAGSTROM, W. O. (1967), 'Sponsored and Contest Mobility of American Academic Scientists', *Sociology of Education*, 40: 24–38.

—— (1982), 'Scientific Consensus and Academic Status Attainment Patterns', *Sociology of Education*, 55: 183–96.

KANTER, R. M. (1977), *Men and Women of the Corporation*, (New York: Basic).

KERCKHOFF, A. C., and GLENNIE, E. (1999), 'The Matthew Effect in American Education', *Research in Sociology of Education and Socialization*, 12: 35–66.

KRACKHARDT, D. (1990), 'Assessing the Political Landscape: Structure, Cognition, and Power in Organizations', *Administrative Science Quarterly*, 35 (2): 342–69.

LEAHEY, E. (2004), 'The Role of Status in Evaluating Research: The Case of Data Editing', *Social Science Research*, 33: 521–37.

LONG, J. S. (1978), 'Productivity and Academic Position in the Scientific Career', *American Sociological Review*, 43: 889–908.

LYNN, F. B. (2006), 'Quality Uncertainty and Professional Status: A Study of Mathematicians and Economists', Ph.D. diss. (Harvard University).

MARCUSE, H. (1991), *One-dimensional Man: Studies in the Ideology of Advanced Industrialized Society*, 2nd edn. (London: Routledge).

MARSDEN, P. V. (1982), 'Brokerage Behavior in Restricted Exchange Networks', in P. V. Marsden and N. Lin (eds.), *Social Structure and Network Analysis* (London: Sage), 201–18.

MARX, K. [1867] (1990), *Capital: A Critique of Political Economy*, trans. Ben Fowkes and introd. Ernest Mandel (New York: Penguin).

MAYHEW, B. (1980), 'Structuralism vs. Individualism, 1. Shadowboxing in the Dark', *Social Forces*, 59 (2): 335–75.

MERTON, R. K. (1968), 'Matthew Effect in Science', *Science*, 159: 56–63.

OLLIVIER, M. (2004), 'Towards a Structural Theory of Status Inequality', in Arne L. Kalleberg et al. (eds.), *Research in Social Stratification and Mobility* (Oxford: Elsevier).

PHILLIPS, D. J. (2001), 'The Promotion Paradox: Organizational Mortality and Employee Promotion Chances in Silicon Valley Law Firms, 1946–1996', *American Journal of Sociology*, 106: 1058–98.

PODOLNY, J. M. (1993), 'A Status-based Model of Market Competition', *American Journal of Sociology*, 984: 829–72.

—— and PHILLIPS, D. J. (1996), 'The Dynamics of Organizational Status', *Industrial and Corporate Change*, 5 (2): 453–71.

—— STUART, T. E., and HANNAN, M. T. (1996), 'Networks, Knowledge, and Niches: Competition in the Worldwide Semiconductor Industry, 1984–1991', *American Journal of Sociology*, 102: 659–89.

RAO, H., DAVIS, G. F., and WARD, A. (2000), 'Embeddedness, Social Identity and Mobility: Why Firms Leave the NASDAQ and Join the New York Stock Exchange', *Administrative Science Quarterly*, 45: 268–92.

RESKIN, B. F. (1979), 'Academic Sponsorship and Scientists' Careers', *Sociology of Education*, 52: 129–46.

RIDGEWAY, C. L. (1984), 'Dominance, Performance, and Status in Groups', *Advances in Group Processes*, 1: 59–93.

—— (1991), 'The Social Construction of Status Value: Gender and Other Nominal Characteristics', *Social Forces*, 702: 367–86.

—— and BALKWELL, J. W. (1997), 'Group Processes and the Diffusion of Status Beliefs', *Social Psychology Quarterly*, 60: 14–31.

—— and ERICKSON, K. G. (2000), 'Creating and Spreading Status Beliefs', *American Journal of Sociology*, 106: 579–615.

Ross, J. S., et al. (2006), 'Effect of Blinded Peer Review on Abstract Acceptance', *Journal of the American Medical Association*, 295: 1675–80.

Salganik, M. J., Dodds, P. S., and Watts, D. J. (2006), 'Experimental Study of Inequality and Unpredictability in an Artificial Cultural Market', *Science*, 311: 854–6.

Simmel, G. (1978), *Philosophy of Money*, trans. Tom Bottomore and David Frisby (Boston, Mass.: Routledge & Kegan Paul).

Spence, M. (1973), 'Job Market Signaling', *Quarterly Journal of Economics*, 87: 355–74.

Stuart, T. E., Hoang, H., and Hybels, R. C. (1999), 'Interorganizational Endorsements and the Performance of Entrepreneurial Ventures', *Administrative Science Quarterly*, 44: 315–49.

Walberg, H. J., and Tsai, S. L. (1983), 'Matthew Effects in Education', *American Educational Research Journal*, 20: 359–73.

White, H. C. (1981), 'Where Do Markets Come From?', *American Journal of Sociology*, 87 (3): 517–47.

——Boorman, S. A., and Brieger, R. L. (1976), 'Social Structures from Networks, 1. Blockmodels of Roles and Positions', *American Journal of Sociology*, 81 (4): 730–80.

Whyte, W. F. (1943), *Street Corner Society: The Social Structure of an Italian Slum* (Chicago, Ill.: University of Chicago Press).

Zuckerman, E. W. (1999), 'The Categorical Imperative: Securities Analysts and the Illegitimacy Discount', *American Journal of Sociology*, 104: 1398–438.

——(2000), 'Focusing the Corporate Product: Securities Analysts and De-diversification', *Administrative Science Quarterly*, 45: 591–619.

CHAPTER 24

DOMINANCE HIERARCHIES*

IVAN CHASE
W. BRENT LINDQUIST

INTRODUCTION

VIRTUALLY all human groups show some form of hierarchical organization. Hierarchies are top-to-bottom social orders in which some individuals rank higher than others on authority, influence, material goods, or prestige. Some examples of more formal hierarchical organizations are businesses, governments, churches, political organizations, and armies. Less formal hierarchies are found in groups of men in hunter-gatherer bands deciding how to divide the meat from an animal just killed, male and female relatives in tribal societies deciding whom a woman should marry, gangs in urban settings, and friends picking an activity to do together. Hierarchies serve to provide orderly access to monetary and other material rewards, to diminish conflict and violence within groups (but they may help accentuate conflict between groups), to channel the flow of information, to assign tasks and areas of responsibility, to indicate lines of authority in choosing courses of action, and to specify the kinds of interactions that can occur among individuals. Without hierarchies, large groups, organizations, and nation-states could not operate, and even the functioning of smaller groups would be fraught with difficulties. Consequently,

* We thank Peter Bearman, Stefan Cover, Peter Hedström, Roger Masters, and Andrea Tyree for comments on earlier drafts and Stephen Nash and Paul St Denis for help with the illustrations.

human social life as we know it would be impossible without the presence and operation of hierarchical structures.

While centralized authorities, acting on purpose, usually design the structures of the more formal hierarchies, the structures of the less formal hierarchies often emerge spontaneously without explicit decisions about the overall structure by the participants. Surprisingly, even without conscious design, these hierarchy structures often take the same, typical form across many groups of the same type. For example, the dominance hierarchies in groups of both younger and older children often take what is known as a linear structure (defined below), friendship networks across cultures and age groups tend toward a series of ranked cliques with members of each clique mutually choosing one another, and task-oriented groups have a few members that speak and are spoken to often while most other members have low rates of participation (Bales et al. 1951; Bales 1953; J. A. Davis 1970; Holland and Leinhard 1970; Savin-Williams 1980; Johnsen 1985).

In this chapter we ask how these informal hierarchies develop their typical structures. How is it that different groups develop the same kinds of hierarchy structures, even when the structures arise spontaneously, without being imposed by central authority? What mechanisms generate these hierarchy structures? Do these mechanisms reflect differences among individuals or their actions during hierarchy formation? What theoretical models exist to explain the structural forms of hierarchies, and what are the levels of support for the different models? Can understanding the development of hierarchies provide more general insight into the evolution of other kinds of social structures in small groups?

We begin this exploration of these questions in a way that is unusual for sociology: we first look at theoretical models for the explanation of dominance hierarchies ('pecking orders') in small groups of animals, before considering hierarchies in small groups of humans. We do this for several reasons: First, and perhaps surprisingly, as we shall show, explanations for the structure of hierarchies in animals have to be sociological, not biological. We shall demonstrate that even the relatively simple hierarchy structures in animals such as fish and chickens have to be generated by social processes and are not just simple reflections of differences in the physicality of individuals. Second, hierarchies in human small groups are often similar in structure to those in animals. We will indicate that dominance relationships in animal hierarchies usually take transitive configurations; consequently such hierarchies have what are termed 'linear' structures. While the structures of human friendship networks, participation in task-oriented groups, and dominance hierarchies in pre-schoolers and adolescents are not always perfectly linear, the component relationships are often highly transitive and the resulting structures tend toward linearity. Third, both animal behaviorists and sociologists have spent enormous amounts of energy in trying to discover the micro-dynamics of social organization in small groups. The micro-dynamics that animal behaviorists have suggested are responsible for the forms of animal hierarchies are often similar to those that sociologists have suggested for human hierarchies, but the role of these dynamics has been more rigorously evaluated in the case of animal hierarchies. We can use these animal evaluations as clues to the effectiveness of similar dynamics to explain the forms of human hierarchies. Fourth, it is easier to perform rigorous tests of theoretical models for animal hierarchies than it is for human ones; we can carry out careful experiments, manipulate variables, and perform controlled observations more quickly and less expensively in animals. Consequently, we can determine what kinds of models, mechanisms, data, and methods are most effective in understanding animal hierarchies, and we can use this knowledge to help in understanding the formation of human hierarchies in small groups.

Our plan for this chapter is as follows. We shall describe dominance relationships and dominance hierarchies in animal groups, evaluate the various theoretical models that biologists and sociologists have proposed to explain the structural forms of these hierarchies, outline a new type of model for animal hierarchies that avoids some of the problems inherent in the earlier models, and then compare current models for human small-group hierarchies with those for animal hierarchies. We shall conclude that both our new model and current experimental work on animals indicate, ironically, that animals generate their hierarchies through richer and more sociologically sophisticated dynamics than those proposed in the current models for humans.

24.1 Background Information: Dominance Relationships, Dominance Hierarchies, and the Structural Form of Hierarchies in Animals

If a small group of, say, four or five animals of a species that forms dominance hierarchies is assembled for observation, after a few minutes of exploring their new enclosure they will begin to have aggressive interactions with one another. These interactions usually involve two animals at a time, often begin with threat gestures—a fish flaring its gill covers at another or a chicken raising its head above that of another—and then evolve to include physical contact—pecks, bites, slaps, etc. depending upon the species. In a day or so the aggressive physical contacts between the animals decrease, and stable dominance relationships and a stable dominance hierarchy emerge. In a stable dominance relationship, one animal in a pair consistently directs aggressive acts at the other who is consistently subordinate and does not return those acts.

Taken together, the dominance relationships in all pairs in a group constitute the dominance hierarchy. These hierarchies are often linear in form. In a linear hierarchy, one animal dominates all the others, a second dominates all but the top one, and so on down to the last animal that is dominated by all the others. An enormous range of species commonly form linear hierarchy structures, despite great differences in the environments in which they live, levels of intelligence, relatedness on the evolutionary tree, and, indeed, whether or not they possess culture. These species include some insects, some crustaceans, and a large variety of fish, birds, and mammals, including human children and adolescents (Addison and Simmel 1970; Vannini and Sardini 1971; Wilson 1975; Savin-Williams 1980; Hausfater, Altmann, and Altmann 1982; Nelissen 1985; Barkan et al. 1986; Heinze 1990; Post 1992; Goessmann, Hemelrijk, and Huber 2000). In other species, such as baboons, chimpanzees, wolves, and dolphins, and in older humans, individuals form both temporary and long-lasting coalitions, and the resulting hierarchies are too complex to be labeled as simple, linear structures. Concentrating only on animals showing linear hierarchies, we ask: What forces, what organizing principles, what mechanisms can explain the occurrence of the same structural form in so many diverse species? Can one common theoretical approach account for linearity in all these species, or do we need different approaches for different species; say, biological ones for some of the 'lower' animals and psychological or sociological ones for the 'higher' animals? In the next section of this chapter we review the three main theoretical approaches that researchers have proposed to account for the common presence of linear structures.

24.2 The Main Theoretical Approaches

24.2.1 The prior-attributes hypothesis

The prior-attributes hypothesis was the first theoretical approach formulated to explain linear hierarchy structures. It proposes that linear hierarchies are simply reflections of differences in attributes related to dominance that individuals have before they join groups. For example, if dominance were determined by some combination of weight, hormone level, and level of aggressiveness, the animal ranking highest on this measure would take the top position in the hierarchy when its group was assembled, the animal ranking second-highest would take the next-to-the-top

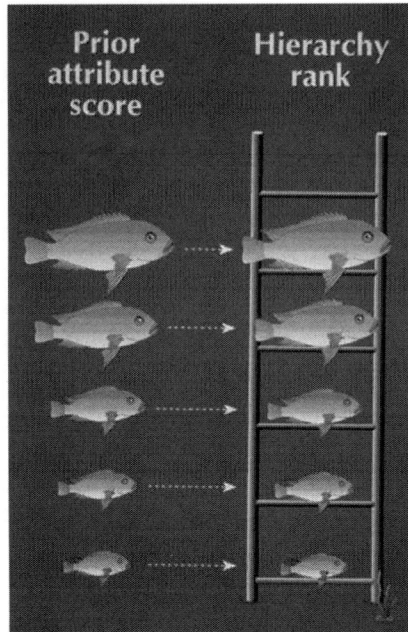

Fig. 24.1 The prior-attributes hypothesis (size indicates relative
prior-attribute value)

position, and so on (see Fig. 24.1). Under this theory, hierarchies are linear because individuals can be linearly ranked on attribute scores.

At first glance the prior-attributes hypothesis has great intuitive appeal. First, animal behaviorists have found that individual scores on many attributes, including genetic, physiological, physical, behavioral, and experiential ones, are correlated with positions in hierarchies (Clutton-Brock, Albon, and Guinness 1984; Beacham 1988; Jackson and Winnegrad 1988; Raleigh et al. 1991; Drews 1993; Holenkamp and Smale 1993; Sapolsky and Share 1994). Second, the hypothesis has great adaptability, since different sets of attributes can be used, as considered appropriate, with different species—say, genetic and physical differences for fish and behavioral and experiential ones for monkeys. Third, dominance hierarchies would seem to be the ideal candidate for a type of social organization based upon individual differences: the very idea of a pecking order conjures up visions of a struggle based upon differences of might and main. Fourth, and perhaps even more fundamentally, the prior-attributes hypothesis is a prime example of the methodological individualism that is so pervasive in explaining social outcomes in the social and behavioral sciences. In animal behavior, this assumption of methodological individualism fits perfectly with the prevailing theoretical assumption that evolution works most directly upon individuals rather than aggregations of animals. But is the individual-differences hypothesis an adequate account for the formation of linear hierarchies in animals?

Although some early ethologists suggested that hierarchy structures might not be based upon individual differences, Rapoport (1950) and, especially, Landau (1951) carried out the first serious examinations of the prior-attributes hypothesis. They examined the mathematical and statistical conditions required to produce linear hierarchy structures from differences in prior attributes. Chase (1974) extended their work using simpler mathematical techniques. Chase found that little-recognized, but stringent, mathematical and statistical requirements were needed to generate hierarchies even near linear in structure. These requirements include extremely high correlation coefficients (0.9 or higher) between the attribute scores of individuals and their ranks in a hierarchy, and 'unusual' probability distributions for animals winning pairwise contests (one individual with a 0.95 probability of defeating everyone else, a second with a 0.95 probability of dominating all but the first individual, and so on). An examination of the available data indicated that the required conditions were rarely or never met (Chase 1974).

More recently Chase et al. (2002) carried out an experimental evaluation of the prior-attributes hypothesis. In a first experiment, twenty-two groups, each of four cichlid fish, were assembled, the groups were allowed to form stable dominance hierarchies (which in almost all cases were linear), the individuals in the groups were separated for two weeks, and, finally, the groups were reassembled and allowed to form second hierarchies (which again were overwhelmingly linear). The idea behind this experiment was to let the fish form their hierarchies using whatever individual attributes were important (including ones unknown to the researchers), to 'rewind their tape' by separating them for a period of time sufficient to forget their previous relationships in their groups, and then to reassemble them to reform hierarchies. If the hierarchies were formed on the basis of individual differences, and if those differences were reasonably robust across the two-week period, the researchers reasoned that a large percentage of the groups should have identical first and second hierarchies; that is, the individuals should have the same rank positions in both hierarchies. On the other hand, if other mechanisms were involved, the percentage of groups with identical hierarchies should be low, and that is indeed what the researchers found. Only 27 percent of the groups re-formed second hierarchies identical to their first hierarchies. Of the remaining 73 percent that re-formed different second hierarchies: in 36 percent of the groups two fish switched positions upon re-forming the hierarchy; in 18 percent three fish were in different positions; and in the final 18 percent all four of the fish had different positions in the second hierarchy! While having 27 percent of the groups re-form with identical hierarchies was above the level expected by chance, thus indicating some apparent influence of differences in attributes, this percentage was much below what would have been expected if differences in attributes were the primary mechanism for generating linear structures. Some other mechanism had a principle role in producing linear hierarchies: linear hierarchy structures were robust, but the positions of individuals within them were labile.

An alternative explanation, that the animals in a group changed ranks on some attribute from the time of formation of the first hierarchy to the second, results in a complicated argument not supported by empirical findings. For example, if the animals readily changed ranks on attribute scores, a considerable number of dominance relationships should have been unstable and/or intransitive when they were observed. This was not the case. (See Chase et al. 2002 for more details of this argument.) In addition, in another experiment, when pairs of fish were tested in the same way (meeting to form a dominance relationship, separation for two weeks, and meeting to form a second relationship), they almost always replicated their initial relationships, thus suggesting that their rank on attributes did not reverse (Chase, Tovey, and Murch 2003).

In order to determine what other mechanisms might be involved in producing linear hierarchies, a second experiment was carried out by forming hierarchies using two different treatments. In the first treatment, round-robin competition, the fish in a group met to form dominance relationships only as isolated pairs, out of sight of the other members of their group. All pairs of a group met, so that the overall hierarchy structure for a group could be determined. In this treatment, the fish could not use mechanisms that involved social interaction: they could not observe the interactions among other fish and they could not 'take advantage' of their own wins by quickly attacking other group members or suffer defeats made more possible by earlier losses. In the second treatment, group assembly, the fish in a group met together, at the same time, in one tank. In this treatment, the fish could use whatever mechanisms involving social interaction of which they might be capable: observations of others' interactions, inferences about those interactions, reactions to their earlier wins and losses, etc. The researchers reasoned that if some of the mechanisms generating linear hierarchies were social in nature, then a higher percentage of the hierarchies formed through group assembly should be linear than those formed through round-robin competition. They found that in groups of four and five fish, over 90 percent of the hierarchies established through group assembly were linear while only about half of those established through round-robin competition were. Taken together, this mathematical and experimental work suggests that prior individual differences are not the mechanisms explaining linear structures, even in 'simple' animals such as chickens and fish.

24.2.2 The jigsaw-puzzle model

The second theoretical approach suggested to explain the common occurrence of linear hierarchy structures was the jigsaw-puzzle model (Chase 1982a, 1982b). Rather than conceiving of linear hierarchies as a collection of individuals ranked by the number of other group members that they dominated, as did the prior-attributes hypothesis, the jigsaw-puzzle model makes a fundamental departure and views linear hierarchies as *networks* of dominance relationships. More specifically and mathematically, these were networks in which all possible subgroups of three individuals (component triads) had transitive dominance relationships. In a transitive relationship, if A dominates B and B dominates C, A also dominates C. The idea behind the jigsaw-puzzle model is that an overall linear-hierarchy structure is generated by sequences of interactions producing transitive dominance relationships in component triads.

Chase (1982*a*, 1982*b*) noted that there are only four possible sequences for the first two dominance relationships in a component triad (barring reversal of any relationship already formed). These are shown in Figure 24.2. While all these sequences are logically possible, and each would be equally likely if dominance relationships in triads formed randomly (i.e. each possible pairwise relationship had a 50 percent probability of occurring), the sequences have very different implications for transitivity in dominance relationships and consequently for the formation of linear hierarchies. Two of the sequence patterns, 'double dominance' and 'double subordinance,' guarantee transitive dominance relationship regardless of the direction that the third dominance relationship takes when it fills in. The other two sequence patterns, 'bystander dominates initial dominant' and 'initial subordinate dominates bystander,' can give rise to either transitive or intransitive relationships, depending upon the direction of the third relationship. For example, in double dominance, if B later dominates C, the triad is transitive with A > B, B > C, and A > C; or if C later dominates B, it is also transitive with A > C, C > B, and A > B. On the other hand, in bystander dominates initial dominant, for example, if B later dominates C, the relationship in the triad is intransitive (or cyclical) with A > B, B > C, and C > A; but if C later dominates B, the triad is transitive with C > A, A > B, and C > B.

In an initial study of twenty-four groups of three hens, Chase (1982*a*, 1982*b*) found that the two sequences guaranteeing transitivity, double dominance and double subordinance, occurred in 91 percent of the groups while the other two sequences only occurred in 9 percent. As noted above, if the relationships had formed randomly, each sequence pattern would have occurred in about 25 percent of the groups. In a second experiment, testing the model in groups of four hens (with four component triads per group), the sequence patterns ensuring transitivity again occurred in the overwhelming majority (87 percent) of the component triads (Chase 1982*a*, 1982*b*).

Following Chase's initial work with hens, other researchers confirmed that a wide variety of other species—rhesus monkeys, Japanese macaques, Harris sparrows, crayfish, and ants—also used sequences ensuring transitivity at high rates (Mendoza and Barchas 1983; Barchas and Mendoza 1984; Eaton 1984; Chase and Rohwer 1987; Goessmann, Hemelrijk, and Huber 2000; Heinze, personal communication).

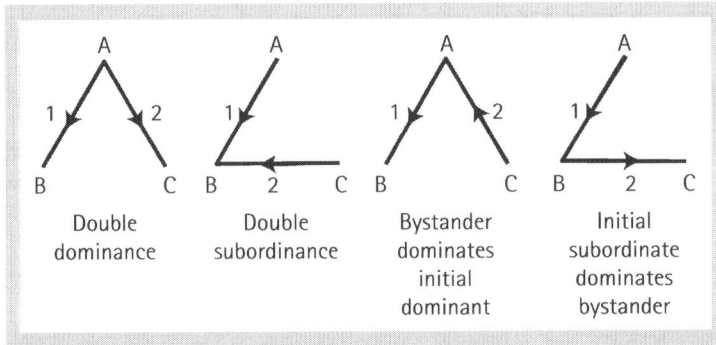

Fig. 24.2 The four possible sequences for the first two domin-ance relationships in a component triad. In all cases the first established relationship is between A and B, with A identi-fied as the aggressor (dominant) and B as the subordinate. C is the third animal (bystander) with whom a relationship is established

These findings indicated that the jigsaw-puzzle model had found a poten-tial solution to the classic micro-to-macro problem in sociology (Coleman 1986; Hedström 2005)—how to link the actions of individuals to social-system outcomes—albeit it had done so for animals in quite small groups. In doing so, it suggested that common social forms—linear dominance hierarchies—might be the result of abstractly equivalent modes of social interaction, even across groups that were evolutionarily distinct and whose individuals appeared to have little in common. However, the jigsaw-puzzle model has a serious problem. It only provides snapshots of sequences of interaction in triads and does not follow how relation-ships fill in and change over time, if they do, on the way to forming stable linear hierarchies.

24.2.3 Winner–loser–bystander models

Winner–loser–bystander (WLB) models are the third theoretical approach pro-posed to explain the presence of linear hierarchies. This approach derives from the jigsaw-puzzle model (Chase 1982a, 1982b) but concentrates on individual-level mechanisms, rather than the interaction-process mechanisms of the jigsaw-puzzle model itself. Chase (1982a, 1982b) suggested that what he called winner, loser, and bystander effects could help explain why sequences ensuring transi-tivity predominated while those not doing so were rare. In a winner effect, an individual winning an earlier dominance encounter has an increased probability of winning a subsequent encounter with another individual; in a loser effect, an individual losing an earlier encounter has a decreased probability of winning a second one; and in a bystander effect, an individual observing an encounter between two other individuals alters its probability of winning, depending on its observations, when it later meets either the winner or the loser. Double dominance, one of the sequences ensuring transitivity, could be explained, for example, as follows: After A dominates B it is very likely to dominate C because of a winner effect on its part and/or a bystander effect on C's part. Similarly, the occurrence of initial subordinate dominates bystander, one of the sequences not ensuring transitivity, would be rare, since after A dominates B, B would be unlikely to dominate C because of a loser effect on its (B's) part and a bystander effect on C's part.

At first WLB models appeared to be a very promising approach as researchers found these effects in a great variety of species (see Chase, Bartolomeo, and Dugatkin 1994 and Chase, Tovey, and Murch 2003 and the literature reviewed there). Based upon this empirical work, both sociologists and animal behaviorists developed mathematical models and computer simulations to show that these effects, singly or in combination, could, in principle, generate highly linear hierarchies (Fararo and Skvoretz 1988; Skvoretz, Faust, and Fararo 1996; Dugatkin 1997; Bonabeau, Theraulaz, and Deneubourg 1999; Hemelrijk 1999). With the proper choice of parameters and probability functions for determining winners and losers, schedules for pairs meeting and interacting, these models can produce one individual that, eventually, is very likely to win against all others when it encounters them; one that is very likely to win against all but the first individual; and so on. These models use feedback procedures from records of wins and losses to dynamically update the dominance ability of individuals and to clearly differentiate them by these updated abilities. In essence, WLB explanations of linear hierarchy structure are very much like those involving prior attributes, but now the attributes are dynamic ones. Like the prior-attributes hypothesis, WLB models view a linear hierarchy as a set of *individuals* differentiated by some social quality—the number of individuals in the group that they are aggressive toward—and not as a small social system or a network of relationships.

A study by Chase, Tovey, and Murch (2003) first indicated a serious problem with the WLB models. The research documenting winner and loser effects had been carried out in isolated dyads in which a previous winner or loser met another individual in isolation. When they investigated the loser effect in isolated dyads of fish versus socially embedded ones—that is, pairs within groups of size three or four—they found that while there was a strong loser effect in the isolated dyads, there was no significant effect in the socially embedded ones. More recently, Lindquist and Chase (2008) evaluated the mathematical formulations and core assumptions of three of the most prominent winner–loser models in the animal-behavior literature. Overall, they found little support for either the mathematical formulations or the core assumptions of these models.

24.3 A New Approach to Explaining Linear Hierarchy Structures: The Interaction-Process Model

Given the problems with the three earlier approaches, we now outline a new approach to account for linear hierarchies—the interaction-process (IP) model. This is an action theory in that it attempts to explain the development of linear structures on the basis of the behavioral actions by individuals, but it does not describe those actions as emanating from separate individuals as do most action theories (Coleman 1990; Hedström 2005). Rather, like the jigsaw-puzzle model, the IP approach sees actions as occurring in the smaller social components of a larger group, particularly in dyads and triads, although larger components may play a role. The IP model is a descriptive explanation of hierarchy formation; it indicates the micro-level interaction processes that lead to and ensure linear structures, but it does not account for the reasons that individuals use those particular processes. The IP model provides a 'how' rather than a 'why' explanation.

Below we outline the IP model. The actions that the model describes assume considerable cognitive awareness, flexibility, and sophistication, perhaps supported by intentions and preferences, even on the part of 'simple' animals. Consequently, we review experimental research that independently supports these assumptions. The model requires different methodological techniques for collecting, visualizing, and analyzing data than are usually used in studying small-group hierarchies. We briefly discuss these techniques and suggest that they might be generalized to study various kinds of social structures in small groups of humans and other animals. Finally, we discuss why we think that it is not possible now, and perhaps not in principle, to reduce the IP approach to one based upon the actions of individuals themselves. This assumption distinguishes the IP model from the jigsaw-puzzle approach, which did assume that interaction sequences could ultimately be explained in terms of individual actions and effects.

The IP model was developed through micro-level reanalysis of data on hierarchy formation in groups of four hens—data consisting of every aggressive action involving physical contact among the hens over a course of two days from introduction through the formation of stable, overwhelmingly linear hierarchies (Chase 1982a, 1982b). The model describes several characteristic processes that promote the efficient and robust formation of linear structures. By 'efficient' we mean that a process decreases the number of interactions that need to occur in order to reach or be assured of reaching a linear structure. By 'robust,' we mean that a process promotes the return of a hierarchy structure to linear form whenever it assumes a non-linear form. There are three characteristic processes that promote efficiency—(1) low rates of pair-relationship reversals, (2) high rates of formation of transitive initial relationships, and (3) high rates of formation of configurations that guarantee transitivity in component triads—and one feature that promotes robustness: rapid conversion of intransitive dominance relationships to transitive ones. In describing interaction processes, we will assume that each single attack establishes a dominance relationship or reverses a previous one; that is, if A attacks B then A dominates B, and if, sometime later, B attacks A, B then dominates A. We do this in order to concentrate on the micro-dynamics of interaction leading to hierarchy formation; a coarser definition of dominance relationships, say one involving a number of successive attacks, would miss some of the important forms of interaction that we describe below.

24.3.1 Reversals in dominance-relationship formation

Consider two groups of animals, each forming a dominance hierarchy. In the first group assume there are many counterattacks in the dyads, interaction patterns that we call pair-flips, in which existing dominance relationships reverse, i.e. an animal A attacks B, then B attacks A, and so on, with similar attack reversals happening in other pairs. Eventually, the pair-flips cease, and stable relationships are established. In the second group there are no pair-flips at all. Relationship formation is much more efficient in the second group, since stable relationships are formed immediately, and never reversed, while those in the first group flip back and forth before becoming stable.

Overall, the hens formed relationships with a high level of efficiency. Of the 7,257 aggressive acts recorded in the 84 dyads (14 groups with 6 dyads per group), only 138 interactions (1.9 percent) involved a pair-flip, and two groups by themselves accounted for 60 of these dyadic reversals. Of the 138 pair-flips, one-half took place within the first 60 interactions occurring after the groups were introduced on the first day of observation. These data raise an interesting question: Do small groups of humans and other animals also have low rates of pair-flips in establishing dominance hierarchies and other network structures? Preliminary data collected in the first author's laboratory suggest that isolated pairs of fish have much higher rates of relationship reversals than do pairs socially embedded within large groups, and perhaps this finding may also carry over to humans and other animals forming hierarchies and other kinds of social structures in small groups.

24.3.2 Initial formation of transitive relationships in component triads

Again, consider two groups forming hierarchies. In the first, assume some of the component triads initially form intransitive dominance relationships and some form transitive ones. Eventually, the intransitive relationships convert to transitive relationships by flipping one of their dominance relationships, while those initially transitive remain so. In the second group, assume all of the component triads initially form, and retain, transitive relationships. We would say that the second group reached a linear hierarchy in a more efficient manner than the first, since no relationships needed to be reversed in the second in order to develop a linear structure.

The groups of hens had very high rates of formation of transitive initial relationships in the component triads. Of the 56 component triads in the groups (14 groups with 4 triads each) only 2 (3.6 percent) were initially intransitive. If the dominance relationships in the groups had formed randomly, 25 percent (about 14) component triads would have been intransitive; our finding of just 2 is highly statistically significant ($p \leq 1.9 \cdot 10^{-5}$, binomial test).

24.3.3 Configurations of the first two relationships in component triads guaranteeing transitivity

Again, consider two groups. In one group, the first two relationships in some component triads form in configurations that allow either transitivity or intransitivity while the relationships in other triads form via configurations that guarantee transitivity (see Fig. 24.2 and discussion of the jigsaw-puzzle model). Eventually, the third relationships in the triads that could be either transitive or intransitive fill in so as to produce only transitive triads, and the dominance hierarchy becomes linear. In group two, all of the component triads fill in via configurations that ensure transitivity. We would say that the second group reached linearity in a more efficient manner than did the first because in the second group a linear structure was an assured outcome even before all relationships were defined.

In the hen data, of the 56 component triads, 41 (73 percent) filled in with configurations guaranteeing transitivity, while 15 (27 percent) did not. If relationships had formed randomly, 50 percent would have formed via configurations ensuring transitivity. The deviation from random is significant ($p < 10^{-3}$, X^2 test, d.f. = 3). This analysis is not, of course, completely independent of the one in Section 24.3.2. The analysis here accentuates the fact that in many triads the first two relationships ensure initial transitive configurations even before the third relationship is in place. This analysis is also very similar to the analysis described in the jigsaw-puzzle-model section; here we use a finer-grained definition for dominance relationships.

24.3.4 Conversion of intransitive dominance relationships to transitive ones

Again, consider two groups, in both of which the animals efficiently establish a linear hierarchy using the three interaction processes that we have just mentioned.

Assume further that in one component triad of each group an animal then reverses an existing relationship in such a manner as to convert a previously transitive relationship to an intransitive one. Both groups now have a nonlinear hierarchy. Assume that this nonlinear hierarchy remains in place in the first group (because the triad in question retains its intransitive relationship) while in the second group the intransitive relationship is quickly converted back to a transitive one (by reversing one of the relationships in the intransitive triad). The hierarchy-formation process in group two is more robust than in group one (since group two quickly regained its linear structure).

Although not noted in earlier analyses of the data (Chase 1982a, 1982b, 1985), many of the component triads in the hen groups did develop intransitive relationships after initially forming transitive ones (recall that only 2 of 56 triads initially established intransitive relationships). A total of 15 triads (27 percent) became intransitive at some point over the two days of observation (the 2 initially intransitive ones plus 13 that became intransitive after initially forming as transitive). All but one of these triads with intransitive relationships ultimately converted to transitive ones over the time that the hens were observed. The one exception developed an intransitive relationship shortly before observations terminated on the final day and had little time to convert before the experiment ended.

We measured how long an intransitive triad lasted in terms of the number of aggressive interactions that occurred in the group until the intransitive triad was converted to transitive. The average length of time that an intransitive triad lasted was extremely short: 5.2 interactions. By comparison the average length that a transitive triad lasted (before being converted into an intransitive one or into a different transitive triad) was 54.3 interactions—more than 10 times longer than an intransitive triad lasted! A similar analysis covering the first day of the experiment using clock time (rather than interaction count) also showed that transitive triads lasted about 10 times longer than intransitive ones. On average, intransitive relationships were much less stable than transitive ones, rapidly reverting to transitive configurations. Although a large fraction of the triads in the hen groups did develop intransitive relationships, and thus the hierarchies in the groups deviated from linear structures, all the groups but one regained their linear structures (by the end of the period of observation), and they usually did so quickly.

24.3.5 Independent experimental evidence concerning animal abilities and interaction processes

In order to carry out the kinds of interaction processes that we have described, animals presumably require some basic abilities of social cognition: recognition of other individuals, perception of the interactions of other individuals, and making inferences about the interactions of other individuals. There is ample experimental evidence for all these abilities. Animals across a broad range of species that form dominance hierarchies—including insects, crustaceans, fish, birds, and mammals—are able to identify one another as individuals (Todd, Atema, and Bardach 1967; Brown and Colgan 1986; Cheney and Seyfarth 1990; Karavanich and Atema 1998; Tibbetts 2002; D'Eath and Keeling 2003; D'Ettorre and Heinze 2005; Gherardi and Atema 2005; Lai et al. 2005; McLeman et al. 2005); even fruit flies can remember previous opponents after thirty minutes of separation (Yurkovic et al. 2006)!

Animals of many species monitor the interactions of others of their species and change their behavior in various ways according to what they see. For example, fish change their hormonal profiles after watching the contests of others (Oliveira et al. 2001), act differently when they meet those they have seen win versus those they have seen lose (Oliveira, McGregor, and Latruffe 1998), and are more 'interested' in the contests of individuals with which they have previously interacted than of those with which they have not interacted (Amell, personal communication). The experimental evidence also demonstrates that a variety of species, including birds and fish, have the ability to infer transitivity in dominance relationships (Gillian 1981; Fersen et al. 1991; Davis 1992; Roberts and Phelps 1994; Steirn, Weaver, and Zentall 1995; Bond, Kamil, and Balda 2003; Lazareva 2004; Paz-y-Mino et al. 2004; Grosenick et al. 2007). For example, recent work by Amell (personal communication) in the first author's lab shows that if fish B dominates fish C, and then C observes fish A dominating B from behind a one-way mirror, C is much more likely to use lower levels of aggressive behavior and to lose to A when they meet than is a control fish (i.e. one that has had identical past experiences and watches some fish X dominate Y but has no previous relationship with Y). Current research, again by Amell, provides experimental confirmation of the instability of intransitive relationships. If the interactions of three fish are manipulated so that they form an intransitive relationship when they meet as separate dyads, their relationship quickly converts to, and remains, a transitive one when all three fish are placed together in the same tank (Amell, personal communication). All this evidence provides strong independent support that animals of many species have the cognitive abilities necessary for, and do carry out the kinds of interaction processes that we have suggested are responsible for, the formation and maintenance of linear hierarchy structures.

24.3.6 Recording data and discovering features of interaction

In order to use the IP approach, researchers must record micro-level interaction data and then discover and analyze the patterns in this data by appropriate methods. For the hens, we recorded micro-level interactions on a PC as they occurred in real

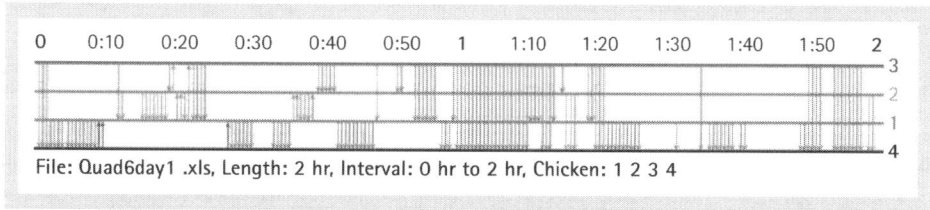

File: Quad6day1 .xls, Length: 2 hr, Interval: 0 hr to 2 hr, Chicken: 1 2 3 4

Fig. 24.3 Music–notation summary of the interactions observed during the first two hours of the first day of observations on group Q6. Horizontal lines represent individuals, ordered by dominance rank. Hen identification numbers are given at the end of each line. Each aggressive act between individuals is indicated by a vertical arrow from the line representing the initiator to the receiver's line. The time in minutes and hours since the assembly of the group is shown above the graph

time. More recently we have used a voice-recognition program for data input. If interactions are very rapid it may be necessary to make video recordings. We used a technique called music notation and several methods for following the evolution of relationships in triads and whole groups in order to find the interaction patterns we have reported with the IP model. Music notation is a technique that graphically displays detailed records of interaction in compact form so that researchers can visually recognize features of interaction for further analysis. (See Chase 2006 and Lindquist and Chase 2008 for further discussion and examples.) Figure 24.3 is a black-and-white version of an excerpt from the music-notation graph for one of the hen groups; the use of color enhances the technique. Tracking the developmental history of component triads allowed us to see how relationships filled in and how long a triad remained in transitive versus intransitive configurations. Following the evolution of relationships in a whole group enabled us to follow the hierarchy in a group as it went from having no relationships, to one relationship, and so on until it finally reached a linear structure (see Lindquist and Chase 2008 for more information on techniques for following the development history of groups in 'network state-space'). All of these methods have application beyond the IP model and can be used more generally for thinking about the development of network structures and the processes of interaction that might lead to those structures.

24.3.7 Theory of action: individual behaviors or interaction processes?

We have explained how micro-level behavioral mechanisms produce a macro-level social outcome, but we have departed from the usual type of theory of action in analytical sociology in doing so by describing the mechanisms as interactions processes in dyads and triads, instead of behaviors produced by individuals. Why have we made this departure? The answer lies in what we believe to be the inherent and irreducible randomness—the wide variation—in the behavior of individuals, and thus groups, in establishing hierarchies. For example, although 13 of 14 groups of hens developed linear hierarchies and had them at the end of the second day of observation, no two groups reached and maintained their linear hierarchies in quite the same way. In two groups individuals had no pair-flips, formed initially transitive triads, and retained their transitive relationships throughout both days of observation. In three other groups triads formed transitively, and although there were a few pair-flips, triads remained transitive. In the other nine groups, the path to linearity was tortuous: individuals reversed their relationships more often, component triads alternated between transitive and intransitive configurations, and the resulting hierarchy structures alternated between linear and nonlinear before stabilizing in linear form. In one group, one triad made over twenty transitions through transitive and intransitive states. In some groups the future highest-ranking hen emerged by quickly dominating all the others, but in other groups this was not so. (In one group the hen that was initially at the bottom of the hierarchy eventually rose to the highest rank.)

While the aim of the three hierarchy models previously discussed is simply to account for linear structures, we developed the IP approach in response to this randomness and variation: to discover mechanisms that generate linear structures *in spite of* the great variability existing at the individual and group levels. We wanted to discover how it was that different groups and different individuals could take different roads on the way to hierarchy formation and still reach the same destination—even if they sometimes wandered in the wilderness for a while. The IP model does this by describing micro-level interaction processes of sufficient abstraction (Hedström 2005) that they can be used in the investigation of hierarchy formation across many species of animals and, one hopes, in young children.

The micro-level nature of these features of interaction makes them difficult to reduce to pure individual-level processes. In order to do this, we would have to develop an individual-level theory that could account for each interaction that occurred in a group during hierarchy formation. Such a theory would have to deal with the enormous number of contingencies that affect which act will occur next in a group establishing a hierarchy—the spatial layout of the animals, their previous interactions, their physiological states, their memories of what actions took place previously, their motivational states, and so on. We believe that a theory of this sort is beyond our current level of scientific knowledge, even for the 'simpler' animals, not to mention humans, and that it may be something that will never be possible. Even dealing with the (gravitational) interactions among three or more inanimate objects, where the proper equations are already known, has proven to be extremely difficult! However, as demonstrated by the IP model, it is certainly within our capabilities, aided by the new methods described above for investigating interactions, to find features of interaction that do lead to the generation of linear hierarchies. We suggest that an IP approach may also prove helpful, if researchers gather the requisite data, to understand how networks and other social structures in small groups develop their characteristic structures.

24.4 MODELS FOR THE DEVELOPMENT OF STATUS HIERARCHIES IN HUMANS

In the Introduction to this chapter we indicated that informal hierarchies are widespread in human small groups, and that despite the lack of centralized decisions by the participants, a particular kind of hierarchy often takes the same structural forms across many different groups. We indicated that we wanted to explore the question of how informal hierarchies developed their typical structures by first looking at a parallel but simpler case: the development of linear dominance hierarchies in animal groups. We have now done so, and we have shown that theoretical models broadly based upon differences among individuals—either resulting from attributes that they possess before joining groups or from dynamically updated qualities that they develop during group formation—are not sufficient to explain the formation of linear structures. Instead of individual-level models, we have argued that explanations based upon micro-level dynamics of interaction assuming considerable sophistication in social cognition on the part of animals are more satisfactory. We now review some of the recent formal models for the development of hierarchies in human small groups. After this review, we compare the human and IP models. In brief, we find that the recent human models resemble the older, individual-oriented animal models in their theoretical approach, kinds of mechanisms suggested, and types of data that they attempt to fit.

Most of the recent formal models for the formation of hierarchies in human small groups have been influenced directly or in part by work in the 'expectation states' area (Berger, Cohen, and Zelditch 1966). Fişek, Berger, and Norman (1991) developed the first of these models. In their models, individuals develop expectations on the ability of other group members to aid in accomplishing group goals—for example, dependent upon their status outside the group (occupation, race, gender, etc.) or from differential standing as a result of interaction within the group. Building on this work, Fararo, Skvoretz, and their associates extended the expectation-states idea and combined it with tools from the study of social networks to develop an extensive series of models to account for hierarchies in both humans and animals (Fararo and Skvoretz 1988; Skvoretz and Fararo 1996; Skvoretz, Faust, and Fararo 1996). One of their innovations was to take the concept of bystander effects from animal models and use it in their models for humans: bystanders observed the actions of others, they could take actions towards those they observed interacting, and those interacting could take actions toward the bystanders. Some of their models also show another important innovation: rather than predicting a final-equilibrium structure for a status hierarchy, these models describe a dynamic process by which a hierarchy is generated.

24.4.1 Gould's model

Gould (2002) made the next major step in the development of models for human hierarchies. This model assumes the most sophisticated levels of individual social awareness and reactions of any of the major human models, and we review it in some detail in preparation for comparing it and the other human models to the IP approach. Gould begins by noting two alternative theoretical positions in the explanation of status hierarchies in humans. One theoretical position sees hierarchies as 'a natural or *emergent* phenomenon reflecting underlying variations in individual qualities' and the other sees hierarchies as being 'artificially imposed or *enacted* by interested parties' (Gould 2002: 1145). The first position is similar to the prior-attributes hypothesis, and the second has a rough resemblance to the bystander part of the WLB model. His aim is to create a model that bridges the gap between these two theoretical positions. In his model, individuals make evaluations of other group members (or, alternatively, choose or make attachments to other group members) that are dependent upon two aspects of the qualities of those members: (1) their scores on some easily recognizable individual-attribute measure and (2) the social evaluations of those individuals by other group members. In evaluating other group members, an individual also considers how each member will evaluate him/her: 'ego is drawn to match his or her attachments to group-level attributions of status (which themselves are merely the aggregate patterns of attachments), but this impulse is tempered by the desire for reciprocation from alter' (Gould 2002: 1170). Individuals with higher attribute scores tend to get higher evaluations, and these evaluations are further increased by positive feedback. Evaluations are expressed empirically by measures such as whom an individual chooses as a friend or talks to. A recipient of many such choices has higher status than one receiving fewer.

Although Gould's model can, in theory, predict specific structures of status hierarchies (e.g. actual numerical levels of attachment patterns), he does not use it to do so because he cannot easily estimate the values of some of the parameters in the mathematical formulation of the model. Instead, he manipulates the equations (takes derivatives, etc.) to derive a number of formal propositions about the attachment profiles of individuals, pairs, and groups. He then tests these propositions using three empirical data sets: Bales's study of verbal communication in task groups (1956); the observations of Blatz et al. of physical interactions among the Dionne quintuplets (1937); and Newcomb's study of friendship ratings in a college fraternity (1961). He checks whether the kinds of attachment patterns predicted by the propositions hold at statistically significant levels in the data sets. For example, one proposition, expressed informally, is that higher-status group members will direct weaker levels of attachment to lower-status members than vice versa. Overall, he finds that most of the patterns described in the propositions appear at statistically significant levels in the empirical data, and he concludes that there is a high level of support for his model.

24.4.2 Comparison of the human and interaction-process models

Overall, there is considerable agreement on goals and the general nature of the mechanisms that account for hierarchy formation in the human and IP models. Both types of models aim to explain the structural forms of hierarchies through mechanisms assuming that individuals are cognizant of, and influenced by, the actions of other group members. However, beyond this general similarity there are marked differences in the specific types of mechanisms, units of analysis, approaches to deriving explanations, kinds of data utilized, and acknowledgment of variability in the two models. These differences are largely dictated by the types of mechanisms that the models use. In the human models the mechanisms that generate hierarchy structures are *individual-level* ones—an individual 'attacks' or chooses other individuals depending upon such things as differences in attributes and the observed behaviors and choices of other group members. In the IP model, the mechanisms that generate hierarchy structures are the dynamics of micro-level interaction in *pairs* and *triads* such as lack of pair-flips, filling in component triads with initially transitive relationships, and speedy conversion of intransitive to transitive relationships. It seems particularly ironic that the mechanisms in the IP model, based upon data from chickens, suggest that individuals make inferences about chains of relationships involving three individuals, while the mechanisms in the human models only assume that individuals make inferences about relationships in pairs. Thus, even Gould's and Fararo and Skvoretz's models, which assume some of the most socially sophisticated actions on the part of individuals for the human models, fall short in incorporating the types of inferences that animals are verified to have and that the IP model finds necessary to explain their comparatively simple hierarchy structures.

The differences in how the two kinds of models were formulated help to explain the differences in the kinds of mechanisms that they use. In formulating the IP model we took what might be called an 'engineering' approach. We carefully observed and recorded the behavior of individuals forming hierarchies, and used this data set in developing our ideas of how the machinery of hierarchies might work. Given the richness of this data set, we were able to explore a variety of possible mechanisms based upon both individual actions and interaction processes. To do this we needed a set of methods that were different from most of those used for models of human hierarchies. In the end, as described above, we formulated a model based upon interaction processes.

In contrast, the method for formulating the human models was a 'reverse engineering' approach: the researcher relied upon reports of final-outcome structures for hierarchies and assorted experimental findings about groups reported in the literature in order to infer how the structures might have been produced. But the problem was that the machinery producing the hierarchies was no longer visible. Although both Fararo and Skvoretz's and Gould's models proposed that hierarchies got their structures through individual-level micro-dynamical processes, the data were not available in the literature to determine whether these processes actually occurred (but see Skvoretz and Fararo 1996 and Gould 2002 for some attempts to treat coarse-scale dynamics). We suggest that this way of developing models obscures and underestimates the richness, variability, and cognitive sophistication of human behavior in forming hierarchies and other kinds of social structures in small groups.

Finally, the two types of models are different in their acknowledgment of variation in the actions of individuals during hierarchy formation. The human models are not explicitly concerned with individual variability, and, indeed, with the lack of data on the micro-dynamics of individual behavior during hierarchy formation, it would be difficult for them to be so. Putting aside the daunting problem of estimating parameter values, the human models aim to predict a specific hierarchy structure for a specific group. The IP model has a different orientation. It acknowledges that there is great variation in the behavior of individuals during hierarchy formation, and, as a result, it attempts to find mechanisms that ensure linear hierarchy structures across groups in spite of that variation. In short, while the human models ignore the problem of individual variability, the IP models treats it as the core problem to be solved in understanding how hierarchies develop their characteristic structural form.

Conclusion

The essence of what we have done in this chapter is to point out that there are two fundamentally different theories for the forces that produce social organization in small groups of humans and animals. One theory maintains that these forces reside within individuals: in their various kinds of personal differences and in the various kinds of actions that they take within their groups. This is the concept behind the prior-attributes hypothesis, WLB models, and the various models for human status hierarchies. The other theory holds that these forces reside in features of interaction that occur during the group-formation process and that individual-level actions are too variable and unpredictable to be the basis for a satisfactory explanation of social structures in small groups. If the second theory is a more adequate view of social organization, it has fundamental implications for how we study the formation of hierarchies, networks, and other kinds of structures in small groups: the kinds of data that we collect, the kinds of methods we use for recording and analyzing data, and the kinds of models that we develop.

REFERENCES

ADDISON, W. E., and SIMMEL, E. C. (1970), 'The Relationship between Dominance and Leadership in a Flock of Ewes', *Bulletin of the Psychonomic Society*, 15: 303–5.

AMELL, S., personal communication.

BALES, R. F. (1953), 'The Equilibrium Problem in Small Groups', in T. Parsons, R. F. Bales, and E. A. Shils (eds.), *Working Papers in the Theory of Action* (Glencoe, Ill.: Free Press), 111–65.

—— (1956), 'Task Status and Likeability as a Function of Talking and Listening in Decision-Making Groups', in L. D. White (ed.), *The State of the Social Sciences* (Chicago Ill.: University of Chicago Press), 148–61.

—— et al. (1951), 'Channels of Communication in Small Groups', *American Sociological Review*, 16: 461–8.

BARCHAS, P. R., and MENDOZA, S. P. (1984), 'Emergent Hierarchical Relationships in Rhesus Macaques: An Application of Chase's Model', in P. R. Barchas (ed.), *Social Hierarchies: Essays Toward a Sociophysiological Perspective* (Westport, Conn.: Greenwood).

BARKAN, C. P. L., et al. (1986), 'Social Dominance in Communal Mexican Jays *Aphelocoma-Ultramarina*', *Animal Behaviour*, 34: 175–87.

BEACHAM, J. L. (1988), 'The Relative Importance of Body Size and Aggressive Experience as Determinants of Dominance in Pumpkinseed Sunfish, *Lepomis-gibbosus*', *Animal Behaviour*, 36: 621–3.

BERGER, J., COHEN, B. P., and ZELDITCH, M. (1966), 'Status Characteristics and Expectation States', in J. Berger, M. Zelditch, and B. Anderson (eds.), *Sociological Theories in Progress*, i (Boston, Mass.: Houghton Mifflin), 29–46.

BLATZ, W. E., et al. (1937), *Collected Studies of the Dionne Quintuplets* (Toronto: University of Toronto Press).

BONABEAU, E., THERAULAZ, G., and DENEUBOURG, J.-L. (1999), 'Dominance Orders in Animal Societies: The Self-organization Hypothesis Revisited', *Bulletin of Mathematical Biology*, 61: 727–57.

Bond, A. B., Kamil, A. C., and Balda, R. P. (2003), 'Social Complexity and Transitive Inference in Corvids', *Animal Behaviour*, 65: 479–87.

Brown, J. A., and Colgan, P. W. (1986), 'Individual and Species Recognition in Centrachid Fishes: Evidence and Hypotheses', *Behavioral Ecology and Sociobiology*, 19: 373–9.

Chase, I. D. (1974), 'Models of Hierarchy Formation in Animal Societies', *Behavioral Science*, 19: 374–82.

—— (1982a), 'Behavioral Sequences during Dominance Hierarchy Formation in Chickens', *Science*, 216 (4544): 439–40.

—— (1982b), 'Dynamics of Hierarchy Formation: The Sequential Development of Dominance Relationships', *Behaviour*, 80: 218–40.

—— (1985), 'The Sequential Analysis of Aggressive Acts during Hierarchy Formation: An Application of the "Jigsaw Puzzle" Approach', *Animal Behaviour*, 33: 86–100.

—— (2006), 'Music Notation: A New Method for Visualizing Social Interaction in Animals and Humans', *Frontiers in Zoology*, 3: 18.

—— and Rohwer, S. (1987), 'Two Methods for Quantifying the Development of Dominance Hierarchies in Large Groups with Applications to Harris' Sparrows', *Animal Behaviour*, 35: 1113–28.

—— Bartolomeo, C., and Dugatkin, L. A. (1994), 'Aggressive Interactions and Intercontest Interval: How Long Do Winners Keep Winning', *Animal Behaviour*, 48 (2): 393–00.

—— Tovey, C., and Murch, P. (2003), 'Two's Company, Three's a Crowd: Differences in Dominance Relationships in Isolated Versus Socially Embedded Pairs of Fish', *Behaviour*, 140: 1193–217.

—— et al. (2002), 'Individual Differences Versus Social Dynamics in the Formation of Animal Dominance Hierarchies', *Proceedings of the National Academy of Sciences of the USA*, 99 (8): 5744–9.

Cheney, D. L., and Seyfarth, R. M. (1990), *How Monkeys See the World: Inside the Mind of Another Species* (Chicago, Ill.: University of Chicago Press).

Clutton-Brock, T. H., Albon, S. D., and Guinness, F. E. (1984), 'Maternal Dominance, Breeding Success and Birth Sex-ratios in Red Deer', *Nature*, 308 (5957): 358–60.

Coleman, J. S. (1986), 'Social Theory, Social Research, and a Theory of Action', *American Journal of Sociology*, 91 (6): 1309–35.

—— (1990), 'Commentary: Social Institutions and Social theory', *American Sociological Review*, 55 (3): 333–9.

Davis, H. (1992), 'Transitive Inference in Rats (*Rattus norvegicus*)', *Journal of Comparative Psychology*, 106: 342–9.

Davis, J. A. (1970), 'Clustering and Hierarchy in Interpersonal Relations—Testing 2 Graph-theoretical Models on 742 Sociomatrices', *American Sociological Review*, 35 (5): 843–51.

D'Eath, R. B., and Keeling, L. J. (2003), 'Social Discrimination and Aggression by Laying Hens in Large Groups: From Peck Orders to Social Tolerance', *Applied Animal Behaviour Science*, 84: 197–212.

D'Ettorre, P., and Heinze, J. (2005), 'Individual Recognition in Ant Queens', *Current Biology*, 15: 2170–4.

Drews, C. (1993), 'The Concept and Definition of Dominance in Animal Behavior', *Behaviour*, 125: 283–313.

DUGATKIN, L. A. (1997), 'Winner and Loser Effects and the Structure of Dominance Hierarchies', *Behavioral Ecology*, 8 (6): 583–7.

EATON, G. G. (1984), 'Aggression in Adult Male Primates: A Comparison of Confined Japanese Macaques and Free-ranging Olive Baboons', *International Journal of Primatology*, 5 (2): 145–60.

FARARO, T. J., and SKVORETZ, J. (1988), 'Dynamics of the Formation of Stable Dominance Structures', in M. Webster and M. Foschi (eds.), *Status Generalization: New Theory and Research* (Stanford, Calif.: Stanford University Press).

FERSEN, L. VON, et al. (1991), 'Transitive Inference Formation in Pigeons', *Journal of Experimental Psychology: Animal Behavior Processes*, 17: 334–41.

FIŞEK, M. H., BERGER, J., and NORMAN, R. Z. (1991), 'Participation in Heterogeneous and Homogeneous Groups: A Theoretical Integration', *American Journal of Sociology*, 97 (1): 114–42.

GHERARDI, F., and ATEMA, J. (2005), 'Memory of Social Partners in Hermit Crab Dominance', *Ethology*, 111 (3): 271–85.

GILLIAN, D. J. (1981), 'Reasoning in the Chimpanzee, II. Transitive Inference', *Journal of Experimental Psychology: Animal Behavior Processes*, 7: 87–108.

GOESSMANN, C., HEMELRIJK, C., and HUBER, R. (2000), 'The Formation and Maintenance of Crayfish Hierarchies: Behavioral and Self-structuring Properties', *Behavioral Ecology and Sociobiology*, 48 (6): 418–28.

GOULD, R. V. (2002), 'The Origins of Status Hierarchies: A Formal Theory and Empirical Test', *American Journal of Sociology*, 107 (5): 1143–78.

GROSENICK, L., CLEMENT, T. S., and FERNALD, R. D. (2007), 'Fish Can Infer Social Rank by Observation Alone', *Nature*, 445: 429–32.

HAUSFATER, G., ALTMANN, J., and ALTMANN, S. (1982), 'Long-term Consistency of Dominance Relations among Female Baboons (*Papio-cynocephalus*)', *Science*, 217 (4561): 752–5.

HEDSTRÖM, P. (2005), *Dissecting the Social* (Cambridge: Cambridge University Press).

HEINZE, J. (1990), 'Dominance Behavior Among Ant Females', *Naturwissenschaften*, 77: 41–3.

—— personal communication.

HEMELRIJK, C. K. (1999), 'An Individual-orientated Model of the Emergence of Despotic and Egalitarian Societies', *Proceedings of the Royal Society of London*, B 266: 361–9.

HOLENKAMP, K. E., and SMALE, L. (1993), 'Ontogeny of Dominance in Free-living Spotted Hyenas: Juvenile Rank Relations with Other Immature Individuals', *Animal Behaviour*, 46 (3): 451–66.

HOLLAND, P. W., and LEINHARD, S. (1970), 'Method for Detecting Structure in Sociometric Data', *American Journal of Sociology*, 76 (3): 492–513.

JACKSON, W. M., and WINNEGRAD, R. L. (1988), 'Linearity in Dominance Hierarchies: A Second Look at the Individual Attributes Model', *Animal Behaviour*, 36: 1237–40.

JOHNSEN, E. C. (1985), 'Network Macrostructure Models for the Davis-Leinhardt Set of Empirical Sociomatrices', *Social Networks*, 7 (3): 203–24.

KARAVANICH, C., and ATEMA, J. (1998), 'Individual Recognition and Memory in Lobster Dominance', *Animal Behaviour*, 56: 1553–60.

LAI, W.-S., et al. (2005), 'Recognition of Familiar Individuals in Golden Hamsters: A New Method and Functional Neuroanatomy', *Journal of Neuroscience*, 25: 11239–47.

LANDAU, H. G. (1951), 'On Dominance Relations and Structures of Animal Societies', *Bulletin of Mathematical Biophysics*, 13: 1–19.

LAZAREVA, O. F. (2004), 'Transitive Responding in Hooded Crow Requires Linearly Ordered Stimuli', *Journal of the Experimental Analysis of Behavior*, 82: 1–19.

LINDQUIST, W. B., and CHASE, I. D. (2008), 'Data-based Analysis of Winner–Loser Models of Hierarchy Formation in Animals', Stony Brook University, Department of Applied Mathematics and Statistics report SUNYSB-AMS-07-06, Stony Brook, N.Y.

MCLEMAN, M. A., et al. (2005), 'Discrimination of Conspecifics by Juvenile Domestic Pigs, *Sus scrofa*', *Animal Behaviour*, 70: 451–61.

MENDOZA, S. P., and BARCHAS, P. R. (1983), 'Behavioral Processes Leading to Linear Status Hierarchies Following Group Formation in Rhesus Monkeys', *Journal of Human Evolution*, 12 (2): 185–92.

NELISSEN, M. H. J. (1985), 'Structure of the Dominance Hierarchy and Dominance Determining Group Factors in *Melanochromic auratus* (Pices, Cichlidae)', *Behaviour*, 94: 85–107.

NEWCOMB, T. M. (1961), *The Acquaintance Process* (New York: Holt, Rinehart & Winston).

OLIVEIRA, R. F., MCGREGOR, P. K., and LATRUFFE, C. (1998), 'Know Thine Enemy: Fighting Fish Gather Information from Observing Conspecific Interactions', *Proceedings of the Royal Society of London Series B-Biological Sciences*, 265 (1401): 1045–49.

——et al. (2001), 'Watching Fights Raises Fish Hormone Levels—Cichlid Fish Wrestling for Dominance Induce an Androgen Surge in Male Spectators', *Nature*, 409 (6819): 475.

PAZ-Y-MINO, G., et al. (2004), 'Pinyon Jays use Transitive Inference to Predict Social Dominance', *Nature*, 430 (7001): 778–81.

POST, W. (1992), 'Dominance and Mating Success in Male Boat-tailed Grackles', *Animal Behaviour*, 44 (5): 917–29.

RALEIGH, M. J., et al. (1991), 'Serotonergic Mechanisms Promote Dominance Acquisition in Adult Male Vervet Monkeys', *Brain Research*, 559 (2): 181–90.

RAPOPORT, A. (1950), 'Outline of a Mathematical Theory of Peck Right', *Biometrics*, 6 (3): 330–41.

ROBERTS, W. A., and PHELPS, M. T. (1994), 'Transitive Inference in Rats: A Test of the Spatial Coding Hypothesis', *Psychological Science*, 5: 368–74.

SAPOLSKY, R. M., and SHARE, L. J. (1994), 'Rank-related Differences in Cardiovascular Function Among Wild Baboons: Role of Sensitivity to Glucocorticoids', *American Journal of Primatology*, 32 (4): 261–75.

SAVIN-WILLIAMS, R. C. (1980), 'Dominance Hierarchies in Groups of Middle to Late Adolescent Males', *Journal of Youth and Adolescence*, 9 (1): 75–85.

SKVORETZ, J., and FARARO, T. J. (1996), 'Status and Participation in Task Groups: A Dynamic Network Model', *American Journal of Sociology*, 101 (5): 1366–414.

——FAUST, K., and FARARO, T. J. (1996), 'Social Structure, Networks, and E-state Structuralism Models', *Journal of Mathematical Sociology*, 21 (1–2): 57–76.

STEIRN, J. N., WEAVER, J. E., and ZENTALL, T. R. (1995), 'Transitive Inference in Pigeons: Simplified Procedures and a Test of Value Transfer Theory', *Animal Learning and Behavior*, 23: 76–82.

TIBBETTS, E. A. (2002), 'Visual Signals of Individual Identity in the Wasp *Polistes fuscatus*', *Proceedings of the Royal Society of London* B 269: 1423–8.

Todd, J. H., Atema, J., and Bardach, J. E. (1967), 'Chemical Communication in Social Behavior of a Fish, the Yellow Bullhead (*Ictalurus natalis*)', *Science*, 158: 672–3.

Vannini, M., and Sardini, A. (1971), 'Aggressivity and Dominance in River Crab *Potomon fluviantile* (Herbst)', *Monitore Zoologico Italiano*, 5: 173–213.

Wilson, E. O. (1975), *Sociobiology* (Cambridge, Mass.: Harvard University Press).

Yurkovic, A., et al. (2006), 'Learning and Memory Associated with Aggression in *Drosophila melanogaster*', *Proceedings of the National Academy of Sciences of the USA*, 103: 17519–24.

CHAPTER 25

......

CONFLICT*

......

STATHIS KALYVAS

INTRODUCTION

......

CONSIDER Iraq between 2003 and 2008, the site of overlapping violent civil conflicts. There is no denying the centrality of the 'sectarian' division, pitting Shia against Sunni Iraqis. Nevertheless, this was hardly the only type of violence in Iraq. In the south, Shiite factions fought each other; in the west and around the capital Bagdhad, rival Sunni factions faced off; and in the north, Sunni Kurds clashed with Sunni Arabs. In fact, a multitude of political actors emerged since the 2003 US invasion, including insurgent groups of various persuasions, political parties, religious factions, local militias, semiautonomous military and police units, militarized tribes and subtribes, and criminal gangs. The political landscape is characterized by a high level of fragmentation, with many groups switching sides, most notably former Sunni insurgents who joined US forces. A journalist described a gloomy reality where 'the lives of most Iraqis are dominated by a complex array of militias and gangs that are ruthlessly competing with one another, and whose motives for killing are more often economic or personal than religious or ideological' (Packer 2007: 58).

Even 'sectarian violence' turns out to be far from an uncontested category. Journalists point to a variety of sordid motivations underlying this violence, including bad blood between neighbors or the desire to expropriate a neighbor's house; they refer to 'the very intimate nature of the war in Iraq—a war in which your enemies are often people you've known much of your life; in which your neighbors are often

* I am grateful to Meredith Rolfe for her excellent comments on the first draft of this chapter.

behind the crimes committed against you; in which every slight, every misdeed, every injustice is recorded and the desire for vengeance runs deep' (Parker 2007).

Extreme fragmentation and confusion surrounding motives are hardly specific to Iraq. Many violent internal conflicts are characterized by a high level of complexity and fluidity, with a proliferation of actors and with motivations varying depending on the vantage point. Local and self-interested motivations at the micro level appear to coexist uneasily with abstract and general motivations at the macro level. In fact, violent internal conflict tends to give rise to two apparently contradictory observations.

On the one hand, much of the violence taking place in contexts characterized by intense political and social conflict is described as the outcome of abstract group-level dynamics (e.g. Horowitz 1985). In fact, group-level descriptions (e.g. 'Serbs versus Albanians'; 'Sunni versus Shia Iraqis or Lebanese') inform the theoretical connection between violent action on the ground and its macro-level antecedents. This link is best encapsulated by the concept of polarization, which refers to the intensity of divisions between groups, 'when a large number of conflict group members attach overwhelming importance to the issues at stake, or manifest strongly held antagonistic beliefs and emotions toward the opposing segment, or both' (Nordlinger 1972: 9).

On the other hand, the magnification of one's focus often shows specific acts of violence to be intimate, exercised between people who know each other personally—in many cases between peers. Violence in the context of civil war, more particularly, is frequently exercised among people who share everyday ties of social and spatial interaction, such as neighborhood or kinship. This explains the commonality of the term 'fratricide' and the frequent references to the biblical story of Abel and Cain. Furthermore, intimate violence often appears to be based on trivial everyday motivations rather than abstract enmity. In fact, there is a close connection between the intimate character of violence and the local setting within which it takes place. For example, Spencer (2000: 134) describes how the JVP (Janatha Vimukthi Peramuna: People's Liberation Front) insurgency in Sri Lanka 'permeated the capillary relations of everyday interaction: your political opponents would be neighbors usually, kin often, former friends sometimes.'

Are these two views, abstract enmity and intimate conflict, as contradictory as they appear to be? Are the insights derived from close observation due to an observer's particular vantage point or do they carry broader theoretical implications? Is it possible to reconcile the intimate and local dimension of violence revealed by detailed observation with the focus on abstract group violence that informs most theorizing on this subject? Is it possible to connect individual-level and group-level actions? If yes, how?

In this chapter I argue in favor of an analytical approach to conflict that reconciles these apparently contradictory insights. This approach accepts that agency is located simultaneously at different levels of aggregation; it explains how conflict causes action and the formation of collective identities, much as collective identities give rise to conflict and action. Put otherwise, an analytical approach to the study of conflict demonstrates and incorporates the fundamentally interactive, bidirectional, or *endogenous* relation of conflict and action. Unpacking this relationship requires a clear understanding of the link between individual and group action in the production of conflict.

This chapter is divided in four main sections. In the first I review some of the challenges raised by the study of conflict, discuss popular theorizations, and outline key arguments. In the second section I turn to interpersonal conflict as a way to illustrate the application of an analytical approach to individual-level dynamics; in the third section I focus on ethnic and class conflict in order to discuss the application of this approach to group-level dynamics; and in the fourth section, I turn to civil war and discuss the links between individual-level and group-level logics.

25.1 CONFLICT

Conflict can be defined very broadly as an outcome of the 'purposeful interaction among two or more parties in a competitive setting' (Oberschall 1978: 291). In his influential analysis of conflict, Georg Simmel (1955: 14) described conflict as 'one of the most vivid interactions' among humans, whose causes could be traced to 'dissociating' factors such as 'hate, envy, need, [and] desire.' Although conflict has acquired a negative connotation, it is not perceived as necessarily dysfunctional. Simmel (1955) and Coser (1956) argued convincingly that conflict is functional from a social point of view, because it is an expression of the plural views and interests that exist in society, and its resolution allows the emergence of unity from conflicting multiplicity.

Conflict is as old as human history—and so the history of reflecting on conflict is also old. Simplifying what is an enormous literature, it is possible to discern a major divide between approaches stressing the role of groups, and arguments focusing primarily on individuals. This chapter argues against this dichotomy and makes the case for a theoretically and empirically explicit connection between individual and group action. Achieving such a connection allows us to grasp the fundamentally bidirectional or endogenous relation between conflict and action; it allows us to connect agency at different levels of aggregation, thus resolving the puzzle of contradictory motivations; and it finally allows us to grasp the 'creative' dimension of conflict which shapes individual and collective identities.

Conflict takes a wild multiplicity of forms, from disputes between spouses and neighbors, to wars between states. Because its forms are so varied, conflict has been divided into different types and studied accordingly. Perhaps the most common distinction is between violent and nonviolent conflict (Brubaker and Laitin 1998).

Nonviolent conflict covers, most obviously, politics as a general category. Harold Lasswell's 1936 book carries a title that still serves as a popular definition: *Politics: Who Gets What, When, How*. In this vein, democracy is seen as a way of managing conflict; that is, of transforming what is potentially violent conflict into a nonviolent activity. Seen from this perspective, the entire discipline of political science is preoccupied with the study of political and social conflict and its management, with Hobbes's *Leviathan* being an early, yet foundational, example.

Beyond the study of how institutions 'tame' politics by eliminating its potential for violence, a particularly fertile field of scholarly research on nonviolent conflict has been the study of 'contentious action'—a term referring to nonviolent forms of collective protest such as mass demonstrations and strikes (McAdam, Tarrow, and Tilly 2001).

It would be fair to say that violent conflict has always exercised considerable fascination over researchers. Three types of violent conflict, in particular, have attracted sustained scholarly attention: criminal violence, riots and pogroms, and war in all its varied forms. 'Deviant' behavior has been the object of considerable study and the specialized field of criminology (Sampson and Laub 1992; Birkbeck and LaFree 1993). Research on riots and pogroms (often defined as 'ethnic') has taken off in recent years; in particular, studies of Hindu–Muslim riots in India by Varshney (2003) and Wilkinson (2006) have moved our understanding of this phenomenon onto a new plane.

Scale is the main distinguishing characteristic between criminal violence and ethnic riots, on the one hand, and war, on the other. Though violent criminal activity can range from individual (e.g. a single homicide) to collective (e.g. clashes between organized gangs or between gangs and state forces), it rarely reaches the level of collective mobilization usually associated with war. Likewise, fatalities caused by ethnic riots, while considerable, typically fail to reach major-war levels. War is usually defined as large-scale organized violence between political units (Levy 1983), a definition that applies primarily to international war. Internal or civil war, the most common form of armed conflict since 1945, has been defined as armed combat within the boundaries of a recognized sovereign entity between parties subject to a common authority at the outset of the hostilities (Kalyvas 2006). Operational definitions of both international and civil war rely on a fatality threshold—usually 1,000 battle-related fatalities (Singer and Small 1972).

Unsurprisingly, there has been considerable fragmentation in the study of conflict. Crime is studied by criminologists who are active in the discipline of sociology; international war has been the province of either historians or political scientists associated with the subfield of international relations; and civil war has been the province primarily of political-science scholars focusing on domestic politics, and hence the subfield of comparative politics.[1] Additional distinctions cut through these divisions. For instance, anthropologists have focused on the local level and social psychologists on the individual level; the study of war onset has been differentiated from that of war termination; and so on. As a result, theories, methodologies, and data sources have diverged considerably, thus giving rise to a fragmented field of inquiry.

Underlining this fragmentation in the study of conflict is a fundamental methodological divide between two styles of research. One approach, dominant in sociology and political science, adopts a group-level perspective (a) taking groups as exogenously given and fixed and (b) deriving individual interactions directly from group interactions. This has been the standard approach in studies of class conflict (Dahrendorf 1959; Moore 1966), as well as ethnic conflict (Horowitz 1985; Petersen 2002). To use the example of present-day conflict in Iraq, these approaches begin by positing groups in conflict (Shia, Sunni, Kurd) and proceed to interpret individual actions as resulting from this overarching conflict. This type of analysis tends to misinterpret a great deal of the conflict and violence on the ground, missing how the violence shapes individual and collective identities and contributes to the escalation of conflict.

The alternative approach, dominant in social psychology and economics, adopts an individual-level perspective which assumes that collective-level conflict is an aggregation of individual-level tendencies or choices. Using evidence from laboratory experiments, social psychologists have argued that individuals have a natural tendency to aggregate in groups, which then become embroiled in conflicts (Tajfel and Turner [1979] 2004). In this view, conflicts emerge primarily from the stickiness of the individual association with these groups rather than past hostility or a conflict of interests. It is the omnipresent human tendency toward intergroup discrimination favoring the in-group (the so-called 'in-group bias') which is at the root of conflict. In contrast, economists tend to see groups as concatenations of individuals making rational choices based on their economic interests. Conflict emerges once similar individual interests, be they political or economic in nature (Downs 1957) or ethnic (Caselli and Coleman 2006), aggregate into collective ones.

Although psychological and economic approaches differ in their fundamental epistemology, they reach an understanding of group conflict that parallels that of sociological approaches. To return to the example of Iraq, psychological and economic approaches would interpret the current conflict in much the same vein as sociological ones, with the difference that they would provide a general theory for individual participation in group activities, something lacking from the latter. Hence, despite their epistemological differences, the dominant approaches to the study of conflict tend to neglect the dynamic relation between individuals and groups and, therefore, the potentially endogenous relation between conflict and action.

There is an alternative, however—one that specifies microfoundations and focuses on the process of interaction between individual and group action. Recent examples include the analysis by Fearon and Laitin (1996) of interethnic cooperation and the research of Fehr and Gachter (2000) on the role of norms of fairness and reciprocity for in-group cooperation. The former argue that intragroup disciplining of group members who misbehave toward outsiders explains the relative scarcity of intergroup conflict; the latter use laboratory experiments to show that individuals are willing to disregard considerable costs so as to discipline group members attempting to free-ride out of group collective action.

This recent research trend (which focuses on cooperation more than conflict) adopts an analytical strategy combining two elements. First is theoretical disaggregation or microfoundational analysis, following the seminal work of Thomas Schelling (1978); in Coleman's (1990: 503) formulation: 'Any theory of action requires a theory of the elementary actor. The elementary actor is the wellspring of action, no matter how complex are the structures through which action takes place.' Second is empirical disaggregation, which entails the empirical testing of micromechanisms in order to show how individual and collective actors connect with each other.

To show the benefits of this analytical strategy on the study of conflict, I discuss three types of conflict: (a) interpersonal conflict, (b) ethnic and class conflict, and (c) civil wars. Each section is anchored in one key work: Roger Gould's *Collision of Wills*, Adam Przeworski's *Capitalism and Social Democracy*, and Stathis Kalyvas's *The Logic of Violence in Civil War*. The objective is to illustrate diverse yet consistent strategies of theoretical and empirical disaggregation and to show how they help us come to grips with the endogenous dynamics that characterize individual and group conflict. Furthermore, I wish to show how these different types of conflict, usually treated in isolation, can benefit from a more integrated approach.

25.2 INTERPERSONAL CONFLICT—INDIVIDUAL-LEVEL DYNAMICS

In *Collision of Wills* Roger Gould endeavors to build a theory of interpersonal conflict and specify its links to group conflict. The originality of his undertaking is straightforward: interpersonal conflict has generally been studied as a self-contained topic. Conversely, large-scale social conflicts, articulated along macro cleavages and relating to a key political dimension such as class or ethnicity, have generally not been empirically connected to individual dynamics.[2]

Gould focuses on dynamics: his central motivating puzzle is the transformation of conflict from individual to collective and from nonviolent to violent—how to explain the fact that some interpersonal disputes escalate into violence despite arising from trivial motives such as minor debts, derisive remarks, or insults. Indeed, such violence is often described as 'senseless.' In other words, the goal is to account for the enormous gap between the trivial character of the dispute and the violence of the outcome. In fact, considerable research in the field of criminology suggests that criminal homicide tends to be intimate; a large part of nonpredatory common murder implicates relatives, friends, or at least acquaintances. Furthermore, the relationship between victims and assailants tends to be horizontal: people often kill their mates, friends, and acquaintances rather than their bosses (Black 1976; Katz 1988; Black 1993; Decker 1993).[3]

The answer to this puzzle lies in a specific mechanism: repeated interaction between individuals generates more or less formal social ranking; yet these emerging hierarchies can be highly consequential. For instance, honor is a reflection of informal, yet powerful, hierarchies. Conflict emerges when these hierarchies are challenged; and they are challenged when they appear to be ambiguous—either because previously well-established relations between individuals have changed or because new definitions of social status have emerged. The main implication is that conflict is likely to erupt among peers—people whose social status is comparable— rather than among people who are located on the opposite ends of the social spectrum. In short, Gould predicts that closeness and similarity, rather than distance and difference, are at the root of interpersonal violent conflict. This prediction challenges the social-psychological literature.

In turn, a number of testable implications are derived from this empirical prediction. They include the correlation between the outbreak of violent conflict and (a) the symmetry of relationships, (b) the ambiguity of hierarchy, and (c) (more remotely) political instability. The empirical tests take place at multiple levels of aggregation and are based on several distinct bodies of data, including a statistical analysis of homicides in two American and two Indian districts. The main causal variables are the presence of verbal arguments prior to the eruption of violence and the ambiguity of the hierarchical relations between perpetrator and victim. Gould finds that where hierarchy is ambiguous verbal disputes are more likely to escalate into homicides.

The next step consists in exploring the degree to which this argument can be generalized to group conflict. Gould reasons through analogy: groups relate to each other in the same fashion as individuals do. The analog of individual symmetry is group solidarity; that is, the willingness of individuals to sacrifice something for the group's well-being. When solidarity within the group appears to be in question, a rival group is likely to challenge it so as to move up the hierarchical ladder. This argument is ingeniously tested with data from nineteenth-century Corsica, an island society characterized by two dimensions that rarely overlap: on the one hand, extensive premodern practices of blood feud or vendetta and, on the other hand, a modern police and judicial bureaucracy that were able to collect reliable data. Gould asks whether interpersonal violence always escalates into group violence, as one would expect in a blood-feuding society. Surprisingly, he finds that only a small proportion of interpersonal violent confrontations escalate into group violence. However, those that escalate into group violence do exhibit characteristics that are consistent with his theoretical expectations. An interesting and important empirical finding is that of all cases of group violence studied, only one-fifth turned out to have escalated from interpersonal violence. This finding points to the heterogeneity of conflict: some conflicts begin at the group level and then escalate among individuals while others begin among individuals and escalate up to the group level.

Though Gould's account is not rationalist, it is analytical. Individuals are the main building block and group interactions are predicated on individual choices which are embedded in social relationships. Intergroup violence is unpacked and intragroup dynamics are connected to intergroup conflict, an insight taken successfully by recent research in different settings (e.g. Lawrence 2007). However, Gould follows the sociological tradition that takes groups to be exogenously given and fixed. Individual membership is not a choice, and the scaling from individual-level dynamics to group-level dynamics remains fuzzy, which is why the argument's scope conditions exclude large-scale violence.

In short, Gould supplies an analytical account of interpersonal conflict and its escalation into violence based on sound empirical microfoundations, yet he limits his analysis to individuals and small groups. A final question emerges. Is it possible to expand this type of analysis to take into account large-group conflict, while also moving away from the assumption that groups are stable and fixed? Is it possible to build a theoretically and empirically sound micro-level analysis of conflict that generalizes to macro-level conflict?

25.3 ETHNIC AND CLASS CONFLICT— GROUP-LEVEL DYNAMICS

Moving up the ladder from interpersonal to group conflict we encounter two important streams of research, one focusing on ethnic conflict and the other on class conflict. Let me begin with a discussion of ethnic conflict. Initially developed in the aftermath of decolonization, this literature is undergoing a renaissance following the end of the cold war and the realization that ethnic conflict is, after all, quite alive. It is impossible to summarize this very extensive body of work. Nevertheless, one can point to a number of important traditions.

One tradition has focused on the development of nationalism and national identity in Europe and has emphasized a variety of processes, most notably modernization and urbanization (Deutsch 1953) and urban/rural conflict in multiethnic empires (Gellner 1983). Another tradition has looked into the postcolonial world (Horowitz 1985) and, unlike the former, has approached ethnic identity as given rather than constructed. Ethnic conflict emerges either in the process of construction of ethnic and national identities or in the process of competition between groups already formed in pursuit of resources, political power, or status.

With few exceptions, this literature has focused on group-level dynamics (e.g. Petersen 2002; Varshney 2003; Wilkinson 2006). Even those trying to unpack groups have primarily looked less at followers and more at leaders or 'elites,' often framed as 'political entrepreneurs' who are stirring ethnic hatred and conflict, either in pursuit of personal political power (Figueiredo and Weingast 1999) or because they misinterpret the intentions of their ethnic rivals under conditions of heightened uncertainty, in what is known as a 'security dilemma' (Posen 1993). In these accounts, individuals tend to be bundled into an undifferentiated mass that responds to fear by engaging in violence. As pointed out above, Fearon and Laitin (1996) focus on individuals by reversing the standard question of ethnic conflict and asking why ethnic conflict is so rare (and ethnic peace so frequent) compared to its actual possibility given the number of extant ethnic groups. They argue that a powerful mechanism of 'in-group policing' exists, whereby the group punishes its members who misbehave toward members of another group; as a result cooperation tends to prevail over defection.

Class conflict occupied the center of the field of political sociology, perhaps until the end of the cold war. Influenced by either the historical analysis of cleavages which relates the type of salient political division in a country to the historical process of state- and nation-building (Lipset and Rokkan 1967), or the Marxist perspective of class struggle as a reflection of the unequal distribution of the means of production, combined with an analysis of class coalitions (Moore 1966), this body of research sought to explain the variation in intensity of class conflict across societies, as well as its outcomes. The focus was squarely placed on groups; individuals were assumed to belong to groups based on their 'objective' economic interests.

A key concept in explaining the emergence of group conflict, whether ethnic, class, religious, or ideological, is polarization, which comes with a variety of adjectives: it can be of an ideological, religious, class, or ethnic nature. Polarization entails an interaction between groups that simultaneously display high internal homogeneity and high external heterogeneity (Esteban and Ray 1994). Populations clustered around a small number of distant but equally large poles, this intuition goes, are likely to clash. The underlining mechanism is dislike so intense as to cancel even fraternal ties, imagined or real. Groups thus signaled by collective identities produce conflict. This is what Buruma (2002: 12) has in mind when he writes of 'what gets the blood boiling, what makes people do unspeakable things to their neighbors. It is the fuel used by agitators to set whole countries on fire.' Although polarized conflicts entail issues of material distribution, they can escalate so as to be 'no longer over specific gains or losses but over conceptions of moral right and over the interpretation of history and human destiny' (Lipset and Rokkan 1967: 11). They can turn, in other words, into 'the kind of intense and divisive politics one may refer to by the name of *absolute politics*' (Perez-Díaz 1993: 6). Seen from this perspective, conflict constitutes the very essence of politics. The *political*, as Schmitt (1976) argued, is the most extreme antagonism pitting one fighting collectivity of people against another; politics is but the reflection of the fundamental distinction between friend and enemy. Hence, war is just the natural expression of enmity; as Lenin pointed out, civil war in a class-based society is but an extension of the class struggle in it (in Martin 1995: 61); and because, as Bobbio (1992: 303) observed, the relationship between a just war and a just enemy is inverse, i.e. a war is just when the enemy is unjust, unjust enemies need no mercy. As a result, the fundamental insight of this argument is that violence is secreted from deep divisions and that barbaric violence is the inevitable result of polarized conflict which constitutes the very essence of politics.

Though plausible, this argument faces four important challenges. First, and most obviously, it wildly overpredicts violent conflict (Fearon and Laitin 1996). Second, it entails a kind of backward reasoning, from on-the-ground violence to the factors that are believed to have produced it in the first place. Linking polarization between groups on the one hand and violence on the other implies an underlying causal claim that both predicts the relevant perpetrator–victim dyad and assigns a motive to the violence. For example, the relevant dyad in a class war includes the owners of capital and the owners of labor. In an ethnic war this dyad includes members of different ethnic groups. The argument follows a two-step logic. First a group is targeted because of its position on the relevant cleavage dimension, and subsequently individuals belonging to this group are victimized because of their membership in this group. Hence, this argument explains simultaneously group conflict and interpersonal violence. The problem is that this causal link is generally assumed rather than demonstrated empirically. We observe a specific action, e.g. an Iraqi Shia victimizing an Iraqi Sunni, and conclude that these individuals are fully intercheangable (i.e. they are irrelevant *qua* individuals), and that this particular action is the outcome of an abstract group-level conflict—in this particular instance of sectarian conflict. Third, this argument carries an important empirical implication; namely, that the highest form of domestic political conflict, civil war, is caused by deep group divisions. However, there exists a significant body of empirical research suggesting that high levels of social, religious, or ethnic polarization fail to explain the outbreak of civil war; they appear to be neither a necessary nor a sufficient condition (e.g. Laitin 2001; Collier et al. 2003). Furthermore, the absence of a good indicator for polarization has concealed the fact that, as empirical evidence suggests, even in societies that are deeply polarized, only a minority of the population can really be described as holding tightly to one pole or the other; the majority tends to remain either weakly committed or uncommitted, part of a 'grey zone' between the two poles (Malefakis 1996: 26; Seidman 2002). When more systematic data are available, as in Yugoslavia, the link between prewar group-level polarization and war appears tenuous. From a cross-sectional perspective, there was an inverse relationship between prewar polarization and civil war, with Bosnia scoring very high on interethnic tolerance (Hodson, Sekulic, and Massey 1994); from a temporal perspective, there was little change in mass indicators of nationalist attitudes in Croatia from 1984 to 1989, suggesting that polarization increased just before and immediately after the civil war erupted (Sekulic 2005). Fourth, this argument implies that conflicts with deep pre-existing cleavages should be, *ceteris paribus*, more barbaric than civil wars motivated by more shallow cleavages. Likewise, variation in levels of violence within the same civil war should covary with the depth of cleavages. Existing empirical evidence points to an absence of correlation between deeply divided societies and highly intense civil wars—or between subnational variation of deep division and intensity of violence (Bosch Sánchez 1983; Casanova 1985: 59; Ortiz Sarmiento 1990: 22; Wood 2003). At the same time, recent and more rigorous empirical research uncovers a relation between high levels of prewar electoral competition and violence (but no relation between domination and subjection and violence) (Balcells 2007).

To be sure, rigorous empirical research on these issues is still in its infancy. Nevertheless, it is suggestive, especially when considered in light of the following methodological critique. Violence may be erroneously linked to prewar polarization via a variety of inference biases, including the extrapolation from the aggregate to the individual level and the privileging of target information over base-rate information. For example, Boudon (1988) has shown that even in a homogeneous society of equals it is possible to generate processes of competition (and hence violence) which would on the aggregate level appear as having been generated by deep cleavages. Likewise it has been pointed out that competition effects between groups may be merely by-products of a selection bias: even in a world where ethnicity plays no role whatsoever in defining either the likely interactions among individuals or the proclivity of individuals to engage in violence, we would still see significant violence, wrongly perceived as resulting from ethnic competition (Dion 1997).

Among the efforts to recast the study of class conflict away from unquestioned group-level assumptions, Adam Przeworski's *Capitalism and Social Democracy* stands out. Przeworski sought to specify the microfoundations of class conflict in nineteenth-century Europe; he promoted an ambitious agenda, also pioneered by Elster (1985) and Roemer (1986), which consisted in reconstructing Marxist theory using modern analytical tools and in a way consistent with advances in microeconomic theory and the principles of methodological individualism.

Influenced by the work of the Italian thinker Antonio Gramsci, Przeworski departs from many of the standard assumptions underlying classic Marxist theory. He challenges the premise that individual identities, individual interests, and individual actions[4] could be derived from 'objective' group interests—in this case from class. He thus elaborates a 'constructivist' perspective *avant la lettre* (and in a field other than ethnicity), by arguing that individuals have multiple options when it comes to social and political identities (1985: 100):

> [T]he division of a society into classes does not necessarily result in the organiza-
> tion of politics in terms of class. Nor is the experience of class the only one which
> is objective. If 'objective' means experience that is inherited by individuals and is
> independent of individual will, then being a Catholic today in Italy is an objective
> experience, as is being a Black in the United States, or a woman in France. The people
> who perpetuate their existence by selling their capacity to work for a wage are also
> men or women, Catholics or Protestants, Northerners or Southerners. They are also
> consumers, taxpayers, parents and city-dwellers. They may become mobilized into
> politics as workers, but they may also become Catholic workers, Catholics, or Bavarian
> Catholics.

In turn, these identity options are likely to shape an individual's self-perception of what her interests are and, therefore, her willingness to mobilize and participate in political and social conflicts. In other words, individual choices help determine the likelihood of conflict. But, then, what helps determine these individual choices in the first place? Przeworski demonstrates that rather than deriving from production relations and the class structure, these choices are shaped by the organizational choices of political parties. It is the mobilizing of parties that creates and sustains individual identities and hence both their perceptions of what their interests are as well as their subsequent actions. This is not the classic Downsian view of parties as vote-maximizing political machines that seek to position themselves as close to the median voter as possible, but the Gramscian view of parties as engaged in the construction of 'hegemony'; that is, actively molding the perceptions and consciousness of the masses—a point that resonates with the European political history of the turn of the nineteenth and twentieth centuries. Insofar as mobilization raises the likelihood of conflict, this perspective points to a view whereby political-party activity was at the root of conflict not just in the traditional view of party competition but also in the deeper process of cleavage and identity construction and transformation. Hence a key empirical question: How did the young European democracies avert mass violent conflict?

Part of the answer is obviously related to structure: The strategic choices of political parties are constrained by structural conditions and their strategic implications, that is the 'real conflicts of interest and values that divide society at any particular moment' (Przeworski 1985: 129), and the strategies of their rivals. A less obvious part of the answer points to the role of democratic institutions within which political parties mobilized voters.

Three implications follow. First, initial choices over party strategy, such as whether to participate or not in electoral contests, ended up having long-term, and often unintended, effects on group formation and group-based action. Ideology often shifted as the result of these initial choices. Hence, participation in elections which was initially an instrumental and self-interested strategy in the context of high levels of conflict ended up reducing the likelihood of conflict.[5] Second, democracy can be reconceptualized as an institutional mechanism permitting the realization of concessions by the capitalists toward the organized workers, thus preempting conflict. It is, in other words, a game that may predetermine the players' strategies based on their resources (i.e. 'structure') but one that does not predetermine the exact outcome; instead it attaches probabilities to outcomes such that the range of possible outcomes varies significantly. Because democratic institutions 'institutionalize uncertainty' (Przeworski 1991), they succeed in drawing in new actors. Losers in elections comply because future victory remains a possibility; violent conflict is prevented and democracy becomes a 'self-enforcing institution.' Third, this analysis also allows the reconceptualization of legitimacy as 'the correspondence between the uses of force and rules which specify when it can and should be used' (1985: 141). Consent, in this perspective, is but the reflection of a deliberate set of choices under specific constraints. Repression is always 'off the equilibrium path.' We pay taxes in great part because we are aware of the risk of sanction if we don't. The fact that violence is not observed does not imply that it does not matter—the contrary: it matters because it does not manifest itself. In the context of a capitalist system, it is possible to determine the a posteriori material conditions under which workers will consent, and even predict, as Przeworski does, what the levels of militancy will be. Social democracy can be, therefore, understood as the optimal answer of individual workers given a set of constraints. Consent emerges from bargains in a specific institutional context; the material bases of class-conflict mitigation are both explicit and predictable.

To summarize, by endogenizing individual identities and actions into a larger game with clear rules (democratic institutions) and a given distribution of resources (capitalism) and constraints (the possibility of repression for a certain level of worker militancy), Przeworski was able to derive some powerful implications (e.g. that democratic institutions are self-enforcing). This line of research has proven extremely fertile, as indicated by recent global-level studies by Boix (2003), and Acemoglu and Robinson (2006). To be sure, Przeworski's analysis is primarily theoretical; his empirical tests are conducted at a highly aggregate level and are indirect. Indeed, Burawoy (1989) was correct to point out that the main weakness of this analysis (unlike Gould's) is the absence of a direct empirical test of the theoretical microfoundations.

The contrast between Gould and Przeworski is obvious: the former focuses on small-scale conflict, takes large groups as fixed, specifies how nonviolent conflict escalates into violence, and tests his microfoundations; the latter focuses on large-scale conflict, shows how groups are formed, specifies how institutions contain conflict, and posits only theoretical microfoundations. Both works, however, share a fundamental similarity: they assume a unidirectional causal effect. Gould demonstrates how interpersonal conflict spills over into small-scale collective conflict, while Przeworski shows that large-scale collective conflict shapes individual action. Hence the question: Is it possible to build a theoretically and empirically sound micro-level analysis of conflict that generalizes to macro-level conflict, and vice versa, without having to resort to assumptions about exogenously fixed groups? This is the theoretical challenge taken up by Kalyvas in *The Logic of Violence in Civil War* (2006).

25.4 VIOLENT CONFLICT/ENDOGENOUS DYNAMICS

Kalyvas (2006) investigates the dynamics of violent conflict in the context of civil war and attempts to resolve the apparent contradiction between the group-level theorization of the causes of large-scale violent conflict on the one hand, and the individual- and local-level dynamics revealed by close observation on the other.

Given the difficulty of empirically testing hypotheses about the relation between social cleavages and conflict intensity (due to the difficulty of measuring the depth of cleavages independently from conflict intensity), a common practice has been to derive deep group-level divisions from violence on the ground. In other words, if violence is horrific, this must mean that social cleavages run extremely deep. However, this raises a classic problem of endogeneity, for we know that violence typically causes identities to form or sharpen and conflicts to deepen. Thucydides (3.83–4) remarked, in the context of the civil conflict in the Greek *polis* of Corcyra, on 'the violent fanaticism which came into play *once* the struggle had broken out. . . . *As the result* of these revolutions, there was a general deterioration of character throughout the Greek world. . . . Society *had become* divided into two ideologically hostile camps, and each side viewed the other with suspicion' (emphasis added). More recently, Girard (1977) reminded us that as rivalry becomes acute, the rivals tend to forget its initial cause and instead become more fascinated with one another; as a result, the rivalry is purified of any external stake and becomes a matter of pure rivalry and prestige.

Indeed, violence may emerge from dynamics that inhere in civil wars and are either indirectly connected or totally unconnected to prewar polarization via two processes: endogenous polarization and endogenous violence. Most group-level arguments assume the distribution of popular support during a civil war to be a faithful reflection of (prewar) cleavages; in times of high polarization, the 'carrying capacity' of political actors reaches its maximum value, producing an almost total overlap between the goals of political actors and the goals of the population they claim to represent. Hence, landless peasants naturally support leftist insurgents and landowners right-wing governments; Tamils join the Tamil Tigers and Sinhalas side with Sri Lanka's government; Catholics support the IRA and Protestants the Unionists, and so on. In other words, support is fixed and given exogenously with respect to the war; hence, determining its distribution requires only access to census data.

However, as the discussion above has pointed out, 'groups,' be they economic, ethnic, ideological, or religious, do not exist as such. What can be observed instead are organizations, usually armed ones, making claims on behalf of groups that may be more or less homogeneous and more or less fragmented. In fact, many of their actions are intended precisely to mobilize and homogenize these groups, a fact consistent with the observation that insurgent violence in many ethnic rebellions 'is usually directed primarily against their own people, in order to ensure their support for the revolt, however reluctant or however passive' (Paget 1967: 32). Although initial predispositions and preferences that flow directly from prewar politics are present at the onset of a civil war, they also tend to shift as a result of its dynamics. Sometimes the direction of the shift is toward 'harder' group identities, but sometimes new cleavages and identities emerge. For example, Tilly (1964: 305, 330) shows that whereas the initial configuration of parties in southern Anjou during the French Revolution ran along class lines and had crystallized 'long before' the outbreak of the counterrevolutionary rebellion, in 1793 'participation in the counterrevolution cut boldly across class lines. Therefore, no simple scheme of class alignment can account adequately for the division of forces in 1793.'

Beyond polarization, violence may also be endogenous to the war in the sense of being unconnected to the causes of war. War acquires 'a life of its own.' Cycles of retaliation, the emphasis on violent resolution of disputes, brutalization, a new war economy, these are all factors that produce violence independent of the initial conflict that caused the eruption of the war in the first place.

In short, the universalization of the distinction between friend and enemy implied by group-level analysis is often a consequence of the war, a by-product of its violence. The responses of political actors and individuals to the dynamics of war (and the responses to their responses) shape violence, the war, and the prospects for peace in a way that is often quite independent of the proximate causes of the conflict. Acknowledging that both violence and polarization can be endogenous to war implies an understanding of the institutional environment within which violence unfolds, very much as the analysis of class conflict in late-nineteenth-century Europe called for an understanding of democracy rather than just an understanding of class.

Kalyvas (2006) develops a theory of the informal institutions of civil war; his primary aim is to account for the subnational variation in violence across space and political actors—in other words, his is a theory that aims to predict where violence will erupt and by whom it will be exercised, conditional on a civil war being on. The starting point is a theory of irregular war rather than a theory of group conflict. This war, commonly referred to as 'guerrilla war,'[6] results in territorial fragmentation into geographical zones that are either monopolistically controlled by rival actors or whose sovereignty is 'shared.' The type of sovereignty or control that prevails in a given region affects the type of strategies followed by armed actors. These actors try to shape popular support in their favor ('collaboration') and deter collaboration with their rival ('defection'). As the conflict matures, control is increasingly likely to shape collaboration, because armed actors who enjoy substantial territorial control can protect civilians who live on that territory—both from their rivals and from themselves, thus providing survival-oriented civilians with a strong incentive to collaborate with them, irrespective of their true or initial preferences. In this sense, and consistent with what Coleman (1990: 179) calls 'power theory,' collaboration is largely endogenous to control, though, of course, high rates of collaboration spawned by control at a given point in time are likely to reinforce it in the future. Violence is bounded by the nature of sovereignty exercised by each political actor and generally must be selective (or personalized) rather than indiscriminate (or group-level)—which tends to be counterproductive (Coleman 1990: 502).

Selective violence requires private information which is asymmetrically distributed among organizations and local civilians: only the latter may know who the defectors are and they have a choice to denounce them or not. Denunciation constitutes a key link between individuals and armed actors; this is precisely the mechanism that turns often trivial interpersonal and local disputes into violence. Given armed actors who maximize territorial control subject to specific resources and choose whether to use violence or not, and individual civilians who maximize various benefits subject to survival and choose whether to denounce their neighbors or not, it is possible to predict both the distribution of selective violence across geographical zones of control and the armed actor likely to resort to violence in a specific zone. Kalyvas provides an empirical test of these predictions.

Besides producing specific predictions about the distribution of violence, this model entails two implications that speak directly to the issues raised above. The first one extends Gould's insights about the logic of interpersonal violence to the kind of large-scale violence associated with civil wars. The second one allows the integration of on-the-ground local dynamics and group-level politics, which are typically considered to be contradictory.

First, it is possible to connect a great deal of the violence perpetrated by armed actors and interpersonal conflict between individuals. The key lies in the observation that denunciations are often malicious and loosely related to the cleavage motivating the conflict. That is, individuals exploit the high demand for information to settle local and interpersonal conflicts which may bear little or no relation to the political conflict raging around them. Malicious denunciation turns out to be closely related to interpersonal conflict in contexts of 'organic' (rather than 'mechanical') solidarity: small-scale, face-to-face social settings, where people develop dense interpersonal interactions, living and working together in daily mutual dependency, rivalry, and love. These include tight-knit neighborhoods, villages and small towns, apartment buildings, family businesses, and work environments. Surprisingly, socially egalitarian settings that lack deep ethnic, religious, or class divisions appear not to be as adverse to denunciation as one would expect. Indeed, denunciation is often horizontal (Gellately 1991; Fitzpatrick 1994). Relatively homogeneous, tight-knit, and egalitarian social settings may be prone to high levels of denunciation for two distinct reasons: 'symmetry' and 'concentration.'

Consistent with Gould, symmetric contexts foster denunciation, via the mechanisms of fear of status loss and envy. Social hierarchies in such contexts tend to be fluid (people are ranked in relation to others in terms of subtle gradations) and open to modification (unlike with castes or rigid strata). Competition for status ('face' or 'honor') is open, daily, and intense; it generates humiliation, shaming, and 'loss of face'—usually experienced as among the worst things that can happen to a person. This is also consistent with Simmel's remark (1955: 43–4) that similarity breeds intense conflict and that people who have many common features often do one another worse wrong than complete strangers do.

The other factor is 'concentration,' which refers to the dense overlap of social interaction in small and closed settings. Concentration is associated with denunciation through two related mechanisms. First, the number of interactions between individuals is high, hence the likelihood that interpersonal conflicts and grievances will emerge. Conflicts in dense environments tend to be intense, Simmel (1955: 44–5) has suggested, because the depth of relations between persons in intimate relationships who quarrel causes 'not a single contact, not a single word, not a single activity or pain' to remain isolated. It is no coincidence that name-calling, character assassination, and gossip, which Barthes (1977: 169) aptly called 'murder by language,' are prevalent in dense social environments. Second, dense contexts entail the presence of an audience for every interaction. The higher the number, and the greater the density of interactions among the members of a group, the greater the opportunity to directly observe each other's behavior (Hechter 1987: 154; Gambetta 1993: 168). In short, dense communities fit the Spanish saying 'small village, big hell.' It is true that the existence of institutions that defuse conflicts simmering under the surface of dense environments has often led observers to interpret them as being solidaristic. However, anthropologists have pointed to their fundamentally dual nature: they are simultaneously conflictual and solidaristic (Gilmore 1987).

The second implication of the model concerns an ill-understood puzzle whereby conflicts and violence on the ground often seem more related to local issues rather than the 'master cleavage' that drives the civil war at the national level. As suggested above, many instances of violence taking place in the context of an ethnic conflict turn out to be motivated by the kind of daily interpersonal or local disputes that are unrelated to the larger conflict. This disjunction takes place even when local cleavages are usually framed in the discursive terminology of the master cleavage.

Two interpretations have been offered to explain this disjunction. The first one, inspired by group-level intuitions, views local conflicts as purely epiphenomenal of the larger cleavages. To be sure, they are often 'contaminated' by local elements, but they are not autonomous of the larger cleavages. The real agents are groups. This view should be qualified in light of massive micro-level evidence (Kalyvas 2006: ch. 11) and must become the object of empirical investigation as opposed to simple assertion. The second interpretation takes the opposite stand: because of the breakdown of order, all violence is personal and local. Since neither actors nor observers can possibly make sense of such wild diversity and complexity, they simplify, or 'emplot' them (Ricoeur 1984) by referring to core issues and cleavages which are compelling but ultimately misleading constructions unrelated to the action on the ground. Both interpretations are problematic.

This disjunction can be elucidated once it is recognized that the loci of agency spawned by civil war are multiple—hence the confusing diversity and ambiguity of motives and identities observed. In other words, the fusion and interaction between dynamics at the group level and the individual level (or the 'center' and the 'periphery') are fundamental rather than incidental to civil war, a matter of essence rather than noise. A key insight from the discussion of denunciation is that individuals and local communities involved in the war tend to take advantage of the prevailing situation to settle private and local conflicts whose relation to the grand causes of the war or the goals of the belligerents is often tenuous. Under normal circumstances these conflicts are regulated and do not result in violent conflict. We hardly think of them as connected to political violence in general and civil war in particular. Civil wars alter this reality by allowing for the exchange of information for violent action. This perspective provides a key missing link between the public and private spheres, and between master cleavages and local cleavages. Civil war can be analyzed as a process that transforms the political actors' quest for victory and power and the local or individual actors' quest for personal and local advantage into a joint process of violence. Departing from both practices of deriving the local from the central and ignoring the central, it is possible to identify a key mechanism linking elite and local dynamics: 'alliance.' This mechanism entails a set of transactions between supralocal and local actors, whereby the former supply the latter with external muscle, thus allowing them to win decisive local advantage; in exchange supralocal actors recruit and motivate supporters at the local level. Viewed from this perspective, violence is a key resource for collective action. In the long run, and with iterations, the process of alliance may produce a durable and endogenous shift in identities.

This perspective allows the reconceptualization of 'master' cleavages as symbolic formations that simplify, streamline, and incorporate a bewildering variety of local conflicts. The concept of alliance allows us to reintroduce complexity, yet in a theoretically tractable way. Civil wars are concatenations of multiple and often disparate local cleavages, more or less loosely arrayed around the master cleavage. In turn, this cleavage is often influenced by global trends that explain why the same insurgent groups may represent themselves as socialist during the cold war, ethnic nationalist after its end, or Islamist after the World Trade Center attacks.

The mechanism of alliance points to a critical dilemma for both central and local actors. On the one hand, central actors must mobilize at the local level—even when their ideological agenda is universalistic and, thus, opposed to localism. At the same time, to be effective they must also transcend particularism and localism. On the other hand, local actors resist their absorption into centralized and hierarchical structures—both organizational and discursive. Though instrumentally tied to the master cleavage, they strive to remain distinct and maintain their autonomy. The history of many revolutionary movements is a tale of the tension between these conflicting goals. Seen from this perspective, civil war is a process of political and administrative 'normalization,' and state-building is an externality of civil war.

Determining when and how such alliances emerge calls for fine-grained research. For instance, a recurring pattern is that losers in local conflicts are more likely to move first allying with outside forces. If this is true, civil war is particularly destabilizing, since it supplies new opportunities to losers in local power conflicts who are seeking an opportunity for *revanche*. Empirically, alliance is consistent with the intimate and often malicious nature of selective violence, the endogeneity of cleavages to the war, and the limited visibility of local cleavages after the war. Once a war has ended, the master narrative of the conflict provides a handy way to *ex post facto* simplify, streamline, and ultimately erase the war's complexities, contradictions, and ambiguities. An interesting implication is that what differentiates modern insurgencies from premodern rebellions (but also some post-cold-war insurgencies) is the absence of sophisticated elites with a 'global' discourse.

CONCLUSION

The relevance of alliance as a mechanism linking local cleavages into a conflict's master cleavage is twofold: first, it allows for a theoretical understanding of large-scale conflict that incorporates rather than ignores the puzzle of the disjunction between individual-level and group-level dynamics—and the extensive ambiguity that surrounds this process. Second, it turns the individual/group-level interface into a central issue and forces us to rethink precisely the modalities linking distinct actors and motivations. Recognizing the existence of a concatenation of multiple and disparate local cleavages allows the exploration of the relation between the individual and the group levels—a possibility precluded by the prevailing understanding of cleavage.[7]

It is possible, therefore, to reconcile within the same analytical framework, but without bundling them, two sets of dynamics that have been approached as being contradictory to each other: group-level and individual-level action. The theoretical advantage of the mechanism of alliance is that it allows for multiple rather than unitary actors, agency located in *both* center and periphery rather than only in either one, and a variety of preferences and identities as opposed to a common and overarching one. The main implication is that identity labels should be treated with caution and not projected on individual actions from the level of the group.

The discussion of the mechanism of alliance in civil-war contexts is illustrative. It is possible to come up with a substantial number of micromechanisms depending on the question investigated and the context studied. By adopting an analytical strategy of theoretical and empirical disaggregation of the constitutive elements of conflict, such as cleavages, groups, or identities, and by making microfoundations explicit, we can arrive at an improved understanding of the causes and consequences of conflict: one that recognizes the dynamic interaction between conflict and action, and between individuals and groups. This approach allows us to relax the usual assumptions of unitary and exogenously given groups, bypass the dichotomy of individual and group-based perspectives, integrate the interpersonal and local dimensions of violent conflict with its collective dimension, and focus on the dynamic and bidirectional relationship between groups and individuals. In short, the analytical approach to the study of conflict opens up a vast and exciting research agenda, combining abstract theorization with rich empirical evidence, while countering the disciplinary and subdisciplinary fragmentation that has undermined the effective study of conflict.

Notes

1. The emerging field of terrorism studies is primarily associated with the discipline of political science as well, as is the study of genocide and ethnic cleansing.

2. Economic theories begin with theorizations of individual dynamics, yet their empirical tests tend to stay at the level of group dynamics and the mechanisms linking individuals and groups are not empirically tested.

3. For example, in 2002, 43 percent of all murder victims in the USA were related to or acquainted with their assailants, whereas only 14 percent of victims were murdered by strangers (43 percent of victims had an unknown relationship to their murderer) (US Department of Justice).

4. In this respect, Przeworski's analysis goes beyond the standard Olsonian collective-action problem, which posits the potential impossibility of action despite interest in its favor.

5. Kalyvas (2000) has argued that a similar mechanism could be triggered in Muslim polities.

6. Keep in mind that irregular or guerrilla war is not the only type of civil war.

7. In fact, surrogate warfare has a long history in international politics, from the days of the Roman Empire up until the cold war and its aftermath. Yet we have generally failed to conceptualize civil war as a concatenation of multiple surrogate wars.

REFERENCES

ACEMOGLU, D., and ROBINSON, J. A. (2006), *Economic Origins of Dictatorship and Democracy* (New York: Cambridge University Press).

BALCELLS, L. (2007), 'Rivalry and Revenge: *Killing Civilians in the Spanish Civil War*', Estudios/working papers CEACS, no. 233.

BARTHES, R. (1977), *Roland Barthes* (New York: Hill and Wang).

BIRKBECK, C., and LAFREE, G. (1993), 'The Situational Analysis of Crime and Deviance', *Annual Review of Sociology*, 19: 113–37.

BLACK, D. J. (1976), *The Behavior of Law* (New York: Academic).

—— (1993), *The Social Structure of Right and Wrong* (San Diego, Calif.: Academic).

BOBBIO, N. (1992), 'Guerra Civile?', *Teoria Politica*, 1–2: 297–307.

BOIX, C. (2003), *Democracy and Redistribution* (New York: Cambridge University Press).

BOSCH SÁNCHEZ, A. (1983), *Ugetistas y Libertarios: Guerra Civil y Revolución en el Pais Valenciano, 1936–1939* (Valencia: Instituto Alfons el Magnanim).

BOUDON, R. (1988), 'The Logic of Relative Frustration', in M. Taylor (ed.), *Rationality and Revolution* (Cambridge: Cambridge University Press), 245–67.

BRUBAKER, R., and LAITIN, D. D. (1998), 'Ethnic and Nationalist Violence', *Annual Review of Sociology*, 24: 243–52.

BURAWOY, M. (1989), 'Marxism Without Microfoundations: Przeworski's Critique of Social Democracy', *Socialist Review*, 89: 53–86.

BURUMA, I. (2002), 'The Blood Lust of Identity', *New York Review of Books*, 11 April, pp. 12–14.

CASANOVA, J. (1985), *Anarquismo y Revolución Social en la Socieadad Aragonesa, 1936–1938* (Madrid: Siglo XXI).

CASELLI, F., and COLEMAN, W. J. (2006), 'On the Theory of Ethnic Conflict', NBER working paper no. 12125.

COLEMAN, J. S. (1990), *Foundations of Social Theory* (Cambridge, Mass.: Harvard University Press).

COLLIER, P., et al. (2003), *Breaking the Conflict Trap: Civil War and Development Policy* (Washington, D.C.: World Bank/Oxford University Press).

COSER, L. A. (1956), *The Functions of Social Conflict* (Glencoe, Ill.: Free Press).

DAHRENDORF, R. (1959), *Class and Class Conflict in Industrial Society* (Stanford, Calif.: Stanford University Press).

DECKER, S. H. (1993), 'Exploring Victim–Offender Relationships in Homicide: The Role of Individual and Event Characteristics', *Justice Quarterly*, 10: 585–612.

DEUTSCH, K. W. (1953), *Nationalism and Social Communication: An Inquiry into the Foundations of Nationality* (New York: Wiley).

DION, D. (1997), 'Competition and Ethnic Conflict: Artifactual?', *Journal of Conflict Resolution*, 41: 638–48.

DOWNS, A. (1957), *An Economic Theory of Democracy* (New York: Harper).

ELSTER, J. (1985), *Making Sense of Marx* (Cambridge: Cambridge University Press).

ESTEBAN, J., and RAY, D. (1994), 'On the Measurement of Polarization', *Econometrica*, 62: 819–52.

FEARON, J. D., and LAITIN, D. (1996), 'Explaining Interethnic Cooperation', *American Political Science Review*, 90: 715–35.

FEHR, E., and GACHTER, S. (2000), 'Fairness and Retaliation: The Economics of Reciprocity', *Journal of Economic Perspectives*, 14: 159–81.

FIGUEIREDO, R. DE, and WEINGAST, B. R. (1999), 'The Rationality of Fear: Political Opportunism and Ethnic Conflict', in B. Walter and R. Snyder (eds.), *Civil Wars, Insecurity, and Intervention* (New York: Columbia University Press), 262–302.

FITZPATRICK, S. (1994), *Stalin's Peasants: Resistance and Survival in the Russian Village After Collectivization* (New York: Oxford University Press).

GAMBETTA, D. (1993), *The Sicilian Mafia: The Business of Private Protection* (Cambridge, Mass.: Harvard University Press).

GELLATELY, R. (1991), *The Gestapo and German Society: Enforcing Racial Policy, 1933–1945* (Oxford: Oxford University Press).

GELLNER, E. (1983), *Nations and Nationalism* (Oxford: Blackwell).

GILMORE, D. D. (1987), *Aggression and Community: Paradoxes of Audalusian Culture* (New Haven, Conn.: Yale University Press).

GIRARD, R. (1977), *Violence and the Sacred* (Baltimore, Md.: Johns Hopkins University Press).

GOULD, R. (2003), *Collision of Wills: How Ambiguitiy about Social Rank Breeds Conflict* (Chicago, Ill.: University of Chicago Press).

HECHTER, M. (1987), *Principles of Group Solidarity* (Berkeley, Calif.: University of California Press).

HODSON, R., SEKULIC, D., and MASSEY, G. (1994), 'National Tolerance in the Former Yugoslavia', *American Journal of Sociology*, 99: 1535–58.

HOROWITZ, D. L. (1985), *Ethnic Groups in Conflict* (Berkeley, Calif.: University of California Press).

KALYVAS, S. N. (2000), 'Commitment Problems in Emerging Democracies: The Case of Religious Parties', *Comparative Politics*, 32: 379–99.

—— (2006), *The Logic of Violence in Civil War* (New York: Cambridge University Press).

KATZ, J. (1988), *Seductions of Crime: A Chilling Exploration of the Criminal Mind—from Juvenile Delinquency to Cold-blooded Murder* (New York: Basic).

LAITIN, D. (2001), 'Secessionist Rebellion in the Former Soviet Union', *Comparative Political Studies*, 34: 839–61.

LASSWELL, H. D. (1936), *Politics: Who Gets What, When, How* (New York/London: Whittlesey).

LAWRENCE, A. (2007), *Imperial Rule and the Politics of Nationalism*, Ph.D. thesis (University of Chicago).

LEVY, J. S. (1983), *War in the Modern Great Power System, 1495–1975* (Lexington, Ky.: Kentucky University Press).

LIPSET, S. M., and ROKKAN, S. (1967), 'Cleavage Structures, Party Systems, and Voter Alignments: An Introduction', in S. M. Lipset and S. Rokkan (eds.), *Party Systems and Voter Alignments: Cross-National Perspectives* (New York: Free Press), 1–64.

MCADAM, D., TARROW, S., and TILLY, C. (2001), *Dynamics of Contention* (New York: Cambridge University Press).

MALEFAKIS, E. (1996), 'Aspectos históricos y teóricos de la guerra', in E. Malefakis (ed.), *La Guerra de España (1936–1939)* (Madrid: Taurus), 11–47.

MARTIN, J. C. (1995), 'Guerre civile et modernité: le cas de la Révolution', in J. C. Martin (ed.), *La guerre civile entre histoire et mémoire* (Nantes: Ouest).

MOORE, B., JUN. (1966), *Social Origins of Dictatorship and Democracy: Lord and Peasant in the Making of the Modern World* (Boston, Mass.: Beacon).

NORDLINGER, E. A. (1972), 'Conflict Regulation in Divided Societies', Occasional Papers in International Affairs no. 29, Center for International Affairs, Harvard University.

OBERSCHALL, A. (1978), 'Theories of Social Conflict', *Annual Review of Sociology*, 4: 291–315.

ORTIZ SARMIENTO, C. M. (1990), *La violence en Colombie: Racines historiques et sociales*, (Paris: L'Harmatan).

PACKER, G. (2007), 'Planning for Defeat', *New Yorker*, 17 September, pp. 56–65.

PAGET, J. (1967), *Counter-insurgency Operations: Techniques of Guerrilla Warfare* (New York: Walker).

PARKER, N. (2007), 'Iraq's War Makes Intimates Enemies', *Los Angeles Times*, 16 September; at <http://www.latimes.com/news/nationworld/world/la-fg-realworld16sep16, 1,7704935,full.story?ctrack=5&cset=true>, accessed 2008.

PEREZ-DÍAZ, V. M. (1993), *The Return of Civil Society: The Emergence of Democratic Spain* (Cambridge, Mass: Harvard University Press).

PETERSEN, R. D. (2002), *Understanding Ethnic Violence: Fear, Hatred, and Resentment in Twentieth-century Eastern Europe* (New York: Cambridge University Press).

POSEN, B. R. (1993), 'The Security Dilemma and Ethnic Conflict', *Survival*, 35: 27–47.

PRZEWORSKI, A. (1985), *Capitalism and Social Democracy* (Cambridge: Cambridge University Press).

—— (1991), *Democracy and the Market: Political and Economic Reforms in Eastern Europe and Latin America* (Cambridge: Cambridge University Press).

RICOEUR, P. (1984), *Time and Narrative* (Chicago, Ill.: University of Chicago Press).

ROEMER, J. (1986), *Analytical Marxism* (Cambridge: Cambridge University Press).

SAMPSON, R. J., and LAUB, J. H. (1992), 'Crime and Deviance in the Life Course', *Annual Review of Sociology*, 18: 63–84.

SCHELLING, T. C. (1978), *Micromotives and Macrobehavior* (New York: Norton).

SCHMITT, C. (1976), *The Concept of the Political* (New Brunswick, N.J.: Rutgers University Press).

SEIDMAN, M. (2002), *Republic of Egos: A Social History of the Spanish Civil War* (Madison, Wisc.: University of Wisconsin Press).

SEKULIC, D. (2005), 'Structural Determinants of Nationalism in Croatia', unpublished paper.

SIMMEL, G. (1955), *Conflict and the Web of Group Affiliations* (New York: Free Press).

SINGER, J. D., and SMALL, M. (1972), *The Wages of War, 1816–1965: A Statistical Handbook* (New York: Wiley).

SPENCER, J. (2000), 'On Not Becoming a "Terrorist": Problems of Memory, Agency, and Community in the Sri Lankan Conflict', in V. Das, et al. (eds.), *Violence and Subjectivity* (Berkeley, Calif.: University of California Press), 120–40.

TAJFEL, H., and TURNER, J. C. [1979] (2004), 'An Integrative Theory of Intergroup Conflict', in M. J. Hatch and M. Schultz (eds.), *Organizational Identity: A Reader* (Oxford: Oxford University Press), 56–65.

THUCYDIDES (1972), *History of the Peloponnesian War*, trans. Rex Warner (London: Penguin).

TILLY, C. (1964), *The Vendée* (Cambridge, Mass.: Harvard University Press).

US Department of Justice, Bureau of Justice Statistics; at <http://www.ojp.usdoj.gov/bjs/cvict_c.htm>, accessed 2008.

VARSHNEY, A. (2003), *Ethnic Conflict and Civic Life: Hindus and Muslims in India* (New Haven, Conn.: Yale University Press).

WILKINSON, S. I. (2006), *Votes and Violence: Electoral Competition and Ethnic Riots in India* (New York: Cambridge University Press).

WOOD, E. J. (2003), *Insurgent Collective Action and Civil War in El Salvador* (New York: Cambridge University Press).

PART IV

····································

PERSPECTIVES FROM OTHER FIELDS AND APPROACHES

····································

CHAPTER 26

GAME THEORY*

RICHARD BREEN

INTRODUCTION

IN the past fifty years game theory has swept all before it in many social sciences, most notably in economics, but also political science, law, and social psychology. Yet in sociology it has not attained anything like a dominant position and continues to be a minority interest. This is despite the fact that game theory analyzes the interactions between agents,[1] and is thus the closest thing we have to a method that embodies Weber's famous definition of sociology as the study of social action, where 'action is social insofar as its subjective meaning takes account of the behavior of others and is thereby oriented in its course' (Weber 1978: 4). Indeed, Elster (1982: 477) advanced the claim that 'if one accepts that interaction is the essence of social life, then . . . game theory provides solid microfoundations for the study of social structure and social change.'

Several arguments have been made to explain sociologists' lack of interest in game theory (for example, Petersen 1994); broadly speaking, sociologists seem to find the general idea of games quite attractive, but do not like the assumptions which support the formal analysis of games. Some of these assumptions are not always a necessary part of game theory: agents need not be motivated only by egoistic interests, they need not be hyperrational, and they need not have complete information about the game and those they are playing against. So objections on these bases are not objections to game theory as such but to particular applications

* Thanks to Scott Boorman, Peter Hedström, and Chris Winship for comments on earlier drafts of this chapter.

of it. But other elements of games are essential and present difficulties to many sociologists. According to Swedberg (2001: 305), Jessie Bernard, one of the pioneers of game theory in sociology, pointed to the problem of determining the rules and payoffs when seeking to apply game theory to real-world problems, and thirty years later the same point was made by Kreps (1990*b*: ch. 5). He noted that whereas game theory addresses questions of strategic interaction in situations governed by closely specified rules or 'protocols,' many situations of interest to social scientists lack these. Real interactions may be much more loosely structured, lacking menus of strategies and well-defined payoff functions.

But should we therefore conclude that game theory has nothing to offer sociologists? Like any theory, game theory makes assumptions in order to develop simplified models of the real world; it may indeed be the case that what interests us are real-world situations in which people do not seem to have strategies or clear ideas about payoffs, but it may be helpful to analyze such situations as if they did. However, game theory need not be restricted in this way; as I show below, it can be extended to incorporate all kinds of uncertainty on the part of the players, including uncertainty over the game's payoffs. So in this chapter I argue that, contrary to what I take to be conventional wisdom, game theory has enormous and as yet largely unrealized potential for sociology and particularly for analytical sociology. I want to suggest two ways that game theory can realize its potential: as a tool to think with, and as a method for addressing the way in which macro-level outcomes can be derived from micro-level interactions.

As many scientists have recognized, posing a question in the right way is the key to answering it. Framing the question correctly usually involves conceptualizing the problem in such a way that the most important elements are brought into focus and the less important details are put to one side. When we are concerned with situations that involve interactions between agents, trying to cast the problem in the form of a game can be an effective way of doing this. Theories simplify reality and a tractable game is usually a radical simplification. In the end, a game may or may not be adequate to capture the salient features of the phenomenon, but, even if it is not, it shows what other elements need to be included to attain adequacy. In other words, using games as conceptualizing devices entails a strategy of starting from the simple and making things more complex only where this is necessary. In this sense, games are 'good to think with.' But there is another sense in which this is true. Game theory is full of smart ideas, and several sociologists have taken these ideas and applied them to empirical phenomena even though they have not constructed, much less sought to solve, a formal game. The value of this approach can be judged by whether the use of game-theoretic concepts adds explanatory power.

Analytical sociologists are supposed to be interested in explaining systemic outcomes, not individual behavior, and yet, as every analytical sociologist (and every economist) knows, it is often difficult to move from the level of individual actions to that of system-level phenomena, except in those cases where the latter is just the straightforward aggregation of individual actions.[2] Game theory is the only formal analytical method that we have of generating aggregate outcomes from complex interactions. Thus, one of the major uses of game theory in sociology should be to show how these aggregate or systemic outcomes can be so derived. This is hardly a novel suggestion: Swedberg and Augier (2003) quote the anthropologist Fredrik Barth: 'the Theory of Games is . . . a model whereby one may generate forms according to the rules of strategy . . . and these forms . . . may then be compared to the empirical patterns which one has observed' (Barth 1966). Sociologists have sought to do this, and we shall see examples later. This project shades into the use of computer simulations, which can be employed for the same purpose, though with the important difference that the relationship between the inputs (individual actions) and output (aggregate or system-level phenomena) is much more transparent in games than it usually is in simulations.

The bulk of this chapter will present examples of how sociologists have used game theory for the purposes of thinking and for the derivation of system-level outcomes. But to begin with, and in order to understand what these sociologists have been up to, I shall need to spend a few paragraphs presenting some basic game-theoretic ideas.

26.1 GAME THEORY: SOME BASIC CONCEPTS

I find it useful to think of noncooperative games[3] as falling into one of three varieties: classical game theory, evolutionary game theory, and behavioral game theory. In all varieties a game involves two or more players, each of whom has one or more moves in the game, at which they can choose among two or more possible actions. The game ends with a set of payoffs to each player, and these payoffs are functions of the actions chosen in the course of the game by all the players. Each player is said to follow a strategy, which is the set of actions the player chooses each time she gets a move. Classical game theory assumes forward-looking rational agents who choose their strategies on the basis of beliefs about the consequences of doing so. Agents are assumed to be rational and capable of carrying out any computations necessary in order to find the payoff-maximizing strategy. All players are assumed to know the game and each player knows that all other players know this. They know the sequence of moves and the actions available to all players and in games of complete information they know the payoffs to all players. In games of imperfect information a player might not know all the moves that have previously been made in the game, and in games of incomplete information a player might not know the payoffs of another player. In contrast, in evolutionary games different strategies are assumed to diffuse within a population through imitation. Behavioral games might be described as classical game theory in which the 'rational choice' assumptions about agents are replaced with more psychologically accurate models of how humans make decisions, update their beliefs, discount the future, and suchlike.

The conventional solution concept in a game is the Nash equilibrium; this arises when each player's strategy is the best response strategy to the other players' strategies. In other words, at a Nash equilibrium no player could do better by unilaterally changing her strategy. A result due to John Nash tells us that any game with a finite number of players and a finite number of strategies has at least one Nash equilibrium in pure or mixed strategies. A mixed strategy is a probability distribution over the player's set of possible pure strategies that makes her opponent indifferent between his possible pure strategies. It is fair comment to say that they are highly counterintuitive in one-shot games, though not in repeated games.

A long-standing problem for game theorists (and some sociologists) is not the existence of equilibrium but the fact that many games have multiple Nash equilibria. In response, game theorists have come up with other definitions of equilibrium that are more restrictive.[4] Another approach is to say that a particular equilibrium is chosen because of some exogenous reason. One well-known argument of this kind is Schelling's idea (1960) of a 'focal point.' This is an action which, out of all possible actions, seems like the most natural or sensible one. Imagine that two people are told to meet each other in a particular city at a particular date and time, but they are not told exactly where they should meet. In this case there is a very large number of equilibria (all the places that they could both meet) and so the equilibrium-selection problem seems impossible. A focal point, in this case, would be some location that would seem the most obvious place in which two strangers would look for each other in the city. That such focal points do indeed exist for this problem has been repeatedly verified experimentally. But they cannot exist for all coordination problems, and another solution that has been proposed is the existence of explicit norms: indeed, some writers use the terms 'norm' and 'coordination device' or 'convention' interchangeably (though a useful attempt to distinguish social norms from conventions is made by Bicchieri 2006).

In his review, Swedberg (2001: 316) claims, with some justification, that current game-theoretic research in sociology 'falls in the general category of social dilemma research.' The prisoner's dilemma (PD) is the canonical representation of this problem, and the free-rider and collective-action problems which it makes transparent have given rise to work based on deductive theory, computer simulation, and, to a much lesser extent, empirical research. But if the original PD and so-called N-person PD are the most widely used elements of classical game theory in contemporary sociology, they are not the only ones, and, indeed, other areas may hold more promise not least because they have not been so extensively utilized.

One such area is signaling games. These rest on the idea of 'types,' and this concept plays a central role in much game theory because it allows one to model uncertainty among players about what other players will do. Typically, a player in a game can be one of several types which differ in their payoffs. A player, A, faced with a player, B, whose type she does not know, must have beliefs about B's type because B's type determines what B will do and thus the payoffs to A's own choice of action. Thus, A's beliefs enter as a crucial part of her strategy. In the course of a game, beliefs can be updated. This is normally done using Bayes' rule, but the underlying idea is simple: A knows the equilibrium strategies of all possible B types and so, by observing what actions B takes, she can modify her beliefs about which type she is facing. But B knows this and in a signaling game the signaler (B in this example) may seek to persuade the receiver (A) that he is of one particular type rather than another. He does this because he knows the strategies that the receiver will play against all types of sender and he wants to instill in the receiver a belief such that the actions that the receiver takes will be most favorable to the sender. To make things concrete, suppose A is an investor and B is a would-be entrepreneur. B wants A to invest in his business but A believes that only people who are already successful (who are of the successful type, s) are worth investing in, and she will not invest in someone she believes to be of the unsuccessful type (u). B may be of either type but he wants to persuade R he is of type s. Emitting the signal that he is the 'better' type is costly if he is really a u-type—perhaps because this involves turning up to the meeting with R in a very expensive car, wearing very expensive clothes, or pretending to have first-hand experience of a successful business.

The important issue in signaling games is whether s-types and u-types will both signal that they are of the same type or whether the signals they send will allow the receiver to distinguish between them. This depends on the receiver's initial belief, on the costs of signaling, and on the payoffs to the different types. If the receiver's prior belief that the sender is of type s is high, and if the costs of signaling are low, both u-types and s-types will signal that they are s-types: this is called a pooling equilibrium. A pooling equilibrium may also arise if the costs of signaling that one is an s-type are too high regardless of one's true type (as in Spence's market-signaling model, 1973): in this case everyone will signal that they are a u-type. Only in cases where the costs of signaling that one is an s-type are such that s-types will so signal but u-types will not will each type signal truthfully and so reveal their hitherto private information about their type: this is a separating equilibrium. Another possible outcome is a so-called semipooling or semiseparating equilibrium, in which all the s-types signal that they are s-types and some of the u-types do too (or all the u-types do some of the time). This idea is capable of many applications. Consider the example of designing assessments of candidates, such as interviews. The ideal interview question will neither be too difficult nor too easy; rather, it will be difficult for those who are unsuited to the job but not for those who will do the job well. If all the interview questions are too easy or too difficult, it will not be possible for the good candidates to reveal themselves.

26.2 EVOLUTIONARY GAME THEORY

Classical game theory makes some strong assumptions about players or agents: that they know the structure of the game, that they have common knowledge about each other, that they can form and update, via Bayes' rule, probability distributions over different possible types, and suchlike. One of the initially appealing things about evolutionary game theory is that it seems to rest on much weaker assumptions. It works through the idea that more successful strategies spread in a population of players either (in biological applications) through reproduction (the success of the strategy is measured in terms of the reproductive fitness of those who follow it) or (in social-science applications) imitation (more successful strategies are adopted by players at a rate proportional to their success relative to other strategies). Table 26.1 shows a simple example (originally presented by Maynard-Smith and Price 1974).

In this game each player (R for row, C for column) has two possible strategies, called 'hawk' and 'dove.' When a hawk meets a dove, the hawk does very well (getting a payoff of 2) and the dove does very badly (getting zero). When two doves meet, the outcome is good for them both, but when two hawks meet the outcome is very bad for both of them. A real-world basis for this game would be that hawk and dove are strategies that can be used in deciding the allocation of resources, with hawk being an aggressive strategy, and dove a cooperative strategy. Hawks prey on doves but two hawks will fight, inflicting damage on each other. By contrast, two doves will reach an amicable settlement.

Imagine the hawk–dove game played only once with two players as in Table 26.1: then there are three Nash equilibria: R plays H and C plays D; R plays D and C plays H; and $p = 1/3$, where p is the probability of each player playing H in a mixed

Table 26.1 Hawk-and-dove game

		C (column player)	
		Hawk	Dove
R (row player)	Hawk	−2, −2	2, 0
	Dove	0, 2	1, 1

strategy. But now think of the game being played repeatedly among a population of agents and let p be the proportion of the population playing hawk. Under the assumption of random mixing of types throughout the population, the expected utility to any single agent from playing hawk is

$$U(H) = p(-2) + (1 - p)2 = 2 - 4p$$

and from playing dove

$$U(D) = p0 + (1 - p)1 = 1 - p.$$

These two will be equal when p = 1/3, and any player will then be indifferent between playing hawk or dove. If the proportion playing hawk were less than 1/3, U(H) > U(D): that is, it would be better to play hawk. The attractiveness of hawk is that it does very well against those who play dove, but the danger lies in meeting another hawk. If p < 1/3 this danger is small and so it pays to play hawk and take the small risk of meeting another hawk. But if p > 1/3 this danger is too great and so it is better to play dove. It is true that someone playing dove will fare badly against the many hawks in the population, but, nevertheless, a dove who meets a hawk does better than a hawk who meets a hawk. All members of the population will gradually discover this and they will adjust their strategy until the population comprises one-third playing hawk and two-thirds playing dove. They do not need to know the parameters of the game; rather, the population reaches an equilibrium distribution of hawks and doves through a process of individual trial and error.[5] This equilibrium is an evolutionarily stable strategy or ESS. An ESS is a refinement of Nash equilibrium: all ESSs are Nash equilibria but not all Nash equilibria are ESSs. Either of two conditions is required for an equilibrium to be an ESS. If strategy I is an ESS, then the first condition states that the expected payoff to playing I against someone else playing I must be greater than the expected payoff to playing another strategy, J, against someone else playing I. If this condition does not hold then we move on to the second, which says that the payoff to playing I against I must be equal to the payoff to playing J against I (so this is just the first condition stated as an equality) but the payoff to playing I against J must exceed that to playing J against J. The idea of an ESS is that it is a strategy (I in this case) that cannot be invaded by another strategy (J) either because I always does better than J when facing I (first condition) or because if I and J do equally against I, I does better than J against J (second condition).

This concept of equilibrium is one of the most attractive things about evolutionary game theory. An ESS is a 'stable stationary point of a dynamical system' (Gintis 2007: 2) and it does not rest on any of those assumptions about the players' rationality (such as subgame perfection) that are required to support the equilibrium refinements of Nash equilibrium in classical games.

26.3 BEHAVIORAL GAME THEORY

The main difference between classical and behavioral game theory concerns the way that the players are conceptualized. Behavioral game theory replaces the assumptions about agents derived from rational choice with agents endowed with a more realistic psychology. The evidence for this comes mainly from experiments, and the major differences from classical game theory concern how agents learn (they are not assumed always to be able to employ Bayes' rule); how they discount the future (they do not always discount exponentially) and how much foresight they have; and how they react to the actions taken by other players. Particular attention has been given to the role of fairness as an element in players' utility function which, under certain conditions, leads them to act in a cooperative fashion even when this is not what a purely self-regarding rational agent would do.

The absence of sociological studies that make explicit use of evolutionary or behavioral game theory (though see below) is surely something of a paradox. As I pointed out at the start of this chapter, many sociologists find the idea of game theory attractive but they balk at the details—and at no detail more than the assumptions about rational agents that derive from classical game theory (for example, see the comments by White 1992: 201–2).

26.4 INFORMAL SOCIOLOGICAL APPLICATIONS: GAME THEORY AS A WAY OF THINKING

Mackie (1996) analyzes the persistence of female foot-binding in imperial China and female genital mutilation (FGM) in Africa in terms of a coordination game. He uses the example of a two-player game with two actions available to each player, as shown in Table 26.2. Here there are two equilibria: U, L and D, R. The former is superior though either is preferable to U, R or D, L. Mackie argues that societies practicing foot-binding or FGM are caught in the inferior (D, R) equilibrium. Men and women both prefer marriage to not being married, but the convention stipulates that men will only marry women who have been foot-bound or genitally mutilated. This is a game with two possible equilibria and the equilibrium-selection problem is solved by convention: 'However the custom originated, as soon as women believed that men would not marry an unmutilated woman, and men believed that an unmutilated woman would not be a faithful

Table 26.2 Coordination game

		C (column player)	
		L	R
R (row player)	U	2, 2	0, 0
	D	0, 0	1, 1

partner in marriage...expectations were mutually concordant and a self-enforcing convention was locked in' (Mackie 1996: 1008). Mackie explains the origins of the practice by the demands of high-status men in polygynous societies for assurance that they were in fact the father of their wives' children; mutilation of women was, according to Mackie, a way of providing this assurance. As a practice it diffused from high-status marriages to the rest of society even though, for monogamous men at the bottom of the hierarchy, 'fidelity-assurance costs' were minimal. The problem is to shift the convention to the other, superior, equilibrium, in which women are not mutilated and men do not expect them to be in order to marry them. Mackie suggests a number of strategies that might be pursued to bring this about, including a program to educate people about the real costs of foot-binding and so change the payoffs to the game.

Mackie does not develop a formal game-theoretic model of FGM; in particular, the evolution of the practice and how it diffused from the upper strata of society is not included in the game and the proposed solutions are not formally modeled either (though some use is made of Schelling diagrams). Nevertheless, the paper is a good example of the use of game theory as a tool to think with: a complicated phenomenon is persuasively modeled using a simple game, and this helps us to grasp the central features of the phenomenon and suggest some ways of addressing it.

Another example of game theory being employed as a way of addressing a phenomenon is Gambetta's work on trust. Bacharach and Gambetta (2001) reformulate the problem of trust using concepts from signaling games. For them, the problem of trust concerns whether the person to be trusted (the 'trustee') is of the correct 'type'—the trustworthy type, in this case. The issue then becomes one of how the truster can determine the trustee's type, given that there are likely to be untrustworthy types who would like to pass themselves off as trustworthy in order to abuse the truster's trust. Thus, what Bacharach and Gambetta call the 'primary problem of trust' (Can agent A trust agent B?) is transformed into the secondary problem of trust (Can agent A trust the signs of trustworthiness that she receives from B?). They draw on the different equilibria of signaling games (pooling, separating, semiseparating) to codify the different possible outcomes of trust situations. Signaling theory 'provides a framework for analyzing, in a wide if somewhat idealized class of cases... signaling of both information and deliberately misleading kinds. It thus serves as a basis for an analytical account of the secondary problem of trust' (Bacharach and Gambetta 2001: 161). Bacharach and Gambetta seek to go beyond the abstract model by examining specific ways in which signals are used and inferred, and this task is also taken up by Gambetta and Hamill (2005). They use the ideas of signaling equilibria to look at how taxi drivers in dangerous cities determine who it is safe to pick up, how bona fide customers try to signal their trustworthiness, and how untrustworthy customers seek to mimic these signals.[6] As with Mackie's work, here game-theoretic ideas are being used to organize and illustrate sociological phenomena, with productive consequences.[7]

Perhaps the best example of using game theory as a tool to think with is behavioral game theory itself, because here games provide the basis of experimental designs to try to get at the psychology of how human agents make decisions in strategic contexts (Camerer 2004 provides a good summary). Behavioral game theorists have developed new games, and adapted existing ones (notably the ultimatum game and the dictator game but also the trust game and the prisoner's dilemma) for this purpose. Their basic approach might be said to be the successive refinement of the design of experimental games in order to isolate exactly what behavioral dispositions of human players need to be assumed in order to explain the observations of earlier experiments. For example, is cooperative behavior (which would not be predicted under rational-choice assumptions about players) observed because of the fear of punishment or because players are altruistic? Fehr and Gintis (2007) is a useful summary of much of the experimental research on fairness.

26.5 DERIVING AGGREGATE DISTRIBUTIONS AND EXPLAINING AGGREGATE OUTCOMES

In this section I review three recent papers that have used game theory in a more formal way in order to derive aggregate properties from a social system comprising interacting agents. In all cases this is done by setting up the interactions between agents as a game and finding the equilibrium (or equilibria) of the game and assessing its goodness of fit, in either a formal or informal way, to observed data.

Montgomery (1998) uses some basic game-theoretic ideas to model the observed characteristics of interactions between manufacturers and contractors in the New York City garment industry, as described by Uzzi (1996). He goes beyond conventional classical game theory in seeking to show how role theorists might construct games in which the players are roles, rather than individuals. Because manufacturers and contractors are effectively playing a finitely repeated prisoner's dilemma, game theory would predict only one equilibrium: mutual defection. Yet what was observed, and what Montgomery sought to explain, were, first, that manufacturers and contractors begin to cooperate 'only if a mutual friend "primes" the relationship'; second, that there is a trial phase during which 'exchange partners maintain a calculative orientation focused narrowly on economic goals' after which they 'adopt heuristic decision making and become motivated by friendship as well as profit'; and, finally, that they cooperate even in the endgame (Montgomery 1998: 96).[8]

The game that Montgomery constructs allows manufacturers and contractors to play as businessmen (who engage in rational calculation) or as friends (who follow a rule of 'always cooperate'), and one player can induce the other to be a friend by cooperating for a sufficient number of plays of the game, even when the other player is defecting. Provided that a 'sufficient number' is small enough, relative to the duration of the entire game, and that the players care enough about future payoffs, a cooperative equilibrium which includes endgame cooperation is possible, given that the players play a mixed strategy (Montgomery 1998: 110–11). Montgomery proposes a quite simple 'meta-rule' for how different roles are evoked.

Whereas Montgomery starts with the findings of a specific empirical investigation in mind, Breen and Cooke (2005) begin with something more akin to a stylized (but largely accurate) fact. They develop a model and then try to test the model's implications against data. Their aim is to explain why the gendered division of domestic labor has proved so resistant to change despite the growth in married women's labor-force participation. To do this they develop an extension of the trust game in which if a woman decides to marry a man, the latter may either cooperate in domestic tasks or defect, and if he defects, she is then faced with the choice of accepting this situation or divorcing him. They model uncertainty in the marriage market by assuming that there are three types of men and three types of women, and an individual's type is not revealed to his or her spouse until after the marriage. They justify the assumptions concerning types and the lack of information about a spouse's type until after marriage by referring to a number of empirical studies (Breen and Cooke 2005: 45, 48); their assumptions are simplifications whose purpose is to capture the salient features shaping the division of domestic labor. They derive the full set of equilibria of the game (technically these are 'perfect Bayesian equilibria,' which are defined in terms not only of the players' strategies but also their beliefs about the type of their potential or actual spouse) and they show that which equilibrium emerges depends on the distribution of types in the population (or, more strictly, players' prior beliefs about this distribution). This suggests that the conditions for a more equal division of domestic labor (as evidenced by those equilibria in which men cooperate rather than defect) are not only a greater proportion of economically autonomous women within the society as a whole but also a sufficiently large proportion of men who, if faced with an economically autonomous woman, would rather participate in domestic tasks than endure marital breakdown. In other words, what is required is both greater material

gender equality for the majority of women and an evolution in men's gender ideology. These predictions are tested using aggregate data from twenty-two countries
and found to be supported (although, as the authors themselves point out, the test
should be regarded as indicative rather than definitive).

Gould (2002) develops a formal model of how status hierarchies emerge. Individuals accord status to others on the basis of their evaluation of the other's 'quality.'
This perception of quality is held to be a weighted sum of some exogenously
determined quality (which we might call true quality, as seen in someone's abilities,
contributions, and so on) and the status accorded to the other by everyone else,
which functions as a signal of quality. The latter captures an important aspect
of status hierarchies: individuals may be accorded status just because they are
accorded status by everyone else (Gould 2002: 1147). This self-reinforcing characteristic of status hierarchies generates a positive-feedback mechanism, but its effects
are then dampened (so ensuring an interior equilibrium in Gould's model) by the
symmetry effect; that is to say, all else equal we prefer to accord status to those
who reciprocate, and so how much status we accord to high-status people who
do not reciprocate is restricted. Conditional on how much weight they give to the
judgments of others, agents in the model pick the optimum amount of status they
accord to each of the other agents. A Nash equilibrium exists, and Gould derives
from this a set of propositions, which he then tests on three data sets, and finds that
all of them are supported. One important aspect of the model is that it explains
how small differences in true quality can be magnified by the endogenous social-
influence effect. 'In other words, it can be simultaneously true . . . that competitive
processes distribute rewards as a function of individual qualities, and . . . that these
rewards are nevertheless filtered through structural positions that distribute advantage unevenly' (Gould 2002: 1170–1). The paper is interesting not least because it
marries classical-game-theory assumptions about agents' ability to find equilibrium
strategies to the idea that agents form beliefs by observing the actions of others.

26.6 EVOLUTIONARY GAMES

This idea of learning from the actions of others (usually called 'observational learning') underlies a very influential paper by Bikhchandani, Hirshleifer, and Welch
(1998). In their model, agents are trying to learn whether the true state of the world
is X or ~X. The state of the world determines the payoffs to two possible actions,
A (which is better in state X) and B (better in state ~X). Each agent receives some
private information about which state is true in the form of a 'noisy signal.' The
agent gets the signal, either P or Q: P is more likely if X is true, Q if ~X is the true

state, but the noise in the signal means that there is some small probability that an agent could get Q if X were true and P if ~X were. Agents are therefore uncertain about the true state of the world. Nevertheless, if agents could see many signals they could use Bayes' rule to deduce the true state of the world (provided that they knew the prior probability of getting each signal conditional on whichever state of the world was true and that they had initial probabilities as to which state was true). But agents only observe what other agents do. The model supposes that agents act in sequence: agent 1 receives a signal, P or Q, then acts (A or B); then agent 2 follows, having seen which action agent 1 took, and so on. Bikhchandani, Hirshleifer, and Welch show that once any two successive agents take the same action, all later agents will do the same thing. They call this a cascade. To see roughly how it works, imagine that the first agent does A; this must mean that his signal was P. Suppose that agent 2 does A also; this could mean that her signal was P, so reinforcing what she learned from agent 1. But it could also have been that her signal was Q, in which case she would have chosen A or B at random (because she knew there had been one signal of P and one of Q). Agent 3 would like to infer which signal B is most likely to have got. The answer is P, because agent 2's probability of playing A given that she got P(= 1) is greater than her probability of playing A given that she got Q(= 1/2). Suppose agent 3's signal is Q, he will nevertheless play A too, based on the calculation that he knows that there has been one signal of P (agent 1's signal) and one of Q (his own signal) and another signal that was more probably P than Q. So agent 3 acts against his own signal; indeed, agent 3's signal has no effect on his choice of A or B. It follows that agent 4 and later agents will all also play A, and they will do this even if every one of them receives the signal Q.

Although the sequential setup seems rather restrictive, and although the authors do not undertake any formal empirical tests, the model is both interesting and suggestive. It shows, for example, how, in situations of high uncertainty, an action taken by one agent can have a very large impact if other agents interpret this as a sign that he is better informed than they are and so imitate his action. The model is also informative about how easily fads and fashions can be started and how people may adopt some fashionable practice even when doing so goes against their own private belief. Cascades are common in situations in which individuals are unsure about the value of the signals they receive (as in the fairy tale of the emperor's new clothes), or can be persuaded to doubt them (as in the Asch 1955 social-conformity experiment), or believe that particular individuals receive better signals (possess more accurate information). In some situations of uncertainty agents infer that a first mover must be better informed simply because he or she moved first.

Games that involve learning by observing the actions of others are evolutionary games. Evolutionary games crop up quite often in sociology, though they might not always be recognized as such. In fact, they underlie one of the areas of most intense activity in sociology over the past twenty years; namely, the study of social or endogenous interactions. This is immediately evident when we consider that

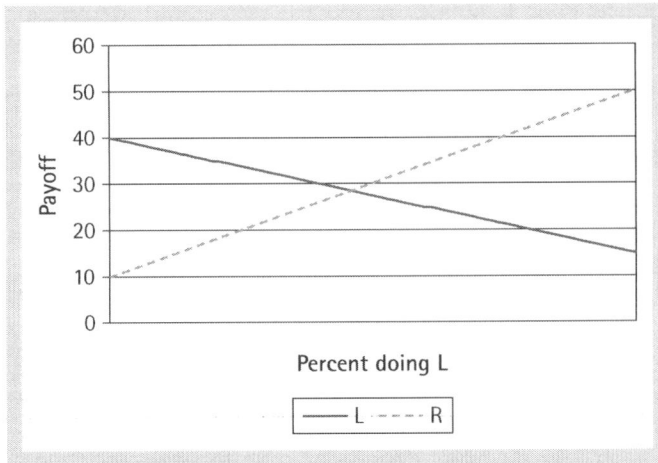

Fig. 26.1 Schelling diagram (from Schelling 1978)

these models are based on the idea that the frequency or proportion of others who perform an action A influences the likelihood that any particular agent will perform A.[9] Much of the credit for making recent generations of social scientists aware of social-interaction effects is due to Thomas Schelling, particularly *Micromotives and Macrobehavior* (1978). Here Schelling dealt with situations of binary choice in which an individual's choice of action depends on the actions taken by others. He illustrated his discussion with what is now known as a 'Schelling diagram.' Figure 26.1 is an example (taken from Schelling 1978: ch. 7, fig. 15).

In Figure 26.1 the two possible actions are R and L. The x-axis shows the percentage who do L and the y-axis shows the returns to an action. The downward sloping line shows the returns to doing L as a function of the percentage doing L, and the upward sloping line shows the returns to doing R as a function of the percentage doing L. This diagram represents a situation in which an agent wants to do the opposite to what everyone else does: L and R might be choosing to visit alternative unspoiled scenic locations; if everyone wants to go to L it is better to go to R and vice versa. The equilibrium distribution of agents choosing L and R occurs at the point where the L and R lines intersect (and so the returns to L and R are equal). This is the unique ESS of this game, though it is not the unique Nash equilibrium.

Now consider the case in which everyone wants to do what everyone else does. Figure 26.1 will also serve to show this situation if we simply relabel the lines, so that the returns to L are increasing in the number who do L and the returns to R are increasing in the number who choose R. According to Schelling the equilibria are X = 0 and X = 100. An example is that the attractiveness of playing football rather than doing homework increases as the number of other children who are playing football instead of doing their homework increases. There are two equilibria—everyone plays football or everyone does their homework—but there is no equilibrium at which some do their homework and some play football. Yet this intersection is a Nash equilibrium; it is not, however, an ESS (whereas both $X = 0$ and $X = 100$ are).[10]

The same concept of the equilibrium of a dynamical system underlies social-interaction models and evolutionary games. However, sociologists tend to pay little attention to the concept of equilibrium. The basic idea of endogenous interaction models—namely, that what others do may influence an agent's choice of action—has entered sociology as another kind of explanatory variable. Elaborations of the basic-population-level Schelling (and other related) models have involved allowing for heterogeneity among agents in terms of measured and hypothesized (e.g. Granovetter 1978) factors and in their susceptibility to the influence of others. All these ideas are found in applications of Strang and Tuma's individual-level event-history-diffusion models (1993). Event-history-diffusion models for example treat the number who have already made the particular transition in question (or some function of this) as a variable to predict the conditional probability that an agent who is at risk will make the transition. The hypotheses tested are concerned with whether such an effect exists, what its functional form is, and similar, but this is quite some way from the central idea in evolutionary game theory, and in Schelling diagrams, of seeking to explain why a system settles into, or is drawn towards, some particular state(s) and what that state is.

An important exception to this is much of the work that uses game theory together with simulation models to address public goods and other similar questions. The starting point for much of this work was Axelrod's *The Evolution of Cooperation* (1984), and since then a number of sociologists have made important contributions. I do not review that work here because several reviews already exist (Swedberg 2001; Macy and Willer 2002; Macy and Flache, this volume). Not all of the work in this area draws explicitly on game theory, but a good example of a paper that makes evident the link between game theory and simulation is Heckathorn (1996).

Finally, formal applications of behavioral games, which seem to hold out a lot of promise for sociology, are in fact absent from the field. In some cases (as in Montgomery's paper summarized earlier) modifications are made to the players of the game that move them in the direction of possessing a more plausible psychology, but I know of no substantive application in sociology that, in its depiction of the players, draws on experimental results about how humans judge and decide. An example of how sociologists might do this, however, can be found in a paper by Dufwenberg (2002).

Dufwenberg's 'marital-investment game' is, like Breen and Cooke's 'marriage game,' a variant of the trust game, but in this case the wife decides whether the couple will invest heavily in the husband's education, at the expense of the wife's, or whether they will invest equally, but modestly, in the education of both. If the latter, then each partner gets a modest return ($a > 0$). If the former, the husband decides whether to stay with his wife or divorce her. If he stays with her, they share the fruits of his education (they each get $b > a$) and if he divorces her he gets c ($c > b$) and she gets zero.[11] The question the paper addresses is: What investment will couples make? If this were a classical game the answer would be immediately evident: because, by subgame perfection, an educated husband would always divorce his wife, she will never want to invest in educating her husband. But in this game Dufwenberg introduces the (empirically warranted) idea that the more the husband believes that his wife trusts him, the more guilt he will feel if he divorces her. (This is an example of a psychological game: Geanakoplos, Pearce, and Stacchetti 1989.) Provided that the husband is sufficiently influenced by feelings of guilt, equilibria can emerge in which couples do indeed invest in the education of the husband. What is particularly interesting in this example, however, is that because the players are rational, the wife can induce in the husband beliefs about how much she trusts him, simply by deciding that they should invest in his education. This paper includes no empirical tests of the model, but it does provide an account which is at least plausible and provides a useful illustration of how games with more realistic depictions of agents might be constructed and solved.

26.7 Hurdles

Many social scientists view behavioral games, and particularly evolutionary games, as more promising approaches for explaining macro-level phenomena than classical game theory. Compared with classical game theory, evolutionary game theory rests on the simple premise that more successful strategies spread through a population by imitation. However, this may be a slow process, making empirical tests difficult or impossible. Many applications of evolutionary game theory construct a game that gives rise to the outcome of interest (very often this is some form of cooperative behavior as in Skyrms 1996), but this is far from showing that the outcome really was the result of this game. For that we would need empirical evidence, or else it would have to be shown that the hypothesized game was the only way in which the outcome could have been generated (though this criticism is hardly limited to explanations using evolutionary game theory).

A further difficulty with evolutionary games and, by extension, models of social interactions is their dependence on particular forms of learning which usually cannot be empirically verified. It is assumed that people imitate others, or change their behavior in response to the outcomes they have received. Yet a great deal depends on exactly how this happens. As Young (1998: 27) notes, how individuals adapt their behavior in response to others' behavior is 'a key building block...yet the truth is that we do not yet have adequate data (let alone an accepted theory) about how individuals actually make such decisions.' Crucially, whether or not a process reaches equilibrium is highly dependent on the kind of adaptation assumed.

CONCLUSIONS

An argument for the importance of game theory might seem to be redundant. Not only has it swept through several of the social (as well as the biological) sciences, but also topics dear to the hearts of sociologists, such as norms, coordination devices, conventions, and so on, are almost impossible to think about without casting them in the framework of a game. Yet there remains skepticism within sociology towards game theory and so I have presented some examples to show how sociologists have used it both as a means of conceptualizing a problem or issue and as a way of determining an aggregate, macro-level outcome as the consequence of the inter-action of individual agents. The examples illustrate the flexibility of game theory: the use of different types as a way of introducing uncertainty into the model; the use of signaling as a means of modeling how people try to induce beliefs in others; the ability to distinguish between individual agents and the roles they play; and so forth. Furthermore, although the use of game theory commits one to accounting for action in terms of individual beliefs, desires, and opportunities, it does not entail the necessary acceptance of any of the postulates of hard-line rational choice—that agents are only motivated by narrowly defined self-interest and that they can make inferences and judgments in a hyperrational fashion. Dufwenberg's paper shows how game theory can depict agents in a more flexible fashion and evolutionary games show us that equilibria can be reached via imitation and learning by agents without the assumption of rational, strategic calculation. All these are characteris-tics that should commend game theory to analytical sociologists.

NOTES

1. These can be persons or organizations or nations, but the choice of such an elemen-tary unit of analysis is a matter of convenience: the units are elementary because we believe that decomposing them further would not be useful given our explanatory goal.
2. This would be the case, for example, in class differences in educational attainment. These are the aggregation of individual educational choices that we might reasonably model as being made without reference to the choices of others (as in Breen and Goldthorpe 1997).
3. Cooperative games are a different kettle of fish and they have had no impact on sociology in recent times.
4. The point here is that some Nash equilibria admit of nonrational strategies on the part of one or more players; refinements to the Nash equilibrium seek to rule these out as solutions to the game. These refinements include subgame perfection and Cho and Kreps's 'intuitive criterion' (1987).
5. But in an evolutionary contest this is not the only possible outcome. Hawks might evolve advance warning capabilities that helped to avoid encounters with

other-hawks. Then the population could support a larger proportion of hawks than in the proposed equilibrium. This leads naturally to the idea of local interactions, which is taken up further in the text.

6. But the same idea—of signaling one's type and of the possibility of deception—has run through sociology for a very long time. Erving Goffman's work (e.g. 1959) might be read as presenting many examples of signaling, though I am unaware of any work that recasts his insights into a mathematical form.

7. But signaling games have also been used by sociologists in a more formal and thoroughgoing way. Smith and Varese (2001) use a signaling game to model how fake Russian Mafiosi seek to present themselves as the real thing to businessmen whom they are trying to extort, while seeking to avoid the attention of the real Russian Mafia. They solve the game for its equilibria and they consider the circumstances under which each equilibrium will arise and describe their features (for example, whether both real and fake Mafiosi demand money, whether the fakes will be prepared to use violence, and so on). Schroeder and Rojas (2002) use a signaling game to model interactions between sexual partners who are trying to signal that they are not infected with HIV. The authors use the game to model the dynamics of an HIV infection in a population.

8. Some elements of what Uzzi reports could be explained using a model of reputation (Kreps 1990a). This would include cooperation in the endgame and, possibly, the role of the mutual friend, who might be seen as providing reputational information, much like the law merchant in Milgrom, North, and Weingast's analysis (1990) of the Champagne Fairs.

9. Sometimes attempts are made to specify the mechanisms by which this happens, and the usual typology is that the actions of others influence individual agents' preferences or their beliefs or their opportunities (or, indeed, more than one of these). See, for example, Manski (2000) and Hedström (2005: 47).

10. We can find the Nash equilibria if we think of the figure as representing a coordination game with payoff s to both players if they both do R and t if they both do L and zero otherwise. Then there are three Nash equilibria: both do R, both do L and each does R with probability $t/(s + t)$.

11. The assumption that the husband gets everything is not necessary; what is required is that the wife's payoff in the event of divorce is less than a.

REFERENCES

Asch, S. E. (1955), 'Opinions and Social Pressure', *Scientific American*, 193: 33–5.

Axelrod, R. (1984), *The Evolution of Cooperation* (New York: Basic).

Bacharach, M., and Gambetta, D. (2001), 'Trust in Signs', in K. S. Cook (ed.), *Trust in Society* (New York: Russell Sage).

Barth, F. (1966), 'Models of Social Organization, I–III', in Barth, *Process and Form in Social Life*, i (London: Routledge & Kegan Paul), 32–75.

Bicchieri, C. (2006), *The Grammar of Society: The Nature and Dynamics of Social Norms* (Cambridge: Cambridge University Press).

BIKHCHANDANI, S., HIRSHLEIFER, D., and WELCH, I. (1998), 'Learning from the Behavior of Others: Conformity, Fads and Informational Cascades', *Journal of Economic Perspectives*, 12: 151–70.

BREEN, R., and COOKE, L. P. (2005), 'The Persistence of the Gendered Division of Domestic Labour', *European Sociological Review*, 21 (1): 43–57.

—— and GOLDTHORPE, J. H. (1997), 'Explaining Educational Differentials: Towards a Formal Rational Action Theory', *Rationality and Society*, 9: 275–305.

CAMERER, C. F. (2004), 'Behavioral Game Theory: Predicting Human Behavior in Strategic Situations', in C. F. Camerer, G. Loewenstein, and M. Rabin (eds.), *Advances in Behavioral Economics* (New York: Russel Sage), 374–92.

CHO, I. K., and KREPS, D. M. (1987), 'Signaling Games and Stable Equilibria', *Quarterly Journal of Economics*, 102: 179–222.

DUFWENBERG, M. (2002), 'Marital Investments, Time Consistency and Emotions', *Journal of Economic Behavior and Organization*, 48: 57–69.

ELSTER, J. (1982), 'Marxism, Functionalism and Game Theory', *Theory and Society*, 11: 453–82.

FEHR, E., and GINTIS, H. (2007), 'Human Motivation and Social Cooperation: Experimental and Analytical Foundations', *Annual Review of Sociology*, 33: 43–64.

GAMBETTA, D., and HAMILL, H. (2005), *Streetwise: How Taxi Drivers Establish their Customers' Trustworthiness* (New York: Russell Sage).

GEANAKOPLOS, J., PEARCE, D., and STACCHETTI, E. (1989), 'Psychological Games and Sequential Rationality', *Games and Economic Behavior*, 1: 60–79.

GINTIS, H. (2007), 'A framework for the Unification of the Behavioural Sciences', *Behavioral and Brain Sciences*, 30: 1–61.

GOFFMAN, E. (1959), *The Presentation of Self in Everyday Life* (New York: Doubleday).

GOULD, R. V. (2002), 'The Origins of Status Hierarchies: A Formal Theory and Empirical Test', *American Journal of Sociology*, 107: 1143–78.

GRANOVETTER, M. (1978), 'Threshold Models of Collective Behavior', *American Journal of Sociology*, 83: 1420–43.

HECKATHORN, D. D. (1996), 'The Dynamics and Dilemmas of Collective Action', *American Sociological Review*, 61: 250–77.

HEDSTRÖM, P. (2005), *Dissecting the Social: On the Principles of Analytical Sociology* (Cambridge: Cambridge University Press).

KREPS, D. M. (1990a), 'Corporate Culture and Economic Theory', in J. E. Alt and K. A. Shepsle (eds.), *Perspectives on Positive Political Economy* (Cambridge: Cambridge University Press), 90–143.

—— (1990b), *Game Theory and Economic Modelling* (Oxford: Oxford University Press).

MACKIE, G. (1996), 'Ending Footbinding and Infibulation: A Convention Account', *American Sociological Review*, 61 (6): 999–1017.

MACY, M. W., and FLACHE, A. (2009), 'Social Dynamics from the Bottom Up: Agent-based Models of Social Interaction', *The Oxford Handbook of Analytical Sociology* (Oxford: Oxford University Press).

—— and WILLER, R. (2002), 'From Factors to Actors: Computational Sociology and Agent-based Modeling', *Annual Review of Sociology*, 28: 143–66.

MANSKI, C. F. (2000), 'Economic Analysis of Social Interactions', *Journal of Economic Perspectives*, 14: 115–36.

MAYNARD-SMITH, J., and PRICE, G. (1974), 'The Theory of Games and the Evolution of Animal Conflict', *Journal of Theoretical Biology*, 47: 209–21.

MILGROM, P. R., NORTH, D. C., and WEINGAST, B. R. (1990), 'The Role of Institutions in the Revival of Trade: The Law Merchant, Private Judges and the Champagne Fairs', *Economics and Politics*, 2 (1): 1–24.

MONTGOMERY, J. D. (1998), 'Toward a Role-theoretic Conception of Embeddedness', *American Journal of Sociology*, 104: 92–125.

PETERSEN, T. (1994), 'The Promise of Game Theory in Sociology', *Contemporary Sociology*, 23: 498–502.

SCHELLING, T. C. (1960), *The Strategy of Conflict* (Cambridge, Mass.: Harvard University Press).

—— (1978), *Micromotives and Macrobehavior* (New York: Norton).

SCHROEDER, K. J., and ROJAS, F. G., (2002), 'A Game-theoretical Analysis of Sexually Transmitted Disease Epidemics', *Rationality and Society*, 14: 353–83.

SKYRMS, B. (1996), *Evolution of the Social Contract* (Cambridge: Cambridge University Press).

SMITH, A., and VARESE, F. (2001), 'Payment, Protection and Punishment: the Role of Information and Reputation in the Mafia', *Rationality and Society*, 13 (3): 349–93.

SPENCE, A. M. (1973), 'Job Market Signaling', *Quarterly Journal of Economics*, 87: 355–74.

STRANG, D., and TUMA, N. B. (1993), 'Spatial and Temporal Heterogeneity in Diffusion', *American Journal of Sociology*, 99: 614–39.

SWEDBERG, R. (2001), 'Sociology and Game Theory: Contemporary and Historical Perspectives', *Theory and Society*, 30: 301–35.

—— and AUGIER, M. (2003), 'Game Theory and Sociology: Landmarks in Game Theory from a Sociological Perspective', *History of Economic Ideas*, 11: 15–42.

UZZI, B. (1996), 'The Sources and Consequences of Embeddedness for the Economic Performance of Organizations: The Network Effect', *American Sociological Review*, 61: 674–98.

WEBER, M. [1922–3] (1978), *Economy and Society*, ed. G. Roth and C. Wittich (Berkeley, Calif.: University of California Press).

WHITE, H. C. (1992), *Identity and Control: A Structural Theory of Social Action* (Princeton, N.J.: Princeton University Press).

YOUNG, H. P. (1998), *Individual Strategy and Social Structure*, (Princeton, N.J.: Princeton University Press).

CHAPTER 27

EXPERIMENTS

IRIS BOHNET

INTRODUCTION

THE goal of this chapter is to provide a review of game-theoretic experiments run in the laboratory on topics of particular interest to analytical sociologists. Although there is an important experimental tradition in sociology, during the last two decades there has been an explosion of experimental work in economics that seems to be of direct relevance to analytical sociology but is not yet well known in the field. This chapter gives a way into this literature and a flavor of what this research has to offer.

Most of the studies discussed belong to the new field of 'behavioral economics,' which is grounded in economics but has been heavily influenced by psychology. (For recent reviews see Kagel and Roth 1995; Camerer 2003.) While this chapter includes about forty references to work from other disciplines than economics, it cannot do justice to the rich tradition of experimental work in psychology or sociology. In the spirit of cross-disciplinary fertilization, its focus is behavioral economics, acknowledging, however, that sociologists have relied on experimental approaches for a long time, and often have been among the first to employ experiments to study a specific phenomenon. For example, Gerald Marwell and Ruth Ames initiated the first systematic experimental-research program on the determinants of the voluntary provision of public goods, in the late 1970s. Marwell and Ames (1979, 1980) suggested that they were studying 'a fundamental sociological question: when will a collectivity act to maximize its collective interest even though such behavior conflicts with a course of action that would maximize the short-term interests of each individual separately.' The research team examined the effect of a rather large number of important variables on voluntary contributions: group size, experience of the subjects, provision points, distribution of resources, the heterogeneity of benefits, the divisibility of the public goods, strength of induced preferences, and the economics training of the subjects (the latter being a question still disputed in the experimental community).

Experiments are run for many reasons. They are a useful tool for testing the validity of normative theories, for discovering behavioral regularities that allow for a more accurate description of how people behave, and for 'test-bedding' specific designs and mechanisms for prescriptive advice. Some researchers focus on the normative aspects or description only; many try to combine all dimensions.

Experiments are conducted in the laboratory and in the field, with the former typically involving students as subjects and the latter focusing on people in their naturally occurring environments. In the extreme case, subjects in field experiments are not aware that they are participants in an experiment. Recent examples include fund-raising experiments where potential donors were not aware that how they were being asked whether they would be willing to make a contribution was part of an experimental manipulation (e.g. Croson and Shang 2005; Karlan and List 2007; and, for a review, Harrison and List 2004).

Hybrids between the two approaches include laboratory studies with nonstandard subject pools and/or in nonstandard locations. For example, as a result of an interdisciplinary collaboration between several anthropologists and economists, bargaining and public-goods experiments have been run in various small-scale societies across the world, such as the Machiguenga farmers in Peru or the Lamelara whalers in Indonesia (Henrich et al. 2004). Cardenas and Carpenter (2007) survey the evidence on trust and public goods experiments run in developing countries and show how they can shed new light on issues related to development.

Laboratory experiments allow for a maximum of internal control. Such control is useful if the researcher wishes to examine theoretical predictions, that are often sensitive to a large number of design variables. Game-theoretic predictions, for example, typically depend on the choices and information available to the players, how players value outcomes, or in which order they move, etc.; other theories may be sensitive to other parameters, such as the status of the various players or the communication channels available to them; but all theories have in common that they outline a specific set of assumptions under which the predictions ought to work. The laboratory is unique in its ability to create such environments, allowing the researcher not only to test theories but also to identify how sensitive the outcome is to changes in the environment. By manipulating one variable at a time—for example, the number of players involved or the number of choice options available—the researcher learns how generalizable theoretical predictions are.

Clearly, the degree to which experimental results based on student subjects playing in a controlled environment for relatively small stakes generalize to naturally occurring settings outside of the laboratory is an important question for experimentalists to address. First steps have been taken, but many more need to follow to increase external validity (see Levitt and List 2007 for a critical discussion). Important steps include: running of experiments with nonstandard and sometimes representative subject pools (e.g. for a representative sample of the German population and trust games see Fehr 2002); increasing stake sizes to sometimes several months' income (e.g. Cameron 1999); and deepening the social context in which experiments take place by, for example, allowing participants to talk to each other (for an early example see Dawes, McTavish, and Shaklee 1977). A few researchers have examined external validity by directly testing to what degree experimental behavior is related to the corresponding behavior in naturally occurring settings. For example, Karlan (2005) ran trust experiments with members of a microfinance organization in Peru and measured the correlation between trustworthiness in the trust game and the repayment of loans. Greig and Bohnet (2009) ran public-goods games with slum dwellers in Kenya and looked at how contributions to the experimental public good were correlated with participation in 'harambee,' the Swahili word for 'let's pull together,' and ROSCAs, which are groups of individuals who make regular contributions to a fund which is given in whole or in part to each contributor in turn. ROSCA members are indeed more likely to contribute to the experimental public good.

While making experiments more realistic and, in particular, more embedded in a social context is certainly desirable, it comes at a price. The more closely an experiment represents a naturally occurring environment, the less clear will be the theoretical predictions. Elegant theories include only a few principles. Elegant experimental designs build on these principles and are able to identify which principle is at fault in case the prediction turns out to be wrong. Decisions are usually posed in abstract terms, not because abstraction helps understand reality but rather because it helps understand and improve theory by identifying the relevant deviations that then inspire new theory. Take the elusive concept of trust as an example. Trust is studied in all of the social sciences. Experimentalists have come up with a clever way to define and measure it: If a person is willing to lend money to someone who does not have to pay her back (but might feel morally obliged to do so), the person is said to trust. Her counterpart is said to behave trustworthily if he returns the money.

This chapter presents experimental research that we hope will be useful for sociologists, and in particular those sociologists interested in questions of cooperation, collective action, and social order. Game-theoretic experiments can shed new light on social norms of fairness and cooperativeness. We take social norms to be standards of behavior based on widely shared beliefs on how one should behave in a given situation (Elster 1989; Coleman 1990), or, as Michael Hechter and Karl-Dieter

Opp (2001: xi) put it: 'Norms are cultural phenomena that prescribe and proscribe behavior in specific circumstances. As such, they have long been considered to be at least partly responsible for regulating social behavior.'

This chapter is organized as follows. In Section 27.1 we first discuss some key methodological considerations and then present an example highlighting how experiments primarily control by design rather than by relying on statistical, socio-, psycho-, or econometric tools (although these tools sometimes complement an experimental analysis). Section 26.2 focuses on social norms of fairness and cooperativeness and looks at how norms can be measured experimentally, how they become salient, and what experiments tell us on how norm-abiding behavior can be sustained.

27.1 METHODOLOGY

An experimenter has many design choices to make. She will be guided by the purpose the experiment should serve, primarily normative, descriptive, or prescriptive, but also by the norms that apply to her particular discipline. For example, for nonobvious reasons, different norms of procedure apply to experiments in economics and in psychology. Because the author is an experimental economist, the focus of this chapter will be the norms relevant in economics, but deviations from psychology will be indicated. Section 27.1.1 presents an overview of some crucial questions of design. Section 27.1.2 gives an example which illustrates how experimenters control for alternative explanations by design.

27.1.1 Experimental design

We focus on seven key elements of design: incentives, social context, language, repetition, common knowledge, control group, and empirical analysis.

Incentives

Value is induced using monetary payments linked to performance. Experimental economists prefer this incentive scheme to relying on subjects' intrinsic motivation or some other extrinsic motivator, such as chocolate, because most people like more money most of the time while the degree of intrinsic motivation or the preference intensity for chocolate may vary more substantially among people. Psychologists typically do not reward their subjects for performance (although participation in experiments often is a course requirement for psychology students). The debate to what degree incentives matter is ongoing. Several studies suggest that paying subjects their earnings decreases the variance of responses (e.g. Smith and Walker 1993; Camerer and Hogarth 1999). Performance-based incentives seem to be most important in judgment and decision-making tasks, where there are returns to thinking harder. They are less relevant for either very easy or very difficult tasks (see e.g. the joint work by a psychologist and an economist, Hertwig and Ortmann 2001). Note that monetary payoffs are useful for both those who believe that people in fact have money-maximizing preferences and want to test theoretical predictions based on the money-maximization assumption as well as those who do not believe that preferences can be equated with monetary payoffs, as it allows them to measure how behavior deviates from an income-maximizing strategy. Fehr and Schmidt (2002) discuss recent experiments examining social preferences, such as altruism or inequity aversion.

Social context

Typically, care is taken in economic experiments to preserve a subject's anonymity. Experiments that guarantee between-subjects anonymity have been referred to as 'single-blind' while experiments that also preserve a subject's anonymity vis-à-vis the experimenter have been referred to as 'double-blind.' A number of studies have compared single- and double-blind treatments, with mixed results. In some cases double-blindness mattered (e.g Hoffman, McCabe, and Smith 1996), in others it did not (e.g. Bolton, Katok, and Zwick 1998). While the final verdict on the importance of subject–experimenter anonymity is still out, the importance of between-subjects anonymity is well established. Generally, people care more about others when they know their identity, often referred to as the 'identifiable-victim effect,' following Schelling (1968), but the variance of responses also increases. If identification is mutual, that is everyone knows everyone else's identity in the game, subjects seem to fear social sanctions after the experiment, leading them to converge to whatever the social norm of behavior happens to be in a given context (e.g. Bohnet and Frey 1999a, 1999b, explained in more detail below).

Language

Experimental economists typically use abstract language to describe subjects' choices. For example, a participant in a prisoner's-dilemma game is not asked whether she is willing to cooperate with her counterpart or not but rather is confronted with two options to choose from, A and B, one representing cooperation and one defection. Such abstraction is not meant to capture naturally occurring situations but rather to provide a benchmark against which the effects of specific 'frames' can be measured. A large literature on individual choice, building on Kahneman and Tversky (1979), has shown that theoretically equivalent choices may elicit different responses when presented differently. For example, defaults matter. When indicating their valuation for a public good, such as a park, people tend to indicate higher 'values' when asked how much they would have to be compensated for giving it up ('willingness to accept') than when asked how much they would be willing to pay for keeping it ('willingness to pay'). (For a review of this and related effects see Thaler 1992.) People also entrust another person with less money when asked how much they are trusting than when asked how much they are distrusting the other person. In the former version of the game, the standard trust game, the default is no trust, in the latter version, the distrust game, it is full trust (Bohnet and Meier 2007). Thus, in contrast to most of the literature (summarized in Lewicki, McAllister, and Bies 1998) but in accordance with Luhmann (1979) and Lewicki and his colleagues (1998: 444), Bohnet and Meier show experimentally that 'low distrust is not the same thing as high trust, and high distrust is not the same thing as low trust.'

Repetition

Depending on the research question, games are played 'one-shot' or repeated over several rounds. Repetition allows for learning, often itself the subject of inquiry, and reputation-building. To separate the two potential influences on behavior, experiments are typically run using either a 'stranger' or a 'partner' protocol. In the former, subjects are either matched with a new counterpart in each round or randomly matched with someone in each round, without subjects knowing whether a given counterpart is a new or a repeat match (which should be a low-probability event in any case). Such repeated one-shot games enable subjects to learn over time and the researcher to study equilibration dynamics, a topic of particular interest to economists. In the 'partner' design, subjects are matched with the same person over several rounds. This allows for reputation-building and the examination of repeated-game effects (e.g. Kreps et al. 1982; Axelrod 1984; Taylor 1987).

Common knowledge

Typically, the same set of instructions is handed out to all experimental participants. Experimentalists often go to great lengths to ensure that all subjects understand the instructions (e.g. by administering a quiz before the start of the experiment) and that knowledge is shared among all participants (e.g. by reading instructions out loud). Establishing 'common knowledge' is of particular importance to game-theoretic inquiries because theoretical predictions build on what subjects know everyone else knows, and what everyone else knows everyone else knows, etc. More generally, the norm in experimental economics but not in experimental psychology is not to deceive subjects. Thus, 'common knowledge' includes the experimenter. For example, subjects can count on being paired with another experimental participant rather than a preprogrammed computer or a confederate when told so. The no-deception rule is rather strictly enforced by laboratories and economics journals.

Control group

Depending on the design, a subject may or may not serve as her own control group. In within-subject designs, often used in psychology but rarely in economics, a single subject is confronted with different treatment conditions. To avoid order effects, the order in which the subject is exposed to the various treatment conditions is varied and taken into account in statistical analyses (with order dummies). Within-subject designs automatically control for individual differences, often a substantial source of variation, and thus are statistically very powerful. In between-subjects designs, a given subject is observed in one treatment condition only, and comparisons are made across groups. If individual differences are a concern, they are controlled for econometrically. Both designs have advantages and disadvantages. In within-subject designs, subjects may anchor on the first decision and not fully adjust to the new circumstances in a different treatment; or they may be more sensitive to the differences in conditions knowing the counterfactual. In between-subjects designs, individual differences may swamp the treatment effects without the researcher being able to tease apart the specific reasons due to limited statistical power. Unfortunately, little is known about the size of these problems.

Empirical analysis

Much like in physics, controlling by experimental design means stripping down to the bare essentials, running a control treatment, and then reintroducing variables of interest one at a time. Fischbacher (2007) offers an excellent toolbox for programming experiments: z-Tree. (Many of the experiments discussed here were programmed using z-Tree.) Controlling by design differs from econometric approaches, which control for various influences on behavior by measuring the marginal effect of one variable by holding everything else constant. Sometimes, experimental outcomes are analyzed using econometric techniques. To what degree an experimenter wants to employ advanced statistical tools to analyze her data is her choice. Sophistication also varies with the experimental school one is affiliated with. For example, the German tradition, following the Nobel prize winner Reinhardt Selten, focuses on sophisticated experimental designs but is reluctant to impose structure on the data by using, for example, regression analysis. Finally, also much like in physics, one experiment is only rarely able to give a conclusive answer. Series of experiments are necessary to achieve reliable conclusions.

27.1.2 An example: controlling by experimental design

Trust has been studied across many disciplines (e.g. Kramer and Cook 2003; Ostrom and Walker 2003; and, specifically for experiments on trust, see the reviews by Cook and Cooper 2003 and Bohnet 2008). We adopt the definition of trust proposed by a cross-disciplinary review, as 'a psychological state composing the intention to accept vulnerability based on positive expectations of the intentions or behavior of another' (Rousseau et al. 1998: 395). It is often assumed that a person's willingness to accept vulnerability is closely associated with her willingness to take risk (for example, within philosophy see Luhmann 1979; within economics see Ben-Ner and Putterman 2001; within sociology see Cook and Cooper 2003). Hardin (2002) is critical of approaches that equate trust with a gamble or a risky investment. Experimental evidence on the relationship between risk preferences and trust behavior is mixed. Eckel and Wilson (2004) and Ashraf, Bohnet, and Piankov (2006) find hardly any evidence that subjects' risk preferences, as revealed in risky-choice tasks, are correlated with trust decisions in trust games; Schechter (2007) reports rather strong correlation coefficients.

Bohnet and Zeckhauser (2004a) and Bohnet et al. (2008) introduced a new experimental framework to disentangle willingness to trust from willingness to take risk. In contrast to the earlier approaches, it does not rely on correlation or regression analysis to determine the relationship between willingness to take risk and willingness to trust. Rather, it controls risk preferences by experimental design. It also argues that any approach wanting to measure the relevance of risk preferences for trust decisions has to control for social preferences. Risky choices and trust decisions do not only vary in the agent of uncertainty, nature or people, but also in who is affected by one's decision. In a standard risky-choice task it is the decision maker. In a standard trust game it is the decision maker and her counterpart(s). Thus, to build the bridge between a standard risky-choice task and a decision involving trust, we need a new game that offers the same payoffs and probabilities as a trust game but differs in who the agent of uncertainty is. We present the experimental design here and then show how experimental results can lead to questions of institutional design and differences across groups.

An experimental design disentangling willingness to trust from willingness to take risk

Taking a binary-choice trust game (Camerer and Weigelt 1988; Dasgupta 1988) as our baseline, we designed the risky-dictator game. The only difference between the two games is that in the risky-dictator game, nature (a chance device) rather than another person is the agent of uncertainty. To calibrate risk acceptance in the two games, we employed a novel methodology that is incentive compatible—that is, should induce people to reveal their preferences truthfully. Rather than asking decision makers to choose between trust (the risky option in the risky-dictator game) and a sure alternative, we asked them how high the probability of meeting a trustworthy counterpart (getting a good lottery outcome) would minimally have to be for them to be willing to trust (take risk). This 'minimum acceptable probability' (MAP) was then compared with the true value of meeting a trustworthy counterpart (getting the good lottery outcome), resulting from all counterparts' choices in the trust game (being predetermined in the lottery based on the counterparts' choices).

Our principal hypothesis was that it is fundamentally different to trust another person than to rely on a random device that offers the same outcomes: people are averse to being betrayed. Thus, we conjectured that we would see higher MAPs in the trust game than in the risky-dictator game. Our prediction is independent of people's estimates of the likelihood of trustworthiness. Presumably, everyone would be more inclined to trust when the odds of betrayal are low than when they are high. However, for a given probability of betrayal, some people may choose to trust and others may not.

We found that people demand significantly higher MAPs in the trust game than in the risky-dictator game. This indicates *betrayal aversion*. Willingness to trust cannot be equated with willingness to take risk. People care about why the outcome came to be and dislike making themselves vulnerable to the actions of another person more than to natural circumstances. Thus far, our research has shown that betrayal aversion is a broad-based phenomenon: in all countries studied—Brazil, China, Kuwait, Oman, Switzerland, Turkey, the United Arab Emirates, the USA— experimental participants disliked being betrayed by another person more than losing a lottery with the same odds and payoffs (Bohnet et al. 2008). Nonetheless, there are systematic individual and cross-cultural differences in the degree of betrayal aversion.

Motivational heterogeneity

Demographic characteristics mediate in important ways how institutions affect behavior. In a subsequent study, Hong and Bohnet (2007) examined whether betrayal aversion varied by status. Status has been defined as holding 'high rank on some dimension that is held by society to be important' (Ball and Eckel 1996: 381) and as 'the outcome of an evaluation of attributes that produces differences in respect and prominence' (Keltner, Gruenfeld, and Anderson 2003: 266). We focused on four status dimensions: sex, race, religion, and age. WOMPs—white, older, male, Protestant decision makers—were more averse to betrayal than their respective counterparts, which is in line with what status theories predict. Unbalanced power relations, such as between the trusting and the trusted parties, are unstable and are likely to lead to a variety of 'cost reduction' actions or 'balancing operations' (Emerson 1962: 33). High-status decision makers confronted with the decision of whether or not to trust were likely to choose a balancing action that increased their control; namely, quitting the relationship. As Emerson described, 'the denial of dependency involved in this balancing operation will have the effect of moving actors away from relations which are unbalanced to their disadvantage' (Emerson 1962: 36; see, more generally, Ridgeway and Berger 1986).

In our cross-cultural research comparing subjects in western and Gulf countries we found that, for example, Emiratis were significantly more betrayal averse than Americans. More generally, in the Gulf region people seemed to look for mechanisms decreasing the likelihood rather than the cost of betrayal, such as, for example, repetition and reputation.

Questions of institutional design

The existence of and systematic differences in betrayal aversion across groups has implications for institutional design. If people are betrayal averse, arrangements compensating the victims of betrayal for the material losses experienced will not effectively foster trust. For example, in most contractual arrangements in western countries damages are thought to compensate the decision maker for the injury caused by a counterpart, making the potential victim of breach equally financially well off whether the contract is performed or breached. Even where the legal system falls short, for example when transaction costs are large, commercial insurance may protect a contracting party for losses ranging from breach of contract (surety bonds) to employee theft (fidelity bonding). The more betrayal averse a person is, the less effective are institutions that decrease the risk of material losses rather than the risk of betrayal.

To further explore this question we sought to capture how people respond to changes in the institutional environment, specifically the cost and the likelihood of betrayal, experimentally. We introduced the concept of the elasticity of trust, which measures how much more people are willing to trust for given changes in either the cost or the likelihood of betrayal (Bohnet, Hermann, and Zeckhauser forthcoming). We found that trust was very inelastic to both changes in the three Gulf countries studied while subjects in the western countries responded much more strongly to such changes. For many decision makers in the Gulf countries almost absolute certainty of trustworthiness was required to make them willing to trust. Group-based societal organization founded on long-standing relationships, prevalent in the Gulf, can substantially reduce the social uncertainty involved in trust. Within groups, repeated interactions are likely, information on reputation spreads quickly, monitoring is comparatively cheap, social sanctions help maintain commitments, and loyalty brings high levels of reliability. Differences in the elasticity of trust across nations help explain why some countries are more likely than others to engage in business and contractual arrangements with strangers. They also help us understand differences in negotiation and conflict-resolution styles.

For some groups conflicts may be resolved once all parties have been compensated for the losses incurred. For others, broken promises, violations of obligations, and contractual transgressions impose substantial costs of the type that are not easily compensated, indeed may not be reparable.

27.2 SOCIAL NORMS OF FAIRNESS AND COOPERATIVENESS

Social norms of fairness and cooperativeness can be studied in the laboratory by observing whether behavior converges to what the experimenters believe the social norm in a specific context to be. Sometimes this approach is complemented by asking subjects after the experiment about their expectations and/or about what the right behavior would have been. While experimenters are often reluctant to rely on questionnaires, these can shed additional light on a specific behavioral pattern.

We present examples examining the norm of reciprocity in Part 27.2.1. Reciprocity may be thought of as an intention-based fairness norm where people base their judgments not only on outcomes but also on how those outcomes came to be and what that process tells them about their counterpart's intentions (e.g. Rabin 1993). Many believe that reciprocity is a universal social norm. For example, Gouldner, one of the first to point out the importance of this norm, wrote: 'A norm of reciprocity is, I suspect, no less universal and important an element of culture than the incest taboo,' but its 'concrete formulations may vary with time and place' (1960: 171).

Part 27.2.2 focuses on the norms of equity and equality, two outcome-based fairness norms, and examines contextual factors that make these distributive norms salient, or, as Thomas Schelling (1960) would put it, turn them into focal points. In Part 26.2.3 we focus on the effect of three institutional interventions—reputation, selection, and punishment—on norm-abiding behavior.

27.2.1 Measuring the norm of reciprocity

Reciprocity is an internalized norm, inducing people to respond to kindness with kindness and to unkindness with unkindness, even if it is not in a person's material self-interest to do so. A number of recent theoretical models in economics, building on Rabin (1993), suggest proximate mechanisms driving such behavior. Reciprocity differs fundamentally from cooperation in repeated games, where reputational concerns can enforce 'cooperation' (see e.g. Kreps et al. 1982; Axelrod 1984). Reciprocity helps explain why people respond to above-market-clearing wages with above-standard effort (see e.g. Akerlof 1982), contribute to public goods (see e.g. Ledyard 1995), and reward trust with trustworthiness even in one-shot interactions (see e.g. Berg et al. 1995). The norm of reciprocity helps parties achieve efficient outcomes even if contracts are incomplete and legal enforcement is absent (see e.g. Ostrom 1998).

To measure reciprocity and distinguish it from behavior motivated by repeated-game incentives, most experiments are run one-shot between strangers. Experimental paradigms used to study reciprocity include various versions of (sequential) social dilemmas, for example the (sequential) prisoner's dilemma, public goods (Marwell and Ames 1979), gift exchange (Fehr, Gächter, and Kirchsteiger 1997), and investment games (see e.g. Bert, Dickhaut, and McCabe 1995). We focus on investment and public-goods games here. In the investment game, first and second movers are each endowed with an amount of money, S. The first mover can send any amount $X \leq S$ to the second mover. X is multiplied by $k > 1$ by the experimenter to capture the efficiency-increasing potential of this transaction. Second movers thus receive kX and then decide how much of it, $Y \leq S + kX$, to return to their first mover. The final payoffs are $S - X + Y$ for the first mover and $S + kX - Y$ for the second mover. X is commonly referred to as 'trust,' Y/X measures 'trustworthiness' (trustworthiness is precluded when first movers send zero), and the relationship between trust and trustworthiness indicates 'reciprocity.' A second mover is said to behave according to a norm of *conditional reciprocity* if trustworthiness increases with trust—that is, if the return ratio Y/X is increasing in X (see e.g. Camerer and Fehr 2004). A second mover behaves according to a norm of *balanced reciprocity* if trustworthiness does not vary with trust that is, if the return ratio Y/X equals 1 for all values of X (Greig and Bohnet 2008).

Investment-game experiments conducted in the developed world typically find support for conditional reciprocity: the more trust second movers are offered, the higher the return ratio. (For a review see Camerer 2003.) Thus, often the money-maximizing strategy is to send everything (see e.g. Pillutla, Malhotra, and Murnighan 2003 for American subjects). To examine whether conditional reciprocity is a broad-based phenomenon and to what degree the concrete formulation may vary with place, Greig and Bohnet (2008) ran investment-game experiments in a context different from the typical environment studied so far: a slum in Nairobi, Kenya. This context is characterized by informal enforcement due to repeated interactions typical of 'reciprocal-exchange economies.' In a reciprocal-exchange economy people exchange goods, services, or money in repeated interactions in order to insure against income and cost shocks and smooth consumption over time. Contracts are informally enforced by norms of balanced reciprocity, which obligate future quid-pro-quo repayment of (often interest-free) loans (see e.g. Thomas and Worrall 2002).

If the norm of balanced reciprocity were internalized, trust and trustworthiness should not be related in the investment game. Second movers should return exactly what was sent, making the first mover wholly independent of how much was sent, and first movers should anticipate this. If Nairobi slum dwellers adhere to (expectations of) the norm of balanced reciprocity in our one-shot 'investment game,' the game we use is clearly a misnomer in this context because the expected return on trust is zero. The norm of balanced reciprocity—and expectations thereof—leaves amounts sent completely up to first movers' intrinsic willingness to comply with the norm and/or their social (and risk) preferences.

The authors found strong evidence of the norm of balanced reciprocity in the investment game conducted in Nairobi: first movers expected the norm to apply, i.e. to be made whole; second movers generally conformed to the norm, i.e. returned the amount sent (although a minority deviated from the norm and returned less than the amount sent); and, finally, most everyone indicated in a post-experimental questionnaire that they would conform to the norm of balanced reciprocity independent of the amount sent. Reviewing the evidence from other investment-game experiments run in developing countries, Greig and Bohnet (2008) note that they may have detected a pattern that more generally applies in economies based on reciprocal exchange.

The norm of reciprocity also suggests that subjects are *conditionally cooperative* in public-goods games (e.g. Fischbacher, Gächter, and Fehr 2001). Subjects cooperate, i.e. contribute to the public good or participate in collective action, if (they believe that) others cooperate as well. They respond to defection with defection. To examine conditional cooperation, Fischbacher et al. (2001) elicited subjects' willingness to contribute to a public good conditional on the average contribution of the other group members. Groups consisted of four members, and each member could contribute up to about six dollars to the public good. A selfish player should not contribute anything in this environment. The authors found that, in fact, 30 percent of the subjects conformed to the rational-actor model assuming selfish, money-maximizing preferences; 50 percent contributed conditionally cooperatively and increased their contributions with the average contribution of the other three group members; the rest of the subjects played a mixture of strategies.

While a majority of subjects is conditionally cooperative in many experiments, this does not suffice to sustain cooperation. Conditional cooperators respond to the selfish players by decreasing their contributions as well, leading to a breakdown of cooperation over time. (For reviews of the evidence see Dawes and Thaler 1988; Ledyard 1995.) Sanctions or credible sanction threats are required to motivate the minority of selfish players to contribute.

27.2.2 Salience of distributive social norms

Social norms may be more likely to be activated when a decision is taken in a social context—for example, where communication between participants is possible and/or where social comparisons are available, making it easier to determine what norm-deviant behavior is.

Social context

One might assume that the greater the extent to which a decision is taken in a social context, the more relevant social norms become. Al Roth (1995: 295), for example, argued that 'face-to-face interactions call into play all of the social training we are endowed with.' Thus, a relatively large number of experimental studies have examined the impact of face-to-face communication on behavior, often focusing on cooperation in social dilemmas or prosocial behavior in dictator games. Sally (1995) provides a meta-analysis of the impact of communication on cooperation, showing that communication exhibits a statistically and economically significant effect on people's willingness to cooperate. The dictator game (Kahneman, Knetsch, and Thaler 1986; Forsythe et al. 1994) is characterized by the interaction of two players, the dictator and the recipient. The dictator is asked to allocate a sum previously received from the experimenter between herself and the recipient, deciding unilaterally about the allocation of the money. The dictator game thus tests whether subjects are willing to pass some amount of money on to a second person even where the recipient has no sanctioning power. (Compare the ultimatum game, discussed below, where the recipient may reject the share received, in which case neither of the two players gets anything.)

To better understand to what degree communication activates social norms, Bohnet and Frey (1999a, 1999b) decomposed communication into talk and identification. They expected mutual identification to activate social norms and talk to induce more interaction-specific rules. Mutual identification strengthens social or cultural propensities for specific behavior and allows for social sanctions to become relevant. Drawing analogy to the focal point adduced by Schelling (1960) on which the players of a game can agree in the absence of communication, they called the respective meeting point a 'Schelling norm.' For example, the Schelling norm of fairness is equal division in most societies. (For empirical evidence see e.g. Young 1994; Brams and Taylor 1996.)

Talk, while not excluding social sanctions, allows more information to be transferred and therefore more scope for actually abandoning these norms. It leads to a divergence of behavior corresponding to the heterogeneous composition of the group of individuals involved. The interaction is transformed into a personal relationship where norms can be substituted by interaction-specific solutions.

The authors found for prisoner's dilemma and dictator games that while both talk and mutual identification increased prosocial behavior, mutual identification led to a convergence to the social norm while communication increased the variance in behavior. Identification, however, had yet another effect. Apart from activating social norms, it also decreased the social distance between the participants, thereby allowing empathy for the other person(s) to exist. The 'other' was no longer some unknown individual from some anonymous crowd but a specific human being, an 'identifiable victim' (Schelling 1968). Standing by and neglecting a specific child who has fallen into a well is much more difficult than not rescuing an unspecified statistical life—for example, an anonymous starving child. Charities have long recognized the importance of a victim's identifiability and try to decrease social distance between donors and recipients by various means.

In order to discriminate between prosocial behavior motivated by reciprocity and by closeness, Bohnet and Frey (1999b) compared mutual identification with one-way identification where the 'victims' did not know the identity of their potential benefactors. As social sanctions were excluded in the latter treatment, no convergence to the social norm was expected. The authors found that dictators converged to offering an equal split in a dictator game where the dictator and the recipient could visually identify each other but no such convergence was found in an otherwise analogous game where only dictators could identify recipients. While mean offers were almost identical, 71 percent of the dictators split the pie equally in the former but only 16 percent of the dictators sent half of their endowment in the latter treatment condition.

Social comparisons

A large body of research in psychology and sociology, building on Festinger (1954), suggests that 'social comparisons' provide information on what is the 'right behavior' in a certain context. The term 'social comparisons' refers to information on others in like circumstances. This reference group has received relatively little attention in the literally thousands of experimental studies on bargaining. Recent theoretical models on fairness and reciprocity focus almost exclusively on the relationship between the two bargainers. (For a survey see Fehr and Schmidt 2002.) But parties to a negotiation may make comparisons other than to their bargaining counterpart. In salary negotiations, for example, prospective employees typically do not compare their wage (or wage less reservation price) with the surplus the employer reaps from their employ, but rather with the wages of similarly situated employees.

Bohnet and Zeckhauser (2004b) used the ultimatum game, probably the most studied bargaining game, to investigate the role of social comparisons between responders. In the standard ultimatum game a proposer first allocates a fixed amount of money, the 'pie,' between herself and a responder. The responder can either accept or reject the proposer's offer. If he accepts, the deal stays as proposed; if he rejects, both earn zero. The subgame-perfect-equilibrium prediction is for the proposer to offer ε, the smallest possible amount, and for the responder to accept. When social comparisons are given, offers should gravitate towards the 'right behavior,' and rejection rates should rise where there are deviations from such behavior. Earlier studies on social comparisons in bargaining typically informed people on one other offer. Knowledge of one other offer had only modest effects. A randomly chosen 'other' may not 'cause an individual to change her belief regarding what constitutes the appropriate or correct behavior' (Cason and Mui 1998: 262). In contrast, we informed our responders on the average offer, which we expected to be more likely to establish a social norm.

Social norms raise questions of coordination. In contrast to earlier studies, we posed that social comparisons in bargaining are linked to problems of coordination. If social comparisons establish a social norm about which responders care, proposers can no longer take advantage of reference-point ambiguity. If all other proposers made a small offer, the reference point would be low and a given proposer could afford to offer less as well—but successful collusion is unlikely within large groups of proposers who do not know each other and cannot communicate. More likely, such proposers will tend toward a focal point that comes to serve as the norm. As the modal offer in the standard ultimatum game is typically an equal division, we expected social comparisons to reinforce the role of this focal point. (Note that while the focal point is an equal split in the standard ultimatum game in most western societies, this does not need to be the case. If proposers earned the right to allocate the money, for example, they feel entitled to keep more than half of the pie, which responders accept—see Hoffman and Spitzer 1985. Substantially different norms have been found to guide behavior in ultimatum games in some of the small-scale societies studied by Henrich et al. 2004.)

We found that proposers made higher offers and were more likely to offer an equal split when social comparisons were provided than when they were not. Responders were more likely to reject a given offer with social comparisons than without. Social comparisons activated the norm of equity: responders expected to be treated like others in like circumstances.

To assess the economic significance of these effects and provide a metric, we compared social-comparison effects with another well-established factor in informational conditions, asymmetric information on the size of the pie (see e.g. Croson 1996). We chose to compare effects of social comparison with impacts of pie-size knowledge because we believed that both were important characteristics in real-world bargaining. Note that many experimenters choose to study the effect of one institutional change at a time, which makes between-study comparisons challenging, since many variables will change between experiments (subject pool, incentives, information conditions, etc.). Our approach allowed us to directly compare the magnitude of two important institutional effects, for specific parameter values. It follows in an experimental tradition that focuses on institutional comparisons (see Ostrom, Gardner, and Walker 1994).

Knowing comparable offers increased offers by a similar magnitude, as did knowing the pie size. Social comparisons gain in importance over time, especially when responders do not know the size of the pie. They enable responders to hold proposers accountable to the norm of equity, both with respect to other responders and with respect to the share their proposers keep. Our results do not suggest that responders do not care about their bargaining counterpart, but they do suggest that in addition to these considerations, responders are also concerned that they be treated equivalently to others in like circumstances, and that proposers are aware of this.

Our preliminary conclusion, based on a limited number of experiments, is that social comparisons facilitate attention to the social norm. In our design, the social norm, an equal split, improved the responders' lot. More generally, social comparisons decrease the distance between an offer and the norm. Whether social comparisons favor proposers or responders, employers or workers, sellers or buyers, will depend on a variety of contextual factors that help establish norms.

27.2.3 Sustainability of norm-abiding behavior

Norm-abiding behavior may be more likely to be sustained when repeated game or reputation incentives are available, when reciprocally minded or conditional cooperators can self-select into groups of similar types, or when conditional cooperators can punish defectors. We examine both the short-term and the long-term effects of these institutional mechanisms.

Reputation

Reputation systems may provide incentives for trustworthiness and trust. Direct reputation-building may occur in repeated games where pairs of subjects play the same stage game repeatedly ('partner' treatment), but repeat transactions are not necessarily the rule in today's global economy. In population games where agents are randomly rematched in every period, indirect-reputation systems are a potential substitute for personal interactions—provided information about others' past behavior is available. On eBay, for example, buyers are willing to pay a premium of 8.1 percent of the selling price to a seller with an established good reputation (Resnick et al. 2006).

Bohnet and Huck (2004) examined to what degree indirect reputation-building substitutes for direct reputation-building in repeat interactions in the short run and analyzed the effects these environments have on behavior in the long run. So far, most earlier experimental studies have focused on one-shot and repeat interactions in the short run. (For a survey see Andreoni and Croson 2008.) We compared the effects of direct and indirect reputation-building in a binary-choice trust game similar to the game described in Section 27.1.2, but repeated it several times. Importantly, we tested the effect of reputation in the short run when reputational incentives were present, and in the long run where subjects were confronted with a one-shot repeated game environment with strangers. For the long run, all orthodox models predict the same behavior. We should see low (or zero) levels of trust and trustworthiness in all treatments, since incentives for building a reputation have been removed. Orthodox models predict that history does not matter. If, on the other hand, reputation-based interactions 'crowd in' (see below) trust and trustworthiness by evoking specific norms of behavior, differences between the treatments might be observed. Theoretically, such long-term effects require changes in preferences (see Bohnet, Frey, and Huck 2001 for a theoretical model) or, alternatively, inertia in adjustment and learning (see e.g. Erev and Roth 1998).

We found that direct- and indirect-reputation systems increased trust and trustworthiness in the short run. Subjects strongly responded to the direct-reputation-building opportunities in a repeated game. With indirect reputation-building, second movers appeared to respond more strongly to the institutional environment than first movers. The benefits of this more complex and less familiar environment may not be as obvious as the advantages of repeat interactions, which may help explain why many consumers do not trust internet-based transactions using indirect-reputation systems such as on eBay (see e.g. Kollock 1999). Our results suggest that they may be too pessimistic.

Finally, and perhaps most importantly, there were significant history effects. In particular, second movers were more likely to reciprocate trust after having been exposed to a partner treatment. The partner treatment was the most effective institutional arrangement to foster trust and trustworthiness in the short *and* in the long run. Indeed, it appeared as if experiencing the intimate partner relationship bred genuine trustworthiness. This might have important implications for issues in institutional design and education. Interactions in small close-knit groups may have long-lasting beneficial consequences.

Selection

Normally, subjects are assigned to experimental conditions. What if experimental participants can choose which game they want to play? Will they be able to self-select into the groups most compatible with their preferences? Will conditional cooperators be able to separate from defectors, thus being able to sustain cooperation over time? Bohnet and Kübler (2005) investigated whether auctioning off the right to play a prisoner's-dilemma game, in which the cost of unilateral cooperation was lower than in the status quo version, increased cooperation rates. Put differently, we provided an insurance mechanism for conditional cooperators in case their cooperation was not reciprocated, thus decreasing what sometimes is referred to as 'fear' (Rapoport 1967). While the two games have the same Nash equilibrium, the different out-of-equilibrium payoffs may provide a means of sorting, allowing conditional cooperators to self-select into the 'insured' and selfish players to choose the standard version of the game.

After the auction significantly more subjects cooperated in the insured prisoner's dilemma than in the status quo prisoner's dilemma, whereas there was no difference between cooperation rates if the two versions of the game were randomly assigned to participants. However, sorting was incomplete, and cooperators were always mixed with money maximizers who 'took advantage' of the other's willingness to cooperate and caused cooperation to deteriorate over time.

Successful sorting mechanisms are rare in these kinds of environments. In Ehrhart and Keser's public-goods experiment (1999), where subjects could leave their groups to form new ones, 'cooperating subjects are on the run from less cooperative ones who follow them around' (p. 9). As cooperative subjects formed new groups, hoping to meet other cooperators, egoists constantly invaded and decreased cooperation rates over time. Sorting seems to be more successful if combined with other mechanisms. Using a similar approach to Erhart and Keser (1999), Page, Putterman, and Unel (2005) found that endogenous group formation was more successful if subjects could choose other group members based on their past contributions, significantly increasing contributions and efficiency. The decrease in contributions over time could be stopped if such endogenous group formation was combined with the ability to punish free riders. Thus, while perfect sorting is hard to achieve in the short run, if it works in the short run, it is also likely to lead to sustainable norm-abiding behavior in the long run.

Punishment

Norm-abiding people are able to force others to conform to the norm when they have sanctioning opportunities available. A number of social-dilemma experiments with sanctioning opportunities have been conducted (e.g. Yamagishi 1986; Ostrom 2000; Fehr and Gachter 2002). While the studies differ in detail, the typical setup is as follows: groups of n subjects (where $n > 2$) participate in an anonymous public-goods experiment for a number of rounds. In each round, each participant decides how much to contribute to the public good. All group members are then informed of everyone else's decision. (Subjects remain anonymous, being identified by code numbers only.) Finally, subjects can punish other group members. Punishment typically is costly, both for the punisher as well as for the punished.

The introduction of a sanctioning opportunity dramatically increases contributions to the public good, which often approach 100 percent during the game. Subjects typically focus their punishment on those who contribute less than average, with punishments increasing with the deviation from the group average. The punishment opportunity not only disciplines selfish players but also helps conditional cooperators contribute, as it generates a belief that others will contribute as well. Note that punishing others typically is costly, both in naturally occurring settings as well as in the laboratory. The effectiveness of a sanctioning opportunity depends on these costs. The larger they are, the fewer and weaker the sanctions will be. Thus, as norm enforcement (and norm adherence) becomes more costly, norms are more likely to break down.

More elaborate approaches examining the existence and influence of social norms include third parties who observe how players interact and then can impose penalties for norm-deviant behavior. Importantly, the third parties' payoffs are not related to the players' behavior, the experiments are run one-shot and anonymously, and punishment typically is costly for the third party. Thus, the third party does not derive any material benefits from punishing. Rather, the intrinsic benefits from punishing norm violations have to outweigh the third party's material benefits from not doing anything for such a 'disinterested' third party to punish norm violations.

Fehr and Fischbacher (2004) conducted prisoner's-dilemma games in which third parties were able to punish whoever they wanted to. They found that a majority of third parties was willing to punish defectors, while cooperators were hardly punished. Specifically, 46 percent of third parties punished unilateral defectors (and spent a bit more than a dollar on punishment) and 21 percent punished mutual defectors (spending about twenty cents on punishment); 8 percent punished unilateral cooperators (spending basically nothing on punishment) and 4 percent punished mutual cooperators (spending basically nothing on punishment). This punishment pattern suggests a norm of conditional cooperation where a third party is particularly annoyed by defectors whose counterpart cooperates.

While sanctions seem to be a very effective means to enforce norm-abiding behavior in the short run, the evidence on long-term effects is more ambiguous. Fehr and Gächter (2003) ran their public-goods games both with and without a sanctioning opportunity with the same subjects. Participants who first had sanctions available were less likely to cooperate in future rounds where no sanctions were available than the subjects in the control treatment who had not experienced sanctions beforehand. More generally, Bohnet, Frey, and Huck (2001) showed theoretically and experimentally for trust interactions that institutions increasing the expected costs of defection or betrayal, such as sanctions, need not lead to more norm-abiding behavior. In addition to changing incentives, institutional constraints may undermine or foster internalized norms. We refer to these dynamics as 'crowding out' and 'crowding in' respectively. Our model predicted that economic incentives have a nonmonotonic effect on behavior: second movers reciprocate trust when the expected sanction is large enough to deter betrayal *and* when it is small enough to *not* encourage the first mover to offer trust. Low-range expected sanctions crowd in reciprocity. Medium-range expected sanctions crowd out reciprocity.

To test our theoretical predictions experimentally, we employed a standard binary-choice trust game but added a third stage to the game. In case of betrayal, there was some chance that trustworthy behavior would be externally enforced. If the expected value of a sanction is large enough to deter, intrinsic reciprocity is substituted by extrinsic incentives. The theory predicted that second movers perform not because this is what they want to do but because it pays to do so. When expected sanctions are too small to deter, two scenarios are possible: sanctions can be so small that it never pays to trust a money-maximizing second mover, or they can be large enough that in expectation it pays to trust a money-maximizing second mover even though he always breaches. Our theory predicted that in the first scenario first movers have an incentive to look for and identify the intrinsically reciprocal second movers. Only reciprocal types will be offered trust, and in the long run will be better off than money-maximizing types. (For a related argument see Bacharach and Gambetta 2001.) Reciprocity is crowded in because in the end it pays to reward trust. In contrast, in the second scenario first movers offer trust even to a money-maximizing second mover who, in the long run, will be better off than intrinsically reciprocally minded types. Reciprocity is crowded out because in the end it pays to betray. Our model's predictions were supported in the laboratory.

Stronger institutional constraints or 'more law' do not necessarily increase trustworthiness even if they increase the expected cost of betrayal. If extrinsic incentives are large enough to deter and outweigh any loss in internalized norms, trustworthiness increases. However, when incentives do not satisfy this condition, they may lead to less trustworthiness than without any external intervention because they destroy the intrinsic motivation to reciprocate trust.

Similar negative effects of sanctions on cooperation and trustworthiness have been found by Tenbrunsel and Messick (1999) and Gneezy and Rustichini (2000). Sitkin and Roth (1993: 376) observed that 'legalistic remedies can erode the interpersonal foundations of a relationship they are intended to bolster because they replace reliance on an individual's goodwill with objective, formal requirements.' Similarly, Yamagishi, Cook, and Watabe (1998) suggested that people living in legalistic institutional environments may lose the capacity for intrinsic trustworthiness because interpersonal trust is replaced by institutional trust.

CONCLUSIONS

This chapter provides an introduction to the experimental approach as employed in behavioral game theory. It summarizes some key aspects of experimental design and shows how economic experiments can be useful for better understanding social norms of fairness and cooperativeness. In particular, it looks at how such norms can be measured in the laboratory, under which conditions they become salient, and which institutions make norm-abiding behavior sustainable.

The chapter can only discuss a small subset of the questions sociologists are interested in. There are many other social norms (see e.g. the discussion in Hechter and Opp 2001), experimental approaches that do not rely on the design guidelines dominant in economics (see e.g. Cook and Cooper 2003), and other topics discussed in this book which could be experimentally explored. Our goal is to give the reader a taste of the experimental approach as used in behavioral game theory, and the potential it offers.

Fascinating new developments include experiments in neuroscience. For example, to better understand what might motivate some of the behaviors discussed in this chapter, such as the dislike of inequality, unfair treatment, or betrayal, neuroscientific studies are searching for their neural locus. In Sanfey et al.'s fMRI study of ultimatum bargaining (2003), very unfair offers activated three regions of the brain: insula cortex, dorsolateral prefrontal cortex, and anterior cingulate. The insula is an area typically activated when negative emotions like pain and disgust are experienced. The prefrontal cortex is associated with deliberate decisions and executive control. Knoch et al. (2006) experimentally disrupted the dorsolateral prefrontal cortex. As a result, subjects in the treatment group made the same fairness judgments as the control group but did not behave according to them but rather acted more selfishly. Kosfeld et al. (2005) dispensed the neuropeptide oxytocin, which has been shown to promote prosocial behavior in animals, to their subjects to better understand betrayal aversion. Subjects given oxytocin took the social risk involved in trusting more readily, but not the natural risk involved in a risky-choice task. Camerer, Loewenstein, and Prelec (2005) provide an excellent review of the relationship between neuroscience and economics.

Other important developments include a closer analysis of how social norms of fairness and cooperativeness interact with institutions and social context to determine aggregate outcomes. While an abundance of empirical evidence suggests that people generally are both boundedly rational and boundedly selfish, there is also substantial heterogeneity among people, with some individuals coming close to the predictions of a rational-actor model. The question thus is how social interactions among *heterogenous individuals* shape aggregate outcomes under specific circumstances.

Camerer and Fehr (2006) offer first insights: cooperative aggregate outcomes are likely if prosocial individuals (even if they are in the minority) can generate incentives for selfish individuals (who might be in the majority) to copy their behavior and behave cooperatively. An example is the sequential prisoner's dilemma, where a selfish first mover knows that a reciprocally minded second mover will only cooperate if she cooperates first, thus inducing her to act cooperatively and generate a cooperative outcome. Noncooperative aggregate outcomes will likely result if selfish individuals can generate incentives for prosocial types to mimic their behavior. The simultaneous prisoner's dilemma is an example. There is no incentive for selfish types to cooperate and thus reciprocally minded subjects will not cooperate either.

This interaction between such 'micromotives,' the rules of the game, and 'macrobehavior' (to paraphrase the Noble prize winner Thomas Schelling's book, 1978) invites collaboration between sociologists, psychologists, and economists. This chapter was written in the hope that the experimental approach may build a bridge between these disciplines.

References

AKERLOF, G. A. (1982), 'Labor Contracts as Partial Gift Exchange', *Quarterly Journal of Economics*, 97: 543–69.

ANDREONI, J., and CROSON, R. (2008), 'Partners Versus Strangers: Random Rematching in Public Goods Experiments', in C. Plott and V. Smith (eds.), *Handbook of Experimental Economic Results* (North Holland: Elsevier), 776–83.

ASHRAF, N., BOHNET, I., and PIANKOV, N. (2006), 'Decomposing Trust and Trustworthiness', *Experimental Economics*, 9: 193–208.

AXELROD, R. (1984), *The Evolution of Cooperation* (New York: Basic).

BACHARACH, M., and GAMBETTA, D. (2001), 'Trust in Signs', in K. Cook (ed.), *Trust in Society* (New York: Russell Sage), 148–84.

BALL, S. B., and ECKEL, C. C. (1996), 'Buying Status: Experimental Evidence on Status in Negotiation', *Psychology & Marketing*, 13: 381–405.

BEN-NER, A., and PUTTERMAN, L. (2001), 'Trusting and Trustworthiness', *Boston University Law Review*, 81: 523–51.

BERG, J., DICKHAUT, J., and McCABE, K. A. (1995), 'Trust, Reciprocity, and Social History', *Games and Economic Behavior*, 10: 290–307.

BOHNET, I. (2008), 'Trust in Experiments', in S. Durlauf and L. Blume (eds.), *The New Palgrave Dictionary of Economics*, 2nd edn. Palgrave Macmillan. The New Palgrave Dictionary of Economics Online.

—— and FREY, B. S. (1999*a*), 'The Sound of Silence in Prisoner's Dilemma and Dictator Games', *Journal of Economic Behavior and Organization*, 38: 43–57.

—— (1999*b*), 'Social Distance and Other-regarding Behavior in Dictator Games: Comment', *American Economic Review*, 89: 335–40.

—— and HUCK, S. (2004), 'Repetition and Reputation: Implications for Trust and Trustworthiness When Institutions Change', *American Economic Review*, 94: 362–6.

—— and KÜBLER, D. (2005), 'Compensating the Cooperators: Is Sorting in the Prisoner's Dilemma Possible?', *Journal of Economic Behavior and Organization*, 56: 61–76.

—— and MEIER, S. (2007), 'Deciding to Distrust', working paper, Kennedy School of Government, Harvard University.

—— and ZECKHAUSER, R. (2004*a*), 'Trust, Risk and Betrayal', *Journal of Economic Behavior and Organization*, 55: 467–84.

—— —— (2004*b*), 'Social Comparisons in Ultimatum Bargaining', *Scandinavian Journal of Economics*, 106: 495–510.

—— FREY, B. S., and HUCK, S. (2001), 'More Order with Less Law: On Contract Enforcement, Trust and Crowding', *American Political Science Review*, 95: 131–44.

—— GREIG, F., HERMANN, B. and ZECKHAUSER, R. (2008), 'Betrayal Aversion: Evidence from Brazil, China, Turkey, Switzerland, Oman, and the United States', *American Economic Review*, 98 (1): 294–310.

—— HERMANN, B., and ZECKHAUSER, R., 'The Requirements for Trust in Gulf and Western Countries', *Quarterly Journal of Economics* (forthcoming).

BOLTON, G., KATOK, E., and ZWICK, R. (1998), 'Dictator Game Giving: Rules of Fairness Versus Acts of Kindness', *International Journal of Game Theory*, 27: 269–99.

BRAMS, S. J., and TAYLOR, A. D. (1996), *Fair Division: From Cake-cutting to Dispute Resolution* (Cambridge: Cambridge University Press).

CAMERER, C. (2003), *Behavioral Game Theory* (Princeton, N.J.: Princeton University Press).

——and FEHR, E. (2004), 'Measuring Social Norms and Preferences Using Experimental Games: A Guide for Social Scientists', in J. Henrich, et al. (eds.), *Foundations of Human Sociality* (Oxford: Oxford University Press), 55–96.

————(2006), 'When Does "Economic Man" Dominate Social Behavior?', *Science*, 311: 47–52.

——and HOGARTH, R. M. (1999), 'The Effects of Financial Incentives in Economics Experiments: A Review and Capital–Labor–Production Framework', *Journal of Risk and Uncertainty*, 18: 7–42.

——and WEIGELT, K. (1988), 'Experimental Tests of a Sequential Equilibrium Reputation Model', *Econometrica*, 56: 1–36.

——LOEWENSTEIN, G., and PRELEC, D. (2005), 'Neuroeconomics: How Neuroscience can Inform Economics', *Journal of Economic Literature*, 43: 9–64.

CAMERON, L. A. (1999), 'Raising the Stakes in the Ultimatum Game: Experimental Evidence from Indonesia', *Economic Inquiry*, 27: 47–59.

CARDENAS, J.-C., and CARPENTER, J. (2007), 'Behavioral Development Economics: Lessons from Field Labs in the Developing World', *Journal of Development Studies*, 44 (3): 337–64.

CASON, T. N., and MUI, V.-L. (1998), 'Social Influence in the Sequential Dictator Game', *Journal of Mathematical Psychology*, 42: 248–65.

COLEMAN, J. (1990), *Foundations of Social Theory* (Cambridge, Mass.: Harvard University Press).

COOK, K. S., and COOPER, R. M. (2003), 'Experimental Studies of Cooperation, Trust, and Social Exchange', in E. Ostrom and J. Walker (eds.), *Trust and Reciprocity* (New York: Russell Sage), 209–44.

CROSON, R. (1996), 'Information in Ultimatum Games: An Experimental Study', *Journal of Economic Behavior and Organization*, 30: 197–212.

——and SHANG, J. (2005), 'Field Experiments in Charitable Contribution: The Impact of Social Influence on the Voluntary Contribution of Public Goods', working paper, Wharton School, University of Pennsylvania.

DASGUPTA, P. (1988), 'Trust as Commodity', in D. Gambetta (ed.), *Trust: Making and Breaking Cooperative Relations* (Oxford: Blackwell), 49–72.

DAWES, R., and THALER, R. (1988), 'Cooperation', *Journal of Economic Perspectives*, 2: 187–97.

——McTAVISH, J., and SHAKLEE, H. (1977), 'Behavior, Communication, and Assumptions about Other People's Behavior in a Commons Dilemma Situation', *Journal of Personality and Social Psychology*, 35: 1–11.

ECKEL, C. C., and WILSON, R. K. (2004), 'Is Trust a Risky Decision?', *Journal of Economic Behavior and Organization*, 55 (4): 447–65.

EHRHART, K.-M., and KESER, C. (1999), 'Mobility and Cooperation: On the Run', working paper, CIRANO, University of Montreal.

ELSTER, J. (1989), *The Cement of Society: A Study of Social Order* (Cambridge: Cambridge University Press).

EMERSON, R. M. (1962), 'Power-dependence Relations', *American Sociological Review*, 27: 31–41.

EREV, I., and ROTH, A. E. (1998), 'Predicting How People Play Games: Reinforcement Learning in Experimental Games with Unique, Mixed Strategy Equilibria', *American Economic Review*, 88: 848–81.

FEHR, E., and FISCHBACHER, U. (2004), 'Third-party Punishment and Social Norms', *Evolution and Human Behavior*, 25: 63–87.

—— and GÄCHTER, S. (2002), 'Cooperation and Punishment in Public Goods Experiments', *American Economic Review*, 90: 980–94.

———— (2003), 'Do Incentive Contracts Crowd Out Voluntary Cooperation?', working paper, Institute for Empirical Research in Economics, University of Zurich.

—— and SCHMIDT, K. (2002), 'Theories of Fairness and Reciprocity—Evidence and Economic Applications', in M. Dewatripont, L. Hansen, and S. Turnovsky (eds.), *Advances in Economics and Econometrics* (Cambridge: Cambridge University Press), 208–57.

—— GÄCHTER, S., and KIRCHSTEIGER, G. (1997), 'Reciprocity as a Contract Enforcement Device: Experimental Evidence', *Econometrica*, 64: 833–60.

—— et al. (2002), 'A Nation-wide Laboratory: Examining Trust and Trustworthiness by Integrating Behavioral Experiments into Representative Surveys', *Schmollers Jahrbuch*, 122: 519–42.

FESTINGER, L. (1954), 'A Theory of Social Comparison Processes', *Human Relations*, 7: 117–40.

FISCHBACHER, U. (2007), 'Z-Tree: Zurich Toolbox for Ready-made Economic Experiments', *Experimental Economics*, 10: 171–78.

—— GÄCHTER, S., and FEHR, E. (2001), 'Are People Conditionally Cooperative? Evidence from a Public Goods Experiment', *Economics Letters*, 71: 397–404.

FORSYTHE, R., et al. (1994), 'Fairness in Simple Bargaining Experiments', *Games and Economic Behavior*, 6: 347–69.

GNEEZY, U., and RUSTICHINI, A. (2000), 'Pay Enough or Don't Pay At All', *Quarterly Journal of Economics*, 115: 791–810.

GOULDNER, A. (1960), 'The Norm of Reciprocity', *American Sociological Review*, 25: 161–78.

GREIG, F., and BOHNET, I. (2008), 'Is There Reciprocity in a Reciprocal-exchange Economy? Evidence of Gendered Norms from a Slum in Nairobi, Kenya', *Economic Inquiry*, 46 (1): 77–83.

———— (2009), 'Exploring Gendered Behavior in the Field with Experiments: Why Public Goods are Provided by Women in a Nairobi Slum', *Journal of Economic Behavior and Organization*. Forthcoming.

HARDIN, R. (2002), *Trust and Trustworthiness* (New York: Russell Sage).

HARRISON, G., and LIST, J. A. (2004), 'Field Experiments', *Journal of Economic Literature*, 42: 1013–59.

HECHTER, M., and OPP, K. D. (2001) (eds.), *Social Norms* (New York: Russell Sage).

HENRICH, J., et al. (2004) (eds.), *Foundations of Human Sociality* (Oxford: Oxford University Press).

HERTWIG, R., and ORTMANN, A. (2001), 'Experimental Practices in Economics: A Methodological Challenge for Psychologists?', *Behavioral and Brain Sciences*, 24: 383–403.

HOFFMAN, E., and SPITZER, M. L. (1985), 'Entitlements, Rights and Fairness: An Experimental Examination of Subjects' Concepts of Distributive Justice', *Journal of Legal Studies*, 14: 259–97.

Hoffman, E., McCabe, K., and Smith, V. (1996), 'Social Distance and Other-regarding Behavior in Dictator Games', *American Economic Review*, 86: 653–60.

Hong, K., and Bohnet, I. (2007), 'Status and Distrust: The Relevance of Inequality and Betrayal Aversion', *Journal of Economic Psychology*, 28: 197–213.

Kagel, J. H., and Roth, A. E. (1995) (eds.), *Handbook of Experimental Economics* (Princeton, N.J.: Princeton University Press).

Kahneman, D., and Tversky, A. (1979), 'Prospect Theory: An Analysis of Decision under Risk', *Econometrica*, 47: 263–91.

——Knetsch, J., and Thaler, R. (1986), 'Fairness and the Assumptions of Economics', *Journal of Business*, 59: 285–300.

Karlan, D. (2005), 'Using Experimental Economics to Measure Social Capital and Predict Financial Decisions', *American Economic Review*, 95: 1688–99.

——and List, J. A. (2007), 'Does Price Matter in Charitable Giving? Evidence from a Large-scale Natural Field Experiment', *American Economic Review*, 97 (5): 1774–93.

Keltner, D., Gruenfeld, D. H., and Anderson, C. (2003), 'Power, Approach, and Inhibition', *Psychological Review*, 110: 265–84.

Knoch D., et al. (2006), 'Diminishing Reciprocal Fairness by Disrupting the Right Prefrontal Cortex', *Science*, 314: 829–32.

Kollock, P. (1999), 'The Production of Trust in Online Markets', in E. J. Lawler, et al. (eds.), *Advances in Group Processes* (Greenwich, Conn.: JAI).

Kosfeld, M., et al. (2005), 'Oxytocin Increases Trust in Humans', *Nature*, 435: 673–6.

Kramer, R. M., and Cook, K. S. (2003) (eds.), *Trust and Distrust in Organizations* (New York: Russell Sage).

Kreps, D., et al. (1982), 'Rational Cooperation in the Finitely Repeated Prisoner's Dilemma', *Journal of Economic Theory*, 27: 245–52.

Ledyard, J. (1995), 'Public Goods: A Survey of Experimental Research', in J. Kagel and A. Roth (eds.), *Handbook of Experimental Economics*, (Princeton, N.J.: Princeton University Press), 111–94.

Levitt, S. D., and List, J. A. (2007), 'What Do Laboratory Experiments Measuring Social Preferences Tell Us About the Real World', *Journal of Economic Perspectives*, 21 (2): 153–74.

Lewicki, R. J., McAllister, D. J., and Bies, R. (1998), 'Trust and Distrust: New Relationships and Realities', *Academy of Management Review*, 23: 438–58.

Luhmann, N. (1979), *Trust and Power* (Chichester: Wiley).

Marwell, G., and Ames, R. E. (1979), 'Experiments on the Provision of Public Goods, I: Resources, Interest, Group Size, and the Free-rider Problem', *American Journal of Sociology*, 84: 1335–60.

————(1980), 'Experiments on the Provision of Public Goods, II: Provision Points, Stakes, Experience, and the Free-rider Problem', *American Journal of Sociology*, 85: 926–37.

Ostrom, E., (1998), 'A Behavioral Approach to the Rational Choice Theory of Collective Action: Presidential Address, American Political Science Association, 1997', *American Political Science Review*, 92: 1–22.

——(2000), 'Collective Action and the Evolution of Social Norms', *Journal of Economic Perspectives*, 14: 137–58.

——and Walker, J. (2003) (eds.), *Trust and Reciprocity* (New York: Russell Sage).

——Gardner, R., and Walker, J. (1994), *Rules, Games, and Common-pool Resources* (Ann Arbor, Mich.: University of Michigan Press).

PAGE, T., PUTTERMAN, L., and UNEL, B. (2005), 'Voluntary Association in Public Goods Experiments: Reciprocity, Mimicry and Efficiency', *Economic Journal*, 115: 1032–53.

PILLUTLA, M. M., MALHOTRA, D., and MURNIGHAN, J. K. (2003), 'Attributions of Trust and the Calculus of Reciprocity', *Journal of Experimental Social Psychology*, 39: 448–55.

RABIN, M. (1993), 'Incorporating Fairness into Game Theory and Economics', *American Economic Review*, 83: 1281–302.

RAPOPORT, A. (1967), 'A Note on the "Index of Cooperation" for the Prisoner's Dilemma', *Journal of Conflict Resolution*, 11: 101–3.

RESNICK, P., et al. (2006), 'The Value of Reputation on eBay: A Controlled Experiment', *Experimental Economics*, 9: 79–101.

RIDGEWAY, C. L., and BERGER, J. (1986), 'Expectations, Legitimating, and Dominance Behavior in Task Groups', *American Sociological Review*, 51: 603–17.

ROTH, A. E. (1995), 'Bargaining Experiments', in J. Kagel and A. Roth (eds.), *Handbook of Experimental Economics* (Princeton, N.J.: Princeton University Press), 253–348.

ROUSSEAU, D., et al. (1998), 'Not So Different After All: A Cross-discipline View of Trust', *Academy of Management Review*, 23: 393–404.

SALLY, D. (1995), 'Conversation and Cooperation in Social Dilemmas', *Rationality and Society*, 7: 58–92.

SANFEY A. G., et al. (2003), 'The Neural Basis of Economic Decision-making in the Ultimatum Game', *Science*, 300: 1755–8.

SCHECHTER, L. (2007), 'Traditional Trust Measurement and the Risk Confounded: An Experiment in Rural Paraguay', *Journal of Economic Behavior and Organization*, 62 (2): 272–92.

SCHELLING, T. C. (1960), *The Strategy of Conflict* (Oxford: Oxford University Press).

—— (1968), 'The Life You Save May Be Your Own', in S. Chase (ed.), *Problems in Public Expenditure Analysis* (Washington, D.C.: Brookings Institution), 127–62.

—— (1978), *Micromotives and Macrobehavior* (New York: Norton).

SITKIN, S. B., and ROTH, N. L. (1993), 'Explaining the Limited Effectiveness of Legalistic "Remedies" for Trust/Distrust', *Organization Science*, 4: 367–92.

SMITH, V. L. and WALKER, J. M. (1993), 'Rewards, Experience and Decisions Costs in First Price Auctions', *Economic Inquiry*, 31: 237–44.

TAYLOR, M. (1987), *The Possibility of Cooperation* (New York: Cambridge University Press).

TENBRUNSEL, A. E., and MESSICK, D. M. (1999), 'Sanction Systems, Decision Frames and Cooperation', *Administrative Science Quarterly*, 44: 684–707.

THALER, R. (1992), *The Winner's Curse: Anomalies and Paradoxes of Economic Life* (New York: Free Press).

THOMAS, J. P., and WORRALL, T. (2002), 'Gift-giving, Quasi-credit and Reciprocity', *Rationality and Society*, 14: 308–52.

YAMAGISHI, T. (1986), 'The Provision of a Sanctioning System as a Public Good', *Journal of Personality and Social Psychology*, 51: 32–42.

—— COOK, K. S., and WATABE, M. (1998), 'Uncertainty, Trust and Commitment Formation in the Unites States and Japan', *American Journal of Sociology*, 194: 165–94.

YOUNG, H. P. (1994), *Equity: In Theory and Practice* (Princeton, N.J.: Princeton University Press).

C H A P T E R   28

....

SURVEYS

....

H A N N A H   B R Ü C K N E R

INTRODUCTION

....

SURVEYS are arguably the most widely used method of data-gathering in the social sciences.[1] For example, more than half of the articles (55 percent) published between 1995 and 2005 in the *American Sociological Review* and 39 percent of those published in the *American Journal of Sociology* used survey data in one way or another.[2] In the special issue of the journal *Science* on 'Frontiers in the Social Sciences' the increasing availability of nationally representative longitudinal survey data is mentioned as one of six developments that hold promise for scientific progress (Butz and Torrey 2006). Yet surveys, together with advances in computing, are sometimes held responsible for the kind of 'variable-centered sociology' analytical sociology ought to overcome—typically, work that produces associations between independent variables and outcomes at the individual level that are at best ambiguous and at worst meaningless with respect to the causal mechanisms that account for the measured associations (Sørensen 1998; Hedström 2005: 109). Obviously surveys are just one tool in the arsenal of empirical methods available to sociologists. As such, survey data cannot be better than the use we are putting them to and their usefulness is further limited by the skills we bring to bear on collecting and analyzing survey data. Perhaps less obvious is the answer to the question of whether there is something inherent in the method itself that limits its usefulness for analytical sociology. It is worth reflecting on the history of the modern sample survey as a starting point for thinking about these issues.

Initially motivated by the desire to achieve accurate predictions, social scientists developed probability-sampling designs that could measure the distribution of some characteristic of a given population with great precision. Ironically, the development of the survey method that greatly improved its descriptive power is also associated with the downfall of quantitative sociology into variable-centered sociology. Many classic studies that used surveys, including the work of the Chicago School, the Middletown studies (Lynd and Lynd 1929), and the Marienthal project (Jahoda, Lazarsfeld, and Zeisel 1971), were community-based. They often used survey in conjunction with other data-collection methods to produce rich and analytically meaningful imagery of the social processes in these communities. The price such studies paid was lack of generalizability—Middletown was certainly a quintessential town but perhaps not necessarily one that represented America's diversity even back then.

The modern sample survey, in contrast, achieved representativeness, that is accuracy in estimating population characteristics, precisely by stripping away the social context that was the focus in the community studies. The ideal-typical random-sampling technique consists in collecting sampling-unit identifiers for the target population in a sampling frame and randomly drawing a sample; the data will give an estimate of a population characteristic with known precision depending on the distribution of the attribute in question and the sample size. In the absence of a comprehensive sampling frame such as a population register, most population studies in the USA and elsewhere use multistage cluster sampling. It is more efficient and much easier to sample geographic units, schools, or neighborhoods first, and then select multiple respondents within each sampled cluster point. Population samples will typically sample households in a second step, and then randomly select one member in each household. The role of communities and households, to name only two relevant social settings, was hence reduced to providing a sampling frame, and the clustering of individuals in such contexts became a nuisance for calculating the correct population estimates[3] rather than a source of data in its own right.[4] Social contexts, however, are the raw material for interaction-based explanations as well as the arenas in which interdependent action takes place. Part of the answer of how to engage in analytical sociology with survey data is therefore located in sampling design. Although this chapter is not primarily about sampling, designing surveys usually involves selecting survey respondents in some way, which turns out to be important for realizing analytical ambitions. In addition to who to select for surveying, there are two other basic design elements: (1) How to ask questions, and (2) What to do with the answers. I will barely touch on the first. It would be impossible to answer that question in a single chapter with any kind of specificity without focusing on a particular substantive area. I will discuss the second question at length.

Survey researchers use the collection of attributes, behaviors, and orientations of the sampled individuals (variables) to build statistical models of some outcome in question. The shortcomings of this approach in comparison with a mechanism-based explanatory strategy are discussed at length in Hedström—most importantly, the gulf between social theory and statistical explanations (2005: ch. 5). There is not much else one can do with survey data.[5] The question is thus whether surveys inherently imply variable-centered explanatory strategies and should therefore be discounted by analytical sociologists. The answer given in this chapter is a decisive *no*. On the contrary, I will argue here that surveys are essential for the project of analytical sociology. First, surveys provide social facts, or empirical regularities that analytical sociology aims to explain. In fact, in many situations surveys are the only way to acquire such empirical regularities. Surveys are uniquely suited for the task of abstracting and dissecting a 'complex totality into its constituent entities and activities and then [bringing] into focus what is believed to be its most essential elements' (Hedström 2005: 2). Second, surveys can be and have been used to empirically study social mechanisms. Doing so in fact always involves measuring variables and typically also entails building statistical models. Needless to say, neither variables nor statistical modeling as such make for nonanalytical sociology. Much of this chapter will discuss aspects of survey design that enable the study of mechanisms. In particular, there are often no feasible alternatives to surveys for finding out who interacts with whom in what ways and systematically relating that to beliefs, actions, and outcomes. While the search for interaction-based explanations is currently not regularly embedded in the design of surveys, it is certainly possible to do so. And third, survey data are better suited than data collected by many other methods to the analysis, comparison, and simulation of macro effects or aggregation and are therefore critical for studying interdependent action.

28.1 SOCIAL FACTS AND SOCIAL MECHANISMS

The descriptive strength of surveys is extremely useful in producing starting points for analytical sociology; namely, empirical regularities and distributions of the raw material for causal explanations, such as actors' beliefs, norms, behavior, and resources. We need surveys because our perceptions of how the world works, what others do and think, and so on are fundamentally structured by local and personal experience. That empirical regularities are subject to interpretation and contestation is evidenced in the many disagreements among social scientists about 'what happens'—for example, in the form of disagreements about social change. It certainly makes a difference for understanding the social whether people are more or less likely to marry than twenty or thirty years ago, whether education is more or less important in structuring income inequality, whether parents' socioeconomic status is more or less important in structuring their offsprings' opportunities, and so on. The (analytical) question of whether women's increasing educational attainment and labor-force participation reduce marriage rates is first and foremost premised on an empirically observable decline in marriage rates. Among the many possible examples of survey-based research that has yielded social facts that speak directly to (or against) prominent social theory, one might think of an elegant paper by Oppenheimer (1994) which engages Becker's analysis of the division of labor in the family (1981) and shows that neither the historical trend in marriage behavior nor the empirical realities of contemporary households in the USA are consistent with major predictions arising from Becker's theory. Similarly, predictions about broad changes in the life course long diagnosed by modernization theorists are only partially borne out by long-range empirical analyses (Hillmert 2005; Brückner and Mayer 2005; Fussel and Furstenberg 2005). Conducting a debate about the causes and consequences of such issues without reference to data is largely futile. The first and crucial step in explaining such trends is to show what is actually going on. Surveys provide the principle avenue to produce such data.

As with all empirical work, the capacity of surveys to provide social facts in support of social theory is crucially dependent on appropriate research design and processing. The details of how surveys measure elementary concepts such as earnings, race and ethnicity, household structure, let alone complex concepts such as marriage rates, gender-role attitudes, or educational aspirations are surprisingly complex and often too tedious to be adequately reported or understood (Martin 1983; Brückner 1995; Fowler 1995; Snipp 2003). Analytical sociology will have to embrace such complexity fully in order to make sense of the facts. The income and earnings decompositions described below, for example, are useful only to the extent that the groups that are compared constitute social categories that are meaningful across time and space and measurable with respect to the hypotheses to be tested. Generally, and for research on processes of social change in particular, the principal problem for surveys is to capture the relevant concepts involved in the social process of interest. Social change in basic living arrangements such as the composition of households, in the occupational structure, and in institutional systems such as schools complicates the production of facts (Martin 1983).

Furthermore, as language usage evolves, frames of reference and meanings change as well. For example, researchers interested in racial attitudes and subjective constructions of race face the problem of ever-increasing sensitivity with respect to how we talk about race. Thus, questionnaire items that—however imperfectly—measured racism in the seventies and eighties have now become obsolete (Brückner, Morning, and Nelson 2007). The producers of long-range surveys are loath to change measurement instruments, because that reduces comparability of data over time. Unfortunately, not changing the instruments may result in misrepresenting or missing the process altogether.

In this sense, a survey's virtue is its vice: constructing questionnaires forces one to come up with clear definitions of what one wants to measure, and the way in which it is done is there to see for all who care to look. However, what is actually measured in the field may depend on who is asked, and may be subject to variability in meaning, as well as to change over time, because the way in which meaning is expressed and communicated changes as well. In method parlance, surveys trade generalizability for validity, and therefore those interested in analyzing survey data ought to be aware of the dangers of reification of concepts. Facts are not given, or are somehow out there waiting to be analyzed. Facts of the kind that are of interest here are always constructed by those collecting, processing, and analyzing the data and thus are subject to local myopia as well. Analytical sociologists, rather than discounting the survey method, ought to take on (and have had) a critical role in guiding survey research to collect the right data. The remainder of this chapter should be read with these caveats in mind.

An important current arena of contestation of facts in which survey data play a large role is the discussion about causes of rising social inequality. Decomposition analyzes that compare inequalities within and between social groups, occupations, education groups, localities, economic sectors, and so on provide information on the sources of inequality. For example, a plausible theory about rising inequality is that women's rising educational attainment and labor-force participation together with increasing educational homogamy accounts for (part of) the increase in inequality of household incomes. The idea is that inequality rises because dual-earner households are more common and more likely to contain two well-educated earners, so that earnings capacities are more concentrated within households, increasing the gap between working-class one-earner households and others. This theory can be tested with survey data and, at least for the UK through the period between 1970 and 1990, has been largely refuted (Breen and Salazar 2009). Similar analyzes regarding the effects of demographic and economic trends have generally shown that many popular theories about the causes of rising inequality are not consistent with the available data (Morris and Western 1999; Western, Bloome, and Percheski 2008).

The descriptive work on income inequality dissects the trend into its 'constituent entities' (Hedström 2005: 2) such as the erosion of blue-collar wages at the lower end of the income distribution (Morris and Western 1999) and runaway compensation at the top (Piketty and Saez 2003). These components may be explained by different mechanisms or be part of a single process. The decomposition of trends in earnings inequality, such as the comparison of white and African American workers as well as workers in different sectors (Morgan and McKerrow 2004) and in different class positions (Morgan and Cha 2007) is consistent with hypotheses derived from Sørensen's rent-based explanation of inequality (Sørensen 1996, 2000), pointing to the destruction of rent-extraction capacities of workers and to a transfer of earnings from rank-and-file workers to managers and professionals.

Given Hedström's critique it is useful at this point to raise the question of whether and how this work constitutes analytical sociology. I have argued that dissecting processes in this manner is part and parcel of isolating the mechanism(s) that account for it. Clearly, homogamy requires interaction, and rent destruction is an action-based explanation for inequality, so why is there even a question? It seems to me that the problem is not in the fact that rent destruction is not measured directly (the presence of the mechanism is inferred from the analysis of who gets what).[6] While inferences of this kind may have their own problems, the question of how directly mechanisms are measured does not seem to make or break analytical sociology.[7] Neither is it especially problematic to impute intentional explanations in these cases; that is, to understand why actors do what they do when they destroy rents or marry others with similar educational attainment. However, Hedström also insists that '[t]o understand why actors do what they do is not sufficient [...] we must also seek to explain why, acting as they do, they bring about the social outcomes they do' (2005: 5)—the 'social' here referring to the idea that sociologists ought not to be interested in explaining individuals' actions per se but in understanding change (or, I might add, absence of change) 'at the social level.'

In the examples given above we do not learn whether rent destruction is simply the sum of a myriad of mutually independent micro processes at the local level or whether there are interdependencies. For example, rent destruction in one industry (for contingent reasons, or as part of a global or national restructuring process) may trigger supply- or demand-related changes in other industries that are unaffected by the first process, suggesting a kind of vacancy chain. As an aside, it is perhaps in order to point out that one nevertheless stands to learn a great deal about social inequality from the work described above. Be that as it may, the way in which actions aggregate or influence each other is a key component of analytical sociology in Hedström's version. Such aggregation or multiplier effects are the focus in the following discussion.

The decomposition of distributions in these studies is used to ask counterfactual questions: If factor X (say, household structure, marital homogamy, or residential segregation) had not changed over time and everything else had stayed the same, how would the distribution of Y (say, income or educational achievement) look? The problem here is of course that, generally, everything else would *not* stay the same if X had not changed.[8] For example, the gender gap in wages obtains in a social structure in which men and women are occupationally segregated. We may use survey data to estimate how the gender gap would look if occupational segregation were absent, but it is likely that reassigning half or more of the workforce to different occupations, even if it were possible, would have considerable impact on all parameters implicated in the model, including the wage structure within and across occupations. Such dynamics are an important component of analytical sociology and are here conceptualized as the aggregation problem—because the focus shifts from individual-level effects (a person with attribute X changes jobs) to interdependent effects (many persons with attribute X change jobs) and hence to aggregate (emergent) properties of the system. In other words, making multivariate analyses more analytical entails a theoretical model of how actions at the micro level reproduce or change the macro level and vice versa. This has important implications for survey design, which I will illustrate here with two examples.

In the first example, Breen and Cooke (2005) use aggregate, internationally comparative survey data on gender-role attitudes to test predictions from a game-theoretical model that explains the persistence of the gendered household division of labor. The model assumes that men and women have preferences regarding the division of labor in the household that vary from traditional (gendered) to modern (ungendered), and that partner choices take place under the condition of uncertainty regarding one's (potential) partner's preference. Some people value a traditional division of labor over marriage and some value a modern role division over marriage. The third group are adjusters, who prefer one over the other but would not forgo marriage if a partner with whom to realize their preference is not available. The game-theoretical model suggests and the survey data show that variation in the proportion of nontraditional women by itself does not produce aggregate changes in the division of household labor. Such changes come about only when a country has a sizeable proportion both of adjuster men and of non-traditional women.

The difference between this analysis and the usual variable-centered approach is clearly in the explicit attention to matching of preferences in couples under the condition of uncertainty about the preferences of potential partners as a mechanism, and aggregation over the population. The model predicts that individuals' gender-role attitudes affect the marital division of labor appreciably only if the distribution of attitudes in the population passes a threshold that allows for enough pairings of people who prefer (or adjust to) a less-gendered division of labor. To empirically test their model, Breen and Cooke studied cross-sectional variation between countries based on a conventional random-sampling approach.[9] The implication for survey design is that the data have to be rich enough to aggregate across the relevant social contexts, and that there is variation in the aggregate properties, be it over time or between contexts.

A second example is the context-dependent effect of virginity pledges on sexual behavior (Bearman and Brückner 2001). The mechanism proposed is that pledging works like a selective incentive in the context of an identity movement. Taking a virginity pledge affects adolescents' behavior most when they are embedded in an interacting community of others that constitutes a meaningful identity for pledgers. Where too many pledgers were around, however, pledging ceased to be a basis for identity and behavioral effects declined. Similarly, adolescents were most at risk of taking a virginity pledge in schools with some but not too many pledgers. Thus, the proposed mechanism suggested two things: a specific functional form for the contextual effect (number of pledgers in the environment) and a cross-level interaction effect. To test this idea it was necessary to measure the properties of the relevant social context for adolescents—in this case, schools. In fact, the context effect appeared significant only in those schools that were the focal point for social organization in friendship networks.

Both examples, in my view, constitute interaction-based explanations for the outcome of interest. The contextual measures are not simply another variable that contributes to variation in the outcome—they add information about the dynamics of the process. Both examples also illustrate the unique contribution surveys can make to analytical sociology, compared to other data-collection methods. In the case of the virginity pledge, not only is it hard to imagine how one would randomly assign adolescents to pledging in the context of an experiment; what is more, the findings suggest that such a procedure would not result in the same effect because random assignment precludes the interacting community of pledgers that is the basis for the effect of pledging. In fact, experiments are designed to remove the effect of any interaction-based factors that are not built into the experimental stimulus itself, and thus may eliminate from view precisely what is interesting to the analytical sociologist. Finally, ethnographic work very rarely achieves the scale and perspective that enabled the findings discussed in this section. Ethnographic data would be able to directly reveal the formation of pledge identities in a given community—that is, we could know what pledging really means to those engaging in it; however, it is much less likely that such data would be available over time; the data will not contain precise measurement of the prevalence of pledging and subsequent behavior (unless combined with surveys); and they will rarely afford comparisons between a wide range of contexts. Thus, ethnographic data would not allow testing the hypothesis regarding the functional form of the contextual effect (curvilinear) and therefore would likely be silent on aggregation effects. The next section will discuss more in-depth ideas about how to design surveys that enable interaction-based explanations.

28.2 SURVEY DESIGN AND INTERACTION-BASED EXPLANATION

To exploit the full potential for interaction-based explanations, surveys have to fan out from individuals to their significant others, peers, to the focal points of social organizations they are embedded in, and sample those others and their social connections as well. Longitudinal data, here understood as the observation of the same units over time, is equally important—both for disentangling compositional change and unit-specific change (one important aspect of aggregation), and for disentangling selection effects from social influence. An exceptional example of such a survey design is the Longitudinal Study of Adolescent Health (Udry and Bearman 1997) that collected data on students, their siblings and parents, friends, and schools.[10] A unique and centrally important feature of these data is that global, school-based network data were collected at baseline, yielding rich information about the social context of adolescent behavior. These data have been used to explore the effect of composition and structure of friendship networks as well as school context on sexual behavior (Bearman and Brückner 1999, 2001; Adamczyk and Felson 2005; Fletcher 2007), deviance (Haynie 2001; Mangino 2005), and suicide ideation (Bearman and Moody 2004; Lee 2006), and many other behaviors and outcomes. Some of these papers attempt to measure the normative climate in peer groups by aggregating resources, behavior, aspirations, and attitudes at various levels of social organization. The mechanisms that are inferred to be at work are simple: friends exert pressure to conform to expectations; they provide role models and opportunity structures (Bearman and Brückner 1999).

Often, surveys collect data on ego-networks and use survey respondents as informants about their interaction partners. While this is better than nothing, in many situations it will be problematic because such information may be unreliable and biased. We may be interested in information about significant others that even in close relationships is not easily disclosed. For example, people are notoriously unaware of how much money their spouses make or whether or not their children are sexually active (Brückner and Bearman 2003). It is also well known that we tend to think that our friends are more similar to us than they in fact are. Even more importantly, data on more remote social contacts, such as friends of friends or 'weak ties,' is extremely difficult to collect through focal respondents alone but quite important for many outcomes of interest (Bearman and Brückner 1999). Nevertheless, Granovetter's concept of weak ties (1973) and other network metaphors have generated many instances of analytical sociology, some of which are based on surveys (Wegener 1991; Bearman 2005). People find jobs and other important information through ties that bridge small worlds, through acquaintances, distant relatives, or friends of friends rather than through their close significant others, because such weak ties are more likely to yield nonredundant information. This literature is a happy instance where the mechanism (diffusion of information through network ties) coincides directly with the strategy for data collection. We can ask people how they obtained a job and analyze their answers directly. Sociologists have invented ingenuous methods that, sometimes indirectly, measure network size, reach, density, and other concepts that represent access to network resources from ego-network data (Bernard et al. 1984; Killworth et al. 1990; Marsden 1990). In other instances, interaction-based explanations require more complex survey designs because the attributes and networks of respondents' network partners are of interest as well. Respondent-driven sampling, perhaps combined with traditional sampling of multiple starting points, is an efficient (and sometimes the only) method to recruit significant alters for each ego. Thus, Add Health randomly sampled individuals within social contexts (here, schools) and then recruited their parents and siblings into the study.

Christakis and Fowler's recent study of obesity among the participants of the thirty-two-year long Framington Heart Study is another interesting example. The names of relatives and friends and their relationship to the participant were originally recorded for the purpose of securing follow-up in subsequent waves. Because all participants lived in the same community and the alters listed in the contact sheets were study participants themselves, it was possible to construct a community network from these data and to show that obesity spread through the network in ways that point to social influences rather than genetic causes at the heart of the epidemic. As with Add Health, recruiting a large number of participants situated in the community was crucial for providing an interaction-based explanation.

In addition to aggregation from individual-level responses, survey data is often augmented with contextual data from censuses, observational studies, or ethnographies to characterize communities. The Project on Human Development in Chicago Neighborhoods, for example, combines survey data with systematic unobtrusive observation, in-depth interviews with relevant community members, census data, and other government statistics to explain variation in outcomes such as crime rates and child development (Raudenbush and Sampson 1999).[11] One crucial step in such a multilevel design is to identify the social geography of the relevant social context where such outcomes are produced. Administrative units such as census tracts or zip codes may not coincide with real-social-interaction patterns at all (Grannis 1998). In the Chicago example, the researchers used multiple methods to divide the city into 370 neighborhoods that subsequently served as primary sampling units for the survey components. Survey respondents serve as informants both about themselves and about their social context through aggregation at the neighborhood level. Furthermore, these data allow the modeling of interdependencies between neighborhoods as well; for example, the question of whether changes in one context affect crime rates in the adjacent neighborhoods. Censuses themselves will likely be extremely useful in this regard in the future, to the extent that the complete data, rather than just random samples, are available and samples can be linked across households, family trees, and census years. Complete and linked data are made available for some periods for the USA, Canada, Great Britain, Iceland, and Norway through the North Atlantic Population Project.[12]

The extensions to the survey method discussed so far have fundamental implications for survey design. The widespread use of clustered sampling designs in survey research, taken together with a renewed focus on social context, carry the potential to make surveys more and more useful for analytical sociology. What is needed to realize this potential, however, is to 'scale up' sample sizes. Raudenbush and Sampson (1999) discuss the question of sample sizes suitable for achieving reliable estimation of neighborhood characteristics and modeling between-neighborhood variability. As it turns out, the most efficient sampling strategy for multilevel analysis involves increasing the number of clusters sampled at stage 1 after identifying the minimal number of individuals within each cluster needed for reliable aggregate measures. Where collection of global-network data is important, one does of course need saturated samples within contexts.

In any case, it should be clear that analytically useful surveys will often imply much larger samples than conventional surveys that typically generalize from 1,500–2,000 respondents to the US residential population. The collection of global-network data also poses a challenge for surveys because it is necessary to identify the social topography of the target population. Schools may be the focal point of social organization for adolescents, and, conveniently, have rosters with lists of potential friends that are needed for global-network data, but, even so, in the Add Health sample more than half of black females' opposite-sex friends were not in their school and therefore were not recruited into the sample. Observing social networks over time and targeting less salient types of ties is also fraught with difficulty (Bernard et al. 1984). Surveys are not well suited to continuous monitoring of social interaction. Longitudinal network data based on surveys, where available at all, are (usually short) series of snapshots. Prospective analyses that relate network properties to other constructs of interest then may face the problem of time-ordering, much like cross-sectional research. For the most salient types of relationships, such as romantic partners, it is possible, if difficult, to collect data on relationship formation and dissolution retrospectively; but it may be difficult to determine when a friendship started or ended, and impossible to remember the timing of less intimate relations. Unobtrusive observation of network ties, for example by monitoring communication networks and other traces of social contacts, is better able to capture networks-in-formation. Such data, if available, may usefully be combined with survey data, where the survey data could provide information on node attributes and behavior. There are many ways to enrich survey data by embedding other data-collection methods within survey designs or vice versa. The remainder of this section will give a brief flavor of how this has been used to address some weaknesses in the survey method.

While surveys can provide much information on a great many things, even the most comprehensive survey design is likely to leave gaping holes regarding subjective understandings of respondents—concepts such as identity, meaning, and reasoning. The defining feature of surveys is to standardize the questions (and, most often, answers) that are posed to respondents. Whether respondents have a uniform understanding of the meaning of these questions is another animal altogether (Brückner 1995). For example, Smith (1981) found that respondents had very different things in mind when asked about their confidence in the scientific community. Many had no referent at all in mind, others thought about particular fields such as medicine, atomic energy, electricity, the space program, even their own local community. Confidence in the scientific community was greatest among those who had no referent in mind or thought about the space program.

People confronted with an issue they have never or not recently thought about might not be able to answer a question in a meaningful way. John Zaller suggests that respondents construct answers to survey questions (and elect candidates) 'on the fly' (1992: 1) based on ideas that happen to be salient to them at the moment. Because of conversation norms, respondents will answer questions by making educated guesses even though they have no knowledge whatsoever about an issue. Especially when a 'don't know' category is not provided, respondents confronted with a policy question about which they know nothing may try to infer hints from the question-and-answer categories in a way that may be quite unrelated to the issue at stake (Schuman and Presser 1980; Converse and Presser 1986). Individuals define the importance of discussion matters according to the network partners they talk to, rather than the other way round, as is intended by the ego name generator in the General Social Survey (Bearman and Parigi 2004).

These examples illustrate the principal weakness of survey data: their relatively low validity or superficiality with respect to subjective states and meaning. Assessing validity in this vein is generally achieved by combining survey methods with qualitative approaches or experiments to figure out what the answers to survey questions really mean. Many survey instruments are based on qualitative fieldwork. Beyond the validation of measurement instruments, combining qualitative and quantitative methods has substantive applications. Combining data from surveys with fieldwork, observation, focus groups, or in-depth interviews ('triangulation') can be used to enrich findings from surveys with accounts of subjects' understandings in order to integrate divergent perspectives on the same process; to elaborate the meaning of quantitative relationships on the ground or to explain unexpected findings in quantitative research; and to discover mechanisms that one method by itself cannot reveal (see e.g. Merton, Fiske, and Kendall [1956] 1990). Many organizational studies combine surveys with comparative fieldwork or case studies. For example, Ely (1996) shows with a combination of survey data and qualitative interviewing how the proportional representation of women in the workplace, a contextual effect long thought to be associated with women's career chances in organizations, is implicated in the social construction of gender identity and gender difference among lawyers. Merton, Fiske, and Kendall ([1956] 1990) developed a manual of interviewing techniques designed to make sense of relationships found in quantitative research, which, in Sørensen's words, is also a 'codification of procedures for developing theory from the analysis of patterns of evidence' (1991: 518). In other words, in this division of labor surveys provide 'patterns of evidence' and more qualitative data provide material for understanding why actors act the way they act.

This, of course, presupposes that one can learn about causes of action by talking to the actors. I am not convinced that one can always learn about causes of empirical regularities by asking people why they act in the way they act. For example, we may be at a loss to explain complex behavior such as our partner choices even to our most significant others, let alone to a survey interviewer. Nevertheless, individuals' partner choices produce empirical regularities that can and have been studied with survey data, uncovering interaction patterns that are not usually transparent to the individuals making their choices. People choose partners in diffuse and haphazard ways—perhaps we were present when a person made a funny joke and laughing together leads to more interaction that escalates into a romantic tie. The pattern emerges in the aggregate, when mysteriously (to the actors on the ground) the 'right' people with matching class and education backgrounds find each other (Waller 1937). Another example of a mechanism in partner choice that is at work outside the consciousness of actors comes from Add Health. Bearman, Moody, and Stovel (2004) use simulations to discover the parameter that accounts for the observed structure of the network of romantic and sexual relations in a high school. As it turns out, a single parameter, specifically the near-absence of cycles of four, accounts for the structure of the network. While adolescents are probably unaware of this, they avoid dating their partner's former partner's partner. The result is a spanning-tree-like network component that connects a large proportion of adolescents, with strong implications for diffusion of information or communicative diseases that are not transparent to adolescents and others concerned with their well-being. It strikes me as unlikely that asking adolescents why they date or do not date others would yield much insight about the formation and the structure of the network. In sum, while 'why' questions in surveys may yield interesting data in some instances, they often do not help shed light on mechanisms (Fowler 1995). In other words, reasons for action and causes of action are not the same. Here, again, getting at the mechanism that produced the aggregate outcome crucially depended on being able to map the global network—that is, to gather information about realized and absent ties. Similarly, mapping the range of available options or choice sets could illuminate studies of other processes of matching, including segregation in housing and job markets.[13]

Two other ways of enriching survey data should be mentioned. First, experiments embedded in surveys have long been used for measurement and validation purposes—for example, to assess the effects of question-wording and -sequencing (Converse and Presser 1986) or to unobtrusively measure sensitive constructs such as racism (Kuklinski, Cobb, and Gilens 1997), beliefs about genetic bases for racial inequality (Brückner, Morning, and Nelson 2007), or sexual behavior (Lauman et al. 1994). Manipulation of the context in which respondents are presented with the survey instruments can illuminate how attitudes and preferences are formed and changed and could therefore provide an excellent instrument for analytical sociologists interested in cognitive and social processes in the formation of subjective states.[14]

Second, the information-technology revolution has produced a wealth of data that is probably largely untapped for research purposes (with the possible exception of some Scandinavian countries)—ranging from administrative data from social-security systems and payrolls to grade report cards, medical records, consumption data, satellite images, and online friendship or dating networks. Social-security and personnel databases are highly valuable because they provide continuous measurement of key constructs, such as wages. Online contacts that leave behind retrievable traces could similarly provide continuous measurement of contact networks, as well as 'instant' global-network data. While such data are often 'thin,' they can be usefully enriched with survey data if a mechanism for matching the data is available. The use of such data could unburden surveys considerably and leave valuable interview time for other things.

28.3 Causal Inference

To varying degrees, all the examples cited above make explicit statements about causal mechanisms that account for the observed data. A discussion of the problem of causal inference with observational data is therefore useful. It will necessarily be brief, but there are many recent comprehensive treatments (among others, Frank 1998, 2006; Morgan and Winship 2007; Hong and Raudenbush 2005; Morgan and Harding 2006; Winship and Morgan 1999; see also Rubin 1974; Rosenbaum and Rubin 1983). Unobserved heterogeneity of individuals and selection bias are ubiquitous threats to internal validity in survey research. Researchers in the variable-based tradition may prudently refrain from making causal statements, although their findings will inevitably be interpreted in causal terms. Analytical sociologists cannot afford to do so. Neither can they afford to limit their research to questions that lend themselves to designing randomized experiments. Randomized experiments neutralize selection effects because random assignment of the causal variable of interest assures that there is no relationship between the prior experiences and characteristics of study participants and the presence or absence of the putative cause. However, these prior experiences are often exactly the fabric of interaction-based explanations. It is generally not feasible or even possible to randomly assign people to neighborhoods, networks, schools, occupations, and group memberships, let alone childbearing, taking a virginity pledge, or moving to another country. But even if this were possible, the causal effect of the variable of interest, if any, will probably differ from what it would be in the real world of the actors where causes are embedded in social interaction and in the life histories of individuals.

Experimental designs are also likely to neutralize aggregate emergent properties that can be crucially important in shaping the process of interest. Just like counterfactuals derived from survey research, generalizations from randomized experiments are problematic even when the process of interest is meaningfully conceptualized as a treatment. School-voucher or welfare-to-work programs may yield encouraging results in local evaluation experiments, but when those programs are implemented on a more comprehensive scale they might run into problems simply because there are now more families with vouchers than good schools which have room, and too many former welfare recipients looking for jobs. It is of course theoretically possible to design large-scale experiments with subexperiments that vary context (such as the proportion of people receiving the treatment) to get at aggregation effects. Because experiments require a great deal of control over the implementation of the experimental conditions and the selection of the experimental and control groups, however, doing so may be prohibitively expensive and require a degree of organization and power that researchers do not ordinarily possess. For all these reasons, experiments are often not an alternative to observational data.

Causal inference presupposes three things. The putative cause and effect have to be associated with each other, there must be no endogeneity present (for example, selection effects), often expressed as correct time-ordering of cause and effect, and there must be no other factors that may explain the association (unobserved heterogeneity). The first line of defense for inference from survey data is multivariate models that attempt to control for factors that may render the association of interest spurious. Multivariate models mimic the randomization in experiments; that is, the goal is to make the observed units equal to each other, except for the presence of the putative cause. Frank (2000, 2006) has developed an elegant way to assess the potential impact of omitted variable bias on the estimate for the causal variable of interest.

Much recent work on selectivity has focused on propensity methods for causal inference. The basic idea is to model actors' propensity to receive the treatment and to use that propensity in models of the outcome. Propensity scores are used as control variables or weights in regression models of the outcome, and in analyses where actors are matched or stratified according to their estimated propensity. The relationship between treatment and outcome is then compared among units with equal propensity to receive the treatment, under the assumption that any remaining (unobserved) differences are ignorable. (For a cogent discussion and comparison of different approaches see Morgan 2001.) Unfortunately, propensity scores are problematic for modeling processes with strong social selectivity (Stolzenberg and Relles 1997). There may not be enough people around who have received the treatment in spite of low propensities, and none with high propensities who did not receive it. For example, in a hypersegregated school system it will be impossible to analyze school effects with propensity-score methods because all the variation of propensity scores is between schools and none within schools. In other words, it will be impossible to match students with different treatment status based on their propensity to attend certain schools. Examining the data with respect to balance in the propensities is therefore crucially important.

Even though many potential causes of interest to sociologists do not lend themselves easily to being conceptualized as treatment, the method has been applied to such causes as well. It would perhaps be desirable to adjust the language in the literature to reflect the reality that actor attributes and behavior such as gender, race, civic participation, sexual activity, and so on are not experimental treatments, and that the resulting propensities reflect predispositions of these actors to end up in specific social situations only in the best case. Propensity models are often treated as the kitchen sink, in the sense that everything conceivable that is measured is introduced in the multivariate models that generate propensity scores with the goal of making the units that serve as controls as similar as possible to those in the 'experimental' group—that is, they are just another instance of variable-based sociology, with the added convenience of savings in degrees of freedom in the outcome model. Like experiments, propensity-score methodology tends to direct attention away from social action and interaction in its focus on a single causal variable. A more analytical approach to processes of social selection is needed to make propensity-score methodology useful for sociology and for causal inference.

The second line of defense for inference from survey data is longitudinal data: measuring the putative cause before the effect occurs at the very least ensures that the outcome is not causing the putative effect. Furthermore, relating changes in the putative cause to changes in the outcome alone goes a long way towards controlling selection effects. Fixed-effects models remove the effect of unobserved heterogeneity on the model parameters for factors that do not change over time. (For an overview see DiPrete and Forristal 1994; Halaby 2004.) Essentially, units serve as their own controls, absorbing the impact of time-invariant unmeasured characteristics on the estimates in the model. In a similar vein, unmeasured predispositions can be effectively absorbed by prior outcome measures, and in some instances such models are able to replicate estimates from experimental-study designs (Glazerman, Levy, and Myers 2003; Frank 2006).

Note that both approaches require multiple repeated measurements. Fixed-effects models are only identified if the number of measurements exceeds the parameters in the model. Using prior outcomes as controls to strengthen causal inference requires at least three time points, because measurement error in the repeated outcome measures is correlated, resulting in biased and unreliable estimates. When multiple repeated measures are available, the measurement error can be estimated and removed from the model (Raudenbush and Bryk 2002). In sum, longitudinal data is essential for causal inference with survey data. It goes without saying that designing longitudinal surveys requires the utmost care and attention to the temporal patterns of the processes involved.

CONCLUSION: IMPLICATIONS

In sum, analytical sociologists can take advantage of the widespread use of surveys in sociology in several ways. I argued that surveys can and do provide useful data when anchored appropriately in time and social space. Explanations of action almost always require longitudinal data of some kind. The most useful survey designs will also incorporate data about the social contexts of actors at multiple levels of social organization; most importantly, social networks, families, organizations, etc. Triangulation of surveys with other kinds of (contextual) data and hybrid designs that combine surveys with experiments, observation, and qualitative methods have much promise. Such extensions to the survey method can provide insights into how beliefs, values, and emotions, as well as actors' understandings and identities, come about and can be measured appropriately.

In the final analysis, surveys provide information about mechanisms such as social influence in the form of correlations between constructs—we don't actually see it happen, as we might in a more narrative approach. In the case of virginity pledges, the relationship that is observed is consistent with the proposed mechanism (identity-movement participation) and we can measure participation directly, in contrast to a pledge identity as a subjective state and what it means to the actors. Christakis and Fowler (2007) inferred changes in norms about body weight as a mechanism that accounts for the spread of obesity but observed the correlation between gaining weight and having obese friends. Such inferences will be more credible if the underlying theoretical model has specificity and depth; that is, if it suggests specific relationships and accounts for a broad range of instances of the phenomenon in question. Sørensen (1998) has pointed out that there is no reason why these relationships should be linear, and in the case of interdependent action that implies multiplier and threshold effects they will be nonlinear for sure. Analytical sociologists, rather than shunning surveys, should embrace surveys' capacities to provide data that is rich and precise enough to model such relationships. In a world where the organization of the social sciences often results in a strict separation of the activities and roles of theorists, researchers, and methodologists, surveys' potential to yield useful material for analytical sociology remains underused (Sørensen 1991). Theory without empirical referents will rarely be specific enough; mathematical models without substantive referents are not helpful; and researchers without theoretical referents and knowledge of mathematical models will rarely and only serendipitously collect the data that is needed for analytical sociology. In this sense, surveys are—just like any other empirical method—a tool that is made useful primarily by the skill and sociological imagination of the user.

Notes

1. Surveys are here understood as data-collection efforts that proceed by asking questions of individuals. Typically, these questions are structured and standardized to ensure uniform measurement across individuals. Answers tend to be preformatted as well, although open-ended questions are frequently employed. Unless specified otherwise, this chapter is written with well-designed surveys in mind; that is, surveys that exploit the strengths of the method and avoid its weaknesses to the extent possible.

2. These numbers were calculated from coding articles in all issues published between January 1995 and December 2005. An article was coded as using survey data if its principal empirical focus was based on survey data; that is, simple references to findings from surveys were not counted and are even more common in the discipline.

3. In theory, and depending on the number of clusters/observations sampled, estimated standard errors ought to be adjusted for clustered sample designs, because people within a cluster tend to be more similar to each other than to those in other clusters that are not in the sample. Therefore, variability may be underestimated in cluster samples without appropriate adjustments.

4. Under the definition given in n. 1, surveys do not have to be based on samples. The census, for example, is a survey even if sampling is not (yet) employed.

5. It is possible to use survey data to build case-comparative studies; that is, to look at individuals as cases (wholes) rather than as collections of variables. Rich typologies are one example that goes beyond the variable strategy. My guess is that such strategies are rarely used for explanatory purposes, although in some cases rich typologies will be used as variables in statistical models. Here the case-comparative component is classificatory rather than explanatory in nature and serves to create a more meaningful variable (examples are found in Bearman and Brückner 1999; Stovel, Bearman, and Savage 1997).

6. Direct evidence for processes like wage discrimination, exclusion, rent destruction, or income transfers is difficult to observe with survey data. One reason is that actors are either not aware of what is going on or have reason to keep their knowledge to themselves. Furthermore, such processes may not be intelligible at the individual level even though conflict and bargaining processes are happening around individuals, because the component mechanisms (in this case, transfer of income or destruction of institutions that reduce income inequality) acquire meaning (increasing inequality) only in the aggregate. Here surveys are useful to evaluate the outcome (earnings distributions), but at least some of the processes by which inequality is produced must be studied with other methods, including ethnography and case-comparative studies, perhaps in conjunction with survey data. (For a recent example see Fernandez 1994.)

7. Hedström (2005) gives a contextual effect of unemployment as an example for interaction-based explanations of outcomes, where youth are more at risk of becoming or staying unemployed when many others in their social world are

unemployed as well. This, too, is an indirect measure of mechanisms that increase unemployment risk.

8. One way to make these counterfactuals more realistic is to explicitly model interdependence of parameters in the form of interaction effects (e.g. Breen and Salazar 2009; Maralani 2008). Another related idea is to use empirical regularities produced by the analysis of survey data to provide realistic inputs into simulation studies of action-based models (Hedström 2005: ch. 5).

9. A stronger design might have sampled individuals at risk for marriage and followed them over time with specific attention to the formation of preferences in marriage markets. In the absence of such data, the paper takes preferences as a given.

10. See also <http://www.cpc.unc.edu/projects/addhealth>, accessed 2008.

11. For more information see <http://www.icpsr.umich.edu/PHDCN>, accessed 2008.

12. For more information see <http://www.nappdata.org>, accessed 2008.

13. I am grateful to Elizabeth Bruch for pointing this out to me during a discussion of an earlier version of this chapter.

14. For an overview see Sniderman and Grob (1996). Many recent applications can be found on the webpage of 'Timesharing Experiments in the Social Sciences,' an NSF-funded infrastructure project that supports experiments in multipurpose population surveys at <http://experimentcentral.org>, accessed 2008.

References

ADAMCZYK, A., and FELSON, J. (2006), 'Friends' Religiosity and First Sex', *Social Science Research*, 354: 924–47.

BEARMAN, P. S. (2005), *Doormen* (Chicago, Ill.: University of Chicago Press).

—— and BRÜCKNER, H. (1999), *Power in Numbers: Peer Effects on Adolescent Girls' Sexual Debut and Pregnancy* (Washington, D.C.: National Campaign to Prevent Teen Pregnancy).

—— —— (2001), 'Promising the Future: Virginity Pledges and First Intercourse', *American Journal of Sociology*, 104: 859–912.

—— and MOODY, J. (2004), 'Suicide and Friendships among American Adolescents', *American Journal of Public Health*, 94: 89–95.

—— and PARIGI, P. (2004), 'Cloning Headless Frogs and Other Important Matters: Conversation Topics and Network Structure', *Social Forces*, 832: 535–57.

—— MOODY, J., and STOVEL, K. (2004), 'Chains of Affection: The Structure of Adolescent Romantic and Sexual Networks', *American Journal of Sociology*, 110 (1): 44–91.

BECKER, G. S. (1981), *A Treatise on the Family* (Cambridge, Mass.: Harvard University Press).

BERNARD, H. R., SHELLEY, G. A., and KILLWORTH, P. (1987), 'How Much of a Network does the GSS and RSW Dredge Up?', *Social Networks*, 9: 49–63.

—— et al. (1984), 'The Problem of Informant Accuracy: The Validity of Retrospective Data', *Annual Review of Anthropology*, 13: 495–517.

BREEN, R., and COOKE, L. P. (2005), 'The Persistence of the Gendered Division of Domestic Labour', *European Sociological Review*, 21: 43–57.

—— and SALAZAR, L. (2009), 'Has Increased Women's Educational Attainment Led to Greater Earnings Inequality in the United Kingdom? A Multivariate Decomposition Analysis', *European Sociological Review*, 25: 1–15.

BRÜCKNER, H. (1995), *Surveys Don't Lie, People Do? An Analysis of Data Quality in a Retrospective Life Course Study* (Berlin: Max Planck Institute for Human Development).

—— and BEARMAN, P. S. (2003), 'Dating Behavior and Sexual Activity Among Young Adolescents', in B. Albert, S. Brown, and C. M. Flanigan (eds.), *Fourteen and Younger: The Sexual Behavior of Young Adolescents* (Washington, D.C.: Campaign to Prevent Teen Pregnancy), 31–56.

—— and MAYER, K. U. (2005), 'The De-standardization of the Life Course: What It Might Mean and If It Means Anything Whether It Actually Took Place', *Advances in Life Course Research*, 9: 27–54.

—— MORNING, A., and NELSON, A. (2007), 'When "No" Means "Yes": Measuring Social Desirability Effects on the Expression of Biological Concepts of Race', unpublished manuscript.

BUTZ, W. P., and TORREY, B. B. (2006), 'Some Frontiers in Social Science', *Science*, 312 (5782): 1898–900.

CHRISTAKIS, N., and FOWLER, J. (2007), 'The Spread of Obesity in a Large Social Network over Thirty-two Years', *New England Journal of Medicine*, 3754: 370–9.

CONVERSE, J. M., and PRESSER, S. (1986), *Survey Questions: Handcrafting the Standardized Questionnaire* (Newbury Park, Calif.: Sage).

DiPRETE, T. A., and FORRISTAL, J. D. (1994), 'Multilevel Models: Methods and Substance', *Annual Review of Sociology*, 20: 331–57.

ELY, R. J. (1996), 'The Power in Demography: Women's Social Constructions of Gender Identity at Work', *Academy of Management Journal*, 383: 589–634.

FERNANDEZ, R. M. (1994), 'Race, Space, and Job Accessibility: Evidence from a Plant Relocation', *Economic Geography*, 70: 390–416.

FLETCHER, J. M. (2007), 'Social Multipliers in Sexual Initiation Decisions Among US High School Students', *Demography*, 442: 373–88.

FOWLER, F. J. (1995), *Improving Survey Questions: Design and Evaluation* (Newbury Park, Calif.: Sage).

FRANK, K. A. (1998), 'The Social Context of Schooling: Quantitative Methods', *Review of Research in Education*, 23: 171–216.

—— (2000), 'Impact of a Confounding Variable on the Inference of a Regression Coefficient', *Sociological Methods and Research*, 292: 147–94.

—— (2006), 'Introduction to Causal Inference', unpublished manuscript.

FUSSEL, E., and FURSTENBERG, F. F. (2005), 'The Transition to Adulthood during the Twentieth Century', in R. Settersten, jun., F. Furstenberg, and R. Rumbaut (eds.), *On the Frontier of Adulthood: Theory, Research, and Public Policy* (Chicago, Ill.: University of Chicago Press), 29–75.

GLAZERMAN, S., LEVY, D. M., and MYERS, D. (2003), 'Nonexperimental Versus Experimental Estimates of Earnings Impacts', *Annals of the American Academy of Political and Social Science*, 589: 63–93.

GRANNIS, R. (1998), 'The Importance of Trivial Streets: Residential Streets and Residential Segregation', *American Journal of Sociology*, 103: 1530–64.

GRANOVETTER, M. S. (1973), 'The Strength of Weak Ties', *American Journal of Sociology*, 78 (6): 1360–80.

HALABY, C. N. (2004), 'Panel Models in Sociological Research: Theory into Practice', *Annual Review of Sociology*, 30: 507–44.

HAYNIE, D. (2001), 'Delinquent Peers Revisited: Does Network Structure Matter?', *American Journal of Sociology*, 106: 1013–57.

HEDSTRÖM, P. (2005), *Dissecting the Social: On the Principles of Analytical Sociology* (Cambridge: Cambridge University Press).

HILLMERT, S. (2005), 'From Old to New Structures: A Long-term Comparison of the Transition to Adulthood in West and East Germany', *Advances in Life Course Research*, 9: 151–73.

HONG, G. L., and RAUDENBUSH, S. W. (2005), 'Effects of Kindergarten Retention Policy on Children's Cognitive Growth in Reading and Mathematics', *Educational Evaluation and Policy Analysis*, 273: 205–24.

JAHODA, M., LAZARSFELD, P. F., and ZEISEL, H. (1971), *Marienthal: The Sociography of an Unemployed Community* [*Arbeitslosen von Marienthal*] (Chicago, Ill.: Aldine/Atherton).

KILLWORTH, P. D., et al. (1990), 'Comparing Four Different Methods for Measuring Personal Social Networks', *Social Networks*, 12: 179–215.

KUKLINSKI, J. H., COBB, M. D., and GILENS, M. (1997), 'Racial Attitudes and the "New South"', *Journal of Politics*, 59: 323–49.

LAUMANN, E. O., et al. (1994), *The Social Organization of Sexuality: Sexual Practices in the United States* (Chicago, Ill.: University of Chicago Press).

LEE, J. K., (2006), 'Normative Dissonance and Anomie: A Prospective Microlevel Model of Adolescent Suicide Ideation', *Yale Journal of Sociology*, 6: 139–78.

LYND, R. S., and LYND, H. M. (1929), *Middletown: A Study in Contemporary American Culture* (New York: Harcourt, Brace).

MANGINO, W. (2005), 'Serious Delinquency among Adolescents: Openness, Social Capital, and Durkheim's Types of Suicide', Ph.D. thesis (Yale University).

MARALANI, V. (2008), 'Black–White Differences in Educational Reproduction', unpublished manuscript, University of Pennsylvania.

MARSDEN, P. V. (1990), 'Network Data and Measurement', *Annual Review of Sociology*, 16: 435–63.

MARTIN, E. (1983), 'Surveys as Social Indicators: Problems in Monitoring Trends', in P. H. Rossi, J. D. Wright, and A. B. Anderson (eds.), *Handbook of Survey Research* (New York: Academic).

Merton, R. K., Fiske, M., and Kendall, P. [1956] (1990), *The Focused Interview* (New York: Free Press).

MORGAN, S. L. (2001), 'Counterfactuals, Causal Effect Heterogeneity, and the Catholic School Effect on Learning', *Sociology of Education*, 74: 341–74.

—— and CHA, Y. (2007), 'Rent and the Evolution of Inequality in Late Industrial United States', *American Behavioral Scientist*, 50: 677–701.

—— and HARDING, D. J. (2006), 'Matching Estimators of Causal Effects: Prospects and Pitfalls in Theory and Practice', *Sociological Methods & Research*, 351: 3–60.

—— and McKERROW, M. W. (2004), 'Social Class, Rent Destruction, and the Earnings of Black and White Men, 1982–2000', *Research in Social Stratification and Mobility*, 21: 215–51.

—— and WINSHIP, C. (2007), *Counterfactuals and Causal Inference: Methods and Principles for Social Research* (Cambridge: Cambridge University Press).

MORRIS, M., and WESTERN, B. (1999), 'Inequality in Earnings at the Close of the Twentieth Century', *Annual Review of Sociology*, 25: 623–57.

OPPENHEIMER, V. K. (1994), 'Women's Rising Employment and the Future of the Family in Industrial Societies', *Population and Development Review*, 20 (2): 293–342.

PIKETTY, T., and SAEZ, E. (2003), 'Income Inequality in the United States, 1913–1998', *Quarterly Journal of Economics*, 1181: 1–39.

RAUDENBUSH, S. W., and BRYK, A. S. (2002), *Hierarchical Linear Models: Applications and Data Analysis Methods*, 2nd edn. (Newbury Park, Calif.: Sage).

——and SAMPSON, R. J. (1999), 'Ecometrics: Toward a Science of Assessing Ecological Settings, with Application to the Systematic Social Observation of Neighborhoods', *Sociological Methodology*, 29: 1–41.

ROSENBAUM, P. R., and RUBIN, D. B. (1983), 'The Central Role of the Propensity Score in Observational Studies for Causal Effects', *Biometrika*, 701: 41–55.

RUBIN, D. B. (1974), 'Estimating Causal Effects of Treatments in Randomized and Nonrandomized Studies', *Journal of Educational Psychology*, 665: 688–701.

SCHUMAN, H., and PRESSER, S. (1980), 'Public Opinion and Public Ignorance: The Fine Line between Attitudes and Nonattidudes', *American Journal of Sociology*, 855: 1214–25.

SMITH, T. W. (1981), 'Can We Have Confidence in Confidence? Revisited', in D. Johnston (ed.), *Measurement of Subjective Phenomena* (Washington, D.C.: Government Printing Office).

SNIDERMAN, P. M., and GROB, D. B. (1996), 'Innovations in Experimental Design in Attitude Surveys', *Annual Review of Sociology*, 22: 377–99.

——et al. (1991), 'The New Racism', *American Journal of Political Science*, 35: 423–47.

SNIPP, C. M. (2003), 'Racial Measurement in the American Census: Past Practices and Implications for the Future', *Annual Review of Sociology*, 29: 563–88.

SØRENSON, A. B. (1991), 'Merton and Methodology', *Contemporary Sociology*, 20: 516–19.

——(1996), 'The Structural Basis of Social Inequality', *American Journal of Sociology*, 101: 1333–65.

——(1998), 'Theoretical Mechanisms and the Empirical Study of Social Processes', in P. Hedström and R. Swedberg (eds.), *Social Mechanisms: An Analytical Approach to Social Theory* (Cambridge: Cambridge University Press), 238–66.

——(2000), 'Toward a Sounder Basis for Class Analysis', *American Journal of Sociology*, 105: 1523–58.

STOLZENBERG, R. M., and RELLES, D. A. (1997), 'Tools for Intuition about Sample Selection Bias and its Correction', *American Sociological Review*, 62: 494–507.

STOVEL, K., BEARMAN, P. S., and SAVAGE, M. (1997), 'Ascription into Achievement: Models of Career Systems at Lloyds Bank, 1890–1970', *American Jouranl of Sociology*, 102: 358–99.

UDRY, J., and BEARMAN, P. S. (1997), 'New Methods for New Perspectives on Adolescent Sexual Behavior', in Richard Jessor (ed.), *New Perspectives on Adolescent Sexual Behavior* (Cambridge: Cambridge University Press), 240–69.

WALLER, W. (1937), 'The Rating and Dating Complex', *American Sociological Review*, 2: 727–34.

WEGENER, B. (1991), 'Job Mobility and Social Ties: Social Resources, Prior Job, and Status Attainment', *American Sociological Review*, 56: 60–71.

WESTERN, B., BLOOME, D., and PERCHESKI, C. (2008), 'Inequality Among American Families with Children, 1975 to 2005', *American Sociological Review*, 73 (6): 903–20.

WINSHIP, C., and MORGAN, S. L. (1999), 'The Estimation of Causal Effects from Observational Data', *Annual Review of Sociology*, 25: 659–706.

ZALLER, J. (1992), *The Nature and Origins of Mass Opinion* (Cambridge: Cambridge University Press).

CHAPTER 29

....

ANALYTIC
ETHNOGRAPHY*

....

DIANE VAUGHAN

INTRODUCTION

....

ANALYTICAL sociology is designed to bridge the gap between theory and empirical research by incorporating action-based theories into explanations of macro-
level phenomena (Hedström 2005). Because understanding macro-level outcomes
is the goal, the principles of analytical sociology primarily have been used by
mathematically oriented scholars employing statistical analyses, simulation models,
experiments, and mathematical models, as most of the chapters in this volume
indicate. Ironically, the fundamental principles of analytical sociology are the
essence of ethnography. Analytical sociology urges a turning away from variable-
centered approaches toward strategies that produce explanations of events and
outcomes by revealing the mechanisms that generate the observed relationships.
It is designed to examine key social processes and break them down into their
primary components, showing how they work together to produce outcomes.
The focus shifts from variables to actors, actions, and the 'cogs and wheels' that

 * For helpful comments on an earlier version of this chapter I thank Karen Barkey, Howie Becker,
Larissa Buchholtz, Diego Gambetta, Jack Katz, Debra Minkoff, Loic Wacquant, and the editors of
this book.

respond to and reproduce social phenomena. Arriving at explanation is the goal. In crucial ways, however, ethnography marches to a different drummer. Moreover, although all ethnography has important characteristics in common, within it are vastly different approaches to the social. No single work can be taken as representative.

How then might we understand ethnography in relation to analytical sociology? This chapter offers no primer on ethnography, nor does it revisit methodological debates or reiterate the instrumental view of ethnography as a supplemental data-collection method for generating hypotheses related to analytical sociology. Instead, I will focus specifically on the unique contribution ethnography has made and can make to accomplishing two of the key principles of analytical sociology: (1) developing theoretical explanations by identifying mechanisms that connect actors, action, and outcomes, and (2) bridging the micro, meso, and macro levels of analysis in those explanations. I will show that analytic ethnography has historically developed mechanism-based explanations going beyond the micro level and has more in common with analytical sociology than is usually assumed. My purpose is to give empirical direction for theoretical integration between the two as a way to advance explanations that link micro, meso, and macro levels of analysis.

Establishing ethnography's contribution to building mechanism-based explanations requires examining developments in ethnography that probably are unfamiliar to analytical sociologists and other nonpractitioners of the craft. Even ethnographers have not examined these developments in any systematic way. I begin by isolating 'analytic ethnography' (Lofland 1971) from the varieties of ethnography practiced, because it provides the primary basis for exchange between ethnography and analytical sociology. Second, and contradicting the conventional view of ethnography as limited to micro-level explanations, I demonstrate how analytic ethnography has developed mechanism-based explanations at all levels of analysis. Third, I compare analytic ethnography to analytical sociology (Hedström 2005) to establish the compatibility of the two, despite different understandings about the appropriate methods for studying the social. Finally, I consider the role analytic ethnography can play in advancing mechanism-based explanations that link actors, actions, and social outcomes. I demonstrate how theoretical integration can be achieved first within analytic ethnography, then between analytic ethnography and analytical sociology. To illustrate both, I consider how the signaling research of Vaughan (1983, 1986, 1996, 2002), Podolny (1993, 2005), Bacharach and Gambetta (2001), and Gambetta and Hamill (2005), authors in this volume using different methods, levels, and units of analysis, might be integrated to elaborate explanations of outcomes in which signals are the mechanism.

29.1 ANALYTIC ETHNOGRAPHY

What is analytic ethnography? No doubt most ethnographers would argue, and correctly, that all ethnography is analytic. This general point of agreement stands in contrast to a more recent history of contentious debate between ethnographers about the specifics of what ethnography is and how it should be done. The practice of ethnography has diversified into different fieldwork traditions, each with its own approach and epistemological assumptions (see e.g. Adler and Adler 1995; Atkinson et al. 2001; DeVault 2007). To complicate matters further, recent research investigating claims about the proliferation of ethnography found that the words 'ethnography', 'participant observation', and 'fieldwork'—terms traditionally used by ethnographers to refer to closely related practices—have been used loosely, mainly by people who do not do ethnographic work (Culyba, Heimer, and Petty 2004).

Given this diversity, it is important to begin by locating analytic ethnography within ethnography. For purposes of this chapter, ethnography is defined as participant observation: research conducted by situating oneself in a social setting to observe and analyze individual interaction in order to understand some complex social process, event, activity, or outcome. Developing explanations requires extensive time in the setting—long enough to recognize patterns of interaction and distinctive social practices—so the duration of the observations cannot be known in advance. Explanation proceeds inductively by iteration between theory and data that revises theory. It is more than a method, however. It is a perspective committed to understanding a particular social world in terms of the meanings it has for the people who inhabit it. Because individual interpretation, meaning, and action are shaped by the social, the empirical focus is interaction within its social context. Social context is multilayered; to study it, the ethnographer carves it up according to the people, places, groups, organizations, or institutions relevant to explaining the problem. But context is not just background for some main event. The social context may either provide an explanation of some interaction, or interaction may explain some aspect of social context.

Currently two strands of ethnography with opposing epistemologies are dominant: analytic and critical. Analytic ethnography is our focus. However, critical ethnography has historic importance, not just for the experimental methods and cultural analysis it has produced, but because analytic ethnography has clarified its boundaries and methods as a result of it. By analytic ethnography, I mean an approach to field observations and interpretation of individual interaction that involves careful collection of data and evidence-backed arguments. It relies on systematic methods and standards, assumes that causes and explanations can be found, proceeds inductively to formulate explanations of outcomes, and holds theory and theoretical explanation as core objectives. The analysis developed is conceptually elaborated, based on interrogating the relationship between concepts, theory, and data, and aims for generic explanations of events, activities, and social processes.

In the 1960s and early 1970s ethnographers generally agreed that all ethnography was analytic ethnography, as defined above. Several ethnographers wrote about data-gathering, analysis, and theorizing, laying down a set of principles that became guidelines for other ethnographers. These writers challenged and criticized quantitative methods and grand theory, yet at the same time they adopted many of the tenets of positivism and the goal of developing theory. Their efforts aimed at training new ethnographers but also at gaining legitimacy for qualitative work criticized for its looseness and lack of systemicity in a discipline dominated by quantitative research and scientific methods. Two contributions received a lasting place in the canon: Blumer's 'sensitizing concepts' (1954), and Glaser and Strauss's grounded theory (1967). Of greatest impact was the Glaser and Strauss book, which was an exegesis on developing general theory by adhering to procedures of scientific method. Glaser and Strauss proposed a system for theory generation that was inductive, evidence-based, and developed by constant comparison between data and the nascent explanation. They identified two types of theory. Substantive theory is an explanation of an individual case that focuses on an empirical area, such as homelessness or patient care, with the goal of explaining the case. Formal theory is an explanation resulting from a conceptual or theory-based inquiry, developed by comparing cases and advancing an explanation that generalizes across cases. Encompassing these developments and affirming rigorous standards, the term 'analytic ethnography' first appeared in the literature in Lofland (1971).

The consensus that all ethnography was analytic ethnography dissolved in the late 1970s. Concurrent with the cultural turn in anthropology, history, and literature, a new genre of qualitative research took hold. Critical ethnography (also known as interpretive or postmodern ethnography) rejected the positivist tenets of objectivism and the search for causes, instead asserting subjectivism, language, and discourse as key to understanding the meanings upon which individual actions were based. The new work was opposed to analytic ethnography's evidence-based assumptions and theoretical goals, its standard research strategies, and exclusionary research and writing practices (for a review, see Adler and Adler 1995). Critical ethnography eventually achieved an impact on analytic ethnography, visible in the appearance of first-person writing and practices reflecting a new awareness of bias and power relations between ethnographers and the people whose lives they entered. However, its commitment to evidence-based theory remained the same. Analytic ethnographers responded to the challenge by increasing their emphasis on rigor, systematic methods, and their search for generic, data-based theoretical explanations. For example, Katz (1983) reclaimed the quantitative lexicon of reliability, representativeness, reactivity, and replicability by showing how fieldwork embodied these very scientific standards. An all-encompassing textbook of systematic methods for qualitative data analysis appeared (Miles and Huberman 1984).

In 1985 Lofland clarified analytic ethnography in the midst of the alternative critical approaches by then available to ethnographers. He reiterated the goal of general theory: the identification of generic propositions that reflected the social-analytic categories that the data at hand exemplified (1985: 40). Significant historically was his reminder that ethnographers were in the business of science and the production of general explanations that went beyond the individual case. However, Lofland had not gone far enough (Snow, Morrill, and Anderson 2003). The purpose of analytic ethnography was general explanation, but Lofland had said nothing about how to get from generic propositions to theory. Even as analytic ethnography had flourished and systematic methods were deployed, Glaser and Strauss's emphasis (1967) on going from particulars to a general explanation had apparently been lost. They had distinguished two kinds of explanation: substantive theory, which was achieving an explanation of the empirical case under investigation, and formal theory, or achieving a general explanation that not only encompassed the case at hand but developed by case comparison to generalize to other cases of similar phenomena. As practiced by most analytic ethnographers, however, the constant-comparative method that Glaser and Strauss advocated was reduced to the constant comparison between data and theory, thus dropping the comparison with other cases. Substantive theory, not formal theory, was the usual product (Strauss 1995).

These two trends continue to typify analytic ethnography today: the effort to teach and practice systematic methods has flourished, a most notable contribution being Emerson, Fretz, and Shaw's *Writing Ethnographic Field Notes* (1995), and substantive theory is most often the product of an analysis. The result has been a proliferation of research guided by the standards of analytic ethnography, but diverse in many important ways, with little coherence within the specialty. Explanatory theory remains the goal, but analytic ethnographers have different understandings about what theory is, how it is to be achieved, the appropriate unit and level of analysis, and even the meaning of generalizability (Culyba, Heimer, and Petty 2004: 381). These differences have generated intense debates within the community of analytic ethnographers about what ethnography is and how to go about it (e.g. Anderson 2002; Duneier 2002; Newman 2002; Wacquant 2002). However, the heterogeneity within analytic ethnography has had a good result: an extensive body of research exists identifying mechanisms and providing explanations at micro, meso, and macro levels of analysis. The next section demonstrates how, in combination, both substantive theory and formal theory have produced mechanism-based explanations at all levels of analysis, thus establishing the basis for our later discussion of theoretical integration within analytic ethnography and between analytic ethnography and analytical sociology.

29.2 VARIETIES OF ANALYTIC ETHNOGRAPHY: LINKING ACTION, MECHANISMS, AND OUTCOMES IN EXPLANATION

Since the 1940s and 1950s, analytic ethnographers have generated hundreds of mechanism-based explanations at all levels of analysis. Consider the classics. Contradicting the view that ethnography is limited to micro-level explanations, many classic ethnographies produced substantive theories explaining meso outcomes. For example, Whyte's *Street Corner Society* (1943) identified reciprocal obligations between individuals as the mechanism explaining the structure of the corner gang, the racket and police organizations, and political organizations in the Italian North End of Boston.

'Network' was not yet the accepted terminology when Dalton (1959) identified the mechanisms that produced 'cliques' in bureaucratic organizations, then showed how competition, conflict, and cooperation between the cliques were mechanisms producing organization survival. Similarly, Becker (1982) identified cooperative networks of different specializations as the mechanisms producing art, but 'conventions'—basic knowledge shared by all who participate in the art world—played a role in linking actors and actions to produce the networks. In actor-network theory, the mechanism generating network formation and collective activity was 'translation': an entrepreneurial actor defines the problem, interests others, enrolls participants, and mobilizes action (Callon 1986; Latour 1987, 1988). But entities also have agency. Thus, the 'boundary object'—an idea, a bacteria, a mosquito—could also be a mechanism triggering network formation (Star and Griesemer 1989). Undoubtedly, the best-known substantive theory of a macro outcome is Willis's classic (1977) explaining the reproduction of social class. He identified the mechanisms by which 'working class lads get working class jobs.' By their opposition to school authority and their refusal to master the curricula, they disqualified themselves from educational credentials and reproduced themselves as a working class.

In contemporary ethnographies producing substantive theory, mechanism-based explanations that make micro–macro connections are so numerous they defy examination in a chapter of this length.[1] Instead, I turn now to contemporary exemplars of formal theory in order to make a set of more detailed analytical points. Focusing on formal theory has two advantages: first, formal theory is the strongest example because it is based upon case comparisons that show how particular mechanisms have *regularly* produced similar outcomes over time. Second, it is expedient as a selection criterion because efforts to transform substantive theory into formal theory are few. To draw attention to the production of mechanism-based explanations at a variety of levels of analysis, I present the exemplars in this order: micro, then macro, and finally a micro–meso–macro–explanation. I will first indicate, very schematically, the organizing principles of each exemplar: theoretical orientation, level and unit of analysis, and method. Then I show the mechanism-based explanation as it was developed and elaborated to generalize across cases, successively developing formal theory—one of considerable scope, range, and conceptual complexity, with a degree of specificity that encompasses variability (Strauss 1995: 17).

29.2.1 Katz: a theory of situational transcendence

Theoretical orientation; unit and level of analysis; method: A phenomenologist and symbolic interactionist, Katz's theoretical orientation directs his attention to actors, mechanisms, and outcomes, all at the micro level. The causes of the outcomes to be explained can be found in aspects of the immediate situation. Explanation, for Katz, resides in uncovering the meanings grounded in the subject's experience of the moment. Emotion is the mechanism linking actors and actions to outcomes. Emotions are an actor's way of sensing the meanings currently present in the immediate situation. Conditions antecedent to the situation, such as social class, gender, and race, are irrelevant 'background' factors that 'fail to address the lived experience' of social life. Thus, his unit of analysis is individual interaction, isolated from individual social location, previous experience, history, culture, or structure. His method is to develop formal theory by cross-case comparison: analyzing similar phenomena in different social settings.

Mechanism-based explanation: In *Seductions of Crime: Moral and Sensual Attractions of Doing Evil* (1988) Katz develops a formal theory to explain all varieties of crime. He compares six cases: each chapter builds an explanation of one type of crime from many examples by combining ethnography, interviews, and published historical, biographical, and research accounts. In each, the circumstances of the situation challenge the actor's sense of identity and place in the world. The resulting emotion drives the criminal act such that at the moment of its commission the crime becomes morally justified—a sensible, satisfying, compelling action that allows the offender to transcend the situation.

In violent crimes, emotions—humiliation, degradation, frustration—produce a 'socially transcendent rage' that compels the person to act. Committed in defense of social identity, the crime at the moment of commission restores the offender's sense of self in relation to others. Reinforcing Katz's claim for a theory explaining all kinds of crime, he varies social class, showing how middle-class and upper-class people are seduced by the situation in property crime and white-collar crime. For example, college students shoplift not for material reasons but because of the power of the object, its availability, the ease of taking it, and the emotional thrill of transcending the mundane by getting away with a forbidden act. Thus, based on these cross-case comparisons, Katz stakes his claim that his theory generalizes to the crimes of all social classes.

29.2.2 Burawoy: the extended-case method

Theoretical orientation; unit and level of analysis; method: A Marxist, Burawoy's theoretical orientation directs his attention to macro-level outcomes: specifically, reproduction or change of economic systems. Taking factory jobs, he studied the micro processes of four large-scale historical transformations: decolonization, the transition to organized capitalism, the Soviet transition to socialism, and the transition from socialism to market capitalism. The mechanism responsible for linking actors, action, and outcomes was the social organization and regulation of work. His unit of analysis was the shop floor, analyzed within history and the economic forces of production. He used the extended-case method (Burawoy 1998), so called because a case (1) extends into history and into the future, as each day in the field shows the evolving situation, (2) extends from micro processes to macro-level forces, and (3) extends theory by comparison with other cases.

Mechanism-based explanation: In *Manufacturing Consent* (1979) Burawoy found that the possibility of working-class revolutions was not constrained by the super-structure, as Marxists posited, but in the workplace. The factory coordinated the interests of workers and management in the pursuit of profit so that consent, not dissent, was the product. The organization and regulation of work was the mechanism that produced the consent of workers to work. The trade union gave legitimacy to contracts and protected the rights of individuals, eliciting consent to the factory order. The piece-rate system guaranteed a minimum wage and job security. Together, they gave workers incentive and opportunity to establish counternorms to protect themselves from some of the deprivations of the job. Consequently, at the micro level work was constituted as a game in which workers cooperated to 'make out,' which, ironically, resulted in the factory meeting its production goals. In this way, advanced capitalism reproduced itself.

Using comparisons to proceed from this substantive theory toward formal theory, Burawoy investigated whether work was organized and regulated differently in Eastern Europe, so that dissent rather than consent was the product. Ethnographies of factories in different political economies explored variation within and between capitalism and state socialism (Burawoy 2009). The comparisons affirmed that the organization and regulation of work was the mechanism that produced either dissent or consent of workers to work, and thus the development (or not) of counterpower movements to effect social change.

29.2.3 Bourdieu: a theory of practice

Theoretical orientation; unit and level of analysis; method: Bourdieu was eclectic, combining Marx, Weber, and structural anthropology with attention to the body and practices in everyday life. His focus was the macro level: power, domination, and reproduction or change of social hierarchy. The mechanism linking actors and actions to outcomes was habitus: a subjective set of dispositions comprised of lasting patterns of thought, perception, and behavior (Bourdieu [1980] 1990). Habitus is acquired by individuals or groups through internalization of culture or social structures such as class, family, occupation, education. They become embodied, providing a set of practical skills, enacted without thinking. His method for developing formal theory was cross-case analysis: analyzing similar phenomena in different social settings. Sallaz and Zavisca (2007) trace its evolution chronologically: social structure and social action from the Kabyle; the reproduction of inequality in education in France; social inequality in cultural production and consumption; the theory of the state through language, education, and housing. His unit of analysis varied, depending on the case he was examining. An experienced anthropologist, even when relying primarily on survey research his ethnographic insights dominate the analysis (Wacquant 2004b).

Mechanism-based explanation: In *Distinction* ([1979] 1984), Bourdieu shows how an individual's cultural practices can either maintain or increase position in the system of class domination. Class is enacted in tastes for food, ritual practices of serving, the formality of the meal, preferences for glassware and crockery, and the use of the body in consumption. Taste itself becomes embodied, its enactment 'revealing the deepest dispositions of the habitus' ([1979] 1984: 190). For Bourdieu, the dynamic relationship between habitus, field, and capital is essential to explaining persistence or change in structures of inequality. The field is a highly competitive site structured by power relationships, where people jockey for resources, status, and control over outcomes. Forms of capital— economic, social, cultural, symbolic—are a determinant of success for individuals. In response to the conditions they encounter, actors internalize sets of dispositions and actions (habitus) consonant with the norms of the field, thereby tending to reproduce its power structure. In *Distinction*, class-cultural practices constitute a system of status signals, differentiating the working class from the bourgeoisie, thereby limiting mobility, maintaining class position, and reproducing inequality.

In European scholarship applying his theory to other cases, it has been verified frequently. In American sociology, however, field, habitus, and capital have seldom been joined in a single analysis (Sallaz and Zavisca 2007; Emirbayer and Johnson 2008). Instead, each concept has had a separate path of elaboration (see e.g. Martin 2003). Habitus may be the concept least investigated empirically, and rarely as the linking mechanism between micro and macro levels of analysis that Bourdieu intended. (For American exceptions see Vaughan 1996; Hallett 2003; Wacquant 2004*a*; Desmond 2007; Kahn 2008.)

29.2.4 Vaughan: analogical theorizing

Theoretical orientation; unit and level of analysis; method: Analogical theorizing generates micro-, meso-, and macro-level explanations. It is influenced by sociological theory indicating that action is situated in layered structures, culture, and history, which affect interpretation, meaning, and action at the local level. Meso-level structures—neighborhoods, complex organizations, groups—transform historical institutional imperatives, shaping cultural understandings to fit the local situation. Thus, the unit of analysis is individual actors and interaction, situated within meso- and macro-level contexts. Analogical theorizing is based on Simmel's formal sociology, which urges sociologists to extract form from content to find common processes and structures in similar activities across different social settings. It calls for cross-case (hospitals, schools, families) rather than same-case (all hospitals) comparison. Lovers break up as con men cool out marks as bosses fire employees as children terminate monopoly games (Vaughan 1986: 188–195).[2]

A case is chosen as a possible example of some phenomenon. The starting theory or concept is used heuristically, as a tool for sorting the data to identify both analogies and differences. Procedures are in place to guard against force-fitting the data to the theory (Vaughan 1992, 2004). The result may confirm, refute, or elaborate the starting theory, which, in its modified form, guides analysis of the next example. Additional cases are chosen that vary in size, complexity, and function, intentionally producing data at different levels of analysis in order to develop a micro–meso–macro explanation. Findings of either reproduction or change are possible. Although the emphasis is on identifying micro–meso–macro connections, analogical theorizing is theoretically and methodologically neutral, and thus could be used with qualitative and quantitative research at any level of analysis, as I will show at pp. 702–6.

Mechanism-based explanation: Vaughan's 'The Social Organization of Dissent' investigated 'individual organization members who resist authority, speaking out against illegal, illegitimate, or immoral actions in or by the organization to which they belong, alerting other actors who might help effect some change' (unpublished manuscript, ch. 5). Comparing the prison snitch, corporate whistle-blowers, and dissent against sex-discrimination in hiring, sexual harassment in the workplace, and domestic violence showed the mechanisms that produced or repressed dissent across cases. In the prison, the workplace, and the family, the same bundle of five mechanisms appeared. Social location, power-dependence relations, norms of loyalty, organizational retaliation, and social support interacted: willingness to dissent varied as these conditions varied. For example, social support, when present, was an 'enabler' of dissent, when absent, a 'silencer.' Macro-level contingencies, such as structured gender inequalities, and legal and normative standards also affected the production of dissent.

To sum: Analytic ethnography has a long history of building mechanism-based explanations linking actors, actions, and outcomes at all levels of analysis. Close examination of formal theory exemplars showed that analytic ethnography comes wrapped in very different packages (see Table 29.1). The heterogeneity in analytic ethnography is not an indicator of an undisciplined specialty, however. Rather, each exemplar differs in the theoretical orientation of the author, demonstrating that mechanism-based explanations have been achieved using very different theoretical approaches. Each has been driven by its author's theory of how society works, which in turn affects the unit of analysis, the level of analysis, and the level of explanation that the ethnographer produces.

The same is true for substantive theory. Since each ethnographer's process is ordered by some overarching theory or theories about how the world works, and since theoretical orientation determines the level of explanation, analytic ethnographers have produced mechanism-based explanations at every level of the multi-layered social context. Not all analytic ethnographers are committed to explaining macro-level outcomes. However, the examples of substantive theories and formal theories, in combination, show how the varieties of analytic ethnography bridge these layers, filling in the intersection of social processes and structures at micro, meso, and macro levels of analysis. This ability of analytic ethnography to identify mechanisms that link actions to outcomes at all levels of analysis is central to understanding how it meshes with the goal of analytical sociology to develop explanations that bridge the distance between theories of macro–micro relations and research that does the same. To establish the basis for such integration, next I examine the compatibility of these two approaches, usually viewed as oppositional and incompatible.

29.3 THE COMPATIBILITY OF ANALYTIC ETHNOGRAPHY AND ANALYTICAL SOCIOLOGY

Recall that analytical sociology is designed to escape the limits of variable analysis in quantitative sociology by examining key social processes and breaking them down into their primary components, showing how they work together to produce social outcomes. Providing plausible causal accounts of why things happen is a goal,

Table 29.1 Formal theory mechanism-based explanations

Ethnographer	Theoretical Orientation	Unit of Analysis	Mechanism	Outcome	Level of Explanation
Katz	Symbolic Interaction	Situation	Emotion	Crime	Micro–Micro
Burawoy	Marx	Workplace	Social Organization of Work	Reproduction or Change: Economic System	Micro–Macro
Bourdieu	Marx, Weber, Anthropology, Body, Practice	Position of Individual in Field or Social Space	Habitus	Reproduction or Change: Hierarchy, Domination	Micro–Macro
Vaughan	Eclectic	Position of Individual in Meso-Structure; Macro-Context	Problem-Dependent	Reproduction or Change	Micro–Meso–Macro

despite internal disputes about the meaning of explanation. Examining analytic ethnography in relation to analytical sociology's more specific principles establishes the compatibility of the two approaches by showing how, using very different methods, analytic ethnography uses the same principles to arrive at explanations of the social. Those principles are explanation, dissection and abstraction, precision and clarity, and a theory of action (Hedström 2005).

29.3.1 Principles: similarities and differences

Explanation: The position of analytical sociology is that the best explanation for the social sciences is mechanism-based. Mechanisms are the 'constellation of entities and activities, typically actors and their actions, that are linked to one another in such a way that they regularly bring about the type of phenomenon we seek to explain' (Hedström 2005: 2). As we have seen, mechanisms also are the core concern of analytic ethnography. Empirical work breaks down social processes into key components to see how they effect social outcomes. Explanation requires detailed description: the two go hand in hand (Katz 2001*b*). Detailed description renders mechanisms observable. They may be micro-, meso-, or macro-level, or some combination.

Dissection and abstraction: For analytical sociology, dissection and abstraction are tools for decomposing complex social processes in order to identify the mechanisms that drive social outcomes. Dissection isolates the constituent entities; abstraction selects from them those most essential to understanding the phenomenon of interest. Analytic ethnography relies upon the same sorting and sifting practices to identify mechanisms that produce social regularities. Observations are recorded in detailed field notes, often supplemented by interviews, documents, and/or archival materials. Close, careful attention to data and its accurate depiction of social life is the essence of explanation. It is the complexity and amount of descriptive data, often difficult to sort into patterns, that makes dissection and abstraction essential tools for explanation. After gathering descriptions, the focus shifts to the analytic: reorganization of data into explanatory lines through iterative processing of theory and data. Description is made useful by conversion into theoretical specification. This process Katz describes as going from 'how' to 'why' (2001*b*). 'Abstraction,' however, applies in a second way for those analytical ethnographers who strive for formal theory. After isolating the essential patterns and deriving substantive theory, they abstract further from the substantive explanation to build formal theory generalizing beyond the individual case.

Precision and clarity: For analytical sociology, achieving precision and clarity includes identifying details and conveying them through operational and conceptual definitions that can be easily grasped (Hedström 2005). Otherwise mechanisms remain obscure and explanation is not achieved; the relationship between one activity, event, or phenomenon and another will not be conveyed. For analytic ethnography, precision and clarity also depend on moving from the detailed data to clear operational and conceptual definitions. Precision and clarity are obtained by (1) accurate description so that both patterns and exceptions are clear; (2) analytic induction, a research logic for data analysis that requires continually adjusting a developing explanation to take into account anomalies that contradict hypotheses until a perfect relationship between data and theory is reached (Lindesmith 1947; Katz 2001a); (3) constant comparison between theory and data (Glaser and Strauss 1967) in the individual case and in some instances cross-case comparison also, depending on the researcher's interest in formal theory or substantive theory; and (4) presenting results that provide strong empirical evidence to support analysis and conclusions.

Operational definitions and conceptual definitions are integral to every analysis, although their use and centrality in the written analysis may vary. First, concepts may be used to set up the research problem by defining the social setting conceptually and stating the theoretical and empirical boundaries for investigation. Second, a known concept may guide the data analysis, its development, and theory elaboration. Third, a new concept may be created as an outcome of the data analysis. Finally, several concepts may be joined in a formal theory that initially frames the data analysis, then is revised as a result of the findings.

A theory of action: The stated goal of analytical sociology is not just achieving explanation, but achieving explanation that links actors, actions, and outcomes. This requires a theory of action that explains what actors do. Analytic ethnography also shares this goal. However, the two approaches disagree on methodological strategies and theoretical assumptions for achieving a theory of action. Ironically, this difference turns out to be the crux of a productive relation between them.

Most often in analytical sociology the empirical focus is on the structures of interaction that are the outcome of individual interaction, not the actors, actions, and interactions themselves (but see Gambetta, this volume). The theory of action precedes the analysis, guiding it by positing the mechanisms likely to have brought about the outcomes to be explained. Consequently, making the connection between actions and outcomes relies on a rational-choice assumption. Because the focus is structures of interaction, analytical sociology differentiates itself from other rational-choice-based approaches; it is 'structural individualism,' not methodological individualism (Hedström 2005: 5 n. 4). About actors and actions, the question asked is 'why, acting as they do, they bring about the social outcomes that they do' (2005: 5). Social outcomes are defined as changes in collective properties brought about by the structures of interaction. Thus, the outcomes to be explained are structural, either at the meso or macro level of analysis. Often, social change is the outcome to be explained.

In contrast to analytical sociology, actors, action, and interaction are directly observed in analytic ethnography. The assumption is that individual choice is rational, but the social context shapes what is perceived as rational at a given moment. Although this constitutes the major divergence between analytic ethnography and analytical sociology, it also is the most important basis for exchange between them. Because the social context is multilayered, analytic ethnographers have directly linked actors and actions to micro, meso, and macro outcomes, as we have seen. Research has verified both reproduction and change. The contributions analytic ethnography has made to mechanism-based explanations across levels of analysis are the foundation for theoretical integration: building mechanism-based explanations that connect actors and actions to social outcomes *within* analytic ethnography and *between* analytic ethnography and analytical sociology. The next section will illustrate this potential.

29.4 THEORETICAL INTEGRATION: SIGNALS AS MECHANISMS

Analogical theorizing has a role to play in advancing mechanism-based explanations both within analytic ethnography and between it and analytical sociology. Eclectic in orientation, it is a tool for theory-building by case comparison regardless of qualitative or quantitative method. The premise behind cross-case rather than same-case comparison is that theory and concepts developed at one level of analysis can be used heuristically to examine social relations at another. This is so because all socially organized forms have structures and processes in common—division of labor, stratification, conflict, hierarchy, cooperation, culture, socialization (Vaughan 1992). Therefore, theoretical integration could be achieved two ways.

One would be separate projects within analytical sociology and analytic ethnography to advance mechanism-based explanations at the *same* level of analysis. In analytical sociology, for example, research could investigate how the same mechanisms (e.g. those associated with networks) operate across different substantive problems, or how different mechanisms are involved in producing the same (or similar) social outcomes. In analytic ethnography, cross-case comparison at the same level of analysis could begin to move substantive theory toward formal theory. For example, research using actor-network theory has never been integrated to identify similarities and differences found. Theoretical integration at the same level of analysis is an important precursor to the second means of achieving theoretical integration: comparing research on similar phenomena, in different social settings, at *different* levels of analysis. The result would be the development of mechanism-based explanations linking actors to outcomes that span micro, meso, and macro levels of analysis, both within analytic ethnography and between it and analytical sociology. I will demonstrate this second approach by showing how signals as a mechanism can be found in multiple contexts at multiple levels of observation. First, the signaling examples will show how theoretical integration across levels of analysis can be achieved within analytic ethnography (Vaughan 1983, 1986, 1996). Then, to show theoretical integration between analytic ethnography and analytical sociology, I extend my findings on signals to research by analytical sociologists (Podolny 1993, 2005; Bacharach and Gambetta 2001; Gambetta and Hamill 2005).

In substantively unrelated research—corporate malfeasance (Vaughan 1983), the deterioration of intimate relationships (Vaughan 1986), and NASA's flawed decision to launch the space shuttle *Challenger* (Vaughan 1996)—signals were a mechanism contributing to harmful outcomes. Comparison was not part of the original design; I did not suspect that the cases had analogous patterns nor that signals would be a part of the explanation. The misconduct case was not an ethnography but important because signaling theory (Spence 1974) became part of its sociological explanation, which then led to its ethnographic elaboration in the two subsequent cases. Because the three cases were organizations varying in size, complexity, and function, each case produced data at different levels of analysis. The result was theoretical integration across levels of analysis: a mechanism-based theory of mistake and unanticipated consequences that connected micro, meso, and macro levels of analysis.

In the first case (Vaughan 1983), a prominent drugstore chain made over 50,000 false Medicaid claims, submitted them on computer tapes, and received reimbursement from the state welfare department. The scheme went on for three years. Why were the false claims not detected? The explanation lay in the characteristics of organizations, how they exchange information, and how information (signals) was interpreted. Spence (1974) explained how organizations discriminated among multiple job applicants in hiring decisions. To reduce costs, firms used a shortcut method that relied on signals as indicators of quality and competence. Various signals (education, recommendation letters) thus became the basis of decision-making. Spence's theory fit my data: many claims were submitted; the welfare department's computerized screening system checked for predesignated signals to separate good claims from bad. Because signals varied, they could be manipulated, making fraud possible. Discovery was prevented by 'structural secrecy'—the nature of organizational exchange, structure, and division of labor interfered with the sending, receiving, and interpretation of information—so the fraud continued. It was discovered accidentally during investigation of another matter.

Intimate relationships are the smallest organizations we create. Their endings are not sudden breaks but gradual transitions during which identity and social networks are transformed (Vaughan 1986). The main pattern is that one person, whom I called the initiator, becomes unhappy and begins leaving the relationship socially and psychologically long before the other person. How was it possible for one person to get so far away without the other noticing and acting? Surprisingly, the uncoupling process was analogous to the fraud case: both had long incubation periods that were littered with warning signs that were either misinterpreted or ignored. This case provided micro-level data that added to the structural explanation in the first case by revealing the process of sending, receiving, and interpreting signals. The initiator's signals were embedded in patterns of information that diffused their import: they appeared mixed, weak, and routine. In addition, the partner had a positive view of the relationship, and thus focused on the positive signals, not the negative. Structural secrecy again played a role. The relationship's patterns of exchange, structure, and division of labor affected the partner's interpretative work. Typically, initiators only sent an undeniable strong signal when they were ready to go. By that time, the relationship was difficult—if not impossible—to salvage.

The *Challenger* research (Vaughan 1996) inquired into the organizational contribution to the technical failure. Why, for years before the accident, had NASA repeatedly launched despite recurring anomalies on the O-rings, the shuttle part that failed? The analysis revealed a now familiar pattern: the accident was preceded by a long incubation period filled with warning signals that were either misinterpreted or ignored. This case produced data that gave a micro-, meso-, and macro-level explanation showing signals as a mechanism producing the outcome. At the micro level, as launch data accumulated O-ring anomalies occurred in a pattern of information indicating they were operating as expected: signals appeared mixed, weak, and routine. At the meso level, structural secrecy created by organizational exchange, hierarchy, division of labor, and evidentiary rules obscured the seriousness of these early warning signs. At the macro level, decisions to continue launching were reinforced by production pressures generated by the White House, Congress, and international relations, resulting in a frame of reference focusing on the good signals, not the anomalies. The result was 'the normalization of deviance': technical anomalies that outsiders viewed after the accident as clear signals of danger were viewed as normal and acceptable to insiders as launch decisions were being made.

The cross-comparison demonstrates theoretical integration within analytic ethnography: it led to a Bourdieusian theory of signals and interpretive work that included micro-, meso-, and macro-level factors (see Vaughan 2002). It verified signals as a mechanism in producing mistakes in organizations that varied in size, complexity, and function. It exposed the dynamics of signals as a mechanism and the process of sending, receiving, and interpreting them. It showed that signals can be interpreted differently, their meaning affected by their embeddedness in a stream of information, organization characteristics, history and previous understandings, actions by actors in the institutional environment, and the social location of the interpreter. Because the meaning of a signal varies, depending on the social context and the worldview of the interpreter, falsification, mistake, and unintended consequences can occur. Further, the comparison shows that the ethnographic project is uniquely positioned to identify mechanisms linking actors to macro-level outcomes because the relation between micro, meso, and macro levels of analysis can be—and is—observed, traced, and documented in what people say and do in local situations. For example, a NASA engineer's statement, 'No one has to tell me schedule is important when I see people working 24 hours a day, 7 days a week,' captures the impact of NASA's competitive institutional environment on organizational practices and thus on the individual engineers.

To consider theoretical integration with analytical sociology, we extend the above findings about signals to the research of Podolny and Gambetta. The signaling comparison is especially apt because it shows how a theory developed in a mathematically oriented rational-choice specialty (economics), can be elaborated into sociological explanations of signals as a mechanism operating in different social settings, across levels of analysis. Podolny (1993, 2005) conceptualizes status as a signal of quality and investigates market mechanisms for sustaining the status-ordering in a market. He hypothesizes that rational consumers will rely on status as an indicator of quality in order to reduce their uncertainty in markets. Making rational-choice assumptions and working at the macro level, he examines status dynamics in industries, comparing investment banking, wine, shipping, venture capital, and semiconductors (Podolny 2005). One finding is that signals are inseparable from context: reputational information is situated in the pattern of ties among a group of actors.

Bacharach and Gambetta (2001) reconceptualize signaling theory to analyze trust games. Using ethnography and interviews to understand how taxi drivers establish a customer's trustworthiness, Gambetta and Hamill (2005) examine customers' mimicry and falsification of signals and taxi drivers' rational and nonrational reasoning (unfounded beliefs, unfounded stereotypes) in identifying and interpreting signals to resolve uncertainty about trustworthiness. They alter the rational-choice assumption that incentives in the form of rewards and penalties motivate the customer; instead Gambetta defines trustworthiness as the product of customer attributes conveyed to and interpreted by the taxi driver as signals. Consistent with signaling theory in economics, costs figure into the trust game: reliability of a signal is based on calculating the cost of attaining it legitimately.

The above summaries of Podolny, Gambetta, and Vaughan suggest how integration of theory and research on signals between analytic ethnography and analytical sociology might proceed. Analogical comparison is justified because, uniformly and consistent with use of the concept in economics, Podolny, Gambetta, and Vaughan all treat signals as information, examining how decisions are made under conditions of uncertainty, and all found signals operating as a mechanism. In contrast to its use in economics, in all three signals are inseparable from context. However, it is the differences between the three signaling projects that promote theory elaboration and integration between the two disciplinary specialties. The research by Podolny, Gambetta, and Vaughan could be subject to systematic in-depth comparison, searching for analogies and differences, that begins to articulate a general theory of signaling that merges levels of analysis. Space prevents such a comparison here, but we can identify some directions that would advance mechanism-based explanations.

Whereas typically analytical sociology examines structures of interaction rather than interaction itself (Hedström 2005), analytic ethnography supplies data about interaction within social context. Variation in signals sent over time, their embeddedness in information streams, institutional and organizational effects, and the social location of the interpreter show the dynamics and uncertainty that underlie the production of trust and the status-ordering of a market. What is the relevance of mixed, weak, and routine signals or the sequential interjection of new signals in a social context over time for the research of Podolny and Gambetta? Both Gambetta and Vaughan raise the possibility of mistake and unintended consequences. How might this affect market stability? What relevance might the normalization of deviance have for both trust relations and market stability, in light of uncertainty and variation in signals and their interpretation? All three projects are either explicitly or implicitly about risk, so another possibility is to incorporate signals as mechanisms into a theory of risk that stands up across the three substantive problems summarized here. Above are only a few of the possible ways that analytic ethnography and analytical sociology could be joined. My purpose has been to be suggestive, rather than definitive. Nonetheless, the examples indicate the potential for theoretical integration both within analytic ethnography and between it and analytical sociology, thus advancing the development of mechanism-based explanations that span micro, meso, and macro levels of analysis.

Conclusion

The purpose of this chapter has been to demonstrate the unique contribution that analytic ethnography has made and can make to accomplishing the two key principles of analytical sociology: (1) building mechanism-based explanations that connect actors, actions, and outcomes, and (2) bridging the micro–meso–macro levels of analysis in those explanations. I began by defining ethnography and locating analytic ethnography within it as an evidence-based, theory-building enterprise. Then, using examples from substantive theory and formal theory, I showed the contribution analytic ethnographers have made to identifying mechanisms that connect actors, actions, and outcomes at all three levels of analysis. Next, to establish the empirical basis for theoretical integration between the two specialties, I showed their compatibility, describing how they achieve the same principles. The single divergence—a theory of action—is crucial to exchange between the two. Finally, I addressed the critical issue of theoretical integration. Demonstrating analogical theorizing as a useful tool, I showed how analytic ethnography produced an analysis of signals as a mechanism that incorporated micro, meso, and macro factors to explain outcomes. Finally, I extended those results to signaling research in analytical sociology to show how theory building might occur.

My point has been that analytic ethnography has more in common with analytical sociology than is usually assumed, has consistently and reliably identified mechanisms that link actors to outcomes at all levels of analysis, and that theoretical integration both within analytic ethnography and between it and analytical sociology is a productive way to advance mechanism-based explanations that link micro, meso, and macro levels of analysis. Obstacles exist, however. Currently, there is lack of integration both within analytical ethnography as well as between it and analytical sociology. Little effort has been put to accumulating results within each specialty in a systematic way. For many scholars of both specialties this integrative direction requires altering a commitment to substantive theory and thus how research is conducted. Typically, the emphasis is on moving forward with the next substantive project, not integrating the findings from the last into the next, so formal theory is not the outcome. Moreover, integrating micro, meso, and macro levels of the social in explanations has not been a common goal. This condition has structural origins. Although theory classes instruct that the essence of society is the nexus of structure and agency, our tendency is to specialize in a method that best captures either the macro or micro level of analysis but not both, due to department specialty, mentor influence, personal capability and preference, and the desire to get a job in a discipline where specialization is rewarded. Although research methods classes encourage mixed methods, how to combine them to make empirical connections across levels of analysis is not typically taught.

Many scholars bridge the micro–macro gap by framing micro-level projects in literature describing relevant macro-level factors or the reverse, but empirical demonstrations of the connection between the two are more rare and tend to be qualitative. An obstacle specific to ethnography is that ethnographers work, often alone, on distinctive problems in unique settings that make finding generalities across projects difficult. If achieving integration within each approach is complex and challenging, how then might we pursue a productive relationship between analytic ethnography and analytical sociology in making micro–macro connections? Although the structural obstacles described above suggest that ultimately bridging the gap between theories of macro–micro relations and research depends upon structural change in the discipline, the example of signals as mechanisms suggests that crossing intradisciplinary boundaries to bridge the micro–macro gap may be easier than imagined. Most promising in the signaling example is that three sociologists independently read across disciplinary boundaries to discover and use an economic theory that helped explain their data, which led to examination of signals as a mechanism in multiple contexts at multiple levels of analysis in sociology. Even if general theory remains elusive, the exchange of ideas, theories, and concepts between analytic ethnography and analytical sociology would be productive. Some of the central interests of analytical sociology are networks, informal rules and social norms, and the desires, benefits, and structured opportunities of individuals (Hedström 2005). These all can be and have been studied by analytic ethnographers. Network ties, for example, can be examined using individuals, families, organizations, or nation-states (or subunits within them) as the units of analysis. Dalton's intra- and interorganizational 'cliques' (1959), Latour's actor-network theory (1987), Becker's conventions (1982), and the concept of boundary object (Star and Griesemer 1989) hold hypotheses for network research in analytical sociology.

It is this bridging ability of analytic ethnography that is the essence of theoretical integration, both within the specialty and between it and analytical sociology. Analytic ethnography cannot explain large-scale social outcomes, as does analytical sociology, but it has developed mechanism-based explanations of both reproduction and change at the macro level. Also, it can make micro–meso–macro-level connections and has accumulated data at all levels of analysis (see note 1). Analytical sociology examines the structures of interaction. The strength of analytic ethnography is revealing the complexity of actors, actions, and interactions—the mechanisms *behind* the mechanisms that contribute to the macro-level change and stability that are the focus of analytical sociology. Theorists have long argued that the social is explained by the intersection of micro- and macro-level factors. Mechanisms are the linchpin of that relationship. The examples of mechanism-based explanations presented here allow a more empirically grounded consideration of what micro–macro integration might entail and how we might proceed. Further, the similarities and differences between analytical sociology and analytic ethnography described in this chapter suggest that a productive exchange relationship would make more complete explanations possible.

Notes

1. See e.g. Halle 1984; DeVault 1991; Diamond 1992; Bourgois 1995; Morrill 1995; Salzinger 2003; Newman 2004; Auyero 2005; Espiritu 2005; Grasmuck 2005; Smith 2005; Desmond 2007; Sherman 2007.
2. Several well-known analytic ethnographers have developed theory by cross-case comparison without describing their method (see e.g. Goffman 1961; also Katz 1988). Of

those ethnographers who have, none has acknowledged the role of analogy (Eisenhardt 1989: 540–1; Strauss and Corbin 1994; Morrill 1995; Strauss 1995; Snow, Morrill, and Anderson 2003; Zerubavel 2007).

References

Adler, P., and Adler, P. (1995), 'The Demography of Ethnography', *Journal of Contemporary Ethnography*, 24: 3–29.

Anderson, E. (2002), 'The Ideologically Driven Critique', *American Journal of Sociology*, 107 (6): 1533–50.

Atkinson, P., et al. (2001) (eds.), *Handbook of Ethnography* (Thousand Oaks, Calif.: Sage).

Auyero, J. (2005), *Routine Politics and Violence in Argentina* (New York: Cambridge University Press).

Bacharach, M., and Gambetta, D. (2001), 'Trust in Signs', in K. S. Cook (ed.), *Trust in Society* (New York: Russell Sage).

Becker, H. S. (1982), *Art Worlds* (Berkeley, Calif.: University of California Press).

Blumer, H. (1954), 'What is Wrong with Social Theory?', *American Sociological Review*, 19: 3–10.

Bourdieu, P. [1979] (1984), *Distinction* (Cambridge, Mass.: Harvard University Press).

—— [1980] (1990), *The Logic of Practice* (Stanford, Calif.: Stanford University Press).

Bourgois, P. (1995), *In Search of Respect* (New York: Cambridge University Press).

Burawoy, M. (1979), *Manufacturing Consent* (Chicago, Ill.: University of Chicago Press).

—— (1998), 'The Extended Case Method', *Sociological Theory*, 16: 4–33.

—— (2009), *The Extended Case Method: Four Countries, Four Decades, Four Great Transformations, and One Theoretical Tradition* (Berkeley, Calif.: University of California Press).

Callon, M. (1986), 'Some Elements of a Sociology of Translation', in J. Law (ed.), *Power, Action, and Belief* (Keele: Methuen), 196–229.

Culyba, R. J., Heimer, C. A., and Petty, J. C. (2004), 'The Ethnographic Turn', *Qualitative Sociology*, 27 (4): 365–90.

Dalton, M. (1959), *Men Who Manage* (New York: J. Wiley).

Desmond, M. (2007), *On the Fireline* (Chicago, Ill.: University of Chicago Press).

DeVault, M. L. (1991), *Feeding the Family* (Chicago, Ill.: University of Chicago Press).

—— (2007), 'Knowledge From the Field', in C. Calhoun (ed.), *Sociology in America: A History* (Chicago, Ill.: University of Chicago Press).

Diamond, T. (1992), *Making Grey Gold* (Chicago, Ill.: University of Chicago Press).

Duneier, M. (2002), 'What Kind of Combat Sport is Sociology?', *American Journal of Sociology*, 107 (6): 1551–76.

Eisenhardt, K. M. (1989), 'Building Theories from Case Study Research', *Academy of Management Review*, 14 (4): 532–50.

Emerson, R. M., Fretz, R. I., and Shaw, L. L. (1995), *Writing Ethnographic Fieldnotes* (Chicago, Ill.: University of Chicago Press).

Emirbayer, M., and Johnson, V. (2008), 'Bourdieu and Organizational Analysis', *Theory and Society*, 37 (1): 1–44.

Espiritu, Y. (2005), *Home Bound* (Berkeley Calif.: University of California Press).

GAMBETTA, D., and HAMILL, H. (2005), *Streetwise* (New York: Russell Sage).

GLASER, B. G., and STRAUSS, A. L. (1967), *The Discovery of Grounded Theory* (Chicago, Ill.: Aldine).

GOFFMAN, E. (1961), *Asylums* (Garden City, N.Y.: Anchor).

GRASMUCK, S. (2005), *Protecting Home* (Piscataway, N.J.: Rutgers University Press).

HALLE, D. (1984), *America's Working Man* (Chicago, Ill.: University of Chicago Press).

HALLETT, T. (2003), 'Symbolic Power and Organization Culture', *Sociological Theory*, 21 (2): 128–49.

HEDSTRÖM. P. (2005), *Dissecting the Social* (Cambridge: Cambridge University Press).

KAHN, S. (2008), *The Production of Privilege*, Ph.D. thesis (University of Wisconsin).

KATZ, J. (1983), 'A Theory of Qualitative Methodology', in R. E. Emerson (ed.), *Contemporary Field Research* (Boston, Mass.: Little, Brown), 127–48.

—— (1988), *Seductions of Crime* (Chicago, Ill.: University of Chicago Press).

—— (2001*a*), 'Analytic Induction', in N. J. Smelser and P. B. Baltes (eds.), *International Encyclopedia of the Social and Behavioral Sciences* (Oxford: Elsevier).

—— (2001*b*), 'From How to Why on Luminous Description and Causal Inference in Ethnography (Part 1)', *Ethnography*, 2 (4): 443–73; (Part 2), *Ethnography*, 3 (1): 63–90.

LATOUR, B. (1987), *Science in Action* (Cambridge, Mass.: Harvard University Press).

—— (1988), *The Pasteurization of France* (Cambridge, Mass.: Harvard University Press).

LINDESMITH, A. R. (1947), *Opiate Addiction* (Bloomington, Ind.: Principia).

LOFLAND, J. (1971), *Analyzing Social Settings* (Belmont, Calif.: Wadsworth).

—— (1985), 'Analytic Ethnography', *Journal of Contemporary Ethnography*, 24: 30–67.

MARTIN, J. L. (2003), 'What Is Field Theory?', *American Journal of Sociology*, 109: 1–49.

MILES, M. B., and HUBERMAN, A. M. (1984), *Qualitative Data Analysis* (Beverly Hills, Calif.: Sage).

MORRILL, C. (1995), *The Executive Way* (Chicago, Ill.: University of Chicago Press).

NEWMAN, K. (2002), 'No Shame', *American Journal of Sociology*, 107 (6): 1577–600.

—— (2004), *Rampage: The Social Organization of School Shootings* (New York: Basic).

PODOLNY, J. M. (1993), 'A Status-based Model of Market Competition', *American Journal of Sociology*, 98: 829–72.

—— (2005), *Status Signals* (Princeton, N.J.: Princeton University Press).

SALLAZ, J. J., and ZAVISCA, J. (2007), 'Bourdieu in American Sociology, 1980–2004', *Annual Review of Sociology*, 33: 21–41.

SALZINGER, L. (2003), *Genders in Production* (Berkeley, Calif.: University of California Press).

SHERMAN, R. (2007), *Class Acts* (Berkeley, Calif.: University of California Press).

SNOW, D. A., MORRILL, C., and ANDERSON, L. (2003), 'Elaborating Analytic Ethnography', *Ethnography*, 4 (2): 181–200.

SMITH, D. L. (2005), *Institutional Ethnography* (Lanham, Md.: Alta Mira).

SPENCE, A. M. (1974), *Market Signaling* (Cambridge, Mass.: Harvard University Press).

STAR, S. L., and GRIESEMER, J. R. (1989), 'Institutional Ecology, "Translations", and Boundary Objects', *Social Studies of Science*, 19 (3): 387–420.

STRAUSS, A. L. (1995), 'Notes on the Nature and Development of General Theories', *Qualitative Inquiry*, 1: 7–18.

—— and CORBIN, J. A. (1994), *Basics of Qualitative Research* (Newbury Park, Calif.: Sage).

VAUGHAN, D. (1983), *Controlling Unlawful Organizational Behavior* (Chicago, Ill.: University of Chicago Press).

—— (1986), *Uncoupling* (New York: Oxford University Press).

—— (1992), 'Theory Elaboration', in C. Ragin and H. S. Becker (eds.), *What is a Case? The Foundations of Social Inquiry* (New York: Cambridge University Press), 173–202.

—— (1996), *The Challenger Launch Decision* (Chicago, Ill.: University of Chicago Press).

—— (2002), 'Signals and Interpretive Work', in K. A. Cerulo (ed.), *Culture in Mind* (New York: Routledge).

—— (2004), 'Theorizing Disaster: Analogy, Historical Ethnography, and the Challenger Accident', *Ethnography*, 5 (3): 313–45.

—— *Theorizing: Analogy, Cases, and Comparative Social Organization* (Chicago, Ill.: University of Chicago Press), in progress.

WACQUANT, L. (2002), 'Scrutinizing the Street', *American Journal of Sociology*, 107: 1468–532.

—— (2004*a*), *Body and Soul* (New York: Oxford University Press).

—— (2004*b*) (ed.), 'Pierre Bourdieu in the Field', *Ethnography*, special issue, 5 (4).

WHYTE, W. F. (1943), *Street Corner Society* (Chicago, Ill.: University of Chicago Press).

WILLIS, P. [1977] (1981), *Learning to Labour* (New York: Columbia University Press).

ZERUBAVEL, E. (2007), 'Generally Speaking: The Logic and Mechanics of Social Pattern Analysis', *Sociological Forum*, 22 (2): 131–45.

CHAPTER 30

....

HISTORICAL SOCIOLOGY*

....

KAREN BARKEY

INTRODUCTION

....

WHILE there has been a proliferation of work in the field of historical sociology, it has not always adhered to an original claim by historical sociologists to explain large-scale social processes. Here it is necessary to emphasize both 'explanation,' and 'large-scale social processes,' since both have been questioned. A marriage between historical sociology and analytical sociology would be a desirable goal, one that is already seriously endeavored in some circles. An analytic historical sociology would focus on explaining why phenomena happen and how they happen, rather than relying only on description and interpretation. What analytical sociology brings to the field is an emphasis on an action-oriented sociology which requires that we seek to understand why actors do what they do and how the micro actions link to macro social outcomes towards building middle-range approaches to sociological theory (Hedström 2005).

In this chapter I discuss some of the directions in the field and argue that even though the early generation of historical sociologists were focused on producing explanations for 'large-scale outcomes,' they did so without considering the more meso and micro levels of analysis that link the macro causes to the macro outcomes.

* The author wishes to thank Peter Bearman, Peter Hedström, Frederic Godart, and Michael Biggs for helpful comments.

They also remained aloof from a cultural perspective, denying a chance to integrate structure and culture more fully. Though the field is more differentiated and complex than I represent it here, it still falls into two major groups. One major path which I call comparative historical analysis is well represented by the recent edited volume by Mahoney and Rueschemeyer (2003) and is characterized by historical sociologists and political scientists who seek an explanation for large-scale processes, asking 'big questions,' with research programs embedded in the real social and political phenomena relevant to a changing world. Many scholars initially worked in Marxist, Weberian, or joint agendas with the methodological tools of comparative historical analysis. Later approaches adopted and incorporated institutionalist, rational-choice, and network approaches. In this varied set of strategies many scholars stressed continuing the original agenda of looking for explanations of social processes based on the collection of historical evidence and the repeated working and reworking of the relation between data and theory. Another approach, which I will call the culturalist approach, though quite broad and diverse, overall represents a position removed from straightforward causality, claiming a more radical position than one discussed in the older *Methodenstreit* debate. This approach privileges interpretation, subjectivity and text, language and discourse, and therefore questions the ability to provide scientific explanations for social phenomena.

I briefly review some of these positions to clarify the lay of the land, and to uncover an analytic geography to historical sociology. I then spend the rest of the chapter presenting particular examples of work in historical social science that have come closest to the requirements of analytical sociology. I try to show how we can get additional leverage from an analytical sociology that is resolutely process-oriented, linked in its macro, meso, and micro levels, and where once again the focus can be the explanation of important social-historical processes. The examples demonstrate the manner in which the emphasis on analytical historical sociology can help specify the causality behind processes that have not been clearly interpreted or have been misinterpreted in historical, sociological, and culturally oriented studies.

30.1 COMPARATIVE HISTORICAL ANALYSIS

The field of historical sociology claims many of the illustrious European thinkers of the nineteenth century as its intellectual forebears. In the USA, however, the rise of historical sociology was the result of a small intellectual revolution against the dominance of a Parsonsian paradigm. On the margins of a much more conservative and functionalist field, historical sociology claimed to analyze the large-scale social transformations that affected both western and nonwestern countries. The rise of capitalism, socialism, the revolutionary transformations of the past in Western Europe, and the continuing revolutions of the early twentieth century in colonies and ex-colonies represented issues of vast importance not readily analyzed in sociological circles.

These large-scale transformations were too important, complex, and connected across the globe to be explained by simple functionalist models tested on constrained and confined regions that were taken one at a time. Their insistence on the complexity and diversity of historical trajectories and their use of induction to build middle-range theories as formulated by Merton (1967) was their asset. Therefore, they did not develop a theory of capitalism, but rather produced important statements on the economic organization of the world system (Wallerstein 1974; Brenner 1987); not a theory of large-scale transformation, revolution, or democratization, but various middle-range theoretical statements about a diversity of routes to democracy and revolution (Moore 1966; Anderson 1974a, 1974b; Tilly 1975; Skocpol 1979) or theoretical statements on the nature of nation-building and citizenship (Bendix 1964). They pioneered an entire new expansion of qualitative research, developing an agenda that over the years led to significant knowledge accumulation (Amenta 2003; Goldstone 2003; Mahoney 2003).

As Calhoun (1996) describes, not fully satisfied with their marginal location, historical sociologists engaged in a process of domestication, acquiring the thinking and methodology of their integrated brethren. Their strength lay in the manner in which they were able to combine theory and methods with empirical questions of significance and maintain scientific focus, given the nature of historical evidence. The methodology of comparative work was developed in the 1970s and 1980s to become the major tool of the trade (Pzreworski and Teune 1970; Roth 1971; Smelser 1976; Skocpol and Somers 1980; Skocpol 1984; Ragin 1987). Historical sociologists concentrated on identifying generalizable causal features that explained outcomes across multiple cases. They explained the same or different outcomes across cases through a configuration of variables that were argued to have expected causal effects (Moore 1966; Skocpol 1979; Goldstone 1993). Critiques followed, however, of the flawed conception of time and unilinearity (Abbott 1990), of the independence and equivalence of cases being compared (Sewell 1996), of the greater ontological concerns (Tilly 1997), of the desertion of grand theory (Kiser and Hechter 1991), and others on the small number of cases (King, Keohane and Verba 1994; Goldthorpe 1997, 2000). Such concerns produced a rethinking of the methodology of comparative historical analysis that yielded a variety of directions, combinatorial and unique. Some historical sociologists turned towards a narrative-oriented perspective that promoted the reconsideration of temporality, narratives, and events as the stuff of historical process while others refocused their efforts onto comparisons that were internally reframed within cases along temporal dimensions. The adoption of temporality, events, and narratives was displayed in wide-ranging studies in sociology (Abbott 1990; Sewell 1996; Stryker 1996; Kimeldorf 1998; Stovel 2001) and in the work on analytic narratives in political science (Bates et al. 1998).

A different set of scholars concentrated on the combination of process, social mechanisms, and temporality. These approaches were in no sense novel in historical sociology or sociology more generally. Philip Abrams (1982) in *Historical Sociology* had argued for bringing history and sociology together, since both tried to understand human agency within a process of structuration, as Anthony Giddens was also forcefully doing (1979, 1986, 1987). Arthur Stinchcombe in his *Theoretical Methods in Social History* had already flagged the importance of what he called 'deep causal analogies,' by which he meant finding correspondence between narratives of similar processes, identifying causal analogies between sets of facts, and then building these sets of facts into a cumulative causal analysis of the process at hand (1978). Microeconomic models of strategic action had also been available for some time (Olson [1965] 1971, 1982, 2000; Hechter 1987).

The renewed interest in an analytic direction was clear in some of the rising fields of historical sociology, especially when combined with large-scale comparative questions. For institutionalists the puzzle was to explain long term historical continuity, the reproduction and duration of phenomena, through concepts of institutional inertia and change (Thelen 2003; Pierson 2004), or through process-tracing and analysis (Goldstone 2003; Hall 2003; Mahoney 2003). For network analysis the goal was to reframe the study of society away from categorical attributes of actors towards connectivity-based and positional studies of the structured social relations between individuals (Burt 1980; White 1992; Bearman 1993; Padgett and Ansell 1993; Gould 1995). For analytic-sociology advocates, this has meant a rethinking of mechanism-based explanations and connecting of various levels of analysis (Swedberg and Hedström 1997; Tilly 1998, 2001, 2004; McAdam, Tarrow, and Tilly 2001; Hedström 2005). Another analytic direction took the form of trying to uncover laws of social and political behavior and action (Hechter 1987; Levi 1988; Weingast 1996).

We can also observe a cultural turn in historical sociology, and history, mostly initially inspired by anthropology. Victoria Bonnell and Lynn Hunt claimed a new subfield that combined 'social and cultural modes of analysis in an empirically concrete and yet theoretically informed fashion' (1999: ix). Bonnell and Hunt, but also Sewell and Biernacki skillfully pose their challenge as carrying out a cultural analysis that combines attention to meaning and interpretation as well as explanation. Mostly inspired by Weber, an interpretive comparative-historical program includes a continuous and integrated dialogue between structure and meanings, as well as more insightful uses of temporal processes over time. In a path also set by Reinhard Bendix (1980) and Clifford Geertz (1968), Rogers Brubaker accomplished a path-breaking analysis of French and German citizenship and work on national identity in the post-Soviet republics (1992, 1996). Brubaker has consistently paid attention to the varying conceptions of national identity and citizenship, deriving his explanations about larger macro-institutional outcomes from structural as well as interpretive arguments. Richard Biernacki (1995) studied the impact on economic life of two essentially divergent definitions of the character of labor in Germany and Britain from 1640 to 1914. Here different cultural understandings of how labor was understood and interpreted in national contexts explained the different practices and developments in each country. We can also cite the work of Veljko Vujacic (1996), whose comparison of Serbian and Russian national identity and politics embraced Weberian notions of national self-understanding, or Barkey's analysis (2000) of Hungarian and Romanian nationhood in the interwar era, where the nature of the social and political networks between the state and various institutions, such as education and labor, provided different meanings to what it meant to be a nation. In these works culture is a Weberian *verstehen* formulation that has been integrated into the structural elements of the causal puzzle.

From this initial moderate vision to the new manifestos of cultural sociology (see Steinmetz 1999, 2005; Adams, Clemens, and Orloff 2005) much opposition to comparative historical analysis was utilized to self-consciously demarcate a new position critical of positivism, and to demand a rethinking of the categories of social phenomena that have informed the world we study, such as modernity, capitalism, bureaucratization, and secularization. Those who adopted a stronger culturalist perspective have been ready to dismiss other determinants of social action while privileging a fully constitutive role for culture. So much so that, realizing that the pendulum had swung too far, Sewell, in *Logics of History*, admitted: 'Somehow, at the very time when particularly powerful changes in social and economic structures are manifested even more intently in our daily lives, we cultural historians have ceased not only to grapple with such structures but even to admit their ontological reality' (2005: 520).

Recently, new modes of thinking forced the field out of its more macro moorings to consider a variety of ways of studying social action more concretely, dissecting social processes while respecting their long-term continuity and unfolding. This rethinking is the product of the questions raised with regard to the easy causality used by historical sociologists linking macro states in one particular time to macro outcomes in a later period, without specifying the underlying intermediary mechanisms at work. Moreover, the work of Thomas Shelling brought to light the problems of trying to understand macro-level outcomes without explicitly detailing the micro-level processes that brought them about (1978). Even more critical, he showed the manner in which the micro motives of individuals and the macro behavior of the aggregate might not be the same but coincide as a result of unintended consequences. Such concerns have to resonate more deeply with historical sociologists whose understanding of micro motives of the historical period and setting are incomplete.

Briefly we can cite three major strategies of research that forced historical sociologists toward an increasingly analytical turn: rational choice, network analysis, and institutional analysis. Each of these approaches has self-consciously thought about the linkages between macro-level phenomena and micro-/meso-level actions to 'demonstrate how macro states at one point in time influence individuals' actions, and how these actions bring about new macro states at a later point in time' (Edling and Hedström 2005: 7). Each approach focused on action and mechanisms mediating between structures and action. Given the different perspectives espoused by institutionalists, rational-choice theorists, and network analysts, we have different analytic orientations, sets of mechanisms, and explanations. Yet each subfield has produced significant studies that demonstrated the value of analytical thinking in historical projects. I provide key exemplars of each strategy, focusing on the analytic unpacking they use, the connectivity between levels, and the explanation.

30.2 INSTITUTIONALISM AND NETWORKS IN HISTORICAL STUDIES

30.2.1 Institutions

Especially in political science, the focus on the explanation of political behavior and political outcomes is increasingly located within the study of institutions, since these latter define those who can participate, and shape their preferences and their strategies. The field is divided into rational-choice institutionalism that aspires to uncover the laws of political behavior and historical institutionalism that seeks to understand how political institutions shape the political process. The best studies in rational-choice institutionalism assume that practices and rules that are organizationally embedded are significant in determining the incentives, preferences, and strategies as well as the resources available to actors for political participation. As such they are focused on not simply the micro level of the individual but also the meso level of organizations as structuring the incentives of political actors.

Of Rule and Revenue (1988) by Margaret Levi is a good example of how macrostructural forces determine the micro properties of actors who given certain transaction costs and collective goods engage in bargaining to affect the macro structures in return. When Levi tries to understand the differences in the tax systems that evolved in France and England from the thirteenth century to the end of the seventeenth century (and why English parliamentary rule proved more tax-efficient over time than French absolutism), she stresses how 'policies are the outcome of an exchange between the rules and the various groups who compose the polity,' how rulers had to balance getting monies with maintaining power, how producing revenue required quasi-voluntary compliance, and the importance of the contextual variables such as economic structure, international relations, and 'forms of government' (1988: 11–13). Key to her argument is 'the relative bargaining power of rulers' (p. 17) that depends on the resources they control and the resources those on which they depend control, and the bargains they strike within determinate institutional conditions. She also discusses the transaction costs that come with negotiating agreements with society, and how some institutions, notably parliaments, can reduce them. When the macro situation alters (war, the economy, the international situation, and changes to the form of government), the circumstances of bargaining between the Crown and the society change considerably and with these bargaining and transaction costs rulers seek to manage and reduce in their quest for taxation.

In the case of France and England, she shows convincingly that 'the relatively weaker bargaining position of the English monarchs vis-à-vis their constituents led to concessions that French monarchs did not have to make. However, the Parliament that evolved ultimately enhanced the ability of English monarchs to tax. Parliament provided a forum for conditional cooperation. It engendered quasi-voluntary compliance and reduced transaction costs' (1988: 97).

In a comparison that duplicates the cases but asks a related question of why Jews who had become so valuable to both crowns as economic assets were evicted in 1290 from England and 1306 from France, Barkey and Katznelson use a similar framework (2008). They combine a macro analysis of medieval state-building with the micro dynamics of monarchical strategies regarding taxation. By contrast to the literature stressing the diminished fiscal capacity of the Jews or growing religious animosity based on the transformation in the ambitions and worldview of the Church, crusading, fundamentalist mendicant orders, local religious enthusiasms, and hostility to usury, they show how key features in the making of Europe's pioneering nation-states fundamentally altered the character of kingship and the decisions about resources and legitimacy that monarchs had to make. The economic situation of the Jews was not irreversible (Mundill 1998), and despite the intense religiosity of the period, at no time did the Church either in England or France call for Jewish eviction. Nor did kings simply respond to anti-Jewish mass and elite demands. Instead, kings staunchly shielded 'their' Jews from such external pressures. Therefore, just economic or religious, cultural reasoning is not enough to understand the puzzle of eviction which happened as Levi demonstrates, at the time of the development of different monarchical bargaining power vis-à-vis institutions of Parliament in England and lack thereof in France.

Barkey and Katznelson develop an argument that combines macrohistorical analysis with the micro dynamics of agents' strategies to understand the puzzle of expulsion. They argue the major changes that occurred with the Battle of Bouvines in 1214 sent the two countries on separate trajectories of state-building which affected the character and logic of rule and of public authority by replacing a territorially elastic and inherently feudal system of dynastic rule with situated states, thus including the imperative for rulers to construct regulations for satisfactory engagement with the politically active members of the societies they governed and to make predictable and effective their ability to extract resources for statist purposes.

The transformation from dynasty to states, the alterations to political bargaining, and the changes to taxation proved critical for Jews. Before Bouvines, Jews had been part of dynastic rule, since they were of clear economic advantage. After Bouvines, with the new goals of state-building and the new extractive bargaining relationships with urban and rural society, each regime worked to move away from customary taxation, deeply affecting the fate of Jews. English and French kings sought to make effective and legitimate states, and therefore raised the likelihood that kings would come to choose the expulsion of Jews at the cost of losing a financial asset. After Bouvines, in England the contentious relationship between the Crown and notables claiming rights produced a new type of government with the creation of Parliament as a national institutional site of negotiation between the Crown and political society. Post-Bouvines France, on the other hand, still experienced struggles between kings who sought to create a modern state and the nobility, who sought to rule significant territory by feudal right. The royal effort to impose control, rather than the creation of a powerful national legislature, was also partly the result of the subservience of the French representative forums at the regional and national levels (Elias [1939] 2000; Fawtier 1953; Ertman 1997). Under such conditions, Barkey and Katznelson show that once the calculus of the monarchs shifted after Bouvines, kings came to their rationales for expulsion given their new bargaining power in the context of the institutions and social groups they encountered. In England, the monarch was more readily forced into expelling his Jews, since the new representatives in the Parliament who were burdened by their debt to Jewish moneylenders were much more successful at bargaining with the King. In France, the King made the decision not within the context of a forceful institution but rather as a result of successful bargaining with the various estates in society. He maneuvered to give the different estates a break from taxation after they had contributed to major wars, but only after he was reassured that he had ensured a steady source of taxation for the future from them.

In both cases Barkey and Katznelson show that monarchs arrived at the same decision of expulsion through different processes of bargaining embedded in different conditions, institutions, and financial exigencies. This clearly illustrates the benefit of a stronger linkage between rational choice and historical institutionalism, especially because in historical analysis we have to understand the rational decision maker within the context of the institutions and structural constraints of the period. The decisions of the rulers are strongly embedded in the developing institutions of the time, themselves the outcomes of very different sets of historical and structural relations between the monarchy and the different estates of the two realms. Here the relations between the micro and the macro levels are analyzed, though the intermediary level is not yet fully specified.

Historical institutionalism both is interested in real political outcomes and recognizes institutions as the major mediating variables where politics is played out. Institutions can promote or prevent action, become the site of policy development and contention; in other words, they can become the critical juncture in the unfolding of a political outcome. Institutions here are defined as more or less organized, routinized, and standardized sets of procedures that maintain and reproduce a set of common understandings about the world, and how it functions (Jepperson 1991: 143–7). How do institutions change over time? Scholars are now paying attention to lengthy and large-scale historical processes for extended periods of time, developing strategies for studying how institutions have emerged, evolved, reproduced themselves, and thrived in some contexts and not in others. The rise of historical institutionalism corresponds with a renewed ontological view that many social and political outcomes are the 'result of causal processes in which distant events, sequencing and complex interaction effects play important roles' (Hall 2003: 398).

Two central concepts in historical sociology, path dependence and contingency/conjuncture represent an important tension that is also at the core of the new institutional thinking. Those who believe that institutions are very slow to change endorse the economic work that argues for positive-feedback processes and path dependence, the argument being that once you have engaged down a certain path that has been working and self-reinforcing a reversal of course is quite difficult, therefore institutions often generate slow reproduction or absence of change, implying a lack of contingency (Mahoney 2000, 2001; Pierson 2000, 2004). In these situations the mechanisms that have been most theorized are about cost–benefit analysis as well as mechanisms about power, legitimation, and the functionality of certain sequences (Mahoney 2000; Thelen 2003). In contradistinction to path dependence, the timing and sequence of historical events matter to the way in which paths of political development proceed. The ground-breaking analysis by Alexander Gerschenkron (1962) on the timing of economic development in Western Europe, or the particular configuration and timing of geopolitical and military competition among absolutist states in western Europe, according to Thomas Ertman, take seriously where and when the conjuncture occurs that brings about an alteration in the comparative outcomes across multiple cases.

The tension between contingency and path dependence is best treated by Kathleen Thelen (1999, 2003, 2004), who demonstrates how it is possible for such seemingly contradictory processes of institutional continuity and change to happen together. Her interest is in explaining those institutions that both experience change but also keep many important features of their past. Examples of such institutions could be the English Parliament, the United States Supreme Court, or the national systems of vocational training in the countries she studies. A long-term institutional analysis of the evolution of the German system of vocational training displays the strength of her analytic historical perspective. She studies the emergence of vocational training when the German Handicraft Protection Law came into being in 1897 and established apprenticeship and certification for artisans partly as a tool of the German government to strengthen the artisanal class against the rising working classes. Analyzing the vocational system through the different periods of German history, Thelen demonstrates the manner in which once institutionalized this apprenticeship system remained 'a collectively managed system for monitoring how firms train their workers' (2004: 296) and as such was exploited, emulated, and extended by different governments attesting to institutional flexibility, strength, and continuity.

In understanding Germany today, she argues both for positive-feedback processes, the effects of which were seen in the continuity of a vocational training system, but also for change through specific mechanisms of such change. While the continuity argument is about reinforcing existing sequences and is mostly conceived at the macro level, change for Thelen is where the interaction between levels and dissecting social processes becomes very important. She demonstrates that institutional conversion and layering were operational in Germany—conversion with the appropriation of the training and certification system by industrial and trade-union actors; that is, those who had been excluded before were able to take over and reform the vocational system in the middle of the twentieth century under different circumstances. She also shows how the mechanism of layering works; that is, how, over time, with the growth of private alternatives, institutional innovators adapted and added new features to the old institutional framework when they could not alter what was already entrenched through time. This layering occurred with the additional change of the 1969 law when trade-union participation was added in (2004: 259–64).

In many ways the elegance of Thelen's analysis lies in her demonstration that this system, which was set up in 1897, persisted through several putative historical crises to maintain its basic training structure, and that it also changed because of adaptation and accommodation towards a standardized and centralized vocational training, and towards the incorporation of unions and labor-friendly policies that are present in the system of Germany today (2004). Thelen's analytic feat is in her ability to connect the macro-institutional outcomes of differentiated vocational systems to the social, political, and economic contexts in which sets of actors navigate the general organizational structures and institutions. And the ways in which actors and their actions are linked in the management of institutional contexts help her clarify the mechanisms that are portable to other institutional settings to explain continuity or change. In this way, she combines comparative historical analysis with an institutionalist framework where outcomes and processes are compared and analyzed and mechanisms are found that bridge macro level phenomena to the orientation to action and the manner in which action and actors can reproduce basic mechanisms that bring about the type of phenomenon she tries to explain.

30.2.2 Networks

One of the most important recent developments in historical studies has been the incorporation of network theory and methodology into the reconstruction of the past. The network perspective continues the basic insights of classical sociologists such as Weber, Durkheim, and Simmel, who understood early on that it was not possible to grasp social life just as the aggregated motives and insights of individuals. Rather, we needed to study individuals within their social milieu, to study them as part of a wider social network. This is certainly also Harrison White's insight that 'social reality is in the middle-range order' (2006).

Network analysis accounts for behavior and social processes by using networks of social relations that link actors, or link nodes that could be actors, groups, organizations, or other entities. The relations that tie the nodes are considered independent of the actors' will, values, beliefs, and intentions; and social structure that transpires can be seen as the 'regularities in the patterns of relations among concrete entities; it is *not* a harmony among abstract norms and values or a classification of concrete entities by their attributes' (White, Boorman, and Breiger 1976: 733–4). The network perspective is also inherently historical, since structure is historical, shaping and changing over time, and historical sociology can be at the forefront of forging a more dynamic network analysis. By adopting a network perspective in history, it is possible to bypass many deterministic understandings of structure, individual action, and group attributes and therefore expand our historical reconstruction by allowing the conceptualization of the social world as multilevel networks involving many types of entities, people, organizations, and groups.

30.3 BRINGING HISTORICAL INSTITUTIONALISM TOGETHER WITH NETWORK ANALYSIS

The volume by Mahoney and Rueschemeyer remains powerful in its discussion of comparative historical analysis because it includes institutionalist and network thinking. I strongly believe that comparative historical questions remain key to understanding patterns of variation and difference across cases. Comparative historical analysis helps shape important analytic puzzles that may otherwise escape even the most historically trained eyes. Historical institutionalism studies 'big social and political outcomes,' but encourages process analysis, specifying sequences and studying transformations of different scale and temporality within each case, maintaining the integrity of long-term development, continuity, and change. Finally, network analysis's fundamental insights are at the center of institutionalist thinking, also encouraging to specify the intermediary level at which different structural combinations of relations constitute different social mechanisms. Therefore historical sociology has to remain comparative, institutionalist, and relational at the same time, reinforced by the fact that each of these subfields is most comfortable in an analytic, middle-range approach to sociological theory.

The synthesis that I propose as the basis of an analytic historical sociology remains interested in causal explanations of large-scale social and political outcomes; it moves comfortably between different layers of analysis from the micro level of individuals to constitute the meso-level social networks that in turn inform and lie at the basis of the institutional structures that we study. It is furthermore within these institutional settings that meanings are generated, understandings are shaped that have in turn an impact on how institutions are understood further and programmed. Social actors and social action are at the basis of this inquiry; their actions reproduce, change, and maintain the social networks, social structures, and institutional frameworks that we need to understand as well as impact the cultural meanings within which they operate. The combination of relational with institutionalist historical work is important for such a perspective. But it is even more inclusive, since it engages social action and acknowledges the importance of marrying the dynamics of structure and culture (see Fig. 30.1).

This combination of perspectives can impact many historical inquiries. One such field is that of imperial continuity and change. Empires are political formations that have lasted for very long periods of time and, much more than their rise and decline, they are interesting because of their institutional longevity, the slow-moving aspect of their reproduction that also incorporates significant amounts of change. In *Empire of Difference* (2008) I ask these questions of Ottoman imperial longevity, in comparative perspective, by using the Ottomans' two illustrious predecessors, the Roman and Byzantine empires, and their immediate contemporaries and rivals, the Habsburgs and the Russians. Macrohistorical questions are resolved from a meso, intermediate level of analysis. Often a macrohistorical occurrence such as war or trade causes a chain of events that engage the interface of society—that intermediary space where state actors and social actors meet and resolve their needs, their interests, and ideals, deciding and shaping the outcome that we study. Overall,

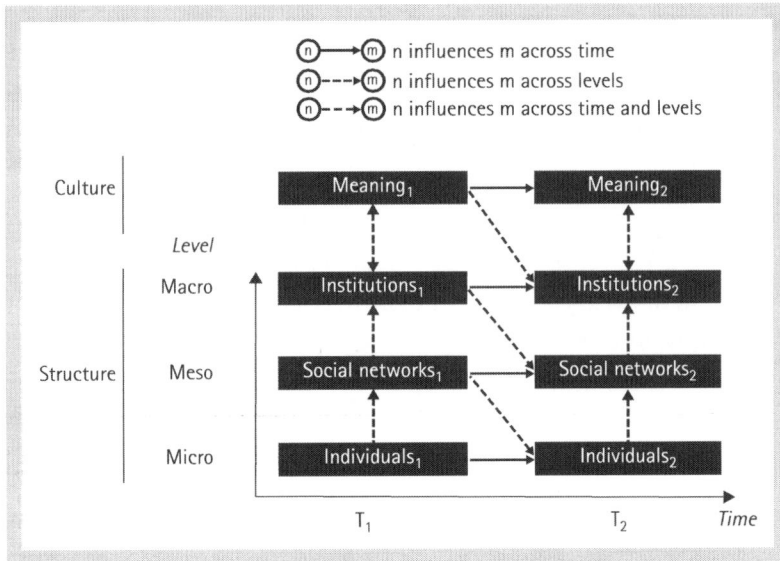

Fig. 30.1 The dynamics of culture and structure (example for two periods, T_1 and T_2)

then, I argue that the answer to the question of the longevity of empire can be found in analyses of the organizations and networks connecting large segmented and constantly changing structures, by focusing on the multivalent, networked, vertical and horizontal linkages and the short-term or durable compacts established between state and social actors. A few anecdotes from *Empire of Difference* can be used to illustrate the fusion between institutional, relational, and comparative fields and the importance of understanding action at different levels of analysis.

One example is that of Ottoman emergence. Traditional narratives have suggested single-minded accounts of the rise of the Turks, their ethnic and religious force, and their ability to overwhelm through Holy War (Wittek 1938; Inalcik 1983, 1994; Koprulu 1992). They emphasize categorical attributes such as religion or ethnicity, structural determinants such as demographic conditions, or a sort of vague cultural-symbiosis effect to explain the swift emergence of the Turks from a small principality to a world-class empire. The results of a comparative analysis of the frontier institutions and their networks of association show that religious and institutional heterogeneity, tolerance, and innovation was at the base of the Ottoman state.

When we study the historical record at the micro level—that is, look for what these leaders were doing, who they were associating with, who were their real partners, and what kinds of organizational structures they encountered and fashioned—what we get from dissecting the actions of the different groups, and drawing the ego networks of leaders is relatively clear. What made possible the rise of Osman as a leader who was able to consolidate a state-like structure around him was both the nature of his horizontal relations and his ability to broker across different previously unconnected groups. In ways reminiscent of the Medicis in the Padgett and Ansell story, this Ottoman leader straddled structural holes among many groups of potential followers, so that when he had consolidated his position he had around him a network of interdependent groups linked to him. Through his actions he connected many different groups, even warring factions, behaving like their broker and resolving social problems arising in his environment. He also extended his reach to many different settlements, communities, and different religious groups, Orthodox Greek, Orthodox Sunni, and heterodox Sufi groups, *akhi* corporations of trade, and non-Muslim religious men of learning, each important groupings that had to lend their support for him to succeed. Brokerage is innovation-producing; it introduces different tactics, practices, and strategies that can be usefully appropriated (Burt 2005). Furthermore, operating in a multivocal institutional environment such as this transitional frontier society with high levels of intermixing, his various declarations were interpreted coherently from multiple perspectives. Osman carried out two crucial tasks of leadership successfully: with brokerage and redistribution of booty from successful warfare, he was able to demand allegiance and transform horizontal relations into vertical relations of command and control. Except for Umur Bey, another leader of the structurally equivalent Aydin emirate, who partly succeeded at the same type of network connections, other leaders were stuck in a much more conservative, hierarchical network, where, rather than brokerage, closure was the rule (Burt 2001, 2005).

The comparative analysis of the network ties of local leaders who were relatively similarly placed in the geography and economic and political structures of the frontier regions demonstrated that those leaders with the ability to broker across religious, ethnic, communal, and economic groupings were clearly more successful at accumulating social capital and using it to their advantage. Resources, manpower, and alliances across religions were the key advantages to have, and Osman's family hoarded them and transformed such privileges into state-building strategies, building armies, and organizations to distribute welfare and tax the population. As such, the emergence of the Ottoman early state through brokerage across networks, mobilizing of different identities, and through strategies of actors embedded in networks is similar to the rise of the Medici through the crafty connection of different Florentine families and the resulting oligarchic-elite formation through marriage cooptation analyzed by Padgett and Ansell (1993). We can see the effectiveness of the more general principles of being at the center of a spoke-like network structure, connecting otherwise segregated groups, and combining strategic action with multivocality in the context of elaborating state-like institutions. Such a perspective is further elaborated by White (2008) and White, Godart, and Corona (2008).

Another example that reinforces the need to understand the processes of institutional continuity and change emerged in the early empire when rulers were faced with choices to make between the existing practices of the conquered populations and their own forms of rule. Again, while traditional historiography emphasized separation, enmity, and the annihilation of the conquered, careful attention to the level of social actors embedded in different networks negotiating across and choosing between institutional practices provides an entirely different picture that explains better the longevity of the empire. In land tenure for example, the early Ottomans mixed Islamic notions of prebendal (timar) benefices with the land distribution that the emperor Diocletian had enacted centuries ago and the Byzantine pronoia system of providing land to aristocrats as salary. The traditional Islamic-imperial land-tenure system insisted on state ownership of land and the distribution of land to state officials in return for military service. The pronoia was adopted in the sense that the form matched well with prebendal office, which also was distributed as a salary to officials, though the Ottomans insisted on the military aspect, and tried to take away such lands from aristocrats for fear they would become entrenched. The Ottomans wanted land to be centrally owned and administered, whereas the pronoia they encountered had become a decentralized institution. Here then we see that some of the structures of land tenure were accepted, yet converted through Ottoman understandings of who owns land in Islam, the sultan as a trust in the name of God. Such negotiation between existing forms and incoming practice is an excellent illustration of the mechanism of layering that Thelen uses to explain Germany's modern adaptation of vocational training systems.

Beyond uncovering divergent explanations that stem from a variety of different sets of actions, the ability to scrutinize micro motives and behaviors in the historical context might yield some unexpected results. While traditional explanations have emphasized centralized rule and warfare as the key to Ottoman rule, I have focused on intermediary network structures that provided the Ottomans with control. When the sheer numbers of military servicemen exceeded the supply of land, Ottomans rotated their prebendal office holders every three years. A by-product of this was increased state control through the segmentation of networks, because landholders who frequently moved did not have the ability to create strong patron–client ties. Looking at the actual registers of land assignment, it is possible to uncover a totally unintentional process that provided the state with even further control over its elites and rural populations.

The prebendal assignment process resulted in a highly fragmented land structure whereby different landholders were assigned adjacent plots. When a prebend-holder died, was dismissed, or went into rotation, his land was returned to a fictitious pool as revenue. It is from this same pool that another deserving prebend-holder was assigned new land. A prebend-holder who had shown prowess at war was rewarded with additional revenue, additional villages, and/or new estates. Yet this process, according to the registers, was quite *ad hoc*, in the sense that there was not much attention paid to the assignment of contiguous land plots. Perhaps it was just impossible, since this continual movement of land, assessed as revenue and therefore parcelled up into villages as revenue, went in and out of possession too fast and too irregularly to keep track of. There has not been any study of landholding patterns in any one period that would map the assignments by landholder. If such a study were carried out, it surely would demonstrate high levels of tenure fragmentation. It is difficult, however, to assign intentionality to the state in such an enterprise. There is no doubt that the state benefited from both the movement and the parcelization. Yet they could not have planned such a tenure structure purposefully. The *ad hoc* aggregation of many individuals coming in and out of a revenue pool led to a significant but unintended outcome of state control. Here, again, we see the workings of an institutional level of landholding practices that helped shape the individual actions and strategies that in turn shaped the networks of segmentation, so crucial to imperial state control.

Although the terminology differs, other scholars have similar interests in connecting the multiple levels of networks and institutions. For example, in his work on historical and contemporary interstate boundaries Gavrilis demonstrates that state borders—traditionally seen as lines between independent states—are actually institutions that operate at multiple levels. At the macro level are the states with their high-level diplomatic agencies and ministries of security that seek to regulate at the micro level access to territory through the control of goods and people. Yet the most important level that determines the stability of a border is the intermediate meso level (2008*a*; 2008*b*). In a study of the Ottoman Empire's nineteenth-century boundary with the new Greek state, Gavrilis demonstrates how Ottoman and Greek border guards, in the process of patrolling and administering the boundary unilaterally, learned to cooperate and trust one another. The guards of each side acted as a joint, bilateral institution and relied more on their counterparts across the border to police against bandits, smugglers, and ethnic insurgents than on their own high-level state agencies. As a result, a meso-level network of Ottoman and Greek border guards effectively policed the border and insulated the Ottoman and Greek capitals from everyday incidents that could have further deteriorated diplomatic relations.

CONCLUSION

Historical sociology has produced a tremendous amount of significant scholarship in the last few decades. It has emerged with a set of important political and social concerns that were thought to be best resolved in historical terms and has since then developed an imposing set of theoretical and methodological perspectives. Each of these perspectives has yearned to develop a more precise and functional tool of social analysis. I have argued that we can find an interesting analytic position in the combination of institutional and relational analysis, where meso-level social networks act as the mediating mechanisms between actions, structures, and institutions and thereby also shape the cultural understandings that create meaning.

References

ABBOTT, A. (1990), 'Conceptions of Time and Events in Social Science Methods: Causal and Narrative Approaches', *Historical Methods*, 23 (4): 141–50.

ABRAMS, P. (1982), *Historical Sociology* (Ithaca, N.Y.: Cornell University Press).

ADAMS, J., CLEMENS, E. S., and ORLOFF, A. S. (2005) (eds.), *Remaking Modernity: Politics, History and Sociology* (Durham, N.C.: Duke University Press).

AMENTA, E. (2003), 'What We Know about the Development of Social Policy: Comparative and Historical Research in Comparative and Historical Perspective', in J. Mahoney and D. Rueshemeyer (eds.), *Comparative Historical Analysis in the Social Sciences* (New York: Cambridge University Press), 91–130.

AMINZADE, R. (1992), 'Historical Sociology and Time', *Sociological Methods and Research*, 20: 459–80.

ANDERSON, P. (1974*a*), *Lineages of the Absolutist State* (London: Verso).

—— (1974*b*), *Passages from Antiquity to Feudalism* (London: Verso).

AZARIAN, R. (2003), *The General Sociology of Harrison White* (Stockholm: Stockholm University).

BARKEY, K. (2000), 'Negotiated Paths to Nationhood: A Comparison of Hungary and Romania in the Early Twentieth Century', *East European Politics and Societies*, 14: 497–531.

—— (2008), *Empire of Difference: The Ottomans in Comparative Perspective* (Cambridge: Cambridge University Press).

—— and KATZNELSON, I. (2008), 'State Making and The Expulsion of Jews from Medieval England and France', unpublished manuscript.

BATES, R., et al. (1998), *Analytic Narratives* (Princeton, N.J.: Princeton University Press).

BEARMAN, P. (1991), 'Desertion as Localism: Army Unit Solidarity and Group Norms in the US Civil War', *Social Forces*, 70: 321–42.

—— (1993), *Relations into Rhetorics: Local Elite Social Structure in Norfolk, England, 1540–1640* (New Brunswick, N.J.: Rutgers University Press).

BENDIX, R. (1964), *Nation-building and Citizenship* (New York: Wiley).

—— (1980), *Kings or People: Power and the Mandate to Rule* (Berkeley, Calif.: University of California Press).

BERMAN, L. (1937), *Histoire des Juifs de France des origines à nos jours* (Paris: Lipschutz).

BIERNACKI, R. (1995), *The Fabrication of Labor in Germany and Britain, 1640–1914* (Berkeley, Calif.: University of California Press).

—— (1999), 'Method and Metaphor after the New Cultural History', in E. V. Bonnell and L. Hunt (eds.), *Beyond the Cultural Turn: New Directions in the Study of Society and Culture* (Berkeley, Calif.: University of California Press), 62–92.

BONNELL, V. E., and HUNT, L. (1999) (eds.), *Beyond the Cultural Turn: New Directions in the Study of Society and Culture* (Berkeley, Calif.: University of California Press).

BRENNER, R. (1987), 'Agrarian Class Structure and the Development of Capitalism: France and England Compared', in T. H. Aston and C. H. E. Philpin (eds.), *The Brenner Debate: Agrarian Class Structure and Economic Development in Pre-industrial Europe* (Cambridge: Cambridge University Press), 10–63.

BRUBAKER, R. (1992), *Citizenship and Nationhood in France and Germany* (Cambridge, Mass.: Harvard University Press).

—— (1996), *Nationalism Reframed: Nationhood and the National Question in the New Europe* (Cambridge: Cambridge University Press).

BURT, R. S. (1980), 'Models of Network Structure', *Annual Review of Sociology*, 6: 79–141.

—— (2001), *Bandwidth and Echo: Trust, Information, and Gossip in Social Networks* (New York: Russell Sage).

—— (2005), *Brokerage and Closure: An Introduction to Social Capital* (Oxford/New York: Oxford University Press).

CALHOUN, C. (1996), 'The Rise and Domestication of Historical Sociology', in T. J. McDonald (ed.), *The Historic Turn in the Human Sciences* (Ann Arbor, Mich.: University of Michigan Press), 305–38.

DIANI, M., and McADAM, D. (2003) (eds.), *Social Movements and Networks: Relational Approaches to Collective Action* (Oxford/New York: Oxford University Press).

EDLING, C., and HEDSTROM, P. (2005), *Analytical Sociology in Tocqueville's Democracy in America*, working paper series, Department of Sociology, University of Stockholm.

ELIAS, N. [1939] (2000), *The Civilizing Process; The History of Manners and State Formation and Civilization* (Oxford: Blackwell).

ELMAN, P. (1937), 'The Economic Causes of the Expulsion of the Jews', *Economic Review*, 7: 145–52.

ERICKSON, B. H. (1997), 'Social Network Analysis: Methods and Applications', *Historical Methods*, 30: 149–59.

ERTMAN, T. (1997), *Birth of the Leviathan: Building States and Regimes in Medieval and Early Modern Europe* (New York: Cambridge University Press).

FAWTIER, R. (1953), 'Parlement d'Angleterre et Etats Generaux de France au Moyen Age', *Comptes Rendus des seances de l'annee, Academie des Inscriptions et Belles Letters*, 30: 275–84.

GAVRILIS, G. (2008a), 'The Greek–Ottoman Frontier as Institution: Locality, and Process (1832–1882)', *American Behavioral Scientist*, 51: 1516–37.

—— (2008b), *The Dynamics of Interstate Boundaries* (Cambridge: Cambridge University Press).

GEERTZ, C. (1968), *Islam Observed: Religious Development in Morocco and Indonesia* (Chicago, Ill.: Chicago University Press).

GERSCHENKRON, A. (1962), *Economic Backwardness in Historical Perspective: A Book of Essays* (Cambridge, Mass.: Harvard University Press).

GIDDENS, A. (1979), *Central Problems in Social Theory: Action, Structure, and Contradiction in Social Analysis* (Berkeley, Calif.: University of California Press).

—— —— (1986), *Constitution of Society: Outline of the Theory of Structuration* (Berkeley, Calif.: University of California Press).

—— (1987), *A Contemporary Critique of Historical Materialism, ii: The Nation-State and Violence* (Berkeley, Calif.: University of California Press).

GOLDSTONE J. A., (1993), *Revolution and Rebellion in the Early Modern World* (Berkeley, Calif.: University of California Press).

—— (2003), 'Comparative Historical Analysis and Knowledge Accumulation in the Study of Revolutions', in J. Mahoney and D. Rueshemeyer (eds.), *Comparative Historical Analysis in the Social Sciences* (New York: Cambridge University Press), 41–90.

GOLDTHORPE, J. H. (1997), 'Current Issues in Comparative Macrosociology: A Debate on Methodological Issues', *Comparative Social Research*, 16: 1–26.

—— (2000), *On Sociology: Numbers, Narratives and the Integration of Research and Theory* (Oxford: Oxford University Press).

GOULD, R. V. (1995), *Insurgent Identities: Class, Community and Protest in Paris from 1848 to the Commune* (Chicago, Ill.: University of Chicago Press).

—— (2003), 'The Uses of Network Tools in Comparative Historical Research', in J. Mahoney and D. Rueshemeyer (eds.), *Comparative Historical Analysis in the Social Sciences* (New York: Cambridge University Press), 241–69.

GRIFFIN, L. J. (1992), 'Temporality, Events and Explanation in Historical Sociology', *Sociological Methods and Research*, 20: 403–27.

HALL, P. (2003), 'Aligning Ontology and Methodology in Comparative Politics', in J. Mahoney and D. Rueshemeyer (eds.), *Comparative Historical Analysis in the Social Sciences* (New York: Cambridge University Press), 373–404.

HECHTER, M. (1987), *Principles of Group Solidarity* (Berkeley/London: University of California Press).

HEDSTRÖM, P. (2005), *Dissecting the Social: On the Principles of Analytic Sociology* (Cambridge, Cambridge University Press).

INALCIK, H. (1983), 'The Question of the Emergence of the Ottoman State', *International Journal of Turkish Studies*, 4: 71–9.

—— (1994), 'The Ottoman State: Economy and Society, 1300–1600', in H. Inalcik and D. Quataert (eds.), *An Economic and Social History of the Ottoman Empire, 1300–1914* (Cambridge: Cambridge University Press).

JEPPERSON, R. L. (1991), 'Institutions, Institutional Effects, and Institutionalism', in W. W. Powell and P. J. Dimaggio (eds.), *The New Institutionalism in Organizational Analysis* (Chicago, Ill.: Chicago University Press).

JORDAN, W. C. (1979), *Louis IX and the Challenge of the Crusade: A Study in Rulership* (Princeton, N.J.: Princeton University Press).

KIMELDORF, H. (1988), *Reds or Rockets? The Making of Radical and Conservative Unions on the Waterfront* (Berkeley, Calif.: University of California Press).

KING, G., KEOHANE, R. O., and VERBA, S. (1994), *Designing Social Inquiry: Scientific Inference in Qualitative Research* (Princeton, N.J.: Princeton University Press).

KISER, E., and HECHTER, M. (1991), 'The Role of General Theory in Comparative Historical Sociology', *American Journal of Sociology*, 97: 1–30.

KOPRULU, F. M. (1992), *The Origins of the Ottoman Empire*, trans. and ed. by L. Gary (Binghampton, N.Y.: State University of New York Press).

LEMERCIER, C. (2005), 'Analyse de reseaux et histoire', *Revue d'histoire moderne et contemporaine*, 52: 88–112.

LEVI, M. (1988), *Of Rule and Revenue* (Berkeley, Calif.: University of California Press).

LEVY, M. (1995), 'Massacre de Juifs en France lors la Deuxieme Croisade', *Archives juives* 28: 89–92.

McAdam, D., Tarrow, S., and Tilly, C. (2001), *Dynamics of Contention* (Cambridge: Cambridge University Press).

McLean, P. D. (2005), 'Patronage, Citizenship, and the Stalled Emergence of the Modern State in Renaissance Florence', *Comparative Studies in Society and History*, 47: 638–64.

Mahoney, J. (2000), 'Path Dependence in Historical Sociology', *Theory and Society*, 29: 507–48.

——(2001), *The Legacies of Liberalism: Path Dependence and Political Regimes in Central America* (Baltimore, Md.: Johns Hopkins University Press).

——(2003), 'Knowledge Accumulation in Comparative Historical Research: The Case of Democracy and Authoritarianism', in J. Mahoney and D. Rueshemeyer (eds.), *Comparative Historical Analysis in the Social Sciences* (New York: Cambridge University Press), 137–74.

——and Rueshemeyer, D. (2003), (eds.), *Comparative Historical Analysis in the Social Sciences* (New York: Cambridge University Press).

Menache, S. (1985), 'Faith, Myth, and Politics: The Stereotype of the Jews and their Expulsion from England and France', *Jewish Quarterly Review*, 75: 351–74.

Merton, R. K. (1967), 'On Sociological Theories of the Middle Range', in his *On Theoretical Sociology* (New York: Free Press).

Moore, B. jun. (1966), *Social Origins of Dictatorship and Democracy* (Boston, Mass.: Beacon).

Mundill, R. R. (1998), *England's Jewish Solution: Experiment and Expulsion, 1262–1290* (Cambridge: Cambridge University Press).

Nahon, G. (1962), 'Contributions à l'histoire de Juifs en France sous Philippe Le Bel', *Revue des Etudes Juives*, 121: 60–81.

Olson, M. [1965] (1971), *The Logic of Collective Action: Public Goods and the Theory of Groups*, rev edn. (Boston, Mass.: Harvard University Press).

——(1982), *The Rise and Decline of Nations: Economic Growth, Stagflation, and Social Rigidities* (New Haven, Conn.: Yale University Press).

——(2000), *Power and Prosperity: Outgrowing Communist and Capitalist Dictatorships* (Oxford: Oxford University Press).

Padgett, J., and Ansell, C. K. (1993), 'Robust Action and the Rise of the Medici, 1400–1434', *American Journal of Sociology*, 98: 1259–1319.

Pantazopoulos, N. J. (1967), *Church and Law in the Balkan Peninsula During the Ottoman Rule* (Thessalonica: Institute of Balkan Studies Press).

Pierson, P. (2000), 'Increasing Returns, Path Dependence, and the Study of Politics', *American Political Science Review*, 94 (2): 251–67.

——(2004), *Politics in Time: History, Institutions, and Social Analysis* (Princeton, N.J.: Princeton University Press).

Przeworski, A., and Teune, H. (1970), *The Logic of Comparative Social Inquiry* (New York: Wiley).

Ragin, C. C. (1987), *The Comparative Method: Moving Beyond Qualitative and Quantitative Strategies* (Berkeley/Los Angeles/London: University of California Press).

Robert, H. B., et al. (1998), *Analytic Narratives* (Princeton, N.J.: Princeton University Press).

Roth, G. (1971), 'Max Weber's Comparative Approach and Historical Typology', in I. Vallier (ed.), *Comparative Methods in Sociology: Essays on Trends and Applications* (Berkeley, Calif.: University of California Press), 75–93.

Schelling, T. (1978), *Micromotives and Microbehavior* (New York/London: Norton).

Sewell, W. H. (1996), 'Historical Events as Transformations of Structures: Inventing Revolution at the Bastille', *Theory and Society*, 25: 841–81.

Sewell, W. H., jun. (1999), 'The Concept(s) of Culture', in V. E. Bonnell and L. Hunt (eds.), *Beyond the Cultural Turn: New Directions in the Study of Society and Culture* (Berkeley, Calif.: University of California Press).

—— (2005), *Logics of History: Social Theory and Social Transformation* (Chicago, Ill.: University of Chicago Press).

Skocpol, T. (1979), *States and Social Revolutions: A Comparative Analysis of France, Russia and China* (Cambridge: Cambridge University Press).

—— (1984) (ed.), *Vision and Method in Historical Sociology* (Cambridge: Cambridge University Press).

—— and Somers, M. (1980), 'The Uses of Comparative History in Macrosocial Inquiry', *Comparative Studies in Society and History*, 22: 174–97.

Smelser, N. (1976), *Comparative Methods in the Social Sciences* (Englewood Cliffs, N.J.: Prentice Hall).

Steinmetz, G. (1999) (ed.), *State/Culture: State Formation after the Cultural Turn* (Ithaca, N.Y./London: Cornell University Press).

—— (2005) (ed.), *The Politics of Method in the Human Sciences: Positivism and Its Epistemological Others* (Durham, N.C.: Duke University Press).

Stinchcombe, A. (1978), *Theoretical Methods in Social History* (New York: Academic).

Stovel, K. (2001), 'Local Sequential Patterns: The Structure of Lynching in the Deep South, 1882–1930', *Social Forces*, 79: 843–80.

Strayer, J. R. (1980), *The Reign of Philip the Fair* (Princeton, N.J.: Princeton University Press).

Stryker, R. (1996), 'Beyond History Versus Theory: Strategic Narrative and Sociological Explanation', *Sociological Methods and Research*, 24: 304–52.

Swedberg, R., and Hedström, P. (1997) (eds.), *Social Mechanisms: An Analytical Approach to Social Theory* (Cambridge: Cambridge University Press).

Thelen, K. (1999), 'Historical Institutionalism in Comparative Politics', *Annual Review of Political Science*, 2: 369–404.

—— (2003), 'How Institutions Evolve: Insights from Comparative Historical Analysis', in J. Mahoney and D. Rueshemeyer (eds.), *Comparative Historical Analysis in the Social Sciences* (New York: Cambridge University Press), 208–40.

—— (2004), *How Institutions Evolve: The Political Economy of Skills in Germany, Britain, the United States, and Japan* (Cambridge: Cambridge University Press).

Tilly, C. (1975) (ed.), *The Formation of National States in Western Europe* (Princeton, N.J.: Princeton University Press).

—— (1997), 'Means and Ends of Comparison in Macrosociology', *Comparative Social Research*, 16: 43–53.

—— (1998), *Durable Inequality* (Berkeley, Calif./London: University of California Press).

—— (2001), 'Mechanisms in Political Processes', *Annual Review of Political Science*, 4: 21–41.

—— (2004), 'Social Boundary Mechanisms', *Philosophy of the Social Sciences*, 34 (2): 211–36.

—— (2005), *Identities, Boundaries and Social Ties* (Boulder, Colo.: Paradigm).

Vujacic, V. (1996), 'Historical Legacies, Nationalist Mobilization, and Political Outcomes in Russia and Serbia: A Weberian View', *Theory and Society*, 25/6: 763–801.

Wallerstein, I. (1974), *The Modern World System*, vol. 1 (Orlando, Fla.: Academic).

WHITE, H. C. (1992), *Identity and Control: A Structural Theory of Social Action* (Princeton, N.J.: Princeton University Press).

—— (2008), *Identity and Control: How Social Formations Emerge* (Princeton, N.J.: Princeton University Press).

—— (2006), 'Identity and Control Revisited', talk given at the New School of Social Research, New York.

—— BOORMAN, S. A., and BREIGER, R. L. (1976) 'Social Structure from Multiple Networks, I', *American Journal of Sociology*, 81: 730–80.

—— GODART, F., and CORONA, V. (2007), 'Mobilizing Identities: Uncertainty and Control in Strategy', *Theory, Culture and Society*, 24 (7–8): 191–212.

WEINGAST, B. (1996), 'Political Institutions: Rational Choice Perspective', in R. E. Goodin and H.-D. Klingemann (eds.), *New Handbook of Political Science* (Oxford: Oxford University Press), 167–90.

WITTEK, P. (1938), *The Rise of the Ottoman Empire* (London: Royal Asiatic Society).

Name Index

Subject Index

Printed in Great Britain
by Amazon.co.uk, Ltd.,
Marston Gate.